Footprint

The travel guide

Mexico

Handbook

The map said it was forty miles, over an all-weather road, but the drive took two and a half hours. The road was a cruel joke, a rutted wash board, insidiously studded with small, kidney-jolting rocks. A fine, drizzling mist splattered the windshield, and the rain intensified the odor of the jungle, which rose like an endless green wall on both sides of the road.

Tim Cahill, *Pecked to Death by Ducks*

Mexico Handbook
First edition
© Footprint Handbooks Ltd 2000

Published by Footprint Handbooks
6 Riverside Court
Lower Bristol Road
Bath BA2 3DZ. England
T +44 (0)1225 469141
F +44 (0)1225 469461
Email discover@footprintbooks.com
Web www.footprintbooks.com

ISBN 1 900949 53 9
CIP DATA: A catalogue record for this
book is available from the British Library

In USA, published by
NTC/Contemporary Publishing Group
4255 West Touhy Avenue, Lincolnwood
(Chicago), Illinois 60712-1975, USA
T 847 679 5500 F 847 679 2494
Email NTCPUB2@AOL.COM

ISBN 0-658-00657-6
Library of Congress Catalog Card
Number 00-132881

Credits

Series editors
Patrick Dawson
Rachel Fielding

Editorial
Editor: Felicity Laughton
Maps: Sarah Sorensen

Production
Additional editorial help: Alan Murphy
and Jo Williams
Typesetting: Richard Ponsford, Emma
Bryers and Leona Bailey
Maps: Kevin Feeney, Robert Lunn, Claire
Benison and Alasdair Dawson
Cover: Camilla Ford

Design
Mytton Williams

Photography
Front cover: Art Directors & Trip
Back cover: Getty One Stone
Inside colour section: Pictures Colour
Library, Impact Photos, Getty One Stone,
Art Directors & Trip, Robert Harding and
Dr Tim Laughton.

Print
Manufactured in Italy by LEGOPRINT

Mexico

UNITED STATES

CUBA

Gulf of Mexico

Pacific Ocean

Gulf of California

BELIZE

GUATEMALA

HONDURAS

NICARAGUA

Tijuana

BAJA CALIFORNIA NORTE

SONORA

BAJA CALIFORNIA SUR

La Paz

Cabo San Lucas

CHIHUAHUA

Copper Canyon

DURANGO

SINALOA

Mazatlán

NAYARIT

Puerto Vallarta

COAHUILA

ZACATECAS

Monterrey

NUEVO LEÓN

TAMAULIPAS

SAN LUIS POTOSI

AGUASCALIENTES

GUANAJUATO

JALISCO

Guadalajara

Manzanillo

COLIMA

MICHOACAN

QUERETARO

HIDALGO

MEXICO

MEXICO CITY

MORELOS

TLAXCALA

PUEBLA

GUERRERO

Acapulco

Zihuatanejo

VERACRUZ

Veracruz

OAXACA

Bahías de Huatulco

TABASCO

CHIAPAS

CAMPECHE

YUCATÁN

Mérida

QUINTANA ROO

Cancún

Cozumel

N

0 km   200
0 miles 200

Contents

Left: A riot of colour at the Xochimilco Fiesta.

4

Right: Girl in traditional dress at the Fiesta de Enero in Chiapa de Corzo, in Chiapas region.

A foot in the door

Highlights

When Cortés was asked what the country looked like, he reputedly crushed a piece of parchment in his fist, released it and said: "That is the map of Mexico." The famed conquistador may have neatly summed up the country's geography, but he certainly wasn't doing much of a selling job for Mexico's considerable appeal. Many countries are described as "an exotic assault on the senses," but Mexico practically defines exotic. Look up the word in the dictionary and it says "see Mexico." Well, okay, it doesn't. But it should.

Come for your senses
Mexico's visual appeal is second to none. The brilliance of the crystal-clear, aquamarine Caribbean sea has to be seen to be believed, as does the massive scale of its Aztec pyramids, Mayan temples and baroque cathedrals, its huge canyons and dense jungles. Mexico may look good, but by God it also smells and tastes good. Surely no one in their right mind could resist a sizzling fajita or a well-mixed margarita cocktail, could they? It all sounds impressive, but Mexico also has its more subtle and mystical charms. Its myriad pre-Hispanic monuments are haunted by the spirits of ancient peoples and there's an intangible, almost spiritual feeling you get when you visit these remnants of Mexico's bloody past.

Big is beautiful
Flying into Mexico City, the largest city in the world, you can't fail to be impressed by the scale of things. Beside the massive main plaza, the Zócalo, and the leaning Cathedral that threatens to collapse on top of it, are the monumental remains of the Templo Mayor, the principal pyramid at the heart of Tenochtitlán, the Aztec capital. These pre-Columbian and colonial buildings are repeatedly painted in the murals of Mexico's big three – the painters Diego Rivera, José Clemente Orozco and David Alfaro Siqueiros – which are to be found in dark cloisters and corridors all over the capital. As well as seeing Rivera's huge mural *Sueño de una tarde dominical en la Alameda Central,* (Dream of a Sunday afternoon in the Alameda Central) make sure you visit the real thing and experience the vibrant park-life of the actual Alameda on a Sunday and the fair at Chapultepec Park at the weekend.

Market forces
Within easy striking distance of the capital, in Michoacan, among the lakes and small volcanic hills of Patzcuáro, Uruapan and Paracutín, is another world unmarked by progress, where people quietly go about their business as they always have, fishing, farming and producing *artesanía*. Two hours to the south of the big smoke the town of Taxco has a sterling reputation for its refined silverwork and presents another opportunity for some retail therapy. You can also visit any number of local markets in out-of-the-way places such as Chilapa and Olinala in Guerrero state, or even enjoy a spell at the witches' market in Catemaco, in Veracruz.

Another fine mass
Some of the most interesting Indian markets are to be found down Chiapas way, around the beautiful town of San Cristóbal de las Casas, one of the most precious jewels in Mexico's tourist crown. San Cristóbal is better known for its startling colonial architecture, in particular its many churches. It was also at the centre of the Zapatista uprising, in 1994. Another fine mass to get into is at Oaxaca, whose Church of Santo Domingo has one of the most ornate gilded altars in the Americas. This showy architecture is repeated in many parts of Mexico. Towns like Zacatecas, Querétaro, San Miguel de Allende and Guanajuato, four or five hours' drive north of Mexico City, have many extravagant Churrigueresque churches and colonial houses.

Left: Detail of wall mural on the Palacio Nacional by the celebrated artist, Diego Rivera, which depicts a traditional Aztec ceremony.
Below: A selection of curious cures, magic potions and religious remedies at the Mercado Sonara.

Above: Bright lights, big city – market stalls outside the cathedral in Oaxaca at Christmas time. *Left*: Taco "belle" serving Mexico's finest at a taco stall in downtown Mexico City.
Next page: A high view over the architectural landscape of Guanajato city.

Below: The Day of the Dead is one of Mexico's most important religious festivals, when the dearly departed are welcomed back from the spirit world to enjoy a last meal with their living relatives. *Right*: The famous murals at Bonampak, lying deep in the jungle, relate the X-rated story of a battle and its bloody aftermath.

Above: El Castillo at Chitchen Itza, one of Mexico's truly awesome sights, and a 'must-see' on any tourist itinerary.
Right: Two of Mexico's greatest icons, the Pope and the Virgin Mary, hang side by side outside the Basilica de Guadaloupe. *Next page*: Two Hacaloleros at the Tlacalolo festival in Guerrero.

The Empires strike back

There are so many archaeological sites in Mexico that the whole place sometimes feels like a gigantic ancient history theme park. There are more pyramids and temples than your average Mexican can shake a cocktail stick at. Even temples within temples, like great architectural Russian dolls. Successive rulers, Maya and Aztec in particular, built upon the pyramids of their immediate ancestors, placing their own higher stamp upon the dynasty. The sheer variety of sites is also astounding, from Tulum in its stunning Caribbean setting, to the brilliantly coloured wall paintings at Bonampak in the jungle, and from the red ornate facades of Mitla to the bizarre Olmec heads in Veracruz.

Myriad pyramids

The term 'ruined out' is sometimes heard amongst travellers in Mexico, but no one should miss the main sites – the so-called "big six".
    Teotihuacan, just outside the capital, is the most monumental site in Latin America, with the biggest pyramids in the world outside Egypt. Its two huge pyramids, the Sun and Moon, are approached by the Avenue of the Dead, which is almost 4 km long. **Monte Alban,** a Zapotec city near Oaxaca, sits atop a fortress-like hill. Its varied pyramidal platforms line the central plaza like a phalanx of giants, each with a different set of curves and postures. **El Tajín,** City of the Totonacas, nestles among the rolling sub-tropical hills near Papantla in northern Veracruz. It has the usual clusters of platforms, pyramids and ball courts, but also has one unique and outstanding feature – a pyramid with hundreds of niches. **Palenque** is many traveller's favourite ancient city, not only because of its position between dense tropical forest on one side and views out over the plains on the other, but because of its remarkable architectural features from the height of the Maya classic period. **Uxmal** and **Chichén Itzá,** not far apart between Mérida and Cancún in the Yucatán Peninsula, are the Pele and Maradona of Mexican archaeology. Each has its own genius, but from different eras, one Maya, the other Toltec-Maya, provoking endless debate as to which is the best. Make sure you see both of them.

Sites for sore eyes

Between 31 October and 2 November, all over Mexico, rural cemetries seem to come alive as villagers set up an all-night vigil to entertain returning souls. These celebrations, known as Day of the Dead and All Saints, are a fascinating spectacle. The ground blazes with candles and orange and red cempasúchil flowers whilst the air is scented with copal. Two of the best places to see it happen are the island of Janitzio and the nearby village of Tzintzuntzan, both on Lake Pátzcuaro. In the cities, the *calavera*, or dancing skeleton, reigns over altars decorated with flowers, tissue paper cut into delicate shapes, food offerings and sugar skulls, while in Mexico City dances and discos are organized for the event. Hardly morbid, is it?

Life and soul of the party

Another great time to be in Mexico is during Easter week, which is a riot of energy and colour. Thousands gather in towns all over the country for processions and passion plays. In some places, like the Ixtapalapa suburb of Mexico City, millions hit the streets to watch an annual crucifixion. Besides the main regional centres there are renowned parades in small towns, amongst them Valle de Allende near Hidalgo de Parral and Huaynamota up in the mountains above Tepic.

Easter 'egg-cess'

Right: Spectacular desert landscape of the Catavina Boulderfield in Northern Baja California. ***Below***: Having a whale of a time in the San Ignacio Lagoon, favourite haunt of these big guys.

Above: Escape "II" paradise on the palm-fringed Playa Carmen beach, at Quintana Roo. ***Right***: Tulum is one of Mexico's most spectacularly sited archaeological treasures, where you can enjoy the best of both worlds. ***Next page***: Close up of masks of animals and gods in San Cristóbal de las Casa, Chiapas.

Thrills, spills and chills

In a way, Mexico has always been synonymous with sports; from that famous leap of Bob Beaman at the Mexico City Olympics in 1968 to the movie reel of young Turks leaping from the cliffs at Acapulco into the crashing waves far below. Today, those of a more adventurous bent still come here, to climb the volcanic peaks which tower over the Central Valley, to spill down the white water of the Antigua and Pescado rivers in Veracruz or ride the tube on the long Pacific coastline. Of course, most people go on holiday to just chill and soak up some rays, and there's no better place than Mexico, which is after all, the land of chilling con carne.

The Caribbean offers superb diving off the Quintana Roo coastline, particularly off Isla Mujeres and Isla Cozumel. Even if you're not diving the water is crystal clear, warm and impossibly blue, and the beaches refreshingly quiet. On the other side of the country is the wild Pacific with its giant rollers, a must for naturals and goofies alike who schlep down here in their droves to catch those waves in places like Puerto Escondido, Oaxaca state, and the length of Baja California. There are beautiful beaches here as well, none more so than Zipolite near Puerto Escondido.

Baja California is like no other part of Mexico. The Sea of Cortez that it shelters is one of the world's richest marine feeding grounds and in many places you can be be horrified by hammerheads, wowed by whales and delight at dolphins – if you go at the right time. The best time to see California Grey Whales is between December and February, but you can see them as late as May or June in some spots. Inland Baja has the rare quiet of an ancient and little disturbed desert landscape, while the Pacific coastline has hundreds of kilometres of deserted beaches and some of the world's best surfing.

One of the very best things about travelling through the Mayan lands of the Yucatán Peninsula is that so often the pre-Columbian architecture is found in such spectacular locations, surrounded by gorgeous scenery, with sometimes even wild natural reserves nearby. Many travellers who visit Tulum leave convinced that this late flowering of Mayan civilization was the one in which they discovered the good life. The ruins sit atop small cliffs above white sand beaches and a perfect blue sea. Just a few kilometres south, is the Sian Ka'an Biosphere Reserve – a savannah, mangrove and marine habitat for many species including big cats, crocodiles, monkeys and manatees.

The Puuc route to Mérida features a trail of classic ruins barely excavated out of the scrub forest, including Edzna, Sayil, Kabah, Labna and Uxmal. Beyond Merida is the Celestún National Park; a wonderful place for seeing flamingoes, pelicans, toucans and many other birds. And at Bonampak and Yaxchilán there's an opportunity to experience a virtually untouched rainforest.

The Copper Canyon, or Cañon de Urique, as it is sometimes known, is so huge that it makes the Grand Canyon look like a crack in the pavement. Creel is one of Mexico's foremost adventure sports bases and ideal for trips to the canyon. Nearby is the sublime gorge of Basaseachi, with a waterfall 311 m high, the highest single fall of water in the whole of North America. The encircling cliffs offer a heady challenge to climbers, and the Chihuahua to Pacific Railway is one of the world's great train rides, travelling through numerous tunnels and across bridges galore, some of which rank among the most spectacular feats of engineering anywhere.

Essentials

2

18

Essentials

Planning your trip

Where to go

Mexico's size makes it impossible for anyone (unless you have unlimited time) to see it all in one go. Fortunately, with so many attractions, and with relatively good transport links, it is not difficult to select a worthwhile variety of options. The Pacific, the Gulf of Mexico and the Caribbean Sea provide thousands of miles of beaches on either side of the country. The bulk of the interior is made up of mountains and plateaux, in the north predominantly arid, but in the south, more densely forested and wet. Added to this are two extremities, the long arm of Baja California in the northwest, and the flat Yucatán Peninsula in the southeast.

For those flying in, there are two main ports of entry to Mexico, the capital and Cancún, and there is one very long and permeable border to the north across which most driving traffic arrives. These suggested routes are orientated, therefore, around the centre, the southeast, and travel down from the north of Mexico. Tijuana and Cancún are about as far apart as Los Angeles and New York and so taking internal flights to link up some of these ground routes is strongly recommended.

Central Mexico Mexico City is one of the world's great capitals and deserves several days stay just to visit its highlights - the Museum of Anthropology, Centro Histórico, Chapultepec Park, Coyoacán, San Angel and Xochimilco among them – and to get a feel for its stirring revolutionary past through the brilliant murals of Orozco, Rivera and Siqueiros.

A relatively short circuit north of Mexico City, possible in a week, is to the colonial heartland, taking in the towns of Querétaro, Guanajuato, San Miguel de Allende and Dolores Hidalgo, architectural gems built on silver wealth. There are other short trips, for those with limited time, within relatively easy reach of the capital. It is possible to explore the towns of Michoacán – Morelia, Pátzcuaro, Uruapan – and the nearby volcano of Paricutín and still have time to reach Guadalajara, Mexico's second city, famed for its *mariachis*, its grand civic buildings and dramatic murals. Given a few more days you can reach the Pacific at Puerto Vallarta for some heavy nightlife or San Blas for easy surfing.

A much underrated circuit would take in the vanilla country and pre-Totonac ruins of El Tajín and then via Veracruz down to the Tuxtlas - Olmec country, the lake at Catemaco and then either into the steamy Papaloapan wetlands *en route* to Oaxaca or back to the capital. This could take 1½-2 weeks.

The south Another indirect route to Oaxaca in a couple of weeks is via Cuernavaca, the silver craft centre and colonial city of Taxco and then down to Acapulco, Puerto Escondido (7½ hours on by bus) and Puerto Angel - a beach-to-beach trail of increasing tranquility.

Oaxaca, just five hours from the capital now that the new toll road is built, is as much of a hub for travellers' routes as the capital. It is worth several days in itself for the nearby ruins and colonial architecture. If you continue southwards, as the majority of backpackers do, then you come to San Cristóbal de las Casas, also worth several days, particularly to experience the surrounding, very Indian, villages. From here, if you have more than a few weeks, you can continue down to Guatemala and sweep back into the Yucatán via Tikal in northern of Guatemala, Belize, and the Mexican Caribbean coast at Quintana Roo, or go directly to the Yucatán via Palenque. Some airlines charge little more to fly into Mexico City and out of Cancún than to return home from the port of entry.

The Mayan routes Arriving by air in Cancún you will probably need at least two weeks to see the Yucatán Peninsula as far as Palenque. The problem is that some backtracking is required.

Whatever happens, try not to miss either the ruins at Tulum, south of Cancún, or at Palenque far out to the west, just over the state border in Chiapas. If you go down to Tulum and are reliant upon buses, it is easiest to return to Cancún before heading out west towards Mérida via the Classic archaeological sites of Chichén Itzá and Uxmal. You could do this northern tip of the peninsula in a week, at a push, but there is enough to see around Palenque – besides the ruins there are the waterfalls of Misol-Há and Agua Azul, and the town is a junction for further travel into the centre and down to Guatemala along the so-called river route via Yaxchilán (with lots to see on the way) – to add at least another week.

Few buses go this way so add a few days for erratic scheduling

An alternative to backtracking all the way to Mérida *en route* for Cancún is to take the road heading east from Escárcega which runs parallel with the Guatemalan border to Chetumal and along which there are several much less visited archaeological sites of the Chenes Maya era. The Caribbean is then yours in your wind down to a flight out of Cancún.

Northern Mexico

The busiest land port of entry is Tijuana and most travellers head down the Baja California Peninsula. Allow at least a week for north to south travel and to see some sites along the way, and longer if you lay up at idyllic beach hang-outs like Playa Santispac on the Bahía Constitución. Once you hit La Paz or the Cape, and have time to continue, you are effectively on an island. The ferry to the mainland is an overnighter.

The second most popular southwards route is that which crosses the border at Ciudad Juárez. It deserves its popularity because it gives access to the Chihuahua-Pacific rail journey and to the Copper Canyon. But note that once you reach the end of the line at Los Mochis you are still a long way from southern Mexico and be prepared for all day or night road travel just to reach the peripheral towns of some of the routes in Central Mexico, such as San Blas or Zacatecas.

An alternative to the Pacific route south is to come the other way up the railway, seeing the best stretch as far as Creel and then visiting the Copper Canyon at Batópilas *en route* to Hidalgo del Parral via Guachochi. Durango is seven hours by road from here and then you are just a few hours from the gems of Zactecas, Guanajuato and other towns in the Colonial Heartland.

The above route takes you through some interesting mining towns and the same goes for the route initiating at Laredo or Reynosa that has Monterrey as its first destination. This may be Mexico's foremost industrial centre but it has some excellent museums and galleries and there are some great national parks just outside the city. The 'ghost town' of Real de Catorce should not be missed on this trail which if followed all the way to Mexico City, taking in the Colonial Heartland, should be given at least 1½ weeks. An alternative route to the capital is along the Gulf and into the Huastec and Totonac region of northern Veracruz where there are some very unusual pre-Columbian ruins.

When to go

If you are not tied to the European or American summer for times when you are able to travel then the best time to go is between October and April when there is virtually no rain. The rainy season works its way up from the south beginning in May and running through until August, September and even October. This is also hurricane season in the Caribbean and on rare occasions the Yucatán and Gulf states get hit. It is not a good time of year for climbing the high volcanoes. But don't be put off by the term 'rainy season' - most years, the rains only really affect travellers for an hour or two a day and, especially in the northern states of Baja, Sonora, Chihuahua and Coahuila, it can remain very hot and dry.

Baja California needs special mention because it is popular at different times of year depending on the type of traveller. During the North American winter, US and

Canadian 'snowbirders' – camper van enthusiasts – come down to escape the cold and then head back when it warms up in the north. This doesn't put any real pressure upon available hotel rooms, but what does is the spring break influx of students, particularly in Baja Norte and in the small oasis towns of Baja Sur. February – March are the best months for whale-watching in the Guerrero Negro area. Mid-April to mid-June is a good time to visit too because it is not too hot and the water is starting to warm up in the Sea of Cortés. October is also good as it is still quiet and the sea is about as warm as it is going to get.

August is holiday time for Mexicans and this can make accommodation scarce in the smaller resorts and in popular places close to Mexico City. Semana Santa (Easter week) witnesses an exodus from parts of the capital, putting pressure on transport to, and hotel space within, many attractive regional towns and villages. The Day of the Dead celebrations at the beginning of November and Christmas holidays can also affect room availability.

Finding out more

All Mexican Government tourist agencies are grouped in the Department of Tourism building at Avenida Masaryk 172, near the corner of Reforma. See under Mexico City for full details. A few cities run municipal tourist offices to help travellers. *Travellers Guide to Mexico*, published annually by the Secretaría de Turismo, lists resorts, attractions, hotels, sports, businesses, etc, US$17. *A calendar of fiestas is published by Mexico This Month*

In a similar vein to the Ruta Maya, but purely Mexican, is the Colonial Cities Schedule, which links 51 cities in eight circuits. Full details are available from the Secretaría de Turismo, T/F52507414.

If you have any complaints about faulty goods or services, go to the *Procuraduría Federal de Protección del Consumidor* of which there is a branch in every city (head office in Mexico City, José Vasconcelos 208, CP 06720, México DF, T57613801/11). Major cities, like Acapulco, also have a Procurador del Turista. The Tourist Office may also help with these, or criminal matters, while the Agente del Ministro Público (Federal or State District Attorney) will also deal with criminal complaints.

Tourist offices overseas **Canada**, 2 Bloor St West, Suite 1801, Toronto, Ontario, M4W 3EZ, T416-9250704. **France**, 4 Rue Notre Dame des Victories, 75002 Paris, T331-40200734. **Germany**, Welsenhuttenplatz 26, D600 Frankfurt am Main 1, T4969-253413. **Italy**, Via Barberini 3, 00187 Rome, T396-4742986. **UK**, Wakefield House, 41 Trinity Square, London EC3N 1DJ, T020-74889392, 0900-1600230 (recorded information). **USA**, 405 Park Avenue, Suite 1401, New York, NY 10022, T212-7557261.

There are telephone numbers that tourists can call to clarify problems. In USA, phone Mexican Turismo, Miami, T1-800-4468277. In North America T1-800-44-MEXICO, for English information for US and Canadian citizens (separate offices in USA and Canada), 24 hours a day, seven days a week. There is a Houston number which anyone can call, T1-713-8808772 for information on surface tourism. In Mexico, tourists can call T01-800-00148 and in Mexico City T56041240. The Secretaría de Turismo has an emergency hot line, open 24 hours a day: T05-52500123/0151.

The Latin American Travel Advisor offers a travel information service including a comprehensive quarterly newsletter (free sample available), country reports sent by email or fax, and a wide selection of travel maps. These provide up-to-date and reliable information on conditions for travel in Mexico as well as for 16 other countries in Central and South America. Individual travel planning assistance is also offered to subscribers. Contact PO Box 17-17-908, Quito, Ecuador, international F593-2562566, USA and Canada toll free F888-2159511, LATA@pi.pro.ec, www.amerispan.com/lata/.

Essentials

Tour operators

In the UK & Ireland

Essentials

In North America

Language

The official language of Mexico is Spanish. Outside of the main tourist centres, travelling without some knowledge of Spanish is a major hindrance. There are also some 50 indigenous languages spoken in Mexico, the most common of which are Nahuatl, Maya, Zapotec and Mixtec.

The National Registration Center for Study Abroad, 823 North 2nd St, PO Box 1393, Milwaukee, WI 53201, USA, T414-2780631, F414-2718884, will advise

Learning Spanish

Essentials

on tuition within a worldwide consortium of language schools. It will also make all arrangements for study in Mexico. The catalogue costs US$3; phone for information and the newsletter. Affiliated schools in Mexico are in San Miguel de Allende, Cuernavaca, Mazatlán, Mérida, Morelia, Guadalajara, Puebla, Acapulco, Mexico City, Aguascalientes, Toluca, Saltillo, Oaxaca. AmeriSpan Unlimited, PO Box 40007, Philadelphia, PA 19106-0007, (USA and Canada) T800-8796640, 215-7511100 (worldwide), F215-7511986, info@amerispan.com, www.amerispan.com, has affiliated schools in eight Mexican cities and also provides many services and advice for travellers.

What to take

Always take more money & fewer clothes than you think you'll need

Everybody has their own preferences, but listed here are those most often mentioned. These include an inflatable travel pillow for neck support and strong shoes (remember that footwear over 9½ English size, or 42 European size, is difficult to find in Mexico). You should also take waterproof clothing and waterproof treatment for leather footwear and wax earplugs, which are vital for long bus trips or noisy hotels. Also important are rubber-thong Japanese-type sandals, which can be worn in showers to avoid athlete's foot, and a sheet sleeping-bag to avoid sleeping on filthy sheets in cheap hotels.

Remember PMT – passport, money, tickets

Other useful things to take with you include: a clothes line, a nailbrush, a vacuum flask, a water bottle, a universal bath- and basin-plug of the flanged type that will fit any waste-pipe (or improvise one from a sheet of thick rubber), string, electrical insulating tape, a Swiss Army knife, an alarm clock for those early-morning bus departures, candles (for frequent power cuts), a torch/flashlight, pocket mirror, pocket calculator, an adaptor, a padlock for the doors of the cheapest hotels (or for tent zip if camping). The most security-conscious may also wish to include a length of chain and padlock for securing luggage to bed or bus/train seat.

A list of useful medicines and health-related items is given at the end of the 'Health' section. To these might be added some lip salve with sun protection, and pre-moistened wipes (such as 'Wet Ones'). Always carry toilet paper, which is especially important on long bus trips. Contact lens wearers: should note that lens solution can be difficult to find in the more remote areas of Mexico.

Before you travel

Getting in

Documents A passport is necessary, but US and Canadian citizens need only show a birth certificate (or for US, a naturalization certificate). Tourists need the free tourist card (FM-T), which

Insurance tips

Insurance companies have tightened up considerably over recent years and it is now almost impossible to claim successfully if you have not followed procedures closely. The problem is that these often involve dealing with the country's red tape which can lead to some inconvenience at best and to serious delays at worst. There is no substitute for suitable precautions against petty crime.

The level of insurance that you carry is often dictated by the sums of medical insurance which you carry. It is inevitably the highest if you go through the USA. Also don't forget to obtain sports extensions if you are going to do sports such as diving, rafting and climbing. Most policies do not cover very high levels of baggage/cash. Don't forget to check whether you can claim on your household insurance. They often have worldwide all risks extensions. Most policies exclude manual work whilst away although working in bars or restaurants is usually alright.

Here are our tips (they apply to most types of policies but always check the details of your own policy before you leave):

1 Take the policy with you (a photocopy will do but make sure it is a complete one).

2 Do not travel against medical advice. It will invalidate your medical insurance cover.

3 There is a 24-hour medical emergency service helpline associated with your insurance. You need to contact them if you require in-patient hospital treatment or you need to return home early. The telephone number is printed on the policy. Make sure you note the time of the call, the person you were talking to and get a reference number. Even better get a receipt from the telephone company showing the number you called.

Should you need to be airlifted home, this is always arranged through the insurance company's representative and the hospital authorities. Ironically this can lead to quite intense discussions which you will not be aware of: the local hospital is often quite keen to keep you!

4 If you have to cancel your trip for whatever reason, contact your travel agent, tour operator or airline without delay.

5 If your property is damaged by an airline, report it immediately and always within three days and get a 'property irregularity report' from them.

6 Claims for baggage left unattended are very rarely settled unless they were left in a securely locked hotel room, apartment, etc; locked in the boot of a car and there is evidence of a forced entry; cash is carried on your person or is in a locked safe or security box.

7 All loss must be reported to the police and/or hotel authorities within 24 hours of discovery and a written report obtained.

8 If medical attention is received for injury or sickness, a medical certificate showing its nature must be obtained, although some companies waive this if only out-patient treatment is required. Keep all receipts in a safe place as they will be needed to substantiate the claim.

9 There may be a date before which claims must be submitted. This is often within 30 days of returning home. It is now usual for companies to want your policy document, proof that you actually travelled (airline ticket or travel agent's confirmation of booking), receipts and written reports (in the event of loss). NB photocopies are not accepted.

can be obtained from any Mexican Consulate or Tourist Commission office, at the Mexican airport on entry, from the offices or on the aircraft of airlines operating into Mexico, and at land borders. Ask for at least 30 days (maximum 180 days); if you say you are in transit you may be charged US$8, with resulting paper work. **NB** Not all Mexican consuls in USA are aware of exact entry requirements; it is best to confirm details with airlines which fly to Mexico. Tourist cards are available for citizens of Western European countries (except Cyprus and Malta), the USA, Canada, Australia, New Zealand, Hungary, Iceland, Japan, Singapore, South Korea, Argentina, Bermuda, Chile, Costa Rica,

Essentials

 Mexico embassies & consulates

Australia, 14 Perth Avenue, Yarralumia, 2600 ACT, Canberra, T61-2 6273-3963, F61-2 6273-1190
Austria, Türkenstrasse 15. 1090, Vienna, T431 310-7383, F431 310-7387
Belgium, Av Franklin Roosvelt 94, 1050 Bruxelles, T322 629-0777, F322 646-8768
Canada, 45 O 'Connor Street, Suite 1500 K1P 1A4, Ottawa, Ont, T613 233-8988, 233-9272, F613 235-9123
Denmark, Strandvejen 64E Hellerup, 2900, Copenhagen, T45 3961-0500, F45)3961-0512
Germany, Adenaueralle 100, 53113, Bonn, T228 914-860, F228 21-1113
Finland, Simonkatu 12 'A', 7th floor, 00100 Helsinki, T3580 694-9400, F3580 694-9411
France, 9, Rue de Longchamp, 75116 Paris, T331 5370-2770, F331 4755-6529
Ireland, 43 Ailesbury Road, Ballsbridge 4, Dublin, T3531 260-0699, F3531 260-0411
Israel, Trade Tower, 25 Hemered St, 5th floor 68125. Tel-Aviv, T9723)516-3938, F9723 516-3711
Italy, Via Lazzaro Spallanzani 16, 00161. Rome, T39-6 440-4400, F(39-6) 440-3876

Norway, Drammensveien 108-B, 0244. Oslo, T47 2243-1165, F47 2244-4352
New Zealand, 111-115 Customhouse Quay, 8th floor, Wellington, T644 472-5555, F644 472-5800
Holland, Nassauplein 17 2585 EB, The Hague, T3170 360-2900, F3170 356-0543
South Africa, PO Box 9077, Pretoria 0001, T27-12 342-5190, F27-12 342-5234
Spain, Carrera de San Jerónimo 46 28014 Madrid, T341 369-2814, F341 420-2292
Switzerland, Bernastrasse 57, 3005, Berne, T4131 351-1875, F4131 351-3492
UK, 42 Hertford Street, Mayfair, London W1Y 7TF, T020-74998586, F020-74954035
USA, 1911 Pennsylvania Ave, NW, 20006 Washington DC, T202 728-1600, F202 728-1698

There are embassies/consulates in most other European countries, many US cities, throughout the Americas, and selected countries elsewhere. Addresses and email numbers can be found on **www.sre.gob.mx/delegaciones/ embajadas.htm**.

Uruguay, Venezuela and Israel. Citizens of other countries need to obtain a visa before travelling. The tourist card is also available at border offices of the American Automobile Association (AAA), which offers this service to members and non-members. There is a multiple entry card valid for all visits within six months for US nationals. The normal validity for other nationals is 90 days, but sometimes only 15-30 days are granted at border crossings; insist you want more if wishing to stay longer. Although technically you are only supposed to stay 180 days a year on a tourist card, one correspondent lived in Mexico for five years on a tourist card, making short visits to the USA three to four times a year, with no problems. Tourist cards are not required for cities close to the US border, such as Tijuana, Mexicali, etc.

If a person under 18 is travelling alone or with one parent, both parents' consent is required, certified by a notary public or authorized by a Consulate. A divorced parent must be able to show custody of a child. (These requirements are not always checked by immigration authorities and do not apply to all nationalities.) Exact details are available from any Mexican Consulate.

Renewal of entry cards or visas must be done at Servicios Migratorios, Homero 1832, Colonia Morales, Mexico City. Only 60 days are given, and you can expect to wait up to 10 days for a replacement tourist card; open Monday-Friday 0930-1400, take metro to Polanco then a taxi. There are also immigration offices at international airpotrts and in cities such as Guadalajara, Oaxaca or Acapulco which can renew tourist cards. To renew a tourist card by leaving the country, you must stay outside Mexico for at least 72 hours. Take travellers' cheques or credit card as proof of finance. The Oaxaca immigration office will renew your tourist card for only 15 days unless you have US$1,000 in cash for one month's stay; credit cards not accepted.

Travellers not carrying tourist cards need visas (South Africans and those nationalities not listed above need a visa), multiple entry not allowed, visa must be renewed before re-entry. Business visitors and technical personnel should apply for the requisite visa and permit. Those entering Mexico to sell or plan investments should obtain form FM3 from the Mexican consulate in their home country; this costs about US$100 and is valid for a year. For a single business trip of less than 30 days, use FMVC which costs nothing. Conducting business on a tourist visa can lead to several hours detention and a heavy fine. (Since 1 April 1994, business visas for US and Canadian citizens are free.) For a Visitante Rentista visa (non-immigrant pensioner) for stays over six months (up to two years) the following are required: passport, proof of income from abroad of US$750 per month (or 400 days of the minimum wage), which is reduced by half if you own a house in Mexico, and your tourist card.

We would warn travellers that there have been several cases of tourist cards not being honoured, or a charge being imposed, or the validity being changed arbitrarily to 60 days or less. In this case, a complaint should be made to the authorities in Mexico City. If, on leaving Mexico, your tourist card is not taken from you, post it to the Mexico City address above. **NB** Do not lose your tourist card. You have to surrender it when you leave the country and not having it will cost you time, worry and/or money (though some US borders crossings are very lax). If you do lose it, contact the nearest immigration office ASAP; a replacement can take a week or more.

If you want to return to Mexico after leaving to visit Belize or Guatemala, remember that you will need a new visa/tourist card if yours is not marked for multiple entry.

At the border crossings with Belize and Guatemala, you may be refused entry into Mexico if you have less than US$200 (or US$350 for each month of intended stay, up to a maximum of 180 days). This restriction does not officially apply to North American and European travellers. If you are carrying more than US$10,000 in cash or travellers' cheques, you must declare it. In most cases on entering Mexico from Belize and Guatemala only 30 days entry is given, possibly renewable for up to 60 days.

Vaccinations A vaccination certificate is required for travellers arriving from countries where yellow fever is present. Otherwise no specific vaccinations are needed to enter Mexico. However, before travelling make sure your tetanus and polio vaccinations are up-to-date. Immunization against hepatitis A and B and typhoid are recommended for people tarvelling to more remote areas, particularly in the south. See Health on page 61.

Customs The luggage of tourist-card holders is often passed unexamined. If flying into Mexico from South America, expect to be thoroughly searched (body and luggage) at the airport. US citizens can take in their own clothing and equipment without paying duty, but all valuable and non-US-made objects (diamonds, cameras, binoculars, typewriters, computers, etc), should be registered at the US Customs office or the port of exit so that duty will not be charged on returning. Radios and television sets must be registered and taken out when leaving. Anyone entering Mexico is allowed to bring in: clothing, footwear and personal cleaning items suitable for the length of stay; camera, or video recorder; books and magazines; one used article of sporting equipment; up to three litres of wine, beer or spirits; 20 packs of cigarettes, or 20 cigars, or 200 grams of tobacco; medicines for personal use. Foreigners who reside legally outside Mexico are also allowed: a portable TV, stereo, 20 records or audio cassettes, a musical instrument, five used toys, fishing tackle, tennis racket, a pair of skis, a boat up to 5m without an engine, camping equipment, a tent. Those entering by trailer, private plane or yacht may also bring a videocassette recorder, bicycle, motorbike and kitchen utensils. Anything additional to this list with a value of over US$300, if entering by land, air or sea, is taxable and must be declared as such (for Mexicans returning by land the value is US$50). This stipulation is rarely invoked for

Essentials

those entering by motor home. Goods imported into Mexico with a value of more than US$1,000 (with the exception of computer equipment, where the limit is US$4,000) have to be handled by an officially appointed agent. One recommended agency is Agencia Promoción y Servicio Aduanal, Durango 111, Colonia Peñón de los Baños T57855769, F57857476, pysasa@aaadam.com.mx, who will arrange everything, including delivery to one's address. The export of goods is relatively simple, but this too is best effected through an accredited agency.

There are no restrictions on the import or export of money apart from gold but foreign gold coins are allowed into the USA only if they are clearly made into jewellery (perforated or otherwise worked on). On return to the USA a person may take from Mexico, free of duty, up to US$100 worth of merchandise for personal use or for personal gifts, every 31 days, if acquired merely as an incident of the trip. One litre of alcoholic drinks may be taken across the border from Mexico (beer is counted as an alcoholic drink); Texas will allow you to pay the small state tax, Arizona will not. All foreign citizens are subject to this law. Archaeological relics may not be taken out of Mexico. US tourists should remember that the US Endangered Species Act, 1973, prohibits importation into the States of products from endangered species, for example tortoise shell. The Department of the Interior issues a leaflet about this. Llama, alpaca, etc, items may be confiscated at the airport for fumigation and it will be necessary to return to the customs area on the Mexico City airport perimeter two to three days later to collect and pay for fumigation. Production of passport will be required and proof that goods are to be re-exported otherwise they may also be subject to import duties.

Money

Currency Until 1 January 1993, the monetary unit was the Mexican peso (represented by an 'S' crossed with a vertical line), divided into 100 centavos. On that date three zeros were eliminated from the peso, so that 1,000 pesos then equalled one new peso. The word 'new' was subsequently dropped and the currency is again referred to as the peso. There are notes for 10, 20, 50, 100, 200 and 500 pesos; coins for 5, 10, 20 and 50 centavos and for 1, 2, 5, 10, 20 and 50 pesos. The one- and two-peso coins and the 10- and 20-peso coins are similar in size; check the number on the coin. Old coins and notes are no longer legal tender.

Travellers' cheques

Casas de cambio may be open longer hours than banks, but they do not offer better exchange rates

The safest way of carrying money is in US$ travellers' cheques which can be changed at most banks and *casas de cambio*. Fees are not charged although the exchange rate will be lower than it is for cash. You may be asked to show your passport or another form of ID. Denominations of US$50 and US$100 are preferable, though you will need a few of US$20. American Express, and Visa US$ travellers' cheques are recommended as the easiest to change and it is also easier to obtain refunds for stolen travellers' cheques with them.

Credit cards

ATMs are now found even in small towns allowing you to travel without carrying large amounts of cash or travellers' cheques

American Express, Mastercard and Visa are generally accepted in Mexico and cash is obtainable with these credit cards at certain banks. Automatic Teller Machines (ATM, *cajero automático*) of Banamex accept Visa, Mastercard and ATM cards of the US Plus and Cirrus ATM networks for withdrawals up to 1,500 pesos. ATM withdrawals on Visa can also be made at branches of Bancomer and Cajeros RED throughout the country. Many banks are affiliated to Mastercard but locations of ATMs should be checked with Mastercard in advance. Visa is more commonly found. There have been repeated instances of Banamex ATMs stating that cash cannot be given, 'try again later', only for the card-holder to find that his/her account has been debited anyway. If you get a receipt saying no cash dispensed, keep it. Emergency phone numbers for Mastercard, T001-800-3077309, and Visa, T95-800-8472911, toll free. **NB** An American Express card

Essentials

Discount flight agents in Australia and New Zealand

Flight Centres, *82 Elizabeth St, Sydney, T13-1600; 205 Queen St, Auckland, T09-309 6171. Also branches in other towns and cities.*
STA Travel, *T1300-360960, www.statravelaus.com.au; 702 Harris St,*

Ultimo, Sydney, and 256 Flinders St, Melbourne. In NZ: 10 High St, Auckland, T09-366 6673. Also in major towns and university campuses.
Travel.com.au, *80 Clarence St, Sydney, T02-929 01500, www.travel.com.au*

issued in Mexico states 'valid only in Mexico', and is used only for peso transactions. All other American Express cards are transacted in US dollars even for employees living in Mexico. Amex travellers' cheques are readily accepted and can easily be purchased with an Amex credit card. If you are enrolled in the Amex Express Cash programme you can withdraw cash with your Amex card from Banco Inverlat ATMs. There is a six percent tax on the use of credit cards. Before you travel, check that your credit cards have not been accidentally demagnetized.

Useful websites For the location of **Visa** ATMs: www.visalatam.com; for **Mastercard**: www.mastercard.com; for **American Express**: www.americanexpress.com; for **Western Union** agents: www.westernunion.com.

Exchange In the border states such as Baja California Norte, the most-used currency is the US dollar, and the Mexican peso is often accepted by stores on the US side of the border. Travellers' cheques from any well-known bank can be cashed in most towns if drawn in US dollars; travellers' cheques in terms of European currencies are harder to cash, and certainly not worth trying to change outside the largest of cities. The free rate of exchange changes daily and varies from bank to bank and even from branch to branch (Banamex usually has the best rates). Until the new day's rate is posted, at any time between 1000 and 1100, yesterday's rate prevails. Many banks, including in Mexico City, only change foreign currency during a limited period (often between 1000 and 1200, but sometimes also 1600-1800 in Banamex), which should be remembered, especially on Friday. Many people pay in their wages on Friday, so longer queues can be expected. *Casas de cambio* are generally quicker than banks for exchange transactions, and stay open later, but their rates may not be as good. Telegraphic transfer of funds within Mexico is not reliable. Beware of short-changing at all times. For information on Western Union services (for USA only), T1-800-3254045.

Student cards Only national, Mexican student cards permit free entry to archaeological sites, museums, etc, see SETEJ page 80. The surest way to get in free is to go on Sunday, when all such places have no entry charge, but are crowded in consequence.

Cost of living Budget travellers should note that there is a definite tourist economy, with high prices and, on occasion, unhelpful service. This can be avoided by seeking out those places used by locals; an understanding of Spanish is useful. In hotels there are sometimes no single rooms, or they cost 80 percent of the price of doubles. As accommodation will probably be your main expense this should be built into your budget if travelling singly. You are advised to check all local prices before booking. VAT (IVA) is charged on all but some basic goods; it is generally 15 percent on almost all consumer goods, including hotel and restaurant bills, but 25 percent is charged on some luxury items.

Doctors and dentists provide good quality care at high prices (taking appropriate insurance is highly recommended). Film is reasonably cheap, but developing is expensive and of poor quality.

Discount flight agents in the UK and Ireland

Council Travel, *28a Poland St, London, W1V 3DB, T020-74377767, www.destinations- group.com*
STA Travel, *86 Old Brompton Rd, London, SW7 3LH, T020-74376262, www.statravel.co.uk They have other branches in London, as well as in Brighton, Bristol, Cambridge, Leeds, Manchester, Newcastle-Upon-Tyne and Oxford and on many University campuses. Specialists in low-cost student/youth flights and tours,*

also good for student IDs and insurance.
Trailfinders, *194 Kensington High Street, London, W8 7RG, T020-79383939.*
Usit Campus, *52 Grosvenor Gardens, London, SW1 0AG, T0870-2401010, www.usitcampus.co.uk Student/youth travel specialists with branches also in Belfast, Brighton, Bristol, Cambridge, Manchester and Oxford. The main Ireland branch is at 19 Aston Quay, Dublin 2, T01-602 1777.*

Getting there

Air

There are several international airports, the two busiest ones being Mexico City and Cancún, both of which receive frequent flights from Europe, North and South America and the Caribbean. For cities other than the capital, see text below for details. For information on the reduced fare Mexiplan, see page 38.

Europe Several airlines have regular direct flights from Europe to Mexico City. Air France and AeroMéxico from Paris; Iberia and AeroMéxico from Madrid; KLM from Amsterdam; British Airways from London (Gatwick); Lufthansa and Delta from Frankfurt (LTU and Condor charter flights from Germany to Mexico City or Cancún); City Bird from Brussels. Aeroflot fly to Mexico City from Moscow via Shannon on Wednesday. Most connecting flights in Europe are through Madrid or Gatwick. Fares vary from airline to airline and according to time of year. Check with an agency for the best deal for when you wish to travel.

USA & Canada From the USA to Mexico City with a variety of airlines including American Airlines, AeroMéxico, Delta, Continental, United, Northwest, Taesa and Americawest. Flights leave from Atlanta, Austin, Boston, Chicago, Dallas, Denver, Detroit, Houston, Laredo, Las Vegas, Los Angeles, McAllen, Miami, Oakland, Ontario (CA), Orlando, Philadelphia, Phoenix, Portland, Salt Lake City, San Antonio (TX), San Diego, San Francisco, San José (CA) and Washington DC. From Canada, Japan Airlines fly from Vancouver, Canadian Airlines and Mexicana fly from Toronto and Mexicana flies from Montreal.

Australia & New Zealand Flights with JAL travel via LA or Vancouver. Qantas-Continental via LA is more direct but more expensive. United Airlines and Air New Zealand–Qantas also travel via LA.

Far East Japan Airlines, twice-weekly flight from Tokyo stops at Vancouver.

Israel Flights with El Al-Continental travel via New York.

Latin America Flights from South and Central America: Lan Chile, AeroMéxico, Mexicana and Lacsa from Santiago, Chile (Lacsa via San José); Mexicana and Lan Chile from Buenos Aires; Lacsa, AeroMéxico, Mexicana from Lima, some flights via Panama City; Lloyd Aéreo Boliviano from Santa Cruz, Bolivia via Panama City; Mexicana from Caracas; Avianca

Discount flight agents in North America

Air Brokers International, 323 Geary St, Suite 411, San Francisco, CA94102, T01-800-883 3273, www.airbrokers.com Consolidator and specialist on RTW and Circle Pacific tickets.

Council Travel, 205 E 42nd St, New York, NY 10017, T1-888-COUNCIL, www. counciltravel.com Student/budget agency with branches in many other US cities.

Discount Airfares Worldwide On-Line, www.etn.nl/discount.htm A hub of consolidator and discount agent links.

International Travel Network/Airlines of the Web, www.itn.net/airlines Online air travel information and reservations.

STA Travel, 5900 Wilshire Blvd, Suite 2110, Los Angeles, CA 90036, T1-800-777 0112, www.sta-travel.com Also branches in New York, San Francisco, Boston, Miami, Chicago, Seattle and Washington DC.

Travel CUTS, 187 College St, Toronto, ON, M5T 1P7, T1-800-667 2887, www.travelcuts.com Specialist in student discount fares, Ids and other travel services. Branches in other Canadian cities.

Travelocity, www.travelocity.com Online consolidator.

Essentials

and Mexicana from Bogotá; Varig from Rio and São Paulo; AeroMéxico also fly from São Paulo; Aviateca, KLM Taca, Aerocaribe, and Mexicana from Guatemala City; Copa from Guayaquil, Managua, Panama City, San Pedro Sula; also Lacsa, Aviateca and Mexicana from Panama; Lacsa, United, Aviateca and Mexicana from San José, Costa Rica; Taca from Tegucigalpa, who fly via San Salvador; Aviateca from Managua and San Salvador.

Caribbean Mexicana and Cubana fly from Havana; Air Jamaica and American Airlines have connecting flights from Kingston and Montego Bay via Miami.

General tips Airlines will only allow a certain weight of luggage without a surcharge; this is normally 30 kg for first class and 20 kg for business and economy classes, but these limits are often not strictly enforced when it is known that the plane is not going to be full. On some flights from the UK special concessions are offered of a 2-piece allowance up to 32 kg, but you may need to request this.

Student/ youth & discount fares Some airlines are flexible on the age limit, others strict. One way and returns available, or 'Open Jaws' (when you fly into one point and return from another). Do not assume that student tickets are the cheapest; though they are often very flexible. **NB** If you foresee returning home at a busy time (eg Christmas-beginning of January, August), a booking is advisable on any type of open-return ticket.

Note that many discount fares require a change of plane at an intermediate point, and a stopover may or may not be permitted, or even obligatory, depending on schedules.

Check whether you are entitled to any refund or re-issued ticket if you lose, or have stolen, a discounted air ticket. Some airlines require the repurchase of a ticket before you can apply for a refund, which will not be given until after the validity of the original ticket has expired. The Iberia group and Air France, for example, operate this costly system. Travel insurance in some cases covers lost tickets.

Road

USA There are many crossings all along the border with the USA. Some are busier than others depending on the number of trucks which pass through. The main crossings are at Tijuana, Mexicali, Nogales, Ciudad Juárez, Piedras Negras, Nuevo Laredo and Matamoros.

Essentials

☞ Airline Websites

AeroCaribe www.aerocaribe.com	**Iberia** www.iberia.com
Aeroflot www.aeroflot.co.uk	**Japan Airlines** www.japanairlines.com
AeroMéxico www.aeromexico.com	**KLM** www.klm.com
Air France www.airfrance.com	**Lacsa** www.grupotaca.com
Air Jamaica www.airjamaica.com	**LanChile** www.lanchile.com
Alitalia www.alitalia.it	**Lufthansa** www.lufthansa.com
American ww.aa.com	**Mexicana** www.mexicana.com
Avianca www.avianca.com.co	**Northwest** www.nwa.com
Aviateca www.flylatinamerica.com/acc _aviateca.html	**Qantas** www.qantas.com
	Taca www.grupotaca.com
British Airways www.britishairways.com	**United** www.ual.com
Canadian www.cdnair.ca	**Varig** www.varig.com.br
City Bird www.citybird.com	
Condor www.condor.de	**NB** www.evasions.com/airlines1.htm has
Continental www.continental.com	a full list of airline website addresses. If you
Copa www.copaair.com	want to hear horror stories from fellow
Cubana www.cubana.cu	travellers about their airline experience, try
Delta www.delta-air.com	www.traveldesk.com!

Guatemala The principal border town is Tapachula, with a crossing over the Talismán Bridge or at Ciudad Hidalgo. A more interesting route is via Ciudad Cuauhtémoc. For road and river travel see the Yucatán Peninsula.

Belize The border crossing at Santa Elena is near Chetumal, where public transport can be arranged. See Chetumal for details.

Touching down

Airport information When arriving in Mexico by air, make sure you fill in the immigration document before joining the queue to have your passport checked. If you are not given one on the plane, find one in the arrivals hall. Also at Mexico City airport you may be subject to a brief interview by the Federal District Health Service; this is in relation to the control of cholera, yellow fever and other diseases.

Airport departure tax US$17.30 on international flights (dollars or pesos accepted); US$10.50 on internal flights; always check when purchasing if departure tax is included in ticket price.

NB VAT is payable on domestic plane tickets bought in Mexico. Domestic tax on Mexican flights is 15 percent, on international flights 3.75 percent.

Rules, customs & etiquette **Clothing** There is little central heating, so warm clothing is needed in winter especially in the north. Four musts are good walking shoes, sun hats, dark glasses, and flip-flops for the hot sandy beaches. Topless bathing is now accepted in parts of Baja California, but ask first, or do as others do. Casual clothes are adequate for most occasions although men may need a jacket and tie in some restaurants. It is difficult to obtain shoes over US size nine and a half, but it is possible to have them made.

Identification It is becoming increasingly common when visiting offices or tourist sites within government buildings to have to present some form of identification (*identificación* or *credencial*, photocopied passport will usually do), to register one's name, and sometimes to leave the ID with the security guard in exchange for a pass.

Essentials

This can be irksome but remember that the people on the door are only doing their job.

Photography There is a charge of US$4-5 for the use of video cameras at historical sites. If you want to use professional equipment, including a tripod, the fee is US$150 per day. In some parts of Mexico, particularly in the southern states, the local people resent being treated as a tourist attraction; always ask their permission before taking a photograph.

Tipping Tipping is more or less on a level of 10-15 percent; the equivalent of US$0.25 per bag for porters, the equivalent of US$0.20 for bell boys, theatre usherettes, and nothing for a taxi driver unless he gives some extra service. It is not necessary to tip the drivers of hired cars.

Orientation

The words *Norte* (north), *Sur* (south), *Poniente* (west) or *Oriente* (east) after the street name in an address tell where the place is in relation to the Zócalo (central square) or to the main church in a town or city. Avenida 3 Poniente, for example, means the avenue is three blocks west of the Zócalo. In some cities, street names seem more complicated: Avenida 3 Sur Poniente, for example, refers to the west end of the street that is three blocks south of the Zócalo.

Prohibitions

Drugs Note that anyone found in possession of narcotics, in however small a quantity, is liable to a minimum prison sentence of 10 years, with a possible one-year wait for a verdict. Narcotics include 'magic mushrooms'.

Smoking Smoking is not allowed on most forms of public transport, including intercity buses, the metro and *colectivos*; there are generally non-smoking areas in the better restaurants. However, the attitude towards smoking is more relaxed than in the USA and some other countries. The price of a pack of cigarettes ranges from US$0.30-US$1.20; most pharmacies stock cigarettes. Mexican brands are available in airport duty free shops but only for US dollars and at a much higher equivalent price. Ordinary airport shops charge up to 30 percent more than standard shops.

Safety & police

Mexico is generally a safe country to visit, although crime is on the increase and precautions over personal safety should be taken, especially in Mexico City. Never carry valuables visibly or in easily picked pockets. Leave passports, tickets and important documents in a hotel safety deposit, not in your room. Underground pedestrian crossings are hiding places for thieves; take extra care at night. Cars are a prime target for theft; never leave possessions visible inside the car and, at night, always park in hotel car parks. There has also been a rapid rise in robbery by taxi drivers in Mexico City, especially after 2200; drivers stop in poorly lit streets where accomplices get in the cab and assault the passenger. Avoid travelling by bus at night particularly in Guerrero, Oaxaca, Veracruz and Chiapas; if at all possible make journeys in daylight. Couples, and even more, women on their own, should avoid lonely beaches. Those on the west coast are gaining a reputation as drug-landing points. The police service has an equivalent to the Green Angels (Angeles Verdes, see 41), the Silver Angels, who help victims of crime to file a report. US citizens should present this report to the nearest embassy or consulate. Otherwise, it is best to avoid the police if at all possible; they are rarely helpful and tend to make complicated situations even worse. Should you come into contact with them, try to stay as calm and polite as possible. Never offer a bribe unless you are fully conversant with the customs of the country (see Warnings page 42).

Speaking Spanish is a great asset for avoiding rip-offs for gringos, especially short changing and overcharging (both rife), and for making the most of cheap *comedores* and market shopping.

Disabled travellers As in most Latin American countries, facilities for disabled travellers are severely lacking. Most airports and hotels and restaurants in major resorts have wheelchair ramps and adapted toilets, but elsewhere they are rare and pavements are often in a poor state of repair. Disabled Mexicans obviously have to cope with these problems, mainly having to rely on the help of others to get around.

But of course only a minority of disabled people are wheelchair-bound and it is now widely acknowledged that disabilities do not stop you from enjoying a great holiday. Some travel companies are beginning to specialize in exciting holidays, tailor-made for individuals depending on their level of disability. For those with access to the internet, a Global Access – Disabled Travel Network Site is www.geocities.com/Paris/1502 It is dedicated to providing travel information for 'disabled adventurers' and includes a number of reviews and tips from members of the public. You might also want to read *Nothing Ventured*, edited by Alison Walsh (Harper Collins), which gives personal accounts of worldwide journeys by disabled travellers, plus advice and listings.

Gay & lesbian travellers Be aware of 'public decency' laws which allow the police much latitude; for as little as holding hands on the beach you can be arrested, even in Acapulco which has many attractions for gay visitors.

Student travellers If you are in full-time education you will be entitled to an International Student Identity Card, which is distributed by student travel offices and travel agencies in 77 countries. The ISIC gives you special prices on all forms of transport and access to a variety of other concessions and services. If you need to find the location of your nearest ISIC office contact: The ISIC Association, Box 9048, 1000 Copenhagen, Denmark T+45-33939303.

Travelling with children
Make sure you pack that favourite toy. Nothing beats a GameBoy unless it's two GameBoys & a link cable

People contemplating overland travel in Mexico with children should remember that a lot of time can be spent waiting for public transport. You should take reading material with you as it is difficult, and expensive to find.

Food can be a problem if the children are not adaptable. It is easier to take biscuits, drinks, bread, etc with you on longer trips than to rely on meal stops where the food may not be to taste. Avocados are safe, easy to eat and nutritious; they can be fed to babies as young as six months and most older children like them. A small immersion heater and jug for making hot drinks is invaluable, but make sure you get a dual-voltage one (110v and 220v).

Fares On long-distance buses children generally pay half or reduced fares. For shorter trips it is cheaper, if less comfortable, to seat small children on your knee. Often there are spare seats which children can occupy after tickets have been collected. In city and local excursion buses, small children generally do not pay a fare, but are not entitled to a seat when paying customers are standing. On sightseeing tours you should always bargain for a family rate – often children can go free.

All airlines charge reduced fares for children under 12 and 10 percent or less for children under two. Double check the child's baggage allowance – some are as low as 7kg. Note that a child travelling free on a long excursion is not always covered by the operator's travel insurance; it is advisable to pay a small premium to arrange cover.

In all hotels, try to negotiate family rates. If charges are per person, always insist that two children will occupy one bed only, therefore counting as one tariff. If rates are per bed, the same applies. In either case you can almost always get a reduced rate at cheaper hotels.

Travel with children can bring you into closer contact with Mexican families and generally presents no special problems – in fact the path is often smoother for family groups. Officials tend to be more amenable where children are concerned and they are pleased if your child knows a little Spanish. Even thieves and pickpockets seem to have some of the traditional respect for families, and may leave you alone because of it!

Touching down

Hours of business The hours of business in Mexico City are extremely variable. All banks are open from 0900 to 1330 from Monday to Friday, some stay open later, and (head offices only) 0900 to 1230 on Saturday. Business offices usually open at 0900 or 1000 and close at 1300 or 1400. They reopen at 1400 or 1500, but senior executives may not return until much later, although they may then stay until after 1900. Other businesses, especially those on the outskirts of the city, and many Government offices, work from 0800 to 1400 or 1500 and then close for the rest of the day. Business hours in other parts of the country vary considerably according to the climate and local custom.

International Direct Dialling code (IDD) 52. Equal tones with long pauses mean it is ringing. Short equal tones with short pauses indicates it is engaged.

Official time US Central Standard Time, six hours behind GMT; Daylight Saving Time, from first Sunday in April to last Sunday in October, five hours behind GMT. Sonora, Sinaloa, Nayarit and Baja California Sur are seven hours behind GMT; Baja California Norte (above 28th Parallel) is eight hours behind GMT (but seven hours behind GMT between 1 April and end October).

Weights and measures The metric system is compulsory.

Essentials

Women travellers

Some women experience problems, whether accompanied or not; others encounter no difficulties at all. You should be aware that unaccompanied Western women will be subject to close scrutiny and exceptional curiosity. Don't be unduly scared – or flattered. Your average Latino would wolf whistle at his own grandmother if she walked past wearing a potato sack for a dress. Simply be prepared for this and try not to over-react. When you set out, err on the side of caution until your instincts have adjusted to the customs of a new culture. If, as a single woman, you can befriend a local woman, you will learn much more about the country you are visiting.

To help minimize unwanted attention, do not wear suggestive clothing. If politeness fails, do not feel bad about showing offence and departing. When accepting a social invitation, make sure that someone knows the address and the time you left. Ask if you can bring a friend (even if you do not intend to do so). A good rule is always to act with confidence, as though you know where you are going, even if you do not. Someone who looks lost is more likely to attract unwanted attention. Do not disclose to strangers where you are staying.

Women travelling alone should take a wedding ring – a fake one if necessary – to prevent being hassled

Where to stay

Sleeping

Hotel prices in the lower and middle categories are still very reasonable by US and European standards. Prices of top and luxury hotels have risen more steeply. Complaints about standards, etc, may be reported to the Department of Tourism, Presidente Masaryk 172, Colonia Polanco, Mexico City, T52501964 and 52508555. English is spoken at the best hotels. There is a hotel (or *hospedaje*) tax, ranging between one percent and four percent, according to the state, although it is generally levied only when a formal bill is issued.

Beware of 'helpfuls' who try to find you a hotel, as prices quoted at the hotel desk rise to give them a commission.

Casas de huéspedes are usually the cheapest places to stay, although they are often dirty with poor plumbing. Usually a flat rate for a room is charged, so sharing works out cheaper. Sleeping out is possible anywhere, but is not advisable in urban areas. Choose a secluded, relatively invisible spot. Mosquito netting (*pabellón*) is available by the metre in textile shops and, sewn into a sheet sleeping bag, is adequate protection against insects.

☞ *Hotel prices and facilities*

LL (over US$150) to A (US$46-65) Hotels in these categories can be found in most of the large cities but especially where there is a strong concentration of tourists or business travellers. They should offer pool, sauna, gym, jacuzzi, all business facilities (including email), several restaurants and bars. A safe box is usually provided in each room. Credit cards are generally accepted and dollars cash changed usually at poor rates.

B (US$31-45) Hotels in this category should provide more than the standard facilities and a fair degree of comfort. Many include a good breakfast and offer extras such as a colour TV, minibar, air conditioning and a swimming pool. They may also provide tourist information and their own transport for airport pickups. Service is generally good and most accept credit cards although a lower rate for cash is often offered.

C (US$21-30) and D (US$12-20) Hotels in these categories range from very comfortable to functional and there are some real bargains to be had. You should expect your own bathroom, constant hot water, a towel, soap and toilet paper. There is sometimes a restaurant and a communal sitting area. In tropical regions rooms are usually equipped with air conditioning although this may be rather old. Hotels used to catering for foreign tourists and backpackers often have luggage storage, money exchange and kitchen facilities.

E (US$7-11) and F (up to US$6) Hotels in these categories are often extremely simple with bedside or ceiling fans, shared bathrooms and little in the way of furniture. Standards of cleanliness may not be high and rooms may also be rented to couples by the hour.

If backpacking, it is best for one of you to watch over bags while the other goes to book a room and pay for it; some hotels are put off by backpacks. During peak season (November-April), it may be hard to find a room and clerks do not always check to see whether a room is vacant. Insist, or if desperate, provide a suitable tip. The week after Semana Santa (Easter) is normally a holiday, so prices remain high, but resorts are not as crowded as the previous week. When using a lift, remember PB stands for ground floor (*Planta Baja*). Discounts on hotel prices can often be arranged in the low season (May-October), but this is more difficult in the Yucatán and Baja California. There is not a great price difference between single and double rooms. Rooms with double beds are usually cheaper than those with two singles. Check-out time from hotels is commonly 1400. When checking into a hotel, always ask if the doors are locked at night, preventing guests from entering if no night guard is posted. Always check the room before paying in advance. Also ask if there is 24-hour running water.

Motels and auto-hotels, especially in central and south Mexico, are not usually places where guests stay the whole night (you can recognize them by curtains over the garage and red and green lights above the door to show if the room is free). If driving, and wishing to avoid a night on the road, they can be quite acceptable (clean, some have hot water, and in the Yucatán they have a/c), and they tend to be cheaper than other 'more respectable' establishments.

Experiment in International Living Ltd, 'Ostesaga', West Malvern Road, Malvern, Worcestershire, WR14 4EN, UK, T01684-562577, F562212, or Ubierstrasse 30, 5300 Bonn 2, Germany, T0228-957220, F0228-358282, can arrange stays with families in Mexico for up to 4 weeks. This is an excellent way to meet people and learn the language.

NB In the highlands, where it can be cold at night especially in winter, many hotels do not have heating; be prepared. The cheaper hotels often provide only one blanket so you may need a sleeping bag. This applies in popular tourist centres such as San Cristóbal de las Casas, Oaxaca and Pátzcuaro.

OMEGA
RESORTS

...the magic of all inclusive

the ocean smiles... Mazatlan

Omega Oceano Palace

The Oceano Palace is a beach-front resort located on the famous golden zone of Mazatlan "Now" offering the convenience of an ALL-INCLUSIVE vacation. The Resort is known for its fun atmosphere and welcomes guests of all ages. Just 30 minutes from the International Airport and 10 minutes from Mazatlan's revitalized downtown.

mexican atmosphere... Puerto Vallarta

Omega Las Palmas Beach Resort

This exciting Resort is nestled right on the beach in the heart of the hotel zone. Only 15 minutes away from downtown, it offers an exciting atmosphere and exceptional beach front accommodations with a unique and authentic Mexican ambiance.

romantic... Puerto Vallarta

Omega San Marino Plaza

Hotel Omega San Marino Plaza is located in the romantic section of Puerto Vallarta, also called Olas Altas or Los Muertos Beach. Surrounded by beautiful tropical mountains, restaurants, shopping areas and cafés. The action is never ending in this quaint city of Puerto Vallarta

www.omegaresorts.com

Blvd. Francisco Medina Ascencio Km. 2.5 Tels (322) 40650 Fax (322) 40543, Puerto Vallarta, Jalisco, Mexico. contactus@omegaresorts.com

Youth hostels 21 *albergues* exist in Mexico, mostly in small towns; they are usually good value and clean. The hostels take YHA members and non-members, who have to pay more. You have to pay a deposit for sheets, pillow and towel; make sure that this is written in the ledger or else you may not get your deposit back. Hostels have lockers for valuables; take good care of your other possessions.

Camping Most sites are called Trailer Parks, but tents are usually allowed. For camping and youth-hostel accommodation, see page 105, *Villas Deportivas Juveniles*. Beware of people stealing clothes, especially when you hang them up after washing. *Playas Públicas*, with a blue and white sign of a palm tree, are beaches where camping is allowed. They are usually cheap, sometimes free and some have shelters and basic amenities. You can often camp in or near National Parks, although you must speak first with the guards, and usually pay a small fee. Paraffin oil (kerosene) for stoves is called *petróleo para lámparas* in Mexico; it is not a very good quality (dirty) and costs about US$0.05 per litre. It is available from an *expendio*, or *despacho de petróleo*, or from a *tlapalería*, but not from gas stations. Methylated spirits is called *alcohol desnaturalizado* or *alcohol del 96* and is available from chemists. Calor gas is widely available, as it is throughout Central America. *Gasolina blanca* may be bought in *ferreterías* (ironmongers) or paint shops; prices vary widely, also ask for Coleman fuel. Alcohol for heating the burner can be obtained from supermarkets. Repairs to stoves at Servis-Coleman at Plaza de San Juan 5, Mexico City. Katadyn water-purifying filters can be bought in Mexico City at: Katadyn/Dispel, Distribuidores de Purificadores y Electrodomésticos, Francisco Javier Olivares Muñoz, Sinaloa 19 PB, Colonia Roma, CP 06700, México DF, T55330600, F52077174, spare parts also available.

Getting around

Air

Note that the majority of internal routes involve a change in Mexico City, for example there is no direct flight Acapulco-Cancún. Promotional packages for local tourism exist, with 30-40 percent discount, operated by hoteliers, restauranteurs, hauliers and AeroMéxico and Mexicana. These may be the best value if going from and returning to the same city. Their tickets are not interchangeable. Mexicana and AeroMéxico in combination offer MexiPlan tickets, which are for a minimum of two coupons covering five zones of the country; the pass is eligible only to those arriving on transatlantic flights, valid 3-90 days and must be purchased before arrival in Mexico. Fares range from US$50-145 per coupon; extra coupons may be bought and reservations may be changed. There are several other airlines flying internal routes (a few with international flights as well), for example Aero California, Aeromar, Aerolitoral, Taesa, Saro, Aviacsa and Aerocaribe.

Bus

Beware of 'scalpers' who try to sell you a seat at a higher price, which you can usually get on a stand-by basis, when somebody doesn't turn up, at the regular price.

Bus services have been upgraded in recent years and are generally organized, clean and prompt. However, the ordinary traveller should not be beguiled into thinking that it is necessary to purchase an expensive ticket in order to travel comfortably. On many routes, the second, or 'normal', class has disappeared. First class is perfectly satisfactory, but there now exist three superior classes, usually called *Primera Plus*, *Futura* and *Ejecutiva*, which offer various degrees of comfort and extra services. Companies offering these services include UNO (recommended) and ETN, as well as the major bus companies. The extras are reclining seats, toilets, drinks, videos, etc. ETN has exceptional buses with very comfortable, extra-wide seats (only three across) but prices are about 35-40 percent above regular first class. The superior classes are probably best for journeys over six hours, but take a warm garment at night because a/c can be very cold. On daytime journeys consider whether you want to see the scenery or a video. If going on an overnight bus, book seats at the front as toilets get very smelly by morning. You must book in advance for buses travelling in the Yucatán Peninsula, especially around Christmas, but it is also advisable to book if going elsewhere. Some companies, for example ADO, are computerized in main cities, so advance reservations can be made. Bus seats are particularly hard to get during school holidays, August and the 15 days up to New Year when many public servants take holidays in all resorts; transport from Mexico City is booked up in advance and hotels are filled, too. If travelling to a popular tourist destination, try to get on the bus at the starting-point of a route; buses are often full at the mid-point of their journeys. Sometimes it helps to talk to the driver, who has two places to use at his discretion behind his seat (don't sit in these until invited). Lock your luggage to the rack with a cycle lock and chain. If protecting luggage with chicken wire it will set off metal detectors used by Cristóbal Colón bus line in southern Mexico. Stowing your luggage on the roof is not advisable on night buses as theft can occur. Luggage racks on both classes of long-distance bus are spacious and will take a rucksack with a little persuasion (either of the rucksack itself, or the bus driver). However well-organized a company (for example ADO), always check that your luggage is on your bus if you are putting it in the hold.

Second-class buses usually operate from a different terminal from first class buses and are often antiques (interesting, but frustrating when they break down) although they may be brand new. They call at towns and villages and go up side roads the first-class buses never touch. They stop quite as often for meals and toilets as their superiors do and, unlike the first-class buses, people get on and off so often that you may be able to obtain a seat after all. Autobuses Unidos (AU) are usually a little cheaper than other services, but they stop more often, including at the roadside when flagged down. They will not stop on curves, walk until you find a straight stretch. It is not unusual to have to stand on these buses. Some second-class seats are bookable (for example in Baja California), others are not; it depends on the company. In general, it is a good idea to take food and drink with you on a long bus ride, as stops may depend on the driver. When a bus stops for refreshment, remember who your driver is and follow him; also memorize your bus' number so you do not miss it when it leaves.

First-class fares are usually 10 percent dearer than second-class ones and the superior classes are even more. On a long journey you can save the price of a hotel room by travelling overnight, but in many areas this is dangerous and not recommended. Some companies give holders of an international student card a 50 percent discount on bus tickets, especially during the summer holiday period; persistence may be required. Look out for special offers, including discounts at some hotel chains. If making a day trip by bus, do not lose your ticket; you will have to show the driver and operator proof that you have paid for the return. There always seem to be many buses leaving in the early morning. All classes of bus invariably leave on time. Buses are often called *camiones*, hence *central camionero* for bus station. A monthly bus guide is available for US$1 (year's subscription) from Guía de Autotransportes de México, Apartado 8929, México 1, DF.

Car

Vehicles may be brought into Mexico on a Tourist Permit for 180 days each year. The **Permits** necessary documents are: passport, birth certificate or naturalization papers; tourist card; vehicle registration (if you do not own the car, a notarised letter from the vehicle's owner, be it the bank, company, whoever, is necessary); a valid driver's licence. National or international driving licences are accepted. The original and two photocopies are required for each. It takes 10 days to extend a permit, so ask for more time than you expect to need. Don't overstay; driving without an extension gets a US$50 fine for the first five days and then rises abruptly to half the value of the car! US$12 is charged for the permit, payable only by credit card (Visa, Mastercard, American Express or Diners Club), not a debit card, in the name of the car owner, as recorded on the vehicle registration. The American Automobile Association (AAA) is permitted to issue Tourist Permits for 'credit card' entry, free to members, US$20 to non-members; in California this service is available only to members. If you do not have a credit card, you have to buy a refundable bond in cash to the value of the vehicle according to its age (a set scale exists), which is repaid on leaving Mexico. The bond is divided into two parts, the bond itself and administration; the latter, accounting for about 43 percent of the total cost, is retained by the authorities; the bond is refunded. The bond is issued by Afianziadora Mexicana at US/Mexican border crossings, or by Sanborn's (see page 41). It may be waived if you are only going to the State of Sonora, under the Sonora Department of Tourism's 'Only Sonora' programme.

English versions of leaflets giving the rules on temporary importation of vehicles state that you must leave at the same crossing by which you entered. The Spanish versions do not say this and in practice it is not so. The temporary importation permit is multiple entry for 180 days; within that period you can enter and leave by whatever crossing, and as often as you like. Remember, though, that you must have a new tourist card or visa for each new entry.

On entry, go to Migración for your tourist card, on which you must state your means of transport. This is the only record of how you entered the country. At the Banjército desk sign an *Importación Temporal de Vehículos / Promesa de retornar vehículo*, which bears all vehicle and credit card details so that, if you sell your car illegally, your credit card account can be debited for the import duty. Next you purchase the *Solicitud de importación temporal*, which costs US$12; it bears a hologram which matches the dated sticker which must be displayed on the windscreen or, on a motorcycle, on some safe surface. Then go to *Copias* to photocopy all necessary documents and papers issued. The sticker and other entry documents must be surrendered on departure. They can only be surrendered at a Mexican border crossing, with date stickers cancelled by Banjército at Immigration. If you neglect to do this, and re-enter Mexico with an expired uncancelled sticker on you car, you will be fined heavily for each 15-day period that has elapsed since the date of expiry. If you intend to return to Mexico within the 180-day period, having surrendered your sticker and documents, keep safe the *Importación Temporal de Vehículos* form, stamped *Cancelado*, as a receipt. If entry papers are lost there can be much delay and expense (including enforcement of the bond) in order to leave the country. Banjércitco (Banco del Ejército) offices at borders are open daily, for 24 hours, except at Naco (daily 0800-2400), Tecate (daily 0800-1600), Tijuana (Monday-Friday 0800-2200, Saturday 0800-1800, Sunday 1200-1600), Columbia, Texas (Monday-Friday 1000-1800), Ojinaga (Monday-Friday 0730-2100, Saturday 0730-1600, Sunday 0800-1600). Each vehicle must have a different licensed driver (that is, you cannot tow another vehicle into Mexico unless it has a separate driver).

On arrival, you have to find the place where car permits are issued; this may not be at the border. If driving into Mexico from California, Nogales is probably the easiest crossing, which means going first into Arizona. The main car documentation point here is Km 21, south of Nogales. Entering at Tijuana, it seems that car entry permits are given at Mexicali (which means taking the very busy Route 2 through Tecate), or, if you drive through Baja California, at the ferry offices in Santa Rosalía or La Paz. This does not apply if you are not going beyond Baja. In Nuevo Laredo permits are issued at a new complex in town, opposite the train station. If crossing from Brownsville to Matamoros and intend staying longer than 10 days, send a fax with car details to immigration at the border three days before leaving the country. Before crossing the border, pick up the fax and show it at the US side of the border. Most visitors to Mexico at this border are just crossing for shopping and only need a 10-day visa.

According to latest official documents, insurance for foreign cars entering Mexico is not mandatory, but it is highly recommended to be insured. Arranging insurance when crossing from the USA is very easy as there are many offices at US border crossings. Policy prices vary enormously between companies, according to age and type of vehicle, etc.

Insurance
In Mexico foreign insurance will not be honoured; you must ensure that the company you insure with will settle accident claims outside Mexico.

Sanborn's Mexican Insurance Service, with offices in every US border town, and many more, will provide comprehensive insurance, including full-year cover, within Mexico and other parts of Latin America, and provides free 'Travelogs' for Mexico and Central America with useful tips. Their head office is Sanborn's Insurance, Travco Services Inc, 2009 S 10th Street, McAllen, TX 78503, T 956-686 3601, F 956-686 0732, toll free 800-222-0158, info@sanbornsinsurance.com, www.sanbornsinsurance.com. *Tepeyac,* with offices in most Mexican cities, and towns and at border crossings (including Tapachula), and in USA (eg in San Diego, Mexican American Insurance Agency, corner of 6th and A streets, downtown, T2337767); *Aseguradora Mexicana SA* (Asemex), with offices in Tijuana, T850301/04, 24 hours, Ensenada, Mexicali, La Paz, and adjusters throughout Baja California and that border zone; *International Gateway Insurance Brokers* (also offers insurance for Mexican residents visiting USA), PO Box 609, Bonita, CA 92002-0609, T619-4223022, F619-4222671; also 2981 North Grande Av, Nogales, T2819141, F2810430; 1155 Larry Mahan, Suite H, El Paso, Texas, T5956544, F5921293; Hidalgo 79F, Riberas del Pilar, Centro Comercial Máscaras, Chapala, Jalisco, T52559, F54316; Escuela Militar de Aviación 60, Chapultepec, Guadalajara, T152992, F341448; Misión de San Diego, No 1517 Despacho 1C, Tijuana, T341446, F341448; Revolución Morelos s/n, Cabo San Lucas, T31174, F30793; Blvd Costera Miguel de la Madrid, Km 10, Plaza Galerías local 3, Manzanillo. *Mex-Insur* in San Diego CA, T4252390, will issue a policy and refund each full 24 hours not used as long as you return over the Mexican/US border. *Points South Caravan Tours*, 11313 Edmonson Avenue, Moreno Valley, CA 92560-5232, T909-2471222 or toll free USA and Canada 1-800-4211394, offers Mexican insurance.

Entering Mexico from Guatemala presents few local insurance problems now that *Tepeyac* (see above), has an office in Tapachula, and *Seguros La Provincial*, of Avenida General Utrillo 10A, upstairs, San Cristóbal de las Casas, have an office in Cuauhtémoc, Avenida Cuauhtémoc 1217 ground floor, Sr García Figueroa, T5-6040500. Otherwise, try *Segumex* in Tuxtla Gutiérrez. In Mexico City, try *Grupo Nacional Provincial*, Río de la Plata 48, T52867732, who have offices in many towns.

British AA and Dutch ANWB members are reminded that there are ties with the AAA, which extends cover to the US and entitles AA members to free travel information including a very useful book and map on Mexico (note that some AAA offices are not open at weekends or on US holidays). Luggage is no longer inspected at the checkpoints along the road where tourist cards and/or car permits are examined.

The only Japanese makes for which spare parts are sold in Mexico are Datsun and Nissan. Most other cars are US makes.

Spare parts

All petrol stations in Mexico are franchised by Petróleos Mexicanos (PEMEX) and fuel costs the same throughout the country except near the US border, where it may be a bit cheaper. All *gasolina* is now unleaded; the old leaded *Nova* is scare, and impossible to find in big cities, where vehicles must have catalytic convertors. Non-leaded petrol is classified either as *Magna*, from the green pumps, or the more expensive *Premium*, from the red ones. Diesel is also available. Petrol stations are not self-service. Make sure the pump is set at zero before your tank is filled and that your filler cap is put back on before you drive off. Specifiy how much you want either in litres or in money; it is normal to give the attendant a small tip.

Petrol (gasoline)

The free assistance service of the Mexican Tourist Department's green jeeps (Angeles Verdes) patrol most of Mexico's main roads. Every state has an Angeles Verdes Hotline

Assistance

and it is advisable to find out the relevant number when entering each state. The drivers speak English, are trained to give first aid and to make minor auto repairs and deal with flat tyres. They carry gasoline and have radio connection. All help is completely free. Gasoline at cost price. If you want your vehicle to be escorted through Mexico City, offer to pay about US$15, and the police will do it for you.

Parking Multi-storey car parks are becoming more common but parking is often to be found right in city centres under the main square. Whenever possible choose hotels with secure overnight parking. Never leave possessions visible inside a parked car.

Road tolls A toll is called a *cuota*, as opposed to a non-toll road, which is a *vía libre*. There are many toll charges, mostly of US$1 to US2, on roads and bridges. Some new freeways bypassing city centres charge US$4-12, or more. Because of the high cost of toll roads, they are often quite empty, which means that good progress can be made on them. With the privatization of many freeways, hefty tolls are charged to road-users (double the car fee for trailers and trucks). Some can be avoided if you seek local, or motoring club (see above) advice on detours around toll gates (follow trucks). This may involve unpaved roads which should not be attempted in the wet. Two advantages of the expensive *super carretera* toll roads are that they are patrolled and safe, even at night, and drivers are insured against accident or breakdown.

In case of accident Do not abandon your vehicle. Call your insurance company immediately to inform it of the accident. Do not leave Mexico without first filing a claim in Mexico. Do not sign any contract or agreement without a representative of the insurance company being present. Always carry with you, in the insured vehicle, your policy identification card and the names of the company's adjusters (these are the recommendations of Asemex). If, in an accident, bodily injury has occurred or the drivers involved cannot agree who is at fault, the vehicles may be impounded. Drivers will be required to stay in the vicinity in cases of serious accidents, the insured being confined to a hotel (or hospital) until the claim is settled (according to Sanborn's). Should parties to an accident be incarcerated, a bail bond will secure release. A helpline for road accidents is available by phoning 02 and asking the operator to connect you to Mexico City T56849715/56849761.

Warnings On all roads, when two vehicles converge from opposite directions, or when a vehicle is behind a slow cart, bicycle, etc, the driver who first flashes his lights has the right of way. This also applies when a bus or truck wishes to turn left across the opposing traffic: if the driver flashes his lights he is claiming right of way and the oncoming traffic must give way. At *Alto* (Halt) signs, all traffic must come to a complete stop. At a crossroad, however, the first person to come to a complete halt then has precedence to cross. This requires a lot of attention to remember your place in the sequence (this is the same system as in the USA). Do not drive at night. If it is unavoidable don't drive fast; farm and wild animals roam freely. Night-time robberies on vehicles are on the increase especially in Guerrero and Oaxaca States. 'Sleeping policemen' or road bumps can be hazardous in towns and villages as often there are no warning signs; they are sometimes marked *zona de topes*, or incorrectly marked as *vibradores*. In most instances, their distinguishing paint has worn away.

Roadworks are usually well marked. If your vehicle breaks down on the highway and you do not have a warning triangle or a piece of red cloth to act as a warning, cut branches from the roadside and lay them in the road some distance in front of and behind your vehicle.

Foreigners may be searched for drugs on the west coast. The following precautions should help towards an incident-free passage of a drug search. Carry copies of all prescriptions for medicines (typed). Keep medicines in the original container. Carry a notice of all medical conditions that need a hypodermic syringe or emergency treatment. Never take packages for another person. Never take hitchers across a border. Always cross a border in your own vehicle. Check your vehicle carefully for suspicious packages secreted by someone other than yourself. If you have bodywork done in Mexico, supervise it yourself and keep records, even photos, of the workshop that did it. Prior to inspections, open all doors, hatches, etc. Put away all money and valuables. Offer no drinks, cigarettes or gifts to the inspectors; accept none. When searched, cooperate with narcotics officers (who wear black and yellow, and have an identity number on a large fob attached to the belt); do not intrude, but watch the proceedings closely.

If you are stopped by police in town for an offence you have not committed and you know you are in the right, do not pay the 'fine' on the spot. Take the policeman's identity number, show him that you have his number and tell him that you will see his chief (*jefe*) at the tourist police headquarters instead. It is also advisable to go to the precinct station anyway whenever a fine is involved, to make sure it is genuine. If stopped in a remote area, it is not advisable to get into a dispute with a policeman; drugs may be planted in your vehicle or problems may occur.

Note that cars must by law display a number/license plate front and back; as this is not the case in some US States, you may have to improvise.

Tourists' cars cannot, by law, be sold in Mexico. This is very strictly applied. You may not leave the country without the car you entered in, except with written government permission with the car (and trailer if you have one) in bond.

If your car breaks down and cannot be repaired, you must donate it to the Mexican people. This is done through the Secretaría de Hacienda. If you have to leave Mexico in a hurry and cannot take the car with you, you have to get permission from the Secretaría de Hacienda which will keep your car until you return.

Further information A useful source of information and advice (whose help we acknowledge here) is the Recreation Vehicle Owner's Association of British Columbia, Box 2977, Vancouver, BC, V6B 3X4 (members receive RV Times publication; Mexican insurance can be arranged for members). RV tours including Mexico are available from RV Adventuretours, 305 West Nolana Loop #2, McAllen, TX78505, USA. Another recommended source of information in Canada is *Mexi-Can Holidays Ltd*, 150-332 Water St, Vancouver, BC V6B 1B6, T604-6853375, F604-6853321. Motorists are referred to: *Clubmex*, PO Box 1646, Bonita, California 91908, USA, T619-5853033, F619-4208133, which publishes a regular newsletter for its members (annual subscription US$35). The newsletter gives useful information and advice for drivers, specialist trips for sport fishing enthusiasts, and some interesting travel articles. Clubmex also arranges insurance for members. *Mexico Travel Monthly Report*, Carolyn Files, Box 1498, Imperial Beach, CA 91933-1498, T/F619-4296566, has also been recommended. *Winter in Mexico Caravans Inc* (a member of The Escapees Club, which issues a bi-monthly newsletter), 101 Rainbow Drive, Livingston, TX77351, T303-7619829, offers advice on caravan trips to Mexico, runs tours for caravanners, including a bird-watching tour, and issues its own bulletin. *RVing in Mexico, Central America and Panamá*, by John and Liz Plaxton (Travel 'N Write, Canada, 1996) has been recommended as full of useful information. Also *Aim*, on retirement and travel in Mexico, Apartado postal 31-70, Guadalajara 45050, Jalisco.

Car hire Car rental is very expensive in Mexico and 15 percent VAT is added to rental costs. Rates will vary from city to city. It can be cheaper to arrange hire in the US or Europe, but rentals booked abroad cannot be guaranteed (though usually they are). Proceed with caution. At some tourist resorts, however, such as Cancún, you can pick up a VW beetle convertible for US$25 per day, which you will not be told about abroad. Renting a vehicle is nearly impossible without a credit card. It is twice as expensive to leave a car at a different point from the starting point than a round trip. Check the spare tyre, that the fuel gauge works and that you have been given a full tank, that the insurance is valid on unmade roads and that you know how the alarm (if fitted) turns off, the car will not go if the alarm is set off. A short length of strong chain and a padlock for securing the boot/trunk are worthwhile for VW beetles (Mexican models are the cheapest cars available for hire but do not come with any frills, a/c, radio, etc).

Bicycle

At first glance a bicycle may not appear to be the most obvious vehicle for a major journey, but given ample time and reasonable energy it most certainly is the best. It can be ridden, carried by almost every form of transport from an aeroplane to a canoe, and can even be lifted across one's shoulders over short distances. Cyclists can be the envy of travellers using more orthodox transport since they can travel at their own pace, explore more remote regions and meet people who are not normally in contact with tourists.

Choosing a bicycle
The choice of bicycle depends on the type and length of expedition being undertaken and on the terrain and road surfaces likely to be encountered. Unless you are planning a journey almost exclusively on paved roads – when a high quality touring bike such as a Dawes Super Galaxy would probably suffice – a mountain bike is strongly recommended. The good quality ones (and the cast iron rule is never to skimp on quality) are incredibly tough and rugged, with low gear ratios for difficult terrain, wide tyres with plenty of tread for good road-holding, cantilever brakes, and a low centre of gravity for improved stability.

Bicycle equipment
A small but comprehensive tool kit (to include chain rivet and crank removers, a spoke key and possibly a block remover), a spare tyre and inner tubes, a puncture repair kit with plenty of extra patches and glue, a set of brake blocks, brake and gear cables and all types of nuts and bolts, at least 12 spokes (best taped to the chain stay), a light oil for the chain (for example Finish-Line Teflon Dry-Lube), tube of waterproof grease, a pump secured by a pump lock, a Blackburn parking block (a most invaluable accessory, cheap and virtually weightless), a cyclometer, a loud bell, and a secure lock and chain. *Richard's Bicycle Book* makes useful reading for even the most mechanically minded.

Luggage & equipment
Strong and waterproof front and back panniers are a must. When packed these are likely to be heavy and should be carried on the strongest racks available. Poor quality racks have ruined many a journey for they take incredible strain on unpaved roads. A top bag cum rucksack (eg Carradice) makes a good addition for use on and off the bike. A Cannondale front bag is good for maps, camera, compass, altimeter, notebook and small tape-recorder. (Other recommended panniers are Ortlieb – front and back – which is waterpoof and almost 'sandproof', Mac-Pac, Madden and Karimoor.) 'Gaffa' tape is excellent for protecting vulnerable parts of panniers and for carrying out all manner of repairs.

All equipment and clothes should be packed in plastic bags to give extra protection against dust and rain. (Also protect all documents, etc carried close to the body from sweat.) Always take the minimum clothing. It's better to buy extra items *en route* when you find you need them. Naturally the choice will depend on whether you are planning a journey through tropical lowlands, deserts, high mountains or a combination, and whether rain is to be expected. Generally it is best to carry several layers of thin light clothes than fewer heavy, bulky ones. Always keep one set of dry clothes, including long trousers, to put on at the end of the day. The incredibly light, strong, waterproof and wind resistant goretex jacket and overtrousers are invaluable. Training shoes can be used for both cycling and walking.

Useful tips
Wind, not hills is the enemy of the cyclist. Try to make the best use of the times of day when there is little; mornings tend to be best but there is no steadfast rule. Take care to avoid dehydration, by drinking regularly. In hot, dry areas with limited supplies of

water, be sure to carry an ample supply. For food, carry the staples (sugar, salt, dried milk, tea, coffee, porridge oats, raisins, dried soups, etc) and supplement these with whatever local foods can be found in the markets. Give your bicycle a thorough daily check for loose nuts, bolts or bearings. See that all parts run smoothly. A good chain should last 2,000 miles, 3,200 km or more, but be sure to keep it as clean as possible – an old toothbrush is good for this – and to oil it lightly from time to time. Always camp out of sight of a road. Remember that thieves are attracted to towns and cities, so when sight-seeing, try to leave your bicycle with someone such as a café owner or a priest. Country people tend to be more honest and are usually friendly and very inquisitive. However, don't take unnecessary risks; always see that your bicycle is secure (most hotels will allow bikes to be kept in rooms). In more remote regions dogs can be vicious; carry a stick or some small stones to frighten them off.

Mexico offers plenty of enjoyable places for riding. The main problems facing cyclists are the heavy traffic which will be encountered on main roads, the poor condition of these roads and the lack of specialized spare parts particularly for mountain bikes. It is possible to find most bike spares in the big cities, but outside these places it is only possible to find the basics: spokes, tyres, tubes, etc. Traffic is particularly bad around Mexico City and on the road between Mazatlán and Guadalajara. The easiest region for cycling is the Gulf of Mexico coast, however, many of the roads are dead flat, straight and generally boring. The mountains may appear intimidating, but gradients are not difficult as clapped-out buses and trucks have to be able to climb them. Consequently, much of the best riding is in the sierra. If cycling in Baja, avoid riding in mid-summer; even during October temperatures can reach 45°C+ and water is very scarce all the time. Also beware of Mexican bike mechanics who will attempt to repair your bike rather than admit that they don't know what they are doing, particularly when it comes to mountain bikes. The toll roads are generally preferable to the ordinary highways for cyclists; there is less traffic, more lanes and a wide paved shoulder. Some toll roads have 'no cyclists' signs but usually the police pay no attention. If you walk your bicycle on the pavement through the toll station you don't have to pay. If using the toll roads, take lots of water as there are few facilities. Cycling on some main roads can be very dangerous; it is useful to fit a rear view mirror.

It is reported that you are allowed to take bicycles on any bus in Mexico, free of charge, and airlines (AeroMéxico for one) should do the same, although they may need to be packed. Some bus drivers, however, will expect a tip when loading the luggage. There are about 20 bicycle shops in Mexico City, one next to the other, on the street that leads from the Mercado Merced towards the Zócalo, Merced metro station. Make sure you insist on quality, known-brand parts, as some of the Mexican brands are made out of inferior/soft material. Most Mexican bicycles have 28-inch wheels, so this size of tyre is easy to find; good 26-inch tyres for road use can be found, but are rare.

The Expedition Advisory Centre, administered by the Royal Geographical Society, 1, Kensington Gore, London SW7 2AR has published a useful monograph entitled *Bicycle Expeditions*, by Paul Vickers. Published in March 1990, it is available direct from the Centre, price £6.50 (postage extra if outside the UK). In the UK there is also the Cyclist's Touring Club, CTC, Cotterell House, 69 Meadrow, Godalming, Surrey, GU7 3HS, T01483-417217, cycling@ctc.org.uk, for touring, and technical information.

Hitchhiking

Hitchhiking is usually possible for single hikers, but apparently less easy for couples. It is generally quick, but not universally safe (seek local advice). Do not, for example, try to hitch in those parts of Guerrero and Oaxaca States where even driving alone is not recommended. In more out of the way parts, short rides from village to village are usually the rule, so progress can be slow. Getting out of big cities is best done by taking a local bus out of town in the direction of the road you intend to take. Ask for the bus to take the *Salida* (exit) to the next city on that road. From Mexico City to the US border, the route via Tula, Ciudad Valles, Ciudad Victoria and the Sierra Madre Oriental, is scenic but slow through the mountains. The quicker route is via Querétaro, San Luis Potosí and Matehuala. Elsewhere, the most difficult stretches are reported to be Acapulco-Puerto Escondido, Santa Cruz-Salina Cruz and Tulum-Chetumal. It is very easy to hitch short distances, such as the last few km to an archaeological site off the main road; offer to pay something, like US$0.50.

Motorbikes

Motor-cycling is good in Mexico as most main roads are in fairly good condition and hotels are usually willing to allow the bike to be parked in a courtyard or patio. In the major tourist centres, such as Acapulco, Puerto Vallarta or Cancún, motorbike parts can be found as there are Honda dealers for bike and jet ski rentals. All Japanese parts are sold only by one shop in Mexico City at extortionate prices (but parts and accessories are easily available in Guatemala at reasonable prices for those travelling there). Recommended for BMW repairs and some parts is BMW Mexico City, Grupo Baviera SA de CV, Calzada de Tlalpan 4585, Apartado postal 22-217-CP 14330, T55734900.

Taxis

To avoid overcharging, the Government has taken control of taxi services from airports to cities and only those with government licences are allowed to carry passengers from the airport. In some cities you do not pay the driver but purchase a ticket from a booth before leaving the airport. No further tipping is then required, except when the driver handles heavy luggage or provides some extra service for you. The same system has been applied at bus stations but it is possible to pay the driver direct. Avoid flagging down taxis in the street at night in Mexico City. It is safer to phone for a *sitio* taxi from your hotel.

Train

Check locally to find out whether trains are running or at: www.ferrocarriles.com.

Much of the passenger equipment in use dates from the forties or fifties. Some railways are being privatized and passenger services have dwindled considerably and may continue to change. Tickets are booked directly at the station. The famous Chihuahua-al-Pacífico, considered one of the worlds greatest railroad, is still running a service (see page 623).

Keeping in touch

Internet
A list of useful websites is given on page 74

It is now de rigeur amongst travellers to get an email address you can access through the internet – such as hotmail. As in many traveller-type places nowadays, internet access in Mexico is extensive and often easier and more reliable than the phone. Every major town now has at least one internet café, with more springing up daily. It has now overtaken post and telephone as the main means of communication with home. It works out much, much cheaper than phoning home. In saying that, the costs do mount up if you use it regularly and if you are travelling on a tight budget, allow a little extra for its access. It is also useful for booking hotels and tours and for checking out information on the web. A list of some (but not all) cybercafés in Mexico can be found at the website of the Asociación Mexicana de Cyber Cafés: www.amcc.org.mx.

Rates are raised periodically in line with the peso's devaluation against the dollar but **Postal services** are reported to vary between towns. They are posted next to the windows where stamps are sold. Rates in pesos are: within Mexico, letters up to 20 grammes $2.60, postcards $1.80; to North and Central America and the Caribbean: letters $3.90 (20 grammes), postcards $2.90; South America and Europe $4.90, postcards $3.50; Asia and Australia $5.50, postcards $4.00. International service has improved and bright red mailboxes, found in many parts of the city, are reliable for letters. Weight limit two kilograms (five kilograms for books) from Mexico to the UK. Surface mail takes about three months to Europe. Small parcel rate is cheaper. Parcel counters often close earlier than other sections of the post office in Mexico. See below for the accelerated service, Mexpost. As for most of Latin America, send printed matter such as magazines registered. Many travellers have recommended that one should not use the post to send film or cherished objects as losses are frequent. Do not seal overseas parcels before visiting the post office, as they have to be inspected before sending. A permit is needed from the Bellas Artes office to send paintings or drawings out of Mexico. Not all these services are obtainable outside Mexico City; delivery times in/from the interior may well be longer than those from Mexico City. Poste Restante ('general delivery' in the US, *lista de correos* in Mexico) functions quite reliably, but you may have to ask under each of your names; mail is sent back after 10 days (for an extension write to the Jefe de la Administración of the post office holding your mail, any other post office will help with this). Address 'favor de retener hasta llegada' on envelope.

Within Mexico many businesses use first and second-class passenger buses to deliver letters and parcels. Each piece is signed for and must be collected at the destination. The service is considered quick and reliable. Should it be necessary to send anything swiftly and safely (in Mexico and other countries), there are many courier firms; the post office's own EMS/Mexpost accelerated service, paid for by weight, is quick and reliable, otherwise the best known is DHL (Mexico City T52270299), but it is about twice the cost of Estrella Blanca (T53686577) or Federal Express (T52289904).

Most public phones take phone cards only (Ladatel) costing 25, 50 or 100 pesos from **Telephone** shops and news kiosks everywhere. AT&T's USA Direct service is available, for **services** information in Mexico dial 412-5537458, ext 359. From LADA phones (see below), dial **01, similar for AT&T credit cards. To use calling cards to Canada T95-800-0101990. Commercially run *casetas*, or booths (for example Computel), where you pay after phoning, are up to twice as expensive as private phones, and charges vary from place to place. Computel's main office is on the 27th floor of the Torre Latinoamericana in Mexico City. They have offices countrywide with long opening hours (if using commercial booths to make credit-card calls, check in advance what charges are imposed). The cost of credit-card calls is not usually posted but has been quoted as follows: to US US$39 for first eight minutes, then US$2 for each subsequent minute. For the UK, it was US$31 for first five minutes, then US$1 for each subsequent minute. However, it would seem that the charges levied may be much higher, so be wary. It is better to call collect from private phones, but better still to use the LADA system. Reverse-charge (collect) calls on LADA can be made from any blue public phone, say you want to *llamar por cobrar*; silver phones are for local and direct long-distance calls, some take coins. Others take foreign credit cards (Visa, Mastercard, not Amex; not all phones that say they take cards accept them, others that say they don't do).

NB Transatlantic calls cannot be made on a 25-peso LADA phone card. LADA numbers are: 01 long distance within Mexico, add city code and number (half-price Sunday); 001 long distance to USA and Canada, add area code and number; 00 to rest of the world, add country code, city code and number; it is not possible to call collect to Germany, but it is possible to Israel. Cheap rates vary according to the country called. For information dial 07 or 611-1100. Foreign calls (through the operator, at least) cannot be made from

1230 on 24 December until the end of Christmas Day. The Directorio Telefónico Nacional Turístico is full of useful information, including LADA details, federal tourist offices, time zones, yellow pages for each state, sights and maps.

Telecommuni- Telégrafos Nacionales maintains the national and international telegraph systems,
cations separate from the Post Office. There is a special office at Balderas 14-18, just near the corner of Colón, in Mexico City to deal with international traffic (open 0800-2300, Metro Hidalgo, exit Calle Basilio Badillo). There are three types of telegraph service: *extra urgente*, *urgente* and *ordinario*; they can only be prepaid, not sent collect. There is a telegraph and telex service available at Mexico City airport. Fax is common in main post offices.

Media **Newspapers** The more important journals are in Mexico City. The most influential
La Jornada publishes a dailies are: *Excelsior, Novedades, El Día, Uno Más Uno; The News,* in English, now available
supplement, Tiempo in all main cities (Grupo Novedades, which comprises *Novedades* and *The News* has a
Libre, on Thursday, web site at www.novedades.com.mx); *The Mexico City Times* (in English, less
listing the week's US-oriented than The News); *El Universal (El Universal Gráfico); El Heraldo; La Jornada*
cultural activities. (more to the left is on-line at unam.netgate.net/jornada); *La Prensa,* a popular tabloid, has the largest circulation. *El Nacional* is the mouthpiece of the Government.

In Guadalajara, *El Occidental, El Informador* and *Siglo 21. The Guadalajara Reporter,* the weekly English-language newspaper, has a monthly on-line edition at www.guadalajara-reporter.com/. *Siglo 21* is on-line at mexplaza.udg.mx/Siglo 21, and *El Informador* at www.infored.com.mx. There are influential weekly magazines *Proceso, Siempre; Epoca,* and *Quehacer Político.* The political satirical weekly is *Los Agachados.*

The New York edition of the *Financial Times* is usually available on the day of issue (from about 1000) at various shops at Mexico City Airport, also from the Casa del Libro, Calle Florencia 37 Zona Rosa, as well as from shops at Hamburgo 141, Zona Rosa and Homero, Polanco. Other British and European papers (two to three days old) are available from the same places.

Food and drink

Food Because of the use of chilli as the principal seasoning in Mexican cooking, it is usually
The best value is perceived as spicy or hot. However, there is another element that is even more
undoubtedly in small, characteristic and which visitors become aware of as they get to know the wide range
family-run places. of Mexican dishes. Maize, or corn, has been a staple crop from oldest times not only in Mexico but in the continent as a whole. Maize can be seen in what is called *antojitos* (light snacks which may be eaten by themselves or as a starter), some of the most common of which are *quesadillas, sopes, tostadas, tlacoyos* and *gorditas,* which consist of various shapes and sizes of *tortillas,* with a variety of fillings and usually garnished with a hot sauce. Tasting such offerings, wrapped in maize, will probably be the visitor's first introduction to Mexican food.

Much has been written since the 1960s about the evolution of Mexican food and the manner of its preparation, and experts suggest that there are three important stages: first, the combination of the indigenous and the Spanish; later, the influence of other European cuisines, notably the French in the 19th century; and finally, the adoption, in the 20th century, of exotic oriental dishes and fast-food from the USA.

Food for most Mexicans represents an integral part of their national identity, and this fact is immediately seen in their desire to offer visitors an excess of the most typical dishes and specialities.

Certain dishes such as *mole* (chicken or turkey prepared in a chilli-based sauce) or *pozole* (a pot-au-feu with a base of maize and stock) are closer to indigenous traditions. Others, however, are of more recent creation, for example the following

Food and drink glossary

Drinks: bebidas
Beer *cerveza*
Coffee *café*
Milk *leche*
Mineral water *agua mineral*
Tea *té*
Wine *vino*

Fish: pescado
Bass *robalo*
Dogfish *cazón*
Dolphin (fish) *dorado*
Grouper *mero*
Red snapper *huachinango*
Trout *trucha*
Tuna *atún*

Fruits: frutas
Avocado *aguacate*
Banana *plátano*
Blackberry *zarzamora*
Coconut *coco*
Guava *guayaba*
Orange *naranja*

Passion fruit *granada*
Pawpaw *papaya*
Pineapple *piña*
Strawberry *fresa*
Tamarind *tamarindo*
Watermelon *sandía*

Meat: carne
Bacon *tocino*
Beef *res*
Chicken *pollo*
Chop *chuleta*
Goat *chivo*
Ham *jamón*
Hamburger *hamburguesa*
Hot dog *perro caliente*
Lamb *cordero*
Liver *hígado*
Pork *puerco*
Ribs *costillas*
Sausage *chorizo/salchicha*
Tenderloin *lomo*
Tongue *lengua*

Seafood: mariscos
Crab *cangrejo*

Lobster *langosta*
Octopus *pulpo*
Shrimps *camarones*
Squid *calamares*

Vegetables: legumbres
Beans *frijoles*
Carrot *zanahoria*
French fries *papas fritas*
Lettuce *lechuga*
Mushrooms *hongos/ champiñones*
Palm hearts *palmito*
Peas *chícharos*
Rice *arroz*
Salad *ensalada*

Others
Bread *pan*
Cheese *queso*
Egg *huevo*
Butter *mantequilla*
Jam *mermelada*
Ice-cream *helado*

Essentials

breakfast dishes, all with eggs: *huevos rancheros* (fried, with spicy sauce on a bed of *tortillas*), *machaca norteña* (scrambled with dried minced beef), *huevos motuleños* (fried with sauce of tomatoes, peas, cheese and fried banana) and *huevos a la mexicana* (scrambled with chilli and tomatoes).

As one travels around Mexico it becomes apparent that in certain provincial cities food takes on a more European aspect, whereas in others it seems to belong to the period when the process of development and integration was still taking place. Furthermore, there are so many regional specialities all over the country that it is difficult to use such a simple term as 'Mexican cooking'.

This is not a complete list by any means, but the visitor should try to sample some of these regional specialities:

Chihuahua *Machaca con huevo*, eggs with dried minced beef
Monterrey and **Coahuila** *Cabrito al pastor*, spit-roast goat; *frijoles charros*, beans with bacon and chilli
Tamaulipas *Carne asada a la tampiqueña*, grilled strips of beef with salad
Tlaxcala *Sopa tlaxcalteca*, soup with mushrooms and *tortilla*, usually spicy
San Luis Potosí *Enchiladas potosinas*, non-spicy coated red tortillas)
Guanajuato *Enchiladas mineras*, large *tortillas* filled with salad of potato, chicken, lettuce and radishes
Michoacán and **Jalisco** *Pozole* (see above), *Birria*, goat-meat
Durango and **Aguascalientes** *Menudo*, tripe
Sinaloa *Chilorio*, loin of pork in chilli sauce
Veracruz *Huachinango a la veracruzana*, red snapper in sauce of tomatoes, olives and onion; *ceviche*, cold marinated fish

Essentials

 ### In search of the best tortillas

The tortilla in Mexico (not to be confused with the tortilla in Spain which is a sort of omelette) consists of unleavened corn dough pressed into a round, thin pancake then cooked on a very hot, un-greased griddle. The unleavened corn dough, called masa, is made from parched corn kernels which are briefly cooked in a solution of slaked lime and water, then left to soak until they are soft enough to be ground into the smooth dough.

Tortillas are the bread of Mexico, a staple served with every meal, and used in an astonishing variety of ways to create numerous kinds of Mexican fast food as well as fine Mexican cuisine. Everything from tacos (tortillas stuffed with various fillings), quesadillas (tortilla filled with cheese or other ingredients before being cooked), tostadas (tortillas fried flat and used as a 'plate' for shredded meat and salad), tostaditas or totopos (tortillas cut up and fried crisp for dipping, known now as nachos) and enchiladas (soft tortillas dipped in hot tomato sauce and used to wrap various fillings).

Tortillas used to be made entirely by hand, and many still are, but with so much demand, more and more tortillas are mass produced by extraordinary assembly line machines which can often be seen in one corner of the market or at the local tortilla factory.

Like bread, not all tortillas are created equal. Anyone who has travelled throughout Mexico notices that the colour, consistency and taste vary. In DF (Mexico City), many tortillas are yellowish and bland, made with basic 'industrial grade' masa. These tortillas are tolerated, even by the millions of people who move in from the country to the capital to work, as a necessary evil of city life, but they are equivalent to plain white sliced bread in North America or Europe. With tortillas, as opposed to white bread, the whiter appearance is often a clue that they will taste better (a dirty yellow colour is also a sign of too much lime in the cooking water).

Among the white and yellow corn tortillas, the different kinds are also partly due to the many kinds of corn grown all over Mexico, some of them more

Yucatán Cochinita pibil, pieces of chicken with hot sweet chilli sauce, wrapped in banana leaves; huevos motuleños (see above); sopa de lima, chicken broth with giblets, fried tortillas, sweet chilli and lime

Chiapas Tamales chiapanecos, maize pancake cooked in banana leaves

Oaxaca Mole negro, as above, but with sauce based on chilli and chocolate; Cecina, beef which has been treated with adobo, a red chilli paste

Puebla Mole (see above); Tinga, beef or chicken meat pulled into fibrous strips in a tomato and chilli sauce; Chile en nogada, stuffed peppers with white almond sauce and red pomegranate seeds, echoing the green, white and red of the Mexican flag

In all the states of the Republic, as well as in Mexico City, there are traces of Mexico's culinary inheritance from Spain, for example albóndigas (meatballs), salpicón (cold cooked beef with salad), picadillo (minced beef with tomatoes and other vegetables), rope vieja (beef pulled into fibrous strips with a tomato-based sauce and peas), caldo de pollo (chicken-based broth with vegetables and seasoned with coriander), sopa Juliana, soups made from lentils (lentejas) or broad beans (habas), croquetas (rissoles), huevos ahogados (hard-boiled eggs in a tomato-based sauce), and, amongst sweet dishes, arroz con leche (rice pudding), flan (crème caramel), torrejas (bread soaked in honey and fried), turrón (nougat) and ate (jelly made from quince – membrillo – or other fruit).

All the main dishes and desserts just mentioned belong to what one may call Mexican 'home cooking', but they are also to be found in what is part of the daily diet for many Mexicans, that is to say the comida corrida. The latter is usually served between 1300-1700, and typically consists of a bowl of caldo de pollo or sopa de pasta

Essentials

commercial and others rather ancient varieties that may be uniquely adapted to a particular mountain elevation, soil, rainfall, amount of sun and length of season.

There are also blue corn tortillas (made from blue masa) which have an almost nutty, slightly heavier taste. Sometimes the blue corn masa harina (flour) used to make these tortillas is greenish or even blackish blue, making for an exotic eating experience.

One of our contributors once conducted a search for the best tortillas within a 100-km radius of Mexico City. He drove from mountain valley to valley, stopping to look at markets, food stalls and corn or maize fields. He found the Chalqueno landrace corn in the fields around Cocotitlán and teosinte, the wild relative of corn, south of Tenango del Aire. Fifteen km east of Highway 115 on the winding road just outside Tlayacapan on the road to Totolapan, he stopped at a line of roadside stands where he had been told that many Mexicans in the know stop en route to the coast. Here, a very white corn is pressed by hand into some of the

freshest, finest, most delicate yet flavoursome tortillas he had tasted. A local farmer led him to his field and to see his secret. It was a variety of corn adapted to this particular valley. It was called ancho which means wide, but which, in the context of corn flavour, has the added connotation of 'full bodied'. Stripping down the silk tassels, the plump ears were filled with the largest kernels of corn he had ever seen. They were not at all uniform, set in neat rows, but each kernel was plump and juicy – up to four times the size of an 'ordinary' kernel of corn.

A small hand tortilla press can be bought for a few pesos in Mexican markets which sell kitchen and hardware. Fresh or frozen masa can be bought at Mexican grocery stores, and sometimes in health food stores in the US. There is also a passable packaged variety of masa flour called masa harina made by Quaker which sells at supermarkets in North America and sometimes in health food stores in Europe. This makes a passable tortilla as well – much better than the packaged, frozen or canned varieties.

(noodles or similar), a plate of rice, a main dish and sometimes a dessert and/or a jug of *agua de frutas* (made with water and fresh fruit).

These menus can be found in middle category restaurants as well as cheaper ones, also inside covered markets, where very often the smaller eating-places are called *fondas*.

To help visitors who are not familiar with Mexican food but who wish to get to know some traditional dishes, we suggest that they start by choosing from:

Sopa de tortilla tomato-based soup with shredded tortillas

Sopa azteca similar but with chilli

Caldo de pollo see above

Caldo tlalpeño *caldo de pollo*, chicken, sometimes with rice, avocado, highly spiced

Guacamole mashed avocado, green tomatoes, with onion, coriander, sometimes with chilli

Ensalada de nopales cactus-leaf salad

Enchiladas verdes fried *tortillas* filled with chicken with green tomato sauce, sprinkled with onion and cream

Enchiladas rojas same with red *mole*

Chilaquiles verdes small fried *tortillas* with green tomato sauce

Chilaquiles rojos same with red tomato sauce

Enfrijoladas fried *tortillas* with a bean-based sauce, with cheese, cream and onion

Mole poblano see above

Pipián chicken or pork in a chilli-based sauce with almonds, peanuts or pumpkin-seeds

Mixiotes chicken or rabbit wrapped in leaves of the maguey

Tamales meat and chilli sauce wrapped in corn dough and then in maize or banana leaves and steamed. Sweet *tamales*, with pineapple, strawberries and nuts are also delicious, while chilli and cheese *tamales* are suitable for vegetarians

Pozole see above

Barbacoa lamb or goat cooked in holes in the ground

Chiles en nogada see above

Tacos rolled up *tortillas* usually filled with chicken or beef, soft or crisp – *doradas* Quesadillas doubled-over *tortillas*, heated, slightly crisp, filled with one or more of beef, chicken, cheese, *rajas* (green peppers), spinach, *flor de calabaza* (pumpkin flower), mashed potato, *chorizo* (spicy sausage), *nopal* (see above) or *huitlacoche* (a fungus that grows in the ear of maize)

NB 'green tomatoes' are not unripe red ones, but a different variety which even when ripe (green), have a slightly bitter taste; in Mexican Spanish the green *tomato* is tomate and the red variety is *jitomate*.

These dishes may be preceded by *tequila, pulque* (a sweet fermented cactus drink), *tepache* (fermented pineapple), accompanied by *aguas de fruta* or Mexican beers, and followed by chocolate, coffee (especially *café de olla* – with cinnamon) and *atole* (sweet maize-based drink with milk).

After these challenges have been successfully met, you might like to progress, and try some of the insects that have, so to speak, found their way into Mexican cooking, for example: *jumiles* (a sort of beetle: eaten alive or fried, by themselves or in *tacos*) from Taxco/Guerrero; *chapulines* (grasshoppers: fried, ditto) from Oaxaca and Puebla, or *gusanos de maguey* (maguey worms: fried and seasoned with garlic, served with *guacamole*), from Tlaxcala.

All these experiences, taken together, will show how broad and yet how regional, how traditional and yet how open to foreign influences, Mexican cooking can be – a far cry indeed from 'Tex-Mex' in London or New York! – and will encourage the traveller to return to find out more – and enjoy the experience.

Usual meals are breakfast (which can consist of several courses), and a heavy lunch between 1400 and 1500. Supper, between 1800 and 2000, is light. Many restaurants give foreigners the menu without the *comida corrida* (set meals), so forcing them to order à la carte at double the price; watch this! Try to avoid eating in restaurants which don't post a menu. Meals in modest establishments cost about US$1.50-2 for breakfast, US$2-3 for set lunch (US$3-5.50 for a special *comida corrida*) and US$5-8 for dinner (generally no set menu). A la carte meals at modest establishments cost about US$7; a very good meal can be had for US$11 at a middle-level establishment. Much higher prices are charged by the classiest restaurants (for example, in Mexico City, US$15-22 medium class, US$30 first class, US$40 luxury). For those who are self-catering, the cost of food in markets and supermarkets is not high. In resort areas the posh hotels include breakfast and dinner in many cases. Check bills and change; even if service is included waiters have been known to deduct a further tip from the change; they will hand it back if challenged. In some restaurants, beer will not be served unless a meal is ordered.

Drink

There are few outdoor drinking places in Mexico except in tourist spots

The beer is good: brands include Dos Equis-XX, Montejo, Bohemia, Sol and Superior. Negra Modelo is a dark beer, it has the same alcohol content as the other beers. Some beer is drunk with lime juice and a salt-rimmed glass, or *michelada* with chilli sauce (both available in Oaxaca). Local wine is cheap and improving in quality; try Domecq, Casa Madero or Santo Tomás; the white sold in *ostionerías*, oyster restaurants, is usually good. Cetto Riesling Fumé has been recommended. The native drinks are *pulque*, the fermented juice of the agave plant (those unaccustomed to it should not over-indulge), *tequila*, made mostly in Jalisco, and *mezcal* from Oaxaca; also distilled from agave plants. *Mezcal* usually has a *gusano de maguey* (worm) in the bottle, considered by Mexicans to be a particular delicacy. Tequila and *mezcal* rarely have an alcoholic content above 40-43 percent; tequila Herradura, Sauza and Cuervo have been recommended. Also available is the Spanish aniseed spirit, *anís*, which is made locally. Imported whiskies and brandies are expensive. Rum is cheap and good. *Puro de caña* (called *chingre* in Chinanteca and *posh* in Chamula) is distilled from sugar cane, stronger than *mezcal* but with less taste; it is found in Oaxaca and Chiapas.

There are always plenty of non-alcoholic soft drinks (*refrescos*) and mineral water (bottled water is available throughout the country in small bottles or more economical large ones which are useful to refill small ones). Fresh juices (as long as they aren't mixed with unpurified water) and milk shakes (*licuados*) are good and usually safe. If you don't like to drink out of a glass ask for a straw, *popote*. Herbal teas, for example chamomile and mint (*manzanilla* and *hierba buena*), are readily available.

Essentials

Shopping

Wandering around the colourful markets and *artesanía* shops is one of the highlights of any visit to Mexico. And the variety of wonderful folk art on offer is mindboggling.

Artesanía in Mexico is an amalgam of ancient and modern design. The stronger
influence, however, is undoubtedly the traditional popular art forms of indigenous
communities the length and breadth of the country which pour into colonial towns
such as Oaxaca, San Cristóbal, Pátzcuaro, and Uruapan. These are convenient market
centres for seeing the superb range of products from functional pots to scary masks
hanging over delicately embroidered robes and gleaming lacquered chests. Almost
everything can be found in Mexico City and most regional capitals have a *Casa de las
Artesanías* with exhibitions, and sometimes sales, of local craftwork. But it is almost
invariably cheaper to buy crafts away from the capital or major tourist centres, perhaps
from the *artesanos* themselves. Bargaining is usually acceptable but don't push it for
what, to you, is only a small amount of money. It is often rewarding to take the time to
visit the villages where the designs were originally conceived and where the *artesanía*
is still made. Here are some of the products on offer and their sites of making.

Crafts

Weaving and textile design has a lineage that is both long and varied. The blouse, of
pre-Hispanic origin, for instance, may be found in almost as many different cuts and
colours as there are towns in Mexico. The comfortable loose shirt and poncho are
ideally suited for the hot days and coolish nights over much of a predominantly
mountainous country, but variations on this practical item of clothing have produced
some classic, related, garment types, generally spun in cotton or wool on the
traditional *telar de cintura*, a waist-high loom, or *telar de pie*, a pedal operated loom
introduced by the Spanish.

Textiles

The *huipil* is a blouse without sleeves, of varying length depending upon the area.
Best places to buy them are San Cristóbal, Tuxtla Gutiérrez (a white cloth). They are
most famous in the towns of Tehuantepec (due to Frida Kahlo's paintings) where they
are often a cherry red or black decorated with large flowers or ribbons.

The *quechquémetl* is a diamond shaped shirt worn by women that covers just the
torso and is woven by indigenous groups in the mountains of Estado de México;
Estado de Puebla, where the brocade is elaborately embroidered; and San Luis Potosí.

Ponchos come in two distinctive types: the *sarape*, which is a long garment, and the
jorongo, which is shorter. They are found all over Mexico but the former is worn
especially in the Valle de Oaxaca, where it is made in Santa Ana del Valle and Teotitlán
del Valle (an elaborate cloak with Grecian designs, butterflies, suns, etc.), and in San

Luis Potosí. *Jorongos* from Tuxtla Gutiérrez are made from black wool.

The birthplace of the classic *rebozo*, a dress drawn at the waist and tassled at the hem, is Santa María del Río, 48 km south of San Luis Potosí where it is a delicate silk garment often bought and stored in a small inlaid chest. A *rebozo* of very fine cotton is made in Tenancingo, 50 km south of Toluca, and in Teotitlán del Valle.

Old Spanish-style dresses are made in Chiapa de Corzo whilst various embroidered textiles including belts and sashes are elaborated in Cuetzalan (Puebla) and the famous *guayabera* shirt is sold in Mérida. Other specialist Yucateca products such as hammocks and *henequen* bags are covered in the relevant chapter.

There are many other woven items on sale in markets. Quite universal is the *morral*, or shoulder bag. Carpets, rugs and bedspreads are found around Oaxaca state.

Masks Textile art is heavily influenced by religious ritual, particularly dances to master natural forces, but as well as being impressively robed, priests, witches and shamans are often masked in the guise of animals such as eagles, jaguars, goats, monkeys, and coyotes, particularly in the states of Guerrero (for example in Chilapa), Sinaloa, Sonora and Nayarit.

Such masks are made from cardboard, wire, wood, hide, tinfoil and other simple materials and decorated with thread, gems, mirrors and crystals. Besides animal spirit invocation they could be related to fiestas such as the Day of the Dead (where the mask might be a cardboard skull or made of sugar), or burlesque, as at the carnaval of Huejotzingo (Puebla) satirising historical and political events specific to a region like the repulsion of the French invasion. At Tepoztlán, (Morelos), where a small pink mask with distorted features is surmounted by a huge hat, again the target is French intervention, this time under Maximilian.

Other places where masks might be sought out in markets local to the site of crafting are Paracho (Michoacán) and Tlaxcala state where the dancer is masked in the appearance of an old man. In Tlaxcala the mask is wooden, the face white and the moustache tiny. Crystal eyes peer out from behind huge eyelashes. At Papantla (Veracruz) black wooden masks stir up African spirits in magic ritual. Devil and clown masks are also commonly found.

San Luis Potosí has the National Museum of the Mask and in the Casa de la Cultura in Morelia there is another collection.

Ceramics Ceramics are generally crafted out of baked clay or plaster and are polished or glazed or polychrome. In some parts such as Michoacán men paint the pieces but in the main pot-making is done by women. Some of the best pots have a brilliant glaze such as the Patambán pottery found in Michoacán and on sale in Uruapan. The green finish comes from the oxidization of copper whilst its fragility comes from 'eggshell' thin clay working. Also outstanding is the *bandera* pottery of Tonalá (Jalisco) decorated in the Mexican national colours.

Another type of ceramic deals with daily events such as the fishermens' life in Tzintzuntzan near Pátzcuaro whilst in Ocotlán de Morelos (Oaxaca) the brilliant colouring is linked to the Day of the Dead celebrations.

There are many unusual forms such as the pineapple-shaped Patambán pieces and the *árboles de vida* (trees of life) of Metepec (Estado de México). Cats are a speciality of Tonalá (Jalisco) whilst Ocumicho in Michoacán produces a range of fantastical animals. Ceramic dolls are made on the Isthmus of Tehuantepec.

Items such as candlesticks are sold in Izúcar de Matamoros and Puebla which also produces decorative ceramic tiles. Large porcelain vases are found in Tlaquepaque (Jalisco) and huge earthenware jars all over Guerrero and in Acatlán de Osorio (Puebla).

The finest china in Mexico, the Maiollica design or Talavera, imported from the Mediterranean, is made in Puebla and Guanajuato and a more practical black pottery is the speciality of San Bartolo Coyotepec (Oaxaca) and Dolores Hidalgo.

Lacquer-ware, known as *maque* or *laca* is a more regionalized craft found in Chiapas, Guerrero and Michoacán. Prior to the Conquest its colouring was derived from naturally occurring pigments but since the Spanish arrived the decoration has been more artificial although more brightly coloured. Some pieces are even inlaid with gold.

Lacquer-ware

In Chiapas the main centre of production is Chiapa de Corzo where the speciality is a large cup made from the wood of the calabash tree and stippled with paint applied by fingertip. There is a Lacquer museum in the town.

Olinalá is the focus of inspiration for *laca* in Guerrero and its influence spreads to other towns such as Temalacacingo, 20 km away, whilst the Sunday market in Chilapa is a good shopping opportunity. Specialities include large chests, boxes, furniture, toys and gourds shaped into fruit and animal figures. Michoacán has the most elaborate lacquer work. Pátzcuaro craftsmen inlay gold to wardrobes, screens, trays and plates. Uruapan is also a good town for purchasing lacquer products.

For silver and gold work, known as *orfebrería*, look under Taxco and the markets in Mexico City. Jade jewellery is made in Michoacán whilst semi-precious stones such as onyx, obsidian, amethyst and turquoise are found in Oaxaca, Puebla, Guerrero, Zacatecas and Querétaro.

Silver & Gold

Leatherwork related to *Charro* (cowboy) culture is sold in many centres, particularly those in ranching country such as Durango and Zacatecas.

The art of paper cutting and pasting, papel picado, flourishes seasonally around the time of the Day of the Dead celebrations, particularly profiles of dancing *calaveras* (skeletons). Papier mâché *calaveras* also spring up at this time. In pre-Hispanic times, paper was sacred as material on which to record histories, cosmologies and social mores. Paper banners were used during religious festivals, and some sacrificial victims carried items of paper as they approached the sacrificial stone.

Holidays and festivals

Sunday is a statutory holiday. Saturday is also observed as a holiday, except by the shops. There is no early-closing day. National holidays are as follows:

New Year (1 January), **Constitution Day** (5 February), **Birthday of Benito Juárez** (21 March), **Maundy Thursday**, **Good Friday** and **Easter Saturday**, Labour Day (1 May), **Bt's Annuattle of Puebla** (5 May), **Presidenal Message** (1 September), **Independence Day** (16 September), **Discovery of America** (Día de la Raza) (12 October), **Day of the Revolution** (20 November), **Christmas Day** (25 December).

The Mexican calendar of religious fiestas lists over 5,000 each year. The most widely celebrated are: **Santos Reyes** (6 January), **Mother's Day** (10 May), **All Souls' Day** (1-2 November) and **Our Lady of Guadalupe** (12 December).

Adventure tourism

Mexico's massive coastline of reefs and swells and expanse of mountain ranges cut by long rivers make it very well suited to outdoor adventure. There is an adventure tourism organization in Mexico City, the Associación Mexicana de Turismo de Aventura y Ecoturismo (AMTAVE), Insurgentes Sur 1981-251, Colonia Guadalupe Inn, Mexico DF.

This is practised off most of Mexico's coastline but two regions, Quintana Roo and Baja California, are particularly noteworthy. The first offers warm water reefs close to the shore and visibility of over 30m. Southern Baja has adventurous diving in deep waters.

Diving

Essentials

Cozumel, in Quintana Roo, has some of the best diving in the world and there are marine parks at Chankanaab and at Palancar Reef with numerous caves and gullies and a horseshoe-shaped diving arena. Also excellent on the west side of the island are Santa Rosa and sites off San Francisco beach. To the southwest are good sites off Laguna Colombia, whilst off Punta Sur there is excellent deep diving. There is concern, however, over the damage to the reef inflicted by the new cruise ship pier, and more of these piers are planned. At Isla Mujeres, also in Quintana Roo, the most dived sites include Los Manchones, La Bandera, a shallow dive south of the island, and El Frío, a deep wreck an hour and a half to the north.

Elsewhere along this Caribbean coast, Punta Nizuc is accessible from Cancún while Akumal is famous for its wrecks such as *El Matancero*, a Spanish galleon. Immediately east of the resort are the Grouper Canyons. This stretch of coastline is perhaps as rich as anywhere in Mexico for variety of marine life. Banco Chinchorro is a magnificent biosphere reserve accessible from Majahual and Xcalak. A full day's boat ride from Progreso, Yucatán, will bring you to the reef system of Arrecife Alacrán.

Southern Baja is warmer than the North but it is still advisable to wear a wetsuit, not least to protect from skin-irritating hydroza oganisms. There are marine forests and a reef at Cabo Pulmo. The rock formations off Pichilingüe are worth seeing and there is a wreck off Isla Espíritu Santo. A fine underwater cavern lies off Isla Cerralvo and the Islas Gaviotas are also dived. If you feel experienced enough to brave the currents off Cabo San Lucas then there are impressive submarine sandfalls to a depth of 65m.

Other centres for diving away from the Baja Peninsula and the Caribbean include Puerto Vallarta; in front of the town, Bahía de Banderas is a good dive training site. Not far away are the Islas Marietas and the reef of the Los Arcos marine park. Puerto Escondido and the Bays of Huatulco offer clear waters which is more than can be said for the Gulf of Mexico although it too has its attractions. Here there is a reef off Veracruz. Best dive sites are at La Blanquilla, Antón Lizardo and there is a wreck at Isla Verde.

A diving organization, the Club de Exploraciones y Deportes Acuáticos de México (CEDAM) is based in Puerto Aventuras.

Surfing Some of the world's most exhilarating surfing can be experienced along Mexico's
The alleged longest Pacific coast. The highlights are the huge Hawaiian-size surf that pounds the Baja
break in the world is at shoreline and the renowned Mexican Pipeline at Puerto Escondido. There are
Bahía de Matanchén numerous possibilities, ranging from developed beaches to remote bays accessible
beside San Blas only by four-wheel drive vehicles. Many are to be found at the estuaries of rivers where sandbars are deposited and points are formed. It is impossible to name all the good beaches; the following is a selection starting in the north.

Isla de Todos Santos in front of Ensenada has big swells. It is much frequented by US surfers and is best in winter. There are 20 good beaches around Playa San Miguel. Punta Mirador beside San José and the beach nearby, km 28, receive some massive waves, particularly in summer. A wetsuit is usually necessary when surfing in Baja.

Mazatlán is the point on the mainland where currents escape the shielding effects of the Peninsula and surfing is possible. As the geographical centre point on Mexico's surfing coast it has been chosen as home to the Surfing Association, PO Box 310. In front of the town Isla de la Piedra is good along with Playa Cerritos just north of the town and also El Caimanero and near Teacapan, 100 km to the south. San Blas is an excellent learning centre. The waves are normally not too big and there are few rocks or dangerous currents. Surfing is best in the spring and summer, particularly between July and October which is when, about three times a year, conditions in the Bahía de Matanchén create a break that links the points at Santa Cruz, Atacama and Isletas beaches. It then becomes possible to surf continuously for more than a mile! South of San Blas, still in Nayarit, are the Playas San Francisco and Sayulita and the Punta de Mita. Up to here only southern currents reach the coast. From Jalisco down northern currents also come into play.

The Colima coast offers good surfing at Boca de Pascuales near Tecomán and at Río Ticla. Before Zihuatanejo are Río Nexpa and Petacalco and, just outside Acapulco, Playa Revolcadero is battered by surf to match its name. Puerto Escondido is, perhaps, the mecca of Mexican surfing. Surfers come here to Playa Zicatela to attempt the pipeline and are duly washed up on the shore.

Sea kayaking

This requires no special prior expertise and you can usually take off on your own in quiet waters for day trips. The simplest kayaks are more like rafts and have no open compartments that you need to worry about flooding. Agencies will assess your experience when renting out more advanced equipment and for longer periods.

The warm waters of the Sea of Cortés off Baja California Sur are kayak heaven. Islas Espíritu Santo and Isla Partida are easily accessible from La Paz and whether in or out of your kayak you can experience a wild party of stingrays, sea-lions, dolphins, porpoises and occasionally grey whales and hammerheads. Further up the coast Loreto is another good base for hiring gear and at Bahía Coyote, near Santispac, on the mainland side of the larger and more encompassing Bahía Concepción, there are many small islands you can explore in a day on calm waters. The Baja Sea Kayak Association is based in La Paz.

Another good spot for kayaking is in the Bahía de Sayulita just north of Puerto Vallarta and around the nearby Islas Marietas. In Veracruz state a popular paddle is to the Isla de los Sacrificios.

Sports fishing

There are resort-based sports fishing fleets along much of Mexico's Pacific coast, from Bahía Kino to Acapulco. At the former there is a fishing tournament at the end of June-beginning of July, and at Manzanillo there is one in February.

Some of the best fishing is in the Sea of Cortés, particularly off La Paz, around Islas Espíritu Santo and Cerralvo, from Loreto, and off the Buena Vista resort (which has boats), near Los Barriles, 60 km south of the Baja Sur capital. Here the high season for many species such as marlín, swordfish, sailfish, roosterfish, dorado, cabrilla and wahoo is May to September. For sierra it is November to January and yellowtail from March to May. There are international competitions in July and August and one in March dedicated to catching yellowtail. Tampico, in the Gulf of Mexico, is the focus for competition fishing for robalo (April), marlín (June) and sábalo (July and August).

Rafting

The variety in Mexico's rafting rivers opens the activity up to all types of traveller. The attraction is not just the run but the trek or rappel to the start and the moments between rapids, drifting in deep canyons beneath hanging tropical forests, some of which contain lesser-known and quite inaccessible ruins. For sheer thrills many of the best are in the centre of the country.

The most popular is the Río Antigua/Pescados in Veracruz. The upper stretch, the Antigua, has some good learning rapids (grade 2) running into grade 3, but, if you have more than one day, the Pescados (the lower Antigua), nearer to Jalcomulco, can give a bigger adrenalin rush with some grade 4 whitewater. Also in Veracruz state, 50 km to the north, is the Río Actopan with grade 3. The biggest rush in the country, however, is on the Barranca Grande and at Cañón Azul where there is excellent quality grade 5 water. To complete the pre-eminence of Veracruz as a rafting destination is the Filo-Bobos. The Alto Filo (grades 4 and 5) and the 25-km-long Tlapacoyan to Palmilla stretch, halfway along which the Bobos enters the Filo, are the areas of most interest to rafter-archaeologists.

In San Luis Potosí state there is the turquoise Santa María, accessible beneath the 105-m-high Cascadas de Tamul and running past several ruins, grades 3 and 4, through dramatic countryside known as the Huasteca Potosina.

The Amacuzac, about an hour and a half from Mexico City in Morelos state, near Taxco, entered at Dos Bocas, has grade 3 and 4 possibilities.

Rafting in Chiapas covers the spectrum from sedate drifting on rivers such as the Lacan-Há through the Lacandó jungle to class 4 and 5 rapids on the Río Jataté which gathers force where the Lacan Tum enters it and gradually diminishes in strength as it nears the Río Usumacinta. The Usumacinta offers compensation in that it flows past the major ruins of Yaxchilán. These rivers, however, are sometimes off-limits because of narco-trafficking and banditry.

An adventurous trip is down the Río Grande from near the border between Chihuahua and Coahuila, opposite Big Bend National Park, through the canyons of Santa Elena, Bacuillas and Mariscal. Fans of the film *Deliverance* might note that there is an 85-mile stretch along which it is impossible to leave the canyon.

The season for whitewater rafting is generally July to September in the centre, when rivers are fuller, but in Chiapas, January and February are preferred because the climate is cooler.

Climbing

Snow climbing is known as 'Alta Montaña' here

The big glaciated volcanoes are within relatively easy reach of Mexico City and climbing them is the best way to get above the throng, although there are few technical routes, crampons, ice-axe and occasionally rope are required for safe ascents.

Now that Popocatépetl (5,452m) and Colima Volcano (3,842m) are sporadically erupting (although it may still be possible to climb El Nevado 4,339m, behind Colima Volcano), Pico de Orizaba (Citlatépetl 5,760m, Mexico's highest volcano) and Iztaccíhuatl (5,286m, the best technical climbing with great views over 'Popo') are the two remaining high altitude challenges. The season is October to May.

There are two good acclimatization climbs before attempting these 5,000-m peaks, Cofre de Perote (Nouhcampatépetl 4,282m) and Nevado de Toluca (Xinantécatl, 4,558m). Further afield, near Tapachula in Chiapas, a worthwhile but little-climbed mountain is the Tacaná Volcano (4,150m).

Rock climbing

This is an increasingly popular sport for Mexicans and there is good to great climbing in most parts of the country. Here are just a few suggestions.

On the outskirts of the capital there are two convenient natural high-rises above the smog: the cliffs at Magdalena Contreras to the southwest and at Naucalpan to the northwest. There are numerous small canyons for weekend-long excursions beyond the borders of the Valley of Mexico: Calixtlahuaca, northwest of Toluca, has easy to moderate routes; Piedra Parada near Ixtapan de la Sal has more difficult walls as there are few fissures in the rock; another site opened up in recent years is Cerro Catedral, 30 km north of Toluca.

Going north of the big smoke, 70 km east of Querétaro, is the Peñón de Bernal, the world's largest monolith after Ayer's Rock. The north face route is 400m in elevation. El Chico national park near Pachuca has excellent climbing as does the Cañón de Zimapán, both in Hidalgo.

You have to go much further north, to Monterrey, for the best rock in Mexico. Near the small town of Hidalgo, is the Potrero Chico big wall, 650m of limestone nirvana. Also near Monterrey are the Cañón de la Huasteca, Independencia and the Cuerno de Toro. There is a top-grade 600-m cliff at El Trono de Angel in Northern Baja California and excellent sea-cliff climbing around the peninsula.

There are two mountain rescue services, the Socorro Alpino de México (SAM) and the Cruz Roja. Their resources are stretched and so take every precaution to avoid getting into difficulties. The Club Alpino Mexicano is based in Mexico City and there are reasonable equipment supply shops here. There is a good snow and rock-climbing magazine, *Aventura Vertical*, featuring the newest and best ascents.

Trekking

The Copper Canyon is a vast wilderness for trekking. Creel is the obvious base but an excellent trek is from Batópilas to Urique - three days in the heat of the *barranca*, through Tarahumara lands - no better way to experience the abyss after you have spent a day or two wondering, from a *mirador* on its rim, what it is like down there. Be careful about where you camp. Ask landowners' permission and don't slow down too much should you stumble across a marijuana plantation.

Best trekking within easy reach of a major city is from Monterrey, particularly in the Cumbres de Monterrey national park. There are several organizations in Mexico City that arrange weekend mountain hiking excursions.

One of the attractions of more remote trekking such as in Oaxaca state and Nayarit is to visit indigenous communities such as Cora and Huichol villages. However, one should be sensitive to local reaction to tourist intrusion. Baja California's petroglyph cave sites can often only be visited on foot, which adds to the mystical experience, but here too remember that most sites are sacred and you should be accompanied by a guide. Seek advice before trekking in Chiapas and Guerrero, both hideouts for rebel groups.

Canyoning Rappel, or abseiling, is often the only way to get down to adventure tourism and so canyoning is frequently a part of any trip. Two of the best locations for this new sport are the Cañadas de Cotlamani, near Jalcomulco in Veracruz and in the Cumbres de Monterrey national park, the *Recorrido de Matacanes* circuit based on the Cascada Lagunillas and a circuit spilling out from the Cascada El Chipitín, known locally as *Recorrido Hidrofobia*. See also caving below.

Caving Caving, or *espeleología*, in Mexico is more than just going down into deep dark holes. Sometimes it is a sport more closely related to canyoning as there are some excellent underground river scrambles. The best of these is probably the 8-km-long Chontalcuatlán, a part of the Cacahuamilpa cave system near Taxco. There is an underground lagoon here in Zacatecolotla cave. Beside the Matacanes river circuit in Nuevo León (see canyoning) there are some large caves, the *Grutas de La Tierrosa, La Cebolla* and *Pterodáctilo*.

For purist potholers there are many vertical caves or *sótanos* (cellars) such as *El Jabalí, El Nogal* and *Tilaco* in the Sierra Gorda de Querétaro and *La Purificación* near Ciudad Victoria. The biggest cave systems are in Chiapas especially around Tuxtla Gutiérrez. One of the best elsewhere is the Sótano de las Golondrinas on the Santa María river, San Luis Potosí (see rafting), but perhaps the most challenging is Pozo Verde, 1,070m deep, near Ocotempa, Puebla.

Aerial sports There are some agencies which specialize in aerial sports. See under 'Specialists in adventure tourism' under the Directory for Mexico City. Guanajuato, Valle de Bravo (for hang-gliding), and Hidalgo state are most often the backdrop.

Responsible tourism

Much has been written about the adverse impacts of tourism on the environment and local communities. It is usually assumed that this only applies to the more excessive end of the travel industry such as the Spanish Costas and Bali. However it now seems that travellers can have an impact at almost any density and this is especially true in areas 'off the beaten track' where local people may not be used to western conventions and lifestyles, and natural environments may be very sensitive.

Of course, tourism can have a beneficial impact and this is something to which every traveller can contribute. Many national parks are part funded by receipts from people who travel to see exotic plants and animals. Similarly, travellers can promote patronage and protection of valuable archaeological sites and heritages through their interest and entrance fees.

However, where visitor pressure is high and/or poorly regulated, damage can occur. This is especially so in parts of the Caribbean where some tour operators are

Essentials

☞ *Eco travelling: a few tips*

Where possible choose a destination, tour operator or hotel with a proven ethical and environmental commitment, and if in doubt ask.

Spend money on locally produced (rather than imported) goods and services and use common sense when bargaining – your few dollars saved may be a week's salary to others.

Use water and electricity carefully – travellers may receive preferential supply while the needs of local communities are overlooked.

Don't give money or sweets to children – it encourages begging – instead give to a recognized project, charity or school.

Learn about local etiquette and culture – consider local norms and behaviour – and dress appropriately for local cultures and situations.

Protect wildlife and other natural resources – don't buy souvenirs or goods made from wildlife unless they are clearly sustainably produced and are not protected under CITES legislation.

Always ask before taking photographs or videos of people.

Consider staying in local, rather than foreign owned, accommodation – the economic benefits for host communities are far greater – and there are far greater opportunities to learn about local culture.

expanding their activities with scant regard for the environment or local communities. It is also unfortunately true that many of the most popular destinations are in ecologically sensitive areas easily disturbed by extra human pressures. The desire to visit sites and communities that are off the beaten track is a driving force for many travellers. However, these are the areas that are often most sensitive to change as a result of increased pressure from visitors. Eventually the very features that tourists travel so far to see may become degraded and so we seek out new sites, discarding the old, and leaving someone else to deal with the plight of local communities and the damaged environment.

Fortunately, there are signs of a new awareness of the responsibilities that the travel industry and its clients need to endorse. For example, some tour operators fund local conservation projects and travellers are now more aware of the impact they may have on host cultures and environments. We can all contribute to the success of what is variously described as responsible, green or alternative tourism. All that is required is a little forethought and consideration. It would be impossible to identify all the possible impacts that might need to be addressed by travellers, but it is worthwhile noting the major areas in which we can all take a more responsible attitude in the countries we visit. These include, changes to natural ecosystems (air, water, land, ecology and wildlife), cultural values (beliefs and behaviour) and the built environment (sites of antiquity and archaeological significance). At an individual level, travellers can reduce their impact if greater consideration is given to their activities. Backpacking along the Maya trade routes makes for great stories, but how do local communities cope with the sudden invasive interest in their lives? Will the availability of easy tourist money and gauche behaviour affect them for the worse, possibly diluting the significance of culture and customs? Similarly, have the environmental implications of increased visitor pressure been considered? Litter and disturbance of wildlife might seem to be small issues and, on an individual scale they probably are, however multiplied several fold they become more serious (as the Inca Trail in Peru can attest).

Some of these impacts are caused by factors beyond the direct control of travellers, such as the management and operation of a hotel chain. Even here it is possible to voice concern about damaging activities and an increasing number of hotels and travel operators are taking 'green concerns' seriously, even if it is only to protect their share of the market.

Environmental legislation Legislation is increasingly being enacted to control damage to the environment, and in some cases this can have a bearing on travellers. The establishment of national parks may involve rules and guidelines for visitors and these should always be followed. In addition there may be local or national laws controlling behaviour and use of natural resources (especially wildlife) that are being increasingly enforced. If in doubt, ask. Finally, international legislation, principally the Convention on International Trade in Endangered Species of Wild Fauna and Flora (CITES), may affect travellers.

CITES aims to control the trade in live specimens of endangered plants and animals and also 'recognizable parts or derivatives' of protected species. Sale of Black Coral, Turtle Shells, Protected Orchids and other wildlife is strictly controlled by signatories of the convention. The full list of protected wildlife varies, so if you feel the need to purchase souvenirs and trinkets derived from wildlife, it would be prudent to check whether they are protected. Mexico is a signatory of CITES. In addition, most European countries, the USA and Canada are signatories of CITES. Importation of CITES protected species into these countries can lead to heavy fines, confiscation of goods and even imprisonment. Information on the status of legislation and protective measures can be obtained from Traffic International, UK office, 219C Huntingdon Rd, Cambridge, CB3 0DL, T01223-277427, F01223-277237, traffic @wcmc.org.uk.

Green travel companies and information The increasing awareness of the environmental impact of travel and tourism has led to a range of advice and information services as well as spawning specialist travel companies who claim to provide 'responsible travel' for clients. This is an expanding field and the veracity of claims needs to be substantiated in some cases. The following organizations and publications can provide useful information for those with an interest in pursuing responsible travel opportunities.

Organizations GREEN GLOBE, a membership organization, advises anyone involved in the travel industry on environmental policy, T UK 01223-890250, F890258, 101453.3077@compuserve.com; also on this number is Environmental Travel Solutions Ltd. **Tourism Concern** Aims to promote a greater understanding of the impact of tourism on host communities and environments; Southlands College, Wimbledon Parkside, London SW19 5NN, T UK-0181-9440464, tourconcern@gn.apc.org, www.gn.apc. org/ tourismconcern. **Rethinking Tourism Project**, PO Box 581938, Minneapolis, MN 55458-1938, USA, T612-5210098, RTProject@aol.com. **Centre for the Advancement of Responsive Travel** CART has a range of publications available as well as information on alternative holiday destinations, T UK-01732-352757.

Health

Staying healthy in Mexico is straightforward. With the following advice and precautions you should keep as healthy as you do at home. Most visitors return home having experienced no problems at all beyond an upset stomach. However, in Mexico the health risks are different from those encountered in Europe or the USA. It also depends on how you travel, and where. There are clear health differences in the various countries of Latin America and between the risks for the business traveller, who stays in international class hotels in large cities, the backpacker who is trekking from country to country and the tourist who heads for the beach. There are no hard and fast rules to follow: you will often have to make your own judgement on the healthiness or otherwise of your surroundings. There are English- (or other foreign language) speaking doctors in most major cities who have particular experience in dealing with locally occurring diseases. Your Embassy representative will often be able to give you the name of local reputable doctors and most of the better hotels have a doctor on standby. If you do fall ill and cannot find a recommended doctor, try the Outpatient Department of a hospital. The Social Security hospitals are restricted to members, but will take visitors in emergencies; they are more up to date than the Centros de Salud and Hospitales Civiles found in most centres, which are very cheap and open to everyone. There are many homeopathic physicians in all parts of Mexico. It is worth remembering that, apart from mosquitoes, the most dangerous animals are men, be they bandits or behind steering wheels. Think carefully about violent confrontations and wear a seat belt if you are lucky enough to have one available to you.

Before travelling

Take out medical insurance. Make sure it covers all eventualities especially evacuation to your home country by a medically equipped plane. You should have a dental check up, obtain a spare glasses prescription, a spare oral contraceptive prescription (or enough pills to last) and, if you suffer from a chronic illness (such as diabetes, high blood pressure, ear or sinus troubles, cardio-pulmonary disease or nervous disorder), you should arrange for a check up with your doctor. He will be able at the same time to provide you with a letter explaining the details of your disability in English and if possible Spanish. Check the current practice for malaria prophylaxis (prevention) in Mexico. If you are on regular medication, make sure you have enough to cover the period of your travel.

Children More preparation is probably necessary for babies and children than for an adult and perhaps a little more care should be taken when travelling to remote areas where health services are primitive. This is because children can be become more rapidly ill than adults (although, on the other hand, they often recover more quickly). Diarrhoea and vomiting are the most common problems, so take the usual precautions, but more intensively. Breastfeeding is best and most convenient for babies, but powdered milk is generally available and so are baby foods in most countries. Papaya, bananas and avocados are all nutritious and can be cleanly prepared. The treatment of diarrhoea is the same as it is for adults, except that it should start earlier and be continued with more persistence. Children get dehydrated very quickly in hot countries and can become drowsy and uncooperative unless cajoled to drink water or juice plus salts. Upper respiratory infections, such as colds, catarrh and middle ear infections are also common and if your child suffers from these normally, take some antibiotics against the possibility. Outer ear infections after swimming are also common and antibiotic eardrops will help. Wet wipes are always useful and sometimes difficult to find, as, in some extremely remote places, are disposable nappies.

Medicines & There is very little control on the sale of drugs and medicines. You may be able to buy
what to take any and every drug in pharmacies without a prescription. Be wary of this because pharmacists can be poorly trained and might sell you drugs that are unsuitable, dangerous or old. Many drugs and medicines are manufactured under licence from American or European companies, so the trade names may be familiar to you. This means you do not have to carry a whole chest of medicines with you, but remember that the shelf life of some items, especially vaccines and antibiotics, is markedly reduced in hot conditions. Buy your supplies at the better outlets where there are more refrigerators, even though they are more expensive, and check the expiry date of all preparations you buy. Immigration officials occasionally confiscate scheduled drugs (Lomotil is an example) if they are not accompanied by a doctor's prescription. Self-medication may be forced on you by circumstances so the following information contains the names of drugs and medicines which you may find useful in an emergency or in out-of-the-way places.

Sunglasses: a type designed for intense sunlight; **Earplugs**: for sleeping on aeroplanes and in noisy hotels; **Suntan cream**: with a high protection factor; **Insect repellent**: containing DET for preference; **Mosquito net**: lightweight, permethrin-impregnated; **Tablets**: for travel sickness; **Tampons**: can be expensive; **Condoms**; **Contraceptives**; **Water sterilizing tablets**; **Antimalarial tablets**; **Anti-infective ointment**: eg Cetrimide; **Dusting powder for feet etc**: containing fungicide; **Antacid tablets**: for indigestion; **Sachets of rehydration salts plus anti-diarrhoea preparations**; **Painkillers**: such as paracetamol or aspirin; **Antibiotics**: for diarrhoea etc. **First Aid Kit**: Small pack containing a few sterile syringes and needles and disposable gloves. The risk of catching hepatitis, etc from a dirty needle used for injection is now negligible, but you may feel safer carrying your own supplies – available from camping shops and at airports.

Medical Kit check list

Smallpox vaccination is no longer required anywhere in the world and cholera vaccination is no longer recognized as necessary or effective for international travel by the World Health Organisation. Nevertheless, some immigration officials are still demanding proof of vaccination against cholera in Latin America and in some countries outside Latin America, following the outbreak of the disease which originated in Peru in 1990-91 and subsequently affected most surrounding countries. Although it is very unlikely to affect visitors to Latin America, the cholera epidemic continues to make its greatest impact in poor areas where water supplies are polluted and food hygiene practices are insanitary. Not surprisingly, cholera is on the increase in Mexico.

Vaccination & immunisation

Vaccination against the following diseases is recommended:

Yellow Fever This is a live vaccination not to be given to children under nine months or persons allergic to eggs. Immunity lasts for 10 years, an International Certificate of Yellow Fever Vaccination will be given and should be kept because it is sometimes asked for. Yellow fever is very rare in Latin America, but the vaccination is practically without side effects and almost totally protective.

Typhoid A number of new vaccines against this condition are now available; the older TAB and monovalent typhoid vaccines are being phased out. The newer, eg Typhim Vi, cause less side effects, but are more expensive. For those who do not like injections, there are now oral vaccines.

Poliomyelitis Despite its decline in the world this remains a serious disease if caught and is easy to protect against. There are live oral vaccines and in some countries injected vaccines. Whichever one you choose it is a good idea to have a booster every 3-5 years if visiting developing countries regularly.

Tetanus & other routine vaccinations One dose should be given with a booster at six weeks and another at six months and 10 yearly boosters thereafter are recommended. Children should already be properly protected against diphtheria, poliomyelitis and pertussis (whooping cough), measles and HIB all of which can be more serious infections in Latin America than at home. Measles, mumps and rubella vaccine is also given to children throughout the world, but those teenage girls who have not had rubella (German measles) should be tested and vaccinated. Hepatitis B vaccination for babies is now routine in some countries. Consult your doctor for advice on tuberculosis inoculation: the disease is still widespread.

Infectious Hepatitis This is less of a problem for travellers than it used to be because of the development of two extremely effective vaccines against the A and B form of the disease. It remains common, however, in Mexico. A combined hepatitis A & B vaccine is now licensed and has been available since 1997 – one jab covers both diseases.

Other vaccinations These might be considered in the case of epidemics eg meningitis. There is an effective vaccination against rabies, which should be considered by all travellers, especially those going through remote areas or if there is a particular occupational risk, eg for zoologists or veterinarians.

Further information Further information on health risks abroad, vaccinations, etc may be available from a local travel clinic. If you wish to take specific drugs with you such as antibiotics, these are best prescribed by your own doctor. Be aware, however, that not all doctors are experts on the health problems of remote countries. More detailed or more up-to-date information than local doctors can provide is available from various sources. In the UK there are hospital departments specializing in tropical diseases in London, Liverpool, Birmingham and Glasgow and the Malaria Reference Laboratory at the London School of Hygiene and Tropical Medicine provides advice about malaria, T0891-600350. In the USA the local Public Health Services can give such information and information is available centrally from the Centres for Disease Control (CDC) in Atlanta, T404-3324559, www.cdc.gov. In Canada contact IAMAT, 40 Regal Rd, Guelph, Ontario, M6E 1B8.

There are in addition computerized databases which can be accessed for destination-specific, up-to-the-minute information. In the UK there is MASTA (Medical Advisory Service to Travellers Abroad), T020 78375540, F0113 2387575, www.masta.org and Travax (Glasgow, T0141-9467120 ext 247). MASTA will also send by post a health brief on Mexico if ordered on T09068 224100. Other information on medical problems overseas can be obtained from the book by Dr Richard Dawood (Editor) – *Travellers' Health, How to Stay Healthy Abroad* (Oxford University Press, 1992 £7.99). We strongly recommend the new, revised and updated edition (publication imminent), especially to the intrepid traveller heading for the more out of the way places. General advice is also available in the UK in *Health Information for Overseas Travel* (Department of Health) available from HMSO and *International Travel and Health* (WHO). Handbooks on First Aid are produced by the British & American Red Cross and by St John's Ambulance (UK).

On the way

For most travellers a trip to Mexico means a long air flight. If this crosses time zones then jetlag can be a problem. The main symptoms are tiredness and sleepiness at inconvenient times and, conversely, a tendency to wake up in the middle of the night feeling like you want your breakfast. Most find that the problem is worse when flying in an easterly direction. The best way to get over jetlag is to try to force yourself into the new time zone as strictly as possible. This may involve, on a westward flight, trying to stay awake until your normal bedtime and on an eastward flight, forgetting that you have lost some sleep on the way out and going to bed relatively early but near your normal time on the evening after you arrive. The symptoms of jetlag may be helped by keeping up your fluid intake on the journey, but not with alcohol. The hormone melatonin seems to reduce the symptoms of jetlag but is not presently licensed in most of Europe although it can be obtained from health food stores in the USA.

On long-haul flights it is also important to stretch your legs at least every hour to prevent slowing of the circulation and the possible development of blood clots. Drinking plenty of non-alcoholic fluids also helps.

If travelling by boat then sea sickness can be a problem – this is dealt with in the usual way by taking anti motion-sickness pills or by wearing travel sickness wristbands.

Staying healthy on arrival

Intestinal upsets The thought of catching a stomach bug worries visitors but there have been great improvements in food hygiene and most such infections are preventable. Travellers' diarrhoea and vomiting is due, most of the time, to food poisoning, usually passed on by the insanitary habits of food handlers. As a general rule the cleaner your surroundings and the smarter the restaurant, the less likely you are to suffer.

Foods to avoid: uncooked, undercooked, partially cooked or reheated meat, fish, eggs, raw vegetables and salads, especially when they have been left out and exposed to flies. Food sold on the streets and in cheap cafés, especially in Mexico City, may be dangerous. Women who are breast-feeding should avoid eating chilli. Stick to fresh food that has been cooked from raw just before eating and make sure you peel fruit yourself. Wash and dry your hands before eating – disposable wet-wipe tissues are useful for this.

Shellfish eaten raw are risky and at certain times of the year some fish and shellfish concentrate toxins from their environment and cause various kinds of food poisoning. The local authorities notify the public not to eat these foods. Do not ignore the warning. Heat treated milk (UHT) pasteurized or sterilized is becoming more available in Latin America as is pasteurized cheese. On the whole matured or processed cheeses are safer than the fresh varieties. Fresh unpasteurized milk can be a source of food poisoning germs, tuberculosis and brucellosis. This applies equally to ice-cream, yoghurt and cheese made from unpasteurized milk, so avoid these home-made products – the factory made ones are probably safer.

Tap water Use bottled or mineral water for drinking, except in hotels which normally provide *agua de garrafón* (purified drinking water). Take care with ice; make sure it is made from *agua purificada*. Coffee water is not necessarily boiled. Bottled water is available everywhere and is safe, although you must make sure that somebody is not filling bottles from the tap and hammering on a new crown cap. Tehuacán mineral water is sold all over Mexico; both plain and flavoured are first class. Water-sterilizing tablets and water purification solution, Microdyn, can be bought at pharmacies.

This is usually caused by eating food which has been contaminated by food poisoning germs. Drinking water is rarely the culprit. Sea water or river water is more likely to be contaminated by sewage and so swimming in such dilute effluent can also be a cause.

Travellers' diarrhoea

Infection with various organisms can give rise to travellers' diarrhoea. They may be viruses, bacteria, eg Escherichia coli (probably the most common cause worldwide), protozoa (such as Amoeba and Giardia), Salmonella and cholera. The diarrhoea may come on suddenly or rather slowly. It may be accompanied by vomiting or by severe abdominal pain, and the passage of blood or mucus is a sign of dysentery.

Diagnosis and treatment If you can time the onset of the diarrhoea to the minute ('acute') then it is probably due to a virus or a bacterium and/or the onset of dysentery. The treatment, in addition to rehydration, is an antibiotic such as ciprofloxacin 500 milograms every 12 hours; the drug is now widely available and there are many similar ones.

Locals recommend Imecol for 'Moctezuma's Revenge' (the very common diarrhoea).

If the diarrhoea comes on slowly or intermittently ('sub-acute') then it is more likely to be protozoal, ie caused by an amoeba or giardia. Antibiotics such as ciprofloxacin will have little effect. These cases are best treated by a doctor as is any outbreak of diarrhoea continuing for more than three days. Sometimes blood is passed in amoebic dysentery and for this you should certainly seek medical help. If this is not available then the best treatment is probably tinidazole (Fasigyn) one tablet four times a day for three days. If there are severe stomach cramps, the following drugs may help but are not very useful in the management of acute diarrhoea: loperamide (Imodium) and diphenoxylate with atropine (Lomotil). They should not be given to children.

Any kind of diarrhoea, whether or not accompanied by vomiting, responds well to the replacement of water and salts, taken as frequent sips of some kind of rehydration solution. There are proprietary preparations consisting of sachets of powder which you dissolve in boiled water, or you can make your own by adding half a teaspoonful of salt (3.5 grams) and four tablespoonfuls of sugar (40 grams) to a litre of boiled water.

Thus the linchpins of treatment for diarrhoea are rest, fluid and salt replacement, antibiotics such as ciprofloxacin for the bacterial types and special diagnostic tests and medical treatment for the amoeba and giardia infections. Salmonella infections and cholera, although rare, can be devastating diseases and it would be wise to get to a hospital as soon as possible if these are suspected.

Fasting, peculiar diets and the consumption of large quantities of yoghurt have not been found useful in calming travellers' diarrhoea or in rehabilitating inflamed bowels. Oral rehydration has, on the other hand, been a life saving technique especially in children, and should always be practised, whatever other treatment you use. As there is some evidence that alcohol and milk might prolong diarrhoea they should be avoided during and immediately after an attack. So should chillies!

Diarrhoea occurring day after day for long periods of time (chronic diarrhoea) is notoriously resistant to amateur attempts at treatment and again warrants proper diagnostic tests (most towns with reasonable sized hospitals have laboratories for stool samples). There are ways of preventing travellers' diarrhoea for short periods of time by taking antibiotics, but this is not a foolproof technique and should not be used other than in exceptional circumstances. Doxycycline is possibly the best drug. Some preventatives such as Enterovioform can have serious side effects if taken for long periods.

Paradoxically, constipation is also common, probably induced by dietary change, inadequate fluid intake in hot places and long bus journeys. Simple laxatives are useful in the short-term and bulky foods such as maize, beans and plenty of fruit are also useful.

Water purification There are a number of ways of purifying water in order to make it safe to drink. Dirty water should first be strained through a filter bag (camping shops) and then boiled or treated. Bringing water to a rolling boil at sea level is sufficient to make the water safe for drinking, but at higher altitudes you have to boil the water for a few minutes longer to ensure that all the microbes are killed (20 minutes is recommended in Mexico City).

There are sterilizing methods that can be used and there are proprietary preparations containing chlorine (eg Puritabs) or iodine (eg Pota Aqua) compounds. Chlorine compounds generally do not kill protozoa (eg Giardia).

There are a number of water filters now on the market available in personal and expedition size. They work either on mechanical or chemical principles, or may do both. Make sure you take the spare parts or spare chemicals with you and do not believe everything the manufacturers say.

High altitude Spending time at high altitude in Latin America, especially in the tropics, is usually a pleasure – it is not so hot, there are no insects and the air is clear and spring-like. Travelling to high altitudes, however, can cause medical problems, all of which can be prevented if care is taken.

Heavy eating and drinking of alcohol is unwise in the capital because of its altitude; avoid strenuous physical exercise for the first few days until you are acclimatized. Some people experience nosebleeds in Guadalajara and Mexico City because of altitude and pollution; they cease with fresh air.

On reaching heights above about 3,000 metres, heart pounding and shortness of breath, especially on exertion, are a normal response to the lack of oxygen in the air. A condition called acute mountain sickness can also affect visitors. It is more likely to affect those who ascend rapidly. This takes a few hours or days to come on and its symptoms are: a bad headache; extreme tiredness; sometimes dizziness; loss of appetite and frequently nausea and vomiting. Insomnia is common and is often associated with a suffocating feeling when lying in bed. Keen observers may note that their breathing rate tends to wax and wane at night and that their face tends to be puffy in the mornings – this is all part of the syndrome. Anyone can get this condition and past experience is not always a good guide: the author, having spent years in Peru travelling constantly between sea level and very high altitude never suffered symptoms, then was severely affected whilst climbing Kilimanjaro in Tanzania.

The treatment of acute mountain sickness is simple – rest, painkillers (preferably not aspirin-based) for the headache and anti-sickness pills for vomiting. Oxygen is actually not much help, except at very high altitude. Various local panaceas – Coramina glucosada, Effortil, Micoren are popular in Latin America.

To prevent the condition: on arrival at places over 3,000 metres have a few hours rest in a chair and avoid alcohol, cigarettes and heavy food. If the symptoms are severe and prolonged, it is best to descend to a lower altitude and to reascend slowly or in stages. If this is impossible because of shortage of time, or if you are going so high that acute mountain sickness is very likely, then the drug acetazolamide (Diamox) can be used as a preventative and continued during the ascent. There is good evidence of the value of this drug in the prevention of soroche, but some people do experience peculiar side effects. The usual dose is 500 milograms of the slow release preparation each night, starting the night before ascending above 3,000 metres.

Watch out for sunburn at high altitude. The ultraviolet rays are extremely powerful. The air is also excessively dry at high altitude and you might find that your skin dries out and the inside of your nose becomes crusted. Use a moisturiser for the skin and some vaseline wiped into the nostrils. Some people find contact lenses irritate because of the dry air. It is unwise to ascend to high altitude if you are pregnant, especially in the first three months, or if you have a history of heart, lung or blood disease, including sickle cell.

A more unusual condition can affect mountaineers who ascend rapidly to high altitude – acute pulmonary oedema. Residents at altitude sometimes experience this when returning to the mountains from time spent at the coast. This condition is often preceded by acute mountain sickness and comes on quite rapidly with severe breathlessness, noisy breathing, cough, blueness of the lips and frothing at the mouth. Anybody who develops this must be brought down as soon as possible, given oxygen and taken to hospital.

A rapid descent from high places will make sinus problems and middle-ear infections worse and might make your teeth ache. Lastly, don't fly to altitude within 24 hours of scuba diving. You might suffer from 'the bends'.

Heat & cold

Full acclimatization to high temperatures takes about two weeks. During this period it is normal to feel a bit apathetic, especially if the relative humidity is high. Drink plenty of water (up to 15 litres a day are required when working physically hard in the tropics), use salt on your food and avoid extreme exertion. Tepid showers are more cooling than hot or cold ones. Large hats do not cool you down, but do prevent sunburn. Remember that, especially in the highlands, there can be a large and sudden drop in temperature between sun and shade and between night and day, so dress accordingly. Warm jackets or woollens are essential after dark at high altitude. Loose cotton is still the best material when the weather is hot.

Air pollution

Many large cities are notorious for their poor air quality; Mexico City and Guadalajara for example. Expect sore throats and itchy eyes. Sufferers from asthma or bronchitis may have to increase their regular maintenance treatment.

Insects

These are mostly more of a nuisance than a serious hazard and with a bit of preparation, you can prevent being bitten entirely. Some, such as mosquitoes are, of course, carriers of potentially serious diseases, so it is sensible to avoid being bitten as much as possible. Sleep off the ground and use a mosquito net or some kind of insecticide. Preparations containing pyrethrum or synthetic pyrethroids are safe. They are available as aerosols or pumps and the best way to use these is to spray the room thoroughly in all areas (follow the instructions rather than the insects) and then shut the door for a while, re-entering when the smell has dispersed. Mosquito coils release insecticide as they burn slowly. They are widely available and useful out of doors. Tablets of insecticide which are placed on a heated mat plugged into a wall socket are probably the most effective. They fill the room with insecticidal fumes in the same way as aerosols or coils.

You can also use insect repellents, most of which are effective against a wide range of pests. The most common and effective is diethyl metatoluamide (DET). DET liquid is best for arms and face (take care around eyes and with spectacles – DET dissolves plastic). Aerosol spray is good for clothes and ankles and liquid DET can be dissolved in water and used to impregnate cotton clothes and mosquito nets. Some repellents now contain DET and permethrin, an insecticide. Impregnated wrist and ankle bands can also be useful.

If you are bitten or stung, itching may be relieved by cool baths, antihistamine tablets (care with alcohol or driving) or mild corticosteriod creams, eg hydrocortisone (great care should be exercised: never use if there is any hint of infection). Careful scratching of all your bites once a day can be surprisingly effective. Calamine lotion and cream have limited effectiveness and antihistamine creams are not generally recommended – they can cause allergies themselves. Bites which become infected should be treated with a local antiseptic or antibiotic cream such as cetrimide, as should any infected sores or scratches.

When living rough, infestations of the skin with body lice (crabs) and scabies are easy to pick up. Use whatever local commercial preparation is recommended for lice and scabies. Crotamiton cream (Eurax) alleviates itching and also kills a number of skin parasites. Malathion lotion five percent (Prioderm) kills lice effectively, but avoid the use of the toxic agricultural preparation of malathion, more often used to commit suicide.

Ticks   Ticks usually attach themselves to the lower parts of the body often after walking in areas where cattle have grazed. They take a while to attach themselves strongly, but swell up as they start to suck blood. The important thing is to remove them gently, so that they do not leave their head parts in your skin because this can cause a nasty allergic reaction some days later. Do not use petrol, vaseline, lighted cigarettes etc to remove the tick, but, with a pair of tweezers remove the beast gently by gripping it at the attached (head) end and rock it out in very much the same way that a tooth is extracted. Certain tropical flies which lay their eggs under the skin of sheep and cattle also occasionally do the same thing to humans with the unpleasant result that a maggot grows under the skin and pops up as a boil or pimple. The best way to remove these is to cover the boil with oil, vaseline or nail varnish so as to stop the maggot breathing, then to squeeze it out gently the next day.

Other animal   It is a very rare event indeed for travellers, but if you are unlucky (or careless) enough to
bites & stings   be bitten by a venomous snake, spider, scorpion or sea creature, try to identify the creature, without putting yourself in further danger. Snake bites in particular are very frightening, but in fact rarely poisonous – even venomous snakes bite without injecting venom. What you might expect if bitten are: fright, swelling, pain and bruising around the bite and soreness of the regional lymph glands, perhaps nausea, vomiting and a fever. Signs of serious poisoning would be the following symptoms: numbness and tingling of the face, muscular spasms, convulsions, shortness of breath or a failure of the blood to clot, causing generalized bleeding. Victims should be taken to a hospital or a doctor without delay. Commercial snake bite and scorpion kits are available, but are usually only useful for the specific types of snake or scorpion. Most serum has to be given intravenously so it is not much good equipping yourself with it unless you are used to making injections into veins. It is best to rely on local practice in these cases, because the particular creatures will be known about locally and appropriate treatment can be given.

Reassure and comfort the victim frequently. Immobilize the limb by a bandage or a splint or by getting the person to lie still. Do not slash the bite area and try to suck out the poison because this sort of heroism does more harm than good. If you know how to use a tourniquet in these circumstances, you will not need this advice. If you are not experienced, do not apply a tourniquet.

Treatment of snake bite

Avoid walking in snake territory in bare feet or sandals – wear proper shoes or boots. If you encounter a snake stay put until it slithers away, and do not investigate a wounded snake. Spiders and scorpions may be found in the more basic hotels. If stung, rest and take plenty of fluids and call a doctor. The best precaution is to keep beds away from the walls and look inside your shoes and under the toilet seat every morning.

Precautions

Essentials

Certain tropical sea fish when trodden upon inject venom into bathers' feet. This can be exceptionally painful. Wear plastic shoes when you go bathing if such creatures are reported. The pain can be relieved by immersing the foot in extremely hot water for as long as the pain persists.

Marine bites & stings

The burning power of the tropical sun, especially at high altitude, is phenomenal. Always wear a wide brimmed hat and use some form of suncream or lotion on untanned skin. Normal temperate zone suntan lotions (protection factor up to seven) are not much good; you need to use the types designed specifically for the tropics or for mountaineers or skiers with protection factors up to 15 or above. These are often not available in remoter areas. Glare from the sun can cause conjunctivitis, so wear sunglasses especially on tropical beaches, where high protection factor sunscreen should also be used.

Sunburn

AIDS is increasing throughout the region and is not wholly confined to the well-known high-risk sections of the population, ie homosexual men, intravenous drug abusers and children of infected mothers. Heterosexual transmission is now the dominant mode and so the main risk to travellers is from casual sex. The same precautions should be taken as with any sexually transmitted disease. The AIDS virus (HIV) can be passed by unsterilized needles which have been previously used to inject an HIV positive patient, but the risk of this is negligible. It would, however, be sensible to check that needles have been properly sterilized or disposable needles have been used. If you wish to take your own disposable needles, be prepared to explain what they are for. The risk of receiving a blood transfusion with blood infected with the HIV virus is greater than from dirty needles because of the amount of fluid exchanged. Supplies of blood for transfusion should now be screened for HIV in all reputable hospitals, so again the risk is very small indeed. Catching the AIDS virus does not always produce an illness in itself (although it may do). The only way to be sure if you feel you have been put at risk is to have a blood test for HIV antibodies on your return to a place where there are reliable laboratory facilities. The test does not become positive for some weeks.

AIDS

In Central America malaria is theoretically confined to coastal and jungle zones, but is now on the increase again. Mosquitoes do not thrive above 2,500 metres, so you are safe at altitude. There are different varieties of malaria, some resistant to the normal drugs. Make local enquiries if you intend to visit possibly infected zones and use a prophylactic regime. Start taking the tablets a few days before exposure and continue to take them for six weeks after leaving the malarial zone. Remember to give the drugs to babies and children also. Opinion varies on the precise drugs and dosage to be used for protection. All the drugs may have some side effects and it is important to balance the risk of catching the disease against the (albeit rare) side effects. The increasing complexity of the subject is such that as the malarial parasite becomes immune to the

Malaria

new generation of drugs it has made concentration on the physical prevention of being bitten by mosquitoes more important. This involves the use of long sleeved shirts or blouses and long trousers, repellents and nets. Clothes are now available impregnated with the insecticide permethrin or deltamethrin or it is possible to impregnate the clothes yourself. Wide meshed nets impregnated with permethrin are also available, are lighter to carry and less claustrophobic to sleep in.

Prophylaxis and treatment If your itinerary takes you into a malarial area, seek expert advice before you go on a suitable prophylactic regime. This is especially true for pregnant women who are particularly prone to catch malaria. You can still catch the disease even when sticking to a proper regime, although it is unlikely. Advice and malaria pills can be obtained from San Luis Potosí 199, the sixth floor, Colonia Roma Norte, Mexico City, 0900-1400 (chloroquine is available cheaply in most large pharmacies under the brand name Aralen; mefloquire-larium, is not available). If you do develop symptoms (high fever, shivering, headache, sometimes diarrhoea), seek medical advice immediately. If this is not possible and there is a great likelihood of malaria, the treatment is as follows:

If the local strain is likely to be sensitive to it, then the treatment is Chloroquine, a single dose of four tablets (600 milograms) followed by two tablets (300 milograms) in six hours and 300 milograms each day following.

If it is falciparum malaria or the type is in doubt, take local advice. Various combinations of drugs are being used such as Quinine, Tetracycline or Halofantrine. If falciparum malaria is definitely diagnosed, it is wise to get to a good hospital as treatment can be complex and the illness very serious.

Infectious The main symptoms are pains in the stomach, lack of appetite, lassitude and **hepatitis** yellowness of the eyes and skin. Medically speaking there are two main types. The less **(jaundice)** serious, but more common is hepatitis A for which the best protection is the careful preparation of food, the avoidance of contaminated drinking water and scrupulous attention to toilet hygiene. The other, more serious, version is hepatitis B which is acquired usually as a sexually transmitted disease or by blood transfusion. It is less commonly transmitted by injections with unclean needles and possibly by insect bites. The symptoms are the same as for hepatitis A. The incubation period is much longer (up to six months compared with six weeks) and there are more likely to be complications.

Hepatitis A can be protected against with gamma globulin. It should be obtained from a reputable source and is certainly useful for travellers who intend to live rough. You should have a shot before leaving and have it repeated every six months. The dose of gamma globulin depends on the concentration of the particular preparation used, so the manufacturer's advice should be taken. The injection should be given as close as possible to your departure and, as the dose depends on the time you are likely to spend in potentially affected areas, the manufacturer's instructions should be followed. Gamma globulin has really been superseded now by a proper vaccination against hepatitis A (Havrix), which gives immunity lasting up to 10 years. After that, boosters are required. Havrix monodose is now widely available as is junior Havrix. The vaccination has negligible side effects and is extremely effective. Gamma globulin injection can be a bit painful, but it is cheaper than Havrix and may be more readily available in some places.

Hepatitis B can be effectively prevented by a specific vaccine (Engerix) – three shots over six months before travelling. If you have had jaundice in the past it would be worthwhile having a blood test to see if you are immune to either of these two types, because this might avoid the necessity and costs of vaccination or gamma globulin. There are other kinds of viral hepatitis (C, E, G, etc) which are fairly similar to A and B, but vaccines are not available as yet.

Other afflictions

Athlete's Foot This and other fungal skin infections are best treated with tolnaftate or clotrimazole.

Chagas' Disease (South American trypanosomiasis) This is a chronic disease, very rarely caught by travellers and difficult to treat. It is transmitted by the simultaneous biting and excreting of the Reduvid bug, also known as the Vinchuca or Barbeiro. Somewhat resembling a small cockroach, this nocturnal bug lives in poor adobe houses with dirt floors often frequented by opossums. If you cannot avoid such accommodation, sleep off the floor with a candle lit, use a mosquito net, keep as much of your skin covered as possible, and use DET repellent or a spray insecticide. If you are bitten overnight (the bites are painless) do not scratch them, but wash thoroughly with soap and water.

Dengue Fever This is increasing worldwide, including in Mexico and Central American countries and the Caribbean. It can be completely prevented by avoiding mosquito bites in the same way as malaria. No vaccine is available. Dengue is an unpleasant and painful disease, which causes a high temperature and body pains; visitors are spared the more serious forms (haemorrhagic types) which are a problem for local people who have been exposed to the disease more than once. There is no specific treatment for dengue – just pain killers and rest. Seek advice on where the Aedes mosquitoe is present and take precautions against being bitten (see page 70).

Intestinal Worms These are common and the more serious ones, such as hookworm, can be contracted from walking barefoot on infested earth or beaches. Some cause an itchy rash on the feet, 'cutaneous larva migrans'. Schistosomiasis (bilharzia) is also present in some lakes – take local advice before swimming in them.

Leptospirosis Various forms of leptospirosis occur, transmitted by a bacterium which is excreted in rodent urine. Fresh water and moist soil harbour the organisms which enter the body through cuts and scratches. If you suffer from any form of prolonged fever consult a doctor.

Prickly heat A very common intensely itchy rash is avoided by frequent washing and by wearing loose clothing. It is cured by allowing skin to dry off (through use of powder and spending two nights in an air-conditioned hotel!).

Psychological Disorders First time exposure to countries where sections of the population live in extreme poverty or squalor can cause odd psychological reactions in visitors, or what is more commonly known as culture shock. So can the incessant pestering, especially of women, which is unfortunately common in some of these countries. Simply be prepared for this and try not to over-react.

Rabies Remember that rabies is endemic, so avoid dogs that are behaving strangely and cover your toes at night from the vampire bats, which also carry the disease. If you are bitten by a domestic or wild animal, do not leave things to chance: scrub the wound with soap and water and/or disinfectant, try to have the animal captured (within limits) or at least determine its ownership, where possible, and seek medical assistance at once. The course of treatment depends on whether you have already been satisfactorily vaccinated against rabies. If you have (this is worthwhile if you are spending lengths of time in developing countries) then some further doses of vaccine are all that is required. Human diploid vaccine is the best, but expensive: other, older kinds of vaccine, such as that derived from duck embryos may be the only types available. These are effective, much cheaper and interchangeable generally with the human derived types. If not already vaccinated then anti rabies serum (immunoglobulin) may be required in addition. It is important to finish the course of treatment whether the animal survives or not.

Typhus This can still occur and is carried by ticks. There is usually a reaction at the site of the bite and a fever. Seek medical advice.

Other tropical diseases and problems found in jungle areas are usually transmitted by biting insects. They are often related to African diseases and were probably introduced by the slave labour trade. Onchocerciasis (river blindness) carried by blackflies is found in parts of Mexico. Leishmaniasis (Espundia) is carried by sandflies and causes a sore that will not heal or a severe nasal infection. Wearing long trousers and a long sleeved shirt in infected areas protects against these flies. DET is also effective. Epidemics of meningitis occur from time-to-time. Be careful about swimming in piranha or caribe infested rivers. It is a good idea not to swim naked: the Candiru fish can follow urine currents and become lodged in body orifices. Swimwear offers some protection.

When you return home

Remember to take your antimalarial tablets for six weeks after leaving the malarial area. If you have had attacks of diarrhoea it is worth having a stool specimen tested in case you have picked up amoebas. If you have been living rough, blood tests may be worthwhile to detect worms and other parasites. If you have been exposed to Bilharzia (schistosomiasis) by swimming in lakes, etc, check by means of a blood test when you get home, but leave it for six weeks because the test is slow to become positive. Report any untoward symptoms to your doctor and tell him exactly where you have been and, if you know, what the likelihood is of having contracted the disease to which you were exposed.

The above information has been compiled for us by Dr David Snashall, who is presently Senior Lecturer in Occupational Health at the United Medical Schools of Guy's & St Thomas' Hospitals in London and Chief Medical Advisor of the British Foreign and Commonwealth Office. He has travelled extensively in Central and South America and the Caribbean, worked in Peru and in East Africa and keeps in close touch with developments in preventative and tropical medicine.

Further reading

Travellers wanting more information than we have space to provide, on archaeological sites for instance, would do well to use the widely available *Panorama Guides* and the *Easy Guides* written by Richard Bloomgarden, with plans and good illustrations. Also available are Miniguides to archaeological and historical sites, published in various languages by INAH, US$0.75 each. You will appreciate archaeological sites much more if you do some research before visiting them. Do not expect to find leaflets or books at the sites, stock up before you visit. For ornithologists: *A Field Guide to Mexican Birds*, Peterson and Chalif, Houghton Mifflin, 1973, has been recommended; *Finding Birds in Mexico*, by Ernest P Edwards, Box AQ, Sweet Briar, Virginia 24595, USA, is recommended as detailed and thorough. Two books by Rudi Robins are: *One-day Car Trips from Mexico City*, and *Weekend Trips to Cities near Mexico City*. Highly recommended, practical and entertaining is *The People's Guide to Mexico* by Carl Franz (John Muir Publications, Santa Fe, NM), now in its eighth edition, 1990; there is also a *People's Guide Travel Letter.* Another publication *Back Country Mexico, A Traveller's Guide and Phrase Book,* by Bob Burlison and David H Riskind (University of Texas Press, Box 7819, Austin, Texas, 78713-7819), has also been recommended. *Mexico From The Driver's Seat,* by Mike Nelson, is published by Sanborn's (see Motoring, above). Also *Hidden Mexico* by Rebecca Brüns.

Recommended reading for the Maya archaeological area: *The Maya,* by MD Coe (Pelican Books, or large format edition, Thames and Hudson); C Bruce Hunter, *A Guide to Ancient Mayan Ruins* (University of Oklahoma Press, 1986); Joyce Kelly, *An Archaeological Guide to Mexico's Yucatán Peninsula (the states of Yucatán, Quintana Roo and Campeche)* published by University of Oklahoma Press, Norman and London, 1993, with maps, photos, 364 pages, accessible, informative and very good. *More Maya Missions. Exploring Colonial Chiapas,* written and illustrated by Richard D Perry (Espadaña Press, PO Box 31067, Santa Barbara, CA 93130, USA) is the latest in a series; also published, *Maya Missions (in Yucatán)* and *Mexico's Fortress Monasteries (Central Mexico and Oaxaca).* For the Puuc region, *Guide to Puuc Region,* Prof Gualberto Zapata Alonzo (US$7.30), has been recommended. For a contemporary account of travel in the Maya region, see *Time among the Maya,* by Ronald Wright. Perhaps the most descriptive of travel in the region is John L Stephens, *Incidents of Travel in Central America, Chiapas and Yucatán,* with illustrations by Frederick Catherwood (several editions exist). *Western Mexico: A Traveller's Treasury,* by Tony Burton (Editorial Agata, Guadalajara), has also been suggested for further reading. For a short guide to the people, politics, geography, history, economy and culture, *In Focus, Mexico* by John Ross is recommended as part of the In Focus series published by Latin America Bureau in 1996, ISBN 1 899365 05 2.

The Mexican Government Tourist Highway map is available free of charge at tourist offices (when in stock). If driving from the USA you get a free map if you buy your insurance at Sanborn's in the border cities. The official map printers, Detenal, produce the only good large-scale maps of the country.   **Maps**

Guía Roji publish a wide range of regional maps, city plans and gazettes, available at most bookshops. The Dirección General de Oceanografía, Calle Medellín 10, near Insurgentes metro station, sells excellent maps of the entire coastline of Mexico. Good detailed maps of states of Mexico and the country itself from Dirección General de Geografía y Meteorología, Avenida Observatorio 192, México 18, DF, T55151527 (go to Observatorio metro station and up Calle Sur 114, then turn right a short distance down Avenida Observatorio). Best road maps of Mexican states, free, on polite written request, from Director General de Programación, Xola 1755, 8th floor, México 12 DF (building is on the corner of Xola with Avenida Universidad). Mapas Turísticos de México has Mexican (stocks Detenal maps) and world-maps; permanent exhibition at Río Rhin 29,

Essentials

Colonia Cuauhtémoc, México 5 DF, T5662177. Maps are also available from Instituto Nacional de Estadística, Geografía e Informática (INEGI), which has branches in Mexico City (see page 79) and in state capitals (US$3 per sheet). Pemex road atlas, *Atlas de Carreteras y Ciudades Turísticas*, US$5 in bookshops (for example Sanborns), has 20 pages of city maps, almost every road one may need, contour lines, points of interest, service stations, etc (it is rarely on sale in Pemex stations), recommended. Similar, and good, is *The Green Guide*. As well as its maps of Mexico City and Baja California, ITM of Vancouver (PO Box 2290, Vancouver, BC, V6B 3W5, Canada) publish a map of Mexico (1:3,300,000, 1993-94), Mexico: South (1:1,000,000, 1992-93) and Yucatán (1:1,000,000, third edition, 1993-95). The Mexican Automobile Association (AMA) is at Orizaba 7, 06700 México DF, T52088329, F55116285; they sell an indispensable road guide, with good maps and very useful lists of hotels, with current prices. The ANA (Asociación Nacional Automobilística) sells similar but not such good material; offices in Insurgentes (Metro Insurgentes) and Avenida Jalisco 27, México 18 DF. For road conditions consult the AMA, which is quite reliable. The AAA road map is fine for major roads, less good off the beaten track. Also recommended, maps published by HFET SA, Fresas 27, Colonia del Valle, México DF, T55592310/ 55592320, Mexico City, Estado de México and Mapectual Road Atlas of the whole country, US$6 (from Sanborns). The best road map obtainable outside the country is Berndtson & Berndtson Yucatán 1:1,000,000, plastic coated, but already outdated (as they all are) by an ambitious road building programme undertaken by Pemex (rural roads) and the Federal government.

Mexico on the web

US Library of Congress Study: Mexico lcweb2.loc.gov/frd/cs/mxtoc.html Excellent starting point for learning about Mexico. Includes facts at a glance and sections on ethnicity, history and government.

Mexico Tourist Board www.mexico-travel.com. This is a pretty good site as far as tourist boards go.

Mexicanwave www.mexicanwave.com. A well constructed site which is updated daily. As well as current affairs, it has feature articles and advice on travel in Mexico. Look out for the forum where comments from fellow travellers are exchanged. A good one to keep in your 'favourites'.

Mexico Web www.mexicoweb.com/

World Travel Guide - Mexico www.wtgonline.com/data/mex/mex.asp Overview of Mexico for travellers, with useful "Essentials" section with facts on visas, public holidays, money and health.

GORP: Basic Mexico www.gorp.com/gorp/location/latamer/mexico.htm. Overview of the country, with lots of detailed information including some good suggestions and tips on more adventurous travel.

Mexico Reference desk www.lanic.utexas.edu/la/Mexico/. A huge site containing a variety of information about Mexico ranging from anthropology to sport and trade. Rather academic in tone, it is nevertheless an excellent source for background information.

Cyber cafés www.amcc.org.mx. The Asociación Mexicana de Cyber Cafés site lists some (but not all) cyber cafés in Mexico. If this is not available, www.cybercaptive.com is a good alternative.

Mexico City

3

Mexico City

Mexico City, the capital, founded by the Spaniards in 1521, was built upon the remains of Tenochtitlán, the Aztec capital. Although very little remains of that island city, the one that replaced it is equally impressive. It is colourful, bawdy, gaudy, vibrant, cultured, noisy, sometimes dangerous, but always fascinating. It will enthrall. The Valley of Mexico, the basin in which it lies, is about 110 km long by 30 km wide. Rimming this valley is a sentinel-like chain of peaks of the Sierra Nevada mountains.

Although one of the largest in the world, Mexico City is not intimidating; those visitors who surrender themselves to its rhythm fare very well. But you will need to allocate sufficient time to do it justice, especially the Centro Histórico, best managed on foot with the occasional break for a refresco (soft drink). With so much to offer architecture, magnificent church interiors, museums and murals full of the optimism of the post-Revolution period, the centre invites you to drift around savouring its delights (and, unfortunately, its pollution).

There is music, dance and theatre in parks and plazas round every corner. Spend the weekend exploring the suburbs of San Angel, Coyoacán and Xochimilco, and in the evening stroll around Plaza Garibaldi and watch the many mariachi bands vie with each other to make themselves heard. It is great fun.

Phone code: 5
Colour map 3, grid B5
Population: 20m
Altitude: 2,240m

About one in four of Mexico's population live in this city, which has over half the country's manufacturing employment and much of the nation's industrial smog (the worst months being December to February). Measures such as closing the huge Pemex refinery have reduced lead and sulphur dioxide emissions to acceptable levels, but the ozone level is occasionally dangerous. Common ailments are a burning sensation in the eyes (contact-lens wearers take note) and nose, and a sore throat. Citizens are advised by the local authorities not to smoke and not to take outdoor exercise. The English-language dailies, *The*

Mexico City orientation

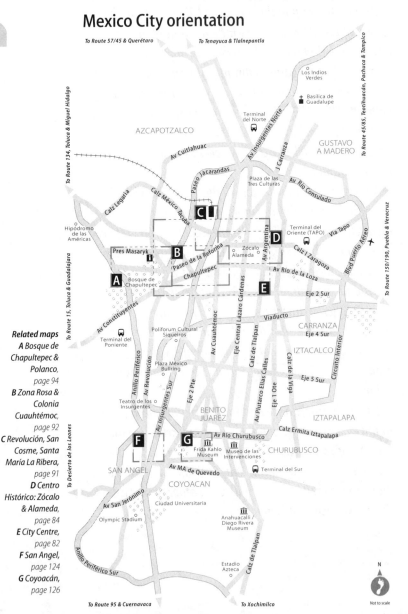

Related maps

A Bosque de Chapultepec & Polanco, page 94

B Zona Rosa & Colonia Cuauhtémoc, page 92

C Revolución, San Cosme, Santa María La Ribera, page 91

D Centro Histórico: Zócalo & Alameda, page 84

E City Centre, page 82

F San Angel, page 124

G Coyoacán, page 126

News and the *Mexico City Times* give analysis of the air quality, with warnings and advice.

The city suffers from a fever of demolition and rebuilding, especially since the heavy damage caused by the September 1985 earthquake. This was concentrated along the Paseo de la Reforma, Avenida Juárez, the Alameda, and various suburbs and residential districts. About 20,000 people are believed to have lost their lives, largely in multi-storey housing and government-controlled buildings, including Juárez hospital in which there were about 3,000 fatalities.

Mexico City has long burst its ancient boundaries and spread; some of the new residential suburbs are most imaginatively planned, though there are many appalling shanty-towns. Like all big centres it is faced with a fearsome traffic problem, despite the building of inner and outer ring roads (the Circuito Interior and the Periférico). Nine metro lines now operate, plus the *tren ligero* in the south and the *tren férreo* in the east. There is a large traffic-free area east of the Zócalo.

Ins and outs

Mexico City is well served by air and road, less well connected by rail. The airport is about 12 km from the city centre. For details of international scheduled flights see Essentials, page 30, and for airport information see page 117. Domestic flights go to all major towns in Mexico. There are 4 long distance bus terminals, north, south, east and west, according to the regions they serve. The railway station is fairly central but services are unreliable. Passenger services operate from Saltillo in the north and Veracruz on the east coast.

Getting there
See also Transport, page 113

Traffic is congested and you are not recommended to try and drive round Mexico City. The metro is the most convenient form of public transport and is easy and cheap to use, see page 113. It is also less polluted than the alternatives, such as buses and taxis. Most sights are within easy walking distance of a metro station. Take care in the centre at quiet times (eg Sunday afternoon) and in Chapultepec, where Sunday is the safest day. At night you are advised to phone for a taxi.

Getting around

You will find, as you explore the city, that you use two thoroughfares more than any others. The most famous is Paseo de la Reforma, with a tree-shaded, wide centre section and two side lanes. It skirts the north edge of the Bosque de Chapultepec and then runs diagonally northeast past the Centro Histórico and on towards the Basílica de Guadalupe, still fairly wide but without side lanes. The other and longer thoroughfare is Av Insurgentes, a diagonal north-south artery about 35 km long. Reforma and Insurgentes bisect at a *plazuela* with a statue of Cuauhtémoc, the last of the Aztec emperors. Other important thoroughfares are the Eje Central (Lázaro Cárdenas), which runs south to north only from the Circuito Interior (near the Olympic swimming pool) via Bellas Artes and the Latin American Tower, through Tlatelolco, past the Terminal del Norte (North Bus Terminal) and beyond; the Calzada de Tlalpan, which runs north to south from near the city centre, past the Terminal del Sur (South Bus Terminal) and leads out of the city towards Cuernavaca; the Circuito Interior, which encircles most of the city at an average distance of about 5 km from the centre; further out is the Periférico; and crossing from the east, near the airport, and joining the Periférico in the west is the Viaducto Miguel Alemán.

Orientation

Maps Instituto Nacional de Estadística Geografía e Informática (INEGI) sells maps and has information, branches in each state capital and in the Distrito Federal in the arcade below the traffic roundabout at Insurgentes (where the metro station is), open

Mexico City

0800-1600, all maps available, but only one index for consultation. The Automobile Club's (AMA) street map is good, but hard to find. Good maps of the city from *HFET* (see **Maps**, page 73), *Guía Roji* (an excellent A to Z, US$14), *Ciudad de Mexico, mapa turístico* (Quimera Editores, 1999, 1:10,000, US$8.75) and *Trillas Tourist Guide* (US$6.50, recommended). Street vendors on Zócalo and in kiosks sell a large city map for US$3. Good large postcard/maps of Coyoacán, La Alameda Central and San Angel are available at many museums and bookshops. **SETEJ** (Mexican Students' Union), Hamburgo 301, Zona Rosa, metro Sevilla, issues student cards, required to buy hostel cards, T52110743 or 52116636, and deals with ISIS insurance. To obtain a national student card you need 3 photos, passport, confirmation of student status and US$7. Open Mon-Fri 0900-1800, Sat 0900-1400.

Tourist offices   The *Mexican Secretariat of Tourism* (Secretaría de Turismo) is at Masaryk 172, 5th floor, between Hegel and Emerson, Colonia Polanco (reached by bus No 32), T52508555, ext 116, F52542636, emergency hot line T52500123/0151. The amount and quality of printed information available varies enormously, although it is possible to book hotels in other parts of the country. The tourist office produces a telephone directory in English and French. Better information is available at tourist information centres operated by the Mexico City Government at the following points: *Mexico City airport*, Sala B; *Amberes* 54, Zona Rosa. *Terminal de Autobuses del Norte*, main entrance. *Terminal Oriente TAPO* bus station, at the end of tunnel 1; in the *Delegación Coyoacán*, Plaza Hidalgo, Coyoacán; in the *Casa de la Cultura de San Angel*, corner of Revolución and Francisco I Madero, San Angel; *Embarcadero Nativitas*, Xochimilco; and opposite *Hemiciclo a Juárez*, Alameda Central. You may refer complaints here, or to the tourist police, in blue uniforms, who are reported to be very friendly. Articles from the various craft displays can be bought. Free maps not always available, but try Cámara de Comercio de la Ciudad de México, Información Turística, open Mon-Fri 0900-1400, 1500-1800, at Reforma 42, which provides maps and brochures of the city (apparently for government employees only); may otherwise be got from Department of Public Works; or buy in bookshops. Bus and metro maps available. Information bureau outside Insurgentes metro station and on Juárez, just east of Paseo de la Reforma (closed Sun). Tourist information can be dialled between 0800 and 2000 (bilingual operator) on T55259380. For problems, eg theft, fraud, abuse of power by officials, T55160490, Protectur. Also try the *Agencia Especializada en Asuntos de Turista*, Florencia 20, Colonia Juárez, English spoken, very helpful. The attorney general's office for crimes against tourists: T56258761 (Zona Rosa)/56258763 (airport). A weekly magazine, *The Gazer/El Mirón* gives basic information and tips for Mexico City and elsewhere in Mexico. Also *Mexico City Daily Bulletin*, free from most hotels, good listings, exchange rate information unreliable. The magazine *Dónde* (US$2) gives general information, details on hotels, restaurants, crafts and entertainment. *Concierge* is a monthly tourist guide in English and Spanish with information on Mexico City.

Climate   Because of the altitude the climate is mild and exhilarating save for a few days in mid-winter. The normal annual rainfall is 660mm and most of it falls, usually in the late afternoon, between May and Oct. Even in summer the temperature at night is rarely above 13°C and in winter there can be sharp frosts. Despite this, central heating is not common.

Sights

In the following description we start at the Zócalo (main square) and the
streets around it, and move in the general direction of the West, to the Palacio
de Bellas Artes, through the Alameda Central, down Reforma, skirting the
Zona Rosa, until we come to Chapultepec Park. Once the fashionable area, the
Zona Rosa has recently been replaced by **Polanco**, north of Chapultepec, a
luxury residential area with many interesting art galleries and shops. It does
not suffer from the tourists that crowd the Zona Rosa and other chic areas.
Many old houses have carved stone façades, tiled roofs and gardens, especially
on Calle Horacio, a pretty street lined with trees and parks.

Sightseeing in & around the city can easily take up 10 days

Mexico City

Historical centre

Much of the **Centro Histórico** has been refurbished; this is roughly a rectangle
from Alhóndiga/Santísma, east of the Zócalo, to Guerrero, west of the
Alameda; República de Honduras by Plaza Garibaldi, north of the Alameda, to
Arcos de Belén/Izazaga south of the Alameda and Zócalo. Calle Tacuba is
especially fine; street vendors have been banished from it. The *Guía Peatonal*
of Sacbé (US$1.15) is recommended, giving eight suggested walking routes, all
starting from metro stations. Two ways of familiarizing oneself quickly with
the Centro Histórico are to take a trip (US$5 for 45 minutes) on a 1910-type
street car (every 30 minutes from the Museo de la Ciudad de México, Pino
Suárez, or from in front of the Palacio de Bellas Artes), or to ride on a form of
rickshaw (*bici-taxi*) from the Zócalo, US$1.65 for 30 minutes.

The great main square, or Plaza Mayor, centre of the oldest part, is always alive
with people and often vivid with official ceremonies and celebrations, also
with demonstrations and marches. The flag in the centre of the square is raised
at 0600 (0500 in winter), and taken down, with ceremony, at 1800 each day
(1700 in winter). On the north side, on the site of the Great Teocalli or temple
of the Aztecs, is the Cathedral.

Zócalo

This is the largest and oldest cathedral in Latin America. It was first built in 1525
and rebuilding began in 1573; it was consecrated in 1667 and finished in 1813. It
is singularly harmonious considering the many architects employed and time
taken to build it. Restoration work on the exterior has been completed but work
continues inside. The Cathedral has been subject to subsidence over many years
and a lengthy programme of work is under way to build new foundations. A
plumb line hanging from the cupola and a notice board by the west entrance give
some idea of the extent of the problem. The massive scaffolding inside the
Cathedral serves as a preventive measure. There is an underground crypt
reached by stairs in the west wing of the main part of the building (closed for restoration since 1993). Next to the Cathedral is the **Sagrario Metropolitano**,
1769, with fine churrigueresque façade. Unlike the Cathedral, it was built on the
remains of an Aztec pyramid and is more stable than the former.

Cathedral

To the side of the Cathedral are the Aztec ruins of the **Templo Mayor** or
Teocalli, which were discovered in 1978 when public works were being carried
out. They make a very worthwhile visit, especially since the Aztecs built a new
temple every 52 years, and seven have been identified on top of each other. The
Museo Arqueológico del Sitio was opened in 1987 behind the temple to
house various sculptures found in the main pyramid of Tenochtitlán and six

Templo Mayor

Mexico City centre

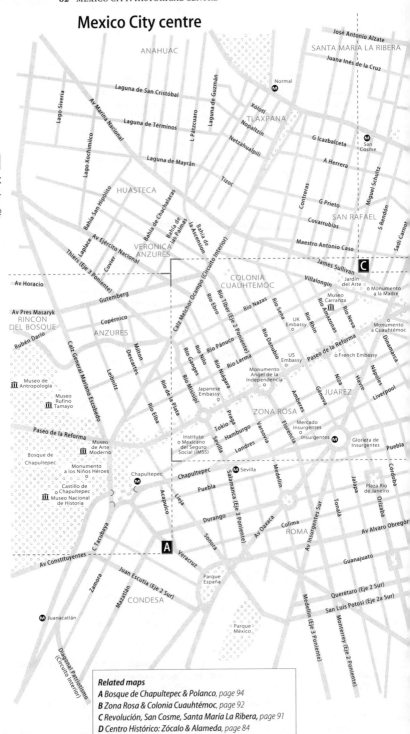

Mexico City

Related maps
A *Bosque de Chapultepec & Polanco*, page 94
B *Zona Rosa & Colonia Cuauhtémoc*, page 92
C *Revolución, San Cosme, Santa María La Ribera*, page 91
D *Centro Histórico: Zócalo & Alameda*, page 84

Mexico City

others, including a huge, circular monolith representing the dismembered body of Coyolxauhqui, who was killed by her brother Huitzilopochtli, the Aztec tutelary god, and many other objects. The Templo Mayor and museum are at Seminario 4 y Guatemala, entrance in the northeast corner of the Zócalo. There is a café, bookshop and left luggage office, and TV displays in the halls with English subtitles. ■ *0900-1730 daily except Mon, last tickets at 1700, museum and temple US$2, free Sun, US$1.25 to take photos, US$3.00 to use video camera; guided tours in Spanish Tue-Fri 0930-1800, Sat 0930-1300, in English Tue-Sat 1000 and 1200, US$0.85 pp (sometimes cancelled at short notice).*

North of the Zócalo On Calle Justo Sierra, north of Cathedral between Guatemala and San Ildefonso, is the **Mexican Geographical Society** (No 19), in whose courtyard is a bust of Humboldt and a statue of Benito Juárez, plus a display of documents and maps

Centro Histórico: Zócalo & Alameda

■ Sleeping	7 Catedral *B5*	14 Frimont *B1*
1 Atlanta *A4*	8 Concordia *C3*	15 Galicia *A3*
2 Avenida *C3*	9 Congreso *B4*	16 Habana *B4*
3 Canadá *B4*	10 Cortés *B2*	17 Howard Johnson Gran
4 Cancún *C1*	11 Cuba *B4*	Hotel de México *C4*
5 Capitol *C3*	12 El Salvador *C3*	18 Isabel la Católica *C4*
6 Carlton *B1*	13 Fleming *C2*	19 Jena *B1*

(ask at the door to be shown in); opposite are the **Anfiteatro Simón Bolívar**, with murals of his life in the lobby and an attractive theatre, and the former **Colegio San Ildefonso**, built 1749 as the Jesuit School of San Ildefonso in splendid baroque (it later became the Escuela Nacional Preparatoria). There are important frescoes by Orozco (including *Revolutionary Trinity* and *The Trench*) and, in the Anfiteatro Bolívar, by Diego Rivera (*Creation*) and Fernando Leal, all of which are in excellent condition. There is another Leal mural, *Lord of Chalma*, in the stairwell separating the two floors of Orozco works, as well as Jean Charlot's *Massacre in the Templo Mayor*. In a stairwell of the Colegio Chico there are experimental murals by Siqueiros. The whole interior has been magnificently restored. There are occasional important temporary exhibitions. More Orozco frescoes can be seen at the Biblioteca Iberoamericana on Cuba between República de Brasil and Argentina (for more information on the muralists and

Mexico City

their work, see page 99-101). Just along the road is the **Museo de la Caricatura**, Calle de Donceles 97. Housed in the former Colegio de Cristo, this collection includes works by contemporary cartoonists as well as the influential artist José Guadalupe Posada, famous for using skeletal images in his caricatures. ■ *Tue-Sun, 1000-1800, US$0.70.*

The **Secretaría de Educación Pública**, on Argentina 28, three blocks from the Zócalo, was built in 1922. It contains frescoes by a number of painters and includes some of Diego Rivera's masterpieces, painted between 1923 and 1928, illustrating the lives and sufferings of the common people, as well as satirising the rich. Look out for *Día de Muertos* (Day of the Dead) on the ground floor (far left in second courtyard) and, on the first floor, *El pan nuestro* (Our Daily Bread) showing the poor at supper, *El banquete de Wall Street*(The Wall Street Banquet), and the splendidly restored *La cena del capitalista* (The Capitalist's Supper). ■ *Daily, 1000-1800, free.* A long passageway connects the Secretaría with the older Ex-Aduana de Santo Domingo where there is a dynamic Siqueiros mural *Patriots and Parricides*. ■ *Mon-Sun 1100-1800, except Wed 1100-2100, US$2, Sun US$1.30.*

Plaza Santo Domingo, two blocks north of the Cathedral, is an intimate little plaza surrounded by fine colonial buildings. There is the Antigua Aduana (former customs house) on the east side; the Portales de Santo Domingo, on the west side, where public scribes and owners of small hand-operated printing presses still carry on their business; the church of Santo Domingo, in Mexican baroque, 1737, on the north side (note the carving on the doors and façade); and the old Edificio de la Inquisición, where the tribunals of the Inquisition were held, at the northeast corner. By standing on tiptoe in the men's room one can see – if tall enough – through the window into the prison cells of the Inquisition, which are not yet open to the public. It became the Escuela Nacional de la Medicina and is now the **Museo de la Medicina Mexicana**, Brasil 33. There is a remarkable staircase in the patio and it also has a theatre. The nearby streets contain some fine examples of colonial architecture.

Two blocks east of Santo Domingo are the church and convent of **San Pedro y San Pablo** (1603), both massive structures and now turned over to secular use. A block north is the Mercado Rodríguez, a public market with striking mural decorations.

The **Church of Loreto**, built 1816 and now tilting badly, but being restored, is on a square of the same name, surrounded by colonial buildings. Its façade is a remarkable example of 'primitive' or 'radical' neoclassicism.

La Santísima Trinidad (1677, remodelled 1755), a little further south, on Moneda, should be seen for its fine towers and the rich carvings on its façade. **Museo José Luis Cuevas**, Academia 13, in a large colonial building. It houses a permanent collection of paintings, drawings and sculptures (one is two storeys high) by the controversial, contemporary Cuevas (**NB** the Sala Erótica), and temporary exhibitions. ■ *Tue-Fri 1000-1830, Sat-Sun 1000-1730, US$1.*

La Merced

For details of museums far from the centre, see under Suburbs, page 129

The **Mercado Merced** (metro Merced), said to be the largest market in all the Americas, dates back over 400 years. Its activities spread over several blocks and it is well worth a visit. In the northern quarter of this market are the ruins of La Merced monastery; the fine 18th-century patio is almost all that survives; the courtyard, on Avenida Uruguay, between Calle Talavera and Calle Jesús María, opposite No 171, is nearly restored. **Museo Legislativo** is inside the Palacio Legislativo on Avenida Congreso de la Unión 66, entrance in Sidar y Rivorosa, Metro Candelaria east of La Merced. It shows the development of the legislative processes in Mexico from pre-Hispanic times to the 20th century. ■ *1000-1800, closed Mon, free.*

Heading back towards the centre the oldest hospital in continental America, **Jesús Nazareno**, is at 20 de Noviembre 82. It was founded in 1526 by Cortés and was remodelled in 1928, save for the patio and staircase. Cortés' bones have been kept since 1794 in the adjoining church, on the corner of Pino Suárez and República de El Salvador, diagonally opposite the Museo de la Ciudad (see page 100). Further south, **Museo de la Charrería**, on Isabel la Católica esquina José María Izazaga, is close to Metro Isabel la Católica. It is small, with interesting artefacts and history of the *charro*. Information labels are in Spanish, English and French. ■ *Free.*

Museo de la Ciudad, on Avenida Pino Suárez and República de El Salvador, two blocks south of the Zócalo, shows the geology of the city and has life-size figures in period costumes showing the history of different peoples before Cortés. It also has a photographic exhibition of the construction of the metro system. The permanent exhibition is sometimes inaccessible during temporary shows. In the attic above the museum is the studio of Joaquín Clausell, with walls covered with impressionist miniatures. ■ *Tue-Thu, free.* Two blocks south of this museum at Mesones 139 is the **Anglican (Episcopal) Cathedral**, called the Catedral de San José de Gracia. Built in 1642 as a Roman Catholic church, it was given by the Benito Juárez government to the Episcopal Mission in Mexico. Juárez himself often attended services in it.

The National Palace takes up the whole of the eastern side of the Zócalo. Built **Palacio** on the site of the Palace of Moctezuma and rebuilt in 1692 in colonial baroque, **Nacional** it has a façade of the red volcanic stone called *tezontle*; the top floor was added by President Calles in the 1920s. It houses various government departments. Over the central door hangs the Liberty Bell, rung at 2300 on 15 September by the President, who commemorates Mexican Independence from Spain and gives the multitude the *Grito* – '¡Viva México!'

The staircase leading to the first floor of the inner courtyard and two of the walls of the first floor are decorated with frescoes by Diego Rivera. The right-hand panel on the staircase (1929) depicts pre-Hispanic Mexico; the large central panel (275.17 sq m and started 1929, finished 1935) shows the History of Mexico from 1521 to 1930 and the panel on the left is known as *El mundo de hoy y de mañana* (The World Today and Tomorrow, 1934). The first fresco (4.92 x 9.71 m) on the first floor is known variously as *La Gran Tenochtitlán* and *El mercado de Tlatelolco* (1945), and shows the market of Tlatelolco against a background of the ancient city of Tenochtitlán. There follow representations of various indigenous cultures – Purépecha, Mixteca-Zapoteca, Totonaca and Huasteca (the last showing the cultivation and worship of maize), culminating in the final fresco, which shows in narrative form the arrival of Hernán Cortés in Veracruz. These murals were done between 1942 and 1951. There are guides who are knowledgeable and who speak English. They also sell postcards of the murals, but much better reproductions of the same works are available in most museums in the city. The Juárez Museum which used to be on the first floor, has been moved to Avenida Higalgo 79.

On the first and second floors of the Palacio Nacional, on the left as one enters the great courtyard, an area formerly occupied by government offices has been transformed into elegant galleries open to the public housing temporary exhibitions. Across from the main entrance and beyond the courtyard is a pleasant open-air area which the public can also visit. **Museo de las Culturas**, Moneda 13, behind the Palacio Nacional holds exhibitions from countries worldwide and has some historical information. ■ *0930-1800, closed Sun, free.*

Mexico City

The **Suprema Corte de Justicia de la Nación**, opposite Palacio Nacional, on the southeast corner of the Zócalo, has frescoes by Orozco (*National Riches* and *Proletarian Struggle*). ■ *Closes at 1400*. The ornate building in the southwest corner of the Zócalo is the **Antiguo Ayuntamiento** (City Hall), which is now used for ceremonial purposes and is where visiting dignitaries are granted the Keys of the City.

On the west side of the Zócalo are the Portales de los Mercaderes (Arcades of the Merchants), which have been very busy since they were built in 1524. North of them, opposite the Cathedral, is the **Monte de Piedad** (National Pawnshop), established in the 18th century and housed in a 16th-century building. Prices are government controlled and bargains are often found. Auctions are held each Friday at 1000 (first, second and third Friday for jewellery and watches, fourth for everything else), US dollars accepted.

Zócalo to Alameda Avenida Madero leads from the Zócalo west to the Alameda. On it is the late 16th-century **La Profesa** church with a fine high altar and a leaning tower. The 18th-century **Palacio de Iturbide**, Avenida Madero 17, once the home of Emperor Agustín (1821-23), has been restored and has a clear plastic roof. Wander around, it is now a bank head office. The **Museo Serfín**, Madero 33, displays indigenous costumes in two rooms. ■ *Tue-Sun, 1000-1700. Free.*

The 16th-century **Casa de los Azulejos** (House of Tiles) is near the Alameda on Avenida Madero. It is brilliantly faced with blue and white 18th-century Puebla tiles. Occupied by the Zapatista army during the Revolution, it is now home to *Sanborn's Restaurant*. The staircase walls are covered with an Orozco fresco *Omniscience* (1925). Opposite is the **Church of San Francisco**, founded in 1525 by the 'Apostles of Mexico', the first 12 Franciscans to reach the country. It was by far the most important church in colonial days, attended by the Viceroys themselves. Cortés' body rested here for some time, as did 'Emperor' Iturbide's.

Beyond San Francisco church, Eje Central Lázaro Cárdenas, formerly Calle San Juan de Letrán, leads south towards **Colegio Las Vizcaínas**, at Plaza Las Vizcaínas, built in 1734 as a school for girls; some of it is still used as such, but some of it has become slum tenements. In spite of neglect, it is still the best example of colonial secular baroque architecture in the city. ■ *Not open to the public; permission to visit sometimes given.*

The **Palacio de Minería** (1797), Tacuba 9, is a fine old building, now restored and once more level on its foundations. From 1910 to 1954 it was the Escuela Nacional de Ingeniería; there is a permanent exhibition of meteorites from all over Mexico (up to 14 tonnes). ■ *Free.* There are cheap concerts on Sunday at 1700, upstairs. Moved from the Plaza de la Reforma to Plaza Manuel Tolsá opposite the Palacio is the great equestrian statue, *El Caballito*, of King Charles IV, cast in 1802; it weighs 26 tonnes and is the second-largest bronze casting in the world.

The **Museo Nacional de Arte**, Tacuba 8, is opposite Palacio de Minería, near the main Post Office. It was built in 1904 and designed by the Italian architect, Silvio Contri, as the Palacio de Comunicaciones. The building has magnificent staircases made by the Florentine firm Pignone. It houses a large collection of Mexican paintings, drawings, sculptures and ceramics dating from the 16th century to 1950. It has the largest number of paintings (more than 100) by José María Velasco in Mexico City, as well as works by Miguel Cabrera, Gerardo Murillo, Rivera, Orozco, Siqueiros, Tamayo and Anguiano. There is also a giftshop. ■ *Tue-Sun, 1000-1730. US$2.00, Sun free.* The **Escuela Nacional de Artes Plásticas** at the corner of Academia and Moneda, houses about 50 modern Mexican paintings.

On the corner of Tacuba and the Eje Central (Lázaro Cárdenas) is the magnificent **Correo Central** (Post Office), commissioned 1902, completed 1907. The postal museum on the first floor with exhibits from mid-18th century is well worth a visit. ■ *Mon-Fri 0900-1800, Sat 1000-1400, free.*

The Palacio was refurbished, inside and out, in 1994 to celebrate its diamond jubilee; the garden in front of the marble apron has been laid out as originally designed. A large, showy building, interesting for Art Deco lovers (see the fabulous stained-glass skylight in the roof), it houses a museum, theatre, a *cafetería* at mezzanine level (light, serving average continental food at moderate prices) and an excellent bookshop on the arts. The museum has old and contemporary paintings, prints, sculptures, and handicrafts. There are spirited Riveras in the room of oils and watercolours. Other frescoes are by Orozco, Tamayo and Siqueiros. ■ *Daily, 1000-2000; Sun, 1000-1900, US$2, free Sun and with ISIC.* There are also prestigious temporary fine art exhibitions (no extra charge). On the top floor is a museum of architecture which holds temporary exhibitions and and shows the building's history. The most remarkable thing about the theatre is its glass curtain designed by Tiffany. It is solemnly raised and lowered before each performance of the Ballet Folclórico de México. The Palacio is listing badly, for it has sunk 4m since it was built. Operas are performed and there are frequent orchestral concerts. ■ *Performances by the **Ballet Folclórico de México** are on Sun, 0930 and 2100, and on Wed at 2100 (check press for details); you must book in advance. Tickets US$12 on the balcony, US$20 and US$25 (cheap balcony seats are not recommended because you see only a third of the stage set, although you can see the performers). Tickets are on sale from 1100; hotels, agencies, etc only sell the most expensive; cheaper tickets only at the theatre.* There are cheap concerts at 1200 on Sunday, and also at Teatro Hidalgo, behind Bellas Artes on Hidalgo, at the same time, book in advance. Concessions of 50 percent are available for students and teachers (show documents at counter on right before going to the box office).

Palacio de Bellas Artes
The fresco by Rivera is a copy of the one rubbed out in disapproval at Radio City, New York.

Across the road is the **Torre Latinoamericana** which has a viewing platform with telescopes on the 44th floor. The *cafetería* is poor, but try the Coca-Cola with lemon ice-cream. ■ *0900-2300, US$3.50 to go up.* This great glass tower dominates the gardens of the **Alameda Central**, once the Aztec market and later the place of execution for the Spanish Inquisition. Beneath the broken shade of eucalyptus, cypress and ragged palms, wide paths link fountains and heroic statues. It became a popular area for all social classes to stroll casually in the 19th century. It is now much more a common thoroughfare, with many temporary stalls at certain festive times of year. On Sunday afternoons it is a popular walking-place for young women in domestic service. The park is illuminated at night. There is much rebuilding going on in this area which was badly affected by the 1985 earthquake.

The Alameda

Along the south side of the Alameda runs Avenida Juárez, a broad street with a mixture of old and new buildings. Opposite the Palacio de Bellas Artes, is a building known as **La Nacional**, which was Mexico City's first skyscraper in the 1930s. Look carefully at its perpendicularity, a result of the 1985 earthquake.

Also on the south side of the Alameda is the **Hemiciclo a Juárez**, designed by Guillermo de Heredia in white marble, inaugurated in 1910 to mark the centenary of Independence. Opposite, the colonial church of Corpus Christi is used to display and sell folk arts and crafts. Further west a sunken section of the pavement shelters the **Plaza de las Esculturas** (1998), with 19th-century sculptures. A stroll down Calle Dolores, a busy and fascinating street, leads to the market of San Juan. Three blocks west on Plaza Ciudadela, is a large

Mexico City

colonial building, **La Ciudadela**, dating from 1700. It has been used for all kinds of purposes but is now a library. On the other side of the Plaza, the **Mercado de la Ciudadela** sells crafts from all over Mexico.

Diego Rivera's huge (15m by 4.80m) and fascinating mural, the *Sueño de una Tarde Dominical en la Alameda Central*, was removed from the earthquake-damaged *Hotel del Prado* on Avenida Juárez in 1985 and now occupies its own purpose-built museum, the **Museo Mural Diego Rivera**, on the north side of the Jardín de la Solidaridad at the west end of the Alameda Central. One of Rivera's finest works, it presents a pageant of Mexican history from the Conquest up to the 1940s with vivid portraits of national and foreign figures, heroes and villains as well as characters from everyday life. It is highly recommended. ■ *Tue-Sun 1000-1800, US$1, free for students with ISIC card.*

Around the corner from the Museo Mural, on Dr Mora, 7, is the **Pinacoteca Virreinal**, in the former church of San Diego (1621), a gallery containing colonial and religious paintings of the 16th-18th centuries. ■ *Tue-Sun 1000-1800. Free.*

On the northern side of the Alameda, on Avenida Hidalgo, is the Jardín Morelos, flanked by two old churches: **Santa Veracruz** (1730) to the right and **San Juan de Dios** to the left. The latter has a richly carved baroque exterior; its image of San Antonio de Padua is visited by those who are broken-hearted from love. The **Franz Mayer** museum is located next to this church, in the former Hospital de San Juan de Dios, which was built in the 17th century. Recently rebuilt and exquisitely restored, it houses a library and an important decorative arts collection of ceramics, glass, silver, time pieces, furniture and textiles, as well as Mexican and European paintings from the 16th-20th centuries. Its cloister, with a pleasant *cafetería*, is an oasis of peace in the heart of the city. ■ *1000-1700 except Mon; US$1.15 (US$0.30 if only visiting the cloister), free Tue.* On the same side of Hidalgo, next to the Franz Mayer, is the **Museo de la Estampa** (Museum of Engraving). ■ *1000-1700 (closed Mon), US$1.50.* A little further west, just before Metro Hidalgo, is the former Augustine Hospice (1780) of Santo Tomás de Villanueva, now the **Hotel Cortés**.

Plaza Garibaldi

On one side of Plaza Garibaldi is a gigantic eating hall, different stalls sell different courses, very entertaining.

About four blocks north of the Post Office off Eje Central Lázaro Cárdenas is Plaza Garibaldi, a must, especially on Friday and Saturday night, when up to 200 *mariachis* in their traditional costume of huge sombrero, tight silver-embroidered trousers, pistol and *sarape*, will play your favourite Mexican serenade for US$5 (for a bad one) to US$10 (for a good one). If you arrive by taxi you will be besieged. The whole square throbs with life and the packed bars are cheerful, though there is some danger from thieves and pickpockets, particularly after dark. The **Lagunilla** market is held about four blocks northeast of the plaza, a hive of activity particularly on Sundays.

Plaza de las Tres Culturas

Further north still Lázaro Cárdenas leads to Santa María la Redonda, at the end of which is Plaza Santiago de Tlatelolco, next oldest plaza to the Zócalo. Here was the main market of the Aztecs, and on it, in 1524, the Franciscans built a huge church and convent. This is now known as the Plaza de las Tres Culturas, which shows elements of Aztec, colonial and modern architecture. The Aztec ruins have been restored and the magnificent Franciscan church of Santiago Tlatelolco, completed 1609, is now the focus of the massive, multi-storey Nonoalco-Tlatelolco housing scheme (heavily damaged in the 1985 earthquake), a garden city within a city, with pedestrian and wheeled traffic entirely separate. In October 1968, the Plaza de las Tres Culturas was the scene of serious disturbances between the authorities and students, in which a large number of students were killed (see *The Other Mexico* by Octavio Paz, or *La Noche de Tlatelolco* by Elena Poniatowska, Biblioteca Era, 1971 – *Massacre in Mexico* in

English – and the very readable, and startling, *68* by Paco Ignacio Taibo II, 1991, in Spanish).

From Plaza de las Tres Culturas return south along Reforma. At the corner of Juárez and Reforma is the Lotería Nacional building. Draws are held three times a week, at 2000: an interesting scene, open to the public. Also at this site is a large yellow sculpture known as **El Caballito** after the original equestrian

Revolución, San Cosme, Santa María la Ribera

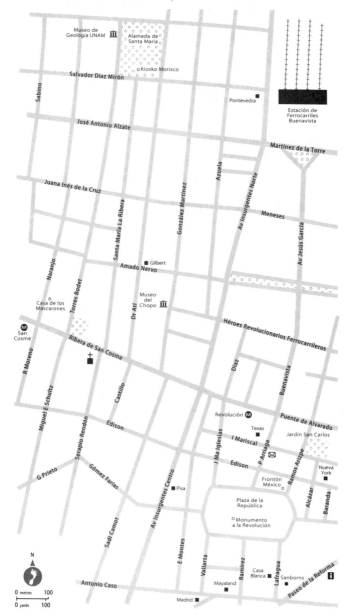

statue that stands in front of the Palacio de Minería (see above).

Beyond Plaza de la Reforma is the **Monumento a la Revolución**, a great copper dome, soaring above supporting columns set on the largest triumphal arches in the world. Beneath the monument is the **Museo Nacional de la Revolución**, which deals with the period 1867-1917, is very interesting and has lots of exhibits, original photographs and videos. ■ *Tue-Sun, 1000-1700, US$1.50.*

The Museo de San Carlos, Puente de Alvarado 50 (Metro Revolución), a 19th-century palace, has fine Mexican colonial painting and a first-class collection of European paintings. It is the former home of Señora Calderón de la Barca who wrote *Life in Mexico* while living there. ■ *Closed Tue, US$2.* It can be reached by crossing Reforma near Metro Hidalgo.

Santa María la Ribera & San Cosme
see map on page 91

These are two wards north of Metro San Cosme which became fashionable residential areas in the late 19th century, and many elegant, if neglected façades are to be seen. On the corner of Ribera de San Cosme and Naranjo next to San Cosme metro note the **Casa de los Mascarones**. Built in 1766, this was the country house of the Conde del Valle de Orizaba, later the Escuela Nacional de Música. Recently restored, it now houses a university computer centre. The **Museo Universitario del Chopo**, Enrique González Martínez 10, between Metro San Cosme and Insurgentes, is near Insurgentes Norte. It holds contemporary international photography and art exhibitions in a church-like building designed by Eiffel. ■ *Wed-Sun 1000-1400, 1600-1900.* In the pleasant

Zona Rosa & Colonia Cuauhtémoc

N

0 metres 200
0 yards 200

■ **Sleeping**	6 Ejecutivo *B5*	12 María Isabel Sheraton *C2*
1 Aristos *C3*	7 Imperial *A6*	13 Plaza Madrid *A5*
2 Calinda Genève *C4*	8 Krystal *D3*	14 Reforma *B5*
3 Casa González *B3*	9 Mallorca *A4*	15 Royal *D3*
4 Century *D3*	10 Marco Polo *C3*	16 Sevilla *A4*
5 Crowne Plaza *A6*	11 María Cristina *B4*	17 Suites Amberes *D3*

Alameda de Santa María, between Pino and Torres Bodet, stands an extraordinary Moorish pavilion designed by Mexicans for the Paris Exhibition in 1889. On its return to Mexico, the *kiosko* was placed in the Alameda Central before being transferred to its present site in 1910. On the west side of this square, on Torres Bodet, is the **Museo del Instituto Geológico**; apart from its collection of fossils and minerals (and magnificent early 20th-century showcases), the building itself (1904) is worth a visit for its swirling wrought-iron staircases and unusual stained-glass windows of mining scenes by Zettler (Munich and Mexico). ■ *Tue-Sun 1000-1700, free.*

Parque Sullivan

Popularly known as Jardín del Arte, Parque Sullivan is reached by going up Paseo de la Reforma to the intersection with Insurgentes, and then west two blocks between Calle Sullivan and Calle Villalongín. Here, each Sunday afternoon, there is a display of paintings, engravings and sculptures near the Monumento a La Madre, packed with sightseers and buyers; everything is for sale (beware of thieves).

Mexico City

Paseo de la Reforma

The wide and handsome Paseo de la Reforma continues to the Bosque de Chapultepec. It is lined with shops, offices, hotels, restaurants and some striking modern buildings: the *Hotel Crowne Plaza*, the Mexican Stock Exchange (*Bolsa de Valores*) and the *Hotel María Cristina*, as well as a red-and-black cuboid office structure on the left. Along it are monuments to Columbus, Cuauhtémoc and, at the intersection with Tiber/Florencia, a 45-m marble column supports the golden form of a female angel representing Independence. Known as 'El Angel' or 'El Angelito' to the Mexicans, the statue fell to the ground in the 1956 earthquake. This is a favourite spot for demonstrations, sporting and national celebrations. One block north of Reforma, the **Museo Carranza**, Lerma y Amazonas, is a museum with items linked to the life of this revolutionery and constitutionalist, and to the Revolution itself. Worth a visit. And just south of Reforma, the **Museo de Cera de la Ciudad de México** (Wax Museum) is in a remarkable house at Londres 6. ■ *1100-1900 daily.*

Zona Rosa

The famous **Zona Rosa** (Pink Zone) lies to the south of Reforma, bounded approximately by Reforma, Sevilla, Avenida Chapultepec and Insurgentes Sur. This was formerly Mexico City's West End, ie the area with the most fashionable stores, restaurants, nightclubs (but no theatres). It suffered considerable damage in the 1985 earthquake, and subsequently lost ground to Polanco (see below). In recent times it has seen a revival, and is once again a very pleasant area in which to stroll, shop (or window-shop) and dine, as there are many open-air or half-covered restaurants. **Casasola Archive**, Praga 16, T5649214, holds amazing photos of the revolutionary period, with reproductions for sale. Be careful, though, as thieves operate in this area, particularly with foreign tourists in their sights, and it is not to be recommended late at night especially at the weekends.

Just before Chapultepec Park, on the left, is the Secretaría de Salud (health) building. Unfortunately, Rivera's frescoes in this building cannot be seen by the public, who can view only the stained-glass windows on the staircases.

Bosque de Chapultepec

The park with its thousands of *ahuehuete* trees (so sacred to the Aztecs), is beautiful and is now being kept litter-free and well policed (park closes at 1700). The best day to visit is Sunday when it is all much more colourful (and more crowded). The park is divided into three sections: the first, the eastern-most, was a wood inhabited by the Toltecs and Aztecs. Most of the interesting sites are in this section (see below).

Bosque de Chapultepec & Polanco

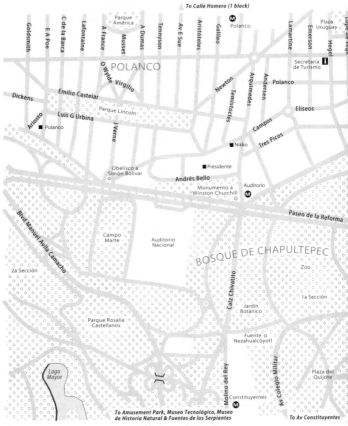

The second section, west of Boulevard Manuel Avila Camacho, was added in 1964. It has a large **amusement park**. There is a wonderful section for children and another for adults and huge roller coasters including the *Montaña Rusa*, one of the world's largest, bridle paths and polo grounds. ◼ *Wed, Fri and weekends, 1030-2000, US$1. Montaña Rusa Sat and Sun only, US$0.40.* Diego Rivera's famous fountain, the **Fuente de Tláloc**, is near the children's amusement park. Close by are the Fuentes de las Serpientes (Snake Fountains). There are two museums in this section: the **Museo Tecnológico** is free; it is operated by the Federal Electricity Commission with touchable exhibits which demonstrate electrical and energy principles. It is located beside the roller coasters. The **Museo de Historia Natural** is beside the Lago Menor of the second section. ◼ *1000-1700, Tue-Sun.* Both the Lago Menor and Lago Mayor are popular for boating; on the shore of each is a restaurant.

The third section, which was added in 1974, stretches a long way beyond the Panteón Civil de Dolores (cemetery), and has little to interest the tourist.

The first section contains a maze of pathways, the **Plaza del Quijote** and **Monumento a los Niños Héroes** (frequently visited by foreign heads of state, see box page 96), a large lake and a smaller one (with an outdoor theatre used for performances of *Swan Lake* and similar), shaded areas, and stalls selling snacks

Mexico City

The Young Butterflies of Grasshopper Hill

It was believed, in pre-Hispanic times, that those warriors who had died in battle would become butterflies and accompany the Sun on his daily emergence on the eastern horizon until they reached noon. Chapultepec, dominating the park of the same name, means Grasshopper Hill. A castle, now a museum, crowns it; in 1847, however, it was the Mexican Military College, where young cadets were trained to be officers in the Mexican Army. On 13 September of that year, the US forces had already made impressive advances, especially after the Battle of Churubusco. Victory at Chapultepec was guaranteed to lead to the capture of Mexico City. As the US forces prepared for the attack, preparations were being made at San Angel and Mixcoac to execute those members of the St Patrick's Battalion who had been captured at Churubusco and convicted of desertion. At Mixcoac, Colonel Harney, the officer entrusted to oversee the executions of the prisoners from Tacubaya, had them ready with nooses around their necks, but decided that they should

remain where they were until a US victory was proclaimed by raising the American flag over Chapultepec Castle.

Several attempts to take the hill were repulsed. The battle raged and the prisoners awaiting execution at Mixcoac slumped on the wagons with the nooses around their necks. They had been there for about four hours when finally the US army gained the heights. As they swept through the castle a number of the teenage cadets threw themselves from the walls rather than surrender (some reports indicate that they were wrapped in the Mexican Flag). They are known as the Niños Héroes, the Heroic Youths. Visitors to Mexico will notice that almost every city or town has a street named Los Niños Héroes de Chapultepec. Will these young heroes have joined their pre-Hispanic counterparts and become the butterflies who accompanied the Sun? And might they have been joined by the prisoners who were finally executed when Colonel Harney saw the US flag soar above Chapultepec Castle? Perhaps.

of all kinds, especially at weekends. There is also a **zoo** with giant pandas and other animals from around the world; it is well laid out, the cages are spacious and most animals seem content. ■ *Free, closed Mon, shuts 1630.* The official residence of the President, **Los Pinos**, is also situated in the first section.

At the top of a hill, and visible from afar (a long climb on foot; train to the top US$0.20, return journey) is the imposing **Castillo de Chapultepec**, with a view over the Valley of Mexico from its beautiful balconies. It now houses the **Museo Nacional de Historia** but its rooms were once used by the Emperor Maximilian and the Empress Carlota during their brief reign. There is an impressive mural by Siqueiros, *From the Dictatorship of Porfirio Díaz to the Revolution* (in Sala XIII, near the entrance) and a notable mural by O'Gorman on the theme of Independence as well as several by Camarena. ■ *0900-1700, US$4.35, free on Sun; long queues on Sun, closed Mon.* Free classical music concerts are given on Sunday at 1200 by the Bellas Artes Chamber Orchestra; arrive early for a seat.

Halfway down the hill is the **Galería de Historia**, which has dioramas, with tape-recorded explanations of Mexican history, and photographs of the 1910 Revolution. Just below the castle are the remains of the famous Arbol de Moctezuma, known locally as *El Sargento*. This immense tree, which has a circumference of 14m, was about 60m high before it was cut down to 10m.

Also in the first section of the Bosque de Chapultepec and on the same side of Reforma as Chapultepec castle, is the **Museo de Arte Moderno**, which has a permanent collection of modern Mexican art and which regularly stages temporary national and international exhibitions. It consists of two circular buildings pleasantly set among trees with sculptures in the grounds. The temporary exhibitions are usually held in the smaller of the two buildings; entrance through the larger one. The delightfully light architecture of the larger building is balanced by a heavy, marble staircase, with a curious acoustic effect on the central landing under a translucent dome, which must have been unplanned. There is a good bookshop, gift shop and an open-air cafeteria behind the first building. A free galleries map and monthly calendar of exhibitions is availaible here and at other museums and galleries. ■ *1100-1800 daily except Mon. US$1.50, free with ISIC card.*

The **Museo Rufino Tamayo** (on the other side of Reforma, cross near the Museo de Arte Moderno, on the way to the Anthropological Museum) has a fine collection of works by Rufino Tamayo and shows contemporary Mexican and other painters. The interior space of the museum is unusual in that it is difficult to know which floor one is on. ■ *1000-1700, closed Mon, US$2, free to students with ISIC card.*

Mexico City

The crowning glory of Chapultepec Park was built by architect Pedro Ramírez Vásquez to house a vast collection illustrating pre-Conquest Mexican culture. It has a 350m façade and an immense patio shaded by a gigantic concrete mushroom measuring 4,200 sq m, the world's largest concrete and steel expanse supported by a single pillar. The largest exhibit (8½ m high, weighing 167 tonnes) is the image of Tlaloc, the rain god, removed (accompanied by protesting cloud bursts) from near the town of Texcoco to the museum. Upstairs is a display of folk costumes, which may be closed Sunday. Attractions include *voladores* and Maya musicians. After more than 10 years, 140 invaluable objects have been returned to the museum; they had been stolen by some rich young people and had been kept in a cupboard in their parents' house in downtown Mexico City.

Museo Nacional de Antropología

The museum is very well organized; each major culture that contributed to the evolution of Mesoamerican civilization is well represented in its own room or *Sala*: Pre-Classic, Teotihuacán, Toltec, Aztec, Oaxaca, Gulf Coast, Maya, Northwestern and Western Mexico. It might be an idea to leave your visit until after you have seen as many of the archaeological sights as possible. You will then understand how each item functioned within the specific culture. Two areas are often missed by visitors: the Torres Bodet Auditorium where visiting archaeologists, art historians, anthropologists, etc, give seminars, often in English and usually free; the Temporary Exhibitions Hall is also worth checking out; it can make a pleasant change when they offer an exhibition unrelated to pre-Hispanic culture.

Because of the enormous number of exhibits to be examined, please allow enough time to do justice to the museum; it is exhausting.

The Biblioteca Nacional de Historia y Antropología is upstairs; access is by means of a staircase to the left as you enter the foyer. It contains a wealth of pre-Hispanic and early-colonial documents. Although admittance is not always possible, those with a special interest in ancient documents (see the facsimile of the Dresden Codex) could ask to speak with the senior librarian, who is charming and probably the most knowledgeable person in this field in Mexico. ■ *Tue-Sat, 0900-1900 and Sun, 1000-1800 (library 0900-2130). US$2.50 except Sun (free, and very crowded; arrive early). Free to those with Mexican student card. Now has some written explanations in English. An audio guide available in English, US$4, including payment on Sun, describes 130 of the exhibits. Guided tours in English or Spanish free with a minimum of 5 people. Ask for the parts you want to see as each tour only visits 2 of 23 halls. Excellent audio-visual introduction free (lasts 1 hr, includes 3D models). If you want to see everything, you need at least 2 days. Permission to photograph (no tripod or flash allowed) US$1, US$5 for video camera. On sale are English and Spanish books plus a few in French and German, and guides to Mexican ruins including maps. Guide books of the museum itself cost US$10-12. Cafetería on site is good, recommended, particularly for the soup, but pricey with long queues at times. The nearest metro is Auditorio.*

Mexico City

 Modern architecture

The most successful religious architecture in Mexico today is to be found in the churches put up by Enrique de la Mora and Felix Candela; a good example is the chapel they built in 1957 for the Missionaries of the Holy Spirit, in a garden behind high walls at Avenida Universidad 1700, T55135137. (An excellent Candela church, and easy to see, is the Iglesia de la Medalla Milagrosa, Matías Romero e Ixcateopan just to the east of Avenida Universidad at the junction of Avenida División del Norte, Metro División del Norte.) All the churches and chapels built by this team have such lightness and balance that they seem scarcely to rest on their foundations. One of the seminal works of one of Mexico's greatest modern architects, Luis Barragán, is at Los Clubes; take Las Arboledas bus from Chapultepec bus station. See also the objet trouvé mural at the Cine Diana, Paseo de la

Reforma 423 in the centre of the city, and Orozco's great thundercloud of composition, the Apocalypse, at the Church of Jesús Nazareno, Bahía Magdalena 28, Colonia Coltongo, T55871705. Both the Hotel Camino Real in Polanco and the IBM technical centre, Calzada Legaria 853, Colonia Irrigación T52705991, were designed by Ricardo Legorreto, and are well worth seeing. Consult Max Cetto's book on modern Mexican architecture. In this connection, Ciudad Universitaria (see page 128) is also well worth a look.

An example of modern hospital architecture is the huge Centro Médico Benito Juárez on Avenida Cuauhtémoc (corner with Morones Prieto), built after the 1985 earthquake. It contains a small shopping centre, theatre and art exhibition complex (Siglo XXI); entrance from Metro Centro Médico.

The **Auditorio Nacional** (beyond the Museo de Antropología), on the left of Reforma, is a vast modern concert-hall. At the rear there are various theatres, and at the far side is the Campo Marte, a large green sports area, where Prince Charles has played polo.

Polanco
Traffic is frequently very congested; avoid taking taxi if possible

To the right of this section of Reforma, and behind the Museo de Antropología, lies the area known as Polanco. It contains some of the most modern (and conspicuous) hotels in the city, eg the Nikko, Presidente and Camino Real, which are at least worth a walk-in visit. Also here are exclusive private residences, commercial art galleries, fashion stores, expensive restaurants and other establishments which are collectively a monument to the consumer society; one glaring example of this is the huge *Palacio de Hierro* department store and offices along Mazaryk. There are also a couple of fairly unremarkable modern churches. There is little of cultural value, with the exception of the **Sala de Arte Siqueiros** (Tres Picos 29). Metro Polanco on Horacio is centrally situated.

Beyond the Auditorio Nacional, Reforma continues southwest towards the area known as **Lomas de Chapultepec** (or simply 'Lomas'), which gradually rises through broad tree-lined avenues to an altitude which leaves most of the pollution behind. It is mostly residential, with large properties, including many embassies or ambassadorial residences. To the north, taking a right at the Fuente de Petróleos up Boulevard Manuel Avila Camacho, one comes to the modern office and commercial area of **Las Palmas**, while straight ahead, some 8 km further beyond Lomas de Chapultepec and on the way out towards Toluca, lies the district of **Santa Fe** perched on some of the highest ground and therefore in one of the least polluted areas in the city with some extraordinary, futuristic architecture: offices, hotels, banks, university buildings, shopping malls and apartment blocks.

To visit the area from Chapultepec Park take the metro to Chapultepec station. For the **Transport** Museo de Antropología, use metros Chapultepec/Auditorio, or *colectivo* down Reforma marked 'Auditorio'. For Polanco, take a *colectivo* marked Horacio from Metro Chapultepec or Metro Polanco. For 'Las Palmas', take a *colectivo* or bus marked Las Palmas from Antropología. For Lomas de Chapultepec, take a bus marked 'Km 15' or 'Cuajimalpa' from Antropología. These buses start from the bus-station by the exit from metro Chapultepec. To get to Santa Fe, take a *colectivo* marked 'Centro Comercial Santa Fe' from Antropología or a bus from Metro Chapultepec bus station.

Mural sites

Aside from the main centres of mural painting already listed geographically in the text above (Palacio Nacional, Suprema Corte de Justicia, Palacio de Bellas Artes, Museo Mural Diego Rivera, Escuela Nacional Preparatoria-San Ildefonso, Secretaría de Educación and Castillo de Chapultepec and the Polyforum Cultural Siqueiros, see page 123) there are other sites well worth visiting. They all lie within walking distance or short metro ride from the centre. **NB** Tact should be shown when visiting these functioning workplaces – ask permission before heading off into labyrinthine buildings and always check about photo restrictions (invariably flash is prohibited).

See also box, page 100

Mexico City

Before or after visiting the mural sites we recommend one or more of the following: *The Murals of Diego Rivera*, by Desmond Rochfort; London, 1987. *Mexican Muralists*, same author; New York, 1984. *Dreaming with his Eyes Open*, by Patrick Marnham; New York and London, 1998 is an immensely readable though not entirely scholastic life of Diego Rivera, which deals with Orozco, Siqueiros and the other muralists as well as Rivera.

Mercado Abelardo Rodríguez, on Venezuela four blocks northeast of Zócalo, with main entrance on Rodríguez Puebla, is fascinating as one of the only examples of a concerted attempt by a cooperative of artists of varying abilities, under the direction of Diego Rivera, to teach and record the workers' revolution in an actual workers' environment. Today the work of this food market goes on, but the murals, at all the entrances, are largely ignored by traders and tourists alike. Perhaps the most emblematic is *The Markets* by Miguel Tzab on the ceiling above the stairs at the northwest entrance, whilst Ramón Alva Guadarrama's *The Labours of the Field*, at the southeast corner, reflects the market's agricultural base. Most elaborate are the murals of the American Greenwood sisters, Marion

You can obtain a location plan of the murals at the tourist agency on Venezuela 72, beside the Teatro del Pueblo attached to the market

🐎 *Los Tres Grandes*

The story of muralism in Mexico has largely been that of 'Los Tres Grandes', Diego Rivera, Jose Clemente Orozco and David Alfaro Siqueiros, although there were many other artists involved from the start. In 1914 Orozco and Siqueiros were to be found in the Carranza stronghold of Orizaba fomenting social and artistic revolution through the mouthpiece of the pamphlet La Vanguardia. Seven years later, out of the turmoil and divisiveness of the Revolution emerged a need for a visual expression of Mexican identity (mexicanidad) and unity and in 1921 Orozco and Siqueiros answered the call of the Minister of Education, José Vasconcelos, to provide a visual analogue to a rapidly changing Mexico. Rivera was brought onto the team which in buildings like the National Preparatory School and the Ministry of Education attempted to produce a distinctly Mexican form of modernism, on a monumental scale, accessible to the people. These were ideas forged in Orizaba and later clarified in Europe (where Rivera and Siqueiros saw Italian frescoes) but which derived their popular form from paintings on the walls of pulquerías and in the satirical broadsheet engravings of José Guadalupe Posada. Themes were to include Precolumbian society, modern agriculture and medicine and a didactic Mexican history pointing to a mechanized future for the benefit of all. Siqueiros in particular was keen to transform the working practice of artists who would henceforth work as members of co-operatives.

The 'movement' fell apart almost from its inception. There were riots objecting to the communist content of murals and the beginnings of a long ideological and artistic disagreement between Siqueiros and Rivera which would culminate on 28 August 1935 at the Palacio de Bellas Artes with Rivera, brandishing a pistol, storming into a Siqueiros lecture and demanding a debate on what the Mexican Mural Renaissance had all been about! The debate ensued over several days before they agreed to disagree.

Despite the failings of the 'movement' many outstanding murals were painted over a long period. With Siqueiros frequently off the scene, in jail or in exile, Los Tres Grandes became the big two; Rivera carving up much of Mexico City as his territory and Orozco taking on Guadalajara. However, Siqueiros outlasted both of them and carried the torch of Muralism and Revolution into the early 1970s.

and Grace, showing *Industrialization of the Countryside* and *The Mine*, on the stairs either side of the main entrance. Opposite, upstairs, is a relief mural by Isamu Noguchi. Permission to take photos must be gained from the market office behind the restaurant at the southwest entrance.

In the theatre foyer is Antonio Pujol's *Problems of the Worker*, much praised at the time of its completion in 1936. In the cloisters of the confusingly named Patio Diego Rivera, behind the ticket office, is Pablo O'Higgins' tirade against international fascism *The Fight of the Workers Against the Monopolies*.

Next to the Museo Nacional de Arte is the **Cámara de Senadores**, Hipoteca Beride between Donceles and Tacuba, Metro Allende or Bellas Artes, which has a violent mural (1957) by Jorge González Camarena on the history of Mexico, starting with the pre-Cortesian battles between eagle and jaguar warriors.

The **Sindicato Mexicano de Electricistas**, Antonio Caso 45 (west of Cristóbal Colón monument on Reforma), T55350386, has one of Siqueiros' most important murals *Portrait of the Bourgeoisie* (1939-40), located up the second floor stairwell to the left of the entrance. It depicts the revolutionary struggle against international fascism and is considered a seminal work for its use of cinematic montage techniques and viewing points. Before taking photos ask permission in the *secretaría* office on the right at the end of the corridor on the second floor. 15-minute walk away at Altamirano 118, Colonia San Rafael, T55352246, is the **Teatro Jorge Negrete**, in the foyer of which is a later Siqueiros mural *Theatrical Art in the Social Life of Mexico* (1957), precursor in its expression of movement to his mural in Chapultepec Castle. Ask permission to see it in the office at No 128. No photos (nearest metro San Cosme).

At the **Hospital de La Raza** in what was once an outer entrance hall (but is now at the centre of the building) is Rivera's *History of Medicine* (1953) and to the left of the main entrance, in a naturally lit theatre foyer (usually locked but you can see it through the large frontal windows if there is nobody about with keys), is Siqueiros' *For the Complete Safety of All Mexicans at Work* (1952-54). Ask a security guard or at main reception for directions to the murals. Take metro La Raza and from the station head south along the right side of Insurgentes Norte, cross the railway, go straight ahead and then cross the freeway by the footbridge to the hospital. For permission to take photos here and at other medical centres you must ask at the Sede IMSS, Hidalgo 230, Metro Bellas Artes.

Another hospital with a relevant themed mural is the **Centro Médico Nacional**, Avenida Cuauhtémoc, where Siqueiros' *Apology for the Future Victory of Medicine over Cancer* (1958) has been restored following damage in the 1985 earthquake. Since 1996 it has been on display in the waiting area of the oncology building beyond the main entrance building on the right. At the entrance, as you come up the stairs from the metro station Centro Médico, is a mural by Chávez Morado commemorating the rebuilding of the hospital in which many died during the earthquake.

Essentials

Sleeping

Prices of the more expensive hotels do not normally include 15% tax; service is sometimes included. Always check in advance. Reductions are often available; breakfast is rarely included in the room price. There are fair hotel reservation services at the railway station and at the airport; also services for more expensive hotels at bus stations.

■ *on maps*
Price codes:
see inside front cover

LL *Continental Plaza Aeropuerto*, Fundidora Monterrey 89, T52300505, entrance between sections B and C in airport. All facilities. **LL-L** *Ramada Ciudad de México*, Blvd Puerto Aéreo 502, T57858522, F57629934. Free transport to/from airport. A short walk from the airport: **AL** *JR Plaza*, Blvd Puerto Aéreo 390, T57855200, F57843221. Comfortable airport, expensive restaurant, quiet, good rooms with solid furniture, close to metro; next door is **A** *Aeropuerto*, Blvd Aeropuerto 380 (300m from airport over other side of highway), T57855318. Noisy but OK, functional, expensive restaurant, good breakfast.

Hotels at or near the airport

LL *Camino Real*, Mariano Escobedo 700, T52032121, F52506897. **LL** *Century*, Liverpool 152, T57269911, F55257475 (Golden Tulip hotel). **LL** *Clarion Reforma Suites*, Paseo de la Reforma 373, T52078944, F52082719. New. **LL** *Crowne Plaza*, Paseo de la Reforma 1, T51285000, F51285050. **LL** *Fiesta Americana*, Paseo de la Reforma 80, T57051515, F57051313. With restaurants, bars, nightclubs, superior business facilities. **LL** *Flamingos Plaza*, Av Revolución 333, T56270220, F55154850. **LL** *Four Seasons Mexico*, Paseo de la Reforma 500, T52301818, F52301817. Beautiful, excellent restaurant. **LL** *Howard Johnson Gran Hotel de México*, 16 de Septiembre 82 (Zócalo),

Hotels in or near city centre

T55104040, F55122085. Has an incredible foyer, 30's style, 4th floor restaurant and balcony good for Zócalo-watching, especially on Sun morning (breakfast buffet US$10). **LL** *Imperial*, Reforma 64, T55664879. Very good, restaurant, café, bar, 24-hr service, business facilities, etc. **LL** *Krystal*, Liverpool 155, T52289928, F55113490. **LL** *Marco Polo*, Amberes 27, T52070299, F55333727, in the Zona Rosa. Small, select hotel, price reductions at weekends, Mexican, Italian and international cuisine. Recommended. **LL** *María Isabel Sheraton*, Paseo de la Reforma 325, T52073933, F52070684, opposite Angel of Independence. 'Old-fashioned', all facilities, but restaurant overpriced. **LL** *Marquis*, Paseo de la Reforma 465, Col Cuauhtémoc, T52113600, F52115561. New, all facilities. Recommended. **LL** *Nikko*, Campos Elíseos 204, T52801111, F52809191. **LL** *Presidente*, Campos Elíseos 218, T53277700, F53277737. Good location, exercise room. **LL** *Royal Zona Rosa*, Amberes 78, T52289918, F55143330. Good. **LL** *Westin Galería Plaza*, Hamburgo 195, T52110014, F52075867. Three restaurants, rooftop pool and gym.

AL *Aristos*, Paseo de la Reforma 276, T52110112, F55256783. **AL** *Casa Blanca*, Lafragua 7 (1 block from Reforma and Revolución monument), T57051300, F57054197. Modern. **AL** *Cortés* (Best Western), Av Hidalgo 85, T55182184, F55121863. This is the only baroque-style hotel in Mexico City, a former pilgrims' guesthouse, with a pleasant patio, TV, good bathroom, no a/c or pool, quiet, good yet touristy floor show, good food. **AL** *Geneve Quality Inn*, Londres 130, T52110071, F52087422. Pleasant dining area. **AL** *Plaza Madrid*, Madrid 15, T57050836, F57050961. **AL** *Majestic* (Best Western), Madero 73 on Zócalo, T55218609, F55126262. Interesting rooms, lots of tiles, carved wooden beams, large beds, quiet rooms overlook courtyard, magnificent breakfast in 7th floor restaurant with excellent views of centre. **AL** *María Cristina*, Lerma 31, T55669688, F55923447. Attractive colonial-style, comfortable, helpful, safe parking. Recommended (book well in advance). **AL** *Ritz* (Best Western), Madero 30, T55181340, F55183466. **A** *Del Angel*, Río Lerma 154, T55331032. **A** *Ejecutivo*, Viena 8, T55666422, staff helpful. Recommended. **A** *Metropol*, Luis Moya 39, T51086601, F55121273. Good, clean, safe, touristy, average restaurant, good value. Recommended. **A** *Regente*, París 9, T55668933. Clean, friendly, noisy at front. Restaurant. **A** *Royal Plaza*, Parroquia 1056, corner with Cuauhtémoc, T56058943 (**B** at weekends). **A** *Viena*, Marsella 28 (close to Juárez market and Cuauhtémoc metro), T55660700. Quiet, Swiss decor, garage, dining room. Recommended.

B *Brasilia*, near Terminal del Norte bus station, on Av Cien Metros 48-25, T55878577, F53682714. Excellent modern hotel, king-size bed, TV. 24-hr traffic jam in front. **B** *Cancún*, Donato Guerra 24, T55666083, F55666488. Restaurant, safe, noisy. Recommended. **B** *Catedral*, Donceles 95, T55182532, F55124344, behind Cathedral. Clean, spacious, good service. Recommended. **B** *Fleming*, Revillagigedo 35, T55104530. Good value, central. **B** *Jena*, Jesús Terán 12. New, central. Recommended (but not the travel agency on the premises). **B** *Lepanto*, Guerrero 90. TV, phone, modern, attractive, good restaurant. **B** *Mallorca*, Serapio Rendón 119, T55664833. Clean, reasonable. **B** *Mayaland*, Maestro Antonio Caso 23, T55666066. With bath, good value, good restaurant. **B** *Palace*, Ignacio Ramírez 7, T55662400. Very friendly, good restaurant. **B** *Polanco*, Edgar Poe 8, T52808082, near Chapultepec. Dark, quiet, good restaurant. **B** *Premier*, Atenas 72, T55662701. Good location, clean, front rooms noisy, will store bags. **B** *Prim*, Versalles 46, T55924600, F55924835. Clean, good in all respects. **B** *Del Principado*, Londres 42, Zona Rosa (near Metro Insurgentes), T55332944. Clean, rooms at back better, good restaurant. **B** *San Francisco*, Luis Moya 11, T55218960, F55108831, just off Alameda. Great views, friendly, excellent value, takes credit cards, good set meals. **B** *Sevilla*, Serapio Rendón 126 and Sullivan, T55910522. Restaurant, garage, reasonable (not to be confused with **AL** *Sevilla Palace*, Reforma 105, T55668877, which is smart). **B** *Vasco de Quiroga*,

Londres 15 y Berlín, 3 mins walk from Zona Rosa, T55462614, F55352257. Clean, friendly, very good (ask for room away from the generator), restaurant downstairs.

C *Astor*, Antonio Caso 83, near Sullivan Park. New, clean, restaurant. Recommended. **C** *Canadá*, Av 5 de Mayo 47, T55182106, F55211233, closest metro station Allende. With bath, hot water, TV, collect calls can be made for US$1, good value, friendly, helpful, no restaurant. **C** *Capitol*, Uruguay 12, T55181750, F55211149. Attractive lobby, recently remodelled, TV, bath, clean, friendly, don't miss the restaurant in the same building: *El Malecón*. **C** *Casa González*, Lerma y Sena 69 (near British Embassy), T55143302. Full board available, shower, English spoken by Sr González, clean, quiet and friendly, no credit cards. Recommended. **C** *Congreso*, Allende 18, T55109888. With bath, hot water, good, central, clean, quiet, TV, garage. **C** *Galicia*, Honduras 11, T55297791. Good. **C** *Gilbert*, Amado Nervo 37, Col Buenavista, Mex 4 DF, T55479260. Good location but a bit spooky at night. **C** *Gillow*, 5 de Mayo e Isabel la Católica 17, T55181440, F55122078. Central, large, clean, best rooms on 6th floor, many services, attractive, hospitable, good value, mediocre restaurant. **C** *La Villa de los Quijotes*, Moctezuma 20, near Basílica de Guadalupe (Metro La Villa), T55771088. Modern, quiet, clean, expensive restaurant. **C** *Marlowe*, Independencia 17, T55219540, F55186862. Clean, modern, finished to a high standard, safe parking, lift, restaurant good but service is slow (tourist office at airport refers many travellers here – if this one is too expensive, the cheaper *Concordia*, see below, is round the corner). **C** *Nueva York*, Edison 45. Large, clean rooms, expensive restaurants. **C** *Parador Washington*, Dinamarca 42 y Londres. With bath, clean, safe area, café next door. **C** *Pisa*, Insurgentes Nte 58. Recommended. **C** *Uxmal*, Madrid 13, quite close to Zona Rosa. Clean rooms, same owner as more expensive *Madrid*, next door, see **AL** category above. With access to their better facilities. Recommended.

D *Antillas*, Blvd Domínguez 34, T55265674. With bath and TV, friendly, stores luggage. **D** *Atlanta*, corner of Blvd Domínguez and Allende, T55181201. Good, clean, quiet if you ask for a room away from street, friendly, luggage store. **D** *Avenida*, Lázaro Cárdenas 38 (Bellas Artes metro), T55181007. With bath, central, friendly, will store luggage, good value, cheapest hotel that can be booked at airport. Recommended. **D** *Buenos Aires*, Av 5 de Mayo. Safe, friendly, TV, stores luggage, hot water. **D** *Florida*, Belisario Domínguez 57. TV, shower, clean. Recommended. **D** *Lafayette*, Motolinia 40 and 16 de Septiembre. With bath, and TV, good, clean, quiet (pedestrian precinct), but check rooms, there's a variety of sizes. **D** *Principal*, Bolívar 29. With bath, central, OK, friendly owner. **D** *San Antonio*, 2nd Callejón, 5 de Mayo 29, T55129906. Clean, pleasant, popular, friendly, TV in room. Recommended. **D** *Toledo*, López 22 (Bellas Artes Metro), T55213249. With bath, TV. Warmly recommended.

Near Metro Allende
The best of the cheaper hotels are in the old part of town between the Zócalo & the Alameda

D-E *Cuba*, on Cuba 69, T55181380. With bath, TV, good beds but sheets too small, noisy. **D-E** *Habana*, República de Cuba 77 (near metro Allende). Spacious rooms, huge beds, renovated, very clean, phone, TV, friendly and helpful staff. Highly recommended. **D-E** *Isabel la Católica* on street of the same name, No 63, T55181213, F55211233. Pleasant, popular, clean, helpful, safe (taxi drivers must register at desk before taking passengers), roof terrace, large shabby rooms with bath and hot water (some without windows), central, a bit noisy, fax service, quite good restaurant, luggage held, rooms on top floor with shared bathroom are cheaper. Recommended. **D-E** *Washington*, Av 5 de Mayo 54. Clean, small rooms, cable TV.

E *La Marina*, Allende 30 y Blvd Domínguez. Clean, comfortable, safe, friendly, TV, hot water, will store luggage. Recommended. **E** *Rioja*, Av 5 de Mayo 45, next door to *Canadá*, see above. T55218333. Shared or private baths, reliable hot water, clean, popular, luggage store, well placed. Recommended. Opposite are **E** *Juárez*, in small

Mexico City

alley on 5 de Mayo 17, 1 min walk from Zócalo, T55126929. Ask for room with window, safe, clean, with bath, phone, radio, TV. Recommended. **F** *Pensión del Centro*, Cuba 74, apt 203 y Chile, Centro Histórico, T55120832, paic@data.net.mx. Laundry, luggage store, email service, 4-bed dorms. **F** *Princess*, Cuba 55. With bath, good value, TV, fairly secure, front rooms noisy. **F** *República*, Cuba 57, T55129517. With bath, hot water, rooms upstairs quieter, 3 blocks from Bellas Artes. Recommended. **F** *Zamora*, Av 5 de Mayo 50. Clean, cheap, hot water, OK.

North of the Zócalo **D** *Hostel Catedral*, Guatemala 4, T55181726, F55103442, www.remaj.com. New hostel just behind the Cathedral, 209 beds (private rooms and dorms), restaurant, kitchen, laundry, internet centre, secure storage, travel agency has booking service. **E** *Tuxpán*, on Colombia, near Brasil. Modern, clean, TV, hot shower. **E** *Azores*, Brasil 25, T55215220. Large rooms, TV, a/c. **F** *Río de Janeiro*, on Brasil, near Colombia. Dirty, noisy.

North of Metro Hildago **D** *Managua*, on Plaza de la Iglesia de San Fernando. With bath, phone, TV, good location, car park, very friendly, run down. **D** *Mina*, José T Salgado 18, esq Mina, T57031682. Modern, clean, TV, large beds. **D** *Monaco* opposite, Guerrero 12, T55668333. Comfortable, TV, modern, good service. Almost behind is **D** *La Fuente*, Orozco y Berra 10, T55669122. Bath, TV, garage, bar (noisy bar opposite). **D** *Detroit*, Zaragoza 55, T55911088. Hot shower, central, clean, has parking. **D** *Savoy*, Zaragoza 10, T55664611, near Hidalgo metro. Convenient for Zócalo, with bath and hot water, clean, phone, TV, modernized, good value.

North of Plaza de la República **C** *Oxford*, Ignacio Mariscal 67, T55660500. Very clean, radio and satellite TV, helpful, but short stay. **C** *Texas*, Ignacio Mariscal 129, T55644626. With bath, clean, hot water, small rooms, good breakfasts. **D** *América*, Buena Vista 4 (near Revolución metro). With bath, hot water, TV, good service. Recommended. **D** *Frimont*, Jesús Terán 35, T57054169. Clean, central. **D** *Royalty*, Jesús Terán 21, opposite *Hotel Jena*. With bath, TV, clean, very quiet, near Hidalgo metro. **E** *Carlton*, Ignacio Mariscal 32-bis, T55662911. Getting rough around the edges, small rooms but some with fine views, rooms at front noisy, good restaurant. Recommended. **E** *El Paraíso*, Ignacio Mariscal 99, T55668077. Hot water, clean, private bath, TV, phone, recently renovated. Friendly. **E** *Pennsylvania*, Ignacio Mariscal 15, T55350070. With bath, clean, TV. **E-F** *Casa de los Amigos*, Ignacio Mariscal 132. T57050521/0646, near train and bus station (metro Revolución). In dormitory, **D-E** in double room, pay 2 nights in advance, use of kitchen, recommended, maximum 15-day stay, separation of sexes, run by Quakers for Quakers, or development-work related travellers, other travellers taken only if space is available, good information on volunteer work, travel and language schools, breakfast US$2.50 (weekdays only) and laundry facilities on roof, safe-keeping for luggage, English library, references or advance booking recommended.

Near the train station **D** *Encino*, Av Insurgentes, 1 block from the railway station. Clean, private bath. **D** *Pontevedra*, Insurgentes Nte opposite railway station. Bath, hot water, TV, clean, helpful, will store luggage. **D** *Santander*, Arista 22, not far from railway station. With bath, good value and service, clean. **D** *Nueva Estación*, Zaragoza opposite Buenavista station. With bath, clean, quiet, friendly, colour TV. **D** *Yale*, Mosqueta 200, 5 mins walk from Buenavista station. Showers, toilet, large room with TV and phone, very good value. Recommended. **E** *Atoyac*, Eje de Guerrero 161, Col Guerrero, 200m from metro. Clean, friendly, safe.

South of the Zócalo **D** *Concordia*, Uruguay 13. Clean, hot water, friendly, some rooms airless, lift, phone, noisy. **D** *El Roble*, Uruguay y Pino Suárez. Bath, TV, restaurant closes early. Recommended. **D** *El Salvador*, República de El Salvador 16, T55211247, near Zócalo. Modern, clean, laundry, safe, parking, good value. **D** *Monte Carlo*, Uruguay 69, T55181418/55212559/55219363 (D H Lawrence's hotel). Elegant, clean, friendly owner (also suites), with bath, hot water, good about storing luggage, safe car park inside the hotel premises, US$3.45, rooms in front noisy, even rooms at the back vibrate with noise from disco 2230-0300 Wed-Sat, can make collect calls abroad from room. Refuses to take bookings without payment in advance, also has mosquito-net problems. **F** *San Pedro*, Mesones 126 and Pino Suárez. With bath, TV, tiny rooms, clean (but the occasional cockroach) and friendly. Good value.

D *Danky*, Donato Guerra 10, T55469960/61. With bath, central, hot water, phone, clean, easy parking. Recommended. **E** *Fornos*, Revillagigedo 92, near Balderas metro, 10 mins walk to Alameda. Extremely clean, bathroom, TV, radio, smarter bigger rooms for **D**, restaurant, large, indoor car park, friendly staff, Dutch-speaking, Spanish owner, very good value. Highly recommended. **E** *Meave*, Meave 6, esq Lázaro Cárdenas, T55216712. Bath, TV, clean, quiet, very friendly, ground floor rooms rented by hour, but very discreet. Recommended.

South of the Alameda

B *Suites Quinta Palo Verde*, Cerro del Otate 20, Col Romero de Terreros (México 21 DF) T55543575. Pleasant, diplomatic residence turned guesthouse, near the University; run by a veterinary surgeon, Miguel Angel, very friendly, speaks English and German, but the dogs are sometimes noisy. *Suites Amberes*, Amberes 64, Zona Rosa, T55331306, F52071509. Kitchenette, good value (US$150 per day and the equivalent of US$105 a day, for a week's stay). Recommended. *Suites Havre*, Havre 74, T55335670, near Zona Rosa. 56 suites with kitchen, phone and service. Recommended for longer stays. *Club Med* head office for Club Med and *Villas Arqueológicas* reservations, Masaryk 183, Col Polanco, México 11570, T52033086/3833.

Longer stays

Campo Escuela Nacional de Tantoco, Km 29.5 on road Mexico-City to Toluca, T55122279. Cabins and campsite. The Dirección de Villas Deportivas Juveniles, address below (Condep), has details of campsites throughout the country; site in the capital, T56655027. They have either camping, or camping and dormitory accommodation on sites with additional facilities, including luggage lockers; ask in advance what documentation is required. The nearest trailer park is *Pepe's* in Tepotzotlán (see page 145), 43 km north of the capital (address: Eva Sámano de López Mateos 62, T58760515/0616, in Mexico City, *Mallorca Travel Service*, Paseo de la Reforma 105, T57052424, F57052673); it costs about US$12 a night, 55 pads with full hook-ups, very friendly, clean, hot showers, Canadian run. Recommended (owner has a hotel in Mexico City if you want to leave your trailer here and stay in the capital).

Campsites
If you want to bring your car into the city, find a cheap hotel where you can park and leave it, while you explore the city by bus, metro or on foot. Or try camping in the parking lot of the Museum of Anthropology.

Asociación Mexicana de Albergues de la Juventud, Madero 6, Oficina 314, México 1, DF. Write for information. There is a similar organization, Comisión Nacional del Deporte (Condep), which runs the *Villas Deportivas Juveniles* (see above); information office at Glorieta del Metro Insurgentes, local C-11, T55252916/55331291. Condep will make reservations for groups of 10 or more; to qualify you must be between 8 and 65 and have a *Tarjeta Plan Verde* membership card, US$6, valid 2 years, obtainable within 24 hrs from office at Tlalpan 583, esq Soria, metro Xola, or a IYHF card. See also SETEJ, below, for information on hotels and other establishments offering lodging for students. HOME, Tabasco 303, Col Roma, T/F55112698, US$8 per night.

Youth hostels

Eating

All the best hotels have good restaurants. The number and variety of restaurants is vast; the following is a small selection.

Note the *Hotel Majestic's* Mexican breakfast, Sat and Sun till 1200, excellent, go to terrace on seventh floor, otherwise food mediocre, live music. *San Angel Inn*, Las Palmas 50, in San Angel. Excellent and very popular, so book well in advance (San Angel can

Mexican food

Mexico City

be reached by bus along Insurgentes or by metro to Barranca del Muerto and bus 5 along Revolución). *Hostelería Santo Domingo*, Belisario Domínguez, 2 blocks west of Plaza Santo Domingo. Good food and service, excellent music, the oldest restaurant in the city. *La Plancha Azteca*, Río Lerma 54. Good *tacos* and *tortas*, moderate prices. *La Puerta del Angel*, Varsovia y Londres. Local food and specializing in American cuts, very good. *Fonda del Recuerdo*, Bahía de las Palmas 39A, México 17, DF. Excellent *mole poblano,* with music. *Club de Periodistas de México*, F Mata 8, near 5 de Mayo, open to public. OK. *Bar La Opera*, 5 de Mayo near Bellas Artes. Good atmosphere, expensive, see Pancho Villa's bullet-hole in ceiling (cocktails made with foreign spirits are 3 times as expensive as tequila). *Cardenal*, Palma 23. Food, service and music (from 1530) is outstanding, 1930s ambience. *Casa Zavala*, Bolívar y Uruguay. Cheap, large selection of dishes. *El Huequito*, Bolívar 58. Casual, friendly, cheap meals for US\$2. *Focolare*, Hamburgo 87 (swank and high priced). *Taquería Lobo Bobo*, Insurgentes Sur 2117. Excellent food, quite cheap, very friendly. *Nadja*, Mesones 65, near Pino Suárez. Typical food, set menu for US\$1.30, large portions, friendly. Recommended. A very old restaurant with stunning tile décor and not touristy is the *Café Tacuba*, Tacuba 28. It specializes in Mexican food, very good *enchiladas*, excellent meat dishes, *tamales* and fruit desserts, good service, live music, very popular with local business people. Highly recommended. *Los Girasoles*, corner of Tacuba and Gante. Mexican cuisine, makes a cover charge of US\$1.20 which is not mentioned in the menu. Reasonable food. *La Casa de las Sirenas*, Tacuba y Seminario, behind the Cathedral. Mexican menu. Excellent food and service. Recommended. *México Viejo*, Tacuba 86 (near Zócalo). Excellent breakfast, not touristy, pricey. *El Refugio*, Liverpool 166. Tourist-oriented, good desserts, check bill carefully. *Doneraky*, Nuevo León y Laredo (Col Condesa). Good *tacos*. Recommended. *Don Albis*, Tomás Edison 100. Delicious, large, cheap meals, popular with office workers. *La Luna*, Oslo y Copenhaguen, Zona Rosa. Mostly Mexican, good breakfasts. *El Perro de Enfrente*, Copenhague. Excellent food and service. Recommended. *Casa Neri*, Bélgica 211, Col Portales. Excellent authentic cooking, Oaxacan specialities, huge *comida corrida* for US\$4. *La Lupe*, Industria, Metro Coyoacán. Leafy patio, good and cheap, open till 1800. Almost everywhere are American-style restaurant chains, eg *Vips*, *Toks*, *El Portón*, *Lyni's* and *Sanborns*, offering Mexican and international food, clean and reliable, but by no means cheap by local standards (breakfast US\$3.50, lunch US\$7).

International   *Delmonico's*, Londres 87 and 16 de Septiembre 82. Elegant. *Jena*, Morelos 110. Deservedly famous, *à la carte*, expensive. *La Cava*, Insurgentes Sur 2465. Excellent food and steaks, lavishly decorated as an old French tavern, moderate. *Andreson's*, Reforma 400. Very good atmosphere, excellent local menu, not cheap. *Keops*, Hamburgo 146, near Amberes in Zona Rosa, T55256706. Reasonable food, good live music. Also in Zona Rosa are *La Calesa de Londres*, Londres 102. Good meat. *Carousel Internacional*, Hamburgo and Niza. Very popular drinking-hole for smartly dressed Mexicans, resident *mariachi*, food not gourmet but fun atmosphere, about US\$15 pp. *Trevi*, Dr Mora y Colón (west end of Alameda). Italian/US/Mexican, reasonable prices. *Milomita*, Mesones 87, Centro, 0800-2000. Specializes in American cuts of meat.

US & other Latin American   *Sanborn's*. Thirty-six locations (known as the foreigners' home-from-home), soda fountain, drugstore, restaurant, English, German and Spanish-language magazines, handicrafts, chocolates, etc, try their restaurant in the famous 16th-century *Casa de los Azulejos*, the 'house of tiles' at Av Madero 17, poor service, but many delicious local dishes in beautiful high-ceilinged room, about US\$10-15 pp without wine (also has handicraft shops in basement and first floor). *Café El Popular* next door to Hotel Zamora on 5 de Mayo. *New York Deli and Bagel*, Av Revolución 1321, just south of metro Barranca del Muerto, 0800-0100. Good coffee and full meals available. Many US chain fast-food restaurants (eg *Burger Boy* for good value breakfasts, *McDonalds* and

Dunkin Donuts on Madero). *Rincón Gaucho*, Insurgentes Sur 1162. Argentine food. Also Argentine, *Esquina La Pibe*, two locations just off Madero, OK. *El Patio del Gaucho*, Uruguay. Moderate prices, attentive service, good *asado*. Recommended.

Del Cid, Humboldt 61. Castilian with medieval menu. *El Faro*, Belgrado y Reforma, Zona Rosa. Very good, US$25-30 per head, closed in evenings except Thu and Fri, closed Sat. *Mesón del Castellano*, Bolívar y Uruguay, T5186080. Good atmosphere, plentiful and not too dear, excellent steaks. Highly recommended. *Centro Catalán*, Bolívar 31, open 1100-1700 only. Excellent *paella* and other Spanish cuisine (2nd floor). *Centro Castellano*, on Uruguay. Excellent, cheap, try the steaks. *Vasco*, Madero 6, 1st Floor. *Mesón del Perro Andaluz*, Copenhague 26, and Luis P Ogazón 89. Very pleasant.

Spanish

French cuisine at *Le Gourmet*, Dakota 155. Said to be most expensive restaurant in Mexico, and also said to be worth it! *Ambassadeurs*, Paseo de la Reforma 12. Swank and high priced. *Les Moustaches*, Río Sena 88 (second most expensive in town, probably). *Bellinghausen*, Londres y Niza. Excellent food, lunch only, another branch *Casa Bell*, Praga 14, T5115733. Smaller, identical menu, old house, elegant. Recommended. *Chalet Suizo*, Niza 37. Very popular with tourists, specializes in Swiss and German food, moderate. *Grotto Ticino*, Florencia 33. Swiss food. Recommended. *Rivoli*, Hamburgo 123. A gourmet's delight, high-priced. *Café Konditori*, Génova 61. Danish open sandwiches. *La Gondola*, Génova. Great pasta. *La Casserole*, Insurgentes Sur 1880, near Núcleo Radio Mil building. French. *Sir Winston Churchill*, Avila Camacho 67. Serves British food, expensive, smart, popular.

Other European

Mr Lee, Independencia 19-B. Chinese, seafood, good food, value and service. *Dinastía Lee*, Independencia y Dolores. Reasonable Chinese food, open 0800-2400. *Chen Wan*, Bolívar 104. Large portions, set meal US$2-3.

Oriental

La Costa Azul, López 127 y Delicias. Central, good, cold lighting, reasonable prices. *Marisquito*, near Congress on Donceles 12. Very good.

Seafood

Restaurante Vegetariano, Filomeno Mata 13, open until 2000, Sun 0900-1900. Good *menú del día* US$3. *Chalet Vegetariano*, near Dr Río de la Loza. *El Bosque*, Hamburgo 15 between Berlín and Dinamarca. Recommended. Vegetarian restaurant at Motolinia 31, near Madero, is open Mon-Sat 1300-1800. Reasonably priced. *Karl*, on Amberes near junction Londres. Excellent buffet lunch and dinner. *Saks*, Insurgentes Sur 1641, close to Teatro Insurgentes. Very good. *Yug*, Varsovia 3. Cheap vegetarian, 4-course set lunch US$3.50. *Super Soya*, Tacuba, metro Allende. Good juices and fruit salads, health food shop. Health food shop, *Alimentos Naturales*, close to Metro Revolución, on P Arriaga. Health food shops in other metro stations.

Vegetarian
The best place to buy natural products is in the San Juan market (see Markets below), including tofu (queso de soya).

In the lower price ranges: *La Parrilla Suiza*, Arquimedes y Presidente Masaryk. For grilled meats, *alambres*, *sopa de tortilla* and other meat-and-cheese dishes, very popular, especially 1400-1600, service fair, moderately priced. *The City Bistro*, Lope de Vega 341, north of Horacio. Serves finest English and international cuisine, also stunningly inventive dishes, moderately priced. *Zeco*, Sudermann 336, T55315211. Mexican-Italian. Very good, middle price range, wines expensive. (*Addetto*, Av Revolución 1382, Col Guadalupe Inn, T5625434. Same ownership.) *El Buen Comer Marcelín*, Edgar Allan Poe 50, T52035337. Mainly French, very good. *Cambalache*, Arquimedes north of Presidente Masaryk. Argentine steakhouse, good steaks, wide selection of wines, cosy atmosphere, not as expensive as *El Rincón Argentino*, Presidente Masaryk 181, which is very expensive. For *tacos* and other *tortilla*-based dishes: *Los Tacos*, Newton just south of Horacio. Inexpensive. *Chilango's*, Molière between Ejército Nacional and Homero. Good value and service, MTV videos. Recommended.

Polanco

El Tizoncito, south of Ejército Nacional just west of Pabellón Polanco mall. Very popular at lunchtime. *El Jarocho*, Homero between Emerson and Hegel. Informal, eat-at-counter place, inexpensive. *Embers*, Séneca y Ejército Nacional. 43 types of excellent hamburger, good French fries. Recommended.

Cafés Many economical restaurants on 5 de Mayo, eg *Café La Blanca* at No 40. Popular and busy atmosphere, good expresso coffee, open for Sun breakfast and early on weekdays. Recommended. *Torta Brava*, near Zócalo. Good *comida*, friendly. *París*, No 10. Good breakfast and dinner. *Popular*, No 52 between Alameda and Zócalo, on corner of alley to *Hotel Juárez*. Cheap, rushed, 24 hrs, meeting place. *Gili's Pollo*, opposite *Hotel Rioja*. Excellent chicken, eat in or takeaway. *El 20 de Bolívar*, Bolívar 20. Excellent service and highly recommended for breakfasts. *Klein's*, Av Madero with Simón Bolívar. Buffet US$3.30. *Comida Económica Verónica*, República de Cuba, 2 doors from *Hotel Habana* (No 77). For tasty breakfasts and set *comida corrida*, very hot *chilaquiles*, good value and delightful staff. Recommended. *La Rosita*, 2a Callejón de Allende 14-C. Cheap and good. *El Reloj*, 5 de Febrero 50. Good *comida* and *à la carte*. *Rex*, 5 de Febrero 40, near Zócalo. Good *café con leche* and cheap *comidas*. *Shakey's*, Monte de Piedad (at the Zócalo). Self-service, large helpings of pizza and chicken. *Pastelería Madrid*, 5 de Febrero 25, 1 block from *Hotel Isabel la Católica*. Good pastries and breakfasts. *Bamerette*, Av Juárez 52 (*Hotel Bamer*). Excellent breakfast. Good small restaurants on Uruguay, near *Hotel Monte Carlo*. The *Maple*, next to *Hotel Roble* at No 109, has been recommended for its *comida*, and *Pancho* (No 84), for its breakfasts, cheap meals and service. *Flor*, San Jerónimo 100, near *Hotel Ambar*. Recommended for breakfast, non-touristy atmosphere, cheap. *Tic Tac*, Av Balderas. Very good *comida corrida*. *La Habana*, Bucareli y Morelos. Not cheap but good food and excellent coffee. Another centre for small restaurants is Pasaje Jacarandas, off Génova 44: *Llave de Oro* and many others. *La Casa del Pavo*, Motolinia near 16 de Septiembre. Clean, courteous, excellent *comida corrida*. Also Motilinia between 5 de Mayo and Tacuba. Cheap *cafeterías* on Belisario Domínguez. *Gaby's*, Liverpool y Nápoles. Excellent Italian-style coffee, décor of old coffee machines, etc. *Duca d'Este*, Av Florencia y Hamburgo. Good coffee and pastries. *Il Mangiare*, opposite Poliforum Cultural Siqueiros (see page 123). Very good sandwiches. *El Núcleo*, Lerma y Marne. Excellent fruit salads, breakfasts and lunches, closes 1800 and all day Sun. *Zenón*, corner of Madero 65 and Palma. Trendy décor, average Mexican food, *comida corrida* US$1.50-US$3.50. *Enanos de Tapanco y Café*, Orizaba 161, between Querétaro and San Luis Potosí. Great coffee, warm friendly atmosphere. Good breakfasts can be had at *Woolworth*, 16 de Septiembre. *Dulcería de Celaya*, 5 de Mayo 39. Good candy store and lovely old premises. Good bakeries on 16 de Noviembre, near Zócalo. Also *Panadería La Vasconia*, Tacuba 73. Good, also sells cheap chicken and fries. *Jugos California* on Guerrero by Hidalgo metro. Good juices. *Roxy*, Montes de Oca y Mazatlán, Col Condesa. Good ice cream. Good juices and sandwiches at the *Juguería* on 5 de Mayo, next to *Hotel Rioja*. *El Sol*, Gómez Farías 67, Col San Rafael. Frequented by journalists, superb Mexican cuisine, *comida corrida* US$2. See page 120, Internet for cybercafés.

Bars *Bar Jardín*, in the *Hotel Reforma*. *El Morroco*, Conjunto Marrakesh, Florencia 36.
There are many safe gay bars in the Zona Rosa in the area between Niza and Florencia, north of Londres — *Casino*, Isabel la Católica, near *Sanborn's*. Superb painted glass doors and lavish interior, also has Spanish restaurant. *Abundio*, Zaragoza y Mosqueta. Very friendly, free food. *Yuppies Sports Bar*, Génova. Expensive but good atmosphere. *Guadalupana*, near Plaza Hidalgo, Coyoacán.

Entertainment

For all cultural events, consult *Tiempo Libre*, every Thu from news stands, US$1, or monthly programme pamphlets from Bellas Artes bookshop.

Cabarets & nightclubs

Every large hotel has one. ***El Patio***, Atenas 9. ***Passepartout***, Hamburgo. ***La Madelón***, Florencia 36. ***Brasileirinho***, León 160. There are many discotheques in the better hotels and scattered throughout town.

Cinemas

A number show non-Hollywood films in original language (Spanish subtitles); check *Tiempo Libre* magazine, or *Mexico City News* for details. Some recommended cinemas are: ***Cineteca Nacional***, Metro Coyoacán (excellent bookshop on the cinema and related topics, library). ***Cinematógrafo del Chopo***, Dr Atl, non-commercial films daily 1700 and 1930, US$1; good cinema in Ciudad Universitaria; ***Cine Latino***, Av Reforma between the statue of Cuauhtémoc and El Angel. ***Cine Versalles***, Versalles (side street off Av Reforma, near statue of Cuauhtémoc). ***Cine Electra***, Río Guadalquivir (near El Angel). ***Cine Diana***, Av Reforma, at the end where Parque Chapultepec starts. ***Cine Palacio Chino***, in the Chinese *barrio* south of Av Juárez (also interesting for restaurants). The sound is often very low on subtitled films, only option is to sit near speakers at front. Most cinemas, except *Cineteca Nacional*, charge half-price on Wed.

Folk music

A fine place for light refreshments and music is the ***Hostería del Bohemio***, formerly the San Hipólito monastery, near Reforma on Av Hidalgo 107, metro Hidalgo: poetry and music every night from 1700 to 2200, light snacks and refreshments US$4 minimum, expensive but no cover charge.

Theatres

Spectaculars (eg presidential inauguration) are often staged in the Auditorio Nacional itself.

Palacio de Bellas Artes (for ballet, songs, dances, also concerts 2-3 times a week, see page 89), ***Fábregas***, ***Lírico***, ***Iris***, ***Sullivan***, ***Alarcón***, ***Hidalgo***, ***Urueta***, ***San Rafael*** and ***Insurgentes*** in town and a cluster of theatres around the Auditorio Nacional in Chapultepec Park (check at Tourist Office for details of cheap programmes). Also in Chapultepec Park is the Audiorama (behind the Castle on the Constituyentes side) where one may listen to recorded classical music in a small open amphitheatre in a charming wooded glade. A request book is provided, for the following day. There may be a free performance of a play in one of the parks by the Teatro Trashumante (Nomadic Theatre). Variety show nightly with singers, dancers, comedians, magicians and ventriloquists, very popular with locals, at ***Teatro la Blanquita***, on Av Lázaro Cárdenas Sur near Plaza Garibaldi. The ***Teatro de la Ciudad***, Donceles 36 (T55102197 and 55102942) has the Ballet Folklórico Nacional Aztlán, US$3-US$15 for tickets, very good shows Sun morning and Wed.

Festivals

Just as much fun, and probably safer, is the Grito which takes place at the same time in the Plaza in Coyoacán.

The largest is the Independence celebration on **15 September**, when the President gives the *Grito*: 'Viva México' from the Palacio Nacional on the Zócalo at 2300, and rings the Liberty Bell (now, sadly, electronic!). This is followed by fireworks, and on **16 September** (0900-1400) there are military and traditional regional parades in the Zócalo and surrounding streets – great atmosphere.

Shopping

Mexican **jewellery** and hand-made **silver** can be bought everywhere. Among the good silver shops are ***Sanborn's***, ***Calpini***, ***Prieto***, and ***Vendome***. ***Joyería Sobre Diseño*** (local 159) at the Ciudadela Market is helpful and will produce personalized jewellery cheaply. There are also good buys in perfumes, quality leather, and suede articles. ***De Sol*** on 16 de Septiembre, and on Periférico Sur, T58068427, for cheap food, drinks, clothes, domestic goods, etc. With the extension of the ring roads around the city, **hypermarkets** are being set up: there are 2, ***Perisur*** in the south of the city (with *Liverpool*, *Sears*, *Sanborn's* and *Palacio de Hierro*), open Tue-Fri 1100-2000, Sat 1100-2100; and ***Plaza Satélite*** in the north (with *Sumesa*, *Sears* and *Liverpool*), open on Sun. There is an ISSSTE supermarket in Tres Guerras, 2 blocks from metro Balderas and 1 block from Bucareli. **Luggage repairs** (moderate prices) at Rinconada de Jesús 15-G, opposite Museo de la Ciudad de México on Pino Suárez, but opening times can be unreliable; better try the shop in Callejón del Parque del Conde off Pino Suárez opposite Hospital de Jesús church. At Pino Suárez metro station are several shops selling *charro* clothing and equipment (leggings, boots, spurs, bags, saddles, etc), eg *Casa Iturriaga*. Recommended. Many small **tailors** are found in and around República de Brasil; suits made to measure in a week or less at a fraction of European prices. Guatemalan Refugee shop, Yosemite 45, Col Nápoles, off Insurgentes Sur, T5232114. **Art supplies** *Casa Bernstein*, República de El Salvador 66.

Bookshops Many good ones in the city centre, especially along Av Juárez, Madero and Donceles, also along Miguel Angel de Quevedo (Coyoacán/San Angel – Metro Miguel Angel de Quevedo). Good chain of literary and art bookshops called *Libros y Arte* in the Palacio de Bellas Artes, the airport (area D), the Centro Nacional de Las Artes, the Cineteca Nacional, Coyoacán (Av Hidalgo), Museo del Carmen (San Angel) and the Museo Nacional de las Culturas (Moneda 13, Centro). Several shops belonging to the *Gandhi* chain (large selection, keen prices), two large branches on Miguel Angel de Quevedo, another opposite Palacio de Bellas Artes. One of the most famous bookshops is *El Parnaso*, Jardín Centenario, Coyoacán (its coffee is equally well known). Others include *Librería Británica*, Serapio Rendón 125 (near Parque Sullivan, west of Monumento Cuauhtémoc on Reforma), also Madero 30-A (limited range of titles in English). The *American Bookstore* (Madero 25, also on Revolución – 5-min bus ride south from metro Barranca del Muerte), is much better in this and other respects – large stocks of Penguins and Pelicans, low mark up. For inexpensive editions in Spanish look out for branches of the *Librería del Sótano* (Av Juárez, Antonio Caso, Miguel Angel de Quevedo), and of the *Fondo de Cultura Económico* (Miguel Angel de Quevedo). *Librería Madero*, Madero 12, good, also stocks antiquarian books. *Libros, Libros, Libros*, Monte Ararat 220, Lomas Barrilaco, T55404778, hundreds of hardback and paperback English titles; the shop at the entrance to the Templo Mayor has a good selection of travel books and guides in many languages. *Nueva Librería Francesa*, Hamburgo 172, T55251173/1213. *Librería Italiana*, Plaza Río de Janeiro 53, Col Roma, T55116180. The *Sanborn* chain has the largest selection of English-language magazines in the country, also stocks some best-selling paperbacks in English. *Casa Libros*, Monte Athos 355, Lomas, large stock of second-hand English books, the shop is staffed by volunteers, gifts of books welcome, all proceeds to the American Benevolent Society. *Libros y Discos*, Madero 1. Plenty of Spanish bookshops on Argentina and many open-shelf bookstores in the underpass between metros Zócalo and Pino Suárez. *UNAM* bookshop has a comprehensive range. Second-hand book market on Independencia just past junction with Eje Lázaro Cárdenas has some English books; also Puente de Alvarado, 100m from Metro Hidalgo, and Dr Bernard 42, Metro Niños Héroes. Second-hand Spanish and antiquarian booksellers on Donceles between Palma and República de Brasil, about 1½ blocks from Zócalo. *La Torre de Papel*, Filomeno Mata 6-A, in Club de Periodistas, sells newspapers from all over Mexico and USA. See also **Newspapers**, page 48.

Posters An interesting collection of shops/stores all selling posters – of all sorts and qualities – is to be found in Justo Sierra (behind the Templo Mayor). The prices are very keen. Also, here you can have your posters mounted onto lightweight wooden frames which are then laminated. Many places to choose from, one of the best being Amoxcalli, Justo Sierra 25.

Cycle shops *Tecno-Bici*, Av Manuel Acuña 27 (Camarones metro station, line 7), stocks almost all cycle spares, parts, highly recommended. *Benolto*, near Polanco metro, stocks almost all cycle spares. Another good shop is between San Antonio and Mixcoac metro stations. The Escuela Médico Militar, near Pino Suárez metro station, has a very good shop, stocking all the best-known international makes for spare parts. For excellent cycle repairs, see under Coyoacán, page 128.

Handicrafts

Fonart, Fondo Nacional para el Fomento de las Artesanías, a state organization founded in 1974 in order to rescue, promote and diffuse the traditional crafts of Mexico. Main showroom at Av Patriotismo 594 (Metro Mixcoac), T55981666, branches at Av Juárez 89 (Metro Hidalgo), Londres 136 (Zona Rosa) and Coyoacán (Presidente Carranza 115). Competitive prices, superb quality. *The Mercado de Artesanías Finas Indios Verdes* is at Galería Reforma Nte SA, González Bocanegra 44 (corner of Reforma Norte, near statue of Cuitláhuac, Tlatelolco); good prices and quality but no bargaining. For onyx, *Müllers*, Londres y Florencia, near Insurgentes metro, good chess sets. For Talavera pottery from Puebla, *Uriarte*, Emilio Castelar 95-E, Polanco, T52822699, and Pabellón Altavista, Calzada Desierto de los Leones 52 D-6, San Angel, T56163119, www. talavera.com. There is an annual **national craft fair** in Mexico City, first week in December.

Markets

San Juan market, Ayuntamiento and Arandas, near Salto del Agua metro, good prices for handicrafts, especially leather goods and silver (also cheap fruit and health food); open Mon-Sat 0900-1900, Sun 0900-1600 (but don't go before 1000). The *Plaza Ciudadela* market (Mercado Central de Artesanías, open 1100-1800 weekdays, Sun 1100-1400), beside Balderas 95 between Ayuntamiento y Plaza Morelos, government-sponsored, fixed prices, good selection, reasonable and uncrowded, is cheaper than San Juan, but not for leather; craftsmen from all Mexico have set up workshops here (best for papier maché, lacquer, pottery and Guatemalan goods) but prices are still cheaper in places of origin. *Mercado Lagunilla* near Glorieta Cuitláhuac (take *colectivo* from Metro Hidalgo) is a flea market where antique and collectable bargains are sometimes to be found, also a lot of rubbish (open daily, but Sun best day). The market, which covers several blocks, now has all sorts of merchandise, including a wider range of non-silver jewellery; good atmosphere. Mercado Insurgentes in Calle Londres, Zona Rosa, good for silver, but other things expensive, stallholders pester visitors, only place where they do so. There is a market in every district selling pottery, glassware, textiles, *sarapes* and jewellery. Try also *San Angel Bazar del Sábado*, (see page 125), although expensive, many items are exclusive to it; good leather belts, crafts and silver; open Sat only from about 1100. Mexican tinware and lacquer are found everywhere. Vast fruit and veg market, *Mercado Merced* (see page 86), Metro Merced. A few blocks away on Fray Servando Teresa de Mier (nearest metro Fray Servando) lies the fascinating *Mercado Sonora*: secret potions and remedies, animals and birds as well as *artesanías*. *Buena Vista craft market*, Aldama 187 y Degollado (nearest metro Guerrero), excellent quality (open 0900-1800, Sun 0900-1400). Also on Aldama, No 211, between Sol and Luna, the *Tianguis del Chopo* is held on Sat, 1000-1600, selling clothes, records, etc, frequented by hippies, punks, rockers, and police. You can bargain in the markets and smaller shops. *Jamaica* market, Jamaica metro, line 4, has a huge variety of fruits and vegetables, also flowers, pottery, and canaries, parrots, geese, and ducks, indoor and outdoor halls.

Photography

Kodak film (Ektachrome, not Kodachrome) is produced in Mexico and is not expensive. Imported film is also available (eg Agfa slide film US$6). Cheapest film reported to be on Av Madero, eg 36 Slide Kodak Ektachrome costs US$4.50, but shop around. The price for slide film does not include processing. Small shops around República de Chile and Tacuba are cheaper than larger ones south of Av 5 de Mayo, but it may be worth paying more for good quality prints. Special offers abound, quality is good, prints normally ready in 45 mins (no express charge), slides up to 48 hrs. *Laboratorio Mexicano del Imagen*, Carlos B Zetina 34, Col Hipodromo Condesa, T5155540, excellent quality, fast service, normal prices. Several shops sell slide and print film (Fuji and Kodak) on Donceles, near Zócalo. **Camera repairs** *Vanta*, Gabriel Barreda 93, Col San Rafael, metro San Cosme, T55665566. Mon-Fri 1000-1400 and 1530-1730.

Mexico City

Sports

Charreadas (Cowboy displays) *Rancho Grande de la Villa*, at very top of Insurgentes Nte (from metro Indios Verdes, walk north beyond bus station and keep asking), Sun 1100-1500, US$1.30.

Football Sun midday, Aztec and Olympic stadia (former has a great atmosphere at football matches, latter has a Rivera mural of the history of Mexican sport); also Thu (2100) and Sat (1700). Tickets from US$3.35 at Olympic Stadium. To Aztec Stadium take metro to Taxqueña terminus, then tram *en route* to Xochimilco to Estadio station; about 75 mins from Zócalo. To Olympic Stadium take bus down Insurgentes marked 'CU' (Ciudad Universitaria), or metro to Universidad terminus, then local bus (US$0.35) or taxi (US$1); leave Zócalo at 1045 for 1200 kick-off.

Golf At *Chapultepec Golf Club* and *Churubusco Country Club*. These are private clubs, open to visitors only if accompanied by a member. Green fees are US$20 upwards.

Horse races *Hipódromo de las Américas*, west of Blvd Manuel Avila Camacho, off Av Conscriptos. Beautiful track with infield lagoons and flamingos, and plenty of atmosphere. Was in financial difficulties. Best to check whether it is open with Tourist Office, T52500123.

Hiking Every weekend with the Alpino and Everest clubs. *Club de Exploraciones de México*, Juan A Mateos 146, Col Obrero (Metro Chabacano), DF 06800, T55785730, 1930-2400 Wed or Fri, organizes several walks in and around the city on Sat and Sun, cheap equipment hire, slideshow Wed. *Club Alpino Mexicano*, Córdoba 234, Col Roma (Metro Hospital General), T/F55749683, open Mon-Fri 1000-2000, Sat 1000-1500, small shop (if club door is closed ask here for access). José María Aguayo Estrada, club president, very helpful; also arrange (free) mountain hiking at weekends, run ice climbing courses. **Equipment suppliers** *Vertimania*, Federico T de la Chica 12, Plaza Versailles, Local 11-B, Col Satélite, T/F53935287. More central is *Deportes Rubens*, Venustiano Carranza 17, T55185636, F55128312. **Stove repair** *Servicio Coleman*, Marqués Sterling 23.

Climbing wall *Rocadromo*, Lindavista, T7525674. Further reading: *Iztaccíhuatl, Toluca and Colima* by Alfredo Careaga Pardave; *Mexico's Volcanoes* by R Secord.

Ice-skating Pista de Hielo San Jerónimo, Av Contreras 300, Col San Jerónimo, Metro Barranca del Muerto then bus to arena, T6831625, full-sized rink, crowded, closed Mon, US$3.50. *Pista de Hielo de Galerías Reforma*, Carretera México-Toluca 1725, Lomas Palo Alto, T2593543, US$3.50, small rink, not crowded.

Jai-Alai Events with the foremost players in the world every day except Fri at the Frontón México across from Monumento a la Revolución, from 2000 (1900 Sun) till 2400 (closed Mon), entry US$7, drinks expensive. It seats 4,000. Jackets and ties are needed for admission. Restaurant *El Rincón Pampero*. The people in the red caps are the *corredores*, who place the bets. Pari-mutuel betting. Also Frontón Metropolitano, on Bahía de Todos los Santos, near junction of Gutemberg and Calzada Melchor Ocampo.

Swimming Agua Caliente, Las Termas, Elba, Centro Deportivo Chapultepec and others.

Tour operators

Shop around as prices vary considerably. Deals regularly found in Europe or the US are rare

Use a travel agent that has been recommended to you (if possible), as not all are efficient or reliable. One of the most reliable is *Cultours*, Guanajuato 72 (Col Roma), T52640854/1004/1076, F52640919, highly recommended, good for flights to Europe, Central and South America, and for changing flight dates, English spoken, ask for

Icarus Monk. ***Thomas Cook***, Campos Elíseos 345, Col Polanco, travellers' cheques agency only. ***Wagons-Lits***, Av Juárez 88, F55181180 (reported to be closed all day Sat), also Av de las Palmas 731, T55400579, very helpful and knowledgeable. ***Grey Line Tours***, Londres 166, T52081163, reasonably priced tours, car hire, produces *This is Mexico* book (free). ***American Express***, Reforma 234 y Havre, T55330380, open Mon-Fri 0900-1800, Sat 0900-1300, charges US$3-4 for *Poste Restante* if you do not have their travellers' cheques and US$1 if no card or cheques are held for other services, service slow but helpful.

   Mundo Joven Travel Shop, Insurgentes Sur 1510 (on the corner of Río Churubusco), T56628244, F56631556, issues ISIC card, agents for International Youth Hostel Federation, hostellingmexico@remaj.com. ***Corresponsales de Hoteles***, Blvd Centro 224-4, T53603356, for hotel reservations (upmarket). ***Hadad Viajes***, Torres Adalid 205, oficina 602, Col de Valle, T56870488. ***Asatej***, Insurgentes Sur 421, Local B.10, Col Hipódromo Condesa, T55740899, F55743462, ve@ve.com.mx. ***Humboldt Tours***, José María Velasco 34, San José Insurgentes, T56609152/6650, F56600735, one of Mexico's leading tour operators, good for individual tours as well as groups, multilingual staff. ***Viajes Tirol***, José Ma Rico 212, Depto 503, T55345582/3323/1765, English and German spoken, recommended. ***Turisjoven***, Tuxpan 54-903 (Metro Chilpancingo). For cheap tickets to Cuba, ask in agencies around Hamburgo. ***W Tours and Travel***, T56821718/1607, are also recommended. Finding a cheap flight to Europe is difficult. Try ***Vacation Planning***, Copenhague 21-203, Zona Rosa, T55111604. ***Beltravel***, Londres 51, Zona Rosa; ***Viajes de Alba***, Villalongín 20-2, Col Cuauhtémoc, T57054180. We have been informed that it is difficult to find a travel agent open for business in Mexico City at weekends or on bank holidays.

The Asociación Mexicana de Turismo de Aventura y Ecoturismo (AMTAVE) regulates and promotes many of the agencies listed below. Not all areas of adventure sport come under their umbrella, for instance specialist diving agencies remain unattached to any Mexico-based organization, as diving is a mainly regional activity. *Río y Montaña*, Prado Norte 450-T, Lomas de Chapultepec, T/F55202041, sea kayaking, rafting (Ríos Pescados-Antigua stretch, Filo Bobos, Usumacinta, Santa María, Río Grande, Jatate); climbing expertise – Alfonso de la Parra, one of the guides, has climbed Everest. *Al Aire Libre*, Centro Comercial Interlomas, Local 2122, Lomas Anáhuac Huixquilucan, T2919217, rafting (Ríos Pescados-Antigua, Santa María, Amacuzac), climbing, caving (Chontalcuatlán, Zacatecoltla, La Joya), ballooning, parapenting. *Intercontinental Adventures*, Homero 526-801, Col Polanco, T52254400, F52554465/52540381, email: adventu@mps net.com.mx, run by Agustín Arroyo who is president of AMTAVE, operates mainly in Veracruz, historical tours, rafting and sea kayaking, represents *México Verde* agency (see under Guadalajara tour operators) in Mexico City. *Ecogrupos de México*, Centro Comercial Plaza Inn, Insurgentes Sur 1971251, T56619121, F56627354, nature tours eg butterfly habitats.

Specialists in adventure tourism

Transport

Car hire *Budget Rent Auto*, Reforma 60; *Hertz*, Revillagigedo 2; *Avis*, Medellín 14; *VW*, Av Chapultepec 284-6; *National Car Rental*, Insurgentes Sur 1883; *Auto Rent*, Reforma Nte 604; quick service at Av Chapultepec 168, T55335335 (57629892 airport); *Pamara*, Hamburgo 135, T55255572, 200 km free mileage; *Odin*, Balderas 24-A; and many local firms, which tend to be cheaper. It is generally cheaper to hire in the US or Europe. **NB** When driving in the capital you must check which *día sin auto hoy no circula* applies to your vehicle's number plate; if your car is on the street when its number is prohibited, you could be fined US$80. This should not apply to foreign-licensed cars. The regulation covers the state of México besides the Distrito Federal. The ban applies to the last digit of your number plate: Mon 5,6; Tue 7,8; Wed 3,4; Thu 1,2; Fri 9,0. Occasionally,

Local
See also Ins & outs, page 79

Mexico City

when contamination levels are even worse than usual, the programme runs at week-ends too: Sat, all even numbers and 0; Sun, all odd numbers. Normally, you can drive freely in 'greater' Mexico City on Sat, Sun and between 2200 and 0500 all week.

City buses Buses have been coordinated into one system: odd numbers run north-south, evens east-west. Fares on large buses, which display routes on the

Mexico City metro

Mexico City

N

Not to scale

windscreen are US$0.15, exact fare only. There are 60 direct routes and 48 feeder (SARO) routes. Thieves and pickpockets haunt the buses plying along Reforma and Juárez. A most useful route for tourists (and well-known to thieves, so don't take anything you don't require immediately) is No 76 which runs from Uruguay (about the level of the Juárez Monument at Parque Alameda) along Paseo de la Reforma, beside Chapultepec Park. A *Peribus* service goes round the entire Anillo Periférico (see Traffic System.) Trolley buses also charge US$0.15. *Colectivos* run on fixed routes, often between metro stations and other known landmarks; destination and route displayed on the windscreen. Avoid the smaller, white VW Combis which do not have catalytic converters and which can be unpleasant. *Colectivos* can be hailed almost anywhere and stop anywhere (press the button or say '*Bajan*'); this can make long journeys slow. If a bus runs on the same route, it is preferable as it has fixed stops. Fares are US$0.20 up to 5 km, US$0.25 up to 10 km and US$0.35 beyond.

Metro An efficient, modern system (virtually impossible to get lost) and the best method of getting around the city, especially when the pollution is bad. Trains are fast, frequent, clean and quiet although overcrowded at certain times (eg early morning, 1400-1500 and 1830-2000). Pino Suárez, Hidalgo and Autobuses del Norte are particularly infamous for thieves. Between 1800 and 2100 men are separated from women and children at Pino Suárez and certain other central stations. Two pieces of medium-sized luggage are permitted. Music is played quietly at the stations. Tickets cost 1.80 pesos, buy several to avoid queueing, check train direction before entering turnstile or you may have to pay again. **NB** Lines 1, 2, 3 and A open 0500-0030 Mon-Fri, 0600-0130 Sat and 0700-0030 Sun and holidays; the other lines open 1 hr later on weekdays (same hours on weekends and holidays). Do not take photos or make sound-recordings in the metro without obtaining a permit and a uniformed escort from metro police, or you could be arrested. For lost property enquire at Oficina de Objetos Extraviados at Chabacano (intersection of lines 2, 8 and 9), open Mon-Fri only.

There is a metro information service at Insurgentes station on the Pink Line 1 which dispenses maps, and most

Beware of pickpocketing at any time on the metro, many reports; the police are not as helpful as the vigilancias

Line		
1		
2		& Tren Ligero
3		
4		
5		
6		
7		
8		
9		
A		Metro Férreo
B		

Mexico City

interchange stations have information kiosks. The *Atlas de Carreteras*, US$1.65 has a map of Mexico City, its centre and the metro lines marked. *Pronto's* map of the metropolitan area displays the metro clearly. Good metro and bus maps at the Anthropology Museum, US$1.25. *Guía práctica del Metro*, US$9, explains all the station symbols; also *Guía cultural del Metro*, US$3, both for sale at Zócalo station. All the stations have a symbol, eg the grasshopper signifying Chapultepec.

There are 9 lines in service. **1** from Observatorio (by Chapultepec Park) to Pantitlán in the eastern suburbs (pink). It goes under Av Chapultepec and not far from the lower half of Paseo de la Reforma, the Mercado Merced, and 3 km from the airport. **2**, from Cuatro Caminos in the northwest to the Zócalo and then south above ground to Taxqueña (blue); **3**, from Indios Verdes south to the University City (olive; free bus service to Insurgentes); **4**, from Santa Anita on the southeast side to Martín Carrera in the northeast (turquoise); **5**, from Pantitlán, via Terminal Aérea (which is within walking distance of gate A of the airport, but some distance from the international gates – opens 0600), up to Politécnico (yellow; if using La Raza to connect with Line 3, note that there is a long walk between Lines 5 and 3, through the Tunnel of Knowledge); **6**, from El Rosario in the northwest to Martín Carrera in the northeast (red); **7**, from El Rosario in the northwest to Barranca del Muerto in the southwest (orange); **8**, the newest, runs from Garibaldi (north of Bellas Artes, Line 2), through Chabacano (Line 9) and Santa Anita (Line 4), to Constitución de 1917 in the southeast (green). **9** parallels Line 1 to the south, running from Tacubaya in the west (where there are interesting paintings in the station) to Pantitlán in the east (brown).

In addition to the numbered lines: running southeast from Pantitlán, Line A, the *metro férreo* goes as far as La Paz, 10 stations in all. From Taxqueña the *tren ligero* goes as far as Xochimilco, a very convenient way to this popular destination. Line B, from Buenavista to Ciudad Azteca in Ecatepec, north of the city, is now partially open and should be completed by the end of 2000.

At the Zócalo metro station there is an interesting permanent exhibit about the city. At Pino Suárez, the station has been built around a small restored Aztec temple. **Art in the metro**: Line 1, Pino Suárez and Tacubaya; Line 2, Bellas Artes and Panteones; Line 3, La Raza, scientific display in the Tunnel of Knowledge, and south of Coyoacán; Line 4, Santa Anita; Line 5, Terminal Aérea; Line 6, all stations, Line 7, Barranca del Muerto; Line 9, Mixuca.

Taxis There are 3 types: *1) turismo taxis* which operate from first-class hotels, the Museo Nacional de Antropología, etc – are the most expensive. *2) Taxis from sitios (fixed ranks)*, from bus terminals, railway station and other locations; no meters. About double the normal price but safer. You pay in advance at a booth (check your change); they charge on a zone basis, US$4.60 for up to 4 km, rising to US$22 for up to 22 km (the same system applies at the airport – see below). *3) Taxis on unfixed routes are green* (lead-free petrol) and can be flagged down anywhere; tariffs US$0.35 plus 5 cents for each 250m or 45 seconds; between 2200 and 0600 they charge 20% extra. They have meters (check they are working properly and set at zero); if you do not bargain before getting in, or if the driver does not know the route well, the meter will be switched on, which usually works out cheaper than negotiating a price. Some drivers refuse to use their meter after 1800. Note that radiotelephone taxis and those with catalytic converters have a basic fee of 2.50 pesos. Drivers often do not know where the street you want is; try to give the name of the intersection between two streets rather than a number, because the city's numbering can be erratic. A tip is not normally expected, except when special help has been given. For information, or complaints, T56055520/6727/5388/6894; if complaining, make sure you take the taxi's ID number. Another type of taxi travel, the tricycle, is now being encouraged to counter exhaust pollution, and is a good way to see the architecture of the centre.

Driving in Mexico City

If you are brave enough to drive in Mexico City, you should be aware that this has to be undertaken with immense alertness and a sense of daring. There are, in theory, traffic regulations, but these are interpreted extremely liberally where not ignored totally; 'lawless roads' is not too far off the mark. The most important rule of the road observed by most drivers in Mexico City is to fill any space ahead, or to the left or right, even if only slightly ahead, which seems to be empty; this leads to endless changes of lanes in thoroughfares such as the Eje Central or Tlalpan. Direction indicators are not normally used, and when used do not necessarily mean that the vehicle will behave as indicated. Traffic lights are observed, with some licence; the custom in the USA of filtering right when at red is frequently observed, but the same custom is applied to going straight ahead or even turning right across the bows of other traffic. Cyclists and motorcyclists do not observe one-way restrictions; and in many broad streets there are special lanes intended for buses or trolley-buses travelling in the opposite direction – and they suddenly appear at great speed.

Mexico City

Warning Lone travellers, especially female, are advised to take only official taxis from hotels or ordered by phone. If you have to hail a taxi in the street, choose one with a licence plate beginning with S, not L. There have been reports of rapes, muggings, robbery, etc, particularly at night. Tourist Police advise that you make note of registration and taxi numbers before getting in.

Traffic system The city has two ring roads, the Anillo Periférico through what used to be the city outskirts, and the Circuito Interior running within its circumference. You can cross the city via Viaducto and Periférico but only with a *small* motorhome or car. In the centre, there is a system of Ejes Viales. It consists of a series of freeways laid out in a grid pattern, spreading from the Eje Central Lázaro Cárdenas; the latter serves as a focal point for numbering (Eje 2 Pte, Eje I Ote, etc). Norte, Sur, Oriente, Poniente refer to the roads' position in relation to the Eje Central. The system is remarkably clear in its signposting with special symbols for telephones, information points, tram stops, etc. Beware of the tram lines – trams, buses, emergency services and folk in a hurry come down at high speed; and as often as not this lane goes against the normal flow of traffic! Bicycles are permitted to go the wrong way on all roads, which also 'adds to the spice of life'. Traffic police at most busy corners direct the flow of traffic (some visitors find Mexico City driving a nightmare). Traffic can be extremely heavy and, at certain times, very slow moving. You must, however, have a good city map (see maps, page 79).

Eje Central Lázaro Cárdenas used to be called San Juan de Letrán

Air The airport terminal is divided into sections, each designated by a letter. A row of shops and offices outside each section contains various services. Section **A**: national arrivals; post office, city of Mexico tourist office, exit to taxis and metro, INAH shop, telecommunications office. Between **A** and **B**: AeroMéxico; Bancomer ATM. Outside **B**: Banamex. Between **B** and **C**: entrance to *Continental Plaza* hotel, *casa de cambio*. **C** Mexicana; map shop. Ladatel phones just after C (Ladatel cards are sold at many outlets in the airport). Between **C** and **D**: Exposición Diego Rivera exhibition hall. **C-D**: Other national airline offices; bookshop. **D**: national and international departures; *cambio* opposite. By D are more national airline desks, long-distance phones, a bar and restaurant. From D you have to leave the building to get to **E**: international arrivals; car hire offices, exchange (Banamex), 24-hr luggage lockers (US$2.50 per day). **F**: international check-in; banks. Upstairs at E-F are shops, fast-food restaurants (mostly US-style), exchange and phones. Pesos may be bought at any of the bank branches liberally spread from A to F. Most foreign currencies or travellers' cheques accepted, also most credit cards. The rate can vary considerably, so shop around. When buying dollars (and

Long distance
See also Transport, page 113

other 'hard' currency, when available), **Coberturas Mexicanas** almost always offers the best rates (Local 1, section D and local 8/9, section E). Only US$500 may be changed back into dollars after passing through immigration and customs when leaving. Exchange facilities in E or F (particularly on the upper floor) are less crowded. Banks and *casas de cambio* between them provide a 24-hr service. Phone calls from the airport may be made at many locations, but you have to keep trying all the phones to find one in operation that will accept the method of payment you wish to use. Look for the Lada *multitarjeta* phones. There is a phone office at the far end of section F, which accepts Amex and, in theory, Visa, Mastercard and other cards. It is very expensive though.

Fixed-price taxis by zone, buy tickets from booths at exits by A, E and F; you can buy tickets before passing customs but they are cheaper outside the duty free area; rates range from US$5 upwards, according to distance (per vehicle, not per person), drivers may not know, or may be unwilling to go to, cheaper hotels. For losses or complaints about airport taxis, T55713600 Ext 2299; for reservations T55719344/57848642, 0800-0200. The fixed-price taxi system is efficient and safe. A cheaper alternative (about 50%) if one doesn't have too much luggage is to cross the Blvd Puerto Aéreo by the Metro Terminal Aérea and flag down an ordinary taxi outside the *Ramada* hotel. There are regular buses from the city centre to the airport (eg No 20, along north side of Alameda), but the drawback is that you have to take one to Calzada Ignacio Zaragoza and transfer to trolley bus at the Boulevard Puerto Aéreo (ie at Metro Terminal Aerea). Buses to airport may be caught every 45 mins until 0100 from outside *Hotel De Carlo*, Plaza de la República 35. It takes 1 hr from downtown (and in the rush hour, most of the day, it is jam-packed), but you can take baggage if you can squeeze it in. To get to the airport cheaply, take metro to Terminal Aérea and walk, or take metro to Blvd Puerto Aéreo and then a *pesero* marked 'Oceanía', which will leave you at the Terminal metro station. Avoid rush hours especially if you have luggage. There are airport information kiosks at *Salas* A, D, E and F. There is a hotel desk before passing through customs. The tourist office at A has phones for calling hotels, no charge, helpful, but Spanish only. The travel agency at east exit will book hotels or reconfirm flights, charges 5 pesos. For air freight contact the Agencia Aduanales, Plazuela Hermanos, Colima 114, Mon-Fri 0900-1700, US$5.75 per kilo.

Trains The Buenavista central station (a spacious building) is on Insurgentes Norte, junction Alzate with Mosqueta, nearest metro Revolución or Guerrero. Left luggage for US$1 per piece per day, open 0630-2130. *Cafetería* reasonable. At the station there are long-distance phone and fax services and an information desk. The only passenger services are to Saltillo in the north on Mon, Wed, Fri at 0900, arriving 2355, returning Tue, Thu, Sat, 0235-1900, and to Veracruz daily at 0845 and 2015 (arriving 1915 and 0600), returning 0820 and 2200 (arriving 1940 and 0800).These services are subject to change or cancellation. A monthly timetable, *Rutas Ferroviarias*, is available from the station (Departamento de Tráfico de Pasajeros) and from ticket offices. Reservations T5976177, 5 lines; information T55471084/1097. If planning a train journey, find out in advance whether the service is actually running, the departure time, which floor the ticket will be sold on and when, and arrive 1 hr in advance. In general, first-class tickets can be bought in advance, second-class are only available on the day. **NB** Lost or stolen tickets will not be replaced.

See map on page 78, for location of terminals

For details of bus services, see destinations in text

Buses At all bus stations there are many counters for the bus companies, not all are manned and it is essential to ask which is selling tickets for the destination you want (don't take notice boards at face value). On the whole, the bus stations are clean and well organized. Book ahead where possible. Buses to destinations in north Mexico, including US borders, leave from **Terminal del Norte**, Av Cien Metros 4907, which has a *casa de cambio*, 24-hr cafés, left luggage, pharmacy, bakery and phone offices for long-distance calls (often closed and poorly informed, very high charges). The bus station is on metro line 5 at Autobuses del Norte. City buses marked Cien Metros or Central del Norte go directly there. **Terminal del Sur**, at corner of Tlalpan 2205 across from metro Taxqueña (line 2), serves Cuernavaca, Acapulco and Zihuatanejo areas. Direct buses to centre (Donceles) from Terminal del Sur, and an express bus connects the Sur and Norte terminals. It is difficult to get tickets to the south, book as soon as possible; the terminal for the south is chaotic. The **Terminal Poniente** is situated opposite the Observatorio station of line 1 of the metro, to serve the west of Mexico. You can go to the centre by bus from the *urbano* outside the bus station, Terminal Poniente (US$0.10). The **Terminal Oriente**, known as **TAPO**, Calzada Ignacio Zaragoza (Metro San Lázaro, Line 1) for buses to Veracruz, Yucatán and southeast, including Oaxaca and Puebla (2 hrs). It has a tourist information office open from 0900; luggage lockers, US$2.65 per day, key is left with guard; post office, *farmacia* changes travellers' cheques. To **Guatemala**, from TAPO, take a bus to Tapachula, Comitán or Ciudad Cuauhtémoc, pesos only accepted.

There are also buses departing from Mexico City airport (outside Sala D), to Puebla, Toluca, Cuernavaca and Querétaro, very convenient. Buy ticket from driver.

All bus terminals operate taxis with voucher system and there are long queues (check change carefully at the taxi office). It is much easier to pay the driver, although beware of extra charges. In the confusion at the terminals some drivers move each other's cabs to get out of the line faster and may take your voucher and disappear. Fares are given under **Taxis** above. The terminals are connected by metro, but this is not a good option at rush hours, or if carrying too much luggage. Advance booking is recommended for all trips, and very early reservation if going to *fiestas* during Holy Week, etc. At Christmas, many Central American students return home via Tapachula, and buses from Mexico City are booked solid for 2 weeks before, except for those lines which do not make reservations. You must go and queue at the bus stations which can involve a long wait, sometimes 2-2½ hrs. Even if you are travelling, you may sometimes be required to buy a *boleto de andén* (platform ticket) at many bus stations. Note that many bus companies require luggage to be checked in 30 mins in advance of departure.

Bus companies (tickets and bookings) Going north: *Transportes del Norte*, at Av Insurgentes Centro 137, near Reforma (T55875511/5400); depart from Terminal delNorte. *Omnibus de México*, Insurgentes Nte 42, at Héroes Ferrocarrileros (T55676756 and 55675858). *Greyhound* bus, Reforma 27, T55352618/4200, F55353544, closed 1400-1500 and all day Sun; information at Terminal del Norte from Transportes del Norte (Chihuahuenses) or Tres Estrellas bus counters, prices only, no schedules. Going to central states: *Autobuses Anáhuac*, Bernal Díaz 6 (T55910533); Terminal del Norte departures. Going northwest: *ETN*, Terminal del Norte, T55673773, or Terminal Poniente T52730251; *Tres Estrellas de Oro*, Calzada Vallejo 1268 Nte (Col Santa Rosa), T53911139/3021, Terminal del Norte. Going northeast: *ADO*, Av Cien Metros 4907 (T55678455/5322). Beware of ADO selling tickets for buses and then not running the service. Although the ticket will be valid for a later bus, there are then problems with overbooking (your seat number won't be valid). Going south (including Guatemala): *Cristóbal Colón*, Blvd Ignacio Zaragoza 200, T55427263 to 66; from Terminal de Oriente; also *ADO*, Buenavista 9 (T55923600 or 55427192 at terminal). Going southwest: *Estrella de Oro*, Calzada de Tlalpan 2205 (T55498520 to 29).

Directory

The majority are on Paseo de la Reforma: No 325, *Avensa* (T52084998/3018). *Delta*, No 381, T55254840/ 52021608, airport T57623588. *American Airlines*, No 314, T52086396/53999222/ 55713219 (airport). *Avianca*, No 195, T55668588/55463059. *Iberia*, No 24, T55664011/55922988/ 57625844 (airport). *Aero California*, No 332, T52071392. *Alitalia*, No 390-1003, T55335590/1240/1243. *Japan Airlines*, No 295, T55336883/5515, 55718742 (airport). *Canadian Airlines*, No 390, T52076611/3318. On Hamburgo: *Swissair*, No 66, T55336363. *SAS*, No 61,

Airline offices

See page 32 for web addresses

Mexico City

T55330098/0177, 55119872 (airport). *Air Canada*, No 108, p5°, T55112004, 55142516. *Alaska Airlines*, No 213-1004, T55331747/6. *Ecuatoriana de Aviación*, No 213, T55334569, 55141274, 57625199 (airport). *Air France*, Edgar Allan Poe 90, T56276000, airport 55716150. *Mexicana*, Xola 535, Col del Valle, T56604433/4444, 57624011 (airport). *KLM*, Paseo de las Palmas 735, T52024444. *Lufthansa*, Paseo de las Palmas 239, T52028866. *Cubana*, Temístocles 246, Polanco, T52550646/0835. *Continental*, Andrés Bello 45, T55469503, 55357603, 55713661 (airport). *Aeromar*, Sevilla 4, T52076666, 55749211. *Aeroflot*, Insurgentes Sur 569, T55237139. *United Airlines*, Leibnitz 100, loc 23-24, T52501657, 55455147. *AeroMéxico*, Insurgentes Sur 724, T52076311/8233. *British Airways*, Jaime Balmes 8, Los Morales, T53870310. *El Al Israel Airlines*, Paseo de las Palmas, T57351105, 52022243. *Icelandic Airlines*, Durango 103, T55140159, 55116155/8461. *Lacsa*, Río Nazas 135, T555110640, 55250025. *Northwest Airlines*, Reforma y Amberes 312, T55113579, Reforma 300, T55257090. *Pan American Airways*, Plaza Comermex 1-702, T53950022/0077. *Taca*, Morelos 108, Col Juárez, T55468807/8835.

Banks

0930-1700 Mon-Fri,
0900-1300 Sat,
although some
branches open earlier
& close later

Always see if there is a special counter where currency transactions can be effected to avoid standing in queues which can be long, particularly on Fri. It often happens when you are queueing up that bank employees ask you what you are wishing to do (¿*Qué operación quiere hacer?*). This is not a nosey inquiry, but rather a desire to be of assistance. Branches of all major Mexican banks proliferate in most parts of the city. Cash advances on credit cards are easy with good rates. TCs in most major currencies can be cashed at any branch of Bancomer or Banca Serfín without undue delay. Banks do not charge commission for changing TCs. The exchange of foreign currency notes, other than dollars, can be difficult apart from at the airport and main bank branches in the city centre. There are 2 *casas de cambio* at the airport which specialize in obscure currencies. Before buying or selling currency, check the day's exchange rate from a newspaper and then shop around. There is often a great disparity between different banks and *casas de cambio* particularly in times of volatile currency markets. Hotels usually offer very poor rates. *Banco de Comercio* (Bancomer, Visa agent), head office at Av Universidad 1200, also Venustiano Carranza y Bolívar, good quick *cambio*, same rate for cash and TCs. *Banco Nacional de México (Banamex)*, Palmas, Banamex's offices nearby, at Av Isabel la Católica 44, are in a converted baroque palace, ask the porter for a quick look into the magnificent patio. Another worthwhile building is the bank's branch in the Casa Iturbide, where Agustín de Iturbide lived as emperor, at Madero 17 with Gante. *Banco Internacional* recommended, they deal with Mastercard (Carnet) and Visa (usually quicker than Bancomer or Banamex for cash advances against credit card), also *Banca Serfín*, corner of 16 de Septiembre y Bolívar, or Madero 32, near Bolívar. *Citibank*, Paseo de la Reforma 390, for Citicorp TCs, they also give cash advances against credit cards with no commission. *American Express* emergency number, T53262626, platinum, T53262929; also office at Reforma 234 esq Havre, T5330380, will change cheques on Sats, 0930-1330, also open Mon-Fri until 1800 (there are 5 other Amex offices in Mexico City, including Campos Elíseos 204, local 5, Polanco; Centro Comercial Perisur). For more details on Visa and Master Card, see **Credit cards**, page 29. There are many *casas de cambio*, especially on Reforma, Madero and in the centre. Their hours may be more convenient, but their rates can be poor. *Central de Cambios* (Suiza), Madero 58, west of Zócalo and *Casa de Cambio Plus*, Av Juárez, have been recommended for rates. The Perisur shopping centre, Insurgentes and Periférico Sur, has a *casa de cambio* (T56063698) which is usually open until 1900, with a better exchange rate in the morning. See also **Airport** above.

Communications

The symbol @ is called
arroba in Spanish

Internet *Novanet*, Nuevo León 104 y Michoacán, Col Hipódromo (Metro Chilpancingo), T55537503. *Café Java Chat*, Génova 44 K, T5256853/5146856, Zona Rosa (Metro Insurgentes). Mon-Fri 0900-2200, Sat-Sun 1000-2200, US$3.60 per hour, free coffee and soft drinks. *Cyberpuerto*, Alfonso Reyes 238, Col Hipódromo, T52860869. *Café Pedregal*, Av San Jerónimo 630, Col Jardines del Pedregal T56816672. *Internet Station*, Arquímedes 130, local 20 (Metro Polanco) T52806091. *Internet Café* in Plaza Computación at Cárdenas end of Uruguay, US$3.25 per hour, free coffee, soft drinks US$0.60. *Ragnatel*, Centro Comercial Santa Fé, local 472, Col Antigua Mina la Totolapa T52580782. *Interlomas*, Paseo de la Herradura 5, Col Fernando la Herradura, Huixquilucan T52450330. *Cafe@Rock Shop*, Belisario Domínguez 17, Coyoacán, T55543699. *Tarea*, Presidente Carranza esq Tres Cruces, Coyoacán, T56592420. Most of the above open Mon-Sat 1000-2200, but check. Rates US$3-3.30 per hr. *Cybercafé*, Bolívar between República de El Salvador and Viscaínas. Small, very smoky atmosphere, machines very slow, US$5 per hr. *Lafoel Internet Service*, Donceles y Brasil, T55123584.

Post Office Tacuba y Lázaro Cárdenas, opposite Palacio de Bellas Artes, open for letters 0800-2400 Mon-Fri, 0800-2000 Sat, and 0900-1600 Sun. For parcels open 0800-1800 Mon-Fri, Sat 0800-1600. Parcels up to 2 kg (5 kg for books) may be sent. It is an interesting historic building with a stunning interior, worth a visit. Philatelic sales at windows 9 to 12. Mail kept for only 10 days at poste restante window 3, recommended, but closed Sat and Sun (see page 47). If they can't find your mail under the initial of your surname, ask under the initials of any other names you may happen to have. EMS Mexpost, accelerated national and international postage, is available at the central post office, the airport, Zona Rosa, Coyoacán and 13 other post offices in the city; payable by weight. Other post offices (open 0800-1900 Mon-Fri, 0800-1300 Sat) which travellers may find useful: Centre, Nezahualcóyotl 184 and Academia 4; P Arriaga and Ignacio Mariscal, 2 blocks north of Monumento a la Revolución; Zona Rosa, Londres 208; Tlatelolco, Flores Magón 90; San Rafael, Schultz 102; Polanco, Polanco 79A; Lomas de Chapultepec, Prado Nte 525; Buenavista, Aldama 216; San Angel, Dr Gálvez 16; Coyoacán, Higuera 23; Iztapalapa, Calzada Ermita Iztapalapa 1033; Xochimilco, Prolongación Pino 10; also at the airport and bus terminals. In all there are 155 branches in the federal capital, so there is no need to go to the Correo Central.

Telephones See page 47 for details of the LADA phone system. Finding a phone box that works can be a problem. Most public phones take phone cards (Ladatel), costing 20, 50 and 100 pesos, from shops and news kiosks everywhere. Calls abroad can be made from phone booths with credit cards (via LADA system). International calls can easily be made from the phone office in the Terminal del Oriente bus terminal. There are several places, including some shops, all officially listed, with long-distance phones. For information dial 07.

American Community School of Mexico, complete US curriculum to age of 12, Observatorio and Calle Sur 136, T5166720. *American Chamber of Commerce*, Lucerna 78. *Benjamin Franklin Library*, Londres 116 (has *New York Times* 2 days after publication). *Anglo-Mexican Cultural Institute* (with British Council Library), Maestro Antonio Caso 127, T55666144. *British Council*, Lope de Vega 316, Polanco, T52631900, F52631910. *Instituto Italiano*, Francisco Sosa 77, Coyoacán, T55540044/53, has 3-week intensive and painless courses in Spanish, 3 hrs a day. *Goethe-Institut*, Tonalá 43 (Metro Insurgentes), 0900-1300, 1600-1930. *Colegio Alemán*, Alexander V Humboldt, Col Huichapan, Xochimilco CP 16030. *Instituto Francés de la América Latina*, Nazas 43, free films every Thu at 2030.

Cultural centres

Australian Embassy, Plaza Polanco Torre B, Jaime Balmes 11, 10th floor, Colonia Los Morales, T53959988. *Belizean Embassy*, Bernardo de Gálvez 215, Lomas Virreyes, T55201346, F55318115, open 0900-1300 Mon-Fri, visa US$10, takes a day. *British Chamber of Commerce*, Río de la Plata 30, Col Cuauhtémoc, T52560901. *British Embassy*, Río Lerma 71, T52072593/2449 (Apdo 96 bis, Mexico 5), open Mon and Thu 0900-1400 and 1500-1800, Tue, Wed, Fri, 0900-1500. Consular Section at Usumacinta 30, immediately behind main Embassy Building. Reading room in main building; poste restante for 1 month, please address to Consular section, this is not an official service, just a valuable courtesy. *Canadian Embassy*, Schiller 529 (corner Tres Picos), near Anthropology Museum, T57247900, www.canada.org.mx. *Colombian Consulate*, Reforma 195, 3rd floor, will request visa from Bogotá by telegram (which you must pay for) and permission can take up to a month to come through. *Costa Rican Embassy*, Río Póo 113, Col Cuauhtémoc, T55257764 (Metro Insurgentes). *Danish Embassy*, Tres Picos 43, Col Polanco, Apdo Postal 105, CP 11580, T52553405/4145/3339, open Mon-Fri 0900-1300 (nearest metro Auditorio). *Ecuador*, Tennyson 217, T55453141. *Finnish Embassy*, Monte Pelvoux 111, 4th floor, CP11000, T55406036. *French Embassy*, Havre 15, near the Cuauhtémoc monument, T55331360. *German Embassy*, Byron 737, Col Rincón del Bosque, T52805534, 55456655, open 0900-1200. *Greek Consulate*, Paseo de las Palmas 2060, Col Lomas de Reforma, T55966333/6936. *Guatemalan Embassy*, Explanada 1025, Lomas de Chapultepec, CP11000, T55407520/55209249, F52021142, morning only (take No 47 bus from Observatorio to Virreyes, then walk up hill, or No 76 'Km 15.5 por Reforma', or 'por Palmas', or taxi); to visit Guatemala some nationalities need a compulsory visa costing US$10 in US$ cash only (eg Australians and New Zealanders), others need either a free visa (take a passport photo) or a tourist card (issued at the border), the current regulations are given in Guatemala: open 0900-1300 for visas. *Honduran Consulate*, Alfonso Reyes 220, T55156689/52115425 (metro Chilpancingo), visas issued on the spot (no waiting) valid up to 1 year from date of issue, cost varies per nationality, up to US$20 for Australians. *Hon Irish Consulate*, Sylvia Moronadi, San Jerónimo 790a, metro Miguel Angel, T55953333, open Mon-Fri 0900-1700. *Israeli Embassy*, PO Box 25389, T55406340, F52844825. Sierra Madre 215 (nearest metro Auditorio), open Mon-Fri 0900-1200. *Italian Embassy*, Paseo de las Palmas 1994, Col Lomas de Chapultepec, T55963655. *Japanese Embassy*, Apdo Postal 5101, Paseo de la Reforma 395, Col Cuauhtémoc, T52110028. *Netherlands Embassy*, Monte Urales 635-203 (near Fuente de Petróleos), T52028267, F52026148. *New Zealand Embassy*, JL Lagrange 103, 10th floor, Polanco, T52815486, F52815212. *Nicaraguan Consulate*, Payo de Rivera 120, Col Virreyes, Lomas de Chapultepec, T55204421

Embassies & consulates
Check location of embassies & consulates; they tend to move frequently. Most take 24 hrs for visas; check to make sure you have a visa & not just a receipt stamp

Mexico City

(bus 13 along Reforma, get out at Monte Altai and walk south on Monte Athos), visas for 30 days from date of issue, 1 photograph, US$25, plus US$5 if you want it 'on the spot'. *Panamanian Embassy*, Campos Elíseos 111-1, T52504259/4229, near Auditorio metro (visa US$20 for Australians). *Polish Embassy*, Cracovia 40, CP 01000, T55504700. *Salvadorean Embassy*, Monte Altai 320, T52028250, 55200856, metro Auditorio. *Swedish Embassy*, Paseo de las Palmas 1375. *Swiss Embassy*, Edificio Torre Optima, Paseo de las Palmas 405, 11th floor, Col Lomas de Chapultepec, T55208535, open 0900-1200 Mon-Fri. *USA Embassy*, Reforma 305, Col Cuauhtémoc, T52110042, F55119980, open Mon-Fri 0830-1730, if requiring a visa for the States, it is best to get it in your home country.

Medical services **Hospitals** *American British Cowdray Hospital*, (also known as El Hospital Inglés, or ABC), on Observatorio past Calle Sur 136. T52775000 (emergency: 55158359); very helpful. **Medical services** *Dr César Calva Pellicer* (who speaks English, French and German), Copenhague 24, 3rd floor, T55142529. *Dr Smythe*, Campos Elíseos 81, T5457861, recommended by US and Canadian Embassies. For any medical services you can also go to the *Clínica Prensa*, US$1.20 for consultation, subsidized medicines. *Hospital de Jesús Nazareno*, 20 de Noviembre 82, Spanish-speaking, friendly, drugs prescribed cheaply. It is a historical monument (see page 87). Most embassies have a list of recommended doctors and dentists who speak languages other than Spanish. Good dentist in south of city: *Dr Ricardo Rosas Maldonado*, Calzada de Tlalpan 1320 (metro Portales), T55399608. **Pharmacies** *Farmacia Homeopática*, Mesones 111-B. *Farmacia Nosarco*, corner of 5 de Febrero and República de El Salvador, stocks wide range of drugs for stomach bugs and tropical diseases, may give 21% discount. *Sanborn's* chain and *El Fénix* discount pharmacies are the largest chains with the most complete selection (the *Sanborn's* behind the Post Office stocks gamma globulin). Many supermarkets have good pharmacies. **Vaccination centre** Benjamín Hill 14, near Metro Juanacatlán (Line 1). Open Mon-Fri 0830-1430, 1530-2030, avoid last 30 mins, also open on Sat from 0830-1430; typhoid free (this is free all over Mexico), cholera and yellow fever (Tue and Fri only) US$2; will give a prescription for gamma globulin. For hepatitis shots you have to buy gamma globulin in a pharmacy (make sure it's been refrigerated) and then an injection there (cheap but not always clean), or at a doctor's surgery or the ABC Hospital (see above). Gamma globulin is hard to find (see **Pharmacies** above); try Hospital Santa Elena, Querétaro 58, Col Roma, T55747711, about US$50 for a vaccination. Malaria prophylaxis and advice free from San Luis Potosí 199, 6th floor, Col Roma Nte, 0900-1400, or from the Centro de Salud near metro Chabacano, opposite Comercial Mexicano supermarket – no typhoid vaccinations here (ask at Centro de Salud Benjamín Hill, which does not supply malaria pills). It seems that paludrine is not available in Mexico, only chloroquine.

Language schools The UNAM has excellent classes of Spanish tuition and Mexican culture: *Centro de Enseñanza para Extranjeros*, US$200 for 6 weeks, 5 different levels, free additional courses in culture, free use of medical service, swimming pool, library, a student card from here allows free entry to all national monuments and museums and half price on many bus lines (eg ADO during summer vacations). See also **Learning Spanish**, page 23, and **Cultural centres** above.

Laundry Laundry on Río Danubio, between Lerma and Pánuco and at Chapultepec and Toledo, near Sevilla metro, expensive. *Lavandería* at Chapultepec y Toledo. *Lavandería Automática Edison*, Edison 91 (nearest metro Revolución), between José María Iglesias y Ponciano Arriaga, Col Tabacalera (centre). Mon-Fri 0900-1900, Sat 0900-1800. Has automatic machines, US$1.50 per 3 kg, US$1.50 drying. Also at Parque España 14 and Antonio Caso 82, near British Council, US$4 for 3kg, quick service. Dry cleaning shops (*tintorerías* or *lavado en seco*) are plentiful. Typical charges: jacket or skirt US$1.10, suit US$2.20, can take up to 48 hrs.

Places of worship **English-speaking** Roman Catholic, St Patrick's, Bondojito 248, Tacubaya, T55151993; Evangelical Union, Reforma 1870, Lomas de Chapultepec, T55200436; Baptist, Capital City Baptist Church, Calle Sur 138 y Bondojito, T55161862; Lutheran, Church of the Good Shepherd, Paseo de Palmas 1910, T55961034; Anglican, Mexican Anglican Cathedral, Mesones 139 (see page 87) has services in Spanish, for services in English, Christ Church, Monte Escandinavos 405, Lomas de Chapultepec, T52020949 (services at 0800 and 1000, sung Eucharist, take bus Reforma Km 15 or Km 16 to Monte Alti, then down hill off opposite side of the road); First Church of Christ Scientist, 21 Dante, Col Anzures. Jewish, Beth Israel, Virreyes 1140, Lomas Virreyes, Nidche Israel (Orthodox), Acapulco 70, near Chapultepec metro.

Customs Dirección General de Aduanas, 20 de Noviembre 195, T57092900. **Delegation building** Av Central, the Ministry of Public Works is the place to report a theft; take a long book. **Immigration** Servicios Migratorios, of the Secretaría de Gobernación, Homero 1832, Colonia Morales, Mon-Fri 0930-1330, get there early, long queues, no English spoken. The office is not easy to get to (it's one block before you get to the Periférico, on the left along Homero); the best way from most directions is to go to metro Polanco and take a taxi (US$1). There is a *colectivo* which leaves Metro Chapultepec (marked 'Horacio' or sometimes even 'Inmigración' which also passes Polanco metro station; get off at the terminus which is outside Gobernación; return *pesero* from the same place. Here you can extend tourist cards for stays over 90 days or replace lost cards; new card will be given in 10 days; you may be given 10 days to leave the country. This is also where one has to come to exchange a tourist card for a student's visa and for any other immigration matter concerning foreigners. It is essential to be armed with a lot of patience, and to attend with a Spanish-speaker if one doesn't speak the language. The normal procedure is to fill out a form indicating which service you need; you are then given a receipt with a number. A telephone number is available to see if one's application has been completed; ask, as it changes. For enquiries about the progress of your application, call T53872400.

Useful addresses

Mexico City (sidebar)

Mexico City suburbs

When you have exhausted the centre of Mexico City, or perhaps when it has exhausted you, the suburbs, most of which are easily reached, have much to offer in the way of museums, colonial architecture, markets, shops, restaurants and parks. At Xochimilco you can float in a colourful boat and enjoy a picnic on the banks of the chinampas, or floating gardens. At La Villa you can visit Mexico's most venerated shrine. The enormous university should not be missed, nor should the botanical gardens. Try a glass of the fermented sap of the agave maguey or take in a theatrical performance at Coyoacán.

Heading out of the city centre along Insurgentes towards the delightful suburbs, or *colonias*, of San Angel and Coyoacán, there are several sites which should not be missed. A little to the west of where Insurgentes crosses Chapultepec, and on Avenida Chapultepec itself between Calle Praga and Calle Varsovia, are the remains of the old aqueduct built in 1779. The **Polyforum Cultural Siqueiros** on Insurgentes Sur includes a handicraft shop and an art museum, with huge frescoes by Siqueiros, one of the largest in the world, inside the ovoid dome. ■ *Closed for lunch. Frescoes US$0.40; 1000-1900.* Next door is the *Hotel de México* skyscraper, which is now Mexico's World Trade Centre.

Insurgentes Sur

A little further south is the **Plaza México**, the largest bullring in the world, with capacity for some 55,000 spectators. It is situated in the **Ciudad de los Deportes**, just off Insurgentes Sur, Metro San Antonio or *colectivo* to junction of Insurgentes Sur with Eje 5. With the apprentice season (*temporada chica*), running from May-October, and the *temporada grande*, from November-April, there are bullfights at 1600 or 1630 nearly every Sunday of the year. Alongside Madrid and Seville, the 'México' is one of the world's three most important bullfighting venues. As virtually every great matador comes to fight in Mexico in the winter months, the chances of seeing an important event are high. Useful introductory reading to bullfighting includes Hemingway's *Death in the Afternoon*; Lapierre and Collins *I'll Dress you in Mourning*; and *Matador* magazine. ■ *US$1-18 in the cheaper* sol *(sun) half of the Plaza (binoculars almost essential in the upper rows and recommended in any case); seats in the* sombra *(shade) are more expensive, up to US$35 in the* barreras. *Best to buy tickets, especially for important fights, early on Sat morning from the* taquillas *at the Plaza. Details of what's on from the Plaza itself, T5631659, or in the newspaper* Ovaciones.

Besides the Bull Ring, the Ciudad de los Deportes contains a football stadium with 50,000 capacity, a boxing ring, a cinema, a frontón court for jai-alai, a swimming pool, restaurants, hotels, etc.

Further south still on Avenida Insurgentes Sur at the corner of Mercaderes is a remarkable building by Alejandro Prieto: the **Teatro de Los Insurgentes**, a theatre and opera house seating 1,300 people. The main frontage consists of a high curved wall without windows. This wall is entirely covered with mosaic decoration, the work of Diego Rivera: appropriate figures, scenes, and portraits are composed round the central motif of a gigantic pair of hands holding a mask.

San Angel

Popularly known as **San Angel**, 13 km southwest of the centre, Villa Obregón has narrow, cobble-stone streets, many old homes, huge trees, and the charm of an era now largely past. Most of the distinguished architecture is of the 19th century. See the triple domes of its Iglesia del Carmen, covered with coloured tiles, and of the former Convento del Carmen, now the **Museo Colonial del Carmen**, which houses 17th- and 18th-century furniture and paintings. In the crypt, several mummified bodies are displayed in glass-topped cases. ■ *1000-1700*. See also the beautifully furnished and preserved old house, **Casa del Risco**, near the Bazar del Sábado, on Callejón de la Amargura. ■ *Photographic ID required for entry, Tue-Sun 1000-1700, free.* Also worth a visit is the church of San Jacinto, once belonging to a Dominican convent (1566). The **Museo de Arte Carrillo Gil**, Avenida Revolución 1608, has excellent changing exhibits and a permanent collection including paintings by Orozco and Siqueiros as well as several Diego Rivera Cubist works. There is a good bookshop and *cafetería*. ■ *US$3.35.*

The **Museo Estudio Diego Rivera** (Avenida Altavista y Calle Diego Rivera, opposite Antigua Hacienda de Goicochea – now *San Angel Inn*) is where Rivera and Frida Kahlo lived and worked. It contains several works by Rivera,

San Angel

as well as belongings and memorabilia. The building was designed by Juan O'Gorman. Many tourists come to San Angel on a Saturday to visit the **Bazar del Sábado**, a splendid folk art and curiosity market. Reach San Angel by bus from Chapultepec Park or by metro Line 3 to Miguel Angel de Quevedo. There is a YWCA (ACF) at San Angel, but it is expensive with hot water for two hours in the morning only, and use of kitchen 1800-2200. There are some excellent restaurants: the *San Angel Inn* is first class; good *panadería* by the post office (which is no good for letters abroad). Between San Angel and Coyoacán is the monument to Obregón on the spot where he was assassinated in 1928 (by the junction of Avenida Insurgentes Sur and Arenal). ■ *0900-1400*. The **Centro Cultural San Angel** (on Revolución opposite Museo del Carmen) stages exhibitions, concerts, lectures, etc; **La Carpa Geodésica**, Insurgentes Sur 2135 has theatre of all types from works for children to very avant-garde; the **Centro Cultural Helénico**, Insurgentes 1500, Metro Barranca del Muerto, always has a lively and diversified programme of drama, music and dance.

Excursions

The beautiful **Desierto de los Leones**, a forest of pines and broad-leaved trees, made into a national park, can be reached from Mexico City (24 km) by a fine scenic road from San Angel. In the woods is an old Carmelite monastery begun 1602, finished 1611, abandoned because of cold and damp in 1780. Around are numerous hermitages with several subterranean passages inside and a secret hall with curious acoustic properties. Take a torch.

Alternatively, take an hour's bus ride from Observatorio metro to La Venta and ask the bus driver where to get off for the path to the monastery, which is about a 4 km walk. One can either get there via the paved road or via the beautiful conifer-forest path, but the latter splits frequently so stick to what looks like the main path; or take the fire-break road below the row of shops and cheap restaurants near the main road. Food stalls abound, particularly at weekends when it is crowded. Do not leave valuables in your car and do not walk alone. Many birds may be seen in the valley reached from the picnic area 6 km south of La Venta on Route 15.

Magdalena Contreras has many characteristics of the old Spanish village. Up in the hills in the southwest of the city, it can be reached by *colectivo* or bus from San Angel (or by bus direct from Taxqueña) in about 30-45 minutes. There is an attractive main square and an 18th-century church on the site of an earlier structure. There are *artesanías* and multiple *taquerías*, etc; good *comida corrida* at *Restaurante del Camino* and *Local 29* in the main square. From the bus station behind the church in the village take another bus or *colectivo*, up to **Los Dinamos** (3½ km), site of former pumping stations, now a national park with picnic areas, waterfalls, horse-riding, breathtaking scenery and, above all, clean air. There are *pulquerías* invitingly placed at intervals. If walking, bear in mind that you are quite a lot higher than in the city.

Coyoacán

The oldest part of Mexico City, Coyoacán is the place from which Cortés launched his attack on Tenochtitlán. It is also one of the most beautiful and best-preserved parts of the city, with hundreds of fine buildings from the 16th-19th centuries, elegant tree-lined avenues and carefully tended parks and, in the Jardín Centenario and the Plaza Hidalgo, two very attractive squares. There are no supermarkets, no high-rise buildings, no hotels, no metro stations (see below). It is an area that is best explored on foot.

It is culturally one of the most lively parts of Mexico City and with its attractive cafés and good shops it is much frequented by the inhabitants of the capital, particularly at weekends. From San Angel, one can reach Coyoacán via a delightful walk through Chimalistac, across Avenida Universidad and down Avenida Francisco Sosa; or one can take a bus or *pesero* marked 'Tasqueña' as far as Caballocalco.

Sights

An excellent postcard-cum-pedestrian map of the centre of Coyoacán can be found in local book and gift shops.

From the city centre, it is easiest to take the metro to Viveros, Miguel Angel de Quevedo or General Anaya. Alternatively, take the metro to Coyoacán then *colectivo* for Villa Coapa, which drops you in the historic centre. If coming from Metro Viveros (a large park in which trees are grown for other city parks) or Miguel Angel de Quevedo it is worth making a slight detour in order to walk the length of **Francisco Sosa**, said to be the first urban street laid in Spanish America. At the beginning of this elegant avenue is the 18th-century church of **San Antonio Panzacola** by the side of Río Churubusco; nearby, on Universidad, is the remarkable, beautiful (and modern) chapel of **Nuestra Señora de la Soledad**, built in the grounds of the 19th-century ex-hacienda El Altillo. A little way down, in Salvador Novo, is the **Museo Nacional de la Acuarela** (National Watercolour Museum). The terracotta fronted residence at No 383 is said to have been built by Alvarado. ■ *Tue-Sun, free. Courtyard and garden may be visited 0900-1600 Mon-Fri, no charge, enquire at entrance.* Many fine houses follow, mostly built in the 19th century. **Santa Catarina**, in the square of the same name, is a fine 18th-century church; on Sunday, at about one o'clock, people assemble under the trees to tell stories (all are welcome to attend or participate). In the same square, the **Casa de la Cultura Jesús Reyes Heroles** should not be missed, with its delightful leafy gardens. Just before arriving at the **Jardín Centenario**, with its 16th-century arches, is the 18th-century **Casa de Diego Ordaz**.

The centre of Coyoacán is dominated by the 16th-century church of **San Juan Bautista**, with later additions and a magnificent interior. Jardín Centenario was once the atrium of this 16th-century Franciscan monastery which now houses the *Delegación*. On the north side of Plaza Hidalgo, the **Casa de Cortés**, was in

Coyoacán

Frida Kahlo

The life of Frida Kahlo was not a very happy one; she questioned her European and Mexican background, very much like the artists of an earlier era who were infuenced by styles and subjects originating in the Old World which they attempted to express in New World terms. Frida suffered greatly because the treatment of an accident when she was young went terribly wrong, added to which she and her spouse, Diego Rivera, were not the most compatible of couples. Her anguish is expressed in her paintings on display at the Museo Frida Kahlo.

fact built 244 years after the Conquest, on the site of the Cortés' house. The beautiful 18th-century church of **La Conchita** in a pretty square of the same name is reached by taking Higuera from Plaza Hidalgo; the interior, especially the altarpiece, is magnificent, but the church is normally open only on Friday evenings and Sunday mornings. On the corner of Higuera and Vallarta is what is reputed to be the **Casa de La Malinche**, Cortés' mistress and interpreter.

Admirers of Frida Kahlo will want to visit the **Museo Frida Kahlo**, or Casa Azul, Allende and Londres 247. Two rooms are preserved as lived in by Frida Kahlo and her husband Diego Rivera, and the rest contain drawings and paintings by both. She was very interested in folk art, an interest that is illustrated by the small collection of regional costumes on display. ■ *Tue-Sun 1000-1800, US$1.50, no photos.* In the **Jardín Cultural Frida Kahlo**, near Plaza de La Conchita, there is a striking bronze statue of Frida by the contemporary Mexican sculptor Gabriel Ponzanelli.

La Casa de Trotsky is at Río Churubusco 410, between Gómez Farías and Morelos. This is where the Russian revolutionery lived before he was murdered in the study here in 1940. The house is dark and sombre. There is a tomb in the garden where his ashes were laid. ■ *Tue-Sun 1000-1700, US$1.50, half-price with ISIC card, US$1.50 to take photos.* Also in Coyoacán are the **Museo del Retrato Hablado**, Universidad 1330-C, the **Museo Geles Cabrera**, Xicoténcatl 181, T56883016, which has sculpture (prior appontment needed); and the **Museo del Automóvil**, División del Norte 3752.

To reach the centre of Coyoacán from Metro General Anaya, there is a pleasant walk along Héroes del 47 (one block along on the left is the 16th-century church of **San Lucas**), across División del Norte and down Hidalgo (one block along on the left, and two blocks down San Lucas is the 18th-century church of **San Mateo**). The **Museo Nacional de Culturas Populares** is on Avenida Hidalgo, just off Plaza Hidalgo, and should be seen. It houses permanent and temporary exhibitions, cinema-cum-auditorio and a good bookshop on Mexican culture and folklore. ■ *Tue-Sun 1000-1600, free.*

Coyoacán has several **theatres**, medium and small, and similar establishments, for example the *Coyoacán* and *Usigli* theatres (Eleuterio Méndez, five blocks from Metro General Anaya), the *Foro Cultural de Coyoacán* (Allende; most events free of charge), the *Museo Nacional de Culturas Populares* (Hidalgo), the *Foro Cultural Ana María Hernández* (Pacífico 181), the *Teatro Santa Catarina* (Plaza Santa Catarina), the *Rafael Solana* theatre on Miguel Angel de Quevedo (nearly opposite *Caballocalco*), the *Casa del Teatro*, Vallarta 31 and *Foro de la Conchita*, Vallarta 33. Also note *El Hábito* (Madrid) and *El Hijo del Cuervo* (Jardín Centenario) for avant-garde drama and cabaret, *Los Talleres de Coyoacán* (Francisco Sosa) for dance and ballet, *CADAC* (Centenario) for traditional and experimental drama. On the edge of the Delegación Coyoacán (southeast corner of Churubusco and Tlalpan, Metro General Anaya) is the *Central Nacional de las Artes*, a huge complex of

Mexico City

futuristic buildings dedicated to the training and display of the performing and visual arts. It has a good bookshop, library and *cafeterías*. Details can be found in *Tiempo Libre* and local broadsheets. At weekends there are many open-air events especially in Plaza Hidalgo. Also at weekends is the *artesanía* market, in a site off Plaza Hidalgo, which is well worth a visit. Prices are reasonable and there is lots of potential for bargaining; with the best deals to be had either early or late in the day.

The **Huayamilpas Ecological Park** can be reached by *pesero* from the centre of Coyoacán. The lake and surrounding area are protected by local inhabitants.

Eating There are several pleasant *cafeterías* in the Jardín Centenario, some of which serve light snacks and *antojitos*; the best known is *El Parnaso*, adjacent to the bookshop of the same name. Two of the best-known *cantinas* in Mexico are *La Guadalupana* (Higuera) and the *Puerta del Sol* on Plaza Hidalgo. No shortage of restaurants with *comida corrida*, though prices tend to be higher than in other parts of the city (US$1.75-US$2.50). Very good value are: *Rams*, Hidalgo, almost opposite Museo Nacional de las Culturas Populares, excellent fish, US$1.75; *Fabio's*, overlooking Plaza Hidalgo and the Delegación, credit cards accepted; *Rincón Oaxaqueño*, Carrillo Puerto 12, US$1.75. Good value, too in the *Mercado*, between Malintzin and Xicoténcatl, US$1.15. Possibly the most exquisite *quesadillas* in the whole of Coyoacán are found at local 31 (outside the market, opposite Jardín del Carmen, closed Wed); stall holders are very friendly and fruit and vegetable sellers are ready to explain the names and uses of their goods; frequent musical entertainment particularly lunchtime and weekends. The *Restaurante Vegetariano*, Carranza y Caballocalco, offers an excellent US$5 buffet lunch; *El Morral*, Allende 2, set lunch US$3, double at weekends, no credit cards, quieter upstairs, palatial lavatories. Highly recommended. *Caballocalco*, Plaza Hidalgo. Expensive, but very good, especially for breakfast. There is a *Sanborn's* on Jardín Centenario, near *El Hijo del Cuervo*. *Hacienda de Cortés*, Fernández Leal 74, behind Plaza de la Conchita. Exceptionally pleasant surroundings, large, shaded, outdoor dining area, excellent breakfast, good value, *comida corrida* US$5, try the *sábana de res con chilaquiles verdes*. *Pacífico*, Av Pacífico, in restored 19th-century residence. Specialities include pre-Hispanic dishes, not cheap but good value. *Villa Cristal*, Allende. Excellent *comida corrida*. *La Doña*, Héroes del 47, 141. Elegant restaurant, good value.

Shopping Many gift shops in the area, good taste and prices at *Etra*, on corner of Francisco Sosa opposite Jardín Centenario. *Mayolih*, Aldama with Berlín, 2 blocks from Museo Frida Kahlo; *La Casita* on Higuera. Also on Higuera are *La Rosa de los Vientos* (maps of all parts of the country) and the Post Office with Mexpost service. *Foto Coyoacán*, Francisco Sosa 1, opposite the Arches. Excellent, rapid developing, printing, English, French, German spoken. The best cycle repair in Mexico City is *Hambling González Muller*, Ezequiel Ordóñez 46-1, Col Copilco el Alto, T/F56585591, builds wheels and frames for Mexican racers, reasonable prices, highly recommended. *Sakurafoto*, Plaza Hidalgo, excellent service, English, German spoken. Good range of CDs and tapes at *Gandhi Discos*, Carrillo Puerto 6, excellent prices.

Transport The *pesero* from Metro General Anaya to the centre of Coyoacán is marked 'Santo Domingo', alight at Abasolo or at the Jardín Centenario; it also goes past the Mercado (Malintzin). Alternatively, get off the metro at Ermita and get a *colectivo* (Santo Domingo) from Pirineos, on the west side of Tlalpan just north of the metro station. The *colectivo* passes in front of the Frida Kahlo museum.

Ciudad Universitaria The world famous University City, 18 km from the centre via Insurgentes Sur on the road towards Cuernavaca highway, was founded in 1551. Perhaps the most notable building is the 10-storey **Biblioteca** (library), by Juan O'Gorman, its outside walls iridescent with mosaics telling the story of scientific knowledge, from Aztec astronomy to molecular theory.

The **Rectoría** has a vast, mosaic-covered and semi-sculptured mural by Siqueiros. Across the highway is the **Olympic Stadium**, with seats for 80,000, in shape, colour, and situation a world's wonder, but now closed and run down. Diego Rivera has a sculpture-painting telling the story of Mexican sport. A new complex has been completed beyond the Ciudad Universitaria, including the newspaper library (the **Hemeroteca Nacional**), **Teatro Juan Ruiz de Alarcón**, **Sala Nezahual cóyotl** (concerts etc), bookshop and post office; also the **Museo Universitario Contemporáneo de Arte** and the extraordinary **Espacio Escultórico**, a large circular area of volcanic rock within a circle of cement monoliths; on the opposite side of the road is another large area with many huge sculptures; stick to the path as it is possible to get lost in the vegetation. In the University museum there is an exhibition of traditional masks from all over Mexico. Beyond the Olympic Stadium is the **Jardín Botánico Exterior** which shows all the cactus species in Mexico. ■ *0700-1630, 30-min walk, ask directions.*

The University offers six-week courses (US$200, plus US$35 if you enrol late, good, student card useful).

Transport Take a bus marked CU, along Eje Lázaro Cárdenas; also bus 17, marked Tlalpan, which runs the length of Insurgentes, about 1 hr journey. Another way to the university is on metro Line 3 to Copilco station (20 mins walk to University) or to Universidad station (30 mins walk). At the University City free buses ferry passengers to the different areas of the campus.

Further east, off División del Norte, is **Anahuacalli**, Museo 150, T556174310, which is usually called the **Diego Rivera Museum**. Here is a very fine collection of pre-Columbian sculpture and pottery, effectively displayed in a pseudo-Mayan tomb built for it by Diego Rivera. There is a big display here for the Day of the Dead at the beginning of November. ■ *Tue-Sun 1000-1400, 1500-1800, closed Holy Week, US$1.70, free Sun. The museum is reached by Combi 29 from the Taxqueña metro station to Estadio Azteca, or take the bus marked División del Norte from outside Salto del Agua metro.*

Churubusco

Situated 10 km southeast is Churubusco, which is reached from the Zócalo by Coyoacán or Tlalpan buses, or from General Anaya metro station. The picturesque and partly ruined convent (1762), at General Anaya y 20 de Agosto, is now the **Museo Nacional de las Intervenciones**. It has 17 rooms filled with mementoes, documents, proclamations and pictures recounting foreign invasions, incursions and occupations since Independence and also holds temporary exhibitions. The site of the museum was chosen because it was the scene of a battle when the US Army marched into Mexico City in 1847. ■ *0900-1800, closed Mon, US$3.35, free Sun and holidays.* Next door is the 16th-century church of San Diego, with 17th- and 18th-century additions. Near the church, on the other side of Calzada General Anaya, is the delightful Parque de Churubusco. One block from Tlalpan along Héroes del 47, to the left, is the 18th-century church of San Mateo. There is a golf course at the Churubusco Country Club. Churubusco was for many years the home of Mexico's most important film studios; a smaller-scale operation now exists, devoted to post-production. The new Olympic swimming pool is here. It is near enough to Coyoacán (see page 125) to walk there.

Mexico City

The Saint Patrick's Brigade

One of the many notable features of the Mexican-US War of 1846-48 was the involvement of foreign volunteers who fought on the Mexican side. To this day, the San Patricios, as they came to be known, are regarded as valiant heroes by the Mexicans and cowardly traitors by the US military establishment. Before the war began the Legión Extranjera was formed from European residents in Mexico, and expanded by the addition of deserters, mainly Irish, from the US Army. John Riley from County Galway renamed the unit and gave them their distinctive green flag with an image of the shamrock on one side and one of St Patrick on the other. At the time a lieutenant in the Mexican Army, Riley was a former private soldier in the US Army and had possibly served with the British Army in Canada.

The San Patricios fought in many of the important battles of the war, manifesting both bravery and military competence until they were captured by the US Army at Churubusco, now a suburb of Mexico City. Convicted of desertion, most were hanged at Mixcoac or San Angel in September 1847, but those who had deserted before the outbreak of hostilities were flogged, branded and set free. Riley was among them. After the war he rejoined the Mexican Army in which he continued to serve as a major until 1850, after which time he faded into history.

However, the story of the St Patrick's Brigade has remained sufficiently alive on both sides of the border for a script relating the exploits of its members and entitled One Man's Hero, to be filmed in Hollywood. In the 60s the title role was offered to John Wayne who immediately refused it, clearly concerned about the damage it might do to his image. For those wishing to know further details of the St Patrick's Brigade, a good starting place is Michael Hogan's The Irish Soldiers of Mexico (Fondo Editorial Universitario: Guadalajara, 1998).

Tlalpan A further 6½ km, or direct from San Angel (see page 124), is this suburb with colonial houses, gardens, and near the main square, Plaza de la Constitución, the early 16th-century church of San Agustín with a fine altar and paintings by Cabrera. It can be reached by bus or trolley bus from the Taqueña metro station. The suburb of **Peña Pobre** is 2½ km west, near which, to the northeast, is the **Pyramid of Cuicuilco**, believed to be the oldest in Mexico. The pyramid dates from the fifth or sixth century BC; it is over 100m in diameter but only 25m high. There is an archaeological museum on site, on Insurgentes Sur Km 16 at the intersection with Periférico. ■ *0800-1800, closed Mon.*

South of the city near the Perisur Mall, is an amusement park, formerly called Reino Aventura, for children along Disneyland lines, which is clean, orderly and popular with families.

Xochimilco

Colour map 3 grid B5 Some 20 km to the southeast of the city centre, Xochimilco has many attractions, not least the fact that it lies in an unpolluted area. Easiest access is by bus, *colectivo* or metro to Metro Tasqueña, then (about 20 minutes) *tren ligero*. Get off at the terminal, which is misleadingly named 'Embarcadero' (there are several *embarcaderos*, see map and below).

Xochimilco, 'the place where flowers grow', was an advanced settlement long before the arrival of the Spaniards. Built on a lake, it developed a form of agriculture using *chinampas*, or 'floating gardens'; the area is still a major supplier of fruit and vegetables to Mexico City. The Spaniards recognized its importance and the need to convert the indigenous population; evidence of this is the number of 16th- and 17th-century religious buildings in Xochimilco and in the other 13 *pueblos* which make up the present-day *delegación*, or municipality.

Xochimilco is famous for its canals and colourful punt-like boats, *trajineras*, which bear girls' names. There are seven landing-stages, or *embarcaderos*, in the town, the largest of which are Fernando Celada and Nuevo Nativitas (the latter is where most coach-loads of tourists are set down, large craft-market). All are busy at weekends, especially Sunday afternoon. Official tariffs operate, although prices are sometimes negotiable; a boat taking six passengers costs US$5.75 per hour (a trip of at least 1½ hours is desirable); floating *mariachi* bands will charge US$3.50 per song, marimba groups US$1.50. There are reasonably priced tourist menus (lunch US$2) from passing boats; good, clean and cheap restaurants opposite Fernando Celada (for example *Beto's*, US$2 for lunch); more expensive restaurants are opposite Nuevo Nativitas.

The indisputable architectural jewel of Xochimilco is the church of **San Bernardino de Siena** (begun in 1535, completed 1595; magnificent Renaissance style retable, 1580-90) and its convent (circa 1585). The oldest Spanish-built religious edifice is the tiny chapel of **San Pedro** (1530). Also worthy of mention are **Nuestra Señora de los Dolores de Xaltocán** (17th-century façade, 18th-century retable), **Santa Crucita Analco** and **San Juan Tlaltentli**. All are within walking distance of the centre of Xochimilco.

For those who have an interest in church architecture there is a rich range in the villages to the west, south and east of Xochimilco. The main constraining factor for most travellers will be time (and the pronunciation of some of the names). Churches include **Santa María Tepepan** (1612-21), with a unique decorated earthenware font dated 1599; *tren ligero* Tepepan, walk up 5 de Mayo; **Santiago Tepatcatlalpan** (1770); **San Lucas Xochimanca** (16th century); **San Francisco Tlanepantla** (small 17th-century chapel), village right in the country, superb views; the 16th-century **San Lorenzo Atemoaya**. After **Santa Cruz Acalpixca**, 16th century with a 17th-century façade; near a mediocre Archaeology Museum, are the imposing **San Gregorio Atlapulco** (17th century; 16th-century font), the tiny chapel of **San Luis Tlaxiatemalco** (1633) and the enormous, late 18th-century **Santiago Tulyehualco**. Finally, beyond the boundary of the Delegación Xochimilco, is the church of **San Andrés Míxquic** (second quarter of 16th century; façade 1620; many alterations), built on the site of an earlier temple using some of the original blocks which bear traces of pre-Hispanic designs; it is much-frequented around *Día de los Muertos* (Day of the Dead). All of these villages may be reached by *colectivo* from the centre of Xochimilco, and there is also a bus to Tulyehualco (30 minutes). Eating places are generally limited to stalls with tortas, *tacos* and occasional spit-roasted chicken.

To the north of the town is the **Parque Ecológico**, an extensive area of grassland, lagoons and canals, with not much shade, but lots of birdlife. One can walk beyond the asphalt paths along the canal banks. There is also a punt station. ■ *Daily, 1000-1800, 1000-1700 winter months, US$1.50, children free, over-60s US$0.75. Access from Mexico City: bus, colectivo or tren ligero to the Periférico, then colectivo to Cuemanco; from Xochimilco, bus or colectivo to Periférico, then likewise.*

Museo Dolores Olmedo Patiño, Avenida México 5843, on corner with Antiguo Camino a Xochimilco, one block southwest from La Noria *tren ligero* station, is set in eight acres of beautiful garden and grassland on the site of an old estate, probably dating from the 16th century. Rare Mexican hairless dogs and peacocks parade. It houses 137 works by Diego Rivera, 25 by Frida Kahlo, and an important collection of drawings by Angelina Beloff. There are also pre-Hispanic artefacts, 19th-century antiques and Mexican folk art. Highly recommended. ■ *1000-1800, Tue-Sun, US$1.50, students US$0.75, T55551016.* There is a very pleasant open and covered café and **D** *Hotel Plaza*

Mexico City

El Mesón, Avenida México 64, T56764163. Mixed reports, noisy. Tourist office at Pino 36, open 0800-2100.

Ajusco Another excursion can be made to Ajusco, about 20 km southwest of Mexico City. Catch a bus from Estadio Azteca on Calzada Tlalpan direct to Ajusco. From the summit of the extinct **Volcán Ajusco** (3,929m) there are excellent views on a clear day. The way up is 10 km west of the village, 400m west of where the road branches to Xalatlaco (there is a hut south of the road where the path goes to the mountain). Foothills are also pleasant.

Northern Suburbs

Basílica de In the northern suburbs of Mexico City is the Basílica de Guadalupe, often called **Guadalupe** La Villa de Guadalupe and the most venerated shrine in Mexico. It was here, in December 1531, that the Virgin appeared three times in the guise of an Indian princess to the Indian Juan Diego and imprinted her portrait on his cloak. The cloak is preserved, set in gold, but was moved into the new basilica next door as a massive crack had appeared down the side of the old building. Visitors stand on

Xochimilco

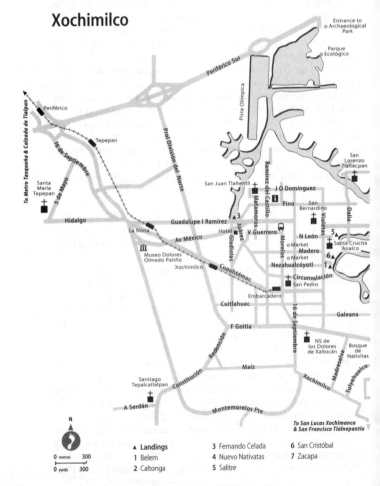

▲ **Landings**	**3** Fernando Celada	**6** San Cristóbal
1 Belem	**4** Nuevo Nativatas	**7** Zacapa
2 Caltonga	**5** Salitre	

a moving platform behind the altar to view the cloak. The huge, modern basilica is impressive and holds over 20,000 people (very crowded on Sunday). The original basilica has been converted into a museum. It still houses the original magnificent altar, but otherwise mostly representations of the image on the cloak, plus interesting painted tin plates offering votive thanks for cures, etc, from about 1860s. ■ *US$3..* A chapel stands over the well which gushed at the spot where the Virgin appeared. The great day here is 12 December, the great night the night before: Indian dance groups provide entertainment in front of the Basílica. There are, in fact, about seven churches in the immediate neighbourhood, including one on the hill above (Iglesia del Cerrito – excellent view of the city, especially at night, free access); most of them are at crazy angles to each other and to the ground, because of subsidence; the subsoil is very soft. The **Templo de los Capuchinos** has been the subject of a remarkable feat of engineering in which one end has been raised 3.375m so that the building is now horizontal. There is a little platform from which to view this work. Buses marked 'La Villa' go close to the site, or you can go by metro to La Villa (Line 6). The Virgin even has her own home page on the Internet, visit her online at Interlupe. http://spin. com.mx/~msalazar.

Tenayuca

The pyramid of Tenayuca, 10 km to the northwest of the city centre, is about 15m high and the best preserved in Mexico. The Aztecs rebuilt this temple every 52 years; this one was last reconstructed about 1507 and is well worth seeing, for it is surrounded with serpents in masonry. ■ *1000-1645, US$1.50.* The easiest way to get there by car from Mexico City centre is to go to Vallejo, 11 km north of the intersection of Insurgentes Norte and Río Consulado. By metro, take the line to the Terminal de Autobuses del Norte (see page 118), La Raza, and catch the bus there. By bus from Tlatelolco, ask the driver and passengers to advise you on arrival as the site is not easily visible. An excursion to Tula (see page 145) may go via Tenayuca. It is not far from the old town of **Tlalnepantla**: see the ancient convent (ask for the *Catedral*) on the Plaza Gustavo Paz, and the church (1583), which contains the first image, a Christ of Mercy, brought to the New World. Two and a half kilometres to the north is the smaller pyramid of **Santa Cecilia Acatitlán**, which is interesting for its restored sanctuary. It is difficult to find; head for the church tower visible from the footbridge over the highway. ■ *US$1.50.*

Av Nuevo León

Craft o Market

4▲

7▲

Archaeological Museum ⏛

Santa Cruz Acalpixca

Xochimilco

San Lorenzo Atemoaya

To San Luis Tlaxialtemalco, San Gregorio Atlapulco, Santiago Tulyehualco & Mixquic

Mexico City

The New Fire Ceremony

Throughout Mesoamerica, two calendars ran concurrently. One, which followed the solar year, consisted of 18 'months' of 20 days, ending with five lost or unlucky days. The second calendar consisted of 260 days, was ritual in nature, and functioned as an almanac. These calendars coincided only every 52 years, when the respective days of both calendars which had started the cycle, were repeated. The whole process was much more complicated than that just described; simply put, the end of each cycle of 52 years was a time of great concern. It was believed that the present era, the Fifth Creation, would end when the next cycle was unable to commence, prevented from doing so by the inability of the priests to provide new fire.

Prior to the arrival of the fateful hour, the priests climbed Huixachtepetl, later known as Cerro de la Estrella, close to Culhuacán and Iztapalapa in Mexico City. Throughout the nation, all fires had been extinguished in anticipation of the moment when either the new cycle would start or the universe would be devoured in the most hideous conflagration. They waited in dread for the appearance of the Pleiades, which would signal the commencement of the most solemn and significant ritual in the Aztec calendar. According to the great chronicler, Fray Bernardino de Sahagún, the Little Goats (the Pleiades) appeared in the centre of the sky at midnight. The priests had gone in procession from the centre of Tenochtitlán to Iztapalapa, and climbed to the top of the hill where there was a small shrine (the remains of the platform on which it stood can easily be reached from Colhuacán) and waited until the Pleiades were directly above. When they observed that they had passed the centre, the priest lit the fire, knowing that the skies (the stars) would not cease to move, and that the world would not end there and they were assured another 52 years before they would again have to contemplate the possible end of the world. At that time, crowds anxiously waited in the neighbouring hilltops and in Tezcoco, Xochimilco and Cuauhtitlán for sight of the New Fire. When it was sighted it was greeted with loud howling.

According to Sahagún, the last New Fire ceremony was celebrated in 1507. The solemnities of 1559 were not observed publicly, because the Spaniards had already begun purging the country of what they saw as barbaric rituals. The New Fire ceremony was solemnized by the priest who ensured a successful outcome by sacrificing a victim in the usual manner, by heart-extraction. But an unusual aspect of this sacrifice was the use of the victim's empty chest as a hearth; the twigs were placed in the hollow where the heart had been, then lit. The fire was then distributed at great speed to the populace.

Los Remedios, a small town 13 km northwest of Mexico City, has in its famous church an image, a foot high, adorned with jewels. See the old aqueduct, with a winding stair leading to the top of two towers. It can be reached by car or by taking the Los Remedios bus at Tacuba metro station. The local *fiesta* starts on 1 September and runs until its climax on 8 September.

At **Naucalpan**, northwest of the city just outside the city boundary on Boulevard Toluca, pre-Classic Olmec-influenced figurines can be seen in the **Museo de la Cultura de Tlatilco**, opposite the *Hotel Naucalpan* on Vía Gustavo Paz. ■ *Closed Mon.* This is said to be the oldest settlement in the Cuenca de México.

Iztapalapa   At the foot of the Cerro de la Estrella, whose top is reached by a paved road or a path through some ruins, is a small museum, a good view of volcanoes and two interesting churches. The Santuario del Calvario (1856), and San Lucas (1664) have original roof timbers restored in the 19th century, with a main door embodying Aztec motifs and a fine interior. The most spectacular of Mexican passion-plays begins at Iztapalapa on Holy Thursday.

Around Mexico City

4

Around Mexico City

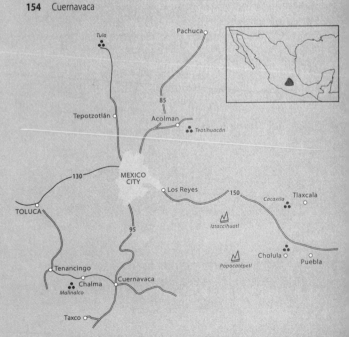

Right in the centre of the country, Mexico City is ideally suited for exploring all around the colonial towns, villages, national parks, pre-Hispanic sites, volcanoes, caves and hot springs that are within easy reach for a day or weekend trip. Everyone heads north to see Mexico's most-visited pyramids at the vast and awe-inspiring site of **Teotihuacán**, 'the place of the gods'. Less crowded are the towering Atlantes at **Tula**, the Toltec capital, and the pretty villages in the hills near **Pachuca** where you can eat Cornish pasties reminiscent of the English who once mined gold in this area. Head west from the capital on Friday, through cool pine forests, for **Toluca's** massive street market, then up into the craters of the extinct Nevado de Toluca volcano or into the fanged serpent's mouth at the Aztec site of Malinalco. South of the capital, charming **Cuernavaca**, 'city of eternal spring', is the weekend resort, where everybody goes to get away from the metropolis and relax. So go during the week if you can, and then on to Tepoztlán and up the Tepozteco, residence of Tepoztecatl, the (drunken) god of pulque. Wander through the pretty up-and-down streets of colonial **Taxco**, wonder at the magnificent Santa Prisca church and stroll from silver shop to silver shop seeking bargains in beautifully worked silver. Snow-capped Popocatépetl, the smoking-mountain warrior, and his princess Iztaccíhuatl rise majestically to the east of the capital en route to **Puebla**, City of the Angels or tucked-away Tlaxcala, delightful capital of Mexico's smallest state. Nearby are the dramatic murals of Cacaxtla and Cholula's artificial 'mountain', in fact the largest pyramid in all Mesoamerica.

North of Mexico City

Beyond the sprawling northern suburbs of Mexico City lie the ancient ruins of Teotihuacán, with their vast pyramids to the sun and moon. At Tula the Toltec architecture bears many similarities with that of Chichén Itzá, in the Yucatán. Make a stop en route at Tepotzotlán, the jewel in the crown of Mexico's colonial history. Further north, near Pachuca, hikers can head for the vast national park at El Chico.

Acolman is 35 km northeast of Mexico City and is easily visited after La Basílica de Guadalupe (see page 132) and on the way to Teotihuacán. It has the formidable fortress-like convent and church of San Agustín. This dates from 1539-60, with much delicate detail on the façade and some interesting murals inside. Note the fine portal and the carved stone cross at the entrance to the atrium. An interesting architectural feature is the open-chapel (see box) just above and to the right of the main entrance. While Mass was being celebrated inside the monastery for the benefit of the Spaniards, the spiritual needs of the indigenous worshippers were catered for by the friar who celebrated the Mass in this tiny balcony chapel. The curator is extremely knowledgeable and helpful; he may show you the inner courtyard where the statue of a chacmool, excavated in recent years in the vicinity of the convent, is exposed to the elements and precariously perched atop a low wall. Acolman can be reached by bus from Indios Verdes metro station, or from the Zócalo.

Teotihuacán

Colour map 3, grid B6
49 km N of Mexico City

This site has some of the most remarkable relics in the world of an ancient civilization. Thought to date from around 300 BC-600 AD, the builders of Teotihuacán, or 'place of the gods', remain a mystery. Where they came from and why the civilization disappeared is pure conjecture. It seems that the city may have housed 250,000 people who were peace-loving but whose influence spread as far as Guatemala. However, the 'peace-loving' theory is constantly being challenged. There are definite indications that human sacrifice was being practiced at Teotihuacán long before the arrival of the Aztecs to the Valley of Mexico. Recent research indicates that an individual from Teotihuacán arrived at Copán in Honduras and usurped the power of the rightful ruler, thus continuing to spread the influence of Teotihuacán throughout the Maya region. Teotihuacán was not just a ceremonial centre; vast areas of enclaves have been excavated showing that, apart from those zones designated as sacred, there were also areas occupied by artisans, labourers, merchants, and representatives of those crafts and professions that contribute to a functioning city. One zone housed merchants from the Maya area, another was occupied by representatives from Monte Albán in Oaxaca. Sometime in the seventh century AD, Teotihuacán was ravaged by fire and may also have been looted, causing an exodus of its inhabitants. So completely was it abandoned that it was left to the Aztecs to give names to its most important features. There are

The Open Chapel of Mexico

The open chapel is one of the most distinctive architectural features of early colonial Mexico. It does not have a direct European prototype; rather, it came into being as a response to a great need, namely, a covered area in which the friar could celebrate the Mass for a congregation of newly-converted Indians. The new Christians numbered many thousands and the friars were few. With no time to build the standard church, the friars decided to use the pre-Conquest custom of open-air worship and developed the open chapel. This could be fronted by a large, usually enclosed, area accommodating a congregation far larger than any church. Because of the extreme climatic conditions, the open chapel in the Yucatán was usually fronted by an enormous ramada, a roof of palm leaves supported by simple wooden poles.

While its form varied considerably from region to region and even from village to village, its function remained constant: to give shelter to the friar celebrating the Mass. Because it was open, the area of the altar could not be consecrated; some open chapels were left unattended for considerable periods, thus inviting desecration. This exigency was met by the portable ara, an oblong slab, consecrated and carried by the friar or one of his acolytes, placed on the altar for the duration of the Mass, then removed and carried to the location of the next service.

As mentioned above, the friars experimented, sometimes with startling and unexpected results, with the form of the open chapel. One form, effective but not repeated to any noticeable extent, was the raised type, such as that at Acolman. It is reminiscent of a small balcony, on the second level of the monastery block, with total command of the large atrio (courtyard) which it overlooks. Perhaps its resemblance to the pre-Hispanic teocalli, the shrine which crowned the pyramids, placing the priest at a higher level than the congregation, prompted the friars to look for a form that separated the old and new religions.

A second form to be tried, and one that was very successful, was the single-cell chapel. This could be square or trapezoidal, backed by a simple wall and covered by a vaulted or flat ceiling. This model, so popular in the Yucatán, left scope for the chapel to be converted to the more standard church by the simple addition of a nave. The open chapel was sometimes embedded in the bulk of the monastery, giving the impression of a huge doorway that leads nowhere. The single-cell model can be seen at Actopan and Jalapa del Marqués.

Now in ruins, the open chapel at Coixlahuaca had flaring buttresses that focussed the attention on the ritual enacted in the rib-vaulted chancel.

Open chapels were also associated with the porticos of monasteries, situated behind one of a series of arches. Those at Atlhuetzía and Tepeyanco are excellent examples of this form. Anyone interested in the open chapel of Mexico should not miss the one at Tlalmanalco, the complexity of which is better experienced than described.

But whatever form it took, the open chapel served its purpose well; it provided an area separated from but close to the congregation in which the priest could celebrate the Mass; a secondary function was to separate the Spanish, who attended Mass in the standard church, from Indian congregations.

In the late 16th and early 17th centuries the open chapel became redundant. Imported diseases and mistreatment caused so great a decline in population that only about a tenth of the numbers living in Mexico at the time of the Conquest survived. Those that remained could easily be accommodated in the standard churches, thus rendering obsolete one of the most innovative architectural features of 16th-century Mexico.

Those interested in further exploration of the form and function of the Open Chapel of Mexico are referred to the excellent The Open-Air Churches of 16th-Century Mexico, John McAndrew, Harvard University Press, 1965.

Around Mexico City

many questions still to be answered about Teotihuacán culture; a recent discovery in 1997 of 50 clay figurines is one more piece in the jigsaw.

Sights

The small pebbles embedded in mortar indicate reconstruction (most of the site apparently!)

There are three main areas: the **Ciudadela**, the **Pyramid of the Sun** and the **Pyramid of the Moon**. The whole is connected by the Avenue of the Dead which runs almost due north for nearly 4 km. To the west lie the sites of Tetitla, Atetelco, Zacuala and Yayahuala (see below). To the northeast lies Tepantitla, with fine frescoes. The old city is traceable over an area of 3½ by 6½ km.

Ins & outs Reckon on about five to eight hours to see the site properly, arrive early before the vast numbers of *ambulantes*, or wandering vendors, selling obsidian, flutes, silver bangles and, in Plaza of the Sun, straw hats, and the big tourist groups at 1100. There is a perimeter road with a number of car parking places – go anticlockwise. If short of time, try to get a lift from a tourist bus to the Pyramid of the Moon car park. This is the most interesting area. Also take food and water as most of the shops are on the west side and you may be some distance from them. There is a handicraft centre with weavings, obsidian carvings and explanations (and tastings) of the production of tequila and mescal.

Capable of holding 60,000 people, the citadel's main feature is the **Temple of Quetzalcoatl** (the Plumed Serpent, Lord of Air and Wind). Go to the east side of the 1 km square. Behind the largest of the temples (take the right hand path) lies an earlier pyramid which has been partially restored. Lining the staircase are huge carved heads of the feathered serpents.

Follow the Avenue of the Dead to the **Plaza of the Sun**. You will pass small grassy mounds which are unexcavated temples. The Plaza contains many buildings, probably for the priests, but is dominated by the massive **Pyramid of the Sun** (64m high, 213 sq m at the base) and covering almost the same space as the Great Pyramid of Cheops in Egypt. The sides are terraced, and wide stairs lead to the summit. The original 4m covering of stone and stucco was removed by mistake in 1910. The view from the top gives a good impression of the whole site. But beware, it is a steep climb, particularly between the third and fourth terrace.

The car park to the north leads to Tepantitla. The murals here depict the rain god Tlaloc. The **museum** (admission included in price of ticket) now lies south of the Pyramid of the Sun. It is well laid out and contains a large model of Teotihuacán in its heyday as well as many beautiful artefacts, recommended. There is an expensive restaurant with indifferent service at the museum which is not always open.

The **Pyramid of the Moon** is about one km further north and on your right a tin roof covers a wall mural of a large, brightly coloured jaguar (the **Jaguar Temple**). The plaza contains the 'A' altars – 11 in a peculiar geometric pattern. The Pyramid is only half the size of the Pyramid of the Sun. The best view of the Avenue of the Dead is from the first level of this pyramid – 48 steep steps – well worth the climb.

To the west of the Plaza of the Moon lies the **Palace of Quetzalpapalotl** (Palace of the Precious Butterfly) where the priests serving the sanctuaries of the Moon lived, which has been restored together with its patio. Note the obsidian inlet into the highly decorated carved pillars. There is a sign here forbidding high heels. Follow the path left under the Palace through the Jaguars' Palace, with catlike murals protected from the sun by green canvas curtains, to the **Temple of the Feathered Shells**. The base of the simple altar is decorated with shells, flowers and eagles.

You will pass several more temples on the west side of the Avenue of the

Dead. If you want to visit the temples of Atetelco, go through the car park opposite the Pyramid of the Sun, turn right past *Restaurant Pirámides Charlies* (reputed to be the best on the site) and turn right along a small track. Alternatively, to get to them from the museum, exit west and walk right up to main road, turning left after crossing the stream. They are well worth a visit: **Tetitla** a walled complex with beautiful frescoes and paintings, **Atetelco** with its three tiny temples and excellent murals and the abandoned sites of **Zacuala** and **Yayahuala**.

At the spring equinox on 21 March the sun is perfectly aligned with the west face of the Pyramid of the Sun; many ad hoc sun worshippers hold unofficial

Teotihuacán

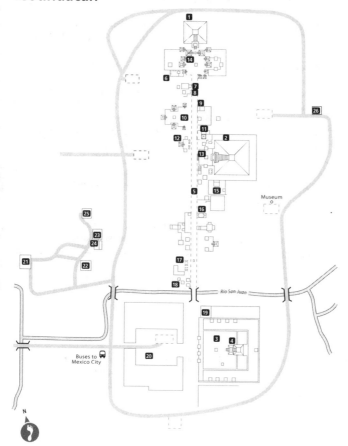

Not to scale

1 Pyramid of the Moon
2 Pyramid of the Sun
3 Ciudadela
4 Temple of Quetzalcoatl
5 Avenue of the Dead
6 Palaces of Quetzalpapalotl,
   Jaguars & Feathered Shells
7 Temple of Agriculture
8 Mural of the Mythological Animals
9 Jaguar Temple & Mural

10 Plaza of the Columns
11 Palace of the Sun
12 Patio of the Four Little Temples
13 Plaza of the Sun
14 Plaza of the Moon
15 House of the Priest
16 Viking Group
17 Avenue of the Dead complex with
   'Superimposed Buildings' group
18 Northwest Cluster

19 Plaza Two
20 Great Compound
21 Palace of Atetelco
22 Palace of Tetitla
23 Palace of Zacuala
24 Patio of Zacuala
25 Palace of Yayahuala
26 Palace of Tepantitla

ceremonies to mark the occasion. This is also Benito Juárez's birthday so entry is free.

■*Daily 0800-1700. If the entrance near the bus stop is not open at 0800 try entrance near the Pyramid of the Moon. US$2.50, cars free, free on Sun (extra charge for videos, tripods not permitted). The outside sites may be closed on Mon. Son et lumière display, US$4 per person (good lumière, not so good son); lasts 45 mins, 1900 in Spanish, 2015 in English (Oct-Jun only); take blanket or rent one. Official guidebook US$1, gives a useful route to follow. The Bloomgarden guide contains a useful map, good description and is recommended. The guide, Ricardo Cervantes (Gorilla), T61415-60540, has been recommended. At weekends students give free guided tours, ask at the entrance.*

Sleeping **AL** *Villas Arqueológicas*, Apdo Postal 44,55800, San Juan Teotihuacán, Estado de México, T60909/60244, F60928; in Mexico City, reservations at Club Med office. Pool.

Transport **Buses** From Terminal del Norte, Gate 8, platform 6 (Autobuses del Norte metro), Mexico City; at least 45 mins, US$2 one way (Pirámides buses are white with a yellow stripe). You can also take the metro to Indios Verdes (last stop on line 3), then a public bus (US$1) to the pyramids. Bus returns from Door 1 (some others from 2 and 3) at Teotihuacán site, supposedly every 30 mins. Some return buses to the capital terminate in the outskirts in rush hour without warning. You can ride back to town with one of the tourist buses for about US$3. Note that the site is more generally known as 'Pirámides' than as 'Teotihuacán'. If driving, the toll on the Autopista Ecatepec-Pirámides is US$3. Tours to Teotihuacán, picking you up at your hotel and usually including the Basílica de Guadalupe (see page 132), normally cost US$30-35, with little time at the site.

The village of **San Juan Teotihuacán** is well worth a visit, if time permits (*pesero* from the road running round the site of the pyramids, US$0.20). It has a magnificent 16th-century church a few blocks down Cuauhtémoc from the square. *Villas Arqeológicas* restaurant is poor for food and service. A good, clean restaurant is *Los Pinos*, in Guadalupe Victoria, one block from the square, *comida corrida* US$1.65. Bus back to Mexico City, Terminal del Norte, or Metro Indios Verdes, US$1.25.

Pachuca

Phone code: 771
Colour map 3, grid B6
Population: 320,000
Altitude: 2,445m

Capital of Hidalgo state, Pachuca is also one of the oldest silver mining centres in Mexico. The Aztecs mined here before the Spaniards came and the hills are honeycombed with old workings and terraced with tailings.

Although the centre is largely modern, there are a number of colonial buildings among its narrow, steep and crooked streets. These include the treasury for the royal tribute, **Las Cajas Reales** (1670), Venustiano Carranza 106, now used as offices; **Las Casas Coloradas** (1785), on Plaza Pedro María Anaya, now the Tribunal Superior de Justicia; and a former **Convento de San Francisco** (1596) on Arista e Hidalgo next to Parque Hidalgo. **Casa de las Artesanías** for Hidalgo state is at the junction of Avenida Revolución and Avenida Juárez. In the Plaza Independencia is a huge clock with four Carrara marble figures. The modern buildings include a notable **theatre**, the **Palacio de Gobierno** (which has a mural depicting ex-President Echeverría's dream of becoming Secretary-General of the UN), and the **Banco de Hidalgo**. The town centre is partly pedestrianized. *Colectivos* run from Julián Carrillo (very frequent, US$0.40) to the large silver-mining camp of Real (or Mineral) del

Monte, picturesque and with steep streets. The **tourist office** is in the clock tower on Plaza Independencia opposite *Hotel Grenfell*.

The **Museo de la Minería** at Mina 110 has an excellent display of the history of mining in Pachuca. ■ *Tue-Sun 1000-1400, 1500-1800. Free.* An outstanding **photographic museum** is in the large cloister on the far side of the convent. ■ *Tue-Sun 1000-1800. Free.* The **Museo Regional de Hidalgo**, in the Centro Cultural Hidalgo, displays chronological exhibits of the state's history. In the complex there is a souvenir shop with reproductions of ceramic and metal anthropological items and recordings of indigenous music, a library and exhibition hall. ■ *Tue-Sun, 0900-1800, may close early on Sun afternoon.*

Museums

Cornish miners settled at **Real del Monte** in the 19th century; their blue-eyed descendants may be seen among the local inhabitants. Note also the Flemish-style gable roofs. At each entry to the town is a mural commemorating the first strike in the Americas, by silver miners in 1776. The Panteón Inglés (English cemetery) is on a wooded hill opposite the town, ask the caretaker for the key. **Mineral del Chico** is a beautiful little town 30 km from Pachuca in **El Chico National Park**. The park has many campsites, which are mostly dirty with no facilities. There is no information or maps at the park headquarters. Mineral del Chico is full of weekend homes for the wealthy of Mexico City. There are huge rock formations covered in pine forests and some splendid walks. Buses run from Pachuca.

Excursions

B *Ciro's*, Independencia. Recommended. C *El Dorado*, Guerrero 721, T42831. Clean, friendly. C *Motel San Antonio*, 6 km from Pachuca on road to Mexico City (ask repeatedly for directions). Spacious rooms, good value, clean, quiet, restaurant. D *De los Baños*, on Plaza Independencia. Rooms not up to standard of entrance, good, friendly and helpful. Recommended. D *Grenfell*, Plaza Independencia 116, T50277. With bath, clean, friendly, pleasant, good value (cheaper without bath, but communal toilets are filthy), bus from bus station passes the door. D *Hidalgo*, Matamoras 503. Recommended. D *Juárez*, Barreda 107. With bath, some rooms without windows, just before Real del Monte, in superb wooded surroundings. F *Colonial*, Guerrero 505. Central.

Sleeping

Casino Español, Everardo Márquez. Old-time favourite. *La Blanca*, next to *Hotel de los Baños*. Local dishes. Recommended. *El Buen Gusto*, Arista y Viaducto Nuevo Hidalgo. Clean, good-value *comida corrida*. *El Rinconcito*, on Juárez. Good cheap food. *Paste* is the local survivor from Cornish miners' days; a good approximation of the real pasty, but a bit peppery! *Pastes Pachuqueños*, Arista 1023. Recommended.

Eating

A four-lane highway now runs from Mexico City to Pachuca via Venta de Carpio, Km 27, from which a road runs east to Acolman, 12 km, and Teotihuacán, another 10 km. If travelling by bus, there are frequent departures from Terminal del Norte.

Transport

Buses   Terminal is outside town; take any bus marked 'Central'.

North and east of Pachuca

North of Pachuca via Atotonilco el Grande, there is a chapel and convent halfway down a beautiful canyon, the impressive **Barranca de Metztitlán** which has a wealth of different varieties of cacti, including the 'hairy old man' cactus, and a huge 17th-century monastery. The death of Ome Tochtli (Two Rabbit) at the hands of Tezcatlipoca (Smoking Mirror) occurred at Metztitlán (see box

Around Mexico City

The gods at Metztitlán

Late in the 16th century, the Spanish authorities carried out a comprehensive census of New Spain. All aspects of indigenous life were explored, including the belief system of the pre-Conquest era. The following is part of the results of the survey for Metztitlán (Close to the Moon).

"Furthermore another fable is told which says that they had as gods two other images, the one named Ome Tochtli, who is the god of wine, and the other, Tezcatlipoca, which is the name of the most important idol who they adored.

It is also said that the idol Tezcatlipoca killed the god of wine, with his consent and agreement, saying that in this manner he was made immortal and were he not to die, all those who drank wine would have to perish. But the death of this Ome Tochtli was like a drunken dream, after which, on returning to himself, he was healthy and well. And by immortalizing him it came about that, from his name, they made the start of the count of their dreams (the tonalpohualli, calendar); because, as will be explained later, the first year they call One Rabbit, and, from there, the history of these

(people) and their pictures proceed by years, which, in all, counted until now, there is no memory nor account of time". (Translated from the Spanish by the editor)

This short extract will give the interested reader some insight into the native ideology at the time of Conquest. The gods had to die to become immortal; Ome Tochtli (Two Rabbit), the generic term for all the pulque gods, of whom they say there were 400, had to die so that drunks would be protected. His death was like a dream, in other words, a drunken stupor, but when he recovered from the hangover, he was well again. To start the present Era, the Fifth Sun, the gods at Teotihuacán had to perform sacrifice by throwing themselves into the fire. They then became the Sun and the Moon. The religion brought by the Spaniards also taught that a god-made man was sacrificed and became immortal, a concept that they were eager to grasp, sometimes with dire results.

That Ome Tochtli was immortalized at Metztitlán indicates that this settlement was important to the pulque cult.

above). Further north on a difficult road is Molango, where there is a restored convent, Nuestra Señora de Loreto. **San Miguel Regla**, 34 km northeast of Pachuca, is a mid-18th century *hacienda* built by the Conde de Regla, and now run as a resort, T91-77154311, or 56800448/ 56516369 (Mexico City) for reservations. It has a fine atmosphere, excellent service, pool, lush gardens, tennis, horse riding and log fires. Highly recommended. A road continues towards **Tulancingo** on the Pachuca-Poza Rica road, Route 130. Seventeen kilometres east of Pachuca, and a further 4 km off Route 130 to the right, is **Epazoyucan**, a village with the interesting convent of San Andrés. After Tulancingo, Route 119 branches off to the right to **Zacatlán**, famous for its apple orchards, plums, pears and cider. Its alpine surroundings include an impressive national park, the **Valle de las Piedras Encimadas** (stacked rocks), where camping is possible. Nearby is **AL** *Posada Campestre al Final de la Senda*, a ranch with weekend accommodation, horse riding and walks, T22-413821 for reservations. Some 16 km south of Zacatlán and about 1½ hours from Puebla (see page 174) is **Chignahuapan**, a leading producer of *sarapes*, surrounded by several curative spas.

Situated 30 km from Tulancingo on Route 130 is *La Cabaña* restaurant, of log cabin construction; thereafter, the road descends with many bends and slow lorries, and in winter there may be fog. At **Huauchinango** an annual flower fair is held in March; 22 km from here is **Xicotepec de Juárez** with **B** *Mi Ranchito*, one of the best small hotels in Mexico and **D** *Italia* near the main square. Along the route are the villages of **Pahuatlán** and **San Pablito**, where sequinned headbands are made, and paintings are done on flattened *amate* bark.

Northwest of Mexico City

About 43 km northwest of Mexico City just off the route to Querétaro is Tepotzotlán, with the splendid Jesuit church of San Francisco Javier in churrigueresque style. There are fine colonial paintings in the convent corridors. The old Jesuit monastery has been converted into the **Museo Nacional del Virreinato**, a comprehensive and well-displayed collection covering all aspects of life under Spanish rule. ■ *1000-1700, closed Mon, US$4.35, Sun free.* It is also a tourist centre with restaurants. There is a big market on Wednesday and Sunday when the town gets very congested; there is a good selection of handicrafts and jewellery, as well as meat, cheese, and other foods. Twenty-eight kilometres northwest is the 18th-century Acueducto del Sitio, 61m at its highest and 438m long.

Tepotzotlán
Phone code: 5
Colour map 3, grid B5

In the third week of December, *pastorelas*, or morality plays, based on the temptation and salvation of Mexican pilgrims voyaging to Bethlehem, are held. Tickets are about US$10 and include a warming punch, the play, a procession and litanies, finishing with a meal, fireworks and music. Contact *Viajes Roca*, Neva 30, Colonia Cuauhtémoc, Mexico City, for tickets.

Sleeping and eating **AL** *Hotel Tepotzotlán*, Industrias, about 3 blocks from centre. TV, restaurant, swimming pool, good views, secure parking. Highly recommended. *Hotel San José*, Zócalo. Nice rooms, poor service and value. *Hostería del Monasterio*. Very good Mexican food and a band on Sun; try their café de olla, coffee with cinnamon. *Restaurant Artesanías*, opposite church. Cheap. Recommended. Also good food at *Brookwell's Posada*.

Transport Buses: from near El Rosario metro station, US$1.50, 1 hr ride. Many Querétaro or Guanajuato buses from Terminal del Norte pass the turn-off at 'Caseta Tepotzotlán' from where one can take a local bus or walk (30 mins) to the town. **NB** Do not confuse Tepotzotlán with Tepoztlán, which is south of Mexico City, near Cuernavaca.

Tula

A half-day excursion from Mexico City can be made to Tula, thought to be the most important Toltec site in Mexico; two ball courts, pyramids, a frieze in colour, and remarkable sculptures over 6m high have been uncovered. There are four huge warriors in black basalt on a pyramid, these are the great Atlantes anthropomorphic pillars. One warrior is a reproduction; the original is on display at the Museo Nacional de Antropología, Mexico City. The platform on which the four warriors stand is encircled by a low relief frieze depicting jaguars and coyotes, and Tlaloc masks adorn the walls. Note the butterfly emblem on the chests of the warriors and the *atlatl* (spear-thrower) held by their sides. The butterfly, so important an element in Toltec iconography, was once more to become associated with the warrior class during the Aztec period (see page 96), when dead warriors became butterflies who escorted the Sun to midday. The museum is well worth visiting and there is a massive fortress-style church, dating from 1553, near the market. **Warning** Assaults have been reported in the ballcourt; be alert at all times, especially in deserted areas of the site. There are no security guards. ■ *Tue-Sun 0930-1630 (museum open Wed-Sun till*

Phone code: 5
Colour map 3, grid B5
65 km N of Mexico City

Around Mexico City

1630). Site and museum, US$2 weekdays, reduction with ISIC card, free Sun and holidays. The small restaurant is not always open. Multilingual guidebooks at entrance, fizzy drinks on sale. The town itself is pleasant, clean and friendly. If driving from Mexico City, take the turn for Actopan before entering Tula, then look for the Parque Nacional sign (and the great statues) on your left.

Sleeping & eating **C** *Hotel Catedral*. Clean, pleasant, TV. *Hotel Sharon*, Callejón de la Cruz 1. Large clean rooms, secure car parking, restaurant, lift. Recommended. *Restaurant la Cabaña*, on main square. Local dishes. Also *Nevería*, with good soup.

Transport **Train** 1½ hrs by train from Buenavista station in Mexico City (from station, walk along track 30 mins to site). Train services are more unreliable since privatisation so check they are still running before making plans.

Bus Tula can also be reached by 1st-class bus, 'Valle de Mesquital', from Terminal del Norte, Av de los Cien Metros, which goes to Tula bus terminal in 2-2½ hrs; US$3.20 each way, every 40 mins 0600-2100; Tula bus terminal is 3 km from the site, take a 'Chapantago' bus (every 20 mins) to the entrance, 5 mins (badly signposted), or a taxi, US$2, or walk, turning right out of the bus station. At the main road, cut diagonally left across road and take first right, which will take you to a bridge over an evil-smelling river. Carry on to the main highway, then turn left. Also bus or car from Actopan, on the Pan-American Highway (see page 602). Tula-Pachuca US$3.30; safe to leave belongings at bus station. Grey Line excursions from Mexico City have been recommended.

West of Mexico City

Head west for a long weekend starting at what is reputed to be the biggest street market in Mexico. Beyond Toluca, a road leads to the top of Mexico's fourth highest mountain but it's a hike to see the lakes in the craters. There are pre-Hispanic sites to visit at Calixtlahuaca, Teotenango and Malinalco and good artesanía in the villages nearby. But leave some time to wind down at the medicinal hot springs of Ixtapan de la Sal or on the lake at Valle de Bravo.

Toluca

From Mexico City to Toluca, 64 km by dual carriageway, head towards **Parque Nacional Miguel Hidalgo**, or **La Marquesa**, which has lakes suitable for watersports and other activities such as hiking. Here also is the turn-off for Chalma and Santiago Tianguistenco from Route 15. There are occasional great panoramic views of the city and the Valley of México during the ascent, smog permitting. Descending into the Basin of Toluca, you will see the proud form of the Toluca volcano dominating the towns and villages that are spread around the base of its piedmont.

Phone code: 72
Colour map 3, grid B5
Population: 600,000
Altitude: 2,639m

Toluca is the capital of the state of México. It is known mostly for its huge Friday market where Indians sell colourful woven baskets, *sarapes*, *rebozos*, pottery and embroidered goods (beware of pickpockets and handbag slashers). The new market is at Paseo Tollocan e Isidro Fabela, spreading over a number of streets, open daily. As well as for textiles, the city is famous for confectionery and for *chorizos* (sausages). It is also a centre of chemical industries which cause pollution. The **tourist office** is at Lerdo de Tejada Pte 101, Edificio Plaza Toluca, 1st floor, T50131. It has a free *Atlas Turístico* of the state of México, including street maps of all towns of interest.

The centre of the city is the **Plaza de los Mártires**, a very open space. On its south side is the **Cathedral**, begun in 1870, but not completed until 1978. Incorporated in its interior is the baroque façade of the 18th-century church of the Tercera Orden. Also on the south side is the **Church of Veracruz**, housing a black Christ and with a very attractive interior. On three sides of the block which contains these two churches are **Los Portales** (Calle Bravo, Calle Hidalgo and Calle Constitución), arcaded shops and restaurants. Northeast of Plaza de los Mártires is a park, Plaza Angel María Garibay, with trees and fountains, on which is the **Museo de Bellas Artes**, formerly the Convento del Carmen, with seven halls of paintings from 18th-century colonial Baroque to the 20th century and temporary exhibitions. A tunnel is said to run from the ex-Convento to all the central churches. ■ *Tue-Sun 1000-1800, US$0.25, concessions half price, booklet US$1.35*. Next door is the **Templo del Carmen**, a neoclassical church with a gold and white interior, and next to that is Plaza España. At the eastern end of Plaza Garibay is the **Cosmovitral** and **Jardín Botánico**. From 1933 to 1975 the building was the 16 de Septiembre market; it

Sights
Watch out for an orange liqueur known as moscos, a local speciality.

was reopened in 1980 as a formal garden in honour of the Japanese Eizi Matuda, who set up the herbarium of Mexico State, with fountains and exhibitions, all bathed in the blues, oranges and reds of the vast stained-glass work of Leopoldo Flores Valdez, a unique sight. ■ *Tue-Sun 0900-1700, US$0.60.* One block west of Plaza Garibay is the **Palacio de Gobierno**. Four blocks west of Los Portales is the **Alameda**, a large park with a statue of Cuauhtémoc and many tall trees; on Sunday morning it is very popular with families strolling among the many stallholders. The entrance is at the junction of Hidalgo and Ocampo. At Ocampo and Morelos is the **Templo de la Merced**. The **Casa de las Artesanías** (Casart), with an excellent display of local artistic products for sale, is at Paseo Tollocán 700. It is more expensive than Mexico City. ■ *Daily 0930-1850.* Ten kilometres south of the city is a good zoo, Zacango.

Excursions From Toluca take a bus north to the pyramids and Aztec seminary of **Calixtlahuaca**, 2 km off the road to Ixtlahuacan. The pyramids are to Quetzalcoatl (circular) and to Tlaloc. They are situated just behind the village, 10 minutes walk from the final bus stop. ■ *US$4.35.* Forty-five minutes north of Toluca by car, near the town of Temoaya, is the Centro Ceremonial Otomí, a modern site for cultural events in a beautiful landscape.

From Toluca to the coast at Ixtapa along Route 134 (see page 398) via Tejupilco, Ciudad Altamirano and La Salitrera, the road is paved but deteriorating in parts, traffic is sparse and the landscape hilly and pleasant.

Toluca

■ Sleeping
1 Colonial
2 Rex
3 San Carlos

● Eating
1 Café L'Ambient
2 Woolworth

Holiday Inn, Carretera a México Km 57.5, T164666, F164099. Restaurant, bar, parking. **Sleeping**
C *San Carlos*, on Hidalgo at Portugal Madero 210, T149422. **C** *Colonial*, Hidalgo Ote 103,
T147066. Pleasant courtyard with stained glass, with bath, clean, TV, cheap food (good
restaurant, closed Sunday). Recommended (bus from Terminal de Autobuses to Centro
passes in front). **D** *Rex*, Matamoros Sur 101, T159300. With bath, hot water, no
restaurant.

■ *on maps*
Price codes:
see inside front cover

On Hidalgo Pte **C** *La Mansión*, No 408, T156578. With hot water, clean, garage,
TV, no restaurant. **E** *Maya*, No 413, no check-in before 2000. Shared bath, hot water,
clean, small rooms without door locks, towels extra. All the above are in the centre,
not many cheap hotels. **D** *Terminal*, adjoining bus terminal, T157960 (prices vary
according to floor). Restaurant next door.

Motels **AL** *Del Rey Inn*, T122122, F122567, Km 63, Mexico City road entrance
(5-star). Resort facilities; on same exit road, **A** *Paseo*, T165730 (4-star) and **AL** *Castel
Plaza Las Fuentes*, Km 57.5, T164666, F164798 (5-star).

Ostionería Escamilla, Rayón Norte 404. Good fish. *San Francisco*, Villada 108. *Café* **Eating**
L'Ambient, Hidalgo 231 Pte. Snacks, meals, quite simple; next door are *Son Jei* and
Panadería Libertad (good pizza takeaway), oriental; opposite, in Los Portales, is *Impala*
for *comida corrida*, coffee. *Woolworth* restaurant, Hidalgo Pte casi Matamoros. Open
Sun from 0930 for good set breakfasts. *Fonda Rosita* in Los Portales central avenue
going through to Plaza de los Mártires. Also open Sun morning, pleasant, Mexican. *Las
Ramblas*, on Constitución side of Los Portales. Mexican food, average.

● *on maps*

Buses Bus station is some distance from the centre; information is difficult to gather **Transport**
inside and all is confusion outside – look for a bus marked 'Centro', US$0.15; from centre to
terminal buses go from, among other places, Ignacio Rayón Norte and Hidalgo Ote, look
for 'Terminal' on window (yellow or orange bus). To Mexico City (Terminal del Occidente,
close to Metro Observatorio), US$2.85, 1 hr. Bus to **Pátzcuaro**, 6 hrs, US$17.50, several
daily; to **Taxco**, 4 buses a day, book in advance, 3 hrs, US$6 with Frontera, a spectacular
journey. To **Morelia**, several buses daily with Herradura de Plata, 4 hrs, US$8.25, ETN
US$14.80. Many buses to **Tenango de Arista** (US$0.65, 30 mins), **Tenancingo** (US$2.25);
also regular buses to **Calixtlahuaca** US$2.50 (1 hr) from platform 7.

Toluca Volcano

A road branches off the Toluca to Valle de Bravo road at Km 75 to the Toluca
volcano, **Nevado de Toluca**, or Xinantécatl. At 4,558m this is the fourth highest mountain in Mexico. The road climbs to the deep blue lakes of the Sun and
the Moon in its two craters, at about 4,270m, from which there is a wide and
awe-inspiring view. It is 27 km from the turning off the main road to the heart
of the craters. During winter it is possible to ski on the slopes; 2 km from the
entrance is an *albergue* with food and cooking facilities. From here it is 10 km
to the entrance to the crater, where there is a smaller *albergue* (cooking facilities, food sold at weekends only, no bathroom or water, dirty), and then a further 6 km to the lakes. A short-cut from the small *albergue* takes 20 minutes to
the crater; it is not possible to drive. At the third refuge, 21 km from the
turn-off is an attendant. Trips to the volcano are very popular at weekends.
You can stay overnight at any of the refuges (**F**), although they are sometimes
closed during the week, and there is a restaurant, but the trip can be done in
one day from Toluca. If walking remember the entrance to the crater is on the
far left side of the volcano.

To reach the Toluca volcano take the first bus to Sultepec from Toluca at
about 0700, every two hours thereafter. Leave the bus where the road to the
radio station branches off, just after Raíces village (US$1), from there it is

about 20 km to the crater, hitching is fairly easy, especially at weekends. Aim to get to the crater by midday, otherwise clouds will cover everything. Visitors must leave by 1700.

Along Route 55 south of Toluca, or reached from it, are a number of most interesting art and craft producing villages, all with fine old churches. The first village is **Metepec**, the pottery-making centre of the valley, 1½ km off the road to Tenango. The clay figurines made here, painted bright fuchsia, purple, green and gold, are unique. This is the source of the 'trees of life and death', the gaudily painted pottery sold in Mexico. Craft workshops are very spread out. Market day is Monday. A recommended place to eat is *Las Cazuelitas*, near the main church. Try the handmade *tortillas*. There is an interesting convent , bus Toluca-Metepec US$0.65.

If you are brave try atepocates; embryo frogs with tomato and chiles, boiled in maize leaves

A detour east off Route 55 or south from Route 15, the Toluca-Mexico City highway, goes to the town of **Santiago Tianguistenco** (*population* 38,000), where there are good *cazuelas*, *metates*, baskets and *sarapes*. Between July and early November displays of wild mushrooms are for sale. Try *gordas* or *tlacoyos*, blue corn stuffed with a broad bean paste. Try restaurant *Mesón del*

Toluca environs

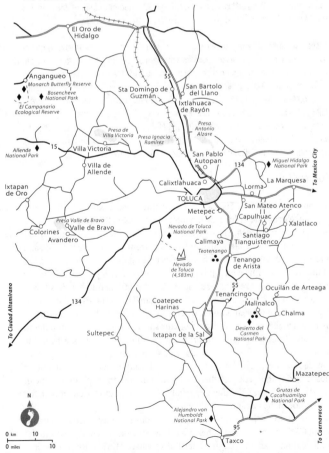

Cid, good regional food, go to kitchen to see choice. Try *sopa de hongos*, mushroom soup. Market day is Wednesday and the town is crowded at weekends.

San Mateo Atenco (*population:* 65,000; *altitude* 2,570m), is situated south of the Toluca-Lerma 'corridor'. Settled in ancient times, it has featured in several important historical moments by virtue of occupying a bridge-head between lagoons: Axayácatl, Hernán Cortés and Hidalgo all passed this way. There is a Franciscan church and monastery, the earliest parts of which date from 1550. The town is famous for its shoes, and leather goods of all descriptions. Excellent bargains are to be had. Market is on Friday and Saturday. On 25 October St Crispin, the patron saint of shoemakers, is honoured in the open chapel of the church in the presence of the local bishop.

Route 55 descends gradually to **Tenango de Arista**, where there are two hotels with a car park alongside the main road, where one can walk (20 minutes) to the ruins of **Teotenango**. The Toluca-Tenango bus costs US$0.65. Teotenango shows the Matlazinca culture and is reminiscent of La Ciudadela at Teotihuacán, with five plazas, 10 structures and one ball court. There is an interesting museum by the ruins; to enter go to the end of town on the right hand side. If you ask the guard, you can pitch a tent at the museum inside the gate. ■ *Entry to museum and ruins US$1.*

Around Mexico City

Tenancingo

Colour map 3, grid B5
Altitude: 1,830m

West of Mexico City, just 48 km south of Toluca, the road descends abruptly through gorges to Tenancingo, which has a soft, warm climate all year round. Thirty minutes by bus to the south along an unpaved road is the magnificent 18th-century Carmelite convent of El Santo Desierto, where they make beautiful *rebozos*. The townspeople themselves weave fine *rebozos* and the fruit wines are delicious and cheap. Overlooking this busy commercial town is a statue of Christ on a hill. The daily market area is two blocks from the bus terminal (continue one block, turn left for two further blocks to the main square); market day is Sunday, with excellent local cheese.

Sleeping and eating Recommended are **D** *Lazo*, Guadalupe Victoria 100, T20083 (1½ blocks straight on from market, away from bus terminal). With clean rooms in annex with shower, leafy courtyard, *El Arbol de la Vida* restaurant. **D** *María Isabel*. Clean, well-lit. **E** *Hotel Jardín*, on main plaza, T20108. With bath, big, airy rooms, restaurant, good value. Good bakery in private house at Guillermo Prieto 302.

Transport Buses: frequent buses to **Toluca**, US$2.25 with *Tres Estrellas del Centro*, 1 hr; also to **Ixtapan de la Sal** US$1 (change here for Taxco US$2.25), **Malinalco**, US$1.50, and **Chalma**.

Malinalco

Phone code: 714
Colour map 3, grid B5

About 11 km east of Tenancingo is Malinalco, from which a path winds up 1 km, 20 minutes, to the partly excavated Malinalco ruins, dating from 1188, certainly one of the most remarkable pre-Hispanic ruins in Mexico. Here is a fantastic rock-cut temple in the side of a mountain which conceals, in its interior, sculptures of eagle and jaguar effigies. Apparently, you can feel movement in the rock if you lie on it or lean against it. The staircase leading to the temple has over 430 steps. The site, which shows Matlatzinca culture with Aztec additions, is very small, but in a commanding position over the valley, and overlooks the town and surrounding wooded hills. ■ *Tue-Sun 1000-1630, US$2, Sun free.*

The site is visible from the town as a ledge on the hillside; the walk up passes a tiny, blue colonial chapel. For an even better view of the ruins carry straight on where the path leading to the ruins branches off to the right. This old road is cobbled in places and rises up the mountainside pretty steeply, arriving (after about 1½ hours walk) at a small shrine with two crosses. It is possible to camp here but there is no water. Breathtaking views can be seen from here off both sides of the ridge. The trail then carries on gently down the other side, past avocado trees, for 20 minutes, to the paved road to Tenancingo, almost opposite a new brick house with arches. It is possible to catch a bus back over the mountains to Malinalco. It would also be much quicker and easier, a downhill walk mostly, to do this whole hike in reverse; catch the bus out, ask for the old road, and walk back.

You should not fail to visit also the Augustinian **Templo y Ex-convento del Divino Salvador** (1552), in the centre of town, the nave of which has a patterned ceiling, while the two-storey cloisters are painted with elaborate, early frescoes. Just below the main square in front of the convent is the market (market day Wednesday). There is a *fiesta* in Malinalco on 6 August.

You can also get to Malinalco from Toluca, or Mexico City, by taking a second class bus to **Chalma**. This is a popular pilgrimage spot and when you get off the bus people will offer to sell you a corona of flowers. From the bus lot, walk up hill, past the market stalls, to the crossroads where blue *colectivos* leave for Malinalco until 2000 (10 km, 20 minutes, US$1).

Sleeping & eating E *Hotel Santa Mónica*, Hidalgo 109. With bath, pretty courtyard, good value. E *Posada Familiar*; cabins for families at north edge of town; camping and trailer park *El Paraíso* opposite the small blue chapel (not well named; no facilities other than one dirty toilet). Eating places include *La Playa* on road to ruins, just off square, with garden, nice place; opposite is *La Salamandra*, good value; trout farm and fishery has a restaurant, superb, bring own supplies of beverages, bread, salad (trout costs US$5-6); also *El Rincón del Convento*, behind the convent on road to square.

Transport A direct road runs from **Tenancingo** to Malinalco, paved to the summit of a range of hills, poor at the summit, then graded to the junction with the Malinalco-San Pedro Zictepec road; pick-up truck or buses run on this direct road hourly, 40 mins, US$2.25 (in Malinalco, bus leaves from corner of Av Progreso and the square). From **Toluca** you can go to Malinalco by leaving the Toluca-Tenancingo road after San Pedro Zictepec, some 12 km north of Tenancingo, which is paved and 28 km long. In Mexico City, buses leave from Terminal del Pte, opposite Observatorio. Buses to Chalma from **Mexico City** leave frequently from Terminal del Pte, 2 hrs, US$3.60 direct. This is also where you make connections if coming from **Cuernavaca** (take a Cuernavaca- Toluca bus to Santa Marta, then wait for a Mexico City or Toluca-Chalma bus).

Ixtapan de la Sal
Phone code: 714
Colour map 3, grid B5

Thirty-two kilometres from Tenancingo on Route 55 is Ixtapan de la Sal, a pleasant leisure resort with medicinal hot springs surrounded by forest. In the centre of this quiet whitewashed town is the municipal spa. ■ *US$1.60. 0700-1800, not always open.* At the edge of town is the privately run Parque Los Trece Lagos which has a train running around it and numerous picnic spots. Private baths charge US$6 for admission only, everything else is extra. For the hedonist there are private 'Roman' baths, for the stiff-limbed a medicinal hot-water pool, mud baths for the vain, an Olympic pool for swimmers, rowing boats and a water slide for the adventurous. The latter is 150m long (prohibited to those over 40). ■ *US$1.55, US$0.90 for two slides, US$2.20 for slides all day, free midweek 1200-1400.* Market day is Sunday and there is a fiesta on the second Friday in Lent.

Sleeping AL *Ixtapan*, Nuevo Ixtapan, T30304. Including food and entertainment. **AL** *Vista Hermosa*, T30092. Next door, full board only, good, friendly. **A** *Kiss* (*Villa Vergel*), Blvd San Román y Av Juárez, T30349, F30842. **B** *Casablanca*, Juárez 615, T30241, F30842. **C** *María Isabel*, T30122. Good. **D** *Guadalajara*. With bath. **D** *Casa de Huéspedes Margarita*, Juárez. Clean. Recommended. **E** *Casa Guille*, José María Morelos. With bath, clean. **E** *Casa Yuyi*. With bath, clean, good; many others.

Eating There are plenty of reasonable restaurants on Av Benito Juárez, most close by 1900. Good value is *Fonda Jardín* on Zócalo.

Transport Car: Ixtapan de la Sal can be reached in about 2 hrs from Mexico City: turn off Route 15, the Toluca highway, at La Marquesa, go through Santiago Tianguistenco and join Route 55 at Tenango. The road goes on to the Grutas de Cacahuamilpa (see page 166) from where you can continue either to Cuernavaca or Taxco. **Buses**: to/from Mexico City 3 hrs, US$5.35, every 30 mins from Terminal Oriente; to Toluca every 30 mins, US$4.20, 2 hrs. Also to Taxco, Coatepec, Cuernavaca.

Tonatico, 5 km past Ixtapan de la Sal, is a much cheaper village with a pleasant municipal *balneario* filled with medicinal hot water supposed to help blood circulation, rhueumatism and other illnesses. There is also a waterslide, open at weekends only, and a cheap hotel (**D**)at the entrance to the *balneario* with bathroom, T10691.

The mountain resort of Valle de Bravo, located on a branch road of Route 134, is a charming old town on the edge of an attractive artificial lake and close to an important Monarch butterfly wintering area. Valle de Bravo's *fiesta* is 26 February to 14 March. There are two direct buses a day Zitácuaro-Valle de Bravo, 1½ hours, US$3.30; hourly buses to Toluca and Mexico City; first-class bus to Toluca, US$3.50.

Sleeping *Loto Azul Resort*, Av Toluca, T20157, F22747. 4-star. *Centro Vacacional ISSEMYM*. Central, pool, restaurant, satisfactory, Independencia 404. **B** *Los Arcos*, Bocanegra 310. Some rooms with excellent view, swimming pool, restaurant (open only at weekends), not very helpful staff (**A**at weekends). **C** *Refugio del Salto*, Fontana Brava. **D** *Blanquita's*, opposite church off main plaza. Basic, fairly clean, OK. **D** *Mary*, main plaza. Hot showers. **C** *Casa Vieja*, Juárez 101, central. Recommended. A few cheap *posadas familiares* around the plaza, ask.

Trailer park Av del Carmen 26, T91726-21972 (or Toluca 91721-21580). Familia Otero, English spoken, 5 hook-ups, 7 dry camping, 3 rentals, small private grounds. Recommended. **NB** Drivers with trailers must approach Avándaro from the Toluca end, no other way is safe because of the hills, narrow streets and town centre.

Eating *Alma Edith*, on Zócalo. One of the few places to be open for breakfast by 0900. Very good, but slow service, good *comida corrida*. *La Estación*, Bocanegra 318. Recommended. Good, cheap food in the *mercado*. Restaurants on pier are expensive. *Los Pericos*, Embarcadero Municipal, T20558. International menu, specialises in fish dishes, 0900-2000.

Ixtapan del Oro is a pleasant town in a valley, 70 km southeast of Zitácuaro. It has a few hotels including **E** *Posada Familiar Portal Moreno*, with bath, clean. A road, mostly dirt, runs between Ixtapan del Oro and Valle de Bravo.

Valle de Bravo
Phone code: 726
Colour map 3, grid B5

This area gets the rich weekend crowd from Mexico City.

Ixtapan del Oro
Population: 20,000

Around Mexico City

South of Mexico City

As in pre-colombian times, Morelos state is still very important to the inhabitants of Mexico City: it is close to the capital and gives access to the tierras calientes and many areas of natural beauty, some of which have been developed as recreational zones for those wishing to escape the hurly-burly of city life. It is the ideal weekend bolt hole for the jaded city dweller and it gives access, via Taxco, to Acapulco, Zihuatanejo, Ixtapa and other resorts on the Pacific Coast.

Cuernavaca

Phone code: 73
Colour map 3, grid B5
Population: 1 million
Altitude: 1,542m

The capital of Morelos State, originally Tlahuica Indian territory, is 724m lower than Mexico City. The nahuatl name, Cuauhnáhuac, means 'adjacent to the Tree'. The temperature never exceeds 27°C nor falls below 10°C and there is almost daily sunshine even during the rainy season. The city has always attracted visitors from the more rigorous highlands and can be overcrowded. The outskirts are dotted with ultra-modern walled homes and some of its charm has been swamped by the city's rapid growth and a new industrial area to the south. The Spaniards captured it in 1521 and Cortés himself, following the custom of the Aztec nobility, lived there.

Ins and outs

Getting there & away
There is a small airport at Cuernavaca with some domestic flights, but most people fly to Mexico City. Buses leave the capital from the Terminal del Sur to one of Cuernavaca's four bus stations, each serving a different bus company (for details see **Transport** page 159). To drive the 89 km to Cuernavaca, follow Insurgentes Sur all the way south beyond Ciudad Universitaria and then take either the fast *cuota* (toll), or the picturesque *libre*. Beyond Cuernavaca, Route 95 and 95D continue south towards Taxco and Acapulco, or you can head east to Tepoztlán, Cuautla and on to the state of Puebla.

Getting around
Most of the sites in Cuernavaca are near the centre of town and are within easy walking distance of each other. Local bus routes can be confusing as they take long, roundabout routes through the *colonias*. Buses marked 'Centro', or 'Buena Vista', all go to the Cathedral. Taxis are plentiful and easy to come by; agree on the price before travelling.

The centre of the city has two adjacent squares, the larger **Zócalo** and the smaller **Alameda**. At the western end of the Zócalo is the Palacio de Gobierno; north of the Zócalo, east of the Alameda is the Centro Las Plazas shopping mall. Heading north from the Alameda, Calle Vicente Guerrero is lined with shops in arcades. Calle Degollado leads down to the main market in a labyrinth of shops and alleys. There is a tourist kiosk on Vicente Guerrero outside *Posada San Angelo*. For cultural activities, go for information to the university building behind the Cathedral on Morelos Sur.

The tierras calientes (warm lands) of Morelos

The tierras calientes *were important contributors to the well-being of Tenochtitlán. Once subjugated, they paid tribute in food-stuffs, labour and, most importantly, an abundance of cotton, either raw or woven. The Aztec rulers wore cloaks of white cotton from Cuauhnáhuac (Cuernavaca). Cotton was a symbol of civilized existence as opposed to the nomadic lifestyle symbolized by animal pelts or apparel woven from the shredded leaf of the agave maguey. Cotton was also used extensively in the production of warrior uniforms and provided padding to protect against the* macana, *the truncheon-like weapon studded with sharp, obsidian chips. Battle shields too were adorned with cotton balls.*

Cuernavaca orientation

Related maps
A Cuernavaca centre, page 156

Sights

The palace Cortés built in 1531 for his second wife stands at the eastern end of the tree-shaded Zócalo; on the rear balcony is a Diego Rivera mural depicting the Conquest of Mexico. It was the seat of the State Legislature until 1967, when the new legislative building opposite was completed; it has now become the **Museo Regional de Historia Cuauhnáhuac**, showing everything from mammoth remains to contemporary Indian culture, explanations are not very logical and most are in Spanish. ■ *1000-1700, closed Mon, US$1.60.* West of the centre, Calle Hidalgo leads to one of the main areas of historical interest in the city.

The Sunday morning Mass at 1100 is accompanied by a special mariachi band. Mariachis also perform on Sunday and Wednesday evenings in the Cathedral

The **Cathedral**, entrance on Hidalgo, near Morelos, finished in 1552, known as Iglesia de la Asunción, stands at one end of an enclosed garden. Some 17th-century murals were discovered during restoration depicting the martyrdom of the Mexican saint San Felipe de Jesús on his journey to Japan. The scenes show monks in open boats, and mass crucifixions. The interior is bathed in different colours from the modern stained-glass windows. At the west end is a stone font full of water; the east end, painted gold, contains the modern altar. In the entrance to the chapel of the Reserva de la Eucarista is a black and white fresco of the crucifixion. There are also two-storey cloisters with painted friezes and a fragment of massed ranks of monks and nuns. By the Cathedral entrance stands the charming small church of the **Tercera Orden** (1529), whose quaint façade carved by Indian craftsmen contains a small figure suspected to be one of the only two known statues of Cortés in Mexico. The other is a mounted statue near the entrance of the *Casino de la Selva* hotel. The gates to the Cathedral and the Tercera Orden are closed each day at 1400.

Cuernavaca centre

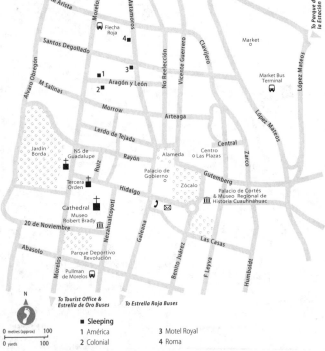

■ Sleeping

1 América	3 Motel Royal
2 Colonial	4 Roma

Beside the Cathedral, in the Casa de la Torre (Calle Nezahualcoyotl 4), is the **Museo Robert Brady**, housing a collection of paintings by, among others, Diego Rivera, Frida Kahlo, Paul Klee and Francisco Toledo. It also has colonial furniture, textiles, pre-Hispanic objects and African art and ceramics and is well worth a visit. Descriptions are in English and Spanish. ■ *1000 to 1800, closed Mon, US$2, café and shop.* The 18th-century **Jardín Borda** on Calle Morelos was a favourite resort of Maximilian and Carlota. It has been restored and is in fine condition. It holds open-air concerts and there are exhibition rooms, café, good bookshop and museum. ■ *1000-1730, closed Mon, US$1.0.* Boats can be rented on the small lake, US$1-2 depending on duration. Next to the Jardín Borda is the neoclassical church of Nuestra Señora de Guadalupe. Two kilometres on the right up Morelos (*pesero*), side by side are the churches of San José Tlaltenango (1521-23) and the early 19th-century Nuestra Señora de la Natividad; bazaar on Sunday, second-hand English books.

The weekend retreat of the ill-fated imperial couple, Casa de Maximiliano, in the Acapatzingo district is now the **Herbolario y Jardín Botánico**, with a peaceful and interesting museum, at Matamoros 200, Colonia Acapatzingo. ■ *Daily 0900-1700, free. To get there take a bus from the centre to Acapatzingo and ask the driver for the Museo del Herbolario, or take a taxi, US$1.75.* Acapatzingo is a pleasant district. The house of David Alfaro Siqueiros, the painter, is now a museum, **Taller Siqueiros**, at Calle Venus 7, a long way east of the centre. It contains lithographs and personal photographs. The very unusual **Teopanzolco** pyramid is to be found just east of the railway station. ■ *1000-1630, US$1.50.* At the pyramid's summit remains of the temple can be seen. Also in the complex are various structures including a circular building, probably dedicated to Quetzalcoatl.

Excursions

Chapultepec Park, southeast of the city centre, has boating facilities, a small zoo, water gardens, with a small admission charge. Also east of the centre is a zoo and recreation centre at **Jungla Mágica**, built around a series of natural springs. The potters' village of **San Antón** is perched above a waterfall a little west of the town, where divers perform on Sundays for small donations. In the vicinity of Cuernavaca are many spas, such as Xochitepec, Atotonilco, Oaxtepec, Temixco, Las Huertas and Los Manantiales at Xicatlocatla.

Essentials

Sleeping
Good value cheap hotels are hard to find

L *Hostería Las Quintas*, Av Díaz Ordáz 9, Col Cantarranas, T183949, F183895. Built in traditional Mexican style, owner has splendid collection of bonsai trees, restaurant, 2 pools, spa, outdoor jacuzzi, magnificent setting, fine reputation. **L** *Misión del Sol*, Av Gral Diego González 31, Col Parres 62550, T210999, F211195 (Toll-free 01-800-9999100), misolmex@mail.giga.com. Spa resort with good sports facilities. Recommended. **L** *Las Mañanitas*, Ricardo Linares 107, T141466/124646, F183672, reyl@infosel.net.mx (one of the best in Mexico). Mexican colonial style, many birds in lovely gardens, excellent food, only Amex accepted, reservation necessary. **AL** *Hacienda de Cortés*, Plaza Kennedy 90, T160867/158844, 16th-century sugar *hacienda*. Magnificent colonial architecture, garden, suites, pool, excellent restaurant, access by car. **AL** *Posada Jacarandas*, Cuauhtémoc 133, T157777, F157888. Garden, restaurant, sports, laundry, safety box, conference hall, parking. **AL** *Posada San Angelo*, Privada la Selva 100, T141499. Restaurant, gardens, pool. **A** *Posada María Cristina*, Francisco Leyva 200, T185767, near Zócalo. Restaurant, pool, garden, secure parking, extensively refurbished. **A** *Suites Paraíso*, Av Domingo Díaz 1100, T133365. Family accommodation. On same avenue, *Villa Bejar*, No 2350, T175000, F174953. Gran Turismo class, all facilities. **A** *Posada Quinta Las Flores*, Tlaquepaque 210, Colonia Las Palmas, T141244/125769, 2 mins walk from Estrella de Oro bus station, 30 mins walk from centre. Includes breakfast, no TV, helpful, pool, gardens, restaurant (set evening meal), small parking space, very pleasant. Highly recommended. **B** *Papagayo*, Motolinia 13, T141711, 5 blocks from Zócalo, 1 block from Estrella Roja bus station. On Fri-Sat rooms are available only if one takes 2 meals a day, on other days price is **C**, room only, pool, gardens, convenient, good value, suitable for families, parking. **B** *Hostería del Sol*, Hidalgo, close to the Palacio de Cortés, T183241. Loaded with charm and authentically Mexican, lots of tiles, courtyards, flowers, etc. Recommended. **C** *Bajo el Volcán*, Humboldt 117, T124873, 187537. Pool, restaurant, fair. **C** *Las Hortensias*, Hidalgo 22, T185265. Takes Visa, pretty courtyard, central, long-distance phone service.

D *Colonial*, Aragón y León 104, T186414. Friendly, pleasant courtyard, clean airy rooms. **D-E** *Roma*, Matamoros 405, T120787. Hot water morning and evening, noisy. Several cheaper hotels in Aragón y León between Morelos and Matamoros: eg **E** *América*, No 111. Safe, good value but noisy, clean, basic; some rent rooms by the hour.

Motels   A *Posada Cuernavaca*, Paseo del Conquistador, T130800. View, restaurant, grounds. **B** *El Verano*, Zapata 602, T170652. **E** *Royal*, Matamoros 19. Hot water 0700-2300, central, clean. Recommended. *Suites OK Motel* with *Restaurant Las Margaritas*, Zapata 71, T131270. Special student and long-term rates, apartments, trailer park, swimming pool and squash courts.

Eating   *Hacienda de Cortés* (see above); *Las Mañanitas*,(see above) Ricardo Linares 107. Beautiful but expensive, only Amex accepted; also *La India Bonita*, Morrow 20. Excellent Mexican food but expensive. *Sushi Itta*, corner Hidalgo and Blvd Juárez. Japanese. On the Zócalo and Alameda: *Villa Roma*, *Café/Pastelería Viena* (expensive); *La Parroquia*, *La Universal* (on corner of Zócalo and Alameda). Next to *La Universal* on the Alameda is *McDonalds*. Also for fast food, *Subway* on Alameda and others in Centro las Plazas. *Parrots*, next to the Museo Regional, opposite which, at Hidalgo y Juárez, are *La Adelita* and *Flash Taco*. *Marco Polo*, opposite Cathedral. Good, Italian, good pizzas, popular meeting place. Recommended. *Vivaldi*, Pericón 102, restaurant and *pastelería*. Very reasonable, popular with locals. There are other *cafés* opposite the Cathedral. Near the Glorieta Niña in Col Las Palmas, *Los Vikingos*, restaurant and a good *pastelería*. There is also a large *panadería pastelería* on this roundabout. Generally, it is not easy to find good, authentic Mexican cooking at reasonable prices. A major exception is *La Pasadita*, Morelos esq Abasolo. Usually an amazingly wide choice at very good prices, quieter upstairs.

Pollo y Más, Galeana. Decent cheap *comida corrida*. *Malvias*, Matamoros, next to *Motel Royal*. Friendly, good value *comida corrida*. *Jugos Hawai* in Centro Las Plazas. Fruit juices are sold from stalls beneath the bandstand on the Zócalo. *Paletas Cuernavaca*, corner Zócalo and Salazar. Terrace with view on the Zócalo. Large choice of ice creams and yogurt.

Shopping   **Bookshop** Second-hand English books at *Guild House*, Tuxtla Gutiérrez, Col Chipitlán, T125197. **Handicrafts market** Behind Palacio de Cortés, moderately priced and interesting silver, textiles and souvenirs. When the tour buses arrive there are lots of handicraft sellers outside the Cathedral gates.

Tour operators   *Marín*, Centro Las Plazas, local 13, Amex agent, changes Amex travellers' cheques but poorer rate than *casas de cambio*, charges US$1 to reconfirm flights. Also in Centro Las Plazas, *Pegaso*, French, Italian, German, English spoken (the sign says), charges US$2 to reconfirm. *Viajes Adelina*, Pasaje Bella Vista, on Zócalo.

Air Flights from Tijuana, Acapulco, Culiacán, Monterrey, Hermosillo and Guadalajara **Transport**
with *Aerolíneas Internacionales.*

Buses Each bus company has its own terminal; *Estrella de Oro* (B5), Morelos Sur 900, Col   *Many minibuses and*
Las Palmas, T123055, 1st class buses to Mexico City, Taxco (0915, 2100), Ixtapa (2145),   *2nd-class buses leave*
Lázaro Cárdenas (2015), Chilpancingo (0900, 1100, 1345, 1630), Aguascalientes (2200),   *from a terminal by the*
Acapulco (7 daily 0715-2230) and Zihuatanejo (2015); this bus station is a US$3.25 taxi   *market (B3).*
ride, or 25 mins walk from the centre. Local buses from the bus station up Morelos, marked
Centro, or Buena Vista, all go to the Cathedral. From the centre take bus on Galeana
marked Palmas. *Pullman de Morelos* has 2 termini: (B1) at Abasolo 106 y Netzahualcóyotl
in the centre, T180907, for Mexico City (*ejecutivo dorado*) every 30 mins from 0530, and
some local departures to Alpuyeca, Tehuixtla, Zacatepec, Jojutla, Grutas de Cacahuamilpa,
and (B4) at 'Casino de la Selva', Plan de Ayala 102, opposite Parque de la Estación, T189205,
for *ejecutivo dorado* to Mexico City and 10 daily buses to Mexico airport (book 24 hrs in
advance at either terminal, US$6). *Flecha Roja* (B1) on Morelos Norte 503 y Arista,
T125797, 2nd class to Mexico City (0530-2100), Taxco (0805-2035), Iguala, Tijuana (via
Guadalajara, Mazatlán, Hermosillo, 1815, 2200), Querétaro (1400), San Luis Potosí (1701),
Nuevo Laredo (via Saltillo, Monterrey, 1615), Acapulco (several daily) and Grutas de
Cacahuamilpa (left luggage open 0700 to 2100 daily, US$0.25 per hr per item). *Estrella
Roja* (B6), Galeana y Cuauhtemotzín, south of the centre, for Cuautla (every 15 mins) via
Yautepec, Matamoros and Puebla (via Izúcar de Matamoros, hourly 0500-1900).

To **Mexico City** 1½ hours, fares US$3.65 ordinary to US$4.25 *ejecutivo dorado*: *Pullman de Morelos* is said to be the most comfortable and fastest, from Terminal del Sur,
Mexico City every 30 mins.

To **Acapulco**, 4 hrs, *Estrella de Oro*, US$14.75 (US$19.50 *plus*). For advance tickets
for Acapulco or other points on the Pacific Coast, be at Estrella de Oro office between
1645 and 1700, 2-3 days before you want to travel, this is when seats are released in
Mexico City and full fare from Mexico City to the coast must be paid. To **Zihuatanejo**,
Estrella de Oro, 1 a day, US$23. To **Taxco**, Flecha Roja, 2nd-class buses, hourly on the
½-hr (not recommended), or Estrella de Oro, 1st class, US$4.25; to **Puebla**, Estrella de
Oro, *gran turismo* service, US$5, 1st class hourly, US$4, 2 stops; **Cuautla** (page 165)
either Estrella Roja every 20 mins, US$1.85, or 2nd class or minibus from market termi-
nal, via Yautepec every hour, 1 hr, interesting trip; go there for long-distance buses
going south (Puebla buses do not stop at Cuautla).

Warning: luggage theft from waiting buses in Cuernavaca is rife; don't ever leave
belongings unattended. Robberies have been reported on the non-toll mountain
road to Taxco and on the road to Mexico City.

Road Warning: On the toll road between Mexico City and Cuernavaca, at Les Tres
Mariás, is a sign to Toluca. Do not be tempted to take this route; it is well-surfaced but
narrow over the pass before leading to the lakes at Zempoala, but thereafter it is almost
impossible to navigate the backroads and villages to Toluca. Among the problems are
livestock on the road, unsigned intersections, signposts to villages not marked on the
Pemex atlas, heavy truck traffic, potholes, *topes* and congested village plazas.

Banks *Cambio Gesta*, Morrow 9, T183750, open 0900-1800. *Divisas de Cuernavaca*, Morrow 12;   **Directory**
many banks in the vicinity of the Zócalo.

Communications Internet: *Axon Cyber Café*, Av Cuauhtémoc 129-B. *California Cybercafé*,
Lerdo de Tejada 10b, Mon-Sat 0800-2000, un 0900-1400, Califcafe@hotmail.com. **Post Office:** on
Hidalgo, just off the Alameda. **Telephone:** Telmex on Hidalgo, just off the Alameda, LADA phones
are outside, almost opposite junction of Nezahualcoyotl. There is a telephone office at *Parrots*
restaurant and bar on the Alameda, next to the Museo Regional.

Language schools Spanish courses start from US$100 per week, plus US$60 registration at
the *Centro de Lengua, Arte e Historia para Extranjeros* at the Universidad Autónoma del Estado
de Morelos, Río Pánuco 20, Col Lomas del Mirador, T161626 (accommodation with families can be
arranged). Private schools charge US$100-150 a week, 5-6 hrs a day and some schools also have a

Around Mexico City

Universidad Internacional
The Center for Bilingual Multicultural Studie

Learn, Live & Love
in
Cuernavaca
World Capital of Learning Spanish

Spanish and Latin-American Culture

Phone: 011 (52-73) 17-10-87, Fax 011 (52-73) 17-05-33
Toll free from:
USA 1 (800) - 932 - 2068 *CANADA* 1 (877) 4 - **MEXIC** - 8 *MEXICO* 1 (800) 770 - UN
www.bilingual-center.com   admission@bilingual-center.com
Contact person: Nicole Sims

US$75-125 registration fee. The peak time for tuition is summer: at other times it may be possible to arrive and negotiate a reduction of up to 25%. There is a co-operative language centre, *Cuauhnáhuac*, Morelos Sur 123, T123673/189275, F182693, inform@cuauhnahuac.edu.mx, intensive Spanish 6 hrs a day and flexible private classes, registration US$70, US$200 per week or US$650 per month high season, US$170 per week, US$560 per month low season, family stays US$18 per day shared room with meals or US$25 single room with meals, efficient, helpful. *Center for Bilingual Multicultural Studies*, Apdo Postal 1520, T171087, F170533 or Los Angeles, LA, T800 9322068, www.bilingual-center.com. *Spanish Language Institute* (SLI), Pradera 208, Col Pradera, T110063 F175294, sli@infosel.net.mx, open 5 days a week, minimum 6 hrs per day, classes start every Mon. *Instituto Fénix*, Salto Chico 3, Col Tlaltenango, T131743, which also has excursions and minor courses in politics, art and music. *Cetlalic*, Madero 721, Col Miraval, Cuernavaca, T170850, F132637, cetlalic@mail.giga.com, themed courses, plus Mexican and Central American history and culture. Non-profit making.Various levels. Small groups (maximum 5 people). Stay with families. Recommended.

Cemanahuac, San Juan 4, Las Palmas, T186407, F125418, 74052.2570@compuserve.com, claims high academic standards, field study, also weaving classes. *Experiencia*, Leyva, Col Las Palmas, T126579, F185209, experiencia@infosel.net.mx, free 'intercambios' (Spanish-English practice sessions) Tue and Wed afternoon, open 5 days a week. *Centro de Artes y Lenguas*, Nueva Tabachín 22-A, T173126/130603, F137352, scale@infosel.net.mx, 5 hrs a day, registration US$100, 1 minimum, classes US$160, US$300 a week accommodation with families including meals. *Cuernavaca Language School*, T175151, F163546, cls@infosel.net.mx, or PO Box 4133, Windham, New Hampshire, T603-4379714, F603-4376412. *Mexican Immersion Centre*, Piñanonas 26, Col Jacarandas, CP 62420, T221083, F157953, mic@axon.com.mx. *Encuentros*, Morelos 36, Col Acapatzingo, CP 62440, T125088, F129800, encuent@infosel.net.mx. *Universal*, JH Preciado 332, Col San Antón, T124902 (Apdo Postal 1-1826), 3 levels of language course, tutorials and mini courses on culture; and *Idel*, Apdo 1271-1, Calz de los Actores 112, Col Atzingo, T/F130157, 5 levels of course. Staying with a local family will be arranged by a school and costs US$12-20 a day including meals; check with individual schools, as this difference in price may apply even if you stay with the same family.

Around Mexico City

Laundry In Las Palmas: *Oaxaca* behind Confía buildings, almost opposite *Restaurante Vikingos*, good. *Euro Klin*, Morelos Sur 700 block, a short way from Glorieta Niña towards centre. There is a good laundry behind the Cathedral.

Tepoztlán

Phone code: 739
Population: 4,000

Tepoztlán, meaning 'where copper abounds', is 24 km northeast of Cuernavaca at the foot of the spectacular **El Tepozteco National Park**, with the small Tepozteco pyramid high up in the mountains. The only way into the park is on foot. It takes 40 minutes to one hour to climb from the car park at the end of Avenida de Tepozteco to the pyramid. The pyramid was dedicated to the pulque deity, Tepoztecatl (see box 163). It is 2 km uphill, strenuous, climb up before the sun is too high, although most of the climb is through trees. The trip is well worth it. The altitude at the top of the pyramid is 2,100m and the view from the top is expansive. Signs remind you on the way that you must pay at the top; five minutes before the entrance a steel ladder has to be scaled. Cold drinks are sold at the entrance for US$1. ■ *Opens anytime between 0900 and 1030, officially 1000-1630, US$3, free with student card.*

Sights
The town has picturesque steep cobbled streets, an outdoor market and a remarkable 16th-century church and convent, María de la Natividad. The Virgin and Child stand upon a crescent moon above the elaborate plateresque portal, no tripod or flash allowed. A mural by Juan Ortega (1887) covers the eastern end of the church. There is a small archaeological museum with objects

Cuernavaca environs

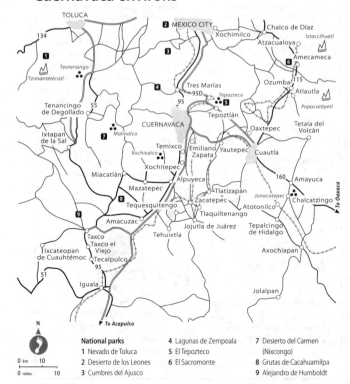

National parks
1 Nevado de Toluca
2 Desierto de los Leones
3 Cumbres del Ajusco

4 Lagunas de Zempoala
5 El Tepozteco
6 El Sacromonte

7 Desierto del Carmen
(Nixcongo)
8 Grutas de Cacahuamilpa
9 Alejandro de Humboldt

Tepoztecatl of Tepoztlán

In recent years, much attention and effort have been expended in analyzing and interpreting the ancient manuscripts of Mexico, both pre-Hispanic and early colonial. A general consensus of agreement is that the contents of these books express very clearly the histories, religion and tribute lists of the peoples who occupied these lands before the advent of the Spaniards. In one such manuscript, the Codex Magliabechiano (there is a facsimile in the Biblioteca Nacional de Antropología e Historia in Mexico City), produced around 1550 but clearly derived from a pre-Hispanic model, a group of 11 gods are beautifully illustrated; they are the Pulque Deities. The first in the series, indicating that he was perceived as a major deity, is Tepoztecatl, He of Tepoztlán. The illustration of Tepoztecatl is accompanied by an explanatory text, which, in pre-Hispanic times would have been unnecessary; the god is accompanied by a toponymic glyph which relates him to Tepoztlán, and the iconography of his clothing makes it clear that he ruled over drunkenness.

The text accompanying Tepoztecatl reads: "This is the figure (illustration) of a great roguery which one village called Tepoztlán had for rite that when an Indian died from drunkenness, the others from this village made a great festival with copper hatchets (the copper hatchet was the symbol for Tepoztlán) with which they chopped firewood. This village is related to Yautepec, vassals of the Sr. Marques del Valle (Cortés)". Translation by the editor.

In and around Tepoztlán there are several geographical features named after pulque deities; this fact, along with the above text, suggests that Tepoztlán was a major pulque centre, probably not for production but for consumption. This suggestion is reinforced by the discovery, very early in the colonial era, of a sculpture strategically placed on a ledge high up on the mountain that overlooks Tepoztlán. Of impressive proportions, the sculpture was the representation of a pulque deity, most likely Tepoztecatl. In pre-Conquest times, pilgrims from as far away as Chiapas and Guatemala came to Tepoztlán to pay homage to this statue. In 1552, the friars who were attempting to wean the inhabitants of Tepoztlán away from their ancient beliefs, cast the sculpture from its ledge down the almost sheer cliff. When it reached the bottom, the friars were dismayed to discover that it had remained intact, thus convincing them that it was the representation of the devil. The sculpture had, in fact, guarded the way to the only known pyramid dedicated to a pulque deity to survive the Conquest. On an elevated plateau close to the summit of Tlahuiltepetl, 'Mountain of Light', the pyramid known as Tepoztecco, 'The Place of Tepoztecatl', affords a stunning view of the surrounding mountains and valleys. It is a temple with a solid pyramidal base and almost perpendicular sides. There are two chambers, one containing a bench that extends around the north, south and east walls of the antechamber. The square or rectangular stone slabs that form the vertical face of the bench are elaborately carved in low relief. They were painted red (red and black are the colours identified with the pulque deities). The symbolism of the engravings is very complex, and while much of it refers to themes unrelated to pulque, the recurring depiction of the yacametztli, the crescent moon nose-plug, always worn by the gods of pulque, leaves no doubt that the temple was dedicated to those deities.

There are reports of numbers of slaves and captives being taken to the summit of Tepoztecco to be sacrificed to Tepoztecatl, an unhappy fate after so difficult a climb. Although pulque has been replaced by beer in Tepoztlán, as in other areas of the Central Highlands, the pulque deities remain a very important element in the folk memory of the town. Appropriately enough, the local bus company is named Ome Tochtli (Two Rabbit), the generic term for the gods of drunkenness.

from all over Mexico behind the church. ■ *Tue-Sun 1000-1800, US$0.75.* There is an arts and crafts market on the plaza at the weekend with a good but expensive selection of handicrafts from Mexico, Guatemala and East Asia. In the first week of November, there is an arts festival with films and concerts held outside and in the main church's cloister. This was the village studied by anthropologist Robert Redfield and later by Oscar Lewis.

Sleeping **A** *Posada del Tepozteco*, T50010, F50323. A very good inn, quiet, old fashioned, with swimming pool, excellent atmosphere and view. Highly recommended. **A** *Hotel Tepoztlán*. Largest hotel, towering over the village, grand pool, popular, crowded at weekends, as they all are. *Hotel Restaurant Anatlán de Quetzalcoatl*, T91739/51880, F51952. Pool, children's park, gardens. **A** *Posada Ali*, Nezahualcóyotl 2 'C', off Av del Tepozteco, T51971. Four rooms, 2 family suites (**AL**) breakfast, pool, fine view. **A** *Casa Iccemanyan*, Familia Berlanga, Calle del Olvido 26, 62520, Tepoztlán, T91-73950096/99. With 3 meals, **B** without meals, monthly rates available, 4 *cabañas*, swimming pool, clothes washing facilities, use of kitchen, laundry, restaurant, English, French and German spoken, beautiful garden. **D** *Mesón del Indio*, Av Revolución 44, no sign, Sr Lara. Basic.

Eating *Los Colorines*, Av del Tepozteco 13-B. Good Mexican vegetarian. Next door is *El Chinelo*. Mexican. *El Jardín del Tepozteco*. Italian, Wed-Sun 1300-2200. *Axitla*, at beginning of path up to Tepozteco, open Fri, Sat, Sun and holidays. *La Costa de San Juan*, by plaza on opposite side of street. Meat and seafood. *Tapatía*, Av Revolución 1910 (just across street from church wall). Good food and pleasant view from 1st floor, takes credit cards. *El Ciruelo*, Zaragoza 17. Quiet, nice décor, popular with wealthy Mexicans.

Transport **Buses** Local bus, *Autobus Verde*, from Cuernavaca market terminal, takes 1 hr to

Mexico City, US$1 (bus returns to Cuernavaca from the top of the Zócalo); bus to Mexico City, US$3.35 1st class, US$3.65 *primera plus*, hourly. There are buses from Tepoztlán to Yautepec (Marigold Hill).

Language schools Tepoztlán is a definite alternative to Cuernavaca. Try *Spanish Communications Institute*, Cuauhtemotzín, T51709, USA T956 994 9977, www.spancom.com.

Directory

Take Route 160 via Yautepec to the semi-tropical town of Cuautla, meaning 'where trees abound'. This crowded weekend resort for the capital is a popular sulphur spring, known as *aguas hediondas* or stinking waters. Tourist Cuautla is divided from locals' Cuautla by a wide river and the locals have the best bargain; it is worth crossing the stream. The plaza is pleasant, traffic-free and well maintained. There is a market in the narrow streets and alleyways around 5 de Mayo. The tourist office is opposite *Hotel Cuautla*, on Av Obregón. The **Casa de la Cultura**, three blocks north of the Zócalo, has useful information and maps. There is a museum and ex-convent next door.

Cuautla
Colour map 3, grid B6
Population: 94,000

Sleeping C *Jardín de Cuautla*, Dos de Mayo 94, opposite Colón bus station. Modern, clean, but bad traffic noise, pool. One block from *Jardín de Cuautla* is **C** *Colonial*. Modern, pool. **D** *Hotel Colón* in Cuautla is on the main square. Good, clean; *Hotel-restaurante Valencia*, 4 blocks north of Cristóbal Colón terminal. **D** *Hotel Madrid*, Los Bravos 27, 11 km from Cuautla. **E** *Hotel España*, Dos de Mayo 22, 3 blocks from bus station. Very good, clean. Recommended. *Casa de Huéspedes Aragón*, Guerrero 72. Hot water, friendly, basic, clean, good value. Recommended. On road to Cuernavaca is the **AL** *Hacienda de Cocoyoc*. An old converted *hacienda* with several swimming pools backed by the mill aqueduct, glorious gardens, 18-hole golf-course, tennis and riding, but isolated, Visa accepted but not Amex, reservations (essential in season) at Centro Comercial El Relox, Local 44, Insurgentes Sur 2374, México 01000 DF, T55507331. **Youth hostel** Unidad Deportiva, T20218, CP 60040.

Eating Try the delicious *lacroyas* and *gorditas*, *tortillas* filled with beans and cheese. Four good restaurants in main square, all serving cheap *comidas*, try the one in the *Hotel Colón*; good restaurant at *Hotel Granada*, Defensa de Aguas 34.

Transport Buses: from **Mexico City** to Cuautla from Terminal del Sur or Terminal del Oriente (Volcanes terminal), 2nd class US$1. Buses from Cuautla at Cristóbal Colón terminal, 5 de Mayo and Zavala, to **Mexico City** hourly US$3.65 1st class, US$4.65 *plus*; *Estrella Roja* 1st class, 2nd class buses or minibuses to **Cuernavaca** at least hourly, 1 hr, US$1.85; to **Oaxaca**, US$14.80, 2 *Cristóbal Colón* buses per day (2nd class 1430 and 1st class 2330), 7-8 hrs, also *ADO*, most overnight and *en route* from Mexico City so book ahead, also try *Fletes y Pasajes* 2nd class buses, or change twice, at Izúcar de Matamoros and Huajuapan. Cristóbal Colón terminal will store luggage until they close at 2200. The 115 road leads to Amecameca (see page 172).

This interesting Olmec sanctuary can be reached from Cuautla. It has an altar, a pyramid and rock carvings, one of which depicts a procession of warriors led by a prisoner with a beard and horned helmet (a Viking, some say), others depict battles between jaguars and men. To get there take Route 160 southeast, direction Izúcar de Matamoros; at Amayuca turn right towards Tepalcingo. Two kilometres down this road turn left towards Jonacatepec and it's 5 km to the village of Chalcatzingo (take a guide). There are buses from Puebla to Amayuca. A taxi from Amayuca costs US$5. Near Jonacatepec are the ruins of Las Pilas. Some 7 km further down the road to Tepalcingo is Atotonilco where there is a *balneario* for swimming (bus from Cuautla).

Chalcatzingo

Around Mexico City

South of Cuernavaca

Alpuyeca, Km 100, has a church with good Indian murals. A road to the left runs to **Lago Tequesquitengo** (*Paraíso Ski Club*) and the lagoon and sulphur baths of **Tehuixtla**. Near the lake a popular resort, with swimming, boating, water skiing and fishing, is **AL** *Hacienda Vista Hermosa*, Hernán Cortés' original *ingenio* (sugar mill), and several lakeside hotels. East of the lake is **Jojutla** and a nearby old Franciscan convent of **Tlaquiltenango** (1540), frequent bus service from Cuernavaca, US$1.75, *Pullman de Morelos*. The route through Jojutla can be used if coming from the coast heading for Cuautla, to avoid Cuernavaca. Enquire locally for road conditions off the major highways.

Xochicalco

At 15 km on the westerly road from Alpuyeca is the right-hand turn to the Xochicalco ruins, 36 km southwest of Cuernavaca, topped by a pyramid on the peak of a rocky hill, dedicated to the Plumed Serpent whose coils enfold the whole building and enclose fine carvings which represent priests. The site is large and needs two to three hours to see it properly.

It was the meeting place of northern and southern cultures and, it is believed, both calendar systems were correlated here.

Xochicalco was at its height between 650 and 900 AD. It is one of the oldest known fortresses in Middle America and a religious centre as well as an important trading point. The name means 'place of the flower house' although now the hilltops are barren. The sides of the Pyramid of the Plumed Serpent are faced with andesite slabs, fitted invisibly without mortar. After the building was finished, reliefs 3-4in deep were carved into the stone as a frieze. There are interesting underground tunnels; one has a shaft to the sky and the centre of the cave. ■ *1100-1400*. There are also ball courts, an avenue 18.5m wide and 46m long, remains of 20 large circular altars and of a palace and dwellings. Xochicalco is well worth the 4 km walk from the bus stop; take a torch for the underground part. There is a new museum about 500m from ruins, a striking edifice incorporating many ecological principles and housing some magnificent items from the ruins, descriptions in Spanish only. There is also a *cafetería*. ■ *US$2, free with ISIC card. Tickets must be bought at the museum, which is open 1000-1700.*

Transport To get to Xochicalco, take a Pullman de Morelos bus from Cuernavaca *en route* to El Rodeo (every 30 mins), Coatlán or Las Grutas; alight at the turn-off, 4 km from the site, then take a *colectivo* taxi, US$0.35-US$1.20 pp, or walk up the hill. From Taxco, take bus to Alpuyeca (US$1.60, 1 hr 40 mins) and pick up bus from Cuernavaca to turn-off, or, taxi from junction at Alpuyeca directly to ruins (12 km, US$2.50).

Cacahuamilpa

From Alpuyeca, a road runs west for 50 km to the Cacahuamilpa caverns known locally as 'Las Grutas'. These are some of the largest caves in North America and are well worth a visit. They have strange stalactite and stalagmite formations; steps lead down from near the entrance to the caverns to the double opening in the mountainside far below, from which an underground river emerges. Guided tours take you 2 km inside; some excursions have gone 6 km; the estimated maximum depth is 16 km. It is worth going with a guided tour, available in Spanish only, as the caves are then lit properly. Don't miss the descent to the river exits at the base of the cliff, called Dos Bocas, which is tranquil and less frequently visited. **Warning** The disease *histoblastose* is present in the bat droppings in the cave (if you breathe in the tiny fungus it can cause a tumour on the lungs); to avoid it you can buy a dentist's face mask (US$0.20) (*cubre boca/protección de dentista*) at a pharmacy; try one opposite bus station. ■*1000-1700, US$2.50, children US$1.50, including 2¼ hours tour, every hour on the hour up to 1600 – crowded after 1100 and at weekends, take a torch.*

Transport Buses: there are direct *Pullman de Morelos* buses from Cuernavaca at 1030 and 1200, returning 1700 and 1830, 1 hr, US$2; also *Flecha Roja*; usually over-crowded at weekends, enquire about schedules for local buses or buses from Taxco to Toluca, which stop there (from Taxco, 30 km, 40 mins).

Taxco

Shortly after Amacuzac, Km 121, a further branch autopista scales moun-tainsides with breathtaking views taking you right to the outskirts of Taxco, a colonial gem, with steep, twisting, cobbled streets and many picturesque build-ings, now wholly dedicated to tourism.

Phone code: 762
Colour map 3, grid C5
Population: 120,000

Ins and outs

For international flights, Mexico City or Acapulco airports are the closest. Some domestic routes are served by Cuernavaca airport. Buses to Taxco leave from Mexico City's Terminal del Sur. You should book onward or return bus tickets to Mexico City on arrival. Some buses en route to Mexico City drop passengers on the main highway, some way from the centre. Taxco is connected to Mexcio City and Acapulco via Route 95 and the fast supercarretera Route 95D.

Getting there & away

Around Mexico City

Combis or taxis will take you up the hill from the bus terminal. Taxco is a fairly small town and, although hilly and cobbled, it is best experienced on foot.

Getting around

The first silver shipped to Spain came from the mines of Taxco. José de la Borda made and spent three fortunes here in the 18th century; he founded the present town and built the magnificent twin-towered, rose-coloured parish church of **Santa Prisca** which soars above everything but the mountains. There are large paintings about Mexican history at the Post Office. The roof of every building is of red tile, every nook or corner in the place is a picture, and even the cobblestone road surfaces have patterns woven in them. It is now a national monument and all modern building is forbidden. Gas stations are outside the city limits. The plaza is 1,700m above sea-level. A good view is had from the **Iglesia de Guadalupe**. There are superb views also from the *Teleférico* to Monte Taxco, US$1.50 return, you can return by bus. The *Teleférico* is reached by microbus along the main street from Santa Prisca. The climate is ideal, never any high winds (for it is protected by huge mountains immediately to the north); never cold and never hot, but sometimes foggy. The processions during Holy Week are spectacular. The main central area is full of shops and shopping tourists; the district between the four-storey Mercado and the Carretera Nacional is quieter and free of tourists. Also qui-eter are those parts up from the main street where the taxis can't go. Wear flat rubber-soled shoes to avoid slithering over the cobbles. **Tourist office** Avenida de los Plateros 1, T22274. ■ *0900-1400 and 1600-2000 every day*. City tours from Tourist Office North, US$35 for up to five people.

Sights

One of the most interesting of Mexican stone-age cultures, the Mezcala or Chontal, is based on the State of Guerrero in which Taxco lies. Its remarkable artefacts, of which there are many imitations, are almost surrealist. The culture remained virtually intact into historic times. The **Museum of the Viceroyalty** (formerly Casa Humboldt), J Ruiz de Alarcón 12, where Baron von Humboldt once stayed has been recently renovated;exhibits include beautiful religious art from Santa Prisca and elsewhere. Ask to see the original sauna (later a pantry) in Sala Humboldt. Descriptions are in English and Spanish. ■ *Tue-Sat 1000-1700, Sun 0900-1500, US$1.00, concessions US$0.50.* The **Casa Figueroa**, the 'House of Tears', so called because the colonial judge who owned it forced Indian labourers to work on it to pay their fines, is now a private house. **Museo Guillermo Spratling**, behind Santa Prisca, is a museum of pre-Hispanic artefacts bought by William Spratling, a North American architect who came to Taxco in the 1920s. His designs in silver helped bring the city

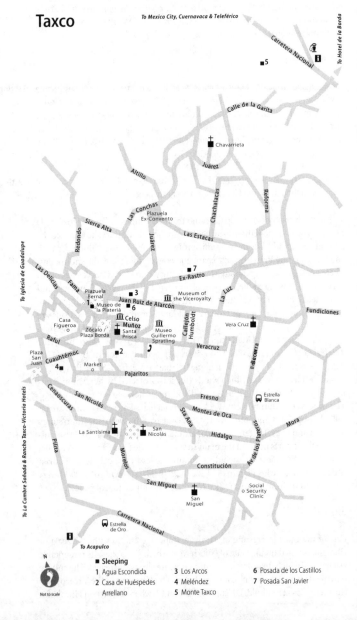

Taxco

■ **Sleeping**
1 Agua Escondida
2 Casa de Huéspedes Arrellano
3 Los Arcos
4 Meléndez
5 Monte Taxco
6 Posada de los Castillos
7 Posada San Javier

N

Not to scale

to world recognition and revived a dwindling industry. On his death bed Spratling donated his collection to the state. ■ *Tue-Sun 1000-1700, US$1.80.* The **Museo de la Platería** is a new museum devoted to modern silverworking, on Plaza Borda 1 ■ *US$0.80*; at the **Platería La Mina** on Avenida de los Plateros you can see mining techniques.

Excursions

Visit *Posada Don Carlos*, Bermeja 6, also Ventana de Taxco in *Hacienda del Solar* for view. *Combi* to Panorámica every 30 minutes from Plaza San Juan, US$0.20, or you can walk up the steep hill from Plaza San Juan for views of the hills and volcanoes. About 20 km out of Taxco a rodeo is held on some Sundays at El Cedrito, costs about US$4-5, tickets in advance from Veterinario Figueroa on Calle Nueva near Flecha Roja terminal.

Twenty-one kilometres from Taxco are the **Acuitlapán** waterfalls; *colectivo* or Flecha Roja bus (US$1.20); 4 km narrow path from nearest village (snakes) to large clear pools for swimming. Taxis about US$7.50 per hour.

To **Cacahuamilpa** for caverns, 40 minutes, see page 166. Buses from 0820 but service erratic, US$1.65, *colectivo* van marked No 1, or take a long white taxi marked 'Grutas' from corner of the bus station, US$3.50. Take an Ixtapan bus from opposite the Flecha Roja bus terminal, US$1.50, one hour, which passes the turn-off to the site, 1 km downhill; Ixtapan-Taxco buses go to the site car park. Alternatively, to return, take bus coming from Toluca at junction, 500m from the caves.

Visit the villages where *amate* pictures are painted (on display at Museum of the Viceroyalty/Casa Humboldt and in the market). **Xalitla** is the most convenient as it is on the old Highway 95 to Acapulco, take a second-class bus there. Villages near Taxco worth a visit include **Taxco el Viejo** (home of many individual jewellery makers), **Tecapulco** (enormous copper-domed church) and **Tehuilotepec** (or '*Tehui*' – ancient church, fine hillside views; chicken *roticería* in main square). At Tecapulco, you can visit the workshop and sales room at Rancho La Cascada, which is reported to have on offer original pieces designed by Antonio Castillo, T76221016, F76225048. Many pieces are inspired by pre-Columbian motifs. Just beyond the entrance to Taxco el Viejo is Rancho Spratling, where the workshop and sales room are open to the public. The pieces here are reportedly more artistic than those on sale in Taxco but also more expensive. These villages are delightfully quiet after Taxco. *Colectivos* leave from near Estrella Blanca bus station. Other villages: Maxela, Ahuelicán, Ahuehuepán and San Juan, past Iguala and before the Río Balsa.

Thirty-three kilometres from Taxco, at Km 55 on the road to Cuernavaca, is Zoofari, T/F209794 (Cuernavaca), a private safari park with many animals roaming free, well worth a visit, ■ *entrance US$5.*

Ixcateopan de Cuauhtémoc (Cuauhtémoc's birthplace), is a beautiful and peaceful village, where most of the buildings, and even the cobblestones, are made of marble. A statue honouring Cuauhtémoc stands at the entrance to the village. To get there, take a *pesero* from the road out of Taxco towards Acapulco, one hour's drive west through beautiful mountain scenery. The old church has been converted into a museum, The skeleton of Cuauhtémoc (Swooping Eagle), the last Aztec Emperor executed by Cortés, is said to rest in the glass-covered tomb, in the place of the altar. 22-23 February is the anniversary of Cuauhtémoc's death, called *Día de la Mexicanidad*. Runners come from Mexico City to Ixcateopan via Taxco, carrying a torch representing the identity of the Mexican people. Aztec dancers (in traditional dress and colourful plumed headdresses) come from all over Mexico to dance all night and most of the following day.

Essentials

Sleeping
■ on maps
Price codes:
see inside front cover

AL *De la Borda*, on left as you enter Taxco, T20225. Largest, all facilities, great views, dearest and best. **AL** *La Cumbre Soñada*, 1500m or so towards Acapulco on a mountain top. Colonial, exquisite. **AL** *La Hacienda del Solar*, Acapulco exit of town, T20323. Recommended. **AL** *Rancho Taxco-Victoria*, Soto la Marina 15, walk to centre. Fantastic view, good restaurant. Recommended. **AL** *Monte Taxco*, on right entering Taxco, T21300, F21428, special prices sometimes available from Mexico City offices, T5259193, F5330314. Spectacular hilltop setting, pool, riding, golf course, beware mosquitoes. **A** *Posada de la Misión*, Cerro de la Misión 32 (Mexico City – Cuernavaca buses stop outside), T20063, F22198. Juan O'Gorman mural, restaurant, good, pool, no a/c, quiet. Recommended. **B** *Posada Don Carlos*, Cerro de Bermeja 6. Converted old mansion, restaurant, good view. **B-C** *Agua Escondida*, near Zócalo at Guillermo Spratling 4, T20726. With bath, nice view, rooftop bar, parking, pool. **C** *Posada San Javier*, down a small street opposite Municipalidad. Clean, lovely garden, pool (sometimes dirty), excellent value, no restaurant. **C** *Meléndez*, near Zócalo, T20006. Best rooms Nos 1 and 19, superb views, visited by jewellery vendors, if booking reconfirm before arrival. **C-D** *Los Arcos*, Juan Ruiz de Alarcón 2, T21836. Reconstructed 17th-century ex-convent, delightful rooftop garden, breakfast available, best rooms for views are 18 and 19, rooms overlooking street are noisy, otherwise recommended. **C-D** *Posada de los Castillos*, Alarcón 7, T23471, off main square. Mexican style, friendly, excellent value. These last two are extremely popular: book ahead where possible.

D-F *Casa de Huéspedes Arrellano*, Pajaritos 23, below Santa Prisca and Plaza Borda. Terrace, quiet at night, with bath, basic, old beds, hot water. **E** *Casa Grande*, Plazuela San Juan 7, T21108. Pleasant, well-furnished but a bit ramshackle, rooms at the top are better, takes credit cards, good value. **E** *El Jumil*, Reforma 6, near Tourist Office North. Without bath, hot water, basic, friendly, but noisy. **E** *Posada Santa Anita*, Av de los Plateros 106, T20752, close to Flecha Roja buses. With hot shower and toilet, cheaper without, very clean, basic, overpriced, noisy at night, friendly, secure parking; the cheapest hotels are in this area. **F** *Central*, round the left hand corner of *Casa de Huéspedes Arrellano*. Shared bath, quite clean, some rooms without windows.

Eating
Restaurants tend to be
pricey

There are many places on the Zócalo: *Alarcón*, overlooking Zócalo. Very good. *Sr Costilla*, next to church on main square. Good drinks and grilled ribs. *Papa's Bar*, on Zócalo. A discotheque and a small pizza place in an arcade. *Bora-Bora*, overlooks Zócalo, Guadalupe y Plaza Borda. Good pizzas. **Pizzería Mario**, Plaza Borda. Beautiful view over city, excellent pizzas, the 1st pizzeria in town, opened 30 years ago, pleasant service. Highly recommended. **La Pagaduría del Rey**, Cerro de Bermeja, T20075. Fabulous panoramic view over city, international menu, excellent food but over-priced wine, main course about US$8, closes 2130, closed Mon. *Restaurant La Ventana* in La Hacienda del Solar, T20587. Wonderful view of the city, Italian and Mexican menu, main course about US$9. Recommended. *La Parroquia*, Plaza Borda 5. Terrace with excellent views, but indifferent food and poor service. *La Hacienda*, Plaza Borda 4 (entrance is off the square). Excellent Mexican food and wine at reasonable prices, chic décor and a nice atmosphere (sit near the door for the comic view of vehicles navigating a 3-point turn to make the sharp corner just outside), fair prices. Exquisite *quesadillas* in the *nevería* on top of the silver shop *Perlita* looking on to the Plaza Borda. *Mi Taverna* next to the Post Office. Excellent Italian food, friendly. *Concha Nuestra*, Plazuela San Juan (above *Hotel Casa Grande*). Mediocre food and poor service, live Latin American music excellent, cheap for breakfasts, other meals pricey.

Around Mexico City

Shopping for silver

Silverwork is a speciality and there are important lead and zinc mines. Vendors will bargain and cheap silver items can often be found. Beware of mistaking the cheapish pretty jewellery, alpaca, an alloy of copper, zinc and nickel, for the real stuff. By law, real silver, defined as 0.925 pure, must be stamped somewhere on the item with the number 925. The downtown shops in general give better value than those on the highway, but the best value is among the booth-holders in the Pasaje de Santa Prisca (from the Zócalo). Prices usually drop in the low season. On the second Sunday in December there is a national silversmiths' competition. The colourful labyrinthine produce and general market beneath the Zócalo is spectacular among Mexican markets; reasonable meals in the many fondas.

NB All silver jewellers must be government-registered. Remember to look for the 925 stamp and, if the piece is large enough, it will also be stamped with the crest of an eagle, and initials of the jeweller. Where the small size of the item does not permit this, a certificate will be provided instead.

Around Mexico City

La Hamburguesa, off Plaza San Juan. Excellent *comida corrida*, US$1.80, home-cooked food, despite name. *De Cruz*, Veracruz. Good Mexican food at low prices. *Armando*, Av Plateros 205, opposite Flecha Roja bus station. Excellent *tacos*. *Pozolería Betty*, Mora 20 (below bus station). Good food includes the local beetle (*jumil*) sauce. Many small restaurants just near *Hotel Meléndez*. *Santa Fe*, Hidalgo 2, opposite *Hotel Santa Prisca*, T21170. Excellent *comida corrida* (US$6) but disappointing *enchiladas*. Used by locals. Cheap *comida corrida* in market and good cheap restaurants on San Nicolás. *Freddie's*, J Ruiz de Alarcón 8, next to Museo de Arte Virreinal. Excellent coffee and cakes.

Festivals There is much festivity in *Semana Santa* (Holy Week); at this time the price of accommodation rises steeply. At any time it is best to book a room in advance because hoteliers tend to quote inflated prices to those without reservations.

Transport **Buses** Taxco is reached from **Mexico City** from the Terminal del Sur, Estrella de Oro, luxury US$10.65, *plus* US$8.65, non-stop, with video, 3 a day, 1st class US$7.65, quick, no overcrowding, 3 a day (2½ hrs); back to Mexico City at 0700, 0900, 1200, but computerized booking allows seat selection in the capital; also Estrella Blanca, many a day, on the hour US$7.50, up to 5 hrs. Buses to **Cuernavaca**; 1st class buses at 0900, 1600, 1800 and 2000 (Estrella de Oro), 2nd class about 5 a day, 1½ hrs (Estrella Blanca), US$3, but can be erratic and crowded (watch out for pickpockets). Little 24-seaters, 'Los Burritos' (also called *Combis*), take you up the hill from the bus terminal on main road, US$0.35, same fare anywhere in town. Spectacular journey to **Toluca**, missing out Mexico City, 2nd class buses only, from Estrella Blanca Terminal, US$6, 3 hrs, change at Toluca for Morelia. To **Acapulco**, Estrella de Oro, or Estrella Blanca, US$11, 5 hrs. Other destinations from Estrella Blanca Terminal include Iguala, Chilpancingo, Iztapan de la Sal and Cuernavaca by old road (via Puente de Ixtla and Alpuyeca).

Directory **Banks** Good rates at *Cambio de Divisar Argentu* on Plazuela San Juan 5. Bancomer, between Plazuela San Juan and Plaza Principal is OK. **Communications** internet: *Azul Cybercafé*, Hidalgo, near Plaza San Juan, Mon-Sat 0900-2200. **Post Office** on Carretera Nacional about 100m east of Estrella de Oro bus terminal. **Laundry** *Lavandería La Cascada*, Delicias 4.

Thirty-six kilometres south of Taxco join the Ruta 95 at **Iguala** (E *Hotel Central*, basic. E *Pasajero*. E *Mary*, OK, enclosed parking. Bus to Taxco US$1, to Cuernavaca US$4.25, to Mexico City from US$9.35 to US$15.35).

East of Mexico City

The drive east of Mexico City is dominated by awe-inspiring views the beautiful and smouldering Popocatépetl. A week-end excursion from Mexico City could be based in busy Puebla, the city of tiles and churches, or in Tlaxcala, La Ciudad Roja (the Red City).

Popocatépetl and Iztaccíhuatl

Colour map 3, grid B6

See transport, page 171

At Km 29 on Route 190 is **Ixtapaluca**, where a road on the right (south) leads to the small town of Amecameca, the starting point for Popocatépetl (5,452m) and Iztaccíhuatl (5,286m). On the way to Amecameca, see the restored 16th-century convent and church at **Chalco**, and the fine church, convent and open-air chapel of the same period at **Tlalmanalco**.

Legend has it that a princess was waiting for her warrior lover to return when news came of his death. Overcome with grief, she poisoned herself and when the warrior returned from battle he took her body to the top of Iztaccíhuatl and jumped into its crater. The three summits of Iztaccíhuatl are the head, breasts and knees of the princess. The saddle between the two volcanoes is reached by car via a paved road up to the Paso de Cortés (25 km from Amecameca) and gives particularly fine views.

Amecameca
Colour map 3, grid B6
Population: 57,000
Altitude: 2,315m
60 km to Mexico City

The Zócalo here is pleasant with good *taco* stands. A road reaches the sanctuary of El Sacromonte, 90m above the town, with magnificent views, a small and very beautiful church built round a cave once inhabited by Fray Martín de Valencia, a *conquistador* who came to Mexico in 1524. It is, after the shrine of Guadalupe, the most sacred place in Mexico and has a much-venerated full-sized image of Santo Entierro weighing only 1½ kg. From the Zócalo, take the exit under the arch and head for the first white station of the cross; the stations lead to the top. Market day is Saturday, and there is an excellent non-touristy market on Sunday. The **tourist office** is near the plaza, open 0900-1500. They can provide information and guides for Iztaccíhuatl.

From Mexico City, take metro to Pantitlán, then a bus or *pesero* to Ixtapaluca. Behind the Mercado Municipal take another *pesero* on the 'Avila Camacho' route and get off at La Vereda (transportation from 0600-2100 daily). For information F55125992.

Sleeping and eating There are 3 hotels, **E**, close to the main plaza (*Ameque*, clean, with bath), and rooms at the *San Carlos* restaurant on the main plaza, **F** with bath, noisy, good, modern, hot water. **Camping** Permitted at the railway station, ask the man in the office (leaving town, it's after the road to Tlamacas, on the right, 1-2 km away).

There are several eating places and a good food market. *San Carlos*, on the main square, good food, set lunch US$1.75. A good-quality *pulque* can be had at the *pulquería* on the main plaza.

Transport Buses: from Mexico City with Cristóbal Colón. Los Volcanes 2nd-class bus 1-1½ hrs journey, US$2, from the Terminal del Oriente; if hitching, take the Calzada Zaragoza, a very dusty road.

Climbing the volcanoes

On Saturdays a pick-up truck leaves the plaza at Amecameca, US$2 per person, for far up the mountain; there are also taxis offering trips to Paso de Cortés, US$15 for two people (but you may be able to negotiate down to half this). Just before the pass, cars (but not pedestrians or taxis) pay US$0.10 entry to the national park. There is a hostel, **E**, at the pass. The road on the other side of the pass to Cholula is rough, steep and sandy (but scenic); a sturdy vehicle is needed. The road beyond the Paso de Cortés to Tlamacas is currently closed. Twice during 1997 there were volcanic eruptions serious enough to cover Mexico City in ash. The authorities have an evacuation plan for some 300,000 people but many villagers on the slopes are suspicious that it is an excuse to take over lands. We suggest that readers seek local advice before planning an ascent.

Popocatépetl has been closed to climbers because of volcanic activity since 1994

The **best time to climb** the volcanoes is between late October and early March when there are clear skies and no rain. From May to October the weather is good before noon; in the afternoons it is bad. Get permission and ask about volcanic activity before you climb.

From Paso de Cortés a road goes left, north along another dirt road which leads past a TV station for 8 km to them parking nearest to the summit of Iztaccíhuatl at La Joya. Near the antennae is a *refugio* called Atzomani, which is the safest place to park, and there is a box (*buzón*) for notifying potential rescue groups of your intended route. From there you find various routes to the summit (12-15 hours return) and three to four refuges to overnight (no furniture, bare floors, dirty). Iztaccíhuatl has been described as "an exhilarating rollercoaster of successive summits". To climb **Iztaccíhuatl** take a taxi to La Joya, from there follow the tracks up the grassy hill on the right, four to six hours to first huts. The first two huts are at 4,750m (places for 30 people), the third at 4,850m (10-15 people), and the last hut is at 5,010m (in poor condition, 10-12 people); the Luis Menéndez hut is the most salubrious. From the last hut it is 2½-3 hours to the top, set off at 0400, over two glaciers. Some rock climbing is required, so crampons and ice-picks are necessary and can be hired in Amecameca.

Iztaccíhuatl

A more technical route starts at the *buzón* and at first descends left into the valley. Walk three to four hours from La Joya to the Ayoloco glacier before which is a *refugio* for eight to 10 people at 4,800m; it is three to four hours to the summit from here. Guides are available in Amecameca and Rigoberto Mendoza has been recommended. The cost is about US$110 and worth it, as walking on glaciers without knowing the conditions is hazardous.

The route to Puebla

The way east begins in the beautiful Valley of Puebla-Tlaxcala. Assuming that the travellers start the journey from Mexico City, we have suggested an early detour to take in Texcoco and the towns and villages in its environs. Those who have already explored the area that in ancient times was known as Acolhuacan will probably want to go directly to Puebla or Tlaxcala: nothing could be easier. There is a steady flow of traffic between the valleys of Mexico and Puebla-Tlaxcala. Whether travelling by car or bus, you can follow the route suggested below. You might want to go directly to Tlaxcala and start from there, although it might be much quicker to take a bus to Puebla, they are

Around Mexico City

far more frequent, then take a *colectivo* from the forecourt of the bus station. It can be fun, especially if you speak some Spanish. Even if you don't, there is no need to be apprehensive: in general, most people are eager to help and, in the main, extremely honest. You will find a number of *colectivos* at the platforms waiting for passengers, and most have their destinations painted on the front of the windscreen. State your destination to any driver and he (they are usually male) will point you to the relevant *colectivo*, which will probably have the name of some village as its destination, but which will be passing through the town you require. Once inside the *colectivo*, have a handful of coins ready and indicate to one of the other passengers that you do not know how much to pay merely by stating your destination. He or she will probably sort through your coins and pay the driver. When they have sorted you out, acknowledge their assistance with a *gracias* or *muy amable*, or even both. And do not be afraid of pronouncing Nahuatl names such as Tlaxcala: the English speaker has less problems than the Spanish speaker. The *tl* sound, as in cattle or bottle, is common in English but unknown in Spanish. The independent driver might like to follow the route described below.

Our description involves a trip along the old road, which goes east along the Puebla road, past the airport and swimming pools, and some spectacular shanty-towns. At Los Reyes, Km 19, a road runs left into a valley containing the now almost completely drained Lake Texcoco, a valley early settled by the *conquistadores*. Along it we come to **Chapingo**, where there is a famous agricultural college with particularly fine frescoes by Rivera in the chapel, *pesero* from General Anaya y San Ciprián or bus from TAPO-Autotransportes Mexico-Texcoco, US$0.70. ■ *Mon-Fri 0900-1800*. Next is Texcoco, which is a good centre for visiting villages in the area. Bus from Mexico City, from Emiliano Zapata 92, near Candelaria metro station or TAPO. Near Chapingo a road runs right to the village of **Huexotla**, with an Aztec wall, ruined fortifications and pyramid, and the 16th-century Franciscan convent of San Luis Obispo. Another road from Texcoco runs through the public park of Molino de las Flores. From the old *hacienda* buildings, now in ruins, a road (right) runs up the hill of Tetzcotzingo, near the top of which are the Baños de Nezahualcóyotl, the poet-prince. **San Miguel de Chiconcuac**, on the road to San Andrés and left at its church, 4 km away, is where Texcoco *sarapes* are woven. Tuesday is market day and there is a rousing *fiesta* in honour of their patron saint on 29 September.

Beyond Ixtapaluca, southeast of Los Reyes on Route 190, the road climbs through pine forests to reach 3,196m, about 63 km from Mexico City, and then descends in a series of sharp bends to the town of **San Martín Texmelucan**, Km 91. The old Franciscan convent here has a beautifully decorated interior, and a former *hacienda* displays weaving and old machinery. The Zócalo is beautiful, with benches covered in ceramic tiles and a central gazebo. Market day is Tuesday. Recommended hotels are **D-E** *Hotel San José*, Pte 115 and **E** *La Granja*, opposite.

Puebla

Phone code: 22
Colour map 3, grid B6
Population: 1,222,177
Altitude: 2,060m

'The city of the angels', Puebla (de los Angeles) is one of Mexico's oldest and most famous cities and the capital of Puebla state. It was founded in 1531 by Fray Julián Garcés who saw angels in a dream indicating where the city should be built, hence its name. This also explains why Puebla wasn't built over Indian ruins like many other colonial cities. Talavera tiles are an outstanding feature of Puebla's architecture and their extensive use on colonial buildings distinguishes it from other colonial cities. Puebla is a charming city, pleasant and friendly and always popular with travellers.

Aeropuerto Hermanos Serdán (PBC) has mostly domestic flights. The CAPU bus station is to the north of the city. Taxis from the terminal to the city centre leave from outside the departure terminal. From the centre to the terminal, take any form of public transport marked 'CAPU'. The train station is a long way from the centre, so before going there check at the tourist office to see if passenger services are running. Puebla is on the main Highway 150 from Mexico City to the Gulf Coast, the same *supercarretera* that branches south, beyond Puebla, to Oaxaca. An important commercial centre, Puebla is also the hub of other lesser routes to towns and villages in the surrounding area.

Getting there & away

Although Puebla is a big city, most of the major sites are around the centre, within easy walking distance of each other. City buses, *colectivos* or taxis will take you to any of the more distant sites.

Getting around

The centre, though still beautifully colonial, is cursed with traffic jams and pollution, except in those shopping streets reserved for pedestrians. Puebla is said to have had 365 churches dating from the early colonial period, one for each day of the year. The din from the church bells was so loud that the residents requested that it be toned down a little since they were driven to distraction on Sundays and Feast days. Some of these churches are quite beautiful and should not be missed.

The **tourist office** is at 5 Ote 3, Avenida Juárez behind the Cathedral, next to the Post Office, T460928, closed Saturday and Sunday. Also at 5 Pte, next to Casa de la Cultura, closed weekends. Administrator of Museums, T327699.

Sights

The **Congreso del Estado** in Calle 5 Pte 128, formerly the Consejo de Justicia, near the post office, is a converted 19th-century Moorish-style town house. The tiled entrance and courtyard are very attractive and it had a theatre inside, shown to visitors on request. It is now the seat of the state government. The Patio de los Azulejos should also be visited; it has fabulous tiled façades on the former almshouses for old retired priests of the order of San Felipe Neri. The colours and designs are beautiful. It is at 11 Pte 110, with a tiny entrance on 16 de Septiembre, which is hard to find. Ring the bell on the top right and you may get a guided tour. Also worth visiting is the **Biblioteca Palafoxiana**, or the library of Bishop Palafox, in the Casa de la Cultura, 5 Ote 5, opposite the Cathedral; it has 46,000 antique volumes. It is in a colonial building with a large courtyard which also houses paintings and art exhibitions. ■ *Open 1000*. Next door at 5 Ote 9 is another attractive building, the **Tribunal Superior de Justicia**, built in 1762; you may go in the courtyard.

The Plaza y Mercado **El Parián** is between Avenida 2 y 4 Ote and Avenida 6 y 8 Norte. On Calle 8 Norte between Avenida 6 Ote and Avenida 4 Ote there are many small shops selling paintings. The area is also notable for onyx souvenir shops. Onyx figures and chess sets are attractive and cheaper than elsewhere, but the *poblanos* are hard bargainers. In the adjoining Barrio del Artista the artists' studios are near to *Hotel Latino*. Live music and refreshments at small *Café del Artista*, Calle 8 Nte y Avenida 6 Ote. Just south at Calle 8 Norte 408 is the *Café Galería Amparo*, which serves light food. The University Arts Centre offers folk dances at various times, look for posters or enquire direct. ■ *free*.

The very tiny glass animal figures make an attractive buy.

Also worth seeing are the church and monastery of **El Carmen**, with its strange façade and beautiful tile work. The **Teatro Principal** (1550), Avenida 8 Ote y Calle 6 Nte, is possibly the oldest in the Americas although it was badly damaged by fire in 1902 and had to be rebuilt. The 17th-century **Academia de**

Around Mexico City

● ●

🐾 China Poblana

This mythical figure, a Chinese princess captured by pirates and abducted to Mexico, is said to have taken to Christianity and good works; her colourful *style of dressing has now become the regional costume; positively dazzling with flowered reds and greens and worn with a strong sparkle of bright beads.*

● ●

las Bellas Artes has a grand staircase and an exhibition of Mexican colonial painting. The Jesuit church of **La Compañía** on Avenida Don Juan de Palafox y Mendoza y 4 Sur, has a plaque in the sacristy showing where China Poblana is said to be buried. Also worth visiting is the house of **Aquiles Serdán** at 6 Ote 206, a leader of the Revolution, preserved as it was during his lifetime. It houses the **Museo de la Revolución Mexicana.** ■ *1000-1630, US$1.* The tiled façade of the **Casa de los Muñecos**, 2 Norte 1, corner of the main square, is famous for its caricatures in tiles of the enemies of the 18th-century builder. Inside, in the **Museo Universitario**, some rooms contain old physics instruments, old seismographs, cameras, telescopes, another has stuffed animals, but most rooms contain religious paintings from the 17th and 18th centuries. ■ *US$1.* Avenida Reforma has many fine buildings, for example No 141, *Hotel Alameda*, which is tiled inside and out. The **Palacio Municipal** is on the north side of the Zócalo. To the right of the entrance is the **Biblioteca del Palacio** (opened 1996) with some tourist information and books on the city. To the left is the **Teatro de la Ciudad**, opened 1995, where music and drama are performed. There is also an art gallery in the same building.

The **Casa del Dean**, 16 de Septiembre y 7 Pte, was built in 1580. The walls of the two remaining rooms are covered with 400-year-old murals in vegetable and mineral dyes, which were discovered in 1953 under layers of wallpaper and paint. After President Miguel de la Madrid visited in 1984, the house, previously used as a cinema, was taken over by the government and opened to the public. The murals were inspired by the poems of the Italian poet and humanist, Petrarch, and are believed to have been painted by Indians under the direction of the Dean, Don Tomás de la Plaza, whose house it was. The murals

Around Mexico City

Puebla centre

N
Not to scale

contain a mixture of classical Greek, pagan (Indian) and Christian themes. About 40 percent have been restored. ■ *US$1 plus tip for the guide if wanted. The current guide, Mariano Díaz, has been recommended.* **NB** Since the earthquake of June 1999, the Casa de Dean is closed and some of the churches are under repair. It is to be hoped that the repairs will have been completed by the time this handbook is published.

On the central arcaded plaza is a fine **Cathedral**, one of the most beautiful and interesting anywhere, notable for its marble floors, onyx and marble statuary and gold-leaf decoration. There are statues flanking the altar which are said to be of an English king and a Scottish queen. The bell tower gives a grand view of the city and snow-capped volcanoes. ■*1030-1230.* In November 1999 it was not permitted to climb the bell tower.

Churches
There are 60 churches in all, many of their domes shining with the glazed tiles for which the city is famous

In the **Capilla del Rosario** of the **Church of Santo Domingo** (1596-1659), 5 de Mayo 407, the baroque displays a beauty of style and prodigality of form which served as an exemplar and inspiration for all later baroque in Mexico. The chapel has very detailed gold leaf all over it inside. The altar of the main church is also decorated with gold leaf with four levels from floor to ceiling of life-size statues of religious figures. There is a strong Indian flavour in Puebla's baroque; this can be seen in the churches of Tonantzintla and Acatepec (see below); it is not so evident, but it is still there, in the opulent decorative work in the Cathedral. Beyond the church, up towards the Fuerte Loreto (see below), there is a spectacular view of the volcanoes.

Other places well worth visiting are the churches of **San Cristóbal** (1687), 4 Norte y 6 Ote, with modern churrigueresque towers and Tonantzintla-like plasterwork inside as well as the 18th-century **San José**, 2 Norte y 18 Ote, with attractive tiled façade and decorated walls around the main doors and

Around Mexico City

Puebla

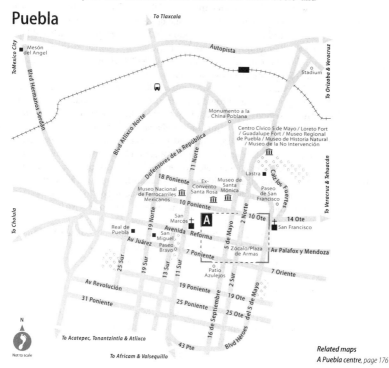

Related maps
A Puebla centre, page 176

beautiful altarpieces inside. One of the most famous and oldest local churches is **San Francisco** at 14 Ote 1009, with a glorious tiled façade and a mummified saint in its side chapel; see also the pearl divers' chapel, given by the poor divers of Veracruz; the church thought it too great a sacrifice but the divers insisted. Since then they believe diving has not claimed a life. The **Capilla de Dolores**, the other side of Boulevard 5 de Mayo from San Francisco, is small but elaborately decorated. **Santa Catalina**, 3 Norte with 2 Pte, has beautiful altarpieces; **Nuestra Señora de la Luz**, 14 Norte and 2 Ote, has a good tiled façade and so has **San Marcos** at Av Reforma and 9 Norte. The Maronite church of **Belén** on 7 Nte and 4 Pte has a lovely old tiled façade and a beautifully tiled interior. The church **La Puerta del Cielo** at the top of the Cerro de San Juan in Colonia La Paz, is modern but in classical style, with over 80 figures of angels inside.

Museums The **Museo de Artesanías del Estado** in the ex-Convento de Santa Rosa (3 Norte 1203) has a priceless collection of 16th-century Talavera tiles on the walls and ceilings of its kitchen, well worth a visit. It was here that the nuns invented the famous *mole poblano*. The museum has a good display of the many crafts produced in the State of Puebla. ■ *Tue-Sun, 1000-1630.*

The fragile-looking and extravagantly ornamented **Casa del Alfeñique** (Sugar Candy House), Av 4 Ote 418, a few blocks from the Cathedral is worth seeing, now the Museo Regional del Estado. ■ *US$0.40.*

Museo Bello, Av 3 Pte 302, is the house of the collector and connoisseur Bello who died in 1938. It has good displays of Chinese porcelain and Talavera pottery and is beautifully furnished. ■ *US$1.10, free Tue and Sun, guided tours, closed Mon.* **Museo de Santa Mónica**, 18 Pte 103, is housed in a former convent where generations of nuns hid after the reform laws of 1857 made the convent illegal. This is where the nuns invented *chiles en nogada.* ■ *1000-1800, closed Mon.* **Museo Amparo**, 2 Sur 708, esquina 9 Ote, has an excellent anthropological exhibition with one of the best pre-Hispanic collections in Mexico and audiovisual explanations in Spanish, English, French and Japanese (take your own headphones, or hire them). Colonial art and furniture is on show upstairs. Recommended. ■ *1000-1800, closed Tue, free guided tour 1200 Sun, US$2, students half price.*

The **Cinco de Mayo Civic Centre**, with a stark statue of Benito Juárez, is, among other things, a regional centre of arts, crafts and folklore. It is near the **Museo Regional de Puebla**, which has magnificent collections but little information. ■ *1000-1700.* Also nearby is the **Museo de Historia Natural**, auditorium, planetarium, fairgrounds and an open-air theatre. In the same area, the forts of Guadalupe and Loreto were the scene of the Battle of Puebla, in which 2,000 Mexican troops defeated Maximilian's 6,000 European troops on 5 May 1862 (although the French returned victorious 10 days later). Hence the reason why 5 May is a holiday in Mexico.Inside the **Fuerte Loreto**, which has views of the city (and of its pollution), is a small museum, **Museo de la No Intervención**, depicting the battle of 1862. ■ *1000-1700, closed Mon, US$1.30.*

For railway enthusiasts there is an outdoor museum, **Museo Nacional de los Ferrocarriles Mexicanos**, displaying old engines and wagons at 11 Norte, between 10 y 14 Pte, in the old Puebla railway station known as El Mexicano.

Excursions

On the Prolongación Av 11 Sur is **Balneario Agua Azul**, in the suburbs, a complex with sulphur springs, playing fields, amusement park etc, popular with families. ■ *Daily 0600-1800. US$3.25, children US$2.25, T431330. Bus from centre, Route 1 on 11 Sur.* Fifteen kilometres south of Puebla lies **Lago**

Valsequillos, with *Africam*, a zoo of free-roaming African animals whose enclosures are nevertheless a bit cramped and uncomfortable. ■ *Daily 1000-1700, US$4.50, children US$4, T358932. Several daily Estrella Roja buses from bus station, US$2.40, round trip. Information from 11 Ote, T460888.* A good one-day excursion is a round trip Puebla-Cacaxtla-Tlaxcala-Tizatlán-Puebla. There is a Volkswagen factory a few kilometres from town. ■ *From 1100, book ahead for guided tours, buses leave from terminal marked VW.*

Essentials

L *Camino Real*, 7 Pte 105, T290909, 91-800-90123, F328993. In ex-Convento de la Concepción, built 1593, beautifully restored, all rooms are different, quiet, bar, restaurant, room service, boutiques, dry cleaning. **AL** *Del Alba*, Blvd Hermanos Serdán 141, T486055. Swimming pool, gardens, Spanish restaurant. **AL** *Mesón del Molino*, Calz del Bosque 10, Col San José del Puente, T305331, 91-800-22612, F305519. Rooms with 2 double beds, some have bathtubs, cable TV, restaurant/bar, small covered pool, chapel with Mass 1300 Sun. **AL** *Real de Puebla* (Best Western), 5 Pte 2522, T489600, F489850. Helpful staff, restaurant open until 2300. **AL-A** *Condado Plaza*, Privada 6B Sur 3106, esq 31 Ote, Zona Dorada, T372733, 91-800-22456, F379305. Cable TV, rooms have modems for computer hook-up, convention halls for 40-300 people. **A** *Del Portal*, Portal Morelos 205, T460211, F323194. Very good, but ask for room away from Zócalo side (noisy), restored colonial, plain rooms, TV, phone, parking across the street. **A** *Lastra*, Calz de Los Fuertes 2633, T359755. Restaurant, pool, games room. **A** *Palacio San Leonardo*, 2 Ote No 211, T460555, F421176. Modern rooms but wonderful colonial entrance hall with adjoining bar/restaurant. **A-C** *Aristos*, Av Reforma 533, esq 7 Sur, T320565, 320529. Good facilities in rooms and bathrooms, gym with sauna, pool, attractive public areas, restaurant, piano bar, cheaper rates at weekends.

B *Posada San Pedro*, 2 Pte 202, T465077, 91-800-22808, F465376. Attractive restaurant, parking. **B-C** *Royalty*, Portal Hidalgo 8, T424740, F424740 ext 113. Pleasant, central, quiet, restaurant good but expensive and service slow, tables outside under the portales where a marimba band sometimes plays. **C** *Cabrera*, 10 Ote 6, T425099, 328525. With shower and phone, clean, quiet in interior rooms, don't be put off by outward appearance of hardware store, no restaurant. **C** *Colonial*, 4 Sur 105, T464199. Across pedestrian street from La Compañía church, old-fashioned and charming, very friendly, colonial style, restaurant, accepts Amex, ask for back room, with bath, TV and phone. **C** *Gilfer*, 2 Ote No 11, T460611, F423485. Attractive, modern building, large rooms, reasonable restaurant, excellent service; next door is **B-C** *Palace*, 2 Ote No 13, T322430, F425599. Price depends on number and size of beds, attractive, modern lobby, *cafetería*, satellite TV, phones, 60 rooms. **C** *Granada*, Blvd de la Pedrera 2303, T320966, F320424. Very close to bus terminal, bus to centre leaves from front door, quiet, comfortable, restaurant, room service, TV in rooms. Also close to the bus terminal **C** *Terminal*, Blvd Carmen Serdán 5101. T205833, F2001275. Modern, on busy main thoroughfare. Even if staying just a night and with luggage, it is still cheaper to take taxis to and from a budget hotel in the centre. **C** *Imperial*, 4 Ote 212, T463825. Good-sized plain rooms with TV and phones, shower, clean, some rooms noisy, laundry, restaurant, gym, parking, 30% discount offered to *Handbook* owners, good value.

D *Alameda*, Reforma 141, close to the Zócalo, T420882. Most rooms windowless, parking, TV, phone, bath, very clean, friendly, good value. **D** *Ritz*, 2 Norte 207 y 4 Ote, T324457, 2 blocks from Zócalo. Reasonable, drab front rooms with balcony quieter, hot water. **D** *San Miguel*, 3 Pte 721, T424860. Carpeted rooms, TV, phone. **D** *Virrey de Mendoza*, Reforma 538, T423903. Old colonial house plain, fairly basic rooms, high ceilings, TV, bath, beautiful wooden staircase. **D-E** *Santander*, 5 Pte 111, T463175,

Sleeping
■ *on maps*
Price codes:
see inside front cover

Around Mexico City

F425792, near Cathedral. Colonial façade, recently renovated, hot showers, clean, simple, big bright rooms towards street, TV, enclosed parking. Recommended. **D-E** *Teresita*, 3 Pte 309, T327072. Small modern rooms, with bath ('comedy showers'), hot water, friendly. **E** *Casa de Huéspedes Los Angeles*, Calle 4 Norte 9. Basic, communal bathrooms, irregular hot water, *comedor*, central. **E** *Embajadores*, 5 de Mayo 603, T322637, 2 blocks from Zócalo. Without bath, limited water and insalubrious. Other cheap places on pedestrian mall on this street **E** *Latino*, Calle 6 Norte 8, T322325, next to Barrio del Artista, basic. **E** *Victoria*, near Zócalo, 3 Pte 306, T328992. Clean, quiet, hot showers. Recommended. **E-F** *Avenida*, 5 Pte 336 between 5 and 3 Sur, 2 blocks from Zócalo. Price depends on number of beds and shared or private bathroom, airy rooms (except those without windows), quiet, friendly, clean, hot water morning and evening, drinking water. Recommended. Several basic *casas de huéspedes*, near markets, very cheap hotel (**F**), 2 blocks south of train station, *20 de Noviembre*. Big rooms, no water 2000 to 0700, clean, bus to town.

Motels LL-AL *Mesón del Angel* (Swiss-run), Hermanos Serdán 807, T243000, F242227, near 1st Puebla interchange on Mexico-Puebla motorway. Possibly best in town, but far from the centre, 192 rooms, a/c, cable TV, conference and banqueting facilities, 2 restaurants, bar, 2 pools, tennis. **B-D** *Panamerican*, Reforma 2114, T485466. Restaurant, no bar, parking. Recommended.

Camping Possible on the extensive university grounds about 8 km south of centre.

Eating **Local specialities** *Mole poblano* chicken or turkey with sauce of chiles, spices, nuts, chocolate and coconut); best at *La Poblanita*, 10 Norte 1404-B, and *Fonda Santa Clara*, 3 Pte 307. Good for local specialities, very popular, often crowded, very good and expensive, second larger location with parking a couple of blocks west on 3 Pte. *Mixiote* is *borrego* (lamb) with chile, wrapped in paper with hot sauce. *Chiles en Nogada* are *poblano chiles* stuffed with minced meat and almonds and topped with a sweet cream sauce made with ground nuts, then topped with pomegranate seeds, best in Jul-Sep, delicious. Calle 6 Ote specializes in shops selling *dulces* (sweets) and *camotes* (candied sweet potatoes). *Nieves*, drinks of alcohol, fruit and milk, are worth trying as are the excellent *empanadas* and *quesadillas*.

The green, white and red colours of chiles en nogada are supposed to represent the Mexican flag

El Vasco, Portal Benito Juárez 105, on Zócalo. Slow, most dishes US$3, US$6 for *plato mexicano*. Several others to choose from on Zócalo, eg *La Princesa*, Portal Juárez 101. Good variety and good prices, breakfast US$2-3, *comida corrida* US$3. *Mac's*. US-style diner, good variety, cheap *comidas* at *Hermilo Nevados*, 2 Ote 408, good value. Recommended. Also *Munich*, 3 Pte y 5 Sur. Many cheap places near main square with menus prominently displayed. *Cafetería La Vaca Negra*, Reforma 106, just off Zócalo. Modern, attractive, part of a chain, meals US$2-7. *Hotel Royalty*, Portal Hidalgo 8. Nice restaurant with meals around US$6-7, *platillos poblanos*, tables under the portales, marimba band plays sometimes. *Mesón Sacristía de la Compañía*, 6 Sur 304, T423554/324513. In the old sacristy, marvellous patio, lots of plants, very cosy. Reasonable prices. *Bajo el Cielo de Jalisco*, Calle 3 sur 507. Recommended. *Mercado El Alto*, in the San Francisco quarter. Beautiful market covered with *azulejos*, with good local cuisine. Breakfast and lunch, 8 different menus. *Woolworth's*, corner of 2 Pte and 5 de Playo, 1½ blocks from northwest corner of Plaza Mayor, 0800-2200. Good range of cheap, reasonable meals and some expensive dishes. *El Vegetariano*, 3 Pte 525 (near *Hotel San Agustín*). Good, serves breakfast. Recommended. *Super-Soya*, 5 de Mayo. Good for fruit salads and juices. Several other good places for *comidas corridas* on 5 de Mayo. *Librería Cafetería Teorema*, Reforma 540, esq 7 Norte. Café, books and art, live music at night, good coffee and snacks, pastries, *platillos mexicanos*. Recommended. *La Gardenia*, Palafox 416. Local dishes, a bit cramped but very good quality, selection and value. Recommended. Several other reasonably priced places nearby. *Cafetería Tres Gallos*, 4 Pte 110. Good coffee and pastries. *Café Britannia*, Reforma 528. Cheap. Recommended. *Jugos y Licuados*, 3 Norte 412. Recommended. *Tony's Tacos*, 3 Nte and Reforma. Quick and very cheap. *La Super Torta de Puebla*, on 3 Pte. Good sandwich bar. *Tepoznieves*, 3 Pte 150 esq 3 Sur. Rustic Mexican décor, serves all varieties of tropical fruit ice cream and sherbet. *La Pasita*, 5 Ote between 2 y 4 Sur, in front of Plaza de los Sapos. The oldest bar in Puebla, sells a drink by the same name, a local speciality. Recommended. *Al Kalifa*, 2 Sur between 15 y 17 Ote. Cheap *tacos*, very good *Taco Arabe*. Recommended.

Festivals *Feria* in **mid-Apr** for 2 weeks. The *Fiesta Palafoxiana* starts on the last Fri in **Sep** until **mid-Nov** for 9 weekends of dancing, music, theatre, exhibitions, etc; some free performances.

Shopping 5 de Mayo is a pedestrian street closed to traffic from the Zócalo to Av 10. The entire block containing the Capilla del Rosario/Templo de Santo Domingo in the southeast corner has been made into a shopping mall (opened 1994), called the Centro Comercial La Victoria after the old La Victoria market. The old market building still exists. Built in 1913, it is a long, narrow building on the 3 Norte side of the mall and on its 2nd floor are many places to eat. The mall is a metal structure, painted green with glass panes. It houses department stores, boutiques and restaurants. **Craft shop** sponsored by the authorities: *Tienda Convento Santa Rosa*, Calle 3 Norte 1203, T28904. The famous Puebla Talavera tiles may be purchased from factories outside Puebla, or from *Taller Uriarte*, Av 4 Pte 911 (spectacular building, tours Mon-Fri 1000-1200, 1700, Sat 1000-1300, morning best). Recommended. *Talavera de la Reyna*, Camino a la Carcaña 2413, Recta a Cholula, T/F845821. Recommended (also in *Hotel Mesón del Angel*); *Centro de Talavera*, Calle 6 Ote 11; *D Aguilar*, 40 Pte 106, opposite Convento de Santa Mónica, and *Casa Rugerio*, 18 Pte 111; *Margarita Guevara*, 20 Pte 30. Mercado Venustiano Carranza, on 11 Nte y 5 Norte, good for *mole*. **Bookshop**: *Librería Británica*, Calle 25 Pte 1705-B, T408549, 374705.

    Bicycle shops There are several shops in 7 Norte, north of 4 Pte. International spare parts.

Sports *Las Termas*, 5 de Mayo 2810, T329562, gay bath house, entry US$2.50, steambaths, sauna, gym; *Lidromasaje*, beer and soft drinks.

Tour operators *American Express*, Centro Comercial Plaza Dorada 2, Héroes 5 de Mayo, locales 21 y 22, T375558, F374221, open Mon-Fri 0900-1800, Sat 0900-1300.

Transport **Local Taxis**: radio taxi service, *Radio Omega*, T406299/406369/406371. New Chevrolet cars, 24-hr service, will deliver packages or pick up food or medicine and deliver it to your hotel.

Long distance Air: Hermanos Serdán airport (PBC) has flights to Guadalajara, León, Mexico City, Monterrey and Tijuana.

Trains: T201664 for information. Micro bus No 1 on Sur 9 goes to station, US$0.35. Trains to **Oaxaca** (2nd class), leave Puebla 0640, 12 hrs, no advance booking, returns from Oaxaca at 0720, superb scenery, crowded. Highly recommended. The line weaves through cactus-laden gorges recalling the Wild West. On clear days one gets a good view of Popocatépetl. There are many food sellers on train. Check that the trains are still running before planning your journey; there have been many cancellations since privatization.

Station is a long way from centre, very run down, in questionable neighbourhood

Buses: new, huge CAPU bus terminal for all buses north of city. From the centre to the terminal, take any form of transport marked 'CAPU', many *colectivos* and buses (route 12) on Av 9 Norte, fare US$1.50 per person flat rate. To the centre from the terminal take *combi* No 14, US$0.30, which stops at 11 Norte and Reforma at Paseo de Bravo (make sure it's a No 14 'directo', there is a No 14 which goes to the suburbs). To reach the terminal, take bus 37 or 21 at Av Camacho. The departure terminal has a *casa de cambio* (open 0900-1830), a Banca Serfín (Mon-Fri) with a 24-hr ATM compatible with Cirrus and Plus networks, *dulcería*, gift and craft shop, newsagent, 24-hr pharmacy, *pastelería*, *cafetería*, *caseta* for long-distance phone calls, tourist information booth, booth selling taxi tickets (US$1.75 to the centre), next to it is a chart showing local bus routes, bathrooms (2 pesos), luggage store (1 peso per hour per bag), open 0700-2230. The arrivals terminal has some shops including small grocery, free bathrooms, long-distance pay phones and taxi ticket booth (but you have to take ramp to the departure terminal to get the taxi). Companies **Autobuses de Oriente (ADO)**, T497144. Mercedes Benz buses, 1st class and 'GL' plus service; **Oro**, T497775, 497177, *gran turismo* or 1st class service; **UNO**, T304014, luxury service, accept Amex; **Estrella Roja**, T497099, 2nd class,1st class and *plus* service; **Cristóbal Colón**, T497144 ext 2860, plus service; **Estrella Blanca**, T497561, 497433, 1st class, *plus* service and Elite; **Autobuses Unidos (AU)**, T497366, 497405, 497967, all 2nd class without toilets.

To **Mexico City**, ADO to TAPO (eastern) terminal at 0445, 0530, then every 20 mins from 0600 to 2145, US$5; to Terminal del Sur every hour from 0635 to 2135, US$5; to Terminal del Norte every 20-40 mins from 0520-2150, US$5, *Estrella Roja* to Mexico City airport every hour from 0300 to 2000, US$7, 2 hrs. To Mexico City 2nd class every 10 mins, US$4, 3 stops, 1st class, several a day US$5, *plus* service US$5.50; *AU*, every 12 mins from 0510 to 2300. To **Tehuacán** direct *ADO* every 30-45 mins from 0600-2100, US$4. To **Oaxaca**, all take new *autopista*, 4 hrs; *ADO* 'GL' *plus* service, 2 daily, US$28.25, 1st class, 5 daily, US$12; *UNO* at 1800, US$18; *AU*, 2nd class. To **Xalapa**, *ADO* 'GL' *plus* service at 0805 and 1700, US$7, 1st class, 8 a day, US$6, 4 hrs; *AU*, 2nd class. To **Villahermosa**, *ADO* 'GL' plus service via autopista, 2200, US$30, 1st class, 1900, 2145, US$25.50; *UNO* at 2100, US$41.25, 8 hrs. To **Reynosa**, *ADO* at 1155, US$31.60. To **Chetumal**, *ADO*, 1145, US$42. To **Mérida**, *ADO*, 2105, US$44. To **Tuxtla Gutiérrez**, *ADO*, 2010, US$30; *UNO*, 2215, US$46, 14 hrs. To **Tapachula**, *UNO*, 1830, US$53, 16 hrs; *Cristóbal Colón*, *plus* service, 2115, US$37.50. To **San Cristóbal de las Casas**, *Cristóbal Colón*, *plus* service, 1715, 1845, 2215, US$36. To **Cuernavaca**, *Oro*, *gran turismo* service, 0700, 1100, 1500, 1900, US$5, 1st class hourly 0600-2000, US$4, 2 stops. To **Nuevo Laredo**, *Estrella Blanca*, 1st class, 1000, US$43. To **Monterrey**, *Estrella Blanca*, 1st class, 1030, US$34.50. To **Matamoros**, *Estrella Blanca*, 1st class, 1330, US$31.50. To **Ciudad Victoria**, *Estrella Blanca*, 1st class, 1030, US$25. To **Acapulco**, *Estrella Blanca*, *plus* service, 2200, US$23.25, 1st class, 1030, 1230, 2130, 2230, 2300, US$20.75. To **Tijuana**, *Estrella Blanca* Elite service, 1400, bypassing Mexico City, goes via Guadalajara (US$31), Tepic, Mazatlán, Nogales (US$85.75) and Tijuana (US$87.25).

Directory
For website addresses, see page 32

Airline offices *Aero California*, Blvd Atlixco 2703, locales B y C, Col Nueva Antequera, T304855. *AeroMéxico*, T91-80090999, 320013/4, Av Juárez 1514, Col La Paz, flight connections at Monterrey. *Aeromar*, at airport, T329633, 329644, 91-80070429. *Mexicana*, Av Juárez 2312, between Calle 23 Sur and 25 Sur, T91-80050220, 485600. *Lufthansa* and *LanChile*, at Av Juárez 2916, Col La Paz, T484400, 301109.

Banks *Bancomer*, 3 Pte 116, changes TCs 0930-1300, good rates. On the Zócalo are *Banco Santander Mexicano*; *Banco Inverlat* at Portal Benito Juárez 109, changes money 0900-1400; and a *casa de cambio* at Portal Hidalgo 6 next to *Hotel Royalty*. On Av Reforma are: *Banamex*, No 135, ATMs accept Cirrus network cards; *Bancomer*, No 113, ATMs accept Visa and Plus network cards; *Banco Bital*, across the street, ATMs accept Plus and Cirrus network cards. All available 24 hrs.

Communications Internet: Colonial building with red/orange bricks and blue and white tiles, also has email service for US$3 per ½ hr; at the *Escuela Sandoval*, on 5 Ote, you can email for US$2 per hr. *Soluciones Alternativas*, Calle 4 Norte 7, 101, 1st flr, no sign, email service US$2 per hr. At the *BUAP University*, Av San Claudio esq 22 Sur, T444404, open Mon-Fri 0700-2100, Sat, Sun 0800-1800, 48PCs, but slow, US$2.50 per hr. **Post Office**: 5 Ote between 16 de Septiembre and 2 Sur, open Mon-Fri, 0800-2000.

Laundry In large commercial centre on Av 21 Pte and Calle 5 Sur, US$4 wash and dry, 3 hrs. Another on 9 Nte, between 2 and 4 Pte, US$2.80 for good service wash.

Medical services Dentist: *Dr A Bustos*, Clínica de Especialidades Dentales, 2 Pte 105-8, T324412, excellent service, recommended. **Doctors**: *Dr Miguel Benítez Cortázar*, 11 Pte 1314, T420556, US$15 per consultation. *Dr Cuauhtémoc Romero López*, same address and phone. **Hospitals**: *Beneficiencia Española*, 19 Norte 1001, T320500. *Betania*, 11 Ote 1826, T358655. *UPAEP*, 5 Pte 715, T466099, F325921, outpatients T328913, 323641. The cheapest is *Universitario de Puebla*, 25 Pte y 13 Sur, T431377, where an outpatient consultation is US$5.

Cholula

This small somnolent town, with the Universidad de las Américas, is one of the strangest-looking in all Mexico. When Cortés arrived, this was a holy centre with 100,000 inhabitants and 400 shrines, or *teocallis*, grouped round the great pyramid of Quetzalcoatl. In its day it was as influential as Teotihuacán. There used to be a series of pyramids built one atop another. When razing them, Cortés vowed to build a chapel for each of the *teocallis* destroyed, but in fact there are no more than about 70.

Phone code: 22
Colour map 3, grid B6
Population: 20,000

Around Mexico City

The excavated pyramid (see box) has 8 km of tunnels and some recently discovered frescoes inside, but only 1 km of tunnel is open to the public, which gives an idea of superimposition (the frescoes are not open to the public). The museum near the tunnel entrance has a copy of the frescoes. ■ *1000-1700, US$2 on weekdays, free on Sun and holidays, guides charge US$6.50, recommended as there are no signs inside (some guides speak English).* From Zócalo follow Avenida Morelos and cross the railway. The 16th-century chapel of **Los Remedios** on top of it gives a fine view. The Franciscan fortress church of **San Gabriel** (1552) is in the plaza. ■ *0600-1200, 1600-1900, Sun 0600-1900.* Next to it is the **Capilla Real**, which has 49 domes. ■ *1000-1200, 1530-1800, Sun 0900-1800.*

Sights

See the Indian statuary and stucco work of the 16th-century church of Santa María de Tonantzintla, or 'the place of our venerable mother', in the neighbouring village of **Tonantzintla**; the church is one of the most beautiful in Mexico. ■ *1000-1800 daily.* It may be reached by paved road from San Francisco **Acatepec**, another village with a beautiful, less ornate 16th-century church, which was recently damaged by fire, although the façade of tiles is still intact.   *Supposedly open 0900-1800 daily, but not always so – key is held by José Ascac, ask for his shop.* These two tiny churches are exquisite and should not be missed; they are resplendent with Poblano tiles and their interiors are a riot of Indian stucco-work and carving. Best light for photography after 1500. Photography *inside* the churches is frowned upon.

Excursions
Some visitors note that regular visiting hours are not strictly observed at Cholula, Acatepec, Tonantzintla and Huejotzingo

One can visit Tonantzintla and Acatepec from Cholula main square with a 'peso-taxi'. Or one can take a combi from Cholula to Acatepec or to Tonantzintla (marked Chilipo or Chipanco, ask which combi goes to the church you want) for US$0.55 from junction of Avenue 5 and Avenue Miguel Alemán. This is two blocks from Zócalo, which is three blocks from tourist office. You can walk the 1 km to the other church, and then take a bus or combi back to Cholula or Puebla. Acatepec from CAPU in Puebla, US$0.45, 30 minutes, bus stops outside the church. The villages are off Highway 190 *en route* from Puebla to Izúcar de Matamoros.

🖙 Tlachihualtepetl-*The man-made mountain of Cholula*

As in other areas of Mexico, the pre-Hispanic pyramid at Cholula is really a series of structures build one on top of the other. Long before the arrival of the Spaniards, this pyramid was known to the people of the area as Tlachihualtepetl, or Mountain Made by Man. Cholula was a sacred city where new regional lords came to be enthroned and priests ordained. On his arrival, Bernal Díaz del Castillo, who accompanied Cortés on the conquest of Mexico and later wrote about it, was astonished at the number of temples to be found in the city. However, this is scarcely surprising as each ward was inhabited by a specific ethnic group which paid homage to its specific tribal god and to whom a temple was dedicated.

The first structure to form the heart of Tlachihualtepetl was erected early in the Christian era; outer layers were superimposed at intervals until sometime in the eighth century, when it took its present form. About 30 years ago excavations at the south of the pyramid revealed a large central plaza bordered by structural bases and monumental stepped terraces. Investigations of the six layers lying beneath these structures revealed that some of the adobe or stucco-surfaced walls were decorated with tablero panel murals of either alternating slanted bands of red, green or yellow, or intertwining bands representing feathers interspersed with starfish-like designs (similar symbols have been found at Teotihuacán). At the lowest of these levels (approximately 7 m below the uppermost structures) a 65m-long structure runs north-south, with an adobe and rough-stone façade facing east to the plaza. Ceramics classified as Cholula II, contemporary with those of Teotihuacán II (200-300 AD) were found, but of even greater interest were the paintings at this level. For their study, a tunnel, 1.5m wide and as high as the murals, was opened along the length of the building. The staircase and base of the superimposed structure had destroyed the middle section of the mural, so that the remaining portions now consist of four panels.

Between Acatepec and Puebla is the superb church of **Tlaxcalantzingo**, with an extravagantly tiled façade, domes and tower. It is worth climbing up on the roof for photographs.

Huejotzingo, Km 106, has the second-oldest church and monastery in Mexico, which was built in 1529 and is now a museum. Market is held on Saturday and Tuesday. There is a dramatic carnival on Shrove Tuesday, portraying the story of Agustín Lorenzo, a famous local bandit. **D** *Hotel Colonial*. Secure but poor value.

Sleeping **B** *Villas Arqueológicas*, 2 Pte 501, T471966, F471508. Behind pyramid, affiliated to *Club Med*. Heated pool, pleasant garden, tennis, French restaurant, rooms have heating, TV, phone, English and French spoken. **C** *Cali Quetzalcoatl*, on Zócalo, Portal Guerrero 11, T474199. Clean. Good restaurant. **C** *Posada Real*, 5 de Mayo 1400, at end of highway from Puebla, 3 blocks from pyramid, T476677. **C-D** *Campestre Los Sauces*, Km 122, Carretera Federal Puebla-Cholula, T471011. Pool, tennis, restaurant/bar, gardens, TV and phone in rooms. **D** *Reforma*, near main square. **D** *Super Motel* on the road from Puebla as you enter town. Each room with private garage, very secure. **E** *Hotel de las Américas*, 14 Ote 6, T470991. Near pyramid, actually a motel, modern with rooms off galleries round paved courtyard (car park), small restaurant, clean, good value. **E** *Trailer Park Las Américas*, 30 Ote 602. Hot showers, secure, as are the furnished apartments. *Motel de la Herradura*, Carretera Federal, T470100. Will not quote rates by phone, close to *Los Sauces*, satellite TV, phones, hot water.

Eating *Restaurant Choloyan*, also handicrafts, Av Morelos. Good, clean, friendly. *Pasta e Pizza*, Portal Guerrero 9B, centre. Try *licuados* at market stalls, fruit and milk and 1 or 2

The discovery of the Cholula murals presented art historians with a wonderful opportunity to readjust their ideas on pre-Hispanic art, dealing as they do with a mainly human activity, rather than the exploits of the gods. Its closest rival would be the mural of Tlalocan at Teotihuacán, depicting humans engaged in a number of activities, some of which appear to be pleasurable, hence the title given to it, which means the Place of Tlaloc, or Heaven. At Cholula, however, the entire mural is devoted to the representation of many human beings in various stages of inebriation, while others, of smaller size to illustrate their lower status, carry huge jars or serve pulque to the imbibers. The drinkers dressed up for the occasion. Many of them wear masks that identify them with a specific animal or bird. This probably related them to specific ethnic groups or settlements. Although almost nude, some of the drinkers wear elaborate headdresses made of fine cotton, which implies that they were high in the social hierarchy of Cholula. The whole ethos of the paintings is one of debauchery and drunkenness. It was probably organized to celebrate planting or harvest.

Of considerable interest is the fact that in the vicinity of Tlachihualtepetl are several villages, San Grabiel Ometusco, San Miguel Papaxtla, Tlilhuacan and Quatlapanca, whose names relate them to specific pulque deities, suggesting that these settlements provided the intoxicating drink for the orgy. The location of Tlachhualtepetl is not accidental; it plays an important role in an astronomical alignment that appears to have extended throughout Mesoamerica. The geographical configurations reflect the heavenly configurations. From the summit of Tlachihualtepetl, the eye is drawn to the Paso de Cortés, that gap between the two mountains that were so sacred to the peoples of the area, Popocatépetl and Iztaccíhuatl.

Reproductions of the paintings of the Pulque Drinkers can be seen in the small museum at the base of the pyramid; it is well worth a visit.

eggs as you wish; *mixiote* is a local dish of lamb or goat barbecued in a bag. Pure drinking water sold behind the public baths, cheaper to fill own receptacle, funnel needed.

Buses Frequent 2nd class Estrella Roja buses from **Puebla** to Cholula US$0.35 from 6 Pte y 13 Norte, 9 km on a new road, 20 mins, also 1st and 2nd class Estrella Roja buses from CAPU bus terminal hourly (be ready to get out, only a quick stop in Cholula); from Cholula take a 'Pueblo Centro' bus to the city centre, or a 'Puebla-CAPU' bus for the terminal; *colectivos* to Cholula, US$0.40. From **Mexico City**, leave for Cholula from Terminal del Oriente with Estrella Roja, every 30 mins, US$3, 2½-3 hrs, 2nd class every 20 mins, a very scenic route through steep wooded hills. Good views of volcanoes. **Transport**

Useful services There is a *casa de cambio* on the corner of the main plaza, and a travel agency in the Los Portales complex on the plaza. **Directory**

Tlaxcala

From Texmelucan a side road leads northeast for 24 km to the once quaint old Indian town of Tlaxcala, with its pleasant centre of simple buildings washed in ochre, pink and yellow, and its vast suburbs. It is the capital of the state of the same name whose wealthy ranchers breed fighting bulls, but whose landless peasantry is still poor. The annual fair is held 29 October-15 November each year. The **tourist office** is at Juárez y Landizábal, and has many maps and leaflets, very helpful, no English spoken.

Phone code: 248
Colour map 3, grid B6
Population: 36,000
Altitude: 2,240m

Sights Dating from 1521 the **Church of San Francisco** is the oldest in Mexico, from whose pulpit the first Christian sermon was preached in New Spain (Mexico). Of course, the sermon would have been for the benefit of the Spanish residents; the Indians would have congregated outside at the open chapel. The severe façade of the church conceals a most sumptuous interior; note the cedar and gold, star-spangled ceiling, and the 'No Photos' sign at the door. Almost next door is the **Museo del Estado de Tlaxcala**, with two floors of interesting historical and artistic exhibits. In the Palacio de Gobierno on the main square are the extremely colourful murals (1966, still incomplete) depicting the indigenous story of Tlaxcala, the history of Mexico and of mankind. ■ *0900-1700, US$1*. A huge market takes place every Saturday. **The Museo de Artes y Tradiciones Populares** is a 'living museum' where Otomi Indians demonstrate traditional arts and customs including the sweat bath, cooking, embroidery, weaving and pulque-making. It is highly recommended. *La Fonda del Museo* restaurant is attached (see below). Two rooms are dedicated to exhibits of local crafts such as bell making and plasterwork covered with goldleaf. ■ *Closed Mon, US$0.60.*

Excursions The **Basílica de Ocotlán** (1541), on a hill in the outskirts of Tlaxcala (a stiff 20-minute climb from Juárez via Guribi and Alcocer, but worth it) commands a view of valley and volcano. It was described by Sacheverell Sitwell as 'the most delicious building in the world', but others have been less impressed. Nevertheless, its façade of lozenge-shaped vermilion bricks framing the white stucco portal and surmounted by two white towers with fretted cornices and salomonic pillars is beautiful. The sumptuous golden interior was worked on for 25 years by the Indian Francisco Miguel.

The ruined pyramid of **Xicoténcatl** at San Esteban de Tizatlán, 5 km outside Tlaxcala, has two sacrificial altars with original colour frescoes preserved under glass. The pictures tell the story of the wars with Aztecs and Chichimecs. Amid the archaeological digs at Tizatlán are a splendid 19th-century church and the 16th-century chapel of San Esteban. To get there, take a *colectivo* to Tizatlán from 1 de Mayo y 20 de Noviembre, Tlaxcala; at the main square, you get out when you see a yellow church dome on the left.

Tlaxcala

La Malinche Volcano, 4,461m, takes its name from the Nahuatl, *matlalcueye*, meaning the greenish-blue skirt. It can be reached from Tlaxcala or Puebla; buses from the market beside the old railway station, Tlaxcala 1½ hours, US$1, one at 0800 and others, return 1800. You go to La Malintzin Centro de Vacaciones at the base of the volcano, now closed to the public. The hike to the summit takes four hours, the descent 1½ (take an ice-axe, altitude is a problem). Alternatively, stay at nearby town of Apizaco. There is a reasonable hotel and restaurant next to the roundabout with a locomotive in the centre and safe parking. It is a good day trip from Puebla. Another route is via Canoa (bus from Puebla, US$0.50). It is a long hike to the top, 10 hours return at a good pace; take warm clothes. Be careful not to be caught on the mountain during an extended rainstorm; it is very easy to lose your way. The volcano could be visited on a two-day trip from Puebla; on the first day reaching the foot of the mountain, where it is possible to set up a tent or rent a four-bed *cabaña* (US$20 per night, firewood can be bought at the office, kitchen with no utensils, shower). On the second day you could climb the volcano, six to seven hours at an easy pace, before returning to Puebla.

Sleeping **A** *Posada San Francisco* (Club Med), Plaza de la Constitución 17, T26022, F26818. Lavishly decorated in colonial style, 2 restaurants, good food, secure parking, swimming pool, tennis courts. Highly recommended. **C** *Alifer*, Morelos 11, uphill from plaza, T25678. Safe parking. **C** *Hotel Albergue de la Loma*, Av Guerrero, T20424. **C** *Hotel San Clemente*, Av Independencia, T21989.

Eating *Los Portales*, main square. *Restaurante del Quijote*, Plaza Xicoténcatl. *La Fonda del Museo* (see above). Serves excellent 4-course traditional meals in a lovely setting. Set lunch US$8. *Oscar's*, Av Juárez, near corner of Zitlalpopocatl. Excellent sandwiches and juices. *La Arboleda*, Lira y Ortega, near square. Good. *The Italian Coffee Company*, Plaza de la Constitución. Very good coffee.

Entertainment *The Cine American*, on Blvd G Valle (continuation of Av Juárez) has 2 for the price of 1 on Wed.

Transport **Buses** Tlaxcala's bus station is about a 10 min walk from the centre. Frequent *Flecha Azul* buses from **Puebla**, central bus station (platform 81/82) between 0600 and 2130, 45 mins, US$1.20. To **Cacaxtla** US$0.40.

Directory **Communications** Internet: *Café Internet*, Independencia 21, south of Av Guerrero. **Laundry** *Servi-Klim*, Av Juárez, 1½ blocks from plaza, dry cleaners, will launder but at dry cleaning prices. *Lavandería Acuario*, Alonsa Escalona 17, between Juárez and Lira y Ortega, 3 kg US$3, self-service 4 kg US$1, 0830-2000.

Cacaxtla

A remarkable series of pre-Columbian frescoes are to be seen at the ruins of Cacaxtla near San Miguel del Milagro, between Texmelucan and Tlaxcala. The colours are still sharp and some of the figures are larger than life size. To protect the paintings from the sun and rain, a huge roof has been constructed. An easily accessible visitors' centre has been opened. There is disappointingly little published information on the site, however. In theory there is a 'per picture' charge for photography, but this is not assiduously collected although flash and tripod are strictly prohibited. ■ *Tue-Sun, 1000-1630, US$2 which also includes access to Xochitecatl. From Puebla take a Flecha Azul bus marked 'Nativitas' from C 10 Pte y C 11 Norte to just beyond Nativitas where a sign on the*

Around Mexico City

right points to San Miguel del Milagro and Cacaxtla (US$1). Walk up the hill (or
colectivo US$0.20) to a large sign with its back to you, turn left here for the ruins.

Excavations over the past few decades have uncovered some of the most interesting and complex murals ever found in Mesoamerica. Much fascinating
material for the art historian has been derived from them, not because the
symbolism and iconography is obscure and difficult to understand, but due to
the motifs and symbols incorporating images which stem from several cultural
traditions. War and peace are expressed in two groups of murals at the site,
The Battle painted on the walls of the substructure of Building B, and the Fertility Deities, registered on the walls of the portico of Building A, represented
by the Man-Jaguar and Man-Bird.

Cacaxtla was strategically located to control the trade route between
Teotihuacán and the lowlands gulf which gave access to Tabasco and
Campeche, a factor that determined its growth and assured the presence of an
imagery that evolved far from its immediate environments. It is very likely that
the paintings were executed or commissioned by the ethnic group known as
the Olmeca-Xicallanca, a warrior-merchant nation who had invaded and subjugated the region of the Valley of Puebla-Tlaxcala. The group is believed to
have been composed of Mixteca, Popoloca (both of the otomanque lingustic
group) and Nahua.

The Battle Scene at Cacaxtla, painted with great verve and realism, depicts
the moment when the battle has been fought and won, and the victors decide
the destiny of the vanquished. Although adorning the walls of Cacaxtla, there
is little to indicate that the battle was fought at that site, except that it was posi-
tioned facing the central plaza to convey a very strong message to the peoples
of the area. These invaders were not to be challenged but rather paid the tribute
due to all victors. Believed to come originally from the area of Laguna de
Términos, in which Xicalango is located, the Olmeca-Xicallanca drew on cultural traits from the lowland Maya, especially from the area bordering on the
Usumacinta river.

The artists portrayed the participants of the battle in a highly naturalistic
way, identifying them as two distinct ethnic groups. The vanquished have
physical characteristics that distinguish them from the victors. Their noses are
aquiline and hooked, they show signs of cranium deformation and their eyes
squint. Their hair is dyed red, long and sometimes with a fringe, although
some sport short hair and part of the head is shaved. All except two who are
barefooted wear jaguar feet or blue bird feathers. Most of the vanquished are
practically nude, except for the two principal characters who are richly attired.
Other iconographical elements that distinguish this group are the symbol for
jade, headdresses made from precious feathers of different lengths, mainly
blue but with yellow and red touches forming a sort of helmet with allusions to
various species of birds from the tropical zones. Apart from a square shield and
a blue lance, they have been divested of their weapons; some are seen to be
attempting to remove arrows from wounds.

The two principal participants are set apart from the rest of the subjugated
group. Although wounded or bound, their great dignity remains intact. They
stand, their bodies proudly front-on with legs apart and firmly planted, and
their heads in profile. They are very likely the military and religious representatives of the group who have been identified as Mayoid, that is, although not
completely Maya, they possess strong cultural characteristics that associate
them with that nation.

The second group, who number about 20, are distinguished by the physical
characteristics of the thin nose and almond eyes. In most cases the hair is black

apart from the two principal characters, whose hair is dyed red. Two elements related to this group are of great importance: the objects they carry and the position of their bodies and feet. They are all standing, in four different menacing postures. They carry lances, dart-throwers, and round shields decorated with feathers. The iconography associated with this group tends to emphasize feline-cult affiliation.

The battle, then, was between two distinct ethnic groups, one with bird affiliations, the other linked to the jaguar, the latter being victorious. They are attired simply in animal skins, mainly jaguar. They are adept at war and their physical characteristics are close those of the Central Highlands. There are sufficient iconographical elements associated with the Mayoid group to indicate their destiny, that they were to be sacrificed.

Although the battle was clearly a conflict that involved two distinct ethnic groups, there are some hieroglyphs affiliated to three different regions of Mesoamerica; the Nahua of the Central Highlands, the Mixteca tradition and that of Xochicalco. However, it has been pointed out that the emphasis is overwhelmingly in favour of the Nahua contingent, therefore the glyphs were addressed to that group. This battle ending in the submission of the Mayoid faction was very probably directed at the peoples of the surrounding area who produced the necessary goods with which to pay tribute to the invading overlords. They must accept their lot or suffer the fate of the Mayoid warriors in the painting. The paintings of the Battle have been dated to around 650 AD.

The subjugated peoples of the region of Cacaxtla would have been sufficiently intimidated by the Battle Scene painted on the walls of substructure of Building B, but they also needed to be encouraged to produce sufficient foodstuffs to feed themselves and the new overlords. This encouragement was provided in the representations of gods of water and fertility, painted on the walls of the portico of Building A, dated to AD 700-800.

There are two paintings on the walls of the portico that lead to a room in Building A. They are accompanied by two acolytes registered on the jambs of the door. The colours are in a wonderful state of preservation, which has suggested that the paintings were buried shortly after they were executed. These murals manifest two distinct pictorial traditions, the Maya and that of Teotihuacán, the latter predominating in compositional structure and hierarchization by dimensions. Conversely, the Maya form is present in the naturalistic representation of the human form, in their proportions and their postures. The motifs are both Maya and Central Highlands. However, though two distinct traditions are present in the murals of the portico of Building A, they do not clash; rather, they merge to produce a new style that is unified and coherent.

The individual represented on the south panel has facial characteristics that are Maya, with squinting eyes and aquiline nose; his body and face are painted black. He is dressed in a cape of black and white feathers and a headdress of a wading bird, linked to his footwear of bird claws. He carries a huge, blue ceremonial bar, usually carried by rulers in the Maya region, with serpent heads at either end. He stands on a feathered serpent.

His counterpart on the north panel is dressed from head to foot in jaguar skin. His cape is of blue feathers. His face, emerging from the jaws of the jaguar, is painted black. He too carries an object that slices diagonally through the painting, but this time it is a bundle of lances from which drops of water descend to the ground. He stands on a jaguar-serpent whose body, similar to the feathered serpent of the south painting, also ends in a spray of quetzal feathers. Both pictures are framed by a wide border full of aquatic creatures that originate on the Gulf Coast and Pacific, as well as rivers and lagoons. The feathered-serpent and jaguar-serpent on which the two protagonists stand represent flowing water, streams or rivers, so necessary to irrigation.

In the south jamb the subject is upright but in a graceful, dancing posture, so reminiscent of many of the individuals depicted on the Maya ceramics of the Classic period. He carries an enormous green conch, from which appears to emerge a Maya individual with long hair and jade adornment. On the north jamb the individual carries a green cup adorned with the image of Tlaloc. Streams and drops of water flow from the cup. In his other hand he carries a blue serpent with blue scrolls and yellow flowers; a plant with two types of yellow flowers emerges from his navel.

The theme of the paintings in the portico of Building A is that of water for cultivation, either temporal or through irrigation. The exchange of symbols, colours and styles in these paintings manifest a syncretism that may be confusing, but which, nevertheless, are easily read. Although the bundle of lances carried by the individual on the north panel have been related to the *xiuhmopilli*, or bundle of reeds which symbolized the tying of 52 years at the New Fire ceremony, there is another explanation. Two great themes that run throughout Mesoamerican ideology are those of warrior and cultivator. The warrior defends the land while the farmer cultivates it. This theme is explicit in the Temple of the Cross at Palenque (see page 264); it is also clear at El Tajín (see page 205) where a warrior nourishes a maguey with his semen. And at Tenochtitlán, the Aztec capital, the Great Pyramid was crowned by shrines dedicated to Huitzilopochtli, patron of the warrior, and Tlaloc, patron of the cultivator.

There are other murals at Cacaxtla, and hopefully more will be uncovered that will provide a fuller picture of the culture that produced paintings that expressed War and Peace at that great site.

Huamantla Thirty miles east of Tlaxcala on Route 136 is Huamantla, an attractive little town (*population* 32,500). The **Museo Nacional de Titeres** (puppet museum) is on Parque Juárez. It has nine rooms of puppets from around the world. All descriptions are in Spanish. ■ *Tue-Sat, 1000-1400, 1600-1800, US$1, students and children US$0.50. Camera US$2.50. Videos can only be used by prior arrangement. Visitors might wish to look at the exhibits before deciding to pay the fee for using a camera.* **Parroquia de San Luis Obispo**, Parque Juárez, lots of gold inside. Also on Parque Juárez is the **Templo Franciscano**, with interesting ceiling paintings, side chapels and a high altar screen painted to look like green marble.

14 August, the eve of the feast of the Assumption, is known locally as *La noche que nadie duerme* (the night when nobody sleeps). Overnight, the people of Huamantla create carpets of flowers and coloured sawdust along 12 km of streets. After a week of festivities there is a **Huamantlada**, a Pamplona-style bull running through the streets of the town.

Cuetzalan

Phone code: 233
Colour map 3, grid B6

It can be very foggy at Cuetzalan, even when it is fine in Puebla

An interesting day trip from Puebla is to Cuetzalan market (via Tetela-Huahuaxtla) which is held on Sunday in the Zócalo (three hours walk up). In the first week of October each year dancers from local villages gather and *voladores* 'fly' from the top of their pole. Nahua Indians sell cradles (*huacales*) for children, machetes and embroidered garments. Women decorate their hair with skeins of wool. The *Día de los Muertos* (2 November) is interesting here. Big clay dogs are made locally, unique stoves which hold large flat clay plates on which *tortillas* are baked and stews are cooked in pots. Also available in nearby

Huitzilán. You can also go via Zaragoza, Zacapoaxtla and Apulco, where you can walk along a path, left of the road, to the fine 35-m waterfall of La Gloria. **C** *Hotel Taselotzin*, a set of cabins, very clean, great views, two beds per cabin, and bathroom (**E** per person per night). Highly recommended. Tourist information is available at Calle Hidalgo y Bravo, helpful, good map.

From Cuetzalan it is a 1½-hour walk to the well-preserved, niched pyramids of Yohualichan (Totonac culture); there are five excavated pyramids, two of them equivalent to that at El Tajín (see page 205), and three still uncovered. There has been earthquake damage, though. Take a bus from Calle Miguel Alvarado Avila y Calle Abosolo, more frequent in morning and market days, to San Antonio and get off at the sign Pirámides Yohualichan (30 minutes, bad road), then walk 2 km to the site. ■ *Closed Mon and Tue, US$2.* In the Cuetzalan area are 32 km of caverns with lakes, rivers and wonderful waterfalls. These include Tzicuilan (follow Calle Emiliano Zapata, east of town) and Atepolihuit (follow Carretera Antigua up to the Campo Deportivo, west of town). Children offer to guide visitors to the ruins and the caves.

Sleeping and eating Several cheap, quite clean hotels, eg **E** *Hotel Rivello*, G Victoria 3, T91-23310139, 1 block from Zócalo, with bath, **F** without, basic, friendly, clean. **E** *Posada Jackelin*, upper end of plaza, near market, behind church, pleasant. **E** *Posada Vicky*, on G Victoria. *Posada Quetzal*, Zaragoza. Good, cheap restaurant. *Yoloxochitl*, 2 de Abril. Good for breakfasts, huge juices. *Casa Elvira Mora*, Hidalgo 54. Recommended. *Villacaiba* for seafood, Francisco Madero 6. *Café-Bazar Galería*, in centre. Good sandwiches and tea, nice garden, English magazines. Recommended.

Transport Direct buses from Puebla (Tezuitecos line only) 5 a day from 0500 to 1530, US$6.50; quite a few return buses, but if none direct go to Zaragoza and change buses there. There are many buses to Zacapoaxtla with frequent connections for Cuetzalan.

South of Puebla

From Puebla, Route 150 continues to **Amozoc**, where tooled leather goods and silver decorations on steel are made, both mostly as outfits for the *charros*, or Mexican cattlemen. Beyond Amozoc lies **Tepeaca** with its late 16th-century monastery, well worth a visit; its weekly market is very extensive. On the main square is Casa de Cortés, where Hernán Cortés signed the second of five *Cartas de Relación* in 1520. ■ *1000-1700.* An old Spanish tower or *rollo* (1580) stands between Tepeaca's main square and the Parroquia. Beyond Tepeaca, 57 km from Puebla, lies **Tecamachalco** where the vast 16th-century Franciscan monastery church has beautiful murals on the choir vault, in late medieval Flemish style, by a local Indian. Language school Escuela de Español en Tecamachalco, run by Patricia O Martínez, Calle 29 Sur 303, Barrio de San Sebastián, Tecamachalco, CP 75480, Apdo Postal 13, T91-24221121, very good; US$70 for one week, four hours a day, possible to live with families. There is a good seafood restaurant; enquire at José Colorado's *tienda* near the school.

This charming town, southeast of Puebla, has a pleasant, sometimes cool, climate. Water from the mineral springs is bottled and sent all over the country by Garci Crespo, San Lorenzo and Peñafiel. From the small dam at Malpaso on the Río Grande, an annual race is held for craft without motors as far as the village of Quiotepec. The central plaza is pleasant and shaded. **Museo de Minerológia Romero** is in the ex-Convento del Carmen, Avenida Reforma, 7 Nte 356. It has one room with a good collection of minerals from all over the world, ■ *0900-1200, 1600-1800, mornings only on Sat, free.* The

Tehuacán
Phone code: 238
Population: 190,000
Altitude: 1,676m

Ayuntamiento on the Zócalo is decorated inside and out with murals and tiles. A short bus ride beyond Peñafiel Spa is the spa of **San Lorenzo** with spring-fed pools surrounded by trees, US$2 entry.

Sleeping B *México*, Reforma Norte and Independencia Pte, 1 block from Zócalo, T20019. With garage, TV, restaurant, renovated colonial building, pool, quiet. **B-C** *Bogh Suites*, 1 Norte 102, northwest side of Zócalo, T23006. New, businessman's hotel, safe parking. **D** *Iberia*, Independencia Ote 217, T31500. With bath, clean, airy, pleasant restaurant, noisy weekends, public parking nearby at reduced fee with voucher from hotel. Recommended. **D** *Inter*, above restaurant of same name, close to bus station (ask there). Hot shower, clean, modern. **E** *Madrid*, 3 Sur 105, T20272, opposite Municipal Library. Comfortable, pleasant courtyard, cheaper without bath. Recommended. Several *casas de huéspedes* along Calle 3 (Norte and Sur) but low standards.

Eating Many eating places on Zócalo with reasonable prices (eg on same corner as Cathedral, good breakfast). The main meal is served at midday in Tehuacán. Try *Restaurant Santander*. Good but pricey. *Cafetería California*, Independencia Ote 108. Excellent juices and *licuados*. *Pizzería Richards*, Reforma Norte 250. Quite good pizzas, good fresh salads; excellent *taco* stands.

Transport ADO bus station on Av Independencia (Pte). Bus direct to **Mexico City**, 5 hrs, US$10; to **Puebla**, 2½ hrs, US$4; to **Oaxaca** (US$10.75, 5½ hrs, *Autobuses Unidos* at 1430, coming from Mexico City, may be full), **Veracruz**, US$7.75, and the Gulf: *Autobuses Unidos*, 2nd class on Calle 2 Ote with several buses daily to Mexico City and Oaxaca. Local bus to **Huajuapan** 3 hrs, US$5; from there, frequent buses to Oaxaca.

From Tehuacán there are two paved roads to Oaxaca: one, very scenic, through Teotitlán del Camino (US$1.65 by second-class bus), and the other, longer but easier to drive, through Huajuapan (see page 400). Railway junction for Oaxaca and Veracruz; no passenger trains on line to Esperanza. Wild maize was first identified by an archaeologist at Coxcatlán Cave nearby. There is an airport.

Teotitlán del Camino, *en route* to Oaxaca, is a glaringly bright town with a military base. Vehicles are stopped occasionally; make sure, if driving, that your papers are in order. From Teotitlán it is possible to drive into the hills to the Indian town of **Huautla de Jiménez**, where the local Mazatec Indians consume the hallucinogenic 'magic' mushrooms made famous by Dr Timothy Leary. Huautla has all four seasons of the year in each day; springlike mornings; wet, foggy afternoons; fresh, autumn evenings; and freezing nights. Hiking in the mountains here is worthwhile. There is the hotel *Olímpico*, **E**, above market, with no sign. It is clean, friendly and simple, with small rooms, bath. You cannot buy food in the town after 2000. Several daily buses to/from Mexico City and Oaxaca (US$6.50) children meet buses offering lodging in their homes. There are many police and military. Drivers may be waved down by people in the road up to Huautla; do not stop for them, they may be robbers.

The road from Tehuacán to the Gulf coast soon begins to climb into the mountains. At Cumbres, 2,300m, there is a wide view: the silvered peak of Citlaltépetl, 'Star Mountain' (or Pica de Orizaba – see page 197) volcano to the northeast, the green valley of Orizaba below. In 10 km the road drops down, through steep curves, sometimes rather misty, to Acultzingo 830m below. The road joins the main toll road from Puebla to Orizaba at Ciudad Mendoza, where it has emerged from the descent through the Cumbres de Maltrata which are usually misty and need to be driven with care and patience. The expensive toll road Puebla-Orizaba is a much safer drive than the route described here; it, too, is scenic.

Veracruz and the Gulf Coast

5

*Most foreign tourists never visit the state of Veracruz; it's off the usual beaten track. Maybe it hasn't got the best beaches in Mexico; but for almost everything else it's hard to beat. Inland, there's adventure tourism with Mexico's highest mountain, deepest caves and fastest rapids. Temperatures rise as the land drops to the green, fertile coastal plain and the endless plantations. To the south, beyond the plains of the vast Papaloapan river, the Tuxtla mountains, tropical and lush, a birdwatcher's paradise, contrast dramatically with the wilderness of the massive oil refineries at Minatitlán and Coatzacoalcos. In **Xalapa**, the lively state capital, don't miss the Anthropology Museum, second only to the one in Mexico City, with exhibits from the region's three major pre-Hispanic civilizations. The descendants of these ancient people still inhabit the region. In the north the Huastecs are best known for their traditional huapango music and falsetto singing. In the vanilla-growing Papantla area, the spectacular volador ritual, an example of surviving Totonac traditions, is performed regularly in Papantla and outside the ruins of **El Tajín**, one of the most magnificent archaeological sites in all America. **Veracruz's** rich cultural mix is what makes it so special. For 300 years, Veracruz was Spain's gateway to the riches of the New World. The arrival of black slaves profoundly influenced the people and culture - most notably the music - of this region. Veracruz is a popular destination for Mexican tourists, who enjoy the famous hospitality of the Veracruzanos, known as jarochos, and the eternally festive, tropical-port atmosphere which crescendoes each spring during the liveliest carnival in all Mexico.*

Mexico City to the Gulf Coast

Much of the area east of Mexico City constituted the eastern tribute quarter conquered by the Mexica, formerly the Aztecs, who derived great wealth from those subject nations that stretched from the Basin of Mexico to the Guatamalan border. Commodities such as cacao, cochineal (obtained from the red insect that was nourished by cacti), jade jewellery, cloaks and rubber poured into Tenochtitlán from these provinces to the east. This, too, was the route along which the *pochtecatl* (merchants) transported the precious feathers of the quetzal, used by the *amanteca* (feather workers) to create elaborate designs in cloaks, shields, and especially headdresses.

By road, the principal route to the coast from Mexico City is paved all the way with no Pemex service station on the road between Puebla and Orizaba, a distance of about 150 km. A new *autopista* (motorway) now runs all the way from Mexico City to Veracruz with four tolls which range from US$4.35 to US$9. If you wish to avoid the toll route, note that the *vía libre* is very congested initially and, at Ixtapaluca, just out of Mexico City, there are a series of *topes* (speed bumps) so high that they are a danger to ordinary saloon cars.

Orizaba

Phone code: 272
Colour map 4, grid B1
Population: 115,000
Altitude: 1,283m

The favourite resort of the Emperor Maximilian lost much of its charm in the 1973 earthquake, when the bullring, many houses and other buildings were lost, and is now heavily industrialized. The setting, however, is lovely. In the distance is the majestic volcanic cone of Orizaba. The town developed because of the natural springs in the valley, some of which are used by the textile and paper industries and others are dammed to form small pools for bathing beside picnic areas; Nogales is the most popular, Ojo de Agua is another. The **Cerro del Borrego**, the hill above the Alameda Park, is a favourite early-morning climb. On the north side of the Zócalo is the market, with a wide variety of local produce and local women in traditional dress, and the

Orizaba

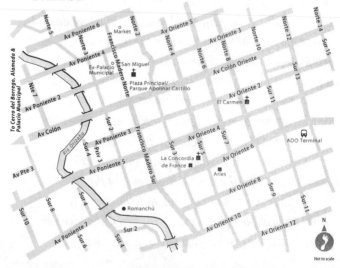

Pico de Orizaba

Also known as Citlaltépetl, *the highest mountain in Mexico (5,760m), it is not too difficult to climb, although acclimatization to altitude is advised and there are some crevasses to be negotiated. About four people a year ski on the glacier, but the surface is unpredictable. From Acatzingo one can go via a paved road to Tlachichuca (35 km, or you can take a bus, every 30 minutes, from Puebla to Tlachichuca). Guides and transport can be arranged: Sr Reyes (F24515019), arranges trips in a four-wheel drive up an appalling road to two huts on the mountain, about US$50, including one night at his house, a former soap factory – very clean (**D** full board), his truck leaves at 1200, three-hour journey, and he picks you up at about 1600, Sr Reyes is well-equipped and keen to give ground support to climbers; Sr Canchola Limón, 3 Poniente 3, Tlachichuca, T15082, charges US$30 for transport to the mountain and pick up, registers your climbing intentions, has equipment, and can provide somebody to guard your equipment at the refugio (two days) for US$13; Sr Espinosa Coba, T15103, is another transporter. Alternatively, stay at **E** Hotel Panchita, Av Benito Juàrez 5, T15035, hot water, bath, restaurant, friendly; **E** Hotel Gerar, 20 de Noviembre 200, with bath; or **E** Hotel Margarita, no sign, then, early in the morning hitch hike to the last village, Villa Hidalgo at 3,000m (about 15 km) or take a taxi, US$10. From there it's about 10 km (2 hrs) to the huts. The huts, one small (sleeps six, water nearby), one larger (sleeps 80, start of north route – normal – or Jamapa glacier route) and colder, are at 4,200m. There is no hut custodian; it's usually fairly empty, except on Saturday night. No food or light, or wood; provide your own. Take a good sleeping bag and warm clothes. Water close at hand, but no cooking facilities. Start from the hut at about 0500, first to reach the glacier at 4,700m, and then a little left to the rim. There is a hazardous section before you get to the Jamapa*

glacier where several icy slopes spill down from its lip and have become a bowling alley for dislodged rocks. Be vigilant. From the rim the summit, marked with a cross, is 100m further on and 40m higher up. Be very careful walking round the rim to the summit. It's about 7-8 hours to the top; the ice is not too steep (about 35-40°), take crampons, if not for the ascent then for the descent which takes only 2½ hours. At the weekend you're more likely to get a lift back to Tlachichuca. 1:50000 maps are available from INEGI information and sales office, eg in Puebla (Av 15 de Mayo 2929), Veracruz or Mexico City.

Volker Huss of Karlsruhe (Germany) informs us of an alternative route up the volcano; this is easier, because there is no glacier and therefore no crevasses, but is best done in the rainy season (April-October), when there is enough snow to cover the loose stone on the final stage. Crampons and ice-axe are necessary. The route is on the south face of the volcano. Stay in Orizaba and take a very early bus to Ciudad Serdán (depart 0530), or stay in Ciudad Serdán. At Serdán bus station take a bus, US$1.50, to San Antonio Atzitzintla, and then taxi US$4 to Texmalaquila; the driver will know the way. Five hours from Texmalaquila is the Fausto González hut at 4,760m (take own food and water). Miguel Quintero in Texmalaquila has mules for luggage transport to the shelter (US$5 per bag). Spend the night there and climb the final 1,000m early in the morning, about five hours. From the top are fine views, with luck even to Veracruz and Mexico City. In the rainy season the summit is usually free of cloud until midday. The entire descent takes six hours and can be done the same day. A recommended guide is Raimund Alvaro Torres, in Orizaba, C Sur 10 574, T27261940. An adventure travel shop on Pte 3 entre Sur 2 y 4, hires equipment and guides but their equipment is old and the guides not very knowledgeable.

many-domed **San Miguel** church (1690-1729). There are several other interesting churches, and there is an Orozco mural in the neo-classical **Palacio Municipal**, formerly the Centro Educativo Obrero on Avenida Colón. The **ex-Palacio Municipal** is the actual cast-iron Belgian pavilion brought piece by piece from France after the famous 19th-century Paris Exhibition, an odd sight. The **Museo de Arte del Estado**, in the Oratorio de San Felipe Neri, 4 Oriente y 23 Sur, has a delightful collection of colonial to contemporary paintings, including, in Sala 3, foreign artists' impressions of Veracruz. ■ *Tue-Sun, 1000-1400, 1600-1900.* The **tourist office** is at Poniente 2, across the river from the Zócalo. open mornings only.

Sleeping **B** *Aries*, Ote 6 No 265, T51116 (nightclub on top floor). **B** *Trueba*, Ote 6 and Sur 11, T42744. Resort facilities. **D** *De France*, Ote 6 No 186, T52311. US$0.25 for parking in courtyard, charming building, clean, comfortable, shower, friendly, reasonable if uninspiring restaurant. **E** *Vallejo*, Madero Norte 242. Dirty, smelly. **F** *América*, on the main street, No 269. Very friendly and good value.

Eating *Romanchú* and *Paso Real*, on the main street, have excellent cuisine. Hare Krishna vegetarian restaurant, *Radha's*, on Sur 4 between Ote 1 and 3. Excellent. The Indian vegetarian restaurant on Sur 5, has an excellent *comida corrida*. Highly recommended. *Crazy Foods*, opposite *Hotel de France*. Good and cheap, nice sandwiches. In the market, try the local morning snack, *memelita picadita*.

Transport Bus to **Mérida**, 1 a day (*ADO*), US$35, 1st class. To **Veracruz**, many buses, US$3.50, 1st class.

South to Zongolica A road leaves Orizaba southwards, up into the mountains of **Zongolica**, a dry, poor and isolated region, cold and inhospitable, inhabited by various groups of Indians who speak Nahuatl, the language of the Aztecs. Zongolica village is a good place to buy *sarapes*; take early bus from Orizaba (ask for direct one) to get clear views of the mountains. Ask about weather conditions before attempting to drive.

Beyond Orizaba, en route to the coast, the scenery is magnificent. The road descends to coffee and sugar cane country and a tropical riot of flowers. It is very pleasant except when a northerly blows, or in the intolerable heat and mugginess of the wet season.

Fortín de las Flores
Colour map 4, grid B1
Km 331

This small town is devoted to growing flowers and exporting them. Sometimes Indian women sell choice blossoms in small baskets made of banana-tree bark. Between Orizaba and Fortín there is a viewpoint looking out over a dramatic gorge, the **Barranca de Metlac**, which plunges down to the river is a cascade of flame trees and luxurient vegetation. The *autopista* from Orizaba to Córdoba passes over this deep valley on a concrete bridge.

Night trains sound their horns when passing Fortín which can be disturbing

Sleeping **B** *Posada la Loma*, Km 333 Carretera Norte 150, T30658. Very attractive, tropical garden with butterflies, distant view of snow-capped volcano in early morning, moderately expensive. There are others, slightly cheaper, which also offer tropical gardens for relaxation.

Córdoba
Phone code: 271
Population: 126,000
Altitude: 923m

Eight kilometres beyond Fortín on in the rich valley of the Río Seco, is this old colonial city, which is also crazy with flowers. Its Zócalo is spacious, leafy and elegant; three sides are arcaded; two of them are lined with tables. On the fourth is an imposing church with a chiming clock. There are several hotels in the Zócalo, which is alive and relaxed at night. In **Portal de Zavallos**, General

Iturbide signed the Treaty of Córdoba in 1821, which was instrumental in freeing Mexico from Spanish colonial rule. There is a local museum at Calle 3, No 303. ■ *1000-1300, 1600-2000.* Córdoba has the highest rainfall in Mexico, but at predictable times. The area grows coffee.

Sleeping **B** *Hotel Layfer*, Av 5 between Calle 9 y 11, T43583/40099. Four-star hotel, swimming pool, gymnasium, video games room, a/c, secure parking, friendly. Highly recommended. **B** *Mansur*, Av 1 y Calle 3, T26600, on square. Smart. **C** *Hostal de Borreña*, Calle 11 308, T20777. Modern, clean, really hot water, some traffic noise but good value. Near the ADO terminal is **C** *Palacio*, Av 3 y Calle 2, T22186. **C** *Marina*, T22600. **C** *Gorbena*, Calle 11 between 3 and 5, large rooms. Recommended. **D** *Iberia*, T21301, **D** *Trescado*, T22366 and *Casa de Huéspedes Regis* are all on Av 2. **E** *Las Carretas*, Av 4 No 512. With bath, clean, noisy, short stay, can wash clothes. Not recommended. *Casa de Huéspedes La Sin Rival* and **E** *La Nueva Querétana* are at 511 and 508 of Av 4, respectively (latter is basic but cheap). **F** *Los Reyes*, Calle 3. Shower, hot water, street rooms double-glazed, street parking OK. Recommended.

Eating *Cantábrico*, Calle 3 No 9, T27646, 1 block from Zócalo. Excellent meat and fish dishes, fine wines and good service, 'worth a trip from Mexico City!' Highly recommended. *El Balcón*, enter through Hotel Zevallos. Balcony overlooking Zócalo. Recommended. *Brujes*, Av 2 No 306. Good *comida corrida*.

Transport **Cars**: Nissan, Chevrolet and Dodge dealers, mechanics all on Calle 11. **Trains**: from Mexico City at 0815, continuing to Veracruz. There may be a 2nd class train for Tierra Blanca (US$1), Medias Aguas (US$3), Coatzacoalcos (US$4), Teapa (US$6.50), Palenque (US$8), Campeche (US$12) and Mérida (US$14), check locally as train services are dwindling. **Buses**: bus station is at the end of Av 6. Direct services to **Veracruz**, 2 hrs, US$4; **Puebla**, 3 hrs, US$7.70; **Mexico City**, hourly, 5 hrs, US$10; to **Coatzacoalcos**, US$13; **Oaxaca** and many others.

Directory **Banks**: *Casa de Cambio* on Av 3 opposite *Bancomer*, recommended.

Córdoba to Veracruz

The direct road from Córdoba to Veracruz is lined, in season, by stalls selling fruit and local honey between Yanga and Cuitláhuac. **Yanga** is a small village named after the leader of a group of escaped black slaves in colonial times. A slightly longer but far more attractive road goes from Fortín de las Flores northwards through Huatusco and Totutla, then swings east to Veracruz. For cyclists, the 125 km from Córdoba to Veracruz has no accommodation *en route*, but is mostly flat, so could be done in one day.

Xalapa

Capital of Veracruz state since 1885 and 132 km from the port, Xalapa (also spelt Jalapa) is in the tierra templada and is a lively town in keeping with its climate. It is yet another 'City of Flowers', with walled gardens, stone-built houses, wide avenues in the newer town and steep cobbled crooked streets in the old. It is a hilly city and the numerous telephone and power lines give it a spaghetti effect.

Phone code: 28
Colour map 4, grid B1
Population: approx 300,000
Altitude: 1,425m

A settlement called Xallac (the place of the sandy waters) is known to have existed here in the 12th century. It has always been a good place to break the journey from the coast to the highlands and, in the 18th century, development was helped by the creation of a huge annual trading fair. There was a passion for building and renovation in the flamboyant gothic style during the first part of the 19th century. The **tourist office** is at Avenida Avila Camacho, T128500, a long walk or short taxi ride from the centre. Look out for *Toma Nota*, a free sheet advertising what is on, available from the shop in front of *Hotel Salmones*. The *Feria de la Primavera* takes place mid-April.

Ins and outs

Getting there & away
There is a small airport serving a few national destinations only, about 15 km south-east of the city, on the Veracruz road. Xalapa is usually reached by bus or car. The new bus station, CAXA, is east of the city centre, with services to Mexico City, Papantla, Poza Rica Puebla, Veracruz and other destinations. Buses to the train station, on the outskirts of town, leave from the market. The Mexico City-Veracruz train stops here, but check that it is still running before making plans. The road from Puebla, Route 140, twists and turns, particularly in the Perote area and is often notriously foggy; if you are driving, avoid it at night if at all possible. From Xalapa to the coast and Veracruz, Route 140 is good.

Getting around
Taxis from the bus station to the centre charge about US$1; buses marked 'Centro' will also take you. Buses marked 'Xalapa' or 'Museo' run north to the Anthropology Museum. To reach the nearby towns of Coatepec and Xico take a bus from Avenida Allende, just west of the city centre.

Sights

The 18th-century **cathedral**, with its sloping floor, has been recently restored. In the northern suburbs of Xalapa, on the road out to Mexico City, is an excellent, modern **Anthropology Museum** showing treasures of the Olmec, Totonac and Huastec coastal cultures. The colossal heads displayed in the museum are Olmec; the museum has the best collection of Olmec monumental stone sculptures in Mexico. ■ *Tue-Sun, 1000-1800, US$1, Tue free, half price for students with ID, guided tours included in fee. To get there take the Tesorería Avila Camacho bus which stops in front of the museum.* The **Pinacoteca Diego Rivera**, Herrera 5 (Zócalo), has a small permanent collection of Rivera's paintings as well as temporary exhibitions. ■ *Tue-Sun 1000-1800, free.* Xalapa has a University; you can take a pleasant stroll round the grounds, known as **El Dique**. Pico de Orizaba is visible from hotel roofs or Parque Juárez very early in the morning, before the haze develops.

Essentials

Sleeping
Cheaper hotels are up the hill from the market, which itself is uphill from Parque Juárez (there is no Zócalo). Town centre hotels are generally noisy

LL *Xalapa*, Victoria y Bustamante, T82222. Good restaurant, excellent bookshop, changes travellers' cheques. **AL** *María Victoria*, Zaragoza 6, T80268. Good. **B-C** *Hostal del Tejar*, 20 de Noviembre Ote 552 esq Av del Tejar, T72459, F83691. A/c, pool, parking. **B-C** *Hotel/Restaurant Mesón del Alférez*, Zaragoza y Sebastián Camacho, T/F186351. Charming, small rooms, free parking opposite, good food. Highly recommended. **C** *Hotel Suites Araucarias*, Avila Camacho 160, T73433. With large window, balcony and view (**D** without), TV, fridge, good cheap restaurant. **C** *México*, Lucio 4, T75030. Clean, with shower, will change dollars.

D *Principal*, Zaragoza 28. Good if a bit shabby, safe parking nearby. **D** *Salmones*, Zaragoza 24, T75435. Excellent view of Orizaba from the roof, good restaurant. Recommended. **E** *Amoro*, near market. No shower but public baths opposite, very clean. **E** *Limón*, Revolución, 100m uphill from cathedral on right hand side. With bath, TV. **E** *Plaza*, Enríquez, T173310. All rooms with private bath and TV, some rooms airless, clean, safe, friendly, will store luggage, good view of Orizaba from the roof.

Recommended. **F** *El Greco*, Av Revolución (opposite cathedral). With bath, hot water, clean.

La Parroquia, Zaragoza 18, and another one on Av Camacho, same menu and prices as famous restaurant of same name in Veracruz. *La Casona del Beaterio*, Zaragoza 20. Good atmosphere, tastefully restored house with patio and bubbling fountain, good breakfast. *Quinto Reyno*, Juárez 67 close to main plaza. Lunches only. Excellent vegetarian with health-food shop, very good service. *La Champion*, Allende, going towards the bus terminal. Vegetation, nice atmosphere, good-value *comida corrida* Mon-Sat. *Café Linda*, Primo de Verdad. Good service and good-value *comida corrida* every day, often live music in the evenings. *Estancia*, opposite Barranquilla. Good food. *Aladino*, Juárez, up from ADO. Excellent Mexican food. *Pizzería*, Ursulo Galván. *La Sopa*, on Diamante, an alleyway just off Enríquez. Great tapas, cheap. Several other small restaurants on Diamante including *La Fonda*, very pleasant upstairs and *El Diamante*. *Fruitlandia* on Abasolo (uphill from Cathedral). Wonderful fresh juices. Health food shops, Ursulo Galván, near Juárez, good bread and yoghurt, another opposite the post office on Zamora. Several good cafés on Carrillo Puerto for good-value *comida corrida*. *La Churrería del Recuerdo*, Victoria 158. Superb, authentic Mexican food at very reasonable prices. No alcohol. Highly recommended.

Eating

The famous Xalapeño (Jalapeño) chilli comes from this region

Centro de Recreación Xalapeño has exhibitions; live music, films and exhibitions in *El Agora*, underneath Parque Juárez; 10 pin bowling, Plaza Cristal, next to cinema. **Cinemas** There are 2 cinemas next to *Hotel Xalapa*, off Camacho; 3-screen cinema in Plaza Cristal; cinemas in the centre tend to show soft porn and gore. **Theatre** *Teatro del Estado*, Avila Camacho; good Balet Folclórico Veracruzano and symphony orchestra. **Nightclubs** *La Tasca*, good music. Recommended. *La Cumbre*, rock.

Entertainment

Crafts *Artesanía* shop on Alfaro, more on Bárcenas, turn off Enríquez into Madero, right again at the top, the owner of *El Tazín* on the corner speaks English. **Books** *Instituto de Antropología*, Benito Juárez, has books in English and Spanish, student ID helps.

Shopping

Veracruz & the Gulf Coast

Xalapa

Tour operators **Travel agents** There are 4 on Camacho: the one nearest Parque Juárez is very helpful.

Transport **Local Bus**: many of the urban creamy yellow buses are for seated passengers only, so they will not stop for you if all the seats are full. Car hire *Automóviles Sánchez*, Av Ignacio de la Llave 14, T79011. Recommended. **Moped hire**: in Camacho US$4-6 per hr, Visa accepted.

Long distance Air: airport 15 km southeast, on Veracruz road.

Trains: railway station on outskirts, buses from near market to get there. **Mexico City-Veracruz** trains stop here but check first as passenger trains, since privatization, are not reliable.

Buses: a new 1st and 2nd class bus station has been built called CAXA; taxi from centre US$1.75. Taxi ticket office outside terminal on lower level. 5 hrs from **Mexico City** by AU or ADO, from the Terminal de Oriente (TAPO). Frequent ADO service to **Veracruz**, US$4, every 20 mins 0700-2000. To **Puebla**, ADO, 'GL' Plus service, US$7, 1st class US$6, 4 hrs, scenic route; also AU 2nd class. To **Coatzacoalcos**, 8 a day, US$17, up to 8 hrs although you will be told 5 hrs. To **Villahermosa**, ADO, 3 a day, 10 hrs. To **Poza Rica**, US$11-14.50, 5 hrs, about every 2 hrs, the coast road is faster, while the impressive route via Teziutlán requires a strong stomach for mountain curves.

Directory **Banks** *Banca Serfín* on Enríquez will change TCs in dollars and other major currencies, *Santander* on Carrillo Puerto changes dollar TCs, *Bancomer* will not. Banks are slow, rates offered are rarely those advertised in the window and money transferred from abroad comes via Mexico City. *American Express* at Viajes Xalapa, Carrillo Puerto 24, T76535, in centre, sells cheques against Amex card but does not change them. *Casa de Cambio*, on right side of Zamora going down hill, English spoken. The liquor shop in Plaza Cristal will change dollars. Rates vary enormously, so shop around. Quick service and good rates at *Dollar Exchange*, Gutiérrez Zamora 36. **Communications Internet:** *Serviexpress*, Zaragoza 14B. *Café Chat* on Camacho opposite Parque Bicentenial, another in shopping arcade off Enríquez. Most charge US$3 per hr. **Post Office:** letters can be sent to the *Lista de Correos* on Diego Leño, friendly post office, and another at the bottom of Zamora. There is a telegraph office next door with *Lista de Correos*. **Telephone:** radio-telephone available opposite *Hotel María Victoria*; long-distance phone in shop on Zaragoza, with a sign outside, others behind the government palace also on Zaragoza. **Laundry** Several on Allende and Ursulo Galván, all charge by weight, usually US$3 per 3kg, some offer same day service, others up to 3 days. **Medical services Dentists:** there are 2 dentists on Ursulo Galván. **Hospitals:** *Nicolás Bravo*.

Excursions from Xalapa Two and a half kilometres along the Coatepec road are lush **botanical gardens** with a small museum. ■ *US$0.20. Take bus from the terminal marked Coatepec Briones, 10 minutes.*

Coatepec, famous for its ice cream, fruit liqueurs and orchids, is a pleasant town and an important centre for the surrounding coffee haciendas. **A** *Posada Coatepec*, Hidalgo 9, Centro, T160544, F160040 (in Mexico City T5142728/2075666). Tastefully modernized colonial house. Reserve in advance, excellent restaurant with Mexican and international cuisine. Highly recommended. Several good cafés and restaurants around the main plaza. Particularly recommended is the seafood at *Casa Bonilla* (Cuauhtémoc 20). ■ *Direct Coatepec bus from Xalapa bus terminal every few minutes, US$0.40, 10 minutes.*

The **Texolo** waterfalls are some 15 km southwest of Xalapa and 5 km from the village of **Xico**, just beyond the town of Coatepec. There is a deep ravine and an old bridge, as well as a good, cheap restaurant at the falls. The old bridge is still visible but a new bridge across the ravine has been built. It is a pleasant place for a cold swim, birdwatching and walking, crowded at weekends. The film *Romancing the Stone* used Texolo as one of its locations. Xico village itself is pretty. ■ *US$0.60 by bus from Xalapa every 30 minutes.*

Hacienda Casa de Santa Anna, was taken over in the Revolution and is now a museum, **Museo Lencero**, with the original furniture. ■ *US$1, Tue-Sun, 1000-1800, no bags allowed inside. By bus from the centre, take Circunvalación bus to Plaza Cristal shopping centre, cross the road and catch bus to Miradores, ask to be put down near the museum. From the stop (by pedestrian bridge) it is a 7-minute walk to the museum.*

Palo Gacho falls are also worth a visit. Take the route 40 from Xalapa, towards Cardel, to Palo Gacho. The waterfalls can be reached on a dirt road next to the church, 4 km steep descent. Avoid weekends.

Naolinco is 30 minutes' ride, 40 km northeast of Xalapa up a winding hilly road. Two waterfalls, with various pools, tumble several thousand feet over steep wooded slopes. *Restaurant La Fuente* serves local food and has a nice garden. *Las Cascadas* has a *mirador* to admire the falls from. Both restaurants are on the way into town. Flocks of *zopilotes* (buzzards) collect late in the afternoon, soaring high up into the thermals.

Two hours northwest from Xalapa is the archaeological site of **Filobobos**. It includes El Cuajilote, a 400m-wide ceremonial centre, and Vega de la Peña, an area of basalt rocks decorated with bas-reliefs, a ball court and several pyramids by the river banks. Abundant wildlife here includes toucans, parrots and otters. At the end of the Veracruz mountain range is the spectacular Encanto waterfall. ■ *Four-wheel drive is recommended for this journey by car: on the outskirts of Tlapacoyan, take the road marked Plan de Arroyas. After half an hour (many bends and hills) you'll see the sign for Filobobos on the left. This is a three-mile dirt track to a refreshment cabin, from where you can walk for 25 minutes to the ruins; follow signs for El Cuajilote. US$2.*

Route 140 towards the capital, renowned for being foggy, continues to climb to Perote, 53 km from Xalapa. **E** *Hotel Central*, near plaza. Quiet, friendly, with bath, TV. **F** *Gran Hotel*, on plaza. Basic, limited water. The **San Carlos fort** here, now a military prison, was built in 1770-77; there is a good view of Cofre de Perote volcano (known, in Aztec times as *Nauhtecuhtli*, Four Times Lord). A road branches north to Teziutlán (**D** *Hotel Valdéz*, hot water, car park), with a Friday market, where good *sarapes* are sold. A local fair, *La Entrega de Inanacatl*, is held in the third week in June. The old convent at **Acatzingo**, 93 km beyond Perote on route 140, is worth seeing. Another 10 km and you join the road to Puebla and Mexico City.

Papantla

Some 40 km inland from Tecolutla is Papantla (Where Banners Abound), built on the top of a hill overlooking the lush plains of northern Veracruz. It was the stronghold of a Totonac rebellion in 1836. Traditional Totonac dress is still seen: the men in baggy white trousers and sailor shirts and the women in lacy white skirts and shawls over embroidered blouses. Papantla is also the centre of one of the world's largest vanilla-producing zones, and the distinctive odour sometimes lingers over the town. Small animal figures, baskets and other fragrant items woven from vanilla bean pods are sold at booths along Highway 180, as well as the essence; packaged in tin boxes, these sachets are widely used to freshen cupboards and drawers. The vanilla is processed in Gutiérrez Zamora, a small town about 30 km east (close to Tecolutla), and a

Phone code: 784
Colour map 3, grid B6
Population: 280,000

'cream of vanilla' liqueur is also produced. The *Fiesta de la Vainilla* is held throughout the area in early June. The **tourist office** is on the first floor of Palacio Municipal, on the Zócalo, T20026 ext 730, F20176, helpful, good local information and maps, bus schedules, English spoken, ■ *Mon-Fri 0900-1400 and 1800-2100.*

Sights The Zócalo, formally known as Plaza Téllez, is bordered by Enríquez on its downhill north edge; on the south uphill side is the **Catedral de Nuestra Señora de la Asunción** (1700) with a remarkable 50m-long mural on its northern wall called *Homenaje a la Cultura Totonaca*, by Teodoro Cano García (1979), with the plumed serpent Quetzalcoatl along its entire length. *Voladores* perform each Sunday at 1100 in the church courtyard and as many as three times daily during the colourful 10 days of Corpus Christi (late May or early June), along with games, fireworks, artistic exhibitions, dances and cock-fights. For a sweeping view of the area, walk up Reforma to the top of the hill where the giant Monumento al Volador was erected in 1988. Murals and mosaic benches in the Zócalo also commemorate Totonac history and their conception of creation. Beside the main plaza is the Mercado Juárez (poultry and vegetables); more interesting is Mercado Hidalgo, 20 de Noviembre off the northwest corner of the Zócalo, where traditional handmade clothing is sold amid fresh produce and livestock. ■ *Daily 0600-2000.*

Sleeping **B** *Premier*, on Zócalo, T21645, F21062. 20 rooms, a/c, phone, TV, hot water, fax service, free car wash. Recommended. **B-C** *Tajín*, Dr Núñez 104, T20121, F21062. 59 rooms,

Papantla

To ADO Bus Terminal

To Poza Rica

Francisco Madero

Bustamante

Rafael Viadama

González Ortega

20 de Noviembre

Olivo

Av Benito Juárez

Pino Suárez

Quintano Roo

S de Mayo

Azueta

2nd Class Terminal
Transportes Papantla

Aquiles Serdán

Farmacia
Aparicio

2

Serfin Bancomer
4 (S) (S) **3**

Enríquez

3 (S)
Banamex

Artes

6

Palacio
Municipal

Zócalo
(Plaza Téllez)

Lázaro Muñoz

J Mina

Castañeda

Reforma

2

Núñez

Núñez

4

Señora de la
Asunción

1

Curando

1

Obispo de las Casas

Mercado
Juárez

Rodolfo Curti

5 Febrero

16 de Septiembre

16 de Septiembre

Transportes Urbanos
-TUSPA (to El Tajín)

Pípila

Centenario

Monumento
al Volador

Ortiz

Cruz Roja

To El Tajín

N

Not to scale

■ Sleeping			● Eating	
1 México	3 Pulido	5 Totonocapan	1 Catedral	3 Piipos
2 Premier	4 Tajín	6 Trujillo	2 Enríquez	4 Sorrente

restaurant with good-value breakfast and bar, fairly clean, hot water, phone, TV, parking, reasonable. **D-E** *Totonocapan*, 20 de Noviembre y Olivo, T21224, F21218. Hot water, TV, a/c, bar/restaurant, good value. **E** *México*, Obispo de Las Casas y Núñez (beyond *Hotel Tajín*, opposite *Cine* Tajín), T20086. Basic, cheapest in town. **E** *Pulido*, Enríquez 205, T20036. Modern, 23 rooms, hot water, fan, noisy, parking. **E** *Trujillo*, 5 de Mayo 401. Rooms with basin, friendly.

Las Brisas del Golfo, Dr Núñez. Reasonable prices and very good. *Sorrento*, Zócalo. Covered in decorative tiles, good, cheap. Recommended. *Enríquez*, on Zócalo. Popular, pleasant, not cheap. *Piipos*, Enríquez 100. Speciality paella. *Catedral*, Núñez y Curado, behind cathedral. Plain, clean, cheap breakfasts and good 'fast' meals, 0630-2100.

Eating

Most open 0700-2400

Taxis Taxi rank on Enríquez between 5 de Mayo and Zócalo and on Juárez.

Buses ADO terminal, Juárez 207, 5 blocks from centre, T20218. To **Mexico City**, 4 a day, 5 hrs via Poza Rica, US$7; **Poza Rica**, 8 daily, 30 mins, US$0.50; to **Xalapa**, 8 daily, 6 hrs, US$6.25; 4 hrs to **Veracruz**, US$14. 2nd class terminal (Transportes Papantla), 20 de Noviembre 200, many services to local destinations, including **El Tajín**, buses leave when full. Occasional minibus to El Tajín from southwest corner of Zócalo, US$2, unreliable schedule about every 1-1½ hrs. Other buses (Transportes Urbano-TUSPA) for El Tajín leave from office on 16 de Septiembre near Obispo de las Casas (US$0.50).

Transport

Banks *Bancomer* and *Banamex*, on Zócalo, 0900-1300, change cash and TCs till 1200. *Serfín*, between the 2, does not change TCs. **Communications** Post Office: Azueta 198, 2nd Floor, Mon-Fri 0900-1300, 1500-1800, Sat 0900-1200. **Medical services** *Farmacia Aparicio*, Enríquez 103, daily 0700-2200. *Hospital Civil*, Madero 518, T20094. **Red Cross**: T20126.

Directory

El Tajín

The great city of El Tajín, 12 km from Papantla, once covered approximately 2,600 acres, at the heart of which are four major groupings of structures: **Tajín proper** covers the valley floor: most of the major temples are located here. This is also the location of most of the carved and plain ball courts as well as ceremonial and market plazas. Apart from being the location of most of the sculpture, this area was the religious and commercial centre of the city. **Tajín Chico** is a huge terraced acropolis dominated by an elaborate multi-storeyed palace and administrative structures for the city's elite. The largest buildings erected at El Tajín are on the upper levels of Tajín Chico. Along with its Annex, the **Building of the Columns** is the greatest architectural complex in the city. It was the special domain of the ruler 13 Rabbit, who governed at the city's zenith. The **West Ridge** is mostly an artificially tiered natural hill. The structures here are thought to be elite residences, modest temples, and, perhaps, small ball courts. The **East Ridge** is very similar to the West Ridge but with fewer structures.

The suggested time scale for El Tajín's construction is AD 300-900, with a great surge of energy around AD 600, the time when Teotihuacán and Monte Albán were experiencing collapse and abandonment. Although impressive, the architecture of El Tajín is less informative than the rich corpus of iconography that decorated the Pyramid of the Niches, the North Ball Court, the South Ball Court and the Building of the Columns. Most of the imagery associated with these structures tells of conquest, ball games, the interplay between this existence and that of the gods, the dignified sacrifice of warriors and ball players and the undignified sacrifice of captive enemy lords. But the ball game was the single most important activity expressed in the imagery of El Tajín, as emphasised by the presence of at least eleven ball courts at the site. The obsession with the ball game and its related iconography suggests that the city was an immense academy where young men were trained in the skills and rules associated with the game. As yet, no evidence supports this suggestion, but it is tempting to speculate that the residences on the East and West Ridges were intended to house young trainees.

Associated almost exclusively with the ball game and players, the cult of the maguey, pulque and pulque deities at El Tajín presents a puzzle, perplexing because the maguey will not grow in the general area. The probability is that the city was the creation of a small enclave of Huastecs rather than the Totonacs who then inhabited and still inhabit the region. The maguey proliferates throughout the Highlands, and in the mythology of the Central Highlands it was a Huastec who drank more than the stipulated four cups, became drunk, stripped naked and had to return in disgrace to his homeland.

El Tajín

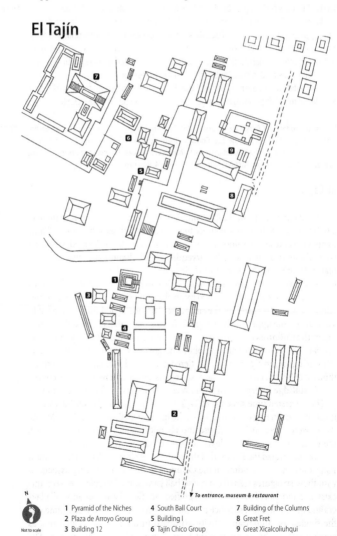

N

Not to scale

▼ To entrance, museum & restaurant

1 Pyramid of the Niches	**4** South Ball Court	**7** Building of the Columns
2 Plaza de Arroyo Group	**5** Building I	**8** Great Fret
3 Building 12	**6** Tajín Chico Group	**9** Great Xicalcoliuhqui

Human Sacrifice at El Tajín

The ferocity of the Spanish conquest of Mexico was due in part to the abhorrence felt by the invaders at the Aztec practice of human sacrifice. Since then, the Aztecs have received a very bad press. However, human sacrifice was practised in Mesoamerica long before the

Aztecs arrived in the Valley of Mexico. Probably nowhere else in this vast area that is now Mexico are there such explicit representations of lives being offered to the gods or to glorify the omnipotence of a ruler than at El Tajín.

The Pyramid of the Niches The form of the Pyramid, one of the earliest structures at El Tajín, is very distinctive, and said to have 365 niches, or one for each day of the year. Dated approximately AD 600, it is crowned with a sanctuary that was lined with engraved panels, one of which shows a cacao plant bearing fruit. Cacao was precious and of great commercial value to the people of the area. There is some evidence that the rulers of Tajín controlled its cultivation in the zones surrounding the site. Another trapezoidal panel depicts a priest or ruler adorned with ball-game accoutrements and holding a knife ready to perform ritual sacrifice, the scene being set within the confines of a ball court. The depiction of a skull at the foot of the executioner indicates sacrifice by decapitation.

The North Ball Court The imagery of the North Ball court is only partially understood. Most of the problems associated with this zone derive from erosion and mutilation of the engravings. Men in bat costumes are a major theme in these panels and suggest influence from the Maya region where men dressed so were common images on ceramics of the Classic period. Also present in the North Ball Court is the imagery of the ball game and human sacrifice.

The South Ball Court The South Ball Court offers a fascinating glimpse into the philosophy that underpinned the whole ritual life of El Tajín. Central to the narrative is the role of the ball player who acts as an intermediary between this world and that of the gods. In the engravings, the ball player is presented to the executioner and decapitated while the gods look on. Two of the panels are bordered with the image of a laughing pulque deity with two bodies, there are many Venus symbols, the death god, Mitlantecuhtli, emerges from an urn of pulque, and many of the known gods of the Mesoamerican pantheon are represented. In some of the painted books of the Central Highlands, the powerful gods Quetzalcoatl and Tezcatlipoca oppose each other in a ball game; at El Tajín, it is possible that the human players represented the earthly aspects of these gods. The imagery of the engravings of the South Ball Court is extremely complex, but it does imply that through the ball game humans can approach the realm of the gods by means of the decapitation of the principal players.

Tajín Chico The Building of the Columns (11th century) is another area with a very complex iconographical narrative. However, where the iconography of the South Ball Court expresses a communion between gods and men, the iconography of the Building of the Columns refers to themes that are much more mundane. The focus of attention is the ruler 13 Rabbit, whose glyph is repeated many times on the surface of the column drums, always with the image of a rabbit and the number 13 expressed by two bars, each counting as five, and three dots. 13 Rabbit has clearly been on a conquest campaign because a number of prisoners are lined up in preparation for the decapitation ritual. They have been divested of almost all their clothes and thus divested of their dignity. They are named by glyphs above or near their persons, which indicates that they were chiefs of opposing polities; the common warrior was rarely identified by name.

Veracruz & the Gulf Coast

Veracruz & the Gulf Coast

 The voladores of El Tajín

Traditionally, on Corpus Christi, Totonac rain dancers erect a 30m mast with a rotating structure at the top of the Pyramid of El Tajín. Four voladores *(flyers)* and a musician climb to the surmounting platform. There the musician dances to his own pipe and drum music, whilst the roped voladores *throw themselves into space to make a dizzy spiral descent, head down, to the ground.* Voladores *are now in attendance every day (during high season, other times just weekends), most of the day, and fly if they think there are enough tourists, donations expected.*

Whereas the warrior/ball player of the South Ball Court approached his death with calm dignity, the prisoners of the Building of the Columns are forced toward the sacrificial block, some held by the hair. Two sacrificial sequences but two very different approaches to death. The narrative of 13 Rabbit is now in the site museum. Although seen and depicted as all-powerful, 13 Rabbit was not omnipotent enough to prevent the destruction of the city and probably the state of El Tajín, which occurred shortly after the engraving of the Building of the Columns was completed. The great centre of the ball game, like so many others, perished, but at whose hands has yet to be discovered.

There is a small modern museum, a cafetería and souvenir shops. In the wet season beware of a large, poisonous creature like a centipede. El Tajín can be visited either from Papantla or from Poza Rica, the oil town, see below. ■ *0800-1800, except mid-Aug 0800-1900. US$2.80, free on Sun. Guidebook US$1.25, available in Museo de Antropología, Mexico City, rarely available on site.*

Four kilometres along a road east of the Río Tecolutla bridge (Puente de Remolino), near Paso de Correo (35 km southeast of Papantla, past Chote), are the Totonac ruins of **Cuyuxquihui**, probably founded around AD 1250, shortly after El Tajín's demise, and later taken over by the Aztecs as a garrison. There is a large pyramid, platforms, altars and a ball court. From Papantla take bus marked 'Joloapan' (every hour, on the hour) from 2nd class bus station.

Poza Rica

Phone code: 782
Colour map 3, grid B6
Population: 210,000

There is little else to recommend Poza Rica, apart from an inordinate number of dentists

Twenty-one kilometres northwest of Papantla is Poza Rica, an ugly oil city, formed out of four old *rancherías*, which happened to lie on top of the then second largest oil strike in the world. It has an old cramped wooden market and a simple mural by O'Higgins (*From Primitive Pre-Hispanic Agricultural Works to the Present Day Oil Industry Development*, 1959) on the outside of the **Palacio Municipal**. The streets are busy, there are several comfortable hotels and bus connections are very good. Flaring gas burn-offs light up the night sky. The tourist office is at the back of the Palacio Municipal on the ground floor, T21390 ext 129, 21338.

Sleeping **B** *Poza Rica Inn*, Carretera a Papantla, Km 4, T31922, F35888. 'Holiday Inn look-alike'. Poor restaurant. **B** *Robert Prince*, Av 6 Norte, 10 Ote, T25455, Col Obrera. **B** *Poza Rica*, 2 Norte, between 0 Ote and 12 Ote, T20134. A Best Western hotel and experienced for what it offers, friendly, credit cards accepted, fairly comfortable, good *comida corrida* in restaurant, if arriving by taxi make sure the driver does not confuse it with the *Poza Rica Inn* outside town. **C** *Nuevo León*, Av Colegio Militar, T20528, opposite market. Rooms quite spacious, fairly clean and quiet. Recommended. **C** *Salinas*, Blvd Ruiz Cortines, 1905, on Cazones road, T20238, F33525. Good, a/c, TV, restaurant, pool, secure parking. **D** *Berlim*, 2 Ote y 6 Norte, T20055. With fan, TV. **E** *Aurora*, Bolívar 4. Basic but quiet and fairly clean. **E** *Fénix*, 6 Norte (near Av Central Ote). Basic, but one of the better cheap places, opposite town centre ADO ticket office in an express mail company office. **E** *San Román*, 8 Norte 5. **E** *San Antonio*, Prolongación 20 de Noviembre (near Plaza), T33784. With bath, fan, friendly. Opposite is **E** *Rossi*, and next door **E** *Casa Blanca*. Bath and TV, cheaper without. **F** *Cárdenas*, Bermúdez y Zaragoza, T26610. Basic, not central.

Lonchería El Petrolero, Plaza Cívica 18 de Marzo y Av Central Ote. Excellent bread **Eating** baked on premises, popular with locals. *Café Manolo*, 10 Ote 60 y 6 Nte. Good breakfast, moderate prices.

Poza Rica

N			
Not to scale			

■ **Sleeping**	4 Fénix	8 Rossi	● **Eating**
1 Aurora	5 Nuevo León	9 San Antonio	1 Café Manolo
2 Berlim	6 Poza Rica	10 San Román	2 Lonchería El Petrolero
3 Casa Blanca	7 Robert Prince		

Transport **Air** Airport **El Tajín**, 3 km south, T22119; several flights daily to Mexico City. **Buses** All buses leave from new terminal referred to as ADO, about 1½ km from centre, take white bus from centre, or taxi, US$1.50. Terminal is divided into ADO (T20085, also office in centre, 6 Nte opposite Hotel Fénix, open daily, hours vary) and all others, good facilities, tourist office. ADO 1st class to **Mexico City** and **Tampico**, 21 daily each, 5 hrs, US$14. Estrella Blanca 2nd class to Mexico City, 23 daily, US$7.25. To **Monterrey**, 4 a day, US$11. To **Veracruz**, 4 hrs, US$11.50. To Xalapa, US$11-14.50, up to 5½ hrs, frequent. To **Pachuca**, Estrella Blanca, 4½ hrs, US$6, change in Tulancingo. To **Tecolutla** (see below), US$2.20, 1¼ hrs. To **Barra de Cazones**, Transportes Papantla or Autotransportes Cazones, 1 hr, US$1.20 (often waits 30 mins in Cazones on way back until bus fills). It is not always necessary to go to bus station to catch your bus: buses to Barra de Cazones leave the terminal but can be picked up as they pass through the centre along Blvd Cortines. To **Papantla** bus may be caught on Av Central Ote by Plaza Cívico 18 de Marzo. To **El Tajín**, buses leave every 20-30 mins 0700-2000 from behind Monumento de la Madre statue, marked Chote or Chote Tajín. Ask driver for fare to Las Ruinas, US$0.50, 20-25 mins, most go to the entrance.

Directory **Airline offices** *AeroMéxico*, Edificio Géminis, Parque Juárez, T26142/28877. *Aeromar*, T43001. **Banks** *Bancomer*, opposite *Hotel Poza Rica*. *Serfín*, 4 Nte y 2 Ote. **Cultural centres** *Casa de la Cultura*, Guatemala 502, T23185. **Laundry** *Yee del Centro*, Prolongación 20 de Noviembre, US$2.50 per 3 kg. **Medical services** Red Cross: Blvd Lázaro Cárdenas 106, T36871.

North of Veracruz

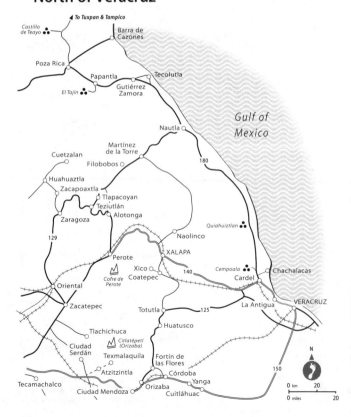

From Poza Rica you can head north to visit the **Castillo de Teayo**, a pyramid with the original sanctuary and interesting carvings on top, buses every 30 minutes, change halfway. 25 km along Route 8 is **Barra de Cazones** (not to be confused with Cazones, the town you pass on the way) with a dirty beach and a less developed, cleaner one on the north side of the river (ferry US$0.25). **B** *Mariner Costa*, on hill above river. Pool, good view over boca. **D** *Estrella del Mar*, north end of south beach. Many restaurants.

Tuxpan

On the north bank of the wide Río Tuxpan, 55 km from Poza Rica, 189 km south of Tampico is Tuxpan, tropical and humid, 12 km from the sea. Essentially a fishing town (shrimps a speciality), it is now decaying from what must have been a beautiful heyday. There's an interesting covered market; fruit sold on the quay. The beach, about 12 km east of town, is at least 10 km long and is reached by taxi or bus from Boulevard Reyes Heroles (marked 'Playa' US$0.50). Few people weekdays, no hasslers, some sandflies; hire deckchairs under banana-leaf shelters for the day (US$2). The **tourist office** is at Av Juárez 20, T40177 ext 117.

Phone code: 783
Colour map 3, grid B6

Sleeping & eating

B *Hotel Florida*, Av Juárez 23, T40650. Clean, hot water. **C** *Plaza Palmas*, on edge of town along bypass route. A/c, tennis, pool, secure parking, clean, boat launch to river, TV, good restaurant, fenced all round compound. Recommended. **C-D** *Riviera*, Blvd Reyes Heroles 17a, T45349. On waterfront, parking, rooms vary in size so check first. **D** *California*, Arteaga 16, T40879. Clean, hot water, good breakfast. **D** *Parroquia*, Berriozábal 4, beside Cathedral, T41630. Clean, friendly, hot water, fan, noisy. **E** *Posada San Ignacio*, Melchor Ocampo 29, 1 block north of plaza, T42905. Clean, with bath, fan, friendly. Recommended. **E** *Tuxpan*, Juárez and Mina, T44110. OK. *Cafetería El Mante*, Juárez beside market. Popular with locals, good *comida corrida*. Also *Bremen*. With a/c, food good and cheap.

Many restaurants line the beach (for example *El Arca*, friendly), with showers for the use of bathers (US$0.35). It is worth asking to hang up a hammock for US$2 per night.

Veracruz & the Gulf Coast

Tuxpan

N
Not to scale

■ Sleeping
1 Florida
2 Parroquia
3 Posada San Ignacio
4 Riviera
5 Tuxpan

● Eating
1 Cafetería El Mante

Entertainment **Nightlife** *Hotel Teján*, over the river, south side, then about 1 km towards the sea. Very plush, good singers but US$6.50 cover charge. *Acropolis*. Disco, dull, no beer. **Cinema** Just off Blvd Reyes Heroles, 1 block east of plaza.

Sports **Watersports** *Aquasport*, 7 km along road to beach, T70259.

Transport **Buses** ADO Terminal, east of market, near north end of bridge. Buses to Mexico City (Terminal del Nte), US$14.80, 6½ hrs via Poza Rica.

Directory **Banks** *Bancomer*, Juárez y Zapata; opposite is *Serfín*.

The coast road

Tecolutla East of Papantla, a side road branches off the main Route 180 to the coast at Tecolutla, a very popular resort on the river of that name, toll bridge US$2.50. A *fiesta* takes place two days before the carnival in Veracruz. Recommended.

Sleeping and eating B *Villas de Palmar*. D *Playa*. Good. D *Tecolutla*, best, and *Marsol* (run-down) are all on the beach. E *Posada Guadalupe* and E *Casa de Huéspedes Malena* (pleasant rooms, clean) are on Av Carlos Prieto, near river landing stage. Other hotels, D, on road to Nautla. *Torre Molina* trailer park, 16 km before Nautla on coastal Route 180 (coming from Veracruz). Electricity, water and sewage disposal, hot showers, bathrooms, swimming pool, on beach, US$10 per vehicle with 2 people. Recommended. *Restaurant Paquita*, next to *Hotel Playa*. Recommended.

Nautla & El Pital Forty-two kilometres further south, Route 180 passes through Nautla (one hotel **E**, recommended, on main street), a pleasant town, but nothing to see or do. Three kilometres before Nautla, Route 131 branches inland to Teziutlán.

El Pital (15 km in from the Gulf along the Nautla River, 80 km southeast of Papantla and named after a nearby village), was identified early in 1994 as the site of an important, sprawling precolumbian seaport (approximately AD 100-600), which lay hidden for centuries under thick rainforest. Now planted over with bananas and oranges, the 100 or more pyramid mounds (some reaching 40m in height) were assumed by plantation workers to be natural hills. Little excavation or clearing has yet been done, but both Teotihuacán -style and local-style ceramics and figurines have been found. Archaeologists believe El Pital may mark the principal end point of an ancient cultural corridor that linked the north central Gulf Coast with the powerful urban centres of Central Mexico. As at nearby El Tajín, ball courts have been discovered, along with stone fragments depicting what may be sacrificed ball players.

The ruins of **Cempoala** are 40 km north of Veracruz. The coastal city was conquered by Cortés and its inhabitants became his allies. The ruins are interesting because of the round stones uniquely used in construction. Sundays can be very crowded. It is a pleasant site and setting and *voladores* are often in attendance. From Veracruz take a picnic. ■ *US$1.40, small museum on site. Take 2nd class bus to Cardel, and then a micro to Cempoala.*

Chachalacas is a beach with a swimming pool and changing facilities (US$1 adults) in an expensive but spotless hotel of the same name. Recommended. Thatched huts; local delicacies sold on beach, including *robalito* fish. It is worth asking the restaurants on the beach to let you hang up your hammock, most have showers and toilets. They charge US$2 if you agree to eat at their restaurant.

Veracruz & the Gulf Coast

La Antigua, the site of what was thought to be Cortés's house, is 1½ km off the road to Cardel, some 30 km north of Veracruz. Take a Cardel bus from the second-class part of the bus station (US$0.40) and get off at La Antigua Caseta, the first toll booth the bus comes to. It is an easy walk from there, 10-15 minutes. The house is worth the visit just to see the large ceiba roots growing all over the walls. There is also an attractive early 16th-century church, the Ermita del Rosario. A small boy at the site gives an excellent tour in Spanish. Boats can be hired on the river. **D** *Hotel Malinche*. Quiet, laid back, peaceful.

Veracruz

Veracruz is a mixture of the very old and the new; there are still many picturesque white-walled buildings and winding side streets. The centre is at the back of the harbour and has something of a fifties feel about it. It is very much a port town, noisy and congested, but lively, full of music and dance, and with a definite Caribbean air.

Phone code: 29
Colour map 4, grid B1
Population: 1mn

The heart of the city is the Plaza de Armas (Zócalo). The square is white-paved, with attractive cast iron lampstands and benches, and surrounded by the cathedral (with an unusual cross, depicted with hands), the Palacio Municipal and colonial-style hotels. The plaza comes alive in the evenings with an impressive combination of the crush of people, colour and marimba music in the floodlit setting. From 15 July to the end of August there is jazz in the Zócalo from 1900. At night too, the *malecón* (seafront) is very lively, and sometimes fire-eaters and other performers entertain the public.

The local craft is tortoise-shell jewellery adorned with silver, but remember that the import of tortoise shell into the USA and many other countries is prohibited.

Ins and outs

Aeropuerto Las Bajadas (VER), about 12 km from the city centre, has flights to Mexico City and other domestic destinations, as well as to Houston and San Antonio in the US, and to Havana, Cuba. There is an efficient shuttle service into town. The bus terminals (first and second class) are about 3 km from the town centre, on Avenida Díaz Mirón (see **Transport** page 167). The train station is five blocks north of the Plaza de Armas, by the docks, but check that passenger services are running before planning your journey. Highways 150 and 150D (*supercarretera*) link Mexico City to the Gulf Coast at the port of Veracruz. Route 180 runs north-south along the coast.

Getting there & away

All places of interest are within easy walking distance of the Plaza de Armas. Frequent buses run along the seafront to Mocambo or Boca del Río during the day, but at night you may have to take a taxi. The **tourist office** in the Palacio Municipal on the Zócalo, T329942, is helpful but they have no hotel price lists or town maps. The Federal office, *en route* to Boca del Río, T321613, has more information.

Getting around

If planning to visit Veracruz or the hills inland (for example Xalapa) between July and September, check the weather forecast because many tropical storms blow themselves out in this region, bringing heavy rain. From October to January the weather tends to be changeable, with cold, damp winds from the north. At this time the beaches and Malecón are empty and many resorts close, except over Christmas and New Year when the tourists flood in and all road transport is booked up five days in advance. Otherwise it is generally hot.

Best time to visit

Background

The principal port of entry for Mexico lies on a low alluvial plain bordering the Gulf coast. Cortés landed near here at Isla de los Sacrificios, on 17 April 1519. The first settlement was called Villa Rica de la Vera Cruz; its location was changed several times, including to La Antigua (see above). The present site was established in 1599.

Culturally, Veracruz is a Caribbean city, home to the *jarocho* costume, dance and music which features harps and guitars. The most famous dances, accompanied by the *conjunto jarocho* dressed in white, are the *bamba* and *zapateado*, with much stamping and lashing of feet related to the flamenco of Andalucía. Mexico's version of the Cuban *danzón* music and the *música tropical* add to the cultural richness. Many cultural events can be seen at the **Instituto Veracruzano de Cultura**, a few blocks from the Zócalo with a good, new café and library; a nice place to relax and mingle with students.

Sights

The food is good, the fishing not bad, and the people noisy and welcoming.

The city's two most interesting buildings are the very fine 17th-century **Palacio Municipal** (1627), on Plaza de Armas, with a splendid façade and courtyard, and the **fortress of San Juan de Ulúa** (1565), on Gallega Island, now joined by a causeway to the mainland. The fortifications failed to deter the buccaneers and San Juan de Ulúa later became a political prison. Mexico's

Veracruz

Related maps
A Veracruz centre,
page 217

'Robin Hood', Chucho el Roto, was imprisoned here, and escaped three times. Benito Juárez was also incarcerated here between 1858 and 1861. In 1915, Venustiano Carranza converted it into a presidential palace. ■ *Take the bus marked Ulúa from Malecón Av República; it is not advisable to walk there. 0900-1700 Tue-Sun, fortress US$1.80.* The **Baluarte de Santiíago**, a bastion which once formed part of the city walls, is at Francisco Canal y Gómez Farías and contains a small prehispanic gold collection recovered from a wreck. ■ *1000-1630, Tue-Sun,* US$2.10. The **aquarium** has moved from the harbour breakwater to a new building at Villa del Mar. There is a large underwater viewing tank for watching sharks and other exotic species. ■ *1000-1900 Mon-Fri, 0900-1900 Sat and Sun, US$4.35.*

The **Museo de la Ciudad**, at Zaragoza 397, has a good, well-displayed collection of photographs; it traces the history of Veracruz from the Conquest to 1910. ■ *0900-1500 Mon-Sat, US$0.35, English booklet available.* Plazuela de la Campana, by Serdán and Zaragoza, is an attractive small square. The **Museo Carranza**, on the *malecón*, has photos of the Revolution, the life of Carranza and his battles against the Huerta régime (the last room shows a picture of Carranza's skeleton and the trajectory of the bullet that killed him). ■ *Tue-Sun 0900-1700, free.* The **Museo Histórico Naval**, Gómez Farías and Morales, has an excellent and extensive collection of naval memorabilia especially 1914 resistance to US invasion. ■ *Mon-Sun 0900-1700, free.*

On the way to Mocambo beach, where the Boulevard Avila Camacho meets Boulevard Ruiz Cortines, is the **Museo Agustín Lara**, *La Casita Blanca*, a must for anyone interested in Mexican popular music. It was the home of the greatest 20th-century Mexican song-writer, Agustín Lara, who wrote more than 700 songs (*Solamente una vez*, *Veracruz*, *Granada*, and *María Bonita* among the most famous), many of which still reverberate around the streets and squares of Veracruz. ■ *US$2, free on Sun. A pianist plays and sings Tue-Sat 1100-1400, 1600-1900, and at other times visitors are welcome to play Lara's piano.*

The beaches along the waterfront, and the sea, are polluted from the heavy shipping. A short bus ride from the fish market takes you to Mocambo beach, which has a superb, 50m swimming pool (with restaurant and bar, admission US$3.30), beach restaurants, Caribbean-style beach huts and dirty sand; the water is quite a bit cleaner though still rather uninviting in colour. There are crabs and mosquitoes and much pestering by sellers. The Gulf is even warmer than the Caribbean. The beach is crowded, and at holiday time cars race up and down,

Beaches
There is a fine, uncrowded beach at Chachalacas, 50 km north (see page 212)

there are loud radios, etc. To Mocambo take a bus marked 'Boca del Río' on Avenida Zaragoza. There is little shade near the beach.

Harbour trips
For excursions north of Veracruz, see page 212

Harbour trips from the *malecón*, US$4 per person for 35 minutes if 15 people turn up. On Sunday, to Mandinga for cheap fresh seafood (big prawns), and local entertainment.

Boca del Río
Some 6 km to the south of Veracruz (*colectivo* from Av Zaragoza) is Boca del Río, beyond Mocambo, on the left bank of the mouth of Río Jamapa. In 1518, the Spaniard Grijalva gave the already existing settlement the name of Río de Banderas as the inhabitants carried small flags in order to transmit messages. Despite commercial and residential development steadily filling up the space between Veracruz and Boca, the latter guards its own identity, and still has the atmosphere of a small village. Worthy of a visit is the church of Santa Ana (1716). Modern buildings of interest include the Palacio Municipal, Teatro del Pueblo, and the Casa de la Cultura but most people come to Boca del Río to eat at one of its many fish restaurants.

A 10-minute bus ride from Boca del Río to the other side of the river is El Conchal, a small residential development overlooking picturesque lagoons with a number of attractive restaurants. The bus continues along a low sandy spit to Punta Antón Lizardo where there is a small village with a few beach restaurants and good sand and bathing.

Sleeping and eating **C** *Zamora*. Comfortable rooms with a/c. **D** *Boulevard*. More expensive hotels are on the coast road (Blvd Avila Camacho and Blvd Miguel Alemán) where the best beaches are (not great-muddy sand).
Boulevard, Blvd I Zaragoza esq Zamora. Expensive. Excellent cheaper restaurants nearby serving large variety of fresh fish. In **El Conchal** *Restaurant El Payán*.

Essentials

Sleeping
Because of the liveliness of the Zócalo at night, hotels rooms overlooking the square can be noisy

■ *on maps*
Price codes:
see inside front cover

AL *Mocambo*, Calzada Ruiz Cortines 4000, T371661, F220212, 8 km out on Mocambo beach. 1930s palace, good service and food. Highly recommended. **A** *Calinda* (formerly *Veracruz*), Av Independencia esq Lerdo, near Zócalo, T311124. Probably the best in the centre. **A** *Emporio*, Paseo del Malecón, Insurgentes Veracruzanos y Xicoténcatl, T320020, F312261. Very good, with bath, swimming pool, inexpensive *comida corrida* and superb buffet breakfast (US$5) Sat-Sun, rather old-fashioned. **A** *Puerto Bello* (aka *Howard Johnson's*), Avila Camacho 1263, T224828, F224835. Good, clean, friendly, most rooms have sea-view. Recommended. **B** *Colonial*, on Zócalo, T320193, F320193. Swimming pool, indoor parking. Recommended. **B** *Hawaii*, Aquiles Serdán 458, T38088, F325524. 'Funky' architecture, comfortable, quiet. **B** *Hostal de Cortés*, 3-star, Avila Camacho y de las Casas, T320065, F315744, hostal@net.iaver.com.mx Convenient for clean beaches, helpful. Recommended.

C *Baluarte*, opposite the small fort of Baluarte, Canal 265, T325842, F325486. Good, clean. Recommended. **C** *Cristóbal Colón*, Avila Camacho 681, T823844. Small, quiet, some rooms with sea-view, balconies, clean. **C** *Ruiz Milán*, Malecón 432 y Gómez Farías, T323777, F322772. Good. **C** *Mar y Tierra*, Figueroa y Malecón, T/F326096. Cheaper in low season, some rooms with balconies overlooking the harbour, restaurant serving good breakfast. **C** *Príncipe*, Collado 195. Some distance from centre, very clean with hot shower and toilet. **C** *Royalty*, Abasolo 34, T322844, F327096. Average, near beach, 20 mins' walk from Zócalo, but noisy as it caters mainly to student groups. Recommended.

D *Casa de Huéspedes*, on Morelia, near Zócalo. With bath, hot water, quiet, clean, use of mosquito net needed, economical restaurant next door. **D** *Central*, Díaz Mirón

1612, T372222, next to ADO bus terminal. Clean, fair, noisy, erratic hot water, friendly, get room at back, especially on 5th floor, laundry facilities. **D** *Concha Dorada*, on Zócalo, T312996, F313246. Very pleasant. **D** *Faro*, 16 de Septiembre 223, near *Hotel Emporio*, T316538, F316176. Good value. **D** *Impala*, Orizaba 658, T370169. With bath, cold water, mosquitoes but clean, near bus station. **D** *Mallorca*, Aquiles Serdán 424 T327549. With bath and fan, radio, newly furnished, very clean. Highly recommended. **D** *Oriente*, M Lerdo 20, T/F312490. Secure parking, clean, friendly, balconies (noisy from street), good fans, some a/c. Recommended. **D** *Santo Domingo*, Aquiles Serdán 481, T316326. With bath, fan, OK, noisy, bakery attached.

E *Amparo*, Aquiles Serdán 482, T322738. With fan, insect screens, clean, hot water, good value. Recommended **E** *Casa de Huéspedes La Tabasqueña*, Av Morelos 325. Fan, new bathrooms, upper rooms less good, front rooms noisy, many others without windows, cheap, clean, safe, helpful. **E** *Hatzin*, Reforma 6 and Avista. Friendly. Recommended. **E** *Marsol de Veracruz*, Av Díaz Mirón 1242, T325399, right from ADO bus station 4 blocks. Quiet, with bath, clean and helpful. Highly recommended. **E** *Paloma*, Av Morales y Reforma, T324260. Clean, basic, fan, friendly, good value. **E** *Santander*, Landero y Coss 123, T324529. With bath and TV, very clean. **E** *Sevilla*, Av Morelos 359, T324246. With fan and TV, negotiate. **F** *Las Nievas*, Tenoya, off Plaza Zamora, T325748. With bath, fan, dark rooms. Many others in port area, reached by bus from the bus terminal.

Trailer park The only trailer park is behind *Hotel Mocambo* (see above). Dry camping, showers and bathrooms dirty, US$6.50 for vehicle and 2 people.

Youth hostel Paso Doña Juana, Municipio de Ursulo Galván, T320878, 2 hrs by bus from town, US$2.30 a night; for information on Villas Deportivas Juveniles, see under Mexico City Campsites.

Veracruz centre

■ Sleeping

1 Amparo	3 Colonial	5 Mar y Tierra
2 Baluarte	4 Emporio	6 Oriente

Veracruz & the Gulf Coast

Eating
● *on maps*

Toros are the local drinks made of eggs, milk, fruit and alcohol, delicious and potent. *La Nueva Parroquia*, on *malecón*, is famous throughout Mexico (it used to be called *Café La Parroquia*, on Plaza de Armas). 2 coffee houses in same block, very popular, excellent coffee and capuccino. In the main market, Cortés y Madero, there are inexpensive restaurants in the mezzanine, overlooking the interior (watch out for extras that you did not order). The fish market has excellent fish and shrimp cocktails, and opposite are *La Garlopa* and *Doña Paz/Normita*. Good seafood. Excellent fresh fish at *Tano's* just off the *malecón*, Mario Molina 20. Highly recommended. There is a good local fish restaurant, *Olímpica*, Zaragoza 250, near the fish market, 2 blocks from the Zócalo. *El Pescador*, for fish, Zaragoza 335 y Morales (not evenings). Good cheap *comida corrida*; and the steakhouse *Submarino Amarillo*, Malecón 472. *La Carreta*, Mariano Arista 574. Highly recommended. *Karen*, Arista 574 between Landero y Coss and Zaragoza. Good fish restaurant. *Café de la Catedral*, Ocampo y Parque Zamora. Large, local, few tourists, try fish stuffed with shrimps. *El Azteca de Cayetano*, Mario Molina 94. *Mondongos de fruta* (a selection of all the fruits in season, plus fruit-flavoured ice) are prepared on a plate; also *Mondongo de Fruta*, M Molina 88. Not cheap but delicious for fruits, juices and ices. An interesting place is *Tiburón*, Landero y Coss 167, esquina Aquiles Serdán, 2 blocks from Zócalo, run by 'Tiburón' González, the 'Rey de la Alegría', or 'Rey Feo' of carnival; the walls are covered in pictures of him and his *comparsas*, dating back to at least 1945. The food is good and inexpensive too. *La Paella*, Plaza de Armas, 138, has its name written into the concrete of the entrance floor as well as a sign. Good *comida corrida*. *Pizza Palace*, Zamora. Buffet 1200-1700, US$5. *Emir Cafetería*, Independencia 1520, near F Canal. Good breakfast. *La Quinta del Son*, on paved side street off Aquiles Serdán. Bar and restaurant, food nothing special but excellent Cuban-style *trova* band in afternoon. *Gran Café del Portal*, opposite Cathedral. Traditional (marimba all day), but not cheap. *La Puerta del Sol*, on Molina, 1 block south of the Zócalo. Friendly bar, cheap beer. *El Tranvía*, General Prim esq Rayón, opposite Parque Zamora. For good value unpretentious food (not just fish). *Le Blé*, coffee house, on road parallel to Blvd Avila Camacho, between F Canal and Rayón. Good décor, fine variety of coffees. *Nevería y Refresquería Aparito*, Aquiles Serdán and Landero y Coss, near fish market. Good for fruit and juices, try *mondongo de frutas*.

Festivals

The *Shrovetide carnival*, 7 weeks before Easter, is said to be Mexico's finest, rivalling those of New Orleans, Brazil and Trinidad. The carnival starts a week before Shrove Tuesday and ends on Ash Wednesday; Sat-Tue are the main days with parades. **NB** At this time of year it can be very difficult to find accommodation (especially on the Sat), or tickets for transportation.

Transport

Air At Las Bajadas (VER), 12 km from the centre, to the capital several flights daily and flights up and down the coast: Monterrey, Tampico, Villahermosa, Ciudad del Carmen, Mérida, Cancún, Tapachula and Tuxtla Gutiérrez. Flights also to Houston, San Antonio and Havana. AeroMexico, García Auly esq Simon Bolivar, between bus station and seafront.

Trains Rail to **Mexico City** Ferrosur: 0830, 'Mexicano' train, arrives 1855; 2200, 'Jarocho' train via Córdoba, arrives 0740, US$9 (US$21 to Córdoba, US$23 to Orizaba, US$57 to Apizaco). There is also a train from Veracruz to Tapachula (arrives 1125, US$16) via Coatzacoalcos (arrives 1840 US$7.50). Coatzacoalcos to Mérida connection at 2000, arrives 1325. Ticket office open 0600-0800, 1600-2030 except Sun and fiestas. Passenger train services are dwindling and times given here must not be relied upon.

Buses The majority of buses are booked solid for 3 days in advance throughout summer and other holiday periods; at other times queues of up to 2 hrs possible at Mexico

City booking offices of bus companies (best company: ADO). Book outward journeys on arrival in Veracruz, as the bus station is some way out of town and there are often long queues. Referred to as ADO, it is divided into 1st and 2nd class; the 1st class part, mostly ADO company, is on the main street, Díaz Mirón y Xalapa, T376790; Autobuses Unidos, mostly 2nd class, is on Lafragua y Xalapa (2 blocks from ADO), T372376. For local buses, get accurate information from the tourist office. Buses to the main bus station along Av 5 de Mayo, marked ADO; and from the station to the centre, blue and white or red and white buses marked Díaz Mirón; pass 1 block from the Zócalo, US$0.35, or *colectivos*, also US$0.35. Taxi to ADO terminal from centre, US$1.50. Bus to **Mexico City**, ADO, US$17.00, US$20.35 *primera plus* (5 hrs), via Xalapa, non-stop, or stops only at Perote, misses out Orizaba, Fortín and Córdoba; to **Villahermosa** US$36 *primera plus* (7½ hrs); to **Puebla**, US$9; to **Oaxaca**, ADO, 7-8 hrs, 0715 and 2200, US$17, US$21.50 *plus* service; to **Mérida** US$43 (16 hrs). To **Xalapa**, frequent departures, 2 hrs, US$4. To Cempoala (see page 212), 2nd class buses from ADO terminal 30 mins to Cardel then *micro*, US$0.40.

Connections with Guatemala   There are no through buses to Guatemala, but there are connecting services. The *directo* train leaves Veracruz 2100 daily for Ixtepec and Tapachula (US$13.25 *primera preferente*); scheduled to take almost 24 hrs, more like 38; not recommended, foul toilets, no lighting, so high likelihood of robbery. Take your own toiletries and food, although there is a restaurant car and food is available at every stop. No sleeping accommodation. Once again, don't rely on these trains without checking first that they are still running. Local bus services run Tapachula-border and border-Guatemala City; quicker than the much more mountainous route further north. Bus Veracruz-**Tapachula** 14 hrs, 1½-hr meal stop (at 0230), 4 10-min station stops, US$30.75, *plus* service US$50, 1900 every night, 13 hrs, video, reclining seats. Alternatively, take ADO bus to Oaxaca, then carry on to Tapachula (12 hrs) by bus. This allows you to stop at intermediate points of your choice. Buy bus tickets out of Veracruz in advance.

Airline offices *AeroMéxico*, García Auly 231, T350142. *Mexicana*, Av 5 de Mayo y Aquiles   **Directory**
Serdán, T322242. **Banks** *Bancomer*, Independencia y Juárez has its own *casa de cambio* for dollars and TCs, good rates, open Mon-Fri 0930-1730, Sat-Sun 1100-1400, also branches at Prim esq Rayón, Blvd Avila Camacho e Iturbide, Centro Comercial Plaza Cristal, Centro Comercial Las Américas, Blvd Ruiz Cortines esq Fraccionamiento Costa de Oro. *Banca Serfín*, Díaz Mirón, 2 blocks from bus station, changes US$ cash and TCs. *Banamex* is at Independencia esq Juárez with branches at 5 de Mayo esq Emparán, Mario Molino and 5 de Mayo, Centro Comercial Las Américas, Plaza Hotel Continental. American Express agency is *Viajes Olymar*, Blvd Avila Camacho 2221, T313406. 2 *casas de cambio*: *La Amistad*, Juárez 112 (behind the hotels on the Zócalo), rates not as good as the banks but much quicker; *Hotel Veracruz* changes money at similar rates.
Communications Internet: *Networld Café*, Callejón Clavijero 173, near Francisco. Canal, Mon-Sat 0900-2100, US$1.25 per hr. *Stationet*, 5 de Mayo, between Lerdo and Zamora, Mon-Sat 0900-2100, US$1 per hr. *Micro Café*, Ruiz Cortines, 100m on from Museo Agustín Lara, Mon-Sat 1000-2300, US$1.80 per hr.   **Post Offices:** main post office by bridge to San Juan de Ulúa fortress, a fine building inaugurated in 1902 by Porfirio Díaz, open 0900-1200 Mon-Fri; also at Palacio Federal, 5 de Mayo y Rayón, 0800-1900. **Embassies & consulates** *US Consular Agency*, Víctimas del 25 de Junio 388, in centre. **Laundry**   Madero 616, US$1.50 per 3 kg, open 0730-2300.

The Papaloapan Region

Route 180 heads southeast from the port of Veracruz along the flat, wet coastal plain through Alvarado and on the Tuxtla mountains and the Isthmus of Tehuantepec. An alternative route is to turn inland through the fertile Papaloapan region and on south into the state of Oaxaca.

Puerto Alvarado is a modern, fishing port 1½ hours south from Veracruz by bus, none too pleasant for women on their own as there are many bars and drunks. **D** *Hotel Lety*. Reasonable but for grim plumbing system. **D** *Hotel del Pastor*. Avoid next-door restaurant. **D** *María Isela*. Quiet, clean with fan. Recommended. Exchange services 1000-1200. Fair/carnival 31 March-5 April. Cross the Río Papaloapan (Butterfly River) by a toll bridge (US$1.70) and go along Route 180 into the sugar-cane area around Lerdo de Tejada and Angel R Cavada. At *El Trópico* shop a dirt road turns left to some quiet beaches such as Salinas and Roca Partida. Only at Easter are the beaches crowded: they are normally the preserve of fishermen using hand nets from small boats. In the dry season (December-May) there is a passable road along the coast.

Alvarado to Tuxtepec

Tlacotalpan
Phone code: 288
Colour map 4, grid B1

There is a famous Candelmas fiesta there on 31 Jan when accommodation is impossible to find

About 15 km from Alvarado a new bridge replaces the old ferry-crossing at Buenavista over the Río Papaloapan, and Route 175 heads southwards to the town of Tlacotalpan where the Papaloapan and San Juan rivers meet. It used to be on an island until the Cabezo and San Cristóbal rivers dried up and it has a secluded feel about it. This small town, once the main town in southern Veracruz, and an important international port in the steamship era, is regarded as the centre of Jarocho culture (an amalgam of Spanish, mainly from Seville, African and indigenous cultures). It has many picturesque streets with one-storey houses all fronted by stuccoed columns and arches painted in various bright colours. There are two churches in the Zócalo, the Parroquia de San Cristóbal and the Capilla de la Candelaria, and a Casa de las Artesanías on Chazaro, 1½ blocks from the Zócalo. The **Museo Salvador Ferrando** contains interesting local 19th-century paintings, furniture, artefacts and Jarocho costume. ■ *US$0.50.* The **tourist office** is on the main plaza, T42050. ■ *Mon-Fri 0800-1400, 1500-1900, Sat-Sun 1000-1400.*

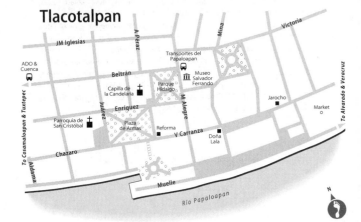

Tlacotalpan

Not to scale

Sleeping and eating **C** *Tlacotalpan*, R Beltrán 35, T/F42063. Clean, a/c, restaurant, good value. **D** *Reforma*, Carranza 2, sometimes known as *Viajero*, T42022. Good. **C** *Posada Doña Lala*, Carranza 11, T42580, F42455. With a/c and TV, good restaurant. **F** *Jarocho*, Carranza 22. Seedy, but large rooms in old house, good view of town from roof. *Restaurant La Flecha*. Excellent *sopa de mariscos* and *jaiba a la tlacotalpina* (crab). Many good fish restaurants with terraces on the riverfront eg *Brisas de Tlacotalpan*.

Transport Buses to/from Veracruz via Alvarado (Rápidos de Papaloapan US$3.10, 2¼ hrs), to Santiago Tuxtla, San Andrés Tuxtla (Cuenca US$2.50, 1½ hrs) and Villahermosa.

Cosamaloapan, some 40 km beyond Tlacotalpan on Route 175, is the local market centre with a number of hotels, and the staging point for most bus lines from Veracruz, Orizaba and Oaxaca (bus station 5 blocks from plaza). One of the largest sugar mills in Mexico is situated just outside the town – Ingenio San Cristóbal – and there is a local airstrip. From Cosamaloapan to Papaloapan the banks on either side of the river are lined with fruit trees. **Chacaltianguis**, on the east bank of the river, reached by car ferry, has houses fronted by columns.

Cosamaloapan
Phone code: 288
Population: 103,000

Sleeping **D** *San Martín*, Hidalgo 304, 1 block from plaza towards main highway, T20888, F20977. Old style, a/c, bar, restaurant. **D** *Roma*, Carranza 101, T21377, F21543. Modern. **E** *Licona*, Carranza, just off plaza. Basic. **E** *Central*, Morelos 302, on plaza, T20108. A/c, restaurant.

Forty kilometres beyond Cosamaloapan is a ferry to Otatitlán, also on the east bank of the river ■ *US$0.25, it leaves whenever there are sufficient passengers*. The town, also known as El Santuario, dates back to early colonial times, its houses with tiled roofs supported by columns (not as impressive as Tlacotalpan), but most interesting is the church. The padre maintains that the gold-patterned dome is the largest unsupported structure of its kind in Mexico, measuring 20m wide and 40m high. El Santuario has one of the three black

Otatitlán

Veracruz & the Gulf Coast

Papaloapan environs

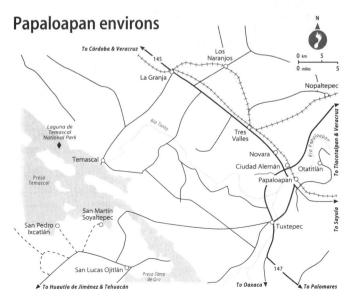

wooden statues of Christ brought over from Spain for the son of Hernán Cortés. During the anti-clerical violence of the 1930s, attempts to burn it failed, although the original head was cut off and now stands in a glass case. The first weekend in May is the saint's day and fair, for which pilgrims flock in from the *sierra* and from the Tuxtlas, many in local dress. (*Restaurant-Bar Pepe* serves delicious but unusual local food. *Restaurant-Bar Ipiranga III* also offers excellent cooking; both by embarkation point). To continue on to Tuxtepec either cross back over the river, or take bus from the plaza to Santa Cruz where there is a bus station at the junction.

At the town of **Papaloapan** on the eastern bank of the river, Route 145 from Orizaba to Rodríguez Clara and Sayula crosses Route 175, the Alvarado to Oaxaca road. On the west bank is the Santa Cruz bus terminal (almost under the railway bridge) where all second-class buses stop. A passenger ferry may be taken from here to Papaloapan (US$0.50). Although Papaloapan is the route centre for the area, the most convenient centre is Tuxtepec, 9 km further south (see below).

Papaloapan to La Tinaja

In the cane cutting season great care should be taken at night for carts travelling on the road with no lights.

Route 145 heads northwest past Tres Valles (cheap, good regional food; annual fair mid-November), and on to **Tierra Blanca**, a railway junction on the Tapachula-Veracruz and Mérida-Córdoba-Mexico City lines (Hotels: **D** *Principal*. Own shower and fan, clean, just above bus station, noisy. **E** *Balún Canán*. Cheap, hot. *Bimbis* restaurant by ADO bus station, good; shopping centre, market, car repairs, including Volkswagen agent). Route 145 passes under a sign saying 'La Puerta del Papaloapan', to join the main Mexico City with Veracruz road (Route 150) at **La Tinaja**, a second-class bus junction, with gasoline, and restaurants (one air-conditioned at service station). Papaloapan to La Tinaja takes about one hour, the road often has a lot of lorries. There are three poorly marked railway crossings on the road, two near La Granja and one near Tierra Blanca. The tarmac is often damaged in the wet season (June-December).

Papaloapan to Sayula

From Papaloapan a paved road runs eastwards to Rodríguez Clara and on to Sayula de Alemán on the Trans-Isthmian road. This road passes through the main pineapple-producing region of Mexico, which has encouraged the development of towns such as **Loma Bonita** (local airstrip, hotels, restaurants and gasoline) and **Villa Isla** (*Hotel La Choca*, restaurant good, railway station, ADO bus terminal, and centre for the rich cattle-producing area that surrounds it).

From Villa Isla a good dirt road runs south to **Playa Vicente** (*Population*: 6,974), another ranching town, located beside a wide river (**F** *Hotel Ros Bal*, clean, safe, fan, good); excellent crayfish may be eaten at the *Restaurant La Candileja*, while the café on the central plaza serves tender steaks. A dirt road leaves the Villa Isla-Playa Vicente road for Abasolo del Valle (*Population*: 2,000), but only reaches to within 7 km. The last few kilometres can be impassable by vehicle in the wet season. The town is set beside a lagoon and the houses are surrounded by fruit trees (no hotels or restaurants). Gasoline can be bought – ask at a shop who has some to sell.

At the crossroads of the Papaloapan-Sayula road about 80 km from Papaloapan, where the south turn is to Villa Isla, the north turn is a paved road which in about 30 minutes will take you past two turnings to the Olmec site at Tres Zapotes and up to Santiago Tuxtla (see page 228).

Route 145 continues east to **Rodríguez Clara**, a compact, thriving town, which is reached by branching off south down a dirt road. There are two hotels, the better is in the centre of the town, **D** *Hotel Roa*; *Restaurant La Mexicana*. Recommended.

Tuxtepec

This is the natural place for a stay in the Papaloapan area. It is an important supply centre in the neighbouring state of Oaxaca, a large commercial city, untouristed and tranquil; prices here are lower than in other parts of Oaxaca. The region has significant agricultural activity, including cattle-raising, sugar cane and pineapple plantations. The local industries are a sugar mill, brewery, and paper mill. The city is built on the left bank of the Río Santo Domingo, a tributary of the Papaloapan. Avenida Independencia, the main commercial avenue, runs along the riverfront and has the market and many shops, as well as several *miradores* offering good views. A small ferry crosses the river from below the viewpoint next to *Hotel Mirador*. The people of Tuxtepec consider themselves more *Jarochos* (i.e. from the state of Veracruz) than *Oaxaqueños*; the mixture of the music and exuberance of Veracruz with the food and handicrafts of Oaxaca is fascinating. The **tourist office**, *Cámara Nacional de Comercio Serytour*, Libertad esq Allende, opposite Parque Juárez, T50886 has limited information.■ *Mon-Fri 0900-1400 and 1700-2000, Sat 0900-1300.*

Phone code: 287
Colour map 4, grid B1
Population: 77,500

Watch out for biting gnats near the river

Parque Benito Juárez, the main plaza, has a monument to the mother and child, an ample Palacio Municipal to the south, and a modern cathedral to the east. Further west is Parque Hidalgo, with a statue of the father of Mexico's independence. The modern Casa de la Cultura, on Daniel Soto by Boulevard Benito Juárez, has a library and an exhibit hall.

Sights

B-C *El Rancho*, Avila Camacho 435, T50588, F50641. With a/c, pool, restaurant, evening entertainment, parking, US motel style. Recommended. **C** *Hacienda*, Blvd Benito

Sleeping

Veracruz & the Gulf Coast

Tuxtepec

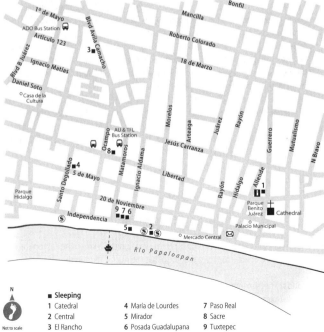

N
Not to scale

■ **Sleeping**
1 Catedral
2 Central
3 El Rancho

4 María de Lourdes
5 Mirador
6 Posada Guadalupana

7 Paso Real
8 Sacre
9 Tuxtepec

Juárez 409, T51500, F51732. With a/c, restaurant, pool, gardens, parking. **C** *Mesón*, Blvd Benito Juárez 1684, T/F51200. With a/c, pool, restaurant. **C-D** *Playa Bruja*, Independencia 1531, T50325. With a/c, pool, cafeteria, parking. **D** *María de Lourdes*, 5 de Mayo 1380, T50410, F50016. A/c, cheaper with fan, hot water, good parking. Recommended. **D** *Mirador*, Independencia 751, T50500. With a/c, hot water, **E** with fan, views of the river, a bit run down but OK, parking. **D** *Posada Guadalupana*, Independencia 584, T/F51195. With a/c, **E** with fan in old wing. **D** *Central*, Independencia 565, T50966, F50801. With a/c. **D** *Sacre*, Libertad 1170 esq Ocampo, T50846. With a/c, **E** with fan. Good. **D** *Posada del Sol*, 20 de Noviembre 1103 y Ocampo, T53737. With a/c, **F** with fan, opposite Fletes y Pasajes terminal. Noisy. **D** *Tuxtepec*, Matamoros 2 esquina Independencia, T50934. With a/c, **E** with fan, hot water, restaurant, good value. Recommended. **E** *Posada la Misión*, Hidalgo 409, T52381. With bath, fan. **E** *Posada La Choca*, Independencia 1713, T50532. Basic. **E-F** *Casa de Huéspedes Ocampo*, Ocampo 285 y Libertad. With bath, fan, friendly. **F** *Avenida*, Independencia 566, T50065. With bath, fan, basic, good value. **F** *Catedral*, Guerrero, near Zócalo, T50764. Very friendly, fan and shower. **F** *Paso Real*, Independencia 826. Very basic, shared bath, dirty.

Eating *Los Caporales*, Independencia 560, 2nd floor. Good value *comida corrida* and à la carte. *El Estero*, Benito Juárez by Independencia. Fish dishes and local cuisine. Excellent. *La Tablita*, Matamoros 2. Good *comida corrida* and à la carte. Long hours. *Mandingo*, 20 de Noviembre. Fish dishes. *Manhattan*, Independencia 49. International food, pricey. *Villa de Carvajal*, Muro Blvd esq Nicolás Bravo, on the riverfront. Seafood and grill. *Taquería Gambrinos*, 5 de Mayo 438, 1½ blocks from Parque Juárez. Excellent *tacos*, very popular, busy every evening. Recommended. *Pizza Viva*, 5 de Mayo 568. Pizza. *Broaster Chicken*, Avila Camacho 400. Fried chicken. *La Mascota de Oro*, 20 de Noviembre 891. Cheap, very friendly. Beer from the barrel can be bought from the bar next to the Palacio Municipal and the best ices are found at *La Movida*.

Sports The Papaloapan River and its tributaries, as well as the Presa Miguel Alemán offer plenty of opportunities for water sports (see Excursions below). **Fishing** The most common species found are *robalo* (sea bass), *mojarra* (carp), and on the Río Tonto (Puente de Caracol), *sábalo* (tarpon). **Boating** Motor boating and rowing is popular on the rivers and artificial lake, popular races are held in the month of May. **Rodeo** Tuxtepec has a *lienzo charro* with capacity for 5,000 spectators, where rodeos are held; this is an important regional tradition.

Festivals The *fiestas patronales* in honour of St John the Baptist are held **Jun 24** and **25**. There are fairs, fireworks and dances, including the *flor de piña* folk dance for which the Papaloapan region is well known. There is also an annual 10-day agricultural and crafts fair, called Expo-Tuxtepec.

Shopping Tuxtepec is a busy commercial centre which attracts shoppers from many nearby towns. There are many clothing stores with good prices.

Tour operators *Sotelo Viajes*, Morelos 118, T52656. *Primore*, Juárez 163, T54344.

Transport **Air** A new airport was opened in 1999 in Loma Bonita, 36 km to the east on the road to Sayula. Veracruz, 165 km to the north, has the main airport in the area.

Roads The Tuxtepec-Palomares road, Route 147, provides a shortcut to the Transístmica, but armed robberies are a danger along this route day and night. The road via Sayula is 20 km longer, but much safer. AU buses covering the route from Tuxtepec to Tehuantepec, Juchitán, and Salina Cruz, take only the Sayula road.

The Papaloapan dams

The river basin drained by the Papaloapan and its tributaries covers some 47,000 sq km, about twice the size of the Netherlands, and is subject to a programme of regional development by the Comisión del Papaloapan. Two large dams, Miguel Alemán and Cerro de Oro, were built to control the sometimes severe flooding of the lower basin. The dams have formed a very large joint lake, *which is quite scenic; the northwestern shore and islands were declared a nature reserve, Parque Natural Laguna de Temascal. A first phase of the Temascal hydroelectric plant by the Presa Alemán was completed in 1959, generating 154 megawatts, a second phase completed in 1996, generates an additional 200 megawatts.*

Buses There is a joint bus station for **ADO**, **AU** and **Cuenca** at Matamoros by Blvd Avila Camacho. Other second class companies have their own stations. To **Oaxaca**, with Cuenca (goes to first class Oaxaca terminal), 8 daily, US$7.60, 7 hrs; second class with Autobuses del Trópico, Libertad esquina Ocampo, 4 daily, US$6.70, 7½ hrs. To **Valle Nacional**, with Autobuses del Trópico, every 15 mins, 0500-2100, US$1.10, 1 hr. To **Mexico City**, with AU, 8 daily, US$19. To **Puebla**, with AU, 6 daily, US$13.80. To **Veracruz**, with Cuenca, frequent daily service, US$5.60. To **San Andrés Tuxtla**, with Cuenca, frequent daily service, US$6.52. To **Juchitán**, **Tehuantepec** and **Salina Cruz**, with AU, 3 nightly, US$9.80 Juchitán, US$10.65 Tehuantepec, US$11.30 Salina Cruz.

Banks *Bancomer*, Independencia 437, Cash and TCs, 0900-1400, complicated. *Bital*, Independencia 895, cash and TCs. *Agencia de Divisas Greco*, Independencia 269, cash and TCs, poor rates, Mon-Fri 0900-1800, Sat 0900-1400. **Communications Internet:** *Tuxcom*, Guerrero esq Muro Blvd, by riverfront, Mon-Sat 0800-2100, Sun 0900-1900. US$1.95 per hr. *Tux-Net*, Morelos 200, Mon-Sat 0900-2100. US$2.15 per hr. **Laundry** *Lava Sec*, Guerrero esq Muro Blvd and Independencia 1683, wash and dry US$3.25 per 4kg load. **Directory**

Excursions from Tuxtepec

The **Presa Miguel Alemán**, a lake formed by the Miguel Alemán and Cerro de Oro dams is very scenic. There are several points of access, the most widely used is that of **Temascal**, a small town near the Alemán dam, with shops and a few places to eat, but no hotels although there is a woman who offers very basic accommodation. Sunday is the most active day in Temascal. Access is via a paved road off the Tuxtepec-Tierra Blanca road. ■ *There is an hourly bus service from Tuxtepec with AU, 0615-1815, US$2, two hours, last bus back from Temascal at 1800*. At one end of the dam, atop a pyramid, is an imposing monument to Miguel Alemán, former president and promoter of the project. To the right of the monument is a small village along the shoreline with thatched huts serving fish and cold drinks; *mojarra* (carp) is the speciality here, brought in by small fishing craft. The same boats can be hired for touring or fishing for approximately US$1.75 per hour. The water by the shore is somewhat dirty; for swimming best take a boat to the island across the bay. There are a number of settlements around the lake and on some islands; Soyaltepec, on an island of the same name, is the closest to Temascal. A nice trip is from Temascal to **San Pedro Ixcatlán**, a Mazatec village to the south ■ *one boat at 1100 daily, US$2.20 per person, 1½ hours*. The crossing is lovely, with many cormorants and herons flying by and spectacular views of the mountains rising abruptly behind the lake. The sun is very strong, with a fierce glare off the water, so take protection. There is a large colonial church in San Pedro, a lovely spot set on a hilltop with fine views of the lake. Nearby, across from a school is **E-F** *Hotel*

Nanguina. With bath, fan, clean, comfortable large rooms, good value, nice terrace with views. There are three simple restaurants in town. The *fiestas patronales* are held on May 14 and 15 when the town gets very crowded. The boat from San Pedro to Temascal goes in the early morning. Shared taxis go from San Pedro along a dirt road to a crossing on the Tuxtepec – Jalapa de Díaz road (30 minutes, US$0.65 per person), from where you can get a pick-up to Jalapa de Díaz (see below, US$0.40 per person) or a bus to Tuxtepec.

The road west of Tuxtepec towards the state of Puebla is quite scenic; along it are a number of towns and villages which maintain an indigenous flavour, *huipiles* and crafts can be found here, especially on market day. The road is paved as far as Jalapa de Díaz and then continues to San Bartolomé Ayautla and Huautla de Jiménez; there is a bus service with AU between Tuxtepec, Ojitlán and Jalapa de Díaz every 30 minutes, 0430-1800, US$1 to Ojitlán, US$2 to Jalapa de Díaz. **San Lucas Ojitlán** is a Chinantec town, 42 km from Tuxtepec, with a hilltop church dominating the surroundings. It is an important regional centre and its Sunday market gathers many people from the nearby villages, this is the best time to see Chinantec women wearing their *huipiles*. **F** *Hotel Gallegos*, off the main street, enquire at the Farmacia Veterinaria. Very basic, no running water. There are also a few basic eating establishments. The local fiesta in honour of Santa Rosa is held the last week in August, when there is much drinking and festivities. **Jalapa de Díaz** (*population* 8,000) is 70 km from Tuxtepec, near the base of Cerro Rabón, a mountain with a spectacular 500m sheer cliff face. The town is built on several small hills, with the church on the highest. The population is mainly Mazatec, the women wear colourful *huipiles* which may be purchased in shops and private homes. **F** Unnamed hotel near the Palacio Municipal, shared bath, very basic. A couple of simple eating establishments and several well-stocked shops. The local fiestas are held in mid-January.

Tuxtepec to Oaxaca

The road from Tuxtepec to Oaxaca, Route 175, is a spectacular steep and winding route, cars need good brakes and it is reported to be difficult for caravans and cyclists; the latter are recommended to take a bus. There are few services and no accommodations *en route*. It is mostly a paved road, but sections near the high passes can at times be badly potholed and rutted. The ride up from Tuxtepec to Oaxaca takes 6-7 hours, a bit less in the opposite direction. From Tuxtepec, at 30m above sea level, the road climbs 30m gradually to Valle Nacional (see below). Just after crossing the Río Valle Nacional it climbs steeply into the Sierra Juárez, reaching the El Mirador pass (2,900m) in 2½ hours. The transition from lush lowland forest to pines is splendid, there are lovely views of the ridges and valley far below (sit on the right if travelling south to Oaxaca). At Cerro Machín, just after the pass, is *Restaurant Yoana*. Good. From here the road drops in two hours to Ixtlán de Juárez and San Pablo Guelatao, the birthplace of Benito Juárez (gas station, restaurants, see Excursions north of Oaxaca, page 427 and box on page 737). The route continues to drop to the dry valley of the Río Manzanillo, at 1,500m, before climbing again to La Cumbre pass (2,700m) from which there are fine views of Oaxaca below, one hour further.

Valle Nacional
Population: 6,244
Colour map 4, grid B1
Altitude: 60m

Set in the beautiful valley of the Río Valle Nacional, 48 km south of Tuxtepec, is the small town of Valle Nacional, which sees few visitors, but offers basic services and excellent opportunities for birding and walking in the surrounding hills. The town is laid out lengthwise along the main road, there is a gas station at the Tuxtepec end; tank-up here on the way to Oaxaca. Nearby are several rubber plantations (for example just across the bridge on the road to Oaxaca) and tappers may be seen at work early in the morning, especially in the dry season. This area had a horrific reputation as the *Valle de los Miserables*, in the era of Porfirio Díaz, for political imprisonment and virtual slavery from which there was no escape; a vivid description of this period can be found in John Kenneth Turner's *Barbarous Mexico* (1911). *Fiestas patronales* of nearby San José are held March 18-19.

Along the scenic Tuxtepec-Valle Nacional road are several recreational opportunities, including **Chiltepec**, a popular bathing spot on the Río Valle Nacional, 22 km from Tuxtepec. Not far from Valle Nacional is a lovely natural spring at **Zuzul**. The setting, by the Soloyapan river and the town of Sola de Vega, is very pretty; although the water is chilly, it is quite pleasant for swimming, free entry, there are a few bars nearby, many people on Sundays and holidays, especially Easter Week. From Valle Nacional, take a Tuxtepec-bound bus as far as La Boca (US$0.33, 20 minutes), then a pick-up truck (US$0.20, 5 minutes) or walk 20 minutes (take the side road right from La Boca, then the first turn-off to the left) to the end of the road at the river's edge, where a motorboat will take you to Zuzul on the other shore (US$0.20). There are other springs nearby. Pick-up trucks also run from La Boca to San Cristóbal and other towns in the valleys to the east of Valle Nacional, you can make some nice day trips in this area. At Ozumacín there is a colonial church in a lovely setting.

Sleeping and eating F *Lourdes Sánchez*, near gas station at north end of town. With bath, fan, good restaurant, basic, family-run, friendly. F *Valle*, off main street. With bath, fan, cold water, parking, basic, family-run, friendly. F Unnamed hotel next door. With bath, cold water, a bit run down. Several simple restaurants and *taquerías* along the main street. One slightly more upscale place at the entrance to town from Tuxtepec.

Transport Buses: to Tuxtepec, every 15 mins throughout the day, US$1.10, 1 hr. To Oaxaca first class terminal, with Cuenca, 8 daily, US$5.90, 6 hrs; to second class terminal, with Autobuses del Trópico or Fletes y Pasajes, 5 daily, US$5.90, 6 hrs.

In the Sierra Juárez, some 50 km south of Valle Nacional, on the road to Oaxaca is a turn-off west for **San Pedro Yolox**, a peaceful Chinantec village, clustered on the side of the mountain, which lies some 20 minutes drive from the main road, along a dirt road. About 25 km further south and 90 km from Oaxaca is **Llano de las Flores**, a huge grassy clearing in the pine forest, with grazing animals and cool scented air; nearby are waterfalls. Wood from these forests is cut for the paper mill in Tuxtepec. As you make the transition from the lowlands to the mountains, the wooden houses with thatched roofs are replaced by adobe or brick homes. 106 km south of Valle Nacional and 65 km north of Oaxaca is Ixtlán de Juárez and a couple of kilometres further south **Guelatao**, the birthplace of Benito Juárez. Thirty kilometres from Oaxaca is **El Punto**, surrounded by pine and oak forest; fruits and flowers are also grown in this area. Near town are a nursery and *Restaurant del Monte*, with nice views, cabins, and tasty soup.

Los Tuxtlas

Back on the coastal Route 180, southeast of Alvarado and the Papaloapan, is Tula where there is a spectacular waterfall, **El Salto de Tula**; a restaurant is set beside the falls. The road then climbs up into the mountainous volcanic area of Los Tuxtlas, known as the Switzerland of Mexico for its mountains and perennial greenness.

Santiago Tuxtla
Phone code: 294
Colour map 4, grid B2

This pleasant town of colonial origin is set on a river. In the main square is the largest known Olmec head, carved in solid stone, and also a museum, Museo Tuxtleco, containing examples of local tools, photos, items used in witchcraft (*brujería*), the first sugar-cane press used in Mexico, and another Olmec head. ■ *Mon-Sat 0900-1800, Sun 0900-1500, tourist info available here.* There is dancing to *jarana* bands in the Christmas fortnight. In June and July, dancers were jaguar masks to perform the *danza de los liseres*.

Travellers with little time to spare may find the trip to Tres Zapotes not worth the effort as there is little to see at the site

The archaeological site of **Tres Zapotes** lies to the west; it is reached by leaving the paved road south towards Villa Isla and taking either the dirt road at Tres Caminos (signposted) in the dry season (a quagmire from May-December), or in the wet season access can be slowly achieved by turning right at about Km 40, called Tibenal, and following the dirt road north to the site of the museum. ■ *0900-1700, US$1.65. (If it is closed, the lady in the nearby shop has a key).* The site, once the centre of the Olmec culture, is 1 km walk (the bus cannot reach Tres Zapotes if rain has swollen the river that the road has to cross). At the museum, there is an Olmec head, also the largest carved stela ever found and stela fragments bearing the New World's oldest Long Count Date, equal to 31 BC. In this region of Mexico are other Olmec sites at Cerro de las Mesas, Laguna de los Cerros, and San Lorenzo Tenochtitlán. The other major Olmec site is further east, at La Venta, in the neighbouring state of Tabasco (see page, 236).

Sleeping and eating C *Hotel Castellanos*, on Plaza, T70300. Hot shower, clean, swimming pool (US$1 for non-residents). Recommended. D *Estancia Olmeca*, No 78 on main highway just north of ADO office, T70737. Clean, friendly, parking. E *Morelos*, Obregón 13 and Morelos, T70474. Family-run, quiet, nicely furnished.

For eating, try *Chazaro*, near bridge over stream, on other side to Morelos. Small, good seafood especially *sopa de mariscos* and *chucumite* (fish). Inexpensive.

South of Veracruz

Transport AU bus from **Veracruz**, 2nd class, 3 hrs, US$2. **Tlacotalpan** with Cuenca US$2.30, 1¼ hrs. To **Tres Zapotes** from Morelos (1 block below ADO), 0700, 0830, 1130, 1300, 1500, 1630.

Banks Exchange at *Banco Comermex* on Plaza, TCs 0900-1330.

Fifteen kilometres beyond lies San Andrés Tuxtla, the largest town of the area, with narrow winding streets, by-passed by a ring road. It has a well-stocked market with Oaxacan foods such at *totopos, carne enchilada*, and *tamales de elote* (crispy tortillas, spicy meat, and cakes of maize-flour steamed in leaves). It is the centre of the cigar trade. One factory beside the main road permits visitors to watch the process and will produce special orders of cigars (*puros*) marked with an individual's name in 30 minutes.

San Andrés Tuxtla
Phone code: 294
Colour map 4, grid B2
Population: 112,000

Sleeping C *Posada San Martín*, Av Juárez 304, T21036. Clean, modern. D *Isabel*, Madero 13, T21617. A/c, OK. D *Posada San José*, Belisario Domínguez 10, T22020, close to plaza. Run by nice family and staff, restaurant, pick-up truck for excursions, 2nd hotel at Monte Pío. F *Catedral*, Pino Suárez and Bocanegra, near Cathedral, T20237. Very nice. D-E *Figueroa*, Pino Suárez 10. Hot water, friendly. D *Colonial*, Pino Suárez opposite *Figueroa*. With bath, hot water, clean. D *del Parque*, Madero 5. A/c, very clean, good restaurant. D *San Andrés*, Madero 6, just off plaza, T20604. Clean, a/c, restaurant, parking, laundry service. D *Zamfer*, ½ block from Zócalo. E *Casa de Huéspedes la Orizabana*, in the centre of town. Without bath, clean, hot water, friendly. E *Juárez*, 400m down street from ADO terminal (No 417, T20974). Clean, friendly.

Eating Near the town centre is the restaurant *La Carreta*, otherwise known as *Guadalajara de Noche*. It appears small from the outside but is large and pleasant inside. Well recommended. Sells *tepache*, a drink made from fermented pineapple, similar in flavour to cider, and *agua de Jamaica*. *La Caperucita*, popular with locals.

Transport Bus: Villahermosa US$11, 6 hrs; to **Mexico City**, 1st class, 9 hrs, US$22. AU to **Catemaco** US$0.50. ADO to **Campeche** US$26, **Frontera** US$13.50, **Cancún** US$44. 13 buses per day to **Tuxtepec**, US$4 via Cosamaloapan.

Directory Tourist office Palacio Municipal, in office of Secretariá de Relaciones Exteriores. **Communications** Internet: *'Ri' Chat*, Constitución Norte 106, near plaza.

Catemaco

A pleasant town with large colonial church and picturesque situation on lake, 13 km from San Andrés Tuxtla (bus service irregular, taxi US$5). There are stalls selling handicrafts from Oaxaca, and boat trips out on the lakes to see the shrine where the Virgin appeared, the spa at Coyamé and the Isla de los Monos (boat owners charge US$30-35 per boat). The Isla de los Monos is home to a colony of macaque monkeys introduced from Thailand for the University of Veracruz. Launches to the island charge US$12.50, or you can pay US$3.20 to be rowed there by local fishermen – cheaper and more peaceful. Many feature films have been made on or around the lake, such as *Medicine Man*, with Sean Connery, which was filmed using the **Nanciyaga** ecological park as a 'jungle' backdrop. Catemaco town is famed for its traditional *brujos* (sorcerers), which have become a great tourist attraction; however, it is a serious business and the Monte del Cerro Blanco, to the north, is the site of their annual reunion.

Phone code: 294
Colour map 4, grid B2
Population: 31,000

There are few streetname signs

Veracruz & the Gulf Coast

Excursions The **Reserva Ecológica Nanciyaga**, T30808, 7 km round the northern shore of the lake, on the road to Coyamé has rainforest with rich birdlife, including toucans.

At Sihuapan, 5 km from Catemaco, is a turning south onto a paved road which leads to the impressive waterfall of Salto de Eyipantla (well worth a visit, especially early morning); there are lots of butterflies. A stairway leads down to the base and a path winds through a small village to the top. Small boys at the restaurant near the falls offer their services as guides. Take second-class AU bus Catemaco-Sihuapan; from 1030 buses leave every 30 minutes from Sihuapan to Eyipantla, otherwise it's a 20-minute walk to Comoapan, then take a taxi for US$2. There are also buses from the plaza in San Andrés Tuxtla.

Sleeping **A** *La Finca*, just outside town, T30430. Pool, attractive grounds, beautiful setting
A number of hotels are beside lake, full at weekends, a/c, comfortable rooms, but poor food and service.
situated at the lakeside **B** *Motel Playa Azul*, 2 km on road to Sontecomapan, T30042. Modern, a/c; in a nice setting, comfortable and shady, with showers. **B-C** *Juros*, Playa 14, T30084. Hot water, café, water-skiing on lake, will allow trailers and use of parking. **C** *Posada Komiapan* (swimming-pool and restaurant), T30063. Very comfortable. **C** *Catemaco*, T30203, F30045. A/c, excellent food and swimming pool, and **C** *Berthangel*, T30411. A/c, satellite TV, similar prices; both on main square.

D *Del Cid*, 1 block from ADO bus terminal. With fan and bath, OK. **D** *Imalca y del Angel*, Independencia and Ocampo, T30412. Parking. **D** *Los Arcos*, T30003. Clean, fan, good value. **D** *del Brujo*, Ocampo y Malecón. Fan, a/c, shower, nice clean rooms, balcony overlooking the lake. Recommended. **E-F** *Acuario*, corner of plaza, T30418. Hot water, parking next to **E** *Loud Pasc*, T30108. **E** *San Francisco*, Matamoros 26. With bath, basic, but good and clean.

Trailer park At Solotepec, by the lake on the road to Playa Azul. US$6.50 per vehicle, very clean, hook-ups, bathrooms. Recommended. Also *La Ceiba*, restaurant and trailer park, Av Malecón, 6 blocks west of Zócalo. By lakeshore, camping and hook-ups, bathrooms with hot water, restaurant and lakeside patio.

Eating On the promenade are a number of good restaurants: *María José*. Best. *Las 7 Brujas*. Wooden restaurant open till 2400, good, try *mojarra* (local fish). *La Julita*, also lets rooms, **E**, with bath, pleasant. Recommended. Opposite Cathedral are *La Pescada*, good fish, US$5 and *Melmar*, popular. *La Ola*, built almost entirely by the owner in local natural materials, and *La Luna*, among others. At the rear of the market, diagonally from the back of *La Luna*, are some inexpensive, good restaurants serving *comida corrida* for US$2-US$2.50, *La Campesina* is recommended. Restaurant on 1st floor opposite church, nice atmosphere. Best value are those not directly on the lake, eg *Los Sauces*, which serves *mojarra*. *Bar El Moreno*, 2 de Abril, at the beach. 'Not too fancy' but good *cuba libres* and live synthesizer music.

Catemaco

Lake Catemaco

N

Not to scale

■ **Sleeping**
1 Acuario
2 Arcos
3 Berthangel
4 Brujo
5 Catemaco
6 Juros
7 Loud Pasc
8 San Francisco

● **Eating**
1 María José

Buses Catemaco can be reached by direct AU 2nd class bus from **Veracruz**, every 10 mins, many stops, 4 hrs, US$6, also ADO 1st class; buses also from **Santiago Tuxtla**, AU 2nd class US$0.70. It is about 120 km northwest of **Minatitlán** (US$4.50) (see below); buses also from/to **Villahermosa**, 6 hrs, US$10 (ADO). To **Tuxtepec**, change in San Andrés Tuxtla. **Coatzalcoalcos** with ADO US$5.50.

Transport

Banks *Bancomer*, opposite Cathedral, open Mon, Wed, Fri 0900-1400.

Directory

To the Gulf Coast

The Gulf Coast may be reached from Catemaco along a dirt road (which can be washed out in winter). It is about 18 km to **Sontecomapan**, crossing over the pass at Buena Vista and looking down to the *laguna* where, it is said, Francis Drake sought refuge. The village of Sontecomapan (*population*: 1,465. *Hotel Sontecomapan*), lies on an entry to the *laguna* and boats may be hired for the 20 minutes' ride out to the bar where the *laguna* meets the sea (US$10 return). A large part of the lagoon is surrounded by mangrove swamp, and the sandy beaches, edged by cliffs, are almost deserted except for local fishermen and groups of pelicans. There are two good restaurants in Sontecomapan. Beaches, such as Jicacal and Playa Hermosa, are accessible to those who enjoy isolation. **Jicacal** can be reached by going straight on from the Catemaco- Sontecomapan road for 9 km on a good dirt road to La Palma where there is a small bridge which is avoided by heavy vehicles; immediately after this take left fork (poor dirt road, there is a bus) for **Montepío**, a pretty location at the mouth of the river (**D** *Posada San José Montepío*, Playas Montepío, T21010. Family-run, also basic rooms to let, **E**, and a restaurant. Recommended). Watch out for a very small sign marked **Playa Hermosa**; road impassable when wet, about 2 km, and then continuing for about 4 km from there. Playa Jicacal is long and open, the first you see as you near the water. The track reaches a T-junction: to the right is Jicacal, to the left Playa Hermosa, *Hotel*, **E** and restaurant. The place is busy at weekends.

It is not recommended to sleep on the beaches (assaults and robberies), although at Easter time many people from the nearby towns camp on the beaches

Coatzacoalcos and Minatitlán

The road from Catemaco heads south to Acayucan then east to Minatitlán and Coatzacoalcos. The latter is the Gulf Coast gateway for the Yucatán Peninsula, 1½ km from the mouth of its wide river. Pemex has a huge oil tanker loading port here. It is hot, humid and lacking in culture, and there is not much to do save watch the river traffic. The river is too polluted for fishing and swimming, and there are less than salubrious discos on the equally polluted beach by the pier at the river mouth; the beach is dangerous at nights, do not sleep there or loiter. Thirty-nine kilometres up river is **Minatitlán**, the oil and petrochemical centre (*population*: 145,000; airport), whose huge oil refinery sends its products by pipeline to Salina Cruz on the Pacific. The road between the two towns carries very heavy industrial traffic. The offshore oil rigs are serviced from Coatzacoalcos. Sulphur is exported from the mines, 69 km away. The air is constantly scented with petrochemical fumes and sometimes ammonia and sulphur compounds. There is a high incidence of lung disease. Not many foreigners visit either town.

Phone code: 921
Colour map 4, grid B2
Population: 186,000

Both cities are often under a pall of smog

Veracruz & the Gulf Coast

Sleeping **Coatzacoalcos** A *Enríquez*, Ignacio de la Llave. Good. **C** *Alex*, JJ Spark 223, T24137.

Very difficult as all hotels are used by oil workers. Don't spend the night on the street if you can't find lodging. Prices double those of hotels elsewhere

With bath, fan, clean, safe parking. **D** *Oliden*, Hidalgo 100. With fan, clean, noisy (other similar hotels in this area). **E** *San Antonio*, Malpica 205, near market. With shower. Several others nearby. *Motel Colima* at Km 5, Carretera Acayucan-Coatzacoalcos. May have rooms if none in Coatzacoalcos; it is clean, in a quiet position, but does have a lot of red-light activity. **Minatitlán** B *César*. **C** *Palazzo* on main street. A/c, credit cards accepted. **C** *Tropical*. With bath, no hot water. **D** *Nacional*, opposite *Palazzo*, Hidalgo 16, T37639. Luggage store, friendly, with bath, fan, hot water, clean. Recommended.

Eating **Coatzacoalcos** *Los Lopitos*, Hidalgo 615. Good *tamales* and *tostadas*. *Mr Kabubu's*. Bar and restaurant, near *Hotel Alex*, good food and drinks. Cheap restaurants on the top floor of the indoor market near the bus terminal. *Cafetería de los Portales*, near main plaza. Very good food and service. By the river here are several cafés, beware of overcharging. **Minatitlan** *El Marino*, behind the colourful church on main plaza. Opens relatively early, very good, clean and friendly service.

Transport **Air** Minatitlán airport (MTT), 30 mins from Coatzacoalcos, 10 mins from Minatitlán. Mexicana to Mexico City and Monterrey. **Trains** Railway station is 5 km from town at Cuatro at end of Puerto Libre bus route and on Playa Palma Sola route, smelly and dingy; irregular bus services. Better walk about 500m to the main road and get a bus there, US$0.25. Train to **Mérida**, via Palenque and Campeche at 2320, arrives 1325, but check whether it is running, service is unreliable. Another station, in the city centre, serves Tapachula, 1910, 16-17 hrs, and Veracruz, 1000, 10½ hrs.

Buses From **Coatzacoalcos** to **Mexico City**, US$26.50; to **Mérida** US$31; to **Córdoba**, US$13; to **Veracruz**, US$12, 7¼ hrs; to **Xalapa**, 8 hrs, US$17 or less, depending on number of stops; to **Ciudad del Carmen**, US$16.50; to **Salina Cruz**, US$12.15; to **Villahermosa**, US$7. The ADO and interurban bus terminal is some way from city centre. Taxi fare about US$1.50 but they will charge more.

From Minatitlán Two terminals, 1st class (ADO) near town centre, 2 blocks from Hidalgo, clean toilets, left luggage. ADO to many destinations. Cristóbal Colón buses leave from Sur, not ADO terminal, in Minatitlán. Taxi between the two, US$1.60. All buses originate in Coatzacoalcos and seat availability is assigned to each destination *en route*. Buses between the 2 town centres are marked *directo*, 40 mins, US$0.60. Those marked *Cantices* go via the airport, 200m walk from bus stop to terminal, much cheaper than US$15 taxis.

Directory **Communications** **Post Office:** Carranza y Lerdo, Coatzacoalcos. Stamps and postage upstairs at Post Office on Hidalgo, Minatitlán.

Thirty nine kilometres east of Coatzacoalcos, on a side road off Route 180 is **Agua Dulce**, where there is a campground, *Rancho Hermanos Graham*. Nice location, full hook-up, cold showers, only one bathroom for whole site, US$6.50 for car and two people.

On the Gulf Coast, further east is **Sánchez Magallanes**, (turn off Route 180 at Las Piedras, 70 km from Coatzacoalcos, signposted), a pleasant, friendly town where you can camp safely on the beach.

Tabasco and Chiapas

6

The states of Tabasco and Chiapas, although very different, merge to form a geographical block that separates Mexico from Guatemala, and from the Yucatán Peninsula. Tabasco is surprisingly flat and much of its territory is swamp and luxuriant jungle. The landscapes of Chiapas, on the other hand, extend from lowland coastal bands to the Chiapas Highlands and the Lacandón Rainforest. The difference in landscape is repeated in the climate. Tabasco is notorious for being hot and humid, while Chiapas' climate is as varied as its geography: hot days and nights by the Pacific coast and cool days and cold nights in the highlands.

Until recently, Tabasco was considered an oil state and held little appeal for the tourist but oil wealth has brought **Villahermosa**, the state capital, a certain self-assurance and vibrancy which invites exploration, and the parks, nature reserves and huge meandering rivers in the eastern and southern regions of the state are beginning to attract visitors. Its lands once gave rise to the first great civilization of Mesoamerica, the Olmec, whose influence was felt through vast zones of Mexico and further afield.

In Chiapas, the land of the Classic Maya (whose descendants still inhabit the highland villages today), the attractions are better known: **San Cristóbal de las Casas** is the end of the line for many travellers who base themselves in this unique Colonial-Indian town while they soak up the atmosphere and explore the jungle waterfalls, the dramatic canyon, the multicoloured lakes, and - highlight of any trip to Mexico - the ruins at **Palenque**, whose jungle setting is probably the most atmospheric and beautiful of all the Mayan sites.

Tabasco & Chiapas

Villahermosa

Phone code: 931
Colour map 4, grid B3
Population: 275,000

Capital of Tabasco state, Villahermosa is on the Río Grijalva, navigable to the sea. It used to be a dirty town, but is now improving, though it is very hot and rainy. **Tourist offices** In the first class bus station (English spoken) and another not far from La Venta park, in Edificio Administrativo Tabasco 2000, at Paseo Grijalva and Paseo Tabasco (T163633, F163632); both good, closed 1300-1600. Many *papelerías* sell a city map for US$0.10.

Villahermosa is heaving under pressure from the oil boom, which is why it is now such an expensive place. Buses to Mexico City are often booked up well in advance, as are hotel rooms, especially during the holiday season (May onwards). Overnight free parking (no facilities) in the Campo de Deportes. It is hard to find swimming facilities in Villahermosa: Ciudad Deportiva pool is for cardholders only. There is a bullring.

Sights The **Cathedral**, ruined in 1973, has been rebuilt, its twin steeples beautifully lit at night; it is not in the centre. There is a warren of modern colonial-style pedestrian malls throughout the central area. The **Centro de Investigaciones de las Culturas Olmecas** (CICOM) is set in a new modern complex with a large public library, expensive restaurant, airline offices and souvenir shops, a few minutes walk south, out of town along the river bank. The **Museo Regional de Antropología Carlos Pellicer**, on three floors, has well laid out displays of Maya and Olmec artefacts, with an excellent bookshop. ■ *0900-2000, closed Mon, US$1.* Two other museums worth visiting are the **Museo de Cultura Popular**, Zaragoza 810. ■ *Daily 0900-2000*, and the **Museo de Historia de Tabasco**, Avenida 27 de Febrero esq Juárez, same hours. At the northwest side of town (west of the downtown area) is **Tabasco 2000**, a futuristic mall/hotel/office area with an original statue of fishermen.

Parque Nacional La Venta In 1925 an expedition of archaeologists discovered huge sculptured human and animal figures, urns and altars in almost impenetrable forest at La Venta, once the centre of the ancient Olmec culture, 120 km west of Villahermosa. In the 1950s the monuments were threatened with destruction by the discovery

Villahermosa

of oil nearby. The poet Carlos Pellicer got them hauled all the way to a woodland area near Villahermosa, now the Parque Nacional de La Venta, Boulevard Adolfo Ruiz Cortines. The park, with scattered lakes, next to a children's playground, is almost opposite the old airport entrance (west of downtown). There, the 33 exhibits are dispersed in various small clearings. The huge heads, one of them weighs 20 tons, are Olmec, a culture which flourished about 1150-150 BC; this is an experience which should not be missed. There is also an excellent zoo with creatures from the Tabasco jungle: monkeys, alligators, deer, wild pigs and birds. ■ *0800-1600, closed Mon, US$1.50. It takes up to two hours to do the park justice; excellent guides, speak Spanish and English (US$6.65 for one hour 10 minutes).* Recommended. There is nothing to see at the original site of La Venta. Outside the park, on the lakeside is an observation tower, **Mirador de las Aguas**, with excellent views. Entry free but only for the fit as there are lots of stairs.

Take a bus marked 'Gracitol' from ADO bus terminal, US$0.30 (don't take a bus going to 'La Venta'; if in doubt, ask). To walk from ADO, left at front entrance, left again at the overpass and straight ahead. Bus Circuito No 1 from outside second-class bus terminal goes past Parque La Venta (taxi to La Venta park US$2). From Parque Juárez in the city, take a 'Fraccionamiento Carrizal' bus and ask to be let off at Parque Tomás Garrido, of which La Venta is a part.

Be sure to take insect repellent for the visit

Northwest of Villahermosa are the Maya ruins of **Comalcalco**, reached by bus (two a day by ADO, 1230 and 1800, US$2.50, or local Souvellera bus, US$2, 1½ hours over paved roads; Souvellera bus leaves from near the bridge where Avenida Universidad crosses Ruiz Cortines, 4-5 blocks north of Central Camionera in Villahermosa). Whichever bus you take, you will need to walk (3 km) or take a taxi to the ruins, US$5. Otherwise, take a taxi as far as the entrance to the park, US$0.50, and walk the rest of the way (1 km). The ruins are unique in Mexico because the palaces and pyramids are built of bricks, long and narrow like ancient Roman bricks, and not of stone. ■ *Daily 1000-1600, US$1.60.* From Comalcalco go to **Paraíso** near the coast; frequent buses run from town to the beach 8 km away. Interesting covered market with good cocoa. **D** *Centro Turístico.* Beach hotel, clean, no hot water, food and drink expensive. Also **E** *Hotel Hidalgo.* In centre, clean.

Excursions

Best is **LL** *Exalaris Hyatt*, Juárez 106, T34444, F55808. All services. **AL** *Holiday Inn Villahermosa Plaza*, Paseo Tabasco 1407, T64400, F64569, 4 km from centre. Restaurant, bar, entertainment. **AL** *Cencali*, Juárez y Paseo Tabasco, T151999, F156600. Excellent breakfast. Highly recommended. **A** *Maya-Tabasco* (Best Western), Blvd Ruiz Cortines 907, T21111, F21133. All services, ask for special offers; sometimes as cheap as **D**. **B** *Don Carlos*, Madero 418, T22493, F24622. Central, clean, helpful, good restaurant (accepts American Express card), nearby parking. **B** *Plaza Independencia*, Independencia 123, T21299, F44724. **C** *Chocos*, Merino 100, T129444, F129649, near ADO terminal. Friendly, clean, a/c. **C** *María Dolores*, Aldama 104. A/c, hot showers, excellent restaurant (closed Sun). **C** *Palma de Mallorca*, Madero 516, T20144. **C** *Ritz*, Madero 1009, T121611. Safe parking. Many other hotels along Madero (eg **D** *La Paz*, central). **D** *Oviedo*, Lerdo 303. Good. **D** *Sofía*, Zaragoza 408, T26055. Central, tolerable but overpriced, a/c. **E** *Madero*, Madero 301, T20516. Damp, good value, some rooms for 4 are cheaper. **E** *Oriente*, Madero 425. Clean, hot shower, fan, good restaurant. Recommended. **E** *San Miguel*, Lerdo 315, T21500. Good value, quiet, clean, shower, fan, very friendly, no windows, run-down. **E** *Tabasco*, Lerdo 317, T20077. Not too clean, cold water, mosquitoes. Several others on Lerdo. Cheap hotels, from **E** per person, on Calle Constitución (come out of main entrance of bus terminal, turn right then 1st left and continue for 5 blocks, but it's the red-light district).

Sleeping
The price difference between a reasonable and a basic hotel can be negligible, so one might as well go for the former

Tabasco & Chiapas

Youth hostel The youth hostel at the back of the Ciudad Deportiva doesn't accept travellers arriving in the evening (4 km southwest of the bus station), CP 80180, T56241.

Eating A good restaurant at *Hotel Madan*, Madero 408. Good breakfast, inexpensive fish dishes, a/c, newspapers, a good and quiet place to escape from the heat. *VIPs*. Next door, reliable and moderately priced. *Cafetería La Terraza*, Reforma 304, in *Hotel Miraflores*. Good breakfast. *Café Casino*, Suárez 530. Good coffee. *Bruno's*, Lerdo y 5 de Mayo. Cheap, good, noisy, good atmosphere. *Café La Barra*, Lerdo, near *Bruno's*. Good coffee, quiet, pleasant. *El Torito Valenzuela*, next to *Hotel Madero*. Mexican specialities, excellent and inexpensive. Highly recommended. *El Fogón*, Av Carlos Pellicer 304A. Good value. *Blanca Mariposa*, near entrance to Parque La Venta. Recommended. *Aquarius*, Javier Mina 309, near Av Méndez. Vegetarian food, juice bar and health food store. Avoid the bad and expensive tourist eating places on and near the river front.

Festivals *Ash Wednesday* is celebrated from 1500 to dusk by the throwing of water in balloon bombs and buckets at anyone who happens to be on the street.

Tour operators *Viajes Villahermosa*, 27 de Febrero 207.

Transport **Local** Taxis run mainly on a fixed-route *colectivo* system (US$1.50 per stop), which can be a problem if you want to go somewhere else. You may have to wait a long time before a driver without fares agrees to take you. **Car hire** *Hertz* car rental is available from the airport. *Agrisa*, M Ocampo esq Paseo Tabasco y Malecón, T129184, good prices, eg US$40 per day including taxes and insurance, but it is expensive to return the car to another city.

Air Airport Carlos R Pérez (VSA), 8 km from town. Flights to Cancún, Ciudad del Carmen, Havana (Cuba), Houston (Texas), Mérida, Mexico City, Monterrey, Oaxaca, San Antonio (Texas), Tampico, Tuxtla Gutiérrez and Veracruz. VW bus to town US$3 per person, taxi US$9.50 for 2.

Buses 1st class, ADO bus terminal is on Javier Mina between Méndez and Lino Merino, 12 blocks north of centre, computerized booking system, staff unhelpful. A taxi to the ADO terminal costs US$6, expensive but hard to avoid. Left luggage at ADO terminal, 0700-2300, US$0.30 per piece per hour, often closed. Alternatively, go to Sra Ana in minute restaurant/shop at Pedro Fuentes 817, 100m from ADO, reliable, open till 2000, small charge made, or, upstairs at 203 Javier Mina, opposite ADO, US$0.10 per piece per hour. Other private luggage depositories by the bus station also make a small charge. The Central Camionera 2nd class bus station is on Avenida Ruiz Cortines, near roundabout with fisherman statue, 1 block east of Javier Mina, opposite Castillo, 4 blocks north of ADO (ie 16 from centre); usually in disarray and it is difficult to get a ticket. Mind your belongings.

Several buses (1st class) to **Mexico City**, US$30, 12 hrs, direct bus leaves 1815 (Cristóbal Colón) or 1650 (ADO) then frequent through the night, expect to wait a few hours for Mexico City buses and at least 30 mins in the ticket queue. To **Xalapa** with ADO, 3 a day, 10 hrs; to **Campeche**, US$16.50 (6 hrs), reservation required; to **Coatzacoalcos**, US$7; to **Tapachula**, US$19.50, 14 hrs. Many buses a day to **Mérida** 8-10 hrs, with ADO, US$19.50, 11 a day, or Cristóbal Colón at 1030 and 2230, US$22; if coming from Oaxaca to make a connection for Mérida, be prepared for long queues as most buses pass through *en route* from México City. To **San Andrés Tuxtla**, 6 hrs, US$12.50. To **San Cristóbal de las Casas**, US$9, 6 hrs; also 2nd class bus with 1 change at Tuxtla, leaves 0800, arrives 2100, fine scenery but treacherous road. To **Puebla**, ADO 'GL' *plus* service via autopista, US$30, 1st class US$25.50; Cristóbal Colón from ADO terminal to **Oaxaca** via Coatzacoalcos and Tehuantepec at 1930 and 2130, 1st class, stops at about 7 places, US$27.50. Bus to **Veracruz**, many a day with ADO, 7 hrs, US$36 *primera plus*; to

Chetumal, US$16, 10 hrs, but the road is now in a very bad state and it can take much longer, 4 buses, erratic service. To **Catazajá**, US$4, 1½ hrs. To **Palenque**, from ADO terminal, US$4.60, 1st class, US$2.50, 2nd class, 2½ hrs, 8 a day in all from 0430 (difficult to get on a bus on Sun). Circuito Maya, US$5.60, ADO; 1st class 1000 (buy ticket day before) and 1700, 1½ hrs. To **Emiliano Zapata** and **Tenosique** (for Río San Pedro crossing into Guatemala, see page 276), buses 0700, 0800, 1330, 3-4 hrs.

Airline offices *AeroMéxico* office, Periférico Carlos Pellicer 511, T26991 (airport 41675). *Mexicana*, Av Madero 109, or Desarrollo Urbano Tabasco 2000, T163785/560101 (airport 21164). *Aerocaribe*, Javier Mina 301-A, T43202 (airport 44695). *Aviacsa*, T65736. **Banks** *Banco Internacional*, Suárez and Lerdo, changes TCs at good rates. *Banamex*, Madero and Reforma. *American Express*, Turismo Nieves, Sarlat 202, T41818. **Communications** *Internet*: *C@fe internet*, Aldama 404-C, lobby of the Hotel Howard Johnson. **Postal services:** Post office on Ignacio in the centre. DHL, parcel courier service, Paseo Tabasco.

Directory

South of Villahermosa

The Maya ruins at Palenque (see page 263), southeast of Villahermosa, are reached by turning off the inland Route 186, at **Playas de Catazajá**, 117 km from Villahermosa. There are no petrol stations until Catazajá; if you look like running out, turn left for **Macuspana**, where there is one. Hotel in Macuspana: **D** *América*. Basic, clean, comfortable, safe parking. Macuspana municipal *fiesta* 15-16 August. Palenque is 26 km away on a good paved but winding road (minibus US$1.15, 30 minutes, taxi US$10).

The road to Huamanguillo goes via **Cárdenas**, 48 km from Villahermosa by dual carriageway, and the headquarters of the Comisión del Grijalva, which is encouraging regional development. It is very hard to find accommodation in Cárdenas. **D** *Hotel Yax-ol*. Cheapest, with bath, a/c, parking, clean, on main plaza. Between Villahermosa and Cárdenas are many stalls selling all varieties of bananas, a speciality of the area.

Twenty kilometres southwest of Villahermosa is the hot and dirty town of **Huimanguillo** (basic hotel *El Carmen*). Continuing up into the Sierra de Huimanguillo the road reaches Malpasito (taxi US$33 from Huimanguillo) where there is a lodge, *El Pava* (reservations at *Hotel El Carmen*). Beyond are the Raudales de Malpaso (cataracts) on Presa Netzahualcóyotl (accommodation, **E**, at ADO bus station, bus service once a day from Huimanguillo). There is a regular launch across the dam (0600, 0700, 0900, 1100 1300, 1500) to Apic-Pac (see page 242) where you can take a pick-up (2½ hours, bumpy road) to Ocozocuautla and on to Tuxtla Gutiérrez (see page 240).

South of Villahermosa on Route 195 this is a nice, clean little town with several hotels and beautiful surroundings. The square is pleasant, and you can swim in the river or in the sulphur pool, El Azufre, and the cavern of Cocona. From Teapa, Tapijulapa on the Chiapas border can be visited, beautiful views.

Teapa

Sleeping and eating C *Quintero*, Eduardo R Bastar 108, T20045, behind Zócalo. A/c, fan, clean, friendly, enthusiastic restaurant. **D** Simple hotel in grounds of El Azufre, entry to pool included, no restaurant. **D** *Jardín*, at the top of the square. Friendly. Recommended. Good restaurant on main square, *El Mirador*. *Familiar*, main street 125. Friendly, not cheap but filling. Recommended.

Transport Buses: There are buses between Teapa and Villahermosa on a paved road, 50 km, 1 hr, US$1.65. Bus to Chiapa de Corzo at 0730, 7 hrs, US$10, lovely, mountainous landscape (see page 245).

Tabasco & Chiapas

Pichucalco
Colour map 4, grid B3

Eighty kilometres southwest of Villahermosa on Route 195 is Pichucalco, an affluent town with a lively and safe atmosphere. The Zócalo is thronged in the evening with people on after-dinner *paseo*. Buses almost every hour to Villahermosa, US$4.

Sleeping and eating There are many good restaurants and bars. **D** *Hotel La Loma*, Francisco Contreras 51, T30052. With bath, a/c, or fan, ample parking, clean (opposite is a cheaper *posada* with resident monkey). **E** *Hotel México*, on left turn from bus station. With bath, fan, clean but musty. *Vila*, on Plaza. **D** *Jardín*, noisy. **D** *La Selva*.

South of Pichucalco on Highway 195 on the way to Tuxtla Gutiérrez, is **Bochil**, an idyllic stopover (**D** *Hotel/Restaurant María Isabel*, 1 Avenida Sur Pte 44, basic but nice, delicious simple food). Highway 195 is fully paved, but narrow and winding with landslides and washouts in the rainy season, high altitudes, beautiful scenery.

Chiapas Heartland

Although in some ways the Chiapas Heartland has fallen victim to the progress bug, it nevertheless seems impervious to the intrusion of outsiders, most of whom are eager to experience a step back in time, or perhaps a time warp. The Lost World feeling is not created by the beautiful aspects of an old colonial town; it is the presence of the indigenous inhabitants and those from the outlying villages who make everything seem timeless. Most visitors will know something about the dreadful treatment they have suffered over centuries, the fundamental cause of the rebellion on 1 January, 1994, which led to the occupation of San Cristóbal by the revolutionaries. What the visitor is unprepared for is the great dignity

Tuxtla Gutiérrez orientation

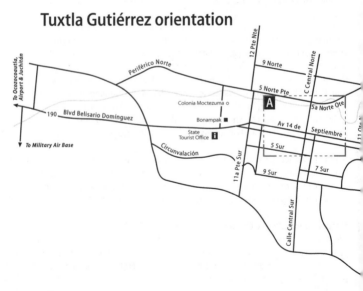

*Related map
A Tuxtla Gutiérrez
centre, page 243*

N

Not to scale

demonstrated by these people who resist the intrusions of outsiders. This dignity is clearly the result of an almost fanatical clinging to ancient traditions in dress, crafts, food, religious practice, festivals and especially languages. As long as they can hold on to their special cultural traits, they cannot be touched. **NB** *Following the EZLN uprising in early 1994, it is advisable to check on political conditions in Chiapas state before travelling in the area. At the time of going to press, there was no fighting between the EZLN and the Mexican army.*

Tuxtla Gutiérrez

The capital of Chiapas is a busy, shabby city without much of interest to the tourist. The main sights are a long way from the centre and too far to walk. There is plenty of budget accommodation a short walk from the first-class ADO terminal. Exit from the main entrance, turn left, past the hotels *Santo Domingo* and *María Teresa* (neither recommended) and head east along Avenida 2 Norte Oriente; go under the underpass (well-policed) beneath the Plaza; as soon as you emerge, there are a number of cheap *posadas* along the continuation of the street.

Phone code: 9
Colour map 4, grid C3
Population: 467,000
Altitude: 522m

The street system here is as follows: Avenidas run from east to west, Calles from north to south. The Avenidas are named according to whether they are north (Norte) or south (Sur) of the Avenida Central and change their names if they are east (Oriente) or west (Poniente) of the Calle Central. The number before Avenida or Calle means the distance from the 'Central' measured in blocks. You know whether it's an Avenida or a Calle by the order of the address: Avenidas have their number, then Sur or Norte followed by east or west; Calles have the east or west position first. For example, 1 Norte Oriente is the eastern part of the first avenue north of Avenida Central; 2 Oriente Norte is the north part of the second street west of Calle Central. It all sounds very complicated, but as long as you check map and road signs very carefully, it is not difficult to navigate your way around the city.

Ins & outs

Tourist offices Boulevard Belisario Domínguez 950, Plaza Instituciones, T6139396/7/8/9. ■ *Mon-Fri 0900-2100, Sat 0900-2000, Sun 0900-1500. Colectivo* from junction of Avenida Central and Calle 2 Oriente. The feast of the Virgen de Guadalupe is celebrated on 12 December.

To Mirador at Sumidero Canyon

Parque Madero, Museo Regional de Chiapas, Botanical Garden & Teatro de la Ciudad

Río Sabinal

To Cahuaré, Chiapa de Corzo & San Cristobal de las Casas

Blvd Angel Albino Corzo

190

Blvd Samuel León Brindis

9 Sur Oriente

Libramiento Sur

Zoo & Museo de Historia Natural

In the Parque Madero at the east end of town (Calzada de los Hombres Ilustres) is the **Museo Regional de Chiapas** with a fine collection of Mayan artefacts. ■ *Daily US$1.25.* Nearby is the **Jardín Botánico** (botanical garden). ■ *Tue-Sun, 0900-1600, free.* Also in this park is the **Teatro de la Ciudad**. There is a superb **zoo** some 3 km south of town up a long hill. The zoo was founded by Dr Miguel Alvarez del Toro, who died in 1996. His philosophy was to provide a free zoo for the children and indigenous people of a low

Sights

economical area. The zoo has always been free, but the new administration proposes a small charge for tourists. At the moment donations are welcome, and recommended to help upkeep the ecological work being carried out. Buying gifts from the shop will not go into the zoo's coffers, as it is privately run. All the animals are regional to Chiapas, except for a few species from other parts of Mexico. The zoo is very large and many of the animals are in open areas, with plenty of room to run about. Monkeys are not in cages, but in areas of trees pruned back so they cannot jump out of the enclosure. Some birds wander around the paths among the visitors. The zoo makes for a very pleasant and educational afternoon. Take mosquito repellent. ■ *Tue-Sun, 0830-1730; in Spanish only, the donations box is in front of the educational centre on the right as you enter the zoo.* The *colectivos* 'Zoológico' and 'Cerro Hueco' from Mercado, Calle 1a Oriente Sur y 7 Sur Oriente, pass the entrance every 20 minutes; taxi US$2.50-3.00 from centre. Town buses charge US$0.20. When returning, catch the bus from the same side you were dropped off as it continues up the hill to the end of the line where it fills up for the return journey.

Excursions Two vast artificial lakes made by dams are worth visiting: **La Angostura**, southeast of Tuxtla, and the **Presa Netzahualcóyotl**, or **Malpaso**, 77 km northwest of the city. You can reach the latter by taking two buses from Tuxtla: the first is for Ocozocoautla; *colectivos* leave all day from Calle 4 Poniente between Avenida 3 y 2 Sur. The second bus goes to Apic-Pac near the lake. Information from the tourist office. Malpaso can also be visited from Cárdenas (see page 239).

Route 190 continues beyond Ocozocoautla (airport for Tuxtla. **D** *Posada San Pedro*, noisy, not recommended) to Cintalapa (**D** *Hotel Leos*, recommended and restaurant. **E** hotel on main street, clean with bath and fan) whence there is a steep climb up an escarpment. Thirty kilometres before Cintalapa a gravel road leads north (last section very rough, only accessible with four-wheel drive with high clearance) to the beautiful waterfall in **El Aguacero National Park** (small sign), which falls several hundred feet down the side of the Río La Venta canyon. There is a small car park at the lip of the canyon; 798 steps lead down to the river and the base of the waterfall. Good camping but no facilities.

Sleeping **AL** *Bonampak* (Best Western), Blvd Belisario Domínguez 180, T6132050, F6122737, west end of town. The social centre, clean, noisy at night, expensive restaurant. **A** *Flamboyant*, Blvd Belisario Domínguez 1081, T6150888, F6191961. Comfortable, good swimming pool. **A** *María Eugenia*, Av Central Ote 507, T6133767/ F6132860. 4-star, restaurant, bar, parking, travel agency. **B** *Gran Hotel Humberto*, Av Central Pte 180, T6122080. Central, a/c, noisy disco. **B-C** *Palace Inn*, Blvd Belisario Domínguez, 4 km from centre, T6150574, F6151042. Generally recommended, lovely garden, pool, noisy videobar. **C** *La Mansión*, 1 Pte Norte 221, T6122151. A/c, bath, safe, clean, but street-facing rooms are noisy and affected by traffic fumes; all centrally located. **C** *Posada del Rey*, 2 Av Norte Ote 310, T6122911. A/c, but damp. **C** *Regional San Marcos*, 1 Sur y 2 Ote Sur 176, T6131940. Cheaper without TV, close to Zócalo, bath, fan or a/c, clean. **C** *Conquistador*, Libramiento Sur Pte, Km 2 (towards the zoo), T6130820.

D *Mar-Inn*, Av 2 Norte Ote 347, T6122715. Pleasant, clean. **D** *Posada de Chiapas*, 2 Sur Pte 243, T6123354. Small rooms with bath, TV, friendly. Opposite Cristóbal Colón bus station are **D** *María Teresa*, 2 Norte Pte 259-B, T6130102, and **E** *Santo Domingo*, with shower, good if you arrive late, but noisy and very basic. **D** *Casa Blanca*, Av 2 Norte Ote, near Plaza Chiapas. OK. **D** *Jas*, Calle Central Sur 665 y Av 6 Sur Ote, T6121554.

Friendly, central, not many foreign tourists, all rooms with phone and colour TV. Recommended. **D** *Catedral*, 1 Norte Ote y 3 Ote Norte. Not very friendly, but has large indoor car park.

E *María Dolores*, 2 Ote Norte 304, between Av 2 y Av 3 Norte Ote, T6123683. Hot water only between 0600 and 1000. **E** *Estrella*, 2 Ote Norte 322, T6123827. With bath, friendly, clean, quiet, comfy, a bit run-down but safe, free drinking water. Recommended. **E** *La Posada*, Av 1 Sur Ote y 5 Ote Sur. With or without bath, laundry facilities, friendly. **E** *Plaza Chiapas*, Av 2 Norte Ote y 2 Ote Norte, T6138365. Clean, with fan and hot shower, most rooms have balconies, good value, good restaurant, enclosed car park. Recommended. **F** *Posada Maya*, 4 Pte Sur 322. Fan, clean. Recommended. *Posada Muñiz*, 2 Sur Ote 245, near 2nd class bus station. Not recommended but useful for early departures. **F** *Santa Elena*, Ote Sur 346. Basic. **F** *Posada del Sol*, 3 Pte Norte, 1 block from Cristóbal Colón buses. With hot shower and fan, good service, good value, basic. Highly recommended. **F** *Tuxtleca*, Av 2 Norte Ote, near *Casa Blanca*. One of the cheapest in town, OK if a bit scruffy.

Youth hostel Calzada Angel Albino Corzo 1800, CP 29070, T6133405. Run-down, meals available.

Motels C *Costa Azul*, Libramiento Sur Ote 3722, T6113364/6113452. Comfy, clean, but everything designed for short-stay couples. **C** *El Sumidero*, Panamericana Km 1093, on left as you enter town from east. A/c, comfortable, but much passing trade. **C** *La Hacienda*, trailer-park-hotel, Belisario Domínguez 1197 (west end of town on Route 190), T6150849. **Camping** US$7-8 per tent, 4 spaces with hook-up, hot

Tuxtla Gutiérrez centre

N

Not to scale

■ **Sleeping**
1 Casa Blanca
2 Catedral
3 Estrella
4 Gran Humberto
5 Jas
6 La Posada
7 María Dolores
8 María Eugenia
9 María Teresa
  & Santo Domingo
10 Mar-Inn
11 Plaza Chiapas
12 Posada Del Rey
13 Posada Muñiz
14 Regional San Marcos

Tabasco & Chiapas

showers, restaurant, minipool, US$13.50 for car and 2 people, a bit noisy and not easily accessible for RVs over 6m, owner speaks English.

Eating *Parrilla La Cabaña*, 2 Ote Norte 250. Excellent *tacos*, very clean. *Los Arcos*, Central Pte 806. Good international food. *Las Pichanchas*. Pretty courtyard, typical food, dancing from Chiapas with *marimba* music between 1400-1700 and 2000-2300, on Av Central Ote 857. Worth trying. *Mina*, Av Central Ote 525, near bus station. Good cheap *comida*. *Café Mesón Manolo*, Av Central Pte 238. Good value, reasonably priced. *Restaurant Imperial*, Av Central Norte. Recommended. *Alameda*, Av 1 Norte 133, near plaza. Good breakfast. *Tuxtla*, Av 2 Norte Pte y Central, near Plaza. Good *comida corrida* and fruit salad. Recommended. Nearby is *Canarios*. Good-value *almuerzos* (late breakfast). *La Parcela*, 2 Ote Sur, near *Hotel Plaza Chiapas*. Good, cheap, good breakfasts. Recommended. *Los Gallos*, Av 2 Norte Pte, 20m from Cristóbal Colón terminal. Open 0700-2400, good and cheap. *Las Delicias*, 2 Norte Pte between Central and 1 Norte Pte, close to Cristóbal Colón terminal. Good breakfasts and snacks. *Pizzería San Marco*, behind Cathedral. Good. *Maryen*, 2 Ote Norte between 1 Norte and Av Central. Good, cheap *tacos*. *El Chato*, opposite *Hotel San Marcos*. One of the few touristy places, *huaraches*, grilled meat, OK, moderate prices. *Nah Yaxal*, 6 Pte Norte, just off Av Central Pte. Vegetarian, modern design, popular with students. *Cantón*, 2 Norte Pte y 6 Pte Norte. Chinese, open 1300-2300. *Café Avenida*, on Av Central just past Aerocaribe office. There are several cheap *taco* places on Calle 2 Ote Norte between 2 Norte and Av Central. Good coffee shop, does cappuccino and espresso. Popular with locals. *Bing*, 1 Sur Pte 1480. Excellent ice cream; many others. Coffee shop below *Hotel Avenida*, Av Central Pte 224. Serves excellent coffee.

Tour operators *Viajes Miramar*, in *Posada del Rey*, 1 Ote Norte 310, T6123983, F6130465, viajesmiramar@infosel.net.mx Good, efficient service for national flight bookings. *Viajes Kali*, Av Central Ote 507 esq 4 Ote. T/F6113175, heugenia@chis1.telmex.net.mx Tours to Sumidero Canyon with English/French/Italian-speaking guide, also books national flights. *Carolina Tours*, Sr José Narváez Valencia (manager), Av Central Pte 1138, T6124281; reliable, recommended; also coffee shop at Av Central Pte 230.

Transport **Local Taxis**: mostly VW beetles, easy to flag down anywhere. US$2 within the centre, US$2.50-3 to the zoo, US$5 to Chiapa de Corzo (for Sumidero Canyon).

Long distance Air: Terán airport is the main one. It is a military airport converted for civilian use. It has no facilities for bad weather, so if there is fog, flights are re-routed to Llano San Juan, further out of town. Always go to Terán first, as transfer to Llano San Juan will be arranged if neccesary. Taxi to Terán US$3. Flights to Hualtulco, Mérida, Mexico City, Oaxaca, Palenque, San Cristóbal de las Casas, Tapachula, Veracruz and Villahermosa.

Buses: Cristóbal Colón 1st class bus terminal is at Av 2 Norte Pte 268 (opposite UNO and Maya de Oro), **Left luggage** at *Juguería* opposite bus station, will guard bag for US$0.50. To **Villahermosa** at 1500, 2300, 8½ hrs, US$10.30, Altos de Chiapas 6 a day between 0700 and 2345; to **Oaxaca** 1130, 1915, 10 hrs, US$18 1st class, US$14 2nd class; to **Puebla**, ADO US$35, departs 1900, Cristóbal Colón 4 a day pm, UNO US$46, 14 hrs; 4 a day pm to **Mexico City**, US$42. Frequent buses 0500-2300 to **San Cristóbal de las Casas**, 2 hrs, US$3 (2nd class US$2 superb mountain journey; *colectivos* from near Av 2 Ote Sur y 2 Sur Ote do the journey for US$2. To **Comitán** 0500 then each hour to 1900 and 1 at 2300, Altos, US$5.80. To **Tapachula**, US$14, 16 a day; there are more 1st class than 2nd class to the Talismán bridge (1st class is less crowded). To **Ciudad Cuauhtémoc**, 7 a day, 0500-2230, US$7.75, including Altos. Oaxaca Pacífico buses to **Salina Cruz**, from 1st class bus terminal. Take travel sickness tablets for Tuxtla-Oaxaca road if you suffer from queasiness. To **Pochutla** at 0935 and 2015, 10 hrs, US$18. To

Palenque, Altos, 6 a day, 0500-2300, US$9, 7 hrs, other buses pass through Palenque. To **Mérida** change at Villahermosa if no direct service at 1530 (Altos), US$26. The scenery between Tuxtla and Mérida is very fine, and the road provides the best route between Chiapas and the Yucatán. To **Córdoba** ADO, 1725, 1900, Cristóbal Colón 2130, US$28.50. To **Tulum** 1230, US$37.50. To **Cancún** 1230, US$39. To **Tonalá** 1615, US$10 (UNO). To **Veracruz** 1930, US$27. To **Chetumal** 1430, US$32.

Airlines *Aviacsa*, Av Central Pte 1144, T6126880/6128081, F6127086, new jets, 40 mins. **Directory** *Aerocaribe*, Av Central Pte 206, T6120020. **Banks** *Bancomer* Av Central Pte y 2 Pte Norte, for Visa and TCs, open 0900-1500. *Banco Bital*, opens 0800, good rates and service. For cheques and cash at 1 Sur Pte 350, near Zócalo. There are ATMs in various branches of Farmacia del Ahorro, all over the city. **Communications Internet:** free at library of Universidad Autónoma de Chiapas, Route 190, 6 km from centre. *Compucentro*, 1 Norte Pte 675, upstairs. US$1.50 per hour, but very slow machines. Post Office: on main square. **Telephone**: international phone calls can be made from 1 Norte, 2 Ote, directly behind post office, 0800-1500, 1700-2100 (1700-2000 Sun). **Useful addresses** Immigration Office 1 Ote Norte.

Sumidero Canyon

An excellent paved road through spectacular scenery, leads to the rim of the tremendous Canyon, over 1,000m deep. Indian warriors, unable to endure the Spanish conquest, hurled themselves into the canyon rather than submit. The canyon is in a national park. ■ *0600-1800*. Camping is permitted outside the gate (bus US$3; taxi fare US$25 return; try to get a group together and negotiate with a *combi* driver to visit the viewpoints on the road into the canyon, US$15 per vehicle, leave from 1 Norte Ote). To get to the first viewpoint only, take *colectivo* marked 'Km 4', get out at the end and walk about 3 km up the road. With your own car, you can drive up to the last *mirador* (restaurant), a 2-3 hour trip, 20 km east of the city. At Cahuaré, 10 km in the direction of Chiapa de Corzo, it is possible to park by the river. If going by bus, US$1.50 each way, get out just past the large bridge on the Chiapa de Corzo road. Boat tours start from below this bridge, where there is also a car park and restaurant serving good seafood. Boat trip into the Sumidero Canyon costs US$6.50 per person foorr the boat for 1½-2 hours; boats leave when full. US$65 to hire boat for private group. Take a sweater, the boats go very fast. From Tuxtla: Taxi to all *miradores* US$18, first *mirador* only US$10. Or taxi to Chiapa de Corzo, US$5, then a *colectivo* boat from there. A licensed taxi service from Tuxtla to the Canyon can be booked at Avenida 1 Sur Pte 1203, T6137033.

Especially recommended at sunset

It is easier to find people to make up numbers in Chiapa de Corzo than in Cahuaré, as the former is a livelier place with more restaurants, launches and other facilities. There is good birdlife but sadly hundreds of plastic water bottles pollute the river. It is not recommended for swimming and besides, there are crocodiles.

Fifteen kilometres on, a colonial town on a bluff overlooking the Grijalva River, is more interesting than Tuxtla: see a fine 16th-century crown-shaped fountain; the 16th-century church of Santo Domingo whose engraved altar is of solid silver; and famous craftsmen in gold, jewellery and lacquer work who travel the fairs.
There is a small lacquer museum. Chiapa de Corzo was a pre-classic and proto-classic Maya site and shares features with early Maya sites in Guatemala; the ruins are behind the Nestlé plant, and some unrestored mounds are on private property in a field near modern houses. There are 1½ and two-hour boat trips along the river to spot crocodiles, turtles, monkeys and hummingbirds, cost US$50 or US$60 for 12 passengers; wait by water's edge, boats soon fill up. Recommended.

Chiapa de Corzo
Phone code: 961
Colour map 4, grid C3
Population: 35,000
Altitude: 456m

Painted and lacquered vessels made of pumpkins are a local speciality

Tabasco & Chiapas

Hardship for Chiapas' Indians

For the visitor to Chiapas, the state's wonders are many: lush tropical jungle, quaint colonial villages, or the modern, prosperous capital, Tuxtla Gutiérrez. However, the peacefulness masks the troubles of the state's indigenous peoples. Their plight was splashed across the world's press with the Zapatista uprising of January 1994 and has remained a photogenic story ever since (see **Recent Politics**, page 741). Chiapas, the southernmost state and one of Mexico's poorest, appears much like its neighbour, Guatemala, and shares many of the same problems. Subsistence has been a way of life for centuries, illiteracy and infant mortality are high, particularly among those who have retained their languages and traditions, shunning the Spanish culture. The Chiapas government estimates that nearly one million Indians live in the state, descendants of the great Maya civilization of 250-900 AD. The Chiapas Indians of today are not a monolith; they are spread out across the state, they do not speak the same language, nor dress alike, have the same customs nor the same types of tribal government.

The Tzotziles and Tzeltales total about 626,000 and live mainly on the plateau and the slopes of the high altitude zones. The Choles number 110,000 and live in the towns of Tila, Tumbalá, Salto de Agua, Sabanilla and Yajalón. The 87,000 Zoques live near the volatile Chichonal volcano. The 66,000 Tojolabales live in Margaritas, Comitán, La Independencia, La Trinitaria and part of Altamirano. On the high mountains and slopes of the Sierra Madre are the 23,000 Mames and the 12,000 Mochós and Kakchikeles. The Lacandones, named after the rain forest they occupy, number only 500 today. Along the border with Guatemala are 21,500 Chujes, Kanjobales and Jacaltecos, although that number includes some refugees still there from the Guatemalan conflict, which ended in a negotiated peace in late 1996.

A minority of the Indians speak Spanish, particularly in the Sierra Madre region and among the Zoques. Many have dropped their típica clothing. Customary positions of authority along with stewardships and standard bearers have been dropped from tribal governance, but medicine men continue to practice. They still celebrate their festivals in ways unique to them and they think about their ancestors as they have for centuries. Many now live in the large cities, some even working for the government, but those who remain in el campo are for the most part, poor. They get by, eating tortillas with salt, some vegetables and occasionally beans. Many who leave for the city end up as domestic servants, labourers or street peddlers. The scarcity of land for the indigenous has been a political issue for many decades and limited land reform merely postponed the crisis which eventually erupted in the 1990s.

Sleeping and eating **D** *Hotel Los Angeles*, on Plaza. Often full, warm shower, fan, beautiful rooms. **C** *La Ceiba*, T6160773. With fan, a/c extra, bath, restaurant, pool. Recommended.

Jardín Turístico on main plaza. Good restaurant, open until 2000 (*plato jardín* is a selection of different regional dishes). Good seafood restaurants by the riverside. Along the pier there are many restaurants, including the *Verónica*. Good food, cheap, slow service. **Bars** Plaza filled with bars playing jukeboxes.

Festivals The *fiestas* here are outstanding; they reach their climax on **20-23 Jan** (in honour of San Sebastián) with a pageant on the river. But there are daylight *fiestas*, *Los Parachicos*, on **15, 17** and **20 Jan**, and the *Chunta fiestas*, at night, from **9-23 Jan**. The *musical parade* is on **19 Jan**. There is another *fiesta* in early Feb and *San Marcos* festival on **25 Apr**, with various *espectáculos*.

Transport Buses from Tuxtla Gutiérrez, Calle 3 Ote Sur, US$0.50, frequent; several buses a day (1 hr) to San Cristóbal de las Casas, 2nd class, US$3.50. Cristóbal Colón to Mexico City, 1815, US$36.50.

The waterfall at the **Cueva de El Chorreadero** is well worth a detour of 1 km (one restaurant here, recommended). The road to the cave is 10 km past Chiapa de Corzo, a few kilometres after you start the climb up into the mountains to get to San Cristóbal. Camping is possible but there are no facilities; take a torch to the cave.

35 km east of Tuxtla, just past Chiapa de Corzo, a road runs north, 294 km, to Villahermosa via Pichucalco (see page 240), paved all the way. If driving to Villahermosa, allow at least 5 hrs for the endless curves and hairpins down from the mountains, a very scenic route, nevertheless.

San Cristóbal de las Casas

One of the most beautiful towns in Mexico, San Cristóbal de las Casas is stunningly located in the fertile Jovel Valley, with the mountains of Huitepec to the west and Tzontehuitz to the east. The city is a charming blend of colonial architecture and indigenous culture, laid out in the colonial period with 21 indigenous barrios on the city's perimeter, which were later integrated into the totally mestizo city which existed by the 18th century. The Indians now form an important part of San Cristóbal's atmosphere, many of them earning a living by selling handicrafts in the town's two markets. The centre is rich in architectural variety, with excellent examples of baroque, neo-classical and plateresque, a Mexican style characterised by the intricate moulding of façades, resembling the work of silversmiths, hence the name, 'like a silversmith's'.

Phone code: 9
Colour map 4, grid C3
Population: 116,729
Altitude: 2,110m

NB: All telephone numbers in the city of San Cristóbal de las Casas should be 7 digits, beginning with 67. The area code is now 9, replacing the former code of 967

Tabasco & Chiapas

Ins and outs

San Cristóbal's new airport is 15 km from town, mostly for local charter flights. There is a first-class bus terminal that services destinations all over Mexico, and two second-class terminals for local buses to destinations within Chiapas and to the Guatemalan border (for details, see Transport page 256). Those travelling to Palenque by car can use the new 210-km paved road which has fine views (avoid night-time journeys because of armed robberies).

Getting there & away

Most places are within walking distance of each other although taxis are available in the town and to the nearby villages; the cheaper *colectivos* run on fixed routes only.

Getting around

Due to its altitude, San Cristóbal has a pleasantly mild climate compared to the hotter Chiapan towns such as Palenque and Tuxtla. During June, July and August, it is warm and sunny in the morning, while in the afternoon it tends to rain, with a sharp drop in temperature. Warm, waterproof clothes are needed, though the heavy rains conveniently stop in the evening, when you can enjoy San Cristóbal's many cheap restaurants and friendly bars and cafés. **Tourist offices** Hidalgo 2, T6786570. Very helpful with all types of information, good maps provided, usually someone there who speaks English. ■ *Mon-Sat 0900-2100, Sun 0900-1400*. There is another office on the main plaza, in the Palacio Municipal, T6780665. Ask here for accommodation in private houses. Infomation on eco tours to Huitepec nature reserve. Good free map of town and surroundings. Maps of San Cristóbal, US$0.35, are also on sale at *Kramsky*, Diego de Mazariegos y 16 de Septiembre, behind Palacio Municipal (one-way traffic shown for Avenida 16 de Septiembre and Avenida Ignacio Allende actually goes in the opposite direction).

San Cristóbal de las Casas

Tabasco & Chiapas

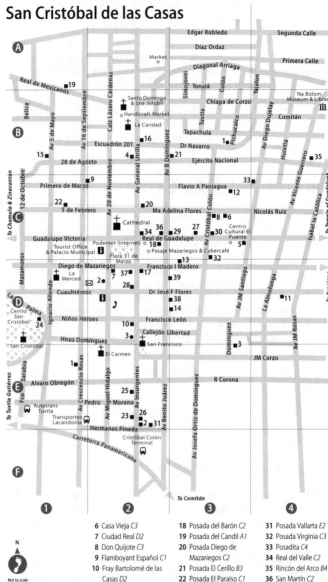

N

Not to scale

■ **Sleeping**
1 Arrecife de Coral *E1*
2 Capri *E2*
3 Casa de Huéspedes Chamula *E3*
4 Casa Mexicana *B2*
5 Casa Real *C3*

6 Casa Vieja *C3*
7 Ciudad Real *D2*
8 Don Quijote *C3*
9 Flamboyant Español *C1*
10 Fray Bartolomé de las Casas *D2*
11 Hospedaje Bed & Breakfast *D4*
12 Jovel *C3*
13 Los Robles *D3*
14 Palacio de Moctezuma *D3*
15 Parador Mexicano *B1*
16 Plaza Santo Domingo *B2*
17 Posada Casa Blanca *D2*

18 Posada del Barón *C2*
19 Posada del Candil *A1*
20 Posada Diego de Mazariegos *C2*
21 Posada El Cerillo *B3*
22 Posada El Paraíso *C1*
23 Posada Insurgente *E2*
24 Posada Los Morales *D1*
25 Posada Lucella *E2*
26 Posada Lupita *E2*
27 Posada Margarita *C3*
28 Posada San Cristóbal *D2*
29 Posada Santiago *C3*
30 Posada Tepeyac *C3*

31 Posada Vallarta *E2*
32 Posada Virginia *C3*
33 Posadita *C4*
34 Real del Valle *C2*
35 Rincón del Arco *B4*
36 San Martín *C2*
37 Santa Clara *D2*
38 Villa Real *D3*
39 Youth Hostel *D3*

● **Eating**
1 La Casa del Pan *B3*
2 La Galería *D2*
3 Madre Tierra *D2*

Sights

In front of the plaza is the neo-classical **Palacio Municipal**, built in 1885. A few steps away is the **Catedral de San Cristóbal**, built in the 16th century, painted in ochre, brown and white, with a baroque pulpit added in the 17th century. Adjacent to the cathedral is the church of **San Nicolás**, which houses the historical archives of the diocese. The building dates from 1613, and is believed to be the only church in Mexico to preserve the original design in the architectural style of indigenous people's churches. Just off the plaza, at the beginning of Insurgentes, is the former **Casa de la Sirena**, now the *Hotel Santa Clara*. Built at the end of the 16th century, this is a rare example of colonial residential architecture in the *plateresque* style. The interior has the four classic corridors of renaissance constructions. Heading off the plaza in the opposite direction, going north up 20 de Noviembre, you reach the **Church and Ex-Convento de Santo Domingo**. By far the most dramatic building in the city, it features an elaborate baroque façade in moulded mortar, especially beautiful when viewed in the late afternoon sun, which picks out the ornate mouldings with salmon pink hues. The church's altarpieces are covered in gold leaf, and the pulpit is intricately carved in a style peculiar to Mexico, known as *churrigueresque*, even more elaborate than the baroque style of Europe. Outside the market is the main handicraft market, with dozens of stalls selling traditional textiles, handmade dolls, wooden toys and jewellery. To the west of the centre, and up a strenuous flight of steps, is the **Templo del Cerrito**, a small church with fine views of the city and the surrounding mountains. The church is so-called (*cerrito* meaning 'small hill') because it is set on an isolated, tree-covered hill. At the other end of the city, to the east, is another little church on a hill, the **Templo de Guadalupe**. This church is used by the indigenous people of the barrio de Guadalupe, the nearest to the centre of the 21 such indigenous neighbourhoods. Each neighbourhood is characterised by the dress of the Indians, depending on which indigenous group they belong to, and by the handicrafts produced by them. Guadalupe is the *barrio* of candle makers, saddle makers, and wooden toy makers. The other *barrios*, such as Mexicanos, the oldest in the city, are further afield and not recommended for unguided visits. The cultural centre **Na Bolom** (see **Museums**) is very helpful for information on all aspects of indigenous culture.

The main square is Plaza 31 de Marzo, with a turn of the century gazebo built during the era of Porfirio Díaz

The **Museo de Los Altos** contains a history of San Cristóbal, with an emphasis on the plight of the indigenous people, as well as a good selection of locally produced textiles. There is a small library with books on Chiapas at the back. Calzada Lázaro Cárdenas, next to Santo Domingo church. ■ *Tue-Sun, 1000-1700. US$2, free on Sun.*

Museums

Na Bolom Museum and Cultural Centre, Vicente Guerrero 33, T6781418, is situated in a neo-classical mansion dating from 1891. Na Bolom was founded in 1951 by the Danish archaeologist Frans Blom and his wife, the Swiss photographer Gertrudis Duby. After the death of Frans Blom in 1963, Na Bolom became a study centre for the universities of Harvard and Stanford, while Gertrudis Duby continued campaigning for the conservation of the Lacandón area. She died in 1993, aged 92, after which the centre has continued to function as a non-profit making organisation dedicated to conserving the Chiapan environment and helping the Lacandón Indians. The photographic archives in the museum contain a detailed visual history of 50 years of daily life of the Maya people with beautifully displayed artefacts, pictures of Lacandón Indians, and information about their present way of life. There are five galleries with collections of pre-Columbian Maya art and colonial religious paintings.

Tabasco & Chiapas

There is a good library, open Monay-Friday 0930-1330, 1630-1900. A handicraft shop sells products made by the indigenous people helped by the centre. ■ *Guided tours Tues-Sun, 1130 in Spanish, 1630 in English. US$2.50 including video, 1½ hours. Recommended. You cannot see the museum on your own. nabolom@sclc.ecosur.mx.*

Na Bolom run various projects, entirely staffed by volunteers. Prospective volunteers spend a minimum of three months, maximum six, at the centre. They must have skills which can be useful to the projects, such as anthropology, organic gardening, or multi-linguists. Volunteers are given help with accommodation and a daily food allowance. Contact Suzanna Paisley for further information. Na Bolom also has 12 rooms to rent in the **B** range (see **Sleeping**). They run tours (Tuesday-Sunday) to San Juan Chamula and San Lorenzo Zinacantán. US$10 per person, good guides, thorough explanations, respectful to indigenous locals.

The **Templo del Carmen**, Crescencio Rosas y Alvaro Obregón, with a unique archery tower in the Moorish style, is the home of the museum of fine art and the El Carmen Cultural Centre. ■ *Tue-Sun 0900-1700. Free.*

The **Centro de Desarrollo de la Medicina Maya**, Salomón González Blanco, has a herb garden with detailed displays on the use of medicinal plants by the Maya for various purposes, including child delivery. ■ *Mon-Fri 0900-1400, 1500-1800, Sat-Sun 1000-1600. US$2.*

NB Check on the situation before you visit the surrounding villages. Travellers are strongly warned not to wander around on their own, especially in the hills surrounding the town where churches are situated, as they could risk assault. Warnings can be seen in some places frequented by tourists. Heed the warning on photographing, casual clothing and courtesy (see page 260).

Excursions

Las Grutas de San Cristóbal (caves), 10 km southeast of the town, contain huge stalagmites and are 2,445m deep but only lit for 750m. ■ *US$0.30.* Refreshments are available. Horses can be hired at Las Grutas for US$13 for a five-hour ride (guide extra) on beautiful trails in the surrounding forest. Some of these are best followed on foot. Yellow diamonds on trees and stones mark the way to beautiful meadows. Stay on the trail to minimize erosion. **NB** Parts of the forest are a military zone. The land next to the caves is taken up by an army football pitch, but once past this, it is possible to walk most of the way back to San Cristóbal through woods and fields. Las Grutas are reached by Autotransportes de Pasaje/31 de Marzo *colectivos* every 15 minutes (0600-1900 US$0.60) from Avenida Benito Juárez 37B, across the Pan-American Highway just south of Cristóbal Colón bus terminal (or take *camioneta* from Pan-American opposite San Diego church 500m east of Cristóbal Colón). *Colectivos* are marked 'San Cristóbal, Teopisca, Ciudad Militar, Villa Las Rosas', or ask for minibus to 'Rancho Nuevo'. To the bus stop take 'San Diego' *colectivo* one block east of Zócalo to the end of Benito Juárez. When you get to Las Grutas, ask the driver to let you out at Km 94; the caves are poorly signed.

Tours from San Cristóbal to the Sumidero Canyon (see page 245) including boat trip cost around US$15.00 with numerous travel agencies, 0900-1600. San Cristóbal can also serve as a base for exploring the Mayan ruins at Palenque (210 km away, see page 263), Bonampak and Yaxchilán, near the Guatelmalan border (see page 271).

Essentials

A *Casa Mexicana*, 28 de Agosto 1, T6780698, F6782627. Cable TV, telephone, indoor patio with fountain, very plush and comfy, same owner as *La Galeria* restaurant. Highly recommended. **A** *Casa Vieja*, María A Flores 27, T6782598, F6786268. Elegant converted colonial house, relaxing, TV, good restaurant hot water, will heat rooms on request if weather cold, parking, laundry service. **A** *Catedral*, Guadalupe Victoria 21, T6785356, F6781363. Pool, solarium. **A** *Flamboyant Español*, 1 de Marzo 16, T6780045. Hot water morning and evening, clean, beautiful coutryard, restaurant, gym, some rooms noisy. **A** *Mansión del Valle*, Diego de Mazariegos 39, T6782582/3, F6782581. Chic, classic colonial building, safe parking. **A** *Parador Ciudad Real*, Diagonal Centenario 32, T6781886, F6782853. West edge of city. **A** *Posada Diego de Mazariegos*, María A Flores 2, T6781825, F6780827, 1 block north of Plaza. Comfortable, quiet, restaurant, live music regularly in the evening in bar *El Jaguar*. Recommended. **B** *Bonampak* (Best Western), Calzada México 5, T6781621, F6781622. Pool, restaurant, bar and excellent travel agency run by Pilar. **B** *Na Bolom*, Vicente Guerrero 33. Beautiful, 12-room guesthouse in cultural centre (see above), bath, fireplace, 3 meals available, lunch and dinner US$5 each with 3 hrs notice. Recommended. **B** *Ciudad Real*, Plaza 31 de Marzo 10, T6780187, F6780469. Clean, good value, TV in rooms, good restaurant, attractive rooms, but noisy parrot talks a lot. **B** *Rincón del Arco*, Ejército Nacional 66, T6781313, F6781568, 8 blocks from centre. Friendly, bar, restaurant. Warmly recommended. **B** *Hotel Mónica*, Insurgentes 33, T6780732, F6782940. Nice patio, restaurant, bar, recommended, and smaller at 5 de Febrero 18, T6781367. **B** *Parador Mexicano*, Av 5 de Mayo 38, T6781515, F6780055. Tennis court, quiet and pleasant. **B** *Posada de los Angeles*, Madero 17, T6781173, F6782581. Very good value, hot water, with bath and TV. **B** *Posada El Paraíso*, Av 5 de Febrero 19, T/F6780085. Mexican-Swiss owned, impeccable rooms varying in size, many open onto pretty patio, excellent restaurant, nearby parking beneath cathedral. Highly recommended. **B** *Santa Clara*, Insurgentes 1, on Plaza, T6781140, F6781041. Colonial style, clean, some rooms noisy, good restaurant, pool bar, pool. Highly recommended. **B-C** *Arrecife de Coral*, Crescencio Rosas 29, T6782125/6782098. Modern, clean, TV, hot water, garden, off-street parking, friendly owners. **B-C** *Plaza Santo Domingo*, Av General Utrilla 35, next to Santo Domingo church, T6781927, F6786514, cielo@sancristobal.podernet.com.mx Nice old building with courtyard, restaurant, bar, safety deposit, money exchange, laundry service, fax service, cable TV.

C *Don Quijote*, Av Cristóbal Colón 7, T6780920, F6780346. Bath, 24-hr hot water, garage, no credit cards. **C** *Molino de La Alborada*, Periférico Sur Km 4, south of airstrip, T6780935. Modern ranch-house and bungalows. **C** *Palacio de Moctezuma*, Juárez 16, T6780352, F6781533. Colonial style, good Mexican food. Highly recommended. **D** *Capri*, Insurgentes 54, T6783018, F6780015, near Cristóbal Colón bus terminal. Clean, helpful. Recommended. **D** *Fray Bartolomé de las Casas*, Insurgentes and Niños Héroes, T6780932, F6783510. Attractive courtyard, with bath, nice rooms (some dark) and patio with *Café Kate*, can be noisy, extra blankets available, safe parking. **D** *Maya Quetzal*, on Pan-American Highway, Km 1171, T6781181, F6780984, adjoining restaurant. **D** *Posada del Barón*, Belisario Domínguez 2. Clean and comfortable, good value. **D** *Posada Los Morales*, Ignacio Allende 17, T6781472. Cottages with open fires (wood US$0.80), kitchen (no pots or pans) and hot showers, beautiful gardens overlook city, parking possible (some cottages are very basic, with no water), beautiful bar/restaurant with live music. **D** *Posada San Cristóbal*, Insurgentes 3 near Plaza, T6786881. With bath, colonial style, renovated, pleasant. **C** *Real del Valle*, Av Real de Guadalupe 14, T6780680, F6783955, next to Plaza. With breakfast, very clean, friendly, avoid noisy room next to kitchen, hot water, laundry, credit cards accepted, parking. **D** *San Martín*, Real de Guadalupe 16, T6780533, near Plaza. Clean, hot water, left-luggage. Highly recommended. **D** *Villa Real*, Av Benito Juárez 8, T6782930. Clean, hot water, luggage deposit, safe. Recommended. **D-E** *Posada El Cerillo*, Av B Domínguez 27, T6781283. Hot showers, laundry facilities, no electricity 1300-1700, reports vary. **D** *Posada Vallarta*, Hermanos Pineda, near Cristóbal Colón bus terminal. Cheaper if you pay for several nights in advance, clean, quiet, hot water, car parking. Recommended.

E *Casa di Gladys* (Privates Gästelhaüs Casa Degli Ospiti), Diego de Mazariegos 65, Apartado Postal 29240, 4 blocks west of Zócalo, or **F** per person in dormitory, patio, hot showers, clean bathrooms, comfortable, breakfast available, Gladys meets Cristóbal Colón buses. Highly recommended. Laundry facilities, horse riding arranged, luggage store. **E** *Hotel de Silvia*, Cuauhtémoc 12. With bath and hot water, small, parking. Recommended. **E** *Posada Casa Blanca*, Insurgentes 6-B, 50m south of Zócalo. With shower, hot water, friendly owner. **E** *Posada Insurgente*, Av Insurgentes 73, T6782435. Clean, refurbished, good bathrooms with hot water, cold rooms, 1 block from Cristóbal Colón station. **E** *Posada Isabel*, Francisco León 54, T6782554, near Av JM Santiago. With hot shower, clean, quiet, good value, parking. Recommended. **E** *Posada Lucella*, Av Insurgentes 55, T6780956, opposite Iglesia Santa Lucía (noisy bells!). Some rooms with bath, hot water, others shared, good value, clean, safe, quiet rooms around patio, large beds. Recommended. **E** *Posada Lupita*, Benito Juárez 12, T6781421. Beds like hammocks, small, enclosed car park, strict controls of hot water and *No ll* (**F**) at Insurgentes 46, T6781019. **E** *Posada Margarita*, Real de Guadalupe 34, T6780957. Private room without bath, spotless, washing and toilets, friendly, hot water, popular with backpackers, often full, attractive restaurant serves good breakfast and dinner (not cheap), wholefood, live music in evenings. Recommended. **E** *Posada San Agustín*. Large rooms, shared bath, family-run, friendly. Recommended. **E** *Posada Santiago*, Real de Guadalupe 32, T6780024. With private bath, clean, hot water, good cafetería. Recommended. **E** *Posada Tepeyac*, Real de Guadalupe 40, 1 block from *Margarita*. With bath, friendly, clean, hot shower, avoid ground floor rooms, dark and gloomy. Otherwise recommended. **E** *Posada Virginia*, Cristóbal Colón y Guadalupe. For 4 in room with bath, hot water, clean. Recommended. **E** *Santo Domingo*, 28 de Agosto 3, 3 blocks north of Zócalo. With bath, **F** without, hot showers, very friendly. **E** *Villa Betania*, Madero 87, T6784467. Not central, airy rooms with bath and fireplace (US$4 extra if you want to light a fire), hot water in morning, clean. Recommended. **E-F** *Jovel*, Flavio Paniagua 28, T6781734. Villa style, roof terrace, clean, quiet, limited hot water, extra blankets available, will store luggage, restaurant, horses for hire, laundry facilities. Recommended. **E-F** *Posada Memetik*, on Dr José Flores 34. Clean, pretty patio, including breakfast. Recommended. **E** *Posada Doña Rosita*, Ejército Nacional 16, 3 blocks from main plaza. **F** Dormitory accommodation, fleas, kitchen and laundry facilities, breakfast US$1, Doña Rosita is very knowledgeable about local affairs and herbal medicine, but you may be moved around to fit in other guests. The herbal medicine course consists of at least 10 hrs of classes, an introduction to vegetarian cooking and 5 meals, costing about US$30. **E** *Posada Lupita*, near bus terminal on Insurgentes. Nice plant-filled courtyard, popular, often full. **E** *Los Robles*, Francisco I Madero y Colón, T6780054. Hot water, own bath, all rooms have 2 beds.

F *Baños Mercederos*, 1 de Marzo 55. Shared quarters, good cheap meals, steam baths (highly recommended, US$2 extra). **F** *Casa de Huéspedes Chamula*, Julio M Corzo 18. Clean, hot showers, washing facilities, friendly, parking, noisy, with shared bath, some rooms without windows. Recommended. **F** *Casa de Huéspedes Santa Lucía*, Clemente Robles 21, T6780315. Shared bath, ask for hot water, refurbished, 1 of the cheapest. Recommended. **F** per person *Ma Adelina Flores 24*, address as name. Including lunch or dinner. **F** *Hospedaje Bed and Breakfast*, Madero 83, 10 mins from

Zócalo. Clean, small breakfast, popular with backpackers. **F** *Posada Casa Real*, Real de Guadalupe 51. Communal bath, clean, friendly. **F** *Posada del Candil*, Real de Mexicanos 7, T6782755. Hot shower, parking, clean, laundry facilities, good value. **F** *Posada Chilam Balam*, Niños Héroes 9. Family-run, hot water, very pleasant. **E** *Posada Maya*, Av Crescencio Rosas 11. Hot water in shared showers, cheap café next door. Recommended. Look on the bulletin board outside the tourist office for guesthouses advertising cheap bed and breakfast. **F** *Posadita*, Flavio Paniagua 30. With bath, clean, laundry facilities. Recommended. Unnamed house at *Real de Guadalupe 28*, no breakfast but use of kitchen, ask owners at their café opposite. **F** *Globetrotters Bed & Breakfast*, Real de Guadalupe, near Av Vicente Guerrero. Shared bath, hot water, laundry, clean, quiet, friendly. Recommended.

Youth Hostels F *Youth Hostel*, Juárez 2. 24-hr hot water, popular with backpackers. **F** *Los Camellos*, Guadalupe 101. Price includes breakfast, popular with backpackers, T6780665. *Qhia*, Tonalá 5. Including breakfast, kitchen, warm water, often full. The main tourist office on the plaza can arrange homestays for US$3-4 per person.

Camping *Rancho San Nicolás*, T6780057, at end of Francisco León, 1½ km east of centre. Beautiful, quiet location, is a trailer park, but do take warm blankets or clothing as the temperature drops greatly at night, hot showers, US$7 for room in *cabaña*, US$5 to camp, US$12 for camper van with 2 people (electricity hook-up), children free, laundry facilities. Recommended. Trailer Park *Bonampak* on Route 190 at west end of town. 22 spaces with full hook-up, hot shower, heated pool in season, restaurant, US$10 per vehicle, US$5 per person. 'White gas' available at small store on corner across from northeast corner of main market (Chiwit).

Expensive *El Teatro*, next to Teatro Municipal on 16 de Septiembre. Good quality French food. There is a good restaurant at *Hotel Ciudad Real*. Rustic setting, good crêpes. *La Parrilla*, Av Belisario Domínguez 32. Excellent grilled meats and cheese, open fire, cowboy décor with saddles as bar stools, closed Mon. Recommended. *La Margarita*, Real de Guadalupe 34. Concerts, good *tacos*. *Los Balcones*, Real de Guadalupe. Friendly, good atmosphere. *Pierre's*, Real de Guadalupe 73. Good-quality French cuisine, will prepare custom dishes given notice.

Eating
● *on maps*

Mid-range *Kau Lom*, Madero, opposite Maya Pakal. Chinese. *Cactus*, Ignacio Allende 25B. Good *burritos* and sandwiches. *El Nuevo Amanecer*, Real de Guadalupe 24D. Vegetarian, good salads. *La Galería*, Hidalgo 3, a few doors from Zócalo. Popular with tourists, best coffee, good breakfast, good pasta, international (many German) newspapers, art gallery, videos at night, pool table, live music at weekends. *El Unicornio*, Av Insurgentes 33a. Good. *Capri*, Insurgentes 16. Good food, set meals at reasonable prices. *Tuluc*, Insurgentes 5, open 0630-2200. Good value especially breakfasts, near Plaza, popular, classical music, art for sale and toys on display (SODAM, see below). Recommended. *Kukulcán*, Insurgentes Sur 3. Mexican food. *El Pavo Real*, Insurgentes 60, near Cristóbal Colón terminal. Regional food. *Sherlock's*, Insurgentes 57. International food, very good value. Recommended. *París-México*, Madero 20. Smart, French cuisine, excellent breakfasts, reasonably priced *comida corrida*, classical music. Not cheap, apart from the 3 daily menus (very good). Highly recommended. *Faisán*, Madero, near Plaza. Good breakfasts, excellent food and service. *Flamingo*, Madero 14. Nice décor, reasonable food (good *paella*). Next door is *El Mirador II*. Good local and international food, excellent *comida corrida* US$3. Recommended. *El Manantial*, 1 de Marzo 11. Good *licuados* and juices. *El Tapanco*, Guadalupe 24B. Good crêpes, friendly. *Shanghai*, 20 de Noviembre 7B, Chinese. *Doña Lolita*, Insurgentes 7. Excellent, cheap, good for breakfast and lunch. *La Langosta*, Madero 9. Seafood.

Tabasco & Chiapas

Cheap *Merendero*, JM Corzo y Insurgentes, OK. *Los Arcos*, Madero 6. Varied menu, family-run, good *comida corrida*, excellent service, closes 2100. Several other cheap, local places on Madero east of Plaza 31 de Marzo. *Fulano*, Madero 12, near Plaza. Excellent set meal. *Maya Pakal*, Madero, 1st block east of Plaza. Excellent 3-course set lunch and dinner, ex-chef of *Madre Tierra*, many vegetarian options, horses for rent to Chamula, book day before T6785911, Francisco Ochoa. *El Huarache Real*, Juárez between Madero y J F Flores, no sign, next to *Todo Especial*. Excellent *huaraches*, a thick kind of *taco* served flat with topping, many varieties. *El Gato Gordo*, Madero and Colón. Cheap set breakfast, crêpes, *tortas*, vegetarian. Unnamed restaurant at *Real de Guadalupe 85*, between Isabel la Católica and Díaz del Castillo. Chiapan specialities are *chalupas*, *tortillas* with beans, pork and vegetables in tomato sauce; also *pan compuesto*, bread with pork, carrots and sauce. *El Suadero*, Insurgentes 69. Very good 3-course *comida corrida*, US$2.50, open till 2300. Very good *panadería*, *Pan Chico*, on Rosales next to *Hotel Casa Mexicana*, excellent bread and cakes. The cheapest places for lunch in San Cristóbal are the stalls in the craft market on Insurgentes. They do set meals for US$1.20, usually beef or chicken. Numerous stalls nearby sell punch, often made with *posh*, the alcoholic brew made by the people of Chamula.

Taco restaurants *Emiliano's Moustache*, Av Crescencio Rosas 7. Popular with Mexicans (no facial hair required). Recommended. *La Salsa Verde*, 2 on 20 de Noviembre. *El Ambar*, Almolonga 43. Friendly, cheap. Recommended. *El Pastorcito de Los Altos*, esq Allende y Clemente Robles. Cheap. *El Pastor Coleto*, Panamericana and Hidalgo, near Pastorcito. Popular with locals. **Health food/vegetarian** *Madre Tierra*, Insurgentes 19 (opposite Franciscan church). Anglo-Mexican owned, European dishes, vegetarian specialities, good breakfasts, wholemeal breads from bakery (also takeaway), pies, brownies, chocolate cheesecake, classical music, popular with travellers, not cheap, good nightlife. Much recommended. *Las Estrellas*, Escuatirón 201. Good cheap food, including vegetarian, good brown bread, try the *caldo Tlalpeño*, nice atmosphere, Mexican/Dutch owned. Recommended. *Café San Cristóbal* on Cuauhtémoc. Good coffee sold in bulk too, chess hangout. *Café Altura*, 20 de Noviembre 4. Vegetarian, organic coffee, music every night. *La Selva Café*, Crescencio Rosas and Cuauhtémoc. 30 types of really delicious organic coffees, owned by growers collective, art gallery, lively in evenings. Good breakfast and cakes. Recommended. *Café Latté*, Real de Guadalupe 24D. *Café Centro*, Real de Guadalupe. Popular for breakfast, good *comida*. *La Casa del Pan*, on B Domínguez and Dr Navarro. Excellent wholemeal bread, breakfasts, live music, closed Mon. Highly recommended but not cheap. *Tortas Tortugas*, Guadalupe Victoria, near corner of Av 20 de Noviembre. Excellent sandwiches. *Pastelería Italiana*, 38A 20 de Noviembre. Very good pastries and coffee. **Cafés** *Todo Natural*, B Domínguez and Madero. Juice bar, huge variety, any combination of fruit, yoghurt and alfalfa, open 0800-2100.

Bars *Las Velas*, Madero, ½ block from plaza. Reggae, Honduran music, sometimes live, happy hour 2000-2200, open till dawn. *Madre Tierra* (see **Eating**) has a bar upstairs open from 2200. *Emiliano's Moustache* (see **Eating**) has a bar open until 0100. *Adobes*, Hidalgo, just off plaza, above a shop. Open Fri and Sat from 2200 until very late. *Los Latinos*, Diego de Mazariegos. Caribbean music.

Entertainment Videos shown at *La Galería*, Hidalgo 3, US$1. *Cine Santa Clara*, Av 16 de Septiembre. International film festival 2nd half Feb. *Cine las Casas*, Guadalupe Victoria 21. International films with subtitles in Spanish. Video films are also shown at Centro Bilingüe in the **Centro Cultural** *El Puente* (see **Cultural centres**, page 257), Real de Guadalupe 55, usually about local issues. Every day except Sunday 3 good films in original version, US$1.25. Film schedules are posted around town.

There is a popular spring festival on Easter Sun and the week after. *La fiesta de* **Festivals**
Guadalupe is celebrated on **12 Dec**.

Part of the ex-convent of Santo Domingo has been converted into a cooperative, *Sna* **Shopping**
Jolobil, selling handicrafts from many Indian villages especially textiles (best quality
and expensive; also concerts by local groups). *Taller Lenateros*, Flavio A Paniagua 54,
T6785174, paper and prints made from natural materials, offers workshops US$6.50
per day. *Weavers Co-op J'pas Joloviletic*, Utrilla 43. *SODAM* (Mutual Aid Society) with
their shop at Casa Utrilla, Utrilla 33, is a co-operative of Indian craftspeople selling
beautiful wooden dolls and toys. Sales go towards a training fund for Chamula Indians, with a workshop based at Yaalboc, a community near San Cristóbal. For local
goods try *Miscelánea Betty*, Utrilla 45, good value. Souvenir markets on Utrilla
between Real de Guadalupe and Dr A Navarro. Amber museum in Plaza Sivan shop,
Utrilla 10, T6783507. Many shops on Av Real de Guadalupe for amber and jade plus
other *artesanías*. The market north of Santo Domingo is worth seeing as well. The craft
market beside Santo Domingo church is soon to be moved to a new covered location
on Insurgentes, at the current location of the smaller craft market in Parque Fray
Bartolomé de las Casas. This would seem an appropriate gesture towards the mainly
indigenous stallholders, as the park was named after the first non-indigenous champion of their cause in the 16th century. Pasaje Mazariegos (in the block bounded by
Real de Guadalupe, Av B Domínguez, Madero and Plaza 31 de Marzo) has luxury
clothes and bookshops, restaurants and travel agents. *Casa de Artesanías*, Niños
Héroes and Hidalgo. Top quality handicrafts. The shop is also a museum.

Bookshops *La Pared*, Hidalgo 2, a few doors down from tourist office. Books in several European languages, many travel books including Footprint South American
Handbook, book exchange, good quality amber jewellery, American owner Dana Gay
is very helpful with local information, also offers phone service. *Feminist bookshop*,
Real de Guadalupe 118. *Soluna*, Real de Guadalupe 13B, has a few English guidebooks, a wide range of Spanish titles and postcards. *Librería Chilam Balam*, Casa
Utrilla, Av Utrilla 33, good range of books, mostly in Spanish, also cassettes of regional
music. *La Quimera*, Real de Guadalupe 24.

Horse hire Carlos, T6781873/6781339. Horses can be hired from *Casa de Huéspedes* **Sports**
Margarita, prices US$16-20 for horse and guide, to Chamula, 5 hrs, US$8, reserve the
day before; or from Sr José Hernández, Calle Elías and Calle 10 (1 block from Av Huixtla
and Chiapa de Corzo, not far from Na Bolom), US$10 for half a day, plus guide
US$11.50; Real de Guadalupe 51A, to Chamula US$6.50, also to Rancho Nuevo and
San José; Francisco Ochón, T6785911, goes to Chamula, US$6.50. The tourist office
also has a list of other stables which hire out horses. Check the saddles; those made of
wood are uncomfortable for long rides if you are not used to them.

Viajes Pakal, Cuauhtémoc 6A, T6782818 F6782819, pakal@sancristobal.podernet. **Tour operators**
com.mx A reliable agency with several branches in other cities. Good for flight bookings, though some require 4 days notice. *Chincultic*, Real de Guadalupe 34, T6780957,
F6787832, viajeschincultic@latinmail.com Very helpful and informative owner
Margarita is the best person to go to for an update on the situation at Lagunas de
Montebello. She runs group tours there (US$17), currently the only safe way to see the
lakes. She also runs tours to the Sumidero Canyon (US$17); also Yaxchilán, Bonampak
and Tikal in Guatemala. *Santa Ana Tours*, Madero, ½ block from plaza, T6780422. Recommended for local and international flight bookings. *Mercedes Hernández Gómez*,
leads tours of local villages, starting at 0900 from kiosk on the Plaza 31 de Mayo (arrive
early), returns about 1500, about US$10 per person, repeatedly recommended.
Mercedes speaks English, is very informative and can be recognized by her long skirts

and flowery umbrella. Many others take tours for same price. *Raúl and Alejandro* (T6783741) who leave from in front of the cathedral at 0930, returning at 1400, in blue VW minibus, US$9, good; *Victor and Verónica* run 4-day camping trips to Lacandón communities, US$192, ask for them at Na Bolom. Recommended. *Héctor Mejía*, T6780545, takes a walking tour (Tue and Thur, 0900, from outside Santo Domingo, US$9, 4 hrs) around cottage industries eg candymaker, dollmaker, toymaker. Longer tours such as to Bonampak and Yaxchilán can be booked by tour operators in San Cristóbal de Las Casas, eg *Yaxchilán Tours*, Guadalupe 26D, but they are much cheaper if booked in Palenque.

Transport **Local** **Taxi**: US$1 anywhere in town, *colectivo* US$0.25. **Bike hire**: *Los Pingüinos* on Av 5 de Mayo 10B, T6780202, open 0915-1430, 1600-1900, rents mountain bikes for US$2 per hour or US$8.50 per day, US$10.50 for 24 hrs. Guided biking tours half or full days, English, German spoken, guide Joel recommended, prices from US$7 to US$12.50, beautiful countryside and knowledgeable guides, highly recommended. *Rodada 28*, on María Adelina Flores, opposite *Hotel Casa Vieja*, open Mon-Sat 0900-1330, 1600-2000, US$1.30 per hour, US$6.50 per day. Bike shops: *Bicipartes*, on Alvaro Obregón and 2 shops on Utrilla between Navarro and Primero de Marzo have a good selection of bike parts. **Car hire**: *Budget*, Mazariegos 36, T6781871.

Long distance **Air**: San Cristóbal has a new airport (SZT) about 15 km from town, Aerocaribe flies to Tuxtla Gutiérrez. There are also charter flights to see Lacanjá, Bonampak and Yaxchilán on the Río Usumacinta, 7 hrs in all (US$100 per person if plane is full, more if not). All with Aerochiapas at airport.

Buses: The 1st class bus terminal serves all destinations in the country. There are 2 other 2nd class terminals across the road, only serving Chiapan destinations. From the 1st class terminal: **Mexico City**, 1350, 1530, 1800, 18 hrs, US$42. **Cancún**, 1430, 1635, 18 hrs, US$37.45. **Mérida**, 0930, 1730, 15 hrs, US$26. **Palenque**, 10 per day, 5 hrs, US$6.50. **Comitán**, 7 per day, 1½ hrs, US$2. **Tuxtla Gutiérrez**, about 12 per day, US$3 (US$5.50 with *Uno* luxury 1st class – with seats which are practically beds, at 1800 and 1445). **Campeche**, 0930, US$20. **Villahermosa**, 1125, 1830, 7 hrs, US$12. **Chetumal**, 1430, 11 hrs, US$26. **Arriaga**, at 1200 via Tuxtla Gutiérrez, US$6. to **Coatzacoalcos** at 0630, US$14.80. **Chiapa de Corzo**, 0800, 0830, 1100, 1400, 2 hrs, US$3.35. Campeche, *servicio plus*, 2100. **Puerto Escondido** *with Cristóbal Colón*, 1st class, 0745, 1815, US$22 (US$23 to **Pochutla**). Tapachula, 9 hrs, 5 a day, 0030-1645, US$14.80. **Puebla** at 1530 and 1730, US$36. Veracruz, 1840, US$39. **Ciudad Cuauhtémoc**, US$5.50. **Cancún**, US$30. **Playa del Carmen**, US$28. **Tulum**, US$26. **Cárdenas**, ADO US$12. Book tickets as far in advance as possible; during Christmas and Holy Week buses are sometimes fully booked for 10 days or more.

Lacandonia 2nd class bus to **Palenque** from 2nd class bus station on Allende (where the 1st class bus station is also), 7 a day between 0100 and 2015, 4-5 hrs, US$5.50 (via Agua Azul, US$5.50); Cristóbal Colón, 1st class service, up to 4 times daily (including at least 1 *servicio plus*) US$7.50, bookings 5 days in advance; Maya de Oro, from Cristóbal Colón terminal, 3 times daily, a/c, videos, non-stop; Rodolfo Figueroa, 5 times a day, US$4.50, a/c. Other buses leave you at **Ocosingo**; Lacandonia, 2nd class to Ocosingo, 3 hrs, US$2.75, Altos at 1725, 1825. Refunds of fares to Palenque when reaching Ocosingo are not rare, and you then have to make your own way. Autotrans Tuxtla, F Sarabia, between Carretera Panamericana and Alvaro Obregón, 2nd class to Palenque, reserved seats, US$5. Minibuses to **Tuxtla Gutiérrez** leave from in front of 1st class bus station, when full, US$1.65.

Buses to Guatemala: *Cristóbal Colón*, south end of Av Insurgentes (left luggage facilities open 0600-2000 excluding Sun and holidays), clean station, direct 1st class buses to the Guatemalan border at **Ciudad Cuauhtémoc**, 170 km, several daily from

0700, 3 hrs, US$3.50 (leave bus at border, not its final destination). 1 ADO bus a day to the border at 1900, book in advance. Altos to Ciudad Cuautémoc/border, 3 a day, US$5. Cristóbal Colón to **Comitán** (if you can't get a bus to the border, take 1 to Comitán and get a pick-up there, US$0.50), hourly from 0700. 87 km (a beautiful, steep route). *Colectivos* also leave for Comitán from outside the Cristóbal Colón bus station, US$2. 2nd class to border with Autotransportes Tuxtla, US$2.75 (do not take 1430 ACL 2nd class, next to Trans Lacandonia, on Carretera Panamericana, it arrives too late for onward transport). For details on crossing the border at La Mesilla see page 280.

Airlines *Aviacsa*, in *Xanav* agency, Pasaje Mazariegos, local 2, Real de Guadalupe, T6784441, F6784384.

Directory

Banks *Casa Margarita* will change dollars and TCs. Banks are usually open for exchange between 0900 and 1300 only, check times. *Bancomer* charges commission, cash advance on Visa, American Express or Citicorp TCs, good rates and service. *Banco Internacional*, Diego de Mazariegos, good rates for cash and TCs (US$ only), fast, efficient, cash advance on Mastercard. *Banamex* changes cheques without commission, 0900-1300. *Banca Serfín* on the Zócalo, changes Euro, Amex, Mastercard, TCs. *Casa de Cambio Lacantún*, Real de Guadalupe 12, open daily 0900-1400, 1600-1900, Sat/Sun 0900-1300 (supposedly, may close early), no commission, at least US$50 must be changed. 24-hr ATM at Bancrecer, 5 de Febrero, adjacent to cathedral. Quetzales can be obtained for pesos or dollars in the *cambio* but better rates are paid at the border.

Communications Internet: *Chisnet*, Juárez between Madero and Dr JF Flores. US$2 per hour, cheapest in town. Open Mon-Sat 1000-1800. Best in the morning, as networks can be oversubscribed in the afternoon. *Podernet*, Real de Guadalupe between General Utrilla and B Domínguez. US$4 per hour, open daily 0900-2130, friendly, convivial but some slow machines. *Tapanco*, 20 de Noviembre and 1 de Marzo. US$4 per hour, free coffee (minimum 1 hr). *Cybercafé*, Pasaje de Mazariegos 14, T87488, F83015. US$4 per hour, 0900-2200. *Zecor*, Av 5 de Mayo 4-bis, US$3.50 per hour. Free ½-hour on the internet at the Telmex office, very slow, poor service, must have identification. **Post Office:** Cuauhtémoc 13, between Rosas and Hidalgo, Mon-Fri 0800-1900, Sat 0900-1300. **Telephone:** *Computel*, Insurgentes 64B, fax, guards luggage; Telmex, Niños Héroes and Hidalgo, also has 24-hr ATM. *La Llamada*, Real de Guadalupe, friendly and helpful. Long-distance phone calls can be made from the *Boutique Santo Domingo* on Utrilla, on corner of Paniagua, takes credit cards, collect call possible; and at shops at Av 16 de Septiembre 22, Madero 75 and Av Insurgentes 60. Phone and fax services available at the Tourist Office in the Plaza. Cheap international calls from 2nd class bus station, no waiting. No operator-assisted phone calls are possible on Sun after 2000 in Chiapas.

Cultural centres The *Casa de Cultura*, opposite El Carmen church on junction of Hermanos Domínguez and Hidalgo, has a busy range of activities on offer: concerts, films, lectures, art exhibitions and conferences. *El Puente*, Real de Guadalupe 55, T6784157, 1 block from the Plaza, has restaurant, internet centre and a small cinema. Check their notice board for forthcoming events. A good place to meet other travellers. *Taller de Artes y Oficios Kun Kun*, Real de Mexicanos 21, T6781417. Exhibits hand-woven woollen textiles made on primitive looms held around the weaver's waist, also ceramics. Some items available to buy. *Casa/Museo de Sergio Castro*, Guadalupe Victoria 47 (6 blocks from plaza), T6784289, excellent collection of indigenous garments, talks (in English, French or Spanish) and slide shows about customs and problems of the indigenous population, open from 1800-2000, best to make appointment, entry free but donations welcome.

Language schools *Centro Cultural El Puente*, Real de Guadalupe 55, Caja Postal 29230, T/F6783723 (Spanish programme), rates range from US$6 per hour to US$8.50 per hour depending on number in class and length of course, home stay programmes available from US$180 per week, registration fee US$100. *Universidad Autónoma de Chiapas*, Av Hidalgo 1, Dpto de Lenguas, offers classes in English, French and Tzotzil. *Instituto Jovel*, María Adelina Flores 21, Apdo Postal 62, T/F6784069, jovel@sancristobal.podernet.com.mx. Group or 1-to-1 classes, homestays arranged, said to be the best school in San Cristóbal as their teachers receive an obligatory 6-week training course.

Laundry *Superklin*, Crescencio Rosas 48, T6783275, US$1.30 per kg, for collection after 5 hrs. *Lavorama* at Guadalupe Victoria 20A; *Lavasor*, Real de Guadalupe 26, US$1.30 per kg, Mon-Sat 0800-2030. *Tinto Clean*, Guadalupe Victoria 20A. Recommended. Clothes washed and mended by Isaiah and friendly staff, B Domínguez 8, near corner of Real de Guadalupe. *Orve*, Belisario Domínguez no 5, T6781802. Open 0800-2000, US$1.20 per kilo, service wash available.

Medical Services *Dra Carmen Ramos*, Av Insurgentes 28, T6781680, or make an appointment through Tourist Office. **Red Cross:** T6780772. Recommended. English-speaking doctor: Dr Roberto Lobato, Guadalupe Victoria 25, T6781910. Regina Centro, 24-hr pharmacy on Diego de Mazariegos and Crescencio Rosas; another on Hidalgo and Chauhtémoc, open 0700-2300, with a homeopathic and natural remedy shop next door.

Useful addresses Immigration: on Carretera Pan Americana and Diagonal Centenario, opposite *Hotel Bonampak*. From Zócalo take Diego de Mazariegos towards west, after crossing bridge take Diagonal on the left towards Highway, 30-min walk. Only 15-day extensions given.

Villages near San Cristóbal

It is best not to take cameras to villages; there are good postcards and photographs on sale

You are recommended to call at Na Bolom (see Museums, above) before visiting the villages, to get information on their cultures and seek advice on the reception you are likely to get. Photography is resisted by some Indians (see below) because they believe the camera steals their souls, and photographing their church is stealing the soul of God, but also it is seen as invasive and sometimes profiteering. Many Indians do not speak Spanish. You can visit the villages of San Juan Chamula, Zinacantán and Tenejapa. While this is a popular excursion, especially when led by a guide (see above), several visitors have felt ashamed at going to look at the villagers as if they were in a zoo; there were many children begging and offering to look after private vehicles in return for not damaging them.

Zinacantán   Zinacantán is reached by VW bus from the market, US$0.75, 30 minutes journey, sometimes with frequent stops while the conductor lights rockets at roadside shrines; taxi US$4. The Zinacantán men wear pink/red jackets with embroidery and tassels, the women a vivid pale blue shawl and navy skirts. Annual festival days here are 6 and 19-22 January, 8-10 August; visitors are welcome. At midday every day the women prepare a communal meal which the men eat in shifts. The main gathering place is around the church; the roof was destroyed by fire (US$0.40 charged for entering church, official ticket from tourist office next door; photography inside is strictly prohibited). There are two museums but both have recently closed because the community felt that they only benefited those most involved in them. Check before planning a visit. **Ik'al Ojov**, off Calle 5 de Febrero, five blocks down Avenida Cristóbal Colón from San Lorenzo church, and one block to the left; the museum includes two traditional *palapas* or huts that people used to live in and there is a small collection of regional costumes. It occasionally holds shows and there is an annual festival on 17 February. Tiny gift shop. Donation requested. The second museum is the **Museo Comunitario Autzetik ta jteklum**, one block from San Lorenzo church, which is run by women from Zinacantán and also has exhibits on local culture.

Chamula   In this Tzotzil village 10 km northwest of San Cristóbal the men wear grey, black or light pink tunics, while the women wear bright blouses with colourful braid and navy or bright blue shawls. One popular excursion is to visit the brightly painted church. A permit (US$1) is needed from the village tourist office and photographing inside the church is absolutely forbidden. There are no pews but family groups sit or kneel on the floor, chanting, with rows of candles lit in front of them, each representing a member of the family and certain significance attached to the colours of the candles. The religion is centred on the 'talking stones', and three idols as well as certain Christian saints. Pagan rituals are held in small huts at the end of August. The pre-Lent festival ends with celebrants running through blazing harvest chaff. This happens just after Easter prayers are held, before the sowing season starts. Festivals in Chamula should *not* be photographed; if you wish to take other shots ask permission, people are not unpleasant, even if they refuse (although children may pester you to take their picture for a small fee). Take great care when visiting this village; some readers found an unreceptive attitude toward tourists.

There are many handicraft stalls on the way up the small hill southwest of the village. This has a good viewpoint of the village and valley. Take the road from the southwest corner of the square, turn left towards the ruined church then up a flight of steps on the left.

To get to Chamula, you can catch a VW bus from the market in San Cristóbal every 20 minutes, last at 1700, last one back at 1900, US$0.70 per person (or taxi, US$4). It is an interesting walk from San Cristóbal to Chamula along the main road to a point 1 km past the crossroads with the Periférico ring road (about 2½ km from town centre); turn right on to an old dirt road, not sign-posted but it is the first fork you come to between some farmhouses. Then head back via the road through the village of Milpoleta, some 8 km downhill; allow five hours for the round trip (one hour for Chamula). Best not done in hot weather. Also, you can hike from Chamula to Zinacantán in 1½ hours: when leaving Chamula, take the track straight ahead instead of turning left onto the San Cristóbal road; turn left on a small hill where the school is (after 30 minutes) and follow a smaller trail through light forest. After an hour you reach the main road 200m before Zinacantán.

NB Signs in Chamula warn that it is dangerous to walk in the area, robberies have occurred between Chamula and both San Cristóbal and Zinacantán. Also seek full advice on any travel outside San Cristóbal de las Casas in the wake of events since early 1994.

Just past the 3 km sign from San Cristóbal, on the road to Chamula, is the **Huitepec** nature reserve. The 2½-km trail is administered by Pronatura-Chiapas. The 135-ha reserve contains grassland, oakwood forest, rising to cloud forest at 2,400m. As well as a wide diversity of plants, there are many birds, including some 50 migratory species and snakes. ■ *0900-1600, Tue-Sun (take combi heading for Chamula from behind market). US$1.25.*

San Cristóbal de las Casas environs

Guided tours restricted to Tue, Thu, Sat 0930-1100. Colectivos go there, US$0.50. Tours can be organized 2-3 days in advance at Pronatura office, María Adelina Flores 21, T6784069.

Tenejapa
Drunkenness is quite open and at times forms part of the rituals

The Thursday market is traditionally fruit and vegetables, but there are a growing number of other stalls. Excellent woven items can be purchased from the weavers' cooperative near the church. They also have a fine collection of old textiles in their regional ethnographic museum adjoining the handicraft shop. The co-operative can also arrange weaving classes. The village is very friendly and many men wear local costume. Few tourists visit Tenejapa (**F** *Hotel Molina*, simple but clean; several *comedores* around the market). Buses leave from San Cristóbal market at 0700 and 1100 (1½ hours journey), and *colectivos* every hour, US$1. Ask permission to take pictures and expect to pay. The market thins out by noon.

Two other excursions can be made, by car or local bus, from San Cristóbal south on the Pan-American Highway (30 minutes by car) to **Amatenango del Valle**, a Tzeltal village where the women make and fire pottery in their yards, and then southeast (15 minutes by car) to **Aguacatenango**, a picturesque village at the foot of a mountain. Continue one hour along this road past Villa Las Rosas (hotel) to **Venustiano Carranza**, where the women wear fine costumes, and there is an extremely good view of the entire valley. There is a good road from Las Rosas to Comitán as an alternative to the Pan-American highway. Frequent buses.

NB Remember that locals are particularly sensitive to proper dress (that is neither men nor women should wear shorts, or revealing clothes) and manners; persistent begging should be countered with courteous, firm replies. It is best not to take cameras to villages; there are good postcards and photographs on sale.

Transport Get to outlying villages by bus or communal VW bus (both very packed); buses leave very early, and often don't return until next day, so you have to stay overnight; lorries are more frequent. To Zinacantán catch also VW bus from market. Buses and *combis* (US$1.50) from the market area to San Andrés Larrainzar (bus at 1000, 1100, 1400, with return same day, US$0.80 1-way) and Tenejapa. Transportes Fray Bartolomé de las Casas has buses to Chanal, Chenalhó (US$15 with taxi, return, 1 hr stay), Pantelhó, Yajalón and villages *en route* to Ocosingo. Transportes Lacandonia on Av Crescencio Rosas also go to the villages of Huixtán, Oxchuc and Yajalón, on the way to Palenque and to Pujiltic, La Mesilla and Venustiano Carranza. If you are in San Cristóbal for a limited period of time it is best to rent a car to see the villages.

Ocosingo
Phone code: 967
Colour map 4, grid C3
Population: 70,000

Palenque (see page 263) can be reached by paved road from San Cristóbal de las Casas, a beautiful ride via Ocosingo, which has a local airport, a colourful market and several hotels (**D** *Central* on Plaza, shower, clean, verandah. **E** *Bodas de Plata*, Av 1 Sur, clean, hot water. **E** *San Jacinto*, just off lower side of Plaza, with bath, hot water, clean, friendly. *Agua Azul*, simple rooms around courtyard, parking; *Posada Morales*) and clean restaurants, including *La Montura*, on the Plaza, good. It was one of the centres of fighting in the Ejército Zapatista de Liberación Nacional uprising in January 1994. Many buses and *colectivos* to Palenque, 2½ hours, US$3.30 and San Cristóbal de Las Casas.

Toniná
It is the perfect place to enjoy the countryside and Maya architecture in peace and quiet, with no crowds

The Maya ruins at Toniná are 12 km from Ocosingo. The road is unpaved but marked with signs once you leave Ocosingo. Beside the road is a marsh, frequented by thousands of swallows in January. A tour from San Cristóbal to Toniná costs US$15, it is possible to drive in an ordinary car, or take a taxi (US$6). To walk from Ocosingo, start in front of the church on the Plaza and follow the signs, or take the 0900 bus from the market to the jungle and get off where the road forks (ask). There is a short cut through the fields: after walking for two hours you come to an official sign with a pyramid on it; don't follow the arrow but take the left fork for about 15 minutes and go through a wooden gate on your right; follow the path for 2-3 km (across a little stream and two more gates, ask farmers when in doubt). You end up in the middle of one of the last classic Maya sites, with the palace high on a hill to your left. It is well worth visiting the ruins, which were excavated by a French government team. The temples are in the Palenque style with internal sanctuaries in the back room, but influences from many different Maya styles of various periods have been found. The huge pyramid complex, seven stone platforms making a man-made hill, is 10m higher than the Temple of the Sun at Teotihuacán and is the tallest pyramidal structure in the Mayan world. Stelae are in very diverse forms, as are wall panels, and some are in styles and in subject unknown at any other Maya site. A beautiful stucco mural was discovered in December 1990. Ask the guardian to show you the second unrestored ballcourt and the sculpture kept at his house. He will show you round the whole site; there is also a small museum. ■ *0900-1600, US$1.30.* (Drinks are available at the site; also toilets and parking.)

Ten minutes walk from Toniná is **C** *Rancho Esmeralda*. Owned by an American couple, *cabañas*, good meals, home-made bread, horse riding. No food or drinks for passers-by.

Some 15 km from Ocosingo on the road to San Cristóbal de las Casas is a beautiful cave with stalagmites, stalactites and bats. It is visible from the road on the left (coming from Ocosingo), close to the road, but look carefully for it. Take a torch/flashlight and walk 15m to a 10m diameter chamber at the end of the cave. Don't touch the geological formations as many stalactites have already been damaged.

Agua Azul and Misol-Há

The series of jungle waterfalls and rapids at Agua Azul run for 7 km and are breathtakingly beautiful. They are easily visited on a day-trip from Palenque. All the travel agencies, as well as many of the hotels, offer a tour there for about US$8, including a visit to the waterfall at Misol-Há (see below). Agua Azul's main swimming area has many restaurants and Indian children selling fruit. Swimming is good, in clear blue water during good weather, in muddy brown water during bad (but still refreshing if very hot, which it usually is). Swimmers should stick to the roped areas where everyone else can see them; the various graves on the steep path up the hill alongside the rapids are testament to the dangers of swimming in those areas. One of the falls is called 'The Liquidizer', an area of white water in which bathing is extremely dangerous. On no account should you enter this stretch of water; many drownings have occurred. Obey the notice posted in an adjacent tree. If you walk some way up the lefthand side of the river you come to uncrowded areas where the river is wider and safer for swimming but do seek local advice about pools away from the main swimming area. Even in the designated areas, the currents are ferocious – the strongest swimmer will not make any progress trying to swim against them. Beware of hidden tree trunks in the water if it is murky. The path on the left of the rapids can be followed for 7 km, with superb views and secluded areas for picnics. There are also several *palapas* for hammocks, and plenty of space for free camping. Violent robberies have been reported and the river bridge is a particularly risky spot. Never go alone, groups of at least four are best. ■ *Entry US$1,*

Tabasco & Chiapas

US$3 for cars. Entry price is included in day trips from Palenque, which allow you to spend at least three hours at Agua Azul. Posada Charito in Palenque does the trip for US$7, marginally less than all the travel agencies. Kim Tours in Palenque town do a day trip taking in Agua Azul, Misol-Há and the Palenque ruins for US$8; a bargain, but a gruelling, hot day of excursions. Eight kilometres from Agua Azul along the river is Agua Clara, a nature reserve with a small zoo, horse-riding and kayaking. Some travel agencies in Palenque include this as part of the day trip. One hotel and restaurant (ask for details at tourist office in Palenque). At Misol-Há there is a stunning waterfall usually visited first on day trips from Palenque. Swimming is possible in the large pool at the bottom of the tumbling cascade of water, but it is better to wait until Agua Azul for a good swim. A narrow path winds around behind the falls, allowing you to stand behind the immense curtain of water and get your camera wet.

Sleeping & eating There are many restaurants and food stalls (if on a tight budget, bring your own). There are 2 places with *cabañas* for hammocks (hammock rental US$1.50 and up, US$3.50 per person in beds in dormitory); if staying, be very careful of your belongings; thefts have been reported. *Camping Agua Azul* is popular and reliable, opposite the parking lot; camping costs US$1.75, US$3.30 for 2 in camper van, and US$0.15 for use of toilets (100m further on are free public toilets), no other facilities. RVs can stay overnight at Agua Azul, using the facilities, without paying extra (as long as you do not leave the park). Plenty of food stalls, 2 restaurants. Follow the path up the falls to a 2nd site, cheaper, less crowded. There are more *cabañas* and nice places to sling a hammock further upstream, all cheaper and less touristy than lower down. *Hamacas Casa Blanca* next to *Comedor El Bosque*, 2 km upstream, big room with mosquito-netted windows, accommodates 10, shared toilet, US$2 per person (US$1.70 with own hammock), free locked luggage store. 750m upstream from *Casa Blanca* is the last house on this path. Here you can sling a hammock for US$1 (US$0.50 with own hammock), friendly family atmosphere, good views, store luggage, basic but good dinner. Recommended. *Restaurant Económico* will rent out a small hut with hammocks, friendly, helpful, excellent food, safe luggage store. At Misol-Há: **D** *cabañas* are for rent and there is a restaurant.

Transport All the travel agencies in Palenque do a cheap tour to both Misol-Há and Agua Azul, about US$8 per person. Many hotels also do a tour for the same price. Most tours allow about ½ hr at Misol-Há and 3-4 hrs at Agua Azul. Bring a swimsuit and plenty of drinking water. *Colectivos* from Hidalgo y Allende, Palenque, for Agua Azul and Misol-Há, 2 a day, US$9; *colectivos* can also be organized between Misol-Há and Agua Azul, in either direction. Taxi US$45 with 2 hours at Agua Azul, or to both falls US$65. Several buses from Palenque daily (direction San Cristóbal de Las Casas or Ocosingo), to crossroads leading to the waterfall, US$3.35, 2nd class, 1½ hrs. From the crossroads walk the 4 km downhill to the falls (or hitch a ride on a minibus for US$0.20). Back from the junction 1400-1600 with Transportes Maya buses. There are buses between San Cristóbal de las Casas and Palenque (to 2nd class bus station, Transportes Maya) which will stop there, but on a number of others you must change at Temo, over 20 km away, north of Ocosingo, which may require a fair wait.

Tabasco & Chiapas

Palenque

Built at the height of the Classic period on a series of artificial terraces surrounded by jungle, Palenque is one of the most beautiful of all the Maya ruins in Mexico. Palenque was clearly built for strategic purposes, with evidence of defensive apertures in some of the retaining walls. In the centre of the site is the Palace, a massive warren of buildings with an asymmetrical tower rising above them, and fine views to the north. The tower was probably used as an astronomical observatory and a watchtower. The outer buildings of the palace have an unusual series of galleries, offering shade from the jungle heat of the site.

From about the fourth century AD, Palenque grew from a small agricultural village to one of the most important cities in the pre-Hispanic world, although it really achieved greatness between AD 600-800. During the long and illustrious reign of Lord Pacal, the city rapidly rose to the first rank of Maya states. The duration of Pacal's reign is still a bone of contention among Mayanists because the remains found in his sarcophagus do not appear to be those of an 81 year-old man, the age implied by the texts in the Temple of the Inscriptions.

It is extremely hot and humid at the ruins especially in the afternoon so it is best to visit as early as possible

Since its discovery, choked by the encroaching jungle that pushed against its walls and climbed the stairs of its temples that had once been climbed by rulers, priests and acolytes, the architecture of Palenque has elicited praise and admiration and begged to be reconstructed. The corbelled vaults, the arrangement of its groupings of buildings, the impression of lightness created by walls broken by pillars and open spaces make Palenque-style architecture unique. It was only later that archaeologists and art historians realized that the architecture of Palenque was created mainly to accommodate the extraordinary sculptures and texts that referred not only to historical individuals and the important events in their lives, but also to mythological beings who endorsed the claims of dynastic continuity, or 'divine right' of the rulers of this great city. The structures most illustrative of this function are the Palace, a group of buildings arranged around four patios to which a tower was later added, the Temple of the Inscriptions that rises above the tomb of Lord Pacal, and the temples of the Group of the Cross, used by Chan Bahlum, Pacal's successor, who made claims in the inscriptions carved on the tablets, pillars and balustrades of these exceptional buildings; claims which, in their audacity, are awe-inspiring.

The Palace and Temple X1 are located in the centre of the site. The Palace stands on an artificial platform about a hundred yards long and thirty feet high. Chan Bahlum's younger brother, Kan Xul, was 57 when he became king. He devoted himself to enlarging the palace, and apparently built the four-storey tower in honour of his dead father. The top of the tower is almost at the level of Pacal's mortuary temple, and on the winter solstice the sun, viewed from here, sets directly above his crypt. Large windows where Maya astronomers could observe and chart the movement of the planets, ancestors of the royal lineage of Palenque, pierce the walls of the tower. Kan-Xul reigned for 18 years before being captured and probably sacrificed by the rulers of Toniná. During his reign Palenque reached its greatest degree of expansion, although recent excavations at the site may prove differently.

The Palace

The Temple of the Inscriptions, along with Temple XII and Temple XIII, lies to the south of the Palace group of buildings and is one of the rare Maya pyramids to have a burial chamber incorporated at the time of its construction. This

Temple of the Inscriptions

Tabasco & Chiapas

building was erected to cover the crypt in which Lord Pacal, the founder of the first ruling dynasty of Palenque, was buried. Discovered in 1952 by Alberto Ruz-Lhuillier, the burial chamber measured 7m long, 7m high and 3.75m across, an incredible achievement considering the weight of the huge pyramid pressing down upon it. According to the inscriptions, Lord Pacal was born in AD 603 and died in AD 684. Inside, Ruz-Lhuillier discovered his bones adorned with jade jewellery. Around the burial chamber are various figures carved in stucco, depicting the Bolontikú, the nine lords of night of Maya mythology. There was a narrow tube alongside the stairs, presumably to give Pacal spiritual access to the outside world. Pacal also left a record of his forbears in the inscriptions. These three great tablets contain one of the longest texts of any Maya monument. There are 620 glyph blocks; they tell of Pacal's ancestors, astronomical events and an astonishing projection into the distant future (AD 4772). One of the last inscriptions reveals that, 132 days after Pacal's death, his son, Chan Bahlum, ascended to power as the new ruler of Palenque.

While finishing his father's funerary monument, Chan Bahlum had himself depicted as a child being presented as heir by his father. The portraits of Chan Bahlum, on the outer pillars of the Temple of the Inscriptions, display features which are both human and divine. He has taken and assumed attributes that rightly belong to the gods, thus ensuring that the heir to the throne was perceived as a divine human.

Sarcophagus lid The sarcophagus, or coffin, is carved out of a solid piece of rock, with a carved slab covering it. Every element in the imagery of the sarcophagus lid is consistent with Maya iconography. It is exquisitely beautiful. The central image is that of Lord Pacal falling back into the fleshless jaws of the earth monster who will transport him to Xibalba, the realm of the dead. A cruciform world-tree rises above the underworld maw. The same world-tree appears on the tablets in the sanctuaries at the backs of the buildings known as the Group of the Cross. A long inscription runs around the edge of the lid which includes a number of dates and personal names that records a dynastic sequence covering almost the whole of the seventh and eight centuries.

Four plugs in the corners of the lid filled the holes used with ropes to lower the lid into place; the plug in the southeast corner had a notch cut in it so that the channel, built into the stairway leading to the upper world, would allow spiritual communion between the dead king and his descendants above. Although the imagery of the sarcophagus lid refers to Pacal's fall into Xibalba, the location of the tower of the palace ensures that he will not remain there. The sun, setting over the crypt on the winter solstice, will have to do battle with the Nine Lords of the Night before re-emerging triumphantly in the east; the nine tiers of the pyramid represent the nine battles to be fought during his downward journey. Pacal, who awaits the sun at the point where the final battle had been fought, will accompany the sun as he re-emerges from Xibalba in the east. Palenque, the westernmost city of the Classic Maya, was in the 'dead zone', which placed it in the perfect position to accommodate the descent of the sun and Lord Pacal into the underworld.

Temples of To the extreme southeast of the centre of the site lie the temples of the Group of
the Cross the Cross and Temple XIV. The buildings known as the Grupo de la Cruz include the Temple of the Sun, with beautiful relief carvings, which would probably have been painted in their day. The three temples in this group all have dramatic roof-combs, originally believed to have a religious significance, although traces of roof-combs have been found on buildings now known to

have been purely residential. In all of the temples there was discovered a huge stone tablet with bas-relief, now removed to the museum, from whose images the name of each temple was taken.

Human and mythological time come together in the inscriptions of these temples. In each tableau carved on the tablets at the back of the temples, Chan Bahlum, the new ruler, receives the regalia of office from his father, Pacal, now in the underworld and shown much smaller than his living son. The shrines in the three temples are dedicated to the Palenque Triad, a sacred trinity linked to the ruling dynasty of the city, whose genealogy is explained in the inscriptions. They were certainly long lived: the parents of the triad were born in 3122 or 3121 BC and the children arrived on October 19, October 23, and November 6, 2360 BC. It has been shown that these were dates of extraordinary astronomical phenomena: the gods were intimately related to heavenly bodies and events. They also provided a mythological origin for the dynasty which is detailed on the three main tablets from the group of the Cross. Rulers died and gods were born in an impressive merging of historical and mythological events. At their completion, the three temples of the Group of the Cross

Palenque archaeological site

Tabasco & Chiapas

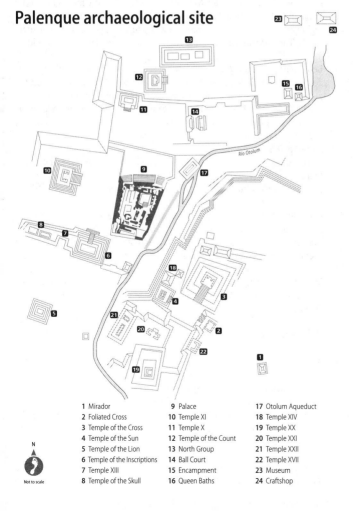

1 Mirador	**9** Palace	**17** Otolum Aqueduct
2 Foliated Cross	**10** Temple XI	**18** Temple XIV
3 Temple of the Cross	**11** Temple X	**19** Temple XX
4 Temple of the Sun	**12** Temple of the Count	**20** Temple XXI
5 Temple of the Lion	**13** North Group	**21** Temple XXII
6 Temple of the Inscriptions	**14** Ball Court	**22** Temple XVII
7 Temple XIII	**15** Encampment	**23** Museum
8 Temple of the Skull	**16** Queen Baths	**24** Craftshop

N

Not to scale

housed the divine sanction for the dynasty as a whole and gave the rationale for its descent through females as well as males.

On each set of balustrades, Chan Bahlum began his text with the birth of the patron god of each temple. On the left side of the stairs, he recorded the time elapsed between the birth of the god and the dedication of the temple. Thus, mythological time and contemporary time were fused. Each temple was named for the central image on its inner tablet. When Chan Bahlum died in 702 after ruling 18 years, his younger brother and heir erected a fourth shrine to record the apotheosis of the departed king (Temple XIV). On these reliefs, Chan Bahlum emerges triumphantly from the underworld and dances toward his mother, Lady Ahpo-Hel.

The lengths to which the rulers of Palenque went to establish legitimacy for their claims of divine right could not guarantee the survival of Palenque after the collapse felt throughout the Classic Maya region, when the building of elite religious structures stopped and stelae where no longer engraved with the details of dynastic events. Toniná, the city that captured and probably sacrificed the Palenque ruler Kan-Xul, outlived the great centre made glorious by Pacal and Chan Bahlum. The last-known dated monument from the Maya region registers 909 AD at the lesser site; it is to be supposed that soon afterwards, Toniná went the way of the other centres of the Classic Maya world.

Behind the public toilets is a path leading to some unexcavated buildings hidden in thick jungle, some of which have trees growing out of their roofs; the path also leads down to a waterfall, providing welcome relief from the heat. ■ *0800-1700. US$2.50, free on Sun. There are lots of handicraft stalls at the main entrance. Colectivos back to the town leave from outside the main entrance, US$0.80, every 15 minutes. From Palenque town, take a colectivo from either of the two points (see Transport).*

The museum is on the way back to the town, with restaurant and gift shop. Many of the stucco carvings retrieved from the site are here, as well as jade pieces of jewellery, funerary urns and ceramics. ■ *Tue-Sun 1000-1700.*

Warning: The ruins are surrounded by thick, mosquito-infested jungle so wear insect repellent and make sure you're up-to-date with your tablets (May-November is the worst time for mosquitoes). It is extremely hot and humid at the ruins especially in the afternoon so it is vest to visit as early as possible.

Readers wishing to learn more about the iconography and writing system of the Classic Maya are referred to: *A Forest of Kings*, L Schele and D Freidel, William Morrow and Company, NY 1990.

Palenque town

Phone code: 934
Colour map 4, grid B4
Population: 22,000

A friendly, colourful little town whose sole *raison d'être* is to accommodate the tourists heading for the famous archaeological site nearby. There is plenty of accommodation for every budget, with dozens of cheap *posadas* around the centre, and a new tourist *barrio*, La Cañada, with more expensive hotels, restaurants and bars. Souvenirs are available at lower prices than elsewhere on the Ruta Maya, making Palenque a convenient place to stop off *en route* to the southerly Chiapan towns of San Cristóbal and Tuxtla Gutiérrez. Travellers coming to Palenque from Mérida, Campeche and other cities in the Yucatán Peninsula will find it much hotter than those places, particularly in June, July and August. The **tourist office** is on Juárez next to the *Artesanía* market. They are very helpful and provide good free map of Palenque and the ruins.■ *Open daily 1000-1200.The Fiesta de Santo Domingo* takes place during the first week in August.

NB Visitors to Palenque and other communities in Chiapas should respect the local customs and dress so as not to offend – footwear and shirts should always be worn.

AL *Maya Toucan*, on road into town, T50290. Swimming pool, a/c, bar, restaurant, lovely views from rooms. **AL** *Motel Chan-Kah Ruinas*, at Km 3 Carretera Ruinas, T51100, F50820. Closest to ruins, cool bungalows, swimming pool fed from river, beautiful gardens, perfectly clean. Recommended. Poor restaurant, with marimba music Fri-Sun, and affiliated to **A** *La Aldea*, road to ruins Km 2.7, T50309, aldea@mex-ico.com Solar-panelled cabins, pool, orchid garden, eco-travel service. To get there, take the *colectivo* towards the ruins and ask to be let off at La Aldea. **AL-C** *Plaza Palenque* (Best Western), Km 27, Carretera Catazajá-Palenque, T50555, F50395. Free transport Mon-Sat 0800-1700, a/c, pool, relaxing, disco, 1½ km from centre, 8 km from ruins. **A** *Misión Palenque*, far end of town in countryside, T50241, F50499. Complete resort, noisy a/c, although poor service in restaurant reported; has a minibus service from Villahermosa airport for about US$20 return (2 hrs journey, avoids backtracking from airport into Villahermosa for transport to Palenque); has courtesy bus to ruins and to airfield for trips to Bonampak and Yaxchilán. **B** *Hotel Maya Tulipanes*, Cañada 6, T50201, F51004. A/c, cable TV, rooms vary in size, price and

Sleeping
It is convenient to stay at hotels near the Pemex service station, as they are also nearer the ruins and the bus stations. (Prices treble around fiesta time)

Tabasco & Chiapas

Palenque

quality, garage, pool, bar/restaurant next door. Recommended. **B-C** *Kashlan*, 5 de Mayo 105, T50297, F50309. With bath, fan or a/c, hot water, quiet, clean, will store luggage, video each pm, mosquito nets, helpful owner Ada Luz Navarro, tours to Agua Azul and Misol-Há falls, US$8 per person, laundry opposite, restaurant with vegetarian food in same building, bus and boat tours to Flores in Guatemala offered. Recommended. **B-C** *Motel Los Leones*, Km 2.5, T50201, F50033. About 5 km before ruins on main road, hot water, a/c, TV, quiet, large restaurant, gringo food.

C *Casa de Pakal*, Juárez 8, T50042, 1 block from Plaza. A/c, good but poor plumbing and not very friendly. **C** *Chan Kah Centro*, corner of Juárez and Independencia, T50318, F50489. A/c, restaurant, street car parking, terrace bar with happy hour. **C** *Hotel La Cañada*, Merle Green 14, T50102, F50446. Very rustic but very clean, with fan, good value, lovely garden, expensive restaurant, the owner, Sr Morales, is an expert on the ruins. **C** *Palenque*, 5 de Mayo 15, off Plaza, T50188, F50030. With bath, a/c restaurant, vast, rambling menage, 'going downhill fast', pool. **D** *Lacroix*, Hidalgo 30, T50014, next to church. With bath, fan, no hot water, some cheaper rooms, pleasant place. **D** *La Posada*, at La Cañada, T50437. Hot water, fans, basic, a little run down but OK, 'designed for young travellers, international ambience', peaceful, luggage store. **D** *Nikte-Há*, Juárez between Allende and Aldama, T 50934. New, modern building, friendly, a/c, TV. **D** *Posada Mallorca*, on highway, T50838. Small rooms, comfortable. **D** *Regional*, Av Juárez 79, T50183, 3 blocks from Plaza. Hot showers (US$1.50 extra), lights located behind fans ensure constant flickering lights, noisy. **D** *Xajlel Jade*, Hidalgo 61, T50463. Clean, comfortable rooms in quiet street, family-run, hot water. Recommended. **D** *Xibalba*, Merle Green 9, T50411, F50392. Spacious rooms, clean, hot water, a/c, fan. Recommended.

E *Avenida*, Juárez 216, T50116. With restaurant, clean, large rooms with fan, parking, but does not display price in rooms so ask for government list to check, no hot showers, some rooms with balcony. **E** *Busil-Ha*, Jiménez 47, between Velasco Suárez and 12 de Octubre, no phone. Same owners as *Posada Charito* (T50121). Family-run, friendly service, nicely furnished rooms. **E** *Casa de Huéspedes León*, Hidalgo (s/n) near junction with Abasolo, T50038. With bath, only cold water, some mosquitoes. **E** *La Selva*, Av Reforma 69. Newly renovated, very good value, same owners as *Posada Charito*, clean. **E** *Los Angeles*, next to ADO terminal. New, hot water, fan, comfortable. Recommended. **E** *Misol-Há*, at Juárez 12, T50092. Fan, with bath, hot water, clean, owner Susana Cuevas speaks English. **E** *Naj K'in*, Hidalgo 72. With bath and fan, hot water 24 hrs, noisy disco nearby, purified water in room and cooler in hallway, safe parking. Excellent value. **E** *Posada Alicia*, Av Manuel Velasco Suárez 59, T50322, between new market and C Novelos. With fan (ask for one), cold water, no towels, cheap, grubby, rooms on left as you enter are cooler, ask for rooms with communal bathroom. **E** *Posada Kin*, Abasolo s/n, 20 de Noviembre y 5 de Mayo T51714, very near Zócalo. Clean doubles with bathroom, fan, tours available, safe and luggage store. **E** *Posada San Francisco*, Hidalgo 113 and Allende. With bath, clean, quiet, no curtains, basic. **E-F** *Posada San Juan*, T50616 (from ADO go up the hill and 1st right, it's on the 4th block on the left). With bath, cheaper without, cold water, and fan, clean, quiet, firm beds, secure locks, nice courtyard, very good for budget accommodation, safe parking available (also near buses, Santo Domingo, 20 de Noviembre 19, T50146, stores luggage). **E** *Posada Shalom*, Av Juárez 156, T50944. New, friendly, clean, noisy, stores luggage. Recommended. **E** *Santa Elena*, Jorge de la Vega. Behind ADO/Cristóbal Colón terminal but still fairly quiet, with bath, good value, clean, simple, fan, safe parking. **E** *Vaca Vieja*, 5 de Mayo 42, T50388, 3 blocks from Plaza. With bath, popular with gringos, good restaurant. **E-F** *Yun-Kax*, Av Corregidora 87 (behind *Santo Domingo*), T50146. Quiet, clean, large rooms, hot water. Recommended. **F** *Johana*, 20 de Noviembre and Allende. Large, clean, airless rooms with fan and bath. **F** per person *Posada Charito*, Av 20 de Noviembre 15B, T50121. Clean, friendly, family-run, very good value, basic, some rooms very airless, ground floor best, laundry service. Opposite is **E-F** *Posada Canek*, 20 de Noviembre. Dearer rooms have bath, all with fan and toilet, very clean, ground floor dormitory near reception noisy, helpful staff, prices are per person and sharing is often required (regardless of sex), fills up early, arrive before 1000 check-out time. Nearby on 20 de Noviembre is **F** *Chacamax*. Small rooms with bath, fan. Ask for a marginally better room upstairs. **E-F** *Posada Nacha'n Ka'an*, 20 de Noviembre 25 por Allende. Recommended.

Camping *Trailer Park Mayabel*, on road to ruins 2 km before entrance (bus from town US$0.30). For caravans and tents, US$8 per vehicle with 2 people. US$2.35 for tent or to sling hammock (an *ambulante* sells hammocks once a day, or you can hire them for an additional US$2.50), palmleaf huts, bathrooms, hot showers, good restaurant but not cheap, nice setting (double room with shower US$12.50), popular so can be noisy, the place is not to everyone's taste; many mosquitoes and many ticks in long grass (we're told they avoid people who eat lots of garlic!). Watch your belongings; management sometimes stores luggage during the day (reluctant to store valuables). At night, around 0100, you can often hear the howler monkeys screaming in the jungle; quite eerie. The path between the campground and the ruins is not open; do not attempt to use this path. *Panchan Camping*, on road to ruins. Cabins (**E**), rent a hammock for US$3 or camp for US$2, hot showers, clean, small pool, vegetarian meals, library, owner is archaeologist and is friendly and informative. Recommended. *Trailer Park María del Mar*, 5 km from Palenque, along road to ruins, T50533. US$12 for 2 in camper van with hook-up, camping US$5, restaurant and swimming pool, cold showers, clean, pretty setting (check that water is turned on). Good swimming at *Calinda Nututún* (entry US$1), 3½ km along Palenque-Ocosingo road, T50100. US$3.30 per person, vehicle free, US$2 per camping site per night, rather run-down, no tent rentals, rooms (**B**) are neglected, toilets and bath; and beautiful lake and waterfall open to the public for a small fee. Misol-Há, 2 km off same road at Km 19, see above.

Eating

Expensive The classier restaurants are in the *barrio* La Cañada, behind the Maya head as you enter the town, eg *El Fogón de Pakal*, Merle Green. Delightful, good and varied menu. *Las Tinajas*, 20 de Noviembre 41 y Abasolo. Good, family-run, excellent food, huge portions. At Km 0.5 on Hidalgo (road to ruins) is *La Selva*. Excellent, smart dress preferred, live music at weekends.

Mid-range *La Quebrada*, Av Juárez 120. Breakfast and reasonably priced meals, fast service. Recommended. *El Patio*, Av Juárez. Cheap set menu, good service. *Merolec*, down street from *La Posada*. Good atmosphere and service. *Lakan-Há*, Juárez 20. Fast, efficient. *El Rodeo*, Juárez 120, near Plaza. Does good breakfasts and meat dishes, popular with travellers. Recommended. *La Ceiba* (Hermanos Cabrera) on Juárez. Good café for breakfast. *Girasoles*, Juárez 189. Roof terrace, very good food and value, good breakfasts. *Francesa*, Juárez, 2 doors down from ADO bus office. Nothing French but reasonable steak and chips. *Pizzería Palenque*, Juárez, T50332. Good pizzas and prices. *Mara*, on 5 de Mayo by the Zócalo. Excellent food, very welcoming. *Mariscos and Pescados*, off Juárez, opposite large *artesanía* market. *Artemio*, Av Hidalgo, near Plaza. Reasonably priced food. Recommended. *Chan Kah*, on Plaza. Good value, accepts credit cards. *Yunuen*, at *Hotel Vaca Vieja*. Generous portions at reasonable prices, good steaks, popular with local ranchers. *California*, Av 5 de Mayo, opposite *Hotel Avenida*, near 2nd class buses. Good value, Mexican specialities. *La Terraza*, Juárez opposite El Rodeo. Very nice terrace overlooking street, good service, varied menu, mainly Mexican specialities. *Restaurante Maya*, Hidalgo and Independencia. Very popular, fills up by 1900, set menu lunches and à-la-carte dinner, mainly Mexican.

Cheap *Los Portales*, Av 20 de Noviembre and Independencia. Cheap, good. Recommended. Good *pollo rostizado* in restaurant inside ADO office. Good *tacos* at food stalls east of Parque Central. Try the ice cream at *Holanda* on Av Juárez s/n, 4 doors west of Banamex, in the centre. **Cafés** Opposite *Hotel Kashlan*, *Café de los Altos*. Good coffee. *El Rinconcito*, Allende, across from *Kashlan*. Good, economical.

Bars *Hard Rock Bar*, 20 de Noviembre esq Plaza. Bar with loud music and many types of Tequila, not part of US-owned Hard Rock Cafe chain. *El Rocamar*, Plaza Independencia and Av 5 de Mayo. Restaurant/bar. Watch your change.

Shopping Av Juárez is lined with souvenir shops selling hammocks, blankets, Maya figurines and hats. Sales staff are much less pushy than in towns in the Yucatán Peninsula, but bargaining is still necessary to get good prices. Near the bus terminal on Juárez is a bag shop selling all types of sports bags, rucksacks and suitcases, prices range from US$2.50 to US$25.

Sports **Horse riding** tours can be booked at the Clínica Dental Zepeda, Avenida Juárez s/n. The dentist is the owner of the horses.

Tour operators *Toniná*, Juárez 105, T50384, or small office on Juárez ½ block from plaza, mixed reports, clarify prices before tour, tours to Bonampak and Yaxchilán, 2 days, US$55 per person. *Yax-Há*, Av Juárez 123, T50798, F50767. English spoken. Recommended. *Shivalva* (Marco A Morales), Merle Green 1, La Cañada, T50411, F50392, tours of Palenque, Yaxchilán, Bonampak, Tikal, Guatemala City, Belize, Copán. *Viajes Mayasol*, Juárez 191, T51006, F50282, mayasol@hotmail.com. Adventure tours to Chacamax River, all-day trek, rafting, lunch US$58. Many other rafting and adventure trips of between 1 and 6 days. *Grupo Turismo Luna*, Allende 6 esq Juárez, T51130, F50210. Flights to Bonampak, Yaxchilán and Flores (Guatemala) in private planes, US$60 per plane, min 4 people. Day trip to Misol-Há and Agua Azul, US$7. Also books flights to Cancún. *Kim Tours*, Juárez opposite *Banamex*. 2-day trip to Yaxchilán and Bonampak US$48, 4-hr jungle walk with swim and visit to ruins with guide, US$15, also adventure trips on the Usumacinta River.

Transport **Air** Aerocaribe flies daily during the high season (twice a week in the low season) to Palenque from Cancún via Flores, Guatemala. There are also flights from Huatulco, Mérida, Oaxaca and Tuxtla Gutiérrez. For flights to Bonampak and Yaxchilán, see above.

Local buses Micro buses run back and forth along the main street, passing the bus station area, to and from the ruins, every 10 mins, US$0.50 (taxi US$5). All bus companies have terminals close to each other at west end of Av Juárez with 20 de Noviembre. **Taxis** charge a flat rate of US$1 within the town.

Colectivos to the ruins run from 2 places, every 15 mins: Allende between Hidalgo and Juárez, and from Allende between 20 de Noviembre and Corregidora. US$0.70, but they pass along the main road and only drop you at the ticket office before the ruins; it is a further 1 km uphill from there, US$0.50. *Colectivos* to Playas de Catazajá (for Escárcega and Campeche) leave from Allende between 20 de Noviembre and Corregidora, US$0.80.

Long distance buses There are 3 bus terminals, 2 smaller 2nd class ones serving destinations in Chiapas state, and the ADO/Cristóbal Colón terminal, with buses to Chiapan destinations as well as longer journeys, all on 1st class buses. **Cancún**, 1st class terminal, 2000, 13 hrs, US$30. 2nd class buses, 2345, US$23. **Campeche**, 1st class terminal, 2345, US$23, 0800 and 2100, 5 hrs, US$13 (*ADO*); 2nd class buses, 2345, US$10. **Escárcega**, 1st class terminal, 1410, 1730, 3 hrs, US$10; 2nd class 2345, US$6. **Mérida**, 1st class terminal, 0800, 2100, 9 hrs, US$20; 2nd class buses, 2345, US$15. **Mexico City**, 1st class terminal, 1800, 2000, 16 hrs, US$41. **Oaxaca**, 1st class terminal, 1730, 15 hrs, US$30 (*ADO*). **San Cristóbal**, 1st class terminal, 0930, 1830, 5 hrs, US$6.50 (also 1st class

Tabasco & Chiapas

service from Lacandonia terminal, 2 doors down, 6 a day, US$6.50); 2nd class buses, same times as Tuxtla, US$5.30; from the Lacandonia terminal, next door to Express Plus, 0530, 0645, 0845, US$5. **Tulum**, 1st class terminal, 2000, 11 hrs, US$26. **Tuxtla Gutiérrez**, 1st class terminal, 0930, 1200, 1830, 6 hrs, US$9.40; 2nd class buses, 3 a day from 0730, US$7. **Villahermosa**, 2nd class buses, 6 per day from 0500, US$4.

NB There are military checks between Palenque and San Cristóbal de las Casas; buses and cars are stopped. If stopped at night in a private car, switch off engine and lights, and switch on the inside light. Always have your passport handy.

Banks Exchange rate only comes through at 1000, then banks open until 1200. *Bancomer*, changes TCs, good rates. *Yax-Há Cambio* on Juárez, open 0700-2000 daily, changes US$ cash and TCs. Next door at No 28, is *Banamex*, open Mon-Fri 0930-1400, slow. *Restaurante El Rodeo* also changes TCs at bank rate. At weekends TCs can be changed at many travel agencies and other shops on Av Juárez; also, the owner at *Farmacia Central* will change US$ at a reasonable rate. ATMs at *Bancomer* and *Banamex*, but with long queues. **Communications** Internet: *Cybercafé*, Independencia between 5 de Mayo and 20 de Noviembre, T51710. Open daily 0900-2100, US$4 per hour, free coffee. Cibernnet@mail.Ciberpal.com.mx **Post Office:** Independencia, next to Palacio Municipal, helpful, open Mon-Fri 0900-1300. **Telephone:** long-distance telephones at ADO bus terminal, cheaper than many other telephone offices; at *Mercería* bookshop in Aldama near Juárez, and a shop by *Hotel Palenque* in Zócalo. **Laundry** Opposite *Hotel Kashlan*, US$2 per 3 kg, mixed reports, open 0800-1930. At the end of Juárez is a laundry, US$3 per 3 kg.

Directory

Yaxchilán and Bonampak

Yaxchilán is a major Classic Maya centre built along a terrace and hills above the Río Usumacinta. The temples are ornately decorated with stucco and stone and the stone lintels are carved with scenes of ceremonies and conquests. There are more howler monkeys than people in Yaxchilán. ■ *0800-1600, US$2.* **Bonampak** was under the political domination of Yaxchilán, built in the late Classic period on the Río Lacanjá, a tributory of the Usumacinta. It is famous for its murals, dated at after AD 800, which relate the story of a battle and the bloody aftermath with the sacrificial torture and execution of prisoners. ■ *0800-1600, free.* Do not visit ruins at night, it is forbidden.

An article in National Geographic, February 1995, reproduces some of the murals with computer enhancement to show their original colours and most of the details.

From around AD 200 to the early 10th century, the era known as the Classic Maya witnessed the growth of many small settlements into great centres noted for wonderful architecture, sculpture, painted ceramics, impressive advances in mathematics and hieroglyphic writings, and the growth of an elite who often created alliances with other polities through marriage. Wide causeways, sacbés, were built between centres enabling the inhabitants to maintain contact with those of other towns. All these great advances came to an end around AD 909, when the Classic Maya civilization collapsed. For many years Mayanists have postulated about the cause of the collapse: some have suggested land exhaustion, others have suggested invasion from the Central Highlands while still others believe in a peasant revolt against the conspicuous consumption of an ever-expanding elite. The painted walls of Structure 1 at Bonampak illustrate well the extravagance indulged in by the elite of this centre on the margins of the Lacandón Rainforest.

The murals at Bonampak are very realistic and expertly executed with an excellent use of colour and available space. Painted on the walls, vault rises and benches of three adjoining but not interconnecting rooms, they describe the rituals surrounding the presentation at court of the future ruler. Some of the rituals were separated by considerable intervals, which adds to the solemnity of the ceremony. It is very possible that the rituals illustrated were only a small

Tabasco & Chiapas

selection of a far greater series of events. The people participating were mainly elite, including the royal family, and a strict hierarchy was observed in which eminent lords were attended by minor nobility.

In Room 1, the celebration opens with the presentation of the young prince, a simple act in which a porter introduces the child to an assembly of lords, dressed for the occasion in white robes. The king, dressed simply, watches from his throne. Also present are two representatives from Yaxchilán, one male and one female. It is probable that the female is the wife or consort of Chaan-Muan, the ruler of Bonampak. After this simple opening, the spectacle begins. Lords are represented dressing in sumptuous clothing and jewellery, musicians appear playing drums, turtle carapaces, rattles and trumpets and they all line up for a procession which will bemuse the peasantry, labourers and artisans waiting outside. We never see the lower orders, but, open-mouthed, we can stand with them to observe the spectacle. The headdresses alone are enough to bedazzle us and the great diversity in the attire of the participants illustrates the wide spectrum of social functions fulfilled by those attending the ceremony. The heir was well launched.

The imagery and text of the sculptured lintels and stelae at nearby Yaxchilán proclaim the right of the heir to accede to the throne while emphasizing the need to take captives to be sacrificed in honour of the king-to-be. This need is echoed in the paintings of Room 2, Structure 1, at Bonampak. A ferocious battle is in progress in which the ruler, Chaan-Muan, proves his right to the throne. In the midst of battle, he shines out heroically. The local warriors pull the hair of those of the opposite side, whose identity is not known. Many captives were taken. In the ensuing scene, the full horror of the fate of those captured by the Maya is illustrated.

On a stepped structure, the ruler Chaan-Muan oversees the torture and mutilation of the captives taken in the recent battle. This event is clearly in the open air and surely witnessed by the inhabitants of Bonampak, whose loyalty is rewarded by admission to the bloody circus. The torture of the captives consisted of mutilation of the hands; some disconsolate individuals hold up their hands dripping blood, while one has clearly been decapitated, his head resting on a bed of leaves. It is to be supposed that the torture of the captives would be followed by death, probably by decapitation. The gods demanded sacrifice, which was provided by the rulers in an extravaganza of bloodletting. What appears to be outright bloodthirstiness was a necessary part of Maya ritual, and probably accepted by all the polities throughout the Classic Maya region. It is very probable that the heir would not have been acceptable without this gory ritual.

The murals of the third room at Bonampak express the events that were meant to close the series of rituals designed to consolidate the claim to the throne by the son of the ruler. At first sight, the paintings that cover the walls of room three of Structure 1 appear to celebrate the sacrifices of the previous depictions in an exuberant public display of music, dance, and perhaps song. The background is a pyramid, and ten elegantly dressed lords dance on different levels, colourful 'dance-wings' sprouting from their hips. The dominant dancer on the uppermost level is believed to be the ruler, Chaan-Muan. However, it has been noted that a very strong element of sacrifice accompanies the extrovert display. In a more private corner, the royal family is portrayed preparing to engage in blood sacrifice; a servant proffers a container to them that holds the sacred bloodletting instruments. There are also indications that the male dancers had already drawn blood by means of penis perforation. As at Yaxchilán, blood endorsed the dynastic claims of the royal family.

Spilling royal blood at Yaxchilán

At Yaxchilán, dynastic succession continued unbroken for about 500 years. It appears that the same bloodline ruled over this city-state throughout this long period. For almost 100 years, from 681 until 771, two rulers, Shield Jaguar and his son, Bird Jaguar, underlined their claim to be descendants of the originator of the royal bloodline through blood sacrifice. The history of these men, their parents, wives, mothers and sometimes in-laws is engraved on lintels and stone tablets (stelae) throughout the city. Similar to Palenque, buildings were erected primarily to function as surfaces on which to register the history of the ruling families.

Descent from the ruler did not guarantee a smooth transition of power to his child. The Heir Apparent had to prove his suitability by engaging in warfare to acquire captives, preferably of high rank, to be tortured and sacrificed in rituals that surrounded the accession ceremonies. However, the sacrifice of captives was not sufficient to prove the worthiness of the pretender. More blood had to flow to accompany the accession of the new ruler.

Engraved on lintels and stelae and confirmed by accompanying texts, the imagery of the vast body of portraits at Yaxchilán attests to the very complex relationship that existed between kings, their wives, mothers and in-laws and blood sacrifice. To prove the suitability of the pretender, the first wife of the ruler is depicted pulling a rope lined with thorns through a hole in her tongue that had been made with a sharp obsidian blade.

The blood flowed. Combined with pre-ritual fasting, the loss of blood provokes the appearance of a vision serpent, out of whose mouth emerges the head of Penis of the Jaguar, the originator of the dynasty. Lady Xoc, the celebrant, has brought him forth to endorse the claims of his descendent. All this is quite explicit in the imagery in the sculptures at Yaxchilán. The sacred blood that flows from the tongue of Lady Xoc falls into a basket of bark-paper, which is saturated and then burned in a censer to honour the gods. This ritual was the privilege and obligation of the royal matrons of this important kingdom. Lady Xoc is also depicted aiding her husband, Shield Jaguar, as he dresses in preparation for battle in which he will surely acquire more captives to be tortured and sacrificed.

In a great public display of his privileges and obligations, the king is also depicted drawing his own blood. But rather than piercing his tongue with an obsidian blade, the ruler uses the sharp sting-ray spine to mutilate his penis in which he cuts three openings and fills them with paper. The royal blood will then be offered in the censer as before. Many depictions of rulers and high-ranking noblemen are explicit in showing the blood-spattered loincloths of those who had performed this ritual.

At Yaxchilán, privileged social status was endorsed by shedding the blood of high-ranking captives, wives and mothers of the rulers, but above all, by the supreme ruler himself.

Tabasco & Chiapas

The rituals portrayed on the walls of Structure 1 at Bonampak are thought to have been performed between 790 and 792, a time when the collapse of the Classic Maya was beginning to be felt. The extravagant use of enormous amounts of fine cloth, expensive jaguar pelts, jade beads and pectorals, elegant costumes, headdresses made from rare feathers, and spondylus shells was not enough to reverse the decadence of the civilization that had produced magnificent works in art, architecture, jewellery, mathematics, astronomy and glyphic writing: within a hundred years, the jungle was to claim it for its own. ■ *0800-1600, free.*

Readers wishing to learn more about the splendid murals at Bonampak are referred to: Mary Ellen Miller, The Murals of Bonampak, Princeton University Press, 1986.

At **Lacanjá** (9 km from Bonampak) there is a community of Lacandón Indians. They have curly hair, rare in Mexico, and wear white gowns. For more details ask at Na-Bolom in San Cristóbal de las Casas. There are four campsites here where you can sling a hammock, *Kin Bor*, *Vicente K'in*, *Carlos Chan Bor* and *Manuel Chan Bor* (best to bring food and mosquito net). Local guides can be hired for hikes in the jungle and to the ruins of Bonampak. Lucas Chambor at the *Casa de Cultura* is a good source of advice. There have been some reports of hostility towards tourists. Transport Lacanjá-Bonampak with locals US$6.50-9. The walk through the jungle is beautiful and crosses several streams. Another walk in the area is to the **Cascadas de Moctuniha** (one hour each way US$6.50 with guide).

Tour operators From Palenque, a 2-day road and river trip to Bonampak and Yaxchilán is sold by travel agencies, US$55 per person, all transport and food included; or 1-day trip to Yaxchilán, US$35; entrance to sites included in cost. Strenuous, but good value: the usual schedule is 4 hrs bus ride to Echeverría/Corozal (mostly tarmac), 1 hr boat to Yaxchilán, next day boat to Echeverría, 1 hr bus to Bonampak turn-off, walk to Bonampak and back, 3-4 hrs bus to Palenque (arriving 2200). *Colectivos Chambala* at Hidalgo y Allende, Palenque, also run 2-day trips, slightly cheaper, again all-inclusive, minimum 6 passengers. Taxis charge US$20 per person for the return trip to Bonampak. Lacandón Indians running an ecotourism project take passengers in 3-wheelers to the ruins (or to Lacanjá Chansayab community), US$7. However you go, take suitable footwear and rain protection for jungle walking, drinking water, insect repellent and passport (there are many military checkpoints). Beware of sandflies, black flies which cause river blindness, and mosquitoes; there is basic accommodation at the site, take hammock and mosquito net. Thieving has been reported.

Transport A new road has been built to **Bonampak**: 2 lanes, paved. Autotransportes Comitán Lagos de Montebello (Manuel Velasco 48, 2 blocks west of plaza, Palenque) buses at 0300, 0430, 0630, 0900 and 2000 all pass the turn-off to Bonampak, US$5.50, check details in advance. Last *colectivo* returning from Echeverría to Palenque passing crossroads for Bonampak at 1500. Buses from Palenque from Chancalá bus terminal every 3 hrs or so, from 0730 to **San Javier**, 3 hrs; *colectivos* US$4. From San Javier, a jungle trail leads to Bonampak, easy to follow but several hours walk with nowhere to stay *en route*. Take your own tent, hammock and sleeping bag as it gets cold at night, as well as food and drink. **Yaxchilán** is reached by 1-hr boat journey from Echeverría; you must register at the immigration office here if you are continuing on to Guatemala. US$67 for up to 4 people, US$92 for more than 5, to hire a motorboat for the round trip. There is no problem finding a boat (max 10 people, cost includes boatman staying overnight), but try to be there before 0900 to give you time to meet other travellers wanting to share launch, you may be able to share with tour parties who arrive from 0900 onwards. It is a beautiful ride, with rewarding ruins at the end of it. The custodian of the ruins is very helpful. Camping is restricted to the INAH site on the Usumacinta.

Air: Flights from Palenque to **Bonampak** and **Yaxchilán**, in light plane for 5, about US$600 per plane, to both places, whole trip 6 hrs. Prices set, list available; Viajes Misol-Há, Juárez 48 at Aldama, T50911, run charter flights to Bonampak and Yaxchilán for US$150 per person return, minimum 4 passengers. ATC Travel Agency, agents for Aviacsa, at Av Juárez and Allende, open 0800-1800 daily except Sun, to Bonampak; book at airport, may be cheaper from Tenosique, best to visit in May – the driest month. **Road**: Bonampak is over 30 km from Frontera Echeverría/Corozal and can be reached from the crossroads to Lacanjá on the road to Echeverría/Corozal.

Routes to Guatemala

There are two main border crossings into Guatemala: one at Ciudad Cuauhtémoc, reached via Rotue 190 from San Cristóbal de las Casas, and the other at Tapachula along the coastal Route 200 from the neighbouring state of Oaxaca. A third option is to cross the border by boat, east of Palenque, along the rivers San Pedro or Usumacinta.

River travel to Guatemala

The Río San Pedro route starts at Tenosique, a friendly place east of Palenque (money exchange at clothing shop, Ortiz y Alvarez at Calle 28 No 404, good rates for dollars to quetzales, poor for dollars to pesos). From here the route takes you by road to La Palma, boat to El Naranjo, in Guatemala, and then road to Flores.

Tenosique & Río San Pedro route

Sleeping and eating D *Rome*, Calle 28, 400, T2151. Clean, will change dollars for residents, bath, not bad. **E** *Azulejos*, Calle 26 416. With bath, fan, clean, hot water, friendly, helpful owner speaks some English, opposite church. **E** *Casa de Huéspedes La Valle*, Calle 19. With bath, clean, good, and others. Excellent and cheap *Taquería Pipirrín*, Calle 26, 512, near *Hotel Azulejos*.

Tour operators For planes to Bonampak contact Sr Quintero, T20099. *Hotel Kashlan*, Palenque, offers 2- and 3-day trips to Flores via Yaxchilán and Bonampak. Reliable and

Tabasco & Chiapas

Guatemala border & Lacandón

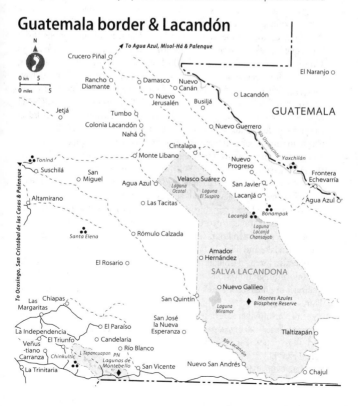

recommended. *Kim Tours*, Av Juárez 27, Palenque, T51499. Do similar trips, 'strenuous but great', US$100 per person. Recommended. Travel agencies in Palenque also do the trip to Flores via La Palma and El Naranjo, US$35-55 per person, 3 passengers minimum (agencies will make up the numbers), departs 0500, arrive Flores 1900; via Corozal/Bethel, US$35 per person, via Yaxchilán and Bonampak, see below, minimum five people. It may take several days before you can join an organized trip in low season. On Av Juárez several agencies offer tours to Flores by minibus and/or taxi, boat and public bus, via Tenosique, La Palma and El Naranjo. You probably won't meet any other travellers. Difficult to find enough people during the low season (otherwise you pay the whole trip yourself), about US70 per person, 16 hrs trip.

Transport You can get to Tenosique from Villahermosa by ADO bus (0430, 0700, 0800, 1330), 4 hrs, from Emiliano Zapata by frequent 1st or 2nd class bus, US$2. From Palenque minibuses Libertad leave from 20 de Noviembre y Allende from 0700 to Emiliano Zapata, 1 hr, US$2.50 (take 0700 to be sure of making the boat at La Palma); and from there to Tenosique at 0800 or 0900, 90 mins, US$2. ADO have a direct bus to Tenosique from Palenque at 0430, 2 hrs, US$3.25. Many travel agents in Palenque organize *colectivos* direct to La Palma at 1000, US$14 per person to connect with the boat to El Naranjo (4 passengers minimum). Alternatively, take a *colectivo* before 0645 to Playas de Catazajá from the stop just up from ADO (US$1.00, 30 mins); get off at the El Crucero de la Playa crossroads on the Villahermosa – Tenosique road and wait for the bus to pass at 0730 (2 hrs to Tenosique, US$2). Similarly, from Tenosique to Palenque, take the Villahermosa bus (every hour or so during the day) as far as El Crucero de la Playa, and then take one of the regular minibuses running to Palenque. Bus also from Mexico City, ADO, 16½ hrs, arrives 0700, US$45.50.

From Tenosique to **La Palma** on the Río San Pedro, orange *colectivos*, starting at 0600 from in front of the market, one hour, US$1, two hours by bus (from Tenosique bus station, which is outside town, take taxi, US$1.70 or *colectivo* to 'Centro', or walk 20 minutes). Taxi to La Palma US$7, shared by all passengers. From La Palma boats leave to El Naranjo (Guatemala) at 0800 (or when they have enough passengers) but timings are very irregular (they wait for a minimum of five passengers before leaving), at least 4½ hours, US$22 (to check boat times, T30811 Rural at the Río San Pedro). Be at the boat one hour early, it sometimes leaves ahead of schedule; if this happens ask around for someone to chase it, US$3-4 per person for three people. If there are fewer than five passengers, the boat may be cancelled, in which case you must either wait for the next one, or hire a *rápido* (US$125, maximum four people). You may be able to arrange a slower boat for up to six people for US$100. In La Palma, two restaurants are poor value; one restaurant will change money at weekends at a reasonable rate.

It is a beautiful boat trip, through mangroves with flocks of white herons and the occasional alligator, dropping people off at homesteads. There is a stop at the border post two hours into the journey to sign out of Mexico, a lovely spot with a lake and lilies. In the rain, your backpack will get wet; take waterproofs and a torch / flashlight. There are no officials on arrival at the jetty in El Naranjo; immigration is a short way uphill on the right (entry will cost US$5 in quetzales or dollars, beware extra unofficial charges at customs); bus tickets to Flores are sold here.

At **El Naranjo** there are hotels (basic) and restaurants (you can wait in a restaurant till the 0100 bus departs, but electricity is turned off at 2200). The grocery store opposite immigration will change dollars into quetzales at a poor rate. From El Naranjo there is a dirt road through the jungle to Flores; buses leave at 0200, 0400, 0600, 1100, 1400 for Flores (minimum 4-5 rough, crowded hours, US$3), or hitchhiking is apparently possible.

The Río Usumacinta route takes you by road to Benemérito (southeast of **Río Usumacinta** Uaxchilán and Bonampak), boat to Sayaxché, Guatemala and then road to **route** Flores. Autotransportes Comitán Lagos de Montebello buses (Avenida Manuel Velasco Suárez, Palenque, three blocks from food market) run daily at 0330, 0530, 0800 to **Benemérito**, on the Mexican side of the Usumacinta, 7-12 hours but will be quicker when the new paved road is completed; basic buses, dreadful road, crowded (it's about half the time in a *camioneta* if you can hitch a ride in one). You must visit immigration, about 3 km from Benemérito, to sign out of Mexico (the bus will wait).

Once in Benemérito where there is a 2100 curfew (two basic *pensiones*), hope for a boat to Guatemala; this may take a couple of days. The boat goes to Sayaxché and should stop at Pipiles for immigration formalities. A trading boat takes two days, US$4-5; a motorized canoe eight hours, US$5-10. From Sayaxché, buses run to Flores.

Alternatively, take the bus Palenque-Frontera Echeverría, now more often known as Puerto Corozal, 1000, four hours by good road, US$5.50; or mini-buses at 0730, 1100, 1400 from 5 de Mayo by *Restaurante El Caimito*, US$4.50 (many travel agencies in Palenque run minibuses on this route, leaving at 0600, to connect with the boat to Bethel, 35 minutes, and on to Flores as below). From Echeverría/Corozal there is a five-minute launch ride to La Técnica, then 20 minutes by bus to Bethel in Guatemala, from where a regular bus service goes to Flores at 1200, five hours. Alternatively launches go directly to Bethel, US$40-45 per boat. At Echeverría/Corozal there is an immigration office; **F** *Posada XX*, nearby, and **F** *Posada Tumbala*, better of the two; near the *embarcadero* are **C** *cabañas* with two double beds, built by the river boat company (Cooperativa Escudo Jaguar de Corozal) and two cheap *comedores*. Coming from Guatemala you may well get stuck at the border as the 0500 Santa Elena-Bethel bus does not connect with buses to Palenque (you may be able to get a lift with a pick-up, or one of the tour buses which start arriving around 1200; bargain hard). Passengers have to wait until 0400 next day. Bus from Frontera Echeverría to Palenque, 0500, US$3 and at 1230, US$5. Many military checkpoints.

San Cristóbal to the border

South of San Cristóbal and heading for Guatemala, follow the 170-km paved **Comitán** road via **Teopisca** (*pensión*, **E**, comfortable; *La Amistad* trailer park, run Phone code: *963* down, one dirty shower and bathroom, no electricity, not recommended), to Colour map *4, grid C4* **Comitán de Domínguez**, a lively, attractive town with a large, shady plaza. Population: *87,000* **Tourist office** On main square, in Palacio Municipal, ground floor. Altitude: *1,580m* ■ *Mon-Fri 1000-1400, 1700-2000*.

Sleeping Accommodation inferior in quality and almost twice the price of San Cristóbal. **B** *Internacional*, Av Domínguez 22, T6720112, near Plaza. Good, decent restaurant. **B** *Los Lagos de Montebello*, T6721092. On Pan-American Highway, Km 1,257. Noisy but good. **B** *Real Balún Canán*, Av 1 Pte Sur 5, T6721094. Restaurant. **E** *Delfín*, Av Domínguez 19-A, T6720013, on Plaza. Small rooms but hot water, helpful and clean. **E** *Posada Panamericana*, Av 1 Pte Norte 2, T6720763. Dirty. 1 block away is **E** *Hospedaje Montebello*. Clean, sunny courtyard, laundry, fax service, friendly. Recommended. **F** *Hospedaje Primavera*, Calle Central Benito Juárez 42, ½ block off Plaza. Room without bath.

Eating *Helen's Enrique*, on Plaza opposite church. Good food in pleasant surroundings. *Nevelandia*, Central Nte 1. Clean. Recommended. *Café Casa de la Cultura*, on

Tabasco & Chiapas

the Plaza. Sandwiches only. **Buffalo Café**, near Plaza, Av Central y Calle Norte. Live music daily at 2030. Several small *comedores* on the Plaza and at market (cheap).

Transport Buses from San Cristóbal de las Casas with Cristóbal Colón, frequent between 0730 and 2030, US$3.75, 2 hrs, last bus back at 1930. One Cristóbal Colón bus goes on to Tuxtla (via San Cristóbal), US$3.50, 4 hrs. Minibuses from Comitán to Tuxtla leave from the Cristóbal Colón bus station. Buses, *combis* and pick-up trucks from Comitán run to the border at Ciudad Cuauhtémoc. Petrol is available in Comitán, in centre of town on east side of Pan-American Highway, and another 2 km south of town, open 24 hrs.

Directory Airline offices: *Aviacsa*, Calle 3 Sur Pte, 12a, T6723519, F6720824, helpful, recommended. **Banks**: *Bancomer*, on Plaza will exchange Amex TCs; 2 others on Plaza, none changes dollars after 1200; also a *casa de cambio*. **Embassies & consulates**: *Guatemalan Consulate*, open Mon-Fri 0800-1200, 1400-1700, Sat 0800-1400 at Calle 1 Sur Pte 26 y Av 2 Pte Sur, T6722669; tourist card US$10 (even for those for whom it should be free), valid 1 year, multiple entry.

Lagunas de Montebello and Chinkultic

Six kilometres south of Comitán take a right turn for the Mayan ruins of **Tenán Puente** (5 km), situated in a forest; there is a shortcut on foot. In 1996 the tomb of a Maya nobleman (1000 AD) was discovered here. The buildings at Tenán are more restored than those at Chinkultic (see below). A road branches off the Pan-American Highway, 16 km further on, to a very beautiful region of vari-coloured lakes and caves, the **Lagunas de Montebello** (a national park). On no account visit the Lagunas alone or stay there the night, because of rapes and robberies at gunpoint (see Sleeping below). Off the road to Montebello, 30 km from the Pan-American Highway, lie the ruins of **Chinkultic**, with temples, ballcourt, carved stone stelae and a *cenote* (deep round lake, good swimming) in beautiful surroundings; from the signpost the ruins are about 3 km

Parque Nacional Lagunas de Montebello

Tabasco & Chiapas

To El Triunfo ▶

To San Antonio Buenavista ▲

Zona Arqueológica Chinkultic
Grutas Cave
Boats for hire
Restaurant & Sleeping Hut
Posada Las Orquideas/ Doña María
Boats for hire
Boats for hire ○ Tziscao
Mexico/Guatemala Border Monument ■ Albergue Turístico

To Pan-American Highway (30 km) for Zona Arqueológica Tenán Puente, Comitán & Tapachula

To Ixcán

GUATEMALA

N
Not to scale

1 Agua de Camarón
2 Cenote Azul
3 Cinco Lagos
4 Lago Chinkultic
5 Lago Montebello
6 Lago Pojoj
7 Lago San Lorenzo
8 Lago Tziscao
9 Laguna Agua Tinta
10 Laguna Bosque Azul
11 Laguna Cacauxti
12 Laguna Caracol
13 Laguna Chanujaba
14 Laguna Encantada
15 Laguna Ensueño
16 Laguna Esmeralda
17 Laguna Internacional
18 Laguna Llalpeh & Agua Pato (seasonal)
19 Laguna Patianú
20 Laguna Subterráneo
21 Laguna Tepancuapan
22 Laguna Yashan

● Restaurants/ Foodstalls

along a dirt road. ■ *Close at 1600, US$3.* Watch and ask for the very small sign and gate where the road to the ruins starts (about 1 km back along the main road, towards Comitán, from Doña María's, see below, don't attempt any short cuts); worth visiting when passing. *Colectivo* from Comitán US$1.

Combi vans or buses marked 'Tziscao' or 'Lagos' to the Lagunas de Montebello National Park (60 km from Comitán, US$1.30 about one hour), via the **Lagunas de Siete Colores** (so-called because the oxides in the water give varieties of colours) leave frequently from Avenida 2 Pte Sur y Calle 3 Sur Poniente, four blocks from the Plaza in Comitán; buses go as far as Laguna Bosque Azul, a one-hour journey. For those with their own transport there are several dirt roads from Comitán to the Lagunas; a recommended route is the one via La Independencia, Buena Vista, La Patria and El Triunfo (beautiful views), eventually joining the road west of the Chinkultic ruins.

Tziscao is 9 km along the road leading right from the park entrance, which is 3 km before Bosque Azul; five buses a day Comitán-Tziscao; the last bus and *colectivo* back connecting with the 1900 bus to San Cristóbal is at 1600. The last *combi* to Comitán is at 1700. A trip to the Lagunas de Siete Colores from Comitán can be done in a day (note that the less accessible lakes are hard to get to even if staying in the vicinity). It is also possible to hire a *combi*, which takes 12 people, to go to the Lakes and Chinkultic for US$15 per hour. A day trip to Chinkultic and the lakes from San Cristóbal de las Casas is also possible, if exhausting (take passport and tourist card with you). The Bosque Azul area is now a reserve. The area is noted for its orchids and birdlife, including the famous *quetzal*; very crowded at weekends and holidays. Horse hire US$4 per hour, if you take a guide you pay for an extra horse.

Tziscao

Sleeping Before planning to spend the night in the area check with the Tourist Office. In 1999 rapes and robberies at gunpoint brought official advice to travellers not to stay the night. There are, as well as picnic areas, an ***Albergue Turístico*** on the shores of Lake Tziscao (10 km, **F** per person, rooms for 4-6, toilet, blankets available, no hot water, reasonable kitchen facilities and bathrooms, excellent, reasonably priced meals, camping including use of hotel facilities; boats for hire, friendly owners, one of whom, Leo, speaks good English and has an intimate knowledge of the region); a small, family-run restaurant at Laguna Bosque Azul with a wooden hut for sleeping, **F**, bring sleeping bag; 2 very basic food shops in the village (best to bring your own food from Comitán market); and there are small caves. Young boys are good guides, take powerful torch. ***Posada Las Orquídeas*** (better known as 'Doña María'), Km 31, on the road to Montebello near Hidalgo and the ruins of Chinkultic, dormitory or cabin, **F** per person, family-run, very basic (no washing facilities, often no water, 2 toilets, urn in a shack) but friendly, small restaurant serving plentiful Mexican food. Next door are *cabañas*/restaurant *El Pino Feliz*. **Youth Hostel** *Las Margaritas*. *Hotel Bosque Bello*, 34 km, reservations in Tuxtla, T6110966, or Comitán T6721702.

NB Some Mexican maps show a road running along the Guatemalan border from Montebello to Bonampak and on to Palenque; this road is not complete and no public transport or other traffic makes the trip.

From Hidalgo you can get to Comitán by pick-up or paying hitchhike for US$1 (not recommended for women); to the Guatemalan border go from Hidalgo to La Trinitaria on Route 190 and catch a bus or pick-up south from there.

Tabasco & Chiapas

Border with Guatemala

Ciudad Cuauhtémoc From Comitán the road winds down to the Guatemalan border at Ciudad Cuauhtémoc via La Trinitaria (near the turn-off to Lagunas de Montebello, restaurant but no hotel). Ciudad Cuauhtémoc, despite its name, is not a city, but just a few buildings; the Cristóbal Colón bus station is opposite Immigration, with an overpriced restaurant and an excellent **E-F** *Hotel Camino Real*. Extremely clean and quiet, changes dollars to pesos. Highly recommended. Be sure to surrender your tourist card and get your exit stamp at Mexican immigration in Ciudad Cuauhtémoc before boarding a pick-up for Guatemalan immigration; you will only have to go back if you don't. A pick-up to the Guatemalan border, 4 km, costs US$0.65 per person. Walk 100m to immigration and customs, open until 2100. Beyond the Guatemalan post at La Mesilla, a beautiful stretch of road, leads 85 km to Huehuetenango. This route is far more interesting than the one through Tapachula; the border crossing at Ciudad Cuauhtémoc is also reported as easier than that at Talismán. Remember that Mexico is one hour ahead of Guatemala.

Entering Mexico from Guatemala Tourist cards and visas are available at the border; recent reports say only 15 days are being given, but extensions are possible in Oaxaca or Mexico City. It is forbidden to bring in fruit and vegetables; rigorous checking at 2 checkpoints to avoid the spread of Mediterranean mosquito.

Crossing by private vehicle Drivers entering Mexico: at the border crossing your vehicle is fumigated, US$7.25, get receipt (if re-entering Mexico, with documents from a previous entry, papers are checked here). Proceed 4 km to Migración to obtain tourist card or visa, or have existing visa checked. Then go to *Banjército* to obtain the necessary papers and windscreen sticker or, if re-entering Mexico, to have existing papers checked. ■ *Mon-Fri 0800-1600, Sat-Sun 0900-1400.*

Exchange Don't change money with the Guatemalan customs officials: the rates they offer are worse than those given by bus drivers or in banks (and these are below the rates inside the country). There is nowhere to change travellers' cheques at the border and bus companies will not accept cheques in payment for fares. 300m after the border, however, you can get good rates for TCs at the *Banco de Café*. The briefcase and dark glasses brigade changes cash on the Guatemalan side only, but you must know in advance what quetzal rates are.

Transport Buses are *de paso* from San Cristóbal so no advance booking is possible. The Cristóbal Colón bus leaves Comitán 0800, 1100 (coming from San Cristóbal) and in pm for the border at Ciudad Cuauhtémoc, fare US$2.75. Autotransportes Tuxtla leave from Comitán (on the main highway at approximately Av 2 Sur) at regular intervals for the border, 1½ hrs. There are at least 8 buses to Comitán 0800-1930 from Ciudad Cuauhtémoc, with 2nd class buses during the evening. Pick-ups charge US$1.55 per person Comitán-border; beware short-changing. From here take a taxi, US$1.65, or *colectivo*, to the Guatemalan side (4 km uphill, minimum 3 people) and get your passport stamped. Cristóbal Colón (terminal near the Pan-American Highway, Comitán) has 1st class buses to **Mexico City** at 0900, 1100 and 1600 (which leave the border 2½ hrs earlier), fare US$40.75 (from Mexico City to Comitán at 1415 and 2040, fully booked 2 hrs in advance); to **Oaxaca** at 0700 and 1900, US$33; to **Tuxtla Gutiérrez** at 0600 and 1600, US$8, and to **Tapachula** (via Arriaga) at 1200 and 2000, US$20. Entering Mexico from Guatemala, to San Cristóbal, direct buses US$3.50, or take a minibus to Comitán, US$1.55; these connect with *combis* at the Autotransportes Tuxtla terminal for San Cristóbal de Las Casas.

Route to Tapachula

Travelling from the neighbouring state of Oaxaca, Routes 190 and 200 merge to cross the Isthmus of Tehuantepec. Accommodation is available at **Zanatepec, C-D** *Posada San Rafael*. Motel. Very comfortable, safe parking. At **Tapanatepec, D** *Motel La Misión* on Highway 190 on northern outskirts, T91971-70140. Fan, hot water, clean, TV, hammock outside each room, affiliated restaurant, very good. This is where Highway 190 heads northeast to Tuxtla Gutiérrez and Highway 200 continues southeast along the coast of Chiapas to the Guatemalan border.

Arriaga is a good stopping place just across the border that separates Oaxaca from Chiapas; many banks around Zócalo for exchange. The road from Arriaga to Tapachula is a four-lane divided freeway.

Arriaga
Phone code: 966
Population: 12,000

Sleeping and eating C *Ik-Lumaal*, near Zócalo. A/c, clean, quiet, good restaurant. *El Parador*, Km 47 on road to Tonalá, T20199. Clean with swimming pool. **D** *Colonial*, Callejón Ferrocarril, next to bus station. Clean, friendly, quiet, limited free parking. **E** *Arbolitos*. Fan, basic, clean, off main road. **F** *Hotel Iris*, Callejón Ferrocarril, near bus station. Bath, fan, basic. *Restaurant Xochimilco*, near bus stations.

Transport Buses: To many destinations, mostly 1st class, to **Mexico City**, US$26.50, 12-13 hrs, at 1645. To **Tuxtla** with Fletes y Pasajes at 1400 and 1600, 4 hrs, US$7. To **Oaxaca**, 6 hrs, US$7.

From Arriaga, Route 200 continues to Tonalá, formerly a very quiet town but now noisy and dirty, with a small museum; good market (bus Tonalá-Tapachula, three hours, US$6.75; also buses to Tuxtla). Beyond Tonalá the road is mostly straight and in perfect condition. This is by far the most direct road for travellers seeking the quickest way from Mexico City to Guatemala.

Tonalá

Sleeping and eating B *Galilea*, Av Hidalgo y Callejón Ote, T6230239. With bath, a/c, good, basic cheap rooms on 1st floor, balconies, on main square, with good restaurants. **D** *Tonalá*, Hidalgo 172, T6230480, opposite museum. **E** *Casa de Huéspedes El Viajero*, Av Matamoros, near market. With bath, rough but OK. **E** *Faro*, 16 de Septiembre 24, near Plaza.
   For eating try *Santa Elena*, at the south end of town, near Cristóbal Colón bus station on outskirts. Good. On the Plaza, *Nora*. Numerous Chinese-named restaurants; good breakfast at restaurants on Zócalo.

Along the coast from Tonalá to Tapachula there are several fine-looking and undeveloped beaches, although waves and currents are dangerous. **Puerto Arista** (17 km south of Tonalá) is now being built up, but it is still a relatively peaceful area with 32 km of clean beach to relax on with no sales people; bus/*colectivo* from Tonalá every hour, 45 minutes, US$0.60, taxi US$2; plenty of buses to Arriaga, US$0.75. Many hotels, motels and restaurants on the beach; hot and in the wet season, sandflies. **B** *Arista Bougainvilla*. With private beach, a/c, pools, restaurant. Some restaurants (closed by 2000) have rooms to rent, eg **F** *Turquesa*, small hotel/restaurant three blocks down on the right from where the road reaches the beach coming from Tonalá and turns right, next to bakery. No fan, basic. **Camping E-F** *José's Camping Cabañas* (ask *colectivo* from Tonalá to take you there, US$0.60 extra), at east edge of town, follow signs. Canadian-run, well organized, clean, laundry, restaurant (including vegetarian), library.

Tabasco & Chiapas

Buses also from Tonalá to **Boca del Cielo** further down the coast, which is good for bathing and has *cabañas* with hammocks, and similarly **Cabeza del Toro**. **Paredón**, on the huge Laguna del Mar Muerto, 14 km west of Tonalá, has excellent seafood and one very basic guest house. You can take a local fishing boat out into the lagoon to swim; the shore stinks because fishermen clean fish on the beach among dogs and pigs. Served by frequent buses.

On the way to Tapachula one passes through **Pijijiapan** where there is the *Hotel Pijijilton*(!) next to the Cristóbal Colón bus station; also **C** *Hotel El Estraneo*. Very nice, parking in courtyard. **E** *Sabrina*. Nice, clean and quiet, safe parking. Many on Route 200, eg **E** *El Navegante Los Reyes* per bed, doubles only. Also **Huixtla**, which has a good market, no tourists (**E** *Casa de Huéspedes Regis*, Independencia Norte 23). From Huixtla, a good, scenic road winds off into the mountains parallel to the border, towards Ciudad Cuauhtémoc and Comitán (see above). *En route* is the small, modern town of **Motozintla de Mendoza** with an attractive zócalo and three hotels: one on the plaza, another, *Rendón*, at Central Norte 415, friendly, parking, limited hot water, noisy; also, cheaper, **D** *Alberto*, Central Norte 305, quiet.

Tapachula

Phone code: 962
Colour map 4, grid C3
Population: 144,000

Tapachula is a pleasant, neat, but expensive, hot commercial town (airport; cinemas in centre). *Avenidas* run north-south, *calles* east-west (Oriente-Poniente). Odd-numbered *calles* are north of Calle Central, odd *avenidas* are east of Avenida Central. It is the road and rail junction for Guatemala (road crossings at the Talismán bridge, or at Ciudad Hidalgo). **Tourist offices** 4 Norte 35, Edificio del Gobierno del Estado, 3rd floor, between 3 and 5 Poniente, T6265470, F6265522. ■ *Mon-Fri, 0900-1500, 1800-2000, helpful.*

Excursions The coastal town of **Puerto Madero**, 18 km from Tapachula (bus US$1.80), is worse than Puerto Arista, because it is more built up and the beaches stink from rubbish being burned. Intense heat in summer. (**E** *Hotel Pegado*. Run down, not recommended. Better is unnamed *hospedaje*, also **E**. **F** *Hotel Puerto Madero*, accommodation in what are really remains of cement block room.) Water defences are being built, but the graveyard is under threat of being washed into the sea. There are many fish restaurants on the beach.

Visit the ruins of **Izapa** (proto-Classic stelae, small museum) just off the road to Talismán; the part of the site on the north is easily visible but a larger portion is on the south side of the highway, about 1 km away, ask caretaker for guidance. These buildings influenced Kaminal Juyú near Guatemala City and are considered archaeologically important as a proto-Mayan site. Some findings from the ruins are displayed in the **Museo Regional del Soconusco** on the west side of the Zócalo in Tapachula. To reach Izapa take *combi* from Unión Progreso bus station. Forty-five kilometres northeast of Tapachula, beyond the turning to Talismán is **Unión Juárez** (**E** *Hotel Alijoat*, hot shower, reasonable restaurant. **E** *Hotel Colonial*; *Restaurant Carmelita* on the square is modest with fair prices). In Unión Juárez you can have your papers stamped and proceed on foot via Talquián to the Guatemalan border at Sibinal. Take a guide.

A worthwhile hike can be made up the **Tacaná volcano** (4,150m), which takes 2-3 days from Unión Juárez. Ask for the road to Chiquihuete; no cars. The Tapachula tourist office can help; in Unión Juárez ask for Sr Umberto Ríos at *Restaurante Montaña*, he will put you in touch with guide Moisés Hernández, who charges US$15 a day. It is possible to stay overnight in Don

Emilio Velásquez' barn half way up, US$2; he offers coffee and *tortillas*. At the top are some *cabañas* in which you sleep for free; sleeping bag essential.

A *Motel Loma Real*, Carretera Costera 200, Km 244, T6261440, 1 km north of city. **Sleeping** Operates as a 1st class hotel, use of swimming pool, cold showers. **C** *Don Miguel*, Calle 1 Pte 18, T6261143. **C** *Posada Michel*, Calle 5 Pte 23, T6252640. A/c. **C** *San Francisco*, Av Central Sur 94, T6261454, F6252114, 15 mins from centre. Good, a/c, large rooms, hot water, TV, restaurant, safe parking. **C** *Santa Julia*, next to Cristóbal Colón terminal, in centre within 1 block of Plaza Central. Bath, phone, TV, a/c, clean, good. **D** *Alpha*, Calle 11 Pte 53, T6265442. Clean, fan, cold shower, similar **D** *Posada de Calú*, Calle 11 Pte 34, T6265659. **D** *Fénix*, Av 4 Norte 19, T6250755. **D** *Tabasco*. With shower, close to 1st-class bus station, poor value but friendly. **E** *Atlántida*, Av 6 Norte between Calle 11 and 13 Pte, T6262136. Helpful, clean, cheaper without window, fans, noisy, safe parking for 2. **E** *Cinco de Mayo*, Calle 5 Pte y Av 12 Norte. With bath (cheaper without), not very clean, convenient for Talismán *colectivos* which leave ½ block away. **E** *Colonial*, Av 4 Norte 31. Attractive courtyard, about 1 block from central square, good value,

Tapachula

Tabasco & Chiapas

clean, safe. **E** *El Retorno*, opposite, on Calle 5 Pte. Unhelpful and noisy. **E** *Hospedaje Madrid*, Av 8 Norte, 43, T6263018. Shared bath. **E** *Hospedaje Santa Cruz*, Calle 11 Pte 36. Clean, fan, bath, no windows in some rooms; all a long way from Cristóbal Colón 2nd class terminal (15-20 blocks). Many hotels along Avs 4, 6, 8 (near Plaza). **E** *Pensión Mary*, Av 4 Norte 28, T6263400. Has cheap *comidas*. **E** *Plaza Guizar*, Av 2 Norte. Old, pleasant, clean, hot water, rooms differ so ask to see more than 1. **E** *Rex*, Av 8 Norte 43, T6250376. Similar. **E** *San Román*, Calle 9 Pte between Av 10 y 12 Norte. Shower, fan, safe motorcycle parking, clean, quiet, friendly, drinks for sale.

Eating   Good restaurant next to Cristóbal Colón terminal and on main square. *Snoopy*, Av 4 no 19. Friendly, excellent *tortas*, breakfasts. *Viva Pizza*, Av Central. Good pizza, reasonable price. Good, cheap chicken on Central Norte. *Heladas Irma*, Calle 13 Pte between Av 4 y 6. Good ice cream.

Shopping   *Rialfer*, supermarket, Blvd Díaz, 2 doors from *Banamex*.

Tour operators   *Viajes Tacaná*, operated by Sr Adolfo Guerrero Chávez, Av 4 Norte no 6, T6263502/6263501/6263245; trips to Izapa ruins, to mountains, beaches and can gain entry to museum when closed.

Transport   **Air**   Flights from Mérida, Mexico City, Tuxtla Gutiérrez, Veracruz daily. *Combis* to airport from Calle 2 Sur No 40, T6251287. From airport to border, minibuses charge US$26 for whole vehicle, so share with others, otherwise take *colectivo* to 2nd class bus terminal and then a bus to Ciudad Hidalgo.

Trains   The passenger service to and from Tapachula was not running when this book went to print. Check locally to see if services have been reinstated.

Buses   Cristóbal Colón bus Mexico City-Guatemala City takes 23 hrs, with a change at the border to Rutas Lima. Mexico City-Tapachula, 20 hrs (Cristóbal Colón 1st class, Av 3 Norte y 17 Ote, T6262880; 2nd class Prolongación 9 Pte s/n, T6261161). To/from Tapachula to **Mexico City**, US$40, 5 a day, all in the afternoon (frequent stops for toilets and food, also frequent police checks, no toilet or a/c on bus) much better to take *plus* service, 1915, US$58. Buses from Mexico City all leave in the afternoon; the 1545 and 1945 go on to Talismán. Bus to **Oaxaca**, Cristóbal Colón and Fipsa (Calle 9 Ote, T6267603) has luggage store, US$19, 14 hrs, many passport checks (Fipsa has 4 a day, continuing to Puebla and Córdoba, take 1830 to see sunrise over the Sierra Madre; also has 2 a day to Mexico City). Cristóbal Colón, plus service to **Puebla**, US$37.50; UNO, US$53, 16 hrs. To **Tehuantepec** and **Salina Cruz** 0915, 8 hrs, US$14.80; to **San Cristóbal de las Casas** and **Tuxtla Gutiérrez** at 1100. The 2nd-class bus station is at Av 3 Norte, Calle 9 Ote. To **Oaxaca**, 10 hrs, US$14.

Directory   **Airlines** *Aviacsa*, Calle Central Nte 52-B, T6263147, T/F6263159. *AeroMéxico*, Av 2 Norte 6, T6263921. *Taesa*, T6263702. **Banks** Avoid the crowds of streetwise little boys at the border; exchange is rather better in the town, bus station gives a good rate (cash only). *Banamex*, Blvd Díaz Ordaz, open 0830-1230, 1400-1600, disagreement over whether TCs are changed. *Bital* is the only bank open Sat, changes TCs. *Casa de Cambio Tapachula*, Av 4 Norte y Calle 3 Pte, changes dollars, TCs, pesos, quetzales, lempiras and colones (open late Mon-Sat), but not recommended, poor rates, very difficult to change money on Sun. Try the supermarket. **Communications** Telephone: several long-distance phone offices, eg *Esther*, Av 5 Norte 46; *La Central*, Av Central Sur 95; *Monaco*, Calle 1 Pte 18. **Embassies & consulates** Guatemalan Consulate, Calle 2 Ote 33 and Av 7 Sur, T6261252, taxi from Cristóbal Colón terminal, US$1. Open Mon-Fri 0800-1600; visa US$10, friendly and quick, take photocopy of passport, photocopier 2 blocks away, the consul may give a visa on Sat if you are willing to pay extra. **Laundry** There is a laundry, at Av Central Norte 99 between Calle 13 y 15 Ote, US$3 wash and dry, 1 hr service, about 2 blocks from Cristóbal Colón bus station, open Sun. Also on Central Norte between Central Ote y Calle 1, opens 0800, closed Sun. **Useful addresses** Migración/Gobernación: Av 14 Norte 57, T6261263.

It is 8 km from Tapachula to the border at the Talismán bridge (open 24 hours a day).

Border with Guatemala-Talismán

Immigration The Mexican customs post is 200m from the Guatemalan one. Exit tax US$0.45. Lots of pushy children offer to help you through border formalities; pay US$2-3 for one, which keeps the others away. **NB** The toilet at immigration at the crossing is dangerous, hold-ups have been reported day or night. **Guatemalan consulate** In Tapachula, above.

Crossing into Guatemala by car can take several hours. If you don't want your car sprayed inside it may cost you a couple of dollars. Do not park in the car park at the control post, it is very expensive. **Driving into Mexico** See **Essentials**, **Motoring**, on the temporary importation of vehicles, page 39. Car papers are issued at the Garita de Aduana on Route 200 out of Tapachula. There is no other road, you can't miss it. Photocopies of documents must be made in town; no facilities at the Garita.

Sleeping There is a *hospedaje* at the border.

Exchange Exchange in town rather than with men standing around customs on the Guatemalan side (check rates before dealing with them, and haggle; there is no bank on the Guatemalan side).

Transport *Combi* vans run from near the Unión y Progreso bus station, about US$1; *colectivo* from outside *Posada de Calú* to Talismán, US$0.60, also from Calle 5 Pte between Avs 12 y 14 Norte. Taxi Tapachula-Talismán, negotiate fare to about US$2. There are few buses between the Talismán bridge and Oaxaca or Mexico City (though they do exist); advisable therefore to travel to Tapachula for connection, delays can occur there at peak times. A taxi from Guatemala to Mexican Immigration will cost US$2, but it may be worth it if you are in a hurry to catch an onward bus. Hitchhikers should note that there is little through international traffic at Talismán bridge.

There is another crossing south of Tapachula, at **Ciudad Hidalgo**, opposite Tecún Umán (you cannot change travellers' cheques here); there are road connections to Coatepeque, Mazatenango and Retalhuleu.

Border with Guatemala-Ciudad Hidalgo

Immigration A few blocks from the town plaza is Mexican Immigration, at the foot of the 1 km-long bridge across the Río Suchiate; cycle taxis cross the bridge for about US$1, pedestrians pay US$0.15.

Transport From Calle 7 Pte between Av 2 Norte and Av Central Norte, Tapachula, buses go to 'Hidalgo', US$1.25.

Tabasco & Chiapas

Yucatán Peninsula

7

Yucatán Peninsula

The Yucatán Peninsula, which includes the states of Campeche, Yucatán and Quintana Roo, is sold to tourists as the land of Maya archaeology and Caribbean beach resorts. And there's no denying it, the warm turquoise sea, fringed with fine white-sand beaches and palm groves of the 'Mayan Riviera' are second to none. And it would be a crime not to tread the beaten path to the sensational ruins at **Chichén Itzá**, **Uxmal** *and* **Tulum**. *But it more than pays to explore beyond the main itineraries to visit some of the lesser-known Maya sites such as Cobá, Edzná or Dzibilchaltún, or the imposing Fraciscan monastery and huge pyramid at* **Izamal**. *There are flamingo feeding grounds at Celestún and Río Lagartos and over 500 other species of birds, many of which are protected in* **Sian Ka'an Biosphere Reserve** *which covers 4,500 sq km of tropical forest, savanna and coastline. Ever since Jacques Cousteau filmed the Palancar Reef in the 1960s, divers have swarmed to the clear waters of* **Cozumel**, *the 'Island of the Swallows', to wonder at the many species of coral, and other underwater plants and creatures at what has become one of the most popular diving centres in the world. Also popular, though more specialized, is diving in the peninsula's many cenotes, or sink holes, including the famous* **Nohooch Nah Chich**, *part of the world's largest underground cave system.*

Yucatán Peninsula

History

After the Maya arrived in Yucatán about 1200BC, they built monumental stone structures during the centuries leading up to the end of the pre-Classic period (250AD). Later they rebuilt their cities, but along different lines, probably because of the arrival of Toltecs in the ninth and 10th centuries. Each city was autonomous, and in rivalry with other cities. Before the Spaniards arrived the Maya had developed a writing system in which the hieroglyphic was somewhere between the pictograph and the letter. Fray Diego de Landa collected their books, wrote a very poor summary, the *Relación de las Cosas de Yucatán*, and with Christian but unscholarlike zeal burnt most of the codices which he never really understood.

The Spaniards found little to please them when they first arrived in the Yucatán: no gold, no concentration of natives; but Mérida was founded in 1542 and the few natives were handed over to the conquerors in *encomiendas*.

Yucatán Peninsula

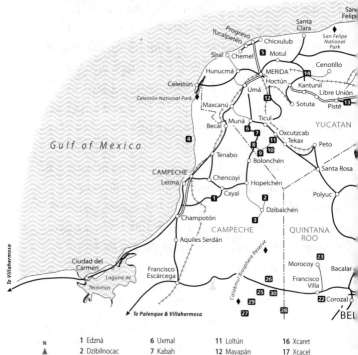

1 Edzná	6 Uxmal	11 Loltún	16 Xcaret
2 Dzibilnocac	7 Kabah	12 Mayapán	17 Xcacel
3 Hochob	8 Sayil	13 Chichén Itzá	18 Tulum
4 Jainu	9 Xlapac	14 Izamal	19 Chumyaxche
5 Dzibilchaltún	10 Labná	15 San Gervasio	20 Tancáh

N
Not to scale

The Spaniards found them difficult to exploit: even as late as 1847 there was a major revolt, fuelled by the inhuman conditions in the *henequén* (sisal) plantations, and the discrimination against the Maya in the towns, but it was the expropriation of the Maya communal lands that was the main source of discontent. In July 1847 a conspiracy against the *Blancos*, or ruling classes from Mexico, was uncovered in Valladolid and one of its leaders, Manuel Antonio Ay, was shot. This precipitated a bloody war, known as the *Guerra de Castas* (Caste War) between the Maya and the *Blancos*. The first act was the massacre of all the non-Maya inhabitants of Tepich, south of Valladolid. The Maya took control of much of the Yucatán, laying siege to Mérida, only to abandon it to sow their crops in 1849. This allowed the governor of Yucatán to counter-attack, driving the Maya by ruthless means into southern Quintana Roo. In Chan Santa Cruz, now called Felipe Carrillo Puerto, one of the Maya leaders, José María Barrera, accompanied by Manuel Nahuat, a ventriloquist, invented the 'talking cross', a cult that attracted thousands of followers. The sect, called Cruzob, established itself and renewed the resistance against the government from Mexico City. It was not until 1901 that the Mexican army retook the Cruzob's domain.

People

The people are divided into two groups: the Maya Indians, the minority, and the *mestizos*. The Maya women wear *huipiles*, or white cotton tunics (silk for *fiestas*) which may reach the ankles and are embroidered round the square neck and bottom hem. Ornaments are mostly gold. A few of the men still wear straight white cotton (occasionally silk) jackets and pants, often with gold or silver buttons, and when working protect this dress with aprons. Carnival is the year's most joyous occasion, with concerts, dances and processions. Yucatán's folk dance is the *Jarana*, the man dancing with his hands behind his back, the woman raising her skirts a little, and with interludes when they pretend to be bullfighting. During pauses in the music the man, in a high falsetto voice, sings *bambas* (compliments) to the woman.

The Maya are a courteous, gentle people. They drink little, except on feast days, speak Mayan, and profess Christianity laced with a more ancient nature worship.

Access to sites and resorts

Many tourists come to the Yucatán, mostly to see the ancient Maya sites and to stay at the new coastal resorts. A good paved road runs from

Yucatán Peninsula

Coatzacoalcos through Villahermosa, Campeche and Mérida (Route 180). An inland road from Villahermosa to Campeche gives easy access to Palenque (see page 263). If time is limited, take a bus from Villahermosa to Chetumal via Escárcega, which can be done overnight as the journey is not very interesting (unless you want to see the Maya ruins off this road, see page 381). From Chetumal travel up the coast to Cancún, then across to Mérida. Route 307 from Chetumal to Cancún and Puerto Juárez and is all paved and in very good condition. Air services from the USA and Mexico City are given under Mérida, Cancún and Cozumel. The state of Quintana Roo is on the eastern side of the Yucatán Peninsula and has recently become the largest tourist area in Mexico with the development of the resort of Cancún, and the parallel growth of Isla Mujeres, Cozumel and the 100-km corridor south of Cancún to Tulum. Growth has been such, in both Yucatán and Quintana Roo, that there are insufficient buses at peak times; old second-class buses may be provided for first-class tickets and second-class buses take far too many standing passengers. There is also a lack of information services. Where beaches are unspoilt they often lack all amenities. Many cheaper hotels are spartan. **Warning**: So many of the tourists coming to the coastal resorts know no Spanish that price hikes and short-changing have become very common there, making those places very expensive if one is not careful. In the peak, winter season, prices are increased anyway, by about 50 percent.

Quintana Roo (and especially Cozumel) is the main area for diving and watersports in the Yucatán Peninsula. A recommended book is *The Dive Sites of Cozumel and the Yucatán* by Lawson Wood (published by New Holland Ltd, 1997, ISBN 1-85368-938-6), which also covers snorkelling and *cenote* diving. However, watersports in Quintana Roo are expensive and touristy, although operators are generally helpful; snorkelling is often organized for large groups. On the more accessible reefs the coral is dying and there are no small coral fishes as a necessary part of the coral life cycle. Further from the shore, though, there is still much reef life to enjoy.

NB The use of tripods for photography at sites is subject to an extra fee of US$3.50, but for using video cameras the fee is US$7.50. Since the major archaeological sites get very crowded, it is best to visit them just before closing time. Note also that in spring and summer temperatures can be very high; take plenty of drinking water and adequate protection against the sun if walking for any length of time (for example around a large Maya site). See page 73 for recommended reading.

Campeche State

Take time out to explore the state of Campeche. Colonial architecture is plentiful, there are several fortified convents and Campeche City itself was fortified to protect its citizens from pirate attacks. The many archaeological sites include: Balamku, Chicanná, Becán, Xpujil, Edzná, Hochob, and Dzibilnocac, most demonstrating the influence of the Chenes architecture. Relax at the resorts of Sihoplaya and Seybaplaya while watching pelicans dive and iguanas scurry. You can try the beaches at Ciudad del Carmen, eat delicious red snapper and buy a cheap, but sturdy, Panama hat. The exhibits at several museums reflect the seafaring nature of the area and the pre-Conquest civilization that occupied these lands. Look out for the fascinating figures that were excavated on the island of Jaina, a necropolis of impressive proportions.

There are two routes to Campeche from the neighbouring state of Tabasco: the inland Highway 186, via Escárcega, with two toll bridges (cost US$4.25), and the slightly longer coastal route through Ciudad del Carmen, Highway 180; both converge at Champotón, 66 km south of Campeche town. Highway 186 passes Villahermosa's modern international airport and runs fast and smooth in a sweeping curve 115 km east to the Palenque turn-off at Playas del Catazajá; beyond, off the highway, is **Emiliano Zapata** (*Fiesta*: 26 October), a busy cattle centre, with Pemex station. There is a mediocre hotel here, painted blue, on a quiet plaza by the river, 200m from the main road. On the main road is restaurant *La Selva*, good food.

Transport   From Emiliano Zapata, all ADO: to **Tenosique**, frequent, 1st at 0700, 0830, 0900, last at 2000, 2100, US$2, 90 mins (plus 2, 2nd class companies); to **Villahermosa**, 17 departures between 0600 and 2000, US$6; to **Mérida**, 5 a day between 0800 and 2100, US$21; to **Escárcega**, 5 between 0630 and 2100, US$5.50; to **Chetumal**, 2130, US$14.

The river town of **Balancán** is a further 60 km northeast and has a small archaeological museum in its Casa de Cultura (**E** *Hotel Delicias*); *fiesta*: 14 December. In 10 km the main highway has crossed the narrow waist of Tabasco state and entered Campeche, a popular destination for hunters and fishermen.

Sleeping   **D** *Ramos*, opposite bus station. With a/c, **E** with fan, reasonable restaurant, friendly. *Bernat Colonial*. All basic.

Francisco Escárcega

Escárcega, as it is commonly known, is a major hub for travellers on their way south to the states of Tabasco and Chiapas, north to Mérida in the state of Yucatán, east to Maya sites in Campeche and Quintana Roo states, and further east to the city of Chetumal. The town itself is not particularly enticing, set on a busy highway with a dusty wild-west atmosphere. If stuck here overnight, all you need to know is that there is a clean budget hotel around the corner from the bus terminal (*Escárcega*, see below), one bank nearby and several cheap restaurants.

Phone code: 982
Colour map 4, grid B4
Population: 20,300

Sleeping **C** *Motel Akim Pech*, on Villahermosa highway. A/c or fans and bath, reasonable rooms, restaurant in motel, another across the street, also Pemex station opposite. **D** *Berta Leticia*, Calle 29 No 28. With bath, fairly clean. **D** *Casa de Huéspedes Lolita* on Chetumal highway at east end of town. Pleasant. **D** *María Isabel*, Justo Sierra 127, T40045. A/c, restaurant, comfortable, back rooms noisy from highway. **D-E** *Escárcega*, Justo Sierra 86, T40186, around the corner from the bus terminal (turn left twice). Clean, bath, parking, hot water, good restaurant, small garden. **D-E** *El Yucateco*, Calle 50 No 42-A, T40065. With or without a/c, central, tidy, fair value. **E** *Las Gemelas*, behind Pemex on Highway 186, west of intersection and ADO. Noisy, decrepit, overpriced. **E** *San Luis*, Calle 28 facing the Zócalo. Simple and lazily maintained.

Eating Not many places used to serving tourists, but there is a good and cheap *lonchería* opposite the bus terminal. For a more expensive meal in a/c surroundings, try *Titanic*, on the corner of the main highway and the road to the train station (first turning on the right after turning right out of the bus terminal). The road to the train station is lined with an extraordinary number of *cantinas* for a town of this size, all of which heave with punters at 3 in the afternoon; their popularity is reflected by the presence of several AA buildings scattered about the town.

Transport **Buses** Most buses from Chetumal or Campeche drop you off at the 2nd class terminal on the main highway. To buy tickets, you have to wait until the outgoing bus has arrived; sit near the ticket office and wait for them to call out your destination, then join the scrum at the ticket office. There is an *ADO* terminal west of the 2nd class terminal, a 20 min walk. From there, 1st class buses go to **Palenque**, several daily, 3 hrs, US$6-10. **Chetumal**; 4 a day, 4 hrs, US$9. **Campeche**; 5 a day, 2 hrs, US$6. From the 2nd class terminal, there are buses to **Playas de Catazajá**, connecting with *colectivos* to Palenque, at 0830, 0930 and 1030, US$5. **Villahermosa**; 1600, 4 hrs, US$9. *Colectivos* to Palenque leave from outside the 2nd class terminal at 1300, US$5.

The coast road

Although Highway 180 via Ciudad del Carmen is narrow, crumbling into the sea in places and usually ignored by tourists intent on visiting Palenque, this journey is a beautiful one and more interesting than the fast toll road inland to Campeche. The road threads its way from Villahermosa 78 km north through marshland and rich cacao, banana and coconut plantations, passing turn-offs to several tiny coastal villages with palm-lined but otherwise mediocre beaches, to the river port of **Frontera** (*Population*: 28,650), from where Graham Greene began the research journey in 1938 that led to the publication of *The Lawless Roads* and later to *The Power and the Glory*. The *Feria Guadalupana* is held from 3-13 December, with an agricultural show, bullfights, *charreadas* and regional dances.

Sleeping and eating in Frontera **D** *Chichén Itzá*, on Plaza. Not very clean, fan, shower, hot water. **E** *San Agustín*. Very basic, fan, no mosquito net. *Restaurant Conquistador*, beside church. Very good.

The road briefly touches the coast at the Tabasco/Campeche state border. It then runs east beside a series of lakes (superb bird watching) to the fishing village of **Zacatal** (93 km), at the entrance to the tarpon-filled **Laguna de Términos** (named for the first Spanish expedition which thought it had reached the end of the 'island' of Yucatán). Just before Zacatal is the lighthouse of **Xicalango**, an important pre-Columbian trading centre. Cortés landed near here in 1519 on his way to Veracruz and was given 20 female slaves, including 'La Malinche', the Indian princess baptized as Doña Marina who, as the Spaniards' interpreter, was to play an important role in the Conquest. A bridge crosses the lake's mouth to Ciudad del Carmen.

Ciudad del Carmen

This is the hot, bursting-at-the-seams principal oil port of the region and is being developed into one of the biggest and most modern on the Gulf. Its important shrimping and prawning fleets are also expanding (good photo possibilities along the trawler-filled docks east of the ferry landing) and much ship building is undertaken. The site was originally established in 1588 by a pirate named McGregor as a lair from which to raid Spanish shipping; it was infamous until the pirates were wiped out by Alfonso Felipe de Andrade in 1717, who then named the town after its patroness, the Virgen del Carmen.

Phone code: 938
Colour map 4, grid B4
Population: 151,400

Carmen is situated on a narrow, largely forested (coconut palm) island, little more than a sandpit, 38 km long and 51 sq km in all. It is joined to the mainland at either end by bridges which are among the longest in the Americas. One, on the east end of the island at Puerto Real, called La Unidad, 3,222m long and built in 1922 (US$1.85 toll), links with Isla Aguada; the other, 3,865m, between Zacatal (mainland) and La Puntilla, was completed in 1994. The town is principally concentrated at the west end of the island and shows few signs of the ugliness often associated with oil-boom centres (the rigs are mainly way off-shore). It is not, as yet, visited by many tourists, but is well worth a detour *en route* to, or from, the Yucatán, and is a good place for those curious to see something of the development of the Mexican fishing and oil industries.

Most streets in the centre are numbered; even numbers generally run west-east, and odd south-north. Calle 20 is the seafront *malecón* and the road to the airport and University is Calle 31. The **tourist office**, on Calle 20 near Calle 23, has little to promote in this non-tourist town; the emphasis is on fishing excursions, a basic street map is available. **Fishing excursions** can be arranged through the *Club de Pesca Nelo Manjárrez,*T20073, at Calle 40 and Calle 61. Coastal lagoons are rich in tarpon *(sábalo)* and bonefish.

The attractive, cream-coloured **Cathedral** (Parroquia de la Virgen del Carmen), begun 1856, is notable for its stained glass. The **Palacio Municipal** and Library, stands on the **Plaza Principal**, or Plaza Zaragoza, a lush square laid out in 1854, near the waterfront, with wooden gazebo (free band concerts Thursday and Sunday evenings), Spanish lanterns, brick walkways and elegant wrought-iron railings from Belgium. There is a modest **Archaeological Museum** in the Liceo Carmelita showing locally excavated items. ■ *US$0.25.* **La Iglesia de Jesús** (1820) opposite Parque Juárez is surrounded by elegant older houses. Nearby is the Barrio del Guanal, the oldest residential quarter, with the church of the **Virgen de la Asunción** (1815) and houses with spacious balconies and tiles brought from Marseilles. Close by is the **Casa de la Cultura** in a French-style building (1860s) with library and temporary exhibitions and concerts.

Sights

There are several good **beaches** with restaurants and watersports, the most scenic is Playa Caracol (southeast of the centre) and the Playa Norte which has extensive white sand and safe bathing. Near the latter is a small zoo with some 50 native species and a family recreation area. Sixteen kilometres along the road to Puerto Real, on Playa Bahamita which runs the rest of the way along the north coast as far as the Unidad bridge, is a *balneario* of the same name (pool and restaurants) from where you can take a boat trip to Laguna de Términos. Beaches are composed of a gritty sand mixed with sea shells and are generally

Yucatán Peninsula

clean, but oil processing does periodically have a bad effect. Campers are warned about the biting chiggers and sharp shells are hard on tents.

Living costs in Carmen tend to be higher than the norm, partly on account of the spending power of the oil workers but also because most commodities have to be brought in. However there are hotels and restaurants in the budget range.

Sleeping
■ *on maps*
Price codes:
see inside front cover

A *EuroHotel*, Calle 22 No 208, T31030. Large and modern, 2 restaurants, pool, a/c, disco, built to accommodate the flow of Pemex traffic. **B** *Hotel del Parque*, Calle 33 No 1. **B** *Isla del Carmen*, Calle 20 No 9, T22350. A/c, restaurant, bar, parking. **B** *Lli-Re*, Calle 32 y 29, T20588. Commercial hotel with large sparsely furnished a/c rooms, TV, servibars, oddly old-fashioned but comfortable, restaurant with good but not cheap fish dishes. **B** *Los Sandes*, Av Periférica. **C** *Aquario*, Calle 51 No 60, T22547. A/c, comfortable. **C** *Lino's*, Calle 31 No 132, T20738. A/c, pool, restaurant, also has 10 RV spaces with electricity hook-ups.

D *Hotel Playa Dorna*, on Playa Norte. Clean, friendly, pool, TV, hot water, 2 strip bars loud and late at weekends. **D** *Zacarías*, Calle 24 No 58, T20121. Modern, some cheaper rooms with fans, brighter a/c rooms are better value. Recommended. **E** *Internacional*, Calle 20 No 21, T21344. Uninspiring outside but clean and friendly, 1 block from Plaza, some a/c. **E** *Casa de Huéspedes Carmen*, Calle 20 No 142, *Villa del Mar*, Calle 20 y 33. There are several **E** range hotels near the ADO bus station on Av Periférica eg *El Ancla*. Simple rooms, TV, a/c, good restaurant in spectacular waterside setting.

Eating
● *on maps*

The better hotels have good restaurants (the shrimp and prawns are especially tasty); others recommended are *Pepe's*, Calle 27 No 15. A/c, attractive seafood dishes. *Vía Veneto*, in the *EuroHotel*. Reasonable prices, good breakfasts. *El Kiosco*, in *Hotel del Parque* with view of Zócalo. Modest prices, eggs, chicken, seafood and Mexican dishes, but not clean, poor service. *La Mesita* , outdoor stand across from ferry landing. Well-prepared shrimp,

Ciudad del Carmen

■ **Sleeping**		
1 El Ancla	5 Technotel	2 Parque Zaragoza
2 Euro		3 Parque Zoológico
3 Lli-Re	▲ **Other**	4 Parroquia de la Virgen
4 Los Sandes	1 Palacio Municipal	del Carmen

Yucatán Peninsula

seafood cocktails, extremely popular all day. *La Fuente*, Calle 20. 24-hr snack bar with view of the Laguna. For 'best coffee in town' try **Café Vadillo** or other tiny cafés along pedestrian walkway (Calle 33) near the Zócalo. Inexpensive snacks also available in the thriving Central Market (Calle 20 y 37, not far northwest of Zócalo). Many bakeries and supermarkets throughout the city, eg *Conasuper*, Calle 20 y 37.

The town's patroness is honoured with a cheerful fiesta each 15-30 **Jun**, bullfights, **Festivals** cultural events, fireworks, etc.

Local Car hire (not cheap): *Auto-Rentas del Carmen*, Calle 33 No 121 (T22376); *Fast* **Transport** (T22306), and *Auto Panamericana*, Calle 22 (T22326).

   Air Carmen's efficient airport (Av Aviación, only 5 km east of the Plaza) has also benefited from the oil traffic with flights daily to Mérida, Mexico City, Poza Rica, Tampico, Veracruz and Villahermosa.

   Buses ADO bus terminal some distance from centre. Take bus or *colectivo* marked 'Renovación' or 'ADO', they leave from around the Zócalo. At least 8 ADO services daily to **Campeche** (3 hrs) and **Mérida** (9 hrs, US$14.80), includes 3 departures between 2100 and 2200 (worth considering if stuck for accommodation); hourly bus to **Villahermosa** via the coast, 3 hrs. A connection can be made to **Palenque** at 2330 or 0400, a slow but worthwhile trip. Buses also travel via **Escárcega**, where connections can be made for Chetumal and Belize.

Airlines Mexicana, Calle 22 y 37, T21171. **Banks** *Banco del Atlántico* or *Banamex*, both at Calle **Directory** 24 y 31. **Communications** Post Office: at Calle 29 y 20, 1 block from the Plaza.

Eleven kilometres beyond Carmen is the *Rancho El Fénix*, with an interesting **Isla Aguada** iguana (*lagarto*) hatchery. Highway 180 runs northeast along the Isla del *Colour map 4, grid B4* Carmen and crosses the bridge to Isla Aguada (**C** *Hotel Tarpon Tropical*. **D** *Motel La Cabaña* and Trailer Park at former boat landing just after the toll bridge. Full hook-up, hot showers, laundry facilities, quiet, US$12 for vehicle and two people), actually a narrow peninsula with more deserted shell-littered beaches on the Gulf shore. The road then undulates its way northeast through tiny fishing villages towards Campeche; there are many offshore oil rigs to be seen. At Sabancuy (85 km from Carmen) a paved road crosses to the Villahermosa-Escárcega highway, 57 km away. Sixty-three bumpy km later, Highway 180 reaches Champotón (see below).

Maya ruins in south Campeche

Three hundred kilometres southeast from Campeche town, and a further 60 **Calakmul** km off the main Escárcega-Chetumal road, the ruins of Calakmul are only accessible by car. The site has been the subject of much attention in recent years, due to the previously concealed scale of the place. It is now believed to be one of the largest archaeological sites in Mesoamerica, and certainly the biggest of all the Maya cities, with somewhere in the region of ten thousand buildings in total, many of them as yet unexplored. There is evidence that Calakmul was begun in 300 BC, and continually added to until 800 AD. At the centre of the site is the Gran Plaza, overlooked by a pyramid whose base covers five acres of ground. One of the buildings grouped around the **Gran Plaza** is believed, due to its curious shape and location, to have been designed for astronomical observation. The **Gran Acrópolis**, the largest of all the structures, is divided into two section: **Plaza Norte**, with the ball court, was used for ceremonies, **Plaza Sur** was used for public activities. The scale of the site is vast, and many of the buildings are still under excavation, which means that information on

Yucatán Peninsula

Calakmul's history is continually being updated. For the latest information, contact INAH in Campeche, T11314, inah@campeche.sureste.com. To reach Calakmul, take Route 186 until Km 95, then turn off at Conhuás, where a paved road leads to the site, 60 km. ■ *US$2.50, free on Sun.*

Xpujil The name means a type of plant similar to a cattail. The architectural style is known as Río Bec, characterized by heavy masonry towers simulating pyramids and temples, usually found rising in pairs at the ends of elongated buildings. The main building at Xpujil features an unusual set of three towers, with rounded corners and steps which are so steep they are unscalable, suggesting they may have been purely decorative. The façade features the open jaws of an enormous reptile in profile on either side of the main entrance, possibly representing Itzamná, the Maya god of creation. Xpujil's main period of activity was 500-750 AD; it began to go into decline around 1100. Major excavation on the third structure was done as recently as 1993, and there are still many unexcavated buildings dotted about the site. It can be very peaceful and quiet in the early mornings, compared with the throng of tourist activity at the more accessible sites such as Chichén Itzá and Uxmal. ■ *0800-1700. US$1.50, free on Sun. US$3 to use a video camera.*

The tiny village of Xpujil on the Chetumal-Escárcega highway, is conveniently located for the three sets of ruins in this area, Xpujil, Becán and Chicanná. There are two hotels and a couple of shops. Guided tours to the more remote sites such as Calakmul and Río Bec can be organized through either of the two hotels listed below, costing about US$20-30 per person for the whole day.

Sleeping C *Calakmul*, 800m from the bus stop, T/F29162. Recently renovated, modern fixtures, good restaurant, quiet, safe, clean. **D** *Mirador*, just past Calakmul. *Cabaña* accommodation. A bit run down, restaurant.

Transport 2nd-class buses from Chetumal and Escárcega stop on the highway in the centre of Xpujil, some 800m east of the 2 hotels. There are 4 buses a day to Escárcega, between 1030 and 1500, 3 hrs, US$4.50. 8 buses a day go to Chetumal, 2 hrs, US$3.50. Change at Escárcega for buses to Palenque or Campeche. 1st class buses will not stop at Xpujil.

Becán Seven kilometres before Xpujil, Becán is another important site in the Río Bec style, its most outstanding feature being a moat, now dry, surrounding the entire city, believed to be one of the oldest defence systems in Mesoamerica. Seven entrance gates cross the moat to the city. The large variety of buildings on the site are a strange combination of decorative towers and fake temples, as well as structures used as shrines and palaces. The twin towers, typical of the Río Bec style, feature on the main structure, set on a pyramid-shaped base supporting a cluster of buildings which seem to have been used for many different functions: religious, administrative and residential. ■ *0800-1700. US$2, free on Sun.*

Chicanná Located 12 km from Xpujil, Chicanná was named upon its discovery in 1966 in reference to Structure II: *chi* – mouth, *can* – serpent, and *ná* – house, 'House of the Serpent's Mouth'. Due to its dimensions and location, Chicanná is considered to have been a small residential centre for the rulers of the ancient regional capital of Becán. It was occupied during the late pre-Classic period (300 BC-250 AD); the final stages of activity at the site have been dated to the post-Classic era (1100 AD). Typical of the Río Bec style are numerous representations of the Maya god Itzamná, or Earth Mother. One of the temples has a dramatic entrance in the shape of a monster's mouth, with fangs jutting out over the lintel and more fangs lining the access stairway. ■ *0800-1700. US$1.50, free on Sun.* A taxi will take you from Xpujil bus stop to Becán and Chicanná for US$10, including waiting time.

Sleeping AL *Hotel Ramada.* Eco-village resort. Discount for members of Sanborn's Amigo Club. Over-priced.

Twenty kilometres southwest of Xpujil, Hormiguero is the site of one of the most important buildings in the Río Bec region, whose elaborate carvings on the façade show an excellent example of the serpent's-mouth entrance, with huge fangs and a gigantic eye.

Hormiguero

In the opposite direction to the other group of sites in this area, Río Bec is south off the main highway, some 10 km along the road to Chetumal. Although the site gave its name to the architectural style seen in this area, there are better examples of it at the ruins listed above. Río Bec is a cluster of several smaller sites, all of which are very difficult to reach without a guide. Guided tours to all the sites in this region can be arranged in Xpujil.

Río Bec

Back near the west coast of Campeche State, Route 261 runs 86 km due north from Escárcega through dense forest to the Gulf of Mexico, where it joins the coastal route at Champotón, a relaxed but run-down fishing and shrimping port spread along the banks of Río Champotón. In pre-Hispanic times it was an important trading link between Guatemala and Central Mexico; Toltec and Maya mingled here, followed by the Spaniards; in fact blood was shed here when Francisco Hernández de Córdoba was fatally wounded in a skirmish with the inhabitants in 1517. On the south side of town can be seen the remnants of a 1719 fort built as a defence against the pirates who frequently raided this coast. The Feast of the Immaculate Conception (8 December) is celebrated with a joyous festival lasting several days.

Champotón
Colour map 4, grid B4
Population: 18,000

Sleeping and eating C *Snook Inn*, Calle 30 No 1, T80088. A/c, fan, pool, owner speaks English, favourite with fishing enthusiasts and bird hunters; for larger game (plentiful in the surrounding jungle) there are 3 primitive but comfortable jungle camps to the south. Recommended guide is José Sansores (*Hotel Castelmar*, Campeche). **D** *Gemenis*, Calle 30 No 10. **E** *Imperial*, Calle 28 No 38. Simple, with fans, river views, regular food. **E** *Casa de Huéspedes*, Calle 30. Clean, basic, big rooms. Recommended. A few unpretentious restaurants, usually seafood menus but *venado* (venison) and *pato* (duck) plentiful in season: *La Palapa*, on the seafront. Covered terrace, speciality is fish stuffed with shrimp, very fresh. Recommended.

Directory Banks Try the *Banco del Atlántico* for currency transactions, open Mon-Fri 0900-1230.

Continuing north, Highways 180 and 261 are combined for 17 km until the latter darts off east on its way to Edzná and Hopelchen (bypassing Campeche, should this be desired). A 66-km toll *autopista*, paralleling Highway 180, just inland from the southern outskirts of Champotón to Campeche, is much quicker than the old highway. Champotón and Seybaplaya are bypassed. But from the old Highway 180, narrow and slow with speed bumps you can reach the resort of **Sihoplaya**. Here is the widely known **C** *Hotel Siho Playa*, T62989. A former sugar hacienda with a beautiful setting and beach facilities, pool, disco/bar, breezy rooms, etc, but, despite remodelling in the past, it has seen

Sihoplaya & Seybaplaya

Yucatán Peninsula

better days; camping possible, US$5; restaurant is overpriced and poor but there is nowhere else to eat nearby; the resort is very popular, nonetheless, with *campechano* families and there are good views from the iguana-covered jetty of pelicans diving for their supper. Regular buses from Campeche US$1. A short distance further north is the larger resort of **Seybaplaya**. This is an attractive place where fishermen mend nets and pelicans dry their wings on posts along the beach. On the Highway is the open-air *Restaurant Veracruz*, serving delicious red snapper (fresh fish at the seafront Public Market is also good value), but in general there is little to explore. Only the *Balneario Payucán* at the north end of the bay makes a special trip worthwhile; this is probably the closest decent beach to Campeche (33 km), although a little isolated, since the water and sand get filthier as one nears the state capital. Nevertheless, there is still much reef life to enjoy.

Campeche

Phone code: 981
Colour map 4, grid B4
Population: 151,000

Highway 180 enters the city as the divided Avenida Resurgimiento, which passes either side of the huge **Monumento al Resurgimiento**, a stone torso holding aloft the torch of Democracy. Originally the trading village of Ah Kim Pech, it was here that the Spaniards, under Francisco Hernández de Córdoba, first disembarked on Mexican soil (22 March 1517) to replenish their water

Campeche

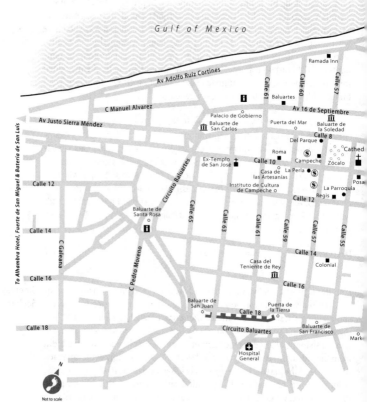

supply. For fear of being attacked by the native population, they quickly left, only to be attacked later by the locals further south in Champotón, where they were forced to land by appalling weather conditions at sea. It was not until 1540 that Francisco de Montejo managed to conquer Ah Kim Pech, after a failed attempt in 1537, and an earlier unsuccessful attempt by his father in 1527. The city of Campeche was founded by Montejo on 4 October, 1541. The export of local dyewoods, *chicle*, timber and other valuable cargoes soon attracted the attention of most of the famous buccaneers, who constantly raided the port from their bases on Isla del Carmen, then known as the Isla de Tris. Combining their fleets for one momentous swoop, they fell upon Campeche on 9 February 1663, wiped out the city and slaughtered its inhabitants. Five years later the Crown began fortifying the site, the first Spanish colonial settlement to be completely walled. Formidable bulwarks, 3 m thick and 'a ship's height', and eight bastions (*baluartes*) were built in the next 36 years. All these fortifications soon put a stop to pirate attacks and Campeche prospered as one of only two Mexican ports (the other was Veracruz) to have had the privilege of conducting international trade. After Mexican Independence from Spain, the city declined into an obscure fishing and logging town. Only with the arrival of a road from the 'mainland' in the 1950s and the oil boom of the 1970s has Campeche begun to see visitors in any numbers, attracted by its historical monuments and relaxed atmosphere (*campechano* has come to mean an easy-going, pleasant person).

Like many of the Yucatán's towns, Campeche's streets in the Old Town are numbered rather than named. Even-numbers run north/south beginning at Calle 8 (no-one knows why) near the *Malecón*, east to Calle 18 inside the walls; odd-numbers run east (inland) from Calle 51 in the north to Calle 65 in the south. Most of the points of interest are within this compact area. The full circuit of the walls is a long walk; buses marked 'Circuito Baluartes' provide a regular service around the perimeter. Running in from the northeast is Avenida Gobernadores, on which are situated the bus and railway stations. The **state tourist office** is on the Malecón in front of the Palacio de Gobierno (walk down Calle 61 towards the sea), T67364/66767. ■ *0800-1600, 1800-2100.* There is a smaller office at Baluarte Santa Rosa, Calle 14. ■ *0800-1230, 1600-2000.*

Of the original walls, seven of the *baluartes* and an ancient fort (now rather dwarfed by two big white hotels on the seafront) remain. Some house museums (see below).

The heart of the city is the Zócalo, where the austere Franciscan **Cathedral** (1540-1705) has an elaborately

Sights

Yucatán Peninsula

carved façade; inside is the Santo Entierro (Holy Burial), a sculpture of Christ on a mahogany sarcophagus with a silver trim. There is plenty of shade under the trees in the Zócalo, and a small pagoda with a snack bar.

Right in front of the Zócalo is the **Baluarte de la Soledad** (see **Museums**), the central bulwark of the city walls, from where you can do a walking tour of the *Circuito Baluartes*, the remains of the city walls. Heading south, you will come to the **Puerta del Mar**, formerly the entrance to those permitted to enter the city from the sea, which used to come up to this point. Next along the *Circuito* is a pair of modern buildings, the **Palacio de Gobierno** and the **Congreso.** The latter looks like a flying saucer, and makes for a bizarre sight when viewed with the 17th-century **Baluarte de San Carlos** in the background. Baluarte de San Carlos now houses a museum (see below). Heading west on the continuation of the *Circuito*, you will pass the **Templo de San José**, on Calle 10, an impressive baroque church with a beautifully tiled façade. It has been de-consecrated, and is now an educational centre. Back on to the *Circuito*, you will come to the **Baluarte de Santa Rosa**, now the home of the tourist information office. Next is **Baluarte de San Juan**, from which a large chunk of the old city wall still extends, protecting you from the noisy traffic on the busy road beyond it. The wall connects with **Puerta de la Tierra**, where a Luz y Sonido (light and Sound) show takes place. ■ *2030, Tue, Fri and Sat (for information, contact the tourist office).* The continuation of the *Circuito* will take you past the **Baluarte de San Francisco**, and then past the market, just outside the line of the city walls. **Baluarte de San Pedro** flanks the northeast corner of the city centre, and now houses a museum (see below). The *circuito* runs down to the northwest tip of the old city, where the **Baluarte de Santiago** houses the Botanical Gardens (see **Museums**).

Further afield from the city walls is the **Batería de San Luis**, 4 km south from the centre along the coast road. This was once a lookout post to catch pirates as they approached the city from a distance. The **Fuerte de San Miguel** 600m inland, is now a museum (see below). A 20-minute walk along Avenida Miguel Alemán from Baluarte de Santiago is the **San Francisco** church, 16th century with wooden altars painted in vermilion and white. Nearby are the **Portales de San Francisco**, a beautifully restored old entrance to the city, with several good restaurants in its shadow.

Museums   **Museo Regional de Campeche**, in the Casa Teniente del Rey, Calle 59 between Calle 14 y Calle 16, charts a history of the state of Campeche since Maya times with interesting displays. ■ *Tue-Sat 0800-1400, 1700-2000, Sun 0900-1300, US$3.*

Museo de la Cultura Maya, in the Fuerte de San Miguel, contains the results of continual excavations at the ruins of Calakmul, including jade masks and a mummified body. ■ *Tue-Fri 0800-2000, US$1.* **Museo de la Escultura Maya**, Baluarte de la Soledad, has three well-laid out rooms of Maya stelae and sculpture. ■ *Tue-Sat 0900-1400, 1600-2000, Sun 0900-1300. US$1.* **Museo Gráfico de la Ciudad**, Baluarte de San Carlos, contains interesting scale models of the 18th-century defences and a collection of colonial arms and seafaring equipment, small library, a fine view from the cannon-studded roof, dungeons and a government-sponsored handicrafts market; for a few pesos, guides will conduct you through underground passageways which once provided escape routes from many of the town's houses (most have now been bricked up). ■ *0900-1300, 1700-2000. Free.* **Exposición de Artesanías**, Baluarte de San Pedro, is a permanent collection of local handicrafts with a shop. ■ *Mon-Fri 0900-1300, 1700-2000. Free.*

Jardín Botánico Xmuch'Haltun, in Baluarte de Santiago, is a small, but perfectly formed collection of tropical plants and flowers in a peaceful setting. ■ *Mon-Sat 0900-1300, 1800-2000, Sun 0900-1300. Free*. **Centro Ecológico de Campeche**, Avenida Escénica s/n, T12528, has a good collection of local wildlife. ■ *Tue-Fri 0900-1300, Sat and Sun 1000-1630.*

The **Fuerte de San Miguel**, on the *Malecón* 4 km southwest, is the most atmospheric of the forts (complete with drawbridge and a moat said to have once contained either crocodiles or skin-burning lime, take your pick!); it houses the **Museo Arqueológico**, with a well-documented display of pre-Columbian exhibits including jade masks and black funeral pottery from Calakmul and recent finds from Jaina. ■ *Tue-Sat, 0900-2000, Sun 0900-1300, US$1. Recommended.*

Excursions

Lerma is virtually a small industrial suburb of Campeche, with large shipyards and fish-processing plants; the afternoon return of the shrimping fleet is a colourful sight. The *Fiesta de Polk Kekén* is held on 6 January, with traditional dances. The nearest beach is Playa Bonita, some 7 km south of Campeche. It gets very packed in the high season with locals, and the water is not very 'bonita' at all, but dirty and polluted. The nearest decent beaches are at Seybaplaya, (see page 300) 20 km south of Campeche. There, the beaches are clean and deserted; take your own food and drink as there are no facilities. Crowded, rickety buses marked 'Lerma' or 'Playa Bonita' run from Campeche, , US$1, 8 km. A short distance to the south is the slightly better but less accessible San Lorenzo beach, rocky and peaceful but littered with cans and bottletops nonetheless.

Yucatán Peninsula

Sleeping

In general, prices are high. Beware of overcharging &, if driving, find a secure car park

AL *Ramada Inn*, Av Ruiz Cortines 51, T62233, F11618. 5-star hotel on the waterfront. **AL** *Alhambra*, Av Resurgimiento 85, T/F66323. 4-star, south end of town, a/c, disco, pool, satellite TV, quiet but popular with Mexican families in summer. **B** *Baluartes*, Av 16 de Septiembre, T63911. Nice, bit run-down, parking for campers, who can use the hotel washrooms, very good restaurant, pool. **C** *Regis*, Calle 12 No 148, between 55 y 57, T63175. Nice setting among cool colonial columns in the centre, bar, good service. **D** *América*, Calle 10 No 252, T64588. Hot water, friendly, no safe deposit, clean, fans but hot, safe parking, with night watchman, at the back of the *Ramada Inn*. **D** *Posada Del Angel*, Calle 10 No 307, T67718 (opposite cathedral). A/c, attractive, some rooms without windows, clean. Recommended. **D** *Autel El Viajero*, López Mateos 177, T65133. Overcharges, but often the only one left with space in the afternoon. **D** *Central*, on Gobernadores opposite ADO bus station. Misleadingly named, a/c, hot water, clean, friendly, noisy. **D** *Colonial*, Calle 14 No 122, T62222. Clean, good, several blocks from Zócalo. **D** *López*, Calle 12 No 189, T62488. Interesting art deco design, clean if a bit musty, with bath, uncomfortable beds, a/c. **E** *Campeche*, Calle 57 No 2, across from the cathedral on the Zócalo, T65183. Fan, cold water, grubby, run-down. **E** *Reforma*, Calle 8 No 257, T64464. Dirty, run-down, upper-floor rooms best, basic. **E** *Roma*, Calle 10 No 54, T63897. Run-down, dirty, dark, difficult parking, not safe (often full). **F** *Hospedaje Teresita*, Calle 53 No 31, 3 blocks northeast of Plaza. Quiet, welcoming, very basic rooms with fans, no hot water.

Camping *Trailer Park Campeche*, on Agustín Melgar and Calle 19, 5 km south of centre, close to the Bay in uninviting suburb of Samulá (signposted). 25 spaces and tent area, full hook-ups, good amenities, cold showers, pleasant site, owners speak some English, US$3.25 per person, US$6.50 for car with 2 people, 'Samulá' bus from market (US$0.15) or a 'Lerma' bus down coast road, get off at Melgar and walk. Tourist office often gives permission to pitch tents in their grounds, as will the Youth Hostel. There is a trailer park near the tourist office, open evenings only, until 2000, no tent or hammock facilities.

Youth hostel Av Agustín Melgar s/n, Col Buenavista, CP 24020, T61302, in the south suburbs, near University, Fuerte San Miguel and Trailer Park, take Samulá or ISSSTE bus from market US$0.15 (ISSSTE bus also from bus station). Segregated dormitories with 4 bunk beds in each room (US$1.50 per person), lovely grounds, pool, *cafetería* (breakfast 0730-0930, lunch 1400-1600, dinner 1930-2130, about US$1.50), clean and friendly, towels provided.

Eating *La Perla*, Calle 10 between 57 and 59. Good fish, busy and popular, venison, squid, locals' haunt, sometimes erratic service, off Plaza. *Mirador*, Calle 8 y 61. Good fish, moderate prices. *Del Parque*, on Zócalo. Good, US$5 meal and drink. *Marganza*, Calle 8. Upmarket, good breakfast and meals, excellent service. *Heladería Bing*, Calle 12 y 59. Good ice-cream. *Av Fénix*, on Juárez where the street bends towards the terminal. Generous breakfasts. Good food in the market, but don't drink the tap water. It is hard to find reasonably priced food before 1800; try the restaurant at the ADO terminal, or *La Parroquia*, Calle 55 No 8. Open 24 hours, good local atmosphere, friendly and clean. Recommended. *Los Portales*, Calle 10 No 86. Authentic local atmosphere, try the *sopa de lima*, open 1900-midnight. *Bar El Portón*, Calle 18 between 61 and 63, near walls. Courtyard, friendly. *Restaurant del Parque*, on the Plaza opposite the Cathedral. Good, cheap seafood.

Campeche is widely-known for its seafood, especially *camarones* (large shrimps), *esmedregal* (black snapper) and *pan de cazón* (baby hammerhead shark sandwiched between corn *tortillas* with black beans). Food stands in the Market serve *tortas*, *tortillas*, *panuchos* and *tamales* but hygiene standards vary widely; barbecued venison is also a marketplace speciality. Fruit is cheap and in great variety; perhaps best to resist the bags of sliced mangoes and peel all fruit yourself. (The word 'cocktail' is said to have originated in Campeche, where 17th-century English pirates enjoyed drinks adorned with palm fronds resembling cocks' tails). *La Pigua*, Av Miguel Alemán, opposite Cine Estela. Seafood in pleasant garden setting. *Lonchería Guayín*, Calle 53 between 16 and 14. Cheap *comida corrida*, good *licuados*, also houses Miguel Angel, spiritualist, fortune teller and feng shui consultant.

Festivals *Feria de San Román*, 2nd 2 weeks of **Sep**. *Fiesta de San Francisco*, **4-13 Oct**. Good *Carnival* in **Feb/Mar**. **7 August** is a *state holiday*.

Shopping Excellent cheap Panama hats *(jipis)*, finely and tightly woven so that they retain their shape even when crushed into your luggage; cheaper at the source in Becal. Handicrafts are generally cheaper than in Mérida. The market, from which most local buses depart, is beside Alameda Park at the south end of Calle 57. Plenty of bargains here, especially Mexican and Maya clothes, hats and shoes, fruit and vegetables; try ice cream, though preferably from a shop rather than a barrow. *Super 10* supermarket behind the post office has an excellent cheap bakery inside. There are souvenir shops along Calle 8, such as *Artesanía Típica Naval* (No 259) with exotic bottled fruit like *nance* and *marañón*, or *El Coral* (No 255) with a large variety of Maya figurines; many high-quality craft items are available from the *Exposición* in the Baluarte San Pedro; *Artesanías Campechanos*, Calle 55 No 25, recommended. Camping and general supplies, and laundrette, at *Superdíaz* supermarket in Akim-Pech shopping area at Av Miguel Alemán y Av Madero, some distance north of the Zócalo. ■ *0800-2100*. *Casa de Artesanía*, Calle 10. Good-quality handicrafts displayed on bizarre Maya dummies, with a mock-up hammock-making cave. Plenty of Panama hats and *huipil* dresses. Set in a colonial patio with a glass covering and a/c, this is a nice place for a cool drink on hot afternoons.

Tour operators *Viajes del Golfo*, Calle 10 No 250 D, T64044/F66154. Tours to Edzná, Calakmul. *Viajes Chicanná*, Av Augustín Melgar, Centro Comercial Triángulo del Sol, Local 12, T13503/F10735. Flight bookings to Cuba, Miami and Central America.

Local Car hire: next to *Hotel Ramada Inn*, Av Ruiz Cortines 51, T62233. *Hertz* and **Transport**
Autorent car rentals at airport (good for neighbourhood excursions).

Long distance Air: modern and efficient airport (CPE) on Porfirio, 10 km northeast.
AeroMéxico direct daily to Mexico City (T65678). If on a budget, walk 100m down service road (Av Aviación) to Av Nacozari, turn right (west) and wait for 'China-Campeche' bus to Zócalo.

Buses: all buses leave from the main terminal on Gobernadores. The following times and prices are for *ADO* buses unless otherwise stated. **Ciudad del Carmen**; 9 a day from 0745, US$8. **Chetumal**; 1200, US$15. **Cancún**; 2200, 2330, US$19. **Escárcega**; 5 a day from 0200, 2 hrs, US$6; Cristóbal Colón, 2210, US$5.50. **Mérida**; 11 a day from 0545-1930, 2½ hrs, US$7; Maya de Oro, 0400, US$8.50; Cristóbal Colón, 2030, US$6.50. **Palenque**, 3 a day from 0030, 5-7 hrs, US$13; Maya de Oro, 2400, US$16; Cristóbal Colón 2210, US$12. **Villahermosa**; 5 a day from 0215, 6½ hrs, US$16. **San Cristóbal de las Casas**; Maya de Oro, 2400, 14 hrs, US$25; Cristóbal Colón, 2210, US$20. **Oaxaca**; 2155, 2400, US$41. There are tourist buses to **Edzná** from Puerta de la Tierra, in front of the market, 0900 and 1400, US$20 return, also cheaper *combis* from the same stop. Buses to **Calakmul** depart from Baluarte de San Pedro, weekends only at 1700. Buses to **Seybaplaya** leave from the tiny Cristo Rey terminal opposite the market, 9 a day from 0615, 45 mins.

Banks *Banamex*, Calle 10 No 15. *Bancomer*, opposite the Baluarte de la Soledad. *Banco del* **Directory**
Atlántico, Calle 50 No 406; open 0900-1300 Mon-Fri; all change TCs and give good service.
American Express, T11010, Calle 59, Edificio Belmar, oficina 5, helpful for lost cheques, etc. Plenty of places to get cash on credit cards and ATMs. **Communications** Internet: *Cybercafé Campeche*, Calle 61 between Calle 10 and 12, open 0900-1300, US$4 per hour; *Telmex*, Calle 8 between Calle 51 y 53, free; Calle 51 No 45, between 12 and 14. *Intertel*, long-distance phones and fax, Calle 57 No 1 between 10 and 12. **Post Office**: Av 16 de Septiembre (*Malecón*) y Calle 53 in Edificio Federal (go to the right upon entry for telegraph service); open Mon-Fri 0800-2000, Sat 0900-1300 for *Lista de Correos*, registered mail, money orders and stamps. **Cultural centres** Casa del Teniente de Rey, on Calle 59 No 38 between 14 and 16, houses the Instituto Nacional de Antropología e Historia (INAH), dedicated to the restoration of Maya ruins in the state of Campeche, as well as supporting local museums. INAH can be visited for information regarding any of the sites in the state. T11314, inah@campeche.sureste.com. *Centro Manik*, Calle 59 No 22 between 12 and 14, T/F62448, opened 1997 in restored house in centre, vegetarian restaurant, bookshop, handicrafts, art gallery, music lessons, conferences, concentrates on ecology, environmentalism and health, also developing ecotourism in southern Campeche. **Hospitals** Red Cross, T52378, emergency T52411. **Laundry** Calle 55 between 12 and 14, US$0.60 per kilogram. **Useful addresses** The *Oficina de Migración* at the Palacio Federal will extend Mexican visas. Take copies of your passport as well as the original.

Maya sites east of Campeche

A number of city remains (mostly in the unfussy Chenes architectural style) are scattered throughout the rainforest and scrub to the east of Campeche; little excavation work has been done and most receive few visitors. Getting to them by the occasional bus service is possible in many cases, but return trips can be tricky. The alternatives are one of the tours run by some luxury hotels and travel agencies in Campeche (see above) or renting a vehicle (preferably with high clearance) in Campeche or Mérida. Whichever way one travels, carrying plenty of drinking water is strongly advised.

The closest site to the state capital is Edzná ('House of Grimaces'), reached by **Edzná**
the highway east to Cayal, then a right turn onto Highway 261 (the road to *Colour map 4, grid B5*
Uxmal, see page 308), a total distance of 61 km. A paved short cut southeast

through China and Poxyaxum (good road) cuts off 11 km; follow Avenida Nacozari out along the railway track. Gracefully situated in a lovely, tranquil valley with thick vegetation on either side, Edzná was a huge ceremonial centre, occupied from about 600 BC to AD 200, built in the simple Chenes style mixed with Puuc, Classical and other influences. The centrepiece is the magnificent, 30m-tall, 60 sq m **Temple of the Five Storeys**, a stepped pyramid consisting of four levels of living quarters for the priests and a shrine and altar at the top; 65 steep steps lead up from the Central Plaza. Opposite is the recently restored **Paal U'na**, Temple of the Moon. Excavations are being carried out on the scores of lesser temples by Guatemalan refugees under the direction of Mexican archaeologists, but most of Edzná's original sprawl remains hidden away under thick vegetation; imagination is still needed to picture the extensive network of irrigation canals and holding basins built by the Maya along the below-sea-level valley. Some of the site's stelae remain in position (two large stone faces with grotesquely squinting eyes are covered by a thatched shelter); others can be seen in various Campeche museums. There is also a good example of a *sacbé* (white road). Edzná is well worth a visit especially in July (exact date varies) when a Maya ceremony to Chac is held, either to encourage or to celebrate the arrival of the rains. ■ *Tue-Sun 0800-1700,*

Edzná

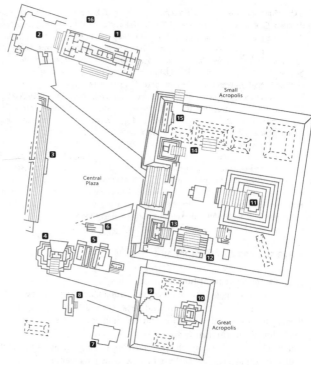

1 Platform of the Knives
2 Annex of the Knives
3 Nohochná
4 South Temple
5 Ball Court
6 North Platform of Ball Court
7 Temple of the Stone Masks
8 Structure 418
9 Structure 419-2
10 Temple of the Stairway with Reliefs
11 Temple of the Five Storeys
12 Temple of the Moon
13 Southwest Temple
14 Northwest Temple
15 Puuc Courtyard
16 Chultún

N

0 metres   50
0 yards   50

US$2, free on Sun; small comedor at the entrance. Local guides available. There is a tourist bus which leaves from Chetumal town wall at 0900, US$10 per person. At weekends take a bus towards Pich from Campeche market place at 0700, 1000 and 1030 (1 hour trip) but it may leave hours late; return buses pass the site (5 mins walk from the Highway) at 0930, 1230 and 1300. In the week, the Pich bus leaves Campeche at 1400, which is only of any use if you are prepared to sleep rough as there is nowhere to stay in the vicinity; hitching back is difficult, but you may get a ride to El Cayal on the road to Uxmal.

Tour operators *Viajes Programados*, Calle 59, Edificio Belmar, in Campeche offers daily 2-hr tours at 1000, US$20; tours from the *Hotel Baluartes*. *Picazh Servicios Turísticos*, Calle 16 No 348 between 357 and 359, T64426, run transport to ruins, with or without guide, US$20. Recommended.

Of the remoter and even less-visited sites beyond Edzná, Hochob and   **Hochob**
Dzibilnocac are the best choices for the non-specialist. **Hochob** is reached by turning right at **Hopelchén** on Highway 261, 85 km east of Campeche. This quiet town has an impressive fortified 16th-century church but only one hotel, **D** *Los Arcos*. A traditional honey and corn festival is held on 13-17 April; another *fiesta* takes place each 3 May on the Día de la Santa Cruz. From here a narrow paved road leads 41 km south to the village of **Dzibalchén**; no hotels but hammock hooks and toilet facilities upon request at the Palacio Municipal, there are some small eating places around the Zócalo. Don Willem Chan will guide tourists to Hochob (he also rents bikes for US$3.50 per day), helpful, speaks English. Directions can be obtained from the church here (run by Americans); essentially you need to travel 18 km southwest on a good dirt road (no public transport, hopeless quagmire in the rainy season) to the village of Chenko, where locals will show the way (4 km through the jungle). Remember to bear left when the road forks; it ends at a small *palapa*, and from here, the ruins are 1 km uphill with a magnificent view over the surrounding forest. Hochob once covered a large area but, as at Edzná, only the hilltop ceremonial centre (the usual Plaza surrounded by elaborately decorated temple buildings) has been properly excavated; although many of these are mounds of rubble, the site is perfect for contemplating deserted yet accessible Maya ruins in solitude and silence. The one-room temple to the right (north) of the plaza is the most famous structure: deep-relief patterns of stylized snakes moulded in stucco across its façade were designed to resemble a mask of the ferocious rain god Chac. A door serves as the mouth. Some concentration is needed to see this due to erosion of the carvings. A fine reconstruction of the building is on display at the Museo de Antropología in Mexico City. ■ *Daily 0800-1700, US$4.35.* Early-morning second-class buses serve Dzibalchén, but, as always, returning to Campeche later in the day is often a matter of luck.

Twenty kilometres northeast of Dzibalchén at Iturbide, this site is one of the   **Dzibilnocac**
largest in Chenes territory. Only three temples have been excavated here (many pyramidal mounds in the forest and roadside *milpas*); the first two are in a bad state of preservation, but the third is worth the visit: a unique narrow edifice with rounded corners and remains of a stucco façade, primitive reliefs and another grim mask of Chac on the top level. Much of the stonework from the extensive site is used by local farmers for huts and fences, keep an eye out in the vegetation for thorns and snakes. ■ *Daily 0800-1700, US$4.35.* A bus leaves Campeche at 0800, 3 hours, return 1245, 1345 and 1600, US$3.35. If driving your own vehicle, well-marked 'km' signs parallel the rocky road to Iturbide (no accommodation); bear right around the tiny Zócalo and its

attendant yellow church and continue (better to walk in the wet season) for 50m, where the right branch of a fork leads to the ruins. Other sites in the region would require four-wheel-drive transport and be likely to appeal only to professional archaeologists.

Jaina The small limestone island of Jaina lies just off the coast, 40 km north of Campeche. Discovered by Morley in 1943, excavations on Jaina have revealed the most extensive Maya burial grounds ever found, over 1,000 interments dating back to AD 652. The bodies of religious and political leaders were carried long distances from all over the Yucatán and Guatemala to be buried beneath the extremely steep **Pyramids of Zacpol** and **Sayasol** on Jaina. The corpses were interred in jars in crouching positions, clutching statues in their folded arms, some with jade stones in their mouths; food, weapons, tools and jewellery accompanied the owner into the afterlife. Terracotta burial offerings (including figurines with movable arms and legs) have provided a revealing picture of Maya customs, dress and living habits; many of these are now on display in Campeche or in the museum at Hecelchakán (see below). The island is Federal property, well guarded and currently closed to visitors. Major restoration and excavation is in progress and the island will reopen in a few years as an accessible tourist attraction.

Campeche to Mérida

There are two routes north from Campeche to Mérida, capital of the state of Yucatán: the so-called *Camino Real, vía corta* or short route (173 km via the shortcut along the railway line to Tenabó), using Highway 180 through Calkiní, Becal and Umán (taken by all first-class and *directo* buses), and the *Ruta Maya* or long route (254 km), Highway 261 through Hopelchén and Muná, which gives access to many of the peninsula's best-known archaeological sites, especially Uxmal (see page 326).

On the direct route, State Highway 24 provides a convenient link from Campeche to Highway 180 at **Tenabó** (36 km against 58 km), from where the well-paved road runs on through rising ground and sleepy villages, each with its traditional Zócalo, solid church and stone houses often made from the materials of nearby Maya ruins, to **Hecelchakán** (18 km, large service station on the bypass), with a 1620 Franciscan church and the rustic Museo Arqueológico del Camino Real on the Zócalo. Although dusty, the museum's five rooms give an informative overview of Mayan cultural development with the help of maps, stelae, a diorama and many Jaina burial artefacts. ■ *Tue-Sat 0900-1400, US$1.85.*

The highway bypasses **Calkiní** (E *Posada del Viajero*, not recommended, in a state of decay; service station) and after 33 km arrives at **Becal** (*Population:* 4,000), the centre for weaving Panama hats, here called *jipis* (pronounced 'hippies') and ubiquitous throughout the Yucatán. Many of the town's families have workshops in cool, moist backyard underground caves, necessary for keeping moist and pliable the shredded leaves of the *jipijapa* palm from which the hats are made; most vendors are happy to give the visitor a tour of their workshop, but are quite zealous in their sales pitches. Prices are better for *jipis* and other locally-woven items (cigarette cases, shoes, belts, etc) in the *Centro Artesanal, Artesanías de Becaleña* (Calle 30 No 210), than in the shops near the Plaza, where the hat is honoured by a hefty sculpture of three concrete *sombreros*! More celebrations of homage take place each 20 May during the *Feria del Jipi*.

Yucatán State

The archaeological sites of Chichen Itzá, Oxkintoc, Uxmal, Kabah and Labná are just a few of the many strewn throughout the state of Yucatán. Try not to miss Dzibilchaltún; the intrusion of European architecture is nowhere more startling than here. The region's many cenotes (deep pools created by the disintegration of the dry land above an underground river) were sacred to the Maya who threw precious jewels, silverware and even humans into their depths; many are perfect for swimming. On the coast, boat trips are organized to observe pelicans, egrets and flamingoes in their natural habitat. It is possible to visit some of the impressive henequén (sisal) haciendas in the more rural areas and admire the showy mansions that line the Paseo de Montejo in Mérida.

Just beyond Becal, *en route* from Campeche, Highway 180 passes under a 19th-century stone arch which is supposed to mark the Campeche/Yucatán border (although nobody seems totally sure of where the line is) and runs 26 km to **Maxcanú**. Here the road to Muná and Ticul branches east (see page 327); a short way down it is the recently restored Maya site of **Oxkintoc**. The Pyramid of the Labyrinth can be entered (take a torch) and there are other ruins, some with figures. ■ *US$3*. Ask for a guide at the village of Calcehtoc which is 4 km from the ruins and from the Grutas de Oxkintoc (no bus service). These, however, cannot compare with the caves at Loltún or Balancanché (see pages 325 and 331). Highway 180 continues north towards Mérida through a region of numerous *cenotes*, soon passing a turn-off to the turn-of-the-century Moorish-style *henequén* (sisal) hacienda at **San Bernardo**, one of a number in the state which can be visited; an interesting colonial museum chronicling the old Yucatán Peninsula tramway system is located in its lush and spacious grounds. Another hacienda is to the east at **Yaxcopoil** on Highway 261, with gigantic machinery, in operation until 1985. ■ *US$1.30*. Running beside the railway, the highway continues 47 km to its junction with the inland route at **Umán**, a *henequén* processing town (*Population: 7,000*) with another large 17th-century church and convent dedicated to St Francis of Assisi; there are many *cenotes* in the flat surrounding limestone plain. Highway 180/261 is a divided four-lane motorway for the final 18 km stretch into Mérida. There is a ring road around the city.

Mérida

The capital of Yucatán state and its colonial heart, Mérida is a bustling, tightly packed city full of colonial buildings in varying states of repair, from the grandiose to the dilapidated. There is continual activity in the centre, with a huge influx of tourists during the high season mingling with busy Meridanos going about their daily business. Although the city has been developed over many years for tourism, there is plenty of local flavour for the traveller to seek out off the beaten track. Attempts to create a sophisticated 'Champs-Elysées' style boulevard in the north of the city at Paseo Montejo have not quite cracked it; the plan almost seems to go against the grain of Mérida's status as an ancient city which has gradually

Phone code: 99
Colour map 4, grid A5
Population: 600,000

Yucatán Peninsula

evolved into a place with its own distinct identity. Mérida is a safe city, with its own tourist police force, recognizable by their brown and white uniforms. It is worth noting that during July and August, although very hot, Mérida is subject to heavy rains during the afternoon. Shoes with a good grip are necessary for the slippery pavement during this time.

Mérida was originally a large Mayan city called Tiho. It was conquered on 6 January, 1542, by Francisco de Montejo. He dismantled the pyramids of the Maya and used the stone as the foundations for the cathedral of San Ildefonso, built 1556-59. For the next 300 years, Mérida remained under Spanish control, unlike the rest of Mexico, which was governed from the capital. During the Caste Wars of 1847-55, Mérida managed to hold out against the marauding forces of indigenous armies, who had defeated the Mexican army in every other city in the Yucatán Peninsula except Campeche. Reinforcements from the centre allowed the Mexicans to regain control of their city, but the price was to relinquish control of the region to Mexico City.

The main **tourist office** is inside the Teatro Peón Contreras, Calle 60 y Calle 57 (just off Parque Hidalgo). ■ *0800-2030 daily.* Very helpful, often staffed by trainees who are very enthusiastic about giving help. There is another tourist office at the airport.

Ins and outs

Getting there All buses from outside Yucatán state arrive at the CAME terminal on Calle 70 between Calle 69 y 71, a few blocks from the centre. There is another bus terminal around the corner on Calle 69, where buses from local destinations such as Uxmal arrive. The airport is situated 8 km from the city, bus 79 takes you to the centre. Taxi to the centre from the airport charge US$9.

Getting around You can see most of Mérida on foot. Although the city is huge, there is not much to concern the tourist outside a few blocks radiating from the main Plaza. The Volkswagen Beetle taxis are expensive, due to their scarcity; fares start at US$3 for a short journey. *Colectivo* buses are difficult to locate; they appear suddenly on the bigger roads in the city, you can flag them down anywhere. They terminate at the market; flat fare US$0.25.

Sights

The city revolves around the large, shady Zócalo, site of the **Cathedral**, completed 1559, the oldest cathedral in Latin America, which has an impressive baroque façade. It contains the Cristo de las Ampollas (Christ of the Blisters), a statue carved from a tree which burned for a whole night after being hit by lightning, without showing any damage at all. Placed in the church at Ichmul, it then suffered only a slight charring (hence the blistering name) when the church was burned to the ground. To the left of the Cathedral on the adjacent side of the Plaza is the **Palacio de Gobierno**, built 1892. It houses a collection of enormous murals by Fernando Castro Pacheco, depicting the struggle of the Maya to integrate with the Spanish. The murals can be viewed until 2000 every day. **Casa de Montejo** is on the south side of the Plaza, a 16th-century palace built by the city's founder, now a branch of Banamex. Away from the main Plaza along Calle 60 is Parque Hidalgo, a charming tree-filled square which borders the 17th-century **Iglesia de Jesús.** A little further along Calle 60 is the **Teatro Peón Contreras** , built at the beginning of the 20th century by an

Mérida

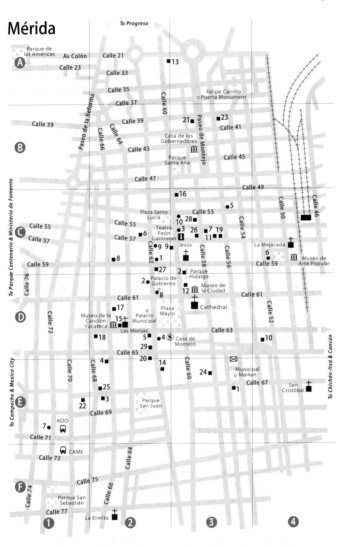

To Progreso

Parque de las Américas

Av Colón

Calle 21

Calle 23

Calle 33

Calle 35

Calle 37

Calle 39

Paseo de la Reforma

Calle 60

Calle 39

Calle 64

Calle 66

■ 13

Felipe Carrillo o Puerta Monument

21 ■

23 ■

Paseo de Montejo

Calle 41

Casa de los Gobernadores

Calle 43

Parque Santa Ana

Calle 45

Calle 47

Calle 49

Calle 50

Calle 46

To Parque Centenario & Ministerio de Fomento

Calle 55

Calle 57

Calle 59

Calle 76

Calle 55

Calle 57

Plaza Santa Lucía

Teatro Peón Contreras

Jesús

Calle 62

■ 16

Calle 53

5 ●

10 ■

28 ■

● 3

26 ■

7 ■ 19 ■

11 ■

Calle 54

6 ■

● 9

● 1

■ 8

27 ■

La Mejorada

Calle 59

6 ●

Museo de Arte Popular

2 ■ Parque Hidalgo

To Parque Centenario & Ministerio de Fomento

Yucatán Peninsula

2 ●

Palacio de Gobierno

● 8

12 ■ Museo de la Ciudad

Calle 61

Calle 56

Calle 58

Calle 61

Calle 52

Calle 72

17 ■

Museo de la Canción Yucateca

15 ■

Palacio Municipal

Plaza Mayor

Cathedral

18 ■

Las Monjas

5 ■

4 ● ⑤ Casa de Montejo

Calle 63

● 10

29 ■

4 ■

20 ■

14 ■

Calle 60

24 ■

✉ Municipal o Market

● 1

Calle 67

San Cristóbal

To Chichén-Itzá & Cancún

Calle 65

Calle 70

Calle 68

25 ■

22 ■

3 ■

Parque San Juan

To Campeche & Mexico City

7 ●

 ADO

Calle 71

Calle 73

 CAME

Calle 64

Calle 75

Calle 66

Parque San Sebastián

Calle 74

Calle 77

La Ermita ■

❶ ❷ ❸ ❹

N

Not to scale

■ Sleeping

1 América *E3*
2 Caribe *C3*
3 Casa Becil *E2*
4 Casa Bowen *E2*
5 Casa de Huéspedes *D2*

6 Castellano *C2*
7 Colón *C3*
8 Del Gobernador *C2*
9 Del Parque *C3*
10 Dolores Alba *D4*
11 Flamingo *C3*
12 Gran *D3*
13 Holiday Inn *A2*
14 La Paz *E2*
15 Las Monjas *D2*
16 Los Aluxes *C3*
17 Margarita *D2*

18 María del Carmen *D2*
19 Mucuy *C3*
20 Oviedo *D2*
21 Palacio Montejo *B3*
22 Pantera Negra *E1*
23 Paseo de Montejo *B3*
24 Peninsular *E3*
25 Posada del Angel *E2*
26 Posada Toledo *C3*
27 Reforma *C2*
28 San Juan *C3*
29 Sevilla *D2*

● Eating

1 Amaro *C2*
2 El Trapiche *D2*
3 El Tucho *C3*
4 Jugos California *D2*
5 La Prosperidad *C3*
6 Los Almendros *C4*
7 Petropolis *E1*
8 Pizza Bella *D2*
9 Pizza Chief *C2*
10 Tianos *C3*

Italian architect, with a neo-classical façade, marble staircase and Italian frescoes.

There are several 16th- and 17th-century churches dotted about the city: **La Mejorada**, behind the Museum of Peninsular Culture (Calle 59 between 48 and 50), **Tercera Orden**, **San Francisco** and **San Cristóbal** (beautiful, in the centre). The **Ermita**, an 18th-century chapel with beautiful grounds, is a lonely, deserted place 10-15 minutes from the centre.

Museums **Museo de Antropología e Historia**, Paseo de Montejo 485, housed in the beautiful neo-classical Palacio Cantón, has an excellent collection of original Maya artefacts from various sites in the Yucatán state. The displays are very well laid out, explanations all in Spanish. Many examples of jade jewellery dredged from *cenotes*, and examples of cosmetically deformed skulls with sharpened teeth. This is a good overview of the history of the Maya. ■ *Tue-Sun 0800-2000. US$2, free on Sun.*

Museo MACAY, Calle 60, on the main Plaza, has a permanent exhibition of Yucatecan artists, with temporary exhibits by contemporary local artists. ■ *Daily 1000-1730. US$2.* **Museo de Arte Popular**, Calle 59 esquina 50, Barrio de la Mejorada, has a permanent exhibition of Mayan art, handicrafts and clothing, with a good souvenir shop attached. ■ *Tue-Sat 0900-2000, Sun 0800-1400. Free.* **Museo de la Canción Yucateca**, Calle 63 between 64 and 66, in the Casa de la Cultura, has an exhibition of objects and instruments relating to the history of music in the region. ■ *Tue-Sat 0900-2000. Free.* **Pinacoteca Juan Gamboa Guzmán**, Calle 59 between Calle 58 and 60, is a gallery showing old and contemporary painting and sculpture. ■ *Tue-Sat 0800-2000, Sun 0800-1400. US$1, Sun free.*

Essentials

Sleeping The prices of hotels are not determined by their location. You can easily find a budget
■ *on map* hotel right near the Plaza, next door to a five-star luxury hotel. If booking into a central hotel, always try to get a room away from the street side, as noise on the narrow streets begins as early as 0500.

There are 2 hotels near the airport: **C** *Alfonso García*, Av Aviación 587 y Calle 53, T842651. **C** *Posada Maya*, Calle 81A No 841 y Av Aviación.

L *Hyatt Regency*, Calle 60 No 344 and Colón, T256722, F257002. Luxury hotel with boutiques, car hire, money exchange, tennis, gym, *Peregrina* restaurant; opposite is a *Fiesta Americana*. **L-AL** *Holiday Inn*, Av Colón No 489 and Montejo, T256877, F247755. All facilities are available. The hotel is elegant but a long way from the centre. **AL** *Best Western María del Carmen*, Calle 63, No 550 esq 68, T239133, F239290. Pool in courtyard with 300-yr-old Ceiba tree, a/c, new wing better than old, good value. **AL** *Calinda Panamericana*, Calle 59, No 455 esq 52, T239111, F248090. Good, expensive, with elaborate courtyard in the Porfirian style, very spacious and airy, ordinary rooms in new building behind, good buffet breakfast, with swimming pool, 5 blocks from centre. **AL** *Casa del Balam*, Calle 60, No 488 esq 57, T248844, F245011 (Mayaland Resort, in USA T305-3446547/ 800-4518891). A/c, close to centre, noisy at front, restaurant, bar, pool, neo-colonial style, facilities rather below 5-star. **AL** *Castellano*, Calle 57, No 513 and 62, T230100. Modern, clean but a bit run-down, friendly, pool. **AL** *El Conquistador*, Paseo del Montejo 458 esq Calle 35, T262155. Modern, specializing in package tours, unhelpful, poor value for independent travellers, good buffet breakfast. **AL** *Los Aluxes*, Calle 60 No 444, T242199. Delightful, pool, restaurants, very convenient, 1st class, 2 large new wings away from traffic noise.

A-C *del Gobernador*, Calle 59, No 533 and 66, T237133, F281590. A/c, bar, restaurant, good pool, excellent value. Highly recommended. **A** *Hotel Paseo de Montejo*, Paseo de Montejo 482, T239033, F239550, montejos@yuc1.telmex.net.mx. Pool, a/c, phone, restaurant, travel agency, shop, events centre. **A** *Palacio Montejo*, Paseo de Montejo 483C, T247644, F282156. Same owners and facilities as above.

B *Aragón*, Calle 57 No 474 between 52 and 54, T240242. A/c, clean, restaurant, good breakfast offering free coffee all day. Good value. **B** *Caribe*, Parque Hidalgo, Calle 59 No 500, T249022. A/c, cheaper with fan, modern, elegant, tasteful patio, tiny pool, helpful. **B** *Gran Hotel*, Parque Hidalgo, Calle 60 No 496, T236963, F247622. Does not accept Amex card, with a/c, TV, hot water, phone, clean, helpful, owner speaks English, Fidel Castro has stayed here frequently, as have other politicians, film and stage stars, expensive restaurant attached, free parking nearby on Calle 61 between 54 and 56 (opposite *Banco BCH*, ask front desk to stamp the parking receipt). **B** *Maya Yucatán*, Calle 58 No 483, T235395, F234642. With bath, a/c, TV, clean, swimming pool, good restaurant. **B** *Reforma*, Calle 59 No 508 esq 62, T247922. Refurbished, swimming pool, nice. **B** *San Juan*, Calle 55 No 497A, T241742. Near Plaza Santa Lucía, restored colonial building with a/c, TV, nice pool, quiet, tasteful furnishings, parking, café. **C** *Casa San Juan*, Calle 62 No 545A between 69 and 71, T236823, F862937, c.sanjuan@sureste.com. Restored 19th-century house with pleasant courtyard, large rooms with bath, a/c, includes breakfast. **C** *Del Parque*, Calle 60 No 497 esq 59, T247844. With bath and a/c, clean, friendly. Recommended. **C** *México*, Calle 60 No 525 esq 67, T247207. Good restaurant, attractive. **C** *Peninsular*, Calle 58 No 519 between 65 and 67, T236996, 1 block from post office and market. A/c, clean, comfortable, convenient, small pool, friendly. **C** *Posada Toledo*, Calle 58, No 487 esq 57, T231690. Good value, central, a/c extra, in charming old house, lots of plants, has paperback exchange. **D** *del Prado*, Calle 50 and 67; **E** with a/c, fan, safe parking, pool. Recommended. **D** *Dolores Alba*, Calle 63, No 464 esq 52 and 54, T285650. Does not take credit cards, rooms with bath and fan, some with a/c (have to pay extra), quiet, friendly, safe parking in courtyard, cool on 1st floor, have to pay for children under 10, good value, good breakfast for US$2.40, 0700-1000, will make reservations for sister establishment at Chichén Itzá; when checked out, will not permit you or your luggage in hotel beyond 2000. **D** *Flamingo*, Calle 57 between 56 and 58 T247755, near Plaza. With private shower, swimming pool, noisy, so get room at the back, clean, helpful, laundry. **D** *Hospedaje San Juan*, 1 block north of arch by Iglesia San Juan. Clean rooms with fan and bath. **D** *Lord*, Calle 63 No 516, T239371, 50m from main Plaza. Small, parking. **D** *María Teresa*, Calle 64 No 529 between 65 and 67, T285194. Friendly, safe, central, with bath and fan, a bit noisy. Some rooms **E**. Recommended. **D** *Mucuy*, Calle 57, No 481 between 56 and 58, T285193. Good, but 1st floor rooms very hot, with shower, use of fridge, washing facilities, efficient, nice gardens. Highly recommended (although owner can be irritable, his wife is nice), but long way from bus station. **D** *Pantera Negra*, Calle 67 No 547B between 68 and 70, T240251. Beautifully restored old colonial house, with cool quiet patio, well-stocked bookshelves, clean, communal bath, very friendly English owner. Recommended. **D** *Posada del Angel*, Calle 67, No 535 between 66 and 68, T232754. Clean, with shower and fan. **D** *San Jorge*, across from ADO bus terminal. With fan and bath, stores luggage, clean, but take interior room as the street is noisy. **D** *Santa Lucía*, Calle 55 No 508, almost opposite Plaza Santa Lucía, T282672. A/c, TV, very clean, parking, small pool, very good value. Recommended. **D-E** *Trinidad Galería*, Calle 60, esq 51, T232463. Hot water, fan, nice atmosphere and arty décor, a bit run down, laundry service, pool, mixed reports. **D-E** *Nacional*, Calle 61 between 54 and 56 (3 blocks from Plaza Mayor), T249255. Large clean rooms with fan, a/c, café, friendly, pool.

E-F *América*, Calle 67 between 60 and 58, T285879. On busy street near market, but warren of rooms at the back are quiet. Cheaper rooms with cold water, nice, comfortable. Best budget deal in Mérida. **E** *Casa Becil*, Calle 67 No 550-C, between 66 and 68.

Convenient for bus station, fan, bath, hot water, clean, safe, popular, breakfast, owner speaks English, quiet, friendly, make you feel at home. Recommended. **E** *Casa Bowen*, restored colonial house (inside better than out), corner of Calle 66 No 521-B, esq 65, near ADO bus station, T286109. Often full at weekends, rooms on the main street noisy, bath, hot water but irregular supply, exchanges dollars, stores luggage, clean, mosquitoes, some rooms with kitchen (but no utensils). Good. **E** *Centenario*, Calle 84 between 59 and 59A, T232532. With bath, friendly, clean, safe. **E** *del Mayab*, Calle 50, No 536A between 65 and 67, T285174. With bath, clean, friendly, tiny pool, car park. **E** *La Paz*, Calle 62 between Calle 65 and 67. Tall, eccentric rooms in old colonial house, some noise in the morning from nearby bus station, but otherwise quiet. **E** *Las Monjas*, Calle 63 and 66A. Clean, quiet, luggage store. Recommended. **E** per person *Latino*, Calle 66, No 505 esq 63, T285827. With fan and shower (water supply problems), friendly and clean, parking outside. **E** per person *Lol-be* Calle 69 between 66 and 68. With bath, fan, friendly. **E** *Margarita*, Calle 66 No 506 and 63, T237236. With shower, clean, good, rooms a bit dark, downstairs near desk noisy, cheaper rooms for 5 (3 beds), friendly. **E** *Meridano*, Calle 54 No 478 between 55 and 57, T232614. Nice courtyard, clean, hot water. **E** *Oviedo*, Calle 62, near main Plaza. With bath, friendly, clean, luggage deposit, quieter rooms at the back. **E** *Posada Central*, Calle 68 between Calle 65 and 67. With bath, clean, good beds, new rooms, parking, luggage store. Recommended. **E** *Rodríguez*, Calle 69, between Calle 54 and 56, T236299. Huge rooms, with bath, central, clean, safe. **E** *San Luis*, Calle 61, No 534 esq 68, T247629. With fan and shower (and US$2.25 for noisy a/c), basic, friendly, patio, pool, restaurant. **E** *Sevilla*, Calle 62 No 511 esq 65, T215258, near Zócalo. Private bath, clean, quiet, fan, but rooms without proper windows.**E** *Trinidad*, Calle 62, No 464 esq 55, T213029. Old house, cheaper rooms with shared bath, hot water, clean bathrooms, tranquil, courtyard, sun roof, lovely garden, can use pool at the other hotel, lots of rules and regulations. Recommended. **F** *Casa de Huéspedes*, Calle 62, No 507 between 63 and 65. Very shabby and faded vestiges of 19th-century features, including the bathrooms, but one of the cheapest options in town, mosquitoes, so take coils or net, pleasant and quiet except at front. **F** *Centenario II*, Calle 69 between 68 and 70, opposite ADO bus station. Fan, small rooms, friendly. **F** *San José*, west of Plaza on Calle 63 No 503. Bath, hot water, basic, clean, friendly, rooms on top floor are baked by the sun, one of the cheapest, popular with locals, will store luggage, good cheap meals available, local speciality Poc Chuc. Recommended.

Camping *Trailer Park Rainbow*, Km 8, on the road to Progreso, is preferable, US$5 for 1 or 2, hot showers. *Oasis Campground*, 3 km from Mérida on Highway 180 to Cancún, F432160. With hook-ups, hot showers, laundry, run-down, US manager, US$7 for car and 2 people.

Eating
● *on map*

Expensive *Pórtico del Peregrino*, Calle 57 between 60 and 62. Dining indoors or in an attractive leafy courtyard, excellent food. *El Mesón*, in *Hotel Caribe*. Pleasant, with tables on the square. *Patio Español*, inside the *Gran Hotel*. Well-cooked and abundant food, local and Spanish specialities, breakfasts. *Tianos*, Calle 59 No 498 esq Calle 60 (outdoor seating). Friendly, touristy, good food, check your change, sometimes live music.

Mid-range *Los Almendros*, Calle 50A No 493 esq 59, in high-vaulted, whitewashed thatched barn. For Yucatán specialities, first rate. *El Tucho*, Calle 60 near University. Good local dishes and occasional live music. A good hotel restaurant for value and cooking is *El Rincón* in *Hotel Caribe*. *Alberto's Continental*, Calle 64 No 482 esq Calle 57. Local, Lebanese and international food, colonial mansion. Recommended. *La Prosperidad*, Calle 53 y 56. Good Yucatecan food, live entertainment at lunchtime. *El Escorpión*, just off Plaza on Calle 61. Good cheap local food. On Parque Hidalgo is

Pizzería Vita Corleone, Calle 59 No 508. Good. The café at the *Gran Chopur* department store serves good food, large portions, a/c. *Amaro*, Calle 59 No 507 between 60 and 62. With open courtyard and covered patio, good food, especially vegetarian, try *chaya* drink from the leaf of the *chaya* tree, their curry, avocado pizza and home-made bread are also very good, open 1200-2200, closed on Sun. *Santa Lucía* Calle 60 between 55 and 57 (near plaza of same name). Moderate prices, good fish dishes, music Fri and Sat.

There are a number of *taco* stands, *pizzerías* and sandwich places in Pasaje Picheta, a small plaza off the Palacio de Gobierno, on the Plaza. *Pizza Chief*, Calle 62 between Calle 57 and 59. Many other branches, good pizzas. *Café Habana*, Calle 59 y Calle 62. International cuisine, a/c, nice atmosphere. *Louvre* (northwest corner). Good, cheap, slow surly service, grubby interior. *Lido*, Calle 62 y 61. Good-value meals and breakfast. *Pizza Bella* on the main Plaza. Good meeting spot, pizzas US$4-7, excellent cappuchino. *Café Restaurante Express*, on Calle 60, at Parque Hidalgo. Breakfast, good *comida*, traditional coffee house where locals meet, nice atmosphere, good food, occasional absence of alcohol due to licence problems.

Cheap *Café Petropolis*, Calle 70 opposite CAME terminal. Existed long before the terminal was built, family-run, sometimes staffed entirely by children, who do a very good job, turkey a speciality, excellent quality, good *horchata* and herb teas. *La Alameda*, Calle 58 No 474 between Calle 57 and 55. Arabic and Mexican cuisine, lunch only, closes at 1800. *Eric's*, Calle 62 between Plaza and Calle 57. Huge sandwiches filled with roast chicken or pork, cheap set breakfast. *El Trapiche*, a few doors down on Calle 62. Excellent pizzas and freshly made juices. *Café Continental*, Calle 60 between 55 and 53. Open 0630-1400, buffet breakfast, nice setting, classical music. Recommended. *Marys*, Calle 63 No 486, between Calle 63 and 58. Mainly Mexican customers. Recommended. *Alameda*. Excellent-value Lebanese food, some vegetarian, can ask for half portions. Recommended. *Mily's*, Calle 59 between 64 and 66. *Comida corrida* for under US$3; *La Pérgola* (both drive-in and tables), at corner Calle 56 and 43. Good veal dishes. Warmly recommended. Also in Colonia Alemán at Calle 24 No 289A. *Los Cardenales*, Calle 69 No 550-A esq 68, close to bus station. Good value, open for breakfast, lunch and dinner. Both *El Ardillo* and *El Viajero*, near bus station, offer good local meals. Cold sliced cooked venison (*venado*) is served in the Municipal Market. *Mil Tortas*, Calle 62 between 65 and 67, good sandwiches. *Tortacos*, Calle 62 y 65. Good Mexican food. Many other *torta* places on Calle 62, but check them carefully for best value and quality. *Kuki's*, Calle 61 esq 62, opposite taxi stand. Very good coffee, snacks, expresso, cookies by the kilo. Highly recommended. Good banana bread and wholemeal rolls at *Pronat* health shop on Calle 59 No 506 esq Calle 62 (but don't have breakfast there). *Café Club*, Calle 55 No 446 between 58 and 60, T231592. Caters for both vegetarian and non-vegetarian, will deliver. *Jugos California*, good fruit salads, Calle 60, in Calle 65, at the main bus station and many other branches all over city. *Bing*, Paseo Montejo 56A y Calle 37, 13 blocks from centre, about 30 different flavours of good ice-cream. Good *panadería* at Calle 65 y 60, banana bread, orange cake. Another good bakery at Calle 62 y 61. Good cheap street fare at Parque Santa Ana, closed middle of day.

There are several good bars on the north side of the Plaza, beer is moderate at US$1.20, though food can be expensive. *Café Expresso*, on Parque Hidalgo, is good for an early evening beer (if they aren't having liquor licence problems). *Panchos*, Calle 59 between Calle 60 and 62. Very touristy, staff in traditional gear, but lively and busy, live music, patio. There are a number of live music venues around Parque Santa Lucía, a couple of blocks from the main plaza. *El Trovador Bohemio*, on the park itself, has folk trios in a tiny 50's Las Vegas-style setting, cover charge US$1, beer US$2. Around the corner on Calle 60 are 2 more music venues. *El Tucho* is a restaurant (see

Bars & nightclubs

above), open till 2100 only, with live music, often guest performers from Cuba. Two doors down towards the Plaza is *El Establo*, upstairs from the street, open 2100-0230. Live local bands, plus occasional Cuban cabaret entertainers. Free entry, drinks US$2 and over.

Entertainment **Theatre** *Teatro Peón Contreras*, Calle 60 with 57. Shows start at 2100, US$4, ballet, etc. The University puts on many theatre and dance productions. **Cinema** There is a cinema showing subtitled films in English on Parque Hidalgo; also *Cine Plaza Internacional*, Calle 58 between 59 and 57. There is a multiscreen cinema in the huge shopping complex Gran Plaza, north of the city; *colectivo* 20 mins from Plaza Mayor. See the free listings magazine *Yucatán Today*, available at hotels and the tourist office, for other evening activities.

Festivals **Carnival** during the week before **Ash Wednesday** (best on Sat). Floats, dancers in regional costume, music and dancing around the Plaza and children dressed in animal suits. On **6 Jan** Mérida celebrates its birthday.

Shopping Many souvenir shops are dotted in the streets around the Plaza. They all specialize in hammocks (see box), they also sell silver jewellery from Tasco, Panama hats (see page 308), *guayabera* shirts, *huaraches* (sandals with car-tyre soles), baskets and Maya figurines. Always bargain hard, the salesmen are pushy, but they expect to receive about half their original asking price. Some of them will even haggle themselves down if you spend long enough in the shop acting indecisively. The golden rule is: don't go into the shop unless you plan to buy something, and go in with a clear idea of what you want. The main handicraft market is on Calle 56 y 67. Bargaining and pushy sales staff as well. There is a smaller handicraft market on Calle 62, one block from the plaza. The *Mercado de Artesanías*, on Calle 67 between 56 and 58, has many nice things, but prices are high and the sales people pushy. Good postcards for sale, though. There are several frequently recommended shops for hammocks (there is little agreement about their respective merits, best to compare them all and let them know you are comparing, shops employing touts do not give very good service or prices): *El Hamaquero*, Calle 58 No 572, between 69 and 71. Popular, but beware the very hard sell. *El Campesino*, the market. Eustaquio Canul Cahum and family, will let you watch the weaving. *El Mayab*, Calle 58 No 553 and 71, friendly, limited choice but good deals available; and *La Poblana*, Calle 65 between 58 and 60, will bargain, especially for sales of more than one, huge stock, a bit curt if not buying there and then; also *Jorge Razu*, Calle 56 No 516B between 63A and 63, very convincing salesman, changes travellers' cheques at good rates. Recommended. *El Aguacate*, Calle 58 No 604, corner of Calle 73. Good hammocks, no hard sell. Recommended. Another branch on Calle 62 opposite *El Trapiche*. Helpful, bargaining possible if buying several items. *Rada*, Calle 60 No 527 between 65 and 67, T241208, F234718. Good. *Santiago*, Calle 70 No 505 between 61 and 63. Very good value. To mail a hammock abroad can be arranged through some shops. Try *La Poblana*, or *El Aguacate* for help with the forms and method of parcelling and addressing. In the market prices are cheaper but quality is lower and sizes smaller. There are licensed vendors on the streets and in the main Plaza; they will bargain and may show you how hammocks are made; some are very persistent. Good silver shops and several antique shops on Calle 60 between 51 and 53. *Bacho Arte Mexicano*, Calle 60 No 466 between Calle 53 and 55. Also sells other jewellery and ornaments. *La Canasta*, No 500. Good range of handicrafts, reasonable prices. Good Panama hats at *El Becaliño*, Calle 65 No 483, esq 56A, diagonally opposite post office. *Paty*, Calle 64 No 549 between Calle 67 and 69. Stocks reputable 'Kary' brand *guayaberas*, also sells hammocks. *Tita*, Calle 59 between 60 and 62. Enthusiastic hard sell, they only sell sisal hammocks, good selection, give demonstrations. *Miniaturas*, Calle 59 no 507A, near Plaza. Traditional folk art, Day of the Dead

Know your hammock

Different materials are available for hammocks. Some you might find are: sisal, very strong, light, hard-wearing but rather scratchy and uncomfortable, identified by its distinctive smell; cotton, soft, flexible, comfortable, not as hard-wearing but good for 4-5 years of everyday use with care. It is not possible to weave cotton and sisal together although you may be told otherwise, so mixtures are unavailable. Cotton/silk mixtures are offered, but will probably be an artificial silk. Nylon, very strong, light but hot in hot weather and cold in cold weather. Never buy your first hammock from a street vendor and never bargain then accept a packaged hammock without checking the size and

quality. The surest way to judge a good hammock is by weight: 1,500 grams (3.3 lbs) is a fine item, under one kilogram (2.2 lbs) is junk (advises Alan Handleman, a US expert). Also, the finer and thinner the strands of material, the more strands there will be, and the more comfortable the hammock. The best hammocks are the so-called 3-ply, but they are difficult to find. There are three sizes: single (sometimes called doble), matrimonial and family (buy a matrimonial at least for comfort). If judging by end-strings, 50 would be sufficient for a child, 150 would suit a medium-sized adult, 250 a couple. Prices vary considerably so shop around and bargain hard.

miniatures, wrestling masks. Calle 62, between Calle 57 y 61, is lined with *guayabera* shops, all of a similar price and quality. Embroidered *huipil* blouses cost about US$25. Good, cheap *guayabera* shop on northwest corner of Parque San Juan, prices half those of the souvenir shops in the centre. Clothes shopping is good along Calle 65 and in the *García Rejón Bazaar*, Calle 65 y 60. Good leather *huaraches* sandals, robust and comfortable, from the market, US$10. Excellent cowboy boots for men and women, maximum size 10, can be bought around the market for US$46. *Casa de las Artesanías*, Calle 63, between 64 and 66, good. There is a big supermarket, *San Francisco de Assisi*, on Calle 67 y 52, well stocked; also *San Francisco de Assisi* at Calle 65, between Av 50 and 52.

Bookshop *Librerías Dante*, Calle 59, No 498 between 58 and 60. Calle 61 between 62 and 64 (near *Lavandería La Fe*) used books.

Cameras and film Repairs on Calle 53 y 62. Mericolor, Calle 67 y 58. Recommended for service and printing; also Kodak on Parque Hidalgo. Many processors around crossing of Calle 59 y 60. Prices are high by international standards.

Camera repairs *Fotolandia*, Calle 62 No 479G y 57, T248223.

Backpack repair *Industria de Petaquera del STE*, Calle 64 No 499, T283175. *Macay*, Pasaje Revolución, beside Cathedral, run by University.

Tour operators *Yucatán Trails*, Calle 62 No 482 between Calle 57 and 59, T282582, F241928, denis@finred.com.mx Tours to all the popular local destinations such as Uxmal, Celestún and Progreso; they do a train trip to Izamal, Sun only, full day with lunch, tour of convent, folklore ballet, guide, trip in horse and cart, US18. *Mayaland Tours*, in *Hotels Casa del Balam*, T263851, and *Fiesta Americana*, T250622, have their own hotel at Chichén Itzá. *Mayan Iniciatic Tours*, Paseo de Montejo 481, T202328, F201912, mayan@yuc1.telmex.net.mx. *Carmen Travel Services*, *Hotel María del Carmen*, Calle 63 No 550 y Calle 68, T239133, 3 other branches.

Transport **Local** **Car hire**: car reservations should be booked well in advance wherever possible; there is a tendency to hand out cars which are in poor condition once the main stock has gone, so check locks, etc, on cheaper models before you leave town. All car hire firms charge around US$40-45 a day although bargains can be found in low season. Cheapest in 1999 was *World Rent a Car*, Calle 60 No 486A, between 55 and 57, T240587, US$40, very fair when car was damaged. *Hertz*, Calle 55, No 479, esq 54, T242834. Most car hire agencies have an office at the airport and, as all share the same counter, negotiating usually takes place. Many agencies also on Calle 60: *Executive*, down from *Gran Hotel*. Good value. *Mexico-Rent-a-Car*. Cheap. *Veloz Rent a Car*, No 488, in lobby of *Hotel Casa del Balam*, good. *Tourist Car Rental*, Calle 60 No 421 between Calle 47 and 45, T246255. *Alamo,* T461623 (airport). *MeriCar*, Calle 41 No 504A between Calle 60 and 62, T240949. *Maya Car*, Paseo Montejo 486 between Calle 41 and 43, T240445. All agencies allow vehicles to be returned to Cancún at an extra charge. Be careful where you park in Mérida, yellow lines mean no parking. **Car service**: *Servicios de Mérida Goodyear*, very helpful and competent, owner speaks English, serves good coffee while you wait for your vehicle. Honest car servicing or quick oil change on Calle 59, near corner of Av 68. **Toll Road**: Tariffs from Mérida: Chichén Itzá, US$4; Valladolid, US$7; Cancún, US$19. The signs for the toll road say *Cuota*, while the old road's signs say *Libre*.

Taxis: There are 2 types: the Volkswagens which you can flag down, prices range from US$3-7; cheaper are the 24-hr radio taxis, T285328/231221, or catch one from their kiosk on Parque Hidalgo. In both types of taxi, establish fare before journey.

Long distance Air: Aeropuerto Rejón (MID), 8 km from town. From Calle 67, 69 and 60, bus 79 goes to the airport, marked 'Aviación', US$0.20, roughly every 20 mins. Taxi US$8, voucher available from airport, you don't pay driver direct; *colectivo* US$2.50. There is a tourist office with a hotel list. No left-luggage facilities. Lots of flights to Mexico City daily, 1¾ hrs. Other internal flights to Acapulco, Cancún, Chetumal, Ciudad del Carmen, Guadalajara, Huatulco, Monterrey, Oaxaca, Palenque, Tapachula, Tijuana, Tuxtla Gutiérrez, Veracruz and Villahermosa. International flights from Belize City, Houston, Miami and Havana. Package tours Mérida-Havana-Mérida are available (be sure to have a confirmed return flight). For return to Mexico ask for details at Secretaría de Migración, Calle 60 No 285. Food and drinks at the airport are very expensive.

Buses: Buses to destinations outside Yucatán state leave from the 1st class terminal at Calle 70 No 555, between Calle 69 and 71 (it is called CAME). The station has lockers; it is open 24 hrs a day. About 20 mins walk to centre, taxi US$2. Most companies have computer booking. Schedules change frequently. The ADO terminal, around the corner, is for Yucatecan destinations, with the single exception of buses to Chichén Itzá, which depart from the CAME terminal. It has nowhere to store luggage. **Mexico City**, US$42, 24-28 hrs, about 6 rest stops (*ADO*, 5 a day); direct Pullman bus Mexico City 2200. **Coatzacoalcos**, 14 hrs, US$31. **Veracruz**, *ADO*, 1430, and 2100, US$43, 16 hrs. **Chetumal**, see Road to Belize below. **Ciudad del Carmen** 8 a day, 1st class, *ADO*, US$14.80, 9 hrs. Buses to **Tulum**, via Chichén Itzá, Valladolid, Cancún and Playa del Carmen, several daily, from main terminal, 6 hrs, US$7, 2nd class, drops you off about 1 km from the ruins. For buses to Uxmal and Chichén Itzá see under those places. Regular 2nd class buses to **Campeche**, with *ATS* (US$4, 3½ hrs) also pass Uxmal, 6 a day between 0630 and 1900; 1st class fare (not via Uxmal), *ADO*, US$6, 8 daily, 2½ hrs. **Puerto Juárez** and **Cancún** (Autobuses de Oriente), every hour 0600 to 2400, US$8 2nd class, US$14 1st class, US$20 *plus*, 4½ hrs. Buses to and from Cancún stop at Calle 50, between Calle 65 and 67. If going to Isla Mujeres, make sure the driver knows you want Puerto Juárez, the bus does not always go there, especially at night. Buses to **Progreso** (US$1.65) with Auto Progreso, leave from the bus station on Calle 62, between Calle 65 and 67 every 15 mins from 0500-2100. To **Valladolid**, US$6-7 1st Express, US$5

2nd class (9 a day). Many buses daily to **Villahermosa**, US$22, 1st class (several from 1030 to 2330) 11 hrs, US$19.50; **Tuxtla Gutiérrez**, 1st class bus daily at 1330 via Villahermosa and Campeche, arrives 0630 next day, US$35 with Autotransportes del Sureste de Yucatán, also with Cristóbal Colón, US$30. Buses to **Palenque** 0800, 2200 (US$23) and 2330 (US$17) from ADO terminal, 8-9 hrs, Cristóbal Colón luxury service US$25; Alternatively take Villahermosa bus to Playas de Catazajá (see page 239), US$16.50, 8½ hrs, then minibus to Palenque, or go to Emiliano Zapata, 5 buses a day US$21, and local bus (see page 293). **Tenosique**, 2115, US$23.35. **San Cristóbal de las Casas**, 1800, US$21 (arr 0800-0900), and another at 0700 (Autotransportes del Sureste de Yucatán); also 2 a day with Cristóbal Colón, 1915 and 2345. Buses to Celestún and Sisal from terminal on Calle 71, between Calle 64 and 66. To **Celestún**, 1st class, US$2.50, 2 hrs, 2nd class, US$2, 2½ hrs, frequent departures. To **Tizimín**, **Cenotillo** and **Izamal** buses leave from Calle 50 between Calle 65 and 67. Route 261, Mérida-Escárcega, paved and in very good condition.

To **Guatemala** take a bus from Mérida to San Cristóbal and change there for Comitán, or to Tenosique for the route to Flores. A more expensive alternative would be to take the bus from Mérida direct to Tuxtla Gutiérrez (times given above), then direct either Tuxtla-Ciudad Cuauhtémoc or to Tapachula.

Road to Belize paved all the way to Chetumal. Bus Mérida-Chetumal US$18.50 luxury, US$16.50, 1st class, takes 7 hrs (Autotransportes del Caribe, Autotransporte Peninsular), US$13 2nd class.

Airline offices *Mexicana* office at Calle 58 No 500 esq 61, T246633, and Paseo Montejo 493, T247421 (airport T461332). *AeroMéxico*, Paseo Montejo 460, T279000, airport T461400. *Taesa*, T202077. *Aviacsa*, T269193/263253. *AeroCaribe*, Paseo Montejo 500B, T286790, airport T461361. *Aviateca*, T243605. **Directory**

Banks *Banamex* (passport necessary), at Calle 56 and 59 (Mon-Fri 0900-1300, 1600-1700), ATM cash machine, quick service, good rates. *Banco del Atlántico*, Calle 61 y 62, quick, good rates. Many banks on Calle 65, off the Plaza. Most have ATM cash machines, open 24 hours, giving cash on Visa or Mastercard with PIN-code. Reliable ATM machine (no queues) at *Inverlat Red Servicaja*, Calle 62 No 513, between 65 and 67. Cash advance on credit cards possible only between 1000 and 1300. *Centro Cambiario*, Calle 61 between Calle 54 and 52. *Casa de Cambio*, Calle 56 No 491 between 57 and 59, open 0900-1700 Mon-Sun. Exchange office on Calle 65 and 62, good rates for TCs, open Mon-Fri 0830-1700, Sat 0830-1400. 2nd branch on Plaza, near Palacio de Gobierno, open daily 0800-2100.

Communications Internet: *ITECH*, Calle 57 No 492 between Calle 56 and 58, US$3 per hour, US$4 for 2 hrs. Open Mon-Fri 0900-1400, 1600-2000, Sat 0900-1400. *Mérida Cyber Coffee*, Paseo Montejo and Calle 45. US$3 per hour, open Mon-Fri 0900-2300, Sat, Sun 1000-2200. *Kaptura*, Calle 62 between Calle 57 and 59, across from *Yucatán Trails*, US$4 per hour, open 0930-1300, 1630-1900. *Cybernet*, Calle 58 between 61 and 59. US$3 per hour, open Mon-Fri 0900-2100, Sat 0900-1400. **Post Office:** Calle 65 and 56, will accept parcels for surface mail to USA only, but don't seal parcels destined overseas; they have to be inspected. For surface mail to Europe try Belize, or mail package to USA, *poste restante*, for collection later if you are heading that way. An airmail parcel to Europe costs US$15 for 5 kg. Also branches at airport (for quick delivery) or on Calle 58. *DHL* on Av Colón offers good service, prices comparable to Post Office prices for air mail packages over 1 kg. **Telephone:** international telephones possible from central bus station, airport, the shop on the corner of Calle 59 and 64, or public telephones, but not from the main telephone exchange. Many phone card and credit card phone booths on squares along Calle 60, but many are out of order. Collect calls can be made on Sat or Sun from the *caseta* opposite central bus station, but beware overcharging (max US$2). Telegrams and faxes from Calle 56, between 65 and 65A (same building as Post Office, entrance at the back), open 0700-1900, Sat 0900-1300. *Tel World* offer long-distance fax service from offices on Calle 60 No 486, between 55 and 57.

Cultural centres *Alliance Française*, Calle 56 No 476 between Calle 55 and 57. Has a busy programme of events, films (Thu 1900), a library and a *cafetería* open all day.

Yucatán Peninsula

Embassies & consulates *British Vice Consul*, also *Belize*, Major A Dutton (retd), MBE, Calle 58-53 No 450, T286152, 0900-1600. Postal address Apdo 89. *USA*, Paseo Montejo 453 y Av Colón, T255011. *Canada*, Av Colón, 309-D, T256419. *Cuba*, Calle 1-C No 277A, between 38 and 40, T444215. *Germany* T252939/811099. *France* T252886. *Switzerland* T272905.

Medical services Hospitals: *Red Cross*, T249813/285391. *Centro Médico de las Américas* (CMA), Calle 54 No 365 between 33A and Av Pérez Ponce. T262619/262732/262354 F264710, emergencies T273199. Affiliated with Mercy Hospital, Miami, Florida, USA. **Doctor:** *Dr A H Puga Navarrete* (speaks English and French), Calle 13 No 210, between Calle 26 and 28, Colonia García Gineres, T250709, open 1600-2000. **Hospital:** *IDEM*, Calle 66, between 67 and 65, open 24 hrs, specializes in dermatology. **Dermatologist:** *Dr José D Cerón Espinosa*, Calle 66 No 524 between 65 and 67, T239938/246653. **Dentist:** *Dr Javier Cámara Patrón*, Calle 17 No 170 between Calle 8 and 10, Colonia García Gineres, T253399. US-trained, English spoken.

Language schools *Instituto Technológico de Hotelería* (ITECH), Calle 57 No 492 between Calle 56 and 58, T240387, dccmid@minter.cieamer.conacyt.mx,www.itech.edu.mx. Courses in Spanish, also courses in local cooking (in Spanish) and Maya culture. Homestays arranged, advanced booking necessary. *Modern Spanish Institute*, Calle 29 No 128 between Calle 26 and 28, Colonia Mexico, T271683, www.modernspanish.com. Courses in Spanish, Maya culture, homestays. *Instituto de Español*, Calle 29, Colonia México, T271683, 4merida@modernspanish.com.

Laundry *Lavandería* on Calle 69, No 541, 2 blocks from bus station, about US$3 a load, 3-hr service. *La Fe*, Calle 61 No 518, between Calle 62 and 64. US$3.30 for 3 kg. Highly recommended (shoe repair next door). Self-service hard to find.

Library English Library at Calle 53 between Calle 66 and 68. Many books on Mexico, used book for sale, bulletin board, magazines, reading patio. ■ *Tue, Thu, Fri 0900-1300, 1400-1900; Mon, Wed, Sat 0900-1300.*

Useful addresses Tourist Police: T252555.

Around Mérida

Celestún
Colour map 4, grid A4

A small, dusty fishing resort much frequented in summer by Mexicans, Celestún stands on the spit of land separating the Río Esperanza estuary from the ocean. The long beach is relatively clean except near the town proper (litter, the morning's fishing rejects, insects, weeds that stick to feet, etc), with clear water ideal for swimming, although rising afternoon winds usually churn up silt and there is little shade; along the beach are many fishing boats bristling with *jimbas* (cane poles), used for catching local octopus. There are beach restaurants with showers. A plain Zócalo watched over by a simple stucco church is the centre for what little happens in town. Cafés (some with hammock space for rent) spill onto the sand, from which parents watch offspring splash in the surf. Even the unmarked post office operating Monday-Friday, 0900-1300, is a private residence the rest of the week.

The immediate region is a National Park, created to protect the thousands of migratory waterfowl (especially flamingoes and pelicans) who inhabit the lagoons; fish, crabs and shrimp also spawn here, and manatees, toucans and crocodiles may sometimes be glimpsed in the quieter waterways. Boat trips to view the wildlife can be arranged with owners at the river bridge 1 km back along the Mérida road (US$35 for one large enough for six to eight people, 1½ hours, bargaining possible). Trips also arranged at *Restaurant Avila*, US$8 per person, 7 to a boat, one to two hours, and from the beach in front of *Hotel María del Carmen*, US$42 per boat, three hours (but much time is spent on the open sea). Ensure in advance that the boatman will cut his motor frequently so as not to scare the birds; morning is the best viewing time as later on flamingoes move deeper into the park. January-March is best time to see them. Also ask to be taken to the freshwater swimming hole. It is often possible to see flamingoes from the bridge early in the morning and the road to it may be alive with egrets, herons and pelicans. Important to wear a hat and use sun-screen. Hourly buses to Mérida 0530-2030, one hour, US$3.

Sleeping **LL** *Eco Paraíso*, Km 10 off the old Sisal Highway, T62100, F62111, burger @mail.internet.com.mx In coconut grove on edge of reserve, pool, tours to surrounding area including flamingoes, turtle nesting, etc. **D** *Gutiérrez*, Calle 12 (the *Malecón*) No 22. Large beds, fans, views, clean. **D** *María del Carmen*. New, spacious and clean. Recommended. **E** *San Julio*, Calle 12 No 92. Large bright rooms and clean bathrooms, owner knowledgeable about the area.

Eating Many beachside restaurants along Calle 12, but be careful of food in the cheaper ones; recommended is *La Playita*, for fried fish, seafood cocktails; bigger menu and more expensive is *Chemas*, for shrimp, oysters and octopus; *Avila* also safe for fried fish. Food stalls along Calle 11 beside the bus station should be approached with caution.

Transport Buses leave every 2 hrs from Calle 71 between 66 and 64 in Mérida, 2-hr journey, US$2.50 1st class, US$2 2nd class.

Twenty-nine kilometres west of Mérida is **Hunucmá**, an oasis in the dry Yucatán, about 30 minutes from the Central Camionera bus station, US$0.50. The road divides here, one branch continuing 63 km west to Celestún, the other running 24 km northwest to the coast at **Sisal**, a languid, faded resort which served as Mérida's port from its earliest days until it was replaced by Progreso last century; the old Customs House still retains some colonial

Yucatán Peninsula

Facilities

15 roomy and comfortably furnished cabins, all with a beautiful view of the emerald green Gulf of Mexico. Surrounded by a coconut grove, at the border of one of the most fascinating Mexican biological reserves, in the middle of our 3 mile virgin beach,

the hotel is fully oriented towards environment protection.
Freshwater swimming pool, spectacular white sand beach covered with thousands of seashells and spacious gardens with exotic coastal dune flora.

Km 10 de la Antigua
Carretera a Sisal
Municipio de Celestún
Yucatán, México

ECO PARAISO

Tel: 52 (991) 621 00/620 60
Fax: 52 (991) 621 11
E-mail: buger@mail.internet.com.mx
www.mexonline.com/eco-paraiso.htm

flavour; snapper and bass fishing from the small wharf is rewarding; the windy beach is acceptable but not in the same league as Celestún's. Sisal's impressive lighthouse, painted in traditional red-and-white, is a private residence and permission must be sought to visit the tower, the expansive view is worth the corkscrew climb. Frequent buses from Mérida (0500-1700), Calle 50 between Calle 65 y 67, two hours, US$1.50. **AL** *Sisal del Mar Hotel Resort*, in USA T800-4510891 or 305-3419173. Luxury accommodation. More modest are **E** *Club Felicidades*, a five-minute walk east of the pier, bathrooms not too clean; **E** *Club de Patos*, similar but a slight improvement; **E** *Los Balnearios*, with shower (cold water) and fan, prickly mattresses; **E** *Yahaira* (**F** low season), large clean rooms. *Restaurant Juanita*, reasonable.

Progreso
Phone code: 993
Population 40,000

Thirty-six kilometres north of Mérida, Progreso has the nearest beach to the city. It is a slow-growing resort town, with the facilities improving to service the increasing number of US cruise ships which arrive every Wednesday. Progreso is famous for its industrial pier, which at 6 km is the longest in the world. It has been closed to the public since someone fell off the end on a moped. The beach is long and clean and the water is shallow and good for swimming.

Sleeping **B** *Siesta Inn*, Calle 40 No 238 between Calle 23 and Calle 25, T51129. Away from the tourist zone, but near the beach, pool, restaurant, bar, TV, a/c. **B-C** *Tropical Suites*, Av Malecón and Calle 20, T51263, F53093. Suites and rooms with cable TV, a/c, sea views. **D** *Real del Mar*, next door to Tropical Suites on the Malecón, T50798. Some rooms with sea views. **C** *Progreso*, Calle 29 No 142, T52478, F52019. Simple rooms in the centre. **E** *Carismar*, Calle 21 No 151A, T52907. 1 block from the beach, sea views, family-run, pleasant. **E-F** *Xcaret*, in front of bus terminal. Basic, friendly, cheaper rooms have fan.

Eating The *Malecón* is lined with seafood restaurants, some with tables on the beach. *Casablanca*, *Capitan Marisco* and *Le Saint Bonnet* have been recommended. For cheaper restaurants, head for the centre of town, near the bus terminal.

Shopping Worth a visit is *Mundo Marino*, Calle 80 s/n, 1 block from the beach, T51380. A souvenir shop whose friendly owner Luis Cámara once caught a great white shark. Many shark-related as well as other marine souvenirs are on sale.

Transport Buses from Mérida leave from the small terminal on Calle 62 between 67 and 65, next to Hotel La Paz, every 10 mins. US$0.80 1-way/US$1.50 return. Return journey every 10 mins until 2200. **Boats** Can be hired to visit the reef of *Los Alacranes* where many ancient wrecks are visible in clear water.

A short bus journey (4 km) west from Progreso are **Puerto Yucalpetén** and **Chelem**, a dusty resort. Balneario Yucalpetén has a beach with lovely shells, but also a large naval base with further construction in progress. **AL** *Fiesta Inn* on the beach and **AL** *Mayaland Club* (Mayaland Resorts, in USA T800-45108891/305-3419173). Villa complex. Yacht marina, changing cabins, beach with gardens and swimming pool. Between the Balneario and Chelem there is a nice hotel with some small bungalows, *Hotel Villanueva* (2 km from village, hot rooms), and also *Costa Maya*, on Calle 29 y Carretera Costera, with restaurant. In Chelem itself is a new hotel, **B** *Las Garzas*, Calle 17 No 742, T244735. A/c, cable TV, bar, good restaurant, private beach club, pool, pleasant. Fish restaurants in Chelem, *Las Palmas* and *El Cocalito*, reasonable, also other small restaurants. Five kilometres east of Progreso is another resort, **Chicxulub**; it has a narrow beach, quiet and peaceful, on which are many boats and much seaweed. Small restaurants sell fried fish by the *ración*, or kilo, served with *tortillas*, mild chilli and *cebolla curtida* (pickled onion). Chicxulub is reputed to be the site of the crater made by a meteorite crash 65 million years ago which caused the extinction of the dinosaurs. The beaches on this coast are often deserted and, between December and February, 'El Norte' wind blows in every 10 days or so, making the water turbid and bringing in cold, rainy weather.

Forty-five kilometres east of Progreso is Telchac Puerto, a laid-back village on **Telchac Puerto** the coast with a luxury hotel and many private beach homes for rent. Not many tourists come here, due to its location. The village has a small plaza, with a lighthouse just off it; there is good swimming in the sea, and there are two large lagoons with interesting wildlife just beyond the village. The ruins of **Xtampu** are nearby, on the road to Progreso, a large site with an impressive pyramid, currently under reconstruction. For years, the locals have been using the stones from this site to build their homes. There is also a catholic church built from the same stone right among the ruins.

Sleeping and eating **AL** *Reef Club*, T74100/74086. Exclusive resort set around a small bay just outside the village, rooms with private terrace, water sports, health spa, nightly entertainment, 2 restaurants, fishing trips, child-minding service, special deals for families. **B** *Casa del Mar*, Apdo 13, Cordemex 97310, Yucatán, T220039, Yuctoday@ finred.com.mx. Maya-style thatched bungalows with modern fittings, kitchen, pool, on the beach. To enquire about renting private homes, contact Miguel Solís Lara, PO Box 102, Progreso, Yucatán, T/F993-54080 www.multired.net.mx/misola. *Bella Mar*, is a seafood restaurant on the beach just outside the village. There are a few restaurants around the plaza serving seafood, eg *Sea Friends*.

Halfway between Mérida and Progreso turn right for the Maya ruins of **Dzibilchaltún** Dzibilchaltún. This unique city, according to carbon dating, was founded as early as 1000 BC. The site is in two halves, connected by a *sacbé* (white road). The most important building is the T**emplo de Las Siete Muñecas** (Seven Dolls, partly restored and on display in the museum) at the east end. At the west end is the ceremonial centre with temples, houses and a large plaza in which the open chapel (see page 139), simple and austere, sticks out like a sore thumb. The evangelizing friars had clearly hi-jacked a pre-Conquest sacred area in which to erect a symbol of the invading religion. At its edge is the **Cenote Xlaca** containing very clear water and 44m deep (you can swim in it, take mask and snorkel as it is full of fascinating fish); there's a very interesting nature trail starting half way between temple and *cenote*; the trail rejoins the *sacbé* half way along. ■ *0800-1700, US$4.50, free with ISIC card*. The museum at entrance by ticket office (site map available). VW *combis* leave from Parque San Juan, corner of Calle 62 y 67A, every one or two hours between 0500 and 1900, stopping at the ruins *en route* to Chablekal, a small village further along the same road. There are also 5 direct buses a day on weekdays, from Parque San Juan, marked 'Tour/Ruta Polígono'; bus returns from site entrance on the hour, passing the junction 15 minutes later, taking 45 minutes from junction to Mérida (US$0.60).

The Convent Route

A popular day trip from Mérida, this tour unfortunately cannot be done on public transport, so a car is necessary. The route takes in Mayan villages and ruins, colonial churches, cathedrals, convents and *cenotes*. It is best to be on the road by 0800 with a full gas tank. Get on the *Periférico* to Ruta 18 (signs say

Yucatán Peninsula

Kanasín, not Ruta 18). At Kanasín *La Susana*, is known especially for local delicacies like *sopa de lima*, *salbutes* and *panuchos*. Clean, excellent service and abundant helpings at reasonable prices. Follow the signs to **Acanceh**. Here you will see the unusual combination of the Grand Pyramid, a colonial church and a modern church, all on the same small plaza (see Tlatelolco in Mexico City; page 90). About four blocks away is the Temple of the Stuccoes, with hieroglyphs. Eight kilometres further south is **Tecoh**, with an ornate church and convent dedicated to the Virgin of the Assumption. There are some impressive carved stones around the altar. The church and convent both stand at the base of a large Maya pyramid. Nearby are the caverns of **Dzab-Náh**; you must take a guide as there are treacherous drops into *cenotes*. Next on the route is **Telchaquillo**, a small village with an austere chapel and a beautiful *cenote* in the plaza, with carved steps for easy access.

Mayapán   A few kilometres off the main road to the right you will find the Maya ruins of Mayapán, a walled city with 4,000 mounds, six of which are in varying stages of restoration. Mayapán, along with Uxmal and Chichén Itzá, once formed a triple alliance, and the site is as big as Chichén Itzá, with some buildings being replicas of those at the latter site. The restoration process is ongoing; the archaeologists can be watched as they unearth more and more new buildings of this large, peaceful, late-Maya site. Mayapán is easily visited by bus from Mérida (every 30 minutes from terminal at Calle 50 y 67 behind the municipal market, one hour, US$1 to Telchaquillo). It can also be reached from Oxcutzcab. Beware of snakes at site. ■ *US$4.35.*

Thirty kilometres along the main road is **Tekit**, a large village containing the church of San Antonio de Padua, with many ornate statues of saints in each of its niches. The next village, 7 km further, is called **Mama**, with the oldest church on the route, famous for its ornate altar and bell-domed roof. Another 9 km is **Chumayel**, where the legendary Mayan document *Chilam Balam* was found. Four kilometres ahead is **Teabo**, with an impressive 17th-century temple. Next comes **Tipikal**, a small village with an austere church.

Maní   Twelve kilometres further on is Maní, the most important stop on this route. Here you will find a large church, convent and museum with explanations in English, Spanish and Mayan. It was here that Fray Diego de Landa ordered many important Maya documents and artefacts to be burned, during an intense period of Franciscan conversion of the Maya people to Christianity. When Fray Diego realised his great error, he set about trying to write down all he could remember of the 27 scrolls and hieroglyphs he had destroyed, along with 5,000 idols, 13 altars, and 127 vases. The text, entitled *Relation of Things in Yucatán*, is still available today, unlike the artefacts. To return to Mérida, head for Ticul, to the west, then follow the main road via Muná.

Ticul   Eighty kilometres south of Mérida, Ticul is a small, pleasant little village
Phone code: 997   known for its *huipiles,* the embroidered white dresses worn by the older Maya
Colour map 4, grid A5   women. You can buy them in the tourist shops in Mérida, but the prices and
Population: 30,000   quality of the ones in Ticul will be much better. It is also a good base for visiting smaller sites in the south of Yucatán state such as Sayil, Kabah, Xlapak and Labná (see below).

Sleeping and eating D *Plaza*, on the Zócalo. Clean, a/c. **D-E** *Sierra Sosa*, Calle 26, near Zócalo, T20008. Cheaper rooms dungeon-like, but friendly, clean and helpful. **E** *San Miguel*, Calle 28 near the market, T20382. Quiet, good value, parking. **E** *Motel*

Buganvillas, on the edge of town on the road to Mérida, T20761. Clean, basic rooms. **E** *Cerro Motor Inn*, also on outskirts, near *Motel Buganvillas*. Run-down. *Los Almendros*, Calle 23. Nice colonial building with patio, good Yucatecan cuisine, reasonable prices. *El Colorín*, near Hotel Sierra Sosa on Calle 26. Cheap local food. *Pizzería La Góndola*, Calle 23. Good, moderately priced pizzas.

Transport There are frequent VW *colectivos* from Parque San Juan, in Mérida, US$2.

Sixteen kilometres southeast of Ticul is Oxkutzcab, a good centre for catching **Oxkutzcab** buses to Chetumal, Muná, Mayapán and Mérida (US$2.20). It is a friendly place with a large market on the side of the Plaza and a church with a 'two-dimensional' façade on the other side of the square.

Sleeping and eating D *Tucanes*. With a/c, **E** with fan, not very clean, by Pemex station. **E** *Casa de Huéspedes*, near bus terminal. Large rooms with bath, TV, fan, friendly. Recommended. *Bermejo*, Calle 51 No 143. **E** *Trujeque*, just south of main Plaza. A/c, TV, clean, good value, discount for stays over a week. **F** *Hotel Rosario*, turn right out of bus station then right again. Double room, shower, cable TV. Hammocks provided in some private houses, usually full, fluent Spanish needed to find them. *Su Cabaña Suiza*, Calle 54 No 101. Good, cheap set lunch, family-run. Recommended. (No money exchange facilities; go to Banco del Atlántico in Tekax, 25 mins away by bus.)

Nearby, to the south, are the caverns and pre-Columbian vestiges at Loltún **Grutas de** (supposedly extending for 8 km). ■ *Caves are open Tue-Sun, 0930, 1100, 1230* **Loltún** *and 1400. US$3 with obligatory guide, one hour 20 mins. Recommended. Caretaker may admit tours on Mon, but no lighting.* Take pick-up (US$0.30) or truck from the market going to Cooperativa (an agricultural town). For return, flag down a passing truck. Alternatively, take a taxi, US$10 (can be visited from Labná on a tour from Mérida). The area around Ticul and Oxcutzcab is intensively farmed with citrus fruits, papayas and mangoes. After Oxkutzcab on Route 184 is **Tekax** with restaurant *La Ermita* serving excellent Yucatecan dishes at reasonable prices. From Tekax a paved road leads to the ruins of **Chacmultún**. From the top you have a beautiful view. There is a caretaker. All the towns between Muná and Peto, 14 km northeast of Tzucacab off Route 184, have large old churches. Beyond the Peto turn-off the scenery is scrub and swamp as far as the Belizean border.

The Puuc Route

These four sites (Kabah, Sayil, Xlapak and Labná) can be visited in a day, as well as Uxmal, on the 'Ruta Puuc' bus, which departs from the 1st class bus station in Mérida every day except Sun at 0800, US$7, entry to sites not included. This is a good whistle-stop tour, but does not give you much time at each of the ruins; if you want to spend longer seeing these sites, it is recommended that you stay overnight in Ticul. ■ *The following sites all cost US$1.70, free on Sun.*

On either side of the main road, 37 km south of Uxmal and often included in **Kabah** tours of the latter, are the ruins of Kabah. On one side there is a fascinating **Palace of Masks** (or *Codz-Poop*), whose façade bears the image of Chac, mesmerically repeated 260 times, the number of days in the Almanac Year. Each mask is made up of 30 units of mosaic stone. Even the central chamber is entered via a huge Chac mask whose curling snout forms the doorstep. On the other side of this wall, beneath the figure of the ruler, Kabal, are impressive carvings on the door arches which depict a man about to be killed, pleading for

Yucatán Peninsula

mercy, and of two men duelling. This side of the road is mostly reconstructed; across the road the outstanding feature is a reconstructed arch marking the start of the *sacbé* (sacred road), which leads all the way to Uxmal, and several stabilized, but unclimbable mounds of collapsed buildings. The style is Classic Puuc. Watch out for snakes and spiders.

Sayil Sayil means 'The Place of the Ants'. Dating from 800-1000 AD, this site has an interesting palace which in its day included 90 bathrooms for some 350 people. The simple, elegant colonnade is reminiscent of the architecture of ancient Greece. The central motif on the upper part of the façade is a broad mask with huge fangs, flanked by two serpents surrounding the grotesque figure of a descending deity. From the upper level of the palace you can see a tiny ruin on the side of a mountain called the Nine Masks.

Xlapak Thirteen kilometres from Sayil, the ruins of Xlapak have not been as extensively restored as the others in this region. There are 14 mounds and three partially restored pyramids.

Labná Labná has a feature which ranks it among the most outstanding sites of the Puuc region: a monumental arch connecting two groups of buildings (now in ruins) which displays an architectural concept unique to this region. Most Maya arches are purely structural, but the one at Labná has been constructed for aesthetic purposes, running right through the façade and clearly meant to be seen from afar. The two façades on either side of the arch differ greatly in their decoration; the one at the entrance is beautifully decorated with delicate latticework and stone carving imitating the wood or palm-frond roofs of Maya huts.

Uxmal

Colour map 4, grid A5 Built during the Classic Period, Uxmal is the most famous of the ruins in the Puuc region. The characteristic features of Maya cities in this region are the quadrangular layout of the buildings, set on raised platforms, and an artificially created underground water-storage system. The **Pyramid of the Sorcerer** is an unusual oval-shaped pyramid set on a large rectangular base; there is evidence that five stages of building were used in its construction. The pyramid is 30m tall, with two temples at the top. It is unfortunately forbidden to walk to the top due to loose stones. The **Nunnery** is set around a large courtyard, with some fine masks of Chaac, the rain god, on the corners of the buildings. The east building of the Nunnery is decorated with double-headed serpents on its cornices. There are some plumed serpents in relief, in excellent condition, on the façade of the west building. The **House of the Governor** is 100m long, and is considered one of the most outstanding buildings in all of Mesoamerica. Two arched passages divide the building into three distinct sections which would probably have been covered over. Above the central entrance is an elaborate trapezoidal motif, with a string of Chaac masks interwoven into a flowing, undulating serpent-like shape extending to the façade's two corners. The stately two-headed jaguar throne in front of the structure suggests a royal or administrative function. The **House of the Turtles** is sober by comparison, its simple walls adorned with carved turtles on the upper cornice, above a short row of tightly-packed columns which resemble the Maya *palapas*, made of sticks with a thatched roof, still used today. The **House of the Doves** is the oldest, and most damaged of the buildings at Uxmal. What remains of it is still impressive: a long, low platform of wide columns topped by clusters of roof-combs, whose similarity to dovecotes gave the building its name. ■ *0800-1800. US$7.50, free on Sunday. Son et Lumière shows cost US$3, in Spanish; rental of translation equipment US$2.50. Shows are at 2000 in summer and 1900 in winter.* There are six buses a day from Mérida, from the terminal on Calle 69 between 68 and 70, US$1.80. Return buses run every two hours, but if you've just missed one, go to the entrance to the site on the main road and wait for a *colectivo*, which will take you to Muná for US$0.50. From there, many buses (US$1.70) and *colectivos* (US$1.40) go to Mérida. Parking at the site costs US$1 for the whole day. Uxmal is 74 km from Mérida, 177 km from Campeche, by a good paved road. If going by car from Mérida, there is a new circular road round the city: follow the signs to Campeche, then Campeche via *ruinas*, then to Muná via Yaxcopoil (long stretch of road with no signposting). Muná-Yaxcopoil is about 34 km.

AL *Misión Uxmal*, T997-62022, F62023, Km 78, 1-2 km from ruins on Mérida road. Rooms a bit dark, pool. **L** *Hacienda Uxmal*, T230275, 300-400m from ruins. Good, efficient and relaxing (3 restaurants open 0800-2200), a/c, gardens, swimming pool (the pottery that decorates the rooms is made by Miguel Zum, Calle 32, Ticul); also owns **L** *Lodge Uxmal*, T230275, at entrance. Comfortable, a/c, bath, TV, fair restaurant. (Mayaland Resorts, Av Colón 502, Mérida T99-250621, F250087). **A** *Club Méditerranée Villa Arqueológica*, Mérida T280644. Beautiful, close to ruins, good and expensive restaurant, excellent service, swimming pool. Recommended. **C** *Rancho Uxmal*, about 4 km north of ruins, T478021. Comfortable rooms, hot and cold water, camping for US$5, pool, reasonable food but not cheap (no taxis to get there). For cheap accommodation, go to Ticul, 28 km away (see below). Restaurant at ruins, good but expensive.

Sleeping & eating
There is no village at Uxmal, just the hotels

Yucatán Peninsula

Uxmal

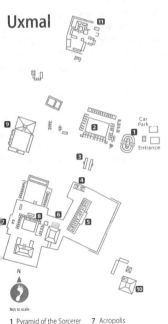

N

Not to scale

1 Pyramid of the Sorcerer
2 Nunnery
3 Ball Court
4 House of the Turtles
5 House of the Governor
6 Great Pyramid
7 Acropolis
8 House of the Doves
9 Cemetery Group
10 Pyramid of the Old Woman
11 North Group

Camping No camping allowed, but there is a campsite, *Sacbé*, at Santa Elena, about 15 km south, between Uxmal and Kabah, on Route 261, Km 127 at south exit of village. Postal address: Portillo, Apdo 5, CP 97860, Ticul, Yucatán. (2nd class buses Mérida-Campeche pass by, ask to be let out at the Campo de Baseball). 9 electric hook-ups (US$7-10 for motor home according to size), big area for tents (US$2.75 per person with tent), *palapas* for hammocks (US$2.65 per person), cars pay US$1, showers, toilets, clothes-washing facilities, also 3 bungalows with ceiling fan (**E**), breakfast, vegetarian lunch and dinner available (US$2.65 each); French and Mexican owners, a beautifully landscaped park, fastidiously clean, and impeccably managed. Highly recommended.

On the road from Uxmal to Mérida is Muná (15 km from Uxmal, 62 from Mérida); delightful square and old church, no hotel, but ask in *Restaurant Katty*, just on plaza, whose owner has two rooms with two double beds at his home, **E**, clean,

Muná

friendly, hot showers. Recommended (restaurant has good, cheap *enchiladas en mole*). Also ask in shops by bus stop in town centre for accommodation in private homes. There is a new direct road (Highway 184 and 293) from Muná to Bacalar, Quintana Roo, just north of Chetumal.

Izamal

Phone code: 995
Colour map 4, grid A5
Population: 15,385

Sixty-eight kilometres east of Mérida is the friendly little town of **Izamal** (reached by direct bus either from Mérida or Valladolid, a good day excursion). Once a major Classic Maya religious site founded by the priest Itzamná, Izamal became one of the centres of the Spanish attempt to Christianize the Maya.

Fray Diego de Landa, the historian of the Spanish conquest of Mérida (of whom there is a statue in the town), founded the huge **convent and church** which now face the main **Plaza de la Constitución**. This building, constructed on top of a Maya pyramid, was begun in 1549 and has the second largest atrium in the world. If you examine carefully the walls that surround the magnificent atrium, you will notice that some of the faced stones are embellished with carvings of Maya origin, confirming that, when they had toppled the pre-Colombian structures, the Spaniards re-used the material to create the imported architecture. There is also a throne built for the Pope's visit in 1993. The image of the Inmaculada Virgen de la Concepción in the magnificent church was made the Reina de Yucatán in 1949, and the patron saint of the state in 1970. Just 2½ blocks away, visible from the convent across a second square and signposted, are the ruins of a great mausoleum known as the **Kinich-Kakmo** pyramid. ■ *0800-1700, free. The entrance is next to the tortilla factory.* You climb the first set of stairs to a broad, tree-covered platform, at the end of which is a further pyramid (still under reconstruction). From the top there is an excellent view of the town and surrounding *henequén* and citrus plantations. Kinich-Kakmo is 195m long, 173m wide and 36m high, the fifth highest in Mexico. In all, 20 Maya structures have been identified in Izamal, several on Calle 27. Another startling feature about the town is that the entire colonial centre, including the convent, the arcaded government offices on Plaza de la Constitución and the arcaded second square, is painted a rich yellow ochre, giving it the nickname of the 'golden city'.

Four blocks up Calle 27, at the junction with Calle 34 is a small church on a square. The front door may be locked, but a little door outside leads to a spiral staircase to the interior gallery (note the wooden poles in the ceilings) and to the roof. The treads on the stairs are very narrow.

Sleeping and eating **C** *Macan-Che*, Calle 22 and Calle 33, T40287. 4 blocks north of the Plaza, pleasant bungalows, breakfast. Recommended. **D** *Kabul*, Plaza de la Constitución. Poor value, cell-like rooms. **E** *Canto*. Basic, Room 1 is best, friendly. *Tumben-Lol*, Calle 22 No 302 between 31 and 33. Yucatecan cuisine. *Kinich-Kakmó*, Calle 27 No 299 between 28 and 30. Near ruins of same name, local food. Several restaurants on Plaza de la Constitución. *Gaby* just off the square on Calle 31. *El Norteño* at bus station. Good, cheap. *Wayane*, near statue of Diego de Landa. Friendly, clean.

Entertainment Activity in town in the evening gets going after 2030.

Shopping **Market**, Calle 31, on Plaza de la Constitución, opposite convent, closes soon after lunch. *Hecho a mano*, Calle 31 No 332 between 36 and 38. Folk art, postcards, textiles, jewellery, papier-mâché masks.

Transport Bus station is on Calle 32 behind government offices, can leave bags. 2nd class to **Mérida**, every 45 mins, 1½ hrs, US$1.50, lovely countryside. Bus station in Mérida, Calle 50 between Calle 65 and 67. 6 a day to/from **Valladolid** (96 km), about 2 hrs, US$2.30-3.

Directory Banks Bank on square with statue to Fray Diego de Landa, south side of convent. **Communications Post Office:** on opposite side of square to convent.

From Izamal one can go by bus to **Cenotillo**, where there are several fine *cenotes* within easy walking distance from the town (avoid the one *in* town), especially **Ucil**, excellent for swimming, and **La Unión**. Take the same bus as for Izamal from Mérida. Past Cenotillo is Espita and then a road forks left to Tizimín (see page 336).

The cemetery of **Hoctún**, on the Mérida-Chichén road, is also worth visiting; indeed it is impossible to miss, there is an 'Empire State Building' on the site. Take a bus from Mérida (last bus back 1700) to see extensive ruins at **Aké**, an unusual structure. Public transport in Mérida is difficult: from an unsigned stop on the corner of Calle 53 y 50, some buses to Tixkokob and Ekmul continue to Aké; ask the driver.

Chichén Itzá

Route 180 runs southeast from Mérida for 120 km to Chichén Itzá where the scrub forest has been cleared from over 5 sq km of ruins. Chichén Itzá means 'Mouth of the well of the water-sorcerer'. The city was built by the Maya in late Classic times (AD 600-900). By the end of the 10th century, the city was more or less abandoned. It was reestablished in the 11th-12th centuries, but much debate surrounds by whom. Whoever the people were, a comparison of some of the architecture with that of Tula, north of Mexico City (see page 145), indicates that they were heavily influenced by the Toltecs of Central Mexico.

The major buildings in the north half display a Toltec influence. Dominating them is **El Castillo**, its top decorated by the symbol of Quetzalcoatl/Kukulcán. The balustrade of the 91 stairs up each of the four sides is also decorated at its base by the head of a plumed, open-mouthed serpent. There is also an interior ascent of 61 steep and narrow steps to a chamber lit by electricity; here the red-painted jaguar which probably served as the throne of the high priest burns bright, its eyes of jade, its fangs of flint (■ *1100-1500, and 1600-1700, closed if raining*). To reach the chamber you have to clamber up very narrow, slippery steps as high as seven tiers of pyramid (count them from the outside) – definitely NOT for the claustrophobic.

There is a **ball court** with grandstand and towering walls, each set with a projecting ring of stone high up; at eye-level is a relief showing the decapitation of the winning captain (sacrifice was an honour; some theories, however, maintain that it was the losing captain who was killed). El Castillo stands at the centre of the northern half of the site, and almost at a right angle to its northern face runs the *sacbé*, sacred way, to the **Cenote Sagrado**, the Well of Sacrifice. Into the Cenote Sagrado were thrown valuable propitiatory objects of all kinds, animals and human sacrifices. The well was first dredged by Edward H Thompson, the US Consul in Mérida, between 1904 and 1907; he accumulated a vast quantity of objects in pottery, jade, copper and gold. In 1962 the well was explored again by an expedition sponsored by the National Geographic Society and some 4,000 further artefacts were recovered, including beads, polished jade, lumps of *copal* resin, small bells, a statuette of rubber latex, another of wood, and a quantity of animal and human bones. Another

Yucatán Peninsula

cenote, the Xtoloc Well, was probably used as a water supply. To the east of El Castillo is the **Temple of the Warriors** with its famous reclining Chacmool statue. This pyramidal platform has now been closed off to avoid erosion.

Old Chichén, where the Maya buildings of the earlier city are found, lies about 500m by path from the main clearing. The famous **El Caracol**, or Observatory, is included in this group, as is the **Casa de las Monjas**, or Nunnery. A footpath to the right of Las Monjas leads to the **Templo de los Tres Dinteles**

Chichén Itzá

Entrance

Car Park

Yucatán Peninsula

N

Not to scale

1 Castillo	7 Well of Sacrifice	12 House of the Deer
2 Ball Court	8 Temple of the Warriors	13 Red House
3 Temple of the Jaguar	& Chacmool Temple	14 El Caracol (Observatory)
4 Platform of the Skulls	9 Group of a Thousand	15 Nunnery
(Tzompantli)	Columns	16 'Church'
5 Platform of Eagles	10 Market	17 Akabdzilo
6 Platform of Venus	11 Tomb of the High Priest	

(the Three Lintels) after 30 minutes walking. It requires at least one day to see the many pyramids, temples, ballcourts and palaces, all of them adorned with astonishing sculptures. Excavation and renovation is still going on. Interesting birdlife and iguanas can also be seen around the ruins. ■ *0800-1700, US$7.50, free Sun and holidays, when it is incredibly crowded, you may leave and re-enter as often as you like on day of issue. Guides charge US$4-6 per person for a 1½-hour tour (they are persistent and go too fast). Recommended guide from Mérida: Miguel Angel Vergara, Centro de Estudios Maya Haltun-Ha, T271172/F267707, PO Box 97148. Guided tours US$37 per group of any size; it is best to try and join one, many languages available. Check at entrance for opening times of the various buildings. Best to arrive before 1030 when the mass of tourists arrives. Son et lumière* (US$5 in English, US$1.35 in Spanish) at Chichén every evening, in Spanish at 1900, and then in English at 2000; nothing like as good as at Uxmal. A tourist centre has been built at the entrance to the ruins with a restaurant, free cinema (short film in English at 1200 and 1600), a small **museum**, books and souvenir shops (if buying slides, check the quality), with exchange facilities at the latter; luggage deposit free. ■ *0800-1700.* Car park US$1.50. Drinks and snacks are available at the entrance (expensive) and at the *Cenote*, also guidebooks and clean toilets at the former. There are more toilets on the way to Old Chichén, and a drinks terrace with film supplies. The site is hot, take a hat, sun cream, sun glasses, shoes with good grip and drinking water. The *Easy Guide* by Richard Bloomgarden is interesting though brief, available in several languages. *Panorama* is the best. José Díaz Bolio's book, although in black and white (and therefore cheaper) is good for background information, but not as a guide to take you round the ruins.

Tours run daily to the Balankanché caves, 3 km east of Chichén Itzá just off the highway. There are archaeological objects, including offerings of pots and *metates* in an extraordinary setting, except for the unavoidable, 'awful' *son et lumière* show (five a day in Spanish; 1100, 1300 and 1500 in English; 1000 in French; it is very damp and hot, so dress accordingly). ■ *0900-1700, US$3.45, free Sun (allow about 45 mins for the 300-m descent), closed Sat and Sun afternoons. The caretaker turns lights on and off, answers questions in Spanish, every hour on the hour, minimum six, maximum 20 persons.* Bus Chichén Itzá or Pisté-Balankanché hourly at a quarter past, US$0.50, taxi US$15.

Grutas de Balankanché

An interesting detour off the Chichén-Mérida highway is to turn in the direction of Yaxcaba at Libre Unión, then after 3 km turn on to a dirt road, singposted to **Xtojil**, a beautiful *cenote* with a Maya platform, which has well-preserved carvings and paintings.

The 3 hotels closest to the ruins are **AL** *Hacienda Chichén*. Once owned by Edward Thompson with charming bungalows. **AL** *Mayaland Hotel*. Including breakfast and dinner, pool, but sometimes no water in it, no a/c, just noisy ceiling fans, but good service and friendly (in USA T800-4518891/305-3419173). **AL** *Villas Arqueológicas*, T985-62830, Apdo Postal 495, Mérida. Pool, tennis, restaurant (expensive and poor). Both are on the other side of the fenced-off ruins from the bus stop; you cannot walk through ruins, either walk all the way round, or take taxi (US$1-1.50). Other hotels are not so close to the ruins: **A** *La Palapa Chichén*. With breakfast and dinner, a few kilometres from the ruins, excellent restaurant, modern, park with animals. **A** *Hotel Misión Chichén Itzá*, Pisté. A/c, pool (disappointing, gloomy, poor restaurant), not easily seen from the road; it has staircases with plumed serpents and a big statue facing north on top. **B** *Sunset Club*, 10 mins walk from Pisté village, 30 mins from Chichén Itzá. Takes credit cards, room with bath, hot water, fan, TV, swimming pool. Recommended. **B-C** *Stardust Posada Annex*, Pisté, about 2 km before the ruins if coming from Mérida

Sleeping
All are expensive for what they offer

(taxi to ruins US$2.50). Good value, especially if you don't want TV or a/c (fans available), swimming pool, popular with German tour groups, average restaurant.

C *Pirámide Inn*, 1½ km from ruins, at the Chichén end of Pisté. Clean but run-down, with good food, swimming pool, friendly English-speaking owner, Trailer Park and camping US$6.50 for 2 plus car in front of hotel, US$4.50 in campground (owned by *Stardust*, see below, but still check in at hotel reception, cold showers). **D** *Dolores Alba*. Small hotel (same family as in Mérida, where you can make advance reservations, advisable in view of long walk from ruins), 2½ km on the road to Puerto Juárez (bus passes it), in need of renovation, with shower and fan, clean, has swimming pool and serves good, expensive meals, English spoken, RVs can park in front for US$5, with use of toilets, shower and pool, free transport to the ruins (be careful if walking along the road from the ruins after dark, there are many trucks speeding by, carry a flashlight/torch).

D *Maya Inn*, on main road to Chichén Itzá. With bath, **E** without, also hammock space, clean. **D** *Posada Chac Mool*. Fan, bath, clean, laundry service, safe parking, a bit noisy. Recommended. **D** *Posada Olalde*, 100m from main road at end of Calle 6. Quiet. **D** *Posada Novelo*, near *Pirámide Inn*. Run by José Novelo who speaks English, guest access to pool and restaurant at nearby *Stardust Inn*. **D** *Posada el Paso*, on main road into village from Chichén. With shower, good value, very friendly, safe parking, nice restaurant. A lot of traffic passes through at night, try to get a room at the back.

There is a small pyramid in the village opposite *Hotel Misión Chichén Itzá*; close by is a huge plumed serpent, part coloured, almost forming a circle at least 20m long. Unfortunately the serpent has been largely destroyed to make way for the *Posada Chac Mool*. There is no sign or public path, climb over gate into scrubland, the serpent will be to right, pyramid to left. The whole construction is an unabashedly modern folly made 25 years ago by a local stone-mason who used to work on the archaeological expeditions.

Eating Mostly poor and overpriced in Chichén itself (cafés inside the ruins are cheaper than the restaurant at the entrance to the ruins, but they are still expensive). *Hotel Restaurant Carrousel* (rooms **D**); *Las Redes*; *Nicte-Ha*, opposite, is cheaper and has chocolate milk shakes; *Fiesta* in Pisté, Calle Principal. Yucatecan specialities, touristy but good. Next door is a place serving good *comida corrida* for US$5.35; *Poxil*, Mérida end of town, for breakfast; *El Paso* in Pisté. Good meals but doesn't open for breakfast as early as it claims. *Sayil* in Pisté. Has good *pollo pibil* for US$2.60. Restaurants in Pisté close 2100-2200.

Shopping Hammocks are sold by *Mario Díaz* (a most interesting character), excellent quality, huge, at his house 500m up the road forking to the left at the centre of the village. 35 km from Chichén is Ebtún, on the road to Valladolid, a sign says 'Hammock sales and repairs'. It is actually a small prison which turns out 1st class cotton or nylon hammocks; haggle with wardens and prisoners; there are no real bargains, but good quality. Silver is sold at orange-coloured shops opposite *Posada Novelo* in Pisté.

Transport **Road** If driving from Mérida, follow Calle 63 (off the Plaza) out as far as the dirt section, where you turn left, then right and right again at the main road, follow until hypermarket on left and make a left turn at the sign for Chichén Itzá. Hitchhiking to Mérida is usually no problem.

Buses Chichén Itzá is easily reached (less so during holiday periods) from Mérida by (ADO) 2nd class, 2½ hrs, US$3 from 0500, bus station on Calle 71 between 64 and 66. 1st class bus, US$4.50. Return tickets from the gift shop near entrance to site. Buses drop off and pick up passengers until 1700 at the top of the coach park opposite entrance to *artesanía* market (thereafter take a taxi to Pisté or *colectivo* to Valladolid for buses). Monday am 2nd class buses may be full with workers from Mérida returning to Cancún. Many buses a day between 0430 and 2300 go to **Cancún** and **Puerto Juárez**, US$6.20. The 1st bus from Pisté to Puerto Juárez is at 0730, 3 hrs. ADO bus office in Pisté is between *Stardust* and *Pirámide Inn*. Budget travellers going on from Mérida to Isla Mujeres or Cozumel should visit Chichén from Valladolid (see below), although if you plan to go through in a day you can store luggage at the visitors' centre. Buses from **Valladolid** go every hour to the site, the 0715 bus reaches the ruins at 0800 when they open, and you can return by standing on the main road 1 km from the entrance to the ruins and flagging down any bus going straight through. *Colectivo* entrance-Valladolid, US$1.65. Bus Pisté-Valladolid US$1.50; Pisté-**Tulum**, 1 bus only at 1300, US$4. Chichén Itzá-Tulum, bus at 1330 and 1445, 4 hrs, very crowded.

Banks Bank in Pisté, *Banamex*, open 0900-1300. **Communications** Telephone: international calls may be placed from *Teléfonos de México*, opposite *Hotel Xaybe*. — **Directory**

Valladolid

Situated roughly half way between Mérida and Cancún, Valladolid is a pleasant little town, until now untouched by tourism. Its proximity to the famous ruins of Chichén Itzá, however, means that Valladolid has been earmarked for extensive development by the Mexican government. Construction is under way of a new international airport at Kaná, in the deserted land near Chichén Itzá, which will open Valladolid's doors to a much larger influx of travellers than the trickle it receives at the moment, and two new luxury hotels are being built on the outskirts of the town. This doesn't mean that the area will receive a Cancún-like transformation, because the airport will be for those travellers in search of the historic-cultural aspects of this area, as opposed to the golden beaches and nightclubs of Quintana Roo.

Phone code: 985
Colour map 4, grid A6
Population: 19,300

Yucatán Peninsula

Valladolid is set around a large plaza, flanked by the imposing Franciscan cathedral. Most of the hotels are clustered around the centre, as well as numerous restaurants catering for all budgets, favouring the lower end. There is a slightly medieval feel to the city, with some of the streets tapering off into mud tracks. The Vallisoletanos, as they are known, are friendlier than their Meridano neighbours, and Valladolid's location makes it an ideal place to settle for a few days, while exploring the ruins of Chichén Itzá, the fishing village of Río Lagartos on the north coast, and the two beautiful *cenotes* in the area, one of which is right in the town itself, on Calle 36 y 39.

The **tourist office**, on the southeast corner of the plaza, is not very helpful but they give a useful map. Much more helpful information from **Antonio 'Negro' Aguilar**, on Calle 44 No 195. Something of a local celebrity, he was a baseball champion in the 50s and 60s, playing for the Leones de Yucatán and the Washington Senators. He was also the Chief of Police in Valladolid for three years. Now semi-retired, he runs a shop selling sports equipment, rents bicycles and rents very cheap accommodation (see below). He is glad to offer information on any of the tourist attractions in the area; if cycling around, he will personally draw you a map of the best route you should take. Antonio also does tours in a minivan to the ruins at Ek-Balam, minimum four people, US$3 per person.

Cenote Zací is an artificially lit *cenote* where you can swim, except when it is occasionally prohibited due to algae in the water. There is a thatched-roof restaurant and lighted promenades. The *cenote* is right in town, on Calle 36 — **Sights**

between Calle 37 and 39. ■ *0800-1800, US$2, half price for children.* There is a small town **museum** on Calle 41, housed in Santa Ana church, with displays showing the history of rural Yucatán and some exhibits from recent excavations at the ruins of *Ek-Balam.* ■ *Free.*

Seven kilometres from Valladolid is the beautiful **Cenote X-Kekén** at Dzitnup, the name by which it is more commonly known. It is stunningly lit with electric lights, the only natural light source being a tiny hole in the cavernous ceiling dripping with stalagtites. Swimming is excellent, the water is cool, clean and refreshing, and harmless bats zip around overhead. Exploratory walks can also be made through the many tunnels leading off the *cenote,* for which you will need a torch. ■ *0800-1800, entry US$1.20. Colectivos* leave hourly from in front of Hotel María Guadalupe, US$1, they return until 1800, after which you will have to get a taxi back to Valladolid, US$4. Alternatively, hire a bicycle from Antonio Aguilar (see above) and cycle there, 25 minutes. Antonio will explain the best route before you set off.

Sleeping   **B** *Mesón del Marqués*, north side of Plaza Principal, T91985, F622680. Amex, only credit card, cash payment in advance, a/c, with bath, on square, with good but pricey restaurant and shop (helpful for information), cable TV, swimming pool, excellent value. Recommended. **C** *María de la Luz*, Calle 42 No 193-C, Plaza Principal, T62071. Takes Visa, good, a/c, swimming pool (non-residents, US$0.50), excellent restaurant, buffet breakfast US$3.50, *comida corrida* US$5, closes at 2230.

   D *Posada Osorio*, Calle 40 between 35 and 33. Clean, quiet. **D** *San Clemente*, Calle 42 No 206, T62208. With a/c, spacious, quiet, clean, has car park, TV, small swimming

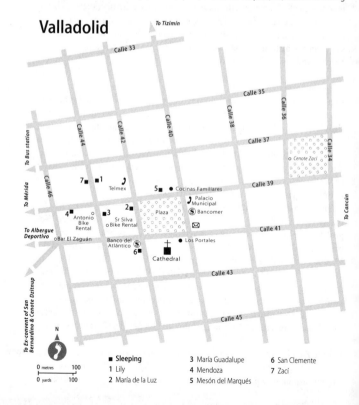

Valladolid

pool, restaurant, opposite cathedral, in centre of town. Recommended. **D** *Zací*, Calle 44 No 191. A/c, cheaper with fan, TV, good pool with café beside it, clean, quiet. **D** *María Guadalupe*, Calle 44 No 198, T62068. Quiet, fan, clean, good value, hot water, washing facilities, parking. Recommended. **D-E** *Maya*, Calle 41 No 231, between 48 and 50, T62069. Fan or a/c, clean, quiet, good value, laundry service, also runs good restaurant 2 doors away. **E** *Hotel Mendoza*, Calle 39 No 294 between Calle 44 and 46. Recommended. **E** *Lily*, Calle 44. Hot shower, cheaper with shared bath, fan, basic, not too clean, good location, laundry facilities, motorcycle parking US$3, friendly. **F** *Antonio 'Negro' Aguilar* rents rooms for 2, 3 or 4 people. The best budget deal in the town, clean, spacious rooms on a quiet street, garden, volleyball/basketball court, small pool. The rooms are on Calle 41 No 225, but you need to book them at Aguilar's shop on Calle 44 No 195, T62125. If the shop is closed, knock on the door of the house next door on the right of the shop. **F** per person *Sr Silva* (see **Transport**: bike hire), rents large, airy rooms with fan and bathroom. Recommended.

Eating
Los Portales, on southeast corner of main square. Very good and cheap. *La Sirenita*, Calle 41 No 168-A, a few blocks east of main square. Highly recommended for seafood, popular, only open to 1800, closed Sun. Next to *Hotel Lily* are *Panadería La Central* and *Taquería La Principal*. Marginally cheaper food at the *Cocinas Familiares*, Yucatecan food, pizzas, burgers, etc, northeast corner of Plaza Principal, next to *Mesón del Marqués*, try the *Janet*, half way back. Cheap meals in the market, Calle 37, 2 blocks east of the Cenote Zací. There is a well-stocked supermarket on the road between the centre and bus station. **Cafés** Nice café on the corner of Calle 40 and 39, off the plaza. Open till late but doesn't serve alcohol. **Bars** *El Zaguán*, Calle 41 and 41A, 2 blocks west of the Plaza. One of the few places serving alcohol without a meal, nice setting in plant-filled courtyard, music, open until about 0300.

Shopping
Quality cheap leather goods from *Mercado de Artesanías*, Calle 39 between 42 and 44.

Transport
Bike hire Antonio Aguilar (see page 333) rents bicycles, US$0.50 per hour, US$3 for the whole day (8 hrs).

Buses The main bus terminal is on Calle 37 and Calle 54. **Mérida**, 9 buses a day with various companies, 2½ hrs, US$6-7. **Cancún** *Express Oriente*, 9 a day, 2 hrs, US$6, *Avante* 3 a day, US$6. **Chichén Itzá**, 10 a day, 45 mins, US$1.20. **Tizimín** (for Río Lagartos), 10 a day, 2 hrs, US$1.50 (for some strange reason it costs the same for a return ticket to Tizimín, make sure you ask for it if planning to return to Valladolid). **Izamal** 2 a day, 2 hrs, US$2.60. **Playa del Carmen** 9 a day, 4 hrs, US$6.

Directory
Banks *Bancomer* on east side of square, changes TCs between 0900 and 1330. *Banco del Atlántico*, corner of Calle 41 and 42, quick service for TCs, from 1000. *Banco del Sureste* has a branch in the shopping centre on Calle 39, 5 blocks west from the Plaza. Open Mon-Fri 0900-2100, Sat and Sun 0900-1400, 1700-1930. **Communications** Internet *Internet café* on corner of Calle 46 and 37, open Mon-Sat 1000-2100. Another, *Oriente*, on Calle 39 next to huge supermarket. **Post Office:** on east side of Plaza, 0800-1500 (does not accept parcels for abroad). **Telephones:** Telmex phone office on Calle 42, just north of square; expensive Computel offices at bus station and next to *Hotel San Clemente*; Ladatel phonecards can be bought from *farmacias* for use in phone booths. **Laundry** *Teresita*, Calle 33 between 40 and 42, US$6 for 5½ kg.

North of Valladolid

Ek-Balam
Twenty-five kilometres north of Valladolid are the recently opened Maya ruins of Ek-Balam meaning 'Black Jaguar'. The ruins contain an impressive series of temples, sacrificial altars and residential buildings grouped around a large central plaza. The main temple, known as 'The Tower', is an immaculate

seven-tiered staircase leading up to a flattened area with the remains of a temple. The views are stunning, and because they are not on the tourist trail, these ruins can be viewed at leisure, without the presence of hordes of tour groups from Cancún. ■ *0800-1700, US$2, free on Sun.* To get there by car, take Route 295 north out of Valladolid. Just after the village of Temozón, take the turning on the right for Santa Rita. The ruins are some 5 km further on. A recommended way for those without a car is to hire a bike, take it on the roof of a *colectivo* leaving for Temozón from outside the Hotel María Guadalupe, and ask to be dropped off at the turning for Ek-Balam. From there, cycle the remaining 12 km to the ruins. There are also minivans to Ek-Balam run by Antonio Aguilar (see page 333).

Tizimín Tizimín is a dirty, scruffy little town *en route* for Río Lagartos, where you will have to change buses. If stuck, there are several cheap *posadas* and restaurants, but with frequent buses to Río Lagartos, there should be no need to stay the night here.

Sleeping and eating There are several hotels, eg **D** *San Jorge*, on main plaza. A/c, good value. **D** *San Carlos*, 2 blocks from main square. With bath, fan, clean, good. **D** *Tizimín*, on main square. **D** *Posada* next to church. There is a good but expensive restaurant, *Tres Reyes*, also *Los Portales*, on main square, and others, including many serving cheap *menú del día* around the Plaza.

Entertainment On the edge of town is a vast pink disco, popular with Meridanos.

Transport There are 2 terminals side by side. If coming from Valladolid *en route* to Río Lagartos, you will need to walk to the other terminal. Río Lagartos, 7 per day, 1½ hrs, US$2. Valladolid, 10 per day, 1 hr, US$1.50. Mérida, several daily, 4 hrs, US$4. There are also buses to Cancún, Felipe Carrillo Puerto and Chetumal.

Communications Telephone: long-distance phone at Calle 50 No 410, just off Plaza.

Río Lagartos
Colour map 4, grid A5
Population: 3,000

An attractive little fishing village on the north coast of Yucatán state, whose main attraction is the massive biosphere reserve containing thousands of pink flamingoes, as well as 25 other species of birds. The people of Río Lagartos are extremely friendly and very welcoming to tourists, who are few and far between, due to the distances involved in getting there. The only route is on the paved road from Valladolid; access from Cancún is by boat only, a journey mainly made by tradesmen ferrying fish to the resort. Development in Río Lagartos, however, is on the horizon. The former *posada* is being refurbished as an expensive hotel, and the so-far unspoilt *malecón* could easily be the home to luxury yachts in the not-too-distant future.

Excursions Boat trips to see the flamingo reserve can be easily arranged by walking down to the harbour and taking your pick from the many offers you'll receive from boatmen. You will get a longer trip with less people, due to the decreased weight in the boat. As well as flamingoes, there are 25 other species of bird, some very rare, in the 68-km reserve. Make sure your boatman takes you to the larger colony of flamingoes near **Las Coloradas** (15 km), recognisable by a large salt mound on the horizon, rather than the smaller groups of birds along the river. A good boatman will cut the engine as you near the flamingoes, and propel the boat using a stick to avoid frightening the birds. Early morning boat trips can be arranged in Río Lagartos to see the flamingoes. ■ *US$35, in 8-9 seater, 2½-4 hours, cheaper in five-seater, fix the price before embarking; in* *mid-week few people go so there is no chance of negotiating, but boat owners are more flexible on where they go; at weekends it is very busy, so it may be easier to get a party together and reduce costs.* There are often only a few pairs of birds feeding in the lagoons east of Las Coloradas; ask for Adriano who is a good guide and bird expert, or for Manuel at the Río Lagartos bus stop. Make sure you are taken to the furthest breeding grounds, to see most flamingoes, and pelicans. Another recommended boatman is Edgardo, in the doctor's house next to the bus station. He has a boat with shade for up to six people, and takes you well into the main colony, with frequent stops to observe the flamingoes and take photographs. If there are only two people in the boat, he will take you to the beach opposite the village on the way back, where there is good swimming. A trip to the beach from the village will cost US$5 return. The boatmen either wait for you, or come and pick you up whenever you want. There is also a road around the main congregating area. Check before going whether the flamingoes are there, they usually nest here during May-June and stay through July-August. (Salt mining is disturbing their habitat). There is not a lot else here, certainly no accommodation, but if you are stuck for food, eat inexpensively at the *Casino* (ask locals).

Fifteen minutes walk east from the Río Lagartos harbour is an *ojo de agua*, a pool of sulphurous water for bathing, supplied by an underground *cenote*. The waters are supposed to have curative properties – locals say it is better than Viagra.

Buses run from Río Lagartos to **San Felipe** (13 km), where you can bathe in the sea; access to the beach here, too, is by boat only; there is basic accommodation in the old cinema, **F**, ask in the shop *Floresita*; also houses for rent; Miguel arranges boat trips to the beach (US$3), he lives next door to the old cinema; good cheap seafood at *El Payaso* restaurant; on the waterfront is *La Playa* restaurant, recommended; on a small island with ruins of a Maya pyramid, beware of rattlesnakes.

Sleeping and eating The *Hotel Nefertiti* will soon be renamed and upgraded to the **B-C** range. There are 3 **E** rooms for rent at the house of Tere and Miguel, near the harbour (ask at the bus terminal). Very nicely furnished, double and triple rooms, 1 with an extra hammock, sea views. Recommended. For a fishing village, seafood is not spectacular, as most of the good fish is sold to restaurants in Mérida and Cancún. *Isla Contoy*, Calle 19 No 134, average seafood, not cheap for the quality. *Los Negritos*, off the Plaza, moderately priced seafood. There are a couple of smaller restaurants around the Plaza, and a grocery shop, useful for stocking up on supplies for the boat trip to see the flamingoes, which usually departs around 0600 in the morning.

Festivals 12 Dec, Virgen de María de la Guadalupe. The whole village converges on the chapel built in 1976 on the site of a vision of the Virgin Mary by a local non-believer, who suddenly died, along with his dog, shortly after receiving the vision. **17 Jul** there is a big local *fiesta*, with music, food and dancing in the Plaza.

Transport There are frequent buses from Tizimín (see above), and it is possible to get to Río Lagartos and back in a day from Valladolid, if you leave on the 0630 or 0730 bus (taxi Tizimín-Río Lagartos US$25, driver may negotiate) and last bus back from Río Lagartos at 1730.

El Cuyo

The road goes east along the coast on to El Cuyo, rough and sandy, but passable. El Cuyo has a shark-fishing harbour. Fishermen cannot sell (co-op) but can barter fish. Fry your shark steak with garlic, onions and lime juice. El Cuyo is a very quiet, friendly place with a beach where swimming is safe (there is less

Yucatán Peninsula

seaweed in the water the further from town you go towards the Caribbean). *La Conchita* restaurant (good-value meals) has *cabañas* with bath, double bed and hammock (**D**). Opposite *La Conchita* bread is sold after 1700. From Tizimín there are *combis* (US$2.70, 1½ hours) and buses (slower, four times a day) to El Cuyo, or take a *combi* to Colonia and hitch from there.

Holbox Island
Colour map 4, grid A6

The beach is at the opposite end of the island to the ferry, 10 minutes walk

Also north of Valladolid, turning off the road to Puerto Juárez after Nuevo Xcan (see page 373), is Holbox Island. Buses to **Chiquilá** for boats, three times a day, also direct from Tizimín at 1130, connecting with the ferry, US$2.20. The ferry leaves for Holbox 0600 and 1430, one hour, US$1, returning to Chiquilá at 0500 and 1300. A bus to Mérida connects with the 0500 ferry. If you miss the ferry a fisherman will probably take you (for about US$14). You can leave your car in the care of the harbour master for a small charge; his house is east of the dock. Take water with you if possible. During 'El Norte' season, the water is turbid and the beach is littered with seaweed.

Sleeping *Delfín Palapas*, on the beach, T848603. 'Expensive but nice'. **E** *Hotel Holbox* at dock. Clean, quiet, cold water, friendly. House with 3 doors, ½ block from plaza, rooms, some beds, mostly for hammocks, very basic, very cheap, outdoor toilet, no shower, noisy, meals available which are recommended; rooms at pink house off plaza, **D**, clean, with bath. *Cabañas*, **D**, usually occupied; take blankets and hammock (ask at fishermen's houses where you can put up), and lots of mosquito repellent. **Camping** Best camping on beach east of village (north side of island).

Eating *Lonchería*, on Plaza. Restaurant on main road open for dinner. All bars close 1900. Bakery with fresh bread daily, good. Fish is generally expensive.

Entertainment **Disco**: Opens 2230, admission US$2.75.

There are five more uninhabited islands beyond Holbox. Beware of sharks and barracuda, though very few nasty occurrences have been reported. Off the rough and mostly unpopulated bulge of the Yucatán coastline are several islands, once notorious for contraband. Beware of mosquitoes in the area.

Quintana Roo

Known worldwide as Mexico's most famous resort, Cancún is not the only attraction the state of Quintana Roo has to offer. There are several other luxury resorts and, in contrast to Cancún, Isla Mujeres provides a much more laid-back atmosphere for the weary traveller. Diving is famous in Cozumel, and other watersports can be enjoyed at almost any point along the coastlines of Quintana Roo, which also has its fair share of interesting archaeological sites. See the Temple of the Diving God at sunset in Tulum and visit the 32 sites on Cozumel Island. There is also Xcaret, Cobá and Xpujil to be explored. Those interested in wildlife will enjoy the sanctuary on Isla Contoy or the Sian Ka'an Biosphere Reserve.

Cancún

In 1970, when Cancún was discovered by the Mexican tourist board, it was an inaccessible strip of barren land with beautiful beaches; the only road went straight past Cancún to Puerto Juárez for the ferry to Isla Mujeres, which had been a national tourist destination since the 1950s. Massive international investment and government sponsorship saw the luxury resort of Cancún completed within 25 years. The 25-km hotel zone, set on a narrow strip of land in the shape of a number seven alongside the coast, is an ultra-modern American-style boulevard, with five-star hotels, high-tech nightclubs, high-class shopping malls, and branches of Macdonalds, Burger King and Planet Hollywood.

Phone code: *98*
Colour map 4, grid A6
Population: *500,000*

Yucatán Peninsula

Two and a half million visitors arrive in Cancún every year, staying in a total of 24,000 rooms in the hotel zone alone, a figure expected to rise to 37,000 in the next few years. The prices are geared towards the wealthy US package tourist, and the atmosphere at night is not unlike Las Vegas, but without the casinos or the glamour. Every hotel has its own strip of beach; the beaches are supposedly public, but locals complain of being refused entry to some of them if not lodged in the hotel.

During July and August, peak tourist season for European travellers, the rains can be very heavy during the afternoon. This is true for the whole of the Yucatán Peninsula

Ins and outs

Cancún airport is 16 km south of the city. There are 2 terminals, but only the main one is used for international departures and arrivals. *Colectivo* taxi to the Hotel Zone or the centre costs US$9; pay at the kiosk outside airport. Drivers go via the Hotel Zone, but must take you to whichever part of the city centre you want. If going to the centre, make sure you know the name and address of your hotel before you get in the taxi, or the driver will offer to take you to a budget hotel of his own choice. Buses go to the centre via Av Tulum every half hour from the airport. Taxi to the airport from the centre US$10. Buses go from several stops, marked 'Aeropuerto', along Av Tulum, every ½ hour, US$0.50. There is a tourist information kiosk in the airport, and a *casa de cambio* with poor rates.

Getting there

Ruta 1 and Ruta 2 buses go from the centre to the Hotel Zone, US$0.50; Ruta 1 runs 24 hrs and goes via Av Tulum; Ruta 2 runs 0500-0330 and goes via Av Cobá to the bus

Getting around

terminal. Buses to the hotel zone can be caught from many stops along Av Tulum. Buses to Puerto Juárez leave from outside Cinema Royal, across Av Tulum from the bus terminal, US$0.50. To get around in the centre, get on a bus at Plaza 2000 and ask the driver if he's going to Mercado 28; those buses go along Av Yaxchilán; all others go to the hotel zone. Taxis are cheap and abundant in Cancún. Flat rate for anywhere within the centre is US$1-1.50; hotel zone from centre US$3; Puerto Juárez US$3. Many taxis stop at El Crucero, the junction of Av Tulum and Av López Portillo outside Plaza 2000, but there are often queues.

Cancún City is a world apart from the hotel zone. It evolved from temporary shacks housing the thousands of builders working on the hotel zone, and is now a massive city with very little character. Architecture has not had a role to play in its geography; there is no definite centre, unlike most Mexican cities, in fact visitors may feel as if they are always on the outskirts, groping their way

Cancún environs

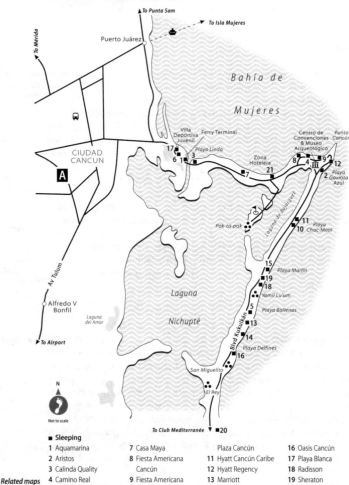

N

Not to scale

■ **Sleeping**

1 Aquamarina	7 Casa Maya	Plaza Cancún	16 Oasis Cancún
2 Aristos	8 Fiesta Americana	11 Hyatt Cancún Caribe	17 Playa Blanca
3 Calinda Quality	Cancún	12 Hyatt Regency	18 Radisson
4 Camino Real	9 Fiesta Americana	13 Marriott	19 Sheraton
5 Cancún Palace	Coral Beach	14 Meliá Cancún	20 Solymar
6 Carrousel	10 Fiesta Americana	15 Meliá Turquesa	21 Stouffer Presidente

Related maps
A Cancún centre,
page 343

towards a non-existent zócalo. Hastily cobbled together over the last 25 years, the extent of town planning has merely been to name the broad avenues and narrow streets as they have appeared over the years. The main avenue is Tulum, formerly the highway running through the city when it was first conceived. It is now the location of the handicraft market, the main shops, banks and the tourist office. There are also restaurants, but the better ones are along Av Yaxchilán, which is also the main centre for nightlife.

The cheaper end of the city, and a good area for budget travellers to base themselves, is around the junction of Av Tulum and Av López Portillo, known locally as El Crucero. The rest of the city is fairly expensive, but not as much as the hotel zone. The city is laid out in *supermanzanas* (SM), the blocks of streets between avenues, with smaller *manzanas* (M), or blocks, within them. Often the address you are given is, for example, SM24, M6, L3. L stands for *lote*, and is the precise number of the building within its *manzana*. This can lead to confusion when walking about, as the streets also have names, often not mentioned in the addresses. Look closely at street signs and you will see the SM and the M numbers. Taxi drivers generally respond better to addresses based on the *manzana* system. More confusion arises from the fact that most side streets are named in pairs; they rejoin the main avenue after forming a U shape. If you can't find what you're looking for, walk to the end of the street and find the continuation (right or left) leading back to the main avenue. The **tourist office** is at Av Tulum 26, in a building which also houses local government offices. Typically for Quintana Roo state, it is not very helpful; most tourists seem to get palmed off with a glossy pocket guide to Cancún full of adverts for expensive restaurants. A slightly better map can be found in *Cancún Tips*, a free magazine available in most hotels.

Essentials

Hotels in the hotel zone cost upwards of US$50, mostly much more, and are best arranged as part of a package holiday. The centre (or Downtown, as it is known locally) has many cheaper options, but prices are still higher than other parts of the Yucatán Peninsula. **NB** El Crucero, location of some of the budget hotels, is said by locals to be safe during the day, but unsafe at night.

Sleeping
■ *on map*
Price codes:
see inside front cover

Hotels in the hotel zone The following have all the features of a luxury hotel, including extensive watersports and activities; distance from the centre is marked in kilometres.

Some of these hotels have special offers during Jul and Aug, listed in Riviera Maya Hotels Guide, available free at the airport

LL Range: *Caesar Park Cancún*, Km 17, T818000. *Camino Real*, Km 9, T830100. *Cancún Palace*, Km 15, T850533. *Sheraton Cancún Resort and Towers*, Km 10.5, PO Box 834, Cancún, T831988, F850202. *Casa Maya*, Km 5.5, T830555. *Club Mediterranée*, Km 21.5, T852409. *Hyatt Cancún Caribe*, Km 11, T830044. *Hyatt Regency*, Km 9, T830966. *Meliá Cancún*, Km 15, T851114. *Meliá Turquesa*, Km 12, T832544. *The Ritz Carlton*, Km 14, T850808. **L Range**: *Blue Bay Village*, Km 3.5, T830344. *Carrousel*, Km 4.3, T830513. *Holiday Inn Express*, Km 7.5, T832200. *Mexhotel Resort*, Km 19.5, T850361. *Solymar*, Km 19, T851811. *Pirámides Cancún*, Km 12.5, T851333. *Stouffer Presidente*, Km 8, T830200, F832515. *Miramar Misión Park Plaza*, Km 20.5, T831755, F831136. *Playa Blanca*, Km 3.5, T830071, F830904. Resort facilities. *Krystal*, Km 3.5, T831133, F831790. *Oasis Cancún*, Km 16.5, T850867, F850131. Huge hotel but well separated to give intimate feel, nice pool, helpful staff. Slightly less expensive: *Aristos*, T830011, F830078. *Calinda Quality Cancún Beach*, T830800, F831857, and *Calinda Viva*, same phone, F832087. *Club Lagoon Marina*, T831101, F831326. Also represented are 3 hotels in the *Fiesta Americana* chain, *Days Inn*, *Marriott*, *Radisson* (2). There are many more hotels, suites and villas. At the southern end of the island is the *Club Méditerranée* with its customary facilities T842409, F842090. **AL Range**: *Carisa y Palma*, Km 9.5, T5830211. *Aquamarina*, Km 4.5, T831344, F831751. *Cancún Clipper Club*, Km 9, T834001, F831731. *Blue Lagoon*, Km 7.8, T/F 831215. *Kin-Ha*, Km 8, T832377, F832147.

Hotels in the centre   Many hotels, especially the budget ones, tend to be full during Jul. It is best to get to them as early as possible in the morning, or try to make a reservation if planning to return to Cancún after a trip to the interior or Isla Mujeres.

AL *Margaritas*, Yaxchilán y Jazmines, T/F849333. Modern, efficient service. **AL** *Best Western*, Av Tulum y Uxmal, lote 19, T841377, F846352, plazache@ cancun.rce.com.mx   Pool, a/c, car rental, airport transfer, restaurant. **AL** *Suites Plaza Sol*, Av Yaxchilán 31, SM22, T/F879293. 24-hr room service, a/c, pool, elegant décor. **A** *Antillano*, Tulum y Claveles 1, T841132, F841878. Pool, cable TV, a/c, boutique, travel agency, laundry, bar. **A** *Bonampak*, Av Bonampak 225, SM4, M9, Lotes 48-51, T/F840280. Travel agency, cable TV, supermarket, restaurant, laundry service, pool, a/c, near hotel zone. **A** *Caribe Internacional*, at the junction of Yaxchilán and Sunyaxchén, T843499, F841993. **A** *El Rey del Caribe*, Av Uxmal esq Náder, SM2A, T842028, F849857, reycarib@cancun.com.mx. A/c, gardens, parking, pool, jacuzzi. **A** *Howard Johnson Kokai*, Av Uxmal 26, SM 2A, T843218, F844335. Cable TV, pool, travel agency, free shuttle to beach, rooftop solarium and jacuzzi, nightclub. **A** *María de Lourdes*, Av Yaxchilán 80, SM22, M14, T844744, F841242. Pool, cable TV, restaurant, bar, laundry. **A** *Mexhotel*, Av Yaxchilán 31, SM22, T843078, F843478. Central, a/c, laundry, restaurant, cable TV.

   B *Batab*, Chichén Itza 52, SM23, T843822, F843821. A/c, cable TV, beach club, restaurant, bar. **B** *Cancún Handall*, Tulum y Jaleb, SM20, T841412. Fan, a/c. **B** *Cancún Rosa*, Margaritas 2, local 10, T842873, F840623. Close to bus terminal. A/c, TV, phone, comfortable rooms. **B** *El Alux*, Av Uxmal 21, T840662, turn left and first right from bus station. A/c with bath, clean, TV, some rooms cheaper, good value. Recommended. **B** *Hacienda*, Sunyaxchén 38-40. A/c, TV. **C** *Coral*, Sunyaxchén 30 (towards post office), T842901. *Cotty*, Av Uxmal 44, T840550, near bus station. A/c, TV, clean. **C** *Hotel Palma*, Palmeras. Huge rooms, clean. Recommended. **C** *Lucy*, Gladiolas 25, between Tulum and Yaxchilán, T844165. A/c, kitchenettes, takes credit cards. **C** *Novotel*, Av Tulum y Azucenas, T842999, F843162, close to bus station. Rooms start at under US$30 with fan, but rise to **B** range with a/c, popular, noisy on Av Tulum side. **C** *Parador*, Av Tulum 26, T841310, F849712, close to bus terminal. Some rooms noisy, inefficient, a/c, TV, phone, pool, restaurant attached, clean. **C** *Rivemar*, Av Tulum 49-51 y Crisantemos, T841708. A/c, phone, TV. **C** *Villa Maya Cancún*, Uxmal 20 y Rubia, T842829, F841762. A/c, pool; *La Francesa* bakery next door. **C** *Villa Rossana*, Av Yaxchilán opposite *Mexhotel*, Lotes 67, 68, 69, T841943. Popular, central and spacious, good location. **C-D** *Jerusalem*, Av Tulum 64, T840506. Cheaper with fan, on busy avenue near bus terminal.

The following budget hotels all come with fan and private bathroom unless otherwise stated: **D** *Azteca*, Av López Portillo. Hot water, good, cheap restaurant next door. **D** *Colonial*, Tulipanes 22 y Av Tulum, T841535. A/c, with bath, cheaper with fan, quiet, TV, phone, poor service, not too clean. **D** *Guadalupe*, Av López Portillo, SM65, M2, L6, (NE corner of Crucero) T845740. Quiet, small, clean. **D** *Jardín*, SM64, M14, Lote 20, No 37, T848704. Clean, friendly, a bit noisy. **D** *María Isabel*, Palmera 59, T849015, near bus station and Av Tulum. Fan and a/c, hot water, TV, small and clean, friendly, helpful, will store luggage, avoid rooms backing onto noisy air shaft. **D** *San Carlos*, Cedro 14, T840786, near bus terminal. Cramped, shabby rooms, upper floors better but hot, OK if desperate. **D** *Tankah*, **C** with a/c, TV. Recommended. **D** *Tropical Caribe*, Cedro 10 (2nd turning onto Cedro from bus terminal), T411442. Old building, passing local

Cancún centre

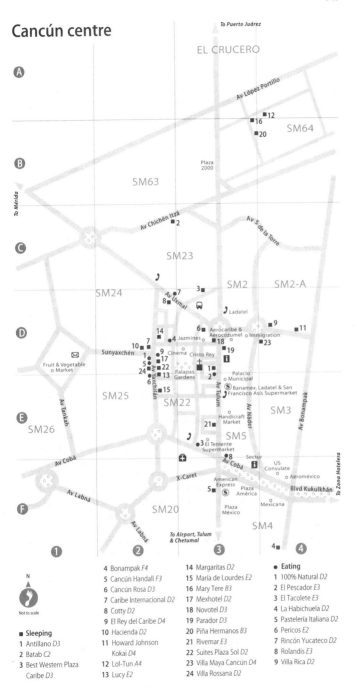

To Puerto Juárez

EL CRUCERO

Av López Portillo

SM64

Plaza
2000

SM63

To Merida

Av Chichén Itzá

Av S de la Torre

SM23

SM24

SM2

SM2-A

Av Uxmal

Ladatel

Aerocaribe &
Aerocozumel

Immigration

Jazmines

Cristo Rey

Sunyaxchén

Cinema

Fruit & Vegetable
Market

Palapas
Gardens

Palacio
Municipal

SM25

SM22

Banamex, Ladatel & San
Francisco Asís Supermarket

Av Tankah

SM26

Handicraft
Market

SM3

SM5

Av Bonampak

El Teniente
Supermarket

Av Cobá

X-Caret

Sectur

US
Consulate

Av Cobá

Aeroméxico

American
Express

Plaza
América

Blvd Kukulkhán

To Zona Hotelera

Av Labná

SM20

Plaza
México

Mexicana

Av Labná

SM4

To Airport, Tulum
& Chetumal

N

Not to scale

■ Sleeping
1 Antillano *D3*
2 Batab *C2*
3 Best Western Plaza
Caribe *D3*

4 Bonampak *F4*
5 Cancún Handall *F3*
6 Cancún Rosa *D3*
7 Caribe Internacional *D2*
8 Cotty *D2*
9 El Rey del Caribe *D4*
10 Hacienda *D2*
11 Howard Johnson
Kokai *D4*
12 Lol-Tun *A4*
13 Lucy *E2*

14 Margaritas *D2*
15 María de Lourdes *E2*
16 Mary Tere *B3*
17 Mexhotel *D2*
18 Novotel *D3*
19 Parador *D3*
20 Piña Hermanos *B3*
21 Rivemar *E3*
22 Suites Plaza Sol *D2*
23 Villa Maya Cancún *D4*
24 Villa Rossana *D2*

● Eating
1 100% Natural *D2*
2 El Pescador *E3*
3 El Tacolete *E3*
4 La Habichuela *D2*
5 Pastelería Italiana *D2*
6 Pericos *E2*
7 Rincón Yucateco *D2*
8 Rolandis *E3*
9 Villa Rica *D2*

trade, OK. **D** per person *De Valle*, Av Uxmal (near Av Chichén Itzá). Noisy club next door but clean, OK. **D** *Uxmal*, Av Uxmal 111, T842266. Fan, hot water, quiet, not too clean.

The following 4 hotels are all in a *barrio* near the Crucero. Walk to Plaza 2000, 500m north of the bus terminal on Av Tulum; directly opposite is Calle 10, which leads into Supermanzana 64, where there are also cheap restaurants (if going by taxi, ask for 'Supermanzana 64'). **D** *Alda*, next door to *Piña Hermanos*. Seedy, poky, no sign, OK as last resort. **D** *Lol-Tun*, SM64, M12, L21, T843205. A bit shabby, noisy, OK, good service. *Mary Tere*, SM64, M6, L1, 2, 3, T840496. Large, chaotic service, busy, OK. **D** *Piña Hermanos*, Calle 7 No 35, SM64, M6, L14, T842150. The best budget deal in Cancún, very clean, nice decor, restaurant, friendly staff. Highly recommended.

Camping Not permitted in Cancún town except at the Villa Deportiva youth hostel. There is a trailer park, *Rainbow*, just south of the airport. *El Meco Loco*, campground, 2 km north of passenger ferry to Isla Mujeres. Full hook-ups for RVs, good showers, small store, access to small beach, buses into town. **Youth hostel E** *Villa Deportiva Juvenil*, is at Km 3.2 Blvd Kukulkán, T831337, on the beach, 5 mins walk from the bridge towards Cancún town, next to *Club Verano Beat*. Dormitory-style, price per person, US$10 deposit, 10% discount with membership card, 8 people per room, friendly, basic, dirty, plumbing unreliable, sketchy locker facilities, camping US$5.

Eating
● *on map*

The hotel zone is lined with expensive restaurants, with every type of international cuisine imaginable, but with a predominance of Tex-Mex and Italian. Restaurants in the centre are cheaper, and the accent is on local food. Av Yaxchilán has many restaurants in the mid-price range, as well as a few budget *loncherías*; Av Uxmal is slightly cheaper, with more street stalls.

Restaurants in the centre Expensive: *Rolandis*, Av Cobá 12. Italian, also branch on hotel zone at Km 9. *Matilda*, Plaza Las Américas, Av Tulum 260. French bistro style, freshly baked bread. *La Habichuela*, Margaritas 25. Caribbean seafood, tropical garden setting, jazz music. *Pericos*, Av Yaxchilán 71. Themed *Mexican*, staff in fancy dress, lively atmosphere. *El Pescador*, Tulipanes 28. Good seafood but expensive. **Mid-price**: *Villa Rica*, Yaxchilán 35. Veracruz seafood specialities, live band, good service. *Ciao*, Yaxchilán 37, SM22. *Tacos*, pizzas, touristy, live music, garden, happy hour. *100% Natural*, Yaxchilán y Sunyaxchén. Some vegetarian dishes, seafood, healthy breakfasts. *Los Almendros*, Bonampak 60. Good Yucatecan food. *El Tacolote*, Cobá 19. *Tacos*, good variety. *La Placita*, Yaxchilán 12. Good local food, good service. *La Doña*, on Av Yaxchilán between Av Uxmal and Av Sunyaxchén. Good cheap breakfast, and lunch, clean, a/c, friendly. *Rincón Yucateca*, Av Uxmal 24, opposite *Hotel Cotty*. Good Mexican breakfasts, popular. *Pop*, next to *Hotel Parador*. For quicker-type food, good value. *Torta y Torta*, Av Tulum (opposite *McDonalds*). Good juices, cheap. *Bing*, Av Tulum y Uxmal, close to Banpais bank. Best ice cream. *Piemonte Pizzería*, Av Yaxchilán 52. Good food and value, appetizing aperitifs on the house. Recommended. *Las Tejas*, Av Uxmal, just before Calle Laurel. Good food at reasonable prices. On Av Tulum, *Olé Olé*. Good meat, friendly. *Comida Casera*, Av Uxmal opposite bus terminal. Good coffee. *La Chiquita del Caribe*, Av Xel-Há at Mercado 28. Great seafood, good value. Recommended. **Cheap**: the cheapest area for dinner is SM64, opposite Plaza 2000. Popular with locals, especially on Sun when it is hard to get a table, there are 4 or 5 small family-run restaurants serving local specialities. *Comida corrida* for as little as US$2. Mercado 28 (see map) is the best budget option for breakfast or lunch, with many cheap outdoor and indoor *loncherías* serving *comida corrida*, very popular with locals, quick service. *Mr Greek*, Uxmal 40 between Yaxchilán and Tulum. Outdoor stand with authentic Greek food and *tacos*. *Los Huaraches*, on Uxmal opposite

Yaxchilán. Fast food, cheap *empanada* specials after 1300. *Pastelería Italiana*, Yaxchilán, just before turning of Sunyaxchén. Excellent coffee and pastries, friendly. A few other cheap eateries along Yaxchilán, tucked away between the pricey themed restaurants, some open during the day only. *Jaguari*, in the Zona Hotelera. Brazilian, opens 1700, set price, has been recommended.

A night out in the hotel zone will set you back anywhere between US$20 and US$50. There are many nightclubs, most of them branches of US-run chains throughout Mexico. Attendance tends towards 16-21 year-old Americans, who can drink under age here. The clubs all try to outdo each other by offering wild and wacky entertainment; this usually involves drinking and dancing competitions, all with very little connection with Mexico. *Señor Frogs* is one of the most popular, while *La Boom* is said to be the 'craziest'. The only place for a cheap beer is right opposite *Señor Frogs*, where there is a grocery store selling beer which you can drink at the tables outside. They also sell pizzas, and there is a burger stall open from 2300.

    In Cancún City, there are cheaper and more down-to-earth nightclubs, where you might even hear a bit of local music, if you're lucky. Av Yaxchilán has several nightclubs and bars, the most popular with locals being *Bum-Bum*, which has a dress code, and is open till late. *Blue Bar*, next to *Restaurant Villa Rica*, fills up about 11pm, open till very late. Many of the restaurants along Av Yaxchilán will serve a beer without ordering any food.

Bars & nightclubs

Cinemas: the main one is Cine Royal, on Av Tulum near the bus terminal. *Multiplex*, showing mostly Hollywood blockbusters with Spanish subtitles, entry US$2.30. There are a couple of smaller cinemas near the Crucero, one of them, on Calle 10, SM64, shows vintage Mexican gangster films in Spanish. There is also a multiplex cinema in the Zona Hotelera at Plaza Kukulcán.

Entertainment

There are several US-style shopping malls in the Zona Hotelera, the main one being Plaza Kukulcán, with over 200 shops, restaurants, a bowling alley and video games. It is open from 1000-2200, and the prices are high for most things, including souvenirs. The main 'handicraft' market in the centre is on Av Tulum near Plaza Las Américas; it is a huge network of stalls, all selling exactly the same merchandise: silver jewellery from Taxco, ceramic Maya figurines, hammocks, jade chess sets. Prices are hiked up to the limit, so bargain hard: most vendors expect to get half what they originally ask for. The market called Mercado 23 (at the end of Calle Cedro, off Av Tulum) has cheaper souvenirs and less aggressive salesmen, but the quality is shoddy; *guayabera* shirts are available on one of the stalls. The only bookshop in the city is the modestly stocked *Fama*, on Av Tulum, which mostly sells glossy books on the Maya and American thrillers. Several new smoking shops have appeared, cashing in on the craze for Cuban cigars; these are all located on or just off Av Tulum. Cheaper clothes shops than the hotel zone can be found at the north end of Av Tulum, near Plaza 2000. Pricey leather goods, clothes and jewellery can be bought in Plaza 2000 shopping mall.

Shopping

A variety of watersports can be organized on the beaches along the hotel zone, including parasailing, water-skiing, windsurfing and jet-skiing.

Sport

Colors Travel, Av Yaxchilán 7C, SM24, T877929, colors@correoweb.com Very friendly and helpful owner Martha Reyes Sangri; all-inclusive package deals to Río Lagartos and Ek-Balam with guides in various languages; overnight trip by plane to Tikal ruins in Guatemala; flights to Cuba, many other trips, reliable service. *Mayan Destinations*, Cobá 31, Edificio Monaco, SM22, T844308. All the usual destinations, such as Chichén Itzá, Xcaret, Tulum, as well as flights to Cuba. Many others in the centre and at larger hotels. Most hotels on the hotel zone have their own travel agency. *American Express*, Av Tulum 208, esq Agua, SM 4, T845441, F846942.

Tour operators

Transport **Car hire**: *Budget Rent-a-Car* in Cancún has been recommended for good service. A 4-door Nissan Sentra, a/c, can be hired for US$24 per day from *Budget* at the airport, insurance US$15. *Avis*, Plaza Caracol, cheapest but still expensive. There are many car hire agencies, with offices on Av Tulum, in the Zona Hotelera and at the airport; look out for special deals, but check vehicles carefully. Beware of overcharging and read any documents carefully before you sign. Rates vary enormously, from US$40 to US$80 a day for a VW Golf (VW Beetles are cheaper), larger cars and jeeps available. Car parking: do not leave cars parked in side streets; there is a high risk of theft. Use the parking lot on Av Uxmal.

Air Cancún airport (CUN) is 16 km south of the town (very expensive shops and restaurant, exchange facilities, double check your money, especially at busy times, poor rates too, 2 hotel reservation agencies, no rooms under US$45). 2 terminals, Main and South (or 'FBO' building), white shuttle minibuses between them. From Cancún, domestic destinations include Chetumal, Chichén Itzá, Cozumel, Guadalajara, Mérida, Mexico City, Monterrey, Oaxaca, Palenque, Tijuana, Tuxtla Gutiérrez, Veracruz and Villahermosa. International flights: Albany (US Air); Amsterdam (Martinair); Atlanta (AeroMéxico); Barcelona (Iberia); Belize City (Aero Caribe); Buenos Aires (Mexicana, Aerolíneas Argentinas); Charlotte (US Air); Cologne/Bonn (Condor); Dallas (American Airlines, AeroMéxico); Dusseldorf (LTU); Flores, Guatemala (Aero Caribe, Mayan World Airlines, Aviateca); Frankfurt (LTU, Condor); Guatemala City (Aviateca, Mayan World Airlines); Havana (Aero Caribe, Cubana); Houston (Continental, AeroMéxico); Indianapolis (American Trans Air); Lima (Mexicana); London (British Airways); Los Angeles (AeroMéxico, Mexicana, Northwest Airlines); Madrid (Iberia); Memphis (Northwest); Miami (American Airlines, Mexicana, AeroMéxico, Iberia); Munich (Condor); New Orleans (AeroMéxico, Lacsa); New York (AeroMéxico, Continental, US Air); Panama City (LAB); Philadelphia (American Airlines, US Air); Rio de Janeiro (Varig); St Louis, Missouri (TWA); San Antonio (Continental); San Francisco (Mexicana); San José (Lacsa); Santa Cruz, Bolivia (LAB); Santiago (Lan Chile); São Paulo (Varig); Tampa (Northwest); Vienna (Lauda Air); Washington DC (Continental). Many charters from Europe and North America. Reconfirm flights at a travel agent, they charge, but it is easier than phoning.

Buses Cancún bus terminal, at the junction of Av Tulum and Uxmal, is small but very well organized. It is divided into two halves: the west section is for 2nd-class bus services, while the east section handles the 1st-class traffic. Left luggage is found in the 2nd-class section. The bus station is the hub for routes west to Mérida and south to Tulum and Chetumal, open 24 hrs, left luggage US$0.60 for 24 hrs. Many services to **Mérida**, 4 hrs, ranging from *Plus* with TV, a/c, etc, US$20, to 1st class US$14, to 2nd class US$8; all services call at **Valladolid**, US$6.20 1st class, US$5.00 2nd class; to **Chichén Itzá**, many buses, starting at 0630, Expreso de Oriente 1st class to Mérida, US$6.20, 2½ hrs. Expreso de Oriente also has services to **Tizimín** (3 hrs, US$6), Izamal, Cenotillo and Chiquilá. Caribe Express (T74173/4) has a 1330 service to **Campeche** via Mérida, US$38. Caribe Inter 3 times a day to Mérida via Felipe Carrillo Puerto, calling at Polyuc, Peto, Tekax, Oxkutzcab, Ticul, Muná and Umán. To **San Cristóbal**, 3 a day, US$30, 18 hrs. To **Villahermosa**, US$60. Autotransportes del Oriente to **Playa del Carmen** have been recommended, 2nd class, US$2.25. Inter Playa Express every 30 mins to **Puerto Morelos**, US$1, **Playa del Carmen**, US$2.25 and **Xcaret**, US$2.25; 3 times daily to **Puerto Aventuras**, US$2.50, **Akumal**, US$3, **Xel-Há**, US$3.30 and **Tulum**, US$4.25. Other services to Playa del Carmen and Tulum are more expensive, eg 1st class *Caribe Inter* to Playa del Carmen US$3, 2nd class US$2.35, and US$4.75 to Tulum. Last bus to Playa del Carmen 2000, first bus to Tulum 0430. These services are *en route* to **Chetumal** (US$17 luxury, US$13.50 1st class, US$10 2nd, 5 hrs). The 0800 departure for Chetumal arrives for connection to Flores. Several other services to Chetumal, include Caribe Express, deluxe service with a/c.

Ferries and cruises The ferry to Isla Mujeres is much cheaper from Puerto Juárez (see below). The one from Cancún departs from Playa Linda Pier, at the mainland side of the bridge across Canal Nichupté, about 4 km from centre, opposite the *Calinda Quality Cancún Beach*. Playa Linda has shops, agencies for boat trips, a snack bar and Computel. The ferry leaves 9 times a day between 0900 and 1645, US$12.50 return, 20 mins journey. Returns 7 times a day between 0900 and 1700. Trips to Isla Mujeres, with snorkelling, bar, shopping, start at US$27.50, or US$35 with meal. *M/V Aqua II* has all-inclusive day cruises to Isla Mujeres starting from US$44 (sometimes discounts for user of the *Handbook*), T871909. Boat trips: *Nautibus*, a vessel with seats below the waterline, makes trips to the reefs, 1½ hrs, a good way to see fish, Playa Linda dock, T833552. There are a number of other cruises on offer. *Atlantis* submarines offer trips in a 48-passenger vessel to explore natural and man-made reefs off Cancún. For more information contact Robert Theofel on T834963.

Airline offices *Aerocaribe* and *Aerocozumel*, Av Cobá 5, Plaza América SM4, T842000. *AeroMéxico*, Av Cobá 80, SM3, T843571. *American Airlines*, Aeropuerto, T834460. *Aviacsa*, Av Cobá 37, SM4, T874211. *Aviateca*, Av Cobá 5, Plaza América SM4, T874110. *Continental*, Aeropuerto, T860006. *Cubana de Aviación*, Av Yaxchilán 23, T877373. *Iberia*, Aeropuerto, T860243. *Lacsa*, Av Cobá 5, Plaza América SM4, T873101. *Mexicana*, Av Cobá 39, T874444.

Directory

See page 32, for Airline websites

Banks There are 11 Mexican banks along Av Tulum, all in SMs 4 and 5. American Express, for changing their own TCs at better rates than anywhere else, is on Av Tulum, just south of Av Cobá. Many *casas de cambio* in the centre, mainly around the bus terminal and along Av Tulum. *Casas de cambio* in the hotel zone give slightly lower rates for TCs than those in the centre.

Communications Internet: *Cyberbar*, Av Yaxchilán 23, US$4 per hour, open daily 1000-0500; also branch on hotel zone opposite *Hotel Royal Mayan*, US$9 per hour, open 1100-2300. *Cancún*

Yucatán Peninsula

Internet, entrance to Mercado 28, US$3.50 per hour. *Café Internet*, Av Tulum, next to Comercial Mexicano. *Sybcom*, Av Nader 42, SM2A. *Nutrinet*, Uxmal 19, Local 6-A Central. Mon-Sat 0900-2130, Sun 1200-1900. **Post office**: at the end of Av Sunyaxchén, near Mercado 28, open Mon-Fri 0800-1900, Sat 0900-1300. **Telephones:** many public phones everywhere, phone cards available from general stores and pharmacies, for US$2, $3 and $5. Collect calls can be made without a card. Also many public phones designed for international calls, which take coins and credit cards. **Fax:** at Post Office, Mon-Sat, and at San Francisco de Asís shopping mall, Mon-Sat until 2200.

Cultural centres *Casa Tabasco*, Av Tulum 230, displays and handicrafts for sale from the state of Tabasco, a good place to go if bored of the same old souvenirs in Cancún.

Embassies & consulates the following consulates are in the hotel zone: *Canada*, Plaza Caracol, 3rd floor, T833360. *France*, Hotel Casa Turquesa, T852924. *Netherlands*, Hotel Presidente, T830200. *Spain*, Oasis Corporativo, T832466. *Sweden*, Switzerland, Hotel Caesar Park, T818013. *UK*, Hotel Royal Caribbean, T810100. *US*, Plaza Caracol, 3rd floor, T830272. The following consulates are in the centre: *Austria*, Cantera 4, SM15, T875896. *Germany*, Punta Conoco 36, SM24, T841898. *Finland*, Nader 28, SM2, T841557. *Italy*, Alcatraces 39, SM22, T841261.

Hospitals *American Hospital* (24-hr) Viento 15, Centre, T846068. *Total Assist* (24-hr) Claveles 5, Centre, T841092/848116. *American Medical Centre*, Plaza Quetzal, Zona Hotelera Km 8, T830113.

Language schools *El Bosque del Caribe*, Calle Piña 1, SM25, T841038, F845888, bcaribe@mail.cancun-language.com.mx

Laundry *Alborada*, Nader 5, behind Tourist Information building on Av Tulum. *Cox-boh*, Av Tankah 26, SM24.

Immigration office is on the corner of Av Nader and Av Uxmal.

Excursions

Punta Sam A strip of coastline north of Punta Sam is officially part of Isla Mujeres. It is being developed as a luxury resort, but without the high-rise buildings of Cancún's hotel zone. Accommodation will be in luxury bunga-lows and *cabañas*. The first of these, now completed, is **AL** *Villas Chalet Maya*, Km 9 Punta Sam Highway (for reservations, contact COMITSA, Km 12.5, Zona Hotelera, Cancún, T851418, F851498). Ocean views, elaborate eth-nic interiors, pool, beach, restaurant.

Puerto Juárez About 3 km north of Cancún, Puerto Juárez is the dock for the cheaper ferry services to Isla Mujeres; there is also a bus terminal, but services are more fre-quent from Cancún. There are many buses between Cancún and Puerto Juárez, for example No 8 opposite the bus terminal (US$0.70), but when the ferries arrive from Isla Mujeres there are many more taxis than buses (taxi fare should be no more than US$2, beware overcharging).

Sleeping and eating **A** *Hotel Caribel*. Resort complex, with bath and fan; in the same price range is *San Marcos*. Other hotels include **D** *Kan Che*, 1st hotel on right coming from Cancún. Fan, clean, swimming pool on beach, good value. *Posada Hermanos Sánchez*, 100m from bus terminal, on road to Cancún. **D** *Fuente Azul*, opposite the dock. **E** *Pina Hermanos*, SM 68, M 6, Lote 14, Puerto Juárez, T842150, 10 mins from Cancún by bus depot. Excellent value, friendly, clean, secure. *Cabañas Punta Sam*, on the beach. Clean, comfortable, **D** with bath (**C** in high season). Possi-ble to camp, with permission, on the beach near the restaurant next door. A big trailer park has been built opposite *Punta Sam*, 150 spaces, camping **F** per person, shop selling basic commodities. Irregular bus service there, or hitchhike from Puerto Juárez. Check to see if restaurant is open evenings. Take mosquito repellent.

Restaurants *Natz Ti Ha* and *Mandinga* by the ferry dock in Puerto Juárez, serve breakfast.

Transport Buses: Regular buses to Cancún from outside the ferry dock, US$0.50. On the whole it is better to catch outgoing buses to more distant destinations in Cancún rather than in Puerto Juárez as there are more of them.

Ferry to Isla Mujeres There are 2 types of ferry: the more expensive costs US$2.20 and leaves Puerto Juárez every 45 mins between 0500 and 1830. Passengers are packed inside; badly functioning a/c makes for a hot and airless journey of 30 mins. The cheaper ferry is in an open-decked boat with cool breezes, much nicer but slightly slower journey, 45 mins, cost US$1, departures every 2 hours. Car ferries leave from Punta Sam 5 times a day from 0800, US$7-8 per car, US$1.50 passengers, 45 mins. There is a luggage store, 0800-1800, and a tourist information desk at the jetty.

Isla Mujeres

A refreshing antidote to the urban sprawl of Cancún, Isla Mujeres is a good place to relax for a few days away from the hurly-burly of package tourism. The island is especially nice in the evening, when all the Cancún day-trippers have gone. The town is strictly low-rise, with brightly coloured buildings giving it the feel of a Caribbean island such as Trinidad. The island's laws prohibit the construction of any building higher than three floors, and US franchises such as Macdonalds and Walmart are not allowed to open branches here.

Phone code: 987
Colour map 4, grid A6

There are several good beaches on Isla Mujeres, the best being **Playa Cocos** on the north west coast, five minutes walk from the town. Further south, there are several places to swim, snorkel and observe marine life. Restaurants and nightspots are plentiful, good quality and cheaper than those on the mainland, and the people are friendlier. There are several ways to explore the island: you can rent a golf cart, many of which chug around the streets all day, good for families; mopeds and bicycles are cheap and plentiful to rent, and a public bus runs all the way from the town to El Paraíso, almost at the southern tip of the island.

The name Isla Mujeres refers to the large number of clay female idols found by the Spaniards here in 1518. The island contains the only known Maya shrine to a female deity: Ixchel, goddess of the moon and fertility. Sadly, the ruins of the shrine at the southern tip of the island have recently been bought by developers. They will be made into part of a new tourist complex like Xcaret, and locals are furious at having to pay a fee to view them. The tourist office, Rueda Medina, opposite the ferry dock, is very helpful. ■ *Mon-Fri 0900-2100, Sat 0900-1400.* The immigration office is next door.

Most of the sights south of the town can be seen in a day. The first of these, 5 km from the town, is the **Turtle Farm**, T70595, with hundreds of sea turtles weighing from 6oz to 600lbs in a humane setting. ■ *Daily 0900-1700, US$1.* To get there, take the bus to the final stop, Playa Paraíso, double back and walk five minutes along the main road.

Sights

At the centre of the island are the curious remains of a pirate's domain, called **Casa de Mundaca**. A big, new arch gate marks its entrance. Paths have been laid out among the large trees, but all that remains of the estate (called Vista Alegre) are one small building and a circular garden with raised beds, a well and a gateway. Fermín Mundaca, more of a slave-trader than a buccaneer, built Vista Alegre for the teenage girl he loved. She rejected him and he died, broken-hearted, in Mérida. His epitaph there reads *Como eres, yo fui; como*

Yucatán Peninsula

soy, tu serás ('what you are I was; what I am you shall be'). See the poignant little carving on the garden side of the gate, *La entrada de La Trigueña* (the girl's nickname). To get there, get off the bus at the final stop, and turn the opposite way to the beach; the house is a short walk away.

El Garrafón, a snorkelling centre 7 km from the town, is being developed into a luxury resort in the style of Xcaret, on the mainland. Snorkelling is still possible, US$2, lockers US$2, plus deposit, equipment rental available. There is a 39-ft bronze cross submerged offshore, trips to snorkel around it cost US$13, 1½ hours, no lunch. There is an expensive restaurant and bar at El Garrafón, and a small beach. The snorkelling is good past the pier, along a reef with some dead coral. Large numbers of different coloured fish can be seen at very close range. If you want to walk to El Garrafón from the bus stop at Playa Paraíso, take the second path on the right to the beach from the main road. The first path leads through Restaurant Playa Paraíso, which charges US$1 for the privilege of walking through their premises to the beach. Playa Paraíso is an expensive mini-resort for Cancún day-trippers; there is a swimming-with-sharks option, during which harmless nurse sharks are treated cruelly so that tourists can have their picture taken with them. Once on the beach, you can walk all the way to El Garrafón along the coast, though it gets very rocky for the final part. It is easier to go as far as the cluster of beach villas, then cut through one of them (ask for permission) to the main road. The whole walk takes about half an hour. When you arrive at El Garrafón, turn right at the building site, go down the hill to Hotel Garrafón del Castillo, which is the entrance to the snorkelling centre.

A further 15 minutes walk from El Garrafón, at the tip of the island, are the ruins of the Maya shrine to Ixchel, goddess of fertility. Unfortunately, these are no longer free to visit. They have been bought and developed as part of the El Garrafón 'National Park', and it now costs US$3.50 just to see the ruins. Only a thin strip of land overlooking a rocky, unswimable bit of the Atlantic Ocean has been left by the developers for free public access at this tip of the island.

Excursions A small island north of Isla Mujeres, **Isla Contoy** has been designated as a bird and wildlife sanctuary, with good birdwatching. Trips can be arranged through many agencies; the specialist is Ricardo Gaitán, at Av Madero 16, T70434. His trips include snorkelling, fishing and a fish lunch. Many touts around the main dock will offer trips to Isla Contoy for around US$50 for a full day.

Isla Mujeres town

0 metres 100
0 yards 100

➤ **To Puerto Juárez**

■ **Sleeping**
1 Belmar & Pizzería Rolandi
2 Berny
3 Cabañas María del Mar
4 Caribe Maya
5 Condominio Nautibeach
6 El Caracol
7 Isleño
8 Las Palmas
9 María José
10 Osorio
11 Perlas del Caribe
12 Poc-Na
13 Posada del Mar
14 Rocamar & Chen Huayo Restaurant
15 Rocas del Caribe
16 Xul-Há

● **Eating**
1 Balcón de Arriba
2 Gomar
3 Loncherías
4 Los Abuelos
5 Miramar
6 Poc-chuc

AL *Hi-Na-Ha*, on a secluded tip of land south of the town, T/F70615. Private suites on the beach, kitchen, living and dining areas, private terrace. **AL** *Posada del Mar*, Av Rueda 15, T20212. Has pleasant terrace but expensive drinks, restaurant for residents only, price includes meals. **A** *Belmar*, Av Hidalgo 110 between Madero and Abasolo, T70430, F70429. A/c, TV, restaurant *Pizza Rolandi* downstairs. **A** *Condominio Nautibeach*, on Playa Los Cocos, T70606. 2-bed apartments, a/c, pool, right on beach facing the sunset. **A** *El Mesón del Bucanero*, Hidalgo 11, T20210, F20126. All rooms with fan. **A** *Las Perlas del Caribe*, Caribbean side of town. Clean, a/c, pool. Recommended. **B** *Cabañas María del Mar*, overlooks Coco beach. A/c, lovely beach bar with hammocks and rocking chairs for 2. **B** *Francis Arlene*, Guerrero 7, T/F 70310. Modern, pleasant, efficient service. **B** *Rocamar*, Nicolás Bravo y Zona Marítima, T/F 70101. On the eastern side, quiet, nice views.

C *Berny*, Juárez y Abasolo, T20025. With bath and fan, basic, problems with water supply, swimming pool, long-distance calls possible, residents only, but does not honour confirmed reservations unless a deposit for 1 night's stay has been made. **C** *Casa Maya*, Zazil-Ha (near Playa Los Cocos) T/F 70045. Bungalows right next to

Sleeping

Isla Mujeres & Quintana Roo coast

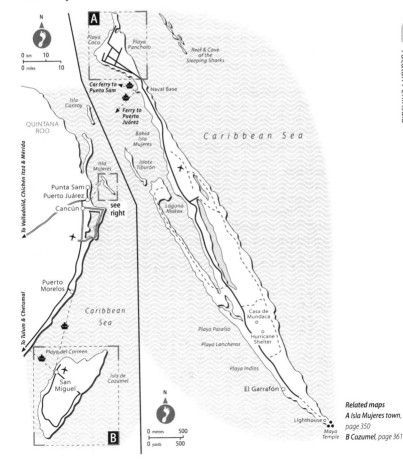

Related maps
A Isla Mujeres town,
page 350
B Cozumel, page 361

Yucatán Peninsula

beach, palm trees garden, kitchen, restaurant. **C** *El Caracol*, Matamoros 5, T70150, F70547. Cheaper with fan, hot water, terrace balcony, stoves for guests' use, bar, coffee shop, laundry, central, clean, good value. **C** *El Paso*, Morelos 13. With bath, clean, facing the pier. **C** *Isla Mujeres*, next to church. With bath, renovated, run by pleasant Englishman. **C** *Rocas del Caribe*, Madero 2, 100m from ocean. Cool rooms, big balcony, clean, good service. **C** *Vistalmar*, on promenade about 300m left from ferry dock (**D** for longer stays). Ask for rooms on top floor, bath, balcony, fan, insect screens, good value.

D *Caribe Maya*, Madero 9. Central, modern, a/c, cheaper with fan, very clean and comfy. **D** *Carmelina*, Guerrero 4, T70006. Central, with bath and a/c, clean, safe, but no toilet paper, soap, blankets or hot water, unfriendly family, rents bikes and snorkelling gear, advance payment for room required daily. **D** *Isleño*, Madero and Guerrero. Very clean, with bath, cheaper without, helpful. **D** *Las Palmas*, Guerrero 20. Central, 2 blocks from north beach, good, clean. **D** *María José*, Madero 25, T20130. Clean, fans, friendly, scooter hire. **D** *Osorio*, Madero, 1 block from waterfront. Clean, fan, with bath and hot water, friendly, reception closes at 2100. Recommended. *La Reina* bakery nearby. **D** *Posada Suemi*, Matamoros 12, T70122. Nice, recently opened, family-run, clean, well-furnished rooms, 3 to a room for US$5 extra. Recommended. **D** *San Jorge*, Juárez between López Mateos and Matamoros. Recently renovated, small, quiet, friendly. Recommended. **D** *Xul-Há*, on Hidalgo towards north beach. With fan.

F (per person) *Poc-Na Hostel*, top end of Matamoros on the northeast coast, T70090. Mixed-sex dormitories, 6-14 to a room, also 2 double rooms (**E**), sheets US$0.30 extra, restaurant, busy, often booked up in summer and Dec.

Eating **Expensive** *Rolandis*, Hidalgo. Italian, terrace overlooking street, busy. *Bucanero*, Hidalgo, opposite *Rolandis*. Steak, seafood, terrace, classy. *Miramar*, Rueda Medina opposite ferry dock. Seafood, Mexican. *Lo Lo Lorena*, Guerrero 7, esq Matamoros. Authentic French bistro, lobster, shrimp, also has international dishes. *Gomar*, Hidalgo y Madero. Large veranda, Mexican and US-style food, touristy.

Mid-range *El Balcón de Arriba*, Hidalgo 12, above souvenir shop. Varied menu, excellent fish and seafood, some vegetarian and tempura dishes, very friendly staff, large portions. Highly recommended. *Velázquez*, on the beach next to the ferry dock. Excellent fresh seafood (except the shrimp), tables on the sand. *Mirita*, Rueda Medina opposite ferry dock. Seafood, Yucatecan dishes, good value. *Manolos*, Juárez. Small, nice décor, seafood, barbecue, baked potatoes. *Pizzería Los Amigos*, Hidalgo. Small, with 2 tables outside, excellent pizzas and pasta. *All Natural*, Plaza Karlita on Hidalgo. Speciality grilled fish, many varieties, some vegetarian dishes.

Cheap *Poc-Chuc*, Juárez y Madero. Very good local food, big portions, good *tortas*. Next door is *La Susanita*. Excellent home cooking, friendly locals' place; when closed it is the family's living room. *Los Abuelos*, next door to *Los Amigos Pizzería* on Hidalgo. Basic interior, but excellent local food; try the *plato mexicano* or the *plato regional*. There are 4 *loncherías* at the northwest end of Guerrero, open till 1800. Good for breakfast, snacks and lunch. All serve the same local fare at similar prices. Opposite is *Lonchería Chely*, similar food and prices. *Chen Huayo*, end of Hidalgo opposite Zocalo. Good Yucatecan lunch, but poor breakfast.

Cafés *Café Sienna*, corner of Madero and Rueda Medina. Good café, organic coffee from Chiapas, cappuccino, latte, etc, fine views of the harbour. *La Casita*, Madero between Hidalgo and Juárez. Fresh coffee and croissants, bagels, also has internet facility at US$4 per hour.

Bars Most of the bars have a permanent happy hour, with 2 drinks for the price of 1. Not particularly good value, since the prices are double the usual. It works out if 2 people are having the same drink: simply order one! *Daniel's*, Hidalgo between Madero and Morelos. Very popular (and loudest) in the early evening, live music every night. *Kokonuts*, Hidalgo 65, towards beach from centre. Most popular in town, fills up after 2200, dance floor, happy hour, young crowd. Further along towards the beach is *Chile Locos*, more sedate than Kokonuts, with live marimba music. *La Palapa*, on Playa Los Cocos. Cocktails and snacks, busy during the day until everyone leaves the beach, then fills up again after midnight. There is sometimes live music at *La Taverna*, on the harbour near the ferry dock. Nice location on wooden stilts in the sea, but the venue is having difficulty competing with the popularity of places in the centre like *Daniel's* and *Kokonuts*.

Festivals Between **1-12 Dec** there is a *fiesta* for the Virgin of Guadalupe, fireworks, dances until 0400 in the Plaza. In **Oct** there is a festival of music, with groups from Mexico and the USA performing in the main square.

Shopping **Souvenirs**: Av Hidalgo is lined with souvenir shops, most of them selling the same things: ceramic Maya figurines and masks; hammocks; blankets; and silver jewellery from Taxco. Bargaining is obligatory – try and get the desired item for half the original asking price, which is what the vendors expect to receive. There are more souvenir shops along the harbour front, where the salesmen are more pushy, and more shops along Av Morelos. **Jewellery**: *Van Cleef & Arpels*, Av Morelos esq Juárez. A very expensive centre for gold and silver jewellery with diamonds, sapphires and rubies. **Books**: *Cosmic Cosas*, Matamoros 82, T70806. New and used books bought, sold and exchanged, CDs, internet café, US-run, good place to meet fellow travellers. **Cigars**: *Tobacco & Co*, Hidalgo 14. Cuban cigars and smoking paraphernalia. There are several other shops in the centre selling Cuban cigars. **Supermarkets**: The largest supermarket is on the Zócalo; there is a smaller one on Juárez between Morelos and Bravo.

Sport **Scuba diving and snorkelling**: There are various reefs for diving and snorkelling, as well as a sunken cross specifically placed in deep water for divers to explore (see above). **Dive centres** *Sea Hawk*, Zazil-Ha (behind *Hotel Na-Balam*) T/F70296. Certified PADI instructors, 2-tank dive US$50, introductory course including shallow dive US$75. Also snorkelling trips, US$20, and fishing trips, US$150 including bait, tackle and refreshments. *Coral*, Av Matamoros 13A, T70763, F70371, coral@coralscubadivecenter.com The only dive centre on the island affiliated with PADI, over 20 years experience, bilingual staff, over 50 local dive sites, including reef, adventure or Ultrafreeze options. *Bahía*, Av Rueda Medina 166, opposite the ferry dock, T70340. Snorkelling trips depart from the ferry dock daily between 1000 and 1100. They include 2 hrs snorkelling in various spots and lunch, returning at 1430. US$150pp. Lots of touts along the seafront, who will tell you that the snorkelling centre at El Garrafón is closed. It is not.

Tour operators *Prisma Tours*, Av Juárez 22, T/F70938. Tours to Tulum, Cobá, Chichén Itzá, Uxmal, Sian Ka'an in a/c vans. Also cheap and reliable airport transfer from Cancún Airport-Puerto Juárez. *Tercer Milenio*, Abasolo 46, between Juárez and Hidalgo, T70795, F70794. Tours to archaeological sites in Quintana Roo, airport transfer, high-class van rental, reservations for cruises, golf cart, moped and car rental, scuba diving, flights to Cuba, Belize, Guatemala.

Transport There is a public **bus** which runs from the ferry dock to Playa Paraíso every half an hour, US$0.25. A **taxi** doing the same journey will cost US$1-2, taxi from town to El Garrafón US$3.40. For the return journey, sharing a taxi will work out marginally more

Yucatán Peninsula

expensive than the bus for four people. A taxi from El Garrafón to the bus stop at Playa Paraíso is US$1.

There are several places renting **golf carts**, eg *Ciros*, on Matamoros near Playa Cocos. Rates are generally US$40-50 per day. A credit card is usually required as a deposit. **Mopeds**: many touts along Hidalgo offer similar rates: US$6 per hour, US$20 full day. *Sport Bike*, Av Juárez y Morelos, has good bikes. *Cárdenas*, Av Guerrero 105, T/F 70079, for mopeds and golf carts. **Bicycles** are usually offered by the same places as mopeds for about US$6 per day.

Air The small airstrip in the middle of the island is mainly used for private planes. Flights can be booked to Cancún and Chichén Itzá through *Mundaca Travel*, on Hidalgo, T70025, F70076.

Ferry For information on ferries to and from the island, see page 349.

Directory **Banks** *Banco del Atlántico*, Av Juárez 5. *Banca Serfín*, Av Juárez 3. Both can get very busy. Good rates, varying daily, are offered by several *casas de cambio* on Av Hidalgo. The one opposite *Rolandis* is open daily 0900-2100. **Communications** Internet: *Compuisla*, Av Abasolo 11. Open daily 0800-2200, also fax service. *Café Internet*, Plaza Karlita, Av Hidalgo. US$4 per hour, lots of computers, a/c. *La Casita*, Madero 10. US$4 per hour, only 4 computers, open Mon-Fri 0730-2130. The Post Office is at the end of Guerrero towards the beach. Phone cards can be bought at some of the souvenir shops along Hidalgo. International calls and faxes at *Gold & Silver*, Av Hidalgo 58. **Laundry** Tim Pho, Juárez y Abasolo. **Medical services** Dr Antonio Salas, Hidalgo, next to *Farmacia*, T70477/70021. 24-hrs, house calls, English spoken, air ambulance. Dr Antonio Torres, Av Matamoros esq Guerrero, T70050. 24-hrs, English and German spoken.

Puerto Morelos

Phone code: 987
Colour map 4, grid A6

A quiet little village 34 km south of Cancún, Puerto Morelos is a nice place to stop over *en route* to larger towns further south, such as Playa del Carmen. The village is really just a large plaza right on the seafront with a couple of streets going off it. If on arrival at Cancún airport you don't wish to spend the night in the city, you can get a taxi directly to Puerto Morelos. This is also the place to catch the car ferry to the island of Cozumel. The *Sinaltur* office on the plaza offers snorkelling, kayak and fishing trips. *Goyos*, just north of the plaza, offers jungle adventures and rooms for rent, erratic hours maintained.

Sleeping & eating
L-AL *Caribbean Reef Club*, just past the car ferry dock on the beach, T10162. Luxury resort hotel with organized watersports and a pool. Next door is **A** *Rancho Libertad*, T10181. Thatched *cabañas*, price includes breakfast, scuba diving and skorkelling gear for rent. **A** *Hacienda Morelos*, on the seafront, T10015. Nice rooms with sea views. **D** *Posada Amor*, opposite the beach, T10033, F10178. Very pleasant, well-built *cabañas* with good mosquito nets, the cheaper ones have outdoor communal showers, good restaurant, prices are reduced considerably out of season, ie Feb-Jun/Sep-Nov. Recommended. There are several restaurants on the plaza, eg *Palapa*, with good seafood.

Transport
There are buses to Cancún and Playa del Carmen every half hour. Buses depart from the main road, taxi to bus stop US$3. Car ferries to Cozumel depart twice a day at 0600 and 1500, the dock is 500m south of the plaza. Taxi from Cancún airport to Puerto Morelos, US$25-35.

Directory
Communications There is an internet café on the corner of the plaza opposite *Posada Amor*, US$8 per hour, open Mon-Sat 1000-1400, 1600-2100.

Playa del Carmen

A pleasant little town on the beach which still maintains some of the charms of its former existence as a fishing village. Recent development for tourism has been rapid, but Playa, as it is known locally, has not had the high-rise treatment of Cancún, 64 km away. The beach is dazzling white, with crystal-clear shallow water, ideal for swimming, and further out there is good scuba diving. There is accommodation for every budget, and plenty of good restaurants and bars of every description. Many travellers choose Playa as their base for trips to the ruins of Tulum in the south, and archaeological sites such as Cobá in the interior.

Phone code: 987
Colour map 4, grid A6
Population: 45,000

The town is laid out in a grid system, with the main centre of tourist activity based on Avenida 5, pedestrianized, one block from and parallel with the beach. This is where the more expensive hotels and restaurants are, as well as being the centre for nightlife. Cheaper accommodation can be found up Avenida Juárez and further north of the beach. **Tourist information** is scant, but the kiosk on the main plaza will provide a copy of *Destination Playa del Carmen*, a useful guide with maps produced by US residents.

Most luxurious is **L** *Continental Plaza Playacar*, T30100, F30105. A huge new development just south of the ferry terminal, excellent in every respect, non-residents can use swimming pool, no charge; in the same development as this 5-star hotel is the 5-star **L** *Diamond Resort*, Apdo Postal 149, T30340, F30348, and the 4-star **AL** *Caribbean Villages*, T30434, F30437. Both all-inclusive club operations, the latter in the middle of the golf course; there are also villas for rent (**LL-A**), Apdo Postal 139, Playa del Carmen, T/F30148. Also based at Playacar (and equally luxurious) are two all-inclusive clubs run by Viva Resorts: *Viva Maya* and the slightly smaller *Viva Azteca*. Both are in our **L-AL** range. Details from the Viva Resorts, Apdo Postal 340, T31400, F31424 or in the USA, T800 8989968, F809 221-6806, www.vivaresorts.com **L** *Las Palapas*, at north end of bay north of Playa, T22977, F41668 (Mexico City F53798641). Breakfast and dinner included, cabins with hammocks outside, good. **L** *Mosquito Blue*, Av 5 between Calle 12 and Calle 14, T31245, F31337. Pool, minibar, TV, phone, king-size beds, beautiful courtyard restaurant. **AL** *Alhambra*, Calle 8 Norte, on corner with the beach, T30735, F30699, olas@cancun.com.mx All rooms with balcony or sea view, family-run, French and English spoken. Recommended. **AL** *Cabañas Capitán Lafitte*, at Km 297/8, north of Playa del Carmen. Very good, pool, excellent cheap restaurant on barren beach; under same ownership is **AL** *Shangri-Lá Caribe*, T22888, 7 km south, closer to town (at north end of the bay north of Playa). Cabins, equally good, excellent beach with diving (Cyan-Ha, PADI) and snorkelling, sailing, easy birdwatching beside hotel. **AL** *Jungla Caribe*, Av 5 y Calle 8, T30650. Modern, nice restaurant. **AL** *Las Molcas*, T30070, near ferry pier. Pool, a bit shabby, friendly staff, interesting architecture, its open-air restaurant across street is good and reasonable. **AL** *Panchos*, Av 5 y Calle 12, T30328, F32222. King-size beds, tropical garden, pool, continental breakfast included. On the beach is **AL** *Pelícano*, T30997. Including good breakfast, impersonal. **AL** *Quinta Mija*, Av 5 y Calle 14, T/F 30111, quinta@ playadelcarmen.com.mx Condos with kitchenette (more expensive) and rooms in lush landscaped gardens with funky architecture, wood carvings, pool, outdoor restaurant, rooftop sundecks. Next door is **AL** *El Tukan Condotel*, T30417, F30668 info@el-tukan.com. Jungle-style setting, luxury secluded pool, bar, restaurant, airport shuttle, exchange facilities. **AL** *Treetops*, Calle 8 between Av 5 and the beach, T30351, treetops@ playadelcarmen.com Includes contintental breakfast, minibar, pool, nice staff. **AL** *Villa Catarina*, Calle Privada Norte between Calle 12 and Calle 14 Norte, T32098, F32097. Well-built *cabañas* in a jungly garden setting, also an exclusive treetop apartment with its own pool, **LL**, and rooms available in **A** range. At the north end

Sleeping
■ *on map*
Prices quoted are for the high season – Jul/Aug and Dec; during the low season prices will drop by about 25%

of town, on a popular stretch of beach between Calle 12 y 14, is **AL-B** *Blue Parrot*, T30083, F44564 (reservations in USA 904-7756660, toll free 800-6343547). Price depends on type of room and facilities, has bungalows, no a/c, with excellent bar (Happy Hour 2200) and café, volleyball court, deep-sea fishing expeditions. Highly

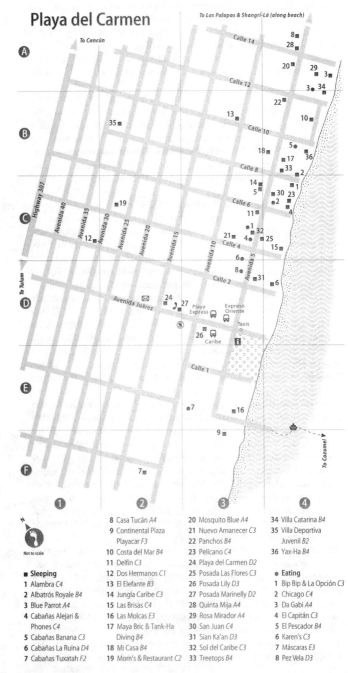

Playa del Carmen

To Las Palapas & Shangri-Lá (along beach)

To Cancún

Yucatán Peninsula

Not to scale

recommended. **A** *Albatrós Royale*, on the beach, T30001. Clean, very good, no pool. **A** *El Marlín Azul*, Km 296. Swimming pool, good food. **A** *Hotel Maranatha*, Av Juárez between Av 30 and 35, T30143, F30038 (US Res T1-800-3298388). Luxury with all facilities. **A** *Moongate*, end of Av 5, opposite *El Tukan Condotel*, T31949. Mixture of Maya/Chinese architecture with enchanted garden and castle, all rooms with balcony. **A** *San Juan*, Av 5 No 165, T30647. Including continental breakfast. **A** *Sol del Caribe*, Av 5 No 156 between Calle 4 and Calle 6, T30958, F32755. Fridge, microwave, cafeteria, cable TV, sea views.

B *Azul Profundo*, next to *Blue Parrot*. With bath and balcony. **B** *Costa del Mar*, T30058, on little road by beach between Calle 10 and 12. Clean, restaurant (disappointing) and bar, pool. **B** *Marasol*, Calle 6. Clean, balconies overlooking sea. **B** *Mom's*, Av 30 y Calle 4, T30315, about 5 blocks from bus station or beach. Clean, comfortable, small pool, good restaurant with Chinese home cooking and plenty of vegetables. **B** *Rosa Mirador*, behind the *Blue Parrot*, **AL** in high season. Hot showers, fan, best views from 3rd floor, owner Alberto speaks English. Recommended. **B-F** *Cabañas Alejari*, Calle 6 going down to beach, T30374. Very nice, shop has long-distance phones. **B-C** *Cabañas Banana*, Av 5 between Calle 6 and 8, T30036. Cabins and rooms, kitchenettes. **B-C** *Casa de Gopala*, Calle 2 Norte and Av 10 Norte (PO Box 154), T/F30054. Bath and fan, 150m from beach, quiet and central, American/Mexican owned, large rooms, quiet and comfortable. Recommended. **B-C** *El Acuario*, Av 25 Norte between 2 and 4 Norte. Large rooms, some with kitchen, a/c, pool. *Yax-Ha* cabins, on the beach, via Av 5 by Calle 10. Price depends on size and season. Excellent.

C *Cabañas Tuxatah*, 2 minutes from sea, 2 blocks south from Av Juárez (Apdo 45, T30025). German owner, Maria Weltin, speaks English and French. Bath, clean, comfortable, hot water, laundry service, beautiful gardens, breakfast US$4. Recommended. **C** *Delfín*, Av 5 y Calle 6, T30176. With bath. **C** *Maya Bric*, Av 5, between Calle 8 and 10, T30011. Hot water, clean, friendly, pool, *Tank-Ha* dive shop (see below). **C** *Nuevo Amanecer*, Calle 4, west of Av 5. Very attractive, fans, hot water, hammocks, mosquito nets, clean, laundry area, poolroom, helpful. Recommended. **C** *Posada Freud*, Av 5 between Calle 8 and 10 Nte, T/F30601. With bath, fan, some with kitchenette, *palapa*-style, quiet, clean, Austrian owner, simpler rooms without bath available priced at **D-E**. Recommended. **C** *Posada Las Flores*, Av 5 between Calle 4 and Calle 6. Popular, friendly, courtyard, near beach. **C** *Posada Xaman-Ha*, Av 10, quiet, very friendly. Recommended. **C** *Sian Ka'an*, Av 5 y Calle 2, T30203, 100m from bus station. Modern rooms with balcony, clean. Recommended. Others in the **C** range include *El Elefante*, Calle 10 between Av 10 and 15, T30262. With bath, modern but basic, and *Playa del Carmen*, Av Juárez, between Calle 10 y 15, T30293, opposite bank. **C-D** *Castillo Verde*, Calle 26 between Av 5 and 10, T/F30990, 10 mins from centre at north end of town. With bath, hot water, garden, free coffee, Swiss-German owned. **C-D** *La Palma*, Av Juárez between Calle 10 and Calle 15, T65173. TV, hot water. **D** *Casa Tucán*, Calle 4 Norte, between 10 and 15 Av Norte, T/F30283. Nice patio, small but clean rooms. **D** *Dos Hermanos*, Av 30 between Calle 2 Bis y Calle 4 Norte. Rooms at back quiet, hot water, fan, clean. Recommended. **D** *El Bucanero*, Av 25 and Calle 4, T31454. Comfortable rooms away from the noisy centre. **D** *Posada Marinelly*, Av Juárez between Calle 10 and Calle 15. Near the centre, some rooms noisy, very clean, nice staff, family-run, good cheap café downstairs. **D** *Posada Melodia*, Calle 4 between Av 25 and Av 30, T30335. A/c, hot water, TV, in-house doctor. **D** *Posada Lily*, Av Juárez at Caribe bus stop. With shower, fan, safe, clean, but noisy in the morning and cell-like rooms. Under same ownership **C-D** *Posada Papagayo*, Av 15 between Calle 4 and 6. Fan and bath, mosquito net, very nicely furnished rooms, friendly. Highly recommended. **D** *Posada Marixchel*, Calle 30 and 1 Sur, T20823. Shower, safe, fan, clean. Recommended. **D** *Posada Mar Caribe*, Av 15. Small, friendly. Recommended.

Yucatán Peninsula

E *Posada Fernández*, Av 10 opposite Calle 1. Bath, hot water and fan, friendly. Recommended. **E-F** *Cabañas La Ruina*, at the beach end of Calle 2. Popular, crowded, noisy, clean, lots of options and prices, from 2 to 3-bedded cabins, hammock space under *palapa*, with or without security locker, hammock in open air, camping US$3, space for vehicles and camper vans, linen rental, bath extra, cooking facilities. A good budget option. **E-F** *Mi Casa* (painted red), Av 5 opposite *Maya Bric*. Also apartments (**E**) with kitchenette, patchy mosquito net, fan, well-furnished, bath, cold water, owner speaks German, English and Spanish, nice garden. Recommended. Lots of new places going up, none under US$10 a night. Small apartments on Av 5, esq Calle 6. Approximately US$200 per month, with kitchen; also rooms near basketball court, US$100 per month.

Youth Hostel F *Villa Deportiva Juvenil*, 5 blocks up from Av 5, on Calle 8 Norte, T5252548, camping, in dormitory (hot with only 2 fans and a lot of beds), for up to 4 in cabin with fan and private shower, comfortable, with basketball court, clean, difficult to find, especially after dark, but it is signposted. Recommended.

Camping See above under *La Ruina* and *Villa Deportiva Juvenil*; also **Camping Las Brisas** at the beach end of Calle 4. *Punta Bete*, 10 km north, the right-hand one of 3 campsites at the end of a 5-km road, on beach. US$3 for tent, also 2 restaurants and *cabañas*. *Outback*, small trailer park on beach at end of Calle 6. US$10 for car and 2 people.

Eating Expensive *Idea Pasta*, Av 5 between Calle 12 and Calle 14. Good Italian, seafood. *Panchos*, Av 5 between Calle 10 and Calle 12. Traditional Mexican food, speciality international flambées and flaming Spanish coffee. *Abraxas*, Av 5 between Calle 10 and Calle 12. Traditional European cuisine. *El Provenzal*, Av 5 and Calle 14, in *Hotel Quinta Mija*. Mediterranean cuisine, garden setting. *Jazzy Cat*, Calle 6 between Av 5 and Av 10. Rib roasts, oven-baked lasagne, homemade pasta. *Limones*, Av 5 and Calle 6. Good food, popular.

Mid-range *Máscaras*, on square. Highly recommended. Also on the square, *El Tacolote*. Tacos, etc, and *Las Piñatas*. *Da Gabi*, just up Calle 12 from *Blue Parrot*, good pastas, Mexican dishes, breakfast buffet, also has rooms in **C** range. Next to *Cabañas Yax-Ha* is *Il Pescadore*. Fish, has a variety of beers. *Tarraya*, on seafront. Seafood, closes 2100. Recommended. On or near Avenida 5: *Pez Vela*, Av 5 y Calle 2. Good atmosphere, food, drinks and music (closed 1500-1700). *Pollo Caribe*, near bus station between Calle 2 and Juárez. Set chicken menu for US$2, good, closes early when chicken runs out. Recommended. *La Parrilla*, Av 5 y Calle 8. Large portions, good service, live music every night, popular. *Buenos Aires*, Calle 6 Norte between Av 5 and Av 10, on Plaza Playa. Speciality Argentine meats, run by Argentines, nice for a change from Mexican food. *La Choza*, Av 5 between Av Juárez and Calle 2. Good breakfasts, Tex-Mex dinners. *Bip Bip*, Av Constituyentes between Av 5 and the beach. Good pizzas. *Media Luna*, Av 5 between Calle 8 and Calle 10. Excellent vegetarian and seafood. *Sabor*, Calle 4 and Av 5. Vegetarian and health food, bakery. *The Lazy Lizard*, Av 5 between Calle 2 and Calle 4. Canadian-run, US-style food, burgers. *Yaxche*, Calle 8 between Av 5 and Av 10. Traditional Maya cuisine. *Karen's Pizza*, Av 5 between Calle 2 and 4. Pizzas, Mexican dishes, cable TV, popular. *Le Bistro*, Calle 2. Good French cheese/Caribbean chicken and wine. Recommended. *Los Almendros*, Calle 6 and Av 10. Excellent Mexican food, friendly. Recommended. *La Choza*, 5 Av between Juárez and Calle 2. Great food, set menus. *El Chino*, Calle 4 Norte between Calle 10 and 15. Popular with Mexicans, seafood, Yucatán specialities, good breakfast, inexpensive, friendly.

Cheap *Lonchería Maquech*, Calle 1 between Av 5 and 10. Set lunch daily, cheap, friendly. Recommended. *El Correo*, just beyond *Posada Fernández*. Mexican, cheap, excellent *menú del día* and *pollo pibil*. Recommended. *Tacos Senjansen*, Av Juárez between Calle 10 and Calle 15. Nice open-air café under *Posada Marinelly*, for good breakfast and snacks. *Cielito Lindo*, Av 20 s/n y Av Juárez. Good filling meals, varied menu, popular with locals, surly staff. Nice *palapa* (no name) for snacks, on Av 20 Norte and Calle 2 Norte. Popular with locals. *Taquería el Poblano*, Av. Juárez between Calle 15 and 20. Mexican food. Reccomended. *Pizza y Pasta de Fofo*, Calle 4 between Av 5 and 10. Recommended.

Cafés & bakeries *Coffee Press*, Calle 2 between Av 5 and the beach. Espresso, cappuccino, latte, breakfast. *Java Joe's*, Av 5 between Calle 10 and 12. Italian and gourmet coffees, sandwiches, pastries. *Panadería del Caribe*, Av 5 between Calle 4 and 2. For breads and cakes. *Panificadora del Carmen*, Av 30, just before Youth Hostel. Excellent, open until 2300, has a café/restaurant at the side called *La Concha*. *Zermat Bakery* at extreme end of pedestrian Calle Norte, 5 blocks from bus station. Recommended for pastries.

Bars *The Blue Parrot Inn*, Calle 12 y Av 1, next to beach. Live music every night, happy hour 1700-2000 and 2200-2400. *Zulu*, Av 5 between Calle 6 and 8. Contemporary European music, Thai food. *Tapas Bar*, Av 10 y Calle 8. Cocktail bar open till 0100, satellite TV.

Bars & nightclubs

Nightclubs *Señor Frogs*, by the pier. Part of large chain throughout Mexico, live reggae and karaoke, open from 2200 till late. *Fiesta Latina*, Calle 8 y Av 25. Live Latin music and ballet show. *Buena Onda*, Av 5 between Calle 26 and Calle 28. Live music, salsa, funk, reggae. *Espiral*, Av 5 off the main plaza. House and techno.

Lots of souvenir shops clustered around the plaza, pricey. Cheaper shops, for day-to-day items, can be found on Av Juárez. There is a cheap *panadería* at the beginning of Av Juárez. For developing photos and buying film, there are several places along Av 5. Recommended jeweller is *Joyera Cobá*, Av 5.

Shopping

Scuba diving: The best is said to be *Abyss*, Calle 12 and the beach, near the *Blue Parrot*, T32164, abyss@playadelcarmen.com Run by fully certified American instructor David Tomlinson, PADI courses cost US$324; 1-tank dive costs US$40, 1-day introductory course US$69, also cave dives and night dives. *Adventures Underwater*, on Plaza, T32647. Diving courses in English, French or Spanish, 3 certified instructors, 1-day beginner course US$60, open water PADI US$350, advanced refresher course US$250, cave diving in 2 *cenotes* US$100. Two other recommended centres are *Tank-Ha*, in *Maya Bric Hotel*, and *Phocea Caribe*, Av 5 between Calle 12 and Calle 14, T31024.

Sport

Classique Travel, Calle 6 between Av 5 and Av 10, T/F 30142, boletaje@ mail.classique.com.mx Long-standing and reliable agency with a branch in Cancún, tours to Chichén Itzá US$72, including transport from hotel, guide, entrance, food, also bookings for national and international flights, helpful staff. *Euro Latino*, Av 5 no 165B, between Calle 6 and 8, T30549, F30550, eurolatino@grupasesores.net.mx An efficiently run agency with young European staff, 2 of their tours are: dawn in Tikal (Guatemala) US$278, including flight, overnight stay in hotel, all meals, all transfers; weekend on Cozumel, including dive (all levels) plus 2 nights and the ferry, US$72.

Tour operators

Buses The *ADO* bus terminal is on Av Juárez between Av 5 and 10. All buses depart from here. The following prices and times are for *ADO* buses (1st class, a/c, usually showing a video on longer journeys); Premier, also 1st class; Maya de Oro, supposed to be 1st class but quality of buses can be poor; San Cristóbal, good 1st class service. **Cancún**, 8 per day, 1 hr 15 mins, ADO US$2.40, Playa Express US$2. **Mérida**, 4 per day, 7 hrs, US$10. **Valladolid**, 0730 and 1115, 3½ hrs, US$6 (most buses going to Mérida stop at Valladolid). **Chichén**

Transport

Yucatán Peninsula

Itzá, 6 per day, 4 hrs, US$7. **Tulum**, 5 per day, 1 hr, US$2. **Xcaret**, frequent service, 10 mins, US$1. **Xel Há**, 2 per day, 1 hr, US$2. **Chetumal**, 8 per day, 5 hrs, US$10. **Mexico City**, 3 per day, 24 hrs, US$54. **San Cristóbal de las Casas**, 3 per day, 16 hrs, US$37.

Taxis Cancún airport US$25. Beware of those who charge only US$5 as they are likely to charge an extra US$20 for luggage. Tours to Tulum and Xel-Há from kiosk by boat dock US$30; tours to Tulum, Xel-Há and Xcaret, 5-6 hrs, US$60; taxi to Xcaret US$6.65. Taxis congregate on the Av Juárez side of the square (Sindicato Lázaro Cárdenas del Río, T30032/30414).

Car hire *Caribetur,* Av 10 No 128 between Calle 2 and 4 Norte, T32292. *Freedom,* Av 5, T31459. *Happy,* Plaza Tucán, Local 6, T31739. *Hertz* T30703. *Budget* T30100.

Transport to Cozumel Ferries depart from the main dock, just off the plaza, every two hours on the hour, 0400-2200, ½ hour, US$6 1-way, buy ticket 1 hr before journey. There are also flights from the nearby airstrip; touts will mingle with the queues for the ferry to get passengers. Flights cost US12.50 1-way, 10 mins.

Directory **Banks** *Bancomer,* Av Juárez between Calle 25 and Calle 30. *Banamex,* Av Juárez between Calle 20 and Calle 25. A few doors down is *Santander. Bancrecer,* Av 5 between Av Juárez and the beach. *Inverlat,* Av 5 between Av Juárez and Calle 2. *Bital,* Av Juárez between Calle 10 and 15, also at Av 30 between Calle 4 and 6. There are several *casas de cambio* along Av 5, which change TCs with no commission. **Communications** Internet: All the cybercafés in town charge the same: US$0.15 per minute. *Cyberia,* Calle 4 y Av 15, 0900-2100. *Atomic,* Calle 8 y Av 5, Mon-Sat 0900-2300, Sun 1200-2000. *Cybersol Systems,* Av 5 between Calle 12 and 14. **Post office** is on Av Juárez y Av 15, open Mon-Fri, 0800-1700, Sat 0900-1300. **Telegraph office** is around the corner on Av 15. **Language schools** *Academia de Español,* 'El Estudiante', Av 15 between Calle 2 and 4, T/F30050. Recommended. Also offer courses in English and German. **Laundry** Av Juárez, 2 blocks from bus station; another on Av 5. *Maya Laundry,* Av 5 between Calle 2 and Calle 4, Mon-Sat 0800-2100. Laundry in by 1000, ready in the afternoon. **Medical services** *International Medical Services,* Dr Victor Macías Orosco, Av 35 between Calle 2 and 4, T30493/31343/31344. 24-hr emergency service, land and air ambulance, ultrasound, most major insurance accepted. *Tourist Divers Medical Centre,* Dr Mario Abarca, Av 10 between Av Juárez and Calle 2, T30512 (24-hr) beeper (98) 844556 code 6092. Air and land ambulance service, hyperbaric and diving medicine, affiliated with South Miami Hospital, all insurance accepted. *Dr E Medina,* at Hotel Molcas, Av 5 y Calle 1, T30134, Cell62144. 24-hr hotel calls. **Dentist:** *Perla de Rocha Torres,* Av 20 Nte s/n between 4 and 6, T30021, speaks English. Recommended. **Useful addresses** *Police station,* Av Juárez, next to the post office, T30291/30242. *Immigration office,* Centro Comercial, Plaza Antigua, Av 10 Sur, T31884.

Cozumel

Phone code: 987
Colour map 4, grid A6
Population: 175,000

The town, San Miguel de Cozumel, is a seedy, overpriced version of Playa del Carmen. Daily tour groups arrive on cruises from Miami and Cancún, and the towns' services seem geared towards this type of tourist, ie expensive diamond and gold shops, Tex-Mex and burger restaurants and US-style bars with satellite TV showing sport. But Cozumel is a mecca for scuba divers, with many beautiful offshore reefs to explore, as well as much interesting wildlife and bird life. Travellers looking for a beach holiday with some nightlife will find the island disappointing compared to Playa del Carmen. There is only one nice beach on the west side, and the eastern, Atlantic coast is far too rugged and choppy for swimming.

Ins and outs

Getting there & away The airport is just north of San Miguel with a minibus shuttle service to the hotels. There are 10-minute flights to and from the airstrip near Playa del Carmen, as well as flights linking to Mexico City, Cancún, Chichén Itzá and Houston (Texas). The passenger ferry from Playa del Carmen runs every two hours (see above), and the car ferry leaves twice daily from Puerto Morelos (see page 354).

Getting around

There are no local buses, but Cozumel town is small enough to visit on foot. To get around the island, there are organized tours or taxis; otherwise, hire a jeep, moped or bicycle.

Sights

The island's only town has very little character, mainly due to the construction of a US air base during the Second World War, whose airfield has now been converted for civilian use. The buildings are mostly modern and functional, with many restaurants and bars cluttering the centre. The outskirts are reserved for large banks and airline offices. There is a variety of accommodation, with a few budget hotels, but mainly focusing on the luxury end of the market.

San Miguel de Cozumel

On the waterfront between Calle 4 and 6, **El Museo de la Isla** provides a well laid-out history of the island. ■ *US$3*. There is a bookshop, art gallery and

Cozumel

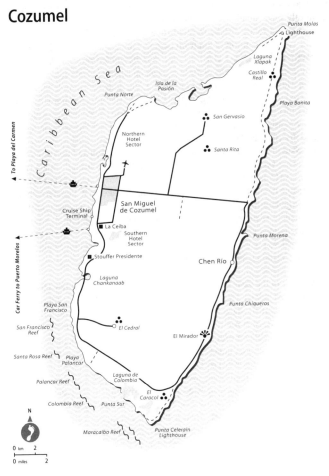

Yucatán Peninsula

rooftop restaurant which has excellent food and views of sunset, good for breakfast, from 0700 ('The Quick' is excellent value). Recommended.

Beaches
The best public beaches are some way from San Miguel town

In the north of the island the beaches are sandy and wide, although those at the Zona Hotel Norte were damaged in 1989 and are smaller than they used to be. At the end of the paved road, walk up the unmade road until it becomes 'dual carriageway'; turn left for the narrow beach, which is a bit dirty. Cleaner beaches are accessible only through the hotels. South of San Miguel, **San Francisco** is good if narrow (clean, very popular, lockers at *Pancho's*, expensive restaurants), but others are generally narrower still and rockier. All the main hotels are on the sheltered west coast. The east, Caribbean coast is rockier, but very picturesque; swimming and diving on the unprotected side is very dangerous owing to ocean underflows. The only safe place is at a sheltered bay at **Chen Río**. Three good (and free) places for snorkelling are the beach in front of *Hotel Las Glorias*, 15 minutes walk south from ferry; you can walk through the hotel's reception. **Playa Corona**, further south, is too far to walk, so hitch or take a taxi. There is a small restaurant and pier; **Xul-Ha**, further south still, has a bar and comfortable beach chairs.

Archaeological sites

There are some 32 archaeological sites on Cozumel; those on the east coast are mostly single buildings (thought to have been lookouts, navigational aids). The easiest to see are the restored ruins of the Maya-Toltec period at **San Gervasio** in the north (7 km from Cozumel town, then 6 km to the left up a paved road, toll US$1). ■ *0700-1700, US$3.50. Guides are on hand, or you can buy a self-guiding booklet at the librería on the square in San Miguel, or at the Flea Market, for US$1.* It is an interesting site, quite spread out, with *sacbés* (sacred roads) between the groups of buildings. There are no large structures, but a nice plaza, an arch, and pigment can be seen in places. It is also a pleasant place to listen to birdsong, see butterflies, animals (if lucky), lizards, landcrabs and insects. **Castillo Real** is one of many sites on the northeastern coast, but the road to this part of the island is in very bad condition and the ruins themselves are very small. **El Cedral** in the southwest (3 km from the main island road) is a two-room temple, overgrown with trees, in the centre of the village of the same name. Behind the temple is a ruin, and next to it a modern church with a green and white façade (an incongruous pairing). In the village are large, permanent shelters for agricultural shows, rug sellers, and locals who pose with *iguanas doradas* (golden iguanas). **El Caracol**, where the sun, in the form of a shell, was worshipped, is 1 km from the southernmost Punta Celarain. At Punta Celarain is an old lighthouse.

Excursions

A circuit of the island on paved roads can easily be done in a day (see **Local Transport** below). Head due east out of San Miguel (take the continuation of Avenida Juárez). Make the detour to San Gervasio before continuing to the Caribbean coast at *Mescalito's* restaurant. Here, turn left for the northern tip (road unsuitable for ordinary vehicles), or right for the south, passing Punta Morena, Chen Río, Punta Chiqueros (restaurant, bathing), El Mirador (a low viewpoint with sea-worn rocks, look out for holes) and Paradise Cove. At this point, the paved road heads west while an unpaved road continues south to Punta Celarain. On the road west, opposite the turn-off to El Cedral, is a sign to *Restaurante Mac y Cía*, an excellent fish restaurant on a lovely beach, popular with dive groups for lunch. Next is Playa San Francisco (see above). A few more kilometres lead to the former *Holiday Inn*, the last big hotel south of San Miguel. Just after this is Parque Chankanab, which used to be an idyllic lagoon behind the beach (9 km from San Miguel). After it became totally spoilt, it was restored as a National Park, with the lagoon, crystal clear again, a botanical garden with local and imported plants, a 'Maya Area' (rather artificial), swimming (ideal for families with young children), snorkelling, dive shops, souvenirs, expensive but good restaurants and lockers (US$2). ■ *0800-1600, US$4, snorkelling mask and fins US$5, use of underwater camera US$25.* Soon the road enters the southern hotel zone at the *Stouffer Presidente*, coming to the cruise ship dock and car ferry port on the outskirts of town.

Essentials

Out of town In the **LL-AL** range: *Meliá Mayan Cozumel*, in northern hotel zone, 5 km from airport, T20072, F21599. *El Cozumeleño*, also in north zone, T20149, F20381. Good, but like all hotels in this area, a bit inconvenient. South of San Miguel are *Stouffer Presidente*, T20322, F21360. 1st class, but some distance from town. *Fiesta Inn*, T22900, F21301, linked to beach by tunnel, and 5 km south, new *Fiesta Cozumel*, 4-star. *La Ceiba*, T20844, F20065. **A** *Tontan*, 3 km north of town (taxi US$1) on waterfront. Pool, clean, safe, snorkelling, cheap restaurant. Recommended.

Sleeping
Prices rise 50% around Christmas

In town In **AL-A** range: *Bahía*, Av Rafael Melgar y Calle 3 Sur (above *Kentucky Fried Chicken*), T20209, F21387. A/c, phone, cable TV, fridge, even-numbered rooms have balcony. Recommended. *Barracuda*, Av Rafael Melgar 628, T20002, F20884. Popular with divers. *Mesón San Miguel*, on the plaza, T20233, F21820. *Plaza Cozumel*, Calle 2 Norte 3, T22711, F20066. A/c, TV, phone, pool, restaurant, car hire, laundry.

B *Hotel del Centro*, Av Juárez 501, corner of Av 25 opposite Pemex, T25471, F20299. Not really central, but in a quiet location not far from it, a/c, pool, TV, modern. **B** *Maya*

Yucatán Peninsula

Cozumel, Calle 5 Sur 4, T20011, F20781. A/c, pool, good value. **B** *Safari*, T20101, F20661. A/c. **B** *Soberanis*, Av Rafael Melgar 471, T20246. A/c, restaurant, terrace bar. **B** *Tamarindo*, Calle 4 Nte 421, between 20 and 25, T/F23614. Bed and breakfast, 3 rooms, shared kitchen, hammocks, dive gear storage and rinse tank, purified drinking water, laundry, safe deposit box, TV, run by Eliane and Jorge, Spanish, English and

San Miguel de Cozumel

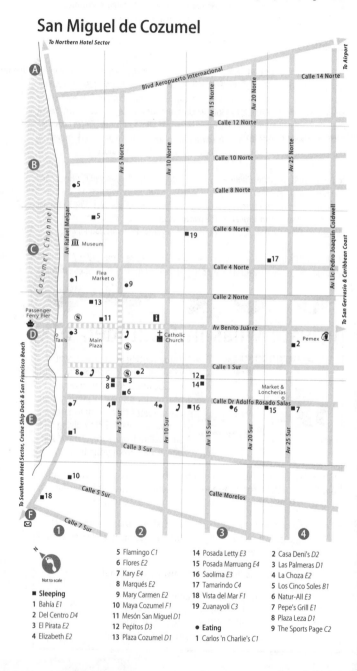

Sleeping
1 Bahía *E1*
2 Del Centro *D4*
3 El Pirata *E2*
4 Elizabeth *E2*
5 Flamingo *C1*
6 Flores *E2*
7 Kary *E4*
8 Marqués *E2*
9 Mary Carmen *E2*
10 Maya Cozumel *F1*
11 Mesón San Miguel *D1*
12 Pepitos *D3*
13 Plaza Cozumel *D1*
14 Posada Letty *E3*
15 Posada Marruang *E4*
16 Saolima *E3*
17 Tamarindo *C4*
18 Vista del Mar *F1*
19 Zuanayoli *C3*

● Eating
1 Carlos 'n Charlie's *C1*
2 Casa Deni's *D2*
3 Las Palmeras *D1*
4 La Choza *E2*
5 Los Cinco Soles *B1*
6 Natur-All *E3*
7 Pepe's Grill *E1*
8 Plaza Leza *D1*
9 The Sports Page *C2*

French spoken, child care on request. **B** *Vista del Mar*, Av Rafael Melgar 45, T20545, near ferry deck. Pool, a/c, restaurant, parking, good value. **C** *Al Marestal*, Calle 10 y 25 Av Norte, T20822. Spacious, clean rooms, fan or a/c, cool showers, swimming pool, very good. **C** *Elizabeth*, Adolfo Rosado Salas 44, T20330. A/c, suites with fridge and stove, also has villas at Calle 3 Sur y Av 25 Sur. 2 doors away is **C-D** *Flores*, A R Salas 72, off plaza, T21429. 50m from the sea, very cheap for central location. A/c, cheaper with fan. **C** *López*, on plaza, Calle Sur 7-A, T20108. Hot showers, clean, main square, no meals. **C** *Marqués*, Av 5 Sur between 1 Sur y A R Salas, T20677. A/c, cheaper with fan. Recommended. Close by are **C** *Mary Carmen* and **C** *El Pirata*. Both cheaper with fan. **C** *Posada Cozumel*, Calle 4 Norte 3, T20314. Pool, showers, a/c, cheaper with fan, clean. **C** *Pepitos*, Av 15 Sur y Calle 1 Sur, T20098, F20201. Very pleasant rooms around a plant-filled courtyard, modern fittings, a/c, fridge in all rooms, free coffee and cookies in the morning. Recommended. **C** *Posada Zuanayoli*, Calle 6 Norte between Av 10 and Av 15 Nte, T20690. Tall, old building in quiet street, TV, modern facilities.

D *Blanquita*, 10 Norte, T21190. Comfortable, clean, friendly, owner speaks English, rents snorkelling gear and motor-scooters. Recommended. **D** *Flamingo*, Calle 6 Norte 81, T21264. Showers, fan, clean, family-run, good value. Recommended. **D** *José de León*, Av Pedro J Coldwell y Calle 17 Sur. Fairly clean, showers. **D** *Kary*, 25 Av Sur y A R Salas, T22011. A/c, showers, pool, clean. **D** *Paraíso Caribe*, 15 Av Norte y Calle 10, fan, showers, clean. **D** *Posada del Charro*, 1 block east of *José de León*, same owner, same facilities. **D** *Posada Letty*, Calle 1 Sur y Av 15 Sur. Clean, hot water, good value. Recommended. **D** *Posada Marruang*, A R Salas 440, between Av 20 Sur and Av 25 Sur, T21678. Very spick and span, large comfortable rooms set back from road; barking dog ensures occasional noise and total security. **D** *Posada de Zorro*, Av Joaquín y Av Juárez, T20790. On busy junction, but cheap and out of the way, in case everywhere else is full. **E** *Saolima*, A R Salas 260, T20886. Clean, fan, showers, hot water. Recommended.

Private **villas** can be rented around the island. Shea and Toni Novakovic have around 40 properties at various prices. Maid service and airport transfer is included. View the properties on their website: www.cozumelvacation.com.

Camping Not permitted although there are 2 suitable sites on the south shore. Try asking for permission at the army base.

Expensive *Morgans*, main square. Elegant, good. *Café del Puerto*, 2nd floor by pier. **Eating** South-Seas style. *El Capi Navegante*, 2 locations: by market for lunch, and Calle 3 y Av 10 Sur. More up-market. Seafood at each. *Pepe's Grill*, waterfront, 2 blocks south of pier. Excellent. *Pancho's Backyard*, Rafael Melgar 27, in *Los Cinco Soles* shopping complex. Mexican food and wine elegantly served, good food. *La Choza*, A R Salas 198. Expensive, Mexico City food. Recommended. *Lobster's Cove*, Av Rafael Melgar 790. Seafood, live music, happy hour 1200-1400. *Prima*, A R Salas, 109. Northern Italian seafood, handmade pasta, brick oven pizzas, non-smoking area.

Mid-range *Las Palmeras*, at the pier (people-watching spot). Very popular for breakfast, opens 0700, always busy. Recommended. *Plaza Leza*, main square. Excellent and reasonable. *Miss Dollar*, A R Salas y Av 20. Good Mexican food, US$2 *comidas*, very friendly. *Karen's Pizza and Grill*, Av 5 Norte between Av Juárez and Calle 2 Norte. Cheap pizza, good. *Western Grill*, Av 5, near Zócalo. Excellent breakfasts. *Gatto Pardo*, Av 10 Sur 121. Good pizzas and try their 'tequila slammers'. *El Moro*, 75 Bis Norte 124, between 4 and 2. Good, closed Thu. *Santiago's Grill*, Av 15 Sur y A R Salas. Excellent, popular with divers; also popular with divers is *Las Tortugas*, Av 10 Norte, just north of square. Good in the evening. *Alfalfa*, Calle 5 Sur, between Rafael Melgar and Av 5.

Mostly vegetarian meals but owner Dawne Detraz expanding with more fish and chicken and health food shop, daily hot special US$3 with salad and drink, excellent coffee, friendly. Highly recommended. *La Yucatequita*, Calle 9 Sur y Av 10 Sur. Genuine Mayan food, closes at 2130, best to go day before and discuss menu. *La Misión*, Av Juárez y Av 10 Norte. Good food, friendly atmosphere. *Acuario*, on beach 6 blocks south of pier. Famous for seafood, aquarium in restaurant (ask to see the tanks at the back). *Carlos n' Charlie's*, restaurant/bar. Popular, 2nd floor on waterfront 2 blocks north of pier. *Mi Chabalita*, Av 10 Sur between Calle 1 Sur and A R Salas. Friendly, cheap and good Mexican food. *Pepe Pelícano*, 2 houses left of *Hotel Saolima*. Cheap and clean. *Casa Deni's*, Calle 1 Sur 164, close to Plaza. Open-air restaurant, very good, moderate prices. *The Sports Page*, Calle 2 Norte y Av 5. US-style, breakfasts, burgers, steaks, lobster, satellite TV, money exchange, phones for USA; US-style breakfasts also at *Los Cocos*, next to ProDive on A R Salas. *Sonora Grill*, Av 15 Nte No 2 between Av Juárez and Calle 2 Norte. Tex-Mex, steaks, seafood. *Los Moros del Morrito*, Av 35 Sur between Calle 3 and Morelos. Typical Yucatecan cuisine and seafood. *Natur-All*, A R Salas No 352, between Av 15 and Av 20. Open for breakfast and lunch only, 0700-1800, no smoking, health food, small portions, soya, yoghurt, fresh salads.

Cheap   There are few eating options for the budget traveller. The cheapest places for breakfast, lunch or an early dinner are the *loncherías* next to the market on A R Salas, between Av 20 and Av 25. There are four of them, all serving fairly good local *comida corrida*, open from 0800-1930.

Bakeries   *Diamond Bakery*, Av 15 y Av 1 Sur. Inconspicuous sign, good bread and pastries, also have a café on the waterfront. *Zermatt*, Av 5 y Calle 4 Norte. Good bakery.

Bars & nightclubs   *Scruffy Murphy's Irish Pub*, A R Salas between Av 10 y Av 15. Also has traditional pub food, eg steak pie. *The Stadium*, Av 5 y Calle 2, 1 block from seafront. American-style sports bar, with live sports via satellite, pool tables and cheap beer deals. *Joe's Lobster Pub & Reggae Bar*, Av 10 No 229, between Av 3 and A R Salas. Live Caribbean music, open till 0330. *Joman's*. Very seedy. *Scaramouche*, Av Rafael Melgar y A R Salas. The best. *Neptuno*, Av Rafael Melgar y Calle 11, south of centre. The last two are state-of-the-art discos, as well as hotel nightclubs.

Shopping   Lots of very expensive diamond and gold shops along the seafront, aimed at the US cruises arriving daily from Miami. Souvenirs are more expensive than Playa del Carmen, with pushy sales staff. The exception is *Exótica*, dockside of the main plaza, for souvenirs, hats, friendly staff. **Film**: 2 shops develop film, both quite expensive (about US$20 for 36 prints). Best to wait till you get home.

Sport   **Golf**   Cozumel putting course, corner of Av 1 Sur and Av 15. Open daily 1100-2300.

Scuba diving   The island is famous for the beauty of its underwater environment. The best reef for scuba diving is **Palancar**, reached only by boat. Also highly recommended are **Santa Rosa** and **Colombia**. There are at least 20 major dive sites. Almost all Cozumel diving is drift diving, so if you are not used to a current, choose an operator you feel comfortable with. There are 2 different types of dive centre: the larger ones, where the divers are taken out to sea in big boats with many passengers; the smaller, more personalised dive shops, with a maximum of 8 people per small boat. The best of the smaller centres is said to be *Deep Blue*, A R Salas 200, esq Av 10 Sur, T/F25653, deepblue@cozumel.com.mx Matt and Deborah, an English/Colombian couple, run the centre. All diving is computerized, the only place on Cozumel where this is used as standard on all dives. As well as the reefs just off the island, *Deep Blue* offer trips to reefs further offshore, including some unusual sites not covered by other dive shops. All PADI and NAUI certifications, eg Open Water Diver US$360; 3-5-day dive packages US$165-250; Cavern & cenote diving, including 2 dives, transport and lunch US$130. Other small dive centres are: *Black Shark*, Av 5 between A R Salas and Calle 3 Sur, T/F25657. *Diving Adventures*, Calle 5 No 2, T23009. *Blue Bubble Divers*, Av 5 Sur, esq Calle 3, T21865. Cozumel has 2 **decompression centres**: *Buceo Médico Mexicano*, Calle 5 Sur No 21B, T22387/21430, immediate localization (24-hr) VHF 16 and 21. It is suported by US$1 per day donations from divers with affiliated operators. *Cozumel Hyperbarics* in Clínica San Miguel, Calle 6 Norte No 135 between Av 5 and Av 10, T23070, VHF channel 65.

Ferinco Travel Tours, T21781. Own airline with flights to all major Maya sites.   **Tour operators**

There is no bus service, but taxis are plentiful. The best way to get around the island is   **Transport** by hired moped or bicycle. Note that the trip to the San Gervasio ruins or the east side of the island is a very strenous ride for all but the most experienced of cyclists; a moped is recommended for either of these journeys. For mopeds, a helmet must be worn, with a US$25 fine for not doing so; get off the road if it starts to rain; always wear sun block for longer journeys, particularly to the exposed east coast. Mopeds cost US$20-25 per day, credit card needed as deposit; bicycles are around US$5 per day, US$20 cash or TC deposit. *Rentadora* Cozumel, Av 10 Sur no 172 between A R Salas y Calle 1 Sur, T21120. *Splash*, Calle 6 Nte, T23977. **Car rental**   There are many agencies, including *Less Pay*, in Hotel Barracuda (see under Sleeping) T24744. *Budget Jeep & Auto*, Av 5 y Calle 2, T20903. *Aguila jeep & Moto*, Calle 11 No 101, T20729.

Air   Cozumel-Mexico City direct with Mexicana, or via Cancún; Continental to Houston; Aerocaribe to Cancún and Chichén Itzá. Aerocaribe and Aerocozumel have almost hourly flights to Cancún.

Airline offices   Most are based at the airport, 2 km north of the town. Aerocozumel T23456.   **Directory** Continental T20847. Mexicana, P Joaquin between A R Salas and Calle 3 Sur, next to Pemex, T20263/22945. **Banks**   4 banks on the main square, all exchange money in morning only, but not at same hours: *Bital*, on Juárez (all with ATM machines), *Bancomer, Banamex, Atlántico. Casas de cambio* on Av 5 Norte and around square, 3.5% commission, open longer hours. **Communications**   Internet: *Internet Cozumel*, Calle 1 Sur esq Av 10 Sur, just off main plaza, US$6 per hour. **Laundry**   *Express*, A R Salas between Av 5 and Av 10, T23655. Coin-op and service washes, US$9 medium load, collection service and dry cleaning. **Post Office:** Av Rafael Melgar y Calle 7 Sur, Mon-Fri 0900-1800, Sat 0900-1200. **Telephone:** Ladatel phones on main square at corner of Av Juárez and Av 5, or on A R Salas, just up from Av 5 Sur, opposite *Roberto's Black Coral Studio* (if working). For calls to the USA, go to *The Sports Page*. Telmex phone offices on the main square next to *Restaurant Plaza Leza*, 0800-2300, and on A R Salas between Av 10 and 15. There are also expensive Computel offices in town, eg at the cruise ship dock. Telephone centre for long distance on corner of Rafael Melgar and Calle 3 Sur. Also public telephone *caseta* at Av 5 esq Calle 2, 0800-1300, 1600-2100. **Medical services**   Hospitals: *Red Cross*, A R Salas between Calle 20 and Calle 25 Sur, T21058. Centro *Médico de Cozumel*, Calle 1 Sur No 101, esq Av 50, T23545/25664/25370. English spoken, international air ambulance, 24-hr emergency service. *Pharmacy*, A R Salas between Av 12 and Av 20. Open 0700-2400. **Dentists:** Dr Hernández, T20656. Dr Mariles, T21352.

Playa del Carmen to Tulum

Back on the mainland, there are some Maya ruins at Xcaret, a turn-off left on   **Xcaret** Route 307 to Tulum, after Playa del Carmen. The Maya site, an ancient port called Polé, was the departure point for voyages to Cozumel. It has now been turned into an overpriced and very tacky theme park catering exclusively for day-trippers. ■ *US$37 (children under five years free)*. This entry fee entitles

👉 *Cenote diving*

There are over 50 cenotes in this area, accessible from Ruta 307 and often well signposted, and cave diving has become very popular. However, it is a specialized sport and unless you have a cave diving qualification, you must be accompanied by a qualified dive master. A cave diving course involves over 12 hours of lectures and a minimum of 14 cave dives using double tanks, costing around US$600. Specialist dive centres offering courses are: Mike Madden's CEDAM Dive Centres, PO Box 1, Puerto Aventuras, T/F98735129; Aquatech, Villas de Rosa, PO Box 25, Aventuras Akumal No 35, Tulum, T/F41271; Akumal Dive Centre, PO Box 1, Akumal, Playa del Carmen, T41259,

F98873164. The above have a 100% safety record. Other operators include Yax-Há Dive Centre, T22888; Akumal Explorers, T22453; Dos Ojos (Divers of the Hidden World), T44081. Some of the best cenotes are 'Carwash', on the Cobá road, good even for beginners, with excellent visibility; 'Dos Ojos', just off Ruta 307 south of Aventuras, the second largest underground cave system in the world; it has a possible link to the Nohoch Nah Chich, the most famous cenote and part of a subterranean system recorded as the world's largest, with over 50 km of surveyed passageways connected to the sea.

you to visit the small ruins, the aviary, the beach, lagoon and inlet, to take an underground river trip (life vest included) and to use all chairs, hammocks and *palapas*. Everything else is extra: food and drink (none may be brought in), snorkel rental (US$7), snorkel lessons, reef trips (US$10), diving, horse riding (US$30) and lockers (for which you have to pay US$1 each time you lock the door). There are also dolphins in pens; you don't actually swim with them, rather they jump or pass over you (US$50). No suntan lotion may be worn in the sea, but there is a film of oils in the sea nonetheless. Buses from Playa del Carmen leave you at the turn-off (US$0.65), by a roadside restaurant which is very clean (accepts Visa). There is a 1 km walk from the entrance to Xcaret. The alternative is to take a taxi, or a tour from Playa del Carmen or Cancún (in a multicoloured bus). You can also walk along the beach from Playa del Carmen, three hours.

Paamul, just south of Playa del Carmen and about 92 km south of Cancún, is a fine beach on a bay, planned for development, with chalets (**C** with bath, fan, terrace for hammocks, comfortable, pretty, clean, recommended) and campsites (recommended). There is snorkelling and diving and a reef a few metres off shore. Second-class buses from Cancún and Playa del Carmen pass.

Akumal
Colour map 4, grid A6

A luxury resort, 102 km south of Cancún, 20 km north of Tulum, Akumal is reached easily by bus from there or from Playa del Carmen (30 minutes). There is a small lagoon 3 km north of Akumal, good snorkelling.

Sleeping and eating **L** *Hotel Club Akumal Caribe*. One of many luxury hotels, villas and condos which can be booked in the US through *Caribbean Fantasy*, PO Box 7606, Loveland, Colorado 80537-0606, caribbfan@aol.com, accommodation is all **LL-AL**. *Akumal Caribe*. Has a restaurant (there is a small supermarket nearby at *Villas Mayas*), poor service, overpriced, no entertainment, excellent beach, with coral reef only 100m offshore. Eat at restaurant marked *Comidas Económicas* outside the gate. **LL** *Club Aventuras Akumal*, T98722887. All inclusive resort owned by Oasis group, small pool, on pleasant beach. **AL** *Villas Mayas*. Bungalows, with bath, comfortable, some with kitchens, on beach, snorkelling equipment for hire, US$6 per day, restaurant with poor service, recommended as base for excursions to Xel-Há, Tulum and Cobá.

Playa Aventuras is a huge beach resort south of Akumal. **LL** *Club Puerto Aventuras*. Another Oasis hotel, sandwiched between the sea and marina, all-inclusive with 309 rooms. Two ferries run daily to Cozumel. Also just south of Akumal are **Chemuyil** (*palapas*, thatched shelters for hammocks, US$4, free shower, expensive restaurant, laundry facilities) and **Xcacel** (campground has water, bathrooms, cold showers and restaurant, very clean, US$2 per person, vehicles free, snorkel hire US$5 a day, beautiful swimming in the bay). Ask guards if you can go on turtle protection patrol at night (May-July).

Laguna Xel-Há

Thirteen kilometres north of Tulum, 122 km from Cancún (bus from Playa del Carmen, 45 minutes), this beautiful clear lagoon is full of fish, but fishing is not allowed as it is a national park. ■ *0800-1630, US$10*. Snorkelling gear can be rented at US$7 for a day, but it is often in poor repair; better to rent from your hotel. Lockers cost US$1. Arrive as early as possible to see fish as the lagoon is full of tourists throughout most of the day. Snorkelling areas are limited by fencing. You need to dive down about 1m because above that level the water is cold and fresh with few fish; below it is the warm, fish-filled salt water). Bungalows, first-class hotels and fast-food restaurants are being built. The food and drink is very expensive. There is a marvellous jungle path to one of the lagoon bays. Xel-Há ruins (known also as **Los Basadres**) are located across the road from the beach of the same name. ■ *US$3.35*. Few tourists but not much to see. You may have to jump the fence to visit; there is a beautiful *cenote* at the end of the ruins where you can have a lovely swim. Small ruins of **Ak** are near Xel-Há. Closer to Tulum, at **Tancáh**, are newly discovered bright post-classical Maya murals, but they are sometimes closed to the public.

Tulum

Tulum

Entrance & Car Park

To Cabañas Zone

N

Not to scale

1 Castillo
2 Main Plaza
3 Temple of the Diving God
4 Temple of the Frescoes

Tulum

Colour map 4, grid A6

The Tulum ruins, Maya-Toltec, are 131 km south of Cancún, 1 km off the main road. They are 12th century, with city walls of white stone atop coastal cliffs. The temples were dedicated to the worship of the Falling God, or the Setting Sun, represented as a falling character over nearly all the west-facing doors (Cozumel was the home of the Rising Sun). The same idea is reflected in the buildings, which are wider at the top than at the bottom.

The main structure is the **Castillo**, which commands a view of both the sea and the forested Quintana Roo lowlands stretching westwards. All the Castillo's openings face west, as do most, but not all, of the doorways at Tulum. Look for the alignment of the **Falling God** on the temple of that name (to the left of the Castillo) with

Yucatán Peninsula

the pillar and the back door in the **House of the Chultún** (the nearest building in the centre group to the entrance). The majority of the main structures are roped off so that you cannot climb the Castillo, nor get close to the surviving frescoes, especially on the **Temple of the Frescoes**. In 1993 the government began a major improvement and conservation programme to improve facilities at the site.

Tulum is these days crowded with tourists (best time to visit is between 0800 and 0900). Take towel and swimsuit if you wish to scramble down from the ruins to one of the two beaches for a swim (the larger of the two is less easy to get to). The reef is from 600m to 1,000m from the shore, so if you wish to snorkel you must either be a strong swimmer, or take a boat trip. ■ *The site is open 0800-1700, entry US$3, parking US$1.50, students with Mexican ID free, Sun free.* There is a tourist complex at the entrance to the ruins. Guide books can be bought in the shops; the *Panorama* guide book is interesting; others are available. Local guides can also be hired. About two hours are needed to view at leisure. The parking area is near Highway 307, and there's a handicraft market. A small train takes you from the parking area to the ruins for US$1, or it is an easy 500-m walk. The paved road continues down the coast to **Boca Paila** and beyond, access by car to this road from the car park is now forbidden. To reach the road south of the ruins, access is possible 1 km from Tulum village.

Public buses drop passengers at El Crucero, a crossroads 500m north of the car park for Tulum Ruinas (an easy walk) where there is an ADO bus terminal which opens for a few hours at 0800; at the crossroads are some hotels, a shop (will exchange travellers' cheques), on the opposite side of the road a naval base and airstrip, and a little way down Highway 307 a Pemex station. The village of **Tulum** is 4 km south of El Crucero. A taxi from the village to the ruins costs US$2.50. It is not very large and has a bus station, a post office but no bank; there are five to six grocery shops, two *panaderías*, a hotel and restaurants.

Tourist office Very good tourist information in the village, next to the police station, 2 blocks north of the bus terminal; Nedza Hualtoyotl is very helpful and informative about the area.

Sleeping & eating
When arriving by bus, get off at El Crucero for the ruins and nearby accommodation. A new hotel is under construction at the site

At El Crucero C *El Faisán y El Venado*. TV, a/c, OK, restaurant serving pizzas, Mexican dishes and very expensive drinks; across the road is **E** *Hotel El Crucero de Tulum*. Much more basic, damp, dirty, but a/c, hot water, staff unhelpful, good restaurant with shop attached. Almost opposite bus stop is a new hotel, **C**, large, clean, a/c, parking, with restaurant (24 hours), good food and service; and *Chilam-Balam*, across the road. Also serves good food.

At Tulum village D-E *Hotel Maya*, near bus stop. A/c or fan, shower, reasonable, restaurant with slow service, small shop, parking in front. Several chicken restaurants and *Leonor's* for fish and Mexican food, good but pricey. *Charlie's*, near *Hotel Maya*. Great atmosphere, décor and food.

Cabañas To reach the following accommodation it is better to get off the bus in town and take a taxi (US$3-5 depending on season), otherwise ½-hr walk from the bus stop. In high season *cabañas* are difficult to get. Establishments are listed according to proximity to the ruins (see map); **E-F** *Cabañas El Mirador*. Small, quiet, cabins (won't rent to singles), hammocks available, camping, 2 showers, use of restaurant toilets (clean), bar and restaurant with excellent views, 10 minutes walk from ruins; next is **E-F** *Santa Fe*. Basic *cabañas*, new toilets and showers, US$1 extra for mosquito net, hammocks or tents, water problems, reported insecure, watch your belongings, has a restaurant, good breakfasts and fish dinners, reggae music, English, French and

Italian spoken, basic toilets, laid-back atmosphere, but cheaper cabins are badly constructed and lack privacy, free camping possible further up the beach. **C-E** *Cabañas Don Armando*, T43856/44539/44437. *Cabañas* for up to 4, prices variable, the best, very popular, staff are friendly and helpful, cheap but limited restaurant with long queues, bar with noisy disco till 0200, certain bus tickets available. **E** *Cabañas Mar Caribe*. Smaller complex than its neighbour *Don Armando*, but a friendly atmosphere, and much more peaceful. Small beachside restaurant. **C-D** *Cabañas Diamante K*, on the beach. Nice bar and restaurant. Recommended. **E** *La Conchita*. Basic *cabañas* on the beach. **D-E** *Punta Piedra*, similar. **B-D** *Nohoch Tunich*, 1 hr walk from ruins. Clean *cabañas*, good food; near the *cabaña* resort are exchange facilities, dive shop and 2 bike rental shops. **AL-A** *Piedra Escondida*. Modern, 2-storey thatched *cabañas*. **D-E** *La Perla*, 5 km south of Tulum. *Cabañas*, camping and restaurant, comfortable, good food, family atmosphere, near beach. Recommended. **B-C** *Zamas Cabañas*. Simple restaurant on beach. Highly recommended. **AL** *Maya Tulum*. Well-equipped huts on secluded beach. **A-B** *Anna y José*, restaurant, 6 km south of ruins. Also has *cabañas* and rooms, some are right on the beach, very clean, comfortable and hospitable. Trips can be arranged to the Sian Ka'an Biosphere Reserve (see page 373). Recommended. **B** *Cabañas Tulum*. Solid stone *cabañas* near the beach, bar and restaurant, electricity until 2200. **AL** *Dos Ceibas*. 9 km from the ruins. Luxury cabins on the edge of the Sian Ka'an Biosphere Reserve. For places to stay in Sian Ka'an Biosphere Reserve, see page 374.

B *Hotel Posada Tulum*, 8 km south of the ruins on the beach. Has an expensive restaurant, hot water (cheaper with cold water), electricity morning and 1800-2300, changes dollars, no credit cards. **E** *Tita Tulum*. Eco hotel, with bath; taxi to Tulum, US$3-5.

Tulum cabañas

To Cancún

El Crucero

Tulum Ruins

Carribbean Sea

El Mirador
Santa Fe
Don Armando
Mar Caribe
Diamante K
La Conchita
Punta Piedra
Nohoch-Tunich
Piedra Escondida

Tulum
Bus Terminal

La Perla

To Cobá

Zamas

Maya Tulum

To Chetumal

Ana y José

Cabañas Tulum

Dos Ceibas

N

0 metres (approx) 500
0 yards (approx) 500

To Sian Ka'an
Biosphere Reserve

Sports

Diving Several dive shops all along the Tulum corridor. See page 368 for cave diving operators and specialist courses. Many untrained snorkelling and diving outfits, take care. *Aktun*, next to *Hotel El Mesón*, 1 km out of Tulum on main road, gunnar.wagner@aktundive.com, German/Mexican-run, experienced NACD and IANTD instructor, very friendly, speaks English, French and Dutch.

Transport

Buses 2nd class buses on the Cancún-Playa del Carmen-Felipe Carrillo Puerto-Chetumal route stop at Tulum; also 3 Inter Playa buses a day from Cancún, US$4.25. Some buses may be full when they reach Tulum; very few buses begin their journeys here. **Felipe Carrillo Puerto**, several between 0600-1200 and 1600-2200, 1 hr, US$2, continuing to **Chetumal**, 2nd class, US$7, 1st class US$8.50, 4 hrs. For **Cobá**, take the Playa del Carmen-Tulum-Cobá-Valladolid bus which passes El Crucero at 0600, 1100 and 1800 (in the other direction buses pass Tulum at 0715 and 1545, all times approximate, may leave 15 mins early). Tulum-Cobá

US$1.35, 45 mins. **Mérida**, several daily, US$7, 2nd class, 6 hrs. **Tizimín** daily at 1400, via Cancún and Valladolid. **Escárcega** and **Córdoba** 0800, **Palenque** US$25. **San Cristóbal**, 1845, often late, US$32. **Villahermosa**, 1630, 2100, US$28. **Mexico City**, 0815, 1315, 2100, US$62. **Veracruz**, 1630. Autobuses del Caribe offices are next door to *Hotel Maya*. Buy tickets here rather than wait for buses at the crossroads, but this still does not ensure getting a seat. It may be better to go to Playa del Carmen (US$1.40) for more connections to nearby destinations. If travelling far, take a bus to Felipe Carrillo Puerto and transfer to ADO there.

Taxis Tulum town to ruins US$3.50; to the *cabañas* US$3.50; to Cobá about US$25.

Bicycles can be hired in the village at US$1 per hour, a good way to visit local centres (*Cristal* and *Escondido* are recommended as much cheaper, US$2, and less commercialized than *Xcaret*).

Directory **Banks** 4 money exchange booths near bus station in Tulum village. TCs can be changed at the offices of the GOPI Construction Company, though not at a very good rate. **Communications** Telephone: long-distance phones in ADO terminal in town; also fax office, F98712009 and bike rental.

Cobá

Colour map 4, grid A6 An important Maya city in the eighth and ninth centuries AD, whose population is estimated to have been between 40,000 and 50,000, Cobá was abandoned for unknown reasons. The present-day village of Cobá lies on either side of Lago Cobá, surrounded by dense jungle, 47 km inland from Tulum. It is a quiet friendly village, with few tourists staying overnight.

The entrance to the ruins of this large but little-excavated city is at the end of the lake between the two parts of the village. A second lake, **Lago Macanxoc**, is within the site. There are turtles and many fish in the lakes. It is a good birdwatching area. Both lakes and their surrounding forest can be seen from the summit of the **Iglesia**, the tallest structure in the **Cobá Group**. There are three other groups of buildings to visit: the **Macanxoc Group**, mainly stelae, about 1½ km from the Cobá Group; **Las Pinturas**, 1 km northeast of Macanxoc, with a temple and the remains of other buildings which had columns in their construction; the **Nohoch Mul Group**, at least another kilometre from Las Pinturas. Nohoch Mul has the tallest pyramid in the northern Yucatán, a magnificent structure, from which the views of the jungle on all sides are superb. You will not find at Cobá the great array of buildings which can be seen at Chichén Itzá or Uxmal, nor the compactness of Tulum. Instead, the delight of the place is the architecture in the jungle, with birds, butterflies, spiders and lizards, and the many uncovered structures which hint at the vastness of the city in its heyday (the urban extension of Cobá is put at some 70 sq km). An unusual feature is the network of ancient roads, known as *sacbés* (white roads), which connect the groups in the site and are known to have extended across the entire Maya Yucatán. Over 40 *sacbés* pass through Cobá, some local, some of great length, such as the 100-km road to Yaxuná in Yucatán state.

At the lake, toucans may be seen very early; also look out for greenish-blue and brown mot-mots in the early morning. The guards at the site are very strict about opening and closing time so it is difficult to gain entry to see the dawn or sunset from a temple.

The paved road into Cobá ends at **Lago Cobá**; to the left are the ruins, to the right *Villas Arqueológicas*. The roads around Cobá are badly potholed. Cobá is becoming more popular as a destination for tourist buses, which come in at

Yucatán Peninsula

1030; arrive before that to avoid the crowds and the heat (ie on the 0430 bus from Valladolid, if not staying in Cobá). Take insect repellent. ■ *0800-1700, US$2.50, free on Sunday*. Guide books: Bloomgarten's *Tulum and Cobá*, and *Descriptive Guide book to Cobá* by Prof Gualberto Zapata Alonzo, which is a little unclear about dates and details, but is still useful and has maps. Free map from *Hotel Restaurant Bocadito*.

B *Villas Arqueológicas* (Club Méditerranée), about 2 km from site on lake shore. Open to non-members, excellent, clean and quiet, a/c, swimming pool, good restaurant with moderate prices, but expensive beer. Do not arrive without a reservation, especially at weekends; on the other hand, making a reservation by phone seems to be practically impossible. In the village, on the street leading to the main road, is **E** *Hotel Restaurant El Bocadito*. Run-down, spartan rooms with fan, intermittent water supply, poor security, good but expensive restaurant (which is popular with tour groups), books and handicrafts for sale. Recommended.

Sleeping

There are plenty of restaurants in the village, on the road to *Villas Arqueológicas* and on the road to the ruins, they are all quite pricey; also a grocery store by *El Bocadito* and souvenir shops. *Nicte-Ha*, good and friendly. *Pirámides*, on corner of track leading to *Villas Arqueológicas*. Highly recommended.

Eating

Local Buses into the village turn round at the road end. There are 3 a day to Valladolid, coming from Playa del Carmen and Tulum, passing through at 0630, 1130 and 1830, 2 hrs to Valladolid, US$2.50; 2 buses a day to Tulum and Playa at 0630 and 1500, US$1 to Tulum. A taxi to Tulum costs around US$25. If you miss the bus there is a taxi to be found at *El Bocadito*.

Transport

Banks *Sterling Store*, opposite entrance to ruins.

Directory

The road linking Tulum with Cobá turns off the main Highway 307 just before Tulum town. This road joins the *vía libre* Valladolid-Cancún road at **Nuevo Xcan**, thus greatly shortening the distance between Chichén Itzá and Tulum (do not take the *cuota* road which no longer exits at Nuevo Xcan). The Cobá-Valladolid bus passes Nuevo Xcan (no hotel but the owner of the shop where the road branches off to Cobá may offer you a room). There is an *aduana* post in Nuevo Xcan which is at the border between Yucatán and Quintana Roo states; police searches are made for those leaving Quintana Roo for items which may transmit plant and other diseases. If going from Valladolid or Cancún to Cobá, follow the *Villas Arqueológicas* sign at Nuevo Xcan. **NB** many maps show a road from Cobá to Chemax, west of Xcan. This road does not exist; the only road from the north to Cobá is from Nuevo Xcan. For drivers, there is no Pemex station between Cancún and Valladolid, or Cancún-Cobá-Tulum, or Valladolid-Cobá- Tulum, all are journeys of 150 km without a fill-up.

Between Nuevo Xcan and Cobá is the tiny village of **Punta Laguna**, which has a lake and forest, preserved through the efforts of ecotourists. Ask for Serapio to show you round; he does not speak English, and depends mainly on tourists for his income.

Sian Ka'an Biosphere Reserve

The Reserve covers 4,500 sq km of the Quintana Roo coast. About one third is covered in tropical forest, one third is savannas and mangrove and one third coastal and marine habitats, including 110 km of barrier reef. Mammals include jaguar, puma, ocelot and other cats, monkeys, tapir, peccaries,

Colour map 4, grid B6

Yucatán Peninsula

manatee and deer; turtles nest on the beaches; there are crocodiles and a wide variety of land and aquatic birds. For all information, go to the office of Los Amigos de Sian Ka'an, Plaza América, Avenida Cobá 5, 3rd floor, suites 48-50, Cancún (Apdo Postal 770, 77500 Cancún, T849583, sian@cancun.rce.com.mx); very helpful. ■ *0900-1500, 1800-2000*. Do not try to get to the reserve independently without a car. *Ecocolors*, Cancún, T/F849580, in collaboration with Los Amigos, run tours to the Reserve, US$115 for a full day, starting at 0700, pick up at hotel, everything included: in winter the tour goes through a canal, in summer it goes birdwatching, in both cases a visit to a Maya ruin, a *cenote*, snorkelling, all equipment, breakfast and evening meal are included. Two-day camping trips can be arranged. Two-hour boat trips through the Biosphere can be taken for US$50. Trips can also be arranged through *Cabañas Ana y José*, near Tulum, US$50, daily except Sunday (see page 371). It is possible to drive into the Reserve from Tulum village as far as Punta Allen (58 km; the road is opposite the turning to Cobá; it is not clearly marked, and the final section is badly potholed); beyond that you need a launch. From the south it is possible to drive to Punta Herrero (unmade road, see **Majahual**, below). No explanations are available for those going independently.

Sleeping At **Punta Allen** is a small fishing village with houses for rent (cooking facilities), and a good, non-touristy restaurant, *La Cantina* (US$3-4 for fish). There are also 2 comfortable *cabañas* at a place called **A** *Rancho Sol Caribe*. With bath, restaurant. Recommended. Reservations to: Diane and Michael Sovereign, Apdo Postal 67, Tulum, CP 77780, T12091, F12092. **Punta Herrero** is 6 hrs from Chetumal, 10 hrs from Cancún; *rancheros* are very hospitable, camping is possible but take all food and plenty of insect repellent.

· In the Reserve, 8 km south of Tulum, are the quiet, pleasant **AL** *Cabañas Los Arrecifes*, with smart chalets on the beach and others behind, cheaper, with good fish restaurant shaped like a ship (no electricity), limited menu. 100m away are **D** *Cabañas de Tulum*, also with good restaurant, clean cabins with shower, electricity 1730-2100; interesting fish in the *cenote* opposite, take taxi there (US$5-6 from ruins car park), empty white beaches. *Pez Maya* and *Boca Paila* are expensive fishing lodges. *Casa Blanca* is an exclusive hotel reached only by small plane. *Rancho Retiro*, camping US$2, food and beer served, very relaxed atmosphere.

Muyil The ruins of Muyil at **Chunyaxché**, three pyramids (partly overgrown), are on the left-hand side of the road to Felipe Carrillo Puerto, 18 km south of Tulum. One of the pyramids is undergoing reconstruction; the other two are relatively untouched. They are very quiet, with interesting birdlife although they are mosquito-infested. ■ *US$4*. Beyond the last pyramid is Laguna Azul, which is good for swimming and snorkelling in blue, clean water (you do not have to pay to visit the pool if you do not visit the pyramids).

Felipe Carrillo Puerto
Colour map 4, grid B6

The cult of the 'talking cross' was founded here. The Santuario de la Cruz Parlante is five blocks west of the Pemex station on Highway 307. The beautiful main square, which has playground equipment for children, is dominated by the Catholic church, built by the Cruzob in the 19th century (see page 291). Legend has it that the unfinished bell tower will only be completed when the descendants of those who heard the talking cross reassert control of the region.

Sleeping and eating *Hotel Carrillo Puerto* has been recommended. **C** *El Faisán y El Venado*, 2 blocks northeast of main square. Mixed reports on cleanliness, but hot water and good-value restaurant, popular with locals. **D** *Tulum*, with better restaurant. **E** *Chan Santa Cruz*, just off the Plaza. Good, basic, clean and friendly (*Restaurante*

24 Horas is open 24 hrs, OK). **E** *Hotel Esquivel*, just off Plaza. Fair, noisy. **D** *San Ignacio*, near Pemex. Good value, a/c, bath, towels, TV, secure car park; next door is restaurant *Danburger Maya*. Good food, reasonable prices, helpful. **F** *María Isabel*, on same road. Clean, friendly, laundry service, quiet, safe parking. *Restaurant Addy*, on main road, south of town. Good, simple. There are a few food shops in the village selling sweet breads, and mineral water.

Tulum to Chetumal

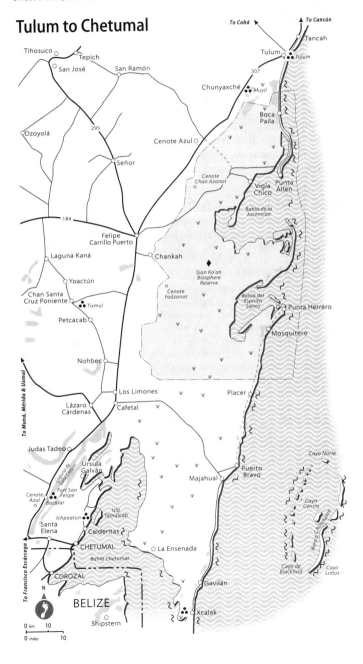

Yucatán Peninsula

Transport Bus station opposite Pemex. Autotransportes del Caribe (Playa Express) to **Cancún** daily from 0600, 1st and 2nd class to **Tulum**, US$2, and **Playa del Carmen** *en route*. Bus Felipe Carrillo Puerto-**Mérida**, via Muná, US$10, 4½ hrs; to **Valladolid**, 2nd class, 2 hrs, US$3.75; to **Chetumal**, 1st class, 2 hrs, US$3.35.

Majahual Further south on Route 307, at Cafetal, is an unpaved road east to Majahual on the coast (56 km from Cafetal), a peaceful, unspoilt place with clear water and beautiful beaches. A *combi* from the bus terminal next to *Hotel Ucum* in Chetumal at 0600, returns 1300. Accommodation at *Restaurant Los Piratas del Caribe*. It is owned by a French family, simple rooms without bath, excellent restaurant, inexpensive. Excursion possible to **Banco Chinchorro** offshore, where there is a coral bank and a white sandy beach.

About 2 km before Majahual a paved road to the left goes to **Puerto Bravo** and on to Placer and **Punta Herrero** (in the Sian Ka'an Biosphere Reserve, see above). 3½ km along this road a right turn goes to the *Sol y Mar* restaurant, with rooms to rent, bathrooms and spaces for RVs, also coconut palms and beach. 10½ km along the Punta Herrero road, again on the right, is *Camidas Trailer Park*, with palm trees, *palapas*, restaurant and restrooms, space for four RVs, US$5 per person, car free.

Xcalak
Colour map 4, grid B6
Population: 250

Across the bay from Chetumal, at the very tip of Quintana Roo, is Xcalak, which may be reached from Chetumal by private launch (two hours), or by the unpaved road from Cafetal to Majahual, then turning south for 55 km (186 km by road from Chetumal, suitable for passenger cars but needs skilled driver). Daily *colectivos* from Chetumal, 0700-1900, 16 de Septiembre 183 y Mahatma Ghandi (T27701), check return times. Bus runs Friday 1600 and Sunday 0600, returning Saturday morning and Sunday afternoon (details from Chetumal tourist office). Xcalak is a fishing village with a few shops with beer and basic supplies and one small restaurant serving Mexican food. A few kilometres north of Xcalak are two hotels, *Costa de Cocos* and *Villa Caracol*, both American-run; the latter is good, with comfortable *cabañas*, though expensive. From here trips can be arranged to the unspoiled islands of Banco Chinchorro or to San Pedro, Belize. *Villa Caracol* has sport fishing and diving facilities. In the village you may be able to rent a boat to explore Chetumal Bay and Banco Chinchorro. Do *not* try to walk from Xcalak along the coast to San Pedro, Belize; the route is virtually impassable.

Chetumal

Phone code: 983
Colour map 4, grid B6
Population: 120,000

State capital of Quintana Roo, Chetumal is a necessary stopover for travellers *en route* to Maya sites in the south of the peninsula, and across the frontier to Guatemala and Belize. Though tourist attractions are thin on the ground, Chetumal does have the advantage of being a small Mexican city not devoted to tourism, and therefore has a more authentic feel than most other towns on the Riviera Maya. It is 240 km south of Tulum. The Chetumal Bay has been designated a Natural Protected Area for manatees, and includes a manatee sanctuary.

The avenues are broad, busy and in the centre lined with huge shops selling cheap imported goods. The main local activity is window-shopping, and the atmosphere is more like a North American city, with the impression of affluence which can be a culture shock to the visitor arriving from the much poorer country of Guatemala. The **tourist offices** at Avenida Miguel Hidalgo 22, 1st floor, esq Carmen Ochoa de Merino, is mainly for trade enquiries. There is very little tourist information in Chetumal; it is usually best to go to a travel agent such as *Tu-Maya* (see below). There is a kiosk in the small plaza on Avenida Héroes and Aguilar, though it is hardly ever staffed, and if so, poorly.

The *paseo* near the waterfront on Sunday night is worth seeing. The State Congress building has a mural showing the history of Quintana Roo. The **Museo de la Cultura Maya**, on Avenida Héroes de Chapultepec by the market, has good models of sites and touchscreen computers explaining the Mayan calendar and glyphs. Although there are few original Maya pieces, it gives an excellent overview; some explanations are in English, guided tours available, and there's a good bookshop with English magazines. ■ *Tue-Thu, 0900-1900, Fri and Sat 0900-2000, Sun 0900-1400, US$1.50. Cold a/c. Highly recommended.*

Sights

AL *Holiday Inn*, Av Héroes 171, T21100. **A** *El Marqués*, Av Lázaro Cárdenas 121, T22998, 5 blocks from centre. Fan, a/c, hot water, restaurant. Recommended. **B** *Los Cocos*, Héroes de Chapultepec 138, T20544. Reductions for AAA members, a/c, pool, restaurant. Recommended. **C** *Real Azteca*, Belice 186, T20720. Cheerful, friendly, but no hot shower. Second floor rooms best, but still not too good. **D** *Caribe Princess*, Av

Sleeping

Chetumal

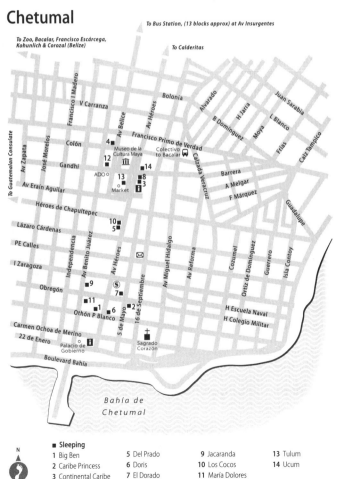

To Bus Station, (13 blocks approx) at Av Insurgentes

To Zoo, Bacalar, Francisco Escárcega, Kohunlich & Corozal (Belize)

To Calderitas

Bahía de Chetumal

Yucatán Peninsula

To Guatemalan Consulate

N

Not to scale

■ **Sleeping**
1 Big Ben
2 Caribe Princess
3 Continental Caribe
4 Cristal
5 Del Prado
6 Doris
7 El Dorado
8 Holiday Inn
9 Jacaranda
10 Los Cocos
11 María Dolores
12 Real Azteca
13 Tulum
14 Ucum

Obregón 168, T20520. A/c, TV, good, very clean, no restaurant. Recommended. **D** *Ucum*, Gandhi 4, T20711. A/c, fan, bath, pleasant, quiet (rooms away from street), expensive laundry, parking in enclosed car park included in price, good value, restaurant next door recommended for *ceviche*. **D-E** *Jacaranda*, Av Obregón 201, T21455. Clean, good, bath, safe parking. **D-E** *Luz María*, Carmen Ochoa de Merino 204, T20202. Friendly but not very clean, owner speaks English. **D-E** *El Dorado*, Av 5 de Mayo 42, T20315. Hot water, a/c, very friendly, quiet. Recommended. **E** *Big Ben*, Héroes 48-A, T20965. Clean, shabby, safe, cheaper rooms for 4, with bath. Arabic restaurant downstairs. **E** *Motel Casablanca*, Alvaro Obregón 312. Clean, quiet, very good value. Recommended. **E** *Crystal*, Colón y Av Belice. Fan, bath, parking. **E** *Doris*, Héroes 49. Seedy, friendly, no hot water, fan. **E** *María Dolores*, Alvaro Obregón 206, T20508. Bath, hot water, fan, clean, windows don't open, noisy, restaurant *Solsimar* downstairs good and popular. Recommended. **E** *Tulum*, Héroes 2, T20518, above market. The noise starts 0530, but clean, with bath and fan, friendly, large rooms. **E-F** *Boston*, Belice 290, between bus station and centre. A/c, not very good. **E-F** *Cuartos Margot*, 5 de Mayo 30. Some with bath, clean, charming. **F** *Ejidal*, Av Independencia between Obregón and Othón P Blanco. With bath, clean. Recommended. Plenty more.

Camping *Sunrise of the Caribbean*, Trailer Park on the road to Calderitas. US$15 for car and 2 people, cold showers, electricity, laundry facilities, *palapas*, boat ramp.

Youth hostel Calzada Veracruz y Alvaro Obregón, referred to as CREA, T23465, CP 77050. Hot water, clean, run-down, friendly, good breakfast, camping US$2. Recommended.

Eating *Lonchería Ivette* on Mahatma Gandhi 154. Cheap snacks. *Pandoja*, Gandhi y 16 de Septiembre. Good food. *Chicho's Lobster House*, Blvd Bahía esq Vicente Guerrero, T27249. Expensive but good seafood, friendly. *Bambino Pizzas*, Othón P Blanco 215. Good. *Sergio Pizza*, Obregón 182. Pizzas, fish, and expensive steak meals, a/c, drinks, excellent service. *Mar Caribe*, 22 de Enero between Madero and Independencia, snacks only. *Hotel Los Cocos*, Good breakfasts, US$5. Several 1 block west of intersection of Héroes and Obregón, eg *Bienvenidos*, good. *Solsimar*, Obregón 206 (closed Sun). Popular, reasonable prices. *El Vaticano*. Popular with locals, good atmosphere, cheap. *Arcada*, Héroes y Zaragoza, open 24 hrs, with mini-market at the back. Another area with many restaurants is about 4 blocks north of market, then 3 blocks west, eg *Barracuda*, good seafood. *Pacho Tec*, small lunch room next to electricity plant, try the chicken broth. Delicious yoghurt ice in shop opposite market. Good juices at *Jugos Xamach*, corner of Salvador y Quintana Roo, friendly local spot. Cheap meals in the market at the top of Av Héroes, but the service is not too good and tourists will be stared at a lot.

Entertainment Try *Safari* roadhouse in Calderitas suburb for enterprising nightlife.

Shopping Shops are open from 0800-1300 and 1800-2000. Avenida Héroes is the main shopping street. Good for foreign foodstuffs – cheaper at the covered market in the outskirts than in the centre. A new commercial centre is being built at the site of the old bus station. *Super San Francisco* supermarket, near bus station, is better than the one behind *Arcada* restaurant.

Tour operators *Tu-Maya*, Av Héroes de Chapultepec 165A, next to Holiday Inn, T20555, F29711. One-day tours to Guatemala, Belize and Calakmul. *Premier*, Av Juárez 83, esq Zaragoza, T23096, F21247, otocarybe@mpsnet.com.mx Eco and adventure tours, car rental. *San Juan Travel Agency*, based at Chetumal bus station, T25110. Leaves 1500 for Flores, arriving 2100.

Taxis no city buses; taxis operate on fixed price routes, US$0.50 on average. Cars with **Transport** light-green licence plates are a form of taxi. **Fuel** Petrol station just outside Chetumal on the road north at the beginning of the road to Escárcega, and another at Xpujil. **Garage** *Talleres Barrera*, helpful, on Primo de Verdad; turn east off Héroes, then past the electrical plant.

Air Airport (CTM) 2½ km from town. Flights to Cancún, Mérida, Belize City (Aerocaribe), Mexico City, Monterrey and Tijuana (Aviacsa, T27765).

Buses The main bus terminal is 3 km out of town at the instersection of Insurgentes y Belice. Modern. Taxi into town US$1.20. There is a bus into the centre from Avenida Belice. Left luggage lockers cost US$0.20 per hour. If buying tickets in advance, go to the ADO office on Av Belice esq Ghandi, 0800-1600. There are often more buses than those marked on the display in the bus station. Always ask at the information desk. Many buses going to the border, US$0.30; taxi from Chetumal to border, 20 mins, US$6 for 2. Long-distance buses are often all booked a day ahead, so avoid unbooked connections. Expect passport checks on buses leaving for Mexican destinations. **Mexico City**, Autobuses del Caribe, 1630 and 2100, 22 hrs, US$45.00. **Villahermosa**, 0800, US$16, 8 hrs, the road is bad and it can take longer; ADO, 3 per day. **Puebla**, US$40; **Escárcega**, 6 departures, 1300-2100, 4 hrs, US$9 1st class, US$7.25 2nd class. **Palenque**, ADO, 1st class at 2215, Maya de Oro, 1st class at 2200, US$20, 9 hrs (2 stops), 2nd class at 2130, US$14.80, otherwise a change is necessary at Emiliano Zapata (bus at 0900, 1300, US$11.50), then change again at Catazajá, or to Catazajá itself (then take a *colectivo*), or Escárcega. **San Cristóbal**, Maya de Oro 1st class, 2300, US$27. Lacandonia has 2nd class bus to San Cristóbal via Palenque at 2130, US$19. **Tuxtla Gutiérrez**, Maya de Oro, 2300, US$30; Cristóbal Colón, 2115, US$26. **Mérida**, 4 per day, luxury US$18.30, US$16.50 1st class (Caribe Express and Autobuses del Caribe), about 7 hrs, 2nd class US$13. **Felipe Carrillo Puerto**, US$3.35, 1½ hrs, many, on excellent road. **Cancún**, 6 hrs, boring road, 10 per day, 0630-0030, luxury US$17, 1st class US$13.50, 2nd class US$12. **Tulum**, several 2nd class from 0630, US$7, 1st class from 0700, 4 hrs, US$8.50. **Playa del Carmen**, 1st class US$10, 2nd class US$7. **Minatitlán**, 12 hrs, US$22.50. There are also buses to Veracruz, Campeche, Villahermosa, Córdoba, Xpujil and Puerto Juárez.

    Colectivos to Bacalar and Francisco Villa (for Kohunlich and Xpujil) depart from the junction of Av Miguel Hidalgo and Francisco Primo de Verdad. Bacalar buses are very frequent (several per hour). To Francisco Villa (US$1.30) and Xpujil (US$4) at 1300 and 1600.

    To **Belize**, Batty Bus from ADO to **Belize City**, 5 per day, schedules change frequently, taking 3½-5 hrs on paved road, US$8.50, in pesos, US dollars or Belize dollars. Money-changers in the bus terminal offer marginally poorer rates than those at the border. Venus Bus to Belize City leaves from the square by Mercado Nuevo on Calzada Veracruz y 2° Circuito Periférico, 3 blocks from main terminal (US$1 taxi ride), morning departures, again frequent schedule changes, first bus leaves at 0600. Be there in good time; they sometimes leave early if full. If intending to stay in Belize City, do not take a bus which arrives at night as it is not recommended to look for a hotel in the dark. Bus **Orange Walk**, 2½ hrs, US$4.50. It is difficult to hitch to the Belizean border. To hitch once inside Belize, it is best to take the *colectivo* from in front of the hospital (1 block from the bus station, ask) marked 'Chetumal-Santa Elena', US$1. *San Juan Travel* at the main bus station has a direct daily service to **Flores** (US$30) and **Tikal** (US$33) in Guatemala, at 1430 from ADO terminal, 8 hrs to Flores, 6 hrs to Tikal.

Airline offices Aerocaribe, Plaza Varudi, Av Héroes 125. **Banks** The banks all close at 1430. **Directory** There are several ATMs. For exchange, *Banamex*, Obregón y Juárez, changes TCs. *Banco Mexicano*, Juárez and Cárdenas, TCs or US$ cash, quick and courteous service. Several on, or near,

Av Héroes with ATMs. Banks do not change quetzales into pesos. Good rates at **Bodegas Blanco** supermarket beside bus terminal; will change US dollars and Belize dollars (only if you spend at least 15% of the total on their groceries!). *Batty Bus* ticket counter will change pesos into Belizean dollars. Try also *Casa Medina*, L Cárdenas. Pemex stations will accept US and Belizean dollars, but at poor rates for the latter. *San Francisco de Assisi* supermarket changes TCs, next to bus station. **Communications** Internet: *Eclipse*, 5 de Mayo 83 between PE Calles and Zaragoza. Open 0930-1500, 1800-2100. Not very friendly but cheap at US$3 per hour. *Los Cebollones*, Calzada Veracruz 452, T29145. Also restaurant and cocktail bar. **Post office** at 16 de Septiembre y PE Calles. Open Mon-Fri 0800-1730, Sat 0900-1300. Packets to be sent abroad must be taken unwrapped to the bus terminal to have them checked by customs before taking them to the post office. Better to wait till another town. Parcel service not available Sat. Western Union office attached to Post office, same hours. **Embassies & consulates** *Guatemala* Av Héroes de Chapultepec 354, T26565. Open for visas, Mon-Fri 0900-1700. Visas to Guatemala not required by nationals of EU, USA and Canada or Mexico and Central America. For other nationals, it is far better to organize your visa, if required, in your home country before travel. *Belize* Hon Consul, Lic Francisco Lechón Rosas, Av Alvaro Obregón 232-1, T20100; visas can take up to 3 weeks to get, and many are only issued in Mexico City. **Laundry** *Lavandería Automática* 'Lava facil', corner of Héroes and Confederación Nacional Campesina. **Medical services** Malaria prophylaxis available from Centro de Salud, opposite hospital (request tablets for *paludismo*).

Frontier with Belize **Customs and Immigration** procedure can be slow particularly at peak holiday times when Belizeans come on charter buses for cheap shopping; over the bridge is Belizean passport control. Visitors who have been to South America recently should check whether they require a health certificate, available from the Centro de Salud at the border. For people entering Mexico, tourist cards are available at the border. It has been reported that only 15 days are given but you can get an additional 30 days at the Servicios Migratorios in Chetumal. Note that fresh fruit cannot be imported into Belize.

Leaving Mexico by car, go to the Mexican immigration office to register your exit and surrender your vehicle permit and tourist card; very straightforward, no charges. Go to the office to obtain compulsory Belizean insurance (also money changing facilities here). Entering Belize, your car will be registered in your passport.

Money is checked on entering Belize. Excess Mexican pesos are easily changed into Belizean dollars with men waiting just beyond customs on the Belize side, but they are not there to meet the early bus. You can change US for Belizean dollar bills in the shops at the border, but this is not necessary as US$ are accepted in Belize. If you can get a good rate (dollars to pesos) in the bank, it is sometimes better to buy Belizean dollars with pesos in *casas de cambio* than to wait until you enter Belize where the US dollar/Belize dollar rate is fixed at 1:2.

Excursions north of Chetumal

Six kilometres north are the stony beaches of **Calderitas**, bus every 30 minutes from Colón, between Belice and Héroes, US$1.80 or taxi, US$5, many fish restaurants. Camping at Calderitas, signposted, OK, US$2.75. Beyond are the unexcavated archaeological sites of **Ichpaatun** (13 km), **Oxtancah** (14 km) and **Nohochmul** (20 km). Sixteen kilometres north on Route 307 to Tulum is the **Laguna de los Milagros**, a beautiful lagoon for swimming. Further on, 34 km north of Chetumal, is **Cenote Azul**, over 70m deep, with a waterside restaurant serving inexpensive and good seafood and regional food (but awful coffee) until 1800. There is also a trailer park (Apartado 88, Chetumal), a relaxing place to camp; other *cenotes* in area. Both the *laguna* and the *cenote* are deserted in the week.

Bacalar About 3 km north of Cenote Azul is the village of **Bacalar** (nice, but not special) on the **Laguna de Siete Colores** which has swimming and skin-diving; *colectivos* from terminal (Suchaa) in Chetumal, corner of Miguel Hidalgo and

Primo de Verdad, from 0700-1900 every 30 minutes, US$1.60, return from plaza when full; also buses from Chetumal bus station every two hours or so, US$1.60. There is a Spanish fort there overlooking a beautiful shallow, clear, fresh-water lagoon, and abundant birdlife on the lakeshore. This is the fort of **San Felipe**, said to have been built around 1729 by the Spanish to defend the area from the English pirates and smugglers of logwood (there is a plaque praying for protection from the British). ■ *US$0.70, small museum*. The British ships roamed the islands and reefs, looting Spanish galleons laden with gold, on their way from Peru to Cuba. There are many old shipwrecks on the reef and around the Banco Chinchorro, 50 km out in the Caribbean (information kindly provided by Coral Pitkin of the *Rancho Encantado*, see below). There is a dock for swimming from north of the plaza, with a restaurant and disco next to it. North of Bacalar a direct road (Route 293) runs to Muná, on the road between Mérida and Uxmal.

Sleeping and eating 3 km north of Bacalar is the resort hotel **AL** *Rancho Encantado*, on the west shore of the lagoon. Half-board also available, Apdo 233, Chetumal, T/F98380427 (USA reservations: T800-505 MAYA (6292) or F505-7762102, PO Box 1256, Taos, New Mexico, www.encantado.com), with private dock, tour boat, canoes and windsurf boards for rent, private cabins with fridge and hammock, very good. At Bacalar is **D** *Hotel América*, 700m north of the bus stop on the plaza (walk in the opposite direction to Chetumal). Recommended. **D** *Hotel Las Lagunas*, about 2 km south of Bacalar (on left-hand side of the road going towards the village). It is very good, wonderful views, helpful, clean, comfortable, hot water, swimming pool and opposite a fresh-water lake; restaurant is poor and overpriced. Several houses rent rooms (**E**) 500m north of the plaza, look for signs on fence. *Restaurant La Esperanza*, 1 block north from plaza. Thatched barn, good seafood, not expensive. 1 cheap place on the plaza, *Punta y Coma*. *Orizaba*, 3 blocks from Zócalo. Inexpensive, large menu including vegetarian. Recommended. Several lakeside bars also serve meals, mostly fish. Camping possible at the end of the road 100m from the lagoon, toilets and shower, US$0.10, but lagoon perfect for washing and swimming. *Balneario Ejidal*, with changing facilities and restaurant (good fried fish). Recommended; gasoline is sold in a side-street.

▲▲▲▲▲▲▲▲▲▲▲▲▲▲▲▲

Uncover the hidden magic of Mexico's Yucatan at Rancho Encantado, eco-resort and retreat center in the Mayan Heartland. Explore ancient temples unknown to the public. Swim and kayak in the crystal waters of Laguna Bacalar, "lake of the 7 colors". Release yourself into a healing array of spa treatments. Hide away in a private hand-crafted cottage on the waterside. Unwind in the soaring lakefront palapa, enjoying regional and international gourmet cuisine.

Luxuriant.
Enchanted.
Undiscovered.

RANCHO ENCANTADO

Visit www.encantado.com
reservations@encantado.com
505.776.5878 fax: 505.776.2102
or call toll-free in the US:
800.505.MAYA (800.505.6292)
Rancho Encantado US Office
PO Box 1256, Taos, NM 87571
▲▲▲▲▲▲▲▲▲▲▲▲▲▲▲▲

West of Chetumal

From Chetumal you can visit the fascinating Mayan ruins that lie on the way (Route 186) to Escárcega, if you have a car. There are few tourists in this area and few facilities. Take plenty of drinking water. About 25 km from Chetumal at **Ucum** (fuel), you can turn off 5 km south to visit **Palmara**, located along the Río Hondo, which borders Belize; there are swimming holes and restaurant.

Kohunlich Just before Francisco Villa (61 km from Chetumal) lie the ruins of **Kohunlich**, 8.4 km south of the main road, 1½ hours walk along a sweltering, unshaded road; take plenty of water. Descriptions in Spanish and English. Every hour or so the van passes for staff working at **AL** *Explorer Kohunlich*, a luxury resort hotel halfway to the ruins, which may give you a lift, but you'll still have 4 km to walk. There are fabulous masks (early Classic, AD 250-500) set on the side of the main pyramid, still bearing red colouring; they are unique of their kind (allow an hour for the site). ■ *US$2*. About 200m west of the turning for Kohunlich is a *Migración* office and a stall selling beer; wait here for buses to Chetumal or Xpujil, which have to stop, but first class will not pick up passengers. *Colectivos* 'Nicolás Bravo' from Chetumal, or bus marked 'Zoh Laguna' from bus station pass the turning.

Dzibanché Other ruins in this area are Dzibanché and **Knichná**. Both are recent excavations and both are accessible down a dirt road off the Chetumal-Morocoy road. The remains of a Maya king have recently been disinterred (June 1999) at Dzibanché, which is thought to have been the largest Maya city in southern Quintana Roo, peaking between 300 and 1200 AD. Its discoverer, Thomas Gann, named it in 1927 after the Maya glyphs he found engraved on the sapodilla wood lintels in Temple VI – *Dzibanché* means 'writing on the wood' in Maya. Later excavations revealed a tomb in Temple I, believed to have belonged to a king because of the number of offerings it contained. This temple is also known as the **Temple of the Owl** because one of the artefacts unearthed was a vase and lid carved with an owl figure. Other important structures are the **Temple of the Cormorants** and **Structure XIII**, known as 'The Captives', due to its friezes depicting prisoners. ■ *Free*. Knichná means 'House of the Sun' in Maya, christened by Thomas Gann in refernece to a glyph he found there. The **Acropolis** is the largest structure. ■ *Free*. To reach these sights follow the Chetumal-Escárcega road, turn off at Km 58 towards Morocoy, 9 km further on. The road to Dzibanché is 2 km down this road, crossing the turning for Knichná.

Other Maya ruins can be visited on the way to Francisco Escárcega in the neighbouring state of Campeche (see page 298-299).

Guerrero, Oaxaca and the Isthmus

8

Guerrero, Oaxaca and the Isthmus

Long before international travel, Hollywood brought
Acapulco to millions of filmgoers with scenes in which
young men with flaming torches would dive off the high cliff
into the crashing waves below. Acapulco became associated
with the jet set, film stars and their inevitable illicit love
affairs. Although it has changed greatly since those days,
Acapulco still retains something of its old mystique and
promises of exotic encounters. Today, there are other resorts
dotting this coastline and challenging Mexico's better-
known playgrounds such as Puerto Vallarta and Cancún.
From Iztapa to Huatulco all the usual beach-holiday
activities are there for the taking: surfing, water-skiing,
parascending and scuba diving or trips in glass-bottomed
boats. And if you want to avoid the crowds, there are still
many beautiful offbeat beaches well away from the mega
resorts. Inland, these states are rugged and remote, until you
come to the attractive university city of Chilpancingo, or
lively, colourful and cosmopolitan **Oaxaca**, where very
pleasant evenings can be spent at the terrace restaurants
'people' watching. Days are filled visiting the magnificent
Santo Domingo church and museum and exploring the
austere archaeological site of **Monte Albán** with its gory
engravings. On a lighter note, take in a performance of the
colourful Guelaguetza. Within easy reach of the city are
several other archaeological sites and many villages where
the descendants of those who built these wonderful
pyramids create some of Mexico's most beautiful and varied
handicrafts. Before crossing the Isthmus to Veracruz, allow a
little time to explore **Tehuantepec**, where you can admire
the Zapotec dress and the white churches of the early
colonial period which dot the landscape.

Guerrero, Oaxaca & the Isthmus

Chilpancingo

Phone Code: 747
Colour map: 3, grid C5
Population: 120,000
Altitude: 1,250m

The journey from Mexico City to Acapulco and the Pacific Coast often includes a stop-off at Cuernavaca, the 'city of eternal spring', see page 154, and a detour to the silver town of Taxco (see page 167). Further south, beyond the Mexcala river, the road passes for some 30 km through the dramatic canyon of Zopilote to reach the university city of Chilpancingo, capital of Guerrero state at Km 302. There is a small but grandly conceived plaza with solid neo-classical buildings and monumental public sculptures commemorating the workers' struggle: *El hombre hacia el futuro* and *El canto al trabajo* by Victor Manuel Contreras. In the **Palacio de Gobierno** there is a museum and murals. The colourful reed bags from the village of Chilapa (see below) are sold in the market. The **Casa de las Artesanías** for Guerrero is on the right-hand side of the old main Mexico City-Acapulco highway. It has a particularly wide selection of lacquer-ware from Olinalá (see below). The local *fiesta* starts on 16 December and lasts a fortnight.

Excursions

Olmec cave paintings can be seen at the **Grutas de Juxtlahuaca** not far from Chilpancingo. To reach the caves, drive to Petaquillas on the non-toll road then take a side road (paved, but poor in parts) through several villages to Colotlipa (*colectivo* from Chilpancingo, see below, US$1.50, 1½ hours). Ask at the restaurant on the corner of the Zócalo for a guide to the caves. They can only be visited with a guide (three hour tour US$25, popular at weekends for groups; if on your own, try for a discount). The limestone cavern is in pristine condition; it has an intricate network of large halls and tunnels, stalagmites and stalactites, a huge underground lake, cave drawings from about 500 AD, a skeleton and artefacts. Take a torch, food and drink and a sweater if going a long way in.

Chilapa, east of Chilpancingo, is accessible by several local buses and is worth a visit (about one hour journey US$2). On Sunday there is an excellent craft market that covers all of the large plaza and surrounding streets, selling especially good-quality and well-priced Olinalá lacquer boxes as well as wood carvings, textiles, leather goods, etc; worth a visit even if you don't buy anything. *Hotel Camino Real* on plaza. *Restaurant Casa Pilla* on other side of plaza, local dishes. Recommended. The **Grutas de Oxtotitlán**, with more Olmec cave paintings, are about 18 km north of Chilapa.

Sleeping & eating

C-D *La Posada Meléndez*. Large rooms, helpful, swimming pool, cheap *comida corrida* in restaurant. Recommended. **D** *María Isabel* and *Cardeña*, both on Madero. **D** *El Portal* on corner of plaza, T50135. **F** *Chilpancingo*, Alemán 8, 50m from Zócalo, T22446. Clean, shower, basic. Small café at back of *Tienda Naturista*, Hidalgo, 2 blocks from plaza. Good yoghurt.

Transport

Buses Cuernavaca-Chilpancingo, Estrella de Oro, US$8.30, or *plus* US$11 (9 a day). Buses Mexico City-Chilpancingo from US$11 to US$23.35, super luxury. To Acapulco with Futura US$3.80; To Taxco with Estrella de Oro US$4.50.

Olinalá

Altitude: 1,350m

This small town is known to most Mexicans for the beautiful lacquered wooden objects made here (boxes, chests, screens, trays, etc), but is visited by few. Situated in the east of the State of Guerrero, it lies in an area of mountains, rivers and ravines, which make access difficult. Most of the population is involved in the production and selling of the lacquer work, which is available from the artisans direct as well as from the more expensive shops on the square. The wood chiefly used is *linaloe*, which gives the objects a gentle fragrance. The lacquering technique includes both the scraping away of layers and applying new ones. Other villages in the area similarly devote themselves

Guerrero, Oaxaca & the Isthmus

almost exclusively to their own *artesanías*. The church on the square is decorated inside with lacquer work. A chapel dedicated to Nuestra Señora de Guadalupe crowns a hill just outside the town, offering striking views. The hill is pyramid-shaped and there are said to be tunnels, but to date no archaeological investigations have been carried out. There are three **F** hotels around the square and a restaurant (no name displayed) above the furniture shop on the main square serves exquisite Mexican cooking.

Transport Buses: direct from Mexico City (Terminal del Sur) via Chilpancingo; also via Izúcar de Matamoros to Tlapa, then local bus. Local bus also from Chilapa. **Road**: there is 1 paved road (1 hr) from the Chilpancingo-Tlapa road; the turning to Olinalá is between the villages of Tlatlauquitepec and Chiepetepec, about 40 km west of Tlapa. There is an unpaved road (4 hrs) from Chiautla to the north, but you have to cross rivers whose bridges are often washed away in the rainy season. A better unpaved road (2½ hrs) from Santa Cruz to the east, near Huamuxtitlán on Route 92, fords the river Tlapaneco, which is feasible for most vehicles except in the rainy season. The scenery is spectacular, with huge bluffs and river valleys, but filling stations are infrequent. If Pemex in Olinalá has no fuel, local shops may sell it. Fill up when you can.

The new section of four-lane toll freeway runs from Iguala west of the old highway as far as Tierra Colorada, where it joins the existing four-lane section to Acapulco. Chilpancingo is bypassed, but there is an exit. This is the third improvement: the first motor road was pushed over the ancient mule trail in 1927, giving Acapulco its first new lease of life in 100 years; when the road was paved and widened in 1954, Acapulco began to boom.

About 20 km from the coast, a branch road goes to the northwest of Acapulco; this is a preferable route for car drivers because it avoids the city chaos. It goes to a point between Pie de la Cuesta and Coyuca, is signed, and has a drugs control point at the junction.

Without stopping, it takes about 3½ hours to drive from the capital to Acapulco on the 406-km four-lane highway. The total toll for the route at eight booths is US$89.

Warning Do not travel by car at night in Guerrero, even on the Mexico City-Acapulco highway and coastal highway. Always set out early to ensure that you reach your destination in daylight. There are many military checkpoints on the highway. *Guerrilleros* have been active in recent years, and there are also problems with highway robbers and stray animals.

Acapulco

Acapulco is the most popular resort in Mexico, particularly in winter and spring. It does not fit everyone's idea of a tropical beach resort. The town stretches for 16 km in a series of bays and cliff coves and is invading the hills. The hotels, of which there are 250, are mostly perched high to catch the breeze, for midday the heat is sizzling; they are filled to overflowing in January and February.

Phone code: 74
Colour map 3, grid C5
Population: 1 million

Ins and outs

Aeropuerto Alvarez Internacional (ACA) is 23 km east of Acapulco. The airport bus takes one hour to town, US$3.35, and the ticket office is outside the terminal. Transportaciones de Pasajeros Aeropuerto shuttle service charge the return trip (*viaje redondo*) when you buy a ticket, so keep it and call 24 hours in advance for a taxi,

Getting there & away

Guerrero, Oaxaca & the Isthmus

US$11 (for further details see transport section, page 393).

The long-distance bus terminal is on Avenida Ejido, reached by bus from Costera Miguel Alemán; allow at least 45 minutes during peak time. Estrella de Oro buses leave from the bus station on Avenida Cuauhtémoc. For people travelling by car, Route 95 connects Acapulco with Mexico City, while Route 200, the Carretera Costera, runs along the coast, west towards Ixtapa-Zihuatanejo and east towards Puerto Escondido, Huatulco and the beaches of Oaxaca.

Getting around The most useful bus route runs the full length of Costera Miguel Alemán, linking the older part of town to the different beaches and hotels. Bus stops on the main thoroughfare are numbered, so find out which number you need to get off at.

The **tourist office** is at *Costera Miguel Alemán*, Playa Hornos, T840599/7621, helpful, but double-check details; useful free magazines, *Aca-Sun* and *Acapulco guide*. Also at *Flechas* bus station, very helpful, will make hotel bookings, but not in cheapest range.

Acapulco has all the paraphernalia of a booming resort: smart shops, nightclubs, red light district, golf club, touts and street vendors and now also air pollution. The famous beaches and expensive hotels are a different world from the streets, hotels and crowded shops and buses of the city centre, which is only two minutes walk away. The Zócalo is lively in the evenings, but the surrounding streets are grimy.

Acapulco Bay

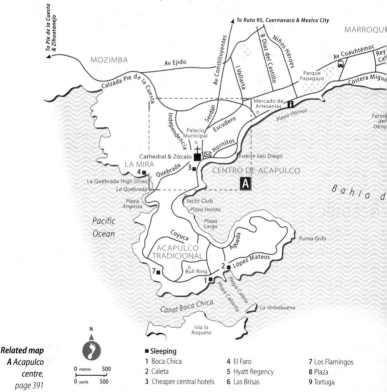

■ Sleeping
1 Boca Chica
2 Caleta
3 Cheaper central hotels
4 El Faro
5 Hyatt Regency
6 Las Brisas
7 Los Flamingos
8 Plaza
9 Tortuga

Guerrero, Oaxaca & the Isthmus

Acapulco in colonial times was the terminal for the Manila convoy. Its main defence, **Fuerte de San Diego**, where the last battle for Mexican Independence was fought, is in the middle of the city and is worth a visit. ■ *1000-1800, Tue and Sun only, free.*

A campaign to tidy up the whole city and its beaches is in process. Acapulco was badly hit by storms in 1997; Hurricane Pauline left more than 111 dead along the coast, dozens missing and 8,000 homeless after mudslides swept away poor areas of the city. Now, however, there is almost no evidence of the damage. There are some 20 beaches, all with fine, golden sand; deckchairs on all beaches, US$0.50; parachute skiing in front of the larger hotels at US$12 for five minutes. Every evening, except Monday, there is a water-skiing display opposite Fuerte de San Diego. The two most popular beaches are the sickle-curved and shielded **Caleta**, with its smooth but dirty water yet clean sands, and the surf-pounded straight beach of **Los Hornos**. Swimmers should look out for motor boats close in shore. At **Playa Revolcadero** development is continuing, with new luxury hotels, new roads and landscaping; it is being called Acapulco Diamante.

At **Playa Icacos** there is a marineland amusement park *Ci-Ci*, with a waterslide, pool with wave-machine and arena with performing dolphins and sea-lions (nothing special). ■ *US$5.70 for whole day, 1000-1800.* Pleasant boat trip across beach to **Puerto Marqués**, US$2 return (or 30 minutes by bus); one can hire small sailing boats there, US$12 per hour. Bay cruises, 2½ hours, from Muelle Yates, US$9, including free bar, at 1100, 1630 and 2230. *Yate Bonanza* has been recommended, stops 30 minutes for swim in bay. Visit the island of **La Roqueta**, in a glass-bottomed boat; tours leave at 1100 and 1300 from Fuerte San Diego and return at 1500 and 1700, US$4; once on the island follow the path which goes over the hill towards the other side of the island (towards the right) where there is a small, secluded and usually empty bay (about 15 minutes walk). Take food and drink with you as it is expensive on the island. Several operators around the bay offer parascending, US$12 for a few minutes. There is an **Aqua Marine museum** on a little island (Yerbabuena) off **Playa Caleta**, with sharks, piranhas, eels and stingrays in an aquarium, and also a swimming pool with water-chute, and breezy bar above. ■ *US$7.*

One sight that should not be missed in Acapulco is that of the amazing cliff divers at **La Quebrada** who plunge 40m into the water below, timing their dives to coincide with the incoming waves. ■ *Daily, US$1.20, at 1915, 2015, 2115 and 2215.*

Beaches

The surf is dangerous on the beach west of the road and the beaches are unsafe at night

To Ruta 95, Cuernavaca & Mexico City
Paseo del Farallón
LAS CUMBRES
ACAPULCO MODERNO
COSTA AZUL
Zona Hotelera
Alemán
Playa Hornos
Convention Centre
La Redonda
Zona Hotelera
ACAPULCO MODERNO
Playa Icacos
Ci Ci Recreation Centre
COLONIA ICACOS
Naval Base
Punta del Guitarrón
PLAYA GUITARRÓN
Carretera Escénica
To Puerto Márquez, Playa Revolcadero & Airport

Guerrero, Oaxaca & the Isthmus

Excursions

Take a local bus to **Pie de la Cuesta**, 12 km, now preferred by many budget travellers to Acapulco itself, but also commercialized. There are several bungalow-hotels and trailer parks (see below), a lagoon (six hours boat trip US$10), sometimes used for laundry, and long, clean, sandy beaches. At Pie de la Cuesta you drink *coco loco*, fortified coconut milk, and watch the sunset from a hammock. You can swim, and fish, the year round. Best free map of Acapulco can be obtained from the desk clerk at *Tortuga Hotel*.

Laguna Coyuca (also known as **La Barra**), is over 10 km long (38 km northwest of Acapulco); strange birds, water hyacinths and tropical flowers and can be explored by motor boat.

Sleeping in Pie de la Cuesta: C *Villa Nirvana*. Canadian/Mexican owners (depending on season) with kitchen, clean, pool, good value. Recommended. D *Casa Blanca*. Rooms for 3, management nice, food good. *Puesta del Sol*, expensive places for hammocks. D *Quinta Dora Trailer Park*. For hammock, managed by American, helpful. The student organization *SETEJ* offers dormitory accommodation, **D**, if one has a valid international student card, at Centro Vacacional, Pie de la Cuesta, 0700-2400.

Essentials

Sleeping A double room in a hotel can cost up to US$200 a night; cheaper for longer stays, but this also means less expensive hotels insist on a double rate even for 1 person and for a minimum period. In the off-season (May-Nov) you can negotiate lower prices even for a single for 1 night. For hotels in our **C** range and above in Acapulco you can make reservations at the bus terminal in Mexico City, helpful; similarly, at the 1st class bus station in Acapulco you can arrange hotel packages, eg 3 nights in 4-star accommodation for US$60. Hotel recommendations, and reservations, made at the bus terminal, often turn out to be dingy downtown hotels.

LL *Elcano*, Costera Miguel Alemán, near golf club, T841950. Many rooms with terrace, pool. **LL** *Villa Vera Raquet Club*, T840333. Luxurious celebrity spot. The fabulous **LL** *Club Residencial de las Brisas*, T841733. A hotel where the services match the astronomical price, it begins at sea-level and reaches up the mountain slope in a series of detached villas and public rooms to a point 300m above sea-level, each room has own or shared swimming pool, guests use pink jeeps to travel to the dining-room and recreation areas. **LL** *Camino Real Diamante*, T812010, on edge of Diamante development at Playa Revolcadero. Luxury resort. **LL-AL** *Acapulco Plaza*, Costera Miguel Alemán 123, T859050. 3 towers, 2 pools, 5 bars, 4 restaurants, a city in itself. **LL-AL** *Hyatt Regency*, next to naval base, Costera Miguel Alemán 1, T842888, F843087. **L** *Acapulco Tortuga*, T848889. Good discounts in low season. **L** *Caleta*, Playa Caleta, T39940. Remodelled. **L** *Romano Days*, T845332, on Costera Miguel Alemán. Many groups. **AL** *Acapulco Imperial*, Costera Miguel Alemán 251, T851918. **AL** *Fiesta Americana Condesa del Mar*, T842828, Costera Miguel Alemán at Playa Condesa. All facilities. **AL** *Maris*, Costera Miguel Alemán y Magallanes, T858440. Very good. The *Acapulco Princess Country Club*, part of the *Acapulco Princess*, T843100, 20 km away on Playa Revolcadero. Highly fashionable, delightful resort, all facilities, taxi to town US$10. **A** *El Cid*, Playa Hornos, T851312. Clean, pool. Recommended. **A** *Los Flamingos*, López Mateos, T820690/2, F839806. One of the finest locations in Acapulco, glorious cliff-top views. In the 1950s it was a retreat for John Wayne, Johnny Weissmuller et al, and the present owner preserves the atmosphere of those days, gardens, pool, restaurant, breakfast included. Highly recommended. **A** *Maralisa*, Alemania s/n, T856677. Smallish and elegant, Arab style, private beach. Recommended.

B *Casa Blanca Tropical*, Cerro de la Pinzona, T821212. With swimming pool. Recommended. **B** *do Brasil*, Costera Miguel Alemán on Playa Hornos, T854364. Shower, TV, all rooms with sea-view balcony, pool, restaurant, bar, travel agency, friendly. Recommended. **B** *Playa Suites*, Costera Miguel Alemán, on beach, suites sleeping up to 6. Good value. **B** *Real del Monte*, Inalambra, T841010. Clean, friendly, on the beach, pool, good food, Playa del Coco opposite new convention centre. *Boca Chica*, Playa Caletillo, T836741. On promontory opposite Isla la Roqueta, pool, clean, direct access to bathing, free drinking water on each floor.

Most cheaper hotels are grouped around the Zócalo, especially on La Paz and Juárez. **C** *Acuario*, Azueta 11, T821784. Popular. **C** *Añorve*, Juárez 17, T822093, 2 blocks off Zócalo. Clean, with bath, front rooms better than back (but can be noisy from street in mornings). **C** *Embassy*, Costera Miguel Alemán, T840273. Clean, a/c, pool. **C** *Fiesta*, Azueta 16, 2 blocks Zócalo, T820019. Clean and nice, with bath, fan. **C** *Misión*, Felipe Valle 12, T823643. Very clean, colonial, close to Zócalo. Recommended.

Opposite *Añorve* is **D** *Colimense*, JM Iglesias II, off Zócalo, T822890. Pleasant, limited parking. **D** *El Tropicano*, Costera Miguel Alemán 150, on Playa Icacos. Clean, a/c, big garden, 2 pools, bars, restaurant, very friendly and helpful. Recommended. **D** *Hospedaje Bienvenidos*, behind Estrella de Oro bus terminal. Clean, safe, sometimes noisy. **D** *Isabel*, La Paz y Valle, near Zócalo, T822191. With fan. Recommended. **D** *Los Pericos*, Costera Miguel Alemán near Playa Honda, T824078. Fan, clean, friendly, pool. Recommended. **D** *Mama Hélène*, who owns 2 hotels in same price range, and offers laundry service, homemade lemonade. **D** *Olivieda*, Costera Miguel Alemán, 1 block from Cathedral. Clean, fan, hot water, great views from top floor rooms. **D** *Sacramento*, Carranza y Valle, T820821. With bath and fan, no towel, soap or loo paper, friendly, noisy, OK, purified water. **D** *San Francisco*, Costera Miguel Alemán 219, T820045, old part of town. Friendly, good value, noisy in front. **D** *Santa Cecilia*, Francisco Madero 7, off Zócalo. With bath and fan, noisy, but otherwise fine. **D** *Santa Lucía*, López Mateos 33, T820441. Family-owned, will negotiate if not full, good value. **D-E** *California*, La Paz 12, T822893, 1½ blocks west of Zócalo. Good value, fan, hot water, pleasant rooms and patio.

Acapulco centre

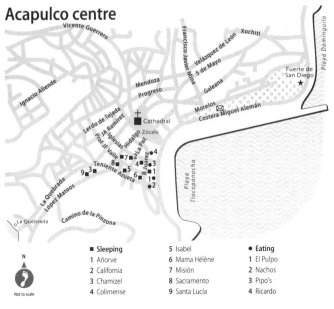

■ Sleeping	5 Isabel	● Eating
1 Añorve	6 Mama Hélène	1 El Pulpo
2 California	7 Misión	2 Nachos
3 Chamizel	8 Sacramento	3 Pipo's
4 Colimense	9 Santa Lucía	4 Ricardo

Not to scale

E *Aca-Plus*, Azueta 11, T831405. With bath and fan, clean, safe. **E** *La Posada*, Azueta 8, near Zócalo. With bath, more expensive in high season. **E** *Paola*, Teniente Azueta, Centro, T826243, 2 blocks from Zócalo. Hot shower, fan, roof terrace with pool, free coffee. Highly recommended. **E-F** *Chamizal*, López Mateos 32, close to Zócalo. Shower, OK.

Many cheap hotels on La Quebrada, basic but clean with fan and bathroom, including **D** *Asturia*, No 45. With bath, no single rooms, clean, friendly, pool, a few cockroaches on lower floor, otherwise recommended. **D** *Betty*, Belisario Domínguez 4, T835092, 5 mins from bus station. With bath, fan, short stay, dirty. Not recommended. Just around corner on same street is **E** *Alberto*, much better. Turn left at *Betty* for several cheap *casas de huéspedes*. **D** *Casa de Huéspedes Aries*, No 30. With bath, nice. **D** *Coral*, No 56, T820756. Good value, friendly, reasonably quiet, small pool. **D** *El Faro*, No 63, T821365. Clean. **E** *Beatriz*, 3 blocks from Flecha Roja terminal, 2 from beach. For more than 1 night, central, fan, shower, pool. **E** *Sagamar*, No 51. With bath, basic, friendly, some English spoken, safe, clean, use mosquito coil.

For longer stays (1 month plus) , try *Amueblados Etel*, Av la Pinzona 92 (near La Quebrada). For self-catering apartments, cheap off-season (before Nov), short stays possible in rooms, **C**, a/c, fan, hot shower, sundeck, large pool. Recommended. **C** *Apartamentos Maraback*, Costera Miguel Alemán. **D** *Amueblos Caletilla Diamante*, López Mateos 28, Las Playas, T827975. Apartments with kitchen, pool, close to beach and market, safe parking.

Camping *Trailer Park El Coloso*, in La Sabana. Small swimming pool. *Trailer Park La Roca* on road from Puerto Márquez to La Sabana. Both secure. *Estacionamiento Juanita* and *Quinta Dora* at Pie de la Cuesta (latter is 13 km up the coast on Highway 200. *Palapas*, bathrooms, cold showers, hook-ups, US$12 for 2 plus car, US$4 just to sling hammock). *Quinta Carla*, Pie de la Cuesta, T601255, *Casa Blanca*, near military base at Laguna Coyuca, and *U Kae Kim*, all US$50 a week upwards, but negotiable. *Acapulco West KDA*, on Barra de Coyuca. Opened 1996, beachfront, security patrol, pool, restaurant, hot showers, laundry, store, volleyball, basketball, Spanish classes, telephones.

Motels **B** *Impala*, T840337. *Bali-Hai*, T857045. *Mónaco*, T856415, all along the Costera Miguel Alemán. **B** *Victoria*, Cristóbal Colón, 1 block behind Costera.

Eating

Fish dishes are a speciality of Acapulco

One of the oldest established and best restaurants is *Pipo's*, Almirante Breton 3 (off Costera near Zócalo). Highly recommended, 2 other branches: Costera esq Plaza Canadá; and Calle Majahua, Puerto Márquez. There are a number of variously priced restaurants along and opposite Playa Condesa, including *Embarcadero* on the Costera Miguel Alemán. Thai/Mexican/US food. Extraordinary décor with waterfalls, bridges, bamboo huts and 'a hall of mirrors on the way to the loo', expensive but worth it for the atmosphere. Many cheap restaurants in the blocks surrounding the Zócalo, especially along Juárez, for example, *El Amigo Miguel* (popular), Juárez 9, near Zócalo, Fixed menu lunch, good. *Nachos*, on Azueta, at corner of Juárez. Popular, excellent prawns. *El Pulpo*, Costera Miguel Alemán 183, 1½ blocks from Zócalo. Good filling breakfasts, friendly. By La Diana roundabout is *Pizza Hut*. Reliable, with 'blissful a/c'. *Italianissimo*. Nearby, decent pizza and garlic bread, average price for area. *Parroquia*, on Zócalo. Excellent. *El Zorrito*, opposite *Ritz Hotel*. Excellent local food with live music, average prices, reputedly popular with Julio Iglesias when he is in town. The *cafetería* at the southeast corner of the Zócalo serves good coffee. Another group of restaurants along Playa Caleta walkway; better value on Caleta beach itself is *La Cabaña*. Good food, delightful setting. Yet another group with mixed prices on the Costera opposite the *Acapulco Plaza Hotel*. 250 or so to select from. *El Mayab*, Costera Miguel Alemán 151. Good value, set meal. Recommended.

There are dozens of discos including *Discoteca Safari*, Costera Miguel Alemán. Free entry, 1 drink obligatory, good ambience; *Disco Beach*, Costera Miguel Alemán, between the *Diana* and *Hotel Fiesta Americana Condesa*. By beach, informal dress, open till 0500, good; every major hotel has at least 1 disco plus bars. Superb varied nightlife always.

Bars & nightclubs

Local Taxis: US$9 an hour; sample fare: Zócalo to Playa Condesa US$3.50. Taxis more expensive from bus terminal, walk half a block round corner and catch one on the street. **Buses**: several bus routes, with 1 running the full length of Costera Miguel Alemán linking the older part of town to the latest hotels, marked 'Caleta-Zócalo-Base', US$0.50, another operating to Playa Caleta. Buses to Pie de la Cuesta, 12 km, 1.50 pesos.

Transport

Long distance Air: Aeropuerto Alvarez Internacional (ACA) 23 km east of Acapulco. Direct connections with New York, Miami, Chicago, Dallas, Houston, Los Angeles, Las Vegas, Memphis, San Fransisco, Tampa and Phoenix by Mexican and US carriers. Condor has a weekly scheduled flight from Frankfurt. There are many charter flights from Europe and North America. Mexico City, 50 mins, also domestic services to Cuernavaca, Culiacán, Guadalajara, Mérida, Monterrey, Oaxaca, Puerto Vallarta and Tijuana. AeroMéxico T847009. Flights to Mexico City are worth booking at least a week in advance, especially in high season.

Buses: bus terminal is on Av Ejido, reached by bus from Costera Miguel Alemán, allow at least 45 mins during peak time. There is a left-luggage office. Estrella de Oro buses leave from the bus station on Av Cuauhtémoc. **Mexico City**, 406 km, 4-5 hrs (1st class or *plus*) – 8 hrs (others); deluxe air-conditioned express buses (*Futura*, highly recommended), US$28.35 and super luxury US$36.65; ordinary bus, US$21.65 1st and US$25.65 *plus*, all-day services from Estación Central de Autobuses del Sur by the Taxqueña metro station, Mexico City, with Estrella de Oro (10 a day, 1 stop) or Flecha Roja (part of Líneas Unidas del Sur, hourly). Taxi to Zócalo, US$5.50; bus, US$0.50. To **Manzanillo**, direct bus US$8.50. Several 1st class buses, Estrella de Oro, 5 hrs, and Flecha Roja buses a day to **Taxco** US$11. To **Cuernavaca**, with Estrella de Oro, 6 hrs, US$14.75-19.50. To **Oaxaca**, no direct bus, change at Puerto Escondido or Pochutla, waiting room and luggage deposit at Pochutla; also via Pinotepa Nacional (1 bus at 2100) but worse road. Bus to **Puerto Escondido** every hour on the ½ hour from 0430-1630, plus 2300, 2400, 0200, US$10.50, and *directo* at 1330 and 2300, US$20, seats bookable, advisable to do so the day before, 7½ hrs, many check-points, bad road; Flecha Roja, Transportes Gacela (US$15.65). To **Tapachula**: take Impala 1st class bus to Huatulco, arriving 1930; from there Cristóbal Colón at 2030 to Salina Cruz, arriving about midnight, then take 1st or 2nd class bus.

Airline offices AeroMéxico and Mexicana offices in Torre Acapulco, Costera Miguel Alemán 1252, Mexicana T841215. *American*, T669248. *Delta*, T800-9022100. *Taesa*, T852488. Condor, T800-5246975. **Communications** Post Office, Costera, 2 blocks south of Zócalo. **Telephones:** public offices will not take collect calls; try from a big hotel (ask around, there will be a surcharge). **Embassies & consulates** *British Consul* (Honorary) Mr DB Gore, MBE, *Hotel Las Brisas*, T846605. *Canadian*, States of Guerrero & Michoacán, Honorary, Mrs Diane McLean de Huerta, T01-7-484-1305. Fax address: local 23, Centro Comercial Marbella, esq Prolongación Farallón y Miguel Alemán. Postal address: Apartado postal 94-C, 39670, Acapulco, Gro. Office hours: Mon-Fri. 0900-1700. *Dutch*, *El Presidente Hotel*, T837148. *Finnish*, Costera Miguel Alemán 500, T847641. *French*, Av Costa Grande 235, T823394. *German*, Antón de Alaminos 46, T847437. *Norwegian*, *Maralisa Hotel*, T843525. *Spanish*, Av Cuauhtémoc y Universidad 2, T857205. *Swedish*, Av Insurgentes 2, T852935. *US*, Club del Sol Hotel, T856600. **Laundry** *Tintorería Bik*, 5 de Mayo. *Lavadín*, José María Iglesias 11a, T822890, next to *Hotel Colimense*, recommended. **Useful addresses Immigration:** Juan Sebastián el Cuno 1, Costa Azul el Lado, T849021, open

Directory

Guerrero, Oaxaca & the Isthmus

0800-1400, take a 'Hornos Base' bus from Miguel Alemán, US$0.20, 30 minutes, visa extensions possible.

Coast northwest of Acapulco

Between Acapulco and Zihuatanejo is **Coyuca de Benítez**, 38 km from Acapulco, near the Laguna Coyuca (see above, Acapulco **Excursions**), a lagoon with little islands. Coyuca is a market town selling exotic fruit, cheap hats and shoes. There is no bank but shops will change US dollars. Take a *combi* from town to La Barra on the lagoon. Pelicans fly by the lagoons, there are passing dolphins and plentiful sardines, and young boys seek turtle eggs. **D** *Parador de los Reyes*. Clean, pool. **E** *Imperial*, off the main square. There is a *jai-alai* palace. The coastal road, Route 200, has many potholed stretches, so take care if driving.

El Carrizal One and a half kilometres beyond Coyuca is a turn-off to El Carrizal (7½ km), a delightful village of some 2,000 people, a short distance from a beautiful beach (many pelicans) with a steep drop-off (unsafe for children), dangerous waves and sharks behind them; good for spotting dolphins and, if you are lucky, whales. There are Frequent VW minibuses from Acapulco or Pie de la Cuesta, US$0.55.

Sleeping and eating Good restaurant (opposite *Hotel-Bungalows El Carrizal*) which has 6 rooms with bath and toilet, **E**, closes early (1800 for food), poor food, not very clean. **E** *Aída*, friendly, but little privacy, more expensive rooms more secure and mosquito-proof, all rooms with bath and fan, Mexican food (good fish). Recommended.

El Morro A couple of kilometres southeast of El Carrizal is El Morro on an unpaved road between the ocean and the lagoon. The waves on the ocean side are very strong, while swimming in the lagoon is excellent. El Morro is a small fishing village (carp) reminiscent of African townships as it is constructed entirely of *palapa* (palm-leaf and wood). Every other house is a 'fish-restaurant', the best are 1 km left along the beach to La Ramada; ask for bungalow rental (**F**), no running water but there is a toilet, mosquito nets on request; *El Mirador* (Jesús and Maty), rooms, canoe hire. One shop sells basic provisions; fruit and vegetables from Coyuca may be available. At El Morro you can rent a canoe for US$2 per hour and sail down river, past El Carrizal; you can also go up river to the lagoon, an all day trip, very beautiful with plenty of birdlife (beware, strong winds blow around midday off the sea). Minibuses run Coyuca-El Carrizal-El Morro.

Tecpan de Galeana & Cavaquito San Jerónimo, 83 km from Acapulco, has an 18th-century parish church; you can make canoe trips up river to restaurants. **Tecpan de Galeana**, 108 km from Acapulco, is a fishing village. Ten kilometres beyond Tecpan is a turn-off to another El Carrizal, which is 7 km from the Pacific Highway. There is some public transport from Tecpan, but plenty of cars go there (the road is rough). Very little accommodation, but plenty of hammock space; there is a beautiful beach and lagoon and the place is very friendly. There is a beach further on at **Cavaquito** where a series of small rivers joins the ocean and there is a large variety of birds and dense vegetation; three restaurants offer fish dishes, there is a reasonable modern hotel, *Club Papanoa*, with lovely views and a camping site; a cheaper, nameless hotel with restaurant on the beach, **E**; and one can also visit the lovely bay of Papanoa.

Guerrero, Oaxaca & the Isthmus

Zihuatanejo

A beautiful fishing port and expensive, commercialized tourist resort 237 km northwest of Acapulco by the paved Route 200, which continues via Barra de Navidad along the Pacific coast to Puerto Vallarta (see page 516). This road goes through coconut plantations where you can buy *tuba*, a drink made from coconut milk fermented on the tree, only slightly alcoholic.

Phone code: 755
Colour map 3, grid C4
Population: 22,000

Despite being spruced up, 'Zihua', as it is called locally, still retains much of its Mexican village charm. There is an Indian handicraft market by the church, some beachside cafés and a small **Museo Arqueológico**, in the old Customs and Immigration building on Av 5 de Mayo. ■ *US$0.70*. At sunset thousands of swallows meet in the air above the local cinema in the centre of town and settle for the night within one minute on the telephone poles. The **Plaza de Toros** is at the town entrance with seasonal *corridas*.

Sights

There are 5 beaches in the bay, including **Playa La Madera**, near town and a bit dirty; better is **Playa La Ropa**, 20 mins walk from centre, with the *Sotavento* and other hotels, and some beach restaurants. Also good is **Playa Las Gatas**, secluded, and a haven for aquatic sports. It can be reached by boat from the centre (US$2 return) or a 20-min walk from La Ropa beach over fishermen-frequented rocks (the boat is much safer, muggings on the path have occurred). Watch out for coconuts falling off the trees! Off the coast there are rock formations, to which divers go, and **Isla Ixtapa**, a nature reserve with numerous restaurants. **Playa Linda**, to the north, is a beautiful beach (no hotels) easily reached by *colectivo* (30 mins). The yacht, *Fandango Zihua*, takes bay cruises from the municipal pier.

Beaches

LL *Villa del Sol*, Playa La Ropa, T42239, F4758, Apdo 84. No children under 12 in high season, very expensive but highly regarded. **AL** *Catalina* and *Sotavento*, Playa La Ropa, T42032, F42975, 105 steps to hotel, same facilities. **AL** *Villas Miramar*, Playa La Madera, T42106, F42149. Suites, pool, lovely gardens. **AL** *Irma*, Playa La Madera, T42025, F43738. Good hotel but not best location.

Sleeping
Difficult to find accommodation in March, and around Christmas/New Year

Zihuatanejo orientation

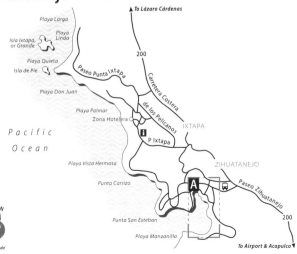

Related map
A Zihuatanejo
centre, page 396

Guerrero, Oaxaca & the Isthmus

A *Avila*, Juan Alvarez 8, T42010. A/c, phone. **A** *Zihuatanejo Centro*, Agustín Ramírez 2, T42669. Bright rooms, a/c. Recommended. **B** *Bungalows Pacíficos*, T42112. Advance reservation necessary, huge terrace, good views. Highly recommended. **B** *Las Urracas*, Playa La Ropa, T42049. Cooking facilities, good value. **B** *Palacios*, T42055, on Playa La Madera. Good. **C** *Imelda*, Catalina González 11, T43199. Clean, no restaurant. Recommended. **C** *Posada Citlali*, Vicente Guerrero 3, T42043.

D *Casa Aurora*, Nicolás Bravo 27. Clean with bath and fan, not all rooms have hot water, and **D** *Casa Bravo*, T42528. **D** *Las Tres Marías*, La Noria 4, T42191, cross the

Zihuatanejo centre

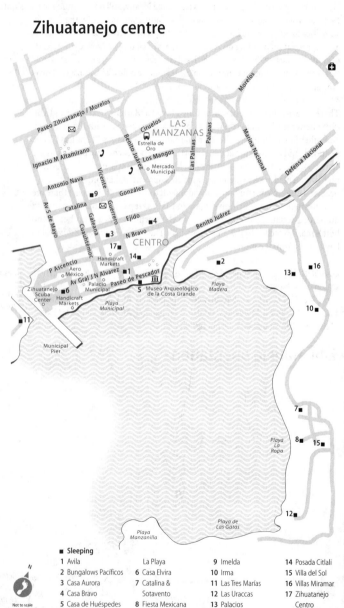

N
Not to scale

■ **Sleeping**

1 Avila
2 Bungalows Pacíficos
3 Casa Aurora
4 Casa Bravo
5 Casa de Huéspedes

La Playa
6 Casa Elvira
7 Catalina &
  Sotavento
8 Fiesta Mexicana

9 Imelda
10 Irma
11 Las Tres Marías
12 Las Uraccas
13 Palacios

14 Posada Citlali
15 Villa del Sol
16 Villas Miramar
17 Zihuatanejo
  Centro

wooden footbridge. Very pleasant with large communal balconies overlooking town and harbour, clean but sparely decorated, tiny baths, nice plants, hotel has an annex at Juan Alvarez 52, part of restaurant, similar rooms and tariffs, best on 2nd floor, note that price doubles during Christmas holidays. **D-E** *Casa La Playa*, on Juan Alvarez. Similar to *Elvira*, but not as good. **E** *Casa Elvira*, hotel-restaurant, on Juan Alvarez, T42061, in older part of town on waterfront. Very basic but clean, fan, with bath, the restaurant is on the beachfront (the place to watch the world go by), good and reasonable. **E** *Rosimar*, Ejido, T42140. Quiet, hot water, some rooms TV.

Youth hostel Av Paseo de las Salinas s/n, CP 40880, T44662.

Playa La Ropa *La Perla*. Very popular, good food, slow service. *Elvira*, by *Hotel Sotavento*. Small, attentive service, good value. *Rossy*. Good, live music at weekends.   **Eating**

Zihuatanejo Many including *El Patio*, 5 de Mayo, beside Catholic church. Excellent food and atmosphere, beautiful patio/garden, live music occasionally. *Il Piccolo*, Nicolás Bravo 22. Restaurant and video bar, excellent value, good pizzas. *Gitano's*. *Coconuts*. Good atmosphere, pricey, dinner only. Recommended. *La Marina*. Popular. Recommended. *Puntarenas*, close to *Hotel Las Tres Marías*. Excellent cooking, friendly, not expensive, popular, slow service. *Stall 27* at marketplace. Very popular, cheap and good, try local lobster for about US$10; most meals cost US$6 or over.

Scuba diving Hire of all equipment and guide from Zihuatanejo Scuba Center,   **Sports**
T42147, English spoken. Off Playa Las Gatas is an underwater wall built, according to legend, by the Tarascan king Calzonzin, to keep the sharks away while he bathed; the wall is fairly massive and can be seen clearly while scuba diving. Many fish too. US$3 a day for mask, snorkel and fins.

Local   Car hire: *Hertz*, Nicolás Bravo and airport, T43050 or F42255; also with offices   **Transport**
at the airport and in Ixtapa hotels: *Avis*, *Budget*, *Dollar*, *Economy*.

Long distance   Air: Ixtapa/Zihuatanejo international airport (ZIH), 20 km from town, T42070/42100. Many flights from Mexico City and others from Guadalajara, Mazatlán and Monterrey, and, in the USA, from Detroit, Houston, Los Angeles, Phoenix and San Francisco. Other destinations via Mexico City.

Buses: Estrella de Oro operates its own terminal on Paseo Palmar, serving Acapulco and **Mexico City**; to the capital 0830, 1130, 1930 (with stops), US$24.20, direct (no stops) at 2000; *Diamante* (wider seats, movie, stewardesses serving free drinks) non-stop 2100, arriving 0600, US$50; *Plus* (wider seats, non-stop) 2200 arriving 0700, US$33. To **Lázaro Cárdenas** at 0600, 1500 and 1900, US$3.65, 2 hrs. Direct to **Acapulco** 0600, US$8, *Plus* at 1630.

The Central de Autobuses is on the Zihuatanejo-Acapulco highway opposite Pemex station (bus from centre US$0.20); 3 lines operate from here, all using good, 32-seater buses. The terminal is clean, with several snackbars. Estrella Blanca: to **Mexico City** almost hourly from 0600-2130, US$24.20; to **Lázaro Cárdenas** daily, for connections further north and to the interior, US$4; to **Manzanillo**, US$15, 9 hrs; to **Acapulco**, US$6 hourly; to **Laredo** at 1730, 30 hrs, US$65. Blancas Fronteras to **Mexico City** 2100 or 2200, US$33 (direct); to **Acapulco** 0100, 0900 and 1700, US$10.65; to **Lázaro Cárdenas** 4 a day, US$4.75; to **Puerto Escondido** and **Huatulco**, 2130, US$34. Cuauhtémoc serves all towns between Zihuatanejo and Acapulco almost ½-hourly from 0400 to 2000. To **Acapulco**, Líneas Unidas del Sur, US$8, leave hourly, recommended. The old Central de Autobuses is half a block from the new; old buses use it, with erratic service to **Mexico City** via the less-used more dangerous road through Altamirano (to be avoided if possible, robberies).

Road: by car from Mexico City via the Toluca-Zihuatanejo highway (430 km) or via the Acapulco-Zihuatanejo highway (405 km). To Acapulco can be done in 3½ hours, but sometimes takes 6 hours. To Lázaro Cárdenas, 103 km, takes 3½ hrs, the road is very bad.

Directory   **Airlines** *AeroMéxico*, T42018/32208/09; Delta (airport), T43386/686; Mexicana, *Hotel Dorado Pacífico*, Ixtapa, T3220810. **Banks** *Banca Serfín* will change TCs at lower commission than in banks in hotel district. *Banamex. Bancomer*. Several *casas de cambio*. **Tourist offices** Tourist Office and Complaints, see under Ixtapa, below. **Useful telephone numbers** Customs at airport: T43262. **Immigration:** T42795. **Ministerio Público:** (to report a crime), T42900. **Police:** T42040. **Red Cross:** (ambulances), T42009.

Ixtapa

Phone code: 755
Colour map 3, grid C4
Population: 32,000

From Zihuatanejo one can drive 7 km or take a bus (US$0.30 from Paseo Zihuatanejo/Morelos) or taxi (US$5, *colectivo*, US$1) to **Ixtapa**, meaning 'where there are salt lakes'. The resort, developed on a large scale, boasts 14 beaches: La Hermosa, Palmar, Don Juan de Dios, Don Juan, Don Rodrigo, Cuata, Quieta, Oliveiro, Linda, Larga, Carey, Pequeña, Cuachalate and Varadero. There are turtles, many species of shellfish and fish, and pelicans at El Morro de los Pericos, which can be seen by launch. There is an island a few metres off Playa Quieta; boats go over at a cost of US$5. Ixtapa has 10 large luxury hotels and a *Club Méditerranée* (all obtain food supplies from Mexico City making food more expensive, as local supplies aren't guaranteed); there is also a shopping complex, golf course, water-ski/parachute skiing and tennis courts. There is a yacht marina and an 18-hole golf club, Palma Real. **Isla Grande** has been developed as a nature park and leisure resort. **NB** The beach can be dangerous with a strong undertow; small children should not be allowed in the sea unaccompanied. Also, there are crocodiles in the beautiful lagoons at the end of the beach. The tourist office is in Ixtapa Shopping Plaza, T31967/68.

Sleeping   **All in LL-A range** *Westin Resort Ixtapa*, T32121, F31091. Spectacular, in a small jungle. *Krystal*, T30333, F30216, book in advance. Highly recommended. *Dorado Pacífico*, T32025, F30126. *Sheraton*, Blvd Ixtapa, T31858, F32438. With panoramic lift, reductions for AAA members. Recommended. *Stouffer Presidente*, T753-30018, F32312. *Aristos*, T31505, the first to open in Ixtapa. *Best Western Posada Real*, next to *Carlos 'n Charlie's Restaurant*, T31745, F31805. *Fontan Ixtapa*, T30003. *Holiday Inn SunSpree Resort*, Blvd Ixtapa, T800-09346, F31991. *Club Med*, Playa Quieta, T743-30742, F743-30393. Taxi between centre and main hotels, US$3.

   Camping *Playa Linda Trailer Park*, on Carretera Playa Linda at *Playa Linda Hotel*, just north of Ixtapa. 50 spaces, full hook-ups, restaurant, recreation hall, baby sitters, on beach, US$14 for 2, comfortable.

Eating   Besides the restaurants in every hotel, there are many others, including *Villa de la Selva*, T30362. Recommended for food and views, book in advance. *El Sombrero*. Mexican, very good. *Montmartre* (French), *Onyx*, *Bogart's* (opposite *Hotel Krystal*), *Gran Tapa*. All more costly than in Zihuatanejo.

Bars & nightlife   Every hotel without exception has at least 1 nightclub/disco and 2 bars.

Transport   **NB for motorists** although paved Highway 134 leads directly from Mexico City and Toluca to Ixtapa, there is no fuel or other supplies after Ciudad Altamirano (188 km, pleasant motel on southwest edge of city, **C** with a/c). This road also runs through remote country, prone to landslides, and there is occasional bandit activity, with unpredictable army check-points (looking for guns and drugs). It is not recommended for non-Spanish speaking, or lone motorists.

The coastal route continues northwest to Lázaro Cárdenas and Playa Azul in Michoacán (see page 478). Twenty kilometres north of Ixtapa is the pleasant little beach town of **Troncones**, with several restaurants and **AL** *Eden*, (evandjim@aol.com). American-run hotel in secluded cove, all rooms with balconies overlooking sea, price includes breakfast, and there is a restaurant serving gourmet Mexican food.

Mexico City to Oaxaca

The express toll road from Mexico City to Oaxaca first runs generally eastwards to Puebla (see page 174), where it turns south to wind through wooded mountains at altitudes of between 1,500 and 1,800m, emerging at last into the warm, red-earth Oaxaca valley. It has been described as a stunning bus ride along a new motorway through cactus-filled valleys and plains. The route described here, however, avoids the new motorway in favour of the less sophisticated but equally attractive Route 190 which continues from Oaxaca to Tehuantepec. The road, although paved throughout and in good condition, serpentines unendingly over the Sierras and is quite beautiful. The alternative coastal route is also very attractive and of especial interest to visitors who wish to engage in the many water sports available. Buses on the new express toll road road now take six hours from Mexico City to Oaxaca. Total road toll Mexico City – Oaxaca, US$30.32.

Route 190 heads south from Puebla to Izúcar de Matamoros (side road to Huaquechula: 16th-century renaissance-cum-plateresque chapel) via Atlixco ('the place lying on the water'), with interesting baroque examples in the Capilla de la Tercera Orden de San Agustín and San Juan de Dios. There is an annual festival, the Atlixcayotl, on San Miguel hill. Nearby, 20 minutes, are the curative springs of **Axocopán**.

Atlixco
Phone code: 244

Sleeping and eating B *Molina de Herrera*, Km 40 of Puebla-Izúcar de Matamoros road, 15 mins from Atlixco, T448171. 50 a/c rooms with satellite TV, pool, restaurant, bar, convention hall for 300 people. C *Mansión Atlixco*, T50691. Highly recommended. E *Hotel Colonial* behind parish church, shared bath. *Restaurant La Taquería*, Avenida Libertad, one block from Plaza, highly recommended.

After Atlixco, Route 190 continues to the town of Izúcar de Matamoros (from *itzocan*, meaning his dirty face), famous for its clay handicrafts, 16th-century convent of Santo Domingo, and two nearby spas, **Los Amatitlanes** (about 6 km away) and **Ojo de Carbón**.

Izúcar de Matamoros
Phone code: 243
Population: 58,000

Sleeping C *Premier*, on Zócalo. D *Hotel Ocampo*, next to bus station. E *Las Fuentes*. Bath and hot water, clean, quiet, TV, courtyard. Recommended. F *La Paz*, off Zócalo. Friendly, clean, basic rooms, hot water. F *Hotel Independencia*, just off Zócalo. OK. *Restaurant Oasis*, Hidalgo, just off Zócalo. Cheap set menu.

A road leads southwest from Izúcar to **Axochiapan**, Morelos state E *Hotel Primavera*, bath, hot water, clean, tiny room, leading to a paved road to the village of **Jolalpan** with the baroque church of Santa María (1553). There are very few restaurants in Jolalpan; ask where you can get a meal. The bus from Axochiapan stops in front of the church in Jolalpan. The road (and bus)

Guerrero, Oaxaca & the Isthmus

Zapotec Indians

The Zapotec language is used by over 300,000 people in the State as a first or second language (about 20 percent of Oaxaca State population speaks only an Indian language). The Zapotec Indians, who weave fantastic toys of grass, have a dance, the Jarabe Tlacolula Zandunga danced by barefoot girls splendid in most becoming coifs, short, brightly coloured skirts and ribbons and long lace petticoats, while the men, all in white with gay handkerchiefs, dance opposite them with their hands behind their backs. Only women, from Tehuantepec or Juchitán, dance the slow and stately Zandunga, costumes gorgeously embroidered on velvet blouse, full skirts with white pleated and starched lace ruffles and huipil.

continues to Atenango del Río in Guerrero state, the last 20-30 km unpaved.

From Izúcar de Matamoros Route 190 switchbacks to Tehuitzingo. Then the landscape is fairly flat to **Acatlán**, a friendly village where black and red clay figures, and palm and flower hats are made.

Sleeping **E** *Plaza*. Clean, hot showers, TV, new, good restaurant. Recommended. **E** *México*. 'Grungy', cockroaches, try elsewhere; *Lux*; *Romano*, both **E**

Carry on to Petlalcingo (restaurant), then ascend to **Huajuapan de León**, an important centre for palm products. To the southeast (12 km) is the Yosocuta Dam with fish farms and recreational facilities. 2nd class bus from Oaxaca to Huajuapan, four a day, US$3.50.

Sleeping *Hotel García Peral*, on the Zócalo. Good restaurant; *Hotel Casablanca*, Amatista 1, Col Vista Hermosa. Also good restaurant (just outside Huajuapan on the road to Oaxaca); **C-D** *Plaza de Angel*. Central, nice, clean. **D** *Playa*, El Centro. Hot water, clean, big windows, good value. **D** *Hotel Bella Vista*. **D** *Colón*. Very good.

After Huajuapan de León, Route 125 leads to **Pinotepa Nacional**. The next town on Route 190 is **Tamazulapan** with a 16th-century church and a pink stone arch in front of the city hall.

Sleeping **D** *Gilda*, one block south of Highway 190. Central, new, large clean rooms, safe parking. **D** *México*, on highway. Modern, clean, has lush courtyard, balconies, good restaurant with *comida corrida*. **D** *Santiago*, without sign, on Zócalo. **E** *Hidalgo*, behind church; restaurant *Coquiz*, on Highway 190, good.

Seventy-two kilometres northwest of Oaxaca on Route 190 is **Yanhuitlán**, with a beautiful 400-year-old church, part of the Santo Domingo monastery, built on a pre-Hispanic platform; it is considered one of the best examples of 16th-century New World Hispanic architecture. Yanhuitlán is in the Sierra Mixteca, where Dominican friars began evangelizing in 1526. Two other important centres in the region were San Juan Bautista at Coixtlahuaca and the open chapel at Teposcolula. The scenery and the altars, the huge convents in such a remote area, are a worthwhile day trip from Oaxaca. The new highway from **Nochixtlán** to Oaxaca (103 km) has been recommended for cyclists: wide hard shoulders and easy gradients.

Sleeping **D** *Mixli*, outskirts at intersection with new highway. Large beds, TV, parking. Recommended but 20 minutes walk from town. **E** *Hotel Sarita*, around corner is **E** *Elazcan*, clean, OK.

Guerrero, Oaxaca & the Isthmus

Oaxaca

Oaxaca, the capital and administrative centre of the State of Oaxaca, is a colourful, charming city; its historical centre was declared a UNESCO World Heritage Trust Site in 1987. The city was founded by the Spanish with the name of Antequera in 1521 on the site where a Zapotec and Mixtec settlement already existed. It gracefully combines its colonial and native roots; fine stone buildings, churches, arcades and airy patios speak for its importance during the colonial period, while its markets, crafts, dances and feast days point to a more indigenous past. There are numerous sights to visit, the highlights for those with very little time include the Santo Domingo church and museum, a market, the Zócalo, and the Monte Albán archaeological site overlooking the town.

Phone code: 951
Colour map 4, grid C1
Population: 300,000
Altitude: 1,546m

Ins and outs

Aeropuerto Xoxocotlán (OAX) is about 9 km south of the city. Airport taxis (*colectivos*) will take you into the city centre. See Transport page 311 for details. The first-class bus terminal is northeast of the Zócalo on Calzada Niños Héroes (some second-class buses also leave from here). The second-class terminal is west of the Zócalo on Calzada Valerio Trujano, near the Central de Abastos market. Autobuses Unidos (AU) have their own terminal northwest of the Zócalo at Prolongación Madero. The train station is on Calzada Madero at the junction with Periférico, 15 minutes walk from the Zócalo, but there are very few, if any, passenger services left.

Getting there & away

Local town minibuses mostly charge US$0.20. For the first-class bus terminal, buses marked 'VW' leave from Avenida Juárez; for the second-class terminal, buses are marked 'Central'. Most of the important sites are in or near the city centre and can be reached on foot.

Getting around

Tourist offices *Sedetur,* Independencia 607 y García Vigil, T5160123, F5160984, info@ oaxaca.gob.mx, oaxaca.gob.mx/sedetur, open 0800-2000 daily, has maps, posters, postcards, information, friendly and very helpful; ask here about the *Tourist Yú'ù* hostel programme in local communities (see Excursions below). **INEGI** (Instituto Nacional de Estadística, Geografía e Informática), Independencia 805 for topographic maps and any statistics about the state.

The Zócalo with its arcades is the heart of town, a pleasant park with a bandstand in the centre and a few food stalls underneath. Because the streets surrounding the Zócalo and the adjacent Alameda de León are closed to traffic, it is very pleasant to sit there or stroll. It is always active, and the surrounding cafés and restaurants are always busy. Free music and dance events are often held in the evenings. Enormous balloons are sold alongside the Cathedral, young and old have a great time tossing them high in the air. In the daytime vendors sell food, in the evening their tourist wares and gardenias. It is especially colourful on Saturday and Sunday nights when Indian women weave and sell their goods. Their weavings and other crafts can also be seen during the week, on Calle Berriozábal behind the Centro Cultural Santo Domingo. Another nice spacious park is Paseo Juárez, also known as El Llano, between Avenida Juárez and Pino Suárez northeast of the Zócalo.

Avenida Independencia is the main street running east-west, the nicer part of the old city is to the north of it; a simpler area, housing the cheaper hotels, lies to the south. Independencia is also a dividing line for the north-south streets, which change names here. Calle Macedonia Alcalá is a cobbled

Guerrero, Oaxaca & the Isthmus

pedestrian walkway which joins the Zócalo with the church of Santo Domingo, many colonial buildings can be seen along this mall; this street and Calle Bustamante, its continuation to the south, are the dividing line for east-west streets, which change names here.

Sights

Worth visiting is the **Palacio de Gobierno**, on the south side of the Zócalo; it has beautiful murals and entry is free. There are often political meetings or protests outside. The **Teatro Macedonio Alcalá**, 5 de Mayo with Independencia, is an elegant theatre from Porfirio Díaz' times, it has a Louis XV-style entrance and white marble staircase; regular performances are held here. Visit also the **Arcos de Xochimilco** on García Vigil, starting at Cosijopi, some eight blocks north of the Zócalo. In this picturesque area are the remains of an aqueduct, cobbled passageways under the arches, flowers and shops. The house of the Maza family, for whom Benito Juárez worked and whose daughter he married, still stands at Independencia 1306 (a plaque marks it). Similarly, a plaque marks the birthplace of Porfirio Díaz at the other end of Independencia, in a building which is now a kindergarten, near La Soledad. DH Lawrence wrote parts of *Mornings in Mexico* in Oaxaca, and revised *The Plumed Serpent*; the house he rented is on Pino Suárez. The bar, *El Favorito*, on 20 de Noviembre, a couple of blocks south of the Zócalo, is supposedly the original that inspired Malcolm Lowry's in his novel *Under the Volcano*. There is a grand view from **Cerro de Fortín**, the hill to the northwest of the centre, here is the Guelaguetza amphitheatre; a monument to Juárez stands on a hillside below. Atop the hill are an observatory and planetarium (shows Monday-Saturday 1230 and 1900, Sunday 1230, 1800 and 1900, US$1.10, students US$0.55); best to take a taxi (about US$3.50) since the walk is dark and deserted. It is a pleasant walk from town to the hill as far as the planetarium and antennas, but muggings have been reported in the trails that go through the woods and the dirt road that goes beyond the antennas towards El Crestón (the hill with the cross); these are not safe day or night, best stay along the main road.

Ciudad de las canteras, the quarries from where the stone for the city's monumental churches and public buildings was extracted, once a huge ugly hole, has been converted into a beautifully landscaped park. It is located on Calzada Niños Héroes de Chapultepec, at the east end of Calzada Eduardo Vasconcelos; several city bus lines go there. There is a small stadium here and the site of the Expo Feria Oaxaca, a fair with rides, craft exhibits, food, and performances, held in July and December (opens 1600, US$0.70).

Churches On the Zócalo is the 17th-century **Cathedral** with a fine baroque façade (watch the raising and lowering of the Mexican flag daily at 0800 and 1800 beside the Cathedral), but the best sight by far, about four blocks from the square up the pedestrianized Calle Macedonio Alcalá, is the church of **Santo Domingo** (closed 1300-1700, no flash photographs allowed) with its adjoining monastery, now the Centro Cultural Santo Domingo (see below). The church is considered one of the best examples of baroque style in Mexico. It first opened to worship in 1608 and was refurbished in the 1950s. Its gold leaf has to be seen to be believed. The ceilings and walls, sculptured and painted white and gold, are stunningly beautiful. There is an extraordinary vaulted decoration under the raised choir, right on the reverse of the façade wall: a number of crowned heads appear on the branches of the genealogical tree of the family of Santo Domingo de Guzmán (died 1221), whose lineage was indirectly related to the royal houses of Castilla and Portugal. The entire ceiling of the central nave is painted. There are also paintings depicting passages of the Old and New Testaments. The Capilla del Rosario, a 17th-century side chapel, depicts the mysteries of the rosary.

The massive 17th-century **Basílica de La Soledad** (between Morelos and Independencia, west of Unión) has fine colonial ironwork and sculpture (including an exquisite Virgen de la Soledad). Its interior is predominantly

Oaxaca

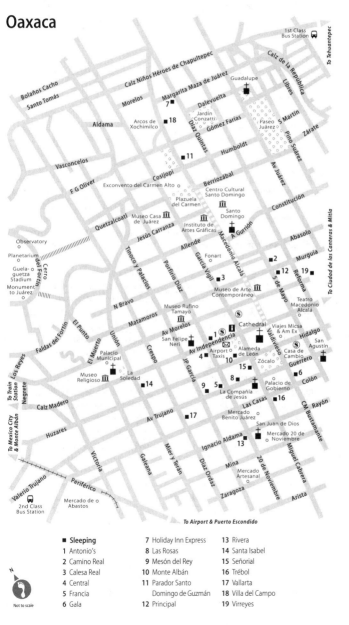

■ Sleeping	7 Holiday Inn Express	13 Rivera
1 Antonio's	8 Las Rosas	14 Santa Isabel
2 Camino Real	9 Mesón del Rey	15 Señorial
3 Calesa Real	10 Monte Albán	16 Trébol
4 Central	11 Parador Santo	17 Vallarta
5 Francia	Domingo de Guzmán	18 Villa del Campo
6 Gala	12 Principal	19 Virreyes

● ●

☞ *Guelaguetza or Lunes del Cerro*

This impressive annual celebration is where all the colour and variety of Oaxaca's many different cultural groups comes together in one place. For those with an interest in native costumes, music and dance, it must not be missed.

The word Guelaguetza *originally means something like 'reciprocity' in Zapotec, the interchange of gifts or favours. Some elements of the celebration may well date from pre-Hispanic times, however the contemporary event is a well-organized large-scale folklore festival. Guelaguetza is heavily promoted by the state government to attract tourism, which it does in great numbers. Estimated revenues totalled US$10mn in 1999.*

The main event is a grand folk-dance show held at the Guelaguetza stadium on the slopes of Cerro del Fortín, on Monday morning. The performance is lively and very colourful, with the city below serving as a spectacular back-drop. Nine different groups are selected each year to represent the principal ethno-linguistic regions of the state.

Among the favourite presentations are always Flor de Piña, *danced by women from the Tuxtepec area with a pineapple on their shoulder, and* Danza de la Pluma, *performed by men from the central valleys using enormous feather head-dresses. The most elaborate costumes are those of the women from the Isthmus of Tehuantepec, including stiffly starched lace resplandores (halos) on their heads. At the end of each performance, gifts are thrown from the stage to the audience – watch out for the pineapples!*

Los Lunes del Cerro are usually the last two Mondays in July, but the exact dates can vary, so prospective visitors should enquire beforehand. Tickets for seats in the lower galleries (A and B) are sold in advance through Sedetur and cost US$30 in 1999. The upper galleries (C and D) are free, line up before 0600, gates open around 0700, the performance begins at 1000 and finishes around 1400. Take a sweater as it is chilly in the morning, but the sun is very strong later on. A sun hat and sun-screen are essential, a pair of binoculars is also helpful in the upper galleries. Drinks and snacks are sold.

In addition to the main event, there are scores of other happenings in Oaxaca at this time of year, ranging from professional cycling races to classical music concerts, a Feria del Mezcal, and several smaller celebrations in nearby villages. Many events are free and a complete programme is available from Sedetur.

On the Saturday before Lunes del Cerro, *at around 1800, participating groups parade down the pedestrian mall on Macedonio Alcalá, from Santo Domingo to the Zócalo. This is a good opportunity to see their splendid costumes close-up and to meet the participants. On Sunday is the election of the Diosa Centeotl (goddess of the new corn), who presides over the following week's festivities. Candidates are chosen based on their knowledge of native traditions.*

On Monday night, following the Guelaguetza, the Donají legend is presented in an elaborate torchlight performance at the same stadium starting around 2000. Donají was a Zapotec princess who fell in love with a Mixtec prince, Nucano, and eventually gave her life for her people. Some claim that the two lovers are buried in the same grave in Cuilapan de Guerrero.

Both the Guelaguetza and Donají pageant are broadcast live on local television. The entire sequence of events is repeated during the second week of the festival, with different groups participating.

● ●

fawn and gold; the plaques on the walls are painted like cross-sections of polished stone. The chandeliers at the sides are supported by angels. The fine façade is made up of stone of different colours, pinks and greens; it is considered the best example of carved stonework in the city. The church was built on the site of the hermitage to San Sebastián; begun in 1582, it was recommenced in 1682 because of earthquakes. It was consecrated in 1690 and the convent was finished in 1697. The **Museo Religioso de la Soledad**, Independencia 107, has a display of religious artefacts; it is at the back of the church. ■ *0900-1400 Mon-Sun, US$0.30 donation requested.* In the small plaza outside the encircling wall, refreshments and offerings are sold. There are elaborate altars at the church of **San Felipe Neri**, Avenida Independencia y García. At **San Juan de Dios**, 20 de Noviembre y Aldama, there is an Indian version in paint of the Conquistadores' arrival in Oaxaca and of an anti-Catholic uprising in 1700. On the ceiling are paintings of the life of Christ. This was the first church in Oaxaca, originally dedicated to Santa Catalina Mártir. The church of **San Agustín**, Armenta y López at Guerrero, has a fine façade, with bas-relief of St Augustine holding the City of God above adoring monks (apparently modelled on that of San Agustín in Mexico City, now the National Library). The church of **La Compañía de Jesús**, Trujano, diagonal to the Zócalo, first built in 1579, has a wooden altarpiece; in the central niche is an image of the Virgin of the Immaculate Conception, hence it is also known as the **Iglesia de la Inmaculada**.

The **Centro Cultural Santo Domingo** is a cultural complex which includes a **Museums** museum, exhibit halls, botanical garden, library, newspaper archives, and bookstore; concerts are also performed here. It is housed in the former convent of Santo Domingo (Macedonio Alcalá y Gurrión), next to the Santo Domingo church. Construction of the convent started in 1575. It was occupied by the Dominican friars from 1608 to 1812. After the expulsion of the church it was occupied by the Mexican army between 1812 and 1972, later it housed the regional museum. Between 1994 and 1998, the convent was very beautifully restored, using only original materials and techniques. The **Museo de las Culturas de Oaxaca**, housed in the Centro Cultural Santo Domingo, and referred to as 'the Louvre of Oaxaca', is a superb museum which requires at least four hours to visit; exhibits are beautifully displayed and explained in Spanish (with plans to implement a system of recorded explanations in other languages); highly recommended. Fourteen galleries cover the history of Oaxaca from pre-Hispanic times to the contemporary period; the archaeology collection includes spectacular riches found in Tomb 7 of Monte Albán. There are also exhibits of different aspects of Oaxacan culture such as crafts, cooking, traditional medicine, etc., as well as temporary exhibits. ■ *1000-2000, closed Mon, US$2.70, free on Sun and holidays, use of video US$3.25.* The **Jardín Etnobotánico**, also in the Centro Cultural, offers free guided tours in Spanish at 1300 and 1800, one hour, sign up in advance, interesting. In high season English tours may be available. This garden aims to preserve different species of plants which are native to southern Mexico and have played and continue to play a role in the lives of different ethnic groups in Oaxaca; you can learn about the different species of *agaves* used to make mezcal, pulque and tequila; the trees used to make crafts; the *grana cochinilla*, an insect that lives in certain cacti and is used to dye cloth; the plants used in folk medicine; and many species more. Also part of the Santo Domingo complex, the **Biblioteca Francisco Burgoa** has a collection of 24,000 ancient volumes dating from 1484. There are temporary exhibits and the library is open to scholars for research. The **Hemeroteca**, corner Reforma and Gurrión, is a newspaper library. ■ *Mon-Fri, 0900-2000, Sat 0900-1700.*

The **Instituto de Artes Gráficas de Oaxaca** (IAGO) housed in an 18th-century building, is almost opposite the Centro Cultural at Alcalá 507; it has interesting exhibition rooms, a very good reference library and beautiful courtyards filled with flowers. ■ *Daily 0730-2200, closed Tue, free, but a donation is appreciated.*

At Alcalá 202 is **Museo de Arte Contemporáneo**, a good exhibition with library and café is housed in a late 17th-century house with a stone façade. ■ *1030-2000 daily, except Tue US$1.10.* The **Museo de Arte Prehispánico Rufino Tamayo**, Morelos 503, has an outstanding display of pre-Columbian artefacts dating from 1250 BC to AD 1100, donated by the Oaxacan painter Rufino Tamayo in 1974. Spanish only and not comprehensive. ■ *1000-1400, 1600-1900, Sun 1000-1500, closed Tue, entry US$1.50.* The **Museo Casa de Juárez**, at García Vigil 609, is where Juárez lived. It contains some of Juárez' possessions, historical documents and some bookbinding tools. ■ *1000-1800, Sun 1000-1700, closed Mon, US$1.40, free Sun and holidays.* The **Museo de Filatelia** Calle Reforma 504, has temporary exhibits, a philatelic library, and tours by appointment. ■ *0900-1900, closed Mon, free.* For photograph exhibits with Oaxacan motives see **Shopping** below.

Markets The colourful markets and varied crafts of Oaxaca are among the foremost attractions of the region. The city has four main markets, all of which are worth a visit; polite bargaining is the rule everywhere. The **Mercado de Abastos** also known as the Central de Abastos, near the second-class bus station is the largest; a cacophony of sights, sounds and aromas, busiest on Saturdays and not to be missed. Prices here tend to be lower than in the smaller markets. Everything imaginable is bought and sold here; look for the *molinos* (mills), where people bring their own mixture of ingredients to be ground into *mole*. In the centre of town is the **Mercado 20 de Noviembre** (Aldama on the corner of 20 de Noviembre), with clean stalls selling prepared foods, cheese and baked goods. Next door, the larger **Mercado Benito Juárez** has a selection of household goods, fruits, vegetables, crafts, and regional products such as *quesillo* (string cheese), bread and chocolate. The **Mercado Artesanal** (Zaragoza and JP García) has a good selection of crafts intended for the tourist trade. Also see **Shopping**, page 413. Smaller but equally interesting markets are found in nearby towns which can be easily reached from Oaxaca. See **Excursions** below.

Safety Oaxaca is a generally safe city; however, sensible precautions are advised. Pickpockets are active in the markets, bus stations, and wherever there are crowds. The Zócalo is usually busy late into the night but the remainder of the city centre is not, so beware of walking to your hotel along deserted streets, especially south of Avenida Indpendencia; when in doubt take a taxi. The main road up to Cerro del Fortín is reasonably safe during the daytime only, but the side roads and trails along the hillside are unsafe day and night. Women should be aware of so-called 'Zócalo boys' or *gavacheros*, local young men who hang around the Zócalo and pick up foreign women in order to get a free meal or other favours.

Excursions

For good hikes, take local bus to San Felipe del Agua, north of the city. To the left of where the buses stop at the end of line is a car parking area, just below it starts a dirt road, follow this road, in five minutes you will reach the San Felipe Park entrance and a booth where you register with the guard. Several trails fan out from here, one follows the river valley, it goes by some picnic areas and a swimming pool, continues upstream crossing the river several times before reaching a waterfall in about one hour. There are longer walks to the mountain to the north, crossing through several vegetation zones, from low dry shrub to pleasant pine forest; allow 5-6 hours to reach the summit.

The Central Valleys of the state of Oaxaca, which surround the capital, make a fine destination for several interesting day-trips or overnight visits. The area features excellent archaeology (Monte Albán, Mitla, and Yagul are but the best-known of many different sites), authentic native towns, their people, markets, crafts, and *fiestas*. There is good walking with impressive views throughout the region, as well as the interesting mineral deposits at Hierve El Agua. The area has good public transport and excursions can easily be organized which combine several of the above attractions. From the ruins at Monte Albán there are paths leading to the valleys below. From the town of Teotitlán del Valle you can walk up to the nearby hills across the river or hike north to the town of Benito Juárez (there are *Tourist Yú'ù* accomodations in both these towns, see sleeping outside Oaxaca below).

Essentials

There are over 160 hotels in Oaxaca in all price categories, and one can usually find some accommodation even at the busiest times of the year. If you wish to stay at a particular hotel however, reservations are recommended during peak holiday periods (Holy Week, Jul-Aug, Christmas and New Year).

Sleeping

LL *Camino Real*, 5 de Mayo 300, T5160611, F5160732. Beautifully converted 16th-century convent of Santa Catalina, very elegant, full service, good pool, restaurant, Fri night show (see Entertainment below). **L** *Casa Oaxaca*, García Vigil 407, T5144173, F5164412. Full service, includes continental breakfast, restaurant, pool. **L** *Fiesta Inn*, Av Universidad 140, 10 min drive from centre towards the coast, T5161122, F5147921. Restaurant, pool, gym. **L** *Holiday Inn Express*, Díaz Quintas 115, T5129200, F5129292, hieoax@oax1.telmex.net.mx. Includes buffet breakfast, full service, a/c, pool, parking, new in 1999. **L** *San Felipe Oaxaca*, Jalisco 15, San Felipe del Agua, in suburb north of town, T5135090, F5135744. Offers transport to the centre, attractive, restaurant, pool. **L** *Victoria*, Lomas del Fortín 1, 15 mins walk from town along the Panamerican Highway Km 545, T5152633, F5152411. Colonial house turned into hotel, bedrooms with showers built round the garden, good value, swimming pool, TV.

AL *Casa Conzatti*, Gómez Farías 218, T5138500. 50 rooms in refurbished colonial house, a/c, safety deposit box, exchange, restaurant, new in 1999. **AL** *Hacienda La Noria*, Periférico 1918 on corner of La Costa, at the south end of town, T5147555, F5165347. Motel-type, pool, restaurant, good and convenient. **AL** *Hostal de la Noria*, Hidalgo 918, T5147844, F5163992, 2 blocks from Zócalo. New colonial style, restaurant, parking. **AL** *Marqués del Valle*, Portal de Clavería, right on the Zócalo by cathedral, T5140688, F5169961, hmarques@oax1.telmex.net.mx. Modern colonial-style, clean, friendly, good restaurant. Recommended. **AL** *Misión de Los Angeles*, Calzada Porfirio Díaz 102, T5151500, F5151680. Motel-style, 2 km from centre, quiet and most attractive, with swimming pool. **AL** *Rivera del Angel*, Mina 518 near Díaz Ordaz, T5166666, F5145405, rivera@antequera.com. Clean, large rooms, good services, pool, tours to ruins (see below). Recommended. **AL** *San Pablo*, M Fiallo 102, T5162553, F5164251. In restored 16th-century convent of San Pablo, luxury suites, a/c, bathtubs, nice courtyard. **AL** *Suites del Centro*, Hidalgo 306, T5168282, F5161549, stcentro@oax1.telmex.net.mx. 1 and 2 bedroom suites, restaurant, parking.

A *Calesa Real*, García Vigil 306, T5165544, F5165347. Modern colonial but many small dark rooms, good but expensive, *Los Arcos* restaurant, parking, central, slow service. **A** *Gala*, Bustamante 103 y Guerrero, southeast corner of Zócalo, T5142251, F5163660. Also suites, cable TV, with a/c, very nice (no elevator). **A** *Parador Santo Domingo de Guzmán*, Alcalá 804, T/F42171 suitesto@anntequera.com/StoDomingoSuites. An all-suite hotel with secure car parking, pool, cable TV. Suites have bedroom, sitting room and kitchen, daily maid included. Recommended. **A-B** *Posada Catarina*, Aldama 325, T5164270, F5165338. Modern colonial, comfortable, nice, refurbished.

B *Anturios*, Privada Emilio Carranza 202, T5130075, F5130122. Clean, friendly, *cafetería*. Recommended. **B-C** *Antonio's*, Independencia 601, T5167227, F5163672, 1 block from Zócalo. Colonial patio, hot water, spotless, good restaurant, closed in evening. **B** *La Casa de María*, Belisario Domínguez 205, Colonia Reforma, T/F5140303. B&B, courtyard, garden. **B** *La Casona del Llano*, Juárez 701, T5147719, F5162219. Nice location across from Paseo Juárez, pleasant, restaurant. **B** *Mesón del Rey*, Trujano 212, T5160033, F5161434, 1 block from Zócalo. Clean, modern, fan, quiet except for street-facing rooms, good value, restaurant and travel agency, no credit cards. **B** *Monte Albán*, Alameda de León 1, T5162777. Friendly, colonial-style, opposite Cathedral, daily folk dance performances (see entertainment below). **B** *Parador San Andrés*, Hidalgo 405, T/F5141011. Comfortable, colonial-style, nice courtyard, new in 1999. **B-C** *Posada del Rosario*, 20 de Noviembre 508, T5164112, F5144911. Large courtyard (several others in same block). **B** *Santa Rosa*, Trujano 201 y 20 de Noviembre, T5146714, F5146715. Fan, TV, phone, restaurant/bar, hot water, laundry, central. Recommended. **B** *Señorial*, Portal de Flores 6 (on Zócalo), T5163933, F5163668. Will store luggage, suites or rooms, with bath, swimming pool, good restaurant, no personal cheques or credit cards, cockroaches. Recommended. **B** *Villa de Campo*, Alcalá 910, T5159652. Rooms and 4 suites, clean, quiet, tiled floors, safe, friendly, parking, pool. **B** *Veracruz*, Chapultepec 1020, T5150511, F5150611, next to ADO bus station. Spotless, welcoming, comfortable, good if you arrive late at night by bus, expensive restaurant.

C *California*, Chapultepec 822, T159500, F5131771, near 1st class bus station. With bath, friendly, pleasant, restaurant. **C** *Del Arbol*, Calzada Madero 131, T5161094, F5142799. Modern, comfortable, bath. **C** *Del Bosque*, exit road to Mitla, T5152122, F5152144. Modern, restaurant. **C** *Ferri*, Las Casas 405, T5145290, F5145292. Modern, comfortable, clean, spacious, secure parking. Recommended. **C** *Francia*, 20 de Noviembre 212, T5164811, F5164251. Around enclosed courtyard, popular, some rooms scruffy without windows, friendly and helpful. Recommended but noisy. **C** *Las Golondrinas*, Tinoco y Palacios 411, T5143298, F5142126. Uphill from centre, 3 courtyards, cash only, pleasant. **C** *Las Rosas*, Trujano 112. Old charm, nice patio, clean, excellent, quiet, friendly, good view from roof. **C** *Maela*, Constitución 206 behind Santo Domingo, T5166022. Fan, TV, parking, nice location. **C** *Posada El Cid*, Pino Suárez 903, near 1st class bus station, T5151070, F5138888. Clean, nice, **D** with shared bath. **C** *Posada de Chencho*, 4a Privada de la Noria 115, T/F5140043. With shower, hot water, quiet, breakfast included, hospitable, enclosed parking. Warmly recommended. **C** *Posada del Centro*, Independencia 403, T/F5161874, posadabb@oax1.telmex.net.mx. Modern colonial, nice, cheaper with shared bath, internet service, new in 1999. **C** *Posada Yagul*, Juárez 106, T/F5143694. Queen size beds, hot water. **C** *Primavera*, Madero 438, T5164508, F5145312. Opposite railway station, with bath, warm water, clean, friendly, good value, front rooms noisy. **C** *Principal*, 5 de Mayo 208, 2 blocks from the Zócalo, T/F5162535. Colonial house, very clean, private shower with hot and cold water, rooms overlooking street are a bit noisy, English spoken, heavily booked. **C-D** *Isabel*, Zaragoza 503, T5162646. With bath, TV, friendly. **C-D** *Jiménez*, Mier y Terán 213, T5140515, F5147960. With bath, TV, nice.

D *Aurora*, Bustamante 212, T5164145, 2 blocks from Zócalo. No private bath. **D** *Hotel Nacional*, 20 de Noviembre, 512, T5162780. With hot water, clean, friendly.

Recommended. **D** *Pasaje*, Mina 302. With bath, parakeets in patio, hot water but you have to ask, clean, provides good town plan. **D** *Posada Margarita*, Labastida 115, near Santo Domingo, T5162802. With bath, hot water, clean, quiet, basic. **D** *Reforma*, Av Reforma 102 between Independencia and Morelos, T/F5160939. Back rooms quieter, upper floors have good views, terrace on roof, friendly, but theft from rooms has been reported. **D** *Regional de Antequera*, Las Casas 901, 5 mins walk from 2nd class bus station, T5166952, F5160118. Pleasant, clean. **D** *Vallarta*, Díaz Ordaz 309, T64967. Clean, good value, enclosed parking, street rooms noisy, good set lunch. **D** *Valle de Oaxaca*, Díaz Ordaz 208, T5163707, F5145203. Clean, comfortable, good restaurant. **D** *Villa Alta*, Cabrera 303, T5162444, 4 blocks from Zócalo. With bath, friendly service, stores luggage, bit run down but still OK. **D** *Yagul*, Mina 103, near Zócalo, T/F5162750. Family atmosphere, use of kitchen on request. **D-E** *Central*, 20 de Noviembre 104, T5165971. With bath, hot water, good value but very noisy, fills up early. **D-E** *La Cabaña*, Mina 203, T5165918. With bath, cheaper without, safe, clean but noisy, hot water 0700-1000, 1700-2100, good value. **D-E** *Posada Las Casas*, Las Casas 507 y Díaz Ordaz, T5162325. Clean, with bath, hot water, cheaper without bath, friendly, good value. Recommended. **D-E** *Virreyes*, Morelos 1001 y Reforma, T5165555. Problems with water, quiet, a bit tatty, rooms on street a bit noisy and unfriendly front desk. Otherwise recommended.

E *Arnel*, Aldama 404, T5152856, F5136285. Homely, pleasant patio, good for meeting people, parking, not central, organize good tours, reservations not always honoured. **E** *Díaz Ordaz*, Díaz Ordaz 316. Basic, water problems. **F** *Hostal Santa Isabel*, Mier y Terán 103, T5142865 (3 blocks from Zócalo). Friendly, kitchen, luggage store, bicycle rental. Recommended. **E** *Lupita*, Díaz Ordaz 314, T5165733. Large, pleasant rooms, upstairs rooms are bright and have mountain views. Recommended. **E-F** *Ninivé*, Periférico 108 and Las Casas, T5144907, across from Mercado Mayorista, near 2nd-class terminal. Basic, shared bath, noisy street. **E** *Posada El Palmar*, JP García 504 and Aldama, T5164335. Cheaper without bath, convenient, friendly, family-run, hot water in morning, only 1 shower upstairs, safe motorcycle parking. **E** *Posada Halcón*, Aldama 316, T5161707. Without bath. Recommended. **E** *San José*, Trujano 412, T5163948. Basic, dirty, cheap, lively, friendly. **E** *Yalalag*, Mina 108, T5162892. Basic, noisy.

Many cheap hotels in the block formed by the streets Mina, Zaragoza, Díaz Ordaz and JP García; also on Trujano 4 blocks from the Zócalo (areas not safe at night).

Long stay *Villa María*, Arteaga 410A, T5165056, F5142562, 5 blocks from the Zócalo. Pleasant modern well-furnished apartments from US$300 per month with 24-hr security, maid service if required, daily rate **B** Recommended.

Youth hostels *Danish Hostel*, Fiallo 305, 5141351. **F** pp in dormitories, full of tourists, friendly, kitchen and laundry facilities, water supply problems, seldom any hot water, stores luggage, purified water, good place to meet travellers, but few Mexicans. Good breakfast. If full you can sling hammock on roof but same price. *Del Valle Youth Hostel*, Humboldt 120-A, T5161863. **F** pp in dorm, **E** for private room with shared bath, 10% discount with ISIC card. *Hostal Guadalupe*, Juárez 409 and Abasolo, T5166365. **F** pp in dorm, **E** for private room with shared bath, separate male and female dorms, hot water, kitchen, laundry, lockers. *Hostal Misión San Pedro*, Juárez y Morelos, T/F5164626. **E-F** pp in dorm, **C** for private room, hot water, kitchen, laundry, TV room. *Villa Deportiva Juvenil*, office at Belisario Domínguez 920, Colonia Reforma, bus from Las Casas and JP García in centre, 5 mins, US$0.15. Cold water, dormitories, clean, friendly, **G** with YHA card, **F** without, sheets and blankets provided.

Camping *Oaxaca Trailer Park*, Violeta 900, Colonia Reforma, north of town off the road to Mitla at a sign marked 'Infonavit' (corner of Pinos and Violetas). US$4.50 for a tent, US$6 for a camper van, secure, clothes washing facilities not always available, try the delicious *tamales* across the road in the green restaurant; bus 'Carmen-Infonavit' from downtown.

Outside Oaxaca On the road to Tehuantepec (Km 9.8): **B** *Hotel Posada Los Arcos*, T/F5175131. Spanish-style motel at San Sebastián Tutla. In 13 towns, throughout the Central Valleys around Oaxaca, there are tourist accomodations known as *Tourist Yú'ù* run by the local communities (**F** pp, US$2.70 to camp). Each house has room with 6 beds, equipped kitchen, bathroom with hot water. For details contact T5160123, F5160984.

Eating

Around the Zócalo Most restaurants on the main square cater for tourists, and are therefore pricey (efficiency and standards depend a bit on how busy they are, but generally they are good). On the west side; *El Jardín*. A nice place to sit and watch all the activity (music, parades, aerobics, etc) in the Zócalo; upstairs is *Asador Vasco*. Live Mexican music in the evening, good food and service. *La Primavera*. Good value meals, international and traditional dishes, good expresso coffee, slow. *La Casa de la Abuela*, upstairs on corner of Zócalo and Alameda de León. On the north side. *El Marqués*. Very slow service. *Pizza, Pasta y Más*. Popular. *El Sagrario*, Valdivieso 120, ½ block north of Zócalo. Varied menu, pizza, bar, live music, no cover charge, open 0800-0200. Recommended. On the east side. *Café El Portal*, Portal Benito Juárez. Good food, quick service. *Café Amarantos* and *Mario's Terranova Restaurant*. Excellent food, friendly and efficient service, pricey. On Hidalgo at northeast corner. *El Mesón*. Buffets 0800-1830, good at US$2.50, breakfast, *comida corrida* poor value, good *tacos*, clean, quick service. Almost opposite is *La Piñata*. Good lunches. *La Casita*, Av Hidalgo 612 near main Post Office, 1st flr. Good food, sample platter of 7 Oaxacan moles, live music. On Bustamante, just south of Zócalo. *Gala*. Good breakfast, opens 0730, not cheap.

Along Macedonio Alcalá walkway *Hostería de Alcalá*, at No 307. Excellent food and quiet atmosphere in colonial courtyard, good service, expensive. *Plaza Garibaldi* at No 303. *María Bonita*, at No 706B. Typical Oaxaca food, small restaurant with pleasant atmosphere, closed Mon. *Alfredo da Roma Pizzería*, at No 400. Expensive wine by the glass. *Pizza Rústica Angelo y Domenico*, Allende y Alcalá, opposite Santo Domingo. Very good, reasonable prices. Recommended. *Quing Long*, at No 407-32, upstairs. Beijing and Szechuan specialities. Expensive.

North of Independencia *Los Arcos*, García Vigil 306 under *Calesa Real* hotel. Good food in pretty setting and friendly service. *Santa Fe*, 5 de Mayo 103, open 0800-2300. Mexican and international dishes, good. Not cheap. *Catedral Restaurant Bar* , corner of García Vigil and Morelos, 1 block from Cathedral. Good for international and local specialities, steaks, good *tamales*, classical music, excellent buffet for US$7. Recommended. *Guitarra, Pan y Vino*, Morelos 511. Regional food, music *soirées*. *Quince Letras*, Abasolo opposite *Hotel Santo Tomás*. Excellent food, friendly service. *Los Chapulines*, Murguia 104. Upscale cooking, good desserts, pricey. *El Sol y la Luna*, Reforma 502. Good international food, not cheap, nice setting, live music Thu-Sun, open evenings only. *Mariscos los Jorges*, Pino Suárez across from Juárez park. Good seafood, outdoor seating, reasonable. *La Verde Antequera*, Matamoros 3 blocks north of Zócalo. Good daily lunch specials, best *comida corrida* in town for US$1. *Los Olmos*, Morelos 403. Regional specialities, popular, friendly. *El Laurel*, Nicolás Bravo 210. Tasty home-style cooking, try the *mole*, open to 1800 Tue-Thu, and to 2200 on Fri and Sat. Not cheap. *Santa Clara*, Reforma and Independencia. Good breakfast, set meal. *Bamby*, García Vigil 205. Cheaper beer than elsewhere, good breakfast. *Arte y*

Oaxacan Cooking

The food of the state of Oaxaca is a fine representation of the complexity and variety of its cultures. The region's cuisine ranges from sublime to highly unusual.

A stroll through any of Oaxaca's markets will quickly bring you into contact with vendors selling chapulines. These small grasshopper-like creatures are fried, turning them bright red, and then served with lime. Another interesting ingredient in the diet is gusanito, a small red worm which is used to make a special sauce or ground with salt to accompany mezcal.

There are local curiosities for vegetarians as well. Flor de calabaza, squash flowers are used in soup, empanadas, or as a garnish. Soup is also prepared from nopales, the young leaves of the prickly-pear cactus.

The most typical regional snacks are tlayudas, huge crispy tortillas, covered with a variety of toppings (beef, sausage, beans, or cheese) and grilled over the coals. Oaxacan string cheese, known as quesillo, is also famous, as is the area's

excellent chocolate, best enjoyed as a hot beverage. A slightly fermented drink made from corn flour is known as atole.

Barbacoa is a pork, lamb, or beef dish combining several different types of chillies and special condiments such as avocado leaves. The colour of the resulting sauce is a very deep red, reminiscent of another platter appropriately called mancha manteles (table-cloth stain).

The essence of Oaxacan cooking however, and the recipes for which the state is most famous, are its many moles, which come in all colours of the rainbow. They are served as sauces accompanying beef, chicken, turkey or pork. The most complex by far is mole negro (black), combining at least 17 different ingredients including cocoa beans and sesame seeds. Mole colorado (red), or just coloradito, is also very typical and quite spicy. Almendrado (also red) is milder and slightly sweet. Mole verde (green) is a bit tangy, while mole amarillo (yellow) rounds out Oaxaca's culinary chromatic spectrum.

Tradición, García Vigil 406. Craft centre with courtyard café, excellent service and food, open Mon-Sat 1100-2200. *Trece Cielos*, Matamoros 101. Good, cheap daily menú. *Tito's*, García Vigil No 116. Good food at very reasonable prices. Several good places for cheap menú del día on Porfirio Díaz, such as *Guidos*. Popular, with cheap pasta and coffee. *El Bicho Pobre II*, Calzada de la República. Lunch only, very popular. Highly recommended.

South of Independencia *Flor de Oaxaca*, Armenta y López 311. Pricey but excellent meals and delicious hot chocolate. *Alameda*, JP García between Trujano and Hidalgo. Excellent regional food, crowded Sun, closes 1800. *El Naranjo*, Trujano 203. In courtyard of 17th-century house, traditional Oaxaca fare, expensive but good, known for its moles. *Café Alex*, Díaz Ordaz 218 y Trujano. Good comida corrida and varied à la carte, coffee and breakfasts, delicious pancakes with fruit, good value. Recommended. *Coronita*, Díaz Ordaz 208 below Hotel Valle de Oaxaca. Tasty lunches, traditional Oaxacan dishes. *Hipocampo's*, Hidalgo 505. Good-value set meals, popular with locals, open late. *Flami*, on Trujano near Zócalo. Good food. *La Quebrada*, Armenta y López. Excellent fish, open only to 1800. *El Paisaje*, 20 de Noviembre. Good, cheap chicken dishes. *Los Canarios*, 20 de Noviembre, near Posada del Rosario. Good comida corrida. *María Cristina's*, in Mercado 20 de Noviembre. Excellent caldos and comidas. *Fiesta*, Las Casas 303. Good for breakfast or comida corrida. *El Shaddai*, Av Hidalgo 121 y Galeano. Family-run, good and cheap. The most authentic Oaxacan food is found in the comedores familiares such as *Clemente*, *Los Almendros*, *La Juchita*, but they are way out of town and could be difficult to get to, or in *comedores populares* in the market. *Makedonia*, Trujano 122 y 20 de Noviembre. Greek food, souvlaki. Japanese restaurant on Fiallo, 100 block.

Vegetarian *Café Fuente y Señor de Salud*, Juárez just north of Morelos. Pleasant, reasonable food. *Arco*, Niños Héroes de Chapultepec opposite ADO bus station. Dearer, loud music. *Manantial Vegetariano*, Tinoco y Palacios 303. Excellent cheap meals, buffet US$4, pleasant patio. Recommended. *Girasoles*, 20 de Noviembre 102. Small, good food. Recommended. *Flor de Loto*, Morelos 509. Good value, clean, vegetarian and Mexican, also breakfast. *La Abeja*, Porfirio Díaz 610 y Carranza. Breakfast and lunch, set meals, bakery, garden setting.

Pizza Nostrana, corner Ignacio Allende and Macedonio Alcalá (close to Santo Domingo church), T40778. 1300-2300. Delicious Italian cuisine. Specializes in vegetarian dishes. Cheap-reasonable prices. *Madre Tierra*, 5 de Mayo 411. Brown bread bakery and delicatessen, vegetarian and imaginative cuisine plus good night life.
Snacks *TLC*, corner of Aldama y García. Excellent *tacos, tortas* and juices in a calm patio setting. *La Gran Torta*, on Independencia opposite Post Office. Small, simple, family-run, cheap, good *pozole* and *tortas*. Good restaurant opposite 1st class bus station, good value, 1 of the only sit-down places among *taco* stands. The most popular place to eat *tlayudas* (oversized tortillas) and other local snacks in the evening is from stalls and restaurants along Aldama, between Cabrera and 20 de Noviembre.

Cafés and Bakeries *French Pastry Shop*, Trujano, 1 block west of Zócalo. Good coffee, pastries, desserts. *Café y Arte Geono*, Macedonio Alcalá 412. Nice garden, good coffee and cakes. *Café Plaza*, 5 de Mayo near Santo Domingo. Courtyard, good coffee. Recommended bakeries and pastry shops are: *Tartamiel*, Trujano, ½ block east of Zócalo; *La Vasconia*, Independencia 907; *La Luna*, Independencia 1105; *Pan Bamby*, García Vigil y Morelos. Good *dulcería* (sweet shop) in the 2nd class bus station. In the Mercado 20 de Noviembre there are *comedores* and lots of stalls selling breads and chocolate. A local bread called *pan de yema*, made with egg-yolk, at the Mercado de Abastos (the *Hermanas Jiménez* bakery is most recommended).

Entertainment **Folk dancing** Guelaguetza-style shows at the following hotels: *Camino Real*, Fri 1900, US$19 includes buffet dinner; *Monte Albán*, nightly at 2030, US$3.50, photography permitted; *Señorial*, most nights of the week; advance booking recommended.

Nightclubs *Snob*, Niños Héroes Chapultepec, young crowd, free Wed; Live salsa at *Rojo Caliente* on Porfirio Díaz; *Candela*, Murguía 413 y Pino Suárez, salsa, merengue, live music from 2200, also restaurant, popular with visitors and locals, cover US$5; *La Tentación*, Murguía between Macedonio Alcalá and García Vigil, salsa, merengue, live music starting 2230, open late, friendly atmosphere, cover US$3.25; *La Cumbanda*, Netzahualcoytl y Eucaliptos, Colonia Reforma, *música tropical*, US$3.80, reduced cover on Thu. *Casa de Mezcal*, in front of the market, popular drinking hole.

Cinemas *Ariel 2000*, Juárez y Berriozabal, subtitled films for US$2, ½ price Mon. *Cine Versalles*, Av Melchor Ocampo, north of Hidalgo (3 blocks east, ½ block north of Zócalo). *Cine Oaxaca*, Morelos near Alcalá; *Plaza Alameda*, Independencia y 20 de Noviembre; another cinema on Trujano, 1 block west of Zócalo.

Sports **Hiking** See **Excursions** above. **Cycling** Pedro's Mountain Bike Rentals, JP García 509, T5143144. **Bird watching** Almost 700 species of birds can be found in the State of Oaxaca. Its strategic location at the junction between North and Central America and its geographic diversity, spanning the Pacific and Atlantic watersheds, result in great diversity. There are birding opportunities in the Central Valleys (San Felipe, Monte Albán, Teotitlán, Yagul), in the mountain range separating the Central Valleys from the Pacific coast, in the coastal lagoons, the thorn forests along Route 190, and in the cloud forests and lowlands of the Atlantic coast (see Valle Nacional). **Public baths** *Baños Reforma*, Reforma 407, open 0700-1800, US$4 for steam-bath for 2, sauna for 1, US$3. **Baños San Rafael**, Tinoco y Palacios 514, Mon-Sat 0600-1800, Sun 0600-1530, hot water. **Caving** Southwest of Oaxaca is San Sebastián de las Grutas, with a large system of caves (see Excursions south of Oaxaca, below).

The most important festival is the *Guelaguetza*, also called *Los Lunes del Cerro*, when a **Festivals** festive atmosphere permeates the city for over 2 weeks at the end of **Jul** (see page 404). *El Señor del Rayo*, a 9-day event in the third week of **Oct**, including excellent fireworks. **2 Nov**, *the Day of the Dead*, is a mixture of festivity and solemn commemoration, best appreciated at the Panteón General (main cemetery); the decoration of family altars is carried to competitive extremes (competition in 5 de Mayo between Santo Domingo and the Zócalo on 1 Nov); traditional wares and foods, representing skulls, skeletons, coffins, etc, are sold in the market. Also celebrated more traditionally, in the outlying villages, especially in the cemetery of Ocotlán. Always ask before photographing. **8-18 Dec** with fine processions centred around the Basílica de la Soledad, patroness of Oaxaca, and throughout the city. On the night of **23 Dec**, *Noche de Rábanos*, outside the Palacio de Gobierno, there is a unique contest of figures carved out of radishes, many groups participate, stands made of flowers and corn stalks have been added in recent years to this old tradition. During the 9 days preceding Christmas, the *Novenas* are held, groups of people go asking for shelter, *posada*, as did Joseph and Mary, and are invited into different homes. This is done in the centre as well as other neighbourhoods like San Felipe (5 km north) and at Xoxo, to the south. The *posadas* culminate on the night of 24 Dec with what is known as *Calendas*, a parade of floats representing allegories from the birth of Christ; every church in town prepares a float honoring their patron saint, the groups from all the parishes converge at the Cathedral at 2300 (best seen from balcony of the restaurants around the Zócalo; go for supper and get a window table). *Buñuelos*, crispy fried dough rings, covered in syrup, are sold and eaten in the streets during a number of festivals, the clay dishes are ceremonially smashed after serving.

Crafts Many crafts are produced throughout the state of Oaxaca, and the artisans are **Shopping** happy to show the visitor how they create their wares. Crafts are sold in nearby villages or they may be purchased in the city of Oaxaca, at the markets listed below. There are endless shopping temptations such as green and black pottery, baskets and bags made from cane and rushes, embroidered shirts, skirts, wooden painted animals called *alebrijes*, hammocks, tooled leather goods, woven wall hangings and rugs. The **Mercado Artesanal** at JP García y Zaragoza has a large selection of all kinds of crafts. The **Mercado Benito Juárez**, in the centre, has a sampling of different wares including a selection of leather bags and straw hats. At the **Mercado de Abastos** you are likely to find better prices, there is a selection of pottery and basketry used by locals and a section with other crafts, but be prepared to spend more time looking, as the market is quite large and spread-out. *Aripo*, on García Vigil 809, T5169211. Government-run, cheaper and better than most, service good, with very good small market nearby on junction of García Vigil and Jesús Carranza, for beautiful coloured belts and clothes. *Arte y Tradición*, García Vigil 406. Superior craft shops, good prices. *Sedetur* (see under **Tourist offices**, page 401), run a shop selling crafts and profits go to the artisans, good prices, recommended. *Casa Breno*, near Santo Domingo church, has unusual textiles and spindles for sale, happy to show visitors around the looms. *Lo Mexicano*, García Vigil, at end furthest from centre, excellent selection of high-quality crafts at reasonable prices, run by young Frenchman. *Pepe*, Av Hidalgo, for jewellery, cheap local crafts. *Yalalag*, 5 de Mayo y Murguía, has good selection of jewellery, rugs and pottery, somewhat overpriced. *Maro*, 5 de Mayo 204 between Morelos y Murguía. Good range of clothes from several regions and some crafts. *El Palacio de las Gemas*, Alcalá 100 block, is recommended for gemstones, good selection at reasonable prices. Cheapest and largest selection of pottery plus a variety of fabrics and sandals at *Productos Típicos de Oaxaca*, Belisario Domínguez 602; city bus near ADO depot goes there. *Casa Aragón*, JP García 503, famous for knives and *machetes*. Fine cream and purple-black pottery (Zapotec and Mixtec designs) available at *Alfarería Jiménez*, Zaragoza 402. Other potteries at Las Casas 614, makers of the Oaxacan daisy design, and Trujano 508, bold flower designs. The nearby village of Atzompa (see excursions north of the city, buses from 2nd class terminal) is worth a visit for its interesting ceramics; local potters are very friendly. *Gilberto Segura* T, 2 Galería de Artesanías, puesto 140, at the *Mercado de Abastos*, makes hammocks to your own design and specification, price depends on size, about US$20 for a single. Sr Leonardo Ruiz of Teotitlán del Valle, has an excellent carpet stall here. *Mujeres Artesanas de las Regiones de Oaxaca* is a regional association of Oaxacan craftswomen with a sales and exhibition store at 5 de Mayo 204, T516067, open daily 0900 to 2000.

Regional food and drink On Mina and 20 de Noviembre, opposite the 20 de Noviembre market, are several mills where they grind cacao beans, almond, sugar and cinnamon into a paste for making delicious hot chocolate, the cacao smell permeates the air in this area. Some of the brands sold are *Mayordomo* (very good), *Guelaguetza*, and *La Soledad*, they all have outlets in several locations in town including the markets and second-class bus station, and there are mills in other locations as well. These same outlets sell Oaxacan *mole*, a thick paste used for preparing sauces. *Mole* and *quesillo,* the regional string cheese, are sold at the Benito Juárez market, where *La Oaxaqueña* stalls are recommended. Also at Mina y 20 de Noviembre is *La Casa del Dulce* sweet shop. Mezcal, the local hard drink (see page 421) is readily available throughout town. There are several mezcal factories on the Mitla road which show the process of making Mezcal and sell it in black pottery bottles.

Bookshops *Librería Universitaria*, Guerrero 104, buys and sells books including English and a few German books. *Proveedora Escolar*, Independencia 1001 y Reforma, large, excellent selection on all subjects, cheaper. *Códice*, Alcalá 403. *Amate*, Alcalá 307, foreign-language books and magazines and a nice selection of books about Oaxaca and Mexico.

Photography *Foto Rivas*, Juárez 605 opposite Parque Juárez and 20 de Noviembre C-502, has an excellent collection of photographs of Oaxacan themes, new and old, also sell postcards and film. *Centro Fotográfico Alvarez Bravo*, Murguía 302, photo exhibits and sales. Likewise at *Galería Nunduá*, Nicolás Bravo 206.

Tour operators There are many in town. Most run the same tours, eg daily to Monte Albán; El Tule, Mitla and, sometimes, another village on this route; city tour; Fri to Coyotepec, Jalietza and Ocotlán; Thu to Cuilapan and Zaachila; Sun to Tlacolula, Mitla and El Tule. Basically, the tours tie in with local markets. Regular day tours run US$11-13 pp; special tours on demand about US$22 per hour for 4 passengers. Judith Reyes at *Arte y Tradición*, García Vigil 406, runs good tours to outlying villages in her VW van, US$8 per hour. *Expediciones Sierra Norte*, T/F5139518, SierraNorte@oaxaca.com, run hiking and mountain biking tours in the Sierra Juárez, north of the town of Benito Juárez. *Tierraventura*, Boca del Monte 110, T/F5143043, tierraventura@yahoo.com, run tours to the highlands (Sierra Juárez, Sierra Mixteca, Hierve el Agua) and coast, US$20-30 per day.

Transport **Local Bus**: buses, mostly US$0. 20. To the first-class bus station, buses marked 'VW' go from Avenida Juárez. Many lines marked 'Central' go by the second-class bus station. To airport US$1.45. **Car hire**: phone ahead to book, a week before if possible. *TTN*, 5 de Mayo 217-7 y Murguía, T5162577; *Hertz*, Portal de Claverías local 7, T5162434, F5160009; *Arrendadora Express*, 20 de Noviembre 204A, T/F5166776, cars motorcycles and bicycles. **Car park**: safe parking at *Estacionamiento La Brisa*, Av Zaragoza y Cabrera, US$3.50 per night, closed Sun.

Long distance Air: The Xoxocotlán (OAX) airport is about 9 km south, direction Ocotepec. The airport taxis (*colectivos*) cost US$1.85 pp. Book at Transportación Terrestre Aeropuerto on Alameda de León No 1-G, opposite the Cathedral in the Zócalo (T5144350) for collection at your hotel to be taken to airport, office open Mon-Sat 0900-1400, 1700-2000, must book at the office. There is also bus service to the airport from *Hotel Rivera de Angel*, T5166666, US$8.70. To **Mexico City** with AeroMéxico, Mexicana, Aerocaribe and Aviacsa, several daily, US$155 1-way (US$128 advance booking), under 1 hr. To **Puerto Escondido** and **Huatulco**, with Aerocaribe, at 1030 and 1705, US$103 1-way (US$85 advance booking), same price both destinations. To **Puerto Escondido** with Aerovega in 7-seater Cesna, daily at 0700, US$70. To **Tuxtla Gutiérrez**, with Aerocaribe at 1210 and 1440, with Aviacsa at 1235, US$146 1-way. To **Tapachula**, with Taesa at 1005, US$100. To **Ciudad Ixtepec** (Tehuantepec Isthmus), with Aerocaribe, at 0840, US$85 1-way. For other destinations it is necessary to make a connection in Mexico City.

Trains: station on Calzada Madero by the corner of Rayón near the Periférico, 15 mins walk from Zócalo, nice stone building. The only passenger train running in 1999 was Oaxaca-Tehuacán-Puebla leaving at 0735, arrives Tehuacán 1540, further 3 hrs to Puebla, US$7.20 to Puebla. There are no advance ticket sales, you must line up before 0600, expect crowds. The train from Puebla to Oaxaca leaves at 0640. Check it is still running before making plans.

Buses: 1st class terminal, also referred to as ADO terminal is northeast of Zócalo on Calzada Niños Héroes de Chapultepec (no luggage office, taxi from centre US$2.50). ADO, Cristóbal Colón, Sur and Cuenca operate from here. Note that many 2nd class buses leave from here too. 2nd class terminal is west of Zócalo on Calzada Valerio Trujano, just west of the Periférico, across from the Central de Abastos, it is referred to as the 'Central Camionera' (has left-luggage office, open until 2100). Some 2nd class companies also offer superior service on some runs. The Autobuses Unidos (AU) terminal (2nd class, 2 levels of service, 1 is very good, modern buses but without a/c) is northwest of the Zócalo at Prolongación Madero, near the road to Puebla (taxi to the centre US$2.50). 1st class terminal is the only one for Villahermosa and the Yucatán. Tickets for ADO, Cristóbal Colón, AU, Sur and Cuenca can also be purchased at Periférico 152, T5163222, by the pedestrian crosswalk across from the Mercado de Abastos. For long-distance travel, you must book in advance; beware of thieves at all bus terminals, but especially on arrival of *plus* services. To **Mexico City**, all 1st class and some 2nd class buses go along the Autopista, the scenery is very nice, 6 hrs; some 2nd class buses go along the old Carretera Federal through the Cañada region, 8-9 hrs. Luxury service: ADO Uno to TAPO (east terminal), 6 daily, US$38.60; ADO Uno to México Terminal del Norte at 2330, US$38.60; ADO GL to TAPO, 7 daily US$27; ADO GL to México Norte, US$27; Cristóbal Colón Uno to TAPO, 6 daily, US$38.60; Cristóbal Colón Plus to TAPO, 5 daily US$27; Cristóbal Colón Plus to México Terminal del Sur at 2330, US$27. 1st class service: ADO to TAPO, hourly 0700-0100, US$23; ADO to México Terminal del Norte, 3 daily, US$23; Cristóbal Colón to TAPO, 4 daily, US$23; Cristóbal Colón to Terminal del Sur, 4 daily, US$23. 2nd class service: AU (AU terminal) to TAPO via Autopista (modern buses), 7 daily, US$20.65; AU to TAPO via old road, 6 daily, US$18.40; SUR (1st class terminal) to TAPO via the old road, 4 daily, US$18.40; Fletes y Pasajes (2nd class terminal) to own terminal near TAPO, via Autopista, 9 daily (stop in Tehuacán and Puebla), US$19.60, 6½ hrs; Fletes y Pasajes, via old road, several daily (many stops), US$16.50. If buses to the capital are fully booked travel via Puebla. It is difficult to get tickets for buses from the capital to Oaxaca on Fri afternoon without booking in advance (you can book in advance and pay on day of travel); bus companies require 1 hr checking-in time in Mexico City on this route. 1st class to **Cuautla**, US$14.80 with ADO, 7 hrs (change there for Cuernavaca and Taxco). To **Puebla**, 1st class and some 2nd class buses take the Autopista, 4 hrs, other

2nd class buses go on the old road, 5-6 hrs; the scenery is very nice in both cases, on the old road, you are likely to be the only foreigner; some through buses do not go into the Puebla CAPU terminal and drop you off at a gas station by the road, this is not safe at night, inquire before booking. Luxury service: ADO Uno, at 1830, US$28.40; ADO GL, 0700 and 1645, US$20; Cristóbal Colón Plus, 1230 and 1600, US$20. 1st class: ADO, 7 daily, US$17; Cristóbal Colón, 5 daily, US$17. 2nd class: AU (AU terminal) via Autopista, 0100, 1030 and 1700, US$15.30 (to Tehuacán US$9.15); AU via old road, 3 daily, US$15.30; Fletes y Pasajes, several daily on both routes, US$13.60; with Cuenca (1st class terminal), 8 daily, US$7.60, 7 hrs, a beautiful ride, sit on the left for views (see page 225); US$5.90 as far as Valle Nacional, 6 hrs. To **Veracruz**, it is 7½ hrs via the Autopista and Orizaba. Luxury service: Cristóbal Colón Plus, at 2330, US$26.40. 1st class: ADO, at 0830 and 2030, US$22.70; 2nd class: Cuenca (1st class terminal) at 0000, US$13.15; AU (AU terminal), at 2230, US$16.80; book early, alternatives are to change at Puebla or go via Tuxtepec. Cristóbal Colón to **Villahermosa**, daily at 1700 and 2100, US$22.70, 14 hrs, book well ahead. To **Mérida**, Cristóbal Colón, Sun at 0900, 16½ hrs.

The route to Chiapas from Oaxaca is via Tehuantepec, the 1st 2 hrs are on very windy roads, don't eat just before travelling. To **Tuxtla Gutiérrez** and **San Cristóbal de las Casas**, luxury service: Cristóbal Colón *Plus*, at 2000, US$26.40, 10½ hrs (Tuxtla); US$27, 12½ hrs (San Cristóbal); 1st class: Cristóbal Colón, at 1930 (both) and 2215 (Tuxtla only), US$20.30 (Tuxtla), US$23.50 (San Cristóbal). 2nd class to Tuxtla only: with Oaxaca-Istmo 4 daily, with Fletes y Pasajes 6 daily, several daytime departures, US$16.30, 10-11 hrs. To **Tapachula**, 1st class, Cristóbal Colón, US$24, 11 hrs; 2nd class, with Fletes y Pasajes. Book well in advance as buses often come almost full from Mexico City. To **Tehuantepec**, scenic, 1st class: Cristóbal Colón, 13 daily, US$9.60, 5½ hrs; 2nd class: with Oaxaca-Istmo and Fletes y Pasajes, every 30 mins 0600-2400, US$7.40, 5½ hrs. To **Ciudad Cuauhtémoc**, US$33, 12 hrs. To **Arriaga** US$7, 6 hrs, 5 a day.

All 1st class services to the Pacific coast go through Tehuantepec in the Isthmus, a long detour, making 2nd class service more convenient for all coastal destinations except Salina Cruz. To **Pochutla**, 1st class: Cristóbal Colón, via Isthmus, 4 daily, US$14.70, 11 hrs; 2nd class: direct route, very scenic, with Oaxaca-Pacífico and Estrella del Valle, direct service (comfortable buses but no a/c) at 0945, 1415 and 2230, US$6.75, 6 hrs; regular service, same companies, every 30 mins throughout the day. Night bus to Puerto Angel, 2315, arrives 0600. To **Puerto Escondido**, 1st class: Cristóbal Colón, via Isthmus, 0100, 0930 and 2400, US$14.80, 12 hrs (night bus via Pochutla 7 hrs); 2nd class: via Pochutla, with Oaxaca-Pacífico and Estrella del Valle, direct service (comfortable buses but no a/c) at 0945, 1415 and 2230, US$7.60, 7 hrs; with Estrella Roja, superior service at 2245, US$8.70, direct service 4 daily, US$7.60; with Tran-Sol via Sola de Vega, at 0600, 1300 and 2200, US$7.60, 7 hrs (Oaxaca-Sola de Vega US$2.70). To **Huatulco**, 1st class: Cristóbal Colón, via Isthmus, 4 daily, US$14.60, 9½ hrs; 2nd class: via Pochutla, with Oaxaca-Pacífico at 2200, 7 hrs, or take a day bus to Pochutla and transfer there.

Directory

For airline websites, see page 32

Airline offices *Mexicana*, Fiallo 102 y Av Independencia, T5168414/5167352 (airport T5115229), Mon-Fri 0900-1900, Sat-Sun 0900-1800. *Aerocaribe*, Hidalgo 1003 esquina Fiallo, T5160266/5160229, Mon-Fri 0900-1930, Sat 0900-1400. *AeroMéxico*, Av Hidalgo 513 Centro, T5163229/5161066 (airport T5115044). *Aviacsa*, Calzada Porfirio Díaz 102-3, Colonia Reforma, T5131809/5131793. *Aerovega*, Alameda de León 1 (in Hotel Monte Albán), T5162777. *Aeromorelos*, Alcalá 501, T5160974.

Banks Get to banks before they open, long queues form. *Bancomer*, on García Vigil, 1 block from Zócalo, exchanges TCs in own *casa de cambio*, 0900-1600, and has cash dispenser for Visa card. *Banco Santander Mexicano*, Independencia 605, cash and TCs, good rates, TCs changed Mon-Fri 0900-1330. *Amex* office *Viajes Micsa*, at Valdivieso 2, T5162700, just off Zócalo, very helpful, but lots of paperwork (no travel reservations). *Interdisa*, Valdivieso near Zócalo, Mon-Sat 0800-2000, Sun 0900-1700, cash, TCs, sells quetzales and exchanges many foreign currencies, also changes

TCs into dollars cash. *Comermex*, on Periférico near Mercado de Abastos, best rates. *Casa de Cambio*, Abasolo 105, 0800-2000 changes TCs. *Casa de Cambio* at Armenta y López, near corner with Hidalgo, 0800-2000 Mon-Sat, shorter hrs on Sun. No problem to change TCs at weekends, many *casas de cambio* around the Zócalo.

Communications Internet: Many cyber cafés including: in the Post Office. Mon-Fri 0800-1900, US$2.50 per ½ hr. *Multitel*, Alcalá 100, internet US$3.25 per hour, fax, long-distance phone. *Multimedia y Sistemas*, Morelos 600 altos. *Café Internet*, Trujano esquina JP García, US$3.25 per hr. *Hi Net*, Plazuela Labastida 115 y Alcalá, US$2.70. *Cybernet*, Juárez 101, T48040. Mon-Sat 100-2200, Sun 1600-2100, US$3.00 per hour. *Negosoft*, Morelos 1010 esquina Juárez, US$1.65. *Makedonia*, Trujano 122 y 20 de Noviembre, US$3.80 per hour. *Milenium*, 5 de Mayo between Gurrión y Abasola. Open 1000-1800. **DHL:** office at Amado Nervo 104D, esq Heróes de Chapultepec, open Mon-Fri 0900-1800, Sat 0900-1400, no credit card payments. **Post Office:** on Alameda de León, Independencia y 20 de Noviembre. **Telephone:** Public card phones are the easiest way to make long-distance calls, otherwise shop around for rates at establishments offering long-distance phone service.

Embassies & consulates *US Consular Agency*, Alcalá 201, suite 204, T5143054. *Canadian Honorary Consulate*, Pino Suárez 700 local 11B, T5133777, F5152147, Mon-Fri, 1100-1400. *Italian Consulate*, Alcaclá 400, T5165058, 1330-2000. *French Consulate*, Portal Benito Juárez 101, T5141900.

Language schools There are many in the city; the following have been recommended: *Vinigulaza*, Abasolo 209, T/F5146426, vinigulaza@infosel.net.mx, small groups, good place to talk with Mexican students, US$3.50 per hour. *Instituto Johann Goethe*, JP García 502, T/F43516, wide variety of courses, eg 4 weeks, 2 hrs a day US$160. *Instituto de Comunicación y Cultura*, M Alcalá 307-12, 2nd Flr, T/F5163443, www.iccoax.com, cultural workshops and field trips included in the programme, US$100 per week, US$350 per month; accommodation can be arranged. *Centro de Idiomas*, Universidad Autónoma Benito Juárez, Burgoa, 5 blocks south of Zócalo, weekly or monthly classes (US$200 per month), or private tuition, very professional and good value for

Guerrero, Oaxaca & the Isthmus

money, recommended. *Becari*, M Bravo 210, Plaza San Cristóbal, T/F5146076, www.mexonline.com/becari.htm, 4 blocks north of Zócalo, US$75 per 15-hr week, fully-qualified teachers, courses including culture, history, literature and politics, with workshops on dancing, cooking or art, flexible programmes, recommended. In addition to Spanish classes, local crafts and culture (including dance, cooking, weaving and pottery) are taught at the *Instituto Cultural Oaxaca*, Av Juárez 909, T5153404/5151323, F5153728, www.inscuoax.com, daily, 4 hrs of formal Spanish teaching are complemented with 2 hrs spent in cultural workshops and 1 hr of informal conversation with a native speaker; US$105 per week, US$400 per month; accommodation can be arranged. See also **Learning Spanish** in **Essentials**.

Laundry *Lavandería Azteca*, Hidalgo 404 between Díaz Ordaz y J P García, Mon-Sat 0830-2000, quick service, delivers to nearby hotels, 3½kg US$3.80. *Lavandería Hidalgo*, Hidalgo esq J P García, Mon-Sat 0800-2000, 3½kg, US$3.80. *ELA, Super Lavandería Automática*, Antonio Roldán 114, Colonia Olímpica, washes and irons.

Libraries *Biblioteca Circulante Benedict Crowel Memorial*, Macedonio Alcalá 305, looks like an apartment block, English lending library with very good English books, a few French and Spanish, also English newspapers (*The News* from Mexico City), used books and magazines for sale (open Mon-Fri, 1000-1300, 1600-1900, Sat 1000-1300), US$13 per year plus US$13 returnable deposit. *The News* is also sold round the Zócalo by newsboys, from mid-morning, or from street vendor at Las Casas y 20 de Noviembre. The *Biblioteca Pública Central*, at Alcalá 200 (no sign) has a lovely courtyard and a reading room with Mexican newspapers and magazines. Next door is the library of the Museo de Arte Contemporáneo. For the libraries at the Centro Cultural Santo Domingo and the Instituto de Artes Gráficas, see Museums above.

Medical Services Pharmacy: 20 de Noviembre y Ignacio Aldama, open till 2300. **Dentist:** *Dra Marta Fernández del Campo*, Armenta y López 215, English-speaking, very friendly, recommended. **Doctor:** *Dr Victor Tenorio*, Clínica del Carmen, Abasolo 215, T62612, close to centre (very good English). *Dr Marco Antonio Callejo* (English-speaking), Belisario Domínguez 115, T53492, surgery 0900-1300, 1700-2000.

Tourist information There are several tourist publications which include travel information, calendars of events, city map, etc: *Oaxaca Times*, English monthly; *Oaxaca*, monthly in Spanish, English and French; *Comunicación*, in Spanish, with a few articles translated to English and French; *Guía Cultural*, published monthly by the Instituto Oaxaqueño de las Culturas, has a complete listing of musical events, exhibitions, conferences, libraries, etc. An excellent reference about art history in the state of Oaxaca is *Historia del Arte de Oaxaca* (Gobierno del Estado de Oaxaca, Instituto Oaxaqueño de las Culturas, 1997, ISBN 968-6951-33-4), a 3 volume set, exhaustive information from the pre-Columbian, colonial and contemporary periods.

Useful addresses Immigration: Periférico 2724 at Rayón, open Mon-Fri 0900-1400, 2nd flr. **Luggage storage:** Servicio Turístico de Guarda Equipaje y Paquetería, Av Tinoco y Palacios 312, Centro, T5160432, open 24 hrs. **Tourist Police:** on Zócalo near Cathedral, friendly and helpful. *Centro de Protección al Turista*, T5167280.

Monte Albán

Colour map 4, grid C1

There are tri-lingual (Spanish, English, and Zapotec) signs throughout the site

Monte Albán is situated about 10 km (20 minutes) west of Oaxaca, on a hilltop dominating the surrounding valley. The ruins were declared a UNESCO World Heritage Trust site in 1987, and additional restoration was carried out between 1992 and 1994, when a museum and visitors centre were built. Monte Albán features pyramids, walls, terraces, tombs, staircases and sculptures of the ancient capital of the Zapotec culture. The place is radiantly colourful during some sunsets, but permission is needed to stay that late (take a torch/flashlight).

Although the city of Monte Albán extended far beyond the confines of the Main Plaza, it is to the latter area that archaeologists, art historians, historians and tourists have looked to assess and interpret the raison d'être of this fascinating site. Constructed 400m up a steep mountain, without immediate access to water or cultivable land, the Main Plaza has at times been considered the site of a regional marketplace or ceremonial centre. The marketplace theory becomes less convincing when access to the site is considered: not only would the visitor have had to haul merchandise up the back-breaking hill, but entrance to the plaza was severely restricted. The modern access roads did not exist in ancient times and the only way into the site was through three narrow passageways, which could easily have been guarded to restrict entry. The modern ramp cuts across what was the ball-court to the southeast of the North Platform. The space at the centre of the Main Plaza would seem ideal for religious ceremonies and rituals: the absence of religious iconography contradicts this interpretation. The imagery at Monte Albán is almost exclusively militaristic, with allusions to tortured captives and captured settlements.

To the right, before getting to the ruins, is Tomb 7, where a fabulous treasure trove was found in 1932; most items are in the Centro Cultural Santo Domingo and the entrance is closed off by a locked gate. Tomb 172 has been left exactly as it was found, with skeleton and urns still in place, but these are not visible. Tombs 7 annd 172 are permanently closed.

The Main Plaza The Main Plaza at Monte Albán is delineated north and south by the two largest structures in the city which have been interpreted as palace and/or public building (North Platform) and temple (South Platform). Apart from these two impressive structures, the ball court and the arrow-shaped building in front of the South Platform, the Main Plaza has 14 other structures, six along the west side of the Plaza, three in the middle and five along the east side. One structure, known as Edificio de los Danzantes (Dancers), has bas-reliefs, glyphs and calender signs (probably fifth century BC). During the period AD 450-600, Monte Albán had 14 districts beyond the confines of the Main Plaza: it has been proposed that each of the 14 structures located within the Main Plaza corresponded with one of the districts outside. Each pertained to a distinct ethnic group or polity, brought together to create a pan-regional confederacy or league. The arrow-shaped structure functioned as a military showcase; it also has astronomical connotations.

The Confederacy The presence of a number of structures in or bordering the Main Plaza that housed representatives of distinct ethnic groups supports the theory that Monte Albán came into being as the site of a confederacy or league. Its neutral position, unrelated to any single polity, lends credence to this suggestion. The absence of religious iconography, which might have favoured one group over the others, emphasizes the secular role of the area, while the presence of the Danzantes sculptures suggests a trophy-gathering group. However, although Monte Albán may have served defensive purposes, the presence of the Danzantes and the captured town glyphs argues for an offensive and expansionist role. In all, about 310 stone slabs depicting captives, some of whom are sexually mutilated with streams of blood (flowers) flowing from the mutilated parts, have been found. Some of these woeful captives are identified by name glyphs, which imply hostilities against some settlement and the capture of its warriors. The fact that most of them are nude denotes the disdain and contempt with which they were treated by their captors: nudity was considered shameful and undignified by the peoples of Mesoamerica. It is very likely that the rulers of Monte Albán were determined to bring into the confederacy as many polities as possible in order to extract tribute which would permit the expansion of the capital. The growth of the confederacy at Monte Albán was a direct response to events in the Valley of Mexico, where

Guerrero, Oaxaca & the Isthmus

Monte Albán

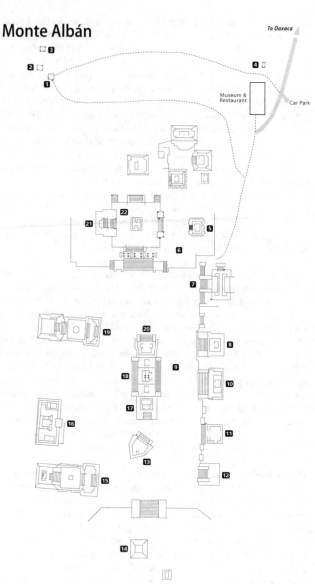

To Oaxaca

Museum & Restaurant

Car Park

N

Not to scale

1 Tomb 104	10 Building P	18 Building H
2 Tomb 103	11 Palace (building S)	19 Complex IV
3 Tomb 172	12 Building Q	20 Building G
4 Tomb 7	13 Observatory (building J)	21 Building B
5 Mound A	14 South Platform	22 Sunken patio
6 North Platform	15 Complex M	
7 Ball court	16 Building of the dancers	
8 Building U	(with building L superimposed)	
9 Chapel	17 Building I	

Mezcal

Produced throughout the dry central valleys of Oaxaca, mezcal has become one of the best-known symbols of the state. This liquor is prepared from the heart of the agave espadín *(Agave angustifolia),* which is widely cultivated for the purpose. Mature plants (12 years old) are selected and first stripped of their swordlike leaves by machete. The hearts are baked in dry ovens – a large pit filled with red-hot coals covered by stones, the agave, and finally a layer of earth. This part of the process gives the drink its characteristic smoky flavour. The baked agave hearts are traditionally ground by teams of oxen and the mash fermented for 10 days in wooden vats. It is then double-distilled with various essences depending on the variety of mezcal. Most famous among these is pechuga, for which raw chicken breasts are hung in the still, a touch apparently much appreciated by the connoisseur. Today some mezcals are flavoured with sweetened fruits, but the original is still drunk straight, accompanied only by lime wedges dipped in sal de gusano – salt into which a special bright red worm has been ground. The squeamish may find some reassurance in the drink's high alcohol content, which is sure to neutralize all the other unusual ingredients!

Teotihuacán was exercising dominion over most of the polities in that area. Although Monte Albán had been developing a policy of offence and capture as early as 200 BC, the growth of the city really gained impetus with the growth of Teotihuacán, whose administrators must have cast an avaricious eye on the rich soil of the Valley of Oaxaca. From the ceramics and architecture analysed at Monte Albán, it is clear that Teotihuacán never realized its ambitions in that area. The confederacy clearly functioned well.

The Collapse Monte Albán reached its maximum size around AD 600, with a population estimated at between 15,000-30,000. Shortly after that date, the city changed dramatically in form and function. There was a decrease in population of nearly 82 percent, the Main Plaza was abandoned and the majority of the people moved nearer to the valley floor, but behind protective walls. They were much closer to major roads, implying that Monte Albán was now becoming more commercially minded and aspired to be self-sufficient, which it had never been in its long history.

The abandonment of the Main Plaza was a direct result of the collapse of the political institution centred there. This collapse has been seen as a consequence of the fact that, beginning early in the seventh century AD, Teotihuacán was already showing signs of decadence. Gaining momentum, the decadence led to the massive abandonment of that great centre. It is unlikely to have been coincidental that the Main Plaza at Monte Albán was abandoned around this time. The removal of the Teotihuacán threat made redundant the confederacy that was so costly to maintain: the collapse was complete.

Readers interested in the archaeology of Monte Albán are referred to: Richard E Blanton, *Monte Albán*, AP, New York, 1978.

The site museum is good, exhibiting stone glyphs and sculptures as well as smaller artifacts; explanations are in Spanish only, and flash photography is prohibited. Informative literature and videos in several languages are sold in the bookstore in the visitors centre, which also houses a small restaurant. (Recommended literature is the Bloomgarden *Easy Guide to Monte Albán* or *Easy Guide to Oaxaca*, covering the city and all the ruins in the valley, with maps. It is available in major hotels or the bookshop at Guerrero 108, and all the ruins.)

Guerrero, Oaxaca & the Isthmus

■ *The ruins are open 0800-1800. Entrance US$2.70, free on Sun and public holidays (and for Mexican students). A charge of US$3 is made to use video cameras; fees for the guides who hang around the site are variable, ask several of them and beware of overcharging. Monte Albán receives many visitors during high season. Most people go in the morning, so it may be easier to catch the afternoon bus.*

Transport To Monte Albán: Autobuses Turísticos depart from *Hotel Rivera del Angel*, Mina 518 near Díaz Ordaz (bus tickets available from hotel lobby) every ½ hr from 0830 to 1600 (schedule may vary with season) fare US$1.50 return, last bus back at 1800; 1½ hrs at the site, allowing not nearly enough time to visit ruins before returning (you are permitted to come back on another tour on 1 ticket for an extra US$1 but you will not, of course, have a reserved seat for your return). Several buses from *Hotel Trébol*, 1 block south of Zócalo, US$1.30, 0930, 1030, returning 1330, 1400. Local city buses marked 'Colonia Monte Albán', US$0.20, pass along the street outside *Hotel Rivera del Angel*, and leave you to walk or hitch the remaining 4 km uphill to the site; nice views but best not to go alone. To give yourself enough time (3 hrs is adequate at the site), you can take the tourist bus to Monte Albán, see the ruins at your leisure, then walk 4 km downhill from the ruins to Colonia Monte Albán and get a city bus back from there. Some prefer to walk up and take the tourist bus back. Taxis charge about US$10 per hour for touring.

Route to Mitla

It is 42 km from Oaxaca to Mitla, on a paved road (Route 190), but with many potholes and occasional flooding. On the way you pass **El Tule** (12 km east of Oaxaca) which in the churchyard has what is reputed the world's largest tree, a savino (*Taxodium mucronatum*), estimated at 2,000 years old. It is 40m high,

Oaxaca environs

42m round at base, weighs an estimated 550 tons, and is fed water by an elabo-rate pipe system. ■ *US$0.25.* Bus from Oaxaca, 2nd class bus station, every 30 minutes, US$0.25, buy ticket on the bus, sit on the left to see the Tule tree; alternatively *colectivos* for surrounding villages leave from near the 2nd class bus station, bus El Tule-Mitla US$0.40. El Tule has a market with good food on sale and *La Sonora* restaurant on eastern edge of town has quite tasty food also *El Milenario* Restaurant at Guerrero 4-A.

Five kilometres east of El Tule along Route 190 is **Tlacochahuaya**, with a 16th-century church and vivid Indian murals; visit the cloisters at the back and see the decorated organ upstairs. ■ *US$0.45 to church.* Carpets and blouses are sold in the market nearby. Bus from Oaxaca second-class terminal, US$0.30.

Another 5 km further, a paved road leads off Route 190 to **Teotitlán del Valle**, where wall hangings and *tapetes* (rugs) are woven, and which is now becoming rather touristy. There is an artesan's market near the church, and a *Museo Comunitario.* ■ *Mon-Sat, 1000-1800, US$0.50.* Since 1999 a *Fiesta 'Antigua' Zapoteca* is celebrated in July, to coincide with the *Guelaguetza* in Oaxaca. 8 September is the feast of *Virgen de la Natividad*, and on 3 May *Fiesta de las Cruces*, when people climb to a cross on a beautiful summit above town (across the river); good hiking at any time of the year. The best prices for weavings are to be had at the stores along the road as you come into town, but they may be even cheaper in Oaxaca where competition is stronger. Buses leave every hour from 0700-2100, from 2nd class bus terminal (US$0.40); the 2nd class bus may provide all the contacts you need to buy all the weavings you want!

Teotitlán del Valle
Make sure you know whether you are getting all wool or a mixture and check the quality. A well-made rug will not ripple when unfolded on the floor.

Sleeping and eating There is a *Tourist Yú'ù* for those wishing to stay overnight, but it is situated far from town, by the turn-off from Route 190. One simple restaurant in town.

Just before the turning for Teotitlán, turn right at Km 23.5 for **Dainzú**, 1 km off the road, a small but important site, which stands out for its complex system of terraces. At the base of the most prominent structure (called Cluster A) are bas reliefs of ball players and priests, similar to the Monte Albán dancers. ■ *Daily 1000-1700, US$1, Sun free.* The nearby site of **Lambityeco** is also well worth visiting, to see several fine and well-preserved stucco heads, ■ *1000-1700, US$1 Sun free.* 2nd class bus Oaxaca-Lambityeco $0.80, bus goes on to Dainzú and back to Oaxaca.

Tlacolula has a most interesting Sunday market and the renowned Capilla del Santo Cristo in the church. The chapel is similar in style to Santo Domingo in Oaxaca, with intricate white and gold stucco, lots of mirrors, silver altar rails and sculptures of martyrs in gruesome detail. Two beheaded saints guard the door to the main nave (*fiesta* 9 October). There is a pleasant walled garden in front of the church. A band plays every evening in the plaza, take a sweater, cold wind most evenings, starts at 1930. The square is colonnaded. On the main street by Parque Juárez is *Casa de Cambio Guelaguetza*, cash only, fair rates. The towns people are renowned for their mezcal preparation. The indoor market next to the church is very interesting; people buy their meat at the stalls and immediately barbecue it on charcoal braziers which run the full length of the market. This appears to be unique. Between the church and the market you might see a local lady selling dried grasshoppers! Tlacolula can be reached by bus from Oaxaca, from the second-class bus station every 10 min-utes, 0600-1900, US$0.80. Taxis stop by the church, except on Sunday when they gather on a street behind the church; ask directions. Tlacolula's bus

Tlacolula

station is just off the main highway, several blocks from the centre; pickpockets are common here, be especially careful at the Sunday market and in the scrum to board the bus.

Sleeping and eating D *Hotel Guish-Bac*, Zaragoza 3, T20080. Clean. **D-E** *Hotel Regis*, Av Juárez 35, T20532. OK. *Hotel Fiesta*, across from gas station at entrance to town. Shared bath, cold water, basic; also a *Tourist Yú'ù*. There are several simple restaurants in town.

Santa Ana del Valle Quality weavings can be found at Santa Ana del Valle (3 km from Tlacolula). The village is peaceful and friendly with a small museum showing ancient textile techniques; ask any villager for the keyholder. Cheap guesthouse. There are two *fiestas*, each lasting three days. One takes place the second week of August, the other at the end of January. There is an important rug market. Sr Alberto Sánchez García, Sor Juana I de la Cruz No 1, sells excellent wool with natural dyes. Turn right just after the school and left at the T-junction at the top of the hill. Sr Sánchez's home is several compounds along on the right with a faded blue metallic gate door. Good prices. Buses leave from Tlacolula every 30 minutes.

Yagul Further east along Route 190 is the turn-off north for Yagul, an outstandingly picturesque archaeologic site where the ball courts priests and quarters are set in a landscape punctuated by candelabra cactus and agave. Yagul was a large Zapotec and later Mixtec religious centre. The ball court is said to be the second largest discovered in Mesoamerica; it also perhaps the most perfect discovered to date. There are fine tombs (take the path from behind the ruins, the last part is steep) and temples, and a superb view from the hill behind the ruins. Recommended. ■ *Daily 0800-1730, US$1.40, free on Sun. Guided tours in English on Tue, US$10, from Oaxaca travel agencies.* Take a bus to Mitla from the Oaxaca seconnd class terminal (see below) and ask to be put down at paved turn-off to Yagul (five minutes after Tlacolula terminal). You will have to walk 1 km uphill from the bus stop to the site (overpriced *Restaurant El Centeotl* half way, open 1100-1900, stock up on water, none at site) and you can return the same way or walk 3 km west to Tlacolula along Route 190 to catch a bus to Oaxaca.

Mitla A further 5 km past the turn-off for Yagul along Route 190, a paved road branches left and leads 4 km to Mitla (meaning 'place of the dead') where there are ruins of four great palaces among minor ones. Some of the archaeology, outside the fenced-in site, can be seen within the present-day town.

Magnificent bas-reliefs, the sculptured designs in the Hall of Mosaics, the Hall of the Columns and, in the depths of a palace, *La Columna de la Muerte* (Column of Death), which people embrace and then measure what they can't reach with their fingers to know how many years they have left to live (rather hard on long-armed people). We have been informed that the column can no longer be embraced but do not know if this is a temporary or permanent arrangement. ■ *Daily 0800-1730, entry US$2 (Sun free, use of video US$3.00), literature sold at entrance.*

By the site, there is a soberly decorated colonial church with four cupolas, built on top of a pre-existing native structure (no access from church to ruins, or vice versa). A small museum (included in entry fee) displays a few artifacts. Crafts and souvenirs are sold at the entrance to the site (bargaining recommended); also on the cobbled road from the town to the ruins are many *artesanía* shops and others selling good mezcal. Away from the ruins the town is very relaxed, there is a pleasant plaza adorned with bright bougainvillea.

Sleeping and eating   D *Hotel y Restaurante Mitla*, on town square, T80112. Private bath, simple, clean, friendly, local food. **D** *Hotel y Restaurante La Zapoteca*, before bridge on road to ruins, T80026. Private bath, hot water, parking, friendly, good food. *María Teresa* restaurant 100m from site towards village. Good *comida corrida*.

Transport   Taxi costs US$10 each to Mitla for 4 sharing, with time to take photographs at Tule and Mitla and to buy souvenirs at ruins, or approximately US$10 per hour for touring as you please. Tours (1000 till 1300, rather rushed) to Tule, Mitla and Tlacolula from Oaxaca agencies, cost US$7.50, not including entry fees. Buses from Oaxaca 2nd class station every 10 mins, 0600-1900, US$0.90, 40 mins; the ruins are 10 mins walk across the village (from the bus stop on the main road, 2 blocks from the square).

From Mitla take a bus to San Lorenzo Albarradas (one hour, US$1). Three **Hierve el Agua** kilometres from there is the village of Hierve el Agua (57 km from Oaxaca). Due to the concentration of minerals, a pre-Hispanic irrigation system and various waterfalls are now petrified over a cliff, forming an enormous stalactite. You can swim in the mineral pools in the dry season. There is a village-run hotel, **E** *Tourist-Yú'ù*, Oaxaca T5160123. Rooms for six people with kitchen, hot water, discounts for students, good restaurant. Recommended. Also several excellent foodstalls (*quesadillas*, etc) above the car park. There are two second-class buses a day from Oaxaca which pass through Hierve El Agua, departing 0810 and 1400, returning around noon and early the following day. A day-trip is possible to Hierve El Agua but transport can be complicated; most visitors recommend staying overnight to have enough time to enjoy the surroundings.

From Mitla the road is paved as far as Ayutla, but an unpaved single track runs from then on to Playa Vicente (see page 222) through beautiful mountain scenery and cloud forest. Four wheel drive recommended. There is no accommodation between Ayutla and Playa Vicente.

Excursions south of Oaxaca

Along Route 175 to Pochutla are several towns which specialize in the production of different crafts. **San Bartolo Coyotepec** 12 km southeast of Oaxaca, is known for its black pottery. There is a crafts market in town or you can purchase from the potters in their homes. Doña Rosa de Nieto accidentally discovered the technique for the black glazed ceramics in the 1930s, her family continues the tradition as do many other potters in town. **San Martín Tilcajete**, 21 km from Oaxaca, 1 km west of the main road, is the centre for the *alebrije* production, animals carved from copal wood, painted in bright colours, often having a supernatural look to them. **Santo Tomás Jalieza**, is the centre for cotton and wool textiles produced with backstrap looms and natural dyes, in the surrounding villages. Blouses, dresses, tablecloths and colourful belts are among the wares sold here, especially during the Friday market.

One of the most important markets in the Central Valleys is held on Fridays at **Ocotlán de Morelos**, 33 km from Oaxaca. There is a great variety of fruits and vegetables, black and red pottery, regional sweets, locally made cutlery and machetes, embroidered goods from nearby San Antonio and a variety of baskets and other products made of reeds and straw (stallholders prefer not to be photographed). The city hall has murals by the well-known painter Rodolfo Morales, who also restored the local church and ex-convent of Santo Domingo. The main festival here is held on the second Sunday in May; in town is *Hotel Posada San Salvador*. Frequent bus service throughout the day from

Miguel Cabrera, next door to *Hotel Villa Alta*, in Oaxaca, US$0.70, 30 minutes, or outside the Mercado de Abastos a steady stream of *colectivos* leave for US$0.70.

Cuilapan Twelve kilometres southwest of Oaxaca is Cuilapan de Guerrero, where there is a vast unfinished 16th-century convent, now in ruins, with a famous nave and columns, and an 'open chapel', whose roof collapsed in an earthquake. The last Zapotec princess, Donaji, daughter of the last ruler Cosijoeza, married a Mixtec prince at Tilantengo and was buried at Cuilapan. On the grave is an inscription with their Christian names, Mariana Cortez and Diego Aguilar. Reached by bus from Oaxaca from second-class bus station, on Calle Bustamante, near Arista (US$0.50).

North of Cuilapan and 6 km west of the main road, is **San Antonio Arrazola**, another town where *alebrijes*, mythical animals made of *copal* wood are sold by the artisans. **Zaachila**, 5 km beyond Cuilapan, was the last capital of the Zapotec empire. Today this town still mantains some of its ancestral traditions which can be experienced in the local cooking (several local restaurants). There is black pottery production, and market day is Thursday. Here are the partially excavated ruins of Zaachila, with two Mixtec tombs; the outer chamber has owls in stucco work and there are carved human figures with skulls for heads inside. No restrictions on flash photography. ■ *US$1.50*. Take bus to Zaachila (US$0.60) which leaves every 30 minutes, then walk to unexcavated ruins in valley.

Eighty kilometres south on Route 131 is **San Sebastián de las Grutas** (about 10 km northwest of El Vado, off the main road) where there is a system of caves. One 400m long cave, with five chambers up to 70m high, has been explored and is open to visitors. Ask for a guide at the Agencia Municipal next to the church. ■ *Guide obligatory, US$1.50*. Near the caves there is a recreational centre and a spring which is the source of the San Sebastián River. Take bus 175 from Oaxaca, terminal at Calle Bustamante, US$0.25 or Solteca buses bound for Sola de Vega from the second-class terminal.

Excursions north of Oaxaca

At **Santa María Atzompa**, 8 km northwest of Oaxaca, at the foot of Monte Albán, green glazed and terracota ceramics are produced, you can see the artisans at work, their wares are sold at La Casa del Artesano; buses from the second-class terminal.

Etla Valley The Etla Valley, along which Route 190 runs, had a number of important settlements in pre-Hispanic times. Seventeen kilometres along this road and 2 km to the west is **San José el Mogote**, an important centre before the rise of Monte Albán; there is a small museum housing the artifacts found at this site. **San Pedro y San Pablo Etla**, 19 km from Oaxaca has an important Wednesday market specializing in Oaxacan foods such as *quesillo* string cheese, *tasajo* (dried meat) and different types of bread; the town has a 17th-century church and convent. At **Santiago Suchilquitongo**, 27 km from Oaxaca and atop a hill, are the ruins of **Huijazoo**, once an important centre which controlled the trade between the Central Valleys and the Cañada region; the local museum has a reproduction of a Huijazoo polychromatic mural, which has been compared to those at Bonampak (see page 271). The town of **San Agustín Etla** (turn-off east from Route 190 at Guadalupe Etla), was once an important industrial centre and in the 19th century it had two large cotton mills; with the introduction of synthetic fibers came a decline to this area. Since 1998, the town has found a new use for the cotton and other natural fibers available in the region, with the production of handmade paper for artists. Cotton, agave fibers, pineapple, nettle, ash, limestone and other raw materials are used in the workshop which welcomes visitors. Further information from the Instituto de Artes Gráficas on Alcalá 507 in Oaxaca city.

The Sierra Norte or Sierra Juárez is a region of beautiful landscapes and great **Sierra Juárez** biological diversity; seven of the nine types of vegetation that exist in Mexico can be found in this area. The region is starting to develop ecotourism with community participation, permits are required to camp on community land. The mountains gradually drop to the Papaloapan valley to the north. There are two access roads, Route 175 from Oaxaca to Tuxtepec, and the small roads that go north from Route 190, past Teotitlán and Santa Ana del Valle (see page 424). *Viajes Rua-Via* in Ixtlán (T5536075), and *Expediciones Sierra Norte* (T/F5139518) and *Tierraventura* (T/F5143043) in Oaxaca run hiking and mountain biking tours in this region. The Oaxaca-Tuxtepec road has been recommended as exhilarating for cyclists.

Along the road to Tuxtepec, 65 km from Oaxaca is the village of **San Pablo de Guelatao**, the birthplace of Benito Juárez. The town is located in the mountainous Sierra Juárez, and can be reached by bus (any service going to Tuxtepec, US$1.50, three hours) along a paved but tortuously winding road (for a more detailed description of this road and area see page 226). Guelatao means 'small lake' and by the shores of this small lake is a statue of Juárez as a shepherd with his lambs. There is also a memorial and a museum to Juárez on the hillside within the village. ■ *US$0.20.* The area is beautiful although the town is rather neglected. A few kilometres north of Guelatao is **Ixtlán de Juárez** (population 2,095), a larger town with a petrol station, hotel, shops, and some simple eating establishments.

The Oaxaca Coast

The 510 km of Oaxaca's Pacific coast, stretching from Guerrero to the west and Chiapas to the east, includes some truly spectacular shoreline and provides most varied opportunities for seaside recreation. Many beaches are still entirely virgin (accessible only on foot or by sea), while others are being developed for various tastes and to varying degrees; a very few have been burnt-out by over-crowding, pollution, drugs, or crime. Palapas, thatched roof shacks, are found all along the coast, these are dwellings or simple restaurants and places to stay. Huatulco is the best-known international resort on the Oaxaca coast, but there are many other popular areas including Puerto Escondido, Puerto Angel, Salina Cruz, and their respective surroundings.

All of the above are linked by Highway 200, the Carretera Costera, fully paved and in generally good condition, with frequent bus service along its entire length, as well as transport to several nationwide destinations. Three main roads connect the coast with the city of Oaxaca and the central valleys of the highlands: Route 131 from Puerto Escondido, Route 175 from Pochutla, and Route 190 (the Panamerican Highway) from Tehuantepec; daytime travel is safest along all of them. There are airports at Puerto Escondido, Huatulco, and near Tehuantepec, with service to Mexico City, Oaxaca and Chiapas.

Guerrero, Oaxaca & the Isthmus

Pinotepa Nacional Santiago Pinotepa Nacional (Population 23,475), the westernmost of Oaxaca's coastal towns is known for its cheerful, witty people, dressed in bright colours, and the happy rhythm of their *chilena* dances. It is 144 km west of Puerto Escondido, 51 km east of Cuajinicuilapa in the state of Guerrero and is linked to the highlands by highway 125 through Putla de Guerrero in the Sierra Mixteca. The local festival, rich in music and dance, is held February 24. From Pinotepa Nacional you can visit the Mixtec Indian village of **Pinotepa de Don Luis** by *camioneta* (US$1, 50 minutes). These leave from beside the Centro de Salud in Pinotepa Nacional, taking paved road, via Tlacamama, to Don Luis (last one back to Pinotepa Nacional at 1300, nowhere to stay). The women there weave beautiful and increasingly rare sarong-like skirts (*chay-ay*), some of which are dyed from the purple of sea snails. They also produce half-gourds incised with various designs. The *ferias* of Don Luis (20 January) and nearby San Juan Colorado (29-30 November) are worth attending for the dancing and availability of handicrafts. Another village, **Huazolotitlán**, is known for mask making; take *camioneta* from near *Hotel Las Palomas*, three blocks from plaza, 40 minutes. *Fiesta*, first Friday in February with masked dancers.

Sleeping **D** *Hotel Carmona*, Porfirio Díaz 127, T5432222. Restaurant, good value but poor laundry service, helpful advice on visiting surrounding villages, parking. **D** *Marisa*, Avenida Juárez 134, near Zócalo, T5432101/F5432696. With bath, more expensive with a/c, **E** with fan. **D** *Las Gaviotas*, 3 Oeste Centro, T5432402/F5432626. Second location Carretera a Acapulco, T5432828. Hot water, TV, restaurant, parking. **D** *Pepes*, Carretera a Acapulco, Km 1, T/F5433602. A/c, restaurant, parking. **E** *Tropical*, Fan, clean, large rooms, quiet, parking.

Transport Buses to Oaxaca, with Cristóbal Colón, 1 daily US$15.90, 9½ hrs; with Oaxaca Pacífico, 2 daily via Pochutla, US$12.00, 9 hrs; with Trans-Sol, 2 daily via Sola de Vega, US$10.90, 8 hrs.

Puerto Escondido

Phone code: 958
Colour map 4, grid C1
Population: 30,000

The town and its surroundings offer some stunningly beautiful beaches with world-class surfing, many facilities for vacationers, and a good base for various interesting excursions. Sadly, however, Puerto Escondido is at risk of becoming a case-study in unsustainable tourism development. It was a small and sleepy fishing village as recently as the 1980s, until the population rapidly increased, perhaps in response to grandiose plans for Acapulco-style development. These never panned-out and tourism instead developed low-rise and haphazardly, none-the-less creating considerable environmental and social impact. Drugs and crime followed, largely ignored by the authorities until an American celebrity (a member of the Kennedy clan) was murdered at the south end of Zicatela beach in 1998. Publicity of the slaying all but wiped-out Puerto Escondido as a destination for US tourists, but also brought home the need to clean up the town. There has since been considerable improvement and, although a good deal remains to be done, it is hoped that better security and more responsible environmental as well as general practices by the area's tourism industry, can still save this very beautiful area.

At present, Puerto Escondido is a bustling and very commercial seaside resort. El Adoquín, the city's pedestrian tourist mall along Avenida Pérez Gasga near the beach (also known as the *Andador Turístico*), teems with vacationing Mexican families in season, sunburnt foreigners and hard-core surfies throughout the year; December-January are the most crowded, May-June are the quietest (and hottest) months. A handful of luxury hotels and resorts are clustered above Playa Bacocho, while Playa Zicatela is ideal for surfers, and the majority of tourist facilities are found in the vicinity of El Adoquín. The real town, where prices are lower and there is less of a hard-sell atmosphere, is located up the hill on the other side of the highway. There is an ample selection of hotels and restaurants in all areas. Many fast-talking '*amigos*' are found at all the nearby beaches and other sites frequented by tourists offering an impressive array of goods and services for sale or hire; be polite and friendly (as are most of the vendors) but also wary, since there is no shortage of overpricing and trickery. **Tourist offices** Sedetur information kiosk at the west end of El Adoquín, very helpful, friendly and knowledgeable about the town and the region, English and French spoken. Sedetur office and information, Avenida Juárez, at the entrance to Playa Bacocho, T5820175, www.ptoescondido. com.mx.

Beaches

The **Playa Principal** abutting El Adoquín pedestrian mall, has the calmest water but it is very close to the city and not clean. A few fishermen still bring in the catch of the day here and a small pier is being built for them and the tourist craft which offer sport fishing and excursions to nearby bays and beaches. Immediately to the south is **Playa Marinero**, with slightly stronger surf (reportedly a good place for beginners), also very built-up with hotels, bars, and restaurants. Further south, past a rocky point called Rocas del Morro, lies the long expanse of **Playa Zicatela**, which claims to be the best surfing beach in Mexico, with the fastest-breaking waves anywhere in the world. It is suitable only for experienced surfers and very dangerous for swimming. To the west of the main bay, past a lovely headland (being built-up with condominiums) and lighthouse, are a series of picturesque bays and beaches, all accessible by road or boat from town. **Playa Manzanillo** and **Puerto Angelito** share the Bahía Puerto Angelito and are the closest, an easy 15 minute walk; they are pretty with reasonably safe swimming but very commercial; every square millimetre of shade is proprietary here. Further west is **Playa Carrizalillo**, with swimming and more gentle surfing than Zicatela, accessible along a steep path. **Playa Bacocho** is next, a long beautiful stretch of less developed beach, where the ocean, alas, is too dangerous for swimming; the luxury hotels have their beach clubs here.

Excursions

Seventy-four kilometres west of Puerto Escondido is the 140,000ha **Lagunas de Chacahua National Park**, a wildlife refuge of sand dunes, interconnected lagoons, mangroves and forest. La Pastoría is the largest lagoon, connected to the sea by an estuary; it has nine islets which harbour thousands of birds, both resident and migratory. On the shores of the lagoon is the village of Chacahua, home to some of the area's small Afro-Mexican population. There is a crocodile hatchery nearby, aimed at preserving this native species. A tour is the easiest way to see the park and learn about its wildlife (see **Tour Companies** below). To go independently you need two days; take a bus to Río Grande (from Carretera Costera and 3ra Norte), then another one to Zapotalito from where there are boats (US$4.50 per person if there are enough passengers) to the village of Chacahua, where you can find very basic accommodations in the **F** price range; take a mosquito net.

Closer and easier to access than Chacahua are the **Lagunas de Manialtepec**, 16 km west of Puerto Escondido, also a good place for bird watching and water sports. Tours are available (see **Tour Companies** below) or take a minibus towards Río Grande (from Carretera Costera and 3ra Norte, US$0.65) or a taxi (US$6). Get off at the village of Manialtepec; at restaurants

Guerrero, Oaxaca & the Isthmus

Isla de Gallo and *Puesta del Sol* you can hire a boat for four persons (US$33.00 for two hours).

Further west along the road to Acapulco, in a cotton growing area 114 km from Puerto Escondido, is **Santiago Jamiltepec** (*Hotel Maris*) where the native Mixtec population processes and weaves cotton with traditional techniques. The Mixtecs are the second largest native group in the state of Oaxaca. Cotton crafts and clothing are sold here. See Pinotepa Nacional, above, for additional excursions in this area.

Santos Reyes Nopala is a mountain town 43 km northeast of Puerto Escondido (*Posada Nopala*). The original Chatino settlement here is believed to date from around 800 BC; stelae can be seen in the municipal palace and the Chatino language is still spoken. Colourful celebrations are held 6-8 January. There are coffee plantations and orchards in the area which can be visited. Tours are available from Puerto Escondido. Further north is **Santa Catarina Juquila** with the Santuario de la Virgen de Juquila, a very popular pilgrimage site; the local *fiesta* is 8 December; there are several hotels here.

NB Safety is an especially important issue in and around Puerto Escondido. A safe and pleasant stay here is possible with the appropriate precautions, but carelessness can have the most severe consequences. Never walk on any beach at night, alone or in groups; armed robbery and rape are serious hazards. Do not walk on deserted beaches even during the daytime and take only a minimum of cash and valuables whenever you leave your hotel. Dogs are another nuisance; beware of packs and do

Puerto Escondido

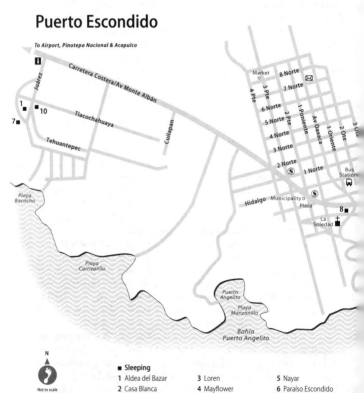

To Airport, Pinotepa Nacional & Acapulco

Carretera Costera/Av Monte Albán

Juárez

Tlacochahuaya

Tehuantepec

Cuilapan

Market

8 Norte
7 Norte
6 Norte
5 Norte
4 Norte
3 Norte
2 Norte
1 Norte

4 Pte
3 Pte
2 Pte
1 Ponente

1 Oriente
Av Oaxaca
2 Ote
3 Ote

Bus Station

Playa Bacocho

Hidalgo   Municipality
Plaza

La Soledad

Playa Carrizalillo

Puerto Angelito
Playa Manzanillo

Bahía Puerto Angelito

N

Not to scale

■ Sleeping
1 Aldea del Bazar
2 Casa Blanca
3 Loren
4 Mayflower
5 Nayar
6 Paraíso Escondido

not contribute to the problem by feeding stray animals. The ocean can also be dangerous (see beaches above) and, finally, beware of sunburn.

Sleeping

Puerto Escondido has more than 85 hotels in all categories, mostly along the beaches. There is little air-conditioning, many of the cheaper hotels have no hot water and cheap *cabañas* may be full of mosquitos, especially in the wet season (Jun-Oct). High season is during Holy Week, the last 2 weeks of Jul, all of Aug, and Nov-Feb; discounts of 10% to 30% may be obtained at other times. Hotels right on El Adoquín may be noisy at weekends and holidays because of nearby discos.

L-AL *Aldea del Bazar*, Av Benito Juárez 7, Bacocho, T5820508/F5821469. A veritable Sultan's palace, complete with Middle Eastern dress for the staff, huge garden with palms, pool, large rooms, good restaurant. Recommended. **L-AL** *Best Western Posada Real*, Blvd Benito Juárez, Bacocho, T5820133/F5820192, posadareal@iserve.net.mx. Very pleasant, lovely gardens, 2 pools, path to beach, a/c, good attentive service. **L-AL** *Days Inn Villa Sol*, Loma Bonita 2, Bacocho, T5820061/F5820350. Courtyard with 2 pools, garden. **AL-A** *La Hacienda*, Atunes 15, Rinconada, T5820279. A/c, luxurious apartments, pool, restaurant, includes breakfast. **A** *Paraíso Escondido*, Unión 10, Centro, T5820444. Away from beach, a/c, pool, colonial style, restaurant open in high season. **AL** *Santa Fe*, Calle del Moro, Playa Marinero, T5820170/F5820260. A/c, pool, very good food, including vegetarian.

B *Barlovento*, Camino al Faro 3, Centro, T5820220/F5820101. Pool, fridge, very comfortable, on the way to the lighthouse, not advisable to walk there at night. Recommended. **B** *Bungalows Zicatela*, Calle del Moro, Playa Marinero, T/F5820798. A/c, cheaper with fan, fridge, pool, small restaurant. **B** *Camino del Sol*, Carretera Costera, Km 1.5, Fraccionamiento Granja El Pescador, T5820243/F5822002. A/c, pool, restaurant, parking. **B** *Fiesta Mexicana*, Blvd Benito Juárez, Bacocho, T/F5820072. Badly damaged by hurricane Paulina and in 1999 still run down. **B** *Nayar*, Av Pérez Gasga 407, Centro, T5820113/F5820319, west of *El Adoquín*. A/c, **C** with fan, big rooms, hot water, pool, safe parking. **B-C** *Arco Iris*, Calle del Moro, Playa Marinero, T5820432, F5821494. Fan, hot water. **B-C** *Bungalows Casa del Mar*, Retorno A6, Fraccionamiento Bacocho, T/F5822377. Equipped bungalows.

C *Beach Hotel Inés*, Calle del Moro, Zicatela. Fan, hot water, pool, restaurant. **C** *Ben Zaa*, 3a Sur 303, T5820523, on hill climbing to the lighthouse. Fan, hot water, pool. **C** *Cabaña del Húngaro*, Carretera Costera, Bacocho, T/F5820823, on road to Acapulco before turn-offs for Bacocho beach. With a/c, hot water, pool, restaurant. **C** *Casa Blanca*, Av Pérez Gasga 905 (Adoquín), T5820168/5821283. Fan, hot water, clean, well furnished, balconies, pool. **C** *Flor de María*, 1st entrance, Playa Marinero, T5820536.

Fan, hot water, pool, restaurant. **C** *Hacienda Revolución*, Andador Revolución 21, Libertad, T5821818, by El Adoquín. Bungalows with fan, hot water, hammocks. **C** *Loren*, Av Pérez Gasga 507, T5820057, F5820591. Pool, fan, hot water, clean, friendly, safe. Recommended. **C** *Rincón del Pacífico*, Av Pérez Gasga 900 (*Adoquín*), T5820056, F5820101. Hot water, on beach, restaurant, very popular, always full. **C** *San Juan*, Felipe Merklin 503, T5820518, F5820612. Some rooms with seaview, fair, small pool, parking.

D *Art and Harry's*, Playa Zicatela. On oceanfront, free use of surfboard, great barbecues, good food. **D** *Bungalows Acuario*, Calle del Moro, Playa Marinero, T5820357, F5821027. Cheaper with shared bath, pool, gym, scuba diving centre, the 1st in the area to treat its waste water. Recommended. **D** *Bungalows María del Mar*, Calle del Moro, Zicatela, T5821091. With fan, pool. **D** *Bungalows Villa Marinero*, Carretera Costera, Playa Marinero, T5820180, F5820716. On seafront, kitchen/eating area, pool, friendly. **D** *Capri*, 1a Sur y 7a Oriente, T5820717, on hill east of the centre. Fine views, with fan, hot water. **D** *Casa Loma*, Camino al Faro opposite Escuela Las Primeras Luces, on road to lighthouse. Popular among fishingmen, cook prepares meals on request (including your catch). **D** *Castillo del Rey*, Av Pérez Gasga, T5820442. Clean, nice rooms, hot water, quiet, good beds, friendly, good value. Highly recommended. **D** *Central*, Av Oaxaca, Centro, T/F5820116, in bus terminal area. Clean, friendly. **D** *Cocoa Beach*, Fundadores esquina Felipe Merklin, T5820428, near the church. Small rooms, mosquito nets, family-run. **D** *Crucero*, Av Pérez Gasga 106, T5820225. Hot water, pool, parking. **D** *El Alemán*, Av Las Brisas, Santa María, Zicatela, T/F5821995. Fan, ocean views, new in 1999. **D** *Liza's Restaurant*, off Carretera Costera, Playa Marinero. Fan, very clean, safe deposit. Highly recommended. **D** *Mayflower*, Andador Libertad, T5820367, F58820422, on pedestrian walkway perpendicular to El Adoquín. With bath, fan, **F** pp in dormitory. **D** *Palacio Azteca*, 1a Norte 108, T5820246, in bus station area. With bath. **D** *Papaya Surf*, Calle del Moro, Zicatela. Fan, mosquito net, hot water, pool. **D** *Roca Mar*, Av Pérez Gasga 601, T5820330. Upper rooms with a/c and balcony, hot water, restaurant. Recommended.

E *Casa de Huéspedes Naxhiely*, Av Pérez Gasga 301. Simple, fairly clean. **E** *Girasol*, Av Oaxaca 403, T/F5821168, in bus station area. With bath, fan, parking. Many other economic hotels in the Centro, near the bus station as well as bungalows and cabins on Playa Zicatela. **E** *Posada de Cortés*, Av Pérez Gasga 218, T/F5820209, on the oceanfront. Small and large basic cabins, take mosquito net. **E** *Ribera del Mar*, Felipe Merklin 205, T/F5820436, behind Iglesia de la Soledad. Fan, hot water, clean, quiet, laundry facilities, good value. **E** *San Rafael*, Av Hidalgo y 2a Oeste, T5821052, near bus stations. Basic, with bath, fan.

Camping *Trailer Park Palmas de Cortés*, Av Pérez Gasga y Andador Azucena, T5820774. Clean bathrooms, shade, US$10.00 per car, US$5.00 per tent. Recommended. *Trailer Park Neptuno*, Av Pérez Gasga, T5820327, on waterfront. Space for vehicles, tents and hammocks, pool, cold showers, electricity, run-down, US10.00 per car with 2 people.

Eating Many restaurants along the main street, Avenida Pérez Gasga, especially on the pedestrian mall: *La Posada del Tiburón*, on the beach. Good food, large portions. *Banana's*, Italian and Mexican. *San Angel*. For fish and international. *Hermann's Best*. Good value, popular. *Mario's Pizzaland*. Excellent pizzas, friendly. *La Galería*. Italian, good pizzas but pricy. *La Estancia*. Good warm service. *La Sardina de Plata*. Popular. *Cappuccino*. Good coffee, fruit salads, some dishes pricy. *Los Crotos*, on the beach. Good varied food, reasonable prices. In Playa Marinero are: *Liza*, off Carretera Costera. Good food, nice location. *La Gota de Vida*, Calle del Moro. International and vegetarian. *Cipriano's Pizza*, Calle del Moro. Italian and regional. *Hotel Santa Fé*. Excellent vegetarian. *El Tabachín*, behind Hotel Santa Fe. Also vegetarian and café. *El Cafecito*,

Calle del Moro, Zicatela. Excellent breakfasts, chocolate bread. Highly recommended. *Super Café Puro*, off top flight of stairs of walkway which starts at the tourist information kiosk. Good for breakfast, pleasant terrace. *Pepe's*, 8a Norte, near market. Great sandwiches. *Carmen's Bakery*, on a path to the beach from main road, Zicatela. Great pastries baked on the premises, also second-hand books and magazines. *Gelatería Giardino*, Av Pérez Gasga 609, just east of El Adoquín. Excellent Italian ice cream and fruit ices, made on the premises, also cappuccino coffee. Highly recommended (closed May-Jun).

Un Tigre Azul, Av Pérez Gasga on El Adoquín, upper floor. Bar, coffee and snacks, nice views. *Tequila Sunrise*, Av Marina Nacional, just west of El Adoquín. Open-air disco, varied music, international crowd. *El Son y la Rumba*, Av Pérez Gasga on El Adoquín. Live salsa. Opposite is *El Tubo*. Disco, popular with local surfers (occasional brawls reported here). *Barfly*. Good music, regular screening of films and videos. *Bar Banana's*, Av Pérez Gasga y Andador Azucena. Drinks and food. *Wipeout*. Rock and techno music. **NB** It is not advisable to stay at bars and discos past 0300. **Entertainment**

Diving The region's coastline offers good opportunities for snorkelling and scuba diving; snorkelling from the beach is easiest at Puerto Angelito. Tours and diving lessons with Jorge Pérez Bravo, *Aventura Submarina*, Av Pérez Gasga at west end of El Adoquín, T/F5822353. You are likely to see turtles and dolphins on the way to the snorkelling and diving sites. Snorkelling 3 hrs, US$22 pp. Diving lessons, US$55 for 1 tank. If you have your certificate, US$38 for 1 tank, US$55 for 2. **Fishing** Boats can be hired for fishing at Playa Principal or through travel agencies for approximately US$27 per hour for up to 4 passengers. **Pelota Mixteca** A modern version of an ancient Mixtec ball game is played on Sat and Sun in Bajos de Chila, 15 mins from Puerto Escondido, on the road to Acapulco (a new field is expected to be operating in town by 2000). In a 9m by 35m court, teams of 5-7 players propel a rubber ball weighing almost 1 kg, using elaborately decorated leather mits which weigh between 3½ and 6 kg. A game can take up to 4 hrs. **Surfing** Playa Zicatela is a surfer's haven, but dangerous for the novice. See beaches above. **Sports**

The city's festivities are held throughout the month of Nov, along with a surfing tournament. In the middle of the month is the *Festival Costeño de la Danza*, when colourful, lively folk dances are performed. The Master World Surf Championship is held in Aug. **Festivals**

Crafts and souvenirs from shops all along El Adoquín, stalls on the main street, east of El Adoquín and on Andador Libertad, a walkway going uphill from about the middle of El Adoquín. Shop around, vendors on the beach are likely to ask for higher prices and you may find better value in shops north of the highway. *Papi's* souvenir shop has a small selection of foreign books for sale or trade. Jewellery with pre-Hispanic motifs from *Oro de Monte Albán*, at west end of *El Adoquín*. Surfing gear and clothing from shops in Zicatela. *Ahorrara*, 3a Poniente y 5a Norte, large well-stocked supermarket. **Shopping**

Several travel agencies for airline reservations and regional tours along El Adoquín. Specialized guides: *Gina Machorro*, a knowledgeable guide, fluent in English and French, offers a 2 hr walking tour of Puerto Escondido in which the visitor is immersed in the local culture and history, US$15 pp, contact through the tourist information kiosk, ginawalkt@ptoescodido.com.mx. Ana Márquez of *Ana's Ecotours* is a certified, recommended guide who speaks English, she is very knowledgeable about birds and knows the region very well; she is the regional representative of *Birds Without Borders*, an international organization concerned with migratory birds. Ana runs tours to all the natural attractions in the area and cultural tours of her native Mixtec community: day trip, US$22-27 pp; contact at *Hotel Rincón del Pacífico*, T5820056, **Tour operators**

Guerrero, Oaxaca & the Isthmus

www.gan.com/TravelAgencies/AnasEcotours. *Michael Malone*, a Canadian ornithologist, is another recommended guide who is in Puerto Escondido Nov-Mar, enquire at the tourism information kiosk about his current contact point. *Margarito* is a Manialtepec resident who takes visitors to the Manialtepec lagoon for US$11.00 pp.

Transport **Air** Airport (PXM) 10 mins drive west of town, orange juice and coffee sold. With Aerocaribe (T5822023), daily from Mexico City at 1140, to Mexico City at 1300, 1 hr, US$87; daily from Oaxaca at 0955 and 1640, to Oaxaca at 1045 and 1820, 30 mins, US$70.00. With Aerovega (T/F5820151) in 7-seat Cesna, daily from Oaxaca at 0700, to Oaxaca at 0900, US$70.00. Airport transport in shared vans (*colectivos*), US$2 pp, T5820030.

Car hire *Budget*, Av Juárez at the entrance to Bacocho, T5820312.

Roads The Sierra Madre del Sur lies between the coast and Oaxaca's central valleys, where the state capital is located. All routes must cross this steep mountain range and are therefore subject to landslides and damage during the rainy periods. Enquire locally as to current conditions. The most direct route between Puerto Escondido and Oaxaca (260 km) is route 131 through Sola de Vega, a paved road. From Puerto Escondido to Oaxaca via Pochutla and Route 200 is 310 km, also fully paved. A third, much longer, alternative (490 km) is Route 190 via Tehuantepec and the Panamerican Highway.

Buses To **Pochutla**, from corner Carretera Costera and Av Oaxaca, every 20 mins, 0500-1900, 1½ hrs, US$1.30. For **Puerto Angel**, **Zipolite** and other beaches: transfer in Pochutla to pick-up or taxi *colectivo*. To **Oaxaca** For better safety, travel only during the daytime and take the direct services which run better vehicles and do not stop to pick up passengers along the way; Oaxaca-Pacífico/Estrella del Valle, Avenida Hidalgo 400 near Avenida Oaxaca, direct service at 0815, 1245, 2215, US$7.60, 7½ hrs, 1st class at 2230, US$8. Cristóbal Colón, 1a norte 207, 3 daily via Tehuantepec, US$14.80, 12 hrs (this 1st class service takes the Isthmus route since it is not allowed to take passengers on the more direct routes where local companies operate). Trans Sol/ Solteca, station near the market, via Sola de Vega, 3 daily, US$7.60, 7 hrs. To **Salina Cruz**, Estrella Blanca, Av Oaxaca, 0730, 1030, 1500, 0000, US$5.50, 5 hrs. To **Acapulco**, Estrella Blanca, a/c service 0430, 0730, 1030, 1230, 2045, 2330, US$19.00, 7 hrs; regular service, hourly 0400-1500, US$26.50. To **Zihuatanejo**, Estrella Blanca, 1 direct bus daily. To **Mexico City**, Estrella Blanca, 1st class at 1930 and 2000, US$33.00, 12 hrs via Acapulco, to travel during the day go to Acapulco and transfer there; Oaxaca-Pacífico/Estrella del Valle, 1st class, at 1745, US$26.00, 12 hrs via Oaxaca, arrives at Fletes y Pasajes terminal near TAPO (east terminal). To **Puebla** Oaxaca-Pacífico/Estrella del Valle, 1st class, at 1745, US$21.00, 10 hrs via Oaxaca, leaves you by the highway, not CAPU. To **Tuxtla Gutiérrez** and **San Cristóbal de las Casas**, Cristóbal Colón, 0845 and 2130, **Tuxtla** US$21.50, 12 hrs, San Cristóbal, US$25.00, 14 hrs. To **Tapachula**, Cristóbal Colón, 2000, US$27.00 14-15 hrs.

Directory **Banks** *Bancomer*, 1a Norte y 2a Poniente, cash and TCs 0800-1400. *Bital*, 1a Norte y 3a Poniente, cash and TCs, cash advance on Visa and MasterCard, Mon-Sat 0800-1900. *Banamex*, Av Pérez Gasga east of El Adoquín, 0900-1300. 2 *Casas de Cambio* on El Adoquín, open till 2000, poor rates. **Communications** Post Office: 7a Norte by Av Oaxaca. **Internet:** *Cibercafé Un Tigre Azul*, on El Adoquín, US$5.40 per hour, coffee, snacks, gift shop, friendly service, open 1100. *Graficom*, Av Pérez Gasga 302, west of El Adoquín, US$5.40 per hour. **Laundry** Lavandería at east end of El Adoquín, US$1 per kg or US$3.25 per load, self service, Mon-Sat, 0900-2100. Another one at Av Pérez Gasga by Hotel Nayar, US$1.5 per kg. **Medical services** Dr Francisco Serrano Severiano, 1a Norte y 2a Poniente, opposite Bancomer, speaks English, 0900-1300, 1700-2000. *Clínica de Especialidades del Puerto*, Av Oaxaca, has been recommended. *Clínica Santa Fe*, Av 5a Poniente. *Farmacia La Moderna*, Av Pérez Gasga 203, T5820214, has a physician in house, open 24 hrs.

Pochutla

Sixty-six kilometres east of Puerto Escondido and 240 km south of Oaxaca is San Pedro Pochutla, a hot supply town with an imposing church set on a small hill. Its pleasant **Plaza de las Golondrinas**, where folks stroll in the cool of the evening, is filled with many singing birds; countless swallows line up on the electric wires here every night. There is a prison in Pochutla, and the inmates carve crafts out of coconut husks for sale by their families and local shops. Pochutla has little of interest but, being at the intersection of Route 175 from Oaxaca, Route 200 from Acapulco to Salina Cruz, and the road to Puerto Angel, it is an important crossroad for bus connections and a good place to change money or stock up on supplies for the beach. Supermarkets and general stores are along Lázaro Cárdenas. The Fiesta de San Pedro takes place on 29-30 June.

Phone code: 958
Colour Map 4, Grid C1
Population: 10,251

Beaches A road runs south of Pochutla 9 km to Puerto Angel, then turns west along the coast past the beaches of **Zipolite**, **San Agustinillo**, and **Mazunte**, each with its own distinct physical and social ambiance. Also along this route are **El Mariposario**, a private butterfly reserve which welcomes visitors, the **Centro Mexicano de la Tortuga**, where sea turtles can be observed, and **Ventanilla**, on a lagoon with birds and crocodiles. Past Ventanilla, the road turns back north to meet Highway 200 at San Antonio. The complete loop takes just over one hour by vehicle and is well served with public transport in both directions (see Transport below). The area's proximity to Huatulco has created a great influx of day-trippers, as well as pressure for further development. The road is reported safe for vehicle travel but less-so for walking between beaches, especially at night. Details of individual beaches are given below.

Thirty kilometres west of Pochutla is the **Criadero de Iguanas Barra del Potrero de Cozoaltepec**, which raises iguanas to repopulate areas in which they have become endangered. Take a bus towards Puerto Escondido and get off at the Río de Cozoaltepec, Km 178; the *iguanario* is just east of the river. Green and black iguanas may be seen. ■ *Daily, free admission but a donation is recommended.*

Excursions

C *Posada San José*, Constitución behind Oaxaca bus terminal, T40153. A/c, small pool, **D** with fan. **D** *Loma Real*, Mina 17 by entrance from Oaxaca, T40645. A/c, cheaper with fan, pool, garden, parking. **D** *Los Portales*, Carretera a Puerto Angel Km 1, T40460. A/c, TV, cheaper with fan. **D** *Costa del Sol*, Av Lázaro Cárdenas 47 (main road), T40318, F40049. A/c, cheaper with fan, restaurant. **D** *Izala*, Lázaro Cárdenas 59, T40115. A/c, cheaper with fan, clean, comfortable. **E** *Pochutla*, Francisco Madero 102, at corner of Plaza, T40003. Bath, ceiling fan, good value. **E** *Santa Cruz*, Lázaro Cárdenas 88, across from Oaxaca terminal, T40116. Fan, basic. **E** *El Patio*, Lázaro Cárdenas, across from market. Fan, basic, parking. **E** *Gloria Estela*, Constitución 23, T40095. Bath, fan, hot water, new in 1999.

Sleeping

San Angel, at Plaza. Nice atmosphere, terrace overlooking park. *Panadería Las 7 Regiones*, Lázaro Cárdenas at Oaxaca end. Recommended.

Eating

Roads Highway 175 from Oaxaca to Pochutla is a very scenic but extremely winding paved road. In the central valleys it goes through the craft towns of **Ocotlán de Morelos** (*Posada San Salvador*) and **Ejutla de Crespo** (*Hotel 6* and several other places to stay), before climbing the Sierra Madre del Sur to its pine-clad ridges and the pass. Just south of the pass is San José del Pacífico, a hamlet with nice views and a restaurant where buses make a rest stop. From here to Pochutla the road descends through

Transport

seemingly endless curves and the vegetation becomes increasingly lush. Tank up in Oaxaca or Pochutla (24-hr gas station) before driving this road.

Local For Puerto Angel, Zipolite, and other beaches, pick-up trucks with benches in back and shared taxis (*colectivos*) do round trips on the coastal road in both directions, these taxis also offer private service (*carreras*); in Pochutla, wait at marked bus stops along the main road. To Puerto Angel, truck US$0.25, *colectivo* US$0.50 pp, taxi US$3-4. To Zipolite, truck US$0.40, *colectivo* US$1, taxi US$6. To Mazunte, truck US$0.50, *colectivo* US$1, taxi US$6. Beware of over-charging, it is especially common in this area. Taxi drivers have been known to wait for unwary visitors and charge US7, Pochutla-Zipolite. To Puerto Escondido, *colectivo* US$3, taxi US$20. To Huatulco, *colectivo* US$1.50, taxi US$10.

Buses **Puerto Escondido**, small buses from side street near church, every 20 mins 0500-1900, US$1.30, 1½ hrs; also with through buses coming from Oaxaca or Salina Cruz. **Huatulco** (La Crucecita), small buses from lane near Oaxaca-Pacífico terminal, every 15 mins 0500-2000, US$0.90, 1 hr. **Salina Cruz**, with Cristóbal Colón, 5 daily; with Estrella Blanca, 3 daily, US7, 3-4 hrs. **Oaxaca**, Oaxaca-Pacífico/Estrella del Valle, direct service 0945, 1415, 2300, US$7.25, 6 hrs. 2nd class service, 14 daily, US$6.20; with Cristóbal Colón via the Isthmus, at 1445 and 1930, US$14.70, 9 hrs. **Tuxtla Gutiérrez**, Cristóbal Colón, 0945 and 2230, US$19, 10 hrs. **Tapachula**, Cristóbal Colón, 2100, US$24, 12 hrs. **Acapulco**, Estrella Blanca, 0600, 1000, 2200, US$19, 8½ hrs. **Mexico City**, Estrella Blanca, 1st class, via Acapulco, 1900, US$36, 12-13 hrs; Oaxaca Pacífico, via Oaxaca, 1800 and 1900, US$24, 12-13 hrs.

Directory **Banks** All on main street: *Bancomer*, 0830-1400, cash and TCs. *Bancrecer*, 0830-1400, cash and TCs. *Bital*, 0830-1700, cash and TCs. **Communications** Email, in a shop on Lázaro Cárdenas, a whopping US$26 per hour! **Medical services** Public hospital just south of town.

Puerto Angel

Colour map 4, grid C1
Population: 2,433

Twenty minutes south of Pochutla along a pretty road which winds through hilly forest country before dropping to the sea is Puerto Angel. Until the 1960s it was a busy port from which coffee and timber were shipped to Asia; with the fall in coffee prices, the local population turned to selling turtle skins until 1990, when this activity was banned in Mexico. Tourism and fishing are currently the main economic activities here. The town lies above a beautiful flask-shaped bay; unfortunately the turquoise water is polluted, but there are hopes for improvement if a planned sewage system is installed. Because of its lovely setting it has been described as 'the ideal place to rest and do nothing'. There is a small navy base here and, atop a nearby hill, the **Universidad del Mar**. The beach right in town is neither clean nor attractive. A short walk away, either along the road or on a concrete path built on the rocks (not safe at night) is **Playa del Panteón**, a small beach in a lovely setting, but crowded with restaurants (touts await visitors on arrival) and many bathers in season. There are cleaner and more tranquil nearby beaches east of town. **Estacahuite**, with simple *cabañas*, 1 km from town, about a 20 minute walk, has good snorkelling (gear rental from hut selling drinks and snacks) but beware of strong waves, currents and sharp coral which can cut you; La Boquilla, with comfortable Canadian-run bungalows, is 3 km away, off a signed track on the road to Pochutla. **Safety** Take extra care in the sea as the currents are very dangerous. Also watch your belongings. There is a *fiesta* on 1 June to celebrate the Día de la Marina and another on 1 October, the Fiesta de San Angel. For transport to and from Puerto Angel see Pochutla above.

B *Angel del Mar*, above Playa del Panteón, T43014. Good views, fan, dirty, run down. **Sleeping**
B *Soraya*, José Vasconcelos corner Av Principal, T43009. A/c, **C** with fan, good views,
parking, money exchange, unfriendly. **C** *Buena Vista*, uphill, T43104. Nice rooms,
clean, renovated in 1999, relaxing but not very friendly. **C** *Villa Florencia*, Av Principal
Virgilio Uribe across from town beach, T/F43044. A/c, cheaper with fan, clean, comfortable, friendly, Italian-Mexican run, restaurant, bar, library. **D** *Cañón Devata*, Playa
del Panteón, T43048, lopezk@spin,com.mx. Clean but dark, lovely setting, booked
continuously, popular with Americans, restaurant. **D** *Casas Penélopes*, on road to
Zipolite and Mazunte. Friendly, beautiful location. Highly recommended. **D** *El Rincón
Sabroso*, T43095. Beautiful views, clean, quiet, friendly, no hot water. **D** *La Cabaña*,
Playa del Panteón, T43105. Fan, clean, friendly, free coffee in the morning. Recommended. **D** *Puesta del Sol*, on road to Playa del Panteón, T43096. Fan, cheaper with
shared bath, clean, restaurant, very friendly, English and German spoken. Recommended. **E** *Anahi*, on road to Playa del Panteón. Fan, basic. **E** *Capy's*, on road to Playa
del Panteón, T43002. Fan, clean, nice restaurant. Recommended. **E** *Casa de
Huéspedes Gladys*, above Soraya, T43050. Clean, fine views, balcony, owner can prepare food. Recommended. **E** *Casa de Huéspedes Gundi y Tomás*. Shared bath, clean,
F in hammocks, good value, popular with travellers, stores luggage, breakfast and
snacks served (cook prepares dinner every day for guests, but expensive), often recommended; Gundi also runs *Pensión El Almendro*, with café (good ice cream) and
library. **E** *Casa de Huéspedes Leal*, T43081. Shared bath, washing facilities, friendly.
Recommended.

Camping   There is a camp ground halfway between Puerto Angel and Pochutla, very
friendly, driveway too steep for large vehicles, US$8.50 for 2 in campervan.
Recommended.

An excellent restaurant at *Villa Florencia* hotel. Good food, Italian and Mexican   **Eating**
dishes, charming place. *Beto's* by turn-off for Playa del Panteón. Good fish (fresh tuna)
and cheap beer, nice views. Nearby are *Capy's*. Good food. *Cañón de Vata*. Also good,
mainly vegetarian. *Pensión Puesta del Sol*. Excellent restaurant. *Mar y Sol*. Cheap,
good seafood. *Sirenita*. Popular for breakfast and bar, friendly. *Cangrejo*, by Naval Base
gate. Popular bar, also good breakfasts and excellent *tacos*. Several fish restaurants

Puerto Angel environs

along the main street; 2 restaurants by fishing harbour, cheap, popular with locals.

Sports Scuba diving with *Hotel La Cabaña*, T430116, experienced instructors, up-to-date equipment, PADI service available. English spoken.

Directory **Banks** Cash and TCs changed at *Hotel Soraya*. Banks in Pochutla. **Communications** Internet: *Caseta Puerto Angel*. C José Vasconcelos 3 (next to *Hotel Soraya*), T43038. **Post office:** next to Agencia Municipal near *Hotel Soraya*.

Zipolite Four kilometres west of Puerto Angel is Zipolite, perhaps the last nude beach in Mexico and once an inspirationally beautiful spot which still attracts many foreign visitors. Sadly, it has become a veritable paradise-lost, notorious for drugs, crime, and violence including murder; it is just acceptably safe to walk along the beach during the daytime but very dangerous at night. The shore is lined with *palapas* offering cheap meals and accommodations (beds from US$3.50 per night, hammocks from US$2.50, shared bath, basic facilities), with informal discos at night. There are also a few more solid structures toward the west end of the beach and a number of establishments had been recommended by visitors in the past, but until the overall public safety situation improves, Zipolite is probably best avoided altogether. The sea can also be very dangerous here. Just past the west end of Zipolite, set in nice forested surroundings is **El Mariposario**, a privately operated butterfly reserve, where many beautiful species, as well as frogs and iguanas, may be seen from inside a net-covered enclosure. ■ *Interesting guided tours in Spanish and English, 0930-1630 daily, entry US$1.50, students US$1, children under 12 US$0.50.*

Another 3 km west lies **San Agustinillo**, a long, pretty beach, with an extraordinary cave in the cliffs. The western end is quite built-up with private homes, simple *cabañas* in the **E** range, and restaurants; nude bathing is prohibited. Swimming is safest at the west end of the beach, surfing best near the centre. There is one larger hotel, **E** *Posada San Agustín*. With private bath, ceiling fan, mosquito net, nice views, friendly.

Mazunte One kilometre further west is Mazunte, perhaps the least developed major beach in the area but rapidly changing, so responsible tourism is especially important here (see **Responsible Tourism**, page 59). The beach is on federal land and drug laws are strictly enforced here; nude bathing is prohibited, the safest swimming is at either end of the bay. At the east end of Mazunte is the **Centro Mexicano de la Tortuga**, a government institute which studies sea turtles and works to conserve these frequently endangered species, as well as to educate visitors and the local population in this regard (interested researchers may contact the director at cmtvasco@ angel.umar.mx). There are interesting viewing tanks to observe many species of turtles underwater. ■ *Guided tours in Spanish and English, open Tue-Sat 1000-1630, Sun 1000-1430, US$2, children under 12 US$1, crowded with tour buses from Huatulco 1100-1300 during high season.* At the west end of Mazunte is *Cosméticos Naturales de Mazunte*, where cosmetics are made with natural ingredients. A trail leads from the west end of the beach to **Punta Cometa**, a spit of land with lovely views of the thundering breakers below, a popular spot to view the sunset, well worth the 30-minute walk.

Sleeping **B** *Altamira*, on a wooded hillside overlooking the west end of the beach. 4 lovely *cabañas*, spacious, clean, comfortable, spectacular views, meals available. Immediately adjacent is *Balam Juyu*. Simpler but in the same splendid setting, breakfast and drinks served. **D-E** *Posada Brisa Marina*, Colonia Roca Blanca, F43070. New large rooms on the beach. Friendly. **E** *Ziga*, at the east end near the *Centro Mexicano de la Tortuga*. Semi-private bath, fan, mosquito net, clean, friendly, family run, nice views, good value. Recommended. Next door is **E** *Porfiria*, basic, friendly, kitchen facilities, small bar. Several *palapas* offer simple accommodation along the middle of the beach.

Eating There are many simple (but not necessarily cheap) restaurants including *Lupita*, at west end of beach. Large portions. *Pizzería Iris*, on track between the west end of the beach and the road. *La Dolce Vita*, on main road at west end. Good Italian cooking including pizza and home-made pasta, pricey. *El Paso*, on main road west of the bridge. Inexpensive and friendly. There are several shops with basic supplies, other items may be brought from Pochutla.

Two kilometres west of Mazunte is a signed turn-off for **Ventanilla**. It is 1½ km from here to the village and visitors information centre on the shores of a lagoon. Tours are run by local residents who are working on a mangrove reforestation project (in 1997 Hurricane Pauline wiped out part of the mangroves here) and have a crocodile farm to repopulate the area. The tour combines a rowing boat ride for up to 10 persons, a visit to the crocodile farm, and a walk on the beach, US$3.25 per person, many birds, crocodiles and iguanas may be seen, guides speak Spanish only. Horse-riding tours along the beach are available for US$5.40 per hour; there are some nice rock formations offshore. Those wishing to spend the night can camp or stay with a family. Simple meals are available in the village.

Huatulco

East of Pochutla (50 km, one hour), and 112 km west of Salina Cruz on the coast road is Huatulco, a meticulously engineered resort complex surrounded by 34,000ha of forest reserve and nine splendid bays. It offers golf, swimming pools, international and Mexican cuisine, nightlife, beaches, watersports, and excursions into the forest. The product is safe, clean, efficient, and claims to be environmentally friendly (see **The Huatulco Experiment**); an international vacation resort in a lovely setting with a mild Mexican flavour. Huatulco's high seasons include Holy Week, July-August, and November-March, with regular charter flights from the USA and Canada during the latter months; prices can be as much as double during these periods.

Phone code: 958
Colour map 4, grid C1

Guerrero, Oaxaca & the Isthmus

   The Huatulco complex encompasses several interconnected towns and development areas; a regular city bus service connects them, and there are many taxis. **Tangolunda**, on the bay of the same name and also known as the Zona Hotelera, is set aside for large luxury hotels and resorts including a Club Mediterranée; it also has the golf course and the most expensive restaurants, souvenir shops, and nightlife. **Chahué**, on the next bay west, where development only began in 1999, has a town park with nothing around it, a marina and a few hotels. Further west (6 km from Tangolunda) is **Santa Cruz Huatulco**, once an ancient Zapotec settlement and Mexico's most important Pacific port during the 16th century (later abandoned). It has the marina where tour boats leave for excursions, as well as facilities for visiting yachts, several upscale hotels, restaurants, shops, and a few luxury homes. An open-air chapel by the beach here, the Capilla de la Santa Cruz, is attractive; nearby is a well-groomed park. A navy base is being built in the vicinity. **La Crucecita**, located 2 km inland, is the functional hub of the Huatulco complex, with housing for the area's employees, bus stations, banks, a small market, ordinary shops, plus the more economical hotels and restaurants. It also doubles as a Mexican town which the tourists can visit, more cosmetic by the manicured Plaza Principal, less so towards the highway. The old-looking, but brand-new Templo de Guadalupe church stands on a small hill next to the plaza. **Santa María Huatulco**, in the mountains 25 km further inland, is a pre-existing town where the municipal offices are located; there is said to be good walking in the area but little else of interest for the visitor. **Tourist office**: Sedetur, Boulevard Benito Juárez near the golf course, Tangolunda, T/F5810176, sedetur6@oaxaca-travel.gob.mx, helpful, informative. On-line information at oaxaca-travel.gob.mx, baysofhuatulco.com.mx

Bays and beaches Huatulco's coastline extends for almost 30 km between the Río Copalita to the east and the Río Coyula to the west. Hills covered in deciduous forest, very green during the rainy season (June-September), yellow and parched in the dry, sweep down to the sea. Nine turquoise bays with 36 beaches line the shore, some bays have road access while others can only be reached by sea. Official prices for boats to one or more beaches are posted at the Santa Cruz Marina, check these and ask around before taking a boat.

From east to west, the first bay is **Bahía Conejos**, with dirt track access, good swimming beaches at either end, some offshore coral towards the west end and a ranch where horses can be hired towards Río Copalita. The luxury hotels at **Bahía Tangolunda** all have their own beach areas spread along a large bay. There is also public access by a dirt road next to the golf course; free parking, public changing rooms, and showers (US$0.20, not always open), but no shade whatsoever on the beach and the slope of the sand is quite steep. The beaches at **Bahía Chahué** are all too steep for swimming. **Bahía Santa Cruz** has the most popular beaches, best suited for swimming and watersports, crowded in high season. **Playa Santa Cruz**, just by the town, is very safe, but packed with restaurants; water skis and other equipment can be rented. Some of the more expensive hotels in La Crucecita have their beach clubs here. Nearby by boat, but a long, hot scenic walk along a winding road (taxi or launch US$1 per person; no bus), is **Playa La Entrega**. It is set on a very beautiful bay and there are spectacular views from above; the snorkelling and swimming are good, but the beach is prone to crowding. Next are **Bahías El Organo** and **El Maguey**, surrounded by many cacti as the names suggest and to which the paved road was being extended in 1999 (no bus service). As you

The bays of Huatulco

Not to scale

The Huatulco Experiment

It has been argued with some justification that mass tourism by any other name is equally harmful to the local physical and social environments. Huatulco claims to be different however, and even the most fundamentalist opponents of industrial-scale resort development might want to consider its unique experiment.

Begun in 1987 and perhaps designed to avoid some of the mistakes of Acapulco or Cancún, it is certainly a contrast to the haphazard development of nearby Puerto Escondido. Huatulco was meticulously planned and executed; the land (34,000 ha comprised mostly of virgin forest) and its spectacular shoreline were all expropriated beforehand by the Mexican federal government. There could be no upward spiral of property values here, nor fragmentation of lots to impede orderly development. With the tiny local population relocated outside the area, there was no social impact to consider and the design concentrated on creating a comprehensive infrastructure in harmony with the natural environment.

A comprehensive infrastructure has certainly been achieved, with an international airport, four-lane divided access roads lined with landscaped greenery, marinas, parks, plazas, public transport, medical facilities, employee housing, commercial areas, sewage systems, huge concrete drainage canals, international courier services, and cellular phones. Huatulco's harmony with its natural environment is a matter of debate, but at least the water looks reasonably clean in the nine bays, and fish swim alongside the bathers and jet-skis, while basket-shaped nests hang from the trees overhead.

Courses on working with tourists are provided for the area's residents, all of whom live directly or indirectly from the industry; the atmosphere is cordial and there is little crime. In fact the only thing Huatulco really lacks is authenticity, but while its detractors may focus on how artificial it all is, its promoters can point out that it works.

In the meantime, the project – which continues to be guided by the federal government agency Fonatur – has not grown as rapidly as expected. There were 'only' 171,000 vistors in 1998 (74 percent Mexicans, 26 percent foreigners), an increase of just one percent from the previous year. Overall, it is probably too soon to properly interpret the results of the Huatulco experiment, to see if it can be both successful and sustainable in the long term, and to know what impact it will have on other parts of the Oaxaca coast.

Guerrero, Oaxaca & the Isthmus

approach Bahía El Organo from the sea, what looks like an Olmec face can be seen on the cliffs above. Playa El Maguey is another popular bathing beach, with calm surf, also suited for watersports and snorkelling. **Bahía Cacaluta** can be reached by a dirt track, the surf is quite strong and boats do not usually land here; there is an island across from the bay surrounded by coral reefs. **Bahía Chachacual** does not have road access, there are six beaches along this bay. **Bahía San Agustín** can be reached by sea or via a dirt road, it is 16 km from Route 200, the turn-off is west of the airport. The beaches here are suitable for bathing, there are *palapas* selling fish and drinks. West of San Agustín, the beaches have a steep slant and the surf is quite strong.

Excursions Full-day boat tours to see the different bays are offered by travel agencies for US$17-27 per person, with stops for swimming, snorkelling and a meal; there are catamarans, sail boats, yachts and small launches. Trips can also be arranged at the Santa Cruz marina directly with the boatsmen, they will most likely speak Spanish only. Some of the bays can also be reached by land, there are tours on all-terrain, quad bikes (*cuatrimotos*).

● ●

 ### Huatulco's legendary cross

● ●

The name Huatulco means 'place of the wood', which refers to a cross planted on the beach, legend tells, by Quetzalcoatl. After resisting efforts to pull it down, it was found to be only a few feet deep when dug up; small crosses were made from it. A more likely history of the cross is told by Michael Turner in his research into Francis Drake's voyages. Until the establishment of Acapulco as the departure point for the Spanish Pacific fleet, Huatulco (Guatulco)

was the main port on the Pacific, its heyday being from about 1537 to 1574. Drake sacked the port on his voyage around the world (1577-80) and Thomas Cavendish raided it in 1587. Cavendish burnt the church to the ground, but the crucifix (La Santa Cruz) survived, thereafter being incorporated into the village's name. The Spanish viceroy ordered Huatulco's abandonment in 1616.

● ●

In the Huatulco area the Sierra Madre del Sur mountains drop from the highest point in the state of Oaxaca (3,750m) right down to the sea. There are ample opportunities for day-hiking, see **Sports** on page 444. In the hills north of Huatulco are a number of coffee plantations which can be visited. Huatulco travel agencies arrange for full-day plantation tours which include a meal with traditional dishes at the farm and bathing in fresh water springs or waterfalls; US$44 per person.

Day trips to the different coastal attractions to the west, including Puerto Angel, Mazunte and Puerto Escondido are offered by travel agencies for US$20. Much ground is covered so it is a long day.

Sleeping
Discounts of up to 50% can be expected in the low season

Tangolunda **LL** *Camino Real Zaashila*, Blvd Benito Juárez 5, T5810460, F5810461, zaa@ caminoreal.com. Includes breakfast, on the beach, large pool. **LL** *Crown Pacific*, Blvd Benito Juárez 8, T5810044, F5810221, cvhuatulco@compuserve.com.mx. All-inclusive suites. **LL** *Gala Royal Maeva*, Blvd. Benito Juárez 4, T5810000, F5810220, rmaevarsvas@huatulco.net.mx. All-inclusive resort, on the beach, several pools, discotheque. **LL** *Quinta Real*, Blvd Benito Juárez 2, T5810428, F5810429. 5-star resort on the beach. **LL-L** *Club Mediterranée*, Bahía Tangolunda west end, T5810038, F5810101. All-inclusive, full board resort, reservations are cheaper if made at Calle Masaryk, Mexico City (not confirmed). Day pass for US$87 gives access to all sports, activities, pools, meals and shows; night pass for US$26 for discotheque and show. **L** *Shereton Resort*, Blvd Benito Juárez, T5810055, F5810113, www.sheraton.com. All-inclusive packages and European plan available, on the beach. **L-AL** *Casa del Mar*, Balcones de Tangolunda 13, T5810102, F5810202. **L-AL** *Plaza Huatulco*, Blvd Benito Juárez 23, T5810035, F5810027. Small luxurious hotel with personalized service. **L-AL** *Villas Coral*, Playa El Arrocito, T/F5810477.

La Crucecita

Chahué **AL** *Posada Chahué*, Mixie y Mixteco, T5870945, F5871240, posadachaue@huatulco.net.mx. A/c, pool, terrace restaurant, **A** with fan.

AL *Real Aligheri*, Mixie 770, Sector R, T5871242, F5871243. Includes American breakfast, pool, restaurant. **AL** *Villablanca*, Blvd Benito Juárez esq Zapoteca, T5870606, F5870660. Pool, restaurant.

Santa Cruz L *Marina Resort*, Tehuantepec 112, T5870963, F5870830, hmarinaresort@huatulco.net.mx. Pools, restaurants, disco. **AL** *Castillo Huatulco*, Blvd Sta Cruz 303, T5870144, F5870131, toll free Mexico 01800-9034900. **AL** *Marlín*, Paseo Mitla 107, T5870055, F5870546, hmarlin@huatulco.net.mx. A/c, pool. **AL** *Meigas Binniguenda*, Blvd Sta Cruz 201, T5870077, F5870284, binniguenda@ huatulco.netmx. Colonial-style, gardens, pool.

La Crucecita AL *Gran Hotel Huatulco*, Carrizal 1406, at the entrance to town, T5870115, 5871346, toll free Mexico 018007127355. A/c, pool. **AL** *Flamboyan*, Gardenia esq Tamarindo, T5870113, 5870121. Includes breakfast, a/c, hot water, pool, beach club, full-board packages including tour of the bays is **LL**, apartments for 4 available. **B** *Busanvi*, Carrizal 601, T5870056. A/c and fan, hot water, apartments with kitchenette, pool. **B** *Misión de los Arcos*, Gardenia 902 y Tamarindo, T/f5870165, losarcos@huatulco.net.mx. A/c, hot water, cheaper with fan, nice rooms. **B** *Las Palmas*, Guamuchil 206, T5870060, F5870057. **B-C** *Suites Begonias*, Bugambilia 503, Plaza Principal, T5870018, F5871390. A/c, cheaper with fan, clean. **C** *Grifer*, Av Carrizal and Guamuchil, T/F5870048. With bath, a/c. **C** *Posada Michelle*, Gardenia 1301, 2nd floor, T/F5870535. A/c, cheaper with fan. **C** *Posada de Rambo*, Guarumbo 307, near main plaza, T5870958. With bath, fan, some with hot water. **C-D** *Posada del Carmen*, Palo Verde 307, T5870593. Nice rooms, cold water, cheaper with 1 double bed. **C-D** *Posada San Agustín*, Carrizal 1102 esq Macuil, T5870368. With bath, fan. **D** *Benimar*, Bugambilia esq Pochote, T5870447. With bath, fan, hot water, simple rooms. **D** *Casa de Huéspedes Koly*, Bugambilia near Plaza, T5871075. With bath, fan.

Camping *Trailer Park Los Mangos*, Blvd Santa Cruz, just where Chahué and Santa Cruz meet.

Tangolunda Luxury restaurants at Tangolunda hotels. *La Pampa Argentina*, Centro Comercial Punta Tangolunda, Blvd Benito Juárez, across from the golf course. For Argentinian-style beef and pasta, pricey. *Don Porfirio*, Blvd Benito Juárez. Fish and seafood specialities, also steak. *Jarro Café*, across from Sheraton. Oaxacan and international cuisine.

Santa Cruz *Mar y Luz*, Bahía Santa Cruz. Seafood specialities. *Jardín del Arte*, Paseo Mitla at *Hotel Marlín*. French and international. *Tipsy's*, Bahía Santa Cruz, by the beach. Seafood, burgers, salads. *Café Huatulco*. Kiosk near the marina, where you can sample regional coffee and snacks.

La Crucecita Cheaper prices, especially as you get away from the plaza, several restaurants along Gardenia including *La Tropicana*, corner Guanacastle. Varied menu. *Oasis Café*, Bugambilia esq Flamboyan and Flamboyan 211, by main plaza. Varied menu, grill, seafood, Oaxacan food. *María Sabina*, Flamboyan 306, by plaza. Grill and lobster. *La Crucecita*, Bugambilia esq Chacah. Breakfast, snacks, set meals. *Los Portales*, Bugambilia 603, Plaza Principal. Breakfast, *tacos* and other snacks, open late. *Don Wilo*, Plaza Principal. Oaxacan specialities and pizza. *El Pato Mojado*, Jazmín. Seafood and regional dishes cooked in wood oven. *Il Giardio del Papa*, Flamboyan 204. Italian, chef was the Pope's cook. *Origami*, Carrizal 504. Japanese food. *El Sabor de Oaxaca*, Guamuchil 206. Regional cooking, Oaxacan *mole*.

Eating

Guerrero, Oaxaca & the Isthmus

Entertainment Several luxury hotels have shows such as the *Sheraton*'s **Fiesta Mexicana with Mariachis**, folk dancing, Mexican buffet, reservations T5810055. La Guelaguetza folklore show at **Noches Oaxaqueñas**, Blvd Benito Juárez, Tangolunda, reservations T5810001. Latin dancing at **Magic Tropic**, Santa Cruz. **Magic Circus**, also in Santa Cruz. European-style disco.

Festivals The *Fiesta del Mar* takes place in the 1st week of Apr, the religious **Fiesta de la Santa Cruz** on 3 May. There is an international sail-fishing tournament during the 1st week of May. The **Fiesta de la Virgen** is on 8 Dec.

Shopping The *Mercado de Artesanías de Santa Cruz*, Blvd Santa Cruz, corner Mitla, has a variety of regional crafts. The **Museo de Artesanías Oaxaqueñas**, Flamboyan 216, Plaza Principal, La Crucecita, also exhibits and sells a variety of Mexican crafts. Crafts can also be found at the **Mercado 3 de Mayo**, food market, on Guanacastle and Bugambilia, in La Crucecita.

Sports **Cycling** A mountain bike is a good way to get around this area and to reach the high points with the many views of the bays. Bike rentals in La Crucecita from restaurants *La Tropicana*, *Gardenia*, and *Guanacastle* near the plaza, US$1.65 per hour and *Origami*, Carrizal 504, US$2.25 per hour. Rentals and cycling tours from *Motor Tours*, *Eco Aventuras* and other agencies (see Tour operators).

Diving and snorkelling There are good snorkelling opportunities on reefs by the beach at La Entrega (Bahía Santa Cruz), Riscalillo (Bahía Cachacual), and San Agustín (Bahía San Agustín). The islands of Cacaluta (Bahía Cacaluta) and La Montosa (Bahía Tangolunda) are also surrounded by reefs with several species of coral, many different organisms can be seen here in relatively shallow water. Snorkel and fins rented at Santa Cruz marina, US$4.35 or through agencies who organize tours. There are good scuba diving opportunities as well, the cliffs that separate the different bays continue underwater an average of 30m; marine life is abundant along these underwater cliffs, there are also shipwrecks to explore. Diving lessons and tours from *Action Sports Marina* (*Sheraton Hotel*), *Buceo Sotavento* (*Hotel Club Plaza Huatulco*) and other agencies. Lessons run about US$82, diving tour if you have your certificate, US$65.

Fishing Launches and yachts can be rented for deep-sea fishing. Yachts charge US$100 per hour, minimal rental 3 hrs. *Paraíso Huatulco* and other agencies can arrange rental.

Golf The Tangolunda golf course offers 18-hole, par-72 golf with nice views of the surroundings. Reservations T5810037, F5810059.

Hiking There are opportunities for hiking in the forested hills to the north of Huatulco. Because part of the forest is deciduous, the experience is very different in the rainy season, when it is green, and in the dry season when the area is brown and even some cacti change from green to violet. The Río Copalita to the north and east of Huatulco is quite scenic. It has waterfalls and rapids, walking here can be combined with a visit to the Punta Celeste Zapotec archaeological site.

Horse-riding Rancho Caballo de Mar, on the shores of the Río Copalita, east of Huatulco and south of Route 200, T5870530, offers riding tours along the river, on forested trails and on the beaches of Bahía de Conejos, US$45 for 3 hrs. Tours can be arranged with agencies in town.

Rafting Several companies run tours down the Copalita and Zimatán rivers, these can be as basic as a float down the river or as challenging as class 4-5 rapids; ask enough questions to find the tour that best suits you. Half-day tours run US$33-40, full day for US$65-76 pp. Note that from Feb-May there may not be enough water. Providers include: *Aventuras Piraguas*, Plaza Oaxaca Local 19, on Flamboyan across from the plaza, La Crucecita, T/F5871333, canoe trips and rafting in up to class 5 rapids. *Copalita River Tours*, Gardenia esquina Palo Verde (*Posada Michelle* lobby), La Crucecita, T/F5870535, kayak and rafting tours. *Huatulco Outfitters*, Plaza Comercial, Punta Tangolunda, T5810315. Rafting.

Rock climbing   There are rock climbing opportunities at Piedra de los Moros a few kilometres north of Route 200, on the road to Pueblo Viejo, the turn-off is west of the Bahías de Huatulco entrance road; by the Copalitilla waterfall, on the Copalita river canyon, 65 km from Huatulco; and in Punta Celeste, at the Botazoo Park, 8 km from Huatulco. Tours available from *Motor Tours*, *Eco Aventuras* and other agencies (see Tour operators).

Water sports   Those looking for wind surfing, sailing, wave running, and water skiing, can rent equipment at the major hotels and beach clubs. Some restaurants at Santa Cruz, such as *Tipsy's*, also rent equipment and have instructors.

Tour operators

Bahías Plus, Carrizal 704, La Crucecita, T/F5870811 and at *Hotel Binniguenda*, Santa Cruz, T/F5870216, bahiasplus@huatulco.net.mex, airline reservations, tours, helpful, American Express representatives on 2nd floor of La Crucecita office.

Paraíso Huatulco, at *Hotel Flamboyan*, La Crucecita, T5870181, F5870190 and at Sheraton Resort, Tangolunda, T5810218 ext 788, Tangolunda, paraiso@ huatulco.net.mx, local and regional tours, diving, fishing, quad bikes. *Motor Tours*, at *Hotel Club Plaza Huatulco*, Tangolunda, T5810024, *Hotel Castillo Huatulco*, Santa Cruz, T5870050, local and regional tours, motorcycles and quad bikes. *Action Sports Marina*, at *Sheraton Resort*, Tangolunda, T5810055, ext 842, F5870537, diving lessons and tours, water sports. *Eco Aventuras*, La Crucecita, T5870669, adventure tours, cycling, rock climbing, kayaking, bird watching. *Jungle Tour*, at *Royal Maeva Hotel*, T5810000 ext 729, *cuatrimotos* tours.

Transport

Local Bus: A city bus runs from corner of Carrizal and Av Oaxaca in La Crucecita to Chahué, Tangolunda and Santa Cruz. 2nd class buses to Pochutla from Blvd Chahué and Riscalillo, La Crucecita, every 15 mins 0500-2000, US$0.90, 1 hr. 2nd class buses to Salina Cruz from Blvd Chahué and Bugambilia, frequent departures, 3 hrs. **Car hire**: *Dollar*, at *Sheraton Hotel*, *Royal Maeva Hotel* and airport, T5871528. *Advantage*, at *Hotel Castillo Huatulco*, Santa Cruz, T5871379. *Pesos*, at *Los Portales* restaurant, main plaza, La Crucecita, T5870070, beach buggies.

Long distance Air: Aeropuerto Bahías de Huatulco (HUX), is located 17 km northwest of Huatulco along Route 200, T5819099; airport van service T5819024, US$27. Taxi US$11, shared taxi (*colectivo*) US$6.50 pp, 20 mins. From Mexico City, Mexicana, daily at 1005 and 1335, returning from Huatulco 1150 and 1520; discounts for advanced purchase. From Oaxaca, Aerocaribe daily at 0700 and 1705, returning from Huatulco at 0750 and 1755. All international flights are charters and run in the boreal winter only.

Buses: Oaxaca, 1st class with Cristóbal Colón, Gardenia corner Ocotillo, La Crucecita, 2 daily, US$15, via Isthmus 8 hrs, luxury *Plus* service at 2100, US$18.50. 2nd class with Oaxaca-Pacífico, Calle Jazmín, La Crucecita, 1 daily, US$8.70, via Pochutla, 7 hrs. **Puerto Escondido**, with Cristóbal Colón, 1st class, 4 daily, US$4.35, 2 hrs; with Estrella Blanca, Gardenia corner Palma Real, La Crucecita, 1st class, 4 daily, US$4.70, 2½ hrs, 2nd class, 3 daily, US$3.50. **Acapulco**, with Estrella Blanca, 1st class, 4 daily, US$21, 9 hrs; 2nd class, 3 daily, US$15.60, 11 hrs. **Salina Cruz**, with Cristóbal Colón, 1st class, 4 daily continuing to Tehuantepec and Juchitán, US$5.60, 2½ hrs; *Plus* service, 2 daily, US$6.50; with Estrella Blanca, 3 daily, US$5.80, 2½ hrs. **Mexico City**, with Cristóbal

Colón, 1st class, 4 daily (arriving at various terminals), US$41, via Isthmus and Oaxaca, 14 hrs: with Estrella Blanca, 1st class, at 1800, US$40, via Acapulco, 13 hrs. **Tuxtla Gutiérrez**, with Cristóbal Colón, 1st class, 1045 and 2330, US$17, 8 hrs. **Tapachula**, with Cristóbal Colón, 1st class, at 2200, US$22, 10 hrs.

Directory **Airline offices** *Mexicana*, Hotel Castillo Huatulco, Santa Cruz, T5870223, airport T5819007. *Aerocaribe*, Hotel Castillo Huatulco, Santa Cruz, T5871220, airport T5810155. **Banks** *Bital*, Bugambilia corner Sabalí, La Crucecita, cash and TCs, cash advances through ATM only. *Bancomer*, Blvd Santa Cruz y Otitlán del Valle, Santa Cruz, cash and TCs. *Inverlat*, Blvd Santa Cruz, Santa Cruz, cash and TCs. *American Express*, Bahías Plus, Carrizal 704, La Crucecita, cash and TCs at good rates, Mon-Sat 0900-1400. *Casa de Cambio*, Guamuchil near the Plaza, La Crucecita, poor rates. **Communications** Internet: *Informática Mare*, Guanacastle 203, 2nd floor, near market, US$6.50 per hour. **Post office:** on Blvd Chahué, at south end of La Crucecita. **Laundry** *Lavandería Abril*, Gardenia 1403 y Pochote, La Crucecita, US$0.75 per kilo. *Lavandería Estrella*, Flamboyan y Carrizal, La Crucecita, US$0.75 per kilo, Mon-Sat, 0800-2100. **Medical services** *Especialidades Médicas Santa Cruz*, Flamboyan at Plaza, La Crucecita, private, English spoken. *Central Médica Huatulco*, Flamboyan 205, La Crucecita, T5870104, private. *IMSS* social security hospital, Blvd Chahué, just south of La Crucecita.

Isthmus of Tehuantepec

From the city of Oaxaca, Route 190 heads southeast towards the Golfo de Tehuantepec and the Pacific. At Km 116, in **San José de Gracia**, is the hotel and restaurant *El Mirador*, **D**. Clean, very friendly, noisy from passing trucks, overlooking a beautiful valley, parking in front. At Km 134 in the village of **El Camarón** is **E** *Hotel Santa Elena*. Clean, friendly, fan and TV. There are some basic restaurants in the village.

Only about 210 km separate the Atlantic and the Pacific at the hot, once heavily jungled Isthmus of Tehuantepec, where the land does not rise more than 250m. This narrowest point of Mexico is also the geographic boundary between North and Central America. There is a railway (freight service only) and a Trans-Isthmian Highway between Salina Cruz and Coatzacoalcos, the terminal cities on the two oceans. The regional airport at Ixtepec has flights to Oaxaca and Mexico City.

The Isthmus has a strong cultural character all of its own. The people are *mestizos* and descendants of several different indigenous groups, but Zapotecs predominate. Once a matriarchal society, Zapotec women continue to play a very important role in local affairs. Their typical dress is most intricate and beautiful, and they are high-pressure saleswomen. The men for the most part work in the fields, or as potters or weavers, or at the Salina Cruz oil refinery.

The Isthmian region of Oaxaca is dominated by three neighbouring cities: Tehuantepec is the smallest and most authentic, Juchitán has the largest and most interesting market, while Salina Cruz is a modern industrial city and port. The climate throughout the area can be oppressive, very hot and quite humid, hence the region's many cultural events usually take place late in the evening. Winds are very strong on and near the Isthmus, because of the inter-mingling of Pacific and Caribbean weather systems. Drivers of high-sided vehicles must take great care.

Salina Cruz

Phone code: 971
Colour map 4, grid C2
Population: 71,464

A modern and industrial city and port, with broad avenues and a large central plaza, Salina Cruz is surrounded by hills and many poor neighbourhoods. The centre is pleasant enough however and, although there is little of outstanding interest here, it offers a good selection of accommodations and services for those breaking a journey or visiting for work. There is a naval base, a large oil refinery and related petrochemical industries, as well as the Pacific terminus of the Transisthmian Railway and the Carretera Transístmica. Salina Cruz is located 17 km south of Tehuantepec and 174 km east of Huatulco, at the junction of the Carretera Transístmica (185) and the Carretera Costera (200). Some of the nearby beaches are quite scenic but oil pollution, high winds, dangerous surf, and sharks all conspire against would-be bathers. Do not park close to the beach, your vehicle may be sandblasted. The **tourist office**, Regiduría de Turismo, is at city hall opposite the plaza. The *Fiesta de la Santa Cruz* is held 3-6 May.

Excursions Ten kilometres to the southeast is a picturesque fishing village with **La Ventosa** beach which, as the name says, is windy. In 1528 the Spanish conquerors established a shipyard here; the old lighthouse, **El Faro de Cortés**, can still be seen. Buses go to the beach every 30 minutes from a corner of the main square. **Sleeping D** *La Posada de Rustrian*. Overlooking the sea, with bath in new block, half in old block, poor value; several other *pensiones* in **D** and **E** ranges. Friendly family at the top of the dirt road coming from Salina Cruz (on the right) and 200m after the first path that leads down to the beach, rents hammocks, US$1 a night, fried fish US$1. *Champas*, or hammocks under thatch shelters by the beach, US$1 a night. The owners serve drinks and food (fish, shrimps, crabs just caught) from early morning on. Prices often high. Many seafood restaurants and bars in town; at the end of the road which crosses the village is a good restaurant under a high palm roof, excellent fish.

Warning It is not safe to wander too far off along the beach alone, nor to sleep on the beach or in your car.

The coast west of Salina Cruz is quite scenic, with several high sand dunes and lagoons; shrimp farms have been set up in this area. Just west of the city is the village of Salinas del Marquez; the beach of **Las Escolleras** in Salinas is popular with locals. Urban bus service from the park in Salina Cruz every 30 minutes.

Sleeping **B** *Lena Real*, Avila Camacho 514, T40085, F43379. A/c, bar. **C** *Costa Real*, Progreso 22, near Avila Camacho, T40293, F45111. A/c, restaurant, parking. **C** *Altagracia*, 5 de Mayo 520, T40726. A/c, bar. **C** *Calendas*, Puerto Angel 408, T/F44574. A/c. **C** *María del Carmen*, Manzanillo 17 and Tampico, T45625, F45421. A/c, modern, nice, **D** with fan. **C** *El Parador*, Carretera Transístmica Km 60, T62951. A/c, pool. Recommended. **C** *Misión San José*, Pacífico 9, T42215. A/c, restaurant, pool. **D** *Pacífico*, Avila Camacho 709, T/F45552. A/c, cheaper with fan, restaurant. **D** *Las Palmas*, Mazatlán 46, T40362, F40357, 1 block from plaza. A/c, clean. **D** *Fuentes*, Avila Camacho 411, T43403. Bath, a/c, **E** with fan. **D** *Magda*, 5 de Mayo 43, T40107, ½ block from Zócalo. Bath, a/c, **E** with fan. **D** *Bugambilias*, 5 de Mayo 24, T44404, F41896. A/c, hot water, **E** with fan. **D** *Posada del Jardín*, Avila Camacho 108, T40162. A/c, bath, **E** with fan. **E** *Ríos*, Wilfrido Cruz 405, T40337. Reasonable.

Eating *El Lugar*, corner of Acapulco and 5 de Mayo on 1st floor, opposite the plaza. Mexican food, good. *Aloha*, Wilfrido Cruz 13-A. Seafood and regional dishes. *Aguascalientes*, Avila Camacho 422. Fish. *Vittorios Pizza*, 5 de Mayo 404. Italian. *Olimpo Pizzas*, Tampico 73. Italian and fish. Several restaurants in outdoor settings along the Carretera Transístmica; many seafood restaurants at La Ventosa beach.

Tour operators *Servicios Turísticos Gilsa*, Tampico 53, T/F44497, airline reservations, transport to airport, helpful.

Guerrero, Oaxaca & the Isthmus

Transport **Air** Regional airport at Ciudad Ixtepec, transport to airport US$9 pp.

Buses Regional service to **Tehuantepec** (US$0.65) and **Juchitán** (US$1.40) every 10 mins with Istmeños, 0500-0000, from Progreso west of Tampico, by train tracks. Frequent 2nd class service to **Huatulco**, 3 hrs. There is a joint bus station for Cristóbal Colón, ADO, AU and Sur at the north end of town, by the Carretera Transístmica. To **Oaxaca**, 1st class: Cristóbal Colón, 8 daily, US$10.20, 6 hrs; 2nd class: Oaxaca-Istmo, 3 daily, US$8.15, 6 hrs. To **Pochutla**, 1st class: Cristóbal Colón, 5 daily; 2nd class: Estrella Blanca, 3 daily, US$7, 3-4 hrs. To **Puerto Escondido**, 2nd class, Estrella Blanca, 4 daily, US$5.50, 5 hrs. To **Tuxtla Gutiérrez** and **San Cristóbal de las Casas**, 2 daily buses come from Oaxaca or Puerto Escondido and are very often full, book well in advance, US$12.30 (Tuxtla), US$15 (San Cristóbal); alternatively, take a 2nd class bus to **Juchitán**, then to Arriaga and from there to Tuxtla and San Cristóbal; a long route. To **Tapachula** by Cristóbal Colón 2nd class, along the coast, 9-10 hrs, 0740 and 2030, US$14.50, 1st class bus at 2000, US$17.60. To **Coatzacoalcos**, US$12.15, 6 hrs.

Directory **Banks** *Bancomer*, Avila Camacho. *Bital*, Avila Camacho and Coatzacoalcos. Both change cash and TCs. **Communications** Internet: service from *Edtzin*, Tampico 40 and *Nautinet*, Tampico 15; both US$2.20 per hour. **Laundry** *Alborada*, Tampico and Guaymas, US$1.65 per kilo. **Medical services** Hospital Civil, Avila Camacho, Centre, T40110.

Tehuantepec

Phone code: 971
Colour map 4, grid C2
Population: 36,888
Altitude: 150m

Santo Domingo Tehuantepec, 257 km from Oaxaca, is a colourful town which conserves the region's indigenous flavour. Robust Zapotec matrons in bright dresses ride standing in the back of motorized tricycles known as *moto-carros*. The town is friendly but not particularly clean. Life moves slowly here, centered on the plaza, which has arcades on one side, and an adjacent market, the best place to admire the Zapotec dress. In the plaza is a statue of Máximo Ramón Ortiz (1816-55) composer of the *zandunga*, the legendary theme music of the Isthmus, which is still very popular. The meandering Río Tehuantepec is two blocks from the plaza, by the highway. Due to the importance of Tehuantepec during the early colonial period, many churches were built here; attractive white churches with coloured trim dot the landscape. Houses are low, in white or pastel shades.

Sights The **Casa de la Cultura** is housed in the 16th-century Dominican ex-convent Rey Cosijopi. The building is quite run-down, but original frescoes can still be seen on some walls. There is a library and some simple exhibits of regional archaeology, history and costumes. Ask the caretaker to open the exhibits for you. The **Museo Casa de la Señora Juana C Romero** is a chalet built entirely with materials brought from France; Sra Romero's great-granddaughter lives there today, ask for permission to visit the house.

Excursions To the northwest of town off the road to Oaxaca, are the unrestored ruins of **Guiengola**, 'the Mexican Machu Picchu', so called because of its lonely location on a mountain. It has walls up to 3m high, running, it is said, for 40 km; there are the remains of two pyramids and a ball court. This last fortress of the Zapotecs was never conquered (*guiengola* is the Zapotec word for fortress); Alvarado and his forces marched past it in 1522. Take the 0500 bus from Tehuantepec towards Oaxaca and get off at the Puente las Tejas bridge (8 km from Tehuantepec); this is the last place to buy water on the way to the ruins. Take the turning at the signpost '*Ruinas Guiengola 7 km*'. Walk 5 km then turn left, uphill, to the car park. From here it is 1½ hours walk to the ruins, there are no facilities or entry fees. Try to return before 0900 because it gets very hot; take plenty of water. Alternatively, take a taxi to the car park and ask the driver to return for you three hours later (US$5.50 each trip), or drive there.

Nine kilometres from Tehuantepec, taking the turn-off at Hotel Calli and going past the *Santa Teresa Trailer Park*, is **Santa María La Mixtequilla**, on the shores of the Tehuantepec river, where many herons can be seen at dawn and dusk. Take the blue Mixtequilla city bus from the Monte de Piedad bus stop in the centre of town.

Sleeping **B** *Calli*, on the road to Juchitán, just north of town, T50085, F51113. A/c, pool, gardens, restaurant, parking. **C** *Guiexhoba*, on the road to Oaxaca, T51714, F51710. A/c, mini-fridge, pool, restaurant, parking. **D** *Donají*, Juárez 10, T50064, F50448, in Centre. A/c, **E** with fan, clean, friendly. Recommended. **D** *Oasis*, Melchor Ocampo 8, T50008, F50835, 1 block from plaza. Good atmosphere, with bath and a/c, **E** with fan, simple, safe parking, owner Julín Contreras is helpful, good information on local history and traditions. **E** *Casa de Huéspedes Istmo*, Hidalgo 31, T50019, 1½ blocks from the main plaza. Quiet, basic, with lovely patio. **E** *Casa de Huéspedes La Tehuanita*, Aldama 62. Fan. **F** *Posada Hasdar*, next to *Oasis*. Fan, shared bath, very basic.

Camping *Santa Teresa Trailer Park*, east side of town, 8 km off Route 190 (take side road at *Hotel Calli* and follow signs or Mixtequilla city bus from the center of town), by sugar cane plantation and mill. US$5.50 for car and 2 people, US$3.80 per tent, cold showers, public conveniences, drinking water, restaurant, lovely mango grove, very friendly owner.

Eating *Café Colonial*, Juana C Romero 66. Good *comida corrida* and *à la carte*, a variety of Mexican dishes, clean, friendly. *Restaurant Scaru*, Leona Vicario 4. Good food, fish and seafood specialities, upscale, nice courtyard and mural. *Nanixe*, at *Hotel Calli*. Good regional and international food. *Guiexhoba*, at *Hotel Guiexhoba*. Also regional and international. *Mariscos Silvia*, Av Juárez by the park. Excellent shrimp, moderate.

Tehuantepec

■ Sleeping	2 Donají	● Eating
1 Casa de Huéspedes Istmo	3 Oasis	1 Café Colonial
	4 Posada Hasdar	2 Scaru

Guerrero, Oaxaca & the Isthmus

Mariscos Angel, 5 de Mayo No 1, by entrance from Salina Cruz. Seafood, moderately priced. Cheap food on top floor of market, here you can get the local specialty, pork or chicken, stuffed with potatoes, but beware of hygiene. The local *quesadillas* made of maize and cheese are delicious; sold at bus stops.

Festivals Festivals and traditions are very important in Tehuantepec. There are many colourful and ceremonious celebrations throughout the year, for which the women don their elaborate embroidered dresses and lace halos, known as *resplandores*. The town is divided into 15 wards, each one has a patron saint. *Fiestas Patronales* are held in each neighbourhood for several days in honour of the local patron, these culminate on the saint's day. In the centre of Tehuantepec the *fiestas* of Santo Domingo are held during the 1st week of **Aug**, in the San José neighbourhood the *fiestas* in honour of St John the Baptist are held during the week leading up to **24 Jun**, and so forth. Another type of celebration are *velas*, very formal dances; the **Vela Zandunga** is held **19 May**, while the **Velas de Agosto** are held throughout the Isthmus in **mid-Aug**, and the **Vela Tehuantepec** is on **26 Dec**.

Transport **Road** Tehuantepec is at the junction of the Carretera Transístmica (185) and Route 190 which connects it with Oaxaca, 257 km away.

Local 3-wheeled motorized rickshaws (*moto-carros*) take locals around town, you have to stand and hold on to the railing.

Long distance **Air**: regional airport in Ciudad Ixtepec.

Buses: regional Istmeños buses leave form the highway (Carretera Cristóbal Colón), by the river, at the end of 5 de Mayo: to **Salina Cruz**, every 10 mins, 0500 to midnight, US$0.65, 45 mins; to *Juchitán*, every 10 mins, 0500 to midnight, US$0.80, 1 hr. There is a joint bus station for Cristóbal Colón, ADO, AU and Sur on the outskirts of town; taxi to Zócalo US$1, *moto-carro* US$0.50 or 15 mins walk (walking not recommended at night). To **San Cristóbal de la Casas** Cristóbal Colón, 0030 and 1400, US$14.50, 6½ hrs. To **Tuxtla Gutiérrez**, Cristóbal Colón, 0030, 1400, 2200, US$11.20, 4½ hrs. To **Tonalá** and **Tapachula**, Cristóbal Colón, 2 nightly, US$7.60 (Tonalá), US$16.50 (Tapachula). Bus to **Arriaga** at 0600, 0800, 1800 to connect to Tonalá (not confirmed). **NB** It is not always possible to get a reservation with Cristóbal Colón in Tehuantepec, for Chiapas destinations; you have a better chance from Salina Cruz (T41441) or Juchitán, where more buses stop. To **Coatzacoalcos** ADO and Sur, 1st class 5 daily, US$11, 6 hrs; 2nd class every 30 mins, US$8.25. To **Oaxaca**, **Pochutla**, and **Puerto Escondido**, Cristóbal Colón, 1st class 4 daily, US$6.20 (Huatulco), US$7.95 (Pochutla), US$10.55 (Puerto Escondido); to Huatulco 2nd class, 0600, 1330, US$4.80. To **Villahermosa**, Cristóbal Colón 1st class, US$14, 8 hrs, 2nd class US$10.50. To **Tuxtepec** and **Veracruz**, AU via Sayula, 1040, 2140, US$10.65, 6 hrs (Tuxtepec), US$19 (Veracruz). To **Cancún**, ADO at 1430, US$54. To **Mexico City**, Cristóbal Colón, *Plus* service, 2030, US$42.60; 1st class, 2000, 2145, US$36.40.

Directory **Banks** *Bital*, Juana C Romero, open 0800-1700. *Bancomer*, 5 de Mayo. *Bancrecer*, 5 de Mayo. All change cash and TCs. **Communications** Internet: service in Salina Cruz or Juchitán. **Tourist offices** SEDETUR regional delegation for the Isthmus, Carretera Transístmica 7, 2nd floor, opposite the petrol station, T51236, F50802. Regiduría de Turismo at Palacio de Gobierno.

Juchitán

Phone code: 971
Colour map 4, grid C2
Population: 62,065

Twenty-seven kilometres from Tehuantepec is the larger and more modern city of Juchitán de Zaragoza, an important commercial and cultural centre on the Isthmus. It has a nice plaza next to impressive colonial municipal buildings and many churches including that of **San Vicente Ferrer**, the city's patron saint. Many Zapotec women here still wear traditional costumes as everyday dress. The **tourist office** is at the Palacio de Gobierno.

Sights

The **Mercado Central 5 de Septiembre** is the largest market on the Isthmus; traditional barter still takes place here. The meat and produce section is dirty, but the crafts section on the second floor is well worth a visit; this is the best place to see the elaborate embroidered Zapotec dresses which sell for up to US$600. In front of the municipal building is the **Corredor de las Flores** where colourful flowers are sold by women in equally colourful outfits. The **Casa de la Cultura** has good art and archaeological exhibits, a library, bookstore (also sells music), and *cafetería*.

Excursions

South of Juchitán and stretching for some 100 km to the east are three very large, shallow lagoons. On the shores of Laguna Superior, the closest one, 10 km south of the city, is the fishing village of **Playa Vicente**; across from here are several scenic islands. In Laguna Mar Muerto, the furthest one to the east, there are salt pans.

About 20 km north of Juchitán along the Ixtepec road are the springs of **Magdalena Tlacotepec** and **Santiago Laollaga**, once the recreational baths of the Zapotec rulers, today these crystalline springs are a favourite swimming spot for all *istmeños*.

Sleeping

C *Don Alex Lena Real*, 16 de Septiembre 48, T11064, F11063. Modern comfortable rooms, a/c, clean, **D** in older wing, cheaper with fan, restaurant. *El Palacio de Gemas*, next door. Recommended for gemstones, good selection at reasonable prices. **C** *López Lena Palace*, 16 de Septiembre 70, T11389, F11388. A/c, restaurant. **C** *Gran Hotel Santo Domingo*, Carretera Transístmica, T11959, F13642. A/c, restaurant, pool, **B** in suite. **D** *La Mansión*, 16 de Septiembre 11, T12055, F11241. A/c, restaurant. **D** *Hotel Casa Río*, has an Indian name, *Coty*, not posted, next to *Casa Río* shop, near market. Clean. **D** *Lidxi Biuxa*, 2 de Abril 79, T11299. A/c, pool. **D** *Alfa*, Carretera Panamericana Km 821, T10327. A/c, bath, cheaper with fan. **D** *Juchitán*, 16 de Septiembre 72, T11065. Simple rooms, a/c, **E** for basic room with fan. **D** *Malla*, across from bus station, T12730. With bath, a/c. **E** *Modelo*, 2 de Abril 64, T11241, near market. With bath, fan, basic. The Casa de Cultura can help if you want to stay with local people and learn about their culture, eg with Florinda Luis Orozco, Callejón de los Leones 18, between Hidalgo and Aldama.

Eating

Casa Grande, Juárez 125, on the main square. In a beautifully restored colonial house, good food, live music. *Café Colón*, Carretera Panamericana, close to the bus station. Good. *Los Chapulines*, 5 de Septiembre esq Morelos. Regional and international food, *comida corrida* and à la carte, a/c. *Deyaurihe*, 5 de Septiembre esquina Aldama. Mexican food, *comida corrida* and à la carte. *Mariscos Angel*, Aldama 100 and 5 de Septiembre. Seafood. *Pizzería La Vianda*, 5 de Septiembre 54-B. Pizza and seafood. *La Tablita*, 5 de Septiembre 15. Regional and other Mexican dishes.

Festivals

Although every birth and wedding is reason for a colourful celebration, best known are the *velas*, formal dances in a decorated setting resembling a European palace, for which the attendees wear traditional dress. Some *velas* also include a *regada de frutas y convite de flores* in which the participants offer gifts of fruits and flowers. There are *velas* throughout the year, the most important ones are held during **May** in honour of San Vicente Ferrer.

Shopping

Regional crafts include embroidered regional costumes, straw and reed basketry, red clay pottery, wooden toys, filigree jewellery, and hammocks.

Guerrero, Oaxaca & the Isthmus

Tour operators *Viajes Zaymar*, 5 de Septiembre 100B, T/F10792, airline bookings.

Transport **Air** The regional airport is at Ciudad Ixtepec.

Road Juchitán is 26 km northeast of Tehuantepec. At La Ventosa, 14 km northeast of Juchitán, the road splits: the Carretera Transístmica (Route 185) continues north towards Coatzacoalcos on the Gulf of Mexico, and the Carretera Costera (Route 200) goes east to San Pedro Tapanatepec, where it splits again, 1 road going to Tuxtla Gutiérrez and the other to Tapachula.

Buses Regional bus service to **Tehuantepec** (US$0.80) and **Salina Cruz** (US$1.40), every 15 mins with Istmeños, 0500-0000, from Prolongación 16 de Septiembre, by the highway to Tehuantepec. Joint bus station for Cristóbal Colón, ADO, Sur and AU at Prolongación 16 de Septiembre, just south of the highway to Tehuantepec. To **Tuxtla Gutiérrez**, Cristóbal Colón, 5 daily, US$10. To **San Cristóbal de las Casas**, Cristóbal Colón, 3 daily, US$13.40. To **Tapachula**, ADO at 0230, US$18; Cristóbal Colón, 2 nightly, US$15.55; Sur 0230 and 1600, US$11.60. To **Oaxaca**, ADO luxury, 3 daily, US$12.50; 1st class: ADO 3 daily, Cristóbal Colón 7 daily, US$10.55, 6 hrs. To **Mexico City**, ADO luxury, at 2145, US$56, ADO 1st class, 1900 and 2100, US$41.40; AU 6 daily US$32. To **Coatzacoalcos**, ADO 13 daily, US$10; Sur, every 20 mins, US$6.50. To **Tuxtepec**, AU at 1115, US$9.80. To **Veracruz**, ADO 0055 and 2130, US$21.30; AU 1115, US$18.30. To **Huatulco**, ADO 0600, US$8.60; Cristóbal Colón, 5 daily, US$7.20; Sur, 3 daily, US$5.55. To **Pochutla** and **Puerto Escondido**, Cristóbal Colón, 4 daily, US$11.52 (Puerto) US$8.90 (Pochutla); Sur, 2330, US$8.90 (Puerto), US$6.85 (Pochutla).

Directory **Banks** *Bancomer*, 16 de Septiembre by the main plaza, Mon-Fri 0830-1400, cash and TCs. *Bital*, 16 de Septiembre y Alvaro Obregón, Mon-Fri 0800-1900, Sat 0900-1400, cash and TCs. **Communications** Internet: *Servitel*, Efraín Gómez and 16 de Septiembre, US$4.35 per hour. *Istmored*, just north of town on the road to Ixtepec, US$3.25 per hour.

A road runs 19 km northwest to **Ciudad Ixtepec** railway junction. South of Ixtepec is a military base and the regional airport.

Sleeping and eating All hotels in the vicinity of the train station: **D** *El Regente Turista*, Nicolás Bravo 10, T/F30237. A/c, restaurant. **D** *Lico*, 16 de Septiembre y Moctezuma, T30424. Bath, a/c. **E** *Casa de Huéspedes San Gerónimo*, close to train station and market. Clean, good. **E** *Panamericano*. Noisy from railway station. **E** *San Juan*, 16 de Septiembre 127. Bath, some with a/c, acceptable. *La Flor del Café*, Av Ferrocarril. Regional food. *La Tropicana*, 16 de Septiembre. Mexican cooking. *La Manzana*, Nicolás Bravo 10. Seafood and international cooking.

Transport **Air**: To **Mexico City**, with Aeromar, 2 daily flights weekdays, 1 daily flight weekends, US$168-US$257. To **Oaxaca**, with Aerocaribe, 1 daily flight at 0935, US$85.

Crossing the Isthmus

From Juchitán, Route 185 crosses the **Isthmus of Tehuantepec** to **Coatzacoalcos**, passing through **Matías Romero**, a quiet town set in the hills, with a less oppressive climate than other parts of the Isthmus. Nearby are some caves. The road across the Isthmus is straight but is not always fast to drive because of high winds (changing air systems from Pacific to Atlantic).

Sleeping and eating C *Real del Istmo*, Carretera Transístmica Km 136, T7221300, F7220088. A/c, safe parking, good restaurant. **D** *Anhe*, Corregidora Sur 202, T7220209, F7220026. In the centre. **D** *Juan Luis*, Carretera Transístmica Km 195, T7220611. Pool, restaurant. **E** *Gil Mary*, Hombres Ilustres 607b, T7220624, F7220224. As well as the restaurant in the Real del Istmo, there is *Piscis*, Guerrero 302. Seafood. *Chava*, 16 de Septiembre, 218. Regional food. *Las Flores*, Carretera Transístmica Km 197. Mexican dishes.

Petrol and food on sale at the half-way point, **Palomares**, where there is a paved road to Tuxtepec (see page 223), 2½ hours drive. A few kilometres south of Palomares a gravelled road enters on the eastern side; this passes under an imposing gateway, *La Puerta de Uxpanapa*, where some 24,500 families are being settled on land reclaimed from the jungle.

Further north the Carretera Transístmica reaches the junction with the Veracruz-Villahermosa Gulf Coast road at **Acayucan**.

Sleeping: **D** *Hotel Joalicia*, Zaragoza 4. **D** *Hotel Ritz*, Av Hidalgo 7, T50024. Shower, fan, noisy, parking. **D** *Los Angeles*. Cheaper without TV, clean, fans, friendly, pool, owners speak some English, space for car inside. **E** *San Miguel*. With bath, hot water and fan, not very attractive, but OK. **E** *Iglesias*, 267 km from Veracruz on toll road (first class buses 'de paso', very hard to get on, 4 hrs to Veracruz, second class 5½ hrs). From Acayucan, continue on Route 180 for Minatitlán, Coatzacoalcos and Villahermosa (Tabasco).

Guerrero, Oaxaca & the Isthmus

Michoacán

9

Michoacán

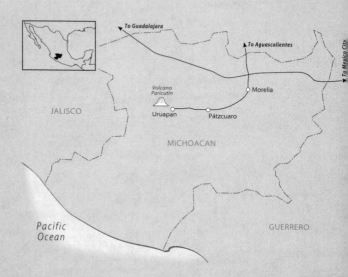

The State of Michoacán, where the Purépecha, or Tarascan Indians live, is a country of deep woods, fine rivers and great lakes. Fruit, game, and fish are abundant.

Visitors are drawn by the **Tarascan customs**, folklore, way of life, craft skills (pottery, wood work and lacquer), music and especially dance. Try and see at least one of the following: they are well worth the effort. Los Viejitos (Old Men; Janitzio, 1 January); Los Sembradores (The Sowers; 2 February); Los Moros (The Moors; Lake Pátzcuaro region, fiestas and carnival); Los Negritos (Black Men; fiestas at Tzintzuntzán); Los Apaches (4 February, at the churches); Las Canacuas (Crown Dance; Uruapan, on Corpus Christi). The Day of the Dead, a very important date in the Mexican calendar of festivals, is especially prominent in Michoacán. Try to be in Pátzcuaro on 1 November when almost every village around the lake honours its dead; it is a festive occasion, but also profoundly spiritual.

One of the most impressive sights in all of Mexico may be experienced at **El Campanario Ecological Reserve** when millions of Monarch butterflies take to the wing.

There are many small pre-Hispanic sites to be explored en route, and the open chapel at **Cuitzeo** should not be missed. Observe craftsmen at Paracho create guitars, violins and mandolins and see chillies drying in the scorching sun at Queréndaro. As elsewhere in Mexico, the colonial architecture will impress and the natural beauty of **Paricutín volcano** will bemuse. A few days relaxing on the almost deserted beaches of **Playa Azul** will prepare you for the next stage of your journey.

Michoacán

Morelia

Phone code: 43
Colour map 3, grid B4
Population: 759,000
Altitude: 1950m
Km 314

Founded in 1541, Morelia, capital of Michoacán state, is a rose-tinted city with grand, attractive colonial buildings, delightful courtyards and shady plazas. It is a quiet, provincial city although the narrow streets suffer from vehicle pollution.

Ins and outs

The airport is about 27 km north of Morelia. Blue-and-white *Aeropuerto* buses will take you to the centre. There is a train station about 2 km from town. Always check that passenger services are still running before planning a journey by train. The bus terminal is close to the town centre, on Eduardo Ruiz between León Guzmán and Gómez Farías. For details see page 462. Morelia is connected by Route 43 to Salamanca, Route 14 to Uruapan and Route 15 to Zamora and Mexico City.

The **tourist office** is inside Palacio Clavijero (south end), Nigromante 79, T128081, F129816, has local hotel information list and map, English spoken. ■ *0800-2000, Mon-Fri, 0900-1900 Sat and Sun.* Also tourist information kiosk at bus terminal, but not always open. Good city maps are available from *Casa de Cambio Troca Mex*, Melchor Ocampo y I Zaragoza and on Guillermo Preito, just south of the Plaza de las Rosas. There are many good language schools in Morelia (see Directory page 463).

Morelia

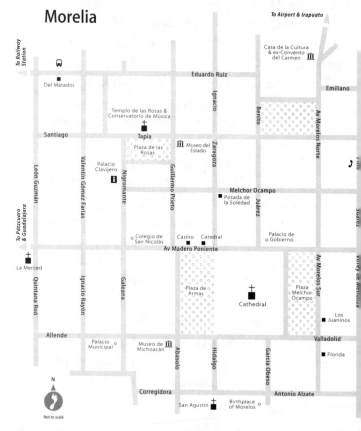

Michoacán

Sights

The **Cathedral** (1640), is set between the two main plazas, with graceful towers and a fine façade, in what is called 'sober baroque'; there are paintings by Juárez in the sacristy. The **Santuario de la Virgen de Guadalupe**, east of the aqueduct, has an ornate interior of terracotta garlands and buds, painted in pastels, like being inside a giant wedding cake. There are four huge oil paintings of the missionaries Christianizing the Indians. Other important churches are the modernized **Templo de la Cruz**, and the 18th-century **Templo de las Rosas** in the delightful plaza of the same name (its ex-Convento now houses the Conservatorio de Música). The oldest of Morelia's churches is the **Templo de San Francisco** of the Spanish Renaissance period, although it lacks many of the decorative features of that style. The **Templo de las Monjas** has an extravagant baroque façade, constructed in 1727. The **Templo de San Agustín** (16th century) has a more Gothic influence but is also imposing.

Even more interesting than the colonial churches are the many fine colonial secular buildings still standing. The Independence hero José María Morelos, the reformer Melchor Ocampo, and the two unfortunate Emperors of Mexico (Agustín de Iturbide and the Archduke Maximilian of Austria) are commemorated by plaques on their houses. **Morelos' birthplace**, at Corregidora 113, is open to visitors, admission free. The **Colegio de San Nicolás** (1540) is the oldest surviving institution of higher education in Latin America. (It has a summer school for foreign students.) Opposite is the **Centro Cultural Universitario**, with many free events. The fine former Jesuit college, now called the **Palacio Clavijero**, corner of Madero and Nigromante contains government offices and an extensive market selling *artesanía* and sweets in the arcades, with a helpful tourist office on the ground floor. Nearby on Avenida Madero is a library with carved wooden balconies and many historical volumes. At the east edge of the downtown area, on the road to Mexico City, are the 224 arches of a ruined **aqueduct**, built in 1788 (walk 11 blocks east from Cathedral along Avenida Madero). Both Banamex and Bancomer have their offices in magnificent old houses on Madero Poniente, near the Plaza; the patio of the former is especially fine. Also notable are the **Law School**, in the former monastery of **San Diego**, next to the Santuario de la Virgen de Guadalupe, past the aqueduct; the **Palacio de Gobierno** (1732-70), facing the Cathedral; the **Palacio Municipal**; and the **Palacio Federal**, built in the 18th century, and formerly a convent. Visit also the churches of **La Merced**, with its

arismo
Plan de Ayala
ata
20 de Noviembre
Alvaro
Belisario
Aquiles Serdán
Obregón
Domínguez
Templo de las Monjas
Palacio Federal
To Aqueduct, Toluca & Mexico City
Madero Oriente
Templo de la Cruz
F Juan D'Sn M
F Alonso
Navarrete
Bartolomé de las Casas
Vasco de Quiroga
San Francisco & Casa de Artesanías
V Santa María
Humboldt
Beau Mon
Corregidora

Michoacán

lovely tower and strange, bulging *estípites* (inverted pyramidal supports), **Las Capuchinas**, Ortega y Montaño, southeast of the centre, which has some Churrigueresque *retablos*, and **Santa María**, on a hilltop south of the city.

Next to the Plaza de Morelos is the Alameda de Calzones, a shady pedestrianized walkway with restored mansions leading three blocks to the **Fuente Tarasca**, a fountain with three bare-chested women holding up a giant basket of fruit.

Thursday and Sunday are market days: specialities are pottery, lacquer, woodcarving, jewellery, blankets and leather sandals; in this connection see the **Casa de Artesanías de Michoacán**, in the ex-Convento de San Francisco, next to the church of the same name; it is full of fine regional products for sale but they are not cheap. The small shops upstairs, some of which have local artisans at work, have better quality crafts than in the shops downstairs. The masks are particularly fine. ■ *The shop on the ground floor is open Monday-Saturday 1000-1500, 1700-2000.*

Museums **Museo de Michoacán**, Calle Allende 305, has a collection of objects relating to the history of Michoacán from prehispanic times to the present day. ■ *0900-1900 daily, 0900-1400 Sun, US$4.35.* The **Casa de la Cultura**, Avenida Morelos Norte, housed in the ex-Convento del Carmen, has a good collection of masks from various regions, and also of crucifixes. The centre hosts arts workshops (nominal fee), daily music and dance performances, exhibitions, etc. ■ *Daily, free.* The **Museo del Estado**, in the house of Iturbide's wife (Casa de la Emperatriz), southeast corner of Jardín de las Rosas, is well worth a visit. Most of the ground floor is dedicated to Tarascan history and culture, lots of information about Michoacán, and, at the front, an old pharmacy with all its bottles, cabinets, scales, etc, intact. ■ *Mon-Sat 0900-1400, 1600-2000, Sun same but closes at 1900, free.* The **Museo Casa de Morelos**, on Morelos Sur, about three blocks south of the Cathedral, has exhibits on the Independence movement and its hero, José María Morelos. ■ *0900-1900, US$1.20.* **Museo de Arte Contemporáneo Alfredo Zalce**, Avenida Acueducto, in a 19th-century French-style building, has temporary exhibitions. ■ *Closes for siesta, reopens 1600, closed Mon.* For a guided tour of the city, contact David, front desk, Villa Montaña Hotel, where there are many other tours on offer, including one to the Monarch Butterfly Reserve (see below).

Parks & zoos There is a fairly good zoo in Parque Juárez, 25 minutes walk south of the centre along Galeana. There is also a Planetarium on Ventura Pte at Ticomete, in the Centro de Convenciones.

Essentials

Sleeping **L** *Fiesta Inn*, Av Ventura Puente, esquina. Av Camelinas (in convention complex), T150050/150023. Very pretty grounds, tennis courts, pools. **AL** *Calinda Holiday Inn*, Av Acueducto, T145969. Colonial-style, modern. **AL** *Holiday Inn*, Av Camelinas 3466, Col Ocolusen, T143100, F150023. Very nice lobby, attractive grounds. **AL** *Los Juaninos*, Morelos Sur 39 centro, T120036, juaninos@mich 1.telmex.net.mx At one time the Episcopal Palace (1685), beautifully restored in 1998, rooftop restaurant overlooking Zócalo. Luxurious. **AL** *Virrey de Mendoza*, Portal Matamoros, T124940, F126719. Superb old-style building, poor restaurant, service could be better, could be cleaner, poor ventilation, ask for room at front with balcony. **A** *Alameda*, Av Madero Pte 313 y Jazmines, T122023, F138727. 'Flashy'. **A** *Posada de la Soledad*, Zaragoza 90 and Ocampo, T121888, F122111. Off the Plaza de Armas and much quieter. Fine courtyards, converted chapel as dining room, TV and fireplaces in rooms, parking opposite (free between 2000 and 0900, otherwise US$1 per hr), good value, María

Some of the cheaper hotels may have water only in the morning; check

Michoacán

Luisa speaks English. Recommended. **B** *Casino*, Best Western, Portal Hidalgo 229, main plaza, T131003, F121252. Clean, hot water, private bath, good restaurant. **B** *Catedral*, Zaragoza 37, T130783, F130467, close to plaza. Spacious, nice bar, restaurant closes quite early. Recommended. **B** *Plaza Morelos*, Glorieta Morelos 31, T124499, F128173. Large, cool, pleasant. **C** *Florida*,Morelos Sur 165, T121819, F121038. Clean, good value. **C** *Valladolid*, Portal Hidalgo 241, on main plaza, T120027, F124663. With bath, good value for its location but a bit drab.

D *del Matador*, E Ruiz 531, opposite bus station, T/F124649. Simple, with bath. **D** *Don Vasco*, Vasco de Quiroga 232, T/F121484. With shower and hot water, clean, safe, some rooms dingy. Recommended. **D** *Mintzicuri*, Vasco de Quiroga 227 (opposite *Don Vasco*), T120590, F120664. Clean, small rooms, hot shower, TV, parking, helpful tourist office. **D** *Posada del Cortijo*, at E Ruiz 673, T129642, F131281. Good value, but small rooms, overlooks the Casa de la Cultura, hot water. **D** *Posada de Luz*, Calle de Trabajo 32, T/F174878. Single rooms dingy.

Cheap hotels on **Morelos Norte**: **D** *Concordia*, Gómez Farías 328, T123052, F242949, round corner from bus station. TV and phone in rooms. **E** *Colonial*, corner with 20 de Noviembre 15, T121897, F131051. Pleasant, lots of hot water, good value. **On Madero Pte**: **D** *San Jorge*, No 719, T124610. With hot shower, clean. **E** *Vallarta*, No 670, T124095, fair. **E** *Fénix*, No 537, T120512. With bath, noisy, clean, cheap. **E** *Posada Lourdes*, No 340, T125603. Basic, clean, quiet, hot water. **F** *Señorial*, Santiago Tapiá 543, 1 block south from bus terminal. Basic, with bath. Cheap *posadas* and *casas de huéspedes* tend to be uninviting, although the half-dozen around the bus station are reported clean and cheap.

On **Santa María hill**, south of the city, with glorious views, are hotels **LL** *Villa Montaña*, Patzimba 201, T140231, F151423. Each room is a house on its own, run by French aristocrats, very expensive but value for money, superb restaurant. **AL** *Villa San José*, Patzimba 77, Col Vista Bella. T/F244545, sanjose@giga.com. Rooms have nice views and fireplaces. Reached only by car. **B** *Vista Bella*, Camino a Santa María s/n, Apdo Postal 135 (for mail), T120248, F140284. Large rooms with wood-burning fireplaces, TVs with VCRs and phones, parking, bar-restaurant, piano bar.

Motels B *Villa Centurión*, on road to Morelos, T132272. Good antiques, pool, TV. **C** *El Parador*, Highway 45, with trailer park. **C** *Las Palmas*, on road to Guadalajara, also trailer park. 2 good trailer parks on Route 126 between Morelia and the capital: *Balneario Las Ajuntas*, after Queréndaro, and *Balneario Atzimba*, hot springs at Zinapécuaro.

Youth hostel Known by its initials *IMJUDE* although some people refer to it as *CREA*, its former initials. At corner of Oaxaca and Chiapas No 180, T133177, 1 km southwest of bus station (walk west to Cuautla, then south along Cuautla to Oaxaca) **F** per person. Camping possible in a forest about 4 km south of centre on unnumbered road signposted to Pátzcuaro.

Café de Conservatorio, on Plaza de las Rosas (opposite music academy). Not cheap but nice atmosphere and tasty cakes. *Quinta Sol*, Aquiles Serdán 729, 5 blocks east of Morelos. Also vegetarian, good *comida corrida*, US$4, served from 1400; both close daily at 1700 and both closed Sunday. *El Viejo Paral*, Madero Ote and Quiroga, for cakes. And *comidas corridas* in an unnamed restaurant on Gómez Farías, on right hand side heading away from bus station, US$1.50. *La Flor de las Mercedes*, León Guzmán. Colonial-style house, beautiful decor, moderate prices. *Woolworth's*, Virrey de Mendoza and Madero. Pretty old building with stone vaulted ceilings. *Pollo-Coa*, Madero Ote 890, near aqueduct. Good food. *Viandas de San José*, Alvaro Obregón 263 and Zapata. Good cheap *comida corrida*, excellent service. Recommended. *Los Pioneros*, Aquiles Serdán y

Eating

The Mercado de Dulces, on Gómez Farías at west end of the Palacio Clavijero, is famous for ates (fruit jams), candies and rompope (an alcoholic drink similar to advocat).

Michoacán

Morelos Nte. Cheap, good local food. *La Bodega de la Iguana*, Av Camelinsa 3636, T144204. Very good traditional cuisine. Highly recommended. *Boca del Río*, Gómez Farías185. Good fish. *Café del Olmo*, Benito Juárez 95. In a nice colonial building. There is a good café in *Casa de la Cultura*, with delicious home-made cakes. *Café Colón*, Aquiles Serdán 265, good coffee.

Entertainment *Peña Bola Suriana*, Allende 355. Live traditional guitar music, open courtyard, small cover charge. Free weekly concerts are held in the Teatro Municipal.

Transport **Air** Many flights daily to and from Mexico City, 50 mins, also to other Mexican destinations: Guadalajara, León, Monterrey, Puerto Vallarta, Tepic, Tijuana, Uruapan and Zacatecas. To USA: Mexicana and Taesa to Chicago; Mexicana to Los Angeles, San Francisco and San José (California); Taesa to Oakland. 27 km from city. Dollar and Budget car rental offices.

Buses The terminal is on Eduardo Ruiz between León Guzmán and Gómez Farías, an easy walk to the town centre. Tourist kiosk, though not always open, restaurants and left luggage.
  Aguascalientes; Primera Plus ("plus" service) 0230, 0805, 1205, 1605, 1705, US$17. **Celaya**; Servicios Coordinados (1st class) 18 per day, US$6. **Colima**; Flecha Amarilla (2nd class) 0740, 1200, US$13.70. **Guadalajara**; ETN (luxury service) 0130, 0630, 0830, 1030, 1230, 1430, 1600, 1700, 1730, 2030, US$19.50. Flecha Amarilla 9 per day, US$10. Primera Plus 0900, 1300, 1530, US$14. By autopista, 0615, 0940, 1815, 2005, 2400. Servicios Coordinados 7 per day, US$11.80. **Guanajuato**; Flecha Amarilla 0650, 0825, 0930, 1330, 1525, US$7.70. Servicios Coordinados 0830, 1130, 1430, US$8. **León**; Flecha Amarilla every ½ hr until 2030, US$7.70. Primera Plus 16 per day, US$9.40. Servicios Coordinados 8 per day, US$8.30. **Manzanillo**; ETN (luxury service) 2230, US$24.50. **Mexico City**; ETN (luxury service) 23 departures daily, US$19.50. Herradura de Plata 25 "plus" departures daily, US$14.50. **Mexico City** (Terminal del Norte); Flecha Amarilla every ½ hr, US$12.50. **Mexico City** (Terminal de Occidente); Autobuses del Occidente (2nd class) every 10 mins. **Monterrey**; Turistar Ejecutivo (luxury service) 1700, US$54.20. **Nogales**; Transportes del Pacífico 2000, US$91.20. **Nuevo Laredo**; Turistar Ejecutivo (luxury service) 1700, US$70.30. Transportes Frontera (first class), 1600, US$50.30. **Pátzcuaro**; Primera Plus 1700, US$26. **Querétaro**; Flecha Amarilla 14 per day, US$7. Primera Plus 9 per day, US$8.60. Servicios Coordinados 15 per day, US$7.70. **San Luis Potosí**; Flecha Amarilla 10 per day, US$15. Primera Plus 0045, 0905, 1105, 1125, 1330, 1635, 2140, 2320, US$18.20. Servicios Coordinados 13 per day, US$16.50. **Tijuana**; Transportes del Pacífico 1530, US$102. **Uruapan**; ETN (luxury service) 1200, 1545, 1800, 1930, US$7. Flecha Amarilla 0730, 1100, 1415, 1730, 2030, US$5.40. Primera Plus 0100, 0540, 1445, 1700, 2200, US$5.80. **Zamora** (by autopista); Primera Plus 0900, 1300, 1530, US$6.20. Servicios Coordinados 9 per day, US$5.

Directory **Airlines** *Aeromar*, T128545; *Taeso*, T134105. **Banks** *Bancomer*, Av Madero Oriente, just off main plaza, VISA, ATM. There is an ATM just east of the Hotel Casino that accepts VISA, MC, and cards of the Plus and Cirrus networks. There is a *Banco Inverlat* ATM next to the bus station at the corner of Eduardo Ruiz and Gómez Farías that accepts American Express cards. **Communications** Internet: *Chatroom Cybercafé*, Nigromante 132A, Mon-Sat 0900-2200, Sun 1200-2100, US$1.60 per hr, spacious, tranquil, a real café. *Inter PC's*, Av Acuaducto 60, T/F120315, 0900-2100, US$1.60, cheaper Sun and 1400-1600 other days. *Shareweb Cybercafé*, Av Madero Ote, 573-c, T122446, mbllanco@morelia.teesa.com; morelia.teesa.com/~shareweb. Mon-Sat 0900-2200, Sun 1400-2200, US$2.20 per hr. *Ceica Computación*, Av. Madero Ote 796. T138546/121510. Charge US$2 per hr. *Cyber Café CEA*, Alvaro Obregón 148. T174381; F174376; cea@michl.telmex.net.mx, www.cea-mex.com. Charge US$1.50 per hr. Open 0930-1400, 1600-1930. *Global Answers*, Fray Antonio de San Miguel 228a, T173531. **Post Office**: in Palacio Federal. Long-distance phone and fax; Gómez Farías 113, near the *mercado de dulces*. Another at

Michoacán

the corner of Zaragosa and Melchor Ocampo. **Medical services** Dentist: *Dr Leopoldo Arroyo Contreras*, Abraham González 35, T120751, near Cathedral. Recommended. **Language schools** *Centro Mexicano de Idiomas*, Calz Fray Antonio de San Miguel 173, T124596, 132796. Intensive weekly classes (US$280 for 1st week); other courses available include handicrafts. Accommodation with families. *Baden-Powell Institute*, Antonio Alzate 565, T124070. From US$6.50 per hr to US$8.50 per hr, depending on length of course, lodging US$12 per day, including 3 meals, courses for all levels, plus cultural, social science and extracurricular courses. Highly recommended. *American Union Academy*, T144577. *Centro Cultural de Lenguas*, T158674/120589. *Instituto Cultural Mexicano Norteamericano*, T153140/153157. (See Learning Spanish in Essentials.) **Laundry** *Lavandería Chapultepec*, Ceballos 881. *Lavandería* on Santiago Tapiá towards bus station.

East of Morelia

The road east of Morelia soon climbs through 50 km of splendid mountain scenery of forests, waterfalls and gorges, to the highest point (Km 253), Puerto Gartan, and **Mil Cumbres** (2,886m), with a magnificent view over mountain and valley, and then descends into a tropical valley. A new, four-lane highway avoids the Mil Cumbres pass.

Another alternative to the Mil Cumbres pass is to take Route 126 from Morelia to **Queréndaro** (**E** *Hotel Imperial*, near church, pleasant rooms and courtyard, hot water, good value. Good *tacos* on main square). At a junction 10 km short of Zinapécuaro, turn right to join Route 15 (to Toluca and Mexico City) at Huajúmbaro. If, instead of turning right you carry straight on, the road climbs and descends to **Maravatío** (hotel) and then turns south and climbs steeply towards **Tlalpujahua**, an old mining town with a museum, several churches, and cobblestoned streets, very picturesque among forests and hills (*Casa de Huéspedes*). From Maravatío, Route 122 goes south to join Route 15 just east of Ciudad Hidalgo. Also from Maravatío, Route 126 to Toluca has been upgraded to a toll road, renamed 15D and is one hour quicker than Route 15 over the mountains.

The pavements here are covered in chillies drying in the blazing sun, and all the shops are filled with large bags of chillies in the season.

Northwest of Maravatío, on the Río Lerma (18th-century bridge), lies the town of **Acámbaro**, founded 1526. It has a Franciscan church of the same date and monastery (finished 1532), with the Capilla de Santa Gracia (mid-16th century) and an ornate fountain. It was the point from which the irrigation system for the whole area was laid out when the town was founded. Acámbaro continues to thrive as an agricultural centre and railway junction. It is also on the main highway from Celaya to Toluca. The mini-diversion from the main route just described can as easily be undertaken starting at Ciudad Hidalgo and ending at Morelia.

Michoacán

Around Morelia

Ciudad Hidalgo
Colour map 3, grid B5
Population: 100,000

Worth a glance is the façade of the 16th-century church at Ciudad Hidalgo. The town is also known for its thermal baths. **C** *Morenita*, T40079. **D** *Hotel Fuente*, Morelos 37, T40518. Some rooms have no keys, clean, showers, no water in the afternoon. **E** *Florida*, damp rooms, garage US$0.50 a night. *Restaurant Manolo*. Inexpensive, good. *Restaurant Lupita's*, excellent, family-run. Also see the old colonial bridge and church at **Tuxpan**, halfway between Cuidad Hidalgo and Zitácuaro; **C** *Ojo de Agua*, T/F41588. **F** *Mara*, on main square. Dirty, hot water, wood stove. *Tuxpan*, Miguel Cabrera, T50058. Noisy. Not far from Tuxpan a side road runs south to the spa of **San José Purúa** at an altitude of 1,800m, in a wild setting of mountains, gorges and woods. The radioactive thermal waters are strong. First-class hotel, beautiful spot, good restaurant, reservations in Mexico City, T55101538/4949. Trailers can park outside the guarded gate (24 hours, tip the guard for security), small charge for entry to grounds. Alternatively, drive down the steep hill to the river, just over the bridge on right to **Agua Amarilla**, a spa where you can camp for a small fee, friendly. Smaller, cheaper hotels lie on the road past the spa and in the town of **Jungapeo**. If driving with a trailer, do not take the downward hill to the village, your brakes may not hold.

Zitácuaro
Colour map 3, grid B5

Zitácuaro is a small town with a pleasant plaza and a good covered market. **Tourist office** Km 4 on the Zitácuaro-Toluca road, T30675.

Sleeping **A** *Villa Monarca Inn*, T35346, F35350, on road to Morelia. Pool. **B** *Rancho San Cayetano*, 3 km out on Huetamo road, T31926. Chalets, friendly, clean. Highly recommended. **B** *Rosales del Valle*, Revolución Sur 56, T31293. OK, some rooms hired by eager lovers. **B** *Salvador*, Hidalgo Pte 7, T31107. Clean and pleasant. **C** *Lorenz*, Av Hidalgo Ote 14, T30991. Quiet, clean, TV, friendly, 9 blocks from bus station. **D** *México*, Revolución Sur 22, T32811. Clean, large rooms with cable TV, parking, restaurant. Recommended. **D** *Florida*. With bath, clean, garage US$0.50 a night. **D** *Colón*. Reasonable, fan, not very quiet, friendly management, can store luggage. **E** *América*, Revolución Sur, 1st block. TV, pleasant, clean. Recommended. **E** *Mary*, on main street. Hot shower, TV, clean; 1 block from *Mary* on same street is unnamed hotel, **F**. Clean, TV, basic. **E** *Posada Michoacán*. Main square, TV, clean, friendly, luggage store.

Buses To **Mexico City**, 3 hrs, US$6; to **Morelia**, hourly, US$4.60, 3½ hrs; to **Guadalajara**, 11 hrs, US$14.80, 409 km (bus station at end of Av Cuauhtémoc, next to market, taxi to centre, US$1).

El Campanario
See box on page 465

North of Zitácuaro, a turning off the main road at Angangueo brings you to a unique site, the wintering grounds of the Monarch butterfly in **El Campanario Ecological Reserve**, above the village of El Rosario. Try to form a small group to go round the reserve. There is a visitors' centre and food kiosks near the entrance. ■ *0900-1700, US$2, plus a tip for your guide (only Spanish spoken).*

North of Morelia

Just north of Morelia there is a good road to two lakeside villages in the neighbouring state of Guanajuato. At **Cuitzeo**, the first one (hotel, *Restaurant Esteban*, by post office), there is a fine Augustinian church and convent (begun in 1550), with a cloister, a huge open chapel, and good choir stalls in the sacristy. The church houses a collection of Mexican graphic art, spanning four centuries, in a gallery in the basement. **Laguna de Cuitzeo**, beside which it stands, is the second largest lake in Mexico; the road crosses it on a causeway. Ecological damage in the past has caused the lake to dry up on occasion. From

Monarch butterflies

There are several trails to see the millions of large orange butterflies, which migrate every year to southeast Canada and northeast USA. Huge clusters of the butterflies hang from branches and on warm days they take to the air in swirling masses of red clouds. Most impressive is the sound of their wings, like a strong breeze blowing through the trees. They leave in March, after which there is nothing to see until the following November/December. **NB** The reserve is at a high altitude and you need to walk a few kilometres (30 minutes) to see the butterflies. Bring warm clothes. It is very cold at night. It gets very busy at weekends, when all the accommodation will be full; best to arrive at the sanctuary when it opens at 0900 to avoid the rush of tourists.

The best base for visiting the reserve is the village of **Angangueo**. From December-March much of the village caters for the influx of butterfly watchers. **C** Albergue Don Bruno, Morelia 92, T60026, good but a little overpriced, nice setting, restaurant. **D** Parakata, Matamoros 7, T80191. **D** La Margarita, Morelia, very clean, highly recommended, owner does tours to butterfly sanctuary. **E** Juárez,

Nacional s/n, T80023, friendly, some rooms damp; **E** Paso de la Monarca, Nacional 20, T80187, large comfortable rooms, hot water, friendly, meals, highly recommended. There are several cafés and restaurants near the plaza, wholesome food, but not gourmet.

Half-hourly local bus (marked Angangueo) from Zitácuaro (Av Santos Degollado Ote, or from bus station on outskirts of town) to Ocampo, one hour, US$0.75, and from Ocampo another local bus (two a day from corner two blocks east of plaza, 1000 and 1200, last one back at 1600, 1¼ hours, US$0.85, 12 km on a mountainous dirt road) to El Rosario, from where it is a 40-minute walk to the Reserve. A truck from Ocampo to the butterfly refuge costs US$17, this can be shared, especially at weekends. All hotels will arrange transport to the Reserve, about US$20 per vehicle, one hour. From Mexico City, Aguila Tours, Amsterdam 291-C, Col Hipódromo Condesa, run tours from early December. Day trips cost around US$100-120. There are four direct buses a day to Mexico City, US$6. To Guadalajara there are three a day, US$13, eight hours.

here one can go through the attractive mountain scenery around **Valle de Santiago** (**D** Hotel Posada de la Parroquia). The second village, 33 km to the north, **Yuriria**, has a large-scale Indian version of the splendid church and convent at Actopan (see page 602). It is on Laguna de Yuriria, which looks like a grassy swamp. (Between Cuitzeo and Yuriria is Moreleón, the clothing distribution centre of Mexico – buses empty here). The road continues to **Salamanca** (hotels, appalling traffic), where one turns left for Irapuato or right for Celaya and Querétaro. Mexico City-Morelia buses from the Terminal del Norte take the freeway to Celaya and then head south through Yuriria and Cuitzeo.

West of Morelia

On the road from Morelia to Zamora, at **Zacapú** (Km 400), see the Franciscan church (1548).

At Quiroga (Km 357), a road turns off right for Pátzcuaro, heart of the Tarascan Indian country. The town is named after Bishop Vasco de Quiroga, who was responsible for most of the Spanish building in the area and for teaching the Indians the various crafts they still practise: work in wool, leather, copper, ceramics and cane; many Indians, few tourists. There is a fair and craft exhibitions in December. The night-time entertainment seems to be driving through town in a pick-up with blaring speakers in the back.

Quiroga
Colour map 3, B4

Quiroga is a good place to buy cheap leather jackets – most shops in town sell them.

Sleeping **C** *Misión don Vasco*, Av Lázaro Cárdenas y Guadalupe Victoria. 3 hotels on main street (Vasco de Quiroga): **D** *Quiroga* and **D** *Tarisco* (was *San Diego*), both modern with parking. **E** *Tarasco*. Colonial-style, courtyard, clean, hot water, pleasant but front rooms noisy. *Cabañas Tzintzuntzan*, Km 6 Quiroga-Pátzcuaro road (Ojo de Agua). Swimming pool, own pier, fully furnished (contact *Hotel Casino*, Morelia, T31003). **Trailer park** 3 km north of town. Old summer residence of a former Mexican president, apparently, wonderful view over Lake Pátzcuaro.

Transport Buses: from Pátzcuaro bus station every 15 mins. Bus Quiroga-Mexico City, US$11, 1st *plus*.

Tzintzuntzan
pronounced rapidly as
sin-sun-san

Colour map 3, grid B4

Tzintzuntzan, was the pre-conquest Tarascan capital; the ruins are just behind the village; a Purépecha ceremonial centre, with five pyramids, is across the road and up the hill (10 minutes walk) from the monastery. ■ *Daily 0900-1700, US$2, Sunday free.* The monastery, on Magdalena, was built in 1533 but closed over 250 years ago. It has been restored, but its frescoes have deteriorated badly. The church bells date from the 16th century; a guard will show you round. In the grounds are some very old olive trees which are still bearing fruit, said to have been planted by Vasco de Quiroga. Fortuitously they were missed in a Spanish edict to destroy all Mexican olive trees when it was thought that Mexican olive oil would compete with Spain's. A most interesting Passion play is given at Tzintzuntzan and *fiestas* are very colourful. Beautiful, hand-painted pottery, displayed everywhere, is very cheap but also brittle. (It is also available in other markets in Mexico.) Other handicrafts on sale include woodcarving, leather and basket-woven Christmas tree ornaments. Good bargaining opportunities.

Transport Bus from Pátzcuaro bus station every 15 mins, US$0.50, same bus as for Quiroga, which is 8 km further on. **NB** If taking the route Uruapan-Pátzcuaro-Morelia, Tzintzuntzan and Quiroga come after Pátzcuaro.

Pátzcuaro

Phone code: 434
Colour map 3, grid B4
Population: 65,000
Altitude: 2,110m

Twenty-three kilometres from Quiroga (cold in the evenings), Pátzcuaro is one of the most picturesque towns in Mexico, with narrow cobbled streets and deep overhanging eaves. The houses are painted white and brown. It is built near Lago de Pátzcuaro, about 50 km in circumference, with Tarascan Indian villages on its shores and many islands.

Ins and outs

Getting there The nearest airports are at Morelia to the east and Uruapan to the west. The train station is distant from town but local buses will take you to the centre. Passenger services are being cut so it is necessary to check before making plans. The bus station is on the outskirts of town. A local bus, *colectivo* or taxi will take you to the centre. Pátzcuaro is connected by Route 14 to Morelia and Uruapan.

The Indians used to come by huge dugout canoes (but now seem to prefer the ferry) for the market, held in the main plaza, shaded by great trees. It is a steep 3-km walk uphill from the lake shore to the plaza; *colectivos* run every few minutes to the Plaza Chica. The **tourist office** is on the north side of the Plaza Grande next to Banca Serfín, friendly, good information, Spanish only. ■ *Mon-Fri 0900-1500, variable in afternoon, usually 1700-1900, Sat-Sun only morning.*

Sights

There are several interesting buildings: the unfinished **La Colegiata** (1603), known locally as La Basílica, with its much venerated Virgin fashioned by an Indian from a paste made with cornstalk pith and said to have been found floating in a canoe. Behind the Basílica there are remains of the pre-Columbian town and of a pyramid in the precincts of the Museo de Artes Populares; the restored Jesuit church of **La Compañía** (and, almost opposite, the early 17th-century church of the **Sagrario**) at the top of Calle Portugal. Behind this street are two more ecclesiastical buildings: the **Colegio Teresiano** and the restored **Templo del Santuario**; on Calle Lerín is the old monastery, with a series of small patios. There are murals by Juan O'Gorman in the **Library**, formerly San Agustín. On Calle Allende is the residence of the first Governor. On Calle Terán is the church of **San Francisco**; nearby is **San Juan de Dios**, on the corner of Calle Romero. Visit also the **Plaza Vasco de Quiroga**. Fifteen minutes walk outside the town is the chapel of **El Calvario**, on the summit of Cerro del Calvario, a hill giving wide views; the views are also good from the old chapel of the **Humilladero**, above the cemetery on the old road to Morelia. This chapel is said to have been built on the spot where the last Tarascan emperor

Pátzcuaro

To Railway Station, Lake Pátzcuaro, Morelia & Uruapan

Michoacán

■ **Sleeping**
1 El Artillero
2 Gran
3 Los Escudos
4 Mansión Iturbe
5 Mesón del Gallo
6 Misión San Manuel
7 Posada de la Rosa
8 Posada de la Salud
9 Posada La Basílica
10 Posada San Rafael

N

Not to scale

knelt in submission to the Spanish Conquistador, Cristóbal de Olid. Do not hike there alone, it is rather isolated.

An 'International Hippy Crafts Market' is held every Saturday and Sunday on the north side of the Plaza Grande.
The very well arranged **Museo de Artes Populares** is in the former Colegio de San Nicolás (1540) and is excellent for seeing regional ceramics, weaving, woodcarving and basketware. ■ *0900-1900 Tue-Sat, 0900-1430 Sun (free), English speaking, friendly guide, US$1.70.* Ask there for the **Casa de los Once Patios**, which contains boutiques selling handicrafts; you can see weavers and painters of lacquerwork in action. See also the attractive Jardín de la Revolución (F Tena y Ponce de León) and, nearby, the old church of the Hospitalito. Friday and also Saturday markets are excellent, often much cheaper than shops. Local specialities such as copperware and woodcarving are widely available. There are good crafts by the intersection of Benigno Serrato and Lerín, near the Basílica. Some stalls open daily on the main square, selling handicrafts, and there is a friendly handicraft shop on the road down to the lake, *Vicky's*, with interesting toys.

Excursions

The best-known island is **Janitzio**, which has been spoilt by the souvenir shops and the tourists (visit during the week if possible). There are many restaurants. It is 45 minutes by motorboat; boats leave when full from 0800 onwards, US$2.50 return from Muelle General; cheaper from Muelle San Pedrito, 500m further on, tickets from office at dock, last boat back (return by any boat) at 2000. It is a 45-minute walk from the centre of Pátzcuaro or take a bus marked 'Lago' from Plaza Bocanegra. There is an unfortunate monument to Morelos crowning a hill on the island, with a mural glorifying Independence inside, which nevertheless affords magnificent views (often queues to climb spiralling stairs inside to the top). ■ *US$0.60.* A circular path goes around the island where there are lots of good restaurants; those on the waterfront charge more than those on the hill, same quality. One hotel **D** *Teru'nukua, T136152,* 50m from *muelle*. Winter is the best time for fishing in the somewhat fish-depleted lake, where Indians traditionally threw nets shaped like dragonflies, now a rather rare event. The Government is planning to improve the lake's water quality, but there are still plenty of places selling white fish on the island, though it is about a quarter of the price in Pátzcuaro.

Another island to visit is **Yunuen**, boat from Muelle General, US$2.70. The island is clean and quiet. There is a *cabaña* (**B**) on the hill with a good restaurant, T21072. During the week there are few *lanchas*, so be sure to arrange a return trip unless you want to spend the night. Bring provisions. On a lakeside estate (formerly the country house of General Lázaro Cárdenas) is the Educational Centre for Community Development in Latin America, better known as *CREFAL* (free films every Wednesday at 1930).

For a truly spectacular view of the lake, the islands and the surrounding countryside, walk to Cerro del Estribo; an ideal site for a quiet picnic. It is a 1½-hour walk to the top from the centre of Pátzcuaro. Follow the cobbled road beyond El Calvario, don't take the dirt tracks off to the left. There are 417 steps to the peak and no buses. Cars go up in the afternoon, the best time for walking. The areas round Pátzcuaro are also recommended for bird watching. If intending to drive around the lake, a high-clearance vehicle is necessary.

From Pátzcuaro, one can also visit Tzintzuntzan and Quiroga by regular bus service. Thirty minutes by local bus from Plaza Chica is **Ihuatzio**, on a peninsula 12 km north of Pátzcuaro town, 8 km from Tzintzuntzan. This was the second most important Tarascan city; two pyramids are well preserved and afford good views of the lake. ■ *US$1.10, leaflets in Spanish or English,*

Michoacán

US$0.40. The pyramids are signposted, 1 km from the village, but the road is very bad. To get to Tzintzuntzan from Ihuatzio, take bus or hitch back to main road and wait for Pátzcuaro-Quiroga bus.

An excursion can be made into the hills to **Santa Clara del Cobre**, a sleepy village with red tiles and overhanging eaves, an attractive square with copper pots filled with flowers along each arcade, and a fine old church. Hand-wrought copper vessels are made here and there is a Museo del Cobre with some excellent examples; it's half a block from the main square. ■ *Closed Mon, free.* There is a Banca Serfín which changes dollars cash and cheques between 1000 and 1200. There is a local *fiesta* here from 12-15 August. Take a bus to Pátzcuaro bus station, then another to Ario de Rosales (every 15 minutes), which passes Santa Clara, US$0.50 each way. Taxi from Pátzcuaro, US$10.50 return with one-hour wait. **C** *Camino Real*, Av Morelos Pte 213, T30281. **D** *Real del Cobre*, Portal Hidalgo 19, T30205. **D** *Oasis*, Portal Allende 144, T30040, both on main square.

Nearby is the pretty **Lago Zirahuén**, where you can take boat trips, eat at lakeside restaurants and visit the huge adobe church. **C** *Motel Zirahuén*, T23600. Attractive, clean, garden restaurant, horse riding. Flecha Amarilla buses leave Pátzcuaro between 0930-1400, 30 minutes direct, last bus back at 1800. Past Santa Clara, on the La Huacana road, after Ario de Rosales, a road to the left descends into the tropics with fine views all the way to Churumuco, where it ends. Pátzcuaro-Ario de Rosales-Nueva Italia-Uruapan-Pátzcuaro is about a six-hour journey through beautiful tropical countryside.

Essentials

Sleeping

Rooms in some hotels are reserved 4 weeks prior to Día de los Muertos, other hotels do not take reservations, so it is pot luck at this time

A *Posada de don Vasco*, Av Lázaro Cárdenas 450, T23971, F20262. 103 rooms, attractive, colonial-style hotel (halfway between lake and town), breakfast good, other meals poor, presents the Dance of the Old Men on Wednesday and Saturday at 2100, no charge, non-residents welcome but drinks very expensive to compensate, also mariachi band. **B** *Las Redes*, Av de las Américas 6, T/F21275. Near lake, 13 rooms, popular restaurant. **B** *Mesón del Cortijo*, Obregón, just off Américas, T21295 F133644. Often fully booked at weekends. Recommended. **C** *Apo-Pau*, between lake and town (closest to town of the non-central hotels), T20601, F24186. Pleasant, friendly.

In the centre AL-B *Mansión Iturbe*, Portal Morelos 59, T20368, F34593, www.mexonline.com/iturbe.htm 14 rooms, English, French and German spoken,

Michoacán

Around Lake Pátzcuaro

Not to scale

beautiful restored 1790 mansion on main plaza, breakfast included, nice décor, satellite TV, cold at night, expensive restaurant, *El Gaucho Viejo*, Argentine *churrasco*, open 1800-2400, Wed-Sun, folk music, 2 other restaurants. Recommended. **A** *Mesón del Gallo*, Dr Coss 20, T21474, F21511. 25 rooms, good value, flower garden, tasteful furnishings. **B** *Misión San Manuel*, Portal Aldama 12 on main plaza, T21313, F21050. Restaurant. Highly recommended. **B** *Posada La Basílica*, Arciga 6, T21108, F20659. 12 rooms, nice restaurant with good views, central. **B** *Posada San Rafael*, Plaza Vasco de Quiroga, T20770. Safe, average restaurant, parking in courtyard. **C** *Fiesta Plaza*, Plaza Bocanegra 24, T22516, F22515. Beautiful interior patio. Good. **C** *Gran Hotel*, Portal Regules 6, on Plaza Bocanegra, T20443 F23090. Small rooms, clean, friendly, pleasant, good food. **C** *Los Escudos*, Portal Hidalgo 73, T/F21290. 17th-century building (*Baile de los Viejitos* every Sat at 2000), ask for room with fireplace, good food. Recommended.

D *Casa de Huéspedes Pátzcuaro*, Ramos 9, T20807. Without bath. **D** *Concordia*, Portal Juárez 31, next to *Posada de la Rosa* at No 29, T20811. With bath and hot water, cheaper without (which means use of toilet, but no bath whatsoever), in poor shape, rooms on plaza noisy. **D** *El Artillero*, Ibarra 22, T21331. With hot water, bath, gloomy, noisy, not too clean or secure, no drinking water, near Zócalo (discounts for long stays paid in advance). **D** *Imperial*, Obregón 21, T20308. Large clean rooms. These are all central. **D** *Posada de la Salud*, Benigno Serrato 9, T20058. Clean, quiet, pleasant, nice garden, excellent value, no hot water during middle of day, some rooms with individual fireplaces. Recommended. **E** *Laguna*, Títere. With bath, cheaper rooms also with bath but no water, buckets outside! **E** *Posada de la Rosa*, Portal Juárez 29 (Plaza Chica). With bath, doors to rooms not very secure, **F** without, parking, colonial style, clean. **E** *Posada La Terraza*, Benito Juárez 46, T21027. Central, gardens, hot water, kind *señora*. Also on Plaza Chica is **E** *Posada San Agustín*, T20442. Very good value, clean, hot water. **E** *Valmen*, Padre Lloreda 34-A, T21151. Good, friendly.

There are many *hospedajes* and hotels near the bus station. Public baths, US$0.50.

Motels and camping **B** *Chalamu*, Pátzcuaro Rd Km 20, T20948 F20948. **B** *Hostería de San Felipe*, Av Lázaro Cárdenas 321, T/F21298. Friendly, clean, fireplaces in rooms, good restaurant (closes 2030). Highly recommended. **B** *San Carlos*, Muelle Col Morelos, T21359. *Villa Pátzcuaro*, Av Lázaro Cárdenas 506, T20767, F22984 (Apdo Postal 206), 1 km from centre. Very quiet, hot water, gardens, lots of birds, tennis, pleasant, also camping and caravan site. *Trailer Park El Pozo*, on lakeside, opposite *Chalamu*, T20937. Hot showers am, large, delightful, well-equipped, US$10, owner speaks English, also camping (take water for drinking from the entrance rather than taps on the trailer pads).

Eating

Local speciality is pescado blanco (white fish), but it is disappearing from menus as a result of over-fishing & pollution

Several lakeside restaurants serve fish dishes, but it is advisable to avoid locally caught fish. Many places close before 2000. Make sure you don't get overcharged in restaurants, some display menus outside which bear no resemblance to the prices inside. *Comida corrida* at restaurants around Plaza Grande and Plaza Chica costs about US$4 and is usually the same each day. *Los Escudos*, Plaza Quiroga. Open till 2200, popular with tourists, try *sopa tarasca* (a flavoursome soup made with toasted *tortillas*, cream and cheese), good value and coffee. Also on this plaza *La Casona*, reasonable prices (cheapest breakfast in town) and *El Primer Piso*. *San Agustín*, Plaza Bocanegra. Friendly, good doughnuts on sale outside in pm. *Mery Lerín*, Benigno Serrato (opposite Basílica). Cheap local dishes. *Mandala*, on Lerín. Vegetarian. OK. *Gran Hotel*, filling *comida corrida*, excellent *café con leche*. Good chicken with vegetables and *enchiladas* over the market (budget restaurants here, usually open in evening). *Don Rafe*, Benito Mendoza. Opens 0800, good. *Restaurant T'irekua*, Plaza Vasco de Quiroga 29. Beautiful patio, peaceful, good breakfast. Recommended. *Cafetería El Buho*, Tejerías 8.

Meals, drinks, slow but very good food, good value, stylish, friendly. Recommended. *Camino Real*, next to Pemex, 100m from *El Pozo Trailer Park*. Very good *comida corrida*, quick service. *Viejo Sam*, Benito Mendoza 8. Good *tortas*. Excellent *paletería* and ice cream parlour at Codallos 24, also sells frozen yoghurt. Fruit and yoghurt for breakfast at *El Patio*, Plaza Vasco de Quiroga 19, T20484. Open 0800-2200, also serves good meals, good service. Recommended. Breakfast available from small stands in the market, usually 0600-0700 (*licuados*, *arroz con leche*, etc). At the Plaza in Erongarícuaro, 17 km clockwise around the lake, is a Hindu vegetarian restaurant at the weekends; also a local crafts fair (take ADO bus from bus or rail station, US$0.65).

1-2 November: *Día de los Muertos* (All Souls' Day), ceremony at midnight, 1 Nov, at **Festivals** almost every village around the lake; if you are in the region at this time it is well worth experiencing. The ceremony is most touristy on Janitzio island and at Tzintzuntzan, but at villages such as Ihuatzio, Jarácuaro and Uranden it is more intimate. The tourist office has leaflets listing all the festivities. The celebrations begin on 31 Oct with the 'Hunting of the Duck', an activity on the verge of disappearing due to the scarcity of ducks. This is followed by the placement of the Altar of the 'Little Angels' on 1 Nov, and concluding with the homage to deceased adults on 2 Nov. These rituals take place mainly in the region around Lake Pátzcuaro and some other Purépecha communities. **6-9 December**, *Virgen de la Salud*, when authentic Tarascan dances are performed in front of the *Basílica*. There is an interesting *fiesta* on **12 December** for the *Virgin de Guadalupe*; on **12 October**, when Columbus reached America, there is also a procession with the Virgin and lots of fireworks. *Carnival* in Feb when the Dance of the Moors is performed.

Massage *Shiatsu Massage*, Stephen Ritter del Castillo, in Tócuaro, 15 minutes by **Sports** bus or taxi clockwise around the lake about halfway to Erongarícuaro, T431-80309, Mon-Fri 0900-1700, excellent, English/Spanish bilingual.

There is a toll road bypassing the town. **Transport**

Buses New bus station (called Central) out of town, with left luggage office, *colectivo* from centre US$0.30, taxi US$1.70. Bus US$0.20 from Plaza Bocanegra. You can pick up buses from large roundabout 1 km north of centre. Taxi US$1.45. To **Mexico City**, Tres Estrellas de Oro, Herradura de Plata (via Morelia – recommended US$15), Pegaso Plus (via Morelia – recommended US$16), Flecha Amarilla to Terminal del Norte US$17, 7½ hrs and Autobuses de Occidente 1st (US$13.60) 5 hrs, and 2nd class buses (US$12.20), 6 hrs. Regular bus service to **Morelia**, 1 hr, US$2.10 with ADO, Herradura de Plata, Galeana and Flecha Amarilla (departs every 30 mins). Buses to **Guadalajara** go through Zamora, US$10 (Flecha Amarilla), 6 hrs; to **Lázaro Cárdenas**, for connections to Zihuatanejo, Acapulco, etc, hourly from 0600, US$12.50, 8 hrs, long but spectacular ride through mountains and lakes (police checks likely); to **Uruapan**, US$2.50 (1 hr); to **Toluca**, 1st class US$17.50, from 0915, 5 hrs. Local buses from corner of market in town to lakeside (*colectivo* to lakeside US$0.25).

Banks *Banamex*, Portal Juárez 32, T23846. *Promex*, Portal Regules 9, T20397. *Serfín*, Portal **Directory** Allende 54, T21000. *Bancomer*, Zaragoza 23, T20334; *cambio* at Benito Mendoza 7, T20240. 4 ATMs in the centre. **Communications** Internet: *México en Línea*, Fed Tena 30-L9, T24566, not a café. **Post Office:** Obregón, 1 block from Plaza Chica, Mon-Sat 0800-1600, Sat 0900-1300. **Medical services** Dentist: Dr Antonio Molina, T23032. Dr Augusto Tena Mora, T22232. **Doctor:** Dr Jorge Asencio Medina, T24038. Dr Javier Hernández and Dra Guadalupe Murillo, T21209. **Pharmacy:** *Gems*, Benito Mendoza 21, T20332, open 0900-2100 daily. **Laundry** *Lavandería 'San Francisco'*, Terán 16, T23939, Mon-Sat 0900-2000.

Michoacán

Uruapan

Phone code: 452
Colour map 3, grid B4
Population: 250,000
Altitude: 1,610m

*The town suffers badly
from traffic fumes*

From Pátzcuaro, the road continues southwest to Uruapan, the 'place where flowers are plentiful'. The most attractive of its three plazas is the **Zócalo** which has the **Jardín de los Mártires** at its west end. Opposite the Jardín is part of the former Collegiate church of San Francisco (17th century with later additions such as an interesting 1960s modern art interior) which houses the attractive **Casa de la Cultura** (small museum upstairs, free, with excellent display of the history of Uruapan). Local crafts can be bought in the *portales* or at the market: There are lacquered bowls and trays, or the delicate woodwork of the Paracho craftsmen, Patamban green pottery and Capácuaro embroideries. At the east end of the Zócalo is the restored hospital, built by Fray Juan de San Miguel in the 16th century; now a ceramics museum, the **Museo La Huatápera**. Adjoining it is a 16th-century chapel now converted into a craft shop. Behind the chapel and museum is the Mercado de Antojitos and, beyond it, the clothes and goods market permanently occupying several streets. The food market has now moved out of the centre to two sites, one at Obregón and Francisco Villa with cheap eateries upstairs, and the other on Calzada Benito Juárez at the end of the goods market that extends up Constitución from the centre. The **tourist office** is on Ayala, between Independencia and Pino Suárez, T47199. ■ *Mon-Sat 0900-1400 and 1600-2000, Sun 1000-1400.*

On M Treviño, between A Isaac and Amado Nervo, there is a house which is just 1½m wide and several stories high, possibly the narrowest building in Mexico.

The town is set beside streams, orchards and waterfalls in the **Parque Nacional Eduardo Ruiz**, cool at night, and well worth a visit. Local foods are sold in the Parque and there is a government-operated trout breeding facility. At the entrance to the Parque, on the corner of Independencia and Culver City, 1 km from the town centre, is a good **Mercado de Artesanías** selling wooden boxes and bracelets ■ *US$0.35.* Walk there or catch a bus one block south of the Zócalo marked 'El Parque'.

Excursions It is 10 km through coffee groves and orchards along Río Cupatitzio (meaning Singing River) to the **Tzararacua Falls** ■ *US$0.25.* There are restaurants at the

Uruapan

■ **Sleeping**
1 Del Parque
2 Villa de Flores

● **Eating**
1 Mundo Feliz

*Related map
A Uruapan
centre,
page 474*

Not to scale

Michoacán

bus stop where you can hire a horse to the falls (US$4 per person); it is not advisable to walk to the falls alone. To extend the trip beyond the falls, cross the stone bridge to the other side of the stream. Take a path to the right which then switches back and heads up the other side of the gorge. After a while you will reach a plateau at the top of the mountain, with good views all around. A well-worn path/stream leads down the other side of the mountain to a more secluded waterfall, from the top of which are many paths down to the river and lake into which the stream flows (a great spot for a swim). There is good camping some 300m below the village under the shelter on the top of a rim, with a view down into the valley to the waterfall (1 km away) and a small lake. A bus (marked Tzararacua, or Zupomita, but ask if it goes all the way) will take you from the Zócalo at Uruapan to Tzararacua, US$1 (15-25 minutes), weekends and public holidays only. Alternatively, try to buy a ticket to Tzararacua on the bus to Apatzinguán (which passes the falls) and ask the driver to let you off. If on a tight schedule, take a taxi.

Parque Cholinde, 1½ km out of town (all uphill – take a bus), has a swimming pool. ■ *US$1.30*. Colibrí Nurseries are nearby. For **Balneario Caracha** (frequent buses), alight at crossroads by sign, then walk 1 km on road to pools, a delightful place, with restaurant, hotel, several pools and beautiful gardens. ■ *Daily, US$2*. **Tingambato** ruins, with a pyramid and a ball court, are half way along the road to Pátzcuaro, about 2 km downhill from Tingambato town.

A *Victoria*, Cupatitzio 13, T36700 F39662. Good, quiet, restaurant and garage. **B** *Concordia* on main plaza, T30500, F30500. Has nice restaurant. **B** *El Tarasco*, Independencia 2, T41500. Pool, lovely, good restaurant, moderate prices. **B** *Plaza Uruapan*, Ocampo 64, T30333 F33980. Good, clean, large rooms. **B** *Villa de Flores*, Emilio Carranza 15, west of centre, T21650. Quiet, pleasantly furnished, lovely flowers. Recommended.

C *Atzimbal*, Francisco Villa, T44325 F44153(street where the *mariachis* are waiting). Modern, Recommended. On main plaza, **C** *Nuevo Hotel Alameda*, Av 5 de Febrero, T34100. With bath, clean, TV, good value. **C** *del Parque*, Av Independencia 124. With bath, very nice, by entrance to national park, clean, quiet, enclosed parking. Recommended. **D** *Acosta*, opposite bus station. Nearby is **E** *Sandy*. With bath, TV, basic and **E** per person *Betty's*. With bath. **D** *Capri*, Portal Santos Degollado, by market. Friendly. **D** *Los Tres Caballeros*, Constitución 50, T47170. Walk out front door into market. **D** *Mi Solar*, Juan Delgado 10, T20912. Good value, hot water, clean. Recommended. **E** *Moderno*, main plaza. Lovely building, with bath, water spasmodic, friendly, very basic. **E** *Oseguera*, main plaza. Dirty but good hot shower.

Sleeping

Motels **A** *Mansión del Cupatitzio*, on the road to Guadalajara, T32100. Swimming pool, patio, restaurant, good souvenir shop. Outstanding. **B** *Paricutín*, Juárez 295, T20303. Well maintained. **B** *Pie de la Sierra*, Km 4 Carretera a Carapán, on north outskirts, T42510. Good moderately priced restaurant. **B** *Las Cabañas*, Km 1 on road to Mexico City, near the bus terminal, T34777. Clean, local bus until 2200. One trailer park which takes small units only.

La Pérgola, on plaza. Good breakfasts and coffee. Recommended. *Café Tradicional de Uruapan*, just off Plaza, on same side as *Hotel Villa de Flores*. Freshly ground coffee, home-made chocolates, light meals. Recommended. *Calypso*, Alvaro Obregón 2A. Excellent cakes and hamburgers, ask for local speciality: *agua fresca de rompope*. Locals eat at open-air food stalls under one roof at back of church, very picturesque. *Café El Sol y La Luna*, Independencia between Zócalo and Parque. Arty/student bar, sometimes live music at weekends. *Monarca*, Cupatitzio opposite Banco Mexicano. Cheap food and yoghurt; good ice cream at *Bing*, Obregón on Plaza. *La Puesta del Sol*,

Eating
Local speciality, cecina, dried meat.

Michoacán

supermarket, Juan Ayala. Has good meals. Cheap meals from *comedores* in the *Mercado de Antojitos*.

Festivals In the 1st week of **April** the Zócalo is filled with pottery and Indians from all the surrounding villages. Around **16 September**, in nearby village of San Juan, to celebrate the saving of an image of Christ from the San Juan church at the time of the Paricutín eruption. The 2 weeks either side of **15 September** are *feria* in Uruapan, too.

Transport **Air** Daily flights from Mexico City, some via Morelia. Also flights from Culiacán, Guadalajara and Tijuana.

Buses Bus station on the northeast edge of town, necessary to get a city bus (US$0.25) into town, finishing at about 2100, or a taxi to the Plaza, US$3. Left luggage, US$0.35 per item for 7 hrs. To **Mexico City**, 9¼ hrs, Flecha Amarilla via Toluca leaves 0845 and then every hour, US$16.25, many stops; others less frequent but quicker, US$18.75. ETN has a deluxe service, US$28, 6 hrs, several a day, hot and cold drinks, clean, good drivers. Omnibus de México has night buses and Tres Estrellas morning departures. To **Morelia**, 2nd class (Flecha Amarilla) US$4.60 (2½ hrs), nice ride. Parhikuni, T38754, 1st class and *plus* with computerized reservations to Morelia, Apatzingán and **Lázaro Cárdenas** US$10.60. To **Colima** with Flecha Amarilla US$13.50, 6 hrs, and to **Los Reyes**, US$2.20, 1¼ hrs with same company. To **Zihuatanejo** (Galeana not recommended, or Occidente) 1st or 2nd class, several a day, 6½ hrs, US$9 (2nd) along winding, intermittently wooded road via Nueva Italia and Arteaga, which turns off just before Playa Azul at La Mira and on to Lázaro Cárdenas on the Río Balsas. From there, frequent buses to Zihuatanejo (see page 395). Bus to **Guadalajara**, several companies, US$10, 4½ hrs, ETN US$17.75. Bus to **Pátzcuaro**, frequent, US$2, 1 hr.

Directory **Airlines** *Aeromar*, T35050; *Taesa*, T70540. **Banks** *Banamex*, Cupatitzio y Morelos, visa agent. *Bancomer*, Carranza y 20 de Noviembre. *Serfín*, Cupatitzio. **Communications** Internet: *Logicentro Cyber Café*, Av Juárez 57, T49494, US$3.70 per hr, open 0900-1400, 1600-2100 Mon-Sat. Also in computer shop in basement of hotel *Plaza*. **Post Office**: Reforma 13. **Telephone & fax:** *Computel*, Ocampo, on plaza, open every day 0700-2200. **Medical services** Red Cross: T40300. **Laundry** Carranza 47, open Mon-Sat 0900-1400 and 1600-2000, US$3.20 service wash. *Mujer Santayo Lavandería*, Michoacán 14, T30876.

Uruapan centre

Paricutín

The volcano of Paricutín can be visited from Uruapan. It started erupting on 20 February 1943, became fiery and violent and rose to a height of 1,300m above the 2,200m-high region, and then died down after several years into a quiet grey mountain (460m) surrounded by a sea of cold lava. The church tower of San Juan, a buried Indian village, thrusting up through cold lava is a fantastic sight. If you are not taking an organized tour (with horses and guides included), Paricutín is best reached by taking a 'Los Reyes' bus on a paved road to Angahuan, 34 km from Uruapan, US$0.85, one hour, nine a day each way (from 0500 to 2000) with Galeana, then hire a horse or mule or walk (one hour). Señores Juan Rivera, Francisco Lázaro (tour is a bit hurried, he lives in the second house on the right, coming from the *albergue*, see below), Atanacio Lázaro and his horse 'Conejo', and Lino Gómez are recommended, but there are a host of other guides at the bus stop. It is definitely worth a guide – essential for the volcano – but it is expensive if you are on your own as you have to pay for the guide's mule too. A full day's excursion with mules to the area costs about US$8-12 per mule, with US$3-4 tip for the guide (six to seven hours); shorter journeys cost less. To go on foot with a guide costs US$10. It is best if you can speak Spanish. It is 3 km from Angahuan to the San Juan ruins, an easy walk: as you stand in the village square with the church in front but a bit to the left, turn right and take the first left after you leave the square and follow this cobbled street with telegraph poles on the left hand side for 750m to a stone pillared gateway and a sight of the ruins. At the gate, turn right down a dirt path which zig-zags downhill, past a plantation to a three forked junction. Take the centre path which winds through the lava field to the church. Alternatively, start at the new hostel from where you can also see the church. Guide on foot to church US$5 per group.

To the crater of the volcano is 10 km, a long, tough walk (also a long day on horseback for the unaccustomed, especially if you get a wooden saddle). Walk westwards round the lava field, through an avocado plantation. Wear good walking shoes with thick soles as the lava is very rough and as sharp as glass in places (some cannot make the last stretch over the tennis-ball size rocks); bear in mind the altitude too, as the return is uphill. It takes seven to nine hours to the volcano and back. The cone itself is rather small and to reach it, there is a stiff 30-minute climb from the base. A path goes around the tip of the crater, where activity has ceased. Take something to drink because it is pretty hot and dusty out on the plains. If going in one day, leave Uruapan by 0800 so that you don't have to rush. Go even earlier in the rainy season as clouds usually build up by midday. Take a sweater for the evening and for the summit where it can be windy and cold after a hot climb. Last bus back to Uruapan at 1900 (but don't rely on it).

Angahuan Much better, though, is to stay the night in Angahuan, where there is an *albergue*, at the Centro Turístico de Angahuan, T50383 or 33934 (Uruapan) **B** *cabañas*, sleep 6, with a log fire, or **E** per person in dormitory with bunk beds (dormitories closed in low season, both have hot showers), meals US$5, restaurant closes 1900 in low season, basic facilities, but clean and peaceful, warm and recommended but service poorer when few people are staying. It can be crowded and noisy at weekends. The *albergue* is signposted from the bus stop and signs are repeated several times *en route*. It takes about a half hour to walk from the bus stop to the *albergue*. The church ruins can be seen from the *albergue*. To reach them just follow the very dusty road downhill; if ever in doubt follow the route with most hoof prints. It is possible to drive to the *albergue* where they try to charge US$1.60 for the free car park. Camping is possible near the hostel. Some families rent out rooms, for example that of

Michoacán

Francisco Lázaro, near the Zócalo, whose son, José, will guide you up the volcano. In the village are shops selling food and drink and there is a good local restaurant in the street behind the church. Two reasonable restaurants are on the road to the *albergue*. There is a water tap near the church; follow the signs. Just outside the village, on the dirt track to the main road, is the cemetery, which is interesting. The local Tarascan Indians still preserve their language. Angahuan is a Purépecha Indian village and in the evening the local radio station broadcasts in Puripeche over a public tannoy system in the plaza until 2200.

Los Reyes
Colour map 3, grid B3

Past Angahuan and Peribán, after the volcano, over a paved road is the little town of Los Reyes; there is good swimming above the electricity generating plant in clear streams (take care not to get sucked down the feed pipe!).

Sleeping C *Arias* behind Cathedral, T20792. Best, clean, friendly. D *Fénix*, T20807. Clean, between bus station and plaza. D *Oasis*, Av Morelos 229, C for a suite. With bath, hot water, clean, pleasant. D *Plaza*, T20666. Not as good as *Arias* but nice, clean, on street facing Cathedral. E *Casa de Huéspedes*. Clean, basic, lovely courtyard, a little further along the same road is E *Villa Rica*. Often no water.

Buses From Uruapan to **Los Reyes** (Galeana, US$2.20) go via Angahuan (US$0.80) (so same frequency), depart from Uruapan bus station, not from the plaza as the tourist office says. Check that you are only charged to Angahuan if not continuing to Los Reyes. Bus from Los Reyes, on Av 5 de Mayo, to **Angahuan**, 1½-2 hrs. Angahuan to Uruapan as above or local bus (US$.75) but it does not go to bus station. Bus to Los Reyes from Guadalajara with Ciénaga de Chapala 4 a day, 4 hrs, US$8.25 1st class.

Zamora
Phone code: 351
Colour map 3, grid B4
Population: 135,000

Zamora (58 km east of Jiquilpan) is an agricultural centre founded in 1540. There is a large, interesting gothic-style church in the centre, the Catedral Inconclusa, started in 1898, work suspended during the Revolution, now with a projected completion date of 2000. There are several other, fine churches,

and a market on Corregidora. Much of the area around the plaza is pedestrianised. Nearby is tiny Laguna de Camécuaro, with boats for hire, restaurants and wandering musicians; popular at holiday times.

Sleeping **C** *Fénix*, Madero Sur 401, T20266 F20150. Clean, swimming pool, poor ventilation, pleasant balconies. **D** *Amalia*, Hidalgo 194, T21327. Pleasant, some rooms noisy, restaurant OK. **D-E** *Posada Fénix*, Esquina Morelos y Corregidora, 1 block from Zócalo. Rooms of varying quality, nice owner (also owns *Fénix* – see above), good laundry service. **E** *Posada Marena*. Simple, clean; other cheap *hospedajes* near market, none very clean. **F** *Hotel 5 de Mayo* – cheapest in centre. **E** *Jasmín*, 2 km on road to Morelia, opposite Pemex. With bath, clean, noisy, used a lot by truckers. **Motel**: **A3** *Jérico*, Km 3 on La Barca road just north of town, T25252. Swimming pool, restaurant.

Eating *El Campanario*, Nervo 22, off main square. Recommended. *Carnes Toluca*, Madero Sur and Leonardo, and *Antigua Carnes Toluca* over the road. Not much more than meat, but plenty of it.

Transport Bus station at north edge of town, local bus to centre US$0.25, taxi US$3.50, from centre to bus station from 5 de Mayo in front of Catedral Inconclusa. Bus to **Mexico City**, 1st *plus*, US$16.50, 1st US$14.20. To **Guadalajara**, US$11, and US$10 to **Morelia**. To **Pátzcuaro**, 2½ hrs, with Via 2000. To Tamazula for **Ciudad Guzmán**, 3½-4 hrs, US$6.

Directory **Communications**: **Internet**: In small mall on Morelos, between Colón and Ocampo. **Tourist office**: Morelos Sur 76, T24015.

Southeast of Zamora, on Route 15, is **Carapán** (**E** *Motel La Hacienda*. Friendly, clean, cold water, good restaurant), a crossroads at which a road goes north to **La Piedad de Cabadas**, a pleasant stopping place on the old toll road between Guadalajara and Mexico City (**D** *Hotel Mansión Imperial*. Parking. **E** *San Sebastián*. Central, hot water, old but nice, parking across the street. **E** *Gran Hotel*. On main street, OK. *Restaurant El Patio*, near church. Very good, dish of the day good value).

At Carapán a branch road runs 32 km south through pine woods to Paracho, a **Paracho** quaint, very traditional Indian village of small wooden houses; in every other one craftsmen make guitars, violins and mandolins worth from US$15 to US$1,500. A recommended workshop is that of Ramiro Castillo, Av Independencia 259, Galeana 38, good value, friendly. Bargaining possible in all workshops. On the main plaza is the *Casa para el Arte y la Cultura Purépecha* with information, library, shops, etc. There is a guitar museum and concert hall, main venue for a famous week-long guitar festival in the second week of August (free concerts). There are buses to/from Uruapan US$.80, 45 minutes. Also to Morelia via Pátzcuaro.

Sleeping and eating **D** *Hermelinda*, in centre. **E** hotel on main road south of town, hot water morning only. Eating places include *La Casona*, on main Plaza, quiet; *Café D'Gribet*, on main street, cheap and good snacks. Try local pancakes.

West of Zamora and south of Laguna de Chapala, you come to **Jiquilpan** (on Route 110 to Colima). There are frescoes by Orozco in the library, which was formerly a church. At least five hotels. **D** *Posada Palmira*, on main street. Pleasant, clean, good restaurant. **E** *Imperial*, on main street. Good value. **E** *Colonial Mendoza*, Route 15 in the centre. With bath, clean, good value, but noisy. Good, cheap, street foodstalls in the town.

Michoacán

The Pacific coast of Michoacán

Playa Azul
Colour map 3, grid C4

*Beware of the large
waves at Playa Azul & of
dangerous currents;
always check with locals
if particular beaches
are safe*

The Pacific coast of Michoacán is only just coming under development. From Uruapan, Route 37 goes to Playa Azul, 350 km northwest of Acapulco (bus US$9, 10½ hours minimum) and 122 km from Zihuatanejo (see page 395). Playa Azul is a coconut-and-hammock resort (reported dirty and dilapidated) frequented much more by Mexicans than foreigners, with a few large hotels. The town of La Mira, on the main road, is larger than Playa Azul. Forty kilometres of excellent deserted beaches stretch to the north of Playa Azul. At night there is much beautiful phosphorescence at the water's edge.

Sleeping and eating D *El Delfín*, Venustiano Carranza s/n, T60007. No a/c, clean, pleasant, swimming pool. D *Hotel del Pacífico*. Opposite beach, with bath, fan, clean, hammocks on roof, friendly. A bit run-down but recommended. E *Costa de Oro*, Francisco I Madero s/n, T60982. Clean, with fan, safe parking. Recommended. *Hotel Playa Azul*, Venustiano Carranza s/n, T60024/88, F60090. Has a trailer park with 20 spaces, full hook-up, bathrooms, cold shower, 2 pools, bar and restaurant, US$13 for car and 2 people. Many small fish restaurants along beach, but most close early; *Martita*. Highly recommended. Tap and shower water seems to smell of petrol.

Transport Buses: these ply up and down the coast road, stopping at the road junction 4 km from Plaza Azul. *Colectivos* take you between town and junction. If driving north it is 5 hrs to Tecomán (where the road from Colima comes down to the coast).

Lázaro Cárdenas
Colour map 3, grid C4

Lázaro Cárdenas is the connecting point for buses from Uruapan, Manzanillo and Zihuatanejo. There is a **tourist office** at Nicolás Bravo 475, T21547, in the *Hotel Casablanca* building.

Sleeping and eating C *Hotel de la Curva*, Vicente Guerrero esq Nicolás Bravo, T736569, F23237. D *Sol del Pacífico*, Javier Mina 178, T20660, F70490. E *Viña del Mar*, Javier Mina 352, T/F20415. Avoid E *Hotel Sam Sam*, near terminal; go to *Capri*, Juan Alvarez 237, T20551, or *Costa Azul*, 5 de Mayo 276, T20780, both E with bath, or E *Verónica*, Javier Mina 47, T20254, 2 blocks on left as you leave bus station. Friendly, pleasant, noisy, restaurant in front part of hotel has nice atmosphere but indifferent food; several eating places in streets near bus terminal. **Transport** Galeana to Manzanillo 7¾ hrs, US$10; to Uruapan, US$10.75, 6½ hrs; to Guadalajara, US$21.50 with La Línea; to Mexico City from 2nd US$17, 1st US$36.65 to US$43.35, luxury; Flecha Roja to Zihuatanejo, 2 hrs, US$3.65). If possible, book tickets in advance at the bus terminal for all journeys.

Caleta de Campos
76 km northwest up the coast from Playa Azul. Watch out for elaborate, if dangerous fireworks at fiesta time.

Buses continue along the coast road to La Mira, then a short distance to Caleta de Campos. In this poor village perched above a beautiful bay, there is little to eat other than seafood. D *Hotel Yuritzi*. With bath, a/c, TV, E without, clean, no hot water, good views from front, changes travellers' cheques at reasonable rates. E *Los Arcos*. With bath, good views from most rooms; *cabañas* with hammock space at US$1 per person, northwest of village, where Río Nexpa reaches the coast. At beach here, five minutes from the village, there are bars and restaurants, popular with surfers. Be careful swimming, there are strong currents. Fiesta: 10-13 December; at 0200 on the 13th El Torito, a bull mask and sculpture loaded with fireworks appears.

Avoid night-time driving in this area as hold ups have been reported

Eighty-six kilometres further up the coast, to the northwest, is **Maruata**, unspoilt and beautiful. This is a turtle conservation area. There are floods in the rainy season and the river has washed away some of the beach. There are *cabañas* for rent (**F**) and *palapas* under which you can camp. For southbound traffic seeking Maruata, road signs are inadequate.

10

Guadalajara to the Pacific Coast

Guadalajara to the Pacific Coast

If it's the Mexican stereotype you're after, then the State of Jalisco is the place to head for. This is where you'll find the original town of Tequila, the lasso-swinging charros, the swirling Jarabe Tapatío, or Mexican hat dance, and the romantic mariachis, those roving musicians dressed in fine, tight-trousered gala suits and massive sombreros of early 19th-century rural gentry. All these originated in Jalisco, but there are other attractions worth making a song and dance about. **Guadalajara**, *the state capital, is today a huge, modern metropolis. But the 'pearl of the west' has a magnificent and very Spanish core with elegant, shady plazas, impressive colonial architecture, some fine museum and the vast San Juan de Dios market. Nearby, you can visit Tlaquepaque or Tonalá, both famous craft centres, take a boat ride on Mexico's largest lake, climb the dormant Nevado de Colima, cool off in the pine forests around the delightful old town of Tapalpa, or visit one (or all twelve) of the distilleries in Mexico's most famous small town,* **Tequila**. *Jalisco is also gateway to the Pacific coast and the mega resort of Puerto Vallarta on the vast Bahía de Banderas, one of the largest bays in the world. But there are other beautiful and secluded beaches both north and south of Vallarta. Up the coast, in the neighbouring state of Nayarit, sleepy* **San Blas** *is a mecca for surfers and bird watchers. Away from the resorts, remote in the Sierra Madre Occidental, live the Cora and Huichol Indians. The latter are renowned for their stunningly beautiful chaquira beadwork and colourful nierika yarn paintings as well as for the ancestral ritual which takes them hundreds of miles every year on a pilgrimage to the sacred peyote grounds near Real de Catorce to collect the hallucinogenic cactus.*

Guadalajara

Phone code: 3
Colour map 3, grid B3
Population: 5,000,000
Altitude: 1,650m

Guadalajara, Mexico's second city, founded on 14 February 1542 and capital of Jalisco state, is 573 km from Mexico City, and warmer than the capital. Graceful colonial arcades, or portales, flank scores of old plazas and shaded parks. Efforts are being made (within a limited budget) to preserve the colonial atmosphere and restore noteworthy buildings. It is now illegal to modify the façades of colonial buildings in the centre.

During the past 25 years the city has developed to the west of Avenida Chapultepec, where the best shops and residential neighbourhoods are now located. The climate is mild, and clear all through the year, although in summer it can be thundery at night. Pollution from vehicles can be bad downtown and the winter is the worst time for smog. However, afternoons are usually clear and sunny and during the rainy summer season smog is no problem.

Ins and outs

Getting there Aeropuerto Internacional Miguel Hidalgo (GDL) is about 20 km south of the city centre. There are frequent flights to and from Mexico City and other domestic airports as well as to several US destinations. Fixed-rate taxis will take you into the city; no tip necessary. Two local bus routes also service the airport (for details see **Transport** page 498). The new bus terminal is 10 km southeast of the centre; allow at least 30 minutes to get there on one of the luxury bus services (Línea Azul and Línea Cardenal). Confusingly, there are seven modules at the terminal, each serving different bus companies rather than towns or regions within Mexico. The old bus station in the city centre serves towns within 100 km of Guadalajara, mainly with second-class buses. There is a train station at the south end of Calzada de la Independencia, but there are currently no passenger services running. An important commercial centre, Guadalajara is the hub of several major routes heading south to Ciudad Guzmán, Colima and Manzanillo; north to Zacatecas and beyond; east to Mexico City and the towns of the Colonial Heartland; and west to Tepic, Puerto Vallarta and the Pacific Coast.

Getting around Buses and *colectivos* run to most areas of the city although regular services can be frustratingly bad. Trolley buses and the new luxury buses with guaranteed seats on a few fixed routes are a much better option. Guadalajara also has two metro, or rather *tren ligero* lines, one running north-south and the other from west-east of the city. Taxis tend not to use meters so agree on a price before setting off. The most pleasant way of seeing the city is by horse-drawn carriage; these are to be found outside the Museo Regional at the corner of Liceo and Hidalgo.

Tourist offices State and Federal tourist office (*Sectur*), Morelos 102, Plaza Tapatía, T6148686, has information in German and English including good walking tour map of the historic centre, helpful but often understaffed. ■ *Mon-Fri 0900-2000*. There is also a booth in the Palacio de Gobierno, Plaza de Armas. ■ *Mon-Fri 0900-1500, 1800-2000, Sat 0900-1300*. Several other booths staffed by Tourist Police are near many of the main attractions and there is a municipal office at Pedro Moreno 1590, just west of Avenida Chapultepec and Los Arcos, over Avenida Vallarta, T6163332. *Siglo 21* newspaper has a good entertainments section, *Tentaciones*, on Friday, and music, film and art listings every day. The *Instituto Nacional de Estadística, Geografía e Informática*, 16 de Septiembre 670, T6149461, F6583969, has a new, fully computerized office for maps and information. ■ *Mon-Fri 0800-2000*.

The founding of a city

Nuno Beltrán de Guzmán, the founder of the city that is now Guadalajara, named it after his birthplace in Spain, but was less certain about where he wanted it built. Its first location was at Nochistlán, but Guzmán ordered it moved to Tlacotlán and then in 1533 to what is now Tonalá. Still dissatisfied, in 1535 he moved it back to Tlacotlán, but it suffered repeated attacks from the Cazcanes, Tecuejes and Zapoteco Indians. After a particularly bloody massacre, the 26 survivors abandoned what was left of their village and moved to the site of present-day Guadalajara.

Sights

The heart of the city is the Plaza de Armas. On its north side is the **Cathedral**, begun in 1561, finished in 1618, in a medley of styles; its two spires are covered in blue and yellow tiles. There is a reputed Murillo Virgin inside (painted 1650), and the famous *Virgen del Carmen*, painted by Miguel Cabrera, a Zapotec Indian from Oaxaca. In the dome are frescoes of the four gospel writers and in the Capilla del Santísimo are more frescoes and paintings of the Last Supper. From outside you can see the sunset's rays streaming through the dome's stained glass. The Cathedral's west façade is on Plaza de los Laureles, on the north side of which is the **Palacio Municipal** (1952), which contains murals by Gabriel Flores depicting the founding of the city.

Guadalajara is generally a safe city. The centre is not deserted at night and people wander the streets in sociable groups. Normal precautions required against pickpockets but little more. Much safer than many US cities

Also on the Plaza de Armas is the **Palacio de Gobierno** (1643) where in 1810 Hidalgo issued his first proclamation abolishing slavery (plaque). **José Clemente Orozco**'s great murals can be seen on the central staircase; they depict social struggle, dominated by Hidalgo, with the church on the left, fascism on the right and the suffering peasants in the middle. More of Orozco's work can be seen in the **Congreso**, an integral part of the Palacio de Gobierno (entrance free), and in the main **University of Guadalajara** building, on Avenida Juárez y Tolsá (re-named Enrique Díaz de León). Here, in the *Paraninfo* (main hall) is portrayed 'man asleep, man meditating, and man creating'; lie on your back or look in a mirror. The building also houses the **Museo de Arte**. ■ *Small fee, good café.* Other works by this artist can be seen at the University's main Library, Glorieta Normal, and at the massive Hospicio Cabañas near the Mercado Libertad, now known as **Instituto Cultural Cabañas**. The ex-orphanage is a beautiful building with 22 patios, which is floodlit at night. The contents of the former Orozco Museum in Mexico City have been transferred here. Look for *Man of Fire* painted in the dome. Also in the Instituto Cabañas are exhibitions of Mexican and international art and other events, listed under **Entertainment** below. ■ *Tue-Sat 1015-1745, Sun 1015-1445, US$0.80, US$15 to take photos.*

Going east from the Cathedral is the Plaza de la Liberación, with a statue of Hidalgo, where the national flag is raised and lowered daily (with much ceremony). On the north side are the **Museo Regional** (see **Museums** below) and the **Palacio Legislativo** a neo-classical building, remodelled in 1982. ■ *Open to the public 0900 to 1800.* It has a list of the names of all the Constituyentes, from Hidalgo to Otero (1824-57 and 1917). At the eastern end of this plaza is the enormous and fantastically decorated **Teatro Degollado** (1866, see **Entertainment** below), well worth seeing even if you do not go to a performance. ■ *1000-1400.*

A pedestrian mall, **Plaza Tapatía**, has been installed between the Teatro Degollado and the Instituto Cultural Cabañas, crossing the Calzada Independencia, covering 16 blocks. It has beautiful plants, fountains, statuary

The Cristero War

and a tourist office. Facing the Cabañas, on Morelos, is a sculpture in bronze by Rafael Zamarripa of Jalisco's symbol: two lions supporting a tree. The **Mercado Libertad** (locally known as San Juan de Dios, see **Shopping**) is south of Plaza Tapatía and between the market and the Cabañas is a park, with a fine modern sculpture, *The Stampede*, by Jorge de la Peña (1982). Immediately in front of the Instituto Cultural Cabañas are four bronze seats/sculptures by local artist Alejandro Colunga which could be regarded as amusing or macabre, depending on your sense of humour. They include skeletons, an empty man's suit topped by a skull, a large pair of ears, etc.

Other sights worth seeing are the **Parque Alcalde**, Jesús García y Avenida de los Maestros, to the north of the centre; the **Plaza de los Mariachis**, Obregón and Leonardo Vicario, near Mercado Libertad; and the **Templo Expiatorio**, Avenida Enrique Díaz de León y Madero, with fine stained glass and intricate ceiling, gothic style but still unfinished after most of a century. On the way out of the city going north along Calzada Independencia, near the Barranca de Oblatos, a huge canyon, there is a large **zoological garden** with plenty of Central American animals and aviaries in a delightful atmosphere ■ *US$1*. **Selva Mágica** amusement park is inside the zoo; it has a dolphin and seal show three to four times a day. There is also a **Planetarium**.

On Calzada Independencia Sur, at the intersection of Constituyentes and González Gallo is **Parque Agua Azul**. ■ *0800-1900, Tue-Sun, US$0.20*. A park with a good aviary, trees, flowers and fountains, it contains the **Auditorio González Cano**, an outdoor concert bowl with portraits of famous Jalisco musicians, the **Teatro Experimental** and the **Casa de las Artesanías de Jalisco** (see **Crafts** below). On the other side of Calzada Independencia Sur is **Plaza Juárez** with an impressive monument ringed by the flags of other Latin American countries (take bus 52 or 54 up Avenida 16 de Septiembre or 60 or 62 up Calzada Independencia back to centre).

It is worth visiting the architecture faculty of the University of Guadalajara near Parque Mirador (20 minutes by car from centre, or take a bus, see local **Transport** below), which overlooks the canyon.

Churches Other than the Cathedral, churches include: **Santa Mónica** (1718), Santa Mónica y Reforma, which is small, but very elaborate with impressive arches full of gold under a clear atrium and a richly carved façade; **La Merced**, Hidalgo y Pedro Loza, has a beautiful interior with a remarkable number of confessional booths; **El Carmen**, Avenida Juárez 638, whose main altar is surrounded by gilded Corinthian columns; **San José**, Alcalde y Reforma, a 19th-century church with a fine gilded rococo pulpit, has eight pillars in a semicircle around the altar, painted deep red and ochre behind, giving an unusual effect, the overall light blue gives an airy feel; in the plaza outside is a statue of Núñez, defender of the Reforma who was killed in 1858; **San Miguel de Belén**, Hospital 290, enclosed in the Hospital Civil Viejo contains three fine late 18th-century *retablos*; behind the hospital is the **Panteón de Belén**, a

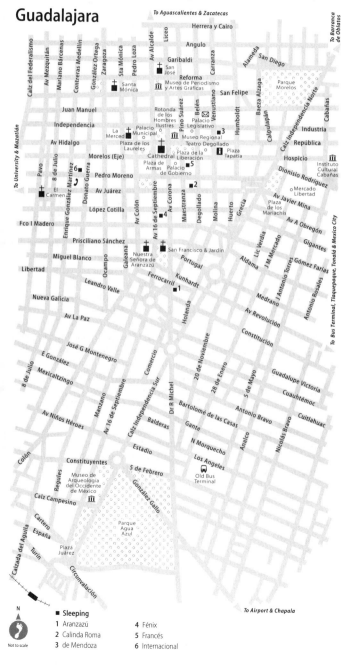

Guadalajara

To Aguascalientes & Zacatecas

To Barranca de Oblatos

To University & Mazatlán

To Bus Terminal, Tlaquepaque, Tonalá & Mexico City

To Airport & Chapala

N

Not to scale

■ Sleeping

1 Aranzazú
2 Calinda Roma
3 de Mendoza
4 Fénix
5 Francés
6 Internacional

Tapatío

The word 'tapatío' is used to describe the people of Guadalajara and sometimes of the State of Jalisco but it is believed to derive from the Indian word tlapatiotl, used in the valley of Atemajac to describe a monetary and commercial unit, equivalent to 'three'. In Guadalajara everything was sold in groups of three. The first known reference to the word tlapatiotl was in the work of Fray Francisco Jiménez, Cuatro libros de la naturaleza y virtudes medicinales de las plantas y animales de la Nueva España ('Four books on the nature and medicinal values of the plants and animals of New Spain'), published in 1615, where the word referred to a commercial unit.

beautiful old cemetery closed to new burials for many years, entrance at Calle Belén 684 at the corner of Eulogio Parra, open until 1500; **San Agustín**, Morelos y Degollado (16th century), is quite plain, with carved stones, music school next door; and **San Francisco Neri** (1550) a three-tiered altar with columns, a feature repeated on the façade. To the north of this last church is the **Jardín San Francisco** (pleasantly shaded, and the starting point for horse-drawn carriages), and to the west is the old church of **Nuestra Señora de Aranzazú**, with three fantastic churrigueresque altarpieces; equally impressive are the coloured ceilings and the finely carved dado, the only light comes from high-up windows and from the open east door. In the shadow of San Francisco is a modern statue to teachers. **María de Gracia**, Carranza and Hidalgo, is another beautiful church. The **Santuario de Guadalupe**, on the corner of Avenida Alcalde and Juan Alvarez, north of the centre is lovely inside; outside, in the Jardín del Santuario, fireworks are let off on 12 December, the day of the Virgin of Guadalupe, with musicians, vendors, games and people celebrating in the plaza.

Museums **Museo de Arqueología del Occidente de México**, Calzada Independencia Sur y Calzada del Campesino (Plaza Juárez) has a very comprehensive collection of objects from Jalisco, Colima and Nayarit, including pottery, ornaments, weapons, figures and illustrations of tombs. A small booklet in English is available. ■ *Mon-Fri 1000-1400, 1600-1800, Sat-Sun 1100-1430, US$0.20.* **Museo Regional de Guadalajara**, Liceo 60, between Hidalgo and Independencia (northeast of Cathedral), T6142227. In an old seminary (1710), with a good prehistoric section (including the complete skeleton of a mammoth found in Jalisco), this museum has an interesting display of shaft tombs, an excellent display of Colima, Nayarit, and Jalisco terracotta figures (but less extensive than the Museo de Arqueología), and possibly the finest display of 17th-18th-century colonial art in Mexico outside the Pinacoteca Virreinal in Mexico City (see page 90). There are also musical instruments, Indian art and one room devoted to the history of Jalisco from the Conquistadores to Iturbide; highly recommended. ■ *Mon-Sat 0900-1745, Sun 0900-1500, US$1.60, free on Sun, Tue, and holidays, free for children and senior citizens.* The **Museo de Periodismo y Artes Gráficas**, Avenida Alcalde 225, between San Felipe and Reforma, T6139285/6, restored and opened in 1994; the building is known as the Casa de los Perros because of two large dog statues on the roof. The first printing shop in Guadalajara was here and the first 'periódico insurgente' (insurgent newspaper) in the Americas, El Despertador Americano was published here in 1810. The museum contains old printing presses, newspapers, etc. When Avenida Alcalde was widened in 1950, the building's façade was moved back 9m. ■ *Tue-Sat 1000-1800, Sun 1100-1500,*

US$0.50, students with ID half price, over 60s free, Sun free. **Museo de la Ciudad**, Calle Independencia 684, in a pretty colonial building with two columned patios, has information on the city from its founding to the present day, including maps and population statistics. ■ *Wed-Sat 1000-1730, Sun 1000-1430, US$0.30, free Sun and for over 60s.* **Albarrán Hunting Museum**, Paseo de los Parques 3530, Colinas de San Javier, has a collection of rare animals from all over the world. ■ *Sat and Sun 1000-1400.* **Casa Museo López Portillo**, Calle Liceo 177, T6132411/2435, formerly the family home of the ex-President, was restored in 1982 when he was in office. It is a colonial house with a large tiled courtyard, and surrounding rooms furnished with 18th and 19th-century Italian and French furniture. It is also used as a cultural centre with classes in music, dance, literature, chess, Indian culture and languages. Across the street at Liceo 166 in another colonial building are the offices of the **Instituto Nacional de Antropología e Historia** (INAH), where there is a library with books on Guadalajara. ■ *1000-1600.* **Casa José Clemente Orozco**, Aurelio Aceves 29, pedestrian street half a block from Los Arcos, was built in the 1940s and donated to the state of Jalisco by the family after the artist's death in 1951. ■ *1000-1600.* Two other museums are the **Museo de Cera**, on the south side of the Plaza de la Liberación, right downtown, on Calle Morelos a couple of doors west of Calle Degollado, and the **Museo del Juguete** (Toy Museum), Hidalgo 1291, esq General Coronado. The **Casa de la Cultura**, Avenida 16 de Septiembre y Constituyentes, holds contemporary art exhibitions and lectures.

Excursions

In a northwest suburb of Guadalajara is the **Basílica de Zapopan**, completed 1690, with a miraculous image of Nuestra Señora, known as *La Generala* on the main altar, given to the Indians in 1542. There is a huge *fiesta* for the Virgen de Zapopan on 12 October. Next door is a museum of Huichol Indian art. ■ *Mon-Fri 1000-1400, Sat-Sun 1000-1300.* At one end of the pedestrian street, Paseo Teopitzintli, leading to the plaza and Basílica, is the colonial-style Arco de Ingreso. The **tourist office** is in the Casa de la Cultura, two blocks behind the Basílica, on Guerrero. ■ *T6330571, Mon-Fri 0900-2100, Sat 0900-1300.* Zapopan is reached by Bus 275 along Avenida Alcalde, or take line 1 of the *tren ligreo* to Avila Camacho stop and pick up Bus 175 to Zapopan. (**NB** There are several different 175s, check with driver that the bus goes all the way to Zapopan.) There is an agricultural fair here in November.

Eight kilometres northeast is the **Barranca de Oblatos**, a 600-m deep canyon. Guides will take you down to see the Río Grande de Santiago cascading at the bottom (except in the dry season). Once described as a stupendous site, it is now rather spoilt by litter and sewage. See especially the Cola de Caballo waterfall and the Parque Mirador Dr Atl. The park is crowded on Sunday. ■ *US$10.* **Balneario Los Comachos**, a large swimming pool with diving boards set on one side of the Barranca de Oblatos, has many terraces with tables and chairs and barbecue pits under mango trees; drinks and snacks are on sale. ■ *US$1.50.*

You can also visit the **Barranca de Huentitán**, access via the Mirador de Huentitán at the end of Calzada Independencia Norte, near the zoological gardens, a tremendous natural site, with interesting flora and better views than at Oblatos. One hour to the bottom (no guide needed) and the river which is straddled by the historic bridge of Huentitán. Buses to Huentitán: 60, 62A, 'Jonilla Centro' from city centre; 44 'Sevilo C Médico', stops 100m short. All buses cost US$0.25.

En Route for Tepic is the **Bosque de la Primavera**, reached by town buses. Pine forests with a hot-water river, ideal for picnics, although increasingly littered. ■ *US$0.50 for a swim*. Good restaurant, *Los Pioneros*, Carretera a Tesistán 2005, esq Avenida Hospital Angel Leaño, with bar, live music, attractions and US 'Wild West' atmosphere.

Tlaquepaque About 7 km southeast of the city centre is the attractive suburb of Tlaquepaque. Calle Independencia runs from Boulevard Tlaquepaque (the main avenue into Guadalajara) to the main plaza where you can see the restored Parroquia de San Pedro Tlaquepaque and the Basílica La Teranensis. Further on is the Parián, a very large, square building occupying most of another plaza, with bars (pretty woodwork and tiling) and kitchens around the perimeter. The rest is an open courtyard with tables and *mariachis*, who play Friday, Saturday, Sunday, 1530 and 2130, also roving *mariachis* play on demand for a fee. The reason most people visit Tlaquepaque is to see the many delightful craft shops (see **Shopping** below). There are a number of good restaurants in Tlaquepaque. *Restaurante Sin Nombre*, Madero 80. In colonial house, seating in courtyard, tropical plants and birds, including peacocks. Nearby, same owner, is *El Pórtico*, also in colonial house on corner of Obregón and Independencia. Other attractive restaurants in colonial houses are *El Patio*, Independencia 186, and *Casa Fuerte*, Independencia 224.

Tonalá Fifteen kilometres southwest of Guadalajara on the road to Mexico City is **Tonalá**, noted for its Sunday and Thursday markets, where you can pick up bargains in pottery, glass and ceramics. The market is held on the central avenue, where all the buses from Guadalajara stop. Calle Benito Juárez intersects this avenue and is a main shopping street. It runs to the main plaza (where it intersects with Calle Madero, the other main shopping street in the centre) and

Guadalajara environs

Related map A Guadalajara, page 485

Not to scale

on another block to the Parroquía de Santiago de Tonalá, a very beautiful church built in the mid-17th century. On the plaza is the cream coloured Iglesia del Sagrado Corazón. The walls are lined with crucifixion paintings. Also on the plaza are the Presidencia Municipal, a pastel blue-green colonial-style building, and the municipal market (food and crafts). For shopping in the centre of town, *Aldana Luna*, at Juárez 194, T6830302, sells wrought-iron furniture; *Plaza Juárez* is a large building at Juárez 141 with several craft shops in it; *Artesanías Nuño*, T6830011, at Juárez 59, sells brightly painted wooden animals. On Madero: there is a *casa de cambio* at No 122; *Restaurant Jalapeños* at No 23 serves pizza, beer and regular meals; **D** *Hotel Tonalá*, opposite, at No 22, is plain but in good shape, some rooms with TV. Another attractive restaurant is *El Rincón del Sol*, at 16 de Septiembre 61, serving steaks and Mexican food.

Four hours north of Guadalajara on the road from Zapopan through San Cristóbal de la Barranca is the small town of **Totatiche** near the Río Tlatenango, founded by the Caxcan Indians but taken over by the Spaniards between 1592-1600. Both Totatiche and neighbouring Temastián were evangelized by Franciscans and the church is in the classical Franciscan style, with a three-tiered tower. In the church is the urn containing the remains of the recently beatified Father Cristóbal Magallanes, who was killed in the Cristero War (see box). Next to the church is the Museo Cristero containing personal effects and furniture. At **Temastián**, 12 km away, the Basílica houses an image of Christ venerated for escaping a lightening bolt which destroyed the cross it was on, known as *El Señor de los Rayos*. The *fiesta*, on 11 January, is celebrated with dancing, parades and rodeos.

Tepatitlán, 79 km northeast of Guadalajara, on the León road, is a small market town with a *charro* centre in an impressive setting with steep hills all around; **Arandas**, further east, has a curious neo-gothic church and a pleasant square with a white wrought-iron bandstand. After Arandas, the road winds tightly up over a range of hills and then down into a long and heavily cultivated valley. It is a five hour journey.

San Miguel El Alto (*population*: 50,000), northeast of Tepatitlán, off Route 80, is an old town, typical of the Jalisco area, where the tradition of the *serenata* is still practiced. On Sunday at 2000, men with confetti and roses line the square while the women promenade. The men signal their interest by throwing confetti on a girl's head; next time around he will offer her a rose. If she is interested she will walk with him round the plaza. At 2200 the police send everyone home and fortunate suitors may be allowed to walk their girlfriends home.

Río Verde

Río Grande de Santiago

TONALA

Av Río Nilo

Central Camionera

To Mexico City

Airport & Chapala

Essentials

LL *Fiesta Americana*, López Mateos at Minerva roundabout, T8253434, 01 (800) 50450, F6303725. Rooms not as grand as the price might suggest, but excellent views from upper floors, and impressive towering hallway. **LL** *Hilton Guadalajara*, T6780505, F6780511, in the Expo Guadalajara Convention Centre, 20 mins from airport, 5 mins from Plaza del Sol, Av de las Rosas 2933, Rinconada del Bosque. 466 rooms, 22 storeys high, luxury, impressive, including breakfast. Opposite Plaza del Sol, is **LL** *Presidente Intercontinental*, López Mateos Sur and Av Moctezuma, T6781237, F6781222. Some deluxe suites with private patio, high-rise tower with built-in shopping centre, cavernous lobby. **LL** *Quinta Real*, Av México 2727 y López Mateos, T6150000, F6301797. Designed as colonial manor, convenient location, good, 78 large, well-furnished rooms, but original art work, good restaurant. **L** *Camino Real*, Vallarta 5005, T1218000, F1218070. 5 pools, tennis, putting green, children's playground, 3 restaurants, bars, conference facilities, some way from the centre. **L** *Holiday Inn Crowne Plaza*, Av López Mateos 2500 Sur, opposite Plaza del Sol shopping centre, T6341034, 01 (800) 36555, F6319393. Restaurant, nightclub, etc.

AL *de Mendoza*, Venustiano Carranza 16, T6134646, 01(800)36126, F6137310, just off Plaza Tapatía. Pleasant, small rooms but pretty colonial-style lobby and restaurant, small pool. Recommended. **AL** *El Tapatío*, Blvd Aeropuerto 4275, T6356050, F6356664, in Tlaquepaque, nearest hotel to airport. Fine view of city, extensive grounds, very attractive and comfortable rooms. **AL-A** *La Villa del Ensueño*, Florida 305, Tlaquepaque, in USA F8185970637, aldez@soca.com. 8 rooms, 2 suites, pool, including breakfast, no smoking, English and Spanish spoken. **A** *Aranzazú*, Av Revolución 110 Pte, T6133232, F6133232 ext 1969. Central, very good. **A** *Fénix*, Av Corona 160, just off López Cotilla, T6145714, F6134005. High-rise block, roof garden with drinks, good restaurant. **A** *Plaza Diana*, Av Circunvalación Agustín Yáñez 2760, T/F6155510. 126 rooms, many refurbished 1995, a/c, TV, restaurant with low-cal menu. **A** *Plaza Génova* (Best Western), Juárez 123, T6137500, F6148253. Including continental breakfast and welcome cocktail, clean, good service, good restaurant. Recommended.

B *del Parque*, Av Juárez 845, T8252800; F8266648. Clean, friendly, courteous, near Parque Revolución, *tren ligero*, University administration. **B** *Francés*, Maestranza 35, T6130917, F6582831. Colonial building with central patio, oldest hotel in the city, built in 1610, have a drink there at 'happy hour' 1800-1900, to enjoy the bygone atmosphere, disco and bar music noisy at night, some rooms small but very good-value penthouse suite (**A**) for 4, with 2 very large bedrooms, living room and kitchen, free parking underneath adjoining Plaza de la Liberación, 3 blocks away. **B** *Hotel Plaza Los Arcos*, Av Vallarta 2456, T6163816, F6151806. 1-bedroom suites, huge hard bed, sitting room, kitchen, good bathroom, very clean, 2-weekly and monthly rates available. **B** *Internacional*, Pedro Moreno 570, T6130330, F6132866. Clean, comfortable, safe. Recommended. **B** *Posada del Sol*, López Mateos Sur 4205, T/F6315205. **B** *Rotonda*, Liceo 130, T/F6141017, central, near Cathedral. Remodelled 19th-century building, attractive, dining area in courtyard, cheap set lunches, nice public areas, rooms OK, with TV, phones, covered parking. **C** *El Parador* at new bus terminal, T6000910, F6000015. Overpriced because of location (does not take Amex), spartan rooms with TV, expensive laundry, clean, noisy, pool, 24-hr café *El Jardín*. **C** *San Francisco Plaza*, Degollado 267, T/F6138954. Many rooms face inwards, street rooms noisy, several patios, hot water, TV, pleasant.

There are cheap hotels along Calzada Independencia (very noisy), on 5 de Febrero and in the 2 blocks north of the old bus station, 28 de Enero and 20 de Noviembre (where there is a small market, good for breakfasts) and the side streets (although rooms can sometimes be filthy, so check). They include **D-E** *Canadá*, Estadio, T6192798, ½ block from old bus station. All rooms with bath, hot water, some with TV, clean, good value (price depends on the section of the hotel, some rooms have been remodelled). **D-E** *Nueva York*, Independencia Sur 43, T/F6173398. With bath, hot water. **E** *Estación*, Calzada Independencia Sur 1297, T6190051, F6190534, across the main boulevard beside train station. Quiet, clean, safe, luggage store, hot water, small, limited restaurant. Recommended. **E** *Royal*, Los Angeles, near old bus terminal. Clean. **F** *León*, Calz Independencia Sur 557. Bath, towel, hot water, clean, staff friendly and helpful. On 5 de Febrero, **E** *San José*, No 116, T/F6191153. **D** *Emperador*, No 530, T6192246. Remodelled, adequate, all rooms have TV and phone, enclosed parking, good public areas, and *Monaco*, No 152. On 20 de Noviembre, *San Carlos*, No 728B, *Praga Central*, No 733A, and *Madrid*, No 775, all **D-E**, good, but rooms on street are noisy.

Other cheap hotels are in the centre, and near Mercado Libertad: several on Javier Mina, eg **D** *Azteca*, 1½ blocks from Mercado Libertad. Clean, parking around the corner (ask at the desk). **D** *Continental*, on Corona. Recommended. **D** *Imperio*, next door. Clean and popular, noisy; other hotels on Corona of similar quality but cheaper. **D** *Janeiro*, Obregón 93, by market. Very clean, good value, cheap laundry service, noisy from *mariachi* music in nearby square. **D** *Maya*, López Cotilla 39, T6144654. With private bath, blankets, pleasant atmosphere. **D** *Posada San Pablo*, Madero 218. Shared bath, hot water, family-run. **D** *Posada Tapatía*, López Cotilla 619, T6149146. Colonial-style house, 2-3 blocks from Federalismo, one of the better budget places, traffic can be a problem. **D-E** *México 70*, Javier Mina, opposite Mercado Libertad. With bath, clean, TV available. **E** *Ana Isabel*, Javier Mina 184, T6177920. Central, TV, not always perfectly clean, tiny rooms but very good value, tell them when you are checking out or room may be relet before you have gone. **E** *González*, behind Mercado Corona, 4 blocks west of cathedral, González Ortega 77. Basic, often full, very friendly, not clean. **E** *Hamilton*, Madero 381. With bath, clean, friendly, good value. **E** *Sevilla*, Prisciliano Sánchez 413, T6149037. Good, clean (4 blocks south of cathedral), owner speaks English, good restaurant (not always open). **F** *del Maestro*, Herrera y Cairo 666, between Mariano Bárcenas and Contreras Medellín, buses from Cathedral 52, 54, 231, from bus station 275, no sign. Not very clean, friendly, OK. **F** *Lisboa*, on corner of Grecia and Juárez in precinct. Shared bath, noisy, but cheap.

Motels AL *Las Américas*, López Mateos Sur 2400, T6314256, F6314415, opposite Plaza del Sol shopping centre. A/c, pool, good. **B** *Del Bosque*, López Mateos Sur 265, T1214700, F1221955. TV and phone in all rooms. **C** *Isabel*, Montenegro 1572, Sector Hidalgo, T/F8262630. Pleasant, pool. There are others at the end of Vallarta, and also along López Mateos near the edge of town, before the *periférico* ring road.

Trailer parks D *La Hacienda*, Circunvalación Pte 66, 16 km out of town, in Col Ciudad Granja, off Av Vallarta on left before you reach *periférico* and head to Tepic, T6271724, F6271724 ext 117. Shaded, pool, clubhouse, hook-ups. Also *San José del Tajo*, 25 km from city on Route 15/80 towards Manzanillo, about 1 km from city boundary. Full hook-up, hot showers, pool, laundry facilities, **D** for vehicle and 2 people, reported in need of repair.

Youth hostel At Prolongación Alcalde 1360, Sector Hidalgo, T8530033, away from centre in a state government complex, entrance gate at intersection of Alcalde and Tamaulipas on east side of Alcalde, office open until 2000. Women's and men's dormitories, bunk beds and lockers which can be padlocked, pillow and blanket, fairly clean, many mosquitoes. Buses 52 and 54 along Av Alcalde from the centre pass the hostel, or bus 275 goes as far as La Normal roundabout, from where it is about 2 blocks north, buses stop between 2200-2300, a taxi from downtown costs US$2-3 but many people walk, about 30 mins. Also *Villa Juvenil Guadalajara II* at Prolongación Federalismo y Lázaro Cárdenas, Unidad Deportiva, CP 44940, T8115628, ask for Arq Abel Buenrostro. Sleeps 90, take Line 1 of *tren ligero* south from centre and get off at Unidad Deportiva.

Guadalajara to the Pacific Coast

Eating
● *on maps*

As can be expected in a city of this size there is a wide variety of restaurants on offer, look in local tourist literature for the latest in International, Mexican, Spanish, Italian, Argentine, Arab, Chinese, Japanese or German cooking. There are also fast food outlets, *pizzerías* and Mexican *cafeterías* and bars. *Carnes Asadas Tolsá*, Enrique Díaz de León 540 and Chapultepec, T8256875. Recommended. *Piaf*, Marsella 126. French cuisine, live music, friendly, closed Sun. Excellent. *Búfalo*, Calderón de la Barca and Av Vallarta. *Tacos* and cheap *comida corrida*, very friendly. *La Banderillas*, Av Alcalde 831. Excellent food at reasonable prices. *El Mexicano*, Plaza Tapatía, Morelos 81. Rustic Mexican décor. Recommended. *Madrid*, Juárez 264 and Corona. Poor service, poor selection of dishes, pricey. *La Catedral del Antojito*, Pedro Moreno 130, a pedestrian street. Colonial style house, restaurant upstairs above bridal gown shops, serves *tacos*, *tortas*, etc, good meal for under US$2. *Café Madoka*, Enrique González Martínez 78, T6133134, just south of Hidalgo. Excellent very early breakfasts, well known for the men who play dominoes there. Friendly, a real gem! Many cheap restaurants in the streets near the old bus station, especially in Calle de Los Angeles, and upstairs in the large Mercado Libertad (San Juan de Dios) in centre, but not always very hygienic here. *La Trattoria*, Niños Héroes 3051. Very good, reasonably priced Italian, very popular (queues form for lunch from 1400). Delicious *carne en su jugo* (beef stew with potatoes, beans, bacon, sausage, onion and avocado, garnished with salsa, onion and coriander) from *Carnes Asadas El Tapatío* in Mercado Libertad (there are 3), or *Carnes Asadas Rigo's*, Independencia 584A, popular. Goat is a speciality, roasted each day and served with radish, onion and chilli. *Karne Garibaldi*, Garibaldi 1306, J Clemente Orozco, Col Sta Teresita. Nice place, serves *carne en su jugo*. For those so inclined, *Lido*, Colón 294 and Miguel Blanco (Plaza San Francisco), serves *criadillas*, bull's testicles. *Cortijo La Venta*, Federación 725, T6171675, open daily 1300-0100. Invites customers to fight small bulls (calves) after their meal (the animals are not harmed, guests might be), restaurant serves meat, soups, salads. *El Ganadero*, on Av Américas. Excellent beef, reasonable prices. *Café Pablo Picasso*, Av Américas 1939, T6361996/6141. Breakfast, lunch, dinner and *tapas*, *galería*, boutique, decorated with photos of Picasso and his work, smart clientèle. Pricey. *Café D'Osio*, around the corner from *Hotel Hamilton*, on corner of Prisciliano Sánchez and Ocampo. Excellent breakfast and vast delicious *tortas*, especially the roast pork, not expensive, open 0900-1800. *El Asadero*, opposite the Basílica in Zapopán suburb (see **Excursions** above). Very good. *La Calle*, Autlán 2, near Galería de Calzado and bus terminal. Expensive but good, with garden. Good *Lonchería* at Morelos 99, by Tourist Office. Try *tortas de lomo doble carne con aguacate* (pork and avocado special). *La Bombilla*, López Cotilla y Penitenciaría. Very good for *churros* and hot chocolate. In the cloister of La Merced is a fast food place, popular with young people. *La Chata*, Francisco Zarco 2277, and *Gemma*, López Mateos Sur 1800, 2 chains serving Mexican food, are usually quite good (*Gemma* has 8 branches in the city and does Guadalajaran *lonches* and *tortas ahogadas*). *La Pianola*, Av México 3220 and several other locations. Good, reasonable prices, serves *chiles en nogada*. Excellent. A good place for fish is *El Delfín Sonriente*, Niños Héroes 2293, T6160216/7441. Nice, attractive. A good Mexican restaurant is *La Gorda*, Juan Alvarez 1336, esq Gen Coronado, Col Sta Teresita. *La Rinconada*, Morelos 86 on Plaza Tapatía. A beautiful colonial building, columned courtyard, carved wood doors, entrées at US$4-8 range, open until 2130, separate bar. Plenty of US fast food places: *Pizza Hut*, *McDonald's*, *Burger King*, *Carl's Junior*, etc, with several outlets.

Bars & nightclubs

La Fuente, Pino Suárez 78. Very popular, mixed clientèle, live music, lots of atmosphere. Many bars serve free *botanas*, snacks, with drinks between 1300 and 1500. Most of these bars are for men only, though. *Botanero el Ciervo*, 20 de Noviembre 797, corner of Calle Los Angeles, opposite old bus station. Two **gay** discos are *SOS*, Av La Paz 1413, and *Mónica's* in Sector Libertad, to the east of the centre. Both are well known locally.

Cinema Average cost of a ticket is US$2. Good quality films, some in English, are shown in the evenings at 1600, 1800, 2000, US$1.25, at the *ciné-teatro* in the *Instituto Cultural Cabañas* (see **Sights** above), which also has a good *cafetería*.

Music Concerts and theatre in the ex-Convento del Carmen. A band plays every Thu at 1800 in the Plaza de Armas, in front of the Palacio de Gobierno, free. Organ recitals in the Cathedral. *Peña Cuicacalli*, Av Niños Héroes almost at corner of Av Chapultepec, T8254690, opens 2000, US$5 cover charge, food and drink available, fills up fast; local groups perform variety of music including Latin American folk music Fri, Sat.

Theatre *Ballet Folklórico de la Universidad de Guadalajara*, every Sun at 1000 in the Teatro Degollado, superb, highly recommended, pre-Hispanic and Mexican-wide dances, and other cultural shows, US$2-10, T6583812, 6144773 (check before you go, if there is another function in the theatre they may perform elsewhere). The theatre is open to the public from 1000-1300 Mon-Fri just to look inside. The *Grupo Folklórico Ciudad de Guadalajara* performs here every Thu at 2000. The *Ballet Folklórico del Instituto Cultural Cabañas* performs Wed 2030, US$4. The Instituto is also an art school, with classes in photography, sculpture, ceramics, literature, music, theatre and dance.

21 March commemorates Benito Juárez' birthday and everything is closed for the day. Ceremonies around his monument at the Parque Agua Azul. In **Jun** the Virgin of Zapopan (see **Excursions** above), leaves her home to spend each night in a different church where fireworks are let off. The virgin has a new car each year but the engine is not started, men pull it through the beautifully decorated streets with ropes. The climax is 12 Oct when the virgin leaves the Cathedral for home, there are great crowds along the route. Throughout the month of **Oct** there is a great *fiesta* with concerts, bullfights, sports and exhibitions of handicrafts from all over Mexico. **12 Dec**, *fiesta* in honour of the Virgin of Guadalupe; Av Alcalde has stalls, music, fair, etc. In Dec there is a Christmas fair at Parque Morelos and hand-made toys are a special feature.

The best shops are no longer in the centre, although a couple of department stores have branches there. The best stores are in the shopping centres, of which there are many, small and large, mainly on the west side. The newest and biggest is La Gran Plaza, 3 floors, with *Sears, Salinas y Rocha*, 12-screen cinema and many smaller shops, between Av Lázaro Cárdenas and Av Vallarta, near where they merge. Plaza México is another large centre, and nearby, with smaller boutiques, is Plaza Bonito. The Plaza del Sol shopping centre, with over 100 shops, is located beyond Chapalita in the south of the city, while the equally modern Plaza Patria, with almost as many shops, is at the north end near the Zapopan suburb. There are many other shopping malls such as the Galería del Calzado (on Av México, several blocks west of Av López Mateos), selling, as the name implies, only shoes. *El Toro Loco*, and *Botas Los Potrillos*, on Morelos by Plaza Tapatía, sell good boots.

The markets, in particular the Mercado Libertad (San Juan de Dios) which has colourful items for souvenirs with lots of Michoacán crafts including Paracho guitars and Sahuayo hats, leather jackets and *huaraches* (sandals) and delicious food upstairs on the 1st level (particularly goat meat, *birria*, also very sweet coconut called *cocada*), fruit juices and other soft drinks. The *tianguis* (Indian market) on Av Guadalupe, Colonia Chapalita, on Fri is of little interest to foreigners, Bus 50 gets you there; the *tianguis* near the University Sports Centre on Calzada Tlaquepaque is on Sun. In Tonalá, market days are Sun and Thu (see **Excursions**).

Bookshops English books available at a reasonable mark up, at *Sanborns*, Av Vallarta 1600 and Gen San Martín, Juárez and 16 de Septiembre, Plaza Bonita and López Mateos Sur 2718 (near Plaza del Sol), also English language magazines. German journals at *Sanborns*, Av Vallarta branch. *Librería Británica*, Av Hidalgo 1796-B, Sector Hidalgo, T6155803, 6155807, F6150935. *Sandi's*, Av Tepeyac 718, Colonia Chapalita,

☞ *The Guadalajara International Book Fair*

Guadalajara is one of the true music capitals of Mexico, famous for its Mariachi Square and street musicians. You frequently find some of the best popular music in town being played by live musicians on street corners or on the move, on the public buses. The graphic arts are also well served here, Guadalajara being the home of many fine examples of Mexican mural art, by José Clemente Orozco, David Alfaro Siqueiros and others.

What is not so well known is that this city is also the site of the third largest book fair in the world, held every year in late November/early December. It takes place in the new Gran Salón de Exposiciones in Guadalajara, and except for the book fairs in Frankfurt and Buenos Aires, there is none more important anywhere. Those others are somewhat stuffy affairs, though, that are unfriendly to the general public and intended mostly for the trade. In Guadalajara everyone is invited, and the book fair festivities go on inside and outside the convention hall. Inside, some 800 publishers from 25 countries may be represented, and writers, agents, publicists, designers and film people of every sort can be seen walking up and down the aisles between exhibits. The general public is welcome (320,000 people attended the fair in 1999) and you can run into the likes of Isabel Allende and Carlos Fuentes, while visiting with all manner of commercial, university and avant-garde presses. Outside the main hall, there are round the clock readings of poetry and fiction, music, celebrations of children's literature, games, food and drink. You can find impromptu street theatre, comedy, improvization, dance, jugglers, fire-eaters, clowns ... anything you wish.

For information, write (in English or Spanish) to FIL Guadalajara, Francia 1747, Colonia Moderna, Guadalajara, Jalisco 44190, Mexico, T523-8100331, F523-8100379, www.fil.com.mex Or write to FIL New York, c/o David Unger, Division of Humanities NAC 6/293, The City College of New York, NY 10031, USA, T212-6507925, F212-6507912, filny@aol.com

T1210863, F6474600, has a good selection of English-language books, including medical textbooks and cards. *Librería México* in Plaza del Sol, local 14, area D, on Av López Mateos side, T1210114, has US magazines and newspapers. *El Libro Antiguo*, Pino Suárez 86, open 1000-2000, mostly Spanish but large selection of English paperbacks. *Librería La Fuente*, Medellín 140, near Juan Manuel in the centre, T6135238, sells used books and magazines in English and Spanish, interesting to browse in, some items quite old, from 1940s and 1950s. Bookshops can be found on López Cotilla, from González Martínez towards 16 de Septiembre.

Crafts Two glass factories at **Tlaquepaque** where the blue, green, amber and amethyst blown-glass articles are made (Bus 275 from the centre goes through Tlaquepaque *en route* to bus station). Calle Independencia is the main shopping street and closed to traffic. The **Museo Regional de la Cerámica** is at Independencia 237. For beautiful, expensive furniture go to *Antigua de México*, Independencia 255, lovely building, used to be a convent, the family has branches in Nogales and Tucson so furniture can be shipped to their shops there. *La Casa Canela*, opposite, sells furniture and crafts, don't miss the colonial kitchen at the back of the house. *Adobe Diseño*, also in a colonial house, sells expensive leather furniture. Visit the shop of *Sergio Bustamante*, who sells his own work (good modern jewellery): expensive but well worth a look, a stream runs through this house with a colonial façade at Independencia 236. Some way from the main shopping area is the *Casa de los Telares*, Hidalgo 1378, where Indian textiles are woven on hand looms. Potters can be watched at work both in Guadalajara and at Tlaquepaque; you may find better bargains at **Tonalá** (pottery and ceramics, some glass), see **Excursions**, above, on market days Thu and Sun; take Bus 275 (see local **Transport** below), bumpy 45 mins journey. Overall, Tlaquepaque is the cheapest and most varied source of the local crafts, with attractive shops set in old colonial villas; best buys: glass, papier mâché goods, leather (cheapest in Mexico), and ceramics. See also the *Tienda Tlaquepaque*, at Av Juárez 267-B, in Tlaquepaque, T6355663. *Casa de Artesanías de Jalisco*, González Gallo 20, T6194664, open 1000-1900 (1400 Sun), in Parque Agua Azul: high quality display (and sale) of handicrafts, ceramics, paintings, handblown glass, dresses, etc (state-subsidized to preserve local culture, reasonably priced but not cheap). There is another shop-cum-exhibition at the *Instituto de Artesanía Jaliscense*, *Casa de Las Artesanías Normal*, Av Alcalde 1221, T6244624.

Bullfights Oct-Mar; *football* throughout year; *charreadas* (cowboy shows) are held **Sports** in mid-Sep at Unión de San Antonio; *lienzo charro* near Parque Agua Azul at Aceves Calindo Lienzo, Sun at 1200. **Baseball** Apr-Sep. **Golf** at Santa Anita, 16 km out on Morelia road, championship course; Rancho Contento, 10 km out on Nogales road; San Isidro, 10 km out on Saltillo road, noted for water hazards; Areas, 8 km out on Chapala road (US$13 during the week, US$20 at weekends is the average price for a round). The *Guadalajara Country Club*, has a beautiful clubhouse and golf course in the middle of the city, near the Plaza Patria shopping centre, Mar Caribe 260, T8173502, phone ahead for start time and to check green fee. **Hiking** club *Colli*, bulletin board Av Juárez 460, details from *Café Madrid*, Juárez 264 or T6233318, 6179248.

Expediciones México Verde, José María Vigil 2406, Colonia Italia Providencia, **Tour operators** T/F6415598, rafting specialists (Ríos Actopan, Jatate, Santa María, Antigua-Pescados, Filobobos, Usumacinta).

Local Horse-drawn carriages US$5 for a short ride or US$7.50 per hr from the Museo **Transport** Regional de Guadalajara at the corner of Liceo and Hidalgo. **Buses**: Tourist Office in Plaza Tapatía has a full list of local buses. If in doubt ask bus driver. Regular buses cost US$0.20, Línea Azul 'luxury' bus US$0.45. Some useful lines: No 275, from Zapopan - Plaza Patria - Glorieta Normal - Av Alcalde - Av 16 de Septiembre - Av Revolución - Tlaquepaque - new bus station - Tonalá (there are different 275s, from A to F, most follow this route, check with driver). Route 707 also goes to Tonalá (silver-blue bus with Tur on the side). Bus 60 goes along Calzada de la Independencia from zoo, passing Estadio Jalisco, Plaza de Toros, Mercado Libertad and Parque Agua Azul to the old bus terminal and the railway station (**NB** if you are going to Parque Mirador, take bus 62 northbound, otherwise 62 has the same route as 60). There is also a new trolley bus that runs along the Calzada de la Independencia to the entrance to the Mirador, better than 60 or 62. For the old bus station, take minibus 174 south along Calzada de la Independencia from Mercado Libertad, or bus 110 south along Av Alcalde. Bus 102 runs from the new bus terminal along Av Revolución, 16 de Septiembre and Prisciliano Sánchez to Mercado Libertad. No 258 or 258A from San Felipe (north of Cathedral) or 258D along Madero go to Plaza del Sol. No 371 runs from Tonalá to Plaza del Sol. A shuttle bus runs between the 2 bus stations. The **Metro**, or *Tren Ligero*, has Línea 1 running under Federalismo from Periférico Sur to Periférico Norte. Línea 2, runs from Juárez station westbound and passes Mercado Libertad. Fare US$0.40, 1-peso coins needed to buy tokens.

Car hire: *Quick*, Av Niños Héroes, esq Manzano, T6142247, VW Sedan US$40 per day, including tax, insurance, 400 km per day; Nissan Tsuru, 4-door, standard shift, a/c, US$52, 500 km included. *Budget*, Av Niños Héroes, esq 16 de septiembre, T6130027, Nissan Tsuru, a/c, US$70 per day, unlimited mileage; Ford Fiesta, US$80, unlimited mileage. *National*, Main office: Niños Heroes 961, by Hotel Carlton, and other offices at the hotels Fiesta Americana, Holiday Inn Select, and the airport, T6147175, VW Sedan, US$35 per day, including 300 km per day; also have Chevy 2-door for same

Guadalajara to the Pacific Coast

Bus timetable from Guadalajara

Guadalajara to the Pacific Coast

destination	module 1	module 2	module 3
Acapulco			
Agua Prieta			
Aguascalientes	PP US$13	ETN US$15	
Ameca			ATM US$3
Arandas			
Autlán			AC US$10
Barra de Navidad			AC US$16
Chihuahua			
Ciudad Guzmán		LL US$6; AS US$6	
Ciudad Juárez			
Ciudad Victoria			
Colima	PP US$10; SC US$8	ETN US$15; LL US$9-11; AO US$8-12; AS US$8	
Culiacán			Eli US$40; TP US$35-40
Cuyatlán		AS US$9	
Durango			
Fresnillo			
Guanajuato	PP US$16	ETN US$16, 3 daily	
Guaymas			Eli US$70; TP US$61-70
Hermosillo			Eli US$75; TP US$65-75
Irapuato	SC US$12		
La Barca	Ci every 30 mins, US$4	AO US$3	
Lagos de Moreno	PP US$11; SC US$10		
Lázaro Cárdenas		LL US$21-24; AO US$18-21; AS US$19	
León	PP US$11; SC US$12	ETN US$17, 8 daily	Eli US$51; TP US$45-51
Los Mochis			
Manzanillo	PP US$12; SC US$12	ETN US$19; LL US$12-14; AS US$11	AC US$19
Mascota			ATM US$7
Matamoros			
Mazamitla		AM US$4, every hr	
Mazatlán (3hrs)			Eli US$27; TP US$24-27
Melaque			AC US$15
Mexicali			Eli US$67; TP US$81-93
Mexico City (6-7 hrs)	PP US$30, every 15 mins	ETN US$39; LL US$27-30; AO US$20-22	Fu US$28
Monterrey			
Morelia	PP US$15; SC US$12	ETN US$20, 2-7 daily; LL US$11-12; AO US$9-12	
Nogales			Eli US$63; TP US$54-85
Nuevo Laredo			
Ocotlán (1hr)	Ci every 30 mins, US$3		
Pátzcuaro		LL US$12	
Pozo Rica			
Puerto Vallarta		ETN US$29, 8 daily	TP US$22
Querétaro	PP US$18; SC US$13	ETN US$22	
Reynosa			
San Blas			
San Juan de los Lagos		ETN US$11	
San Luis Potosí		ETN US$22	
San Miguel de Allende	PP US$17		
Saltillo			
Sayula		AS US$3.25	
Talpa			ATM US$8
Tampico			
Tepatitlán			Eli US$13; TP US$12-13; Fu US$13
Tepic			Eli US$13
Tijuana			Eli US$99; TP US$86-99
Torreón			
Toulca		ETN US$34, 3 daily; AO US$16-18	
Uruapan	PP US$13; SC US$10	ETN US$15; AO US$8-10	
Zacatecas			
Zamora	Ci US$5.50; SC US$6	LL US$6.20-6; AO US$5-6	
Zapotlanejo			

dule 4	module 5	module 6	module 7
			Fu US$48
US$82			
			TE US $13, at 1600
	RA US$4		
			Fu US$55, at 1800; TC/TN US$55; TE US$75, at 1600
		OM US$54	Fu US$72, at 1800; TC/TN US$72; TE US$98, at 1600
	OO/LA US$20-24		
		OM US$9	
US$35			
	RA US$26	OM US$23	Fu US$31
	RA US$17	OM US$20	
US$60			
US$65			
	OO/LA US$6-10		
US$44			
	OO/LA US$30-35	OM US$35	
US$23			
US$81			
	OO/LA US$20-23	OM US$28	Fu US 28; TE US$40, at 2300
		OM US$37	Fu US$37; TE US$49, at 1730-2130
US$76			
		OM US$49	Fu US$49, 1930; TE US$ 39, at 1730, 2100
		OM US$36	
US$19			
	OO/LA US$16		
	OO/LA US$30-34	OM US$34	TE US$61
US$10			
	OO/LA US$11-12	OM US$12	
			TE US$44, at 1900, 2230
		OM US$33	
	OO/LA US$3, every 30 mins		
US$12		OM US$ 13	Fu US$13
US$80			
	RA US$30	OM US$35	Fu US$26, 2200; TC/TN US$35
	RA US$11	OM US$17	Fu US$17
	OO/LA US$3, every 20 mins		

bus company

ATM	ATM
AO	Autobuses de Occidente
AC	Autocamiones Cihuatlán
AS	Autotransportes del Sur
AG	Autotransportes Guadalajara
AM	Autotransportes Mazamitla
Ci	Ciénega
Eli	Elite
ETN	ETN
FA	Flecha Amarilla
Fu	Futura
LL	La Línea
NS	Norte de Sonora
OM	Omnibus de México
OO/LA	Omnibus de Oriente/ Línea Azul
PP	Primera Plus
RA	Rojo de los Altos
SC	Servicios Coordinados
TP	Transportes del Pacífico
TC/TN	Transportes Chihuahuenses
TC/TN	Transportes del Norte
TE	Turistar Ejecutivo

Guadalajara to the Pacific Coast

price. *Avis*, at airport, T6885656, toll free within Mexico 800-2888888, VW Sedan US$40, plus US$18 insurance and 15% tax, unlimited mileage, Chevy US$44, unlimited mileage. *Hertz*, Office at Hotel Quinta Real, other at airport. Others scattered throughout city, T6146162, VW Sedan US$47 per day, unlimited mileage.

Taxis: No meters used. A typical ride in town costs US$2 to US$4. From the centre to the new bus station is about US$6, although if the taxi ticket booths are open at the bus station (and more often than not they aren't) it costs around US$4. A taxi to the airport costs US$10.

Long distance Air: Miguel Hidalgo (GDL), 20 km from town; 3 classes of taxi (*especial, semi-especial and colectivo*) charge fixed rates for 3 city zones; no tip necessary. Bus No 176 'San José del 15', leaves from intersection of Corona and Calzada de la Independencia every 20 mins, US$0.25, grey bus. Autotransportes Guadalajara-Chapala runs 2nd-class buses from old bus terminal every 15 mins, 0655-2125, US$0.35, stop at airport on way to/from Chapala. Many flights daily to and from Mexico City, 65 mins. Connections by air with nearly all domestic airports. US cities served include Chicago, Cincinnati, Dallas, Houston, Jacksonville, Los Angeles, Miami, New York, Oakland, Phoenix, Salt Lake City, San Diego, San Francisco, San José (California).

Buses: New bus station near the El Alamo cloverleaf, 10 km from centre; buses 102 and 275 go to the centre, US$0.25, frequent service (see Local Transport above), journey takes at least 30 mins. There is a new luxury bus service (Línea Azul) running from Zapopan, along Avila Camacho, past Plaza Patria shopping centre to the Glorieta La Normal, south down Av Alcalde, through Tlaquepaque, to the new bus station and ending in Tonalá, seats guaranteed, US$0.45. Another luxury bus service to the centre is Línea Cardenal. No buses after 2230. Bus tickets are sold at 2 offices on Calzada de la Independencia underneath the big fountain on Plaza Tapatía, open 0900-1400, 1600-1900. Because of the distance from the centre of town, it is worth getting your departure information before you go into town. Shop around. It helps to know which company you wish to travel with as their offices are spread over a large area, in 7 modules. All modules have public phones, but only Modules 1 and 2 have long distance, all have left luggage, toilets (some older free ones and some remodelled pay ones), taxi booths, tourist information booths (not always manned), restaurants and shops; outside Module 5 is a map of urban bus routes. A number of bus companies change dollars at rates marginally worse than *casas de cambio*.

The old central bus station, Los Angeles and 28 de Enero, serves towns within 100 km. You have to pay 20 centavos to enter the terminal (open 0545-2215). It has 2 *salas* (wings): A and B, and is shaped like a U. The flat bottom of the U fronts Dr R Michel, where the main entrances are. There is a side entrance to Sala A from Los Angeles and to both A and B from 15 de Febrero via a tunnel. Taxi stands on both sides of the terminal. By the entrances to the *salas* is a Computel outlet with long-distance and fax service. A fax to the USA costs US$2 per min, to Europe US$2.50. There are lots of Ladatel phones for long distance and local calls outside the main entrance, some take coins and others debit cards. There is also a magazine stand selling maps of the city and a shoeshine service in front of the terminal. The shuttle buses to the new bus station leave from here, US$0.20. In Sala A there are 2nd class buses to **Tepatitlán** and **Zapotlanejo** and '*La Penal*' (the prison), with Oriente. 1st class buses to the same destinations leave from the new bus terminal. Buses to **Chapala** (every 30 mins, 0600-2140, US$1.60) and **Ajijic** (every 30 mins, 0700-2100, US$1.80) leave from here with Autotransportes Guadalajara-Chapala. Round trip package to the *balneario* at **San Juan Cosalá**, US$5.25 including admission to the baths. In Sala B, Omnibus de Rivera sells tickets to the same *balneario* for US$1.50 and at La Alteña booth for the *balnearios* **Agua Caliente** and **Chimulco**. A Primera Plus/Servicios Coordinados booth sells tickets to places served by the new bus terminal. Both *salas* have several food stands serving *tortas*, etc, and there are toilets, a luggage store and a magazine stand.

Airline offices *Mexicana*, reservations T6787676, arrival and departure information T6885775, ticket offices: Av Mariano Otero 2353, by Plaza del Sol, T1120011, Av 16 de Septiembre 495, T6148195, Plaza Patria, Local 8H, T6415352, López Cotilla 1552, T6153099/3480, between Av Chapultepec and Américas. *AeroMéxico*, reservations T6690202, airport information T6885098, ticket offices, Av Corona 196 and Plaza del Sol, Local 30, Zona A. *Delta*, López Cotilla 1701, T6303530. *Aero California*, López Cotilla 1423, T8268850. On Av Vallarta: *Air France*, No 1540-103 T6303707), *American*, No 2440 (T6164090 for reservations, T6885518 at airport), *KLM*, No 1390-1005 T8253261, *Continental*, ticket office Astral Plaza, Galerías del *Hotel Presidente Intercontinental*, Locales 8-9, T6474251 reservations, T6885141 airport. *Saro*, Av 16 de Septiembre 334, T91-800-83224. *Taesa*, López Cotilla 1531B, just past Av Chapultepec, reservations T01 (800) 90463. *United*, Plaza Los Arcos, Av Vallarta 2440, local A13, T6169489.

Banks There are many *casas de cambio* on López Cotilla between Independencia and 16 de Septiembre and one in Plaza del Sol. Despite what they say, *casas de cambio* close 1400 or 1500 till 1600, not continuously open 0900-1900. *American Express*, Plaza Los Arcos, Local 1-A, Av Vallarta 2440, esq Francisco García de Quevedo, about 5 blocks east of Minerva roundabout, T6300200, F6157665, open 0900-1800 for the travel agency and 0900-1430, 1600-1800 to change money. Across Prisciliano Sánchez from the Jardín San Francisco is a *Banco Inverlat* with a 24-hr ATM which gives cash on American Express cards if you are enrolled in their Express Cash programme.

Communications **Internet:** Cyber café with Internet access at López Cotilla 773203, 1st floor, southwest corner of Parque Revolución, T8263771, 8263286, F8265610, www.internet-café.com.mx or www.i-set.com.mx/cybercafé They charge US$2.50 per hr for Internet access and give free course in its use; 1 peso per page to print; they receive your email, US$0.60 per page to print out; will notify you when any messages come in; also serve pizza, snacks, beer and soft drinks. Another cyber café is *Arrobba*, Av Lázaro Cárdenas 3286, just west of intersection with López Mateos, open Mon-Sat 1000-2200, internet access US$3.10 per hr, printouts US$0.25, drinks, snacks, salads www.arrobba.com.mx **Post Office:** V Carranza, just behind Palacio de Justicia, open Mon-Fri 0800-1900, Sat 0900-1300. There are also branches at the Mercado Libertad (San Juan de Dios) and at the old bus station, convenient for the cheap hotels. To send parcels abroad go to Aduana Postal in same building as main post office, open Mon-Fri 0800-1300, T6149002. Federal Express has 3 outlets: Av Américas 1395, Plaza del Sol Locales 51-55, Av Washington 1129, next to Bolerama 2000, T8172502, F8172374. United Parcel Service at Av Américas 981, Local 19, T01-80090292. **Telephone:** international collect calls can be made from any coin-box phone kiosk and direct dial calls can be made from LADA pay phones, of which there are many all over the city. You can also make long-distance calls and send faxes from *Computel* outlets: 1 in front of old bus station, 1 on Corona y Madero, opposite *Hotel Fénix*. Another chain, *Copyroyal*, charges 3 times as much for a fax to USA. *Mayahuel*, Paseo Degollado 55 has long-distance service, fax, sells Ladatel cards, postcards and maps. There is a credit card phone at Ramón Corona y Av Juárez, by Cathedral. 2 USA Direct phones, 1 within and 1 beyond the customs barrier at the airport.

Cultural centres *Instituto Goethe*, Morelos 2080 y Calderón de la Barca, T6156147/6160495, F6159717, library, nice garden, newspapers. *Alliance Française*, López Cotilla 1199, Sector Juárez, T8252140, 8255595. *The Instituto Cultural Mexicano-Norteamericano de Jalisco*, Enrique Díaz de León 300, (see below, **Language schools**).

Embassies & consulates *Australia*, López Cotilla 2030, T6157418, F6303479, open 0800-1330, 1500-1800. *Austria*, Montevideo 2695, Colonia Providencia, T6411834, open 0900-1330. *Belgium*, Metalúrgica 2818, Parque Industrial El Alamo, T6704825, F6700346, open Mon-Fri 0900-1400. *Brazil*, Cincinati 130, esq Nueva Orleans, Col La Aurora, next to train station, T6192102, open 0900-1700. *Canada*, trade officer and consul, *Hotel Fiesta Americana*, local 31, T6165642, F615-8665 open 0830-1400 & 1500-1700. *Denmark*, Lázaro Cárdenas 601, 6th floor, T6695515, F6785997, open 0900-1300, 1600-1800. *Dominican Republic*, Colón 632, T6135478, F6145019, open 0900-1400, 1600-1900. *Ecuador*, Morelos 685, esq Pavo, T6131666, F6131729, open 1700-2000. *El Salvador*, Fermín Riestra 1628, between Bélgica and Argentina, Colonia Moderna, T8101061, hours for visas 1230-1400, normally visas will be received the same day. *Finland*, Justo Sierra 2562, 5th floor, T6163623, F6161501, open 0830-1330. *France*, López Mateos Nte 484 entre Herrera y Cairo y Manuel Acuña, T6165516, open 0930-1400. *Germany*, Corona 202, T6139623, F6132609, open 1130-1400. *Great Britain*, Eulogio Parra 2539, T6160629/7616021, F6150197, 0900-1500, 1700-2000. *Guatemala*, Mango 1440, Colonia del Fresno, T8111503, open 1000-1400. *Honduras*,

Directory

Ottawa 1139, Colonia Providencia, T8174998, F8175007, open 1000-1400, 1700-1900. *Israel*, Av Vallarta 2482 Altos, Sector Juárez, T6164554, open 0930-1500. *Italy*, López Mateos Norte 790-1, T6161700, F6162092, open 1100-1400, Tue-Fri. *Netherlands*, Lázaro Cárdenas 601, 6th floor, Zona Industrial, T8112641, F8115386, open 0900-1400, 1630-1900. *Nicaragua*, Eje Central 1024, esq Toreros, Colonia Guadalupe Jardín, behind Club Atlas Chapalita, T6282919, open 1600-1800. *Norway*, Km 5 Antigua Carretera a Chapala 2801, Colonia La Nogalera, T8121411, F8121074, in the building Aceite El Gallo, open 0900-1800. *Perú*, Bogotá 2923, between Terranova and Alberta, Colonia Providencia, T6423009, open 0800-1600. *Spain*, Av Vallarta 2185, T6300450, F6160396, open 0830-1330. *Portugal*, Colimán 277, Ciudad del Sol, T1217714, F6843925. *Sweden*, J Guadalupe Montenegro 1691, T8256767, F8255559, open 0900-1400, 1600-1900. *Switzerland*, Av Revolución 707, Sector Reforma, T6175900, F6173208, open 0800-1400, 1600-1900. *USA*, Progreso 175, T8252700, F6266549.

Language schools *Centro de Estudios para Extranjeros de la Universidad de Guadalajara*, Tomás V Gómez 125, between Justo Sierra and Av México, T6164399/6164382, registration US$85, US$585 for 5 weeks of 4 hrs per day instruction, US$490 for 5 weeks living with a Mexican family with 3 meals a day. *The Universidad Autónoma de Guadalajara (UAG)*, a private university, offers Spanish classes through their Centro Internacional de Idiomas, T6417051, ext 32251, 0800-1800, at Edificio Humanidades 1st floor, on the main campus at Av Patria 1201, Colonia Lomas del Valle, 3a sección, US$350 for 4 weeks of 4 hrs per day instruction, 5 days a week, 7 levels of instruction, each lasting 4 weeks, US$13 per day accommodation and 3 meals with Mexican family. *The Instituto Cultural Mexicano-Norteamericano de Jalisco*, at Enrique Díaz de León 300, T8255838/8252666, US$440 for 6 weeks of 3 hrs per day plus 30 mins conversation, 5 days a week, 5 levels of instruction, cultural lectures on Fri, US$18 per day to live with Mexican family with 3 meals. *Spanish Language School AC*, Ermita 1443 between 12 de Diciembre and Av Las Rosas, Colonia Chapalita, Apdo Postal 5-959, T/F1214774. *Vancouver Language Centre*, Av Vallarta 1151, Colonia América, T8260944, F8252051 (T1-604-6871600-Vancouver), US$150 for 1 week intensive programme. For German and French lessons see **Cultural centres**, above. See also National Registration Center for Study Abroad under Learning Spanish in **Essentials**.

Laundry Aldama 125, US$3.30 per 3 kg load (walk along Independencia towards train station, turn left into Aldama).

Medical services Dentist: *Dr Abraham Waxtein*, Av México 2309, T6151041, speaks English. Doctor: *Dr Daniel Gil Sánchez*, Pablo Neruda 3265, 2nd floor, T6420213, speaks English (1st cosultation, 2½ hrs, including thorough physical, US$50). *Dr Jorge Flores González*, Francisco Rojas González 155 (esq Av México), ground floor, T6166212/6166213/6166217/6167015. Pager: 6784300 code No 8617 (consultation, US$15; call after 1600 to make appointment, recommended). **Hospitals:** good private hospitals are *Hospital del Carmen*, Tarascos 3435, Fraccionamiento Monraz (behind Plaza México), T8130042 (take credit cards). *Hospital San Javier*, Pablo Casals 640 (on the corner of Eulogio Parra and Acueducto), Colonia Providencia, T6690222 (take credit cards). *Hospital Angel Leaño*, off the road to Tesistán, T8343434, affiliated with the University (UAG). A less well-equipped but good hospital near the centre that is also affiliated with the UAG is the *Hospital Ramón Garibay*, Enrique Díaz de León 238, across the street from the Templo Expiatorio, T8255313/8255159/8255115/8255050, inexpensive out-patient clinic with various specialists. Probably the best private laboratory is the *Unidad de Patología*, Av México 2341, T6165410, takes credit cards. For those who cannot afford anything else there are the *Hospital Civil*, T6145501, and the *Nuevo Hospital Civil*, T6189362, F6177177. For *antirrábico* (rabies), T6431917; to receive the vaccine you have to go to Clinic 3 of the Sector Salud, T8233262, at the corner of Circunvalación División del Norte and Calzada Federalismo, across the street from a Telmex office, near the División del Norte Station, Line 1, *tren ligero*; you can also get an AIDS blood test here. *Sidatel* (AIDS), T6137546. **Infectologist:** *Dr J Manuel Ramírez R*, Dom Ermita 103126, Colonia Chapalita, by the intersection of Lázaro Cárdenas and López Mateos, T6477161. **Ophthalmologist:** *Dr Virginia Rivera*, Eulogia Parra 2432, near López Mateos, T6166637/F6164046, English speaking (US$25 for 1st consultation, US$20 for subsequent consultations. Conultations only on Mon, Wed, and Fri between 1600 and 1930). **Pharmacies:** 3 big chains of pharmacies are *Farmacias Guadalajara*, *Benavides* and *ABC*. The *Farmacia Guadalajara* at Av Américas and Morelos has vaccines and harder-to-find drugs, T6155094. Other good pharmacies for hard-to-find drugs are the *Farmacia Especializada*, Av Américas N-252, on corner of Garibaldi, T/F 6154193, and *Farmacia Géminis*, across the street from the *Hospital del Carmen*, T8132874.

Useful services Immigration: Mexican tourist cards can be renewed at the immigration office (1st floor) in the Palacio Federal on Av Alcalde between Juan Alvarez and Hospital, across the avenue from the Santuario de Guadalupe. The Palacio Federal also contains a post and telegraph office and fax service.

Chapala

Chapala town, 64 km to the southeast of Guadalajara on the northern shore of **Laguna de Chapala** (113 km long, 24-32 km wide), has thermal springs, several good and pricey hotels, three golf courses, and is a popular resort particularly with retired North Americans and Mexican day-trippers. Watch women and children play a picture-card game called *Anachuac*.

Phone code: 376
Colour map 3, grid B3

The divided highway from Guadalajara becomes Avenida Francisco Madero in town, with a grassy middle and large trees, *laureles de la India*, giving shade. The avenue ends at the lake. The street that runs along the lakefront, Paseo Ramón Corona, is closed to traffic west of Avenida Madero. The other main street in town is Avenida Hidalgo, one block in from the lake, parallel to Ramón Corona. Avenida Hidalgo going west becomes the road to Ajijic and beyond. Uphill from the *Villa Montecarlo* hotel on Calle Lourdes (cobblestone) is La Iglesia de Lourdes, a small pastel-pink church with a bell tower, facing down the street to the lake. Open during masses on Thursday and at noon on Sunday.

Laguna de Chapala is set in beautiful scenery. There are boats of all kinds for hire, some go to the **Isla de los Alacranes** (restaurant), and there is water-fowl shooting in autumn and winter. Most fish in the lake have been killed by pollution, but the 5cm 'XYZ' fish, called *charales*, are a delicacy similar to whitebait. Beside the lake, four blocks east of Avenida Madero along Paseo Ramón Corona, **Parque de la Cristinia** is worth a visit, it is popular with families at weekends, and there is a swimming pool. Horses can be hired at bargain prices on the beach by the Parque. There is a market on the east side of the Zócalo with stalls selling handicrafts, places to eat, dirty public conveniences (one peso); entrance on street behind the market. The regional **tourist office** is at Aquiles Serdán 26, T53141.

The water level is low because of irrigation demand and it is getting smelly and overgrown at the edges. Lake water must not be drunk.

Sleeping

B-C *Villa Montecarlo*, west edge of town on Av Hidalgo at Calle Lourdes. Family rooms or suites available, beautiful grounds with palms and mangoes, all rooms have phone, bath tub, balcony overlooking lake, pool, tennis, good restaurant, tables outside under massive *laurel de la India* tree. **B** *Lake Chapala Inn*, Paseo Ramón Corona 23, T54786. Breakfast included in price. Recommended. **D** *Chapala Haciendas*, Km 40, Chapala-Guadalajara highway, T52720. Live music Wed and Sat. Unheated pool. **D** *Nido*, Av Madero 202, close to lake, T52116. Brick building, old photos in reception hall, clean, cheaper without TV, accept Visa and MasterCard, good restaurant, swimming pool, parking for motorcycles beside pool. **E** *Casa de Huéspedes Palmitas*, Juárez 531, behind market. TV, hot water, bath, but run down, noisy, cockroaches.

Furnished apartments for rent at Hidalgo 269, information at 274-A, also at Paseo Ramón Corona and Juárez on the lake, 1 block east of Av Madero. Next door at Paseo

Lake Chapala

👉 The Plumed Serpent

In May-July 1923, D H Lawrence lived in Chapala, renting a house called Los Cuentales. The house still stands at Zaragoza 307, although a second floor and some modernization have been added. The church that figures in the last pages of The Plumed Serpent is on the waterfront, its humble façade and interior now covered by a handsome veneer of carved stone. Lawrence's novel, published in 1926, explored Mexican society in the light of the Revolution and there are descriptions of the countryside around Lake Sayula (in reality Lake Chapala) and its 'sperm' coloured, shallow water: "It was a place with a strange atmosphere: stony, hard, broken with round, cruel hills and the many and fluted bunches of the organ-cactus behind the old house, and an ancient road trailing past, deep in ancient dust."

Ramón Corona 16 is a pretty house with large lawn and gardens where rooms are rented by the week or month including morning coffee. Lots of estate agents on Hidalgo, west of Madero, with house or apartment rentals. *Chapala Realty*, Hidalgo 223, T53676, F53528. Helpful.

Trailer park 1 km from the lake between Chapala and Ajijic: *PAL*, Apdo Postal 1-1470, Guadalajara, T53764 or Chapala 60040. US$13 daily, 1st class, pool, good.

Eating *La Leña*, Madero 236. Open air, serves *antojitos* and steaks, bamboo roof; next door is *Che Mary*. Also attractive, outdoor seating. *Café Paris*, Madero 421. Sidewalk tables, popular, *comida corrida* US$3, also breakfast, sandwiches; also on Madero are *El Patio*. Good, cheap, and next door at 405A, *Los Equipales*. Where Madero reaches the lake is a restaurant/bar, *Beer Garden*. Live amplified Mexican music, dancing, tables on the beach. *Bing's* ice cream parlour next door. *Cazadores*, on lake. Old red brick house, *mariachis* sometimes, credit cards accepted. *La Langosta Loca*, Ramón Corona. Seafood; 1 block further is the bar *Centro Botanero Los Caballos Locos*, and 2 doors down is the *Scotland Café*. In part of a colonial house with tables on the front porch and on the back lawn, as well as inside at the bar, open until 0200 or 0300. Several seafood places close by: *El Guayabo*, *El Guayabo Green*, *Cozumel*, *Huichos*, *Acapulquito*, *La Terraza Lupita*. Grocery store on southeast corner of Hidalgo and Madero and another one at Madero 423, next to the plaza.

Festivals On the *Fiesta de Francisco de Asís*, 2-3 Oct, fireworks are displayed and excellent food served in the streets.

Transport **Local Bus**: bus station on Av Madero at corner of Miguel Martínez. Buses from Guadalajara every 30 mins, 0515-2030, 1 hr. 2 blocks south of bus station, minibuses leave every 20 mins for Ajijic, 2 pesos, and San Juan Cosalá, 3 pesos. **Taxi**: stand on Zócalo and at bus station.

Directory **Banks** *Casa de cambio* on Av Madero near *Beer Garden*, open 0830-1700, Mon-Sat. *Banco Bital*, Madero 208, next to *Hotel Nido*, 24-hr ATM taking Visa, MasterCard, and cards of Cirrus and Plus networks. Nearby is a *Banamex* with 24-hr ATMs. *Casa de cambio* at Hidalgo 204 esq Madero, has phone on street for international calls that takes Visa, MasterCard and Amex. *Bancomer* at Hidalgo 212 near Madero, 24-hr ATM taking Visa; across the street is a *Banca Serfín*, 24-hr ATM accepting Visa, MasterCard, Diner's Club, Cirrus and Plus networks. *Lloyds*, Madero 232, is a real estate office, *casa de cambio*, travel agency and *sociedad de inversión*, many Americans keep their money here. **Communications** Postal services: *Mail Box, Etc*, Carretera Chapala-Jocotepec 155, opposite *PAL* Trailer Park, T60747, F60775. Shipping office at Hidalgo 236 uses Federal Express and DHL. Just west of it is the Post Office. At Hidalgo 223 is a UPS office. **Telephones:** Computel on the plaza, long distance and fax, accept Amex, MasterCard, AT&T. Also pay phones for long distance-calls on Zócalo and outside bus station. **Laundry** Zaragoza y Morelos. Dry cleaners at Hidalgo 235A, also repair shoes and other leather items. **Medical services** Clinic: *IMSS* clinic on Niños Héroes between Zaragoza and Cinco de Mayo. Centro de Salud at Flavio Romero de V and Guerrero. **Red Cross:** in Parque de la Cristinia.

Seven kilometres to the west of Chapala, a smaller, once Indian village, has an **Ajijic** arty-crafty American colony with many retired North Americans. The village is pleasant, with cobbled streets, a pretty little plaza and many single-storey villas. One block east of the plaza at the end of Calle Parroquia is the very pretty church of San Andrés, started in 1749. There is also a pretty stone church on the northwest corner of the plaza. On Colón, in the two blocks north of the plaza, are several restaurants, boutiques and galleries. Going south from the plaza, Colón becomes Morelos, crossing Calle Constitución and continuing some five blocks to the lake with lots of restaurants, galleries and shops. The lakeshore has receded about 200m from the original shoreline and it is a bit smelly. The Way of the Cross and a Passion Play are given at Easter in a chapel high above the town. House and garden tours, Thursday 1030, 2½ hrs, US$10, in aid of Lakeside School for the Deaf, T61881 for reservation. Bus from Chapala or taxi US$3.20.

Sleeping B *Hotel Danza del Sol*, T376-60220/61080, or Guadalajara 6218878, Av Lázaro Cárdenas 3260, ground floor. Large complex, nice units and gardens, pool; under same management as **AL** *Real de Chapala*, Paseo del Prado 20, T60007, F60025. Delightful, pleasant gardens. **A** *La Nueva Posada*, Donato Guerra 9, Apdo 30, T61444, F61344. Breakfast included, vast rooms, Canadian management, horseriding, golf, tennis, theatre, gardens, swimming pool, restaurant (large, clean, pretentious, attractive outdoor seating in garden overlooking lake), colonial décor, delightful. **B** *Los Artistas Bed & Breakfast*, Constitución 105, T61027, F60066, artistas@acnet.net. 6 rooms, fireplaces, pool, living room, no credit cards, English and Spanish spoken. **C** *Laguna Bed 'n' Brunch*, Zaragoza 29, T61174, F61188. Good value, clean, comfortable, with bath, parking. **D** *Mariana*, Guadalupe Victoria 10, T62221, 54813. Breakfast available, weekly and monthly rates, all rooms have cable TV. **D** *Las Casitas* (just outside Ajijic, at Carretera Puente 20). Motel-type with kitchen units, pool. Similar is *Las Calandrias* T52819, next door. Furnished apartments, swimming pool. *Mamá Chuy Club*, and *Villa Chello*, on hillside, T376-30013 for both, good, pools, spacious, monthly rentals, good value.

Eating *Los Telares* on main street. Nice, courtyard garden. Clean *lonchería* on plaza, good simple meals, cheap, grilled chicken, used by locals and Americans. *Ajijic*, pavement café on corner of plaza. Cheap drinks, Mexican snacks, hearty *parrillada* Sat, Sun. *Los Girasoles*, 16 de Septiembre 18. Moderately priced, Mexican food in walled courtyard. *Posada Ajijic*, Morelos, opposite pier, T60744. Bar and restaurant, accept credit cards; pier here with fish restaurant at the end, indoor and outdoor seating and bar, used to be over water but stilts are now over dry land. *Bruno's*, on main street. Excellent steaks. Fresh fish shop on plaza and other small food shops.

Directory **Medical services**: Clinics: *Clínica Ajijic*, Carretera Ote 33, T60662/60500, with 24-hr ambulance service, Dr Alfredo Rodríguez Quintana (home T61499). 2 dentists' offices on Colón, just south of plaza. **Useful services**: Post Office: 1 block south of plaza, corner of Colón and Constitución; newspaper shop near plaza sells *Mexico City Times*; small art gallery but few cultural events advertised. On the northwest corner of the plaza is a Computel booth for long-distance phone and fax, open daily, 0800-2100. About ½ block north at Colón 24A is a *lavandería*, US$2 to wash and dry a load. Taxi stand on west side of plaza, next to it is a large map of Ajijic on one side and Chapala on the other, showing businesses and tourist sites. Opposite taxi stand at Colón 29 is a *casa de cambio*. On southwest corner of plaza is Banco Promex with 2 ATMs open 24 hrs, accept Cirrus, Plus, Visa, MasterCard, Diner's Club. *Ajijic Real Estate* at Morelos 4, T62077, is an authorized UPS outlet. *El Ojo del Lago* is a free English-language newspaper, available at hotels and at chapala@infosel.net.mx **Immigration:** Castellanos 4, T62042.

Beyond Ajijic at the western end of the lake is the Indian town of **Jocotepec**, a sizeable agricultural centre (*Population:* 18,000), recently invaded by more cosmopolitan types, little budget accommodation. **D** *Posada del Pescador*, *cabañas* on outskirts. With bedroom, living room, kitchen and bathroom, set in a lovely garden; one other small hotel in town, **E**, bath, not clean. There is a local *fiesta* on 11-18 January. Jocotepec can be reached from Ajijic or from the Mexico-Guadalajara highway. Bus Chapala-Jocotepec US$2, every hour in each direction. The Indians make famous black-and-white *sarapes*. The local ice cream is very good.

Between Ajijic and Jocotepec lies the small town of **San Juan Cosalá**, less prosperous than Ajijic but pleasant, with cobblestone streets and fewer gringos. There are thermal springs (varied temperatures, crowded and noisy at weekends, five pools of different sizes) at **A-B** *Hotel Balneario San Juan Cosalá* (Apdo Postal 181, Chapala, T376-10302, F10222), which has private rooms for bathing with large tiled baths. Sunbathing in private rooms is also possible. Bed and breakfast in clinical modern quarters with bar/restaurant. Rooms to let at **D** *Balneario Paraíso*. Bus service from Chapala. Fish restaurants are squeezed between the carretera and the lake at **Barrenada**, 1 km east of town.

NB Route 80 from Laguna de Chapala to the Pacific Coast at Barra de Navidad is in very poor condition. Route 15 on the southern shore of Laguna de Chapala, which leads to Pátzcuaro (six hours) is in good condition, if slow and winding through the hills.

Forty kilometres due south of Lake Chapala is the colonial town of **Mazamitla** (2,200m), a pleasant place on the side of a range of mountains, but cold at night. It has a charming Zócalo. Hotels, **D** *Posada Alpina*, on square; **E** *Fiesta de Mazamitla*. With bath, clean. Recommended. *La Llorona County Club*, in Sierra del Tigre woods, T6821186. Has *cabañas*, spa-club house and driving range. About 4 km out of town is **Zona Monteverde** with pine forests, small *casitas* for rent, two good restaurants at entrance, T161826; steep hills, access only by car or taxi.

Tapalpa About 130 km south of Guadalajara off Route 54 to Sayula and Ciudad Guzmán is Tapalpa, a very pretty village indeed. It is a 3½ hour drive from Guadalajara. The bus makes several detours into the hills to stop at small places such as Zacoalco (Sunday market) and Amacueca. The road up to Tapalpa is winding and climbs sharply and the air becomes noticeably cooler. The area is becoming increasingly popular as a place for weekend homes. The town itself, with only 11,000 inhabitants, shows ample signs of this influx of prosperity. There are two churches (one with a curious atrium) and an imposing flight of stone steps between them, laid out with fountains and ornamental lamps. Tapalpa is in cattle country; the rodeo is a popular sport at weekends.

The main street is lined with stalls, selling *sarapes* and other tourist goods on Sunday and fresh food the other days of the week. The only local speciality is *ponche*, an improbable blend of tamarind and mezcal which is sold in gallon jars and recommended only for the curious or foolhardy. If you are planning a day trip, get your return ticket as soon as you arrive as the last bus back to Guadalajara (1800 on Sunday) is likely to be full.

Sleeping and eating The more expensive restaurants have tables on balconies overlooking the square – the *Restaurante Posada Hacienda* (which has a US$1 cover charge) is well placed. Others are the *Buena Vista* (which also has rooms) and *La Cabaña*, and all are visited by the *mariachis*. Less grand is the **D** *Hotel Tapalpa*. With huge holes in the floor, but clean and fairly cheap. Some rooms are for hire at *Bungalows Rosita*, and *Posada Hacienda* has nice bungalows with fireplace and small kitchen.

Route 54 continues south through Ciudad Guzmán (formerly Zapotlán) to Colima. Ciudad Guzmán is a mid-19th-century Republican town with wide streets, a huge square, eclectic European-style architecture and a relaxed atmosphere. There are more arcades here than in most Mexican towns, and a central pedestrianised market area. It is a good base for climbing the volcanoes.

Ciudad Guzmán

Sleeping **AL** *Real*, Colón. **B** *Posada San José*, M Chávez Madrueño 135. **C** *Reforma*, Javier Mina 33. **C** *Posada San José*, M Chávez Madrueño 135, T20756 F22786. Phone, TV. **C** *Hacienda Nuera*, Hidalgo 177, T/F21379. Car park. **C-E** *Gran Hotel Zapotlán*, Fed. del Toro 61, on main plaza T20040, F24783. Very reasonable, gym, tennis court. Stores luggage. **D** *Tlayolan*, Javier Mina 33, T23317. Clean, quiet. **E** *Hotel Flamingo*, near main square. Excellent value, very modern, very clean, and quiet. Recommended. **F** *Morelos*, Refugio B de Toscana 12. Run down.

Eating *Juanito*, on main square. Steak dishes, good service. *Bon Appetit*, upstairs on main square. Views of town, excellent chef called Blas Flores, large servings, Japanese, Greek and Continental food. Recommended. *La Flor de Loto*, José Rodón 37C. Vegetarian, cheap soya burgers. *Pilón Burgers* next to *Hotel Flamingo*. Tiny, traditional. On Prisciliano Sánchez there are stalls selling juices, yoghurts and cereals. Good cheap meals in the market (upstairs).

Festivals There is a fair for 2 weeks in **Oct**. On 1st Sun in Oct the festival of San José is celebrated. Farmers march to the church to give presents to the saint, who they believe will bring rain to help their crops grow. There is bull-running through the streets on the 1st Sat in Oct. Famous Mexican singers perform at the local theatre throughout the month.

Transport Buses To Colima 2 hrs, US$3 (Flecha Amarilla); to Uruapan and Morelia involves changes in Tamazula and Zamora. To Tamazula with Trans Tamaz, 1¼ hrs, US$1.40.

Directory Internet: *Podernet*, RB de Toscano 16-A, next to Hotel Morelos, T/F27299, 0900-1400, 1600-2000 Mon-Sat. **Laundry** *José Rodón*, opposite *La Flor de Loto*, cheap.

Colima

The capital of Colima state is a most charming and hospitable town with a 19th-century Moorish-style arcade on the main square and a strange rebuilt gothic ruin on the road beyond the **Cathedral** (late 19th century). Also on the east side of the main square is the **Palacio de Gobierno** which contains interesting murals of the history of Mexico. Both are attractive buildings. Behind them is the Jardín Torres Quintero, another pretty plaza but smaller. Andador Constitución is a pedestrian street, with people selling paintings, several small, attractive restaurants and a state-run artisan's shop at the north end on the corner of Zaragoza. Crossing Zaragoza, Constitución is open to traffic, and one block north on the corner with Vicente Guerrero is the church of **San Felipe de Jesús** (early 18th-century plateresque façade) where Miguel Hidalgo

Phone code: 331
Colour map 3, grid B3
Population: 150,000
Altitude: 494m

☞ *Climbing the volcanoes of Colima*

Colima *volcano (3,842m), which erupted with great loss of life in 1941, and* **El Nevado** *(4,339m) are both near Colima. The former is one of the most exciting climbs in Mexico. They can be climbed by going to Ciudad Guzmán, and taking a bus to the village of Fresnito. Register with the police here before climbing. For El Nevado it is 20 km from Fresnito to the first (more comfortable) hut at 3,500m (beds, take water). A second hut is a bit further on (take the right fork in the road after the first hut). At weekends it may be possible to hitch. From the huts it is a strenuous three-to-four hour hike to the top. From the TV relay station descend to the obvious, sandy track that leads over the saddle towards Pico Nevado. Take the higher track to the stoney ridge. Stick to the right of the* watercourse/rockfall, reaching the ridge which leads up towards the peak.

Sr Agustín Ibarra (T33628, ext 103) organizes day trips to within a two-hour climb of the summit (recommended), US$50 for 10 people to the huts, or 3½-hour horse ride to the refuge with a three-hour climb, US$10 per person. Sr Ibarra's dog Laika is also a great companion! It may be possible to hitch a lift down the next day with the TV maintenance crew who work at the top. The weather in this region is very unpredictable, beware of sudden heavy rains. Sr Ibarra provides homely accommodation in the village; otherwise ask where to camp. There are a couple of shops but only limited supplies. Hotels in Ciudad Guzmán, see text.

was at one time parish priest. There is a public swimming pool in the Parque Regional Metropolitano on Calle Degollado about five to six blocks from southwest corner of the main plaza. **Teatro Hidalgo** on the corner of Degollado, and Morelos, has a pink colonial façade and large carved wooden doors (only open during functions). Parque Núñez, five blocks east of the plaza is also attractive and twice the size of the plaza. South of Parque Núñez, about seven blocks, is Parque Hidalgo, a very large park with tall coconut palms. Young men can be seen climbing the palms to collect coconuts. **Tourist office** Hidalgo, on the corner of 27 de Septiembre, T24360, F28360. Good, but no information on climbing local volcanoes.

Museums **Museo de las Culturas de Occidente María Ahumada**, Calzada Pedro Galván, in the Casa de Cultura complex deserves a visit if only for its ample collection of pre-Hispanic figurines. The region specialized in the production of pottery figures concerned with earthly problems and not cosmological events, as in other areas. ■ *Tue-Sun 0900-1300, 1600-1800.* **Museo de la Máscara, la Danza y el Arte Popular del Occidente**, Calle 27 de Septiembre y Manuel Gallardo, exhibits folklore and handicrafts and has items for sale. The **Museo de la Historia de Colima**, on the Zócalo has a comprehensive collection of pre-Hispanic ceramics; look out for the figurines of dogs which were clearly being fattened for the supper table. The ceramicists attained a high level of perfection in portraying realistically the facial expressions of people engaged in their daily tasks. The museum also has a fair collection of examples of regional craftwork.

Excursions **El Chanal** is an archaeological site, about 15 km to the north of Colima, which has a small pyramid with 36 sculptured figures, discovered in 1944. Another site, closer by, is **La Campana**, just off Avenida Tecnológico, taxi US$1. These largely unexcavated, extant remains include a ballcourt and a few temples and platforms aligned with Colima Volcano 30 km to the north. ■ *US$1.30.*

El Hervidero, 22 km southeast of Colima, is a spa in a natural lake of hot springs which reach 25°C.

Comala, a pretty colonial town with whitewashed adobe buildings near Colima, is worth a few hours visit; bus US$0.25, 20 minutes every ½ hr, from Suburbana bus station. The climate in Comala is somewhat cooler and more comfortable than Colima. The surrounding vegetation is lush with coffee plantations. In the town are two popular restaurants, *Los Portales* and *Comala*, with *mariachis* and local specialities; they are open until 1800. If you sit and drink you will usually be brought complementary food until you wilt from *mariachi* overload. Outside the town on the Colima road is the *Botanero Bucaramanga*, a bar with *botanas* (snacks) and more *mariachis*. Eight kilometres northeast is the Escuela de Artesanía where handmade furniture, painted with fabulous bird designs, and other crafts are manufactured to order. **Suchitlán** (Sunday market) has *Los Portales de Suchitlán*, Galeanas 10, T33954452. Good restaurant selling local specialities. The people here are very small (*chaparrito*) and this is reflected in the size of the doorways. Further down the road, at Km 18 Comala-San Antonio, is *Jacal de San Antonio*, a beautiful, large, open-air restaurant, on top of a hill overlooking a lush valley with the Volcán de Colima in the distance. About 18 km beyond Comala (look out for signposts), is the magnificent 18th-century **Estancia de San Antonio**, set in a green valley with an impressive roman-style aqueduct leading water down from a mountain spring. The road continues up and over a mountain stream; about 1 km further on are **Las Marías**, a private mountain lake used as a picnic site. ■ *Admission US$0.65.*

B-C *Hotel América*, Morelos 162, T29596. A/c, cable TV, phone, largest rooms in new **Sleeping** section, pretty interior gardens, travel agency, steam baths, good restaurant, central, friendly. **C-D** *Ceballos*, Torres Quintero 16, T24449, main square. A fine building with

Colima

To Museo de la Máscara, la Danza y el Arte Popular

To Casa de la Cultura & Museo de las Culturas de Occidente

■ **Sleeping**
1 América   3 Colonial   5 La Merced   7 San Cristóbal
2 Ceballos   4 Flamingos   6 Núñez   8 San Lorenzo

Not to scale

Guadalajara to the Pacific Coast

attractive *portales*, some huge rooms with a/c, clean, good food in restaurant (pricey), secure indoor parking, very good value. Highly recommended. **D** *Rey de Colimán*, on continuation of Medellín on outskirts. Large rooms. *Motel Costeño* on outskirts going towards Manzanillo, T21925. Recommended. **D-E** *Flamingos*, ex-*Gran Hotel*, Av Rey Colimán 18, T22526, near Jardín Núñez. Pleasant small rooms with fan, bath, simple, clean, breakfast expensive, disco below goes on till 0300 on Sat and Sun. **D-E** *La Merced*, Hidalgo 188, T26969. Pretty colonial house with rooms around patio filled with plants, passageway to newer section, entrance at Juárez 82 with reception, all rooms same price, 2 beds cost more than 1, TV, bath. Highly recommended for budget travellers. **E** *Colonial*, Medellín 142, near bus terminal, T30877. Basic. **E** *Núñez*, Juárez 88 at Jardín Núñez, T27030. Basic, dark, with bath. **E-F** *San Cristóbal*, Reforma 98, T20515, near centre. Run down. Many *casas de huéspedes* near Jardín Núñez. **E** *San Lorenzo*, Cuauhtémoc 149, T22000. Parking, modern extension opposite 3 motels coming in from Guadalajara: *María Isabel*, T26262, *Los Candiles*, T23212, and *Villa del Rey*, T22917.

Eating Several restaurants on the Zócalo serve inexpensive meals. *El Trébol* is probably the best, on southwest corner; opposite, on Degollado 67, is nice open-air restaurant on 2nd floor on south side of plaza, overlooking it. *Café de la Plaza*, Portal Medellín 20, beside *Hotel Ceballos*. *Comida corrida* about US$4. *Los Naranjos*, Gabino Barreda 34, ½ block north of Jardín Torres Quintero. Going since 1955, nice, well known. *Samadhi*, Filomeno Medina 125, T32498, opposite *La Sangre de Cristo* church. Vegetarian, good, meal about US$3, good yoghurt and fruit drinks, attractive, large garden with iguanas. *Café Dalí* is in the Casa de la Cultura complex. *Café Colima* is in Parque Corregidora. *Giovannis*, Constitución 58 Norte. Good pizzas and takeaway. *Centro de Nutrición Lakshmi*, Av Madero 265. Good yoghurt and wholemeal bread run by Hari Krishnas. *La Troje*, T22680, on southeast of town heading to Manzanillo. Good, *mariachis*, very Mexican. Try the local sweet *cocada y miel* (coconut and honey in blocks), sold in *dulcerías* (sweet shops).

Festivals *Feria* The annual fair of the region (agriculture, cattle and industry, with much additional festivity) runs from the last Sat of **Oct** until the 1st Sun of **Nov**. Traditional local potions (all the year round) include *Jacalote* (from black maize and pumpkin seeds), *bate* (*chía* and honey), *tuba* (palm tree sap) and *tecuino* (ground, germinated maize).

Transport **Air** Airport (CLQ) 19 km from centre, T44160/49817. Flights to Mexico City and Tijuana available. **Buses** 2 bus stations on the outskirts; 'Suburbana' for buses within Colima state – urban buses and *combis* run to centre, US$0.50, take Routes 1 or 19, or taxi about US$1, and, 'Foránea' for buses out of state, take Route 18 from Jardín Nuñez. Bus companies: ETN; T25899. La Línea; T20508/48179. Primera Plus; T48067. Omnibus de México; T47190. Sur de Jalisco; T20316. Elite; T28499. If going to **Uruapan** it is best to go to **Zamora** (7-8 hrs, although officially 4) and change there. ETN bus to **Guadalajara** US$12, 2½-3 hrs by *autopista*; plus service US$9, regular 1st class US$8, 2nd class US$7, all take *autopista*, non-stop. **Manzanillo**, US$7, 2nd class US$3.20. ETN to **Mexico City**, US$51.65.

Directory **Airline offices** *Aero California*, T44850. *AeroMéxico*, T31340. *Aeromar*, T31340. **Banks** *Banco Inverlat* at Juárez 32 on west side of Jardín Núñez, ATM takes Amex, Visa, Diner's Club. *Casa de cambio* at Morelos and Juárez on southwest corner of same park. *Bancomer* at Madero and Ocampo 3 blocks east of plaza, ATM takes Visa and Plus. *Casa de cambio* across the street. *Banamex* a block south on Ocampo at Hidalgo has an ATM. **Communications** Internet: cyber café in *Plaza Country* on Av Tecnológico, 15 blocks N of centre, Mon-Fri 0900-2200, Sat-Sun 1000-2200, US$1.90 per hr. **Post Office:** Av Francisco I Madero and Gen Núñez, northeast corner of Jardín Núñez. **Telecommunication:** Computel at Morelos 234 on south side for long-distance phone and fax, and at bus station, open 0700-2200, accepts Visa, MasterCard, Amex and AT&T

cards. Fax not always in use. **Laundry** *Lavandería Shell*, 27 de Septiembre 134, open 0900-2000, inexpensive, quick. **Medical services** Hospital: *Hospital Civil*, T20227. **Pharmacy:** *Farmacia Guadalupana* on northeast corner of Jardín Torres Quintero behind Cathedral. Another pharmacy on northeast corner of Zócalo. **Red Cross:** T21451.

Manzanillo

A beautiful, three-hour hilly route runs from Colima to Manzanillo, which has become an important port on the Pacific, since a spectacular 257-km railway has been driven down the sharp slopes of the Sierra Madre through Colima. A new fast toll road has been opened between Guadalajara and Manzanillo, good, double-laned in some sections, but total cost US$17 in tolls. The tolls from Mexico City to Manzanillo total US$55. Occupations for tourists at

Phone code: 333
Colour map 3, grid B2
Population: 150,000

Manzanillo centre

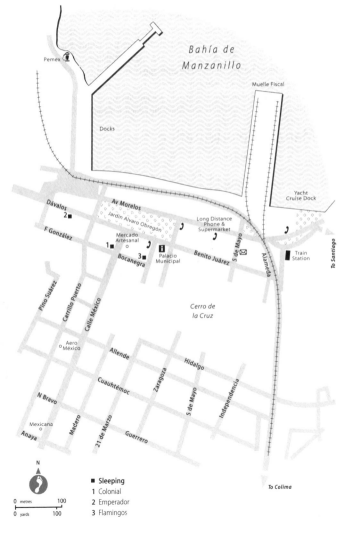

Bahía de Manzanillo

Pemex

Muelle Fiscal

Docks

Yacht Cruise Dock

Dávalos
2 ■

F González

Av Morelos

Jardín Alvaro Obregón

Mercado Artesanal
1 ■

Bocanegra
3 ■

Palacio Municipal

Long Distance Phone & Supermarket

Benito Juárez

5 de Mayo

Alameda

Train Station

To Santiago

Pino Suárez

Carrillo Puerto

Calle México

Aero México

Allende

Cuauhtémoc

Zaragoza

Hidalgo

5 de Mayo

Independencia

Cerro de la Cruz

N Bravo

Mexicana
Anaya

Madero

21 de Marzo

Guerrero

To Colima

N

0 metres 100
0 yards 100

■ Sleeping
1 Colonial
2 Emperador
3 Flamingos

Manzanillo, which is not a touristy town, include deep-sea fishing (US$250 to hire a boat for a day, with beer, *refrescos* and *ceviche*), bathing, and walking in the hills. There is a good snorkelling trip starting at the beach of *Club Las Hadas* (see below), US$40 includes soft drinks and equipment. The water is clear and warm, with lots to see. Trips two to three times daily, last one at 1230. There is a bullring on the outskirts on the road to Colima. The best beach is the lovely crescent of Santiago, 8 km north, but there are three others, all of which are clean, with good swimming. **Tourist offices** Boulevard Miguel de la Madrid 4960, T32277, F31426, halfway along Playa Azul. Tourist helpline (Angeles Verdes) T66600.

Sleeping
■ *on maps*
Price codes:
see inside front cover

LL *Club Las Hadas*, Península de Santiago, T42000. A Moorish fantasy ("architecture crowned by perhaps the most flamboyantly and unabashedly phallic tower ever erected, and the palpable smell of money; should on no account be missed"). **L** *Club Maeva*, Km 12.5 Carretera Santiago-Miramar, T50595. Opposite beach, picturesque, clean rooms with bath and kitchen, meals included in price, several good restaurants. **AL** *La Posada*, Calz Lázaro Cárdenas 201, T31899 near the end of Las Brisas peninsula. US manager, beautifully designed rooms carved into the very rock of an outcrop. **AL** *Roca del Mar*, Playa Azul, T20302. Vacation centre. **B** *Las Brisas Vacation Club*, Av Lázaro Cárdenas 207, T31747/32075. Some a/c, good restaurant.

At **Santiago beach AL** *Playa de Santiago*, T30055. Good, but food expensive. **C** *Anita*, T30161. Built in 1940, has a certain funky charm and it is clean and on the beach. **C** *Parador Marbella*, Blvd M de la Madrid, Km 10, T31103. **C** *Marlyn*, T30107. 3rd floor rooms with balcony overlooking the beach, a bargain. Recommended.

Manzanillo orientation

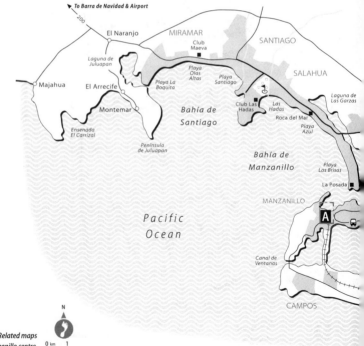

Related maps
A Manzanillo centre,
page 509

At the port **C** *Colonial*, México 100, T21080. Good restaurant, friendly, avoid rooms above the record shop (very loud music). **D** *Casa de Huéspedes Posada Jardín*, Cuauhtémoc. Reasonable. **D** *Emperador*, Dávalos 69, T22374. Good value, good, cheap restaurant. **D** *Flamingos*, 10 de Mayo and Madero, T21037. With bath, quite good. **E** *Casa de Huéspedes Central*, behind bus station. With bath, fan, OK. Visitors can also rent apartments in private condominiums, eg *Villas del Palmar* at Las Hadas, or *Club Santiago*, T50414 (contact Héctor Sandoval at Hectours for information).

Camping At Miramar and Santiago beaches. 4½ km north of Manzanillo is *Trailer Park El Palmar*, T35533. With a large swimming pool, run down, very friendly, coconut palms, US$13 for 2 in camper-van. *La Marmota* trailer park, at junction of Highways 200 and 98. Cold showers, bathrooms, pool, laundry facilities, US$8 per car and 2 people.

Willy's Seafood Restaurant, Playa Azul, on the beach. French owner, primarily seafood, some meat, very good, 3-courses with wine US$15 pp. *Portofino's*, Blvd M de la Madrid, Km 13. Italian, very good pizza; next door is *Plaza de la Perlita*. Good food, live music; also Italian, *Bugatti's*, Crucero Las Brisas. *Carlos and Charlie's*, Blvd M de la Madrid Km 6.9, on the beach. Seafood and ribs, great atmosphere. Good but not cheap food at the 2 *Huerta* restaurants, the original near the centre, and *Huerta II* near the Las Hadas junction. *Johanna*, opposite bus station entrance. Good food, cheap.

Eating
● *on maps*

Local **Car hire**: *National*, Km 9.5 Carreterra Manzanillo-Santiago, T30611. *Budget*, same road, T31445.

Transport

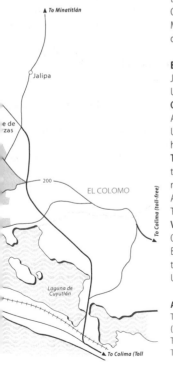

To Minatitlán

Jalipa

e de
zas

200

EL COLOMO

To Colima (toll-free)

Laguna de
Cuyutlán

To Colima (Toll

Long distance **Air**: frequent flights from airport (ZLO) (T31119/ 32525) 19 km from town, to Mexico City and Guadalajara. Other domestic destinations: Chihuahua, Monterrey, Puerto Vallarta and Saltillo. US destinations: Los Angeles.

Buses: to **Miramar**, US$0.50, leave from J J Alcaraz, 'El Tajo'. Several to **Guadalajara**, US$11, or US$23 ETN, 6 hrs. To **Mexico City** with ETN, luxury, US$62, with Autobus de Occidente, 19 hrs, 1st class, US$25. **Barra de Navidad**, US$2.50, 1½ hrs; to **Colima**, US$4, US$7 ETN; to **Tijuana**, US$80, 1st class, 36 hrs. Down the coast to **Lázaro Cárdenas** and crossroads for Playa Azul (see page 478) with Autobus de Occidente or Galeana, 7 hrs. To **Acapulco**, US$8.50. To **Puerto Vallarta**, 1st class with Trans Cihuatlán at 0800 and 1200, 4½ hrs, recommended. Bus terminal in Av Hidalgo outside centre, local buses go there. Taxi to centre US$1.50.

Airlines *Aeromar* T30151. *Aerolitoral* T32424; *Mexicana* T21972. *Aero California* (Boulevard Miguel de La Madrid Km 13.5) T41414. **Medical services** *Hospital Civil*, T24161. **Red Cross**: T65770.

Directory

South of Manzanillo Southeast of Manzanillo is **Tecomán** (*Population:* 68,000) with a delightful atmosphere. **B-C** *Gran Fénix*. Larger rooms have a/c, smaller rooms are noisier but hotel is recommended; unnamed *pensión* on the corner of the Zócalo, if you face the church it is on your left, east. Try the local deep-fried *quesadillas* (*tortillas* filled with cheese). To the west of Tecomán is the small coastal resort of **Cuyutlán**, on the fast highway between Colima and Manzanillo. It has a pleasant, black-sand beach and **D** *Hotel Bucanero*, near the north end of the front. Clean rooms, good restaurant, games room and souvenir shop. Swimming here is excellent and umbrellas and wooden walkways protect feet against the hot sun and sand. The coast road continues southeast to the unspoilt fishing village of **Boca de Apiza** (no hotels but some seafood restaurants). There is abundant bird life at the mouth of the river.

Local police warn against camping in the wild in this area; it is not safe.

The road continues to Playa Azul, Lázaro Cárdenas, Zihuatanejo and Acapulco: for 80 km beyond Manzanillo it is good, then Route 200, through paved, in some parts is in poor condition and for long stretches you cannot see the ocean. In other places there are interesting coastal spots. About one hour south of Tecomán is the village of **San Juan de Lima**, on a small beach; two or three hotels, the furthest south along the beach is very basic, **D**. There are a couple of restaurants, one unnamed, about 200m from the hotels, serving excellent red snapper and shrimp dishes. Halfway between Tecomán and Playa Azul is another uncrowded beach, **Maruata**, where you can ask the restaurant owner if you can camp or sling a hammock (see page 478).

Tecolotlán & Autlán Another road to Manzanillo, Route 80, goes from Guadalajara to the coast, passing the outskirts of several pleasant towns with cobbled streets. The road is fairly trafficked as it plummets from the Sierra Madre to the Pacific. **Tecolotlán**, 200 km northeast of Melaque, is a small town whose Zócalo is 1 km from the highway along rough cobbles. It has a few hotels, eg **D** *Albatros*, one block east of the Zócalo. Modern, clean, with bath, TV. Highly recommended. **Autlán de Navarro**, 115 km from Melaque, is a clean, modern, mid-sized town, with public phones in the Zócalo and several hotels (eg **D** *Palermo*. With bath, pleasant, clean). 74 km from Melaque is **Casimiro Castillo**, a small town with three hotels, including **E** *Costa Azul*. With bath, clean.

Melaque
Phone code: 335

The bay is one of the most beautiful on the Pacific coast, but San Patricio Melaque is very commercialized and crowded at holiday times. An earthquake in 1994 has left a few modern buildings in ruins. A row of hotels along the beach has been made into holiday apartments. The beach is long, shelving and sandy with a rocky coast at each end and pelicans diving for fish. The waves are not so big at San Patricio beach. The week leading up to St Patrick's Day is *fiesta* time, when there are nightly fireworks, dances, rodeos, etc. **Tourist office** Sonora 15, T70100, but better to visit Mari Blanca Pérez at Paraíso Pacífico Tours in *Hotel Barra de Navidad* T55122, F55303, open 0900-1400 May to December and 0900-1800 in winter, very helpful.

Sleeping **L-B** *Villas Camino del Mar*, Apdo Postal 6, San Patricio Melaque, T55207, F55498. Rooms or villas on beach, 2 pools, discounts for long stays, up to 50% for a month, including tax, many US visitors stay all winter. **B** *Bungalows Azteca*, 23 km from Manzanillo airport, for 4 at Calle Avante, T333-70150. With kitchenette, pool, parking. **B** *Royal Costa Sur*, Bahía de Cuastecomate, 2½ km from crossroads at northern edge of town, T/F55085. Tennis court, private beach. *Club Náutico El Dorado*, Gómez Farías 1A, T55239, F55770. Very pleasant, good value, small swimming pool. **C** *Hacienda Melaque*, Morelos 49, T55334. Tennis court, kitchen, pool. **C** *Flamingo*, Vallarta 19. Clean with fan, balconies, water coolers on each floor. Opposite is **D** *Santa*

María, T70338. Friendly. Recommended. **D** *Posada Pablo de Tarso*, Gómez Farías 408, T70117, facing beach. Pretty, galleried building, tiled stairs, antique-style furniture. **D** *San Nicolás*, Gómez Farías 54, T70066, beside Estrella Blanca bus station. Noisy but clean. Off season, very pleasant. **C** *Monterrey*, Gómez Farías 27, T70004, on beach. Clean, fan, bath, parking, superb view. **D** *Bungalows del Tule*, Obregón, T55395. With kitchen. **D** *Posada Clemens*, Gómez Farías, couple of blocks south of plaza and 4 blocks further along. **D** *Santa María*, on beach. **E** *Hidalgo*, Hidalgo off Gómez Farías. Fan, cheapest. OK. *Trailer Park La Playa*, San Patricio Melaque, T70065, in the village, on beach. US$13 for car and 2 people, full hook-up, toilets, cold showers. Follow the 'Melaque' signs and at the end of the main road is a free camping place on the beach at the bay, very good, easily accessible for RVs, popular for vehicles and tents.

Eating *Restaurant Los Pelícanos*, on beach. Overpriced. Many restaurants on beach but most close at 1900. *Koala's at the Beach*, Alvaro Obregón 52, San Patricio, 2 blocks from *Camino del Mar*. Small, good, great food in walled garden compound off dusty street. Canadian/Australian run. *Restaurant Alcatraz*, good food.

Directory Communications: Internet *Cybernet* between beachfront and Gómez Farías, near Hotel Monterrey.

The village of Barra de Navidad, commercial but still pleasant, has a monument to the Spanish ships which set out in 1548 to conquer the Philippines. Barra is 1½ hours from Manzanillo; the beach is beautiful, very good for swimming, but at holiday times it is very crowded and a lot less pleasant. The Colorín liquor store, opposite *Hotel Barra de Navidad*, changes money, sells

Barra de Navidad
Phone code: 333

San Patricio Melaque

stamps and has a mailbox. You can also change money in Cihuatlán (buses every 30 minutes). Bus to Manzanillo, US$2.50, 1½ hours. There is a book exchange on Mazatlán between Sinaloa and Guanajuato. The **tourist office**, is at Jalisco 67, T55100. ■ *Mon-Fri 0900-1700*.

Sleeping **B** *Tropical*, López de Legazpi 96, T70020, on beach. Seedy but pleasant. **C** *Delfín*, Morelos 23, T70068. Very clean, pool, hot water. Highly recommended. Opposite is **C** *Sand's*, Morelos 24, T162859 (Guadalajara) or 70018 (Barra). Bar, clean, some kitchen units, good value, pool. **C** *Hotel Barra de Navidad*, López de Legaspi 250, T70122. With balcony on beach, or bungalows where you can cook, pool, very good value. **D** *Hotel Jalisco*, Av Jalisco 91. Hot water, safe but not very clean, and noisy, nightclub next door with music till 0300. **D** *Marquez*, T55304. Recommended. *San Lorenzo*, Av Sinaloa 87, T70139. Same price and much better, clean, hot water, good restaurant opposite. **E** *Posada Pacífico*, Mazatlán 136, 1 street behind bus terminal. Clean, fan, friendly, good restaurant opposite. **E** *Casa de Huéspedes Caribe*, Av Sonora. Fan, friendly, family-run. Ask about **camping** on beach.

Eating Fish restaurants eg *Antonio* on beach. Many good restaurants on the Pacific side, a couple of good restaurants on the lagoon side. *Velero's*. Delicious snapper and good views. *Ambar*, Veracruz 101. Half of menu vegetarian, real coffee, good breakfast and crêpes, closed lunchtime. Highly recommended. *Pacífico*. Very good barbecued shrimp, and good breakfasts. *Seamaster*, on beach. Best ribs. *Cactus Café*. Best burgers. *Paty's*. Good, cheap, especially for barbecued chicken.

Pretty seaside villages near Barra de Navidad include **La Manzanilla**, 14 km north of Routes 200/80 junction (**D** *Posada de Manzanilla*. Nice. Recommended. *Posada del Cazador*, T70330). Camping possible. South of the village at the end of Los Cocos beach is the **B** hotel and RV trailer park, *Paraíso Miramar*, T321-60434. Pool, gardens, palm huts, restaurant, bar. Three kilometres north of the beach is Boca de Iguanas with two trailer parks: *Boca de Iguanas*, US$7 per person, vehicle free, hook-ups, cold showers, toilets, laundry facilities, clean, pleasant location, and *Tenacatita*, US$9 with hook-ups, US$7 without, cold showers, toilet, laundry facilities, restaurant). For both places take the unpaved road from Highway 200 to the abandoned *Hotel Bahía de Tenacatita*; at the T junction, turn right, pass the hotel, and the campsites are about 500m further on the left. This place is nothing to do with the village of **Tenacatita** which has a perfect beach complete with palm huts and tropical fish among rocks -good for snorkelling (two sections of beach, the bay and oceanside). **D** *Hotel* (no name) in village near beach, or you can sleep on the beach under a palm shelter, but beware mosquitoes. Several kilometres north of Tenacatita is **AL** all-inclusive *Blue Bay*, ex-*Fiesta Americana* resort, Km 20 Carretera Federal 200, T335-15020/15100, F15050. Tennis, watersports, horseriding, disco, pool, gym, credit cards.

Route 200, a little rough in places, links Barra de Navidad with Puerto Vallarta, the second largest resort in Mexico. There are beaches and hotels on this route. In Perula village at the north end of **Chamela** beach, **C** *Hotel Punta Perula*, T333-70190, on beach, Mexican style; *Villa Polonesia Trailer Park*, US$12 for car and two people, full hook-ups, hot showers, on lovely beach (follow signs from Route 200 on unmade road). Recommended. Restaurant on road to trailer park, clean, good food. Pemex at Chamela is closed, no other for miles. 103 km south of Puerto Vallarta and 12 km inland, at the town of **Tomatlán** (not to be confused with Boca de Tomatlán, on the coast), are a few modest hotels (eg **E** *Posada Carmelita*, with bath, clean). Two hours south of Puerto

Barra de Navidad

N

Not to scale

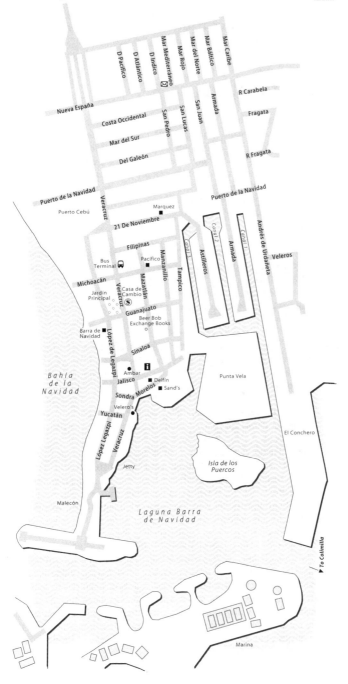

To Melaque, Manzanillo & Guadalajara

D Pacifico

D Atlántico

D Indico

Mar Mediterráneo

Mar Rojo

Mar del Norte

Mar Báltico

Mar Caribe

Armada

R Carabela

Nueva España

Costa Occidental

San Pedro

San Lucas

San Juan

Fragata

Mar del Sur

Del Galeón

R Fragata

Puerto de la Navidad

Veracruz

Puerto de la Navidad

Puerto Cebú

Marquez

Andrés de Urdañeta

Veleros

21 De Noviembre

Canal 2

Canal 1

Filipinas

Astilleros

Armada

Bus Terminal

Pacífico

Manzanillo

Tampico

Michoacán

Mazatlán

Veracruz

Casa de Cambio

Jardín Principal

Guanajuato

Beer Bob Exchange Books

Barra de Navidad

López de Legazpi

Sinaloa

Ambar

Bahía de la Navidad

Jalisco

Delfin

Sand's

Punta Vela

Sondra Morelos

Velero's

Yucatán

López Legazpi

Veracruz

El Conchero

Jetty

Isla de los Puercos

Malecón

Laguna Barra de Navidad

To Colimilla

Marina

Guadalajara to the Pacific Coast

Vallarta is the luxury resort **LL** *Las Alamandas*, T328-55500. Beautiful beach, health club, horse riding, tennis, etc. The resort is 1 km south of Puente San Nicolás on Route 200, turn left towards the coast at sign to Quemaro. Owned by Isobel Goldsmith, it is very exclusive, has been featured in several magazines for the clientèle it attracts and reservations should be made in advance; T020-73731762 in the UK. The excellent **AL** *Hotel Careyes* is *en route*, and several others, **A-B** *El Tecuán*, Carretera 200, Km 32.5, T333-70132. Lovely hotel, gorgeous beach, mediocre bar/restaurant, pool. Highly recommended.

Puerto Vallarta

Phone code: 322
Colour map 3, grid B2
Population: 100,000

A highly commercialized sun-and-sand holiday resort marred by congestion and widespread condominium developments, Puerto Vallarta also has its advantages. The stepped and cobbled streets of the old centre are picturesque, accommodations and restaurants are varied enough to suit everybody, there is much good hiking in the surrounding hills and watersports and diving are easily accessible. Increasingly it has become a base for excursions and for special interest trips including ornithology and whale watching.

Ins and outs

Getting there   The Aeropuerto Internacional Ordaz (PVR), T11325, 6 km north of the town centre, is served by national and international airlines with flights to destinations in Mexico, the USA and Europe (mostly package). The long-distance bus station, almost directly opposite the airport, is a 40-minute ride from town. Puerto Vallarta is on the carretera costera, Route 200, which runs south along the Pacific coast, all the way to the Guatemalan border.

Getting around   Taxis are expensive in Puerto Vallarta. Local buses and colectivos operate on most routes north to Nuevo Vallarta and beyond, and south to Mismaloya and Boca de Tomatlán. Buses marked 'Centro' go through town, while those marked 'Túnel' take the bypass.

The **tourist office**   Morelos 28-A; in the government building on the main square, is very helpful; T30744/20242. Tourist news, tribuna@ pnet.puerto.net.mx

Greater Puerto Vallarta is drawn out along some 25 km of the west-facing curve of the deeply incised Banderas Bay. For ease of reference, it can be split into six sections: **North Central**, the oldest, with the main plaza, Cathedral and seafront Malecón as well as an uninviting strip of pebble/sand beach; **South Central**, across the Río Cuale, is newer but similarly packed with shops and restaurants and bordered by the fine, deep sand of Playa de los Muertos; **South Shore**, where the mountains come to the sea, there are several cove beaches and a scattering of big hotels; **North Hotel Zone**, a long stretch from town towards the cruise ship terminal and the airport, with mediocre beaches, many big hotels and several commercial centres; **Marina Vallarta**, further north, with a dazzling array of craft, a golf course, smart hotels and poor quality beach; you can't walk far because of condominiums built around the marina; **Nuevo Vallarta**, 18 km north of centre, with golf course and marina, in the neighbouring state of Nayarit (time difference), where modern, all-inclusive hotels are strung along miles of white sand beach, far from amenities.

Most travellers will find the central area the most convenient to stay in; its

Puerto Vallarta

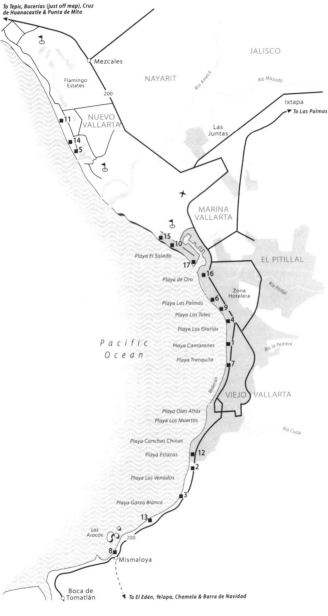

To Tepic, Bucerías (just off map), Cruz
de Huanacaxtle & Punta de Mita

Mezcales

Flamingo
Estates

200

■ 11

**NUEVO
VALLARTA**

■ 14
■ 5

NAYARIT

Río Ameca

JALISCO

Río Mascota

Ixtapa
► To Las Palmas

Las
Juntas

✈

**MARINA
VALLARTA**

EL PITILLAL

■ 15
■ 10

Playa El Salado

■ 17

■ 16

Río Pitillal

Playa de Oro

Zona
Hotelera

■ 6
■ 9

Playa Las Palmas

■ 4

Playa Los Tules

Playa Las Glorias

Río la Pedrera

■ 1

Playa Camarones

Playa Tranquila

■ 7

*P a c i f i c
O c e a n*

Malecón

VIEJO VALLARTA

Playa Olas Altas
Playa Los Muertos

Río Cuale

Playa Conchas Chinas

■ 12

Playa Estacas

■ 2

Playa Los Venados

Playa Garza Blanca

■ 3

■ 13

Los
Arocos

200

■ 8 Mismaloya

Boca de
Tomatlán

► To El Edén, Yelapa, Chamela & Barra de Navidad

N

0 km   10
0 miles   10

■ **Sleeping**	7 Hacienda Buenaventura	13 Presidente
1 Bugambilias Sheraton	8 La Jolla	Intercontinental
2 Camino Real	9 Las Palmas	14 Sierra
3 Casa Grande	10 Marriott Casa Magna	15 Velas Vallarta
4 Continental Plaza	11 Oasis Marival	16 Vista Club Playa
5 Diamond	12 Playa Conchas Chinas	del Oro
6 Fiesta Americana		17 Westin Regina

two halves are divided by the Río Cuale and a narrow island where souvenir shops, cafés and the museum are located. The most dramatic beach in the centre is Playa de los Muertos, apparently named after the murderous activities of pirates in the late 16th century, although the 'dead' tag could apply equally to the fierce undertow or possibly to the pollution which affects this corner of the bay. The authorities are trying to get people to use a sunnier sobriquet: 'Playa del Sol'. Conchas Chinas is probably the best beach close to town, being quiet and clean (at any holiday time, though, every beach is packed); a cobblestone road leads to Conchas Chinas from Route 200, just after *Club Alexandra*.

Excursions

During the rainy season, June-September, some trips are not possible. From November-April, humpback whale watching is organized. A recommended trip including snorkelling is with John Pegueros, who owns the schooner *Elias Mann*. Contact him at Lázaro Cárdenas 27, Apdo Postal 73, Bucerías, Nayarit, CP63732, T329-80060, F80061. Tickets from Marina Vallarta, US$60 includes some meals, starts 0800. See also **Tour operators** below.

Forty kilometres northeast of Puerto Vallarta is the inland village of **Las Palmas**, a typical though unremarkable *pueblo* (buses every 30 minutes, one hour 10 minutes). On the way is the workers' *pueblo* of **Ixtapa**, established by the Montgomery Fruit Co in 1925. Near here are postclassic stone mounds scattered over a wide area.

Ten kilometres south of Puerto Vallarta, along the coast road is **Mismaloya**, where John Huston made *Night of the Iguana* with Richard Burton. A lovely beach backed by a steep subtropical valley, even though the *La Jolla Mismaloya* hotel looms over the sands. The beach is clean and you can hire umbrellas and chairs for the day, US$1; beware of the undertow at low tide. The film set has been developed as *Iguana Park*. There are many condominiums on the north side. You can go horse riding up the valley with Victor, of Rancho Manolo, beside the road bridge, T80018. **Boca de Tomatlán**, 4 km further south, is a quaint and rather down-at-heel fishing village at the river estuary. There are apartments to rent, simple restaurants, a dirty beach and a footbridge across the river. Further round the bay is **Yelapa**, an Indian village with a waterfall, now commercialized with entertainment ranging from live music to rodeo. Tourist water taxi from pier (Los Muertos) US$12 return, leaves 1030, 1100. From fisherman's quay on Malecón (by *Hotel Rosita*, opposite *McDonald's*) US$5 one way, leaves 1130. From Boca de Tomatlán (bus, US$0.30) water taxi from beach is US$3.50 one way, leaves 1030. Organized tours may be better value for anyone wanting to combine such activities as snorkelling at Los Arcos *en route*. **B** *Lagunitas*. Cabin hotel with pool. *Tino's Oasis*. An excellent place to stay, American owned, cheap. Alternatively stay with Mateo and Elenita, **C**, including breakfast, visit their waterfall. Camping available 30 minutes walk up valley, US$4 per person, in beautiful setting, owners Beto and Felicidad (ask for Felicidad's home-made *tortillas*, 'the best in Mexico').

Walk or mountain bike up the Río Cuale valley, through magnificent hills with dense subtropical vegetation, some bathing pools, many birds, a few *ranchitos* and *pueblecitos*. To begin, walk to the eastern extremity of Lázaro Cárdenas, cross the wide bridge and turn sharp right; walk along cobbled street with river on right. Pass Colonia de Buenos Aires and water purification plant; later cross suspension footbridge and continue up rough track with river on left. Two kilometres later, recross the now crystalline Río Cuale via stepping stones. Go as far as you like. 54 km onward is the rustic, ex-mining (silver, gold) village of **Cuale**, with cobbled streets.

Essentials

North Central L *Casa Kimberley*, Zaragoza 445, T21336. Former home of Richard Burton and Elizabeth Taylor, 10 rooms full of memorabilia of the actors, breakfast included, much cheaper in low season. **AL** *Casa del Puente*, by bridge opposite market, T20749. Suites with kitchen in a private villa suspended above river, delightful, book months ahead. **B** *Cuatro Vientos*, Matamoros 520, T20161. Up steep cobbled street from church, lots of steps, great views, restaurant, plunge pool, breakfast included. **C** *Rosita*, Paseo Díaz Ordaz 901, at north end of Malecón, T32000, F32142, hrosita@zonavirtual.com.mx. Puerto Vallarta's original holiday hotel (1948) with pool, on town beach, excellent value and location. Recommended. Its sister hotel 2 blocks north is *Pescador*, Paraguay 1117, esq Uruguay T/F21884, hpescador@pvnet.com.mx **D** *Hotel Escuela*, Hidalgo 300, corner Guerrero, T24910, F30294, is where they teach trainee hotel personnel. A bit clinical, with street noise, but said to be good value. **E** unmarked *hospedaje* at Allende 257, esq Guadalupe, T20986. US owner, Isabel Jordan also has rooms and *cabañas* in Yelapa, more expensive.

Sleeping
■ *on maps,*
pages 517 & 519
Price codes:
see inside front cover

Puerto Vallarta centre

Guadalajara to the Pacific Coast

South Central L *Meza del Mar*, Amapas 380, T24888, F22308. Perched high above Los Muertos beach with slow lifts, balconies remain in shade, small pool, all-inclusive packages. L *Playa Los Arcos*, Olas Altas 380, T20583, F22418. Good location for restaurants, undersized pool terrace overflows to Los Muertos beach. **AL** *Buenaventura*, Av México 1301, T23737, F23546. On shore, fringe of centre, lively holiday hotel. **AL** *Molina de Agua*, Ignacio L Vallarta 130, T21957, F26056. Cabins in pleasant wooded glade on bank of river, a/c, good service, 2 pools. Recommended. **AL** *San Marino Plaza* (formerly the *Oro Verde*, Rodolfo Gómez 111, T20350, F22431, sanmarino@pvnet.com.mx. A/c, pleasant, friendly, standard holiday package, compact pool terrace adjoins Los Muertos beach. **A** *Casa Corazón*, Amapas 326, T/F21371. Hard to find, US-owned hideaway on steep slope down to Los Muertos beach, overpriced but 3 big rooms on top terrace with spectacular views worth the premium, including big breakfast. **B** *Eloisa*, Lázaro Cárdenas 179, T26465, F20286, on square by Playa de los Muertos. A holiday hotel with small pool, most rooms face dim hallways. **B** *Gaviotas*, behind *Eloisa*, Madero 154, Parque Lázaro Cárdenas, T21500, F25516. Faintly colonial, balcony access, glimpses of sea. **B** *Posada de Roger*, Basilio Badillo 237, T20639, F30482. Courtyard arrangement, neat rooms off narrow access balconies, tiny and overpriced, splash pool. **B** *Posada Río Cuale*, Aquiles Serdán 242, near new bridge, T/F20450. Small pool in front garden, not very private, nice, colonial-style rooms. **C** *Gloria del Mar*, Amapas 115, T25143, by Playa de los Muertos. Charmless but clean, convenient holiday base, small rooms.

D *Belmar*, Insurgentes 161, T/F20572. Spartan, ill-lit but friendly, on main road near buses. **D** *Yasmín*, Basilio Badillo 168, T20087. A claustrophobic courtyard arrangement behind *Café Olla*, good value, noisy till at least 2300. There are several cheaper hotels grouped on Francisco I Madero, west of Insurgentes: **D** *Azteca*, No 473, T22750. Probably best of this group. **D** *Villa del Mar*, No 440, T20785. Also satisfactory. **D-E**, and within a few doors are: *Cartagena*, No 428, *Lina*, No 376, T21661. With bath, no hot water, run down, rooms on street noisy. *Bernal*, No 423, T23605. Friendly, large rooms, fan, good showers. Recommended. Cheapest is *El Castillo* at No 273, all convenient for restaurants, a few blocks from long-distance buses.

North Hotel Zone LL *Fiesta Americana*, T42010, F42108. Maintains high service standards in Disneyesque jungly theme. **LL** *Krystal Vallarta*, T40202, F40150. Has suites, apartments, flanking cobbled lanes in Mexican *pueblo* style, amid greenery, fountains, wrought-iron streetlights. **LL** *Sheraton Bugambilias*, T30404, F20500. Dated block on good patch of beach close to downtown, vast but unexciting expanse of grounds. **LL** *Continental Plaza*, Playa Las Glorias, T40123, F45236. In overly cute 'Old Mexico' style. **LL** *Holiday Inn*, T61700, F45683. Unmissable deep mustard edifice shares undersized pool with hulking condominium next door. **LL** *Moranda Casa Grande*, T30916, F24601. All-inclusive, tasteless. **LL** *Qualton Spa*, T44446, F44445. Blocky atrium hotel with crowded pool area extending to beach. **L** *Las Palmas*, Blvd Medina Ascencio, Km 2.5, T40650, F40543. Castaway-on-a-desert-island theme, all rooms with sea view. **AL** *Hacienda Buenaventura*, Paseo de la Marina, T46667, F46242. Modern, with colonial influence, pleasant pool, is nicest in zone but 100m to beach and on main road, discounts out of season. **AL** *Los Pélicanos*, T41010, F41111. Small-scale, rooms enclose central quadrangle with pool, 100m to beach. **AL** *Plaza Las Glorias*, T44444, F46559. Attractive white low-rise, breezy beachfront location. **AL** *Suites del Sol*, Francia y Liverpool, T42541, F42213. Above offices at busy junction on wrong side of road for beach, jumbled open-plan public rooms, tiny pool, large rooms. *Vista Club Playa de Oro*, Av Las Garzas, T46868, F40348. Near cruise ship terminal, a predictable all-inclusive with much manufactured fun, many activities. Cheap hotels are scarce here: **C** *Motel Costa del Sol*, T22055. 300m north of *Sheraton* on the opposite side.

Marina Vallarta LL *Marriott Casa Magna*, T10004, F10760. Grandiose interiors, superb pool, upmarket restaurants. **LL** *Westin Regina*, T11100, F11141. Vibrant colours, imaginative lighting, much cascading water, lush gardens. **LL** *Royal Maeva*, T10200. Big, brassy all-inclusive packages. **LL** *Velas Vallarta*, T10751, F10755. Moorish touches to big, part timeshare hotel with verdant gardens. **AL** *Plaza Iguana*, T10880, F10889. Small pool adjoins marina promenade, 10 mins walk to beach.

Nuevo Vallarta LL *Diamond Resort*, T329-70400, F329-70626. Gaudy, raucous, all-inclusive. **LL** *Sierra*, T329-71300, F329-70800. Colourful building-block hotel, smart, modern, all-inclusive. **L** *Oasis Marival*, T329-70100, F70160. More established and sedate than competitors here, all-inclusive.

Southern shore LL *Camino Real*, Playa de las Estacas, T15000, F16000. On lovely beach 3 km south of centre. **LL** *La Jolla de Mismaloya*, Km 11.5, T80660, F80500. Romantic though overdeveloped setting on filmset beach. **LL** *Presidente Intercontinental*, Km 8.5 Carretera a Barra de Navidad, T80507, F80116. Stylish luxury on quiet, sandy cove. **L** *Majahuitas Resort*, between Quimixto and Yelapa beaches, T322-15808, run by Margot and Lirio González. Including breakfast and dinner, 3 guesthouses, more planned, on cove, sandy beach, rustic furniture, solar energy, riding and snorkelling available, 30% of profits go to indigenous community of Chacala. **AL** *Casa Grande*, Playa Palo María, T21023. Hulking twin towers of all-inclusive fun on crummy beach, 4 km south of centre. **AL** *Playa Conchas Chinas*, Km 2.5 road to Barra de Navidad, T/F15770, about 1 km before *Camino Real*, on west side of road. Spacious rooms with kitchenettes and ocean views.

Camping 2 trailer parks: *Tacho*, on road to Pipala, opposite Marina. 60 spaces but spacious, US$14.50. *Puerto Vallarta*, north of centre, just north of bypass then east 2 blocks. Popular. Also at fishing village of Yelapa, best reached by boat from *Hotel Rosita* at 1130: camp under *palapas* (shelters), about US$4 pp.

South Centre *Posada de Roger*, Basilio Badillo 237. Good courtyard dining, mainly Mexican menu, cheapish. *Café Olla*, lower end Basilio Badillo. Good-value Mexican and barbecue in cramped open-fronted dining room, queues wait for more than an hour in high season, demonstrating a lack of imagination rather than discerning palate. *Puerto Nuevo*, on Badillo. Expensive but good food. *Buengusto*, Rodríguez. Excellent home-cooked Mexican meals. *A Page in the Sun* (café), Olas Altas opposite *Los Arcos* hotel on corner. Coffee is excellent, cakes home-made, second-hand bookshop. *Daiquiri Dick's*, Olas Altas 314, T20566. Restaurant and bar open for breakfast, lunch and dinner, opposite Los Muertos beach, excellent cooking, classical harp and guitar music Sun 1300-1500, about US$18-20 pp. *Las Palapas*, on the beach near Playa de los Muertos. Good food, service, value, décor and atmosphere. *Felipe's*, Prolongación Insurgentes 466, Colonia Alta Vista, T23820, 21434. Beautiful view over town from large balcony, good food and service, can share 1 portion between 2. *Los Arbolitos*, east end of Lázaro Cárdenas, 3 balconied floors above river. Mexican, good atmosphere, moderate prices. *El Dorado*, *palapa* restaurant on Playa de los Muertos. Inexpensive and attractive surroundings but touristy and besieged by belligerent *chiclet* vendors, 3rd-rate musicians, etc. *La Fuente del Puente*, riverfront at old bridge, opposite market. Mexican, colourful, good music, good-value meals but drinks expensive. *Jazz Café/Le Bistro*, by the bridge on Insurgentes. Garden, bamboo, beside river, pleasant for coffee and classical music (piano or harp) in morning, crowded and expensive in evening, many vegetarian dishes, clean. *Café Maximilian*, Olas Altas 380-B, rear part of *Playa Los Arcos*, open 1600-2300, closed Sun. Huge Austrian owner, about US$22 pp meal with wine, clean, efficient, busy, some tables on pavement. Recommended.

Eating
● *on maps*

Guadalajara to the Pacific Coast

North Centre *Pepe's Tacos*, on Honduras, opposite Pemex at northern end of downtown. Cheap, ethnic and delicious in spartan pink/white dining room, open all night. *Juanita's*, Av México 1067. Attracts locals as well as value-seeking gringos, good. *Gaby*, Mina. Small, family-run, eat in garden, excellent food, cheap and clean. *Las Margaritas*, Juárez 512. Forget the queues at the popular gringo restaurants, this one is excellent, moderately priced, cosmopolitan and curiously under-patronized, colonial-style courtyard. Recommended. *Café Amadeus*, Miramar 271, up steps from Guerrero. Classical music, books, board games in delightful whitewashed rooms or balcony perched above old town, coffee, delectable cakes. Recommended. *La Dolce Vita*, midway along Malecón. Hugely popular (queues) Italian and pizza place favoured by package tourists. *Rico Mac Taco*, Av México, corner Uruguay. Busy, cheap and widely popular eatery.

Nightlife *Carlos O'Brian's*, Malecón and Andale, Olas Altas. Attracts a motley crowd of revellers and starts hopping after 2200. Martini types head for *Christine*, at *Hotel Krystal*. For spectacular light show, disco, expensive drinks and cover. Many clubs and late bars throughout central area.

Shopping Endless opportunities, including armies of non-aggressive beach vendors. The flea market is grossly overpriced; the many shops often better value, but not to any great degree. Guadalajara is cheaper for practically everything. The market, by the bridge at the end of Insurgentes, sells silver, clothes and souvenirs as well as meat and fish. Large, well-stocked supermarket nearby. Jewellery at *Olas de Plata*, Francisco Rodríguez 132. Plaza Malecón has 28 curio shops, restaurant, music, etc. *GR* supermarket, Constitución 136, reasonable for basics. Second-hand books, English and some in German, at *Rosas Expresso*, Olas Altas 399.

Tour operators *American Express*, Morelos 660, esq Abasolo, T32955, F32926, town guide available. *Open Air Expeditions*, Guerrero 339, T23310, openair@vivamexico.com, Oscar and Isabel run hiking trips (mountain or waterfall), whale watching (winter), kayaking, birdwatching and other trips from US$40, knowledgeable guides. *Vallarta Adventure*, Edif Marina Golf, local 13-C, Marina Vallarta, T/F10657, boat trips, whale watching, Las Marietas (US$50), Sierra Madre expedition (US$60), jeep safari (US$60), dolphin encounter (US$60), Las Caletas by night or by day (US$50), also scuba diving, PADI certification, a 2-tank dive to Las Marietas, or Las Caletas, with lunch costs US$80, 0900-1630. *Mountain Bike Adventures*, Guerrero 361, T31834, offer trips for cyclists of varying grades of competence, from local environs up to 3-4 days in old silver towns of Sierra Madre, all equipment provided including good, front-suspension bikes, from US$36. *Sierra Madre*, facing the Malecón near Domínguez, are agents for many tours and some of their own, including a long, all-day truck safari to Sierra Madre mountains. *Rancho El Charro*, T40114, horseback expeditions to jungle villages, Sierra Madre silver towns. Independent horse riding guides and horses congregate at lower end of Basilio Badillo; also occasionally at fisherman's wharf, by *Hotel Rosital* for short beach and mountain trips, agree price beforehand. Many agents and hotel tour desks offer boat trips, car hire and tours at big discounts if you accept a timeshare presentation. Worthwhile savings are to be made for those prepared to brazen out the sales pitch, and many do.

Transport **Local Buses**: Mismaloya to Marina, US$0.24, but complicated routing. The main southbound artery through town is México-Morelos-Vallarta, the main northbound is Juárez-Insurgentes. Plaza Lázaro Cárdenas is the main terminal in south of town and starting point for Mismaloya-Boca buses going south. Buses marked 'Olas Altas' go to South Central, those marked 'Hoteles' or 'Aeropuerto' to North Hotel Zone and beyond. Buses are also marked for 'Marina' and 'Mismaloya/Boca' (Boca de Tomatlán). The ones marked 'Centro' go through town, those with 'Túnel' take the bypass. Buses to outlying villages with Medina bus line, terminal at Brasil, between Brasilia and Guatemala, regular (15-20 mins) service to Nuevo Vallarta, San José, San Juan, Bucerías, Manzanilla, Punta de Mita and others. Fares from US$0.75-US$1.50. **Car hire** widely available. **Scooter hire**: opposite *Sheraton*, T21765.

Long distance Air: International Ordaz airport (PVR) 6 km from centre, T11325. If you walk 100m to the highway and catch a local bus to town, it will cost far less than the US$10 taxi fare. International flights from Anchorage (Alaska), Austin (Texas), Boston (MA), Burbank (California), Chicago, Dallas, Denver (Colorado), Frankfurt (Germany), Houston, Los Angeles, New York, Phoenix (Arizona), Portland (Oregon), San Diego (California), San Fransisco, Seattle and Tampa. Mexican destinations served include Mexico City, Guadalajara, Acapulco, Chihuahua, Ciudad Juárez, Morelia, Querétaro, Tijuana, Aguascalientes, León, Los Cabos, Mazatlán and Monterrey.

Buses: all buses leave from bus station almost opposite the airport (turn left when you exit from arrivals, then it's a short walk)), 40 min from centre. Taxis from the airport to the main bus station charge inflated prices. Frequent service to **Guadalajara**, ETN 8 a day, US$21.25, Transportes del Pacífico, 1st class, US$22, also with Elite and Primera Plus. **Tepic**, Transportes del Pacífico, US$9.50. To **Barra de Navidad** and **Manzanillo** with Primera Plus at 0745 and 1200 US$9.50, 4½ hrs and to Barra only with Elite, 0800 and 1300, 4 hrs. Other services to Acapulco, Aguascalientes, Ciudad Guzmán, Ciudad Juárez, Colima, León, Mazatlán, Melaque, Mexico City, Monterrey, Querétaro, Tecomán, Tijuana and Zihuatanejo.

Ferry: For Baja California ferry schedules and fares: www.mexconnect.com/mex/mexicoferryw.html (see page 717).

Directory

Airline offices *AeroMéxico*, T42777. *Alaska Airlines*, T95-800-4260333, or 11350. *American Airlines*, T91-800-90460, or 11799. *America West*, T800-2359292, 800-5336862, or 11333. *Continental*, T91-800-90050, or 11025. *Delta*, T91-800-90221, or 11032. *Taesa*, T50899. *Mexicana*, T48900. *United*, T911-800-00307, 800-4265561. **Banks** *Cambios* on nearly every street in tourist areas. Rates inferior to Guadalajara. Check *Bancomer's cambio* at Juárez 450, for good rates. Like most, it is open every day until late. Numerous banks offer slightly better rates (but slower service) and ATMs for Visa, Mastercard. **Communications** Internet: *Net House CyberCafé*, Ignacio L Vallarta 232, T26953, open 0700-0200, US$5 per hr, charges by the min. *Eclipse* cybercafé, Juárez 208, US$5 per hr, T21755, Mon-Sat 0900-2200, Sun 1000-1400. *Cybercafé*, Juárez 388, US4.50 per hr, T20204, 0900-2300. **Post Office:** Mina between Juárez and Morelos. Long-distance **phone** (*casetas*) and **fax** at Lázaro Cárdenas 267, open daily to 2300, also in lobby of *Hotel Eloísa*, both US$3 per min to Europe. Many shops bear *Larga distancia* sign, check tariffs. **Embassies & consulates** Consulates: *Canada*, Edif Vallarta Plaza, Zaragoza 160, 1st floor, interior 10, T25398, F23517, open 1000-1400. *USA*, T20069/30074. **Laundry** Practically 1 on every block in south central; numerous throughout resort. **Medical services** Doctor: *Dra Irma Gittelson*, Juárez 479, speaks French and English, very helpful. **Emergency:** T915-7247900. **Useful addresses** Immigration: Morelos 600, T11380.

North of Vallarta

The coast road continues in a northerly direction from Puerto Vallarta to Las Varas and then veers eastwards to Compostela where it turns north again towards Tepic. From Puerto Vallarta to Las Varas the road passes some very attractive beach resorts, the first of which is **Bucerías** (*Hotel Playa de Bucerías*, and B *Marlyn*). **Los Veneros**, between Bucerías and Punta de Mita, T10088/10158; is a pretty cove with fairly safe sea bathing where there is a private beach club reached down a 7-km private road through woods to the beach. Entry includes a margarita or non-alcoholic infusion called *jamaica* made from hibiscus petals. The resort is beautifully designed and clean with

There is a time change between Nayarit and Jalisco; the latter is six hours behind GMT, the former, as with all the Pacific coast north of Jalisco, seven hours behind.

two restaurants, bar, café and gardens terraced towards the beach. The food is excellent, no extra charge for sunbeds/umbrellas. Further development is likely and there are plans to introduce horse riding, mountain bikes, watersports, archaeological trail, guided tour and botanical garden. ■ *Daily 1000-1800, entry US$8, you can take a shuttle bus from Los Veneros bus station.* **Punta de Mita**, a fishing village and beach resort at the tip of a peninsula has

Puerto Vallarta environs

fish restaurants, miles of beach and abundant bird life; nearby **A** *Hotel and Trailer Park Piedras Blancas*, good, also camping, US$10, hook-ups US$12-14, restaurants. There is an excellent restaurant at Playa Desileteros, not cheap but delicious food; Medina or Pacífico bus from Puerto Vallarta every 15 minutes. There are boat trips to the nearby **Islas Marietas**, where there are caves and birds. Camping is possible on the beach. Simple accommodation available or stay at the attractive **C** *Quinta del Sol* (beach). **Sayulita** is a beach resort with accommodation and restaurants but the beach is littered (*Trailer Park* highly recommended, on beautiful beach, German owner, very friendly, US$10 per day, also has bungalows, Apdo 5-585, CP 06500, Mexico City T55721335, F53902750, 2½ km off Route 200; *Tía Adriana's* Bed and Breakfast, T/F32751092, November-June, good, central, good value). Then come **San Francisco** (*Costa Azul Resort*, on beach, delightful, pool, apartments, restaurant), Lo de Marcos and Los Ayala. **Rincón de Guayabitos** is being developed as a tourist resort with hotels, holiday village and trailer park (**C** *Coca*, among several hotels and restaurants on a rocky peninsula to the south of the beach). Further on is **Peñita de Jaltemba** (**C** bungalows at north end of town, with clean rooms and kitchen; **C-D** *Hotel Mar Azul*). Route 200 continues to **Las Varas** (**E** *Hotel Contreras*, with fan and bath, clean, small rooms). Las Varas is connected also by good road to San Blas, north up the coast (see page 528). Beaches on the coast road include **Chacala**, nice free beach lined with coconut palms, good swimming, cold showers (restaurant *Delfín*, delicious smoked fish), and reached by an unsurfaced road through jungle.

Turning east at Las Varas, the road leads to **Compostela** (**F** *Hotel Naryt*, with bath, basic but clean) a pleasant small town with an old church, El Señor de la Misericordia, built 1539. From Compostela one can catch an old bus to **Zacualapan**, 1½ hours over a paved road, to visit a small enclosed park with sculptures that have been found in the area, two blocks from main square. Knock on a door to ask for the caretaker who will unlock the gate to the park. Inside there is a small museum. Zacualapan is a pleasant village. At Compostela, the road veers north to Tepic.

Tepic

Capital of Nayarit state, Tepic was founded in 1531 at the foot of the extinct volcano of Sangagüey. It is a clean but slightly scruffy town with much rebuilding going on. There are many little squares, all filled with trees and flowers. The landscape around Tepic is wild and mountainous; access is very difficult. Here live the Huichol and Cora Indians. Their dress is very picturesque; their craftwork – bags (carried only by men), scarves woven in colourful designs, necklaces of tiny beads (*chaquira*) and wall-hangings of brightly coloured wool – is available from souvenir shops (these handicrafts are reported to be cheaper in Guadalajara, at the Casa de Artesanías). You may see them in Tepic but it is best to let Indians approach you when they come to town if you want to purchase any items. **Tourist offices** México 178 Norte, 1 block from Cathedral, T121905, officially open daily, 0900-2000 (in reality not so), English spoken, helpful. *Municipal Tourist Office*, Puebla y Amado Nervo, T165661, F126033, also very helpful. There are also offices at Convento de la Cruz, the airport and bus station.

Phone code: 32
Colour map 3, grid B2
Population: 200,000
Altitude: 900

Guadalajara to the Pacific Coast

The **Cathedral** (1891), with two fine Gothic towers, on the Plaza Principal, has been restored; it is painted primrose yellow, adorned with gold. Worth seeing are the **Palacio Municipal**, painted pink; the **Casa de Amado Nervo**, Zacatecas Norte 281, the house of the great Mexican poet and diplomat.

Sights
The tombs in the cemetery are worth seeing

■ *Mon-Fri 1000-1400, Sat 1000-1300*; the **Museo Regional de Antropología e Historia**, Avenida México 91 Norte, has a fine collection of Aztec and Toltec artefacts and some beautiful religious paintings from the colonial period. ■ *Mon-Fri, 0900-1900, Sat, 0900-1500*; **Museo de Los Cuatro Pueblos**, Hidalgo y Zacatecas, exhibits the work of four indigenous ethnic groups. It is worth visiting to see the colourful artwork, textiles and beadwork of the Coras, Nahuas, Huicholes and Tepehuanos. ■ *Mon-Fri 0900-1400, 1600-1900, Sat-Sun 0900-1400;* **Museo Emilia Ortiz**, Calle Lerdo 192 Poniente has works by this local artist. ■ *Mon-Sat 0900-1400*; and the **Museo de Arte Visual 'Aramara'**, Allende 329 Poniente. ■ *Mon-Fri 0900-1400 and 1600-2000, Sat 0900-1400*. **Plaza de los Constituyentes**, México y Juárez, is flanked on the west side by the **Palacio de Gobierno**. On the summit of a hill south of the centre is the **ex-Convento de la Cruz**.

Sleeping **B** *Real de Don Juan*, Av México 105 Sur, on Plaza de Los Constituyentes, T/F161888. Parking. **B-C** *Bugam Villas*, Av Insurgentes y Libramiento Pte, T180225, F180225. Very comfortable rooms with a/c, TV, pool, garden, restaurant with great food and good wine list. **C** *Fray Junípero Serra*, Lerdo Pte 23, T122525, main square. Comfortable, big rooms, clean, a/c, good restaurant, friendly, good service. Recommended. **C** *Ibarra*, Durango Norte 297A, T123870. Luxurious rooms, with bath and fan (some rooms noisy), and slightly spartan, cheaper rooms without bath, very clean, DHL collection point. **C** *San Jorge*, Lerdo 124, T121324. Very comfortable, good value.

Tepic

To Museo Aramara

Guadalajara to the Pacific Coast

To Main Bus Station, Airport & Guadalajara

N
Not to scale

To San Blas & Mazatlán
To Convento de la Cruz

■ **Sleeping**
1 Altamirano
2 Camarena
3 Fray Junipero Serra
4 Ibarra
5 Real de Don Juan
6 Sarita
7 Sierra de Alicia

● **Eating**
1 Café Farolito
2 El Apacho
3 Tiki Room

C *Villa de las Rosas*, Insurgentes 100, T131800. Fans, friendly, noisy in front, good food, but not clean.

D *Altamirano*, Mina 19 Ote, T127131, near Palacio de Gobierno. Parking, noisy but good value. **D** *Santa Fe*, Calzada de la Cruz 85, near Parque La Loma, a few mins from centre. With TV, clean, comfortable, good restaurant. **D** *Sierra de Alicia*, Av México 180 Norte, T120322, F121309. With fan, tiled stairways, friendly. **E** *Las Américas*, Puebla 317 Norte, T163285. Clean, bath, TV, fan, rooms at back quiet. Recommended. **E** *México*, México 116 Norte, T122354. **E** *Nayarit*, Zapata 190 Pte, T122183. **E** *Sarita*, Bravo 112 Pte, T121333. Clean, TV, restaurant, parking. Good. **E** *Tepic*, Dr Martínez 438, T131377, near bus station outside town. With bath, clean, friendly but noisy. **F** *Pensión Morales*, Insurgentes y Sánchez, 4 blocks from bus station. Clean and friendly, hotel is now closed but family still put up backpackers in what is now a private house. **F** *Camarena*, 4 blocks southeast of Zócalo, San Luis Norte 63. Without bath, clean, friendly.

Motels B *La Loma*, Paseo La Loma 301, T132222. Run down, swimming pool. *Bungalows and Trailer Park Koala*, La Laguna, Santa María del Oro. Has bungalows at US$20, each accommodating up to 4, several trailer sites (US$10) and a large campground. Good cheap meals available. Fishing and waterskiing on nearby lagoon.

Eating *El Apacho*, opposite *Hotel Ibarra*. Good *sopes*, cheap. *El Tripol*, in mall, near plaza. Excellent vegetarian. *Danny O* ice cream shop next door. *Café Farolito*, Zacatecas 129. For *comida corrida*. *Roberto's* and *Chante Clair*. Both good food and near Parque La Loma, closed Sun. *La Terraza*, Mexican and American food, pies, cakes; good vegetarian restaurant at Veracruz 16 Norte, try the granola yoghurts. *Tiki Room*, San Luis Norte opposite *Hotel Camarena*. Restaurant, art gallery, video bar, fun. Restaurant in bus terminal, overpriced. Lots of fish stalls by market on Puebla Norte. The local *huevos rancheros* are extremely *picante* (hot).

Tour operators *Viajes Regina*, tours to San Blas, 8 hrs, US$22.50; Playas de Ensueño, Fri, 8 hrs, US$15.50; Tepic city tour, Mon and Sat, 3 hrs, US$7. *Tovara*, Ignacio Allende 30.

Transport **Air** Airport Amado Nervo (TPQ) with flights to Los Angeles, Mexico City, Tampico and Tijuana daily with Aero California, T161636 or AeroMéxico, T139047.

Trains Station at Prolongación Allende y Jesús García, T134861.

Buses Bus station is a fairly short walk from town centre, T136747; bus from centre to terminal from Puebla Norte by market. At bus station there are phones, including credit card, post office, left luggage and tourist information (not always open). Bus to **San Blas** from main bus terminal and from local bus station on park at Av Victoria y México, from 0615 every hour US$3. To **Guadalajara**, US$12.50, 3 hrs, frequent departures, several companies; **Mazatlán**, 4½ hrs, US$8; to **Los Mochis**, US$32; to **Puerto Vallarta**, 3 hrs, US$6; **Mexico City**, US$30.25.

Directory **Banks** *Casas de cambio* at México 91 and 140 Norte, Mon-Sat 0900-1400, 1600-2000. **Communications Telephones:** credit card phone at Veracruz Norte y Zapata Pte.

Huaynamota One can visit **Cora** villages only by air, as there are no real roads, and it takes at least two days. However, it is possible to visit **Huichol** villages from the small town of **Huaynamota** in the mountains northeast of Tepic. Huaynamota has become much easier to reach with the opening of the Aguamilpa Dam. Boats leave from the west end of the dam at 0900 and 1400 (US$7), stopping at *embarcaderos* for villages along the way. The valley, despite being flooded, is still beautiful, particularly at the narrower parts of the dam where huge boulders hang precariously on clifftops. The *embarcadero* for Huaynamota is at the end of the dam where the Río Atengo feeds in. A community truck meets the launch (US$1.30). It is 8 km up a dirt road to the town which is half populated by Huichol, some of whose traditional houses can be seen on its fringes. There are no hotels. Ask at church or at store (basic supplies) on long south side of plaza for possible lodging. There is a good view over the river valley from the large boulder beside the road at the edge of town. From Huaynamota ask around for guides to Huichol villages four or more hours away. *Semana Santa* (Easter week) is famous, many people from surrounding communities converge on Huaynamota at this time. *Combis* leave for the dam from Tepic at Avenida México just down from Zaragoza, US$2, 1½ hours.

Santa Cruz There are various beaches along the coast west of Tepic. **Santa Cruz**, about 37 km from Tepic, has a rocky beach. No hotels, but there are rental apartments, a camping area and accommodation at *Peter's Shop*, **E**, basic but pleasant and friendly. Simple food available, *Restaurant Belmar*, fish and rice, all reminiscent of the South Seas. There is a shrimp farm nearby. Two buses a day run from San Blas to Santa Cruz, US$1.10, or 2½ hours ride by open-sided lorry, US$0.75.

San Blas

Phone code: 328
Colour map 3, grid B3

This old colonial town, built as a fortress against piracy, is 69 km from Tepic and is overcrowded during US and Mexican summer holidays. Founded in 1768, little is left of the old Spanish fortress, **Basilio**. It is from here that the Spanish set off to colonize Baja California and North America. Above the town are **La Contaduría** (1773), the Spanish counting house ■ *US$.60*, and **La Marinera**, a ruined church. The views over the town, estuaries and mangrove swamps from beside an incredibly ugly statue on the battlements are superb.

In town, near the harbour, is the old **Customs House** (1781-85) and a stone and adobe church (1808-78) on the plaza. Up to the mid-19th century, San Blas was a thriving port and it still has a naval base and a (smelly) harbour.

There are few tourists early in the year or in August when it becomes very hot and there are many mosquitoes, but not on the beach 2 km from the village (although, there are other biting insects, so take repellent anyway). The two worst bugs are *jejenes* or *no sees* during the dry season, and *sancudos* the big black monsters, during the wet season. But don't be too put off, they are diminishing year by year and if you don't linger around vegetation and still water they are not so bad.

Quieter than the town beach (which is dirty) is the extensive and often-deserted **Playa El Rey** on the north side of the estuary of the same name, beyond the lighthouse. Take a boat across the river from just west of the harbour, US$0.60 each way; the boatman works until 1730, but stops at lunchtime. Best to tell him when you want to return so that he knows to look out for your frantic waving from the other bank. The best beach is **Playa de las Islitas** reached by bus marked 'Las Veras' from the bus station, or 'El Llano' from Paredes y Sinaloa, just off the plaza. There is some threat of resort development here, but no signs of it as yet. Seven kilometres from San Blas (taxi US$3) is the beach of **Matanchén**, where there is good swimming but many mosquitoes. Good homemade fruitcakes and bread are sold here. Surfing can be done at these beaches, but rarely at any one time is the surf up at all of them. Check at Juan Bananas (see below, **Surfing**). About three times a year it is possible to surf non-stop for over a mile, from town towards Las Islitas, relaying on a series of point breaks.

Sixteen kilometres south from San Blas is the beautiful **Playa Los Cocos** which is empty except at weekends. The **tourist office**, Mercado, one block from plaza, T50021, has information in English on the history of San Blas as well as a town map. ■ *Mon-Sat 0900-1300, 1800-2000, Sun until 1300.* **NB** Don't wander too far from public beach; tourists have warned against attacks and robberies. The Mexican Navy has a training base in San Blas and there is a strong naval and military presence in town as well as the sound of automatic weapons fire in the afternoon.

Excursions

Four-hour boat trips to see whales and dolphins are available. Ask at the tourist office. Armando is a good guide; he charges US$52 for three people.

It is possible to take a three-hour jungle trip in a boat (bus to *embarcadero* on Matenchén road) to **La Tovara**, a small resort with a fresh-water swimming hole brimming with turtles and catfish, a restaurant, and not much else. The mangrove swamps can be visited on the way to La Tovara. Tour buses leave from the bridge 1 km out of town and cost US$30 for a canoe with six passengers, but it is cheaper to arrange the trip at *Embarcadero El Aguada*. Official prices are posted but it still seems possible to shop around. Away from the swimming hole there are coatis, raccoons, iguanas, turtles, boat-billed herons, egrets and parrots. Avoid fast motorized boats as the motor noise will scare any

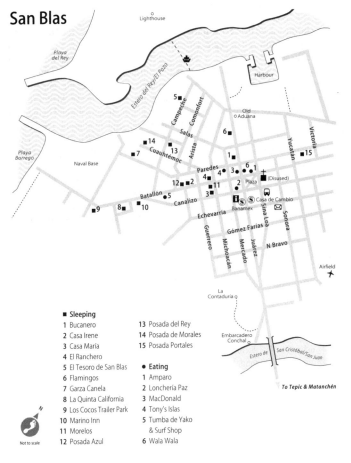

San Blas

■ Sleeping
1 Bucanero
2 Casa Irene
3 Casa María
4 El Ranchero
5 El Tesoro de San Blas
6 Flamingos
7 Garza Canela
8 La Quinta California
9 Los Cocos Trailer Park
10 Marino Inn
11 Morelos
12 Posada Azul
13 Posada del Rey
14 Posada de Morales
15 Posada Portales

● Eating
1 Amparo
2 Lonchería Paz
3 MacDonald
4 Tony's Islas
5 Tumba de Yako
  & Surf Shop
6 Wala Wala

Not to scale

Guadalajara to the Pacific Coast

animals. Tours on foot are even better. Crocodiles are kept in caves along the route. You have to pay US$2 to see the poor, shabby creatures, not recommended. Twilight tours enable naturalists to see pottos and, if very lucky, an ocelot. La Tovara is crowded at midday during the summer. A cheaper 1½-2-hour cruise is also possible from the *Embarcadero El Aguada* (reached by Las Islitas bus – see above), US$17 per boat, but US$4.25 *each* if more than four people; it goes through a tunnel of mangroves, to the swimming hole 20 minutes away. If you take in the crocodile farm the trip is an hour longer, US$23 per boat or US$5.25 per person. When arranging your trip make sure you are told the length of journey and route in advance. You can take a bus from San Blas towards Santa Cruz (see page 528) and get off at Matachén beach (see above). From here, a boat for half-day hire includes the best part of the jungle cruise from San Blas.

Just 3 km east of San Blas is **Singayta** which has a bird sanctuary that is supposed to be very impressive in November and December; very popular with gringo birders. Lucio Rodríguez (T50537) provides eight-hour tours to see (a) crater lake at Santa María del Oro, (b) Mexcaltitán and Santiago Ixquintla, (c) the waterfalls at El Cora/Tecuitata or (d) Ixtlán del Río and Los Toriles. He also tours coffee plantations for about five hours and the petroglyphs and archaeological museum outside Coamiles which also takes about five hours. He can be found at the *Bungalows Tesoro* de San Blas.

The tiny island of **Mexcaltitán**, just 350 m across, can be reached from Highway 15, northwest of Tepic. Turn off to Santiago Ixcuintla, then turn right to Sentispec, from where a dirt road leads to La Batanga on Laguna Mexcaltitán; from Tepic take bus to Santiago Ixcuintla (1½-2 hours) and then *colectivo* to La Batanga (30 minutes). Boats go to the small island (20-minute ride through mangroves). Now a fishing village, Mexcaltitán is reputed to be one of the Aztecs' stopping places, around the end of the 11th century, on the their search for a home and subsequent migration to the central Valley of Mexico. The name means 'near the home of the Mexica'. There is a museum, hotel, **D** *La Ruta Azteca*, and several restaurants. The town's streets are sometimes flooded during the rainy season and the entire village takes to boats. Its *fiesta*, St Peter and St Paul, on 28-29 June, involves a boat race around the island and celebrates the beginning of the shrimp harvest.

The Mirador El Aguila is on Highway 15, 11 km before the junction to San Blas; it overlooks a canyon where many birds can be seen in the morning and the late afternoon.

Sleeping Accommodation becomes scarce and more expensive around Semana Santa and other holidays. A good source of information for alternative rooms and longer stay apartments is Rosa López Castellano who lives at Juárez 5, just off the plaza.

AL *Garza-Canela*, Cuauhtémoc Sur 106, T50112. Very clean, excellent restaurant, small pool, nice garden. Highly recommended. **A** *Flamingos*, Juárez Pte 105, T/F50485. With ceiling fans, huge rooms, colonial, clean, friendly. **B** *Bucanero*, Juárez Pte 75, T50101. With bath and fan, frequented by Americans, food good, pool, lizards abound, noisy discos 3 times a week and bar is open till 0100 with loud music. **B** *Posada del Rey*, Campeche, T50123. Very clean, swimming pool, excellent value. Recommended. *Posada de Morales*, T50023. Also has a swimming pool, more expensive, ½ block from *Posada del Rey*. **C** *Marino Inn*, Batallón, T50340. With a/c, friendly, pool, fair food. **D** *Apartamentos Béjar*, Salas 144. Furnished with daily, weekly or monthly rates, hot water problematic, owner, Rafael Béjar speaks English and is friendly. **D** *Posada Portales*, Paredes 118, T50386. Rooms with *en suite* dining area and fully equipped kitchen, book exchange. Recommended particularly for longer stays. **D** *Morelos*, Batallón 108. With bath, hot water. **D** *María's*, Canalizo s/n (moved from Batallón, same owners as *El Ranchero* and *Morelos*). Fairly clean with cooking, washing and fridge facilities, a bit noisy, no single rooms, friendly. Recommended. **D** *La Quinta California*. Closest to beach, just off Batallón down from *Marino Inn*, T50111. Rooms with well-equipped *en suite* kitchen, free freshly ground coffee in morning, pleasant central court, longer stay discounts, book exchange. Recommended. **D-E** *El Tesoro de San Blas*, 50m south of dock, 5 mins from center. Rooms and villas, hot water, satellite TV, US owners. **D-E** *El Ranchero*, Batallón 102. With bath, laundry service, kitchen. **E** *Casa Irene*, Batallón 122, without sign. Kitchen, friendly. **E** *Posada Azul*, Batallón 126, T50129, 4 blocks from plaza towards beach. 3-bedded rooms with fan and hot water, **F** for simple 2-bedded rooms without bath, cooking facilities.

Camping No camping or sleeping permitted on beaches but several pay campsites available. **Trailer park** at town beach; all trailer parks in the centre are plagued by mosquitoes. The best trailer park is on Los Cocos beach: *Playa Amor*. Good beach, on a narrow strip of land between road to Santa Cruz and cliff, good, popular, 16 km south of town, US$7-10. Next south is **E** *Hotel Delfín*. With bath, balcony, good view, good value; then *Raffles Restaurant* with trailer and camping area attached (no facilities). Last on Los Cocos beach is *Hotel y Restaurante Casa Mañana*, T324-80610 or Tepic T/F321-33565. Austrian-run, good food. Many apartments for rent.

Amparo, on main plaza. Cheap and good. *Tumba de Yako*, on way to beach. **Eating** Yoghurt and health foods, and the original version of *pan de plátano* (banana bread) that is advertised all over town. Also sells banana bread at *Las Islitas*. Recommended. *Tony's 'Islas' restaurant*, good seafood, not cheap, closed Mon. *MacDonald*, Juárez, just off Zócalo. Good breakfast. *Cocodrilo's*, on the square. Good for dinner if a little pricey. *La Familia*, 2 blocks west of the square. Good for lunch or dinner, moderately priced. Plenty of seafood restaurants on the beach; eg *Las Olas*. Good and cheap. Also on Juárez is *Wala Wala*. Good local dishes. *Lonchería Paz*, Canalizo, ½ block off plaza. Cheap.

On Sun women prepare delicious pots of stew for eating al fresco on the plaza.

For art of the Huichol Indians try the *Huichol Cultural Community store*, Juárez 64; it **Shopping** claims to be non-profit making. Great freehand beadwork with glass beads, yarn paintings, decorated masks and scented candles.

Surfing *Tumba de Yako* (see above, **Eating**) rents out boards, US$2.70 per hour, **Sports** US$8 per day, owner, Juan Bananas, was coach to the Mexican surfing team, gives lessons, speaks English. **Mountain Bike** and **Kayak** hire (for estuaries) also from *Tumba de Yako*.

Bus station on corner of Plaza; to **Tepic**, frequent – on hour from 0600, US$4, 1½ hrs. **Transport** To **Guadalajara**, US$10, 8½ hrs.

Banks *Banamex* just off Zócalo, exchange 0830-1000 only. *Comercial de San Blas* on the main **Directory** square will change money, plus commission. **Laundry** 2 blocks down toward the beach from *La Familia*. Will take your clothes and return them, very clean, later or the next day, US$4.44 for about 1½ loads.

Tepic to Guadalajara

The old Route 15 leaves Tepic for Guadalajara. About 50 km from Tepic, off the Guadalajara road, is an attractive area of volcanic lagoons. Take the bus to **Santa María del Oro** for the lagoon of the same name. On the south side of the toll road is the Laguna Tepetiltic and near Chapalilla is another lake at San Pedro Lagunillas. There is a turn-off at Chapalilla to Compostela and Puerto Vallarta. At **Ahuacatlán**, 75 km from Tepic, the 17th-century Ex-Convento de San Juan Evangelista stands on the Plaza Principal; handicrafts are on sale here. Nearby, the village of **Jala** has a festival mid-August. **E** *Hotel Cambero*. From here the **Ceboruco** volcano can be reached in a day. On the main road a lava flow from Ceboruco is visible (*El Ceboruco, Parador Turístico*, with restaurant, information, toilets and shop; buses do not stop here).

Eighty-four kilometres (1¼ hours by bus) from Tepic is **Ixtlán del Río** (**D** *Hotel Colonial*, Hidalgo 45 Pte, very friendly, recommended; *Motel Colón*; cheaper hotels round the Zócalo are *Roma* and *Turista*). There are a few souvenir shops, a Museo Arqueológico in the Palacio Municipal, and a *casa de cambio*. Harvest (maize) festival mid-September. Two kilometres out of town are the ruins of **Los Toriles**, a Toltec ceremonial centre on a warm, wind-swept plain. The main structure is the Temple of Quetzalcoatl, noted for its cruciform windows and circular shape. The ruins have been largely restored and some explanatory notes are posted around the site. There is a caretaker but no real facilities. ■ *US$2.35.* Two kilometres beyond the Los Toriles site is *Motel Hacienda*, with pool. The road climbs out of the valley through uncultivated land, where trees intermix with prickly pear and chaparral cactus.

The journey from Tepic to Guadalajara cannot easily be broken at Ixtlán for sightseeing since buses passing through in either direction tend to be full; the bus on to Guadalajara takes three hours, US$4.25. The route enters the state of Jalisco and, 19 km before Tequila, comes to the town of Magdalena (*Hotel Restaurant Magdalena*), congested with traffic. Nearby there is a small lake. As the bus approaches Tequila there may be opportunities to buy the drink of the same name on board. The blue agave, from which it is distilled, can be seen growing in the pleasant, hilly countryside.

Tequila

Phone code: 374
Colour map 3, grid B3
Population: 33,000
Altitude: 1,300m

A day trip from
Guadalajara is possible

Tequila, 58 km from Guadalajara, is the main place where the famous Mexican drink is distilled. Tours of the distilleries are available (see box page 533) and stores will let you sample different tequilas before you buy. Often around 20 bottles are open for tasting. The town is attractive, a mix of colonial and more modern architecture. It is a pleasant place to stay but there is not much to do other than tour the distilleries and there is little in the way of nightlife. Coming into town from Guadalajara, the road forks at the Pemex station, the right fork is the main highway and the left fork continues into town as Calle Sixto Gorjón, the main commercial street. Buses will let you off here; it is about five blocks to the main plaza. Along Calle Sixto Gorjón there are several liquor stores selling tequila, restaurants where you can eat for under US$5, pharmacies, doctors, dentists and the Rojo de los Altos bus ticket office at No 126A. In the town centre there are two plazas next to each other. On one is the **Templo de Santiago Apóstol**, a large, pretty, old stone building, with a 1930s municipal market next to it. Behind the church is the *Elypsis* discotheque, open at weekends. Also on this plaza is the Post Office and Banamex. About a block behind Banamex where Sixto Gorjón ends, is the entrance to the **Tequila Cuervo distillery**. On the other square is the **Sauza**

"A field of upright swords" – *the making of tequila*

The quote from Paul Theroux's The Old Patagonian Express *describes the swathes of blue agave grown in the dry highlands of the state of Jalisco and a few neighbouring areas. Agave is the raw material for the firewater, tequila, and although there are some 400 varieties of agave, only one, the blue agave, is suitable. The spiky leaves are hacked off and the central core, weighing around 45kg, is crushed and roasted to give the characteristic smell and flavour to the drink. The syrup extracted is then mixed with liquid sugar, fermented for 30-32 hours and then distilled twice. White tequila is the product of a further four months in wooden or stainless steel vats. It can be drunk neat, with a pinch of salt on the back of your hand, followed by a suck on a wedge of lime, or mixed into cocktails such as the famous Margarita. Gold tequila is a blend of white tequila and tequila which has been aged in wooden casks. Añejo, or aged, tequila, is a golden brown from spending at least two years in oak casks. As it ages it becomes smoother and is drunk like a fine brandy or aged rum. Special premium tequila has no sugar added, it is pure agave aged in wooden casks.*

In pre-conquest times, the Indians used the agave sap to brew a mildly alcoholic drink, pulque, which is still drunk today. The Spaniards, however, wanted something more refined and stronger. They developed mezcal and set up distilleries to produce what later became tequila. The first of these was established in 1795 by royal decree of King Charles IV of Spain. It is still in existence today: La Rojena, the distillery of José Cuervo, known by its black crow logo, is the biggest in the country. Around the town of Tequila there are 12 distilleries, of which 10 produce 75 percent of the country's tequila. Tours of the distilleries can be arranged with free samples and of course shopping opportunities. **Tequila Cuervo**, *T6344170, F6348893, in Guadalajara, or T20076 in Tequila (contact Srta Clara Martínez for tours). At* **Tequila Sauza**, *T6790600, F6790690, dating from 1873, you can see the famous fresco illustrating the joys of drinking tequila.* **Herradura**, *T6149657, 6584717, F6140175, 8 km from Tequila, is in an old hacienda outside the village of Amatitlán, which has adobe walls and cobblestone streets and is worth a visit.*

Museo de Tequila at Calle Albino Rojas 22, open until 1400, and the **Presidencia Municipal** with tourist office.

Sleeping **D** *Motel Delicias*, Carretera Internacional 595, on the highway to Guadalajara about 1 km outside Tequila. Best available, TV, off-street parking. **E** *Abasolo*, Abasolo 80. Parts under construction, rooms have TV. **F** *Colonial*, Morelos 52, corner of Sixto Gorjón. Characterless, but central, clean and not run-down, some rooms with private bath. **F** *Morelos*, corner of Morelos and Veracruz, a few blocks from the plaza, above a billiard hall. Basic, ask in bar downstairs if there is no one at the hotel desk. Half-way between Tequila and Guadalajara, in the mountains, is the British-run **LL** *Rancho Río Caliente*, 8 km from the highway, a vegetarian thermal resort (room rates vary according to location), riding and hiking excursions, massages and other personal services extra, taxi from Guadalajara 1 hr, US$25. For reservations in USA, Spa Vacations, PO Box 897, Millbrae, CA 94030, T650-6159543, F650-6150601.

Eating *El Callejón*, Sixto Gorjón 105. Rustic Mexican décor, main courses for under US$5, *antojitos* for less than US$3, hamburgers also available. *El Marinero*, Albino Rojas 16B. Nice seafood restaurant with strolling musicians. *El Sauza*, Juárez 45, beside Banamex. Restaurant/bar, Mexican atmosphere.

Transport **Buses** 2nd class from the old terminal, Sala B, in Guadalajara, Rojo de los Altos, up to 2 hrs, US$2. Return from outside Rojo de los Altos ticket office, Sixto Gorjón, 126A, every 20 mins, 0500-1600, then every 30 mins until 2000. **Taxi** to Guadalajara US$19, plus US$7 in tolls if you take the expressway.

Directory **Banks** *Banamex*, corner of Sixto Gorjón and Juárez, 24-hr ATM accepts Visa, Mastercard, and cards from the Cirrus and Plus networks. *Casa de cambio*, Sixto Gorjón 73, open 0900-1400, 1600-2000, change cash and TCs.

Colonial Heartland

11

Colonial Heartland

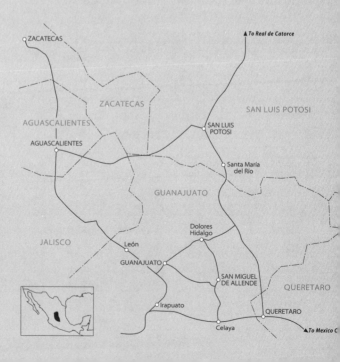

For centuries, the mines of Central Mexico churned out much of the world's silver and a fair amount of gold and precious stones (opals, topazes and amethysts) too. Spanish-style architecture built with the fortunes amassed from silver and gold is at its most opulent and impressive in the magnificent towns and cities of the **Colonial Highlands**. While the mines of Zacatecas, San Luis Potosí and Guanajuato supplied the precious metal to the Spanish crown, the states of Aguascalientes and Querétaro were important supply centres and stopovers on the silver route to the capital and the port of Veracruz. Mining is still important in this area and many of these old cities are today important modern industrial centres, mostly with sprawling suburbs; but they manage to retain at their core the magnificence of their colonial past. The **'ghost towns' of Pozas and Real de Catorce**, once thriving mining centres, have not fared so well, but it is fascinating too to wander through their semi-deserted streets. The years of heavy-handed Spanish rule and obvious inequalities led to discontent, and in the early 19th century this region became the Cuna de la Independencia *(Cradle of Independence)*; nearly every town or village played a part in the break with Spain and there are museums and monuments which tell the story. Colonial rule relied heavily on the work of the missionaries and a tour of the 18th-century **Missions of Querétaro**, well off the beaten track, with a stop-off at the thermal baths and **opal mines of Tequisquiapan**, is well worth the hair-raising '700-curve' drive.

Colonial Heartland

Querétaro

Phone code: 42
Colour map 3, grid B5
Population: 550,000
Altitude: 1,865m

The centre of this sprawling, modern, industrial city, capital of Querétaro state, is old and elegant and dotted with attractive squares and some pedestrianized areas; so much so that it is now protected by UNESCO World Heritage status. There are some of the finest churches, convents and monasteries to explore and museums filled mostly with colonial and religious art.

Getting there & away
There are flights from Mexico City and Monterrey with Aeromar, T241333, and from Guadalajara and Morelia with Aerolitoral, T242788. There are other less-frequent services to and from cities in the north and west of Mexico. Destinations in the south and east are reached from Mexico City. The train station, T121703, is about 1 km north of the city centre, on Avenida Héroes de Nacozari; there are very few passenger services left in Mexico so always check locally before planning a journey by train. The Central Camionera (bus station) is 5 km southeast of the centre, on the south side of the Mexico City - León highway. There are regular services to Mexico City (Terminal del Norte) and to Mexico City Airport (outside Sala D). For details of other destinations see **Transport**, page 541. Querétaro is at the crossroads of Route 57 (San Luis Potosí - Mexico City) and Route 45 to Celaya, León and Aguascalientes.

Getting around
Querétaro centre is reasonably compact and can be managed quite easily on foot; walking tours are very popular. City buses Nos 8 and 19 link the town centre and bus station; make sure they say 'Central Camionera' or 'Terminal de Autobuses'. City buses

Querétaro

Sleeping
1 Hidalgo
2 La Casa de la Marquesa
3 Mesón de Santa Rosa
4 Mirabel
5 Plaza
6 Posada la Academia
7 Posada la Colonial
8 San Agustín

are quite slow and taxis are a not-too-expensive alternative (Radio taxi T122490).

The **State tourist offices**, Pasteur Norte 4, is on Plaza Independencia at junction with Libertad, T121412, F121094.

Querétaro is 215 km from the capital and 1,105 km from the US border at Eagle Pass. Because of the altitude it can be quite cold at night.

The city was founded in 1531 and the name means 'Place of Rocks' in Tarascan. Hidalgo's rising in 1810 was plotted here, and it was also here that Emperor Maximilian surrendered after defeat, was tried, and was shot, on 19 June 1867, on the Cerro de las Campanas (the Hill of Bells), outside the city.

Sights

La Corregidora (Doña Josefa Ortiz de Domínguez, wife of the Corregidor, or Mayor), a member of the group who plotted for independence, masquerading as a society for the study of the fine arts, was able to get word to Father Hidalgo that their plans for revolt had been discovered. Hidalgo immediately gave the cry (*grito*) for Independence. Today, the Grito is given from the balcony of the **Palacio Municipal** (once home of La Corregidora) every 15 September at 1100 (it is echoed on every civic balcony thoughout Mexico on this date). La Corregidora's home may be visited.

The **Santa Rosa de Viterbo** church and monastery was remodelled by Francisco Tresguerras (tours in English). He also reconstructed the **Templo de Santa Clara**, one of the loveliest churches in Mexico. The 16th-century church and monastery of **Santa Cruz** served as the HQ of Maximilian and his forces and later as the Emperor's prison before he faced the firing squad in 1867. There is a good view from the bell tower. The church of **San Felipe**, recently restored, is now the Cathedral. The splendid **Palacio Federal**, once an Augustinian convent with exceptionally fine cloisters, has been restored and houses an art gallery containing some beautiful works. The **Teatro de la República**, by Jardín Obregón, is where Maximilian and his generals were tried, and where the Constitution of 1917 (still in force) was drafted. The **aqueduct**, built in 1726, is very impressive.

Several *andadores* (pedestrian walkways) have been developed, greatly adding to the amenities of the city. The *andadores* replace particular roads in places, for example Avenida 16 de Septiembre becomes Andador de la Corregidora in the centre, and then reverts to its original name. ■*Walking tours can be arranged*

de Mayo
Altamirano
5 de Mayo
Carmona
Tresguerras
gregacion
V Carranza
V Carranza
ndencia
mas
Santa Cruz
Mausoleo de la Corregidora
■3
Rio de la Loza
Pasteur
Av Zaragoza
To Los Arcos
Industria
21 de Marzo
ameda
Artes
Constituyentes
To Mexico City

Colonial Heartland

through the tourist office, daily at 1030 and 1800, 2½ hours, in Spanish but you can ask if an English-speaking guide is available, US$1.80, recommended. City tour plus execution site and Juárez monument, excellent value, from J Guadalupe Velásquez 5, Jardines de Oro, Santa Cruz, T121298, daily at 1130, US$12. On Sun, family excursions leave the Plaza de Armas at 1000.

Museums The important and elegant **Museo Regional** is on the main plaza, known as the Plaza de Armas or as Jardín Obregón (not all its galleries are always open). It contains much material on the Independence movement and the 1864-67 period leading to the imprisonment and death of Maximilian. ■ *0900-1900, closed Mon, free.*

Sleeping **L-AL** *La Casa de la Marquesa*, Madero 41, T120092/120098. Has 3 categories of
■ *on maps* rooms, the cheapest being US$180. Very opulent and lovely lobby. Mid-priced rooms
Price codes: equally opulent. **AL** *Holiday Inn*, Av 5 de Febrero y Pino Suárez, on Highway 57,
see inside front cover T160202, F168902. 5-star, restaurant, bars; also 5-star, **AL***Antigua Hacienda Galindo*, Km 5 on road to Amealco, Apdo Postal 16, T50250/20050, F168902. **AL** *Mesón de la Merced*, 16 de Septiembre Ote 95, Centro, T141498/141499, F145198 (in Mexico City T55142728). Small, elegant. Restaurant with Mexican cuisine. **AL** *Hotel Mesón del Obispo*, Andador 16 de Septiembre, T242464/242465. **AL** *Mirabel*, Constituyentes 2, T143585. Good, garage, restaurant. **AL-A** *Mesón de Santa Rosa*, Pasteur Sur 17, Centro, T242623/242781, F125522 (in Mexico City 55142728). Small, 300-year old inn, tastefully modernized, good restaurant with international and Mexican cuisine. **A** *Real de Minas*, Constituyentes 124, T160444/160257. 4-star. **B** *Casa Blanca*, Constituyentes 69 Pte, T160102, F160100. 4-star.

D *Del Marqués*, Juárez Norte 104, T120414/120554. TV, phone. Clean. **D** *Hidalgo*, Madero 11 Pte, near Zócalo, T120081. With bath, quiet, friendly, excellent value for 2 or more, not so for singles (English owner, Adrian Leece), has restaurant. **D** *Plaza*, Jardín Obregón, T121138. With bath, TV and phone, good location, airy, lovely inner patio, modernized, safe, clean, comfortable. Recommended. **D** *San Agustín*, Pino Suárez 12, T123919/121195. Small.

E *El Cid*, Prolongación Corregidora, T141165. More of a motel, clean, good value. **E** *Corregidora*, Corregidora 138, T140406. Reasonable but noisy. **E** *Posada La Academia*, Pino Suárez 3, just off Plaza Constitución. With bath and TV. Recommended. **E** *Posada La Colonial*, Juárez 19 Sur, T120239. Good value (**F** without bath). **E** *Posada Teresa*, Reforma 51 Ote, T126180. Basic. **E-F** *San Francisco*, Corregidora 144 Sur, T120858. With bath. **F** *Hotel R.J.*, Invierno 21 (extension of Juárez). Basic. **F** *Posada Familiar*, Independencia 22, T120584. Basic but OK, courtyard.

Youth hostel **E** *ex-Convento de la Cruz*, Av del Ejército Republicano, T231120. Running water morning only.

Motels *Posada Campestre*, Madero y Circunvalación, T162728. **AL** *Jurica*, T180022/180262, F180136, edge of town on road to San Luis Potosí, former *hacienda*. With gardens, squash, golf-course, opulent. **AL** *La Mansión*, 6½ km south of town. Excellent dining facilities, gorgeous grounds. **A** *Azteca*, 15 km north on road to San Luis Potosí, T122060. **B** *Flamingo*, on Constituyentes Pte 138, T162093/161972, F155778. Comfortable.

Eating *Mesón Santa Rosa*, Pasteur 17, in hotel of same name. Good but expensive, restored
● *on maps* colonial building. *Fonda del Refugio*, Jardín Corregidora. Pretty but food is poor; *VIPS*, Jardín Obregón (Madero Ote) *Terramar*, where Jardín Obregón and Jardín

Corregidora intersect, top floor of 1870 house. *Lonergan's*, Plaza de Armas. Pleasant café with small art gallery, magazines in English, French and German. *Café del Fondo*, Pino Suárez 9. Nice coffee house. *Mesón del Chucho el Roto* (since 1810), Plaza Independencia. Very popular at night. Serves drinks (alcoholic). Musicians. Absolutely delicious mango mousse, more like a boiled custard, very creamy. *Don Juan*, Plazuela de las Casas. Recommended. *Flor de Querétaro*, on Jardín Obregón, Juárez Norte 5. Good but pricey. *La Cocina Mexicana*, Pino Suárez 17, opposite *Hotel San Agustín*. Cheap and good but rather dark, à la carte better value than *comida corrida*. *Los Tacos de mi General*, Av Reforma y Manuel G Nájera. Cheap and good 4-course *comida corrida*. *Arcangel*, Plaza Chica. Pleasant setting, good food. *Le Bon Vivant*, Pino Suárez. Cheap, good value. Recommended. *Ostionería Tampico*, Corregidora Norte 3. Good cheap fish. *Leo's*, at La Cruz market. Excellent *tacos* and *quesadillas*, popular. *La Mariposa*, A Peralta 7. Excellent coffee, *tortas* and fruit shakes. *Bisquetes*, in arcade of old *Gran Hotel* on Zócalo. Good value. Try local Hidalgo Pinot Noir wine. *Vegetarian restaurant* at Independencia 5, just off Plaza de la Constitución.

Entertainment

Corral de Comedias, Carranza 39, T120765. An original theatre company, colonial surroundings and suppers. *JBJ Disco*, Blvd Zona Dorada, Fracc Los Arcos. *Mariachis* play in the Jardín Corregidora, 16 de Septiembre y Corregidora, in the evenings. The town band plays in the Jardín Obregón on Sun evening, lovely atmosphere.

Festivals

There is a *feria agrícola* from 2nd week of **Dec** until Christmas; bull fights and cock fights. On **New Year's Eve** there is a special market and performances are given in the main street.

Shopping

Stones are cheaper than San Juan del Río, but more expensive than Taxco

There are local opals, amethysts and topazes for sale; remarkable mineral specimens are shaped into spheres, eggs, mushrooms, and then polished until they shine like jewels (US$10-30). Recommended is *Joyería Villalón*, Andador Libertad 24a, for fine opals at good prices. Be careful when buying opals: some dealers keep their stones in humid conditions so they shine when you buy them but soon crack and lose their sheen. **La Cruz market**, 10 mins walk from the centre, is very well stocked, busy and clean. The market is open daily, but on Sun has a *tianguis* (street market).

Transport

Air There are flights from Chihuahua, Durango, Guadalajara, León, Mexico City, Monterrey, Morelia, Puerto Vallarta and Torreón.

Trains The station is not far north of the centre, close to Prolongación Corregidora. No passenger trains are running on the Mexico City-Cuidad Juárez line. There are second-class trains to Mexico City at 1500 on Wed, Fri, and Sun on the Mexico City-Nuevo Laredo line. Trains go to Nuevo Laredo at 1300 on Mon, Wed, and Fri. Check locally for services, trains are not reliable.

Buses Buses aren't allowed in the centre so there are no buses that run from the bus station directly to the centre. A taxi costs about 17 pesos. The bus station has a place for checking luggage that charges 6 pesos per 3 hrs per bag. It also has a restaurant (with a bar upstairs), travel agency, and magazine shop. There are public phones that require debit cards. Public conveniences cost two pesos. The bus station is southeast of city, near Estadio Corregidora, Terminal A, modules 1 and 2, 1st class and *Plus*, Terminal B, modules 3, 4 and 5, 2nd class.

Acapulco: Elite/Futura/Chihuahuenses 2200, 0040, US$31. **Agua Prieta**: Elite/Futura/Chihuahuenses 1215, 2155, US$114. **Aguascalientes**: Omnibus de México (1st class) 1315, 0215, US$14. **Chihuahua**: Omnibus de México 1930, 2030, US$57.50. **Ciudad Juárez**: Elite/Futura/Chihuahuenses 7 per day US$75.50. **Durango**: Omnibus de México 1120, 2100, US$32. **Guadalajara**: ETN (luxury service) 0030, 0700, 1200, 1500, 1700, 1845, US$22. Omnibus de México 0930, 1400, 1715, 2330, 0240, US$17. Servicios Coordinados (1st class) 9 per day, US$17. **Guanajuato**: Omnibus de

Colonial Heartland

México 1030, 2000, US$7. Servicios Coordinados 0800, 1120, 1145, 1700, US$7. **León**: Elite/Futura/Chihuahuenses 0122, 0425, 0655, 0825, 1240, 1615, 1945, US$8.50. Omnibus de México 0240, 0320, US$8.50. Servicios Coordinados 0830, 1100, 1845, $8.30. **Mazatlán**: Elite/Futura/Chihuahuenses 1000, 1210, 1830, US$48.50. **Mexicali**: Elite/Futura/Chihuahuenses 1000, 1210, 1830, US$106. **Mexico City**: Elite/Futura/Chihuahuenses hourly 0600-2100, US$10.50. ETN 32 per day, US$13.50. Omnibus de México 15 per day, US$10.50. **Monterrey**: Elite/Futura/Chihuahuenses 12 per day, US$33. Omnibus de México 1920, 2115, 2300, US$32.50. **Morelia**: Servicios Coordinados 16 per day, US$7.70. **Nogales**: Elite/Futura/Chihuahuenses departure time uncertain, US$107. **Nuevo Laredo**: Elite/Futura/Chihuahuenses 8 per day, US$45. **Piedras Negras**: Elite/Futura/Chihuahuenses (US border) 1540, 1900, 1955, US$54. **Saltillo**: Omnibus de México 2115, US$29. **San Juan de los Lagos**: Omnibus de México 0240, 0320, US$12. **San Luis Potosí**: ETN 1300, 1730, US$11. Omnibus de México 0950, 1150, US$9.50. Servicios Coordinados 16 per day, US$9.50. **San Miguel de Allende**: ETN 1030, 1215, 1550, 1900, US$4.50. Omnibus de México 1020, US$34. **Tijuana**: Elite/Futura/Chihuahuenses (all under same company) 1000, 1210, 1830, US$109.50. **Zacatecas**: Elite/Futura/Chihuahuenses 7 per day, US$19.50. Omnibus de México 0045, 2300, US$19.50.

Primera Plus (*Plus* service): **Mexico City airport**: 13 per day, US$14. **Mexico City** (northern terminal): every 20 mins, US$11. **Puerto Vallarta**: 2015, $40. **Guadalajara**: 1200, 1300, 1400, 1945, 2015, 2230, 0045, US$18. **San Luis Potosí**: 0320, 1510, 1715, 1730, 2015, US$10.50. **León**: 7 per day, US$9. **Morelia**: 1142, 1430, 1725, 1940, US$8.50.

Directory **Airline offices** *Aeromar*, T206936. **Banks** There is a *Banamex ATM* on the Jardín Obregón at Juárez and 16 de Septiembre that accepts Visa, MC, and cards of the Plus and Cirrus networks. There is a *Banco Inverlat ATM* (that should accept AmEx cards) at Corregidora Norte 60. There is a

Querétaro & the Missions

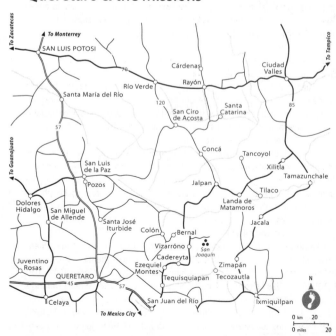

The missions of Querétaro

A little-known feature of Querétaro is the existence of 18th-century missions in the far northeast of the state. They were founded by Fray Junípero de la Serra, who later went on to establish missions in California with names like Nuestra Señora de los Angeles and San Francisco de Asís. He is also said to have planted a miraculous tree in the convent of the Santa Cruz in the city of Querétaro by thrusting his staff into the ground. The tree is apparently the only one of its kind in the world to have cruciform thorns.

All five missions have been restored, and two of them have hotels nearby. The journey itself requires something of a head for heights in that there are said to be 700 curves en route. There is a slightly shorter way, but that has over 1,000 ...

Casa de Cambio at Corregidora Norte 134. **Communications** Internet outlets: *Café Internet Asodi*, Fco. Márquez 219, Col. Las Campanas, T152783. *Café Internet Cibers Pace*, Av. Universidad 297, Col. Las Brujas, T137662. *Café Internet Welo*, Ezequiel Montes 67 Sur (close to corner of Constituyentes) T127272/160250. **Post Office:** Arteaga Pte 5 (inadequate). *DHL*, International courier service, Blvd Zona Dorada 37, Fracc Los Arcos, T142526 or 145256, open Mon-Fri 0900-1800, Sat 0900-1200. **Language schools** Centro Intercultural de Querétaro, Reforma 41, Centro, T/F122831. FEPE (Franco Español para Extranjeros), Luis Pasteur Norte 29, Col. Centro, T120819, info@fepe.edu.mx, www.fepe.edu.mx Only Spanish is spoken; no knowledge of English is necessary. Classes have a maximum of 5 students. 25 hrs per week for US$130. 6 proficiency levels, 100 hrs per level, 4 weeks each. New classes begin every Mon of the year. Also 1-to-1 courses at 12 dollars an hour. 'Spanish for travellers' course is 2 weeks, 5 hrs per day, costs US$265. They offer homestay. A double room costs US$49 pp, a single room costs US$90 per week. Meals are extra: 2 dollars for breakfast, 3 dollars for lunch, and 2 dollars for dinner.

Missions of Querétaro

The road to the **Missions of Querétaro** goes through the small market town of **Ezequiel Montes** (*population:* 5,000), reached either by a road turning northeast from the main highway 21 km east of Querétaro, or by Route 120 from San Juan del Río (see below). Two places of interest off the first-mentioned road are the town of **Colón** (14 km off the road, with 17th-century Templo de Nuestra Señora de los Dolores de Soriana) and **Bernal**, 75 km from Querétaro, a centre for clothing, blankets, wall hangings and carpets made by cottage industry. Near Bernal is the remarkable **Peñón de Bernal**, a massive rocky outcrop 350m high. On the night before and the day of the spring equinox (21 April) there is a festival held here. Local indigenous people believe the mountain is an energy point, because of its distinctive shape, and come to get energy from the first sun of the year. Of its kind, it is considered third after the Rock of Gibraltar and the Sugarloaf Mountain in Rio de Janeiro.

Forty-eight kilometres from Querétaro is San Juan del Río, near where some of the best fighting bulls are raised; the town is a centre for handicrafts, and also for polishing gemstones: opals and amethysts. There is one friendly and reasonable shop, La Guadalupana (16 de Septiembre 5); others are expensive and less friendly. Of the several *balnearios* in San Juan try *Venecia*, which has cold water and is very quiet mid-week (US$1.30).

San Juan del Río
Colour map 3, grid B5

Sleeping AL *Hotel Mansión Galindo*, T20050. Restored hacienda; apparently given by Cortés to his mistress La Malinche, beautiful building. **D** *Hotel Layseca*, Av Juárez 9 Ote. Colonial building, large rooms, nice furniture, excellent, car parking, no restaurant; several picturesque hotels, **D-E** *Estancia*, good, enclosed parking.

Colonial Heartland

Tequisquiapan
Phone code: 427
Colour map 3, grid B5

A branch road runs northeast from San Juan to the picturesque town of Tequisquiapan, with thermal baths, fine climate, watersports, weekend residences and expensive, good hotels. *Artesanías Bugambilia*, a craft shop on the main square, is recommended. Note that the town is deserted from Monday to Thursday and big reductions in hotel prices can be found. On the other hand, there is nothing other than the resort: a good cheap Mexican meal is hard to find. The dam near the town is worth a visit. There is a geyser, at Tecozautla, 1¼ hours from Tequisquiapan. Between San Juan del Río and Tequisquiapan, a small track leads off the main road 4 km to the village of La Trinidad, near which lie some of the opal mines which are still in operation.

Sleeping and eating A *El Relox*, Morelos 8, T30066. Spa pool, open to non-residents. *Maridelphi*, similar price. *Las Cavas*, Paseo Media Luna 8, T30804, F30671. Restaurant *La Chiapaneca*, Carrizal 19. Centre, opposite craft market, very good, reasonably priced, clean.

Transport Buses: San Juan del Río-Tequisquiapan US$1, 20 mins.

Cadereyta
Colour map 3, grid B5

Beyond Tequisquiapan is Cadereyta (Km 75), colonial in style, with two noteworthy churches in the main square, one dedicated to St Peter, the other St Paul. The latter houses an important collection of colonial religious art. Nearby is the Casa de los Alemanes, which has an enormous collection of cacti. There is a petrol station at Cadereyta and another at **Vizarrón**, a local centre for marble.

San Joaquín
Colour map 3, grid B5

The roads to both ruins are steep and the ruins are often swathed in mist

East of Route 120, there are ruins at San Joaquín (Km 138): **Ranas** and **Toluquilla** which have both been only partially excavated. The former receives about 200 visitors a month, the latter only 40 visitors a month. You must register upon arriving and a donation is requested. The sites have been attributed to the Toltecs and the Chichimecs. Ranas is a 30-minute walk from the village and has stupendous views from a series of terraced platforms and pyramids (*entry US$1*); Toluquilla lies 10 km from the village (poorly marked road). Although there were only, at most, 200 inhabitants, there are six ball courts! Tarantulas abound. Fifteen minutes walk from San Joaquín is a beautiful cave (Las Grutas). San Joaquín is famous for the annual Huapango dance festival on 15 April. The village itself is picturesque and has hotels.

Sleeping E *Victoria*, halfway up hill, Av Insurgentes. Basic. **E** *Mesón de Joaquín*, T25315, next to bus park. Good-value rooms for four and a camp-ground with shelters and barbecue stands on the outskirts above the town. **Transport** San Joaquín can be reached in 3 hours by car or bus on a windy road going through desert and then misty pine forests. Flecha Amarilla run six buses a day, earliest from Querétaro 0620, last 1620, US$4; Flecha Azul also run buses San Joaquín-San Juan del Río.

The bends really start after Vizarrón. Much of the journey from here on is through rather arid and yet dramatic terrain with gorges and panoramic views. The high point is called la Puerta del Cielo (Door to the Sky), which is apt enough as you can actually look down on the clouds. As the road begins to descend, so the vegetation becomes more tropical and the weather gets much warmer. Jalpan is only 700m above sea level, Concá 500m. There is a petrol station at Ahuacatlán (Km 166), before Jalpan.

Jalpan
Colour map 3, grid B5

Jalpan, the first of the missions, becomes visible way below in a broad, lush valley. It is the largest of the missions, which are located in valleys that spread out from here. Jalpan was the first to be founded in 1774 and has cloisters as well as the main church. The town itself is picturesque without being spoilt. It makes a good base for day trips to the other missions. Also there are pleasant walks along tree-lined riverbanks. The town museum is worth a visit. ■ *1000-1500, US$0.50.* All the churches are distinguished by the profusion of baroque carving, their superb location and the care with which they have been conserved. They are all different and all worth the trip: **Landa de Matamoros**, 18 km east of Jalpan, **Tilaco**, 25 km beyond Landa to the east, and **Tancoyol**, 37 km to the north of Landa. (The roads are good apart from the last 15 km into Tilaco).

Sleeping and eating D *Posada Fray Junípero*, Ezequiel Montes 124, T121241, opposite church. With bath and TV, clean, friendly, credit cards, colonial style, pool, restaurant, good value but noisy because of bus station. **E** *Posada Aurora*. With bath, hot water, fan, clean, friendly. Recommended.

Las Cazuelas, to right of church. Delicious *tacos*, very clean. *Las Jacarandas*, next to bus station. Good *comida corrida*, reasonably priced, clean. Shrimp cocktails at stalls on plaza.

Transport Buses: 3 direct from Mexico City, US$11, 6 hrs, beautiful trip. Hourly from Jalpan to Landa de Matamoros, US$0.50, 20 mins. To Tilaco and Tancoyol 40-min bus journey to La Lagunita, hourly, then *combis* (on market day, Sat) or hitchhike. To Querétaro every hour, 5 hrs, US$3.50, 2nd class, Flecha Amarilla. To Ciudad Valles, frequent, via Landa de Matamoros and Xilitla, 2nd class, Transporte Vencedor.

Concá
Colour map 3, grid B5

Thirty-eight kilometres northwest of Jalpan is Concá. *Acamaya*, freshwater crayfish, is a local speciality. At the bridge of Concá a hot water river flows into one with cold water. The church is built on a ridge, creating a dramatic skyline when viewed from below. The village is very small with two restaurants and a general store. Hourly bus to Concá from Jalpan, US$1.30. There is a large hotel in its own grounds a few kilometres from the village and mission, again in colonial style with a pool fed by warm spring water.

It is possible to drive from Concá to San Luis Potosí, which is about three hours further on. The journey to Jalpan from Querétaro takes about six hours. At least three days should be allowed to enjoy the tour of the missions.

Xilitla
Phone code: 136
Colour map 3, grid B5

Between Jalpan and Ciudad Valles is the charming village of Xilitla, overlooking a lush tropical valley. Famous for the house (El Castillo) and garden (Las Pozas) of the late Edward James, born 1907, millionaire heir to the Phelps Dodge copper fortune, with connections to the British royal family. Las Pozas is 30 minutes walk from Xilitla and is fascinating with extravagant concrete structures intertwined with exuberant vegetation, waterfalls, birds and butterflies. **Sleeping and eating** at **A-B** *El Castillo*, T52136, 50038, F50055. Includes breakfast, pool, fine views, run by Avery and Leonore Danzinger. Several smaller hotels too. At *Restaurant Los Cayos* (good view), try *enchiladas huastecas* and local coffee. Buses from Jalpan every hour, US$2.30, 2½ hours.

Querétaro to Mexico City

There is a four-lane motorway (US$3 a car) from Irapuato past Querétaro to Mexico City. The Mexico City motorway passes close to Tula and Tepozotlán (see page 145). There are various country clubs along the road. In the state park of El Ocotal is a Swiss-chalet style hotel, **B**, with excellent restaurant.

Colonial Heartland

Celaya

Phone code: *461*
Colour map 3, grid B4
Population: *420,000*
Altitude: *1,800m*

Celaya is famous for its confectionery, especially a caramel spread called *cajeta*, and its churches, built by Mexico's great architect Francisco Eduardo Tresguerras (1759-1833), a native of the town. His best is considered to be **El Carmen**, with a fine tower and dome. He also built a fine bridge over the Río de la Laja. On 12 October 1570 the royal *cédula* was granted to found a town, the Villa de la Purísima Concepción de Zalaya, close to an Otomí settlement known as Nat Tah Hi. Zalaya, or Celaya, was in fact founded on 1 January 1571, but both dates are celebrated locally. Its status was elevated to that of city on 20 October 1655 by King Felipe IV of Spain. The city was located in a productive agricultural region and soon became important as a supply centre for the mines, thereby boosting commerce and making it prosperous. It was an important trading post on the route to Guanajuato, Zacatecas and Guadalajara and for the transport of metals to the capital. The 17th and 18th centuries saw the construction of many great houses and religious buildings and in 1725 a university was founded. Don Miguel Hidalgo y Costilla arrived in Celaya with 40,000 men on 21 September 1810 in his quest for Independence. He lodged in the Mesón de Guadalupe (now the *Hotel Guadalupe*) and received the support of the city, being proclaimed Captain General of the rebel army. He left with 50,000 fighters. Industrialization dates from 1836, when the first factory was built to produce thread and cloth. The railway arrived in 1878, the same year in which the first *cajeta* factory was started. Nowadays industrial enterprises include food processing, mechanical engineering, chemical products and others. The **tourist office**, Casa del Diezmo, Juárez 204, T/F34313, is helpful.

Sights **Templo del Carmen**, built by Tresguerras in 1802-1807, the interior and exterior are neoclassical with a simple elegance, you can see Tresguerras'

Celaya

Colonial Heartland

own paintings inside. **Convento de San Francisco**, one of the largest in the country, the interior is 17th-century baroque; the façade of the cloisters was rebuilt by Tresguerras. **Templo de San Francisco** was rebuilt in 1683 after the original chapel was demolished. The façade is neo-classical and was rebuilt, together with the altars, by Tresguerras between 1810-1820. **Claustro Agustino** dates from the beginning of the 17th century and was the municipal prison until 1961. It is currently the Casa de la Cultura and often has art exhibitions. **Templo de San Agustín** was built in 1609 in the plateresque style. **Templo de la Tercera Orden** is another of Tresguerras' neo-classical works, built in 1820 with marvellous altars. The **Columna de la Independencia** was designed by Tresguerras and was the first monument in the country to celebrate Mexico's freedom in 1828. **Torre Hidráulica**, also known as the **bola de agua** (ball of water), has been adopted as the symbol of the city; it was inaugurated on the centenary of Mexico's Independence from Spain and holds one million litres of water. **Casa del Diezmo**, built at the end of the 17th century, now houses the tourist office. The **Presidencia Municipal** has impressive murals up the stairways in the entrance off the main square, a metamorphosis of people and events in Mexico's history, created in 1980 by local artist Octavio Ocampo González. Another of his murals, showing the evolution of man, is in the library of the **Instituto Tecnológico de Celaya**, on Calle Irrigación. The **Mausoleo de Tresguerras**, is a baroque chapel where the famous architect is buried.

Sleeping

AL *Celaya Plaza*, Blvd López Mateos y Carretera Panamericana, T46260, F46889. 143 rooms, tennis, spa, meeting rooms. **B** *Plaza Bajío Inn*, Libertad 133, T38603, F37353. 80 rooms, central, restaurant, disco, convention facilities, parking, medical service, laundry. **C** *Isabel*, Hidalgo 207, T22096, F33449. Restaurant, bar, laundry, parking. **E** *Guadalupe*, Portal Guadalupe 108, T21839, F29514. Very old hotel with historical connections, central, cheaper rooms without bath.

There are some 30 hotels of different prices & standards; many of the better hotels are outside the centre

Eating

Many restaurants serving steak and others specializing in seafood. *El Caserío*, Blvd López Mateos 1302 Pte, T55608. Spanish cuisine. *La Mansión del Marisco*, Blvd López Mateos 1000, esq Juárez, T55262. Fish and seafood, live music at weekends. *El Mezquital*, Blvd López Mateos 1113 Ote. Meat and traditional barbeque. *Mamma O'Fan*. 3 restaurants, at Benito León 203, Blvd López Mateos 1008 Ote, and Plaza Juárez 127, in Apaseo el Grande. Italian food, pizza, pasta, etc.

Festivals

10-20 Jan is the fiesta of the appearance of the Virgin of Guadalupe in the Tierrasnegras barrio, one of the oldest districts of Celaya. There is drama, dancing, fireworks and eating a typical *antojito*, 'gorditas de Tierrasnegras'. **Easter** is marked by visiting several *balnearios* such as Balnearios Los Arcos y Aguacaliente and others in the area, Cortázar, Villagrán, Juventino Rosas, Apaseo el Grande and Apaseo el Alto. There are processions through the streets, much eating of local delicacies, and on **Easter Sun** Judas is burned in many places in the city. The Virgen del Carmen is celebrated **16 Jul**. The anniversary of the founding of the city is celebrated in **Oct**. The *Day of the Dead* is a movable feast, celebrated in the week leading up to the 2nd Mon in **Nov**, unlike the rest of the country. Since 1844 a Christmas regional fair has been held in the 2nd half of **Dec** with exhibitions of farming, livestock, crafts and cultural and sporting events.

Transport

Six buses a day to Mexico City airport with Primera Plus. There is a 24-hr pharmacy at the bus station. Bus companies serving Celaya: ETN, T28664; Omnibus de México, T23614; Elite, T20533; Tres Estrellas de Oro, T23776; Flecha Amarilla, T22489; Tucán, T36543; Turismos de Celaya, T34280.

Colonial Heartland

Irapuato
Phone code: 462
Population: 475,000
Route 45, Km 315

Irapuato is noted for delicious strawberries, which should on no account be eaten unwashed. It is a prosperous industrial and agricultural town and an important distribution centre. In the town centre, around the **Plaza de los Fundadores** and the **Jardín Hidalgo**, there is a cluster of historic buildings. The **Templo del Hospital** built around 1550, rebuilt 1617, façade completed 1733, is said to have the country's largest chandelier. Outside, the **Cruz Monolítica** commemorates the visit of San Sebastian of Aparicio. The façade of the **Templo de San Francisco**, also known as El Convento (1799), is a mixture of baroque and neo-classical. The huge **Parroquia** (parish church) was rebuilt mid-18th century. The **Presidencia Municipal**, 19th century, incorporates a former 18th-century school, the **Colegio de Enseñanza para Niños**. The fountain, **Fuente de los Delfines** was given to the town by Emperor Maximilian.

Unfortunately, the centre has been invaded by unsightly and incongruous modern buildings. Just off the centre is the 16th-century church of **San José**, with fine examples of American indigenous art. Also the **Templo of Nuestra Señora de Guadalupe** (1890), with its striking late neo-classical gold-leaf-decorated interior.

Sleeping and eating *Hotel Real de Minas*, T62380. Overpriced, with equally over-priced restaurant, on Portal Carrillo Puerto, quiet rooms on church side. *Restaurant El Gaucho*, Díaz Ordaz y Lago.

San Miguel de Allende

Phone code: 415
Colour map 3, grid B4
Population: 150,000
Altitude: 1,850m

A charming old town on a steep hillside facing the broad sweep of the Río Laja and the distant blue of the Guanajuato mountains, is 50 km north of Querétaro by paved road, 90 km from Guanajuato. The city was founded as San Miguel in 1542, and Allende added in honour of the independence patriot born there. Its twisting cobbled streets rise in terraces to the mineral spring of El Chorro, from which the blue and yellow tiled cupolas of some 20 churches can be seen. It has been declared a national monument and all changes in the town are strictly controlled.

Getting there & away
The nearest airport is at Silao, close to León, sometimes called the Aeropuerto del Bajío. The long-distance bus station is west of the town centre along Calle Canal. The town centre can be reached by taxi or bus. The train station is beyond the bus termi-nal; a few second-class passenger trains are still running but check locally before mak-ing plans. San Miguel is on Route 51, between Dolores Hidalgo, Celaya and Querétaro (via Route 57).

Getting around
Most places of interest can be reached from the town centre on foot. Walking tours of old houses and garden leave from the Biblioteca Pública (public library), Insurgentes 25, between Reloj and Hidalgo, T20293. ■ *Sun 1215, 4 hours, US$8.*

There has been a large non-Mexican community here since the 1930s, originally art-ists and writers who came to the art school founded by US artist Stirling Dickinson. The town has a very active cultural scene and cosmopolitan feel to it; the downside is that there are many tourists and a consequent rise in prices. Accommodation and restau-rants are generally more expensive than in other towns. The **tourist office** is on the Plaza next to the church, helpful with finding hotels, English spoken, US$2 for city map.

Sights

The area around Parque Juárez and El Chorro is very picturesque with steep alleyways and women washing clothes in the springs. Social life revolves

Colonial Heartland

around the market and the Jardín, or Plaza Principal, an open-air living room for the whole town. Around it are the colonial **Palacio Municipal**, several hotels, and **La Parroquia** (parish church), adorned in the late 19th century by Zeferino Gutiérrez, an Indian stonemason who provided the austere Franciscan front with a beautiful façade and a Gothic tower. See also the mural in the chapel. The church of **San Felipe Neri**, with its fine baroque façade, is at the southwest end of the market. Notable among the baroque façades and doors rich in churrigueresque details is the **Casa del Mayorazgo de Canal**, and **San Francisco** church, designed by Tresguerras. The convent of **La Concepción**, built in 1734, now houses an art school, the **Centro Cultural Ignacio Ramírez Nigromonte**, locally known as Escuela de Bellas Artes (good cafetería in its courtyard). One of the rooms off the courtyard contains a large mural by Siqueiros, locked up because of vandalism, but you can get the key from the secretary at the entrance. The summer residence of the Condes de Canal, on San Antonio, contains the art school and a language school, the **Instituto Allende**, started by Stirling Dickinson (which has an English-language library and runs Spanish courses, usually without accommodation, but some rooms can be rented – for others, see below). A magnificent view of the city can be gained from the *mirador* on the Querétaro road (the views are also good before you get to the *mirador*).

Excursions

A good all-day hike can be made to the **Palo Huérfano** mountain on the south side of town. Take the road to just before the radio pylon then take the trails to

San Miguel de Allende

■ Sleeping		
1 La Huerta	5 Posada Carmina	9 Rincón del Cielo
2 La Parroquia	6 Posada de San Francisco	10 San Sebastián
3 Mansión del Bosque	7 Posada la Aldea	11 Sautto
4 Parador San Miguel Aristos	8 Quinta Loreto	12 Vista Hermosa Taboada

Colonial Heartland

the summit, where there are oaks and pines. Between San Miguel de Allende and Celaya is **Comonfort** (25 km); from there go 3 km north to Rancho Arias: on a hilltop to the west are pre-Columbian ruins. Cross the river north of the church and climb to the ruins via goat-tracks. **El Charco del Ingenio** Botanical Gardens (reached by taking a bus to El Gigante shopping centre, turn left and continue for 15 minutes, or go up Calle Homobono, a more interesting and attractive route) cover an area of 64ha with lovely views, a deep canyon, an artificial lake and cacti. ■ *US$1, free on Wed.*

Essentials

A good source of information on inexpensive accommodation is the English language paper published weekly by the Anglo-Mexican Library on Insurgentes.

Sleeping
■ *on maps*
Price codes:
see inside front cover
Many weekend visitors
from Mexico City: book
ahead if you can

L *Hotel Antigua Villa Santa Mónica*, Baeza 22 (about 3 blocks from the main plaza), T20451/20427, F20518. Includes breakfast. **AL-A** *Mansión del Bosque*, Aldama 65, T20277. Rooms are heated, some have fireplaces, attractive (high season with 2 meals; low season without meals). **AL** *Casa de Lisa*, Bajada del Chorro 7, T20352. Restored colonial house, with breakfast. **AL** *Casa Luna B&B*, Pila Seca 11, T/F21117, casaluna@unisono.net.mx American-run, excellent breakfast included, beautiful themed rooms, no smoking inside. Highly recommended. **AL** *Misión de los Angeles*, de luxe, 2 km out on Celaya road, T22155. Colonial style, swimming pool, convenient facilities. **AL-A** *Rancho-Hotel El Atascadero*, T20206/20337, F21541, toll-free from within Mexico 8004660000: www.redmex.com/Atascadero, on road to Querétaro. In an old colonial hacienda, family suite (for 4 people) available. Very satisfactory. **AL** *Villa Jacaranda*, Aldama 53, T21015. Central, a couple of blocks behind cathedral, very good restaurant.

A *Casa de las Limas*, Ancha de San Antonio 14, T20853. Restored colonial house, pleasant, breakfast included. **A** *Casa Murphy*, San Antonio Abad 22, T23776/22194/F22188, inside parking. Full use of house, large breakfast included in price. **A** *La Hermita*, Pedro de Vargas 64, T20777. Attractive suites with fireplaces, pool, gardens, used to belong to the comic actor Cantinflas. **A** *Parador San Miguel Aristos*, at Instituto Allende, Ancha de San Antonio 30, T20149. Students given priority, large rooms, some with a fireplace and kitchen, parking US$2. **A** *Posada de San Francisco*, main square, T/F20072/27213. Pleasant, restaurant. **A** *Posada La Aldea*, Ancha de San Antonio, T/F21022/21026. Colonial style, clean, quiet, swimming pool, gardens. **A** *Real de Minas*, Ancha de San Antonio s/n, T22838, F21737. Lovely lobby, rooms average. **A** *Rincón del Cielo*, Correo 10, next to main plaza, T21647/44496. Rooms are very large and have 2 storeys, the bedroom is upstairs with fireplace and huge bathroom with bathtub, living room has wet bar, quite attractive and good value. **AL-B** *Posada Carmina*, Cuna de Allende 7, T20458, F20135. Colonial building, courtyard for meals. Recommended. **B** *Mansión Virreyes*, Canal 19, T20851/23355, F23865. Small, dark rooms. **B** *Mesón San Antonio*, Mesones 80, T20580, F22897. Renovated mansion, clean, friendly, quiet, rooms just so-so. Near Jardín, on Vinaron, **B** *La Siesta*, Salida a Celaya 82, T20207, F23722. Pool (not in use), fireplaces in rooms (US$34 with breakfast). **B-C** *Vista Hermosa Taboada*, Allende 11, T20078/20437, F22638. Very popular, nice old colonial building.

A good source of
information on
inexpensive
accommodation is the
English language paper
published weekly by the
Anglo-Mexican Library
on Insurgentes.

C *Monteverdi*, T21814. Clean, hot water. **C** *Posada La Fuente*, Ancha de San Antonio 95, T20629. Has a few rooms, good food (by arrangement). **C** *Posada de las Monjas*, Canal 37, T20171/26227. With shower, excellent set meals in restaurant, bar, clean and attractive, very good value, a converted convent, also has a few **D** rooms at back if you ask. **C-D** *Hotel Posada 'El Mayorazgo'*, Hidalgo 8, T21309, F23838. If you stay 10 days, the 7th is free. Also rent by the month for US$250 and have 1-bed apartments with kitchen for US$350 per month. **C-D** *Quinta Loreto*, Loreto 13, T20042, F23616.

TV, clean, quiet, swimming pool, pleasant garden, next to Mercado de Artesanías, hot water problems. Good, cheap food, restaurant closed in evening (but beware of mosquitoes). **D** *Casa de Huéspedes*, Mesones 27, T21378. Family atmosphere, clean, hot water, popular, roof garden, nice location, good value. **D** *Hotel La Huerta*, Callejón de Atascadero 9, T44475. Bath, clean, well-furnished, quiet, at the bottom of a dead-end street 4 blocks from the market in woodland, dark and unpleasant at night for lone females walking back, free parking, but watch your valuables. **D** *Posada San Sebastián*, Mesones 7, T20707, near market. With bath, charming, large rooms with fireplace, clean, car park, noisy at front (most rooms at the back), courtyard. Recommended. **D** *Sautto*, Dr Macías 59, T20072. Room with fridge, fireplace and bath, new rooms best, rustic, garden, hot water, parking. Recommended. **E-F** *San Miguel International Hostal*, C Jaime Nuno 28, Col Guadalupe (a long way from the centre). Private rooms for 2 people or bed in dorm, cheaper with a youth hostel card. Shared kitchen, friendly. Another cheap *Casa de Huéspedes* on Animas, just past the market building. **F** *El Nuevo Hostal*, Jaime Nuno 28, T20674. Shared bath, friendly, cosy, clean, kitchen and laundry facilities available.

Motels AL *Villa del Molino*, on road to Mexico City. **B** *Siesta*, on road to Guanajuato, with trailer park, gardens; *KAO campgrounds* further out on same road. Quiet, grassy site, all facilities, pleasant, Dutch owner.

Mesón de San José, Mesones 38. Mexican and international cuisine, vegetarian dishes, excellent breakfasts, nice setting, German/Mexican owners, open 0800-2200, live music Sun, gift shop. Recommended. *Mama Mía*, Umarán, west of main square. Main meals good but not cheap, free live folk music or films in the afternoon, excellent cheap breakfasts. *Café de la Parroquia*, Jesús 11. Good, French owner speaks English. *Casa Mexas*, Canal 15. Good American food, clean, popular with gringos. *L'invito*, near Plaza Principal. Owned by Silvia Bernardini, who taught cuisine in Milan. No reports as yet. *Rincón Español*, opposite Correos. Good *comida corrida*, flamenco at weekends. Recommended. *El Jardín*, San Francisco, close to Plaza. Friendly service, good food, also vegetarian, violinist plays upstairs at weekends for price of a drink. *Flamingos*, Juárez. Good set lunch US$4.50. *La Princesa*, Recreo 5. Set menu 1300-2000, including glass of wine, live music from 2100, cosy cellar atmosphere. *La Vendimie*, Hidalgo. English proprietor, poetry readings Mon afternoon (must book), occasional fish and chips. *El Infierno*, Mesones, just below Plaza Allende. Excellent *sopa azteca*, good value, *menú del día*, US$2.50. *El Tomate*, vegetarian restaurant on Mesones, attractive, spotless, excellent food, generous helpings, not cheap. *Tentenpié*, Allende. Pleasant café/*taquería*. Good cheap chicken restaurant on San Francisco between Juárez and Reloj (roast chicken in windows). *Eclipse*, Hidalgo 15. Vegetarian, *menú del día* US$4. Recommended. *Tío Lucas*, Mesones, opposite Teatro Angela Peralta. Very good. Recommended. *El Buen Café*, Jesús 23, T25807. Good quiche, pies, cakes, and juices.

Eating
● *on maps*

English-language films at *Villa Jacaranda* hotel video bar. US$5 including alcoholic drink and popcorn. *Teatro Angela Peralta*, Mesones 82, has theatre, musical events, and dance. There's a coffee house in the front entrance hall.

Entertainment

End-Jul to mid-Aug, classical chamber music festival, information from Bellas Artes. Main festivals are *Independence Day* (**15-16 Sep**); *Fiesta of San Miguel* (**28 Sep-1 Oct**, with Conchero dancers from many places); *Day of the Dead* (**2 Nov**); the *Christmas Posadas*, celebrated in the traditional colonial manner (**16-24 Dec**); the *pre-Lenten carnival*, *Easter Week*, and *Corpus Christi* (**Jun**). There is a Christmas season musical celebration, started in 1987, which attracts musicians of international level, T20025. *La Pamplonada*, when they let the bulls run loose in the plaza, is held in **Sep** (the exact date varies from year to year).

Festivals

Colonial Heartland

Shopping **Bookshop** *El Colibrí*, Diez de Sollano 30, good selection of French and English books. The English-language daily *The News* is sold on the Jardín. **Handicrafts** Pottery, cotton cloth and brasswork. The Mercado de Artesanías tends to sell tacky souvenirs rather than real handicrafts; prices are high and the selection poor. Tue is the best day for bargains. The shops on Canal have a good selection and quality is high, but so are the prices; bargaining is next to impossible. It may be better to try elsewhere for genuine handicrafts (eg the Ciudadela handicraft market in the capital). *La Casa del Vidrio*, Correo 11, offers an excellent selection of brown-glass items at fair prices (sale prices in the summer, 40% off).

Tour operators *Viajes Vertiz*, on Hidalgo, American Express agent, mail collection and cheque cashing available. Excursions organized by the friends of the local school for handicapped children are US$10 pp, interesting destinations to local ranch or artesans or houses not normally open to the public.

Transport **Trains** The railway station is a long way from the centre, beyond the bus terminal. Both are served by bus. According to the clerk at the ticket office, there are daily trains to Mexico City (2nd class) at 1300 (8½ hrs) and to Nuevo Laredo at 1430. But train services are dwindling so don't rely on them.

Buses The bus station is on the outskirts, regular bus to the centre US$0.25, returns from the market or outside *Posada San Francisco* on the Jardín. A taxi costs about US$1 to the centre. Buses to the centre leave from in front of the terminal. They return from in front of the market.

Aguascalientes; Flecha Armilla (2nd class) 1235, 1435, US$8. **Celaya**; Flecha Armilla every 15 mins, US$2.60. If there are no buses leaving for Guadalajara from San Miguel at the time you want to go, it's best to go to Celaya and catch a bus from there. **Guadalajara**; Primera Plus (*Plus* service) 0730, 0930, 1730, US$22. Servicios Cooridinados (1st class) 1950, US$19.70. **Guanajuato**; Omnibus de Mexico (1st class) 1115, US$4.50. Servicios Cooridinados 1545, 1950, US$4.60. Flecha Armilla 9 per day, US$3.60. **León**; Primera Plus (*Plus* service) 0730, 0930, 1730, US$8. Servicios Cooridinados 1545, 1950, US$7.70. **Mexico City** (northern terminal); Primera Plus 0940, 1600, US$13. Flecha Armilla every 40 mins from 0520 to 2000, US$10.70. **Querétaro**; Flecha Armilla every 40 mins from 0520 to 2000, US$2.60. **San Luis Potosí**; Flecha Armilla 7 per day, US$7.80.

International connections: Autobuses Americanos have daily buses to Laredo, Texas, San Antonio and on to Dallas at 1800. Also daily buses to Houston at 1800. Costs $44.40 to Laredo, Texas and $67 to Dallas. They also have buses on Wed leaving at 1800 to Chicago for $116.

Directory **Banks** *Casa de Cambio Deal* on Correo, opposite Post Office, and on Juárez. **Communications** Internet: *WWW.Punto*, Canal 120, T28124. *La Conexión*, Aldama 1, T/F 21599, 21687, connexion@unisono.net.mx; they charge 10 pesos for blocks of 10 mins. *Border Crossings*, Correo 19, phone, fax, and email service. *Estación Internet*, Recreo 11. There is a long-distance phone service at Diez de Sollano 4, just off the plaza. There are *DHL* and *UPS* agencies across the street from the post office. *Red Com*, Blvd Rosales y Madero, US$3 per hr. **Embassies & consulates** *US Consular Agent*, Plaza Golondrinas arcade, Hernández Macías, interior 111. T22357, emergencies 20068/20653, Mon and Wed 0900-1300. **Language schools** Many of the schools demand payment in US dollars (technically illegal) and you may prefer to arrange private tuition for US$3-4 per hr. *Academia Hispanoamericana*, recommended for language lessons and sessions on Mexican history, folklore, literature, singing and dancing; very helpful; accommodation with families. *Card Game Spanish*, Pilancón 19, T21758, F20135, intensive courses for beginners or intermediate, run by Warren Hardy, the inventor of the Card Game method. See also **Learning Spanish** in Essentials. The library arranges 'amigo' sessions where Mexicans and foreigners can practice English and Spanish for free. Many activities arranged here. **Laundry** On Pasaje de Allende, US$3 wash and dry, same day service; unnamed laundry at Correo 42, good. **Libraries** English-language library on Insurgentes has an excellent selection on Mexico; very extensive bilingual library, with computer centre and English-speaking staff. **Useful addresses** Immigration: 2nd flr Plaza Real del Conde, T22542, 0900-1300. For tourist card extensions, etc, take 2 copies of passport, tourist card and credit card or TCs.

Between San Miguel de Allende and Dolores Hidalgo is the small town of **Atotonilco** Atotonilco, where there is a church, founded in 1740, whose inside walls and ceiling are covered with frescoes. The black, red and grey earth images are unrivalled anywhere for their sheer native exuberance. It was from Atotonilco's church that Padre Hidalgo took the banner of the Virgen de Guadalupe to act as his battle standard.

Sleeping A *Parador El Cortijo*, Apdo Postal 585, San Miguel de Allende, T01-46521700. Very good, pool open to non-residents US$3.30, below the hotel on Querétaro-Dolores Hidalgo road are Las Grutas thermal baths, which belong to the hotel. Take Dolores Hidalgo bus from San Miguel de Allende bus station, or 'Santuario' hourly bus from covered market off Plaza Allende near top of San Miguel: either passes the door.

Thermal Baths Across the river from Atotonilco is the tiny village of San Miguelito. A short distance beyond, natural thermal waters rise from the river bed; local women construct hot tubs, called *arenas*, by piling sand around the springs in which to wash clothes and themselves. There is a spa, the **Balneario Taboada**, between Atotonilco and San Miguel (about 20 minutes bus ride direct from San Miguel market; it is a long walk from the main road, better to go by car or taxi). The spa has a small hot pool, a fine swimming pool and good fishing in a nearby lake – very popular. ■ *Wed-Sun, US$2, café open weekend only*. Near the spa is *Hacienda Taboada* hotel (five-star, large thermal pool, swimming pool, open only to guests – prior booking necessary). Another spa is close by, **Santa Verónica**, with huge clean pool, bus stops outside, recommended. ■ *0900-1800, US$2.50*. From San Miguel de Allende, for either spa, catch bus from Mesones by the market.

Dolores Hidalgo

The home of Padre Hidalgo, 54 km from Guanajuato, is a most attractive, tranquil small town. The main square, or Jardín, is lovely, dominated by a statue of Hidalgo. On one side is the church of **Nuestra Señora de los Dolores** (1712-1778) in which Hidalgo gave *El Grito de la Independencia* (the Cry for Independence from Spain); the façade is impressive, and the churrigueresque side altar pieces, one of gold leaf, one of wood, are more ornate than the main altar. It is not always open. Also on the Jardín are many restaurants, cafés and banks. The **tourist office**, on the main square, can direct you to places making the traditional Talavera tiles which can be seen all over the town and can be bought at very good prices.

Phone code: 418
Colour map 3, grid B4
Population: 135,000

Independence celebrations are held on 15 and 16 September

The **Iglesia de La Asunción**, Puebla y Sonora, has a large tower at one end, a **Sights** dome at the other, with extensive murals and a tiled floor inside. Two blocks away, at Puebla y Jalisco, is Plaza de los Compositores Dolorenses with a bandstand. Between these two sites on Puebla is the post and telegraph office. Visit Hidalgo's house, the **Museo Casa Hidalgo**, Morelos y Hidalgo, a beautiful building with a courtyard and wells, memorabilia and one room almost a shrine to the Father of Independence. ■ *Tue-Sat 1000-1800, Sun 1000-1700, US$4.35.*

Colonial Heartland

The **Museo de la Independencia**, on Zacatecas, was formerly a jail, but now has displays of striking paintings of the path of Independence. ■ *US$0.70.*

Excursions About 5 km southeast of town on a dirt track are the ruins of the **Hacienda de la Erre**, Padre Hidalgo's first stop on the Independence Route after leaving Dolores. The standing walls are only 3-4m high; there are about four rooms with ceilings; the patio, with a lot of litter is overgrown, but the chapel has been rebuilt. Outside is the huge mezquite tree under which Hidalgo is supposed to have said mass for his insurgent troops ■ *free entrance to the untended ruins and grounds.* The walk to the ruins (1½-2 hours) starts from the plaza. Take Calle Guerrero to the east, then Tamaulipas to the main road. Turn left for 1 km to a gravel road on the left on a long curve. Follow this to the Hacienda in a fertile area with plenty of trees; in May there is much colour with the cacti in flower.

Sleeping **C** *Hotel María Dolores*, Av de los Héroes 13, T20517. 2-star. **C** *Posada Las Campanas*, Guerrero 15, T20427. **D** *El Caudillo*, Querétaro 8, just off plaza, opposite the church of Nuestra Señora de los Dolores, T20198. Clean, good value. **D** *Posada Hidalgo*, Hidalgo 15, T/F20477. Clean, dark rooms, TV. **D** *Posada Cocomacán*, T20018, on the Járdin. Pleasant colonial house where Juárez stayed, comfortable, good value, good food, parking. Recommended. **E** *Posada Dolores*, on Yucatán. With bath, clean, OK, small rooms.

Eating *Caballo Blanco*, on Jardín by corner of Hidalgo and Guerrero. Good value. Excellent ice cream at *Helado Torres*, southwest corner of Jardín. *Fruti-Yoghurt*, Hidalgo y Guerrero, just off Jardín. Delicious yoghurt, wholefood cakes and biscuits, also sells homeopathic medicines, etc.

Dolores Hidalgo

Market Tabasco, south side, between Jalisco and Hidalgo. Another market, near *Posada Dolores*, on Yucatán. *Artesanías Castillo*, Ribera del Río (between Hidalgo and Jalisco), beautiful ceramics at low prices. Visit to factory can be arranged. **Shopping**

Buses Bus station is at Hidalgo y Chiapas, 5 mins from main square; has restaurant, toilets, left-luggage, local phones. Frequent buses to Guanajuato, Querétaro (US$3.80), León (US$3.65), Mexico City (US$10.50), San Luis Potosí (US$5) and San Luis de la Paz (US$2). To Aguascalientes, US$6.50, 2nd class, via San Felipe. **Transport**

Guanajuato

The beautiful university city in the central state of Guanajuato, declared a national monument and Unesco World Heritage Zone, has been important for its silver since 1548. Its name derives from the Tarascan Quanax-Huato, 'place of frogs'. It stands in a narrow gorge amid wild and striking scenery; the Guanajuato River which cuts through the city has been covered over and several underground streets opened – an unusual, though often confusing system.

Phone code: 473
Colour map 3, grid B4
Population: 150,000
Altitude: 2,010m

Some streets, like Padre Belaunzarán, are not entirely enclosed; others, such as Hidalgo, are, so they fill with traffic fumes. The Túnel Los Angeles leads from the old subterranean streets to the modern roadway which connects with the Carretera Panorámica and the monument to Pípila (see below). Taking traffic underground has not relieved the congestion of the surface streets, which are steep, twisted and narrow, following the contours of the hills. Some alleys and lanes have steps cut into the rock: one, the **Callejón del Beso** (Alley of the Kiss), is so narrow that, according to legend, two lovers kept apart by their families were able to exchange kisses from opposite balconies. Parking for hotels is often a fair distance away. Over the city looms the shoulder of La Bufa mountain. You can hike to the summit up a trail which takes one hour: from the Pípila monument (see below), follow the main road for about 1 km to the hospital. Walk past the hospital to a power station where the main trail starts; if you pass the quarry, note the quality of the stone masonry on the mason's shelter.

The international Aeropuerto del Bajío (BJX), some 40 km west of Guanajuato, near the town of Silao, has flights to and from destinations in Mexico and the USA. The long-distance bus terminal is on the outskirts southwest of town (for details see Transport page 561); taxis or buses ('centro') will ferry you into town. There is no train service to Guanajuato at present. **Getting there & away**

Although there is a lot to see in Guanajuato, many of the interesting places are along and around Juárez and can be visited on foot in a day or two. Transportes Turísticos de Guanajuato, underneath the Basílica on Plaza de la Paz, T22838, 22134, offer guided tours to some of the interesting sites outside the city. **Getting around**

The **Tourist office (COTUR)** at Plaza de la Paz 14, off to one side of the Basílica, can provide all hotel rates (except the cheapest). They sell maps at reasonable prices and provide some maps free of charge. They also have various booklets and brochures on the city and surrounding areas. State map with town plans can be obtained at the bus station.

Sights

Guanajuato contains a series of fine museums (see below) as well as the most elegant marble-lined public lavatories in Mexico. The best of many colonial churches are **La Compañía** (Jesuit, 1765, by the University), note the brick

Colonial Heartland

ceiling; **San Diego** (1663) on the Jardín de la Unión; the **Parroquia del Inmaculado Corazón de María**, on Juárez, opposite Mercado Hidalgo, has interesting statues on the altar; and the **Basílica** (Cathedral, 1693, on Plaza de la Paz) which has a beautiful yellow interior and an ornately painted vaulted ceiling. **San Roque** (1726) on a small park between Juárez and Pocitos (Plazuela de San Roque), also has a pretty vaulted ceiling. This plaza can be reached by a walkway that goes from the northeast side of the Jardín Reforma. The **Templo de San Francisco** (1671), on Sopeña, is also worth visiting.

Museums   A most interesting building is the massive **Alhóndiga de Granaditas**, built as a granary, turned into a fortress, and now a museum with artefacts from the pre-Colombian and colonial periods. When Father Hidalgo took the city in 1810, the Alhóndiga was the last place to surrender, and there was a wanton slaughter of Spanish soldiers and royalist prisoners. Later when Hidalgo was himself caught and executed, along with three other leaders, in Chihuahua, their severed heads were fixed, in revenge, at the four corners of the Alhóndiga. ■ *US$1.80.*

An unusual sight shown to visitors is of mummified bodies in the small **Museo de las Momias** in the Panteón Municipal, above the city off Tepetapa; buses go there ('Momias', signposted Panteón Municipal, 10 minutes, along Avenida Juárez), but you can walk. It's a gruesome and disturbing spectacle, glass cases of naturally mummified bodies, their mouths gaping from skin contraction, some bodies with shoes and socks on, and, it is claimed, the smallest mummy in the world. ■ *0900-1800, US$2, US$0.75 to take photos, tip the Spanish-speaking guide, long queues on Sun.* The **Museo Iconográfico del Quijote**, opened in 1987 at Manuel Doblado 1, is highly recommended: paintings, drawings, sculptures of the Don (see **Festivals** below for Festival

Guanajuato

Not to scale

■ **Sleeping**
1 Casa Kloster
2 Central
3 Hostería del Frayle
4 Posada San Francisco
5 Posada Santa Fe
6 San Diego

To Túnel Los Angeles
To Bus Station, Celaya & León

Museo Alfredo Dugues
University
Museo del Pueblo
Museo Diego Rivera
Plaza de Paz
Pocitos
Juan Valle
Pedro Lascur
Galarza
Alhóndiga de Granaditas
28 de Septiembre
San Roque
Plazuela San Fernando
Jardín Reforma
Mendizábal
Parroquia del Inmaculado Corazón de María
Plazuela de los Angeles
Juárez
Callejón del Beso
Mercado Hidalgo
To La Valenciana & Dolores Hidalgo
To Calle Insurgencia
To Bus Station, Museo de las Momias, Celaya & León

Cervantino). ■ *Free*. The painter **Diego Rivera** was born at Pocitos 47, now a museum with a permanent collection of his work on various floors, showing his changing styles; on the ground floor are his bed and other household objects; temporary exhibitions also held. ■ *1000, US$1*, recommended. Also on Pocitos, at No 7, just across from the University, is the **Museo del Pueblo** in a beautiful 17th-century mansion; it has one room of work by the muralist José Chávez Morado, a room of selected items of all Mexican art forms and temporary exhibitions. ■ *Tue-Sun, 0900-1900, US$1*. The **Museo Alfredo Dugues**, of natural history, is in the University building. ■ *Mon-Fri, 0900-1400, 1630-1900*. The **University** was founded in 1732; its façade of coloured stone, above a broad staircase, glows richly at sunset. Also in the University is the **Sala Hermenegildo Bustos**, which holds art exhibitions. The School of Mining has a **Museo de Minería** on the Carretera Panorámica, north of the city. ■ *Mon-Fri 0900-1300, 1630-1900*.

Excursions

There is a fine view from the **Monument to Pípila**, the man who fired the door of the Alhóndiga so that the patriots could take it, which crowns the high hill of Hormiguera. Look for the 'Al Pípila' sign. A number of cobbled stairways through picturesque terraces such as Callejón del Calvario, leading off Sopeña go up to the monument. It's a steep but short climb (about 15 minutes). Otherwise take a local bus from Hotel Central, on Juárez. Take a camera for fine panoramic views of the city. The Carretera Panorámica which encircles the city passes the Pípila monument. At its eastern end the Panorámica goes by the **Presa de la Olla**, a favourite picnic spot with good cheap meals available from roadside stalls. From the dam, Paseo de la Olla runs to the city centre, passing mansions of the wealthy silver barons and the **Palacio de Gobierno** (note the use of local stone). Also on the east side of the Panorámica is **Casa de las Leyendas**, with entertainment for children.

Tours of the city and outskirts by minibus cost US$6.15, rising to US$18 for tours out of town and US$40 to the south of the state; if you want a guide in English, prices multiply. The splendid church of **La Valenciana**, one of the most impressive in Mexico, is 5 km out of town on the Dolores Hidalgo road; it was built for the workers of the Valenciana silver mine, once the richest in the world. The church, dedicated to San Cayetano, has three huge, gilt altars, a wooden pulpit of sinuous design, large paintings and a cupola. The style is churrigueresque, done in grey-green and pink stone; the façade is also impressive.

The **Valenciana mine** (1548) is surrounded by a wall with triangular projections on top, said to symbolize

To Presa de la Olla

Colonial Heartland

the crown of the King of Spain. The huge stone walls on the hillside, supported by enormous buttresses, created an artificial level surface from earth excavated higher up the slope. With care you can walk freely in the whole area. Guides are available to take you round (about 30 minutes), interesting. ■ *0900-1700, US$1.* A local 'Valenciana' bus starts in front of *Hotel Mineral de Rayas*, Alhóndiga 7, leaving every 30 minutes during the day, US$0.10, 10 minutes ride; it is a 10-minute walk between church and mine pit-head; don't believe anyone who tells you a taxi is necessary, but don't walk to it along the highway, it is narrow and dangerous. At the mine is a gift shop with a reasonable selection of silver. Also well worth a visit is the Casa del Conde de la Valenciana, formerly the mining company's head office, now an attractive craft shop with pleasant café. If you stay on the 'Valenciana' bus to the end of the line, a church brightly painted and turned into a restaurant, you will see a dirt road to the left which leads to a recreation area with reservoir, picnic ground and several walks into the hills.

At Marfil on the Irapuato road is the former *Hacienda de San Gabriel de Barrera*, now a four-star hotel, (**AL**, T23980, F27460) with 15 patios and gardens, a chapel, museum and colonial furniture (take bus marked 'Marfil' from outside *Hotel Central*, 10 minutes). Thirty kilometres west of Guanajuato is **Cerro Cubilete**, with a statue of Christ the King, and spectacular views of the Bajío; local buses take 1½ hours, US$1.15, 0700, 0900, 1100, 1400, 1600 from Guanajuato (also from Silao for US$0.75). Dormitory at the site (US$1.50) food available, but best to take your own, plus drink (and toilet paper); last bus up leaves at 1600 from Silao and Guanajuato. See also the three local silver mines of Rayas, the city's first mine, La Valenciana (see above) and La Cata. All are to the north of the city, reached from the Carretera Panorámica. It is possible to visit the separating plant at **La Cata**, but visitors are not admitted to the mines. At the old site of La Cata mine (local bus near market), is a church with a magnificent baroque façade and the shrine of El Señor de Villa Seca (the patron of adulterers) with *retablos* and crude drawings of miraculous escapes from harm, mostly due to poor shooting by husbands.

Presa de Insurgentes, a few kilometres up the mountain highway, has a parking area and a couple of tables for picnics; it is a nursery for plants to be planted around the countryside. Four kilometres up a narrow road from **Presa de la Olla** is **Panifiel**, a village with an old church. Children will take visitors into the mission whose doors are held shut against stray animals by a large, round stone just inside the doors (a child's arm is small enough to fit beneath to move the stone). Take lunch.

Fifteen kilometres from Guanajuato on the road to Dolores is **Santa Rosa**; in a story book setting in the forest is **D** *Hotel El Crag*, clean; *Restaurant La Sierra* next door (the Flecha Amarilla bus stops here on the way to Dolores Hidalgo). There are two or three other places, including *Rancho de Enmiedo*, good dried meat specialities and beautiful scenery. The road corkscrews up in spectacular fashion before winding down through impressive rocky outcrops and ravines to the plain on which Dolores Hidalgo stands. The last 10 km or so are very arid.

Sleeping
■ *on maps*
Price codes:
see inside front cover

Hotel rooms can be hard to find after 1400. For holidays and weekends it is advisable to book ahead. However, there are lots of hotel rooms in the city, and in all price ranges. Hotels seem to be somewhat more expensive than in other parts of Mexico, though, and you probably won't find a double for less than ten dollars, and that would be pretty basic. There are frequent water shortages, so that hotels with no reservoirs of their own have no water on certain days; when there is water, do not drink it.

Colonial Heartland

On Dolores Hidalgo road exit **AL** *Castillo de Santa Cecilia*. Tourist-bus haven, T20485, F20153. **AL** *La Casa de los Espíritus Alegres*, ex-Hacienda La Trinidad No 1, Marfil, 3 km from Guanajuato, T/F473-31013. 18th-century hacienda house now owned by US artists, bed and breakfast, library, parking, bus stop close by, no children, pets or smoking. In USA contact Joan Summers, 2817 Smith Grade, Santa Cruz, CA 95060, T408-4230181. On exit road to Irapuato, **AL** *Mission Guanajuato Park Plaza*, Camino Antiguo a Marfil, Km 2.5, T/F23980. Very large rooms. **AL** *Parador San Javier*, Calle San Javier 1, T20650/20944. Very extensive grounds, some rooms have fire-places. **AL-A** *Real de Minas*, Nejayote 17, at city entrance, T21460, F21508 (they will lower their rates if business is slow). Large, attractive rooms, attractive restaurant (prices vary according to time of week). **A** *Posada Santa Fe*, Jardín de la Unión 12, T20084, F24653. Regular rooms are plain but the suites are very attractive with colo-nial-style furniture. Good restaurant on open terrace with excellent service. Tables on the plaza for dining. Recommended. **A** *San Diego*, Jardín de la Unión 1, T21321, F25626. Good bar and restaurant but slow, colonial-style, very pleasant. **A-B** *Paseo de la Presa*, a Best Western hotel, on the Panorámica, not far from Pípila, T23761, F23224. Quiet, good value, fantastic views, small pool, tennis courts. **B** *Hostería del Frayle*, Sopeña 3, next door to Teatro Juárez, T21179. Rooms next to the Teatro are noisy, nice adjoining *Café Veloce*. **C** *La Abadía*, San Matías 50, T/F22464.

On Insurgentes **D** *Alhóndiga*, No 49, T20525. Good, clean, quiet, TV in rooms, park-ing, restaurant *La Estancia*. **D** *del Conde*, Rangel del Alba 1 (next door to Alhóndiga), T21465. TV in rooms, complaints of musty smell in at least one room. With excellent and reasonable restaurant *Mesa de los Reyes* . **D** *Murillo Plaza*, No 9, T21884, F25913. Hot water, phone and TV. **E** *Posada La Condesa*, Plaza de La Paz 60 (west end of plaza), T21462. Small, basic rooms, clean, hot water, drinking water available.

On Alhóndiga **C** *Hotel Sacavón*, No 46A, T24885/26666. Pretty rest/bar. Colonial décor, attractive interior courtyard, nice rooms for price, with TV and phones. **D** *Dos Ríos*, No 29, T20749. TV in rooms, good value, rooms on street noisy. **D** *El Minero*, No 12A, T25251, F24738. Restaurant. **D** *Mineral de Rayas*, No 7, T21967. With bath, clean linen, pool, garage, restaurant, bar and *Danny's Bar*. Recommended.

On Juárez **B** *Hotel Suites Casa de las Manrique*, No 116 (between the Mercado and the Callejón del Beso), T27678, F28306. Large, attractive suites, colonial décor, very good value for price. **C** *El Insurgente*, No 226, T22294/23192. Pleasant, clean, avoid rooms on 4th floor where there is a disco, good breakfasts. **D** *Central*, No 111, T20080, near Cine Reforma. Friendly, good restaurant but noisy for rooms beside it. **D** *Posada del Carmen*, Juárez 111A, T29330. Bath, TV. Recommended. **D** *Posada San Francisco*, corner of Gavira, T22467, F22084. On Zócalo. Good value but outside rooms noisy, no hot water, lovely inner patio. **E** *Posada Juárez*, T22559. Has bathhouse inside (25 pesos). Recommended. **E** *Reforma*, No 113, T20469. With bath, overpriced, little hot water. **F** *Gran Hotel Granaditas* No 109, T21039. With bath, hot showers, clean, friendly, run-down. Other hotels are mostly in our **C** range. Accommodation in private home, **F** pp *Marilú Ordaz*, Barranca 34, T24705. Friendly, 5 mins walk from market.

Elsewhere **B** *La Casa del Quijote*, Pocitos 37, T23923, next to and over the Túnel Santa Fe de Guanajuato. All rooms are suites and have tiled bathtubs, wet bar, and you can ask for a microwave oven to be put in your room. **D** *Posada Molino del Rey*, Campañero 15, T22223, F21040. Simple and quaint. **D-E** *Casa Kloster*, Alonso 32, T20088. Book ahead, good location, very friendly, rooms for 4, a few with private bath, some without windows, clean, very good value. Repeatedly recommended, often full, gardens, no parking (touts in town will say it is shut, but it is not).

Colonial Heartland

Motels Many on Dolores Hidalgo road exit: **A** *Villa de Plata*, T21173. Trailer Park 1 km north of *Mineral de Rayas*, there is a sign on the Carretera Panorámica. Hot showers. **B** *de Los Embajadores*, Paseo Embajadores, T20081. Mexican décor, restaurant, famous Sun lunch. **B** *El Carruaje*. T22140, F21179. **B** *Guanajuato*, T20689. Good pool and food, quiet. Recommended. **B** *Valenciana*, T20799.

Eating
● *on maps*

Tourists are given the à la carte menu; ask for the *menú del día* or *comida corrida* (but they stop serving them early). Reasonable food, *comida corrida* very good value, at *El Retiro*, Sopeña 12, near Jardín de la Unión; also on Sopeña, *Pizzería Mamma Fan* and *La Colmena*. *Pizza Piazza*, Plaza San Fernando and several other locations. Cheap and good. *Cuatro Ranas*, in *Hotel San Diego*, Jardín de la Unión 1. Good location but loud US music and overpriced, reasonable *menú del día*, US$3. *Valadez* on Jardín de la Unión y Sopeña. Excellent *menú del día*; also on Jardín de la Unión, *Bar Luna* and *El Gallo*. Popular with travellers, good. *La Lonja*, on the corner of the Jardín opposite *Hotel San Diego*. Pleasant and lively bar, beers come with complimentary dish of *tacos* with salsa. Meals at *Casino de Guanajuato* on Jardín de la Unión. *La Bohemia*, Alonso, opposite *Casa Kloster*. Overpriced and uninspiring. *Mesón de Marco*, Juárez 25, T27040. 'Rare' Mexican food, flights in balloon offered at US$100. *La Carreta*, Av Juárez about 200m up from Mercado Hidalgo. Mostly chicken, fair. Also on Juárez, *Tasca de los Santos*, Plaza de la Paz. Smart. *Diva's*, Plaza de la Paz 62B. Smart. Highly recommended. *El Zaguán*, Plaza de la Paz 48. Very good and cheap food, entertainment inside courtyard. *Café Truco 7*, Callejón Truco, off Plaza de la Paz. Menu of the day US$2-3, relaxed family atmosphere. Theatre in back room Fri and Sat afternoon. Recommended. *La Flor Alegre* (*casa de pan pizza*), Plazuela de San Fernando 37. Good, clean and cheap. *El Mexicano*, Juárez 214. Good *comida corrida* with dessert and drink. *El Granero*, Juárez 25. Good *comida*, until 1700. *La Mancha*, Galarza 7. Reasonable price. Recommended for *comida corrida*. *Cafetería Nevería*, opposite University. Good, inexpensive. *Vegetariano*, Callejón Calixto 20. Inexpensive, sells wholewheat bread. *Jelly Shot Bar*, below *Hostería del Frayle*. Lovely atmosphere, cheap drinks. Recommended. *El Unicornio Azul* on Plaza Baratillo. Good health food shop, *pan integral*, also sells cosmetic products. Also on Plaza Baratillo is *Café Las Musas*. Good-value breakfast. You can eat well and cheaply in the market (eg *bolillos* – sandwiches, fresh fruit juices) and in the *locales* behind Mercado Hidalgo (some open till 2200; better value on 1st floor; the ladies have been forbidden by their rivals in the covered market to shout the merits of their menus, but their mime is just as engaging). Good *panaderías* also, eg *Panadería Internacional*, Contarranas y Sopeña, sells wholewheat bread. *La Infancia*, *panadería y pastelaría*, Contarranas 57. Delicious, freshly made pastries. Dairy products are safe, all coming from the pasteurizing plant at Silao. Also from Silao come strawberries in Dec.

Entertainment Theatre sketches from classical authors out of doors in lovely old plazas from **Apr-Aug**. *Teatro Juárez* on Sopeña (a magnificent French-type Second Empire building, US$0.50 to view, US$0.35 to take photos), shows art films and has symphony concerts, US$1.50. A band plays in Jardín de la Unión (next to the theatre) 3 times a week. The *Teatro Principal* is on Cantarranas, by Plaza Mexiamora. Two nightclubs have been recommended: *Disco El Grill* on Alonso (100m from *Casa Kloster*) and *Disco Los Comerciales* on Juan Valle.

Festivals Arts festival, the *Festival Cervantino de Guanajuato* (in honour of Cervantes), is an important cultural event in the Spanish-speaking world, encompassing theatre, song and dance. There is a mixture of free, open-air events, and paying events. Internationally famous artists from around the world perform. The festival lasts 2 weeks, is highly recommended and is very crowded; accommodation must be booked in advance (usually held the last 2 weeks in **Oct**, check dates). For information telephone

Guanajuato 20959, or Mexico City 55334121, The International Cervantino Festival, Alvaro Obregón 273, 4th Flr, Colonia Roma, 06700 México DF. *Viernes de las Flores* is held on the Fri before Good Friday, starting with the Dance of the Flowers on Thu night at about 2200 right through the night, adjourning at Jardín de la Unión to exchange flowers. Very colourful and crowded. During the **Christmas** period, students dress up in traditional costumes and wander the streets singing carols and playing music. Groups leave from in front of the theatre at 2030.

Fonart shop opposite La Valenciana church (see above) has an excellent selection of handicrafts; high prices but superb quality. Local pottery can be bought in the *Mercado Hidalgo* (1910), in the centre of town and there is a *Casa de Artesanías* behind the Teatro Juárez (see **Entertainment** above). **Shopping**

Trains Station is off Tepetapa (continuation of Juárez), west of centre. Passenger service no longer runs, although a high-speed trainline linking the whole State of Guanajuato there are plans for. **Transport**

Buses A clean, new bus terminal has opened on the road to Silao, near toll gate, 20 mins from centre by bus, US$0.30. Taxi to centre, US$2.00. Buses leave for the centre from right outside the front of the terminal. Look for 'centro' on the front window of the bus, or the sign above the front window. To get to the bus station from the centre, you pick up buses on Av Juárez in front of the *Hotel Central*, about a block west of the Mercado Hidalgo. The bus stop has a sign saying 'C Camionera'. The bus terminal has a place for storing luggage that charges 8 pesos per 24 hrs per bag and is open from 0700-2000. There is also a post office, long-distance phone and fax service, a couple of stores selling snacks, a magazine shop, and a cafetaría-style restaurant.

There are several booths in the area behind the terminal, where the buses arrive, where you can buy tickets for tours of the city and outlying areas, such as Dolores Hidalgo and San Miguel de Allende. They also have hotel price lists for hotels costing over 200 pesos, and will phone the hotel for you.

Acapulco Expresso Futura (transfer in León), 2100, US$37.80. **Cuidad Juárez**, Omnibus de Mexico (1st class) transferring in León 1015, US$67. **Durango**, Omnibus de Mexico, transferring in León 1300, US$24. **Guadalajara**, Expresso Futura 1630, 2230, US$13.20. Servicios Coordinados (1st class) 0900, 1100, 1200, 1300, 1600, 1900, 2130, 2330 (trip takes a little over 4 hrs), US$15.70. Primera Plus ('plus' service a little better than 1st class) 9 buses per day, US$18.20. They also have buses every hour to Mexico City with a transfer in León costing US$20. **Guadalajara**, ETN (luxury service-have half as many seats as a regular bus and the seats have 45-degree recline and foot rests) 0830, 1230, 1730 (a little over 4 hrs), US$20. **Irapuato**, ETN 0530, 0830, 1145, 1530, 1830, US$2.50. **León**, ETN 0830, 1230, 1730 (45 mins), US$3. **Mexico City**, Expresso Futura 1020,1320, 1700, 2400, US$16.90. Primera Plus 9 buses per day,

Colonial Heartland

US$18.20. ETN 0100, 0530, 0830, 1145, 1430, 1530, 1830 (4½ hr trip), US$22.50. Omnibus de Mexico, transferring in León 1600, 2400 (also Sat, Sun, and Mon at 1100), US$16.90. **Monterrey**, Expresso Futura 1400, 1630, 1830, 1930, 2130, US$33. Omnibus de Mexico, 2100, US34.20. **Morelia**, Servicios Coordinados 0820, 1210, 1620, US$8. **Nuevo Laredo**, Omnibus de Mexico 1930, US$44. **Querétaro**, Servicios Coordinados 0710, 0910, 1220, 1240, 1440, 1820, US$7.50. **Reynosa**, Omnibus de Mexico 2000, US$38.30. **San Luis Potosí**, Flecha Amarilla (2nd class buses) 0720, 1300, 1640, 1940, US$9.90. They also serve many other towns. Omnibus de Mexico 1930, US$10.50. **San Miguel de Allende**, Flecha Amarilla 0700, 0800, 0930, 1100, 1200, 1430, 1615, 1800, US$3.60. Servicios Coordinados 1000, 1330, 1500, 1715, 1915, US$5. Primera Plus 1000, 1330, 1500, 1715, 1915, US$5. **Tijuana**, Expresso Futura 1800, US$85.20.

NB To many destinations it is better to go to León and pick up the more frequent services that go from there (buses every 10 mins Guanajuato-León, US$1.30). Flecha Amarilla have more buses, to more destinations, than other companies in this area; it is not the most reliable company and buses tend to leave when full. Set fare for city buses, US$0.25. Radio Taxi service: T24086/44992, Callejón del Beso #3-B, 24 hr service.

Directory **Banks** *Bancomer, Banca Serfin, Banamex*, 0900-1100. **Communications** Internet: on Alonso 70B, 0900-1800, Mon-Sat, US$5 per hour. **Post Office:** corner of Subida San José, by La Compañía church. **Telephone:** international phone calls from phone booths with coins, or collect. Long-distance offices in Miscelánea Unión shop, by Teatro Principal and on Pocitos, opposite Alhóndiga de Granaditas. **Language schools** Spanish courses: for foreigners at the *University*, T20006, 22662 ext 8001, F27253, email, montesa@quijote.ugto.mx Postal address: Centro de Idiomas, Universidad de Guanajuato, Lascuraín de Retana 5, 36000, Guanajuato, Gto, México. Also at *Instituto Falcón*, Presa 80, T7311084, F7310745, www.institutofalcon.com, good quality instruction. Also at the University are many US exchange students so you can usually find someone who speaks English. See also **Learning Spanish** in Essentials. **Laundry** *Lavandería Internacional*, Alhóndiga 35A, self or service wash (US$3.45). *La Burbuja Express*, Plazuela Baratillo. *Lavandería Automática Internacional*, Manuel Doblado 28, US$3.50; *Lavandería del Centro*, Sopeña 26, US$3.60.

León

Phone code: 47
Colour map 3, grid B4
Population: 1,200,000
Altitude: 1,885m

In the fertile plain of the Gómez River, León is now said to be Mexico's fifth city. Nuño de Guzmán reached the area on 2 December 1530 and subsequently local farms and estates were granted to the Spaniards. Eventually Don Martín Enríquez de Almanza decreed on 12 December 1575 that a city, called León, would be founded if 100 volunteers could be persuaded to live there for 10 years, or a town if only 50 could be found. On 20 January 1576 a town was founded by Dr Juan Bautista de Orozco, and it wasn't until 1830 that León became a city. The business centre is the delightful **Plaza de la Constitución**. There is a **tourist office** in Edificio Cielo 501 on López Mateos Poniente and M Alemán; helpful but limited information (good city map available free at Palacio Municipal).

Sights There is a striking **Palacio Municipal**, a cathedral, many shaded plazas and gardens. The Palacio Municipal is said to have been built as a result of a winning lottery ticket bought by a local doctor! The small **Cathedral** was started by Jesuits in 1744, but they were expelled from Mexico in 1767 by Carlos III. It was eventually finished in 1837 and consecrated in 1866. The **Templo Expiatorio** has been under construction for most of the last century; the catacombs are well worth seeing. ■ *1000-1200 closed Wed.* The **Teatro Doblado**, on Avenida Hermanos Aldama, stages opera, ballet, classical concerts, contemporary theatre and houses art exhibitions. The **Casa de Cultura** also houses exhibitions and is 'buzzing' at night. Also worth seeing is the **Casa de Las Monas** on 5 de Mayo 127-29 where Pancho Villa issued the Agrarian Reform Law on 24 May 1915, and the beautiful **Santuario de Guadalupe**. A new tourist attraction, the **Parque Metropolitano** on Prolongación Morelos, Camino a la Presa, opened in 1995. León is the main shoe centre of the country and is noted for its leather-work, fine silver-trimmed saddles, and *rebozos* (see **Shopping** below).

The Museo de León, on Hermanos Aldama, has art exhibitions. ■ *Tue-Sat,* **Museums** *1000-1400 and 1630-1930, Sun 1000-1400.* The **Museum of Anthropology and History** on Justo Sierra is housed in a beautiful building; the **Explora Science Museum** is on Boulevard Francisco Villa 202, T116711.

Between León and **Silao** (bus from León US$0.70), left off Highway 45 (going **Excursions** south), are the famous swimming pools of **Comanjilla** fed by hot sulphurous springs. There is a luxurious, hacienda-style hotel (**AL**) with restaurant. From Silao take microbus to 'León Centro' and change at Los Sauces for Comanjilla turn-off, well signposted. Eleven kilometres beyond Silao, at Los Infantes, a short side road through the picturesque Marfil canyon leads to Guanajuato.

AL *Fiesta Americana*, Blvd López Mateos 1102 Ote, T136040, F135380. **A** *Camino* **Sleeping** *Real*, López Mateos 1311 Ote, T163939, F163940. **B** *Real de Minas*, López Mateos 2211, T710660, F712400. Recommended. **B** *Estancia*, A López Mateos 1317 Pte, T/F169900. Restaurant recommended. **B** *Condesa*, on Plaza, Portal Bravo 14, T131120, F148210. 3-star. Restaurant recommended. **B** *León*, Madero 113, T141050, F132262. 3-star. **B** *Robert*, López Mateos Ote 1503, T167213. **B** *Roma*, Nuevo Vallarta 202, T/F161500. 3-star. **B** *Señorial*, near Plaza, Juárez 221, T145959. **C** *Fénix*, Comonfort 338. 2-star. *Colón*, 20 de Enero 131. 1-star. **D** *Fundadores*, Ortiz de Domínguez 218, T161727, F166612. Better than similarly priced hotels in centre. **D** *Posada de Fátima*, Belisario Domínguez 205. Clean, central. **D** *Rex*, 5 de Febrero

León

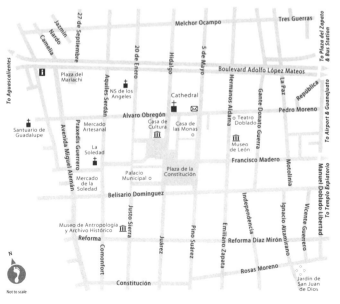

Not to scale

104, near Plaza. Recommended. **D** *Monte Carlo*, Justo Sierra 432. Clean, friendly, central. **D** *Tepeyac*, Obregón 727. 1-star, OK, rooms a bit dark. Also several cheaper hotels near market.

At **Silao** (for airport) **B** *Villa Victoria*, Alvaro Obregón 245, T21831, F22422.

Eating   Several in Colonia Jardines del Moral area in centre, including: *El Jardín de Ling Choy*, López Mateos 2105 Pte, T177507, also *La Pagoda de Ling Choy*, López Mateos 1501 Ote, T149026. Both Chinese. *Kamakura*, Rocío 114, T184383. Japanese. *Lupillos*, López Mateos 2003 Ote, opposite stadium, T711868. Pasta and pizza; also several branches of the US fast food chains. Many restaurants in the Gran Plaza complex next to Macdonalds. Vegetarian snacks at *GFU*, on López Mateos, near IMSS building. *Cadillac*, ½ block from cathedral on Hidalgo. Good *comida corrida* US$5. *Panteón Taurino*, Calzado de Los Héroes 408, T134969. Expensive but worth visiting to see the incredible décor. Look for listings in local guides, lots of places offering seafood, pizzas, Spanish, Oriental, Arab, Argentine, Brazilian and Mexican food.

Nightlife   Lots of **bars** including *JJ Sport*, Rocío 115-A, Jardines del Moral. *Pepe's Pub*, Madero 120, Zona Centro. *Fut-bol Bar*, Hidalgo 923-B, T178020. **Discos** Including *Domus*, López Mateos 2611 Ote, T116614. *Ossy's*, Av Paseo de los Insurgentes, on exit road to Lagos de Moreno, T176880. *La Iguana*, Centro Comercial Insurgentes, Local 4 y 5B, T181416. **Nightclubs** *Piano Bar Maya*, Prolongación Calzada 112, T169734.

Festivals   *Fiesta*: San Sebastián, **19-24 Jan**, very crowded, good fun (if staying outside León, take an early bus out of town when leaving).

Shopping   Several shopping centres: *La Gran Plaza*, Blvd López Mateos 1902 Pte. *Plaza Mayor*, Av de las Torres, corner of Prolongación Morelos. *Plaza León*, Blvd López Mateos 1102 Ote. *Centro Comercial Insurgentes*, Blvd López Mateos y Alud, Jardines del Moral. *Plaza del Zapato*, Hilario Medina y Blvd López Mateos, T146442, for high-quality shoes (cheaper ones in places round the bus station). *Plaza Piel*, Hilario Medina y López Mateos for leather work (also available along Belisario Domínguez).

Tour operators   *Viajes Sindy de León*, 20 de enero 319, T131224, F165080. Recommended. *Jovi de León*, Madero 319 Centro, T145094, F166217. Recommended.

Transport   **Air** New international airport, del Bajío (BJX), 18 km from León, 6 km from Silao: American Airlines to Dallas and Memphis; Mexicana to Chicago; Continental (T185254) to Houston and Orlando; AeroMéxico and Mexicana to Los Angeles; Taesa to Oakland, California; Mexicana to San José, California. Several airlines fly to Mexico City (with connections to international and Mexican destinations), Ciudad Juárez, Durango, San Luis Potosí, Torreón, Puebla, Puerto Vallarta, Querétaro, Tijuana, Monterrey, Chihuahua, Zacatecas, Guadalajara and Morelia. Taxis are expensive to León; either take one to Silao, US$10, and then take a bus to León or Guanajuato, or walk 1½ km to the main road and take a bus from there.

Buses Terminal has post office, long-distance phones, restaurant and shops (street plan on sale, US$2.75). Plenty of buses to **Mexico City**, US$14 (US$28 ETN, T131410), **Querétaro**, US$6. Irapuato and Celaya. Frequent services to **Guanajuato**, 40 mins, US$3 ETN. To **Zacatecas**, 4½ hrs, US$10. To **Poza Rica**, Omnibús de México, T135798, US$21. Same company to **Monterrey**, US$25, and **Guadalajara**, every 30 mins, first at 0600, 4 hrs, US$8, US$16 ETN. Many buses run to **Ciudad Juárez**, US$50. **Durango** US$16.50. **Chihuahua** US$38.50. Primera Plus, T146000; Elite, T169879; Futura, T145451; Turistar Ejecutivo, T145451; Turistar Plus y Estrella Blanca, T145451, 133216; Tres Estrellas de Oro, T169879, 169932.

Road The highway from Mexico City to León is dual carriageway all the way.

Airline offices *AeroMéxico*, Madero 410, T166226, 149667. *Mexicana*, Blvd López Mateos 401 Ote, T149500, 134550. *Taesa*, Pedro Moreno 510 Centro, T143660, 161940. *Continental*, Blvd López Mateos 2307 Pte, T135199, 143937, 91-80090050. **Banks** *Bancomer*, Belisario Domínguez 322, and *Banco Internacional* on the plaza. **Communications** Post Office: on Obregón y 5 de Mayo, open Mon-Fri 0800-1900.

Directory

Aguascalientes

Founded in 1575, capital of its state, the name ('hot waters') comes from its hot mineral springs. An oddity is that the city is built over a network of tunnels dug out by a forgotten people. It has pretty parks, a pleasant climate, delicious fruits, and specializes in drawn-linen threadwork, pottery, and leather goods. Not one of the most attractive colonial cities, shopping malls are as evident as Spanish heritage. The Federal **tourist office** is in Palacio de Gobierno, T60347, F51155. ■ *0800-2000*. The Tourism Development office is at Avenida de La Convención Pte 1626, T125585, F122357. A good town plan is available from the entrance booth of the Palacio Municipal.

Phone code: 49
Colour map 3, grid A4
Population: 750,000
Altitude: 1,987m

Palacio de Gobierno, once the castle home, started in 1665, of the Marqués de Guadalupe, has a splendid courtyard, with decorated arches on two levels. The grand staircase in the centre, built in the 1940s, blends in magnificently with the earlier structure. There are also colourful murals by the Chilean artist Osvaldo Barra, some of the most extensive outside Mexico City and Guadalajara. Among the churches, **San Antonio**, on Zaragoza, should not be missed, neither should the Carmelite **Templo de San Marcos**, with a baroque façade, built 1655-1765 on the site of a chapel which had existed since the mid-16th century, in the barrio of San Marcos west of the centre. Beyond the church of San Marcos is an enormous concrete commercial and leisure complex known as Expo-Plaza which includes the *Fiesta Americana* hotel and new bull-ring. There is much industrial development on the outskirts.

Sights

　　Teatro Morelos, T50097, next to the Cathedral, is where the revolutionary factions led by Pancho Villa, Emiliano Zapata and Venustiano Carranza attempted to find some common ground on which they could all work together. The attempt ended in failure. The **University** is 30 minutes from the city centre. Its administrative offices are in the ex-Convento de San Diego, by the attractive Jardín del Estudiante, and the Parián shopping centre.

　　South of the centre on Boulevard J M Chávez is an aviary, with 50 species of bird, in the **Parque Héroes Mexicanos**. The market is not far away. There is carp fishing at El Jocoqui and Abelardo Rodríguez. The bull ring is on Avenida López Mateos.

Museo de Aguascalientes, Calle Zaragoza 505, by the church of San Antonio, has a collection of contemporary art, including fine paintings by Saturnino Herrán, and works by Orozco, Angel, Montenegro and others. ■ *Daily from 1030, except Sun and Mon*. The **Museo José Guadalupe Posada** is in a gallery by the Templo del Cristo Negro, close to the pleasant Jardín del Encino or Jardín Francisco, on Díaz de León. The museum has a remarkable collection of prints by the artist Posada, best known for his engravings of *calaveras*, macabre skeletal figures illustrating and satirizing the events leading up to the Revolution. There are cultural events in the courtyard on Saturday and Sunday. ■ *Tue-Sun 1030-1900, closed Mon. US$.60.*

Museums

Colonial Heartland

Museo de Arte Contemporáneo, Calle Juan de Montoro, is just east of Plaza. The **Casa de las Artesanías** is also near the main square. The **Casa de la Cultura**, on Venustiano Carranza and Galeana Norte, is a fine colonial building. It holds a display of *artesanía* during the April *feria*. Nearby, on Carranza is the **Museo Regional de Historia**.

Excursions Hacienda de San Blas, 34 km away, contains the **Museo de la Insurgencia**, with murals by Alfredo Zermeño.

Thermal Baths Balneario Ojo Caliente, towards the east end of town beyond the train station, at the end of Calzada Revolución (Alameda), claims to have been founded in 1808. There are some private baths (US$3.50 per hour) and two public pools. Take bus marked 'Alameda'. There are also saunas, squash and tennis courts on the site. At end of Alameda fork right to Deportivo Ojo Caliente, a large complex with several pools, US$0.65. Twenty kilometres north is a thermal swimming pool at **Valladolid** (camping is permitted in the grounds, secure, night watchman in attendance).

Encarnación de Díaz (C *Hotel Casa Blanca*, Anguiano 107 on the plaza, hot water, secure parking nearby, reasonable restaurant) is halfway to **Lagos de Moreno** (Km 425), a charming old town with fine baroque churches. The entry over the bridge, with domes and towers visible on the other side, is

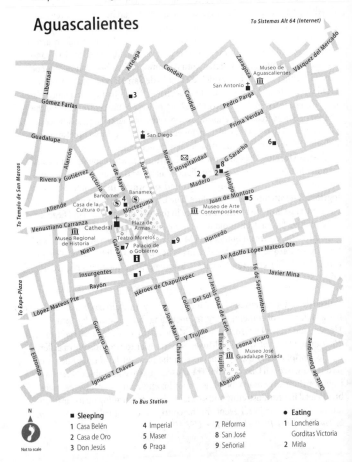

Aguascalientes

To Sistemas Alt 64 (Internet)

Sleeping
1 Casa Belén
2 Casa de Oro
3 Don Jesús
4 Imperial
5 Maser
6 Praga
7 Reforma
8 San José
9 Señorial

Eating
1 Lonchería
  Gorditas Victoria
2 Mitla

N — Not to scale

To Bus Station

particularly impressive. See the ex-convent of the Capuchins and the Teatro Rosas Moreno. The *Feria* is during the last week of July and first of August. Lagos de Moreno has several hotels (on main plaza: **C** *La Traje*; **D** *París*; **D** *Plaza*, best rooms facing the front, small and dark at the back; just off the plaza is **C** *Colonial*; **C** *Victoria*, two blocks away, near river) and restaurants (recommended is *La Rinconada*, colonial building, old photos, on plaza two blocks behind Municipalidad, which is on main plaza, good *enchiladas*). Route 80 heads off right to Guadalajara, 197 km away, and left to Antiguo Morelos via San Luis Potosí. Forty-two kilometres southwest *en route* to Guadalajara and is the colonial town of **San Juan de los Lagos**, a major pilgrimage centre and crowded during Mexican holidays. There is also a fine view on entering this town: as the road descends you see the twin-towered church with its red, blue and yellow tiled dome. San Juan is famous for glazed fruits. There are many hotels in the town.

Sleeping
■ *on maps*
Price codes:
see inside front cover

LL *Elizabeth*, Av de la Convención (inner ring road) 107 Sur, T782926, F782036. **LL** *Fiesta Americana*, on Expo-Plaza, Col Flores, T186010, F186118. **L** *Gran Hotel Hacienda de la Noria*, Av Héroes de Nacozari Sur 1315, Col La Salud, T184343, F185259 (in Mexico City T55142728/52075666). Very comfortable, jacuzzi in all rooms, Mexican, Japanese and international cuisine, gardens, swimming pool. **AL** *De Andrea Alameda*, Alameda esq Av Tecnológico, T184417, F183759. Old hacienda, large rooms, good restaurant. **B** *Hotel Suites Alamo*, Alameda 129, T56885, F185046. Pool. **D** *Imperial*, Moctezuma y 5 de Mayo, T151650, on plaza. Large, sparse rooms. **D** *Praga*, Zaragoza 214, T52357. With TV, OK.

D *Señorial*, Colón 104, T52179. Rooms with phone, helpful lady speaks English. **D-E** *Don Jesús*, Juárez 429, T55598, F84841. Hot water 3 hrs morning and evening, good value. **D** *San José*, Hidalgo 207, T155130. Friendly. At Rep de Brasil 403, **E** *Casa de Huéspedes*, near main plaza, and at No 602, **D** *Gómez*, T70409. Cheap hotels around Juárez market (Av Guadalupe y Guadalupe Victoria), eg **E** *Brasil*, Guadalupe 110, T51106. With bath, quiet. **E** *Casa de Oro*, on Hidalgo 205, next to *San José*. Good. **E** *Maser*, Montoro 303, T53562, 3 blocks from Cathedral. *Comedor* for breakfast. **E** *México*. No bath or hot water. **E** *Reforma*, Nieta y Galeana, 1 block west of main plaza. Colonial-style, large courtyard, rooms a bit dark, friendly, clean. **F** *Casa Belén*, López Mateos y Galeana, T158593. Central, hot water, clean, friendly.

Motels **A** *El Medrano*, Chávez 904, T55500, F68076. **B** *La Cascada*, Chávez 1501, T61411. **Youth hostel** Av de la Convención y Jaime Nuno s/n, CP 20190, T700873.

Eating
Lack of conventional facilities, except in some of the more expensive hotels

Try the area around 5 de Mayo for *pollo rostizado*. Good *comida corrida* at *Sanfer*, Guadalupe Victoria 204, and at *Woolworth* restaurant 1 block away. *Jacalito*, López Mateos, also near Plaza Crystal. Cheap *tortas*, clean. *Lonchería Gorditas Victoria*, popular with locals especially for tacos. *Mitla*, Madero 220. Good breakfast, moderate prices. *Mexicali Rose*, López Mateos. *Comida corrida*, US$10. Also *Freeday*, near Benito Juárez statue. Video bar and restaurant, lively at weekends. *Café Parroquia* on Hidalgo, 1 block west off Madero. Good, cheap. *Jugos Acapulcos*, Allende 106. Good *comida corrida*.

Festivals

The area is famous for viticulture; the local wine is called after San Marcos, and the *feria* in his honour lasts for 3 weeks, starting in the middle of **April**, with processions, cockfights (in Mexico's largest *palenque*, seating 4,000), bullfights, agricultural shows, etc. The Plaza de Armas is lavishly decorated for the occasion. The *feria*, covered by national TV networks, is said to be the biggest in Mexico. Accommodation can be very difficult and prices double during the *feria*. Bullfight also on New Year's Day.

Colonial Heartland

Shopping Many shops sell boots made to order, eg *Zapatería Cervantes*, Guerrero 101 Sur y Nieto, T151943. **Bookshop** *Librería Universal*, Madero 427. **Market** Main one at 5 de Mayo y Unión, large and clean, with toilet on upper floor.

Transport **Air** The airport (AGU) is 21 km from the town centre. Domestic flights to Culiacán, Mexico City, Monclova, Monterrey, Puerto Vallarta, Reynosa, San Luis Potosí, Tijuana and Zacatecas with a variety of airlines. US flights to Los Angeles with AeroMéxico.

Trains Train station at east end of Av Madero (T153858). Bus 17 goes there from Calle Hornedo, 1 block behind *Hotel Reforma*. To Torreón daily 1010, arrives 1930, returns 0900, arrives 1945. Check locally to make sure service is still running.

    Buses Bus station about 1 km south of centre on Av Circunvalación Sur with post office and pharmacy, take city bus from Galeana near López Mateos. To **Guadalajara**, 5 hrs, US$8.25 1st, US$15.50 ETN (luxury service), 5 a day (2 hrs direct with Estrella Blanca). To **Guanajuato** US$4.50 with Flecha Amarilla, 3½ hrs. To **Zacatecas**: US$3, every 30 mins, 1st class US$6, 2½ hrs. To **Ciudad Juárez**, US$46.25. ETN to **Mexico City** US$34, 9 a day, 7 hrs, ordinary fare US$14. To **Tijuana**, Elite, 1530, 2100, US$108; to **Monterrey**, Turistar Ejecutivo US$35 also to **Nuevo Laredo**, US$52, Ciudad Juárez, US$84, **Chihuahua**, US$62; to **Morelia**, Primera Plus, 4 a day, US$17; **León**, 21 a day, US$7; **Puerto Vallarta** at 2230, US$31; **Querétaro**, 8 a day US$15.50; to **San Luis Potosí**, Futura, 16 a day between 0600-2300, US$9.

Directory **Airline offices** *Aero California*, Juan de Montoro 203, T52400. *AeroMéxico*, Madero 474, T61362. *Taesa*, Madero 447, T82698. **Banks** On Plaza Inverlat, *ATM* takes Amex. *Banamex*, ATM. **Communications** Internet: *Sistemas Alt 64*, Vásquez del Mercado 206, T157613, US$2.60 per hr, open 1000-1400, 1600-2100 Mon-Sat, closed Sun. *Acnet*, Edificio Torreplaza Bosques 2nd flr, Av Aguascalientes near University, bus from Rivero Gutiérrez. **Post Office:** Hospitalidad, near El Porián shopping centre. **Cultural centres** *El Centro Cultural Los Arquitos*, Narcozari y Alameda, T170023, formerly a 19th-century bathhouse, restored 1993, museum, bookshop, café. **Medical services** Red Cross: T152055.

Zacatecas

Phone code: 492
Colour map 3, grid A3
Population: 150,000
Altitude: 2,495m

Founded 1548, and capital of Zacatecas state, this picturesque up-and-down mining city is built in a ravine with pink stone houses scattered over the hills. The largest silver mine in the world, processing 10,000 tonnes of ore a day or 220 tonnes of silver, is at Real de Angeles. Silver has bestowed an architectural grandeur on Zacatecas to match that of the state of Guanajuato.

Boulevard López Mateos, a busy highway, runs close to the centre of town from the bus station and down the ravine. The **tourist office**, Hidalgo 403, 2nd floor T23426, F26751 is friendly and helpful; they provide free maps and good hotel information, including cheaper hotels. Ask here about language classes at the University. Also at Obregón 28, T56824.

Sights
Zacatecas is reckoned by many travellers to be the most pleasant town in this part of Mexico

The **Cathedral** (1730-52) has a fine Churrigueresque façade; the **San Agustín** church, with interior carvings, is now being restored, and the Jesuit church of **Santo Domingo** has frescoes in the sacristy by Francisco Antonio Vallejo (ask the sacristan to turn the lights on). Also worth seeing are **Plaza Hidalgo** and its statues; the **Casa Moneda** (better known as the Tesorería), founded 1810; the **Teatro Calderón**, and the **Capilla de Los Remedios** (1728). The **Mina del Edén**, Avenida Torreón y Quebradilla, is an old mine with a short section of mine railway in operation (not a proper train); the tour lasts about one hour,

Colonial Heartland

commentary in fast Spanish. The tour from the main entrance comes out near the *teleférico*, or you can do it the other way around. ■ *US$1.70.* There is also a disco in the mine. ■ *US$10, buy ticket before 2030, varied music.* On the way to the mine note the interesting façade (1738) brought from the hacienda of the Condes de San Mateo, which now adorns the main offices of the local cattle-breeding association.

The **Museo Pedro Coronel**, on Plaza Santo Domingo, houses an excellent collection of European and modern art (including Goya, Hogarth, Miró, Tàpies) as well as folk art from Mexico and around the world (take a guide to make the most of the collections). ■ *1000-1700; closed Thu, US$1.70.* The **Museo Rafael Coronel**, housed in the ex-Convento de San Francisco, has a vast collection of masks and puppets, primarily Mexican, and an attractive garden. ■ *US$1.70, closed Wed.* The **Museo de la Toma de Zacatecas**, on the Cerro de la Bufa, commemorates Pancho Villa's victory over Huerta's forces in 1914. ■ *1000-1700, US$1.10.* The hill, northeast of the city centre, is recommended for views over the city. The light is best in the early morning. It is a pleasant walk though crowded on Sundays. There is also a statue of Villa, an observatory, and the Mausoleo de Los Hombres Ilustres, on the hill. ■ *Cablecar, US$1.10 one way, 1000-1800 (cancelled when windy).* The **Museo Francisco Goitia**, housed in what was once the governor's mansion, is by the Parque General Enrique Estrada, Colonia Sierra de Alicia near the old **Acueducto El Cubo**. The museum has modern paintings by Zacatecans, but its main attractions are the paintings of small-town poverty in Mexico by Francisco Goitia. ■ *1000-1700, Tue-Sun. US$1.70.* **Museo Zacatecano**, east of

Museums

Zacatecas orientation

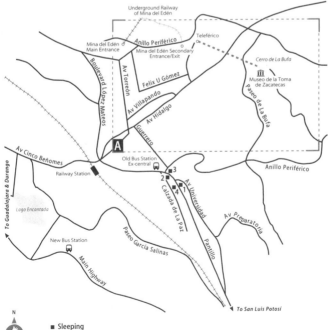

Colonial Heartland

■ Sleeping
1 Colón
2 Gami
3 Howard Johnson 'Plaza'
4 Río Grande

Related map
A Zacatecas, page 570

Not to scale

San Agustín contains religious paintings, Huichol handicrafts and some colonial items. ■ *1000-1700, closed Tue, US$1.*

Excursions Beyond Zacatecas to the east lies the **Convento de Guadalupe**, a national monument, with a fine church and convent, which now houses a **Museum of Colonial Religious Art**. ■ *Tue-Sun 1000-1700, US$3.45.* Next door is the **Museo Regional de Historia**, under development. Frequent buses, No 13, from López Mateos y Salazar, near old terminal, US$0.15, 20 minutes.

Visit also the **Chicomostoc** ruins (also known as **La Quemada**), 56 km south, by taking the 0800 or 1100 Línea Verde bus from main terminal to Adjuntas (about 45 minutes, US$0.60), on the Villanueva road. Then walk 30 minutes through beautiful, silent, nopal-cactus scenery to the ruins, which offer an impressive view. There is the Palace of the Eleven Columns, a Pyramid of the Sun and other remains on a rocky outcrop, in various stages of restoration. In themselves the ruins are not spectacular, but together with the setting they are worth the trip. A museum is being built. Take water. ■ *US$3.35; no information on site, so ask for explanations* (see box page 572). Women are advised to keep at a distance from the caretaker. For the return from the

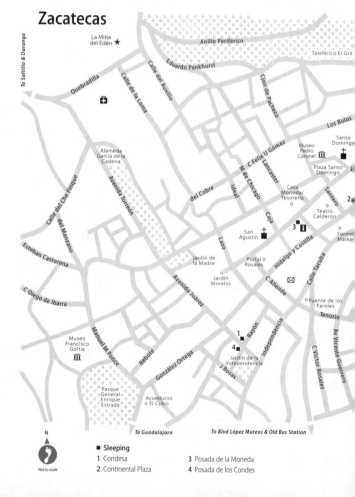

Zacatecas

Colonial Heartland

N
Not to scale

To Saltillo & Durango

La Mina del Edén ★
Anillo Periférico
Teleférico El Gril
Quebradilla
Calle de la Loma
Calle del Auxilio
Eduardo Pankhurst
Cjon de Pacheco
Los Bolos
Alameda García de la Cadena
Santo Domingo
Museo Pedro Coronel 🏛
C Félix U Gómez
M de Chicago
Lancaster
Plaza Santo Domingo
Avenida Torreón
Calle del Che Pinque
del Manzano
del Cobre
Ideal
Caja
Casa Moneda/ Tesorería
Santero
2
Teatro Calderón
Esteban Castorena
Lazo
San Agustín ✝
3 ℹ
Forme Marke
C Diego de Ibarra
Jardín de la Madre
Portal Rosales
Hidalgo y Costilla
C Allende
Calle Tacuba
Avenida Juárez
Jardín Morelos
✉
Fuente de los Faroles
Tenorio
Museo Francisco Goitia 🏛
Manuel M Ponce
Rebote
1 Rayón
4
Independencia
Av Vicente Guerrero
Parque General Enrique Estrada
Acueducto o El Cubo
González Ortega
Jardín de la Independencia
J Rosas
C Víctor Rosales

To Guadalajara
To Blvd López Mateos & Old Bus Station

■ **Sleeping**
1 Condesa
2 Continental Plaza
3 Posada de la Moneda
4 Posada de los Condes

junction at Adjuntas, wait for a bus (possibly a long wait) or hitch back to Zacatecas.

Jerez is an old colonial town about 65 km from Zacatecas, where the wide brimmed *sombrero charro* is still worn. It is worth a visit and is becoming popular with tourists. There are two interesting churches in the town: **La Soledad**, begun 1805, completed later that century, has a baroque façade, but most elaborate are the three gateways – composites of all manner of over-the-top classical styles; **La Inmaculada**, also with a baroque façade, has a neo-Romanesque interior.

Sleeping
■ *on maps*
Price codes:
see inside front cover

L *Quinta Real*, Av González Ortega, T29104. Beautiful, built around old bull ring (said to be the 2nd oldest in Latin America), aqueduct goes past the front door. **AL** *Continental Plaza*, opposite Cathedral, on Av Hidalgo, T26183 (discount offered for AAA members). Recommended. **AL** *Galería*, López Mateos s/n, T23311, near old bus station. Very comfortable. **AL** *Howard Johnson's*, López Mateos y Callejón del Barrio, T23311. **AL** *Mesón de Jobito*, Jardín Juárez 143, Centro, T/F43500 (in Mexico City T55142728/52075666), in heart of Centro Histórico. Small, select hotel, attractive restaurant with international and Mexican cuisine. **A** *Aristos*, Lomas de Soledad, T21788. **A** *María Bonita*, Av López Velarde 319, T24545, F26645. Hot water, heating, very

Colonial Heartland

☞ Chicomostoc: ancestral home of the Chichimeca

The Azteca, instructed by their god, Huitzilopochtli, changed their name to Mexica; they were the final group of a wave of newcomers to arrive in Mesoamerica. They were collectively known as Chichimeca. This was not a wave of immigrants arriving in peace and eager to integrate with the peoples who already occupied the lands. They entered the region violently, either on their own behalf or at the behest of weak polities already resident in the area and in need of the protection that could be achieved by harnessing the strength of these fearless warriors. Over a period of time, the Chichimeca began to take control of much of the Central Highlands, adopted the Nahuatl language, the dress and ways of the peoples they were usurping, and then began to record their ancestral histories as a means of legitimizing their claims to the lands they now occupied. They also had to defend them against other Chichimecas. All these groups looked to Chicomostoc (Chicome=Seven, Ostoc=Cave, Seven Caves) as their original homeland.

The histories of the Chichimeca were usually written as maps, painstakingly prepared and beautifully executed. The maps included individuals, groups and landmarks, all identified by name glyphs. Footprints in long lines indicate the direction of travel; where groups splinter, several lines of footprints proceed in different directions. A number of these maps still exist, most from the early colonial period when those groups subjugated by the Spanish were required to justify their claims to the territories they occupied: they were often used to settle land disputes.

Long before the arrival of the Spanish, Chicomostoc represented the birthplace, or womb, to later generations of Chichimeca, most of whom would never have visited Seven Caves. The maps, as well as legitimizing land claims, provide additional information about the clothes worn by the Chichimeca, the gods who guided each group, the sacrifices made to those gods, and the misfortunes that befell them. In one such map, The Historia Tolteca-Chichimeca, the text describes how, after the fall of Tula (1064) one group of refugees migrated to Cholula, having first approached the authorities there for permission to settle within the jurisdiction of that (then) great city. The lords of the region, the Olmeca-Xicallanca (not to be confused with the archaeological Olmec of La Venta), accepted the refugees but, according to the latter, misused and abused them. Tiring of mistreatment, representatives of the Tolteca-Chichimeca went to Chicomostoc to request the assistance of their kin, which they received. They returned to Cholula, overthrew the Olmeca-Xicallanca, then shared out the lands among themselves and their mercenary cousins. The map is explicit in identifying topographical features, the lands, and who settled where.

The importance of Chicomostoc to the history of the Chichimeca is underlined by the order given by the Huey Tlahtoani (Great Speaker) Motecuhzoma Ilhuicamina to search for the original home of the Azteca/Mexica, the place of the Seven Caves, in the northern plains. This implies that symbolically, Chicomostoc was more important as an ancestral home than the true home of the Azteca/Mexica, Aztlán.

good. **B** *Posada de la Moneda*, near Cathedral, Av Hidalgo 413, T20881, F23693. Nice and clean, but a bit noisy. **B** *Posada Santa Cecilia*, Constitución/San Francisco 4, T52412. Old style, pleasant atmosphere.

   C *Hotel Leo*, short walk from bus station. Good. **D** *Posada de los Condes*, Juárez 107, T21093, F21650. A bit noisy, rooms darkish except those at front with balconies. **D** *Condesa*, opposite *Posada de los Condes*, Av Juárez, T21160. OK, helpful, some rooms quiet with good views of Cerro de la Bufa, cheap restaurant. **D** *Colón*, Av López Velarde 508, T20464. Clean, showers. **D** *Gami*, Av López Mateos 309, T28005. Rooms with TV, OK. **D** *Insurgentes*, Insurgentes 114, off Plaza del Vivar. Without bath, hot showers extra. **D** *Hotel Félix*. Recommended. **D** *Jardín*, on main plaza, T52026. **E** *Barranca*, opposite old bus terminal, López Mateos 401, T21494. Poor value, and noisy traffic. **E** *Conde de Villarreal* (was *Zamora*), Plaza de Zamora 303, T21200. With bath, central, very basic. **E** *Del Parque*, González Ortega 302. Clean, good value. **E** *Morelos*, Morelos 825, T22505. Economical, very basic, shared bath. **E** *Río Grande*, Calzada de la Paz 217, T25349. With bath (**F** without), ask for quiet room on the patio, beautiful view from one side, clean, friendly, hot water, good value. The cheap hotels (very few) are all within 5 mins walk of the old bus station, towards Av Hidalgo.

Motels **B-C** *Hacienda Del Bosque*, T20747, Fortín de la Peña, close to centre so may be noisy. Attractive rooms, good food, has camping facilities and hook-ups, showers and toilets, only for small cars and vans. **C** *Parador Zacatecas*, Pan-American Highway. Excellent.

Youth hostel Parque del Encantado 103, T21151/21891, CP 98000, on bus route to centre from bus station, no singles. Also Av de los Deportes beside Estadio Francisco Villa, CP 98064, T29377.

Trailer park at Morelos junction, about 20 mins northwest of the city, where Route 54 Saltillo-Guadalajara crosses Route 49. Hook-ups, basic, US$8, behind Pemex.

La Cuija, in old Centro Comercial on Av Tacuba. Good food, music, atmosphere. *El Jacalito*, Juárez 18. Excellent *comida corrida* and breakfast. Also on Juárez at 232 is *El Trogadero*. Good Zacatecan dishes. *La Unica Cabaña*, Jardín de la Independencia. Cheap, excellent set meals. *Juana Gallo*, Guanajuato 9. Local dishes. *La Cofradía*, Constitución y San Francisco. Best in town and with moderate prices. *Hotel Mesón de Jobito*, see above, very good food. Recommended. *Burgerlandia*, beside Teatro Calderón. Good. *Mr Laberinto*, Av Hidalgo 338. Luxurious atmosphere, 1970s décor, quite cheap, good breakfast and dinners. Recommended. *Hotel Quinta Real*, address above. Recommended. *Nueva Galicia*, Plazuela Goitia 102. Wide range of Mexican food, also offers delicious Sushi. Recommended. *El Paraíso*, Av Hidalgo y P Goitia, corner of market. Bar/restaurant, nice atmosphere, closed Sun; opposite is *Nueva España*. Bar with loud music, closed Sun. *Chapa Rosa*, Plaza Genaro Codina 112. Good, moderate prices. *La Cantera Musical*, Av Tacuba, Mexican. Good atmosphere, poor a/c, good food but drinks limited after 2000. Good cafés include: *Cafetería La Terraza*, in market on a balcony. Very pleasant, good *malteadas*. *Café Arús*, Centro Comercial, Av Hidalgo. Serves breakfast. *Los Comales*, Hidalgo 611. Good value. *Acrópolis*, opposite Cathedral. 50-year-old café and diner, good breakfast, slow service. *Café Zaz*, Av Hidalgo 201. Several cheap restaurants along Av Independencia. *El Quixote* (at *María Bonita Hotel*), Av López Velarde. Good breakfasts. *Helder*, near old bus station. Excellent breakfasts. Plenty of good coffee shops selling real *expresso* coffee. Many good *tamales* sold on the streets. **Health food** Store at Rayón 413, excellent food at reasonable prices.

Eating
● *on maps*

Spread over most of **Sep**, a rainy month here. There are bullfights on Sun.

Festivals

Interesting shops on Independencia selling hats, riding equipment, fruit and other produce, not touristy. Cheap postcards for sale in the toy shop and stationers on Hidalgo on the right if coming from the Cathedral. Between Hidalgo and Tacuba the elegant 19th-century market building has been converted into a pleasant shopping centre (popular café on balcony, reasonable). The **market** is now dispersed in various locations a few blocks to the southwest. Zacatecas is famous for its *sarapes* and has two delicacies: the local cheese, and *queso de tuna*, a candy made from the fruit of the

Shopping

Colonial Heartland

nopal cactus (do not eat too much, it has laxative properties). Visit the small *tortilla* factories near the station, on the main road. Several good silverware shops around the Cathedral area.

Tour operators *Cantera Tours*, Centro Comercial El Mercado, Av López Velarde 602-6, Local A-21, T29065. *Operadora Zacatecas*, T40050, F43676. Offer several interesting tours. *Viajes Masoco*, Enlace 115, Col Sierra de Alca, T25559, tours to Chicomostoc and Jerez, US$15.50.

Transport **Air** Aeropuerto La Calera (ZCL) 27 km north of city (taxi US$20), flights daily to Mexico City, Tijuana, Guadalajara, Ciudad Juárez, Morelia, Aguascalientes. Direct flights to several US cities: Chicago, Denver, Los Angeles, Oakland, California.

Trains Zacatecas is on the Mexico City-Querétaro-Chihuahua line. Check locally whether there are trains running.

Buses New terminal 4 km north of town; taxi US$1.20; red No 8 buses from Plaza Independencia (US$0.15) or white *camionetas* from Av González Ortega (old bus station on Blvd López Mateos only serves local destinations). To **Durango** with Estrella Blanca, 5 hrs, US$8 (if continuing to Mazatlán, stay the night in Durango in order not to miss the views on the way to the coast), US$13 Omnibus de México, before 1030, then afternoon. To **Chihuahua** via Torreón, 12 hrs, 1st class US$33; **Jiménez**, US$27; to **Hidalgo del Parral** with Transportes Chihuahuenses and Omnibus de México, US$30, 10 hrs; **San Luis Potosí** with Estrella Blanca or Transportes Chihuahuenses, 3½ hrs, US$6. **Ciudad Juárez** 1st class with Omnibus de México at 1930, 11 hrs, US$45; to **Guadalajara**, 6½ hrs, several companies, US$15, but shop around for different journey times (road windy and in poor condition in parts). **Aguascalientes**, every 30 mins, 2½ hrs, US$3, or US$6 1st class. To **León**, 4½ hrs, US$10. To **Mexico City**, 8 hrs, US$25. Apart from buses to Mexico City, Chihuahua and a few other major towns, most routes do not have bookable seats. Frequent buses passing through Jerez back to Zacatecas with Rojo de Los Altos, US$2.20.

Directory **Airline offices** *Mexicana*, T23248. *Taesa*, T20050. **Banks** *Banamex* recommended. *Bancomer* has a Visa cash dispenser and gives cash (pesos) on Visa cards. Both on Av Hidalgo. **Communications** Internet: *Café @rroba*, Félix U Gómez 520 B, 0900-2200, daily, US$2 per hr, chmnet@gauss.logicnet.com.mx. Allende 111. *Cybernovus*, Callejón de Lancaster 100, 1st flr, Mon-Sat 0900-2200. *Internet Café*, Félix y V Cación. **Fax:** service at *Telégrafos*, Av Hidalgo y Juárez. **Cultural centres** *Alianza Francesa*, Callejón del Santero 111, T40348, French film every Tue at 1900 (free). **Language school** *Fénix Language Institute*, T21643. **Laundry** *Lavandería El Indio Triste*, Juan de Tolosa 828, US$.80 per kg. **Medical services** *Santa Elena Clinic*, Av Guerrero, many specialists, consultation, US$15.

San Luis Potosí

Phone code: 48
Colour map 3, grid A4
Population: 850,000
Altitude: 1,880m

423 km from Mexico City, the capital of its state is the centre of a rich mining and agricultural area, which has expanded industrially in recent years. Glazed, many-coloured tiles are a feature of the city; one of its shopping streets, the main plaza, and the domes of many of its churches are covered with them. It became an important centre after the discovery of the famous San Pedro silver mine in the 16th century, and a city in 1658. There is a festival in the second half of August. The **tourist office**, Obregón 520, T129943/125336, is about half a block west of the Plaza de los Fundadores. It's in a beautiful colonial house with lovely gardens. They are very helpful and have good brochures and maps of the city and also of other places to see in the state.

The **Cathedral** is on **Plaza Hidalgo**; it fronts the east side of it, to be exact. It **Sights** has a beautiful exterior of pink cantera (a type of local stone), with very ornately carved bell towers. The interior is also very beautiful. There are rows of stone columns running down the length of each side of the church's interior, each column being about 2m in diameter. Be sure to look up at the vaulted ceiling, because it, too, is very pretty. Also on the east side of the plaza, just north of and adjacent to the Cathedral, is the **Palacio Municipal**. In the interior, over the double branching staircase, you can admire the glasswork representing the city's coat of arms. In the upper floor, the Cabildo Hall has a ceiling painted by Italian artist Erulo Eroli, featuring mythological Christian themes. Do not miss the church of **San Francisco**, which fronts the plaza of the same name. This church is one of the baroque jewels of the city. The construction dates back to 1686. In that year, the work of the beautiful pink limestone façade was begun. But it wasn't until the next century that some of its most important features were added, like the baroque tower and the main altar. The interior is embellished with wonderful paintings, among which the works by Miguel Cabrera and Antonio Torres are the most outstanding. Worthy of admiration is the sacristy, the most magnificent in San Luis Potosí. Another striking piece is the carved stone relief showing a scene from the life of St Francis. Note also the white and blue tiled dome and suspended glass boat in the transept. The **Templo del Carmen**, in **Plaza del Carmen**, has a grand tiled dome, an intricate façade, and a fine pulpit and altar inside. The room to the left of the main altar (as you face it) has another exquisite, very striking altar covered in gold leaf. the **Teatro de la Paz** is next door. The baroque **Capilla de Aranzazú**, behind San Francisco, inside the regional museum (see below), must not be missed; the carved stone framework of the chapel window is one of the most beautiful pieces of baroque art in the city.

San Luis Potosí

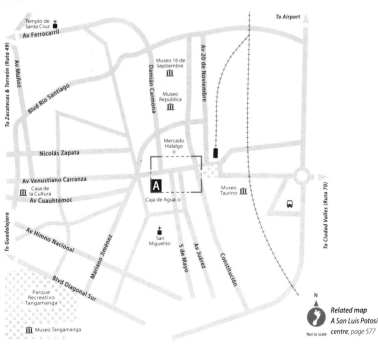

Related map
*A San Luis Potosí
centre*, page 577
Not to scale

Colonial Heartland

Then there is the **Capilla de Loreto** with a baroque façade; the **Templo de San Miguelito**, in the oldest part of the city; **San Agustín**, with its ornate baroque tower; and the startling modern **Iglesia de la Santa Cruz**, in the Industria Aviación district, designed by Enrique de la Mora. The **Palacio de Gobierno**, begun 1789, contains oil-paintings of past governors. There is also the colonial treasury, **Antigua Caja Real**, built 1767. Of great artistic merit are the doors and windows of the chapel, carved in stone in the purist baroque style. Of especial interest is the stairway leading to the first floor. It has very low steps, so that the mules, laden with precious metals, could climb easily. ■ *Some rooms may be visited Mon-Fri 0930-1330.*

Other points of interest are the pedestrian precinct surrounding **Jardín Hidalgo** and the **Caja del Agua** fountain (1835) in Avenida Juárez. **Plaza de San Francisco** is very pleasant. The modern railway station has frescoes by Fernando Leal. The **Teatro Alarcón**, on Calle Abasolo, between Zaragoza and Morelos, is by Tresguerras (see under Celaya, page 546). It is now being used as offices for a miners' union. The **University** was founded in 1804. A scenic road leads to Aguascalientes airport.

Museums The **Museo Regional de Arte Popular**, next to San Francisco church, is housed in what used to be a private residence. Handicrafts from various parts of the state can be seen, including ceramics, woodwork, *rebozos*, textiles, etc. There are also items for sale. ■ *Tue-Sat 1000-1345, 1600-1745; Sun 1000-1400, Mon 1000-1500.* Nearby is **Museo Regional Potosino**, located in the building that originally was a Fransciscan convent. The ground floor has an exhibition of pre-Hispanic artefacts, mainly from the Huastec culture. The wrought-iron collection is outstanding, as well as the collection of handicrafts and ancient handiwork. Upstairs is the Capilla Aranzazú, mentioned above under places of interest. ■ *Tue-Fri 1000-1300, 1500-1800, Sat 1000-1200, Sun 1000-1300.* **La Casa de la Cultura** on Avenida Carranza, halfway between the centre and university, is a very elegant building, made of limestone in a neo-classic style with large and beautiful gardens. Built in 1919 by the architect Joaquín Meade, it was the first residence of Gerardo Meade until 1970, when the state government acquired it to create the Cultural Centre. Now it has on display a selected collection of art works, archaeological pieces and arts and crafts. The annexed **Centre of Historic and Geographical Studies** houses the collection of books and documents owned by Ramón Alcorta Guerrero, who donated it to the city. ■ *Tue-Fri, 1000-1400, 1600-1800, Sat 1000-1400, 1800-2100.* **Museo Nacional de la Máscara**, in what used to be the Palacio Federal, has an excellent collection of masks. The most impressive are the masks used in colonial and pre-Hispanic times in pagan religious ceremonies. ■ *Tue-Fri 1000-1400, 1600-1800, Sat-Sun 1000-1400, US$0.20 plus US$0.20 for use of camera.* In Parque Tangamanga is the **Museo Tangamanga** in an old hacienda, and also a planetarium, observatory and open-air theatre (■ *0600-1800*). In Plaza España, next to the Plaza de Toros, is a **Museo Taurino** (bullfighting museum), east of Alameda on Universidad y Triana. ■ *Tue-Sat 1100-1330, 1730-1930.* **Casa Othón**, Manuel José Othón 225, is the birthplace and home of the poet. ■ *Tue-Fri 0800-1900, Sat and Sun 1000-1300.* **NB** For motorists driving into the centre, parking is very difficult. There is an *estacionamiento* near the police station on Eje Vial, US$1 for 1st hr, US$0.65 for each subsequent hour.

Excursions There are hot springs at Ojo Caliente, Balneario de Lourdes and Gogorrón. **Balneario de Lourdes** (**B** hotel, clean, nice atmosphere, small pool) is south of San Luis Potosí. **Gogorrón** is clean and relaxing, with pools, hot tubs, picnic grounds and campsites. There is a restaurant. A day trip or overnight camp-out is recommended in the lightly wooded hills and meadows near the microwave station (at 2,600m), 40 km east of San Luis Potosí: go 35 km along the Tampico highway and continue up 5 km of cobblestone road to the station. Good views and flora.

B *María Cristina*, Juan Sarabia 110, Altos, T129408, F186417. Modern, clean, small rooms with phone and TV, with restaurant, good value. **B** *Panorama*, Av Venustiano Carranza 315, T121777, F124591. Price includes breakfast and a 20 percent discount in the other meals. Large, attractive rooms. Very good views of the city from the rooms on the upper floors. **C** *Hotel Concordia*, Morelos 705, T120666, F126966. TV and phones in rooms. **C** *Nápoles*, Juan Sarabia 120, T128418/128449, F122260. Good restaurant attached, TV, phones, ceiling fans in rooms. Recommended.

D *Hotel Anáhuac*, Xochitl 140, about 1 block west of the station, T126504/5, F144904. Extra for TV. **D** *Hotel Guadalajara*, Jiménez 253, near train station, T124612/124527. Small rooms with TV and phone; has enclosed parking. **D** *Progreso*, Aldama 415, T120366/120367, less than a block from the Plaza San Francisco. Attractive colonial façade. Rooms are large but rather dark and a little run down. Not bad for the price. **D** *Universidad*, Universidad 1435, between train and bus station. Clean, friendly, hot showers. **D-E** *Jardín Potosí*, Los Bravo 530, T123152. Good, hot water, restaurant. Recommended. **E** *El Principal*, Juan Sarabia opposite *María Cristina*. With bath, OK, loud TV in hall.

Sleeping
Many hotels between the railway station & the cathedral

San Luis Potosí centre

Colonial Heartland

N
Not to scale

■ **Sleeping**
1 Concordia
2 El Principal
3 Jardín
4 María Cristina
5 Nápoles
6 Panorama
7 Progreso

There are several very basic hotels with shared bath by the train station that charge around 35 pesos a night for a double on Jiménez, which really isn't a street, but a sidewalk separated by a 15-m grass median strip from Los Bravo, running parallel to it just to the north, from the train station west a couple of blocks.

Motels All along Highway 57: **L** *Hostal del Quijote*, (now owned by Holiday Inn), Km 420, T181312, F185105, 6 km south on the San Luis Potosí-Mexico City highway. 5-star, convention facilities, one of the best in Mexico. **AL** *Tuna* (Best Western), Highway 80, near exit to Guadalajara, T131207, F111415. Parking, pool, restaurant and bar, near University campus. **A** *Santa Fe*, T125109; all with pools. **C** *Mansión Los Arcos*, a few kilometres south of San Luis Potosí, signposted. With restaurant and safe parking.

Eating   *Los Molinos*, in *Hostal del Quijote*. Excellent, well-served food. *Tokio*, Los Bravo 510. Excellent *comida*. *La Parroquia*, corner of Díaz de León and Carranza, on the Plaza de los Fundadores. In old building but modern inside. Attractive wood panelling. *Comida corrida* costs US$2.70, plus cost of beverage. Good food. *La Posada del Virrey*, on north side of Jardín Hidalgo. The restaurant is in a beautiful covered courtyard of an old colonial building. They also have a dining room facing the plaza. Just west of it is *Helados Bing*. *Café Pacífico*, corner of Los Bravo and Constitución, a couple of blocks from the train station. Open 24 hrs. Dinner costs around US$5. Good hot chocolate. Nice atmosphere. *Restaurant de Mariscos El Pacífico*, across the street from the *Café Pacífico*, at Los Bravo 429. Good *cafetería* at bus station. *Café Florida*, Juan Sarabia 230; many other reasonably priced eating places at western end of Alameda Juan Sarabia.

Shopping   Excellent sweet shop at Galeana 430, next to the Museo Regional Potosino. **Markets** Head north on Hidalgo and you come to Mercado Hidalgo, then Mercado República, and Mercado 16 de Septiembre. Locally made *rebozos* (the best are from Santa María del Río) are for sale in the markets. 3-storey hypermarket, *Chalita*, on Jardín San Juan de Dios between Av Alvaro Obregón and Los Bravo. **Health food store** *Casa de Nutrición*, 5 de Mayo 325, fairly limited.

Transport   **Air** The airport (SLP) is nearly 6 km from the centre. Flights to Chicago, San Antonio (Texas). Many daily to Mexico City, also flights to Aguascalientes, Guadalajara, Monterrey, Tampico.

Trains The station is pretty run down and there are no 1st-class trains passing through. Trains to Nuevo Laredo leave on Mon, Wed, and Fri at 1730. Trains to Mexico City leave on Wed, Fri and Sun at 1030. Check locally to make sure these services are still running.

Buses Bus station on outskirts of town 1½ km from centre. For local buses to the centre, walk out the front door of the terminal and turn right. Walk down the street to the first traffic light. Then take buses heading south on the cross street (ie to your right as you're facing it) marked '1 de Mayo' or 'Los Gómez'.

Luggage can be left at the bus terminal (3 pesos per bag per hour). Snack food, magazines, stationery and typical Mexican sweets are avaiable and there is a booth with long-distance and fax service. There is a taxi ticket booth in the centre of the terminal. Taxis to the centre cost about US$2.

Aguascalientes, Turistar Ejecutivo (luxury service, like ETN) 1100, US$12.30. **Chihuahua**, Omnibus de México (all first class). 9 buses per day, US$46.80. **Ciudad Juárez**, Omnibus de México 9 buses per day, US$64.10. **Durango**, Omnibus de México 1405, 2045, 2330, US$20.80. **Guadalajara**, ETN (luxury service buses have half as many seats as ordinary buses and seats recline 45 degrees and have footrests. They give you a soda and sandwich as you board the bus). 0015, 0230, 0730, 1030, 1230, 1430, 1730, 2030 (4½ hrs), US$22.00. Oriente/Línea Azul (1st class) 0600, 0800, 1200, 1430, 2230, 2320. **Guanajuato**, Omnibus de México 0300, US$11.50. **Laredo**, Autotransportes Tamaulipas (Grupo Senda; all first class except where noted). Only runs on Fri, Sat, and Sun, at 1030 and 2230, US$29.20. **León**, Omnibus de México 0500, US$8.20. **Matehuala** (for Real de Catorce), Autotransportes Tamaulipas 13 buses per day, US$6.90; also 3 2nd-class buses for US$6.30. **León**, Primera Plus (*Plus* service; a little better than 1st class). You can also receive money via Western Union through them, but can't send it. 11 per day, US$49.00. **McAllen, Texas** (via Linares), Autotransportes Tamaulipas 1930 US$28.70. McAllen, Texas (via Monterrey), Autotransportes Tamaulipas 0900, 1105, 2100, 2300, US$28.70. **Mexico City**, Omnibus de México 0045, 0100, 0200, 0300, 0400, 0500, 0600, 0700, 1031 (5 hrs), US$19.30. Primera Plus seven per day (5 hrs), US$20.80. ETN 18 departures daily, US$25.70. Futura (*Plus* service) hourly, US$19.30. Turistar Ejecutivo 0030, 1030, US$25.70. **Monterrey**, Autotransportes Tamaulipas 14 buses per day, US$19.10. Turistar Ejecutivo 2200, US$25.70. **Morelia**, Primera Plus 8 per day, US$18.20. Servicios Coordinarios (1st class) about 15 per day, US$16.50. **Nuevo Laredo**, Turistar Ejecutivo 2200, US$42.30. **Querétaro**, Omnibus de México 1200, 1300, 1400, 1500, 1600, 2000, 2214 (2½ hr trip), US$9.40. Primera Plus 0900, 1145, 1430, US$10.30. Servicios Coordinarios 17 per day, US$9.40. ETN 1630, US$11.00. **Saltillo**, Omnibus de México 2400, US$16.80. **San Juan de los Lagos**, Primera Plus 0800, $9.60. ETN 0730, US$11.50.**San Miguel de Allende**, Flecha Amarilla 0620, 0720, 0920, 1120, 1320, 1745. Also many departures daily to Mexico City, Guanajuato, León, Lagos de Moreno, Dolores Hidalgo, and other cities. **Tijuana**, Turistar Ejecutivo 1530, 1830, US$104.40. **Toluca**, ETN 1630, US$22.50. **Zacatecas**, Omnibus de México 7 buses per day, US$7.80.

Also run other 2nd class buses. Autobuses Americanos; two buses daily, stopping at the following points. **Laredo, Texas** US$29.00; **San Antonio, Texas**, US$44.40; **Dallas, Texas** US$59.00; **Houston, Texas**, US$54.00; 1400, 2200. **Chicago**, US$108.00. Wed. 2230.

Airline offices *Aeromar*, Av Carranza 1160-2; T114671. *AeroMéxico*, T01800-0214010. *Mexicana*, T178836. *United*, T901-800-0030777 (English), 01800-4265561 (Spanish). *Aerocalifornia*, T118050. *Aeroliteral*, T222229. *Mexicana de Aviación*, T178920. **Communications** Internet: *Café Cibernético*, Av Carranza 416. **Post Office:** Morelos y González Ortega. **Health** *Red Cross*, Av Juárez and Diez Gutíerrez, T153332/153635, *Central Hospital* (public), Av Carranza 2395, T130343/130595. **Private Hospitals** *Sociedad de Benificios Española*, Av Carranza 1090, T134048/134050 /134102. *Hospital de Nuestra Señora de la Salud*, Madre Perla 435, Frac Industrias, (4 blocks behind Holiday Inn *Hostal del Quixote*), T245424/245225. *Clínica Díaz Infante*, Arista 730, T123737.

Directory

South of San Luis Potosí, east of the junction with Route 110, is San Luis de la Paz. Nearby is one of Mexico's mining ghost-towns, Pozos, once one of the most important mining centres of Mexico. First you come to the ruins. It's very silent and a complete contrast to Real de Catorce (see below). Many of the mining shafts still remain pristine and very deep. Drive on and you reach the town, where several workshops have pre-Hispanic musical instruments and artefacts for show and sale, all handmade mostly in Pozos; *Camino de Piedra* on Plaza Zaragoza also sells CDs, T-shirts and souvenirs. Particularly helpful is the lady at *Calmecac* near the square, who demonstrates how many of the not-so-obvious instruments work ■ *Mon-Sat 1000-1900*. There is a **Museo Cultural** with a modest display and workshop. ■ *1000-1600*.

Pozos was founded in 1576 when silver was discovered. In the 19th century the population reached 80,000 but following the Revolution most of the foreign (French and Spanish) owners left and the workforce migrated to Mexico

Pozos
Phone code: 48
Colour map 3, grid B5
Altitude: 2,305m

Colonial Heartland

City. After the 1985 earthquake, people who had lost their homes in the capital drifted back. The men now work in Querétaro and the women work at home making clothes to sell in local markets. The population has slowly risen to 2,000. The town is very quiet and the whole area was decreed a historical monument in 1982. There are no rooms to let. Pozos can be reached by bus from San Miguel de Allende (change at San Luis de la Paz) or San José Iturbide.

Real de Catorce

Colour map 3, grid A4
Altitude: 2,765m

Fifty-six kilometres west of Matehuala, an important junction on Route 57, is one of Mexico's most interesting old mining towns, Real de Catorce, founded in 1772. This remarkable city, clustering around the sides of a valley, used to be so quiet that you could hear the river in the canyon, 1,000m below. It is becoming increasingly popular as a tourist destination and new hotels are being built.

To get there, turn left along the Zacatecas road through Cedral. After 27 km turn left off the paved road, on to a cobblestone one. The road passes through Potrero, a big centre for nopal cactus. Some people live in the old mine workings and old buildings. Huichol Indians are seen here occasionally. A silver mine is still being worked at Santana.

Real de Catorce is approached through the Ogarrio tunnel, an old mine gallery widened (only just) to allow trucks through (US$1.65 toll to drive through). It is 2½ km long, and very eerie, with the odd tunnel leading off into the gloom on either side. There is an overtaking bay half way through. A small chapel to the Virgen de los Dolores is by the entrance. The tunnel opens out abruptly into the old city, originally called Real d'Alamos de la Purísima Concepción de los Catorce. Legend has it that 14 bandits hid in nearby caves until the silver was discovered and the town founded. Engineers came from Ireland, Germany and France.

Sights The first church was the **Virgen del Guadalupe** (1779), a little way out of town. Beautiful ceiling paintings remain, as well as the black coffin used for the Mass of the Cuerpo Presente. Many of the images from this church were moved to the **Church of San Francisco** (1817), which is believed to be miraculous. The floor of the church is made of wooden panels, which can be lifted to see the catacombs below. In a room to one side of the main altar are *retablos*, touchingly simple paintings on tin, as votive offerings to the Saint for his intercession. Next to the church is a small but worthwhile museum showing mining equipment, etc. ■ *US$0.10*. In the early 19th century, when the population was about 40,000, Real minted its own coins, which circulated only within the city limits (they are now collectors' items). After the Second World War the population fell dramatically to 400, but it has risen now to about 1,200, since silver is being worked again and tourism is growing. Guided tours are available from the **Casa de la Moneda**, in front of the Cathedral; they include the **Palenque**, an eight-sided amphitheatre built in 1863, which seated 500-600 people (this is otherwise closed to the public). In the Casa de la Moneda you can see silversmiths at work.

There are good hikes in the surrounding mountains. Very peaceful. Take good footwear, sun protection and a jumper. A 30-minute walk takes you to the *pueblo fantasmo* (ghost town) from where there are fine views over the town.

Sleeping **B** *El Coral del Conde*, Morelos, close to Mesón de la Abundancia. 6 rooms, fine furniture, clean, big bathrooms. **B** *Hotel Ruinas Real*, Libertad, next to El Palenque. 10 rooms, restaurant, bar, art gallery, paintings on exhibition may be bought, all rooms are doubles. **D** *Hotel Real*, in a side street. Clean, nice atmosphere, friendly owner, good restaurant. Recommended. **B** *La Puesta del Sol*, on way to cemetery from main square. With bath, TV, beautiful views, poor restaurant. Recommended. **E** *Providencia*, on main street. Hot water, clean, restaurant. Several other hotels, and various restaurants. Accommodation is easy to find: boys greet new arrivals and will guide motorists through the peculiar one-way system (or face a police fine).

Eating

El Eucalyptus, on way to Zócalo. Italian-Swiss run. Excellent homemade pasta, vegetarian food, cakes. Pricey but recommended. Many cheap restaurants on main street and stalls selling *tacos* and hot drinks.

Festivals

There is a pilgrimage here for San Francisco (4 Oct), on foot from Matehuala, overnight on **3 Oct**. Take the local bus from Matehuala to La Paz and join the groups of pilgrims who set out from early evening onwards. The walk takes about 7 hrs, be prepared for rain. It is possible to walk from Matehuala to Real de Catorce, other than on the San Francisco pilgrimage, with the aid of the 1:50,000 map from INEGI (see **Essentials**, page 74). On Good Friday, thousands of visitors gather to watch a lively Passion play 'with almost real Roman soldiers and very colourful Jews and apostles'.

Transport

Trains Real de Catorce can (in theory) be reached from Saltillo or San Luis Potosí by train, but schedules are awkward and trains are often cancelled. The station, called Catorce, is 13 km away. There is one hotel and you can stay in private homes. Jeeps collect passengers from the station (US$16.50 per jeep) and follow a more spectacular route than the minibuses.

Road No fuel on sale in Real de Catorce; there are Pemex Stations before Cedral and at Matehuala.

Buses Many buses a day to Matehuala with Transportes Tamaulipas, from the corner of Guerrero and Mendiz, US$2 one-way. A taxi can be hired nearby for US$25, economic for 4 people; local buses from office 1 block north of the Zócalo.

Colonial Heartland

Northeastern Mexico

12

Northeastern Mexico

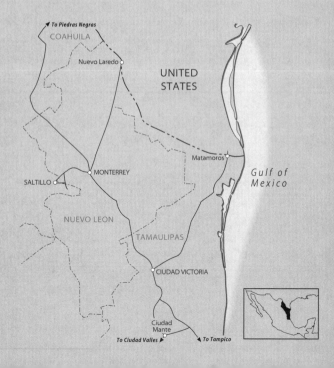

Some of the most crucial battles of the 1846-48 War between Mexico and the United States were fought in the northeast of Mexico. Brownsville and Matamoros experienced the first outbreak of hostilities and it was here that many US troops deserted and joined the Mexican forces, giving rise to the St Patrick's Battalion. Museums in the towns and cities along the way tell this and other stories of the region. On a more contemporary note, the **galleries of Monterrey** are at the cutting edge of modern Mexican art. Here too you can wander around what the regiomontanos - as people from Monterrey are called - claim is the biggest civic square in the world. Outside the city you can explore **Mexico's largest national park**, venture into vast caves with stalactites and stalagmites, try rock climbing on mountains that tower above chasms, or set out on a two-day adventure circuit involving river canyoning, abseiling or swimming through tunnels. Further south, beyond the Tropic of Cancer, you can enjoy tropical bird sanctuaries, jungle and even cloud forest and visit **archaeological sites** of the enigmatic Huastec civilization. And if you've got time, you could even take in some deep-sea fishing before finally reaching Tampico and the Gulf Coast or heading inland to the Colonial Highlands.

Northeastern Mexico

Laredo to Tampico

The Gulf Route from Laredo (by the Pan-American Highway) takes in the major industrial centre of Monterrey and the port of Tampico. The route passes through the coastal state of Tamaulipas before entering Huastec and Otomí Indian regions. Then there is a choice of either continuing south or heading west to the Central Highlands via the old silver-mining centre of Pachuca.

Crossing into Mexico

The first route to be opened was the Gulf Route. Traffic from the central and eastern parts of the United States can enter northeast Mexico through five gateways along the Río Bravo; at **Matamoros**, opposite Brownsville; at **Reynosa** opposite McAllen; at **Ciudad Miguel Alemán**, opposite Roma; at **Nuevo Laredo**, opposite Laredo; and at **Piedras Negras**, opposite Eagle Pass. The roads from these places all converge upon Monterrey (a new toll road from Nuevo Laredo is the quickest route, US$12).

There are alternative roads from Reynosa and Matamoros which join the Nuevo Laredo-Mexico City highway at Montemorelos and Ciudad Victoria, respectively; the latter runs along the tropical Gulf coastal plain and then climbs sharply through the Sierra Madre Oriental to Ciudad Victoria, at 333m.

By car, the best way is over the **Colombia Bridge**, north of Laredo: on Interstate 35, take the exit to Milo (the first exit north of the Tourist Bureau, then take Farm Road 1472 west). This crossing has little traffic and friendly staff, but it does involve a 40-km detour (it is well signposted on the Mexican side). The toll on the international bridge is US$1.25). Once in Mexico, you can continue to Monterrey either on Route 85 via Nuevo Laredo, or by following the railway line via Ciudad Anáhuac and Lampazos.

The direct route is on San Bernardo parallel to Interstate 35 on the west; turn west at Washington, south at Salinas, cross about 10 traffic lights and turn east to the **International bridge**. Do not be directed into the narrow columns: after verbal processing, go three km to the full vehicle processing location at Avenida Cesar López de Lara 1200, opposite the train station. This entails six steps, including photocopying of documents (keep copies), US$2-3, and the bureaucracy described under **Motoring** in Essentials.

If pressed for time, avoid 20 November and other national holidays as there are delays at customs owing to Mexicans visiting the USA in large numbers. Border formalities can take two hours or more.

Crossing points

Laredo/ Nuevo Laredo This is the most important town of the eastern border crossings. Nuevo Laredo is a bit of a tourist trap but it is fun to stroll through the souvenir shops.

Phone code: 87
Colour map 2, grid B5
Population: 400,000

Sleeping (Laredo) The better of the 2 trailer parks is on the east side of Interstate 35, Main Street exit, 10 mins from border. **(Nuevo Laredo)** C *Alameda*, on plaza. C *Dos Laredos*, Matamoros y 15 de Junio. E *Calderón*. With bath, hot water, fan, run-down, friendly. Many **F** hotels, none of which have been recommended. **Motels: A** *Hacienda*, Prolongación Reforma 5530. **B** *Reforma*, Av Guerrero 822. **Shopping** Centro *Artesanal Nuevo Laredo*, Maclovio Herrera 3030, T126399.

Transport Trains To **Mexico City**, US$12 2nd class, US$22 *primera preferente*, daily at 1855, 24 hrs, it can get cold at night, meals on train poor, take your own food, or buy at stations (leaves Mexico City for the border at 0900). Passenger train services in Mexico are being cut since privatization. Always check before planning your route. Information: Av López César de Lara y Mina, Apdo Postal 248, Nuevo Laredo, Tamps, 88000 México, T128097; or PO Box 595, Laredo, Tx78042.

Buses The Nuevo Laredo **bus** station is not near the border; take a bus to the border, then walk across. It is not possible to get a bus from the Laredo Greyhound terminal to the Nuevo Laredo terminal unless you have an onward ticket. Connecting tickets from Houston via Laredo to Monterrey are available, 14 hours. Some buses to Laredo connect with Greyhound buses in the USA. To **Mexico City** with Estrella Blanca/Transportes del Norte 9 buses a day, 16½ hrs, US$42. To **Monterrey** (4 hrs, US$10, departures every hour), **Guadalajara** (18 hrs, US$46.50, 9 a day, Transportes del Norte or Estrella Blanca), to **San Luis Potosí**, US$38, **Tampico**, **Morelia** (17 hrs, US$43).

Banks *UNB Convent* and *Matamoros* charges 1% commission on TCs, it charges pesos, open 0830-1600, Mon-Fri. *IBC*, no commission under US$500. **Communications** Fax: and to receive letter, TCR, Martin and Sandra Reséndez, 820 Juárez, near post office, international service. **Embassies & consulates** *Mexican Consulate*, Farragut and Maine, 4th light on the right after leaving Interstate 35, open 0800-1400 Mon-Fri, helpful. **Useful addresses** Car insurance: *AAA* on San Bernardo Av (Exit 4 on Interstate 35). *Sanborns* on Santa Ursula (Exit 16 on Interstate 35), a bit more expensive, open 24 hours a day. *Johnson's Mexico Insurance*, Tepeyac Agent, Lafayette and Santa Ursula (59 and Interstate 35), US$2.60 per day, open 24 hrs, recommended. **Car tyres:** Tire Center of Laredo Inc, 815 Park, at San Bernardo Av.

After 130 km of grey-green desert, the road from Nuevo Laredo climbs the Mamulique Pass, which it crosses at 700m, and then descends to Monterrey. From Laredo to Monterrey there is a toll road (*cuota*) and a non-toll road (*vía libre*). The latter goes through Sabinas Hidalgo (hotels and museum). There is a toll bypass and a free truck route around Monterrey.

Reynosa is the border town (*Population* 300,000) opposite McAllen.

McAllen/ Reynosa

Phone code: 89

Sleeping **D** *San Carlos*, on the Zócalo. Recommended. **E** *Plaza*. In McAllen on the US side of the border. **E** *Arcade*, corner of Cedar and North 12th St, 2 blocks from Greyhound terminal, south from Valley Transit bus terminal.

Matamoros is a town with a bright and unforbidding museum, designed to let prospective tourists know what they can expect in Mexico. It is well worth a visit. Visas can be obtained in **Brownsville** on the US side of the border from the Mexican Consulate at 940 East Washington. Crossing the border by car here is quick and easy; permission is usually granted for six months (multiple entry) for passengers and vehicle, paperwork takes only about 10 minutes if everything is in order. The return journey is equally easy.

Brownsville/ Matamoros

Phone code: 88
Colour map 2, grid B6
Population: 400,000

Sleeping **C** *Ritz*, Matamoros y Siete. There are 4 motels on the road to the beach, all **B-C**. **Shopping** *Centro Artesanal Matamoros*, Calle 5 Hurtado and Alvaro Obregón, T20384. **Transport Buses** Several lines run 1st-class buses to **Mexico City** in 14 hrs for US$38. Transportes del Norte to **Ciudad Victoria** for US$10.75 (4 hrs).

110 km south of Matamoros is **San Fernando de Presas**, a convenient distance from the border, especially if driving to the USA. **B** *Hotel Las Palomas*, on the highway, is quite good; there is an excellent pizza place, serving more than pizza, near *Hotel América*.

Northeastern Mexico

Eagle Pass/ Piedras Negras, is across the Río Bravo from Eagle Pass, Texas. Beyond Hermanas
Piedras Negras (137 km), the highway begins to climb gradually up to the plateau country.

Phone code: 878 **Shopping** *Centro Artesanal Piedras Negras*, Edif la Estrella, Puerta México, T21087,
Colour map 2, grid B5 *artesanía* shop. **Trains**: Train to Saltillo Tue, Thu, Sat, 0730 arrives 1630, returns Mon,
Population: 150,000 Wed, Fri, 0815, arrives Piedras Negras 1715. Check locally, all passenger services are in a
Altitude: 220m state of flux.

Monclova, 243 km from border, has one of the largest steel mills in Mexico
(*Population: 250,000*). Take in enough gasoline at Monclova to cover the 205
km to Saltillo. Hotel, restaurant and camping prices have risen rapidly.

Saltillo

Phone code: 84 The capital of Coahuila state is a cool, dry popular resort noted for the excellence
Colour map 2, grid C4 of its *sarapes*. Its 18th-century cathedral, a mixture of romanesque,
Population: 650,000 churrigueresque, baroque and plateresque styles, is the best in northern Mexico.
Altitude: 1,600m There is a grand market, as well as good golf, tennis and swimming. College students from the USA attend the popular Summer School (T149541, F149544).

The **Museo de las Aves** (Bird Museum), on Hidalgo y Bolívar 151 (a few
blocks north of *sarape* factory, T140167, contains hundreds of stuffed birds
and a café. ■*Tue-Sat 1000-1800, Sun 1100-1800. Small admission charge.*

Matamoros

Guides available. The house of the artist Juan Antonio Villarreal Ríos, Boulevard Nazario Ortiz Garza, Casa 1, Manzana 1, Colonia Saltillo 400, T152707/151206, has an exhibition in every room of Dali-esque work; visitors are welcome, phone first. ■ *Free*. There are good views from El Cerro del Pueblo overlooking the city. An 87-km road runs east to Monterrey, both toll (US$7) and *vía libre*. You turn right (southwest) for Mexico City.

A short bus ride away is the quaint village of **Arteaga**, with shady parks and a beautiful stream. There are three restaurants at the entrance to the village. Many buses go there from Saltillo.

Sleeping

Several hotels a short distance from the plaza at the intersection of Allende and Aldama, the main streets. Saltillo is a conference centre and has many hotels in the luxury range, several on north end of Boulevard V Carranza north of Boulevard Echeverría Norte eg: *Holiday Inn Eurotel*, No 4100, T151000. *Imperial del Norte*, No 3800, T150011. *Posada San José Inn*, Carranza y Nogal, T152303. Cheaper. *Motel El Paso*, No 3101, T151035. *Huizache*, No 1746, T161000. **AL** *San Jorge*, Manuel Acuña Norte 240, T22222, F29400. In the centre. **B** *Rancho El Marillo*, Prolongación Obregón Sur y Echeverría, T174078. A converted hacienda, excellent value, meals available. **B** *Saade*, Aldama 397 Pte, T129120. **B** *Urdiñola*, G Victoria 211, T40940. Reasonable. **C** *Jardín*, Padre Flores 211, T125916. Basic, cold water, safe motorcycle parking.

D *Hidalgo*, Padre Flores 217, T149853. Without bath, not worth paying for bath in room, cold water only (hot baths open to public and guests for small fee). **E** *Brico*, Ramos Arizpe Pte 552, T125146. Cheap, noisy, clean, tepid water. **E** *El Conde*, Pérez Treviño y Acuña T120136. Several hotels in front of the bus station, eg **D** *Saltillo*, T170237. **E** *Central*, T170004. With bath, ample safe parking, clean, comfy. **F** *Bristol Aldama*, near *Hotel San Jorge*. Recommended.

Motels **L** *Camino Real*, Blvd Los Fundadores 2000, T300000. **A** *La Fuente*, Blvd Los Fundadores, T301599.

Saltillo

■ Sleeping			● Eating	
1 Brico	4 Hidalgo	7 San Jorge	1 Arcasa	4 Victoria
2 Bristol Aldama	5 Jardín	8 Urdiñola	2 El Tapanco	
3 El Conde	6 Saade		3 Señorita Torta	

N
Not to scale

Trailer park Turn right on road into town from Monterrey between *Hotel del Norte* and *Kentucky Fried Chicken*. Hook-ups, toilets, basic.

Eating *El Tapanco*, Allende 225 Sur. Expensive. **Victoria**, Padre Flores 221, by *Hotel Hidalgo*. Has reasonable *comida*. *Café Plaza*, off Plaza de Armas. Good breakfasts. *Señorita Torta*, Hidalgo Sur, 1 block from plaza. *Arcasa*, Victoria. Good local food. *Urdiñola*, next door. Good breakfast. *El Campanario Saloon and Grill*, Ocampo, open noon-midnight. Recommended. Excellent *licuados* (milkshakes) upstairs in the market. Many restaurants and bars in front of the bus station. Drinks and night-time view can be had at the *Rodeway Inn* on the north side of town.

Festivals Local *feria* in 1st half of **Aug**; cheap accommodation impossible to find at this time. Indian dances on**30 May** and **30 Aug**; picturesque ceremonies and bullfights during **Oct** *fiestas*. *Pastorelas*, the story of the Nativity, are performed in the neighbourhood in Christmas week.

Transport **Air** The airport (SLW) is 16 km from town. Flights to Mexico City daily with Mexicana. Aerolitoral flies to Guadalajara and Monterrey.

Trains To Mexico City Tue, Thu, Sat 0235, arrives 1900. To Piedras Negras Mon, Wed, Fri 0815, arrives 1715. Passenger services are being cut right back; check trains are running before making plans.

Buses Terminal is on Blvd Echeverría, 3 km south of centre (yellow bus marked 'Periférico' from Allende y Lerdo de Tejada in centre); minibuses to Pérez Treviño y Allende (for centre) will take luggage. Bus to **Mexico City**, 1st class, US$32, 11 hrs; to **Ciudad Acuña**, 2nd class, US$15, 8 hrs; to **San Luis Potosí**, US$14; to **Parral**, US$22, 9 hrs; to **Monterrey** and **Nuevo Laredo** with Transportes del Norte. For **Torreón**, US$10.50, 3 hrs, all buses originate in Monterrey and tickets are only sold when bus arrives; be prepared to stand.

Directory **Banks** *Bancomer*, Allende y Victoria. *Banamex*, Allende y Ocampo. **Communications Telephones:** long-distance calls from *Café Victoria*, Padre Flores 221, near market. **Tourist office** Blvd Echeverría (ring road) 1560, Edif Torre Saltillo, 11th floor, T151714. Recommended tour guide for Saltillo is *Salvador R Medina*, T174255, F174093.

Saltillo to Matehuala From Saltillo, two roads run south: one to Zacatecas (see page 568) and the other to Matehuala and San Luis Potosí (see page 574). Along the Saltillo-Matehuala section the scenery is worthwhile, as the road winds its way up and down through wooded valleys. The final section to Matehuala passes through undulating scrub country.

There are three Pemex stations between Saltillo and Matehuala, the most northerly one being also a police checkpoint for traffic heading north. Between Matehuala and San Luis Potosí there are frequent Pemex stations. The *vía libre* from Saltillo to San Luis Potosí is good all the way; the turn-off to the *cuota* road is well signposted.

Matehuala is an important road junction. *Fiesta*, 6-20 January.

Sleeping **A** *Motel Trailerpark Las Palmas*, on the north edge of town (Km 617), T20001. Clean, English spoken and paperbacks sold, bowling alley and miniature golf, tours to Real de Catorce (see page 580) arranged. *El Dorado* nearby, T20174. Cheaper. Recommended. *E Alamo*, Guerrero 116, T20017. Hot showers, clean and very pleasant rooms, safe motorcycle parking, friendly. Recommended. *Restaurant La Fontella* in the centre, good regional food.

Transport

Buses To **Real de Catorce**, US$2. **San Luis Potosí**, with Estrella Blanca, 2½ hrs, **Transport** US$6.25. **Mexico City**, US$22, **Monterrey** and **Querétaro**.

From Matehuala you go via the Colonial Heartland route to Mexico City (see chapter 11).

Monterrey

Capital of Nuevo León state and third largest city in Mexico, Monterrey is 253 km south of the border and 915 km from Mexico City. The city is dominated by the Cerro de la Silla (saddle) from the east and the Cerro de las Mitras in the west. It is an important cultural centre in Mexico and there are many fine museums to visit.

Phone code: 8
Colour map 2, grid C5
Population: 3,000,000
Altitude: 538m

Monterrey's population is still growing in spite of its unattractive climate: too hot in summer, too cold in winter, dusty at most times and a shortage of water. Evenings are cool. It now turns out (using cheap gas from near the Texas border and increasingly from the new gas fields in the south) over 75 percent of Mexico's iron and steel, and many other products accompanied by an almost permanent industrial smog. Its streets are congested, its layout seems unplanned and its architecture uninspiring except in the centre which has undergone renewal and remodelling in recent years. The centre lies just north of the Río Santa Catarina. Plaza Zaragoza, Plaza 5 de Mayo, the Explanada de los Héroes and Parque Hundido link with the Gran Plaza to the south to form the **Macro Plaza**, claimed to be the biggest civic square in the world. It runs north-south and is nine blocks long by two blocks wide; its centrepiece is the **Faro de Comercio** (Commerce Beacon). To the east of the Faro is the 18th-century **Cathedral**, badly damaged in the war against the USA in 1846-47, when it was used by Mexican troops as a powder magazine. Running along the west side of the northern part of the Plaza are the Torre Latina, High Court and State Congress; opposite, on the east side are the Biblioteca and the Teatro de La Ciudad, all modern buildings. The Plaza is bordered at its southern end by the **Palacio Municipal**, and at its northern limit is the **Palacio de Gobierno** looking over the Explanada de los Héroes. (There is a clean public convenience beneath the Plaza, on Matamoros between Avenidas Zua Zua and Zaragoza, near the Neptune Fountain.) The older area to the east of the Cathedral is known as the **Barrio Antiguo**.

The city now has a modern and efficient metro system

Ins and outs

Aeropuerto Internacional General Mariano Escobedo (MTY), 24 km from city centre, has flights to cities all over Mexico as well as to the USA, Canada and Cuba. A taxi from the airport to the city centre costs US$8-10. The vast, long-distance bus terminal is north of the city centre on Avenida Colón (Metro Cuauhtémoc). Several major routes converge at Monterrey, connecting the industrial city to the rest of Mexico and to Nuevo Laredo, Reynosa and Matamoros on the US border.

Getting there & away

The Monterrey metro system now has two intersecting lines which run north-south and east-west of the city. Urban buses run to all areas within the city; ask at the tourist office for a bus map (for more details, see **Transport** page 549).

Getting around

The **State Tourist Office** is in the Edificio Kalos, west of the Palacio Municipal, Zaragoza 1300 Sur, Level A-1 T3401080/3444343. Large city maps are available free of charge. An easier to find office is at Padre Mier y Dr Coss on the east side of the Plaza. ■ *Tue-Sun 1000-1700, sometimes closes at lunchtime.* **Official Tourism Service**

(*Osetur*) run tours around the city and Nuevo León, T3471614/3471533. Large city maps available, free. Office by an airport on the highway from Nuevo Laredo, helpful.

Sights

Museums Calle Morelos is a pedestrian-only shopping centre. Its famous **Instituto Tecnológico**, Avenida Garza Sada 2501, has valuable collections of books on 16th-century Mexican history, of rare books printed in Indian tongues, and 2,000 editions of *Don Quixote* in all languages. The new **Museo de la Historia Mexicana** (Mexican History Museum), Dr Coss 445 Sur, off the north end of the Plaza, T3424820, is an excellent interactive museum, good for children. ■ *1100-1900, closed Mon, free Tue.*

Beer, in small bottles, is handed out free in the gardens

The **Museo de Monterrey** is in the grounds of the Cuauhtémoc Brewery, Avenida Alfonso Reyes 2202 Norte (500m north of Metro Central), T3286060. ■ *Tue-Sun 1100-2000, Wed 1000-2000. Visits to brewery Mon-Fri 0930-1530, Sat 0930-1300.* The **Mexican Baseball Hall of Fame** is in part of the museum, as is a **Museum of Modern Art** (temporary shows). ■ *T3285746. Tue-Fri 0930-1700, Sat-Sun 1030-1800.*

Museo de Arte Contemporáneo (MARCO), Zua Zua y PR Jardon, T3424820, is one of the best modern art galleries in Mexico; it holds temporary

Monterrey metro system & main streets

Northeastern Mexico

Related map
A Monterrey centre,
page 594

shows and has a good bookshop. ■ *Wed and Sun 1100-2100, other days 1100-1900, closed Mon. US$2, free Wed.* Two other art galleries with temporary shows are the **Pinacoteca de Nuevo León**, Parque Niños Héroes, T3315462, ■ *Tue-Sun 1000-1800,* and **Centro Cultural de Arte**, Belisario Domínguez 2140 Pte, Col Obispado, T3471128, ■ *Mon-Fri 0900-1300, 1500-1800.*

Museo de Cristal (Museum of Glass), Zaragoza y Magallanes (Metro del Golfo), T3291000 Ext 1219. ■ *0900-1300, 1500-1800, closed Thu.*

Museo de las Culturas Populares, Abasolo 1024, Barrio Antiguo, T3456504. ■ *Tue-Sun 1000-1800.* Also in the centre is the **Museo Metropolitano de Monterrey** in the old Municipal Palace building, Zaragoza s/n between Corregidora and Hidalgo, T3441971. ■ *Mon-Sun 0800-2000.*

The **Centro Cultural Alfa**, in the Garza García suburb, T3565696, has a fine planetarium and an astronomy and physics section with do-it-yourself illustrations of mechanical principles, etc. In a separate building is a Rufino Tamayo stained-glass window. ■ *Tue-Fri 1500-2100, Sat 1400-2100, Sun 1200-2100, closed Mon.* The centre is reached by special bus from the west end of the Alameda, hourly on the hour 1500-2000. Another museum in this locality, with exhibits on the state of Nuevo León, is the **Museo del Centenario**, Libertad 116, esq Morelos San Pedro, Garza García, T3383075. ■ *Mon-Sun 0900-2000.*

The **Alameda Gardens**, between Avenidas Aramberri and Washington, on Avenida Pino Suárez, are a pleasant place to sit. ■ *1000-1700, closed Tue.*

About 2 km west of the centre the **Cerro del Obispado** affords good views, smog permitting. The **Obispado**, former bishops' palace, (1787) is a regional museum. ■ *Sun 1000-1700, Tue-Sat 1000-1300, 1500-1800.* It served as HQ for both Pancho Villa and General Zachary Taylor. Take No 1 bus which stops at the foot of the hill.

Zoo Parque La Pastora, Av Eloy Cavazos, east of centre.

Excursions

In the hills around Monterry is the bathing resort of **Topo Chico**, 6½ km to the northwest; water from its hot springs is bottled and sold throughout Mexico. Reached by a road heading south (extension of Avenia Gómez Morín), is **Chipinque**, an ecological park in the Sierra Madre, with magnificent views of the Monterrey area. It is popular for hiking, mountain biking and climbing, with peaks reaching 2,200m.

López Mateos

Bernardo Reyes

Av Félix Galván

Av Las Américas

Av Ruiz Cortines

To Airport

Av Miguel Alemán

ga

Av Benito Juárez

Palacio Federal

Lerdo de Tejada

Exposición

hapultepec

West of Monterrey, off the Saltillo road, are the **Grutas de García** (about 10 km from Villa García, which is 40 km from Monterrey). The entrance to the caves is 800m up, by cable car, and inside are beautiful stalagmites and stalactites. At the foot of the cable car are a pool and recreational centre. A tour of the caves takes 1½ hours, and it is compulsory to go in a group with a guide. You can take a bus to Villa García, but it is a dusty walk to the caves. On Sunday Transportes Saltillo-Monterrey run a bus to the caves at 0900, 1000 and 1100. Otherwise, take an agency tour, for example *Osetur* (details from *Infotur*); book at *Hotel Ancira*. ■ *Tue, US$3.50*.

Hidalgo is a small town 38 km northwest of Monterrey on the Monclova road (Route 53). Dominating the area are the massive limestone cliffs of **Potrero Chico** (four km west of town, take road leading on from Calle Francisco Villa). There is a noisy recreational park at the foot of the cliffs with *balneario* and restaurants. Passing through the short canyon between 610-m cliffs you come to a peaceful enclosed valley with excellent walking. The cliffs are a magnet for big-wall climbers, particularly during the US winter, and have some of the hardest pitches in the world (up to 5.12d), including the 650-m long *Sendero Luminoso* route on the central pillar of *El Toro*. A sheet guide by Jeff Jackson describing 80 of the best climbs and places to camp is available at the store on the left before you reach the *balneario*. Accommodation **F** at *rancho*. Autobuses Mina leave at hourly intervals from Monterrey bus station to Hidalgo (bus station on plaza).

Another excellent rock-climbing area is at the **Cañón de la Huasteca**, near Santa Catarina, 20 km west of Monterrey along Route 40. The canyon is in the northern part of the Cumbres de Monterrey National Park, where there are prehistoric glyphs.

Monterrey centre

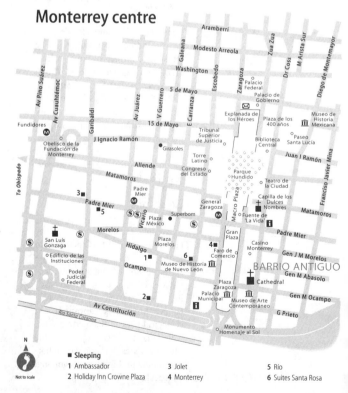

■ Sleeping

1 Ambassador	3 Jolet	5 Río
2 Holiday Inn Crowne Plaza	4 Monterrey	6 Suites Santa Rosa

Northeastern Mexico

Essentials

There are many new hotels in the luxury category in the centre and on radial routes coming into the city (not all listed). Most of the cheap hotels are situated in the area around the bus station (Metros Central and Cuauhtémoc).

Sleeping
■ *on map, page 594*
Price codes: see inside front cover.

L *Crowne Plaza*, Av Constitución 300 Ote, near Plaza Zaragoza, T3196005. Best. **L** *Holiday Inn*, Av Alfonso Reyes 101 Norte, T3766555, also at Av Eugenio Garza Sada 3680 Sur, T3296000, and at Av San Jerónimo 1082, T3896020. **L** *Monterrey*, Morelos 574 Ote, T3454988. **A** *Ambassador*, Hidalgo 310 Ote y Galeana, T3406390. **A** *Jolet*, Padre Mier 201 Pte, T3405505. **A** *Río*, Padre Mier 194 Pte, T3432090. **A** *Royal Courts* (Best Western), Av Alfonso Reyes 314, T3762292. **A** *Suites Santa Rosa*, Escobedo 930 Sur, T3424200.

It is difficult to obtain accommodation because of the constant movement of people travelling north/south

C *Yamallel*, Zaragoza 912, Norte Madero, T753400. Good. **D** *Del Norte*, Juan Méndez y Democracia 260 Pte (north of Av Colón, near bus station) T3752140. TV, a/c. **D** *Posada*, Amado Nervo 1138 Norte, T3722467. With bath, clean. Recommended. Further down same street at Juan Méndez 1518 Norte y Aquiles Serdán is **D** *Monterrey La Silla*, T/F3727579. TV, and opposite at 1515, **B** *La Silla*, its sister hotel. Clean, friendly. Recommended. **D** *Victoria*, Bernardo Reyes 1205 Norte. With bath, parking, a bit noisy. **E** *Estación*, Guadalupe Victoria Pte 1450, T3750755, opposite train station. With bath, a/c. **E** *Nuevo León*, Amado Nervo 1007 Norte by Av Madero. With bath (hot water), dark, seedy, poor value, close to bus station. Many hotels between Colón and Reforma, 2 blocks from the bus station, nothing below US$15.

Motels A *El Paso Autel*, Zaragoza y Martínez. **D** *Motel/Trailerpark Nueva Castilla*, on Highway 85 before Saltillo bypass. 12 spaces for RVs with hook-up, pool, hot showers, reasonable restaurant, clean but drab, US$17 for vehicle and 2 people; several on Nuevo Laredo highway.

Youth hostel Av Madero Ote s/n, Parque Fundidora, CP64000.

There are over 20 eating places around the Zona Rosa and Plaza Zaragoza in the heart of town.

Eating

Vegetarian *Los Girasoles*, Juan Ignacio Ramón 200 Ote (esq Guerrero, 1 block from Juárez). Possibly the best, good value. *Superbom*, Padre Mier. Upstairs, good menú.

Adventure sports: *Asociación de Excursionismo y Montañismo*, Washington Pte 2222-B, Col María Luisa, T3271929 or 3562715 (for Sr Angel Medina). **Baseball**: *Estadio de Baseball Monterrey*, Parque Niños Héroes, T3518022. **Bullfighting**: *Plaza de Toros*, M Barragán y Alfonso Reyes, north of bus station, T3740505. **Football**: *Estadio Tecnológico*, off Av Garza Sada, southeast of centre, T358200; *Estadio Universitario*, Parque Niños Héroes, north of centre, T3762238.

Sports

Local There are 2 **metro** lines and extensions planned. The blue line, the longer, runs south from the suburb of San Bernabé and then makes a right-angle turn traversing the city eastwards passing by the bus and train stations. It connects with the green line (at Cuauhtémoc near the bus station) which runs south into the centre. Tickets bought from machines (2 pesos a ticket, less for more than 1). **Car rental** *Monterrey*, Serafín Peña 740-A Sur, T3446510. *National*, Escobedo Sur 1011 Local 8, T3446363.

Transport

Air Gen Mariano Escobedo airport (MTY), 24 km from centre. Daily flights from Mexico City take 1 hr 20 mins. Many flights to USA (Atlanta, Charlotte, Chicago, Dallas, Dayton, Houston, Huntsville, Las Vegas, Los Angeles, Pensacola, San Antonio), to Havana, Cuba, Toronto, Canada and Mexican cities: Acapulco, Aguascalientes, Cancún, Chihuahua, Ciudad Juárez, Cuernavaca, Culiacán, Durango, Guadalajara,

Hermosillo, La Paz, León, Los Cabos, Mazatlán, Mérida, Monclova, Morelia, Piedras Negras, Puebla, Puerto Vallarta, Querétaro, Saltillo, San Luis Potosí, Tampico, Tijuana Torreón, Veracruz and Villahermosa.

Trains Station on Miguel Nieto Norte (Metro Central) T3510532. Check locally to see if any trains are running.

Buses Terminal on Av Colón, between Calzada B Reyes and Av Pino Suárez (Metro Cuauhtémoc), T3183737. Monterrey-**Mexico City**, US$36, 12½ hrs. A more scenic trip is from Mexico City (northern bus terminal) to **Ciudad Valles**, 10 hrs, from where there are many connecting buses to Monterrey. To **San Luis Potosí**, US$18. To **Nuevo Laredo** departures every hour, 4 hrs, US$12. To **Matamoros**, Transportes del Norte, 4 hrs, US$12. To **Chihuahua** with Transportes del Norte, 8 a day, 12 hrs, US$33. Frequent buses to **Saltillo**, but long queues for tickets. To **Guadalajara**, US$38. To **Tampico**, US$18, 7-8 hrs. To **Torreón**, US$14. To Santiago for Cola de Caballo falls, US$1.65.

NB Motorists if driving Monterrey- Saltillo, there is nothing to indicate you are on the toll-road until it is too late. The toll is US$7. Look for the old road.

Directory **Airline offices** *AeroMéxico*, T435560. *American Airlines*, T403031. *Aviacsa*, T364400. *Mexicana*, T800-7150220. *Taesa*, T597775. *Continental*, T95-800-5379222. **Banks** If stuck without pesos on Sun, the red hotel/restaurant just opposite the bus station changes TCs if you buy something in the restaurant. **Communications** Post Office: *Palacio Federal*, Av 5 de Mayo y Zaragoza (behind Government Palace), T3424003. **Embassies & consulates** *British* (Honorary) Mr Edward Lawrence, Privada de Tamazunchale 104, Colonia del Valle, Garza García, T3337598. *Canadian*, jurisdiction: Nuevo Léon, Coahuila, Tamaulipas. Trade officer and consul: Mr Thomas G Cullen, T3443200/F3443048. Office hours: Mon-Fri 0900-1330 and 1430-1730. Address: Edificio Kalos, Piso C-1, 1300 Sur y Constitución, 64000 Monterrey, NL. *US*, T3452120. *German*, T3385223. *French*, T3364498. *Guatemalan*, T3728648. *Netherlands*, T3425055. *Israeli*, T3361325. *Swedish*, T3463090. *Swiss*, T3383675. **Medical services** *Hospital General de IMSS*, Pino Suárez y J Ramón, T3455355. *Angeles Verdes*, T3402113. **Red Cross**: T3751212.

Monterrey to Ciudad Victoria

Heading south from Monterrey, the road threads through the narrow and lovely Huajuco canyon; from Santiago village a road runs to within 2 km of the Cola de Caballo, or Horsetail Falls, in the **Cumbres de Monterrey** national park, the largest in Mexico. There is a first-class hotel on the way, and you can get a *colectivo*, US$1.65, from the bus stop to the falls, and a horse, US$1.65, to take you to the top of the falls. ■ *US$2.40; cost of guide US$5.* Deeper into the park are other waterfalls, the 75-m Cascada El Chipitín and Cascada Lagunillas. There is a two-day circuit, *Recorrido de Matacanes*, starting at Las Adjuntas, taking in both these falls and involving river canyoning, abseiling and swimming through tunnels. Ask at Asociación de Excursionismo y Montañismo in Monterrey (see above). The road drops gradually into lower and warmer regions, passing through a succession of subtropical valleys with orange groves, banana plantations and vegetable gardens.

At **Montemorelos**, just off the highway, 79 km south of Monterrey, a branch road from the Matamoros-Monterrey highway comes in. Another 53 km takes you to **Linares** (*Population:* 100,000), a fast-expanding town. **B** *Escondido Court*, 1½ km north of Linares on Route 855. Motel, clean, a/c, pool and restaurant. Recommended. **B** *Hotel Guidi*, near the plaza. Buses from Linares to San Luis Potosí, US$16.

A most picturesque 96-km highway runs west from Linares up the lovely Santa Rosa canyon, up and over the Sierra Madre. After Iturbide, turn south on top of the Sierra Madre and continue on a good road through the unspoilt Sierra via La Escondida and Dr Arroyo. Alternatively, stay on the main road for San Roberto, north of Matehuala (see page 590) and join the Highway 57 route from Eagle Pass to Mexico City.

Ciudad Victoria

Capital of Tamaulipas state, at Km 706, is this quiet, clean, unhurried city with a shaded plaza. Here Route 85 from Monterrey and Route 101 from Matamoros meet. It is often used as a stopover.

The **Parque Siglo 21** is the same end of town as the bus station. The centrepiece is a planetarium which looks like a huge red ball that landed on the banks of the Río San Marcos. There is a good view of the sierra from behind the planetarium where there is a large Rosa de los Vientos. Across the river is the Government Plaza, a 12-storey glass tower, the tallest thing in town. Also worth seeing is the state library in a green, tiled, Aztec-style building. The **Centro Cultural Tamaulipas**, Calle 15 and Hidalgo, opposite the Palacio de Gobierno, is a functional, modern building with a library, theatre, art gallery and various cultural functions. The **Museo de Antropología e Historia**, on the plaza, has a good section on the Huastec culture. On top of a hill is a tiny church, the temple of Nuestra Señora de Guadalupe, the patron saint of Mexico. The **tourist office** is on Calle 16 y Rosales near Parque Alameda.

Phone code: 131
Colour map 2, grid C5
Population: 300,000
Altitude: 336 m
The north-south streets (parallel to the Sierra) have names and numbers, the east-west streets have only names

Excursions

Tamatán, a suburb southwest of the centre (plenty of *colectivos*), has a large park with a zoo and a small lake, popular with Mexicans at leisure. Take a *colectivo* to Ejido Libertad for the **Parque Ecológico Los Troncones**, where you can walk along the river and in the hills; there are good swimming holes.

Northeast of Ciudad Victoria is Nueva Ciudad Padilla; nearby is Viejo Padilla, where 'Emperor' Agustín de Iturbide was shot in 1824. Also nearby is Presa Vicente Guerrero, a large lake with good fishing and many tourist facilities.

East of Ciudad Victoria sits the quiet town of **Soto La Marina**, with several places to stay including the new **D** *Hotel María Cristina*, which is good if you want to avoid the large city of Ciudad Victoria. Southwest of Ciudad Victoria, 20 km along Route 101 (towards Jaumave) is a sign to the Zona Arqueológica **El Balcón de Moctezuma**. The site consists of circular buildings and staircases, showing Huastec influence. It is similar to Chicomostoc, La Quemada and Casas Grandes and was a commercial centre in contact with tribes in present-day USA. Ask for the guide Don Gabino, who took part in the excavations completed in June 1990. From the signpost to the Zona Arqueológica it's a 4-km walk, then 100m uphill (a high clearance vehicle can get within 100m and you can park at Altas Cumbres near the site).

Sleeping

A *Santorín* (Best Western), Cristóbal Colón Norte 349, T128938, F128342. A/c, TV, parking, restaurant. **B** *Sierra Gorda*, Hidalgo 990 Ote, T32280. Garage US$0.70 a night. Several **E** hotels by bus station and in the centre. **Motels B** *Panorámica*, Lomas del Santuario, T25506. **D** *Los Monteros*, Plaza Hidalgo, T20300. Downtown. **Trailer Park** *Victoria RV Trailer Park*, Libramiento 101-85, T/F24824. Follow signs, good service, electricity, hot showers; owner (Rosie) has travel information, US$10 for 2 plus vehicle.

Eating

Chavos, Calle 12, Hidalgo y Juárez. All you can eat buffet. *Daddy's* on the plaza. A sort of *Denny's*, with a Mexican touch for the homesick American. Locals congregate at *Café Cantón*, half a block from the plaza on Calle 9.

Transport **Train** Check locally whether rail services are available. **Buses** Terminal is on the outskirts near the ring road northeast of the town centre. Omnibuses Blancos to **Ciudad Valles** (see below) for US$8.50. Bus to **Mexico City** 10 hours, US$26.65.

Ciudad Mante

Phone code: 123
Colour map 3, grid A5

After crossing the Tropic of Cancer the road enters the solid green jungle of the tropical lowlands. 137 km south of Ciudad Victoria is Ciudad Mante (Route 85), which is almost exactly the mid-way point between Matamoros and Mexico City and makes a convenient stopover place. The city is, however, dirty. It has a **Museo de Antropología e Historia**, with objects from the Huastec culture.

Excursions Forty-five kilometres north of Ciudad Mante is the village of **Gómez Farías**, an important centre for ornithological research: the highlands above the village represent the northernmost extent of several tropical vegetation formations. Many tropical bird species reach the northern limit of their range. Gómez Farias is reached by turning west off the main highway, 14 km over a paved road to the town plaza. From there, an easy 2 km walk provides excellent views of bird habitats. A one-hour drive from Ciudad Mante, plus a five-hour walk, leads to **El Cielo Biosphere Reserve** which has four different ecosystems

Ciudad Victoria

at various altitudes, including tropical jungle and cloud forest (about 200m to 2,500m). In the reserve is Canindo Research Station.

South of Ciudad Mante, at Km 548 from Mexico City, is Antiguo Morelos where a road turns off west to San Luis Potosí (see page 574) 314 km, and Guadalajara (see page 482).

Best hotel is probably the **B** *Mante*, Guerrero 500 Norte, T20990. Shaded grounds at north edge of business sector. **D** *Monterrey*, Av Juárez 503 Ote, T21512, in old sector. With bath, hot water, a/c, cable TV, helpful manager speaks English, safe parking, new annex at back, restaurant not so good. Recommended. Several hotels a few blocks south of Zócalo. **Sleeping**

Tampico

Monterrey trains run via Ciudad Victoria to the port of Tampico, on the Gulf of Mexico, definitely not a tourist attraction, reached by a fine road from Ciudad Mante, in a rich sugar-growing area. Tampico was founded in 1522 by Gonzalo de Sandoval but was sacked by pirates in the 17th century and refounded in 1823. It has the faded grandeur of a once prosperous river port and is situated on the northern bank of the Río Pánuco, not far from a large oilfield; there are storage tanks and refineries for miles along the southern bank.

Phone code: 12
Colour map 2, grid A6
Population: 560,000

Fishing (both sea and river) is excellent

To Victoria RV Trailer Park,
Matamoros & Monterrey

Cemetery

Government Tower
& Civic Centre

Legislative Palace, Library &
State Attorney General's Office

To Aiiport & Soto La Marina

To Tampico

The summer heat, rarely above 35°C, is tempered by sea breezes, but June and July are trying. Cold northerlies blow now and again during the winter. There are two pleasant plazas, Plaza de Armas at Colón y Carranza, with squirrels in the trees, and Plaza de la Libertad at Madero y Juárez. There are two interesting buildings on the Plaza de Armas: the **Catedral Santa Iglesia** has an international flavour: a clock from England, an altar from Carrara in Italy and *swastikas* inlaid into the aisle floor. The former **Palacio Municipal** on the northwest corner (now DIF building) is an art nouveau construction. There is a huge, interesting market, but watch your possessions carefully. The **tourist office**, 20 de Noviembre 218, is helpful.

The **Playa de Miramar**, a beach resort, is a tram or bus ride from the city, but is reported dirty. If walking there, go along the breakwater (Escollera Norte) on north side of Río Pánuco, for views of the shipping and to see the monument to Mexican merchant seamen killed in the Second World War. **Laguna del Carpintero**, just north of the centre, is popular for watersports. **Excursions**

Northeastern Mexico

The **Museo de la Cultura Huasteca** in **Ciudad Madero**, an adjacent town, is worth visiting (Instituto Tecnológico, Avenida 1° de Mayo y Sor Juana Inés de la Cruz); take a *colectivo*, 'Madero', from the centre of Tampico to the Zócalo in Ciudad Madero, then another to the Instituto; small but select collection. ■ *1000-1500, except Mon.* Ciudad Madero claims to be Mexico's petroleum capital, with a huge oil refinery.

Sleeping   **AL** *Camino Real*, Av Hidalgo 2000, T38811. **AL** *Impala*, Díaz Mirón 220 Pte, T20990. **AL** *Inglaterra*, Díaz Mirón y Olmos, T92857. **AL** *Mansión Real*, T91515, Colón 104 (near Plaza de Armas). Modern. **B** *Imperial*, López de Lara Sur 201, T25678. With shower, clean, fan, but noisy. **B** *Nuevo León*, Aduana N 107, T24370. With a/c, shower, clean. **B** *Tampico*, Carranza 513, T90057. **C** *Ritz*, on Miramar beach (see above). Deserted at night.

Several cheap hotels near Plaza de la Libertad: **E** *América*, T23478, near market on Olmos. Dirty but safe and friendly. **E** *Hawaii*, Héroes del Cañonero 609 (2 blocks east of Plaza Libertad), T41887. Dark rooms, clean. There are others on this street. **E** *Rex*. Dirty, no hot water. All hotels downtown near market should be treated with discretion; many have a rapid turnover. RVs can stay in the parking lot of the airport, which has public conveniences, US$15 per vehicle, noisy from traffic.

Eating   *Emir*, Olmos between Díaz Mirón and Madero. Good for breakfast. *El Selecto*, opposite market. There are many cheap restaurants in the *Centro Gastronómico Mercado de Comida* east of the market.

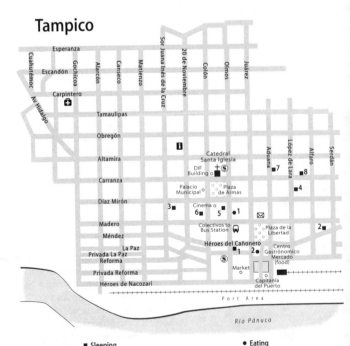

Tampico

■ Sleeping
1 América
2 Hawaii
3 Impala
4 Imperial
5 Inglaterra
6 Mansión Real
7 Nuevo León
8 Tampico

● Eating
1 Emir
2 Selecto

Not to scale

Apr to Aug is the **Deep Sea Fishing** competition season. The main competitions are the *Torneo Internacional de Robalo (bass)* (Apr); *Torneo Internacional de Marlín* (Jun) and *Torneo Internacional del Sábalo (shad)* (Jul and Aug). **Sports**

(Re-)Founders day, beginning of **Apr**. **Festivals**

Air The Francisco Javier Mina Airport (TAM), T280571/72 is 8 km from the centre. Mexicana has daily flights to Mexico City and Aerolitoral flies to San Antonio (Texas), Ciudad del Carmen, Monclova, Monterrey, Piedras Negras, Poza Rica, San Luis Potosí, Torreón, Veracruz and Villahermosa. Aero California flies to Los Angeles via Mexico City, Tepic and Tijuana. Continental Express flies to Dallas and Houston. **Transport**

Train Train station is beside Capitanía del Puerto. Trains Tue, Thu, Sat to Ciudad Victoria 0750, arrives 1240, returns 1440, arrives 1930. However passenger services are being cut so always check before making plans.

Bus Bus station is several km from the centre on Av Ejército Mexicano on the far side of Laguna del Carpintero. *Colectivos* to bus station leave from Olmos between market and plaza. To **Monterrey**, US$19.50, 7-8 hrs; to **Ciudad Valles**, US$5.70; to **Mexico City**, US$18, 9 hrs; to **San Luis Potosí**, US$16, 7 hrs.

Airline offices *Aero California*, T138400. *AeroMéxico*, T170939. *Mexicana*, T139600. **Communications Post Office:** on Madero 309 Ote, T121927. **Embassies & consulates** *German Consul*, 2 de Enero, 102 Sur-A, Hon Consul Dieter Schulze. Postal Address: Apdo 775, T129784/129817. Also deals with British affairs. **Medical services** Red Cross: T21313. **Directory**

A 145-km paved road west from Tampico through the oil camp of **Ebano** joins the Nuevo Laredo-Mexico City highway further south at Ciudad Valles. There are direct buses to Brownsville (Texas). South of Tampico a splendid new bridge was opened in 1988 to replace the ferry to **Villa Cuauhtémoc**. Further south, the coast road, Route 180, enters Veracruz state, leading to Tuxpan, Poza Rica and Veracruz (see Chapter 5). **Routes**

Tampico to the Colonial Heartland

Ciudad Valles, on a winding river is a popular stopover with many hotels. **Museo Regional Huasteco**, Rotarios y Artes (or Peñaloza), is the centre of archaeological and ethnographic research for the Huastec region. ■ *1000-1200, 1400-1800, Mon-Fri*. Visit the market, which is very busy. There are many cheap places to eat *tacos*. **Ciudad Valles**
Phone code: 138
Colour map 4, grid A5
Population: 320,000
Km 476

A *Valles*, T20050, with trailer park. Full hook-up, hot shower, a bit run down, US$10 for 2 in car, on Carretera México-Laredo. **B** *San Fernando*, T20184, on main highway. Clean, large rooms, a/c, TV, parking. **D** *Condesa*, Av Juárez 109, T20015. Clean, basic, fan, friendly, OK. 11 km south of town is campground *El Bañito*. With warm sulphur pools, good restaurant, a bit run down. **Sleeping**

Buses Omnibus Ote to San Luis Potosí for US$7 (4 hrs); Mexico City 10 hrs. **Transport**

With riotous tropical vegetation, Tamazunchale is perhaps the most popular of all the overnight stops on this route. (**B** *Mirador*, good, but passing traffic by night is noisy. **E** *Hotel OK*, cheapest but not recommended.) The potholed road south of here begins a spectacular climb to the highland, winding over the rugged terrain cut by the Río Moctezuma and its tributaries. The highest point on the road is 2,502m. From **Jacala**, Km 279 (two very basic hotels, erratic **Tamazunchale**
Phone code: 136
Colour map 4, grid B6
Population: 150,000
Altitude: 206m
Km 370

Northeastern Mexico

water supply), there is a dizzying view into a chasm. **Zimapán** (*Posada del Rey*, fascinating but very run down, out on the highway), with a charming market place and a small old church in the plaza, is as good a place as any to stay the night. From **Portezuelo** (Km 178 from Mexico City) a paved road runs west to Querétaro (see page 538), 140 km.

Ixmiquilpan
Phone code: 772
Colour map 4, grid B5

An area of 23,300 sq km north and south of Ixmiquilpan (Km 169 from Mexico City), just off the highway, is inhabited by 65,000 Otomí Indians. The beautifully worked Otomí belts and bags may sometimes be bought at the Monday market, and also in the *artesanía* shop in the main street almost opposite the government aid offices.

See early Indian frescoes in the main church, which is one of the 16th-century battlemented Augustinian monastery-churches; the monastery is open to the public. At sunset each day white egrets come to roost in the trees outside the church; it's worth going up on to the battlements to see them swoop down. The church of El Carmen is worth a visit too; it has a lovely west façade and gilded altars inside. There is also a 16th-century bridge over the river and a beautiful walk along the *ahuehuete*-lined banks.

Excursions

Near Ixmiquilpan are several warm swimming pools, both natural and man-made: San Antonio, Dios Padre, Las Humedades, Tzindejé (about 20 minutes from town) and near Tephé (the only warm-water bath, clean. ■ *US$0.40*). The Otomí villages of La Lagunita, La Pechuga and La Bonanza, in a beautiful valley, have no modern conveniences.

The **Barranca de Tolantongo**, 37 km northeast of Ixmiquilpan, is about 1,500m deep with a waterfall and thermal spring; at weekends there is a small eating place. ■ *US$2, car parking US$2 at entrance to recreational area; camping permitted.* To get there take the road towards El Cardonal, then an unpaved turn-off about 3 km before El Cardonal (there is a bus from Pachuca).

Sleeping

C *Hotel Diana*. Rear buildings slightly dearer rooms but much cleaner, safe parking. Recommended. **E** *Hotel/Restaurant Los Portales*, 1 block from main square. Clean, safe parking, mediocre food.

Actopan to Tula

Actopan (Km 119 from the capital) has another fine 16th-century Augustinian church, convent, and an impressive open chapel. (**B** *Hotel Rira*). From Actopan a 56-km branch road runs to one of Mexico's great archaeological sites: Tula, capital of the Toltecs (see page 145).

On the way to Tula there is an interesting co-operative village, **Cruz Azul**, where there are free Sunday-morning concerts at 1000 in front of main market. At Colonia (km 85), a road runs left for 8 km to Pachuca (see page 142). Route 85 continues to Mexico City.

The Northern Highlands

13

The Northern Highlands

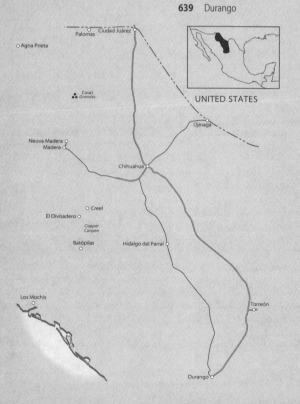

The imposing Sierra Madre highlands of northern Mexico are rarely a destination in themselves, but are usually bypassed, glimpsed at in transit, en route to destinations further south. But these vast landscapes, at times barren and monotonous, hold some of Mexico's most spectacular surprises. The most important archaeological site in Northern Mexico is just a couple of hours' drive south of the border at **Casas Grandes** *or* **Paquimé**, *a maze of multi-storeyed adobe buildings, once a thriving community with over 3,000 inhabitants. Don't expect to see too many dainty little dogs in Chihuahua; this, Mexico's biggest state, is the rugged land of Pancho Villa and there are museums and memorabilia dedicated to the Bandido-turned-Hero of the Revolution, even the bullet-ridden Dodge car he was finally gunned down in. It's dramatic stuff; and so is the* **Chihuahua-al- Pacífico**, *billed as 'the world's most scenic railroad', which wends its way across bridges, through tunnels and over the Sierra Madre down to the Pacific coast at Los Mochis. It's a journey of a lifetime. Hikers will want to stop off at Creel or Divisadero to absorb the views, discover the awe-inspiring landscapes, strange rock formations and wildlife, visit Mexico's tallest waterfall and penetrate the vertiginous depths of the Barranca del Cobre, the* **Copper Canyon**, *vaster by far that Colorado's Grand Canyon. This is the craggy land of the Tarahumara Indians, some 60,000 of them live in the Sierra and you can buy their hand-carved and woven crafts in any of the towns or villages. And if you're still looking for action, why not try some of the Wild-West kind and walk the streets of real Western film sets in the state of Durango.*

The Northern Highlands

Crossing into Mexico: Ciudad Juárez

El Paso/
Ciudad Juárez

From El Paso you can get on a bus outside Gate 9 of the Greyhound terminal and pay the driver (US$5); as you cross the border he should stop and wait for your documents to be processed. On entry you are automatically given 30 days to stay in Mexico, unless you ask for longer. Trolley buses cross the border for short trips. Alternatively you can walk across (US$0.35 toll per person). Walking from Mexico to the USA costs US$0.55 (toll for cars leaving Mexico US$2.05). Border formalities are minimal, although you are likely to have your bags searched on entering the USA on foot because most pedestrians do not carry luggage. If you cross into the USA as a non-US citizen and with a view to leaving the USA by plane, you must ask for an immigration card for when you do leave; you may have problems without one. Remember, also, to have your US visa if you require one. The US Embassy charges US$20 to make an enquiry.

There is a new border crossing at Santa Teresa, New Mexico, just west of El Paso. For trucks and southbound travellers by car, this will avoid the congestion of Ciudad Juárez.

Ciudad Juárez

Phone code: 16
Colour map 2, grid A1
Population: 1,100,000
Altitude: 1,150m

Crossing the border from El Paso, Texas you'll reach Ciudad Juárez, 1,866 km from Mexico City. Ciudad Juárez, and El Paso have over 1.1 million people each; the cross-border industry has made Ciudad Juárez the largest *maquiladora* city in the world. Twin plant assembly and manufacturing operations now supersede tourism and agriculture in the city. **NB** El Paso is on Mountain Standard Time, which is one hour behind Central Standard Time and General Mexican Time.

Ciudad Juárez / El Paso

Related map:
A Ciudad
Juárez detail,
page 609

Juan Gabriel

It would be a pity to have time to kill in Ciudad Juárez and not visit the houses and orphanage owned by Juan Gabriel. If you're interested in Mexican music it's worth the trip. He has written many songs that are known all over Latin America. Most of his youth was spent in Ciudad Juárez, having moved here when he was under a year old (he was born in the state of Michoacán). In the 1970's he wrote songs such as No Vale La Pena, Hasta Que Te Conocí, *and* Yo No Nací Para Amar. *Apparently he started off singing on buses, something you can still do in Mexico but that's prohibited in the US.*

One of the houses is on Avenida Lerdo near the centre. It's a very pretty colonial house that was once owned by a prominent politician. His other house, at the corner of 16 de Septiembre and Colombia, is a huge place with grounds taking up an entire block. According to one taxi driver, this is the house he grew up in when his mother was a servant for the owners. Later, when he made money, he bought it for his mother, a story that endears him to his fans.

The orphanage is near the centre and takes up a city block. It houses around 110 children. They're taught music (many of them have gone on to perform) and they have a doctor there to take care of them. There is also a main avenue named after him that he paid for called Eje Juan Gabriel. It runs about four miles.

The Spanish conquistador Cabeza de Vaca discovered the Paso del Norte (Northern Pass) on the Camino Real. The name was retained until 1888 when Porfirio Díaz renamed the city after Benito Juárez. Today four bridges link the two cities: Santa Fe, for pedestrians and cars leaving Mexico; Stanton Street, for pedestrians and cars leaving USA; Córdova bridge (two-way traffic); and the new Zaragoza toll bridge to the east. The Río Bravo/Grande, which divides the two cities and forms the border, has been canalized and is used for irrigation upstream, so often it has little or no water.

The **tourist office** is on the ground floor of the Presidencia Municipal (City Hall), Malecón y Francisco Villa, on the left as you cross the Sante Fe bridge, T152301/140837.

Sights

In Ciudad Juárez, the **Nuestra Señora de Guadalupe de El Paso del Norte** mission was the first established in the region; the building was completed in 1668. The mission, and the nearby **Cathedral**, are two blocks west of Avenida Juárez on 16 de Septiembre. At the junction of Avenida Juárez and 16 de Septiembre is the Aduana, the former customs building, now the **Museo Histórico**. In Parque Chamizal, just across the Córdova bridge, are the **Museo de Arte Prehispánico**, with exhibits from each Mexican state, the **Botanic Gardens** and a memorial to Benito Juárez. Continuing south down Avenida Lincoln, you come to the Pronaf area with the **Museo de Arte e Historia**. The University Cultural Centre and the **Fonart** artisan centre, which acts as a Mexican 'shop window', are well worth a look for the uninitiated tourist. There are a number of markets in the city and the racetrack is very popular (with dog races in spring and summer). The **Plaza Monumental de Toros**, López Mateos y Triunfo de la República, holds bullfights between April and August, and *charreadas* (rodeos) are held at the **Lienzo Charro**, Av del Charro. The main street is Avenida Juárez, on or near which are most of the souvenir shops, hotels, cheap and expensive restaurants, clubs and bars. The bars and other nightlife cater mostly for El Paso high school students who can drink at 18 in Mexico, but not till 21 in El Paso.

Very few services are open at weekends in El Paso

The Northern Highlands

To the east of **El Paso**, over the border, the **Ysleta Mission** is the oldest in Texas (1680), built by Franciscan monks and Tigua Indians, who have a 'reservation' (more like a suburb) nearby; the Socorro mission (1681) and San Elizario Presidio (1789, rebuilt 1877-87) are in the same direction. There are a number of museums, including the **Americana Museum** in the Civic Centre (which also houses a performing arts centre, convention centre and tourist office), the **Museum of Art** at 1211 Montana, and The **Fort Bliss Air Defence Museum** of the nearby Air Base. Conducted tours of El Paso (US$10 – same price for Ciudad Juárez) usually take in Fort Bliss, the University, the Scenic Drive and the Tigua Reservation. El Paso **tourist office** is in the Civic Centre Plaza, T5340686; also at the airport.

Sleeping **AL** *Calinda Quality Inn*, Calzada Hermanos Escobar 3515, T137250. **AL** *Holiday Inn Express*, Paseo Triunfo de la República 8745, T296000, F296020. **C** *Continental*, Lerdo Sur 112 (downtown), T150084. Clean, TV, noisy, friendly, restaurant good. **C** *Impala*, Lerdo Norte 670, T91160431/0491 Clean, OK. **C** *Parador Juárez*, Miguel Ahumada 615 Sur, T159184; and many others in the upper price ranges. **C** *Santa Fé*, Av Lerdo, opposite *Hotel Impala*, about 10 blocks from the cathedral near the corner of Tlaxcala. **D** *Correo*, Lerdo Sur 250, just across 16 de Septiembre. **D** *Hotel D'Manely*, close to bus station. Go out of the west (taxi) entrance, walk straight ahead across the parking lot to the street, cross the street, and walk left about 2 blocks. Heating, private bath. **D** *Embajador*, 2 blocks from the cathedral on Av Francisco Villa. (According to one taxi driver the *Impala*, *Sante Fe* and *Embajador* are safe; other budget hotels in the centre generally aren't.) **E** *Juárez*, Lerdo Norte 143, close to Stanton St bridge. Comfortable, hot water, good value. **F** *San Luis*, Mariscal y Morelos, 1 block south of, and behind, Cathedral, cheapest but filthy and insecure.

In **El Paso** there are many places to stay, including *Westin Paso del Norte Hotel*, T5343000. Tiffany glass dome, black and pink marble lobby and European chandeliers (the most expensive). **A** *Ramada*, on Oregon, T5443300. Recommended. Also on Oregon, **B** *International Hotel*. With a/c, TV, clean. Recommended. **D** *Gardner*, 311 East Franklin Av, T5323661. Hot water, shared bath, TV and phone in room, rooms with bath available, also serves as **Youth Hostel**. The YMCA no longer rents rooms by the day, only by the month, but the receptionist recommended the **B** *Budget Lodge Motel*, 1301 N Mesa St, T915-5336821. TV and phones in rooms. They take VISA, MC, and AmEx. It is owned and run by Peter and Pamela Riley from Birmingham, UK (very friendly). There are many other motels.

Eating In Juárez, *Taco Cabaña* on Calle de la Peña, next to *Hotel Continental*, and *El Gordo No*
Many eating places *2*, Francisco Madero, ½ block from 16 de Septiembre. Both are good for *tacos* and
either side of the border *burritos* (about US$2-3). *Plaza Lerdo Café*, Lerdo Sur 285 at Galeana. Good breakfasts. *El Saucito*, Lerdo Sur 263. Popular, good breakfasts. *Florida*, Juárez 301, 2 blocks from *Hotel Impala*. Clean, good food and service. There are plenty of Chinese restaurants.

Festivals 2-5 May, *Festival de la Raza*; music, dance, cultural events. **5 May** celebrations on Av Juárez. **15 Sep**, Independence. **Jun-Jul**, *Feria Juárez* in Parque Chamizal.

Shopping Tourist market on Av 16 de Septiembre, 3 blocks past *Hotel Continental* (on opposite side) away from Juárez.

Transport **Local Taxis**: in Juárez, charge by zone, from US$2.75 to US$7.25. You can also negotiate with the driver for hourly rates. The going rate appears to be about US$20 per hour. Some cabs are allowed to cross the border and take you to downtown El Paso; this costs US$30.

Long distance Air: Ciudad Juárez's airport, Abraham González (CJS), is 19 km south of the city (T190734/164363); flights with AeroMéxico, Aerolitoral, Taesa and/or Aero California to Mexico City, Chihuahua, Ciudad Obregón, Culiacán, Durango, Guadalajara, Hermosillo, Ixtapa, León, Los Cabos, Mazatlán, Monterrey, Torreón, Tijuana and Zacatecas. **El Paso's airport (ELP)** is near Fort Bliss and Biggs Field military airbase with flights by American, Delta, America West Airlines and Southwest Airlines to all parts of the USA. There are also flights to El Paso from Chihuahua and Guadalajara. *Colectivo* from Ciudad Juárez airport to El Paso, or El Paso airport, US$15.50.

Trains: Station in Ciudad Juárez is at Eje Vial Juan Gabriel e Insurgentes, a couple of blocks south of junction of Av Juárez and 16 de Septiembre, T122557/149717 (in Mexico) or 5452247 (Amtrak in El Paso). There are currently no passenger trains between Ciudad Juárez and Mexico City and the train station in Juárez is closed.

Road: Sanborns, for insurance and information, 440 Reynolds, El Paso, T915-7793538, F7721795, open Mon-Fri 0830-1700. AAA office: 916 Mesa Av, El Paso.

Buses: Terminal is at Blvd Oscar Flores 4010, T132083, south of the centre. There is a taxi information booth which can give you estimated fares before you approach a driver. From the terminal to centre or Santa Fe bridge, taxi fare is about US$8. If you walk from the terminal to the highway, take any bus going to the right marked *centro* for US$0.30. Shuttle bus to **El Paso** Greyhound Terminal, US$5, hourly. The Greyhound Terminal is right downtown, on the corner of San Antonio and Santa Fe streets, and from there you can get buses to Laredo, Tucson, etc, and connections to all points they serve in the US. They have buses every hour on the half hour to Ciudad Juárez, from 0630 to 2130 that cost US$5. You can buy your ticket on the bus. It stops at the Mexican side of the border for customs and immigration. You can pick up your FM-T (tourist card) there.

The Ciudad Juárez Bus Station is a long rectangular building. On the east side of the terminal is a Sendetel outlet for long-distance phone calls, fax and photocopy, a cafeteria-style restaurant, free public conveniences, a place to check luggage (3 pesos per hour per bag) and a small store selling newspapers, food and drink. On the south side of the terminal is a pharmacy. This is where the buses park to let off and pick up passengers and where you have to go through customs. On the southwest corner of the building is a booth for changing money and travellers' cheques.

On the west side of the building is a juice bar, and a sandwich stand, both with tables and pay toilets (2 pesos). Also

Ciudad Juárez / El Paso detail

■ **Sleeping**
1 Correo
2 Gardner
3 Impala
4 Paso del Norte
5 Santa Fe

Not to scale

on the west side of the building is a taxi booth (tickets cost US$4.80 to the city centre. Exit the west side (the same door you use to get taxis) and cross the parking lot to take any northbound bus to the city centre.

Ticket counters for the various bus lines are on the north side of the terminal.

Chihuahua; Omnibus de México every half hour from 0700 to 0200 the following day (4½ hr trip), US$17. Chihuahenses *Plus* service every hour from 0400-2400, US$17. Turistar Ejecutivo, very comfortable, 1740, 1905, 2115, US$23.50. **Durango**; Omnibus de México 0700, 1145, 1302, 1545, 1800, 1920, 2015, 2125, 2300, US$50. Chihuahuenses *Plus* 0015, 0830, 1245, 1430, 1645, 1830, 1945, 2100, 2200, US$45. **Guadalajara**; Omnibus de México 1000, 1300, 2200, US$72.50. Turistar Ejecutivo 1100, 1740, US$97.50. **León**; Omnibus de México 1100, 1210, 1400, 1725, 2245, US$67. **Matamoros**; Omnibus de México 1630, 2145, US$64. **Mexico City**; Omnibus de México 0800, 1031, 1500, 1700, 2000, 2400 (the 1500 bus takes 22-23 hrs; the rest take 25-26), US$85. Chihuahuenses every 2 hrs, US$85. **Monterrey**; Omnibus de México 1330, 1630, 2145, US$53. Turistar Ejecutivo 1905, US$69.50. **Morelia**; Turistar Ejecutivo 2000, US$103. **Puerto Vallarta**; Chihuahuenses 2330 (trip takes 25-26 hrs), US$93. **Querétaro**; Omnibus de México same as Mexico City schedule, US$75.50. Chihuahuenses every 2 hrs, US$75. **San Luis Potosí**; Omnibus de México same as Mexico City schedule, US$64.50. Chihuahuenses every 2 hrs, US$64.50. **Zacatecas**; Omnibus de México every hour between 0800-2400, US$57. Chihuahuenses every hour from 0400-2400, US$56. Turistar Ejecutivo 1930, US$75.50.

You can also buy tickets with Omnibus de México for points in the US: **Alburquerque**, NM 1000, 1700, 2000, US$25. **Denver, Colorado** 1000, 1900, US$45. **Los Angeles, CA** 1030, 1600, 1845, US$50. **Express Limousine service**: El Paso-Los Angeles, US$40. El Paso-Alburquerque, US$27. The El Paso office is just across the Juárez bridge at 6th and Oregon. Greyhound, El Paso, T5322365. **Turismos Rápidos**, 828 South El Paso, off Santa Fe Bridge, to many US destinations.

Directory **Airline offices** *Aero California*, T183399. *AeroMéxico*, T138719. *Taesa*, T292370. **Banks** In Ciudad Juárez most *cambios* are on Av Juárez and Av de las Américas; there is also a *cambio* at the bus terminal. Rates vary very little, some places charge commission on TCs; some are safer than others. The best and most convenient exchange houses are in El Paso: *Valuta Corp*, 301 Paisano Drive, buys and sells all foreign currencies but at poor rates, wires money transfers, open 24 hrs including holidays, commission charged on all TCs except Amex. *Melek Corp*, 306 Paisano Drive, offers most of the same services as Valuta but only dollars and pesos, not open 24 hrs. *Loren Inc*, 1611 Paisano Drive, much the same, but rates slightly worse. If coming from US Immigration, when you reach Paisano Drive/Highway 62, turn east for these places. In El Paso, banks are closed on Sat. **Communications** Post Office: on corner of Lerdo Sur and Ignacio de la Peña. **Embassies & consulates** *US*, López Mateos 924, Cd Juárez, T134048. *British* (Honorary) Mr CR Maingot, Fresno 185, Campestre Juárez, T75791. *Mexican*, 910, E San Antonio, El Paso, T5334082.

Ciudad Juárez to Chihuahua The road is wide, mostly flat, easy to drive, and not as interesting as the Gulf and Pacific routes. From Ciudad Juárez, for some 50 km along the Río Bravo, there is an oasis which grows cotton of an exceptionally high grade. The next 160 km of the road to Chihuahua are through desert; towns *en route* are Samalayuca (restaurant), at Km 58; **Villa Ahumada** Km 131, *Hotel Cactus*, T42250. **D** *Casa Blanca*, opposite train depot on main street, half a block south of bus terminal. With bath and hot water, room heater, clean. At Km 180 is *Moctezuma* (restaurant). The road leads into grazing lands and the valley of Chihuahua. The Ciudad Juárez-Chihuahua road is an *autopista* with a toll 30 km north of Chihuahua, US$6.30 for cars or pick-ups (the alternative is a long two-sides-of-a-triangle detour to avoid the toll). Recent visitors warn that they had seen only two service stations between Ciudad Juárez and Chihuahua.

Crossing into Mexico: Ojinaga to Chihuahua

Chihuahua may also be reached from the border at Ojinaga: this route is rec- **Presidio/**
ommended not only for the ease of crossing (it is used only by cattle ranchers, **Ojinaga**
no hassles), but also for the spectacular scenery either side of the border.

From Interstate 10 (San Antonio-El Paso), turn southwest after Fort
Stockton on Highway 67. This goes to Alpine, 107 km, no gas *en route*, where
there are eight motels, most on Highway 90. From Alpine it is 42 km to Marfa,
where the film *Giant* was made in 1955 with James Dean, Elizabeth Taylor and
Rock Hudson. In *Motel El Paisano*, T915-7293145, there are signed photos of
the film crew on display; there are two other motels. Fourteen kilometres east
of Marfa on Highway 90 is a viewing point for the Marfa 'Ghost Lights', an
unexplained natural phenomenon. At Marfa, Highway 67 head south 96 km to
Presidio. On the way, look out for two bizarre rock formations, a kneeling elephant with its back to the road, and a profile of Abraham Lincoln. Thirty-two
kilometres from Marfa, the road passes through Shafter, a silver mining ghost
town; no gas is available on this stretch. In Presidio (*Population*: 3,500) is
B *Three Palms Inn*. With bath, a/c, clean, friendly, takes credit cards, pool,
open 0700-2200. **C** *Motel Siesta*. Clean, TV, pool. *Rose's Café*, opposite. Has
good meals for US$6, open 0600-2130, try the 'hot chocolage', good break-
fasts; there are two other restaurants, as well as a bank, post office (*Presidio
Information Center* next door, T915-2294478, 0900-1800), fuel and shops.
Southeast of Presidio is Big Bend National Park; to the northwest is Pinto
Canyon.

Crossing the border Follow signs to Ojinaga; pass US immigration on left (if you
need to, surrender US visa waiver form here). On the Mexican side, a guard will check
your passport. Those with vehicles then park before doing paperwork. Boys selling
chiclets will look after your car/bike, but you can see it through the office windows.
There are separate desks for personal and vehicle papers. Photocopying can be done
for US$1. Get insurance before Presidio, no one sells it there, but you could ask Stella
McKeel Agency, T915-2293221/5. Full details of entry requirement for drivers is given
in **Essentials**, page 39. The border is open 24 hrs.

Leaving Mexico, note that the bus station is 2 km from the border. Make sure all
your papers are stamped correctly.

Essentials Ojinaga has 5 hotels, including **D** *Armendariz*, Zaragoza near Zócalo,
T31198/32241. Clean, safe parking. *Casa de Huéspedes*. Cheap meals at *Lonchería
Avenida* opposite bus station. **Festivals**: 1-4 Jun. Daily buses to/from Chihuahua,
US$6. *Bancomer* on Zócalo, changes TCs, no commission; opposite is *Casa de Cambio
Allende*, cash only, poorer rates.

Forty-two kilometres from Ojinaga on Route 16 towards Chihuahua is **El
Peguis**, overlooking an extraordinary canyon. Also here is a *garita*, where
vehicle papers are checked (in the middle of nowhere). A further 46 km is
Coyame, a village with caves 1 km away; ask for a guide (there is a tourist
complex, thermal springs, *balneario* but no hotel). There is a Pemex station
in Coyame. The road continues in good condition southwest, with no fuel
stations until **Aldama**, 26 km from Chihuahua. This pleasant town has
tree-lined avenues, a shady central square and a church (1876) of pink sand-
stone (hotels, two motels on road to Chihuahua, restaurant *Campestre* opposite the motels, clean, friendly). After Aldama the traffic increases on the way
to the state capital.

Chocolate Cars

> Not a novel candy bar, the term 'carros de chocolate' refers to ilegally imported US vehicles, which are a common sight in parts of Mexico. Of course some cars and pick-up trucks with American licence plates belong to visitors, but many others are owned by Mexicans and have been brought across the northern border without any formalities. They include vehicles which were legally purchased in the US as well others which were stolen. Their new owners then obtain an official-looking sticker for as little as US$5, stating that the car is in the process of being nationalized. This plus the occasional gratuity to transit police is apparently enough to keep them in circulation for years.

Crossing into Mexico: Palomas and Agua Prieta

Columbus/ Palomas
Route 2 runs west from Ciudad Juárez, roughly parallel with the Mexico-US border. Between Juárez and Janos, at the northern end of lateral Mexico 24, is the dusty border town of Palomas, Chihuahua, opposite Columbus, New Mexico. The modern border facilities are open 24 hours. Palomas itself has few attractions apart from limited duty-free shopping for liquor and pharmaceuticals, but Columbus was the site of Pancho Villa's 1916 incursion into New Mexico, which led to reprisals by the forces of American General John J Pershing. **The Columbus Historical Museum**, on the southeast corner of the highway intersection, contains many old photos of Pancho Villa, a copy of his death mask, and one of his sombreros; it also offers exhibits on Villa's sacking and burning of Columbus. There is a small shelf of books on the history of the town that you can browse through. The father of the museum's curator played a part in the battle. ■ *Daily 1000-1600.*

It's three miles from Columbus to the border, south on highway 11. Palomas is just across the border, and you park for free in a paved lot just before the border and walk across. The Mexican immigration office is just on the right as you cross the border. If you're driving, there's also a customs checkpoint at the border crossing. The customs' administrative building is about 60m south of the immigration office, but you'd only need to go there for complaints, etc. New Mexico, unlike Arizona, has no limit on the number of cartons of cigarettes you can bring back to the US with you, so after your first carton, which is duty free, you pay a duty of $2.40 per carton. That's still about one-third of what you'd pay for a carton of cigarettes in the US. Arizona limits you to one carton.

Essentials Reasonable accommodation at **D** *Hotel Restaurant San Francisco*, also **E** *Motel Santa Cruz*. Behind seafood restaurant, opposite gas station. Fairly basic, but less so than the **E** *Hotel Regis*, Av 5 de Mayo. Rooms with shared bath, basic. **E** *Hotel García*, Progreso 950. Basic. On the Columbus side, **A** *Martha's Place*, Main and Lima Sts, T505-5312467, marthas@vtc.net. It has a very attractive lobby and an attractive breakfast area. Price includes breakfast. **C** *Motel Columbus*. **C** *Suncrest Inn*, Highway 11, just north of Highway 9. TV and phones in rooms: just ordinary. **Camping** Excellent, well-maintained sites at *Pancho Villa State Park*, opposite the Columbus Historical Museum, for US$7 per night, additional charge for electrical hook-up. There is no public transport on the US side, but hourly buses connect Palomas with Tres Caminos, where travellers can board buses from Juárez to Nuevo Casas Grandes (see below).

Janos
Colour map 1, grid A5
At the intersection of border Route 2 and Chihuahua Route 10 to Nuevo Casas Grandes is **Janos** (*Restaurant Durango*, de facto bus station at the intersection,

has good inexpensive food; several others at junction, plus **D** *Hotel Restaurant La Fuente*). The landscape between Ciudad Juárez and Nuevo Casas Grandes (see below) is quite barren and, in the winter months, it can be cold.

Near Janos are the northernmost **Mennonite colonies** in Mexico; numerous vendors sell Mennonite cheese, which also has a market in upscale restaurants across the border in New Mexico. The German-speaking Mennonites are very conspicuous, the men in starched overalls and the women in long dresses and leggings, their heads covered with scarves.

Northwest of Janos, via the border Route 2, are the border crossings of **Agua Prieta** (opposite Douglas, Arizona) and **Naco** (adjacent to its Arizona namesake and a short distance south of the historic, picturesque copper mining town of Bisbee). Agua Prieta is growing rapidly with the proliferation of *maquiladoras* on both sides of the border. If possible, avoid crossing in late afternoon, when traffic across the border can be very congested as Mexican labourers return home from Douglas.

Douglas/ Agua Prieta
Colour map 1, grid A5
Population: 80,000

Crossing into Agua Prieta on foot, walk on the right hand side of the road to enter Mexico. There are no obligatory checkpoints if you just want to see Agua Prieta. Otherwise, the **immigration office** for your FM-T (tourist card) is on the right just as you cross the border, and customs is just past it. You also pick up papers for your car here if you're driving, and get auto insurance. If you keep walking straight ahead you'll cross a street which has buses running to the Agua Prieta bus station. Take buses running east which have '13-20', 'Ejidal' or 'P Nuevo' on their front windows. Taxis charge US$3 from the border to the bus station, a 5-10 minute ride. They also charge by the hour: US$20. The main plaza in the centre is the Plaza Azueta, at Avenida 4, between Calle 5 and 6. Fronting it is the Iglesia de Nuestra Señora de Guadalupe.

Agua Prieta is 162 km from Janos via Route 2, which crosses the scenic Sierra San Luis, covered by dense oak-juniper woodland, to the continental divide (elevation 1,820m) at Puerto San Luis, the border between the states of Sonora and Chihuahua. There are outstanding views of the sprawling rangelands to the west. Southbound motorists from the USA must present their papers to Mexican customs at La Joya, a lonely outpost 70 km northwest of Janos.

Both the Agua Prieta and Naco ports of entry are open 24 hours. There is no public transport other than taxi to Naco, Arizona, but there are buses from Naco, Sonora, to Agua Prieta and Nogales. Mexican automobile insurance is not available in Naco, Sonora, but readily obtained at Douglas. The Mexican consulate in Douglas is helpful.

Warning Drug smuggling, auto theft, and other illegal activities are common along the southeastern Arizona border. Watch your belongings and money closely even during 'routine' searches by US Customs officials, whose reputation has been sullied by reports of corruption in recent years. Moreover, the police in Agua Prieta have a bad reputation for stopping drivers for no good reason and trying to extract bribes on the threat of jail.

Sleeping **A** *Motel La Hacienda*, Calle Primera, Av 6, Apdo postal 22 (for mail), T80621/80623, a few blocks from the border (best in town). Heating, TV, etc. **C** *Hotel El Greco*, Calle 3 between Av 2 and 3. **B** *Motel Ruiz* Av 6 between Calle 9 and 10, T82499/85226/85229, F80499. Heating and a/c, hot water, TV and phones in rooms. **C** *Motel Gar-hnos*, Av 21 between Calle 2 and 3. Heating, small restaurant. **C** *Hotel San Francisco*, T85255, Calle 3, between Av 3 and 4. Has cafeteria. **C** *Motel Arizona*, Av 6 between Calle 17 and 18, T82522. Heating, pleasant. **C** *Hotel Yolanda*, corner of

Calle 2 and Av 4, T81253. Has restaurant. **D** *Hotel Vimar*, Calle 8 and Av 2. No heating, private bath. **D** *Hotel Linda*, Calle 4 between Av 7 and 8, T81550. Heat and hot water.

In **Naco**, the only formal accommodation is **D** *Motel Colonial*, which is often full, but the manager may tolerate a night's auto camping within the motel compound.

Accommodation is cheaper in **Douglas**, on the Arizona side. The venerable **B** *Gadsden Hotel*, 1046 G Av, T3644481. A registered historical landmark, has been used as a location for Western films. Fabulous lobby, completely unexpected to find such a place in a border town. Recommended. **C** *Motel 6*. Rates are higher in Bisbee, a very popular tourist destination, but the town offers good value for money. **Camping** RV parks on the Arizona side charge about US$10 per night for vehicle, US$5 for tent camping: *Double Adobe Trailer Park* off Highway 80, *Copper Horse Shoe R V Park* on Highway 666.

Eating In **Agua Prieta**, *El Pollo Loco*, near the plaza, for roasted chicken. 3 seafood restaurants: *Restaurant de Mariscos Hermanos Gómez*, corner of Calle 2 and 6, *Mariscos and Carnes 'La Palapa'*, Calle 6 between Av 11 and 12, and *Mariscos Mazatlán*, corner of Calle 5 and Av 16. In **Naco**: *Restaurant Juárez*. On the Douglas side, restaurant at *Hotel Gadsden* is good and reasonable, but the best selection in the area is at Bisbee, 10 miles north of Naco.

Nightclubs *La Cueva del Greco*, Next to the *Hotel El Greco* mentioned above. With live music and sometimes shows. *El Cid* discoteque, near the *El Greco*. *Yarda's Pub*, Calle 1 between Av 4 and 5. Discoteque with an outside terrace. Those that follow are in the *zona de tolerancia*, or the red-light district. Any cab driver will know how to get there. (Agua Prieta gets a lot of bad press regarding drug violence, so be cautious). *Flamingo Club*, *Quinta Patio Bar*, *El Paraíso Bar*, and *Casa Club Blanca* (gay). All these are close to the corner of Calle 15 and Av 2.

Transport Taxi Armando Chávez, T52162. Recommended. If you are crossing the border, when you come to the first cross street, take a left and the office is just around the corner on the north side of the street.

Buses: The bus station in Agua Prieta is 1 small room with an adequate restaurant called *Don Camione*, and a Sendetel booth with phone and fax service. There is also a counter selling cigarettes, sodas, and a small selection of packaged foods. Luggage can be stored at the entrance to the bathrooms (2.5 pesos per person, regardless of the number of bags that you have).

There are services to: **Bisbee**; Autobuses Crucero $10. **Chihuahua**; Cabellero Azteca (all 2nd class) 0600, 0830, 1000, 1140, 1500, 1700, 2240, US$24. **Ciudad Juárez**; Norte de Sonora 0900, 0930, 2230. **Ciudad Obregón**; Norte de Sonora 2200. **Durango**; Cabellero Azteca (all 2nd class) 1930, $47. **Hermosillo**; Transportes Foráneos 0600, 0800, 1200, US$12. Norte de Sonora 0600, 0800 (1st class) 0900, 1000, 1200, 1600. **Los Angeles**; Autobuses Crucero 0515, 1630, US$65. **Los Mochis**; Norte de Sonora 1330. **Mazatlán**; Norte de Sonora 1045, 1445, 2000. **Mexico City**; Norte de Sonora 1700. **Nogales**; Cabellero Azteca (all 2nd class) 0830, 1100, 1300, 1430, 1630, 2000, US$10. **Phoenix**; Autobuses Crucero 0515, 0815, 1115, 1430, 1630, US$30. **Tijuana**; Norte de Sonora 2030. **Tucson**; Autobuses Crucero $20. **Zacatecas**; Cabellero Azteca (all 2nd class) 2130, US$56.

Another private bus agency is just across the street from the Mexican immigration office as you cross the border and has 4 buses to Tucson at 0915, 1315, 1600 and 1900, US$20.

Douglas has a small bus terminal, 538 14th Street, between Avs F and G, T3642233, operated by Greyhound and Autobuses Crucero. **Tucson**; US$19. **Phoenix**; US$30. *Los Angeles*; US$65. The schedules for all the buses are the same: 0545, 1145, 1515, and 1715. The terminal closes at 1600 so you'd have to wait outside for the 1715 bus.

Directory On the Douglas side, the Chamber of Commerce, T3642477, at 1125 Pan American has good information on Mexico as well as Arizona, with a wealth of maps (including Agua Prieta) and brochures. *Librolandia del Centro*, a bookstore, has a good selection of material on local and regional history. **Banks** There's an exchange house with a Western Union office just before the border crossing on the US side. **Medical services** *Cruz Roja*: corner of Calle 17 and Av 6. From there they can take you to other hospitals. **Pharmacies:** Open 24 hrs: 1 on the corner of Calle 3 and Av 8, and another on the corner of Av 5 and 7. There is also a very large *Farmacia Benavides* on the left side of the street 50 m straight ahead from the border immigration point. **Shopping** There is a large shopping centre at Calle 13 between Av 10 and 13.

During winter Arizona time is the same as Agua Prieta time, but as Arizona doesn't go on daylight saving time, and Mexico does, during the summer Agua Prieta is an hour ahead of Arizona.

Casas Grandes

The archaeological site of Casas Grandes, or Paquimé, can be reached from Chihuahua, Ciudad Juárez or Agua Prieta. **Nuevo Casas Grandes** is a town built around the railway; it is very dusty when dry, the wind blowing clouds of dust down the streets, and when wet the main street becomes a river. There is not much to do, but there are cinemas which show US and Mexican films.

Colour map 2, grid A1

Casas Grandes/Paquimé was probably a trading centre, which reached its peak between 1210 and 1261. The city was destroyed by fire in 1340. Its commercial influence is said to have reached as far as Colorado in the north and into southern Mexico. At its height, it had multi-storeyed buildings; the niches that held the beams for the upper floors are still visible in some structures. A water system, also visible, carried hot water from thermal springs to the north, and acted as drainage. Most of the buildings are of a type of adobe, but some are faced with stone. You can see a ball court and various plazas among the buildings. The site is well tended. Significant archaeological reconstruction is under way at Casas Grandes. About two hours is sufficient to see it all. ■ *1000-1700, US$3.50.* To get there take a yellow bus from outside the furniture shop at 16 de Septiembre y Constitución Pte in , US$0.20, 15 minutes. From the square in Casas Grandes village either take Calle Constitución south out of the square past the school, walk to the end of the road, cross a gully, then straight on for a bit, turn right and you will see the site, or take Avenida Juárez west out of the square and turn left at the sign to Paquimé, 1 km.

Paquimé ceramics, copying the original patterns, either black on black, or beige with intricate red and grey designs, are made in the village of **Mata Ortiz**, 21 km southwest of Nuevo Casas Grandes. Take a bus from Calle Jesús Urueta, west of the railway track, at 1630 (return at 0800), US$2.40.

To reach Casas Grandes from Chihuahua, follow Route 45 towards Ciudad Juárez and take the turn-off near El Sueco (157 km from Chihuahua, 219 from Ciudad Juárez); from here, State Highway 10 to Nuevo Casas Grandes (198 km) passes through Constitución (bus stop), Flores Magón (hotel) and Buenaventura (114 km, a pleasant-looking place). About 100 km from El Sueco a brief section of *camino sinuoso* (twisting roads) affords views of the plains you have just crossed; from Buenaventura the road passes through different valleys, of varying degrees of fertility, the most productive being Buenaventura itself and Lagunillas. Buses from Chihuahua to Nuevo Casas Grandes go either via El Sueco or via Ciudad Cuauhtémoc (see below) and Madera (the Sierra route, see also below), which has some pleasant landscapes. If heading south from the USA via Casas Grandes, you can continue on the Sierra route to Creel on the Chihuahua-Los Mochis railway (see page 623).

B *Motel Hacienda*, Av Juárez 2603, T41046/7/8/9/50. The best, sometimes has Paquimé ceramics on sale. **C** *California*, Constitución Pte 209. Reasonable, takes credit cards, hot water takes a while to come through. **C** *Motel Piñón*, Juárez 605,

Sleeping
In Nuevo Casas Grandes only

The Northern Highlands

T41066. Helpful. **C** *Paquimé*. With fan and a/c, clean, large, pleasant. Recommended. **C** *Parque*, Av Juárez, just past main square heading north. With TV and phone. **D** *Juárez*, Obregón 110, between bus companies. Supposedly hot water, some English spoken, friendly, safe parking, basic bathroom (take your key with you when you go out). *Suite Victoria*, Guadalupe Victoria, 1 block west of Constitución Pte, off 5 de Mayo.

Eating   *Café de la Esquina*, 5 de Mayo y Obregón, near bus offices. Cheap, clean, friendly, popular. *Tacos El Brasero*, Obregón opposite *Hotel Juárez*. Open 24 hrs. *Dinno's Pizza*, Minerva y Constitución Ote, opposite Cine Variedades. Fair, takes credit cards. *Alameda*, next to *Hotel California*. For breakfast and *comida corrida*, average. *Denni's*, Juárez y Jesús Urueta. Mostly steaks, quite good, good service.

Transport   **Buses** All bus offices are on Alvaro Obregón. Several daily to **Ciudad Juárez**, 3 companies, 4 hrs, US$10.60. 3 companies to **Chihuahua**, 5 hrs, US$12.10. Omnibus de México: **Mexico City** once a day via El Sueco, once via Cuauhtémoc. Also to **Monterrey**; Chihuahua Madera to **Cuauhtémoc** and **Madera**; Caballero Azteca to **Agua Prieta** (3 a day), **Hermosillo**, **Tijuana** and **Nogales** (once each).

Directory   **Banks** Banks on 5 de Mayo and Constitución Ote; *Casa de Cambio California* next to hotel of that name. **Communications** Long-distance telephone: at Rivera bus office, on Alvaro Obregón.

Madera

Phone code: 157
Colour map 1, grid B5
Population: 13,000
Altitude: 2,100m

Madera is in the Sierra Madre, surrounded by rugged mountain scenery. It is high enough to receive snow in winter (rainy season September-March, best time to visit May-August). The region around Madera has ample scope for tourism: archaeological sites, bird-watching, hunting, fine landscapes and good infrastructure. By road from the north is via Buenaventura and Gómez Farías. From Chihuahua either turn off Route 16 at La Junta (see below) and take Ruta 37 via Guerrero (*Posada Alicia*; Pemex), or turn off at Ciudad Cuauhtémoc onto Route 65 via Alvaro Obregón (restaurants, Pemex), Bachiniva (restaurants, Pemex) and Soto Maynes (Pemex). Before Gómez Farías, turn west onto Route 180; this takes you through Bavícora, site of George Hearst's ranch (Pemex) and on to Madera.

Sleeping &   **A** *Motel Real del Bosque*, Carretera Chihuahua, Barrio Americano, on main road into
eating   town, T20066, F20538. 3-star, clean, friendly, parking, bar, disco, restaurant, English spoken, manager Angel Leal Estrada is also president of local Comité Pro Turismo, very enthusiastic, tours organized from the hotel (see Excursions below); he is planning to build a backpackers' hostel. **C** *Parador de la Sierra*, Calle 3 and Independencia, T20277. Clean, heating, discount for more than 1 night, off-street parking, restaurant. **C** *María*, Calle 5 y 5 de Mayo. Cheaper rooms available, heating, clean, limited parking, restaurant open 24 hrs. Good. **C** *Mirmay*, Calle 3 y Guerrero, T20944, next to *Café Lo Lobos*. Not too clean. **F** *Motel Maras*, Calle 5 (1 block south of *Mirmay*). Hot water noisy, clean apart from dusty rooms. There are several restaurants in town.

Transport   Madera has an airstrip; call *Motel Real del Bosque* to arrange a landing (Unicom 122.8 and ADF 1300 service). Estrella Blanca bus (T20431) to/from Chihuahua every hour takes 5 hrs, bus stop on Calle 5.

Directory   **Banks** *Banamex*, only place for Visa and Mastercard advances, *Bancomer* and *Banrural* will change dollars (possibly Tcs).

Madera's prosperous past

During the Porfirio Díaz era, two US financiers were granted rights to exploit the area: George Hearst (of the famous newspaper family), who farmed cattle between Madera and Gómez Farías, and William Green. In exchange for building the railway, which runs between Chihuahua, Nuevo Casas Grandes and Ciudad Juárez, Green was allowed to extract timber from the forests. He wished to extend the railway to Cananea (northern Sonora), to take lumber to the mine he owned there, but this section was

never built. In 1904 the first saw mills were in operation. The town developed, with a 66-room hotel, a casino and the largest wooden box-making factory in the world at the time. Green went bankrupt in 1908. During the Revolution, the factories casting iron for the railway turned to making cannon; Pancho Villa ordered two and also permitted the workers to take over management of the factories since the US managers had left. But the factories failed to thrive and eventually the North Americans returned.

Around Madera

Madera is on an important waterfowl migratory route, with white-fronted, blue and snow geese, mallard, pintail, teal, widgeon and redhead duck, and sandhill crane passing through. This does mean that it has become a popular centre for shooting (season mid-November-February), but bird-watching expeditions can be arranged at *Motel Real del Bosque*.

Taking Calle 3 in a northerly direction out of town, the road soon becomes dirt (stony, potholed, good suspension advisable). It parallels the railway to Casas Grandes, passing through pine forest and cultivated fields and heads into the plateau of the Sierra Madre. Twelve kilometres from town, after a sign-post to Nuevo Madera, is a lake and dam, **Presa Penitentes**, to the right. At the water's edge, the clockwise track takes you to the far side where you can fish for rainbow trout. Anticlockwise takes you to a picnic area with restaurant and toilets, children's play area and volleyball pitch. Camping is possible. Behind the dammed part of the lake is a rainbow trout farm where fish can be bought. ■ *Daily 0900-1700.* Water-skiing on the lake (four-hour tour from *Motel Real del Bosque*, US$30, minimum four people; hitchhiking is also possible). Another trout farm and trailer park is under construction near Nuevo Madera.

Back on the main road, you come to a signed turning right to Las Varas, which leads to Casas Grandes (there is another, unsigned turning to Las Varas further on). Straight on is **El Salto**, a 35-m waterfall, best seen after the spring thaw (March-April). The fall is along a track to the left; to see it you have to walk round the rim of a little canyon. It is possible to hike down to the river below (about one hour). Ask at the house on the track to the fall if you want to camp (no facilities).

Four kilometres from the turn-off to El Salto is the entrance to **Cuarenta Casas** (40 houses) 1½ hours from Madera. Cuarenta Casas is a series of cave dwellings, inhabited originally by Indians of the Paquimé culture. Some of the houses have the palet-shaped windows/doorways also seen at Casas Grandes (called here *La Cueva de las Ventanas*); some are two storeys high. There is a good view of the cave houses from the visitors' hut at the entrance. A trail descends to the river before climbing steeply to the cave, a hike that takes 45 minutes-one hour one way. ■ *0900-1600 daily (except 16 Sep), free.* Camping is possible only when personnel are staying the night; there are no facilities other than water. (Tour from *Motel Real del Bosque*, takes six hours, US$65, minimum four people; alternatively, hitchhiking is possible.)

South of Madera is the **Misión Tres Ojitos**, where the Spanish priest, Padre Espronceda, makes ham. The *fiesta* for the Virgen del Rosario takes place on 7 October with rodeos and other activities. Take the road to La Junta from Madera and at the signpost, turn off right. On the dirt road, take the left fork through the village. Go past the church and on the right the Mission is signed (10 km from Madera).

In Madera there is a sign indicating **Zona Arqueológica Huapoca**, going west on Independencia. At Km 13 on this good dirt road is **Lago Campo 3**, shallow and marshy, with wildlife. Camping and picnicking are possible. The lake's name comes from a logging camp. Eighteen kilometres from town you reach an altitude of 2,500m, with stunning views of the Sierra Madre. Plenty of bird-life can be seen from the road. The Huapoca Ranch, a US-owned experimental horse-breeding centre at Km 30, does not take visitors. At Km 41 is the entrance to the **Zona Arqueológica Anasazi**, which contains the **Nido del Aguila** (Eagle's Nest) cave dwellings and the **Cueva del Serpiente** (Serpent's Cave). The 2 km road to the site is terrible and about 300m are impassable (you have to find somewhere to leave your car before the so-called 'car park'). There is no path to the Nido del Aguila, but if you keep to the left slope from the 'car park', you reach first a *mirador*, then the cave around a big bluff. There is another *mirador* further on. A guide is necessary. On the right-hand hillcrest from the 'car park' is the Cueva del Serpiente: a path leads to a sign on a tree, behind which, to the left, is a crevasse. Ten minutes into the crevasse (steep in places) is a set of three chambers and the remains of two others. Follow round on a narrow ledge to 11 more complete chambers and three ruins. All the rooms (covered in graffiti, unfortunately) can be entered; the rows of rooms interconnect and have the typical palet-shaped windows. A strong torch is useful for locating the inner rooms. If you jump up and down, the ground sounds hollow, suggesting that there are more rooms below. The views are magnificent.

At Km 44 is a brightly painted house where, in November-December, they sell cheese. The beautiful valley of the Río Huapoca becomes visible at Km 51. A sign to Aguas Termales at Km 53 leads on another terrible track, to hot springs with a small pool under a waterfall and a cooler section nearer the river (two toilets). The main road then crosses the Puente Huapoca suspension bridge, built in 1950 (a tour this far, including lunch, fishing, and swimming in the rapids, from *Motel Real del Bosque*, 10 hours, costs US$65). **NB** In this area, close any gates that you go through; farmers graze cows and horses on the land, which is private.

Fifty-eight kilometres from Madera is the turn-off to **Cueva Grande**. A clear trail leads in 15 minutes to a waterfall, behind which is the 50-m cave with two complete two-storey houses and some ruins. Visitors can climb to the upper storey and in the ruins see exactly how the constructions were made. Behind the house on the right is a circular trough which was used to store grain. The cave was inhabited from 1060 AD. There are rock pools for swimming by the fall (best March-April) and it is possible, but difficult, to climb to the head of the fall. At the car park you can camp or have a barbecue (but remember if lighting a fire to encircle it with stones; forest fires are a real danger).

Chihuahua

The capital of Chihuahua state and centre of a mining and cattle area, Chihuahua City is 375 km from the border and 1,479 km from the capital. It is mostly a modern and rather run-down industrial city, but has strong historical connections, especially with the Mexican Revolution. Pancho Villa operated in the country around, and once captured the city by disguising his men as peasants going to market. There are also associations with the last days of Independence hero Padre Hidalgo. Summer temperatures often reach 40°C but be prepared for ice at night as late as November. Rain falls from July to September.

Phone Code: 14
Colour map 2, grid B2
Population: 800,000
Altitude: 1,420m

The **tourist offices** in the Palacio de Gobierno T151526, F160032, has general information, maps, pamphlets, etc. ■ *Mon-Fri 0900-1900, Sat-Sun 0900-1400.* The administration office is at Departamento de Comercio y Turismo, Libertad 1300 y Calle 13, 10th floor, T162436. ■ *Mon-Fri 0900-1500.*

The old tower of the **Capilla Real** where Hidalgo awaited his execution is now in the **Palacio Federal** (Libertad y Guerrero). The dungeon (*calabozo*) is quite unremarkable and the Palacio itself is very neglected. The **Palacio de Gobierno**, on the other hand, is in fine condition, with a dramatic set of murals by Aaron Piña Morales depicting Chihuahua's history. There are a number of old mansions (see Museums below) and the Paseo Bolívar area is pleasant. Calle Libertad is for pedestrians only from Plaza Constitución to the Palacio de Gobierno and Palacio Federal. Calle 4 and streets that cross it northwest of Juárez are bustling with market stalls and restaurants. Worth looking at is the **Cathedral** on Plaza Constitución, begun 1717, finished 1789; its Baroque façade dates from 1738, the interior is mostly unadorned, with square columns, glass chandeliers and a carved altarpiece. In the southeast of the town near Calle Zarco are ancient aqueducts. Walk north along Ocampo and over the river for fine views of the city at sunset.

Sights
The local hairless small dog has a constant body temperature of 40°C (104°F), the world's only authentic 'hot dog'

The **Quinta Luz** (1914), Calle 10 No 3014, where Pancho Villa lived, is now the **Museo de la Revolución**, with many old photographs, the car in which Villa was assassinated (looking like a Swiss cheese from all the bullet holes), his death mask and postcards of the assassinated leader, well worth a visit. ■*0900-1300 and 1500-1900, US$1.* The **Museo Regional**, in the former mansion Quinta Gameros at Bolívar 401, has interesting exhibits and extremely fine Art-Nouveau rooms: the dining room, the child's room which features Little Red Riding Hood scenes; the bathroom, with frogs playing among reeds, etc, an exhibition of Paquimé ceramics, as well as temporary exhibitions. ■*Tue-Sun 0900-1300, 1600-1900, US$0.70.* **Museo de Arte e Industria Populares**, Av Reforma 5 (Tarahumara art and lifestyle; shops). ■*Tue-Sat 0900-1300, 1600-1900, free.* The **Museo Casa Juárez**, Juárez y Calle 5 was once the house and office of Benito Juárez. ■*Mon-Fri 0900-1500, 1600-1800.* The **Museo de Arte Sacro**, Libertad y Calle 2. ■*Mon-Fri 1400-1800.*

Museums

For **Santa Eulalia** silver mine, take a blue and white bus from near the old bus station. The bus is marked 'Chihuahua Postillo' and leaves hourly. After visiting the mine (fine views), walk down to Santa Eulalia town where there is a mining museum.

Excursions

AL *Palacio del Sol*, Independencia 500 y Niños Héroes, T166000, F159947. Smart, with Torres del Sol travel agency and Número Uno car rental. Overpriced. **AL** *San Francisco*, Victoria 409, T167770. *Degá* restaurant good for steaks. **B** *El Campanario*, Blvd Díaz Ordaz 1405, southwest of Cathedral, T154545. Good rooms, clean, TV.

Sleeping
■ *on maps*
Price codes:
see inside front cover

The Northern Highlands

Recommended. **C** *Balflo*, Niños Héroes 702, T160300. Modern, poor value. **C** *El Cobre*, Calle 10A y Progreso T151730. With bathroom, hot water, TV, very comfortable, *Bejarano* restaurant good, reasonable laundry.

D *Plaza*, behind cathedral, Calle 4 No 206, T155833. Noisy, quite clean, cold shower, fair, run-down. **D-E** *Reforma*, Victoria 809, T106848. Also colonial-style (including rooms, some floors look unsafe), friendly, clean, fan, hot water, restaurant, TV in reception, safe,

Chihuahua

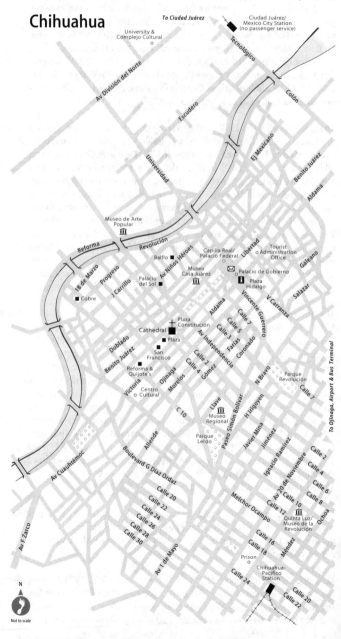

parking next door for cars (US$0.25) or motorbikes in courtyard. Recommended. **D-E** *Cortés*, Gómez Farías 6, near Plaza Constitución, T100471. Clean, quiet, big court-yard, pleasant. **D** *Del Carmen*, Calle 10 No 4, T157096. With hot water, a/c, OK. **E** *San Juan*, Victoria 823, T100035. In old colonial house, but rooms (repairs needed, a bit som-bre) are in another part, reasonable food, water sometimes scarce, friendly. **E** *Roma*, Libertad 1015, T102363. With hot water, run-down (taxi drivers on commission bring tourists here). **E-F** *Posada Aída*, Calle 10 y Av Juárez. With bath and hot water, friendly, helpful, 3 yappy chihuahua dogs! Night porter will watch cars parked outside. Recom-mended (*Cabral* on Calle 10 is not recommended, rooms hired by the hour). **E** *Casa de Huéspedes*, Libertad 1405. With bath, basic but clean, several others in the same street. **E** *Turista*, Juárez 817. With bath, dirty beds, clean bathroom, noisy and damp. The cheaper hotels are in Juárez and its cross-streets; the cheapest are behind the cathedral.

Motels   B *Mirador*, Universidad 1309, T132205. **C** *Nieves*, Tecnológico y Ahuehuetes, T132516.

The smartest and best are in the *Zona Dorada*, northeast of the centre on Juárez, near Colón, eg: *Los Parados de Tomy Vega*, Juárez 3316, *La Calesa*, Juárez y Colón, and *La Olla*, Juárez 3331. Excellent steaks. *La Parilla*, Victoria 450. Recommended. *Quijote's*, Victoria 807. Good food and value, buffet meals till 1700, dinner also, friendly. *Mi Café*, Victoria 1000. Good. *Los Milagros*, Victoria 812. Young people's meeting place, good atmosphere. *La Galatea*, Juárez y Calle 2. Restaurant within department store, recom-mended for breakfast, cheap. *El Gallo*, on Libertad. Good and cheap breakfasts. *Flor de Michoacán*, on Libertad. Serves excellent *licuados*. *Armando's*, Aldama y Guerrero. For snacks, sodas, coffee. *Café Calicanto*, Aldama 411. Good coffee shop. *Café Merino*, Av Juárez y Ocampo. Recommended. *Ostionería de la Monja*, near main Plaza. Good seafood. *Tortas México*, on Independencia, near cathedral. Good break-fasts. *Kosmovita*, Independencia 725. A shop for natural products. Corn on the cob (maize) is cooked and sold on the streets, excellent with cheese, lime, salt and chile. The **market** is between Calle 2 and 6, southeast of Av Niños Héroes, small but good for fruit and vegetables.

Eating
● *on maps*

Cinema   On Universidad near Post Office, shows films from the USA.

Entertainment

Artesanías Tarahumaras, Calle 5 y Doblado 312, T130627. Crafts, baskets, wood-carvings, jewellery.

Shopping

Guillermo Bechman, T30253, arranges stays at cabins above Bahuichivo, near Copper Canyon. *Viajes Flamingo*, Santa Anita Hotel, T91-68121613, F83393, will book train tickets in advance, no commission charged, English spoken. *Turismo Al Mar*, T165950, accommodation and rail packages to Copper Canyon, 5 nights and some meals, US$500 for 2 people. *Turismo Espectacular*, T266460, Elena Flores, speaks English, very helpful.

Tour operators

Local   Taxis work on a zone system. Agree price before boarding, to avoid unpleas-ant surprises. **Town buses** cost US$0.20, go everywhere, ask which one to take. **Bicy-cle spares**: Independencia 807, open 0900-2000.

Transport

Air   Airport Gen Fierro Villalobos (CUU) on Blvd Juan Pablo II, 18 km from centre on road to Ojinaga, T200676. Airport buses collect passengers from hotels, fare US$1.10. Also minibuses. Taxi US$16 (no other transport at night). Flights to Ciudad Juárez, Ciudad Obregón, Culiacán, Guadalajara, Hermosillo, La Paz, Loreto, Los Cabos, Los Mochis, Manzanillo, Mazatlán, Mexico City, Monterrey, Tijuana and Torreón. Aeroméxico to Los Angeles daily, and Aerolitoral to Dallas and El Paso in the USA.

The Northern Highlands

Trains The station for the 631-km Chihuahua-Pacífico railway is 1 block behind the prison (near Av 20 de Noviembre and Blvd Díaz Ordaz – take bus marked Rosario, or walk up Av Independencia, then right along Paseo Bolívar or Av 20 de Noviembre); in the early morning you may have to take a taxi. Information and tickets by post: Departamento Regional de Pasajeros, Apdo Postal 46, Chihuahua, CHIH, México, T157756, F109059. To Los Mochis daily at 0700, arrives 1950, returns 0600 arrives 2050, also Mon, Wed, Fri at 0800, arrives 2225, returns Tue, Thu, Sat 0700, arrives 2325 (see page 623 for details). There is another station (currently freight only) 3 km along Av Niños Héroes, left at Av Colón, which becomes Av Tecnológico, past the river and right along Av División del Norte, T130714.

Buses Bus terminal on Blvd Juan Pablo II, 8 km from centre on way to airport, southeast of town, T202286, 20 mins by bus to centre (US$0.30), or taxi US$4 (fixed price). Buses from centre at Niños Héroes between Ocampo and Calle 10. There is an exchange office (beware short-changing), *cafetería* and left luggage. To **Mexico City** (and intermediate destinations) frequent services with several companies 20 hrs, US$57; **Querétaro**, US$45.50; **San Luis Potosí**, US$36.50; **Aguascalientes**, US$33.50; **Zacatecas**, US$33, 12 hrs; **Durango**, US$32; **Torreón**, US$16.50. 2nd class bus, to **Hidalgo del Parral**, US$7, 1st class US$10.50, 2½ hrs. To **Mazatlán**, 2 companies, US$38, 19 hrs, heart-stopping view. To **Creel**, US$11.50, 4-5 hrs, 9 a day 0700-1730, paved all the way; to **Nuevo Casas Grandes**, see above (note that Chihuahua-Madera buses go either via El Sueco, or via the Sierra). **Nuevo Laredo** at 2030, US$36; also to **Monterrey**, US$33, and **Saltillo**, US$25. To **Guadalajara**, several, US$41, including Estrella Blanca which also goes to **Acapulco**, US$63, and **Puerto Vallarta**, US$58.

Directory **Airline offices** *AeroMéxico*, T156303. **Banks** *Bancomer* on Plaza Constitución offers better rates than *Multibanco Comermex* on same square. *Casa de Cambio Rachasa*, Independencia y Guadalupe Victoria, on Plaza, poorer rates, no commission on cash, 2% on TCs, open Mon-Sat 0900-2100 (also at Aldama 711). *Hernández*, Aldama 410, T162399, Mon-Fri 0900-1400, 1600-1900, Sat 0900-1500. Exchange is available in the bus terminal, but rates are slightly better downtown. **Communications** Internet: *Cyber Café Canaco*, Chamber of Commerce, Av Cuauhtémoc 1800, 2nd flr, US$3.75 per hour. **Telephone**: Libertad, in the Palacio Federal. Also in Central Camionera. Credit card phone outside AeroMéxico office on Guadalupe Victoria, ½ block from Plaza Constitución (towards Carranza). Main phone office on Av Universidad. **Laundry** Ocampo 1412. Julián Carrillo 402.

Ciudad Cuauhtémoc East of La Junta, some 105 km west of Chihuahua, is Ciudad Cuauhtémoc, a town surrounded by 20 or so Mennonite villages (*campos*), which are self-sufficient agricultural communities. The Mexican Mennonites, originally from Belgium, Holland and Germany, arrived from Canada early in the 20th century. Many are blond, blue-eyed and speak old German; they can be seen in town (also in Chihuahua and Nuevo Casas Grandes) selling cheese and vegetables and buying supplies.

Sleeping **A** *Motel Tarahumara Inn*, corner of Allende and Calle 5, T22801/24865. Comfortable, plenty of hot water, good restaurant, travel agency, safe parking, popular, worth booking ahead. Recommended. **E** *Hotel del Norte*, Reforma. Basic, sometimes no hot water.

Buses Bus from Chihuahua US$3.80 every 30 mins after 0700 (hourly 0500-0700); also from Creel. Toll between Ciudad Cuauhtémoc and Chihuahua, US$5.50.

Route 16 leads west from Ciudad Cuauhtémoc via La Junta to the Basaseachi falls which, at 311 m, is the highest single-jump waterfall in North America. The top of the falls is 3 km from town (2 km by dirt road, 1 km by signed trail). A paved road leads to a car park (with *taco* stalls) and *mirador* 1½ km above the falls. From here a path leads to the top of the falls and continues steeply to the pool at the bottom (best to swim in the morning when the sun still strikes the pool). Two thirds of the way to the bottom is the **Mirador Ventana** offering the best viewpoint of the falls. Hitching is difficult here, better to take a tour (US$16). The falls can also be reached from Creel (see below) via San Juanito along a very rough road. Low-bodied cars would be wise to take the longer route from Creel via La Junta, on the Cuauhtémoc road; the San Juanito road is dangerous because there are long straight stretches encouraging speed, but very little traction; via La Junta it is further (195 km from Creel, compared with 125 km from Creel via San Juanito), takes marginally longer at just over three hours, but it is a very good paved road; both routes are scenic. Route 16 goes on through beautiful mountains and forest to **Yepachic**, winding its way through Maycoba, Yécora and **San Nicolás** into Sonora. From San Nicolás the road continues to Hermosillo; it is paved but watch out for rock and mud slides in the rainy season on the older section in the mountains. A heavily potholed road leads south from San Nicolás to the Pacific Highway at Ciudad Obregón. The scenery is beautiful, the services in the villages limited, but you will probably not meet another tourist.

Basaseachi falls
Colour map 1, grid B5

The falls are at their best in July-September

NB Pemex stations are few and far between in this area; there is one 1½ km beyond *Hotel Alma Rosa* (going towards Hermosillo); others are at La Junta, 80 km away, on the Ciudad Cuauhtémoc road and in Anáhuac, on Route 16 *libre*, near Ciudad Cuauhtémoc. There is also Pemex station in Creel.

Sleeping Free camping at trailhead, no water, and near the lookout on the other side of the canyon. Hotels: **C** *Alma Rosa*, 1 km towards Hermosillo. Some new rooms with fire places and oil lamps, TV, electricity 0800-2000, hot water. **E** *Nena*, 'downtown'. Bathroom in room, but no door, no electricity after dark, provides oil lamps. *Deny* also 'downtown'. Has own generator.

Chihuahua to Los Mochis

*The Chihuahua al Pacífico train journey to **Los Mochis** is very spectacular and exciting especially on the descent through the Copper Canyon to the coast beyond Creel: book seats in advance. Sit on the left hand side of the carriage going to Los Mochis. The Primera Especial leaves daily at 0700, supposedly arriving at Creel at about 1125, Divisadero at 1245 (20 minute stop), Bahuichivo at 1430, and Los Mochis at 2050, local time, but delays are common. A reserved seat costs US$49, the fare to Creel is US$22; double check all details as they are subject to frequent change. Bring your own drinking water and toilet paper. Do not take large amounts of cash or jewellery, there are security problems on the railway. There is food at two or three stations along the way including Divisadero.*

A second-class train (*mixto*) to Los Mochis leaves Monday, Wednesday, Friday at 0800, but is often late; tickets are not sold until the first-class train has left (second class only, carriages are good, air-conditioned and comfortable, most windows do not open, and there have been mixed reports on cleanliness, US$10; fare to Creel US$4.50, arrives 1400); it reaches Divisadero at 1530 and Los Mochis at 2225. The most interesting part of the journey is between Creel and Los Mochis. If wishing to see the best scenery, there is little point in taking the train Chihuahua-Creel-Chihuahua (on this stretch, the cheaper train is just as good as the *Primera Especial*). If planning to spend a few days in Creel, there are frequent buses Chihuahua-Creel. Delays are possible in the rainy season.

A US company, DRC Rail Tours (PO Box 671107, Houston, Tx772-671107, T713-6597602, or 800-6597602) sells deluxe rail trips on The South Orient Express, a private train running through the Copper Canyon, using restored vintage carriages. From three to nine-day tours, fares from US$995 per person, double occupancy, to US$2,299; service does not operate beginning January to mid-February, nor end-April to end-September.

West of Chihuahua are high plains, windy and sparsely populated. This is a large apple-growing zone; diesel stoves next to the trunks of some varieties provide the fruit with sufficient heat to ripen. From Chihuahua, the railway and road (Route 16, *cuota* and *libre* after Km 45; the latter is good) cross the Sierra of the Tarahumara Indians, who call themselves the *Raramuri* ('those who run fast'). They were originally cave-dwellers and nomads, but now work as day-labourers in the logging stations and have settled around the mission churches built by the Spanish in the 17th century. Soon after La Junta/López Mateos, a road branches south while Route 16 continues to Hermosillo. The southerly road goes through beautiful scenery to Creel, 90 kilometres from the turning.

Thirty kilometres northeast of Creel the road passes **San Juanito**, a little larger than Creel, with cobblestone streets which are less dusty than other towns in the region. It has an annual *fiesta* on 20-24 June (**C** *Motel Cobre*, very nice rooms).

Creel

Phone code: 145
Colour map 1, grid B5
Population: 5,000
Altitude: 2,356m

Creel (very cold in winter) is the commercial centre of the Tarahumara region, important for its timber and as a tourist centre. Creel is easily reached by car from El Paso or Arizona. The town is named after Enrique Creel (1854-1931), economist and entrepreneur, governor of Chihuahua state in 1907, who initiated the building of the railway and planned to improve the Tarahumara's lives by establishing a colony here. His statue stands in the central square, just below the railway. Around the square are two churches (one of which broadcasts classical music in the evening), the Presidencia Municipal (containing the post office; second door inside on right), Banca Serfín and the Misión Tarahumara. The Misión has maps of the region (US$5 for topographical sheets, US$2.50 for simpler ones), a description of the train ride and other good buys (such as excellent photographs, wood carvings, baskets and books). It acts as a quasi-tourist office. ■ *Mon-Sat 0900-1300, 1500-1800, Sun 0900-1300*. There are several souvenir shops selling Tarahumara weavings, musical instruments, pine-needle baskets, etc. Also on sale are books such as *The National Parks of Northwest Mexico* (also obtainable from R Fisher, PO Box 40092, Tucson, Arizona 85717). Look also for *Tarahumara of the Sierra Madre* by John Kennedy (published by AHM, ISBN 0-88295-614-0).

Sleeping
Make hotel reservations in advance as not many rooms are available

AL *The Lodge at Creel*, Best Western, used to be *Pensión Creel*, Av López Mateos 61, about 1 km from the plaza and railway station, T60071, F60082, Lodgecreel@ infosel.net.mx, including breakfast and dinner. **A** *Motel Cascada Inn*, López Mateos 49, T60253, F60151 (**L** for full board). Clean, parking, restaurant. **B** *Margarita Plaza Mexicana*, Elfido Batista Caro, T60245. Including dinner and breakfast, bar. **B** *Motel Parador La Montaña*, Av López Mateos 44, T145-60075 F60085 (full board available). Will exchange foreign currency at reasonable rates, TV, clean, quiet, restaurant, bar, organizes excursions, safe parking. **B** *Nuevo*, other side of railway from station,

T60022, F60043. Meals overpriced, but nice and clean, some inside rooms dark. *Parador* and *Cascada* have live music most evenings.

C *Korachi*, across railway track from Plaza. In cabin, **C-E** *Cabañas Berti's*, Av López Mateos 31, T60086. Heating, soap and towels, parking, 1 kitchenette, excursions, friendly owner Sr Sergio Arnoldo Rascón plays guitar in local clubs. **D** *Posada de Creel*, 1½ blocks south of station on opposite side of the tracks, T/F145-60142, Apdo Postal 7. Remodelled building, gas fires in rooms, very clean, **E** in room. Not helpful. **F** per person without bath in dormitory. Hot water, helpful, English-speaking managers, coffee served from 0630. Recommended. **F** per person *Casa de Huéspedes Margarita*, López Mateos 11, T60045, between the 2 churches on corner of square. Cheapest in dormitory (packed high season with mattresses on floor) rising to **D**, double with bath, breakfast and dinner included, good communal meals, very popular meeting place (book in advance in high season), Margarita's reps meet arriving passengers, quite pushy, organizes tours (see below), horses can be hired (US$2.50 per hour with guide, lazy horses). Highly recommended (if full, Margarita's sister will put you up for **E** with dinner and breakfast, enjoyable).

A few kilometres out of town, 40 mins drive from station set in high grassland near Cusárare waterfall, is **L** per person *Copper Canyon Sierra Lodge*, (Apdo 3, 33200 Creel, Chihuahua, full board, US reservation, 2741 Paldan St, Auburn Hills, MI48326, T800-7763942, or T810-3407230, F810-3407212). Minimum stay 3 days, closed in Jun,

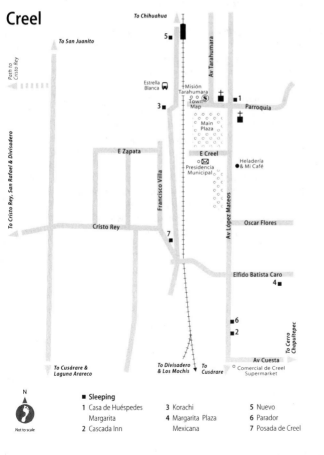

Creel

To Chihuahua

To San Juanito

Path to Cristo Rey

To Cristo Rey, San Rafael & Divisadero

Estrella Blanca
Misión Tarahumara
Town Map
3 ■
5 ■

Av Tarahumara

■ **1**
Parroquia

Main Plaza

E Zapata

E Creel

Francisco Villa

Presidencia Municipal

Heladería & Mi Café

Cristo Rey

7 ■

Oscar Flores

Av López Mateos

Elfido Batista Caro
4 ■

■ **6**
■ **2**

To Cerro Chapultepec

To Cusárare & Laguna Arareco

To Divisadero & Los Mochis

To Cusárare

Av Cuesta
Comercial de Creel Supermarket

N
Not to scale

■ **Sleeping**
1 Casa de Huéspedes Margarita
2 Cascada Inn
3 Korachi
4 Margarita Plaza Mexicana
5 Nuevo
6 Parador
7 Posada de Creel

Tarahumara Indians

This is the country of the long-haired, fleet-footed Tarahumara Indians, able, it is said, to outstrip a galloping horse and to run down birds. A few Indians can be seen in Chihuahua and Nuevo Casas Grandes, mostly women and children and most, sadly, begging. Tarahumara can be seen in much less unfortunate conditions and in greater numbers in Creel and beyond, but note that the Indians are shy, living in remote *ranchos* rather than the towns. 12 December is a festival for the

reservations cannot be made direct at the hotel, minibus to collect travellers, rustic woodstoves and oil-lamps, 8-day packages available; Jesús Manuel is a guide based here. Highly recommended for excellent *burro* hiking trips.

Eating
Water shortages are common

There are plenty of eating places in the town, on López Mateos, eg **Verónica**. Good *comida corrida*, and **Estela**. Also good, open 0800-2100 and on Sun. *Café El Manzano*, beside railway line. Good food. Also many shops selling food (including Mennonite cheese), but few open on Sun. *Panadería* next to *Estela*. There are bars in town, but ask which are the better ones (many are for men only); beers are expensive. *Bar Plaza Mexicana*, on Elfido Batista Caro, owned by *Margarita's* (see hotels). Recommended. Good ice cream shop (*heladería*) on López Mateos between Parroquía and Oscar Flores. Next door is *Mi Café*. Good food, cheap, try the apple *empanadas*, friendly.

Sport

Rock climbing *Expediciones Umarike* (see Bicycle hire below), US$50 per ½ day, at Humira (road to Batópilas), Chapultepec rock (in town) abseil at Basaseachi, bouldering. Generally top rope climbing because of loose volcanic rock. Rents out tents (US$6.50 per night), sleeping bags, stoves.

Tour operators

Tours and rentals: many people hang around the square offering tours in a variety of vehicles, or other means of transport. Roberto Venegas, T60049, has a van. Recommended. **Horses**: for rent at several locations, eg Rarajipa 18 (near *Expediciones Umarike*), US$4 per hour to Cristo Rey statue above town, US$3.20 per hour for 4-5 hr ride to waterfalls. **Bicycle hire**: *Expediciones Umarike*, Av Ferrocarril s/n, north of tracks west of Plaza, PO Box 61, T/F4560212. Run by Arturo Gutiérrez and his Welsh wife Audrey, very friendly, open every day, cosy offices with literature and real coffee, US$6.50 for ½ day, US$10.50 whole day, provide map, good bikes, must deposit ID; longer guided tours available on bike or in four-wheel drive eg to Tararecua Canyon. Also bikes from *Complejo Turístico Arareko*, López Mateos, opposite *Berlis*, US$2 per hour, US$11 per day, poor bikes. Map of town on the wall between Banca Serfín and Misión Tarahumara.

Transport

Trains For schedule see page 623. Station office is open Mon 0800-1000, 1100-1600; Tue-Fri 1000-1600, Sat 1000-1300. From Creel to Los Mochis takes about eight hours on the train.

Buses To **Chihuahua** with Estrella Blanca from 0700-1730, 6 a day, US$11.50, 4-5 hrs. To **Guachochi**, 0700, 1600, US$3. To **Ciudad Juárez** 0800. Buses also to surrounding villages. All leave from outside *Hotel Korachi*, across railway track from square. To **Cusárare** (see below), at 0700, US$1.75, or lift in *Margarita's* transport US$4.50, or hitchhike.

Regular bus to Batópilas US$24 return. Casa Margarita quoted US$30 per person for a return-minimum 6 people. *The Lodge at Creel* charges US$50 per person. Every trip involved an overnight stay in Batópilas; the hotel cost was not included in the rates quoted.

Banks *Banca Serfín*, on the square, very friendly, open 0900-1300, changes dollars cash no commission, but commission charged on TCs (US$1 per cheque), TCs must be authorized by manager, Visa and Mastercard advances, no commission; on Sat and Sun exchange at shops, but at poor rates; some places accept dollars, also at poor rates. **Communications** Post Office: on main square in Presidencia Municipal, no sign. **Telephone:** Long-distance phone office in *Hotel Nuevo*. **Laundry** Pink house opposite side of tracks from square, US$3 per load, 2 hrs, good, Mon-Sat 0900-2000, restricted hrs on Sun. **General stores** also on López Mateos.

Directory

There is a time change (though generally not recognized locally) between Creel (GMT – 6 hrs) and Los Mochis (GMT – 7 hrs).

Creel is an excellent centre for trekking and horse riding. It is also a good centre for reaching several deep canyons, including that of the Río Urique, known as the Barranca del Urique, or del Cobre (the Urique, or Copper Canyon – see below).

Excursions from Creel

From the town, footpaths lead to the Cristo Rey statue, to a viewpoint on Cerro Chapultepec and into the hills around. To see inhabited Tarahumara caves, turn right off the main road south out of town, about five minutes (by car) after the turn-off signed to San Rafael. The woman and her daughters welcome visitors. Further to the south, walk to the San Ignacio Mission, passing the Valle de los Hongos (Valley of the Mushrooms). ■ *US$3.25, entry fee charged by local community.* Continue to **Laguna Arareco** (8 km from Creel), around which one can walk. ■ *US$1.30.* The lake is just off the Creel-Guachochi/Batópilas road.

Just past Laguna Arareco is an unsigned right turn onto a bumpy track which leads, in 1½ hours in a hardy vehicle, to the top of the **Recohauta canyon**. A clear path descends, in an hour or so, to a dry river first, and then the Río Tararécua. Follow the path along the river to where hot springs come out of the canyon's side. A pool has been made. In heavy rain many paths are flooded. The climb back up to the top also takes about an hour (there is loose scree on the path), or you can continue to other hot springs, several hours walk away; camping equipment is essential (look out for the green arrows). Backpacking in the canyon is beautiful and, with a topographical map, original walks are easy to do. There are more trails than shown on maps; if the one you are on leads to a river or house it is not too difficult to find another, but many are vague and some lead to cliff edges.

Twenty kilometres south of Laguna Arareco, is Cusárare ('place of the eagles'), with a Jesuit church (1767) painted by Indians, and a 30m waterfall. ■ *US$1.* To get to the falls, continue 100m after the junction to Cusárare where there is a hotel sign on the right; turn right, pass the hotel and then the bridge, at the junction turn right, about 45 minutes walk; it is not well-signposted. There is very good hiking around Cusárare, but as the Misión in Creel does not stock the Creel/Cusárare topographical map, a guide may be necessary. Sr Reyes Ramírez and his son have been recommended for tours to the canyon, US$20 per day for two people, including guide and two pack donkeys. Allow four days to see the canyon properly, tough hiking. The canyon is hot by day and cold by night. Accommodation is extra. The American guide Cristóbal, at *Margarita's*, has also been recommended.

Cusárare
Colour map 1, grid B6

At Cusárare, the road bifurcates. One branch heads southeast to **Norogachi**, 75 km from Cusárare, with a Tarahumara school and authentic costumes worn on Sunday, typical *fiestas*. This road continues to join the more usual route to Guachochi, which is the southern fork out of Cusárare.

156 km from Creel, Guachochi has a wild west appearance. There is a bank in town. From Guachochi you can walk four hours to the impressive **Barranca de Sinforosa**. Outside the town take the road to the left of a wooden hut; after 6 km take another left turn just after crossing a viaduct, carry on until you

Guachochi
Colour map 1, grid C6

come to a gate on the left side of the road before it veers off to the right. Beyond the gate there is an orchard with a tower in the middle. It seems that you have to cross several sets of barbed wire to get to the canyon. The canyon is not visible until you reach the edge of it. From a point several hundred metres above the Río Verde you can see an unforgettable extended system of immense canyons, grander (according to some) than you can see from El Divisadero or on crossing the Barranca del Cobre. You can descend to the river on a path. This is not advisable for women alone.

Sleeping C *Melina*, Belisario Domínguez 14, T30255. Clean, hot water, bar. **D** *Chaparre*, T30001. Overpriced but good restaurant, bath, TV, hot water. **E** *Orpimel*, in same building as bus station.

Buses To Creel twice daily 0730 and 1330, US$3 (check at *Hotel Korachi* for schedule from Creel); also reached from Hidalgo del Parral, bus leaves for Parral at 0800 and 1200, now paved, but not spectacular.

Copper Canyon

The road south out of Cusárare leads eventually to Batópilas, passing a turn-off to El Tejabán above the **Barranca del Urique/Cobre** (this is claimed to be the 'real' Copper Canyon); **Basíhuare** ('Sash') village, surrounded by pink and white rock formations (40 km from Creel); and the Puente del Río Urique, spanning the Urique Canyon. The climate is ideal for camping. At the junction Creel-Guachochi-Bufa, near Samachique, is a small restaurant/hotel, **F** *La Casita*. Very primitive and romantic. The road is paved as far as the junction but is bumpy from then on. Just after the junction, 3 km down into the valley is **Samachique**, where the *rari-pame* race, kicking a wooden ball for 241 km without rest, often takes 2-3 days and nights in September. Stranded travellers can find a room and food at the bus stop (no more than a shack) in Samachique, which is 1 km off the main route to Batópilas (1330 bus from Guachochi arrives at 1500 after Creel bus has gone through). If wishing to hitch to Batópilas (2½ hour drive) take the right fork as you walk back out of Samachique; it rejoins the route at a junction where you can wait for traffic both coming through and by-passing the village. **Quírare**, 65 km from Creel offers views of the beutiful **Batópilas Canyon**. After Quírare there is an awesome 14-km descent to La Bufa, in the Batópilas canyon, and on to Batópilas, possibly the most scenic road in northern Mexico.

Copper Canyon area

Batópilas

Batópilas, 120 km from Creel, is a little town of 1,100 inhabitants, quiet, palm-fringed, subtropical, delightful and hot, hemmed in by the swirling river and the cactus-studded canyon walls. There are good parties in the Plaza at Christmas and New Year. It is an excellent centre for walking and within easy reach of the Urique Canyon (see box). Horses, pigs, goats and chickens wander freely along the cobblestone streets. Mangoes and other citrus fruits are grown. Europeans arrived here in 1690. The Mina de Guadalupe was discovered in 1780 by Pedro de la Cruz. Batópilas became a thriving silver-mining centre, with mines owned by the Shepard family. Their mansion (near the bridge), abandoned during Pancho Villa's campaign, must be one of the most elaborate adobe houses anywhere, but it is now overgrown and dilapidated. Shepard, whose big strike was La Bufa mine, built houses, bridges and canals around the town. Apparently, Batópilas was the second place in Mexico, after the capital, to receive electricity. Ironically, the town only has electricity from 1800 to midnight, although a new generator is expected. Manuel Gómez Morín, founder of the PAN (National Action Party), lived in Batópilas. His house (now a store) on the main street has a plaque proclaiming the place where he first 'saw the light'. Above the main plaza is the tiny, shady Plaza de la Constitución at the end of town. Three notable houses are the 18th-century Casa Barfusson and Casa Morales and the early 19th-century Casa Bigleer.

Sleeping The owners of the *Copper Canyon Sierra Lodge* in Creel have opened the **LL** *Copper Canyon Riverside Lodge* (US reservations, T800-7763942, F810-3407212). Same prices for full board, closed in Jun, renovated 19th-century hacienda, with gardens, luxurious, full board, drinks with meals and organized trips included). **C** *Mari*. Reservations as for *Parador de la Montaña* in Creel. **D** *Hotel Monse*. Room with 2 double beds. **E** *Batópilas*. Clean, also *Parador Batópilas*, more expensive, but not too much. **E** *Chulavista*, on way into town, owned by Don Mario, near bridge at entrance to village. Clean, hot water, tiny rooms. Basic rooms also at **F** *Restaurant Clarita* and *Sra Monse*, **E-F** – ask prices first – at plaza (she sells Tarahumara violins), rooms with gas lamps. She can give information in English (which she likes to practise on tourists). *Carmen's Youth Hostel*. Basic, good food, friendly.

Eating *Restaurant El Puente Colgante*. New, pleasant and friendly, garden, cold beer, bit pricey. Meals at the private house of Sra Enedina Caraveo de Hernández on Plaza Constitución are good and cheap, large portions. *Restaurant Carolina*, between bridge and centre. Friendly owner, good selection, will prepare a packed lunch, with a group give a time and arrange your own order. Planning to move to Plaza Constitución. In the village there are only basic supplies in shops. The store on the plaza, *Tienda Grande* (Casa Morales), can change travellers' cheques at a poor rate. Bring insect repellent against locally nicknamed 'assassin bug' or bloodsucking insect.

Tour operators Several people in Creel offer trips to Batópilas. A recommended guide is Pedro Estrada Pérez (limited English but patient), T560079. An overnight trip for 4 (minimum) costs US$60 per person, plus lodging and meals, including trip to Jesuit Mission at Satevo (see below). Many hotels arrange tours to some of the places mentioned in this section; prices vary from hotel to hotel, some require a minimum number of people, some provide lunch. Some examples: to Cusárare (US$12-15), mission and falls, and Basíhuare; Recohauta hot springs (US$8 plus US$1.50 entrance); San Ignacio, Valle de los Hongos and Laguna Arareco; to Basaseachi (US$58 includes lunch, minimum 4, from *Parador La Montaña*); Batópilas; Divisadero (US$20, minimum 5, from *Margarita's*). These tours are pricey, but good fun and may involve more walking or

☞ *Batópilas to Urique*

A three-day hike goes from the Batópilas Canyon to Urique (once known as the Camino Real, or Royal Way), from where you can get a ride to Bahuichivo for a train to Creel or Los Mochis.

Routes Batópilas-Cerro Colorado-Piedra Redonda-Cerro El Manzano-La Estación-Los Alisos-Urique. You climb from 500m, reaching 2,200m before descending to Urique at 600m. It can be very hot in the canyons; drink at least four litres of water a day (you can fill up at settlements along the way) and take plenty of sunblock. There are many junctions of paths and so if you are without a guide it is vital to check that you are on the correct route as often as possible (try not to wander into marijuana plantations). One recommendation if you are using the 'Batópilas' survey map (1:50,000 sheet G13A41, covering the entire route, available from the Misión Tarahumara in Creel US$5) is that you take the ridge path (not marked on the 1979 edition) after Cerro El Manzano to La Estación, both for the views and directness.

Horseriding A recommended guide (not cheap) is Librado Balderrama Contreras who will guide you to Urique or to surrounding attractions such as Mesa Quimoba, Mesa de San José and Monerachi. There are several places in town where you can hire mules (with a handler) for carrying gear.

climbing than advertised. Recommended for guided tours deep into the Urique Canyon is *Adventure Specialists*, Inc (president Gary Ziegler), Bear Basin Ranch, Westcliffe, CO 81252 (303/7832519, 800/6218385, ext 648), US$700-800 for 11-day tours from El Paso, vigorous, knowledgeable.

Transport Buses from Creel, Tue, Thu, and Sat at 0700, 5-6 hrs (paved as far as Samachique turn-off) depending on weather, US$9.50, buy ticket the day before, very crowded. Tickets are sold from *Restaurant La Herradura* in the main street; the best time to try is when the bus (white with 'Batópilas' in blue on the side) stands outside from about 1225 having just arrived on its return to Creel, Mon, Wed, and Fri; it leaves Batópilas at 0500 (have a torch handy as it is very dark). Supply lorry leaves for Chihuahua Tue, Thu, Sat at 0600, takes passengers.

Directory Communications: Telephone office on corner of plaza, open 0900-1300, 1500-1900.

Excursions from Batópilas The **Porfirio Díaz Mine** above the bridge into town can be explored to about 3 km into the mountain (take torch); as you get into the mine there is the sickly, sweet smell of bat droppings, after about 1 km the air is thick with disturbed bats. **Satevo**, a 7-km walk from Batópilas along the river, a poor place with 15 houses, two of which sell drinks, has a 350-year-old Jesuit Mission whose dome has been repainted and whose interior is under repair. The mission has flattering acoustics for those who like to sing to themselves. The family next door has the key. ■ *US$ donation appreciated*. The route to Satevo can be driven on a rough jeep track. The surrounding area, but not the town, is inhabited by the Tarahumaras known as *Gentiles* (women don't look at, or talk to, men). If you go 'off road' here, beware of drug cultivation areas. It is possible to walk in the other direction to **Cerro Colorado** and back in a day (8 km, three hours each way, along the road that departs from north side of the bridge). In this tiny village some people still mine for gold, carrying the ore down to the river by donkey where it is ground up in water-powered stone mills. Like Batópilas it has interesting industrial architecture, drainage ditches, tunnels, canals and bridges. You can camp in the schoolyard, or on a small beach 15 minutes before the town. With luck you can hitch to Cerro Colorado, then walk two hours to Munérachi, a remote village, to meet Tarahumara Indians (best to arrange a local guide through Sra Monse on the plaza in Batópilas as drug cultivation in this part of the canyon means some areas are unsafe). At **Cerro Yerbanis** there are amazing views of the Batópilas Canyon.

Beyond Creel, the Chihuahua al Pacífico train passes its highest point, Los Ojitos and, soon after, the Lazo loop, in which the track does a 360° turn. Seventeen kilometres further on is Pitorreal. At Divisadero there is an all-too-brief 20-minute stop to view the canyon and buy souvenirs from the Tarahumara women. Five minutes further on, the train comes to *Hotel Posada Barrancas*. The *Primera Especial* leaves Creel at 1225, US$5, the ordinary train at 1320, US$1, one and a half hours; *Posada Barrancas* is five minutes further on, same fare.

Divisadero
Colour map 1, grid B5

For those who aren't travelling on the train the Barranca de Urique/de Cobre (Urique/Copper Canyon) is quite a long way from Creel. Apart from the access from Batópilas (see box, page 630), or from Bahuichivo (see below), the simplest way to see the canyon is to go to Divisadero or *Posada Barrancas* by rough road, paved halfway from Creel (hitch, no public transport), or by train. To hitch, walk along López Mateos out of Creel to the paved main road; continue for 1 km to the turning to San Rafael and wait for a lift there. Single women should only accept a ride if other women are in the vehicle and ask the women how far they are going. Return to Creel on the slow train at 1700 (or hitch back), or else stay overnight.

Sleeping **A** *Hotel Divisadero Barrancas*, PO Box 661, 31238 Chihuahua, T103330, F156575. Full board and includes 2 tours (to Balancing Rock, see below, and San Luis de Majuachic). 2-3 km by road, 5 mins by train from Divisadero is **A** *Posada Barrancas Mirador*, across the tracks from the old *Posada Barrancas*. New hotel has views from every room, full board, free lemonade on arrival and free *margarita* later, book through *Hotel Santa Anita*, Los Mochis, T681-57046, F681-20046, tours arranged, including hike or horseback trip to a Tarahumara village. Recommended. **A** *Hotel Mansión Tarahumara* (reservations, Av Juárez 1602-A, Chihuahua, T154721, F165444), reached from *Posada Barrancas* station. Full board, good food, lovely rooms, clean, friendly. Reservations are advisable. If you want the train to stop at *Posada Barrancas*, tell a railway official.

C *Casa de Huéspedes Díaz*. Rooms with 2 double beds, hot water on request, prepares meals. **E** *Cabañas*. And bed and breakfast near church, 2 food shops, or, walk 1½ km down the road, past the 'camping' sign to a hamlet of 3 houses. 1st house on left has a rustic room with earth floor and lantern with a double and a single bed, **F**. Breakfast and dinner available with the friendly Gutiérrez family. To hike into the canyon, take the path at the back of their house to a stone wall and stream that leads down into the canyon. Follow trails down to Tarahumara Indian dwellings and interesting mushroom-shaped rocks. Ask locals for *piedras como hongos*. From the canyon rim, the best views are in the late afternoon.

The Balancing Rock is at the edge of the canyon; it wobbles in a stomach-churning way as you stand on it. Reached by *camioneta* from *Hotel Divisadero Barrancas*, or walk 1-2 km from Divisadero (away from Creel) and on the left you will see the wooden entrance gate. From there it is 45 minutes to the rock with stops at the canyon viewing points. Guides are available at the hotel. Car drivers can park outside the entrance, or ask at the hotel for the key to open the gate. Also here is a marked trail for mountain bikes.

Excursions from Divisadero

From *Posada Barrancas Mirador* you can hike down five minutes to a Tarahumara cave dwelling, souvenirs sometimes on sale. You can also hike around the rim to the village.

The canyon can also be reached on foot from Divisadero or *Posada Barrancas*; from the former it is 6 km (walk or hitch) along the dirt road that runs beside the railway to the house of Florencio Manzinas (at the first group of houses you come to). He will hire out donkeys, give directions to the canyon (for a small tip), or will accompany you as guide (more expensive). He also provides food and accommodation in his house, or may let you camp free. From there it's a day's hike along narrow, slippery, often steep and sometimes overgrown trails into the canyon, descending from cool pine forest into gradually more subtropical vegetation as you approach the river and the canyon floor. At this point there are mango, orange and banana trees. Take plenty of water for the hike as, after descending the first section following a stream, you have to go over another hill before getting down to the river, which means several hours without access to water.

Bahuichivo
Colour map 1, grid B5

Twenty-five minutes beyond the *Hotel Posada Barrancas* the Chihuahua al Pacífico reaches **San Rafael**, where there is a 10-minute stop, and then passes the La Laja bridge and tunnel. It is a further 20 minutes to **Cuiteco** which has the **B** *Hotel Cuiteco*, delightful, with a patio which has an unimpeded view of the mountains, quiet, oil lamps, gas stove in courtyard. Next on the line comes Bahuichivo where there is a simple hotel, **E** *Viajero*, restaurant next door, and a few shops; if you don't want to go all the way to Los Mochis you can return from here (Bahuichivo-Creel, 1st class, US$4, three hours). From Bahuichivo to Los Mochis is five hours on the train.

Urique
Colour map 1, grid B5

From Bahuichivo, bus and pick-ups make the five-hour journey to Urique, in the heart of the Barranca de Urique. Before the canyon is the town of Cerocahui, on a meander in the river, with a solid red-stone church (one hotel – **LL** *Mission*, full board, book in Flamingo Travel in Los Mochis). At the lip of the canyon is a *mirador* offering fine views. The road into the canyon is spectacular, only rivalled by the road to Batópilas.

Urique has a hot, subtropical climate, houses sprawl along the river interspersed with citrus groves. 1½ hours walk (7 km) upstream from Urique (crossing to other side by hanging bridge) is the Mission church of Guadalupe Coronal in a small village. Downstream is the village of **Guapalayna** (4,500m) with another old small church. There are two simple hotels, the one on the main street, **F** *Cañón de Urique*, south of centre, is good value. *Restaurant Plaza*, across the main street from the plaza has a garden at the back, and is friendly. No private phones, telephone office on plaza. ■*0800-1300, 1400-1900, Mon-Sat, 0800-1200 Sun. A bus leaves from Urique to return to Bahuichivo at 0800, US$5.50; on arrival and before departure it goes up and down the main street.*

Témoris

Near Témoris, the train track enters a tunnel in which the railway turns through 180°. Témoris, an attractive town 11 km above the train station, in the mining and cattle country of the lower western Sierra Madre, is a good base for visiting working ranches, Tarahumara villages, waterfalls and swimming holes, on foot, horse or mountainbike. *Colectivos* make the trip or you may be able to hitch with local merchants. There are three hotels in the area and several cheap restaurants. *Campamento Adame* (T60750/60612, best to phone in advance), a good choice for backpackers, has *cabañas*, dormitories and tent sites with shower and cooking facilities. Gilberto Adame is friendly and helpful and can arrange trips by whatever mode into the mountains. He also has a bus for local touring. There is a *fiesta* for San Miguel in the last week of September. After Témoris it is a further four hours before the train reaches Los Moches (see page 661).

South from Chihuahua

The first major town southeast of Chihuahua on Route 45, Ciudad Delicias, is the centre of a major agricultural area. There is a **Museo de Paleontología**, Avenida Río Chuvíscar Norte y Círculo de la Plaza de la República, T28513, with fossils from the Zona de Silencio (see below) and from the inland sea that covered the area 80m years ago. At the same address is a cultural centre. ■ *0900-2000, Mon-Sat.*

Ciudad Delicias
Phone code: 14
Colour map 2, grid B2

Sleeping *Casa Grande*, Av 6 Ote 601, T40404. 5-star. *del Norte*, Av Agricultura Norte 5, T20200. 4-star. *Baeza*, Calle 2 Norte 309, T21000. 3-star. *Delicias*, near market. Several others of similar quality nearby.

Markets *Mercado Juárez*, Av del Parque y 3 Norte, local produce and handicrafts, Mon-Sat 0900-2000, Sun 0900-1500. *Mercado Morelos*, Calle 4 Sur 600.

Transport Train Station: Av 7 Ote, T20834. **Buses**: To/from **Chihuahua** hourly, US$3; Omnibus de México, Av 6 y Calle 2 Norte, T21020; Estrella Blanca, Av 6 Norte 300, T21509; Rápidos Delicias, Av 5 Norte 301, T21030.

A small cattle town in a green valley, Ciudad Camargo is quiet except for its eight days of *fiesta* for Santa Rosalía beginning on 4 September, when there are cockfights, horse racing and dancing. There is black bass fishing at the nearby dam lake, and warm sulphur springs 5 km away. A *Hotel Santa Fe*, south edge of town on highway. Very quiet, secure parking, good breakfast, some English spoken. Recommended. **Motel D** *Victoria*, Comonfort y Jiménez. Clean and cheap.

Ciudad Camargo
Phone code: 146
Colour map 2, grid B2

From **Ciudad Jiménez** (1,263 km from Mexico City, **B** *Motel Florido*, hot water) there are two routes south to Fresnillo and Zacatecas: the Central Highway through Durango, or a more direct route via Torreón (237 km from Ciudad Jiménez), passing Escalón (restaurant), **Ceballos** (**E** *Hotel San José*, basic), Yermo (restaurants) and Bermejillo (restaurant), on Route 49.

Between Escalón and Ceballos is the **Zona del Silencio** (the Silent Zone), a highly magnetic area where, it is claimed, electrical appliances fall silent, aircraft radar goes haywire, and so on. It inspires much interest and research but as yet no proof.

Torreón

Torreón is the principal industrial city of La Laguna cotton and wheat district. It is reported hot, polluted and without colonial atmosphere. Here is the **Bolsón de Mayrán**, an oasis of about 28,500 sq km which might be irrigated, but only about 2,000 sq km have been developed and much of that is stricken with drought. On the opposite side of the mostly dry Río Nazas are the two towns of **Gómez Palacio** (*feria* first half of August) and **Ciudad Lerdo**.

Phone code: 17
Colour map 2, grid C3
Population: 700,000
Altitude: 1,137m

Torreón A *Palacio Real*, Morelos 1280, T60000. **A** *Paraíso del Desierto*, Independencia y Jiménez, T61122. Resort. **A** *Río Nazas*. Av Morelos y Treviño. High-rise, very good. **A-D** *Posada de Sol*, Bulevar Revolucionario, opposite La Unidad

Sleeping

The Northern Highlands

de Deportes sports complex. Modern motel, secure parking, small restaurant, bar, hot showers, rooms range from basic, windowless, clean *cabañas* to large, US-style rooms with TV, good value. **D** *Galicia*, Cepeda 273. Good. **D** *Laguna*, Carrillo 333. **D** *Princesa*, Av Morelos near Parque Central. There are a few decent places to eat in the centre.

Gómez Palacio **C** *Motel La Siesta*, Av Madero 320 Nte, T140291/142840. Clean, hot water, safe parking. Good. **D** *Motel La Cabaña*. Hot water. **E** *Colonial*, 3 blocks south of train station. Hot water, bath, only internal locks on doors, basic.

Transport **Air** Torreón airport is 14.5 km from the centre. Services to Chihuahua, Ciudad Juárez, Culiacán, Durango, Guadalajara, Hermosillo, Ixtapa, La Paz, Los Angeles (California), Mazatlán, Mexico City, Monterrey, Piedras Negras, San Antonio (Texas) and Tijuana.

Buses Local buses on Blvd Revolucionario go to all parts of the city. The new Torreón bus station is 5 km south of the city; if coming from the north, drivers allow you to leave the bus in the centre. There is a shuttle service between the centre and the bus station; taxis to centre operate a fixed-fare system. To **Chihuahua**, 6 hrs, US$16.50; to **Tepic**, US$30; to **Ciudad Juárez**, US$30; about 6 a day to **Durango**, 4½ hrs 2nd class. Gómez Palacio has its own bus station, without a shuttle to the centre. City buses outside have frequent services to all three city centres, US$0.33. When leaving either bus terminal, make sure that your bus does not stop at the other terminal; this can cause long delays.

Train Check locally to see whether any passenger services are running.

Between Gómez Palacio and Zacatecas are **Cuencamé** (**D** *Motel la Posta*, hot water, north of town; hotel south of town, **D**, not recommended, damp, dirty,

Chihuahua environs

but has parking; just north of Cuencamé, as you turn off Route 49 onto Route 40 to Durango is *Menudo El Zancas*, 100m on left, a truckers' meal stop open 24 hours, which is excellent, set meal US$3.45), **Río Grande** (D *Hotel Río*) and **Fresnillo**. This last town is the birthplace of the artist Francisco Goitia and musician Manuel M Ponce, with many old buildings and a museum. (C *Motel La Fortuna*, comfortable, hot water; D *Hotel Cuauhtémoc*, basic.)

Hidalgo del Parral

The other route south from Ciudad Jiménez branches 77 km west to Hidalgo del Parral (usually just called Parral), an old mining town with narrow streets, 1,138 km from Mexico City. In 1629, Juan Rangel de Viezma discovered *La Negrita*, the first mine in the area. Now known as *La Prieta*, it overlooks the city from the top of Cerro la Prieta. Rangel founded the town in 1631 under the name of San Juan del Parral; it was renamed Hidalgo in honour of the father of the Revolution in 1833. When Parral was founded, the population consisted of Spaniards, *mestizos*, black slaves from Cuba and Africa, and Indians (who became the workforce for the mining industry). The mine owners were generous benefactors to the city, leaving many beautiful buildings which still stand. On 8 September 1944, severe damage was caused by a flood. The decrease in population, either through drowning or flight, led to a recession.

Phone code: 152
Colour map 2, grid B2
Population: 100,000

The city's history is split between its mining heritage and the fact that Pancho Villa was assassinated here.

Hidalgo del Parral is now a pleasant, safe, affluent city. It has a compact centre with a string of shaded plazas, many bridges over the sinuous, and often dry, Río del Parral, and several churches. A one-way system operates in the centre; drivers should proceed with extreme caution and be wary of obscurely placed traffic lights. There is no tourist office in Parral but advice may be obtained from the Cámara de Comercio, Colegio 28, T20018.

On the Plaza Principal is the **Parroquia de San José**, with a beautiful interior. **Plaza Baca** has a statue to *El Buscador de Ilusiones* (the Dream Seeker), a naked man panning for gold. The **Cathedral** is on this square and, on the opposite side, is the **Templo San Juan de Dios** with an exuberant altarpiece, painted gold. Across the road from the Cathedral is the former *Hotel Hidalgo* (not in use), built in 1905 by mine owner Pedro Alvarado and given to Pancho Villa in the 1920s. Next-door is **Casa Stallforth** (1908), the shop and house of a German family who supplied everything imaginable to the city. It is still a shop, with the original interior. Continuing on Mercaderes, before the bridge, is **Casa Griensen**, now the Colegio Angloamericano Isaac Newton. Griensen, another German, married Alvarado's sister. Behind this house is **Casa Alvarado**, still a private residence, only for viewing from the outside. Crossing the bridge at the end of Mercaderes, you come to the site of Villa's death, on the corner of Plaza Juárez. Also worth seeing is the façade of the **Teatro Hidalgo** on Plazuela Independencia. Just off Avenida Independencia is the **Templo de la Virgen del Rayo** (the Virgin of the Lightning).

Sights

Twenty-one kilometres east of Parral on the Jiménez road is the turning for Talamantes, which is a further 11 km down a dirt road in good condition. Turn right at the square and continue 3 km out of town to the **Ojo de Talamantes**, a warm, natural pool of clear spring water, 2m deep. ■ *Daily, 0900-1800, US$1.* There is also a manmade swimming pool, picnic areas, changing rooms and toilets. Boats, in poor shape, can be rented, US$6 per hour. Bring your own food, not much on sale. The village itself is virtually a ghost town, with the remains of what must have been great estates. No public transport runs to Talamantes.

Excursions

The Northern Highlands

Twenty-six kilometres east of Parral on the Jiménez road, a well-signed road leads 5 km south to **Valle de Allende** (*Population:* 4,000). Originally called Valle de San Bartolomé, it was the site of the first Franciscan mission in Chihuahua, founded in the late 16th century by Fray Agustín Rodríguez. The original monastery building still stands on the main square, but it is unused (it has been used as a *refrigeradora* to store apples). Also on the square is the Parroquia de San Bartolomé and an unsightly Pepsi plant (no longer in production), which replaced the building in which the severed heads of the Independence leaders Hidalgo, Allende, Aldama and Jiménez were deposited for a night on their parade around the country after their execution. The town was renamed after Allende in 1825. Valle de Allende is a beautiful little town with a shaded central square, many colonial-style houses and a number of orchards which produce fruit and walnuts. During Semana Santa (Easter week) there is a re-enactment of Christ carrying the cross to Calvary; all the villagers take part. The artist who painted the murals in the Palacio de Gobierno, Chihuahua, lives here and is setting up an art school and ceramics workshop.

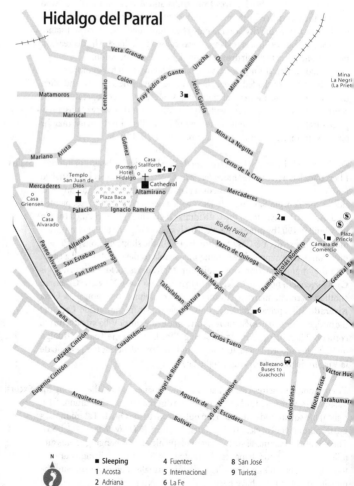

Hidalgo del Parral

■ Sleeping
1 Acosta
2 Adriana
3 Chihuahua
4 Fuentes
5 Internacional
6 La Fe
7 Moreira
8 San José
9 Turista

Outside town is the ruined **Hacienda San Gregorio**, dating from the 19th century. Among the visible features is the *rebote* court, in which a type of squash/rackets was played, using a hard leather bat and a stone ball wrapped in metal (there were a lot of injuries; a gentler form of *rebote* is played in town using a tennis ball and bare hands). The **Balneario El Trébol** is open April-September. There are picnic areas, swimming pools for adults and children, toilets and changing rooms. ■ *US$1*. Behind the Balneario you can swim or fish in the Río Allende. There are rooms to let at *Almacén La Norteña*, Cuauhtémoc 40. Basic but clean, family atmosphere. There is a scheme for private house owners to rent rooms to visitors. Buses from Parral leave from the Central Camionera, last bus back 1800, US$1.30, 30 minutes. There is a Pemex station.

Southwest of Parral are the mining towns of Santa Bárbara and San Francisco el Oro. **Santa Bárbara** was founded in 1567 and a Franciscan mission was set up in 1571. The church on the town square dates from this time. The Museo Comunitario El Minero, on Allende, has many items relating to mining and other objects. ■ *Free*. The town is quite pretty and you can walk to the mine. Buses from Parral (Jesús García) take 30 minutes, US$0.50, half hourly. The bus stops at the Mercado.

Sleeping

B *Adriana*, Colegio 2, between Plaza Principal and Plaza Baca, T22570, F24770. A/c, restaurant, bar, parking. **C** *Acosta*, Agustín Barbachano 3, T20221, F29555, off the Plaza Principal. Quiet, parking for car or motorbike, rooftop terrace with fine view, laundry facilities, very clean, central, friendly, helpful, hot water, excellent value. Recommended. **C** *Moreira*, Jesús García 2, near Cathedral. Unwelcoming. **C** *San José*, Santiago Méndez 5, near Plaza Principal. With bath, safe parking, clean, central. **C** *Turista*, Plazuela Independencia 12, T24489, F24784. Clean, nice.

D *Chihuahua*, Colón 1, off Jesús García. Clean, simple. **D** *Fuentes*, near Plaza Baca. Dirty, dour rooms, restaurant has cheap *comida corrida*. **E** *Margarita*, near bus station. Recommended. **F** *Internacional*, Flores Magón. Basic, friendly, parking, dirty. **F** *La Fe*, Flores Magón 57. Shared bath, dirty.

Eating

La Parroquia in *Hotel San José*. Good-value meals, including breakfast. *Morelos*, Plazuela Morelos 22, off Plaza Principal. Clean, rather expensive, open 0700-2300, Friday and Saturday open 24 hrs. *Café Corales*, Flores Magón opposite Buses Ballezano. Good beef sandwiches. On Independencia: *Nutripan*, No 221. Cakes, pastries and bread, including brown; sliced brown bread at *La Patita*,

The Northern Highlands

The assassination of Pancho Villa

The infamous assassination of Pancho Villa took place in the town centre on 20 July 1923. Villa owned a house on Calle Zaragoza (now a shop called Almacenes Real de Villa, painted bright pink) and was making his way from there to the Hotel Hidalgo, which he also owned, when he was ambushed on Av Juárez. The house chosen by the assassins is now the Museo Pancho Villa. 12 of the 100 bullets fired hit Villa, who was taken immediately to the Hotel Hidalgo. The death mask taken there can be seen in the museum and also in the museum in Chihuahua. His funeral took place the next day and he was buried in the Panteón Municipal; his tomb is still there even though the body has been transferred to Mexico City.
Mon-Fri 0900-2000, Sat 0900-1300.

No 60; wide choice of bread and cakes at *El Parralense*, off Independencia on Calle Los Ojitos.

Shopping Mercado Hidalgo on the corner of Plaza Principal, *comedores*, fruit, vegetables, shoes, etc. Boutiques on Independencia. *Centro Naturista El Vergel*, in front of Casa Alvarado, massage, physiotherapy, natural medicines, herbs and vitamins, etc, for sale. *Homeopathic pharmacy*, 20 de November 90.

Transport **Buses** The bus station is outside town; 20 mins walk, on Av Independencia, east of centre, taxi about US$2. To **Durango**, Transportes Chihuahuenses US$18, 6 hrs. To **Zacatecas**, Omnibus de México, US$30, 9 hrs. To **Chihuahua**, frequent departures, 2½ hrs, US$7 2nd class, US$10.50 1st. Also to **Guachochi** (see page 627). Few bus lines start here so it is difficult to reserve seats. Buses Ballezano to Guachochi leave from office on Carlos Fuero y Flores Magón at 0800, 1230, 1545, US$4.

Directory **Banks** *Banco Unión*, in *Hotel Adriana* complex, exchange until 1200, poor rates, similarly at *Banamex* opposite. Good rates at *Bancomer*, Plaza Principal until 1200. Opposite is *Cambios de Oro*, no commission, good rates, open Mon-Fri 0900-1900, Sat until 1400. *Cambios Palmilla*, Maclovio Herrera 97, Plaza Baca, good rates, open daily 0900-2100. Also at Gasolinera Palmilla on road to Santa Bárbara, 3 km out of town. **Communications Post Office:** on Del Rayo, just over bridge from centre, open 0800-1500.

Routes An alternative route to Parral from Chihuahua is by Highway 24, which turns south from Highway 16, 38 km west of Chihuahua city. It is a lonely road, if shorter than the major road, and in good condition. After 50 km there is a restaurant and Pemex station at the turning to Satevó. At Km 110 is *Centro Trailer El Chamuco*. Restaurant, rooms to let (**C**), clean, hot water. A few kilometres further on is Valle de Zaragoza, with lots of *comedores* and a Pemex station. Then there is nothing until Parral.

Durango environs

Parral to Durango

Route 45, south of Parral, is in good condition all the way to Durango. Pemex is available at Villa de Nieve, just before Canutillo. Here, 3 km down a winding road, well signed, is Pancho Villa's hacienda, with an excellent museum (give a donation to the man who opens the door). Villa was given the hacienda in exchange for promising to lay down his arms and retire to private life (28 July 1920). After the town of Revolución the road becomes dead straight for many kilometres. There is a Pemex station (and a federal document check) at the big crossroads for Torreón.

Cinema enthusiasts can visit the Western sets of *Villa del Oriente* (9 km from Durango) and *Chupaderos* (10½ km), both decaying (especially the latter) but smelling authentically of horse (San Juan del Río buses go there or take a taxi, US$14, which takes you to both sets with a 15-minute stay at each). Also after Rodeo there are some beautiful villages along the river. Four kilometres east off the road, at **San Juan del Río**, is a Pemex station. Halfway down the side road to San Juan is a signed road to Coyotada, off which is a 4 km road to Pancho Villa's birthplace and museum (modest, a few artefacts and photos). ■ *Free, donation welcome.*

Between Rodeo and Durango, is the 'Western landscape' beloved of Hollywood film-makers.

Durango

Victoria de Durango, capital of Durango state was founded in 1563 some 260 km southwest of Torreón and 926 northwest of Mexico City. It is a modernising city but with many beautiful old buildings (see the 18th-century **Casa de los Condes de Suchill**, now Bancomer, on 5 de Febrero, and the French-style **Teatro Ricardo Castro**), a **Cathedral** (1695) and a famous iron-water spring. The main street is Avenida 20 de Noviembre, a wide dominating thoroughfare which reflects the 'wild-west' image of the state of Durango, so often a backdrop to not only Hollywood movies but also the Mexican film industry at its height. There is a small **Cinema Museum** on 16 de Septiembre by Boulevard Dolores del Río, with a good collection of Mexican film posters plus old cameras. ■ *Tue-Sat 1000-1930, Sun 1100-1800, free.* There is a leather goods market, Mercado Gómez Palacio, on Pasteur between 20 de Noviembre and 5 de Febrero. Parque Guadiana at the west edge of town, with huge eucalyptus trees, is a nice place to relax. There are good views of the city from Cerro de Los Remedios; many flights of steps lead up to a chapel. The **tourist office**, on a large roundabout at the edge of the city centre, 20 de Noviembre and Independencia is helpful. There is a *feria* during the first half of July.

Phone code: 18
Colour map 2, grid C2
Population: 600,000
Altitude: 1,924m

Presa Victoria, to the south, can be reached by bus from Durango; one can swim in the lake enclosed by the dam. **Balneario La Florida** on the outskirts is pleasant (take green 'Potreros' bus on Calle Pasteur). Take a bus from Plaza Boca Ortiz to the big hacienda in Ferrería, a 7-km walk along mostly deserted roads leads to the **Mirador la Ventana** with great views.

Excursions

Santiago Papasquiaro is three hours north on Route 23 (on the way, in Canatlán, are Mennonite colonies), **D** *Hotel División del Norte*, Madero 35, T186-20013, in a former convent; the owner's husband was in Pancho Villa's *División del Norte*. *Restaurant Mirador*, across from the market, good food. There are a number of hot springs in the area, Hervideros is the most popular, take the bus to Herreras, then 30 minutes walk. **Tepehuanes**, one hour further on, is a small pleasant town with two hotels. Walk to Purísima and then to a small, spectacular canyon. A dirt road continues to **Guanacevi**, a mining town in the Sierra.

Durango is on the Coast-to-Coast Highway from Mazatlán to Matamoros. The 320-km stretch of road from Durango west to Mazatlán is through splendid mountain scenery. Sixty kilometres from Durango is **El Tecuán Parque Recreativo**, nice forest location, no facilities but camping free. For a day trip, go as far as **El Salto** (96 km), seven buses a day, but go early to get a ticket. The town is dirty and uninviting, but the people are very friendly (**E** *Hotel Diamante*, Francisco I Madero, T60700. Clean, basic, friendly, no running water in room. Recommended).

Between Durango and Zacatecas is **Sombrerete**, a small, lively and pretty colonial silver mining town, which at the height of its prosperity at the end of the 17th century rivalled Zacatecas. The town has 10 good churches and the superb, partially restored Franciscan convent San Mateo, 1567. Next door to it is the elliptical Chapel of the Third Order. (Hotels: **D** *Avenida Real*, clean, restaurant. **E** *Real de Minas*, T493-50340 Clean, comfortable, enclosed parking. **E** *Villa de Llerena*, T4930077, on main plaza. Clean but dark rooms. *La Calera* restaurant, good). 7 km north of the Durango road, 12 km before Sombrerete, is the **Sierra de los Organos** or Valley of the Giants, now a national park, where John Wayne made several of his westerns. It is named after the organ-like basaltic columns which are supposed to resemble organ pipes. There are good hiking possibilities in the area.

Sleeping
■ *on maps*
Price codes:
see inside front cover

AL *Gobernador*, 20 de Noviembre 257 Ote, T131919 F111422. **A** *Fiesta Mexicana*, 20 de Noviembre and Independencia, T121050, F121511. Very pleasant, lots of plants. **A** *Florida Plaza*, 20 de Noviembre and Independencia, T121511. **A** *Motel Los Arcos*, T87777, near bus station, Heróico Colegio Militar 2204, T172216, good restaurant. **B** *Campo México Courts*, 20 de Noviembre extremo Ote, T187744, F183015. Good but restaurant service poor. **B** *Casa Blanca*, 20 de Noviembre 811 Pte, T13599, F14704.

Durango

The Northern Highlands

■ **Sleeping**

1 Casa Blanca
2 Gallo
3 Gobernador

4 Plaza Catedral
5 Posada Durán
6 Posada San Jorge

7 Roma

Nice, big old hotel in the centre, unguarded parking lot. **B** *Posada San Jorge*, Constitución 102 Sur, T13526, F16040. Old colonial building, patio, large rooms, friendly, parking. Recommended. **C** *Reyes*, 20 de Noviembre 220. Clean. **C** *Roma*, 20 de Noviembre 705 Pte, T/F120122. Clean, comfortable.

D *Gallo*, 5 de Febrero 117. With bath, clean, motorcycle parking. Recommended. **D** *Ana Isabel*, 5 de Febrero 219 Ote, T134500. **D** *Reforma*, 5 de Febrero y Madero, T131622. Authentic 60s lobby, clean, comfortable rooms, free indoor parking, good restaurant. Recommended. **D** *Karla*, Pino Suárez opposite bus station, T16348. Small, clean, friendly but noisy. **D** *Pancho Villa*, Pino Suárez 206, opposite bus station, T187311. Clean, pleasant, TV. **D** *Plaza Catedral*, Constitución 216 Sur, T132480. Well-appointed. **D** *Posada Santa Elena*, Negrete 1007 Pte, T127818. Clean, TV, a/c. **D-E** *Posada Durán*, 20 de Noviembre 506 Pte, T12412, colonial inn on Plaza de Armas. Recommended by AAA, good atmosphere, helpful staff. **E** *Oasis*, Zarco between 20 de Noviembre y 5 de Febrero. With bath, hot water, rooms on the top floor have a good view. **E** *Buenos Aires*, Constitución 126 Norte, T123128. Fairly clean.

Youth hostel *Villa Deportiva Juvenil*, Av Heróico Colegio Militar y 20 de Noviembre. Dormitory, gym, pool. **Camping** in the National Park costs about US$3.

Café Salum, 5 de Febrero y Progreso. Good breakfasts, nice. *Cafe La Mancha*, 20 de Noviembre 807 Pte. Relaxed, tables outside at back, cheap lunches. *Mariscos Ramírez*, in front of the market. Good seafood. *La Peña*, Hidalgo 120 north. Friday night is *fiesta* night with local music and singing, very popular. There is a good food store on the first block of Progreso where local foodstuffs are displayed in bulk. *El Zocabón*, on 5 de Febrero, off main plaza. Recommended. *Gorditas Gabino*, Constitución 112 Norte. Very cheap, good. *La Unica*, 20 de Noviembre y Pasteur. Recommended. *Gardy*, F de Urdiñola 239, Nueva Viscaya, T187162. Vegetarian. Theme bar/restaurants on Negrete Pte; *Opera* and *Sloan*, open evenings only.

Eating
● *on maps*

Air Guadalupe Victoria Airport (DGO), 12 km from centre (taxi US$8.50). There are international flights from Chicago (Mexicana), Los Angeles (Aero California) and Tucson (Aerolitoral), and domestic flights from Chihuahua, Ciudad Obregón, Culiacán, Guadalajara, Hermosillo, Ixtapa, Mazatlán, Mexico City, Monterrey, Tijuana (2 per day), and Torreón.

Transport

Buses Bus station out of town: minibus No 2 to centre, US$0.25. Several buses a day cross the Sierra Madre Occidental to **Mazatlán** (Transportes Chihuahuenses, 1st class, 7 hrs, US$14.80), 0400 and 1000. This is recommended if you cannot do the Chihuahua-Los Mochis train journey; sit on left side. 2nd class buses for camera buffs stop more frequently. **Guadalajara**, US$22.25; **Chihuahua**, US$32, 10 hrs. 2nd class bus to **Hidalgo del Parral**, 7 hrs, US$18 with Transportes Chihuahuenses. **Zacatecas**, Omnibus de México, 4½ hours, US$7.75. Town buses stop running early in evening, so try to arrive before dark if you wish to avoid a long walk or taxi ride to the centre.

Airline offices *Mexicana*, T136299, *Aero California*, T177177, 0800-1900. *AeroMéxico*, next to Cathedral, T178828, 0900-1900. **Banks** *Bancomer*, on plaza by Cathedral. *Banamex*, esquina Madero and 5 de Febrero. **Communications** Internet: at 5 de Febrero 203, US$2.50 per hour. *Enter*, Negrete 1314 Pte, T110045, 0900-2100, Mon-Sat, Sun 1200-2100, US$1.70 per hour, bit like a youth club. **Post Office:** Av 20 de Noviembre 500 B Ote.

Directory

The Northern Highlands

The Northwest Coast

14

The Northwest Coast

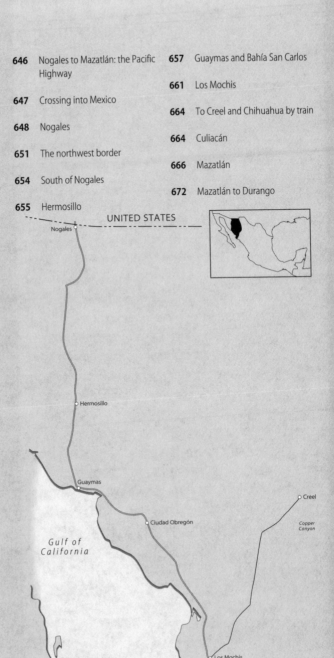

UNITED STATES

Nogales

Hermosillo

Guaymas

Ciudad Obregón

Creel

Copper Canyon

Gulf of California

Los Mochis

To Mazatlán

*The northwest coast of Mexico has much to offer the traveller who, with only a few days to spare, can drift through the scenic **Sierra de Pintos** to the copper-mining centre at Cananea, see the longest sand dunes in North America at Algodones, or brave the desert conditions of the Desierto de Altar. Alternatively, you can enjoy the beaches and watersports of Puerto Peñasco. At the **Pinacate Natural Park** the moonscape of volcanic craters and lava fields is very impressive and so is the wildlife. With a little more time, you can explore the Kino Missions and enjoy sportfishing at Kino Nuevo, participate in fishing tournaments at La Choya and San Carlos or take a boat excursion from Rocky Point. There are many opportunities to take **boat trips** to the islands just off the coast, explore submerged Spanish galleons off Patos Island or perhaps take an overnight ferry to Baja California. Make a detour to the beautiful colonial town of **Alamos**, home of the original Mexican jumping bean, or go to Aduana, where you can visit an old silver mine. Relax in the streets of Los Mochis and enjoy the music of the roaming mariachis before boarding the famous **Copper Canyon train** for the journey of a lifetime. The popularity of Mazatlán as a holiday resort is well established; from here, you can travel northeast to Durango and the Colonial Heartland, or southeast to Tepic and Guadalajara, pleasant resting places if you are travelling on to Mexico City.*

Nogales to Mazatlán: the Pacific Highway

The road along the Pacific Coast gives access to several resorts (for example Guaymas, Mazatlán *and* Puerto Vallarta*), to ferry terminals for Baja California, and to the Los Mochis end of the Chihuahua al Pacífico railway through the Copper Canyon. From Nogales to Guaymas on the Gulf of California, the road runs along the western slopes of the Sierra Madre, whose summits rise to 3,000m. From Guaymas on to Mazatlán it threads along the lowland, with the Sierra Madre Occidental's bold and commanding escarpment to the east. Like the west coasts of all continents between latitudes 20° and 30°, the whole area is desert, but fruitful wherever irrigated by water flowing from the mountains. Summers are very hot, sometimes rainy, but winters are mild and very dry.*

Within the Sierra Madre, nomadic people hunt the many wild animals; along the coasts, available water determines the spots of concentrated settlement and of agriculture. Mexico gets most of its wheat from the southern part of Sonora state, and the irrigated valley bottoms (around Hermosillo) are also used for maize, cotton and beans. Further south, in frost-free Sinaloa and Nayarit, sugar, rice, winter vegetables, tomatoes, and tobacco are grown. The three northern coastal states, Sonora, Sinaloa and Nayarit, make up 21 percent of Mexico's entire area, but include only six percent of its population.

In summer, west coast drivers prefer the Central Route from El Paso, Texas,

The northwest border: Mexicali - Nogales

unless they love heat. It is dangerous to drive on retread tyres over the hot desert. Do not drive at night and never park or sleep along the road.

The Pacific Highway down the coast to Acapulco and Salina Cruz is completely paved but has military searches in the State of Guerrero (for narcotics and arms). There are many motels along the whole route, so that each town of any importance has one or more nearby.

Crossing into Mexico

The Nogales crossing is open 24 hours. Walking into Mexico there's no checkpoint on the Mexican side although there is a customs area that is sometimes staffed and sometimes not. If it is staffed, you push a button and if you get a green light you can pass without being inspected; no such luck if you get a red light. This is how all customs stops operate in Mexico. After you cross the border, if you keep walking straight ahead about 50m you'll get to the immigration office (on your right) where you can pick up your tourist card (FM-T). They aren't available at the bus terminal.

Nogales(USA)/ Nogales

Ideally get a tourist card before crossing the border, at an insurance agent (Jones Associates, linked to International Gateway Insurance, 2981 north Grand Avenida, Nogales, T2819141, F2810430), border town Mexican consulate or tourist office.

It is important to get your tourist card validated before you leave the area. Customs agents at the bus station will turn a blind eye if you get on a bus without a tourist card, but if the bus is stopped for routine checks (frequent) you may get sent back to the border.

To avoid the congestion of the downtown route, motorists are generally advised to use the truck crossing (open 0600-2000, currency exchange available), which is reached by the Mariposa Avenida exit from Interstate 19, 2½ miles north of downtown Nogales, Arizona. Returning from Mexico to the US, follow the sign to the 'Periférico' which avoids the downtown area.

Motor vehicle documents can be obtained at the Mexican Customs post 21 km south of Nogales, on Highway 15 to Santa Ana, along with US insurance (which may also be obtained at the border proper). There is a tourist office and a *casa de cambio* here. You need to have title to the car with you, ie, you can't drive someone else's car into Mexico at least past Km 21. You also need two photocopies of vehicle registration, driver's licence, insurance papers, credit card and visitor's permit (approved), are required; a photocopy machine is available. In the same building as the immigration office on the border is a *Seguros Tepeyac* outlet where you can buy car insurance. If you only want liability, not collison, insurance, they charge US$2.24 per day. To insure a car worth US$7,000 with both liability and collision insurance costs US$5.63 daily. There are also a few other insurance agencies nearby. The *Seguros Tepeyac* agent says there are also agencies at Km 21. Drivers leaving Mexico are advised by a large sign to surrender papers here; this involves crossing the southbound traffic and joining the queues of drivers entering Mexico. It can be chaotic. The post is greatly improved, but has few officers who speak English; high vehicles should avoid the low inspection shed. Those whose destination lies within Sonora State may find these entry procedures are not needed. Check locally (see also **Essentials** page 39).

Nogales

Phone code: 631
Colour map 1, grid A4
Km 2,403 from
Mexico City

Nogales lies astride a mountain pass at 1,120m across from Nogales, Arizona. Population estimates range from 180,000 to 240,000, with another 20,000 on the Arizona side. Nogales is the largest town in the Pimería Alta, the area of southern Arizona and northern Sonora occupied by the Pima Indians at the arrival of the Spaniards. The **Pimería Alta Historical Society**, a block from the border in Nogales, Arizona, has excellent exhibits on the history of the region, a valuable library and archives, and also organizes tours to the Sonoran missions. The staff are a good source of information on the Mexican side. ■ *Weekdays 0900-1700, Sat 1000-1600, and Sun from 1300-1600; no admission charge.* The city's commercial centre is squeezed into a few narrow blocks centred on Avenida Obregón. The town is a mining area and a busy trans-shipment point for fruit and vegetables destined for US supermarkets; walnut groves (*nogales*) and cattle ranches surround it, and the bordertown flavour is that of a miniature Tijuana: liquor stores, glass, silver and leather goods, cheap bars and colourful markets. The **tourist office** is just past the immigration office. The staff are friendly and helpful. They have brochures on many parts of Sonora. Just past the tourist office and to the right is a taxi stand. They charge US$5 to the bus station, which is on the other side of town, across the street from the railroad station. They've privatized the railway and there is no passenger service along the Nogales-Guadalajara route.

Sleeping
B *Fray Marcos de Niza*, Campillo 91. Gaudy but none too good. **C** *Granada*, López Mateos y González, T22911. **C** *Olivia*, Obregón 125, T22200. A/c, TV, reasonable. **D** *Motel Miami*, Campillo and Ingenieros. Friendly, good restaurant. Recommended. There is a wide selection of cheaper hotels on Juárez, a 1-block extension of Av López Mateos between Campillo and the border, 2 blocks from the Mexican port of entry.

Eating
El Greco, upstairs at Obregón and Pierson. Attractive, reasonably priced international menu. Occasionally has live mariachi music. Other recommended restaurants on or near Obregón, including *El Cid* (No 124, good but expensive), *Olivia*, *Casa de María*, *El Toro Steakhouse*. *Café Olga*, Juárez 37 next to bus station. Open all hours. *Elvira's Restaurant*, Obregón 1. Very colourful, relaxed and informal atmosphere. *La Roca*, Elías 91. Secluded, attractive courtyard, live music.

Festivals
Cinco de Mayo festival, lasting 4 days, celebrates the defeat of the French army at Puebla on **5 May** 1862. During the months of **Apr** and **May** the coronation of the Queen of Nogales, Sonora and Arizona, is celebrated with festivities and dances. In May they also hold the *Festival of Flowers*, underlined by music. Very colourful.

Shopping
Nogales is ideally located for cross-border shopping

The wide range of merchandise available is guaranteed to fascinate window shoppers, and the ease with which purchases can be transported to the US encourages casual shoppers to part with their money. No need to change your cash to pesos; US dollars are most welcome here. Buy hand-carved furniture, home furnishings and unusual decorative artefacts from *Antigua de México*, Av Ruiz Cortines 427, or just browse if you have time to kill. At Calle Campanillo 57, the 1st cross street after you pass through the border, *The Lazy Frog Arts and Crafts* will whet your appetite and prepare you for the colourful objects to be found throughout the main shopping zone. On Av Obregón, *El Patio Curios*, No 80, and *Curios Continental*, No 98, have a wide selection of products, as does *Firenze*, No 111. Other stores worth checking out are *Décor de Nogales*, Av Obregón 138 (tinware and ceramics), *La Cucaracha*, Obregón 171, and *Rústicos de México*, Obregón 182. There are many more stores selling quality items aimed directly at the US buyer. Most store owners/managers will assist in the formalities in exporting large items to the US.

Trains There are no passenger services on the Pacific Railway from Nogales to **Transport** Guadalajara any more but this may change; check locally for information.

Buses Nogales' new bus terminal is 8 km south of the city centre, along the highway to Magdalena and Hermosillo; parking US$1 per hour. Taxis at the border ask US$5 to take you to the bus station, but on the return journey the booth selling taxi vouchers charges less than US$4. A local bus, 1 peso, leaves 1 block from the border. Bus 46 from Juárez goes to the terminal (US$0.25). The bus station has a booth to change money. It also has a Computel outlet with fax and long-distance phone service.

Nogales

● ●

☞ Customs checks

There is a customs checkpoint in the terminal. You're allowed to bring in US$50.00 worth of goods duty-free, in addition to those things a tourist would normally carry, such as cameras, clothes, etc. If you fly into Mexico you're allowed *US$300 duty-free. After that you pay 21.67% if the goods are from the US, Canada, or Chile, 22.82% if they're from Colombia, Costa Rica, Venezuela, or Bolivia, and 38.92% if they're from anywhere else.*

● ●

There's a shop selling magazines and some packaged foods and an adequate little restaurant with both Mexican food and burgers and fries (at US$2.50) and pay toilets.

There are 3 bus lines that go into Mexico using the terminal: Norte de Sonora, Transportes del Pacífico, and Elite. They all seem to have high-quality buses; Transportes del Pacífico also runs 2nd-class buses to most of their destinations.

Chihuahua; Elite 0800, 1915, $32.90. **Ciudad Juárez**; Elite 2130. **Ciudad Obregón**; Transportes del Pacífico US$19.30 (1st class), US$16.20 (2nd class). Norte de Sonora 1015, 1330, 1945, US$17.20. Elite 0815, 1300. **Culiacán**; Transportes del Pacífico US$34.60 (1st class), US$30.80 (2nd class). Norte de Sonora 1600, 1830, US$30.80. Elite 1530. **Durango**; Elite 1530, US$53.60. **Guadalajara**; Transportes del Pacífico US$81.80 (1st class), US$68.00 (2nd class). Norte de Sonora 1430, US$71.20. Elite 0730, 0930, 1900, 2045, US$81.80. **Guaymas**; Transportes del Pacífico US$14.70 (1st class), US$11.40 (2nd class). **Hermosillo**; Transportes del Pacífico US$9.90 (1st class), US$9.00 (2nd class). Norte de Sonora 0400, 0830, 1100, 1700, US$9.00. Elite 0600, 0800, 1100, US$10.00. **Los Mochis**; Transportes del Pacífico US$27.30 (1st class), US$24.00 (2nd class). Norte de Sonora 2300, US$24.00. Elite 0030, 1400, 2000. **Mazatlán**; Transportes del Pacífico US$57.00 (1st class), US$46.70 (2nd class). Norte de Sonora 1900, US$49.60. Elite 2130, US$57.00. Also with Ejecutivo to Mazatlán, 3 instead of 4 seats across and about half as many seats for US$62.70 at 1830. **Mexicali**; Norte de Sonora US$24.10. **Mexico City**; Transportes del Pacífico US$105.80 (1st class), US$90.90 (2nd class). They run hourly from 1030 to 2030. Norte de Sonora 0700, 1230, 1730, 2100, US$90.90. Elite 1030, 1300 (via corta), 1330, 1800 (via León), 2330 (via corta), US$105.80. **Puerto Peñasco (Rocky Point)**; Norte de Sonora 1530. **Tepic**; Transportes del Pacífico US$70.00 (1st class), US$60.90 (2nd class). **Tijuana**; Norte de Sonora; 2400, US$33.10, Elite 2045, US$$38.10. **Zacatecas**; Elite 1800, US$61.60.

Another company, Autobuses Crucero, runs buses into the US: **Los Angeles** US$52.00. **Phoenix**; US$19.00. **Tucson**; US$7.00.

To get to the US border, turn left as you leave the building and walk to the 1st traffic light and cross the street you can pick up the buses to the border, referred to by the locals as *La Línea*. The buses run down the same street you'd be walking on. Just past that traffic light is a motel called the **B-C** *Motel Campestre*. Just past that is another private bus terminal for the Tufesa line which run buses down the coast as far as Culiacán (US$33). They have several departures daily and have nice, modern buses.

On the **Arizona** side, 1 block from the port of entry, Citizen Auto Stage Company (T2875628) runs 10 buses daily between Tucson and Nogales (US$6.50); stops at Tucson airport *en route*. Stopovers (no additional charge) are possible to visit Tumacacori mission, north of Nogales. US Greyhound is about ¼ block from the border. If you're entering the US from Mexico, you'll see a ramp and stairs on your left on the street after you've crossed the border. The Grehound station is at the top of the stairs, where you can catch buses to Tucson (US$7) and points beyond. Buses leave for Tucson at 0630, 0900, 1000, 1100, 1400, 1500, 1700, 1800, and 2000. There are smaller vans that leave at 0800, 1200, and 1600. Buses leave for Phoenix, AZ (Arizona's largest city, about 2 hrs north of Tucson) at 0700, 1400, and 1930, US$19.00. They also have buses for **Hermosillo** (US$10) and **Ciudad Obregón** (US$20) that don't require a transfer in

Nogales, Sonora, at 0715, 1215, 0230, 0545, and 0945 which stop across the border on the Mexican side to pick up passengers. The Greyhound bus station is a small, 1-room building with restrooms, lockers, and pay phones. There's a Burger King just behind the bus terminal, and a McDonald's nearby.

Banks *Casa de Cambio Money Exchange*, Campillo y López Mateos. *Casa de Cambio 'El Amigo'*, **Directory**
Campillo y López Mateos local No 14. *Compra-venta de Dólares Serfín*, Av López Mateos y Calle
Pierson 81, 1st floor. *Casa de Cambio 'Maquila'*, Juárez 74. **Health** There's a Farmacia Benavides
behind the immigration office. They give injections. There are several other pharmacies nearby.
According to the tourist office, the best hospital in Nogales (private) is the Hospital del Socorro,
Dirección Granja, T46060. Any taxi driver will know how to get there.

If driving from Nogales to Mazatlán by the four-lane, divided toll road (Route **Road tolls**
15), there are 12 toll gates. The first is 88 km south of Nogales. No motorcycles, bicycles (but see page 45), pedestrians or animals are allowed on the highway, which is fenced and patrolled. The toll stations are well lit, have good public conveniences, fuel and food. The total distance from Nogales to Mazatlán is 1,118 km; the road is being extended beyond Mazatlán so that about 70 per-cent of the entire Nogales-Guadalajara route is now four-lane. The *autopista* sections beyond Mazatlán, for example the sections before and after Tepic, are worth taking for the time they save. It is not possible to list in this guide every toll location and every deviation to avoid it. Most deviations are dirt roads and should not be taken in the rainy season. The high toll cost on this route has contributed to a decline in tourism in Sonora and in Sinaloa. On toll routes and their avoidance, seek advice from US motoring associations and clubs (see page 43) as costs and conditions change rapidly.

The northwest border

Route 2 from Tijuana (see page 685) runs close to the border, going through **San Luis Río**
Mexicali (see page 680), San Luis Río Colorado, Sonoyta, and Caborca to **Colorado**
Santa Ana, where it joins the West Coast Highway (Route 15) to Mexico City. *Colour map 1, grid A2*
East of Mexicali the fast four-lane highway crosses the fertile Mexicali valley to *Population: 134,000*
a toll bridge over the diminished Colorado River, and continues to San Luis Río Colorado, a cheerfully tourist-oriented border town in the 'free zone' and serving cotton country. There are summer bullfights and small nightlife dis-trict like those of the Old West, including a so-called *zona de tolerancia*. Amer-icans cross the border to purchase spectacles, prescription drugs and have dental work done at much lower prices than in the USA. The port of entry is open 24 hours, but there is no public transport from Yuma, 40 km north of the border, in Arizona. **AL** *Hotel San Angel*. *El Rey* and others on Av Obregón, en route to Sonoyta. *Capra*. Budget hotel.

North of San Luis (35 km) is Baja California's last international border-cross- **Algodones**
ing point, the farming town of Algodones. The border is open 0600-2000, but *Colour map 1, grid A2*
motor vehicle documents are processed weekdays only, 0800-1500. The road *Population: 12,000*
north from San Luis skirts the Algodones dunes, the longest in North America. Algodones has one hotel, the rather misnamed **E** *Motel Olímpico*, dozens of souvenir stands, and several decent restaurants. Mexican car insurance is readily available, and there are several *casas de cambio*.

At Andrade, on the California side, the Quechan Indians from the nearby Fort Yuma Reservation operate an RV park and campground (US$12 per site with electricity, US$8 without; including hot showers and access to laundry room). Winter is the peak season, as the town is nearly deserted during the unbearably hot summer. From the west bank of the river, notice the abandoned Hanlon headgate for the Alamo Canal, which burst in 1905 and poured water into California's Imperial Valley for eight months, creating the enormous 'Salton Sea'.

There is public transport hourly between Algodones and Mexicali but, other than taxi, there is none from Yuma, Arizona, to Andrade (although the road has recently been paved and the number of visitors is rapidly increasing). Most people park at the lot operated by Quechan Indians (US$1, but there is plenty of free parking within easy distance of the border, except on the busiest days).

Pozos Nine kilometres south of San Luis is Pozos, which 40 years ago had 60,000 inhabitants, now only 2,500. It has ruins of large buildings, churches, but no hotels. State highway 40 runs south to Riíto (petrol and a few stores) then follows the railway across the edge of the barren Gran Desierto to **El Golfo de Santa Clara**, a good-sized fishing town which has a fish-processing plant, supermarket, general store, church and a couple of eating places. The tidal range at the head of the Gulf is wide but there are good sandy beaches nearby at high tide. There is a public camping area (no facilities) at the end of a 3-km sandy track past the town. The highway is paved, a round-trip from San Luis of 230 km.

Desierto de Altar
This area was used to train US astronauts during the Moon missions

After leaving San Luis Río Colorado, Route 2 crosses the sandy wastes of the Desierto de Altar – Mexico's own mini-Sahara. The road is very narrow in places, watch out for overloaded Mexican trucks. For 150 km there are no facilities (petrol at Los Vidrios), only three houses and an enveloping landscape of sand dunes, cinder cones and a dark lava flow from the Cerro del Pinacate, so extensive that it stands out vividly on photographs from space. All the area around the central range is protected by the **Pinacate Natural Park**. A gravel road 10 km east of Los Vidrios gives access to the northern sector of the park, which contains much wildlife, for example puma, deer, antelope, wild boar, Gila monster, wild sheep, quail and red-tailed eagle. Several volcanic craters, the treacherous lava fields and an interesting cinder mine may also be visited. Visitors must register at the entrance and are restricted to the Cerro Colorado and Elegante Crater area.

Lukeville/ Sonoyta
Colour map 1, grid A3

After a hot and monotonous 200 km from San Luis, Route 2 reaches the sun-bleached bordertown of **Sonoyta**, a short distance from Lukeville, Arizona. (**NB** If coming from Lukeville to San Luis Río Colorado, make sure you turn right (west) at Sonoyta and not left (south) to San Luisito; they are both on Highway 2 but 320 km apart in opposite directions!). Sonoyta has little of interest itself, but there are several American-style accommodations: **C** *Motel Sol de Desierto*. A/c but no heat in some rooms (request extra blankets). **B-C** *Motel San Antonio*. **B** *Motel Excelsior*. Restaurants are few and mediocre at best – the coffee shop at Lukeville is a better alternative. Transportes Norte de Sonora and Tres Estrellas de Oro both run first-class bus services. Water and snacks should be carried at all times in this very arid region, and, if driving your own vehicle, the tank should be kept full and replenished wherever possible. Arizona's picturesque Organ Pipe Cactus National Monument is just across the border from Sonoyta.

The border crossing between Lukeville and Sonoyta is open from 0800 to 2400. Camping is possible at developed sites near the visitor centre at Organ Pipe National Monument for US$8 (US$3 visitor permit is valid for 15 days).

Highway 8 goes southwest from Sonoyta through 100 km of sand dunes; a sign, 'Dunas – 10 km', at Km 80, points along a sandy road which leads to dramatic, desolate inland dunes through mountain-rimmed black lava fields; four-wheel drive is recommended.

One of the most important shrimping ports on the Gulf; the huge shrimp are too expensive for the US market and are mostly exported to Japan. It is very popular with Arizona and California RV drivers for fishing, surfing and the beach. On the north side of the bay, 12 km, is **La Choya**, largely a gringo place, sandy streets, full of trailers and beach cottages, and several fine beaches. Fishing tournaments are held in the Bahía La Choya; Playa de Oro has good surf but Playa Hermosa now suffers from pollution. South of the town is the elite, self-contained community of Las Conchas, with security gate and US-owned beach chalets. Souvenirs are the mirrors, necklaces and figurines locally made from coral, seashells and snail shells. Advertising itself as 'Mexico's tourist resort closest to the US-Mexico border', **Rocky Point** has been developed to cater to the needs of most tourists. The Sierra del Pinacate features impressive and strange-looking hills, reminiscent of a moonscape. Fishing and scuba-diving are well taken care of. On the island of San Jorge, it is possible to observe sea lions, dolphins, and the rare *vaquita*, an endangered species, only to be found in the Upper Gulf of California. It is possible to hire sand motorcycles and buggies. The marina at Rocky Point offers many boat excursions. There is a **tourist office** in Jim-Bur Shopping Centre.

Puerto Peñasco
Colour map 1, grid A2
Population: 60,000

Sleeping **C** *Viña del Mar*, Calle 1 de Junio y Blvd Malecón Kino, T33600. Modern resort, cliffside jacuzzi, video-disco, etc, attractive rooms, good value. **D** *Motel Mar y Sol*, Km 94 on road to Sonoyta. Pleasant gardens, restaurant, a/c, friendly. **D** *Motel Señorial*, T32065, Calle 3 No 81, 1 block from main beach. Good restaurant, dearer upstairs rooms are a/c. **E** *Motel Davis*, Emiliano Zapata 100, T34314. Pleasant.

Camping *Playa de Oro Trailer Resort*, Matamoros 36, T32668, 2 km east. Laundry, boat ramp, 200 sites, US$12 for 2. *Playa Bonita RV Park*, on lovely Playa Bonita, T32596, 245 spaces, restaurant, shop, laundry. *Playa Miramar*, Matamoros y Final Av Campeche, T32351, 105 spaces, laundry, boat ramp, satellite hook-ups. *Pitahaya Trailer Park*, beachfront at *Hotel Villa Granada*, east of town, 25 spaces, full hook-ups, toilets, no showers. Nominal camping fee at *La Choya*, showers.

Eating *Costa Brava Restaurant*, Kino y 1 de Junio. Best in town, modest prices, exotic menu, pleasant. *Café La Cita*, 1 de Junio near the petrol station. Authentic Mexican, budget. *La Curva*, Kino y Comonfort, T33470. Americanized menu, popular, budget prices, little atmosphere. *La Gaviota* coffee shop at *Hotel Viña del Mar*. Good breakfasts and views.

Festivals Navy Day is held in Puerto Peñasco, **29 May-1 Jun**, with a colourful parade, dancing and a widely attended sporting contest.

Shopping *Jim-Bur Shopping Center*, Benito Juárez near railway crossing, is the main commercial hub. Try *El Vaquero* or *El Gift Shop* for souvenirs and camping supplies. Fresh fish from open-air fish market on the Malecón (old town).

Transport **Air**: There is a regular air service to the port and Great Lakes Aviation flies from Albuquerque via Tucson and from Phoenix several times a week.

Directory **Banks**: 2 banks. **Laundry**: *Laundromat Liz*, Altamirano y Simón Morua.

Recently paved State Highway 37 continues southeast, roughly following the rail line to Caborca (180 km) – an alternative to the inland Highway 2 route.

The Northwest Coast

Caborca
Colour map 1, grid A3
Population: 38,000
Altitude: 286m

Route 2 runs from Sonoyta to Caborca (150 km), passing through a number of small towns (San Emeterio, San Luisito) and a more mountainous but still arid land. There is a Customs and Immigration station near Quitovac (28 km south of Sonoyta), where tourist cards and vehicle papers are validated as you enter the Mexican 'mainland'.

Caborca lies on the Mexicali-Benjamín Hill railway in the midst of a gently sloping plain. A Grape Fair is held 21-26 June, with wine exhibitions and an industrial and agricultural show. Caborca's restored Church of Nuestra Señora de la Concepción was one of the 25 missions founded by Padre Kino in Sonora and Arizona between 1687 and 1711. It was also used in 1857 as a fortress during a raid by US renegades under self-styled 'General' Crabb; their defeat is still commemorated by a fair held each 6 April. Caborca is the best base for exploring the Kino missions (see box).

Sleeping A *Motel El Camino.* **C** *Motel San Carlos.* **D** *Hotel San Francisco.* **D** *Hotel Yaqui.* Clean, a/c, TV, service station and general facilities.

Altar to Arizona border

Keep an eye out for semi-wild longhorn cattle along the road to El Sásabe

Highway 2 continues east through **Altar** (café, gas station) to join Highway 15 at **Santa Ana** (*Population:* 12,500), a small town of little note. The *Fiesta de Santa Ana* is held 17-26 July, with horse racing, fireworks, etc. **B** *Motel San Francisco.* A/c, shower, baths, restaurant; motel across the road not so nice, also **B**. There is a Canadian-Mexican trailer park south of town, on the right going south, space for 9-10 trailers, rustic, useful overnight stop. Two kilometres west is San Francisco, with another Kino mission.

From Altar, there is a little-travelled alternative route to El Sásabe, Sonora/Arizona, 110 km southwest of Tucson via Arizona Routes 86 and 286. This is perhaps the most isolated, forlorn and least-frequented legal border crossing between the United States and Mexico. The 98-km dirt road from Altar, which passes west of the Sierra del Carrizal and Sierra San Juan, is passable for any ordinary vehicle except after the heaviest rains (**NB** Mexican maps for Sonora tend to be inaccurate in this area). From Altar, drive 3 km northeast towards Saric and bear left at the clearly signed junction; do not continue on the more inviting paved route unless you wish to visit the Kino mission sites and churches at Oquitoa and Tubutama – although maps show an equivalent dirt road beyond Saric to El Sásabe, there are numerous closed gates, some of them locked, over *ejido* (community) lands.

El Sásabe
Colour map 1, grid A3

The border at El Sásabe is open from 0800 to 2000, but there is no public transport on either side, nor is there any Mexican automobile insurance agency. For information as to road conditions, phone US Customs (T602-8234231); although they appear not to encourage traffic over this route, they will tell you whether vehicles have entered recently from Mexico and what drivers have said about the road.

South of Nogales

Magdalena Valley

South of the border at Nogales, Route 15 passes through the Magdalena Valley. The Cocóspera mines are near **Imuris** and there are famous gold and silver mines near **Magdalena** (*Hotel El Cuervo*, near plaza, **C** without TV, **B** with) which has a great Indian *fiesta* in the first week of October. On the Magdalena bypass is a toll, US$5, avoidable by driving through town (at the north of town heading south, 95 km south of Nogales, keep left to avoid the backstreets). The free road south to Hermosillo becomes 'speed bump alley'. Beyond, the cactus-strewn desert begins.

The Northwest Coast

From Imuris, a major highway junction with numerous inexpensive restaurants, Route 2 heads east (to Naco and Agua Prieta) through the scenic Sierra de Pintos to the historic and still important copper mining centre of **Cananea**. This was the site of a 1906 miners' strike against the American-owned Cananea Consolidated Copper Company, one of the critical events in the last years of the Porfirio Díaz dictatorship. Hundreds of Arizona Rangers crossed the border to join the Sonora militia in putting down the strike, which is commemorated at the Museo de La Lucha Obrera, the former city jail, on Avenida Juárez. There are several motels along the highway.

Back on Route 15, 120 km from Nogales, is Santa Ana, where the road from Tijuana and Mexicali comes in.

Forty-two kilometres south, the Pacific Highway reaches **Benjamín Hill**, where the Mexicali railway joins the main Nogales-Guadalajara track; brightening up this forgettable junction is the Children's Park, with an amusement park, lake, zoo, and a delightful scaled-down children's railway (motel, cheaper than those in Santa Ana, 10 minutes away). For northbound drivers there is a drug search at Benjamín Hill.

There is little of note on the straight run south to Hermosillo through semi-arid farming and rangeland, apart from the little towns of El Oasis and nearby Carbó (on the rail line) – both have petrol supplies; 158 km from Santa Ana the land becomes greener and the irrigated fields and citrus groves begin to enclose.

Hermosillo

Capital of Sonora state, Hermosillo is a modern city, resort town and centre of a rich orchard area. Just east, the Rodríguez Dam captures the fickle flow of the Río Sonora, producing a rich strip of cotton fields, vegetables, melons, oranges and grapes. The local farmers are also big exporters of turkey and beef. Hermosillo's expanding industries draw many people from the hinterland, especially the new Ford assembly plant (manufacturing cars for the US market), as well as electronics and clothing manufacturers. **Tourist office** Palacio de Gobierno, ground floor, T172964.

Phone code: 62
Colour map 1, grid B4
Population: 698,300
Altitude: 237m

Reminders of an illustrious colonial past can be found around the central Plaza Zaragoza (invaded by noisy birds at sunset): the imposing **Catedral de La Asunción** (1779, neo-classical, baroque dome, three naves) and the **Palacio de Gobierno**, with its intricately carved pillars and pediment, historical murals and grandiose statues amid landscaped gardens. Highway 15 sweeps into Hermosillo from the north as a wide boulevard, vibrant in summer with orange-flowering trees, becoming Bulevar Rosales through the commercial centre before exiting south across the ring road (Periférico) for Guaymas (toll at Hermosillo US$5.35). The old traditional quarter is to the east of it, a few blocks southeast of Plaza Zaragoza, where delightful houses and narrow streets wind around the base of Cerro de la Campana (fine views). On the eastern slope is the **Museo de Sonora**. ■ *Wed-Sat 1000-1730, Sun 1000-1530, free.*

Sights

Not far north of downtown (Rosales y Transversal) is **Ciudad Universitaria** (University City), with its modern buildings of Mexican architecture blended tastefully with Moorish and Mission influences. The main building contains a large library auditorium and interesting museum. ■ *Daily 0900-1300, closed holidays.* There is an active fine arts and cultural life, with many events throughout the year open to visitors (check at tourist office for details). Two kilometres south of Plaza Zaragoza, near the Periférico Sur, is the wonderful **Centro Ecológico de Sonora**, a botanical garden and zoo displaying Sonoran and other desert flora and fauna in well-cared-for surroundings.

The Northwest Coast

Sleeping Generally poor standard of hotels, although there are **AL** *Señorial*, Blvd Kino y Guillermo Carpena, T155155, F155093. With a/c, pool, parking, restaurant, bar. **AL** *Holiday Inn* on Blvd Kino 368 (northeast entry highway), T151112. With restaurant, bars, entertainment, etc. **C** *San Alberto*, Serdán y Rosales, T121800. With breakfast, a/c, cable TV, pool, good value. **C-D** *Kino*, Pino Suárez 151, Sur (base of Campana hill), T124599. Popular business hotel, a/c, TV, fridge. **D** *Guaymas Inn*, 5½ km north. With a/c, rooms with shower. **D** *Monte Carlo*, Juárez y Sonora, T12335. With a/c, old, clean, very popular, as is adjoining restaurant. **D** *Washington*, Dr Noriega Pte 68, T131183. With a/c, clean, basic rooms off narrow courts, with bath, best budget hotel, parking for motorbikes. **E** *Casa de los Amigos*, contact the Asociación Sonorense de los Amigos, Felipe Salido 32, Col Centro, T/F170142. Dormitories, living room, library, garden, laundry and kitchen. **E** *Royal*, in centre. With a/c but grubby. A/c is desirable in summer; check that it works before taking room. Cheap hotels and *casas de huéspedes* can be found around Plaza Zaragoza and along Sonora near Matamoros (red-light activity, choose carefully).

Motels **C** *Bugambilia*, Padre Kino 712, T145050. **C** *Motel El Encanto*, Blvd Kino 901. With a/c, phone, TV, comfortable, too close to railway station.

Eating *Jardín Xochimilco*, Obregón 51, Villa de Seris. Very good beef, not cheap. *Mariscos Los Arcos de Hermosillo*, Michel y Ocampo (4 blocks south of Plaza). Fresh seafood, attractive and expensive. *Henry's Restaurant*, Blvd Kino Norte, across the road from *Motel Encanto*. Nice old house, good. *La Huerta*, San Luis Potosí 109. Seafood. *René's Café*, Rosales y Moreno. Good-value lunches, pleasant. *El Rodeo Rosticería*, Dr Noriega Pte 92. Recommended. *San César*, Plutarco Elías Calles 71 Pte. Excellent chop sueys, seafood and expensive 'gringo' food. Mexican specialities better value, open for breakfast.

Transport **Air** The Gen Pesquira/García airport (HMO) is 12 km from town. Daily to Mexico City, AeroMéxico, Mexicana, Aero California and Taesa. Other domestic flights to Chihuahua, Ciudad Juárez, Ciudad Obregón, Cuernavaca, Culiacán, Durango, Guadalajara, Guerrero Negro, La Paz, Los Cabos, Los Mochis, Mazatlán, Mexicali, Monterrey, Tijuana and Torreón. International flights to Los Angeles, Tucson and Phoenix.

Trains Station just off Highway 15, 2½ km north of downtown.

Buses Bus station on Bulevar Transversal 400, north of University; to **Nogales** US$10, 4 hrs, hourly 0230-1830 (Tres Estrellas de Oro, 1st class); to **Agua Prieta**, 7 hrs, US$14, 6 a day (2nd class); **Guaymas**, hourly round the clock, US$6, 2½ hrs; to **Los Mochis**, 1st class, US$22, 7½ hrs through scrubland and wheat fields. Bus to **Tijuana**, US$35 1st class, 11 hrs, there can be long queues, especially near Christmas. Bus to **Mazatlán** 10-12 hrs, US$30. To **Kino**, US$3.35, 4 a day, 2 hrs (2nd class).

Directory **Airline offices** *AeroMéxico*, T168206. *Mexicana*, T171103. *Great Lakes*, T91-80000307. *Taesa*, T173606. **Embassies & consulates** *US Consulate*, T172375 for appointment, Mon-Fri 0900-1700.

Bahía Kino

Phone code: 624
Colour map 1, grid B3

A paved 118-km road runs west past the airport to Bahía Kino, divided into the old, somnolent and somewhat down-at-heel fishing village, and the new **Kino Nuevo**, a 'winter gringoland' of condos, trailer parks and a couple of expensive hotels. Although the public beaches are good, most American visitors come for the sportfishing. The Seri Indians, who used to live across El Canal del Infiernillo (Little Hell Strait) on the mountainous Isla Tiburón (Shark Island), have been

The Kino missions

Padre Eusebio Francisco Kino was the foremost pioneer missionary of northwest Mexico and Baja California. He attempted the first major settlement of the Baja peninsula (San Bruno, 1683); after its failure he was assigned to the mainland, where he blazed a ruta de misiones as far as present-day Tucson. Kino was a versatile and hardy Jesuit of Italian origin – astronomer, cartographer, farmer, physician, navigator, explorer and a man of unlimited faith. Most of his adobe mission buildings were later replaced by substantial Franciscan churches, such as the ones at Pitiquito, Oquitoa and at Magdalena, where his grave was discovered in 1966; the remains are enclosed in glass in situ and the site is a colonial monument. The church of San Ignacio, between Magdalena and Imuris (see below) is in excellent repair, with a wooden spiral staircase of mesquité.

displaced by the navy to the mainland, down a dirt road from Bahía Kino in a settlement at Punta Chueca (no east access). They come into Kino on Saturday and Sunday to sell their ironwood animal sculptures and traditional basketware (not cheap). They may usually be found at the *Posada del Mar Hotel*. For the visitor interested in exploring nature reserves, **Isla Tiburón** is of especial interest. Protected in the nearly 400 sq m preserve, the population of both the big horn sheep and mule deer has grown enormously. On the south end of the island, water depths of 50m or more are common. It is an excellent area not only for scuba diving but also for fishing, and **Dog Bay** provides shelter and ideal anchorage for spending the night. **Isla Patos** (Duck Island), 30 minutes north of Isla Tiburón, offers the opportunity to explore the submerged Spanish vessels that once sailed the Sea of Cortés. Other islands worth visiting are **Alcatraz** (also known as Pelican Island), **Turner**, and **San Esteban**. In Kino Nuevo, a fine **Museo Regional de Arte Seri** has opened on Mar de Cortés, the main boulevard.

Sleeping A *The Anchor House*. Beautiful bed and breakfast house on the beach, American-run, PO Box 80-83340, T20141. *Hotel Posada del Mar*, T181205, F181237. Quality declining. *Hotel Saro*. 5 rooms, on beach. **Camping** On the beaches is possible with or without tent. Camping at one of the trailer parks costs about US$12 a night (eg *Kino Bay RV Park*, Av Mar de Cortés, PO Box 857, Hermosillo, T624-20216/621 -53197). *Islandia Marina Trailer Park*, Puerto Peñasco y Guaymas, US$10, English spoken, hospitable. June Ellen Hayna runs an RV Park, PO Box 50, T20615, also cabins, **B**.

Eating Reasonably priced meals are available in Old Kino at *La Palapa* and *Marlín* restaurants (latter next to *Islandia Marina Trailer Park*). Fresh seafood and snacks. *El Pargo Rojo*. For really good seafood. Recommended.

Directory There is no bank in the area. The nearest is Bancomer in Miguel Alemán, between Kino and Hermosillo, 48 km away.

Guaymas and Bahía San Carlos

At Km 1,867 (from Mexico City) the road reaches the Gulf at the port of **Guaymas** (*Population: 200,000*), on a lovely bay backed by desert mountains; excellent deep-sea fishing, and seafood for the gourmet. Miramar beach, on Bocachibampo Bay with its blue sea sprinkled with green islets, is the resort section. There are watersport events on 10 May. The climate is ideal in winter but unpleasant in summer. The 18th-century church of San Fernando is worth a visit; so too, outside the town, is the 17th-century church of San José de

*Phone code: 622
Colour map 1, grid B4
Guaymas acquired the title 'heroic' in 1935, in memory of the valiant defence by its inhabitants during the French Invasion of 1854*

The Northwest Coast

Guaymas. The port area also boasts some worthy buldings, among which are the Templo del Sagrado Corazón de Jesús, the Banco de Sonora, the Palacio Municipal (constructed in 1899), the Ortiz Barracks and the Antigua Carcel Municipal (old Municipal Prison) constructed in 1900. You can also enjoy an excursion to the cactus forests.

Fifteen kilometres north of Guaymas (or 12 km from Highway 15) is the **Bahía San Carlos**, very Americanized and touristy, where *Catch 22* was filmed. Above the bay a twin-peaked hill, the Tetas de Cabra, is a significant landmark. There is good fishing with an international tournament each July. North of San Carlos further development is taking place on Sonora Bay. Both Miramar and San Carlos beaches are easily reached by bus. The free beaches are dirty. The **tourist office** at Avenida Serdán has lots of pamphlets.

Sleeping: Guaymas B *Ana*, Calle 25 No 135, T20593. With a/c, near cathedral. **B** *Santa Rita*, Serdán and Calle 9. With bath, a/c, clean, good. **E** *América*, Miguel Alemán (Calle 20) y Av 18, T21120. A/c, dirty, noisy. **F** *Casa de Huéspedes Martha*, Calle 13. With bath, fan, hot water, clean, garden. Recommended. **Motels**: **B** *Flamingos*, Carretera Internacional, T20960. **C** *Malibu*, T22244, Carretera Internacional N. At **Miramar Beach**: **AL** *Playa de Cortés*, T11224, F10135. Also has excellent RV park (US$18.50 per day), hot showers, clean, hotel has private beach, pool, restaurant and bar, etc. **A** *Leo's Inn*, at opposite end of the beach, T29490, PO Box 430, Guaymas. **Eating** *Cantón*, Serdán between Calle 20 and 21. Good Chinese. *Todos Comen*, on Serdán. Good food at reasonable prices.

Sleeping and eating: Bahía San Carlos *Condominio Pilar*, check office for rentals, good camp area. **A-B** *Hotel Fiesta San Carlos*, T60229, PO Box 828. Clean, good food (US$10-15), pool. **AL** *Tetakawi Hotel, Suites and RV Park* (Best Western), T60220, F60248, PO Box 71, San Carlos, Guaymas. By beach, swimming pool, bar, snack bar,

Guaymas

The indigenous people of Sonora

The largest concentration of the Yaqui nation is to be found in the Guaymas region: six of the eight ethnic groups that comprise the Yaqui, namely the Vícam, Pótam, Tórim, Belem, Rahum and Huíbiris, reside within the municipality of Guaymas. Etimologically, yaqui means 'Those of the river who speak loudly'. The Yaqui belong to the Cahíta nation and speak the Cahíta language. This was the most numerous nation found by the Spaniards in Sonora. Around 1617 the Spaniards founded the missions of the six ethnic groups of the yaqui: La Natividad del Señor de Vícam, San Ignacio de Tórim, Santísima Trinidad de Pótam, La Asunción de Rahum, Santa Barbara de Huíribis and San Miguel de Belem.

In 1701 the Jesuit missionary Juan Salvatierra founded the mission of San José de la Laguna some kilometres from the bay. Around 1767 the Viceroy Marqués Francisco de Croix ordained the recognition of the Bay of Guaymas so as to include it in the Sonora expedition whose aim was to pacify the Seri and Pimas Altos.

The local history of Guaymas tells of Lola Casanova, a young woman of sound social standing who, during an attack, was carried off by a group of Seri Indians. The chief fell in love with Lola, made her his bride and mother of his children who were heirs to the Seri throne.

---

disco, a/c, cable TV, trailer park rates US$14 per day. Next, after 10 km, is **B-C Creston Motel**. Beach side, clean, good value. **The Country Club**. With hotel and tennis, is extensive. **A-B** *La Posada de San Carlos*. On the beach, very nice. After 10 km from the Highway a road branches to **C** *Dorada Rental Units*, T60307, PO Box 48. On beach, pleasant. **C** *Ferrer Apartments*. Cooking facilities, hot water, pleasant patio, good value. At Km 13 the road forks: left 1 km to 2 secluded bays with limited trailer camping, and right to the new *Marina Real*, the *Howard Johnson Hotel* (trailer park next door) and *Club Mediterranée*, T622-60176, F60070, all on Sonora Bay, and beyond a beach with open camping. **Eating** *Piccolo*. Good pasta, salads, good value. Just over 1 km up a dirt track is *Restaurant Norsa*. Good limited menu, no alcohol. Generally, restaurants are overpriced.

Transport **Air**: The General José M Yáñez airport (GYM) is 5 km from Guaymas on the way to San Carlos. AeroMéxico (T622-20123) has flights to La Paz, Mexico City and Phoenix. Mesa Airlines also fly to Phoenix.

Buses: 1st class bus to **Hermosillo** (2½ hrs, US$6); **Mazatlán**, frequent, 12 hrs, US$30; **Tijuana**, 18 hrs, US$47. To **Culiacán**, 9 hrs, US$16.50. Buses from Empalme to **Los Mochis**/Sufragio with Autotransportes Tufesa, US$9.50, 5½ hrs, T32770.

Ferry: Sematur sail from Guaymas to **Santa Rosalía**, Baja California, 7 hr trip, see schedule, page 717 for details.

Directory 7 km from the Highway, behind the shops, are the post office and police station; the beer depository will sell by the half case. After 10 km are the Pemex station and bank opposite the phone and fax centre.

From Guaymas to Mazatlán is 784 km. There is a toll 8 km west of Empalme, US$5; this is on the toll road which skirts Guaymas completely. An alternative route goes into Guaymas, but forks to avoid the centre from both north and south. A third route goes into the centre of Guaymas which should be avoided unless you have business there. There is another toll at Esperanza, US$5. Then comes Ciudad Obregón, mainly important as the centre of an agricultural

Ciudad Obregón
Phone code: 64
Colour map 1, grid B4
Population: 180,000

region. It is a good place for buying leather goods, such as western boots and saddles.

Sleeping and eating **A** *Motel Valle Grande*, M Alemán y Tetabiate, T40940. **A** *Costa de Oro*, M Alemán 210, T41765. Well-kept and pleasant. **C** *Dora*, California 1016 Sur. **C** *San Jorge*, M Alemán 929 Norte, T49514, F44353. With a/c, TV, restaurant, bar, pool, safe parking, clean, friendly, with colonial Spanish decor; also 2 hotels on street of main bus station (turn right on leaving), 1 block to **D** *La Aduana*. Dirty, cold water, and further down, *Gema*. **Youth hostel**: Laguna de Nainari s/n, CP 85000, ask for bus to Seguro Social – state hospital – and walk round lake to hostal from there; Villas Deportivas Juveniles campsite, T141359. *Café Bibi*, behind Cathedral. Good local food but expensive.

Transport The airport (CEN) is 16 km from town. Flights to Chihuahua, Culiacán, Durango, Guadalajara, Hermosillo, La Paz, Loreto, Los Cabos, Los Mochis and Mexico City. Flights to US cities: Los Angeles and Tucson.

Directory **Airlines**: *AeroMéxico*, T132190. *Great Lakes*, T91-80000307. *Taesa*, T139525.

Navojoa	From Ciudad Obregón to Navojoa is a four-lane highway in poor condition
Phone code: 642	(toll at Navojoa, US$7). Navojoa has the *Motel El Rancho* (T20004) and *Motel*
Colour map 1, grid C5	*del Río* (T20331) and a trailer park in the north of town on Route 15 (run
Population: 200,000	down, shaded, US$10 for full hook-up, US$5 for car or small jeep, dollars pre-ferred to pesos). West of Navojoa, on Huatabampo bay, are the survivors of the Mayo Indians; their festivals are in May.

Alamos

Phone code: 642
Colour map 1, grid C5

The Alamos Music Festival is an annual event held for seven days at the end of January

Fifty-two kilometres into the hills is the delightful old colonial town of Alamos, now declared a national monument. It is set in a once famous mining area fascinating for rock enthusiasts. Although the area was explored by the Spanish in the 1530s, development did not begin for another 100 years when the Jesuits built a mission nearby. In 1683 silver mines were discovered near the village of **Aduana** and the population began to rise. By the 1780s there were over 30,000 people and the town had provided emigrants to settle new towns such as San Francisco and Los Angeles. At the end of the 18th century, silver production was at its peak and Alamos was the world's greatest producer. Political recognition followed, and in 1827 it was made capital of Occidente (Sonora and Sinaloa). However, the mining industry declined in the 19th century and by 1909 most of the mines had closed because of rising costs and revolutions. In 1933 the railroad was abandoned and the population declined to only 1,000 inhabitants. This has since recovered to about 6,200, largely because of US immigration, attracted by the sunny climate, attractive architecture and surroundings, and the proximity of the US border. You can visit the very photogenic old mine site of Aduana, near the village of Minas Nuevas on the road between Navojoa and Alamos, bus US$0.25. There is a good, unnamed restaurant there, American-run, reservations essential, ask in Alamos. The ecological reserve of Cuchijaqui River plays a vital role in the migratory process of a variety of birds on their long trips from north to south and back. Thousands of beautiful birds land here: macaws, parrots, owls, eagles, ducks, etc. Plants and trees of the region include the cedar oak found in deep jungle canyons. Several walking tours of Alamos are offered by the local US community, including a tour of the historical colonial town, and one of the homes and gardens, proceeds are reported to support school children's scholarships. The **Museo Costumbrista** has good explanations of the history of Alamos.

Sleeping **L-AL** *Casa Encantada*, Juárez 20, T80482, F80221, in USA F714-7522331. Courtyard rooms to luxury suites, bed and breakfast, charming, small pool, will find rooms elsewhere if town is 'full'. **AL-A** *Mansión de la Condesa Magdalena*. Same ownership as above, beautifully renovated, clean, quiet, relaxing, colonial rooms, beautiful gardens, excellent food. Recommended. **A** *Posada La Hacienda*, on edge of town. **B** *Los Portales Hotel*, T80111. With beautiful frescoes, on plaza. **D** *Somar*, on the road into Alamos, T80125, Madero 110. *El Caracol Trailer Park*. Rustic, good pool, not always open (US$8.50). Two other trailer parks, *Real de los Alamos*, US$10, with pool (too far to walk from town) and *Dolisa*, Madero 72, T642-80131, US$12, also **B-C** motel, small rooms, a/c, fireplace, with bath, TV.

Transport **Air**: There is a paved, 1,190m landing strip but no scheduled services. **Buses**: Navojoa-Alamos every hour on the half hour from 0630, until 1830, 1 hr, US$2, good road. Bus station for Alamos is about 8 blocks from main bus station in Navoja, but you must ask directions because it is a confusing route. **NB** For drivers heading north, there is a fruit and vegetable checkpoint on entering Sonora state. Toll at Sinaloa border US$5.35. Further toll and drug search 16 km north of Los Mochis, US$3.35.

Los Mochis

Los Mochis, in a sugar cane area, is a fishing resort 25 km from the sea with a US colony. The name is derived either from a local word meaning 'hill like a turtle', or possibly, from 'mocho', meaning one-armed, perhaps after a cowboy thus mutilated. The city was founded in 1904 around a sugar mill built by the American, Benjamin Johnson. His wife was responsible for building the Sagrado Corazón church. The family lost everything in the Revolution. There are plenty of nightspots and bars visited by roaming *mariachis*, who play excellent music. A stairway leads up the hillside behind La Pérgola, a pleasant public park near the city reservoir, for an excellent view of Los Mochis. Toll at Los Mochis US$3.65.

Phone code: 68
Colour map 1, grid C5
Population: 200,000

AL *Santa Anita*, Leyva and Hidalgo, T187046, F120046. Comfortable, clean dining room (good), noisy a/c, stores luggage, mixed reports about *Flamingo* travel agency attached (T121613, F183393), has own bus service to train station, safe garage to leave car while visiting Copper Canyon, US$4 per day; it is usually possible to change dollars. Under same ownership is *Plaza Inn*, on Leyva, the main street; also on this street, **B** *El Dorado*, 20 minutes from centre. A/c, pool, friendly, very good, and *Florida*. **C** *Beltrán*, Hidalgo 281 Pte, T120688, F120710. Noisy a/c, TV, has all travel timetables and will make reservations. Recommended.

Sleeping

D *América*, Allende Sur 655, T121355, F125983. No hot water in early morning, noisy, a/c, has restaurant with good, cheap sandwiches, enclosed parking. **D** *Fénix*, A Flores 365 Sur, T122623, F158948. Safe, clean, wake-up call, very good. **D** *del Valle*, Guillermo Prieto and Independencia, T120105. A/c, bath, OK but pricey. **D** *El Parque*, Obregón 600 Pte, across from Parque Sinaloa, T120260. Fan, US$2 more for a/c. **D** *Hidalgo*, opposite *Beltrán* at No 260 Pte, T123456. Cheap *cafetería*, friendly, occasionally no hot water. **D** *Lorena*, Prieto y Obregón 186 Pte, T120239, F120958. With bath, TV, gloomy, poor value, but good *cafetería*. **D** *Montecarlo*, Independencia y Flores 322 Sur, T121818. Clean, a/c, TV, restaurant, parking. **F** *Los Arcos*, Allende, T123253. Without bath, clean but dingy, fills up quickly, some rooms noisy, more expensive with a/c. **Motel** **D** *Santa Rosa*, López Mateos 1051 Norte. Modest.

The Northwest Coast

Trailer Park *Río Fuerte Trailer Resort*, 16 km north of Los Mochis on Route 15. Good, heated swimming pool, US$10 per car and 2 people, US$14.50 motor home, offers hunting, shooting, fishing expeditions. Recommended. **NB** The Pemex Station 1,500m south of here has a very bad reputation and bad pumps. Ask at *Río Fuerte* which service stations are best, eg the one 16 km south on the right. There is another *Hotel Resort y Trailer Park* on Highway 15 at the turn-off to Topolobampo. Sophisticated, with disco.

Eating *El Farallón*, Flores and Obregón. Good seafood and service, reasonably priced; opposite, on Obregón, is **España**. Very good. **Café León**, Obregón 419. Good meals, including breakfast, cakes, inexpensive. *El Vaquero* in *Hotel Montecarlo*. Recommended. *El Delfín*, on Allende Sur near Obregón. Restaurant and bar, nice atmosphere (owner's husband is a *mariachi* musician). *El Taquito*, Leyva, 1 block from Santa Anita. Open 24 hrs. *Tay-Pak*, near Independencia. Chinese, good clean, reasonably priced. *Chispa*, Leyva Sur 117, near Morelos. Art deco design, clean, good. *Mi Cabaña Tacos*, corner of Obregón y Allende. Popular with locals, friendly. Recommended. *Las Palmeras*. Excellent, reasonably priced. *El Bucanero*. Good seafood. *Birria* is a local beef dish; many places to eat are referred to as a *birriería*.

Transport **Air** Airport Federal (LMM) is 6½ km from town. Flights to Chihuahua, Ciudad Obregón, Culiacán, Guadalajara, Hermosillo, La Paz, Los Cabos, Mazatlán, Mexico City, Monterrey and Tijuana with a variety of airlines. Flights to Los Angeles, Phoenix and Tucson with AeroMéxico and Aero California.

Los Mochis

■ **Sleeping**		**6** Fénix	● **Eating**
1 América		**7** Hidalgo	**1** El Delfín
2 Balderrama		**8** Lorena	**2** El Farallón
3 Beltrán		**9** Los Arcos	**3** España
4 Del Valle		**10** Montecarlo	**4** Mi Cabaña Tacos
5 El Parque		**11** Santa Anita	

N
Not to scale

Trains For **Creel and Chihuahua**, see below. **NB** If coming from Chihuahua and you don't want to stay in Los Mochis, assuming the train is not over-delayed, you can take a night bus to Mazatlán at 2200, arriving 0630. Los Mochis station has toilets and local phones; ticket office is open 1 hour before train leaves. The station is 8 km from town; do not walk there or back in the dark. There is a bus service from 0500, US$0.15 from corner of hotels *Hidalgo* and *Beltrán*, otherwise take the 0500 bus from *Hotel Santa Anita*, US$3.50 (for house guests only), or taxi, of which there is any number going into town after the arrival of the Chihuahua train. Taxis in the centre go from Hidalgo y Leyva; fare to station US$5 per car, bargaining not possible, make sure price quoted is not per person, rip-offs are common. Bus to town from corner of 1st junction from station from 0530.

Buses Each bus company has its own terminal in Los Mochis. **Mexico City**, US$60, 25 hrs. **Guadalajara**, frequent, Tres Estrellas de Oro, 1st class, US$31. **Ciudad Obregón**, US$16.50. **Tijuana**, US$53, several daily up to 24 hrs. **Mazatlán**, 5½ hrs, US$16.50, 1st class, Tres Estrellas de Oro or Transportes Norte de Sonora, hourly, also Estrella Blanca. **Nogales**, US$22, 9 hrs. Elite buses leave every hour until 2200. No reservations can be made for buses north or south at the terminal of Tres Estrellas de Oro and it is difficult to get on buses. Try instead Transportes de Pacífico, 3 blocks away and next to TNS terminal. 1st class bus to **Guaymas** 5½ hrs, US$9.50 with Tufesa. To **Tepic**, US$32, 13 hrs. Local buses to destinations around Sinaloa eg Topolobampo, Guasave, San Blas (Sufragio) and Culiacán leave from Autotransportes del Norte de Sinaloa Terminal near Post Office and Mercado Cuauhtémoc.

Airline offices *Aero California*, T181616. **Banks** *Casa de Cambio Rocha*, T125500, opposite *Hotel Beltrán*; others, and banks, on Leyva. American Express at *Viajes Krystal*, Av Obregón, all services. **Communications** Post Office: Ordóñez Pte, between Prieto y Zaragoza Sur, south of centre, open Mon-Fri 0900-1400,1600-1800. **Laundry** *Lavamatic*, Allende 218; another laundry at Juárez 225. **Medical services** Hospital: *Fátima*, Loaizo 606 Pte, T155703/123312, private, English spoken, maybe a good place to start in an emergency.

Directory

A side road, running southwest from Los Mochis crosses the salt flats to Topolobampo (20 km, 30 minutes). The town is built on a number of hills facing the beautiful bay-and-lagoon-indented coast. In the bay, which has many outlets, there are a number of islands; sunsets here are lovely. Boats can be hired, and fishing trips are available from the jetty. It is difficult to find a beach unless one pays for a private launch. Pemex has a storage facility here and Topolobampo is being developed as a deep-water port. This is as a consequence of the full operation of the Ojinaga (see page 611) – Pacific railway (of which the Los Mochis-Creel-Chihuahua route forms part). Originally conceived in 1872 as an outlet for US goods from Kansas and the south to Japan, the line across the Mexican Sierra was not completed until 1961.

Topolobampo
Phone code: 686
Colour map 1, grid C5

Sleeping **B** *Yacht Hotel*, 3-4 km south of town. Modern, a/c, clean and good food, quiet, good views, but seems to close for the winter. **E** *Estilo Europeo Poama*, at the ferry terminal, 10 mins walk from Los Mochis bus; for other accommodation go to Los Mochis.

Ferry Topolobampo-La Paz, Baja California Sur. For schedule and fares, see page 717. No reservations, buy ticket in Los Mochis (office T183986) or on day of travel at Muelle Topolobampo office, opens 3 hours prior to departure (be there at least 2 hours before sailing) T686-20141, F20035. Travel agency *Viajes Paotán*, Rendón y Angel Flores, can book tickets for you on day of departure. See also page 718.

The Northwest Coast

To Creel and Chihuahua by train

Details of the Copper Canyon and other places passed on the Chihuahua al Pacífico are provided in Chapter 13, pages 623-633

The famous Chihuahua al Pacífico train journey shows the spectacular scenery of the Sierra Madre and the Barranca del Urique/Cobre (Urique/Copper Canyon). The *Servicio Estrella* train should leave daily at 0600 (but often at 0700), US$27 to Creel (about nine hours), US$49 to Chihuahua (about 14 hours, but expect delays). Bring your own toilet paper, food and drinking water. Tickets must be bought in advance, not on the train, either on morning of departure or, in high season (July-August, New Year, Holy Week) a day or more before. Return tickets are valid for 30 days. Tickets can be bought at Flamingo Travel (mixed reports) in *Hotel Santa Anita*, but they will try to persuade you to book into their preferred (expensive) hotels. It may be worth buying tickets from them to avoid long queues at the station. If you are only going as far as Creel buy return tickets as it is impossible to reserve seats from Creel back to Los Mochis. A local bus (US$0.10) leaves from the crossroads near *Hotel Beltrán* for the train station. It departs at 0530, arriving at 0555.

The ordinary train, *Tarahumara*, leaves at 0700, Tuesday, Thursday, Saturday, US$5.50 to Creel, 13 hours, US$10 to Chihuahua, but it is not possible to reserve seats. Second-class trains make many stops but are reasonably comfortable and it is possible to open the windows. On either train, sit on the right for the best views, except when approaching Temoris, then return to the right until the first tunnel after Temoris; thereafter good views can be seen on either side. On the *Primera Especial* the windows do not open so, to take photos, stand between the carriages. Motorists taking the train to Creel have been advised to park in front of the station as there are lights and people at all times. Alternatively, ask for Sr Carlos at the station ticket office, he will guard the car at his home for a modest fee. There is more expensive parking downtown.

El Fuerte

Population: 120,000
Colour map 1, grid C5

This town, 1½ hours by train from Los Mochis, has recently been renovated and has interesting colonial architecture in the centre (it was founded in 1564). The station is 10 km from the town; taxis US$4 per person. *Posada del Hidalgo* is a historical mansion, details from *Hotel Santa Anita* in Los Mochis. **D** *Hotel Oasis*, half a block from Calle Benito Juárez in centre. Not very clean, some rooms better than others, a/c, expensive restaurant. **D** *Hotel San Francisco*. Good value. There is an attractive plaza and good restaurants.

For those travelling on the train, the high, long bridge over the Río Fuerte heralds the beginning of more interesting scenery (this is the first of 37 major bridges); three hours from Los Mochis the first, and longest, of the 86 tunnels is passed, then, 10 minutes later the Chinapas bridge (this is approximately the Sinaloa/Chihuahua border, where clocks go forward an hour).

Culiacán

Phone code: 67
Colour map 1, grid C6
Population: 950,000

Some 210 km beyond Los Mochis, and 1,429 km before Mexico City, Culiacán, the capital of Sinaloa state, was founded in 1531 by Beltrán de Guzmán. It can no longer be called a colonial city, but is attractive and prosperous; it has a university and is an important centre for winter vegetables.

Beaches

The safe beaches of **Altata** are 30 minutes away by paved road. Eighteen kilometres west of Altata on gravel, then sand (passable) is Tambor Beach, with wind and waves, and fewer people than Altata. **Imala**, 25 km northeast by a poor road has thermal baths reaching 40°C.

Culiacán – the place of the curve

In the Nahuatl language, the word Culiacán is rooted in the adjective cultic, something twisted or curved – can is 'place of'. Many students of pre-Hispanic Mexico believe that Culiacán is synonymous with Colhuacán. The toponym Colhuacán proliferated through much of Mesoamerica in the pre-Conquest period. The name was expressed pictorially by the symbol of a curved mountain. The symbol of the curved mountain also identified the nation known as the Colhua, or an individual of that nation. Culiacán is referred to in most of the histories of the Chichimeca, a collection of nations who invaded or were invited into Central Mexico some time around the fall of Teotihuacán: they may even have contributed to the demise of that great centre. The Chichimeca, of whom the Aztecs were the last to enter the Valley of Mexico, forged alliances, usually through marriage, with the remnants of the Toltecs who still inhabited the area. The Toltecs were civilized, as denoted by the cotton clothes they are shown to have worn in the many historical maps created before,

or very soon after, the Conquest. The Chichimeca, on the other hand, were nomadic hunters and gatherers, and depicted themselves as such, wearing animal skins and carrying bows and arrows. The later Chichimecas, in fact, were very proud of their more primitive origins.

The pride the Chichimeca took in these origins is evident in the reference in practically all their histories, oral and pictorial, to Culhuacán, Teoculhuacán (teo-sacred, as in Teotihuacán=Place of the Gods), and even Huecolhuacán, Greater Culhuacán. These are all linked to the Culiacán of Sinaloa. In the Aztec migration history, the journey is instigated by their war god, Huitzilopochtli (Hummingbird-on-the-Left) who speaks to them from a cave in Culiacán urging them to abandon Aztlán. Many believe that Aztlán is an island somewhere off the coast of Sinaloa or even an island in the Laguna de Culiacán. Thus, although Culiacán was officially founded in 1531 by Beltrán de Guzmán, it is very likely that it existed as a settlement long before the arrival of the Spaniards.

Sleeping

A *Executivo*, Madero y Obregón, T139370. C *Del Valle*, Solano 180, T139026. Noisy. Not recommended. D *San Francisco*, Hidalgo 227. With bath, clean, friendly, free parking. E *Louisiana*. **Motels** A *Los Tres Ríos*, 1 km north of town on highway 15. Trailer park, US$10, pool, resort-style, good restaurant. *Pizzería Tivoli*. Good, friendly. C *Los Caminos*, Carretera Internacional y Blvd Leyva Solano, T153300. With a/c, phone, satellite TV, restaurant, pool, nightclub, safe parking, clean rooms.

Transport

Air The Aeropuerto Federal de Bachigualato (CUL) is 10 km from centre. Aero California, T160250; AeroMéxico, T153772; Taesa, T168899 have flights to Acapulco, Aguascalientes, Chihuahua, Ciudad Obregón, Cuernavaca, Durango, Guadalajara, Hermosillo, La Paz, Los Angeles (California), Los Cabos, Los Mochis, Mexico City, Monterrey, Reynosa, Tijuana, Torreón, Tucson (Arizona) and Uruapan.

Buses To **Tepic**, 8¼ hrs, US$12; to **Guaymas**, 9 hrs, US$16.50.

Road North of the city, the north and southbound carriageways are on different levels with no divide (very dangerous). A new toll section of freeway heads nearer to the coast, past Navolato, bypasses Culiacán and rejoins Highway 15 a few km south of that city. Note, though, that this is a very isolated stretch of road and there have been robberies on it at times. Do not drive at night. The area around Culiacán is also a drugs-growing region.

The Northwest Coast

Culiacán to Mazatlan Two thirds of the way between Culiacán and Mazatlán, at the Cruce de Coyotitán, there are two possible side trips off Highway 15: right to the mouth of the Río Piaxtla on the coast where, at **Estación Dimas**, there are petroglyphs, and left up into the *cordillera* to **San Ignacio**, reaching eventually the village of Tepehuaje with hiking possibilities in Los Picachos/Los Frailes (2,511m). Between Coyotitán and Mazatlán, along Highway 15 (good condition) you come to a roadside monument marking the Tropic of Cancer. Toll 27 km north of Mazatlán, US$11.35.

Mazatlán

Phone code: 69
Colour map 3, grid A1
Population: 800,000

Beyond the Tropic of Cancer, 1,089 km from Mexico City, is Mazatlán, spread along a peninsula at the foot of the Sierra Madre. It is the largest Mexican port on the Pacific Ocean and the main industrial and commercial centre in the west. The beauty of its setting and its warm winters have made it a popular resort, but unfortunately with expansion it has lost some of its attraction. It overlooks Olas Altas (High Waves) Bay, which has a very strong current. Entering Mazatlán by sea from Baja shows the city at its most impressive – two pyramid-shaped hills, one with a lighthouse on top, the other the 'rock' of Isla Piedra, guard the harbour entrance.

Ins and outs

Getting there & away

See transport page 671

Aeropuerto General Rafael Buelna (MZT),19 km south, has flights to Mexico City and destinations in northern and western Mexico and in the US. Planes are met by the usual fleet of fixed-fare taxis and microbuses. The main bus station is north of the town centre. First-class buses go to and from most major cities west and north of the capital, while second-class will take you to smaller towns such as San Blas. There is a train station to the east of Mazatlán; confirm that there is a service before planning your journey. A ferry service operates between Mazatlán and La Paz, in Baja California (see page 717 for ferry schedules). For drivers, Routes 15, the coastal road, heads north up to the US border, and south to Tepic then inland to Guadalajara; Route 40 is the picturesque but hair-raising road to Durango.

Getting around Most local buses leave from the market. There is an express service (green and white buses) which runs from the centre along the seafront to the Zona Dorada and beyond. Taxis are readily available and *pulmonias*, taxis that looks like golf carts, will ferry you between the bus station and your hotel.

The **tourist offices** are at Camarón Sábalo, past the main part of the Zona Dorada, in the Banrural building, fourth floor, opposite *Mar Rosa* trailer park and *Holiday Inn*, a long way to go to get information easily obtained at any travel agency or hotel information desk. Information from www.mazcity.com.mx/ homepage.htm; tourist news, www.pacificpearl.com. Mazatlán suffers from severe air pollution from the electric generating plant located between the airport and the town.

Sights

The old part of town is located around **Plaza Machado**, which is on Calle Carnaval. This is far and away the most interesting part of the city. Half a block from the plaza is the **Teatro Peralta**, the 17th-century opera house, which has been restored and reopened to the public. The **Aquarium**, Avenida de los Deportes III, just off the beach, behind *Hotel Las Arenas*, is interesting, and includes sharks and blindfish. ■ *0900, US$3, children US$1.50.* The **Museo**

Arqueológico de Mazatlán, Sixto Osuna 115, half a block from *Hotel Free-man*, is small, covering the state of Sinaloa. Recommended. ■ *US$1, free gallery in same building*. The **Museo de Arte** has a 20th-century collection. ■ *Closes Sun at 1400, US$0.90*.

Beaches

Tourism is now concentrated in the **Zona Dorada**, which includes the beaches of Gaviotas, Los Sábalos, Escondida, Delfín, Cerritos, Cangrejo and Brujas (north of **Playa Brujas** is a rocky area which is good for snorkelling); the area is built up and accommodation is expensive. From Olas Altas, the promenade, lined by hotels with a long beach at its foot, curves northwards around the bay, first as Paseo Claussen, then Avenida del Mar which leads to Avenida Camarón Sábalo in the Zona Dorada (take bus from Juárez – best from in front of market – marked Sábalo Centro US$0.30). The sunsets are superb seen from this side of the peninsula; at this time of day high divers can be watched and the fishermen return to the north beach. There are many good beach bars from which to view the setting sun. Buses from Calle Arriba go to the Zona Dorada for US$0.50.

The lighthouse on El Faro Island is 157m above sea level

Mazatlán

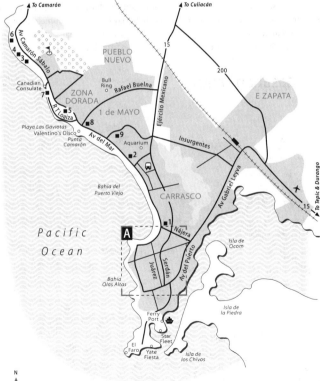

■ **Sleeping**
1 Aguamarina
2 Del Sol
3 El Cid
4 Holiday Inn
5 Los Sábalos
6 Océano Palace
7 Playa Mazatlán
8 San Diego
9 Sands

Related maps
A Mazatlán centre,
page 668

On the other side of the peninsula the Avenida del Puerto promenade overlooks a number of islands. From the ferry terminal at the southern end of Avenida del Puerto, a boat can be taken to **Isla de los Chivos** for US$1; there you can stroll along the beaches and eat at the beach bars. There are more islands in the nearby lagoons, which teem with wildlife. The best beaches, 3-5 km from the city, are easily reached by taxi.

Excursions

To reach **Isla de la Piedra** (which is in fact a peninsula) take a small boat from the south side of town from Armada (naval station near Pacífico brewery, reached by 'Zaragoza' bus from Juárez outside market), regular service, US$1 return ticket. The 30-km beach on the Mazatlán side is now littered but you can walk across the peninsula either side of the hill (10 minutes) to a clean beach where there is good surfing. There is also a ferry that goes from near the lighthouse to the *isla*; runs until 1700. Local *comedores* on the beach provide primitive accommodation, or ask for permission to camp on the beach. Try smoked fish sold on a stick; *Victor's comedor* has been recommended. Beware of sandflies.

Star Fleet boats may be rented at the sports-fishing docks for a cruise round the **Dos Hermanos** rocks, where boobies and many other birds can be seen. A boat excursion on the **Yate Fiesta** cruises out at 1000 or 2000 (with dancing), from second-last bus stop in the direction of Playa del Sur. Refreshments included, and you can see the wildlife in the day time. Four kilometres south of Mazatlán at **El Verde** is a sea turtle reserve in an area of mangroves.

At the foot of the Sierra Madre, 30 minutes from Mazatlán is **LL** *Rancho Las*

Mazatlán centre

Music in Mazatlán

Firmly rooted and extremely popular in the State of Sinaloa is a type of orchestra known as the Banda Sinaloense or Tamborera, which can be seen and heard playing 'Chaparral' at almost any time of day or night in restaurants, dance halls, bars, at family parties or on the street. It usually has from 14 to 16 musicians: four saxophones, four trumpets, clarinets, tuba, 3-4 men on drums and other percussion instruments, including maracas, guiro, and loud, strong voices. It is unabashed, brutal music, loud and lively. One such Banda plays every afternoon at the Chaparral bar, opposite the Conasupo market near the bus

Moras, a converted tequila ranch. Now with six hotel rooms and five villas, tennis courts, pool, laundry service, children's summer camp, restaurant and riding for all abilities (daytime activities for non-residents available), reservations T165044, F165045 (address of office Av Camarón Sábalo 204, Suite 6, Zona Dorada 82110, Mazatlán, or 9297 Siempre Viva Road, Suite 15-474, San Diego, CA 92173, USA). From Route 15, take the road towards La Noria for 9 km, then turn left up dirt road at sign. Highly recommended.

Essentials

Along the northern beach, Av Camarón Sábalo or just off it, all in our **LL-AL** ranges, are: *El Cid*, T133333. Resort, 4 hotels, with *El Caracol* nightclub and *Club 21*. *Holiday Inn*, Camarón Sábalo 696, T132222, F841287, resort facilities. *Los Sábalos*, RT Loaiza 100, T835333. Health Club facilities. *Luna Palace*, T146006 and *Océana Palace*,T130666, north end of Zona Dorada, all-inclusive, www.omegaresorts.com *Playa Mazatlán*, T134455. Good atmosphere. **A** *Las Palmas*, Camarón Sábalo 305, Zona Dorada, PO Box 135, T165664, F165666. Good value. Recommended. **A-C** *Tropicana*, RT Loaiza 27, T838000, F835361. With a/c, shower, large rooms, balconies, filters on taps/faucets for drinking water. Recommended. **B** *Azteca Inn*, Camarón Sábalo, T134477, F137476. Swimming pool.

Sleeping
The expensive hotels are in the area known as the Zona Dorada; budget hotels can be found around Cerro de la Neveria & on Angel Flores, Aquiles Serdán & José Azueta. Ask taxi drivers for the cheaper places

Along Av del Mar, across the road from the beach (front rooms in all are likely to be noisy) are: **AL** *Don Pelayo/Days Inn*, Av del Mar I, III, T831888, F840799. With a/c, TV, pool, parking off street, bar (may be noisy late at night). **AL-A** *Aguamarina*, No 110, T817080, F824624. **B-C** *Sands (Las Arenas)*. With swimming pool, a/c, TV, fridge, garden, good restaurant, on beach. Recommended. **C** *Amigos Plaza*, Av del Mar 900, T830333, F837282, before *Las Brisas*. Some rooms a/c, noisy at weekends, otherwise OK. **C-E** *San Diego*, Av del Mar s/n y Rafael Buelna, T835703. *Las Jacarandas*, Av del Mar 2500, just before Zona Dorada, T841177, F841077. Swimming pool, garden, good value.

Along Olas Altas beach are: **D** *Belmar*, No 166 Sur, T851112, F813428. Modernized but old, a bit run-down, pool. **C-D** *La Siesta*, No 11 Sur, T812640, F137476. With a/c, clean, friendly, safe, very good, nice patio, restaurant: *Shrimp Bucket*.

C *Olas Altas*, Paseo Centenario, T813192. With fan, efficiently run and clean, good views, restaurant. Most of the others are in the downtown area away from the beach front: **C** *Villa del Mar*, Aquiles Serdán 1506, next door at 1510 is a business with fax and email service. **D** *Del Centro*, JM Canizales 705 Pte, T821673, behind cathedral. **D** *Económico*. With bath and fan, noisy, dark but very clean, next to bus station, 500m from main beach. **D** *Milán*, JM Canizales 717. **D** *Posada Familiar Sarita*, Mariano Escobedo. Near beach, colonial. **D-E** *Vialta*, Azueta 2006, 3 blocks from market. With bath and fan, nice central patio, friendly, helpful, comfortable. **E** *San Fernando*, 21 de Marzo 926, T815980. With bath, hot water eventually, very basic, very friendly, car park outside. Recommended. **E** *Casa de Huéspedes El Castillo*, José Azueta 1612, 2 blocks from market. Family atmosphere, big rooms, clean. **E** *Lerma*, Simón Bolívar 5, near beach. With fan and hot showers, friendly, clean, simple, but quiet and cool. Highly recommended. **E** *Roma*, Av Juan Carrasco 127, T823685, 2 blocks from beach. With bath but some rooms noisy, clean. **E** *Zaragoza*, Zaragoza 917, T188937. Old and pretty, with bath, cheap cold drinks, free drinking water, parking for motorbikes.

Camping North of the city there are undeveloped beaches with free overnight camping; some have camped alone, but it is safer in a group (take bus to Sábalos and get out where it turns round). There are at least 10 trailer parks on Playa del Norte/Zona Dorada and on towards the north, including **D** *Casa Blanca Disco*. Cheapest, on beach side, dirty. Big hotels rapidly expanding all along north beach seashore to Mármol.

Motels Strung all along the ocean front. On RT Loaiza: **A** *Los Arcos*, No 214, T/F135066, on beach. **A** *Marley/Suites Lindamar*, No 222, T/F135533, reservations necessary. Recommended. **AL** *La Casa Contenta*, No 224, T134976, F139986. Apartments. **C** *Del Sol*, Av del Mar 200, T814712. Big rooms, with a/c and TV, clean, bright, nice pool, English spoken, motorcyclists allowed to park in front of room, close to aquarium, also have some apartments with kitchen. **C** *Papagayo*, Papagayo 712, T816489. *La Posta Trailer Park* (turn inland at *Valentino's Disco* from northern beach road). Busy, hook-ups at most sites, ½ block off beach, with swimming pool and tent space, lots of shade. **D** *Mar Rosa Trailer Park*, Camarón Sábalo 702 2½ km north of *La Posta*, T136187. Hot water, safe, own beach. Recommended. Three blocks up the road opposite is *San Fernando*. Clean, good, little shade; 4 km north of *Mar Rosa* is **D** *Playa Escondida*, Av Sábalo-Cerritos 999, T880077. Laid back, 236 spaces for RV park, not all have water and electricity, OK (**B-D** in bungalows), pool, volleyball, TV. Beware of theft from trailer parks. If driving to trailer parks north of the city, pass airport on Route 15, avoid left fork 'Centro y Playas'; follow route signed 'Culiacán' but do not go onto the toll road to Culiacán which starts at the Carta Blanca agency. Keep left and 10 km further turn left at sign 'Playa Cerritos'; at beach road turn left again. This leads to **E** *Maravilla Trailer Park*, next to Edificio del DIF, PO Box 1470, Mazatlán, T40400, 35 spaces, hot showers, clean, quiet. *Holiday*, opposite beach, and *Canoa*. Private club, nice, expensive. If coming to Mazatlán from the north turn right at 'Playas Mazatlán Norte' sign on Highway 15; after about 14 km you reach the junction with the Av Camarón Sábalo.

Eating *Mamucas*, Bolívar 404. Seafood expensive. *Shrimp Bucket* and *Señor Frog*, Olas Altas 11 and Av del Mar. Same owners, very famous, popular, good. *La Cumbre*, Benito Juárez and Hidalgo. Few seats, very busy, not many tourists, open 1100-1500. Recommended. *Beach Boys Club*, on Malecón near fisherman's monument. Good-value meals, US-owned. *El Paraíso*, on beach in Zona Dorada. Recommended. *Balneario Playa Norte*, Av del Mar, near monument. Friendly, reasonable prices. Recommended. Also on Av del Mar, Playa Norte, *Bella Mar*. Good, comparatively cheap. Many restaurants along Camaron Sábalo, eg *Villa Italia*. Good varied menu. *Señor Pepper*. Elegant décor, good service, food reasonable. *Doney's*. Good cooking. Recommended. *Lobster Trap*, Camarón Sábalo 307. Good chicken(!). *Mariscos El Camichín*, Paseo Claussen 97. Excellent seafood *parrillada*, good value. Recommended. *Joncol's*, Flores 608 Pte. With a/c, downtown, popular. *Los Comales*, Angel Flores, 2 blocks from Post Office. Good. Best value fish meals, US$4, above the markets near Plaza de la República (bring beer with you from supermarket opposite – not sold in cheap restaurants). Try mixed fish dish, US$15 for 2, very good. *Bar Pacífico*, on main plaza. Excellent *guacamole* and chicken wings, pleasant atmosphere. *Las Cazuelas*, Canizales 273. Good cheap *comedor*, friendly. *Cenaduría el Túnel*, Carnaval Sur 1207, opposite theatre. Excellent chicken *enchiladas*, try *pizzoli*, only open at night, closed Wed. *Pastelería y Cafetería Panamá*, several branches for reasonable meals, pastries, coffee, the one behind the cathedral on Juárez is recommended. *Casa* *del Naturista*, Zaragoza 809. Sells good wholegrain bread. Fast food places, eg *McDonald's*, *Pizza Hut*, are more expensive than in the US. The best deal is at the market where you can get an excellent fish lunch for US$1.50.

Joe's Oyster Bar. Very good disco behind *Hotel Los Sábalos*, open-air, US$10 cover **Entertainment** charge and open bar. *Edgar's Bar*, Aquiles Serdán. One of Mazatlán's oldest drinking joints.

Fishing is the main sport (sailfish, tarpon, marlin, etc). Mazatlán's famous fishing tour- **Sports** nament follows Acapulco's and precedes the one at Guaymas. In the mangrove swamps are egrets, flamingoes, pelicans, cranes, herons, and duck. Nearby at Camarones there is **parasailing**, drawn by motorboats. The northern beach tourist strip offers boat trips to nearby deserted islands, snorkel hire and paragliding. **Bungee jumping** is done at junction Camarón Sábalo y Rafael Buelna opposite *McDonalds*, US$26. Always check with the locals whether **swimming** is safe, since there are strong rip currents in the Pacific which run out to sea and are extremely dangerous. There are **bullfights** at Mazatlán, good view from general seats in the shade (*sombra*), although you can pay much more to get seats in the first 7 rows – Sun at 1600, very touristy.

Explora Tours, Centro Comercial Lomas, Av Camarón Sábalo 204-L-10, T139020, **Tour operators** F161322, very helpful. Recommended. *Zafari Tours*, Paseo Claussen 25, ferry bookings, helpful. *Hudson Tours*, T131764, for mountain biking.

Local Green and white express buses on the 'Sábalo Centro' route run from Playa **Transport** Cerritos to the city centre along the seafront road, US$0.35. Taxis charge an average US$3.50-US$5 between Zona Dorada and city centre. From Bahía del Puerto Viejo to centre, taxi US$1, bus US$0.20. **Car hire** all on Camarón Sábalo: **Budget**, No 402, T132000, F143611. **National**, No 7000, T136000, F139087, US$280 per week. *AGA*, No 316, T144405.

Air Aeropuerto General Rafael Buelna (MZT), 19 km from centre. Taxi, fixed fare US$24 airport-Mazatlán; micro bus US$6 per person. Flights to Mexico City, Guadalajara, La Paz, Durango, Ciudad Juárez, Hermosillo, Los Cabos, Los Mochis, Monterrey, Puerto Vallarta, Querétaro, Tijuana and Torreón. US destinations: Los Angeles, San Francisco, Denver, Seattle, Tucson, San Antonio and Phoenix.

Trains Take 'Insurgentes' bus out to Morelos railway station. Rail privatization has meant that most passenger services have been scrapped.

Buses Terminal at Chachalaco y Ferrusquilla s/n, T812335/815381; take 'Insurgentes' bus from terminal to Av Ejército Mexicano for the centre, via market at Aquiles Serdán; if you cross the boulevard and take bus in the other direction it goes to the railway station (US$0.60); alternatively take a *pulmonía*, a taxi which looks like a golf cart, which costs US$3 to Zona Dorada. Computel outlet open 24 hrs daily at bus station with fax and long-distance phone services. Bus fare to **Mexico City** about US$55, 18 hrs (Tres Estrellas de Oro, T813680, 1st class, express at 2100 a little more expensive; Transportes del Pacífico hourly 1st class slightly cheaper but over 20 hrs, via Irapuato and Querétaro). Elite 1100, 1400, 1945, 2100, US$58. **Mexicali** US$50, Pullman, 21 hrs. **Guadalajara**, several companies, several times a day, US$19.25 (10 hrs). Elite US$26, 7 daily. Ejecutivo (luxury) bus to Guadalajara at 2200, US$38. To **Chihuahua**, US$38 1st class, 19 hrs. To crossroads for **San Blas**, US$8; **Tepic** US$13, Transportes del Pacífico (4½ hrs; Tepic is the best place to make connections to Puerto Vallarta); bus (frequent) to **Los Mochis** (5½ hrs), US$18 with Transportes Norte de Sonora, Estrella Blanca or Autotransportes del Pacífico, tickets available only 45 mins before departure. Autotransportes del Pacífico buses go hourly to Culiacán (US$11) and Los Mochis 0800-2030 via the expressway. To **Navojoa**, US$11 1st class; 2 daily 1st class buses to **Durango**, Futura at 0930, Transportes Chihuahuenses at 1400, 7 hrs, US$15, several 2nd class buses, take a morning bus to see the scenery; **Guaymas**, 12 hrs, US$30. Elite (own waiting room) to **Puerto Vallarta**, 1600, US$20. **Tijuana** 1345, US$80, **Nogales**, 2115, US$58. Bus to **Rosario** US$1.65, you can then (with difficulty) catch bus to Caimanero beach, nearly deserted (see below). Terminal Alamos, Av Guerrero Ote 402, 2 blocks from market, buses to **Alamos** every hour on the half hour.

Tolls Mazatlán to Culiacán US$65. **Cycling** Beware, the road Mazatlán-Tepic-Guadalajara has been described as 'the most dangerous in the world for cyclists'.

Ferry La Paz (Baja California Sur), see schedule, page 717, for other information see under La Paz, Baja California section. Allow plenty of time for booking and customs procedure. Tickets from *Hotel Aguamarina*, Av del Mar 110, with 10% commission, also from travel agents. Ferry terminal is at the southern end of Av del Puerto, quite a way from the centre (take bus marked 'Playa Sur', which also goes from the street corner opposite ferry terminal to Av Ejército Méxicano near bus station). **NB** Ticket office for La Paz ferry opens 0830-1300 only, on day of departure, arrive before 0800, unclaimed reservations on sale at 1100. Don't expect to get vehicle space for same-day departure.

Directory **Airline offices** *Aero California*, T132042. *AeroMéxico*, T841111. *Alaska Airlines*, T95-800-4260333. *Mexicana*, T827722. *United*, T91-800-0030700. **Banks** *Banamex*, Benito Juárez and Angel Flores, also Av Camarón Sábalo 434, 0900-1330, 1530-1730. *Casas de Cambio* on same avenida, Nos 109, 1009 and at junction with Rodolfo T Loaiza; also at R T Loaiza 309. *American Express*, Camarón Sábalo, T130600, open Mon-Fri 0900-1700, Sat 0900-1400, doesn't sell TCs. **Communications** Internet: *Mail Boxes Etc*, Camarón Sábalo 310, T164009, F164011, mail boxes, courier service, fax service, US$3.50 per 15 mins, mailboxes@red2000.com.mx; across the street at Centro Comercial Lomas, *local 9* is another internet outlet, US$5 per 1 hr, T140008. *Netpool*, Olas Altas 81-B, near *Hotel Belmar*, 1000-2100 Mon-Sat, 1400-2000 Sun, US$3.30 per hr. *'Enlaces-Tel internet'*, Angel Flores 912, ½ block from plaza, T811564, Mon-Sat 0800-2000, Sun 0900-1400, US$2.70 per hr. *Pro-Eco Welcome Centre*, US$3.70 per hr, serves organically grown coffee, friendly, sells English-language books, meeting place for Mexicans studying English. *Red 2000*, Plaza Las Américas, email, internet. **Post Office:** Benito Juárez y 21 de Marzo, opposite Palacio Municipal, T812121. DHL is a couple of doors from *Mail Boxes Etc* (see above), 0900-1330, 1500-1800 Mon-Fri, 0830-1330 Sat. **Telephones:** 1 block from American Express; also 21 de Marzo y Juárez. Computel phone and fax service, Aquiles Serdán 1512, T69-850109, F850108. Phone rental, Accetel, Camarón Sábalo 310-4, T165056. There are public phones taking international credit cards all along Camarón Sábalo and Rodolfo T Loaiza in the Zona Dorada for long-distance calls. **Embassies & consulates** *Canada*, *Hotel Playa Mazatlán*, Rodolfo T Loaiza 202, T137320/F146655. *France*, Jacarandas 6, T828552. *Netherlands*, Av Sábalo Cerritos, T135155. *Germany*, Jacarandas 10, T822809. *Italy*, Av Olas Altas 66-105, T814855. *Norway*, F Alcalde 4, T813237. *US*, RT Loaiza, opposite *Hotel Playa Mazatlán*, T/F165889, Mon-Fri 0930-1300, T134455 ext 285. **Hospitals** *Hospital General*, Av Ferrocarril, T840262. *Cruz Roja Mexicana*, Alvaro Obregón 73, T813690. There is a free Red Cross treatment station on Camarón Sábalo, opposite the *Beach Man*. **Laundry** On Av del Mar, between bus station and *Hotel Aguamarina*, also on Benito Juárez near *Hotel Lerma*. **Useful telephone numbers** Emergency: call T06; Red Cross T813690; Ambulance T851451; Police T821867.

Mazatlán to Durango

Twenty-four kilometres beyond Mazatlán, the Coast-to-Coast Highway to Durango (a spectacular stretch in good condition), Torreón, Monterrey and Matamoros turns off left at Villa Unión. Heading east, the road reaches **Concordia**, a delightful colonial town with a well-kept plaza and a splendid church (two **F** hotels, one at each end of town on the main road), then climbs the mountains past **Copala**, another mining ghost town (basic hotel); *Daniel's Restaurant*, open 0900-1700. Copala can be reached by tour bus from Mazatlán or by Auriga pick-up truck from Concordia. On this road, 40 km from Concordia, 3 km before **Santa Lucía**, at La Capilla del Taxte, 1,240m, there is a good German hotel and restaurant, **D**, *Villa Blanca*, T21628. Before reaching **La Ciudad** (one very basic hotel) and the plains, the road goes through a spectacular section, winding through many vertical-sided canyons with partly forested slopes. The road is a phenomenal feat of engineering, as it is cut into the cliff side with steep drops below. At one point, called **El Espinazo del Diablo** (Devil's Spine), the road crosses a narrow bridge (approximately 50m long) with vertical drops either side and superb views to the south and north. After reaching the high plateau, the road passes through heavily logged pine forests to Durango (see page 639). **NB** Cyclists will find this road hard work in this direction, as there are many bends and steep hills. Trucks are frequent but travel at very reduced speeds.

South of Mazatlán

Route 15 continues south from Villa Unión. At **Rosario**, 68 km south of Mazatlán, an old mining town riddled with underground workings, the church is worth a visit (**C** *Hotel Yauco*, 100 m south of Pemex station. Clean but traffic noise. **D** *Hotel Los Morales* - now has new name, unknown - with a/c, **E** with fan, on main highway opposite Pemex, clean, quiet, good bathrooms). There is an attractive and generally clean beach at **Playas El Caimanero**, about 45 km southwest of Rosario. Try the fish. Be careful of hiking around the Baluarte River valley as there are *caimanes*, alligators, hence the name of the beach. South of Rosario and several kilometres north of Escuinapa is **B** *Motel Virginia*, Carretera Internacional Km 1107-1108, T69-532755, good clean, *palapa* restaurant next door, possible trailer parking. There is a good seafood restaurant on the left at the entrance to **Escuinapa** coming from Mazatlán.

In Escuinapa a good road turns off 30 km to the coast at Teacapan. There is a bus that connects the two towns. **Boca de Teacapan**, an inlet from the sea opening into lagoons and the mangrove swamps, is the border between Sinaloa and Nayarit. The area has palm trees, cattle ranches, much bird and animal life, and is an exporter of shrimp and mangoes. The fishing is excellent and you can buy fresh fish directly from the fishermen on Teacapan beach. There are fine beaches such as **Las Cabras**, **La Tambora** and **Los Angeles**. Dolphins can be seen at certain times of year. Buses from Escuinapa; tours from Mazatlán US$45 (for example Marlin Tours, T135301/142690, F164616). The Institute of Archaeology is excavating a 25-m pyramid about six miles east of Rancho Los Angeles; it is hoped that the site will be open to the public shortly.

Teacapan

Sleeping and eating **A** *Rancho Los Angeles*, Teacapan Ecológico (Las Palmas 1-B, Col Los Pinos, Mazatlán, T/F817867). Former home of a drug baron (deceased), 16 km north from Teacapan towards Escuinapa, on beach. Good value, luxurious swimming pool. Recommended. **D** *Hotel Denisse*, on square, T/F69545266, José Morales and Carol Snobel. Clean, next to phone office, noisy, local trips arranged. You can also rent houses with kitchen facilities a few kilometres before Teacapan on the road at Hacienda Los Angeles. There are 3 trailer parks (*Oregon*. US$8, no signs, on beach in town, run-down but one of better places to stay, new Mexican hotel next door; *Las Lupitas*.

US$8, rustic, run-down; another on bay, take road next to *Las Lupitas*. US$3, primitive, pretty setting). *Sr Wayne's Restaurant*. On beach behind *Palmeras Hotel*. Recommended.

South of Escuinapa the road passes several quaint little towns: **Acaponeta** (turn-off for El Novillero beach, large waves and many sandflies), Rosamorada, Tuxpan and Santiago Ixcuintla (several hotels), all with colonial religious buildings and archaeological museums. Nearby is the tiny island of Mexcaltitán and, further south, the beaches at San Blas (see page 528). After Tepic, Route 15 heads inland to Guadalajara (see page 532).

Baja California Peninsula

15

Baja California Peninsula

Baja California (Lower California) is that long narrow arm which dangles southwards from the US border between the Pacific Ocean and the Gulf of California for 1,300 km. It is divided administratively into the states of Baja California and Baja California Sur, with a one-hour time change at the state line. The average width is only 80 km. Rugged and almost uninhabited mountains split its tapering length.

Most tourists flock to brassy Tijuana and the northern beaches, near the USA, and also to the up-market resorts of the southern Cape zone or the colourful carnival in La Paz. But others come to the **wilderness** in between to watch the whales and dolphins, comb the beaches, explore the National Parks, discover the ancient cave paintings, and enjoy the awe-inspiring and ever-changing **desert landscapes**. For them the Peninsula, with its hundreds of kilometres of virgin coastline, is a magical place of blue skies, fresh air, solitude and refuge from the rat race north of the border.

History

Cortés attempted to settle at La Paz in 1534 after one of his expeditions had brought the first Europeans to set foot in Baja, but the land's sterile beauty disguised a chronic lack of food and water; this and sporadic Indian hostility forced the abandonment of most early attempts at settlement. Jesuit missionary fathers arrived at Loreto in 1697 and founded the first of their 20 missions. The Franciscans and then Dominicans took over when the Jesuits were expelled in 1767. The fathers were devoted and untiring in their efforts to convert the peninsula's three ethnic groups, but diseases introduced unknowingly by them and by ships calling along the coasts soon tragically decimated Indian numbers; some Indians remain today, but without tribal organization. Scattered about the *sierras* are the remains of 30 of these missions, some beautifully restored, others no more than eroded adobe foundations. Most are within easy reach from Highway 1, although four-wheel drive is necessary for remoter sites such as San Pedro Mártir and Dolores del Sur.

Today's population of about 2,800,000 has increased by two-thirds in the past decade through migration from Mexico's interior and Central Pacific coast.

Economy

The development of agriculture, tourism and industry, together with migrant labour from California and the opening of the Transpeninsular Highway, have resulted in an upsurge of economic growth and consequently of prices, especially in areas favoured by tourists.

The Morelos Dam on the upper reaches of the Colorado River has turned the Mexicali valley into a major agricultural area: 400,000 acres under irrigation to grow cotton and olives. The San Quintín Valley and the Magdalena Plain are other successful areas where crops have been wrenched from the desert. Industries are encouraged in all border regions by investment incentives; called *maquiladoras*, they are foreign-owned enterprises which import raw materials without duty, manufacture in Mexico and ship the products back to the United States.

Essentials

Food and accommodation tend to be more expensive than they are in the rest of Mexico, but less than in the USA. Tijuana, Ensenada and La Paz all have a good range of duty-free shopping. Stove fuel is impossible to find in Baja California Sur. Beware of overcharging on buses and make a note of departure times of buses in Tijuana or Ensenada when travelling south: between Ensenada and Santa Rosalía it is very difficult to obtain bus timetable information, even at bus stations. Don't ask for menus in English if you can help it, prices often differ from the Spanish version. Always check change, overcharging is rife. Note also that hotels have widely divergent winter and summer rates; between June and November tariffs are normally lower than those given in the text below (especially in expensive places). The US dollar is preferred in most places north of La Paz.

Stretching 1,704 km from Tijuana to Cabo San Lucas, Highway 1 is generally in good repair, although slightly narrow and lacking hard shoulders. Roads in the north are more potholed than those in Baja California Sur. Service stations are placed at adequate intervals along the route, but motorists should fill their tanks at every opportunity and carry spare fuel, particularly if venturing off the main roads. Stations in small towns may not have fuel, or may sell from barrels at inflated prices. The same conditions apply for Highway 5 (Mexicali-San Felipe), Highway 3 (Tecate-Ensenada-San Felipe) and Highway 2 (Tijuana 196, Mexicali-San Luis-Sonoyta). Hitchhiking is difficult, and there is very little public transport off the main highway.

There are only two really comprehensive maps: the road map published by the **Maps** ACSC, which gives highly detailed road distances (but in miles) and conditions, and which is available only to AAA members (the AAA also publishes a *Guide to Baja California* for members only); and International Travel Map (ITM) Production's *Baja California 1:1,000,000* (second edition 1992-93), which includes extra geographical and recreational detail on a topographic base. Many specialist maps and guides are available in book stores in Southern California. Both guidebooks and maps are sadly rare in Baja itself.

There is no immigration check on the Mexican side of the border. The buffer **Border crossing** zone for about 120 km south of the frontier allows US citizens to travel without a tourist card. Some have reported travelling in Baja California Sur without a tourist card. If you are bringing in a vehicle you should try to get a tourist card/vehicle permit in Tijuana (see page 684); if you are travelling beyond Baja California, with or without a vehicle, getting a tourist card in Tijuana will save a lot of trouble later. Immigration authorities are also encountered at Mexicali, Ensenada, Quitovac (28 km south of Sonoyta, Sonora on Highway 2), and when boarding the ferries to cross the Gulf of California. Ferries ply from Pichilingüe (north of La Paz) and Santa Rosalía to various places on the mainland. As a car needs an import permit, make sure you get to the ferry with lots of time and preferably with a reservation if going on the Pichilingüe-Mazatlán ferry (see under La Paz below).

Northern Baja California

Insurance covering bodily injury is **Insurance &** not available locally. Motorcycle **Medical** insurance costs about US$3 a day. If **Services** you require X-ray facilities after an accident it appears that the only place between Tijuana and Los Cabos with X-ray equipment and an on-call technician is Ciudad Constitución.

Crossing into Mexico: Mexicali

The border is open 24 hours a day for **Calexico/** all formalities. Day visitors may pre- **Mexicali** fer to park on the California side, since the extremely congested *The new crossing, 5 km* Avenida Cristóbal Colón in Mexicali, *east of the centre, is* which parallels the frontier fence, is *much quicker for* the only access to the US port of entry. *northbound traffic* Southbound flow is generally better than northbound; entering Mexico, follow the diagonal Calzada López Mateos, which leads to the tourist office and train and bus stations. Mexican automobile insurance is readily available on both sides of the border. There is a duty-free shop at the last set of lights in Calexico (imported alcohol is often expensive in Mexico).

Pedestrians travelling from Mexicali to Calexico should take the underpass beneath Calzada López Mateos, which passes through the utterly indifferent Mexican immigration office before continuing to the US side.

Highway 2 runs east from Mexicali through San Luis Río Colorado, Sonoyta and Caborca to join the Pacific Highway at Santa Ana; see page 654.

Mexicali

Phone code: 65
Colour map 1, grid A1
Population: 850,000

Capital of Baja California, Mexicali is not as geared to tourism as Tijuana and thus retains its busy, business-like border-town flavour. It is a good place to stock up on supplies, cheap clothing and footwear, and souvenirs. The new **Centro Cívico-Comercial**, Calzada López Mateos, is an ambitious urban development comprising government offices, medical school, hospitals, bull-ring, bus station, cinemas, etc.

The **State Tourism Office** is on Calle Comercio, between Reforma and Obregón ('Centro Cívico' bus); better is the **Tourist and Convention Bureau**, Calzada López Mateos y Calle Camelias, helpful, English spoken. ■ *Mon-Fri 0800-1900, Sat 0900-1300.* The Procuraduría de Protección al Turista, which provides legal assistance for visitors, is in the same building as the State Tourism office.

Sights The **City Park**, in the southwest sector, contains a zoo, picnic area and **Museo de Historia Natural**. ■ *Tue-Fri 0900-1700; weekend 0900-1800.* The University of Baja California's **Museo Regional**, Avenida Reforma y Calle L, has interesting exhibits illustrating Baja's archaeology, ethnography and missions. ■ *Tue-Fri 0900-1800, weekend 1000-1500, free.* **Galería de la Ciudad**, Avenida Obregón 1209, between Calle D and E, former state governor's residence, features work of Mexican painters, sculptors and photographers.

Mexicali

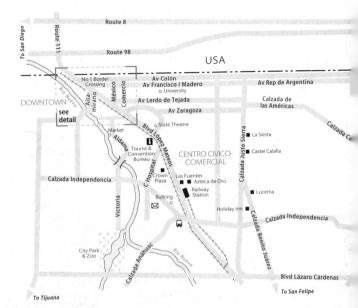

■ *Mon-Fri 0900-2000*. There are *charreadas* (rodeos), held on Sunday during the April-October season, at two separate *charro* grounds on eastern and western outskirts of Mexicali. Mexicali has numerous Chinese restaurants, the legacy of immigration which began in Sonora in the late 19th century.

Calexico, the much smaller city on the California side of the border, is so thoroughly Mexicanized that it can be difficult to find a newspaper from San Diego or Los Angeles. Mexican shoppers flock here for clothing bargains. Mexican Consulate in Calexico: T3573863.

Sleeping

AL *Crowne Plaza*, Blvd López Mateos y Av de los Héroes 201, T573600, F570555. **AL** *Holiday Inn*, Blvd Benito Juárez 2220, T65661300, F664901. A/c, best in town. Also **A** *Castel Calafia*, Calzada Justo Sierra 1495, T682841. A/c, plain but comfortable, dining room. **A** *Lucerna*, Blvd Juárez 2151, T541000. A/c, meeting rooms, bar, nightclub. **B** *Del Norte*, Melgar y Av Francisco Madero, T540575. Some a/c and TV, across from border crossing, pleasant but a little noisy, has free parking for guests and offers discount coupons for breakfast and dinner in its own restaurant. **C** *La Siesta*, Justo Sierra 899, T541100. Reasonable, coffee shop. **D** *Rivera*, near the railway station. A/c, best of the cheaper hotels. *Fortín de las Flores*, Av Cristóbal Colón 612, T524522, and **D** *Las Fuentes*, Blvd López Mateos 1655, T571525. Both with a/c and TV but noisy, tolerable if on a tight budget.

Motels **B-C** *Azteca de Oro*, Industria 600, T571433, opposite the train station and only a few blocks from the bus terminal. A/c, TV, a bit scruffy but convenient. Others around town and in Calexico just across the border around east 4th St. **B-C** *Hotel De Anza*, on the Calexico side. Excellent value for money.

Youth hostel Av Salina Cruz y Coahuila 2050, CP 21050, T551230.

Many good nightclubs on Av Justo Sierra, and on your left as you cross border, several blocks away. **Nightclubs**

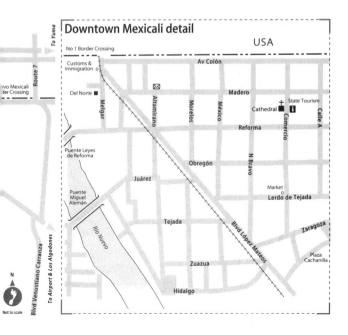

Baja California Peninsula

Transport	**Air** Airport (MXL) 25 km east, Boulevard Aviación. Flights to Mexico City, Guadalajara, Hermosillo, La Paz, Mazatlán, Monterrey, and San Antonio (Texas). Charter services.

Trains The railway station to the south is about 3½ km from the tourist area on the border and Calle 3 bus connects it with the nearby bus terminal. There were no passenger services in 1999. For up-to-date information ask locally or refer to www.trainweb.com/travel; mexican.railspot. com; www.celorio.com/ferro/mexlist.

Buses Ensenada, US$9. **Guadalajara**, US$77. **Hermosillo**, 10 hrs, US$22. **La Paz**, daily 1630, 24 hrs, US$60.50. **Mazatlán**, US$50. **Mexico City**, US$96. **San Felipe**, 3 hrs, 4 a day, US$7. **Santa Rosalía**, US$33. **Tijuana**, 3 hrs, US$16.50 luxury liner, US$6.50 1st class, US$5 2nd class, sit on right for views of the Cantú Grade. All trips leave from the new central bus station (Camionera Central) on Avenida Independencia; 4 major bus companies have their offices here. Autotransportes Tres Estrellas de Oro serves both Baja and the mainland. Golden State buses from Mexicali to Los Angeles (US$40) tickets available at trailer/kiosk across from *Hotel del Norte*. Greyhound from Los Angeles to Calexico (901 Imperial Avenida), US$33, 6 hrs. San Diego to Calexico via El Centro, US$20, 3 to 4 hrs. The 1200 bus from San Diego connects with the Pullman bus to Mazatlán, US$40, 21 hrs. Local buses are cheap, about US$0.55. 'Central Camionera' bus to Civic Centre and bus station.

Directory **Airline offices** *Mexicana*, T535402. *Taesa*, T663921. *AeroMéxico*, T91-800-90999. **Banks** All major banks: currency exchange is only from 0900-1330. *Casas de cambio* in Calexico give a slightly better rate. Several *cambios* on López Mateos.

West of Mexicali The road from Mexicali west to Tijuana is fast and well surfaced, it runs across barren desert flats, below sea level and with organ-pipe cacti in abundance, until reaching the eastern escarpment of the peninsula's spine; it winds its way up the Cantú Grade to **La Rumorosa**, giving expansive, dramatic vistas of desert and mountain. The numerous wrecked trucks and cars which litter the canyons along the Cantú Grade, together with countless crosses, emphasize the need for careful driving and better than adequate brakes. If pulling off the highway for the view, do so only on wide shoulders with good visibility in both directions. La Rumorosa, sited high enough on a boulder-strewn plateau to receive a sprinkling of snow in winter, has a service station. There are three more Pemex stations along the highway before it reaches Tecate after 144 km.

Crossing into Mexico: Tecate

The border crossing is open from 0600-2400. To get to the border immigration facilities, go north three blocks, uphill, from the west side of the Parque. You will pass the theatre. Mexican offices are on the left, Lázaro Cárdenas and Callejón Madero, T40280, US on the right. The orderly and friendly Mexican immigration and customs officers will only process vehicle papers between 0800 and 1600; at other hours, continue to Mexicali or Sonoyta. All documents are obtainable at the border. Tourist cards may also be obtained at the bus terminal. Services to the interior resemble those from Tijuana (Tres Estrellas de Oro to Mexico City, US$93.50). The Baja California **Secretary of Tourism**, opposite the park at Libertad 1305, provides a useful map of the town and other information, T41095. English spoken.

Visitors will find that placid Tecate is more like a Mexican city of the interior than a gaudy border town, perhaps because there is no town centre on the US side. It is a pleasant place to break the journey, especially around the shady Parque Hidalgo, where families promenade on weekends.

Brewing is the most important local industry; the landmark Cervecería Cuauhtémoc, Avenida Hidalgo, which produces Tecate and Carta Blanca beers, offers tours every Saturday at 1115, free. Tours may be arranged at other times, minimum five people. The entry is at the back of the brewery. You can get a free beer straight from the vats at the Jardín (patio) beside the building on Hidalgo. There are also many *maquiladora* industries in Tecate.

Tecate
Phone code: 665
Colour map 1, grid A1
Population: 40,000

Sleeping and eating A *Motel El Dorado*, Juárez 1100, T41102. A/c, central, comfortable; 10 km south of Tecate, on the road to Ensenada, is **A** *Rancho Tecate*, T40011. **C** *Hacienda*, Juárez 861, T41250. A/c, clean. **C** *Paraíso*, Aldrete 83, T41716. **D** *Frontera*, Callejón Madero 131, T41342. Basic but clean and friendly, is probably a step up in quality (Antonio Moller Ponce, who resides here, is knowledgeable on the area's history and ethno-history). Budget-minded travellers may try **E** *Juárez*, Juárez 230. Rooms with or without bath, hot water, rumoured to be a staging post for unauthorized border crossings. Excellent Mexican and Italian specialities at *El Passetto*, Libertad 200 near Parque Hidalgo. *La Escondida*, 174 Callejón Libertad. Popular with locals. Many other good restaurants.

Tecate to Tijuana

The highway continues west past **LL** *Rancho La Puerta*, a spa and physical fitness resort, strictly for the rich, vegetarian meals, petrol station. Leaving the Rodríguez Reservoir behind, Highway 2 enters the industrial suburb of La Mesa and continues into Tijuana as a four-lane boulevard, eventually to become Avenida Revolución, one of the city's main shopping streets.

A new, fast *supercarretera* with much less traffic runs from Tijuana to San Luis Colorado.

Crossing into Mexico: Tijuana

San Diego/ Tijuana

A tourist office at the border gives out maps of the border area explaining money changing, buses, etc.

There is no passport check at the border, although US freeways funnelling 12 lanes of traffic into three on the Mexican side means great congestion, particularly at weekends. A quieter recommended alternative is the **Otay Mesa** crossing (open 0600-2200) 8 km east of Tijuana, reached from the US side by SR-117. Traffic is less frantic and parking much easier, but car insurance and vehicle permit facilities are no longer available here. From the Mexican side it is harder to find: continue on the bypass from Highway 1-D to near the airport and the 'Garita de Otay' sign.

If travelling on into Mexico, don't follow the crowds who cross without visiting immigration: try to deal with US exit formalities and get an entry stamp at the border as it will avoid serious problems later on. Be sure to get an entry stamp on your tourist card as well as your passport. The Migración office is difficult to find: try the right-hand lane marked 'Customs'. When entering with a vehicle or motorcycle you should be able to obtain your tourist card/vehicle permit at this office, then you are supposed to get a stamp from a vehicle registry office about 100m south. The officials will ask for copies of your documents, including the vehicle permit. As they have no photocopier you can look for the copy shop opposite, above a liquor store, or return to the USA, go two blocks north and look for the mailbox rental company opposite the *Jack-in-the-Box*. There is another immigration office for tourist cards and vehicle documents on the right-hand side of Highway 1 as it enters Ensenada. Alternatively, you can forget the stamp and hope you won't be asked for it later (do not do this if going beyond Baja California). If entering by bicycle, go to 'secondary', the immigration area to the right, where an official will process your tourist card to travel beyond Ensenada. Cyclists are not allowed on highway 1-D (the toll road), so head for Highway 1 (*libre*) to Ensenada. Going into the USA, be prepared for tough immigration procedures.

If entering without a vehicle, you can get a tourist card from Tijuana airport or at the bus terminal; there is no passport check at the border but there is a small immigration office for entry stamps. Money-changers operate in the shopping centre 200m from the border and opposite this is the bus stop for the bus terminal. When leaving the USA without a vehicle, you can ask a security guard at the footbridge to take your US entry card to the US immigration office, as there is no passport check on the US side. Otherwise you can send your card to a US consulate. Immigration officials are reluctant to grant visa extensions; you need to get one at your next port of call.

Those visiting Tijuana for the day often find it easier to park on the San Ysidro side and walk 20 minutes across the footbridge to Avenida Revolución and the city centre (parking fees near the border range from US$5 to US$7 per 24 hours). Alternatively, the 'San Diego Trolley' is an entertaining way to reach the border, taking visitors from downtown San Diego to *La Línea* from US$1-3; departures every 15 minutes between 0500 and 0100 (tickets sold from machines at stops). There is a visitor information kiosk at the Trolley's southern terminus.

Tijuana

On the Pacific, in the hills, where 35 million people annually cross the border, fuelling the city's claim to be 'the world's most-visited city', this is the frontline at which the United States and Mexico face up to each other in pleasure and politics. Often criticised as 'not being the real Mexico' it is nevertheless a historic and impassioned place. It came to prominence with Prohibition in the United States in the 1920s when Hollywood stars and thirsty Americans flocked to the sleazy bars and enterprising nightlife of Tijuana and Mexicali, both at this time little more than large villages. Today, tourism is the major industry.

Phone code: 66
Colour map 1, grid A1
Population: 1,800,000

Although countless bars and nightclubs still vie for the visitor's dollar, it is duty-free bargains, horse-racing and inexpensive English-speaking dentists which attract many visitors. It is your last, or first, opportunity to buy craftwork drawn in from all around Mexico. This border area is much more expensive than further south, especially at weekends. Modern Tijuana is Mexico's fourth-largest city and one of the most prosperous. However, a walk along the *barrio* beside the border (don't go alone) to see the breached fence will demonstrate the difference between the first and third worlds.

It is cheaper to fly south from Aeropuerto Rodríguez (TIJ),17 km (20 minutes) from San Diego, CA, than it is from any US airports. For details on destinations and transport to and from the airport, see **Transport**, page 688. The new bus station is 5 km southeast of the town centre at the end of Vía Oriente (at La Mesa); take any local bus marked 'Central Camionera' or 'Buena Vista'. Local buses marked 'La Línea/Centro' go from the bus station to the border.

Getting there & away

    Tijuana is at the junction of Highway 1, from the border down to Cabo San Lucas, at the tip of the Baja California Peninsula, and Highway 2 which runs east to Mexicali, San Luis Río Colorado and on to Ciudad Juárez.

Downtown buses to the border leave from Calle 2 near Revolución. When taking a taxi in Mexico (unless it is a fixed-price airport service), it is often a good idea to agree on a price before travelling (some bargaining may be acceptable).

Getting around

The main **tourist office** is on Plaza Patria, Boulevard Agua Caliente, T880555. ■ *Mon-Fri 1000-1900.* Branch offices are at the airport, the first tollgate on Highway 1-D to Ensenada, and at the Chamber of Commerce, Calle 1 and Avenida Revolución, T881685. Brochures and schematic maps available. English-speaking staff, helpful. ■ *Mon-Fri 0900-1400, 1600-1900; Sat 0900-1300.* The **Procuraduría de Protección al Turista** Chamber of Commerce also offers first aid facilities and public conveniences to visitors in the Government Centre in the Río Tijuana development. ■ *0800-1900.*

Sights

The main drag, Avenida Revolución, runs directly south from the tourist kiosk on the edge of the red-light district, with many bars and restaurants and souvenir shops (generally open 1000-2100). There is, however, more to Tijuana than this hardsell main street to/from the border post. The **Centro Cultural**, Paseo de los Héroes y Avenida Independencia contains the excellent **Museo de las Identidades Mexicanas**, which lets visitors know in no uncertain terms that they are in Mexico. There are also, handicraft shops, restaurant, concert hall, and the ultra-modern spherical Omnimax cinema, T841111, www.cecut.org.mx, where three films are shown on a 180° screen; it is best to

If entering from the USA: it is easier to sightsee in Tijuana without luggage, so stay in San Diego & make a day excursion before travelling on

Baja California Peninsula

sit at the back/top so you don't have to lean too far back. ■ *English perfor-mance 1400 daily, US$4.50, Spanish version 1900, US$3.75.* The **Casa de la Cultura** is a multi-arts cultural centre with a 600-seat theatre. There is a small **Wax Museum** at Calle 1 y Madero with historical figures and movie stars. The Cathedral of **Nuestra Señora de Guadalupe** is at Calle 2. The **Jai-Alai Palace** (Palacio Frontón) is at Avenida Revolución y Calle 7, T852524; games begin at 2000 nightly except Wednesday, spectators may bet on each game. Tijuana has two bullrings: the **Plaza de Toros Monumental** at Playas de Tijuana is the only one in the world built on the sea shore. A few metres away is an obelisk built into the border chain-link fence commemorating the Treaty of Guadalupe Hidalgo, 1848, which fixed the frontier between Mexico and the USA. **El Toreo** bullring is 3 km east of downtown on Bulevar Agua Caliente; *corridas* alternate between the two venues between May and September; Sunday at 1600 sharp. Tickets from US$4.50 in the sun (*sol*) to US$16 in the shade *(sombra)*, T801808. Horse and dog racing is held at the Agua Caliente track, near the Tijuana Country Club. ■ *Horse-racing Sat and Sun from 1200; greyhound meetings Wed-Mon at 1945, Mon, Wed, Fri at 1430. Admission US$0.50, reserved seats US$1. Charreadas* take place each Sunday from May to September at one of four grounds, free. Tourism offices will give up-to-date information.

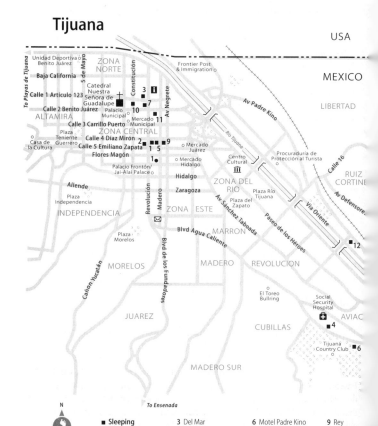

Tijuana

■ Sleeping	3 Del Mar	6 Motel Padre Kino	9 Rey
1 Adelita	4 El Conquistador	7 Nelson	10 San Jorge
2 Caesar	5 La Villa de Zaragoza	8 Paraíso-Radisson	11 St Francis

Essentials

LL *Grand Hotel Tijuana* Blvd Agua Caliente 4500, T817000. Heated pool, suites, etc. First rate. **AL-A** *Country Club*, Blvd Agua Caliente y Tapachula 1, T817733/817692. *Hacienda del Río*, Blvd Sánchez Taboada 10606, T848644, F848620. **AL-A** *La Mesa Inn*, Blvd Díaz Ordaz 50 y Gardenia, T816522, F812871. **AL-A** *Centenario Plaza*, Blvd Agua Caliente 22400, T818183. **AL-A** *Lucerna*, Héroes y Av Rodríguez in new Río Tijuana development, T841000. A/c, pool, piano bar. Popular with business travellers. **AL-A** *Paraíso-Radisson*, Blvd Agua Caliente 1 at the Country Club, T817200. Pool, sauna, bar, a/c, etc. **A-B** *El Conquistador*, Blvd Agua Caliente 700, T817955. Colonial-style, a/c, pool, sauna, disco. **AL** *Plaza Las Glorias*, Blvd Agua Caliente 11553, near the *Paraíso-Radisson*, T817200. A/c, pool, disco, convention centre. **A** *Palacio Azteca*, Highway 1 South, T865301. A/c, modern, cocktail bar, extensively remodelled, in older, congested part of city. **B-C** *Hotel Caesar*, Calle 5 y Av Revolución, T851606. A/c, restaurant, decorated with bullfight posters, unique character. Good. **C** *La Villa de Zaragoza*, Madero 1120 behind the Jai-Alai *frontón*, T851832, F851837. A/c, comfortable. **C** *Nelson*, Av Revolución 502, T854302, F854302. Central, simple clean rooms, coffee shop.

D *Adelita*, Calle 4 2017, Hot showers, cockroaches, basic. **D** *Hotel del Prado*, Calle 5 y Niños Héroes. Acceptable, noisy in parts. **D** *París*, Calle 5 No 1939. Adequate, value-for-money budget hotel. **D** *Rey*, Calle 4 No 2021. Central, old but comfortable. **D** *St Francis*, Benito Juárez 2. More with bath, central. Recommended. **E** *Hotel del Mar*, Calle 1 No 1448, opposite *Nelson*. Central but in a poor section, communal bathroom. Good budget hotel. Recommended nearby are **E** *Hotel Virrey*, Calle Baja California (on edge red-light district); **D** *Rivas*, on Constitución, friendly, clean, a little noisy; **E** *Fénix*, Miguel Martínez 355, TV, T855005; **E** *Machado*, Calle 1 No 1724, restaurant, basic, reasonable; **E** *San Jorge*, Av Constitución 506. Old but clean, basic.

Motels B-C *León*, Calle 7 No 1939, T856320. **C-D** *La Misión*, in Playas de Tijuana near the bullring, T806612. Modern, a/c, restaurant, pool, popular with businessmen. **C** *Kenia*, Coahuila 1714, T384893. Central. **D** *Golf*, T862021, opposite each other on Blvd Agua Caliente, next to *Tijuana Country Club*, both OK, and **D** *Padre Kino*, T864208. An older-type motel.

Youth hostel T832680/822760, Vía Ote y Puente Cuauhtémoc, Zona del Río, far from centre, dirty. Not recommended, inexpensive *cafetería* on premises, open 0700-2300.

LAS CALIFORNIAS

Carretera al Aeropuerto

ALFONSO GARZON

POSTAL

California

TOMAS AQUINO

Acceso Otay Buenavista

BUENAVISTA

Sta Nes

EL CHAMIZAL

To Bus Terminal

20 DE NOVIEMBRE

Consulate

Race Track

To Tecate & Mexicali

● **Eating**
1 Tijuana Tilly's

Baja California Peninsula

Eating *Tijuana Tilly's*. Excellent meal, reasonably priced. *La Leña*, downtown on Av Revolución between Calle 4 and 5. Excellent food and service, beef and Mexican specialities; countless other restaurants, including the new complex near border crossing.

Nightclubs *Flamingos*, south on old road to Ensenada and *Chantecler* are both recommended.

Shopping The Plaza Río Tijuana Shopping Centre, Paseo de Los Héroes, is a new retail development; opposite are the Plaza Fiesta and Plaza del Zapato malls, the latter specializing in footwear. Nearby is the colourful public market. Downtown shopping area is Avs Revolución and Constitución. Bargaining is expected at smaller shops, and everyone except bus drivers is happy to accept US currency.

Transport **Air** Aeropuerto Rodríguez (TIJ), T832102. Lots of flights to Mexico City, also to Acapulco, Aguascalientes, Cancún, Chihuahua, Ciudad Juárez, Ciudad Obregón, Ciudad Victoria, Colima, Cuernavaca, Culiacán, Durango, Guadalajara, Hermosillo, La Paz, León, Los Cabos, Los Mochis, Matamoros, Mazatlán, Mérida, Monterrey, Morelia, Oaxaca, Puebla, Puerto Vallarta, Reynosa, San Luis Potosí, Tampico, Tepic, Torreón, Uruapan and Zacatecas. Also Los Angeles in the USA. Taxi between airport and centre is quoted at US$15 (bargaining may be possible if you walk over the highway beyond the carpark in front of the terminal, or from centre to airport); *colectivo* from airport to border, *La Línea*, US$3.20. Mexicoach run from San Diego to Tijuana airport for US$15; or combination bus to Plaza La Jolla and taxi to airport.

Buses Local buses about US$0.30, taxis ask US$10 (but shouldn't be that much), 'Central Camionera' or 'Buena Vista' buses to bus station, downtown buses to border depart from Calle 2 near Av Revolución. Local buses also go to the border from the bus station, every 30 mins up to 2300, marked 'La Línea/Centro', US$0.50. New bus station is 5 km southeast of centre at the end of Vía Oriente (at La Mesa), T212982. It is very crowded and inefficient; take advantage of toilet facilities as long-distance buses are usually so full of luggage and goods that getting to the toilet at the back is impossible. There is a bank that changes travellers' cheques. Parking at bus terminal US$1 per hour. To **Mexico City** (every couple of hours) 1st class (Tres Estrellas de Oro, T869515/869060), normal about 38-45 hrs, US$100, express US$110, poor, expensive food at stops, *plus* service US$115, or special (with video and more comfort), US$132, 38 hrs. (Transportes del Pacífico, similar fares, express only.) Second class (Transportes del Norte de Sonora), US$86. Other 1st class routes: **Guadalajara**, 36 hrs, US$82.50; **Hermosillo**, 12 hrs, US$35; **Los Mochis**, 22 hrs, US$53, Tres Estrellas de Oro; **Mazatlán**, 29 hrs, US$62.75; **Sonoyta**, US$16.50, **Culiacán**, US$54; **Querétaro**, US$99. By ABC line: **Ensenada**, about hourly 0500-2400, 1½ hrs, US$2.90, bus leaves from behind Centro Comercial at border; **Mexicali**, hourly from 0500-2200, US$6.50 1st class; **San Quintín**, 7 a day, US$7.15; **Santa Rosalía**, 1600, direct, US$37; **La Paz**, 0800, US$60.50, packed full; Autobuses Aragón to La Paz, cheaper, 4 a day, 24 hrs. There are also many services east and south from the old bus station at Av Madero and Calle 1 (Comercio), on the way to the footbridge leading to the border post, eg services to Tecate US$2.20; Mexicali; Rosarito and Ensenada with Autotransportes de Baja California. From Tijuana bus terminal Greyhound has buses every 2 hrs to San Diego via the Otay Mesa crossing, except after 2200, when it uses the Tijuana crossing; coming from San Diego stay on the bus to the main Tijuana terminal, entry stamp given at border (ask driver to get it for you), or at bus station. Long queues for immigration at lunchtime. Fare San Diego-Tijuana US$12.50, 2 hrs. Walk across *La Línea* (border) and catch a Golden State bus to downtown Los Angeles, US$13 (buy ticket inside *McDonalds* restaurant), 12 a day, or take trolley to downtown San Diego and get a Greyhound, US$20, or Amtrak train, US$25, to Los Angeles. Golden State is the cheapest and fastest; its terminal is about 1 km from Greyhound terminal in downtown LA, but stops first at Santa Ana and elsewhere if requested. If travelling beyond Los Angeles, ask about layovers in LA before buying a through ticket. Tijuana is a major transportation centre and schedules are complex and extensive.

Airline offices *Aero California,* Paseo de los Héroes 95, T842100. *AeroMéxico,* T854401. **Directory**
Mexicana, T832851. *Taesa,* T848484. **Banks** Many banks, all dealing in foreign exchange. For Visa TCs, go to *Bancomer.* Better rate than *cambios* but less convenient. Countless *casas de cambio* throughout Tijuana open day and night. Some *cambios* collect a commission (up to 5%), even for cash dollars; ask before changing. **Communications** Internet: At southern end of Av Sánchez Taboada, off parking lot adjacent to Sam's Club. **Telephones:** Computel, Calle 7 y Av Negrete, metered phones, fax, computer facilities. **Embassies & consulates** *Canadian Consul*, Germán Gedovius 5-201, T840461. **France:** Av Revolución 1651, T857177. **Germany:** Av Sánchez Taboada 9210, T801830. **Spain:** Av de los Olivos 305 T865780. **United Kingdom:** Blvd Salinas 1500, T817323. *Mexican Consulate-General,* in San Diego, CA, 549 India St, Mon-Fri 0900-1400, for visas and tourist information. *US Consulate,* Tapachula 96, between Agua Caliente racetrack and the Country Club, Mon-Fri 0800-1630, T6817400. **Emergency telephone numbers** Fire: 135. Police: 134. **Red Cross:** 132; valid for Tijuana, Rosarito, Ensenada, Tecate, Mexicali and San Luis Río Colorado.

South of Tijuana

A dramatic 106-km toll road (Highway 1-D) leads along cliffs overhanging the Pacific to Ensenada; the toll is in three sections of US$2 each. There are emergency phones approximately every 2 km on the toll road. This is the safest route between the two cities and 16 exit points allow access to a number of seaside developments and villages along the coast.

Largest is Rosarito, variously described as a drab resort strung out along the **Rosarito**
old highway, or 'a breath of fresh air after Tijuana', with numerous seafood *Phone code: 661*
restaurants, curio shops, etc. There is a fine swimming beach; horse-riding on *Colour map 1, grid A1*
north and south Rosarito beaches. In March and April accommodation is hard *Population: 50,000*
to find as college students in great numbers take their holiday here. The **tourist office** is at Quinta Plaza Mall, Benito Juárez 96, T20200. ■ *0900-1600 daily.*

Sleeping Many hotels and motels, including **A-B** *Festival Plaza*, Blvd Benito Juárez, T22950, F20224. Deluxe, pool, shopping, 1 block from beach. **A-B** *Quinta del Mar Resort Hotel*, T21145. Pool, sauna, tennis, also condos and town houses with kitchens. *Beachcomber Bar*. Good food, relatively cheap, good for watching the sunset; best is the **A-B** *Rosarito Beach Hotel*, Benito Juárez 31, T20144 (US toll free 1-800-3438582). One of the casinos which opened during Prohibition; its architecture and decoration are worth a look. Several motels in **D** range, including *René's Motel*, T21020. Plain but comfortable. **Camping** Many RV parks nearby eg *Popotla*, T21501; *La Siesta*, T21049.

The coast as far as **Puerto Nuevo** and nearby **Cantamar** (Km 26 and 28) is lightly built-up (toll between Cantamar and Highway 1 US$2.30, none heading towards Cantamar); there are several trailer parks and an amazing number of restaurants specializing in lobster and seafood (impressive is *Jatay*, built on four levels, Puerto Nuevo. There is fine surfing to the north and 'hassle-free' hang-gliding areas south of Cantamar. Eleven kilometres south is an archaeological garden **Plaza del Mar** with an exhibition of pre-Columbian stone art, open to visitors. At **Punta Salsipuedes**, 51 km south of Tijuana by the tollway, a *mirador* affords sweeping views of the rugged Pacific coast and the offshore Todos Santos Islands. The section of Highway 1-D for several kilometres beyond this point is subject to landslides.

Baja California Peninsula

El Sauzal de Rodríguez, 9 km before Ensenada and now almost a part of the city, is a quieter alternative to staying in the port. **E** *Hostal Sauzal* (per person), three blocks from the ocean, T011-52-61746381. Has four-bed dormitory rooms, hot water, storage lockers and a library of books and maps on Baja – good place to stop, chill, and pick up info before rushing down south.

Ensenada

Phone code: 61
Colour map 1, grid A1
Population: 255,700

Baja's third city and leading seaport. Ensenada is a popular place for weekenders from San Diego. There is a tourist village atmosphere at its centre with a lively and very North American nightclub/bar zone at its northern edge. On the harbour fringe is a good locals' fish market with small, cheaper restaurants. Outside of the waterfront centre the town is more commercial with little of interest for party trippers or travellers. It is situated on the northern shore of the Bahía de Todos Santos, whose blue waters sport many dolphins and underline the austere character of a landscape reduced to water, sky and scorched brown earth. Sport and commercial fishing, and agriculture (with canning, wineries, olive growing) are the chief activities. The port itself is rather unattractive and the beach is dirty. The **tourist office** is at Boulevard Costero y Avenida Riviera, on the front just south of the bridge. ■ *Mon-Fri 0900-1900, Sat 1000-1500, Sun 1000-1400*. The **Tourist and Convention Bureau**, Lázaro Cárdenas y Miramar. Helpful; accommodation literature; free copies of *Ensenada News and Views* (monthly English-language paper with information and adverts on northern Baja, Tijuana and Ensenada). ■ *Mon-Sat 0900-1900, Sun 0900-1400*.

Sights

Tourist activity concentrates along Avenida López Mateos and, especially, along its Calle 1 extension north of the drainage channel, where most of the hotels, restaurants and shops are located. The twin white towers of **Nuestra Señora de Guadalupe**, Calle 6, are a prominent landmark; on the seafront boulevard is the new **Plaza Cívica**, a landscaped court containing large busts of Juárez, Hidalgo and Carranza. The **Museo Histórico Regional**, on Gastelum, near Calle 1, has an ethnographic collection on peoples of Mesoamerica. ■ *Closed Mon*. A splendid view over city and bay can be had from the road circling the Chapultepec Hills on the western edge of the business district. Steep but paved access is via the west extension of Calle 2, two blocks from the bus station. The **Bodegas de Santo Tomás**, Avenida Miramar 666, between Calle 6 y 7, T82509, is Mexico's premier winery. ■ *Daily tours at 1100, 1300, 1500, US$2. Charreadas* (rodeos) are held on summer weekends at the *charro* ground at Blancarte y Calle 2. A weekend street market is held from 0700-1700 at Avenida Riveroll y Calle 7; the fish market at the bottom of Avenida Macheros specializes in *tacos de pescado* (a fish finger wrapped in a tortilla!). The *Ensenada Clipper Fleet* runs daily fishing trips from the sportfishing terminal. Also seasonal whale-watching trips and bay and coastal excursions. ■ *0700-1500*. For seasonal whale-watching trips and bay and coastal excursions, contact Ballena Tours, Inc. www.greywhalewatch.com

Sleeping

LL *Las Rosas Hotel and Spa*, on Highway 1, 7 km west of town, T44595, F44310. Suites, spectacular ocean views, pool, sauna, restaurant. **LL-A** *Punta Morro Hotel Suites*, on coast 3 km north of town on Highway 1, T83507, F44490. Rooms have kitchens and fridges, 2 and 3-bedroom apartments available, a/c, pool. **LL** *San Nicolás Resort Hotel*, López Mateos y Av Guadalupe, T61901, F64930, mfoster@compuclub.com.mx; a/c, suites, dining room, disco. In the ranges **AL-A**: *Villa Marina*, Av López Mateos y Blancarte, T83321. Heated pool, coffee shop. *La*

Pinta, Av Floresta y Blvd Bucaneros (**B** Sun-Thu). TV, pool, restaurant. *Quintas Papagayo*, 1½ km north on Highway 1, T44575. Landscaped beach resort complex with all facilities, Hussong's *Pelícano* restaurant attached, seafood and local specialities, 0800-2300. Best value for an Ensenada 'splurge'. **B** *Bahía*, López Mateos, T82101. Balconies, suites, fridges, quiet, clean, parking, a/c, good value, popular. **B** *Misión Santa Isabel*, López Mateos and Castillo, T83616. Pool, suites, Spanish Mission-style, attractive. **D** *América*, López Mateos near State Tourist Office, T61333. Basic, hard beds, kitchenettes, good. **D** *Plaza*, López Mateos 540. Central, plain but clean, rooms facing street noisy. **D** *Ritz*, Av Ruiz y Calle 4 No 381, T40573. Central, a/c, TV, phone, coffee shop, parking. **D** *Royal*, Av Castelum. Bath, parking.

Several cheaper hotels around Miramar and Calle 3, eg **C-E** *Perla del Pacífico*, Av Miramar 229. Quite clean, hot water. **E** *Río*, Av Miramar and Calle 2. Basic, noisy until 0300 when local bars shut. **E** *Pacífico No 1*, Av Gastelum 235. Communal bath. Note that some of the larger hotels have different rates for summer and winter; cheaper tariffs are given above, check first! All hotels are filled in Ensenada at weekends, get in early.

Motels In our **AL-A** ranges: *Ensenada Travelodge*, Av Blancarte 130, T81601. A/c, heated pool, whirlpool, family rates available, restaurant. *Cortés*, López Mateos 1089 y Castillo, T82307, F83904. *Casa del Sol* (Best Western), López Mateos 101, T81570, F82025. A/c, TV, pool, comfortable. *El Cid*, on Fri-Sat, **B** on Sun-Thu, Av López Mateos 993, T82401. Spanish-style building, a/c, fridges, suites available, dining room, lounge, disco. **C** *Balboa*, Guerrero 172 y Cortés, T61077. Modern, comfortable, some way east of downtown. **C** *Villa Fontana*, López Mateos y Blancarte, T83434. Good location, old but large clean rooms, cheerful, English spoken. **D** *Costa Mar*, Av Veracruz 319 at Playa Hermosa (1 km south), ½ block from beach, T66425. TV, phones,

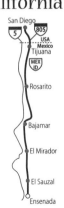

Ensenada centre

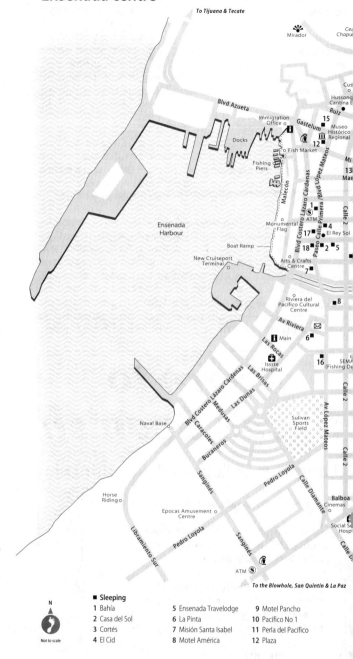

To Tijuana & Tecate

Mirador

Cer
Chapu

Cus

Hussong
Cantina E

Ruiz

Blvd Azueta

Immigration
Office

Gastelum

15

Museo
Histórico
Regional

Docks

12

Fish Market

Mi

13

Mae

Fishing
Piers

Malecón

Blvd Costero Lázaro Cárdenas

Blvd LÓpez Mateos

Paseo Calle Primera

Calle 2

1

ATM

Ensenada
Harbour

Monumental
Flag

17

4

El Rey Sol

Boat Ramp

18

2

5

New Cruiseport
Terminal

Arts & Crafts
Centre

7

8

Riviera del
Pacífico Cultural
Centre

Av Riviera

Main

Las Rocas

6

Issste
Hospital

16

SEM
(Fishing De

Blvd Costero Lázaro Cárdenas

Las Brisas

Las Dunas

Las Medusas

Calle 2

Naval Base

Caracoles

Bucaneros

Sulivan
Sports
Field

Av López Mateos

Calle 2

Sanginés

Pedro Loyola

Calle Diamante

Balboa
Cinemas

Horse
Riding

Epocas Amusement
Centre

Sanginés

Social S
Hosp

Libramiento Sur

Pedro Loyola

Calle L

ATM

To the Blowhole, San Quintín & La Paz

N

Not to scale

■ Sleeping

1 Bahía	5 Ensenada Travelodge	9 Motel Pancho
2 Casa del Sol	6 La Pinta	10 Pacífico No 1
3 Cortés	7 Misión Santa Isabel	11 Perla del Pacífico
4 El Cid	8 Motel América	12 Plaza

Baja California Peninsula

13 Río
14 Ritz
15 Royal
16 San Nicolás Resort
17 Villa Fontana
18 Villa Marina

etc. Agreeable. **E** *Pancho*, Av Alvarado 211. Shabby but clean rooms, opposite the *charro* ground. Cheapest habitable motel in town.

Hostals *Hostal Sausal*, Av L, El Sausal de Rodríguez, 6 miles north of Ensenada. Microbuses every 5 mins to Ensenada. Dorm bed, US$10, including delicious breakfast. Highly recommended.

Trailer parks A great many good trailer parks eg *Campo Playa RV Park*, Blvd Costero y Agustín Sanginés, south of town, US$8-10 per person.

Eating

El Rey Sol, López Mateos 1000 y Blancarte. French/Mexican, elegant, reasonable prices. *Mesón de Don Fernando*, López Mateos. Good breakfasts, *tacos* and seafood, good value. *Cantina Hussong's*, Av Ruiz 113. An institution in both the Californias, more of a bar than a restaurant, open 1000-0100. *Cha-Cha Burgers*, Blvd Costero 609. American-style burgers, fish, chicken, fast food 1000-2200. *Pancho's Place* (don't confuse with *Motel Pancho*), Ejército Nacional (Highway 1) y San Marcos. Well-run, wide menu. Pleasant. *Restaurant Muylam*, Ejército Nacional y Diamante. Seafood and Chinese cuisine, 1200-2400. *China Land*, Riveroll 1149 between Calle 11 and 12. *Sichuan*, Mandarin and Cantonese cuisine, authentic, not cheap, 1200-2300. *El Pollo*, Macheros y Calle 2. Grilled chicken 'Sinaloa style', fast food 1000-2200 every day of year. *Las Brasas*, López Mateos 486, between Ruiz and Gastelum. Barbecue chicken and fish, Mexican specialities, attractive patio dining, 1100-2200, closed Tue. *Mandarin*, López Mateos 2127, between Soto and Balboa (Chinese). Elegant surroundings, good food, expensive, considered to be the best *chifa* in Ensenada. *Lonchería La Terminal*, opposite bus station. Cheap and filling *comida*, good but basic. Several Chinese restaurants on Av Ruiz such as *San San* between Calle 3 and 4.

Transport

Air Airport 8 km south. No scheduled services. **Buses** To Tijuana, US$2.90, 1½ hrs.

Directory **Communications** Internet: *Compuclub*, Av Juárez 1449 with Floresta, Mon-Sat 0900-2100, Sun 1300-2100, US$2.20 per hour, cheaper in evening. **Language School** *Baja California Language College* in the east of the town towards San Quintín, PO Box San Diego, CA 92167, T745688 or USA 1-877-444-2252, www.bajacal.com. Beginners and advance courses on offer with Mexican tutors. Specializes in spanish immersion for business executives, teachers, travellers and students. **Useful addresses** Immigration Office: beside the shipyard, for tourist entry permits.

Southeast to San Felipe
Highway 3 east to San Felipe leaves Ensenada at the Benito Juárez *glorieta* monument as the Calzada Cortés. Twenty-six kilometres out of Ensenada, an 8-km dirt road branches south for a steep descent to the basic resort of **Agua Caliente** (**C** *Hotel Agua Caliente*. Restaurant, bar, closed in winter; adjoining is a campground and large concrete pool heated to 38° by nearby hot springs; access road should not be attempted in wet weather). Free camping at the end of the road 3 km beyond Agua Caliente, no facilities but good hiking in the area.

At Km 39, a paved road leads off 3 km to Ojos Negros, continuing east (graded, dry weather) into scrub-covered foothills. It soon climbs into the ponderosa pine forests of the Sierra de Juárez. The road enters the **Parque Nacional Constitución de 1857** 37 km from Ojos Negros. The jewel of the park is the small Laguna Hanson, a sparkling shallow lake surrounded by Jeffery pines; camping here is delightful, but note that the lake is reduced to a boggy marsh in dry seasons and that the area receives snow in mid-winter. A high-clearance vehicle is necessary for the continuation north out of the park to Highway 2 at El Cóndor, 15 km east of La Rumorosa.

Continue southeast on Highway 3 to Ejido Héroes de la Independencia (Km 92.5), where a graded dirt road runs 8 km northeast to the ruins of Misión Santa Catarina. The mission was founded in 1797 and abandoned after a raid by the Yuman Indians in 1840; the Paipái women in the village often have attractive pottery for sale.

Highway 3 descends along the edge of a green valley to the rapidly developing town of Valle de Trinidad. A reasonable dirt road runs south into the **Parque Nacional Sierra San Pedro Mártir**. Here, *Mike's Sky Rancho* (35 km) is a working ranch which offers motel-style accommodation, a pool, camping and guided trips into the surrounding mountains; rooms **E**, T815514 (Tijuana). Good meals.

After leaving the valley, Highway 3 follows a canyon covered in dense stands of barrel cacti to the **San Matías Pass** between the Sierras Juárez and San Pedro Mártir which leads onto the desolate Valle de San Felipe. The highway turns east and emerges onto open desert hemmed in by arid mountains; 1,985 km from Ensenada it joins Highway 5 at the La Trinidad T-junction, 148 km south of Mexicali and 50 km north of San Felipe.

San Felipe

Phone code: 657
Colour map 1, grid A2
Population: 13,000

On weekends it can become overcrowded and noisy

Paved Highway 5 heads south from Mexicali 196 km to San Felipe, passing at about Km 34 the Cerro Prieto geothermal field. After passing the Río Hardy (one of the peninsula's few permanent rivers) and the **Laguna Salada** (Km 72), a vast dry alkali flat unless turned into a muddy morass by rare falls of rain, the road continues straight across sandy desert until entering San Felipe around a tall, white, double-arched monument. Floods can cut the road across the Laguna Salada; when it is closed, motorists have to use Highway 3 from Ensenada (see above) to get to San Felipe.

San Felipe is a pleasant, tranquil fishing and shrimping port on the Gulf of California with a population of about 13,000. There are about 3,000 North

American RV temporary residents and a further 3,000 on winter weekends. Long a destination for devoted sportfishermen and a weekend retreat for North Americans, San Felipe is now experiencing a second discovery, with new trailer parks and the paving of many of the town's sandy streets. A public library is planned, and a recycling plant, artificial breakwater reef and two golf courses are under construction. Even the *Las Macetas* hotel (the 'grey ghost') may see completion in the near future. There is an airport 8 km south. San Felipe is protected from desert winds by the coastal mountains and is unbearably hot during the summer; in winter the climate is unsurpassed. There is a good view of the wide sandy beach from the Virgin of Guadalupe shrine near the lighthouse. The **tourist office** on Mar de Cortés y Manzanillo, opposite *Motel El Capitán*, T71155 is helpful but has little handout material. ■ *Tue-Sun 0900-1400 and 1600-1800. Navy Day* is celebrated on 1 June with a carnival, street dancing and boat races.

Sleeping

AL *Aquamarina Condohotel and Villas*, 4 km south on Punta Estrella rd. Cheaper Sun-Thu, on beach, pool, attractive rooms, a/c. **AL** *Castel*, Av Misión de Loreto 148, T71282. A/c, 2 pools, tennis, etc. Best in town. **B** *La Trucha Vagabunda*, Mar Báltico, near *Motel Cortés*, T71333. Also a few RV spaces and *Restaurant Alfredo* (Italian), seafood, international cuisine. **B** *Vagabond Inn*, on same street, 3 km south of town. A/c, pool and beach. **B** *Villa del Mar*. Pool, volley-ball court, restaurant. **C** *Fiesta San Felipe*, 9 km south on the airport road. Isolated, every room has Gulf view, tennis, pool, restaurant. VAT (IVA) not included in price. **C** *Riviera*, Av Mar Báltico s/n, 1 km south on coastal bluff, T71185. A/c, pool, spa, restaurant.

Motels B *Chapala*, T71240, on beachfront. Some a/c, free coffee. Clean but pricey. **B** *El Capitán*, Mar de Cortés 298, T71303. A/c, some balconies, pool, lovely *rancho*-style building, hard beds but otherwise OK. **B** *Cortés*, on Av Mar de Cortés, T71055. Beachside esplanade, a/c, pool, *palapas* on beach, launching ramp, disco, restaurant. **C** *El Pescador*, T71044, Mar de Cortés and Calzada Chetumal. A/c, modest but comfortable.

Camping Many trailer parks and campgrounds in town and on coast to north and south, including **D** *El Faro Beach and Trailer Park*, on the bay 18 km south. **E** *Ruben's,* Golfo de California 703, T71442. *Playa Bonita*, Golfo de California 787, T71215. *La Jolla*, *Playa de Laura*, *Mar del Sol,* Av Misión de Loreto, T71088, and the more primitive *Campo Peewee* and *Pete's Camp*, both about 10 km north.

San Felipe

Calle Chetumal

Calle de Ensenada

To Pemex Station & Mexicali (190 km)

Blvd Costero

Motel Chapala

El Capitán

Av Mar de Cortés

Motel Cortés

Riviera

Calz Puerto Vallarta

Mar de Cortés

Av Misión de San Vicente

Av Misión de Loreto

Av Camino del Sur

Av Misión de Santo Tomás

Av Misión del Sur

RV Mar del Sol

Av Central Sur

Av Poniente

Av Oriente Muelle

3 Norte

2 Norte

1 Norte

Calle Oriente

2 Sur

N

Not to scale

To Airport (15 km) & Puertecitos (80 km)

Eating *Green House*, Av Mar de Cortés 132 y Calzada Chetumal. Good food, beef or chicken *fajitas* a speciality, friendly service, cheap breakfasts, 'fish fillet for a fiver'! 0730-0300 daily. *Clam Man's Restaurant*, Calzada Chetumal, 2 blocks west of Pemex station. Used to belong to the late, famous Pasqual 'The Clam Man', oddly decorated, but excellent clams, steamed, fried, barbecued, at budget prices. *Las Misiones* in *Mar del Sol* RV park. Small menu, moderately priced, seafood crêpes a speciality, popular with families, good service. *Las Redes*, Mar de Cortés Sur. *Ruben's Place*, Junípero Serra, both favourites for seafood. *El Toro II*, Chetumal. Mexican and American food, popular for breakfasts; other pleasant places on Av Mar de Cortés: *Corona*, No 348; *El Nido*, No 358, grilled fish and steaks (closed Wed). *Puerto Padre*, Cuban; *George's*, No 336. Steaks, seafood, live music, pleasant, friendly, popular with US residents. Recommended.

Transport **Air** Airport 10 km south of town.

Bus Transportes ABC and TNS buses to **Ensenada**, direct, over the mountains, at 0800 and 1800, 3½ hrs, US$9. Bus to **Mexicali** US$8, 4 a day from 0730, 2 hrs. Hitching to Mexicali is not difficult (much traffic), but beware the desert sun. Bus station is on Mar Báltico near corner of Calzada Chetumal, in town centre.

Directory **Banks** *Bancomer*, Av Mar de Cortés.

South of San Felipe The road south, past the **Valley of the Giants** at Km 21, a desert garden, and **Laguna Percebú** at Km 30 (campsite with bar and restaurant) has been paved as far as **Puertecitos**, a straggling settlement mainly of North American holiday homes. There is an airstrip, a simple grocery store, a Pemex station and *Campo Los Chinos*, US$7 per tent, basic toilets, intermittent water. There is an attractive beach, fishing is good outside the shallow bay and there are several tidal hot springs at the southeast point.

The road continues south along the coast (well graded with improvements continuing, acceptable for standard vehicles), leading to the tranquil **Bahía San Luis Gonzaga**, with the basic resorts of Papá Fernández and Alfonsinas (hotel, **D**, hot water, good but expensive restaurant); the beach here is pure sand and empty. From here, the 'new' road heads west over hills to meet Highway 1 near Laguna Chapala, 53 km south of Cataviña, opening up a circular route through northern Baja California. Between the bay and Highway 1 is *Coco's Corner*, a friendly pit stop, offering meals and, if stranded, basic accommodation.

South from Ensenada

Highway 1 south from Ensenada passes turn-offs to several beach resorts. Just before the agricultural town of **Maneadero**, a paved highway runs 23 km west onto the Punta Banda pensinsula, where you can see **La Bufadora** blowhole, one of the most powerful on the Pacific. Air sucked from a sea-level cave is expelled as high as 16m through a cleft in the cliffs. Concrete steps and viewing platform give easy access. Tourist stalls line the approach road and boys try to charge US$1 for parking (restaurants *Los Panchos* and *La Bufadora*, Mesquite-grilled seafood, *palapa* dining, both 0900 to around sunset). This is one of the easiest side trips off the length of Highway 1.

NB Tourist cards and vehicle documents of those travelling south of Maneadero are supposed to be validated at the immigration checkpoint on the southern outskirts of the town; the roadside office, however, is not always in operation. If you are not stopped, just keep going.

Chaparal-clad slopes begin to close in on the highway as it winds it's way south, passing through the small town of Santo Tomás (**D** *El Palomar Motel*, T/F88002. Adequate but overpriced rooms, restaurant, bar, general store and gas station, RV park with full hook-ups, campsite with swimming pool, clean, refurbished, US$10). Nearby are the ruins of the Dominican Mission of 1791 (local Santo Tomás wine is cheaper out of town). **San Vicente** comes next (**E** *Motel El Cammo*, Highway 1, south of town. Without bath, friendly, OK restaurant), with two Pemex stations, cafés, tyre repairs and several stores). **Colonet**, further south, is a supply centre for surrounding ranches with several services. A dry-weather dirt road runs 12 km west to **San Antonio del Mar** where there are many camping spots amid high dunes fronting a beautiful beach renowned for surf fishing and clam-digging.

Santo Tomás
Colour map 1, grid A1

Fourteen kilometres south of Colonet a reasonable graded road branches east to San Telmo and climbs into the mountains. At 50 km it reaches the **L-AL** *Meling Ranch* (also called *San José*), which offers resort accommodation for about 12 guests. About 15 km beyond San José the road enters the **Parque Nacional Sierra San Pedro Mártir** and climbs through forests (four-wheel drive recommended) to three astronomical observatories perched on the dramatic eastern escarpment of the central range. The view from here is one of the most extensive in North America: east to the Gulf, west to the Pacific, and southeast to the overwhelming granite mass of the **Picacho del Diablo** (3,096m), Baja's highest peak. The higher reaches of the park receive snow in winter. ■ *Small entrance fee. The observatories are not open to visitors.*

San Quintín, 179 km from Ensenada, is a market town which just hasn't quite managed to escape the 'why-stop' effects of the highway rolling through, and remains a 'strip' plan town – long and not very wide. It is almost joined to Lázaro Cárdenas, 5 km south. There are service stations in both centres and San Quintín provides all services. Rising out of the peninsula west of San Quintín Bay is a line of volcanic cinder cones, visible for many kilometres along the highway; the beaches to the south near Santa María are hugely popular with fishermen, campers and beachcombers.

San Quintín
Phone code: 618
Colour map 1, grid A1
Population: 15,000

Sleeping AL *La Pinta*, T/F52878 isolated beachfront location 18 km south of San Quintín then 5 km west on paved road. A/c, TV, balconies, tennis, nearby airstrip, reasonably priced breakfasts, even for non-residents. **E** *Hada's Rooms*, just north of Benito Juárez army camp in Lázaro Cárdenas. Cheapest in town, shabby, basic, sometimes closed when water and electricity are cut off.

Motels A-C *Molino Viejo/The Old Mill* F53376. On site of old English mill, part of an early agricultural scheme, upgraded by new American owners, new wing, new bar and dining room with good food and drink, on bay 6 km west of highway and south of Lázaro Cárdenas, rough access road, some kitchenettes, also one 6-bed dormitory, 15 RV spaces with full hook-up (US$15), camping (US$10), electricity 0800-0900, 1800-2200, various sizes of boat for rent; well-run, cosy. Recommended (in USA, representative is The Baja Outfitter, 223 Via de San Ysidro, Ste 76, San Ysidro, CA 92173, T619-4282779, F619-4286269, or T800-4797962). **C** *Cielito Lindo*, 2 km beyond the *La Pinta Hotel* on south shore of bay. Restaurant, *cafetería*, lounge (dancing Sat nights), electricity Mon-Sat 0700-1100, 1500-2400, Sun 0700-2400, modest but pleasant, US$5 for vehicles to camp overnight (use of showers), last kilometre of access road unpaved, messy after rain. **C** *San Carlos*, by *Muelle Viejo* restaurant. Large rooms, friendly, good value. **D** *Ernesto's*, next door. Rustic, overpriced, popular with fishermen, electricity 0700-2100. **D** *Muelle Viejo*, between *Ernesto's* and the old English cemetery. Restaurant, bad access road, hot showers, bay views. **E** *Chávez*, on highway north of Lázaro Cárdenas. Family-style, clean rooms, TV, plain but good value.

Baja California Peninsula

E *Romo*, about 200m from post office. Clean, OK, convenient if arriving late.
E *Sánchez*, a few kilometres before town in Colonia Guerrero. Large rooms, clean.
E *Uruapan*, at northern end of town. Very clean and friendly.

Camping *Pabellón RV Campground*, 15 km south and 2 km west on coast, 200 spaces. Disposal station, toilets, showers, beach access, no electricity, US$5 per vehicle, great area for clam-digging. *Posada Don Diego*, off highway in Colonia Guerrero (south of town, Km 174). Wide range of facilities, laundry, restaurant, etc, 100 spaces, US$7; at south end of Colonia Guerrero is *Mesón de Don Pepe RV Park*. Smaller and more modest, full hook-ups, restaurant with view of campground so you can watch your tent, US$5. *Campo Lorenzo* is just north of Molino Viejo, 20 spaces, full hook-ups but mostly permanent residents. Trailer park attached to *Cielito Lindo Motel*, comfortable.

Eating *El Alteño*, on highway next to the cinema. Bare but clean roadhouse, fresh seafood and Mexican dishes, *mariachi* music, moderate prices. Closed Jul-Sep. Also on highway: *Viejo San Quintín*, central, good seafood. Just south, on opposite side is *Autotransportes de Baja California, café* where the bus company stops for lunch, reasonably priced and sized meals. *Muelle Viejo*, next to motel. Overlooks old pier, reasonably priced seafood, modest decor. *Mi Lien* on Highway 1, north end of town. Very good Chinese food.

Festivals **20 Nov** *Day of the Revolution*, street parades with school children, bands and the military.

Transport Autotransportes de Baja California. **Ensenada** 3½ hours, **Guerrero Negro** 7 hours, **Santa Rosalía** 9 hours.

El Rosario
Colour map 1, grid B1

After leaving the San Quintín valley, bypassing Santa María (fuel), the Transpeninsular Highway (officially the Carretera Transpeninsular Benito Juárez) runs along the Pacific before darting inland at Rancho El Consuelo. It climbs over a barren spur from which there are fine views, then drops in a succession of tight curves into El Rosario, 58 km from San Quintín. This small, agricultural community has a Pemex station, small supermarket, a basic museum, and meals, including Espinosa's famous lobster *burritos* (expensive and not particularly good) and omelettes; there is also a good *taco* stand outside the grocery store at night. Another 3 km south is a ruined Dominican Mission, founded 1774 upstream, then moved to its present site in 1882; take the graded dirt road to **Punta Baja**, a bold headland on the coast, where there is a solar-powered lighthouse and fishing village.

Sleeping **D** *Motel Rosario*, new motel at south end of town. Small, basic. **D** *Sinai*. Comfortable, very clean, small RV park, friendly owner makes good meals, but beware of overcharging.

Central desert of Baja California

Highway 1 makes a sharp 90° turn at El Rosario and begins to climb continuously into the central plateau; gusty winds increase and astonishingly beautiful desertscapes gradually become populated with many varieties of cacti. Prominent are the stately *cardones*; most intriguing are the strange, twisted *cirios* growing to heights of 6-10m. They are unique to this portion of Baja California as far south as the Vizcaíno Desert, and to a small area of Sonora state on the mainland. At Km 62, a 5-km track branches south to the adobe remains of **Misión San Fernando Velicatá**, the only Franciscan mission in Baja, founded by Padre Serra in 1769. 5 km further on, Rancho El Progreso, offers expensive meals and refreshments (possible to camp behind Rancho, and RV park, fill up with water if possible). The highway is now in the **Parque Natural Desierto Central de Baja California** (not yet officially recognized). About 26 km north of Cataviña a strange region of huge boulders begins, some as big as houses; interspersed by cacti and crouching elephant trees, this area is one of the most picturesque on the peninsula.

Cataviña
Colour map 1, grid B2

Cataviña is only a dozen buildings, with a small grocery store/*Café La Enramada*, the only Pemex station on the 227-km stretch from El Rosario to the Bahía de Los Angeles junction (there are in fact two fuel stations, but do not rely on either having supplies), and the attractive **A** *La Pinta Hotel*, T62601, F63688. A/c, pool, bar, electricity 1800-2400, good restaurant, tennis, 28 rooms. Recommended. Just 2 km north of Cataviña there are easily accessible cave paintings near Km 170 on the Transpeninsular Highway. Attached to *La Pinta* is the *Parque Natural Desierto Central de Baja California Trailer Park*, flush toilets, showers, restaurant, bar, US$3 per site. Another 2 km south of Cataviña is *Rancho Santa Inés*, which has dormitory-style accommodation (**E**), meals and a paved airstrip.

Highway 1 continues southeast through an arid world of boulder-strewn mountains and dry salt lakes. The new graded road to Bahía San Luis Gonzaga (see under South of San Felipe, above) branches off to the east. After skirting the dry bed of Laguna Chapala (natural landing strip at southern end when lake is totally dry), the Transpeninsular Highway arrives at the junction with the paved road east to Bahía de los Angeles (**C** *Parador Punta Prieta*, fair, 20 RV spaces with full hook-ups, few facilities; gas station at junction, fuel supply sometimes unreliable, small store at the junkyard opposite the gas station).

The side road runs 68 km through *cirios* and *datilillo* cactus-landscapes and crosses the Sierra de la Asamblea to Bahía de los Angeles (no public transport but hitchhiking possible), a popular fishing town which, despite a lack of vegetation, is one of Baja's best-known beauty spots. The bay, sheltered by the forbidding slopes of Isla Angel de la Guarda (Baja's largest island), is a haven for boating although winds can be tricky for kayaks and small craft. There is good clamming and oysters. Facilities in town include gas station, bakery, grocery stores, two trailer parks and four restaurants and a paved airstrip. The water supply is inadequate; a water truck visits weekly; electricity is cut off about 2200 nightly. There is also a modest but interesting museum in town, good for information on the many mines and on mining techniques used in the region around the turn of the century. One such mine is the Mina San Juan, high in the mountains 24 km south-southwest, which had its own 2ft-gauge railway and wire-rope tramway down to a smelter at Las Flores as early as 1895; the relic steam locomotive and mine car on display beside the airstrip are from this remarkable mine which returned US$2mn in gold and silver before closing down in 1910.

There are thousands of dolphins in the bay June-December. Some stay all year. There are large colonies of seals and many exotic seabirds. Fishing is excellent. A boat and guide can be rented for US$40 a day; try Raúl, a local fisherman, who speaks English. Camping is free and safe on beach. **La Gringa**, a beautiful beach 13 km north of town, charges a small fee for its many camping sites, pit toilets and rubbish bins.

Bahía de los Angeles
Colour map 1, grid B2
Population: 1,245

The series of tiny beaches at the foot of Cabañas Díaz are good for swimming, but watch out for stingrays when wading

In July and August you can hear the whales breathe as you stand on shore

Sleeping and eating C *Villa Vita Motel*. Modern, a/c, pool, jacuzzi, boat launch, trailer park, electricity 0700-1400, 1700-2000, bar, dining room. **D** *Casa de Díaz*. 15

rooms, restaurant, grocery store, campground, boat rentals, clean but cockroaches, well-run, popular. *Guillermo's Trailer Park*. Flush toilets, showers, restaurant, gift shop, boat ramp and rentals. *Guillermo's* also has a restaurant in a white building on main street, above the gift shop, well-prepared Mexican food, attractive, reservations advised at weekends. *La Playa RV Park*, on beach, similar facilities and tariff (US$4 per site). *Sal y Mauro*, campsite. First gravel road on left before entering town, friendly. Recommended. *Restaurant Las Hamacas*, on north edge of town. Budget café with bay view, slow service, popular for breakfast.

State border: Baja California Sur

The highway now runs due south. Before you enter Baja California Sur you pass Punta Prieta (three stores) and Rosarito (one store and one restaurant) and go through **Villa Jesús María** (gas station, store, cafés) to the 28th parallel. This is the state border between Baja California and Baja California Sur (soaring stylized eagle monument and **A** *Hotel La Pinta*. A/c, pool, dining room, bar, trailer park attached, 60 spaces, full hook-ups, US$5, laundry and gasoline at hotel).

NB Advance clocks one hour to Mountain time when entering Baja California Sur, but note that Northern Baja observes Pacific Daylight Saving Time from first Sunday in April to last Sunday in October; time in both states and California is thus identical during the summer.

Guerrero Negro
Phone code: 115
Colour map 1, grid B2
Population: 9,000

Three kilometres beyond the state line and 4 km west of the highway; 714 km south of Tijuana, 414 km from San Quintín, Guerrero Negro is the halfway point between the US border and La Paz. There are two gas stations, bank (Banamex, does not change travellers' cheques), hospital, cafés, stores, an airport with scheduled services (just north of the Eagle monument), and the headquarters of Exportadora de Sal, the world's largest salt-producing firm. Seawater is evaporated by the sun from thousands of salt ponds south of town; the salt is loaded at the works 11 km southwest of town and barged to a deepwater port on Cedros Island. From there, ore carriers take it to the USA, Canada and Japan; guided tour possible.

Sleeping *San Ignacio*, on road into town from highway. New, clean, good but exact prices unknown as yet. **D** *San José*, opposite bus terminal. Clean, will help to organize whale-watching tours. **E** *Cuartos de Sánchez-Smith*, Barrera, west end of town. Basic rooms, some with showers, cheapest in town. **Motels C** *Cabañas Don Miguel* (same owner and location as *Malarrimo Restaurant*), east end of town. Very clean, TV, fan, quiet. Recommended. **D** *El Morro*, on road into town from highway. Modest, clean. **E** *Las Dunas*, few doors from *El Morro*. Friendly, modest, clean. Recommended. **E** *Gámez*, near city hall, very basic. *Malarrimo Trailer Park*, on highway at east end of town. Flush toilets, showers, bar, US$10 per vehicle, whale-watching tours arranged.

Eating Good restaurant at bus station. *Malarrimo Restaurant-Bar*. Fishing décor, good fish and steak menu, moderate prices, music, open for breakfast, runs whale-watching tours, US$30 per person, including transport to boats and lunch. *El Figón*, next to *Las Dunas*. Good breakfast. *Mario's Restaurant-Bar*, next to *El Morro*. Modest surroundings and fare, disco. Excellent *taco* stall a few blocks towards town from *El Morro*. Good bakery on main street.

Transport Air: airport (GUB), 3 km from town, receives scheduled services only from Hermosillo. There are regular flights to Cedros Island and Bahía Tortugas; information from airfield downtown. **Bus**: To Tijuana, 0830, 1830.

Desierto Vizcaíno

After Guerrero Negro the highway enters the grim Vizcaíno Desert. A paved but badly potholed road branches off due east for 42 km to El Arco and other abandoned mining areas. The road then crosses the peninsula to **San**

Baja California Sur

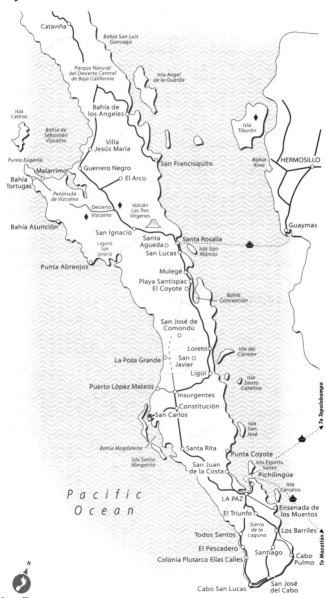

Francisquito on its beautiful bay overlooking the Gulf of California (77 km). It should be stressed that these minor Bajan roads require high-clearance, preferably four-wheel-drive, vehicles carrying adequate equipment and supplies, water and fuel. A new gravel road from Bahía de Los Angeles (135 km) gives easier road access than from El Arco and opens up untouched stretches of the Gulf coast. Southeast of El Arco is the Misión de Santa Gertrudis (1752), some of whose stone ruins have been restored; the chapel is still in use.

Vizcaíno Peninsula
Colour map 1, grid B2

Vizcaíno Peninsula which thrusts into the Pacific south of Guerrero Negro is one of the remotest parts of Baja. Although part of the Vizcaíno Desert, the scenery of the peninsula is varied and interesting; isolated fishcamps dot the silent coast of beautiful coves and untrodden beaches. Until recently only the most hardy ventured into the region; now an improved dry-weather road cuts west through the peninsula to Bahía Tortugas and the rugged headland of Punta Eugenia. It leaves Highway 1, 70 km beyond Guerrero Negro at the Vizcaíno Junction (also called Fundolegal, Pemex station, café, market, pharmacy and auto-parts store; **D** *Motel Olivia* at Vizcaíno. Small rooms with TV, private bath, hot water; nearby is small shop with reasonably priced telephone service). The new road is paved for 8 km to Ejido Díaz Ordaz. It passes Rancho San José (116 km) and the easily missed turn-off to Malarrimo Beach (where beachcombing is unparalleled). After another bumpy 50 km is **Bahía Tortugas**, a surprisingly large place (*Population*: 3,200) considering its remoteness. Many facilities including eating places, health clinic, gas station, airport with services to Isla Cedros and Ensenada, and the small **D-E** *Vera Cruz Motel*. Restaurant, bar, very modest but the only accommodation on the peninsula apart from a trailer park at Campo René, 15 km from Punta Abreojos. Two roads leave the Vizcaíno-Bahía Tortuga road for **Bahía Asunción** (*Population*: 1,600), which has the peninsula's only other gas

Vizcaíno Peninsula

Whale watching

Whale watching is the main attraction on **Laguna Ojo de Liebre**, usually known as **Scammon's Lagoon** after the whaling captain who entered in 1857. California Grey Whales mate and give birth between end-December and February, in several warm-water lagoons on central Baja's Pacific coast. Most leave by the beginning of April, but some stay as late as May or June. They can be seen cavorting and sounding from the old salt wharf 10 km northwest of Guerrero Negro on the Estero San José, or from a designated 'whale watching area' with observation tower on the shore of Scammon's Lagoon, 37 km south of town. The access road branches off Highway 1, 8 km east of the junction (if going by public transport, leave bus at the turn-off and hitch). Local personnel may collect a small fee for camping at the watching area, this pays to keep it clean. The shores of Scammon's Lagoon are part of the **Parque Natural de la Ballena Gris**. The authorities in Guerrero Negro say that boats are not allowed on to the lagoon to watch whales, but pangas are available for hire (US$10 per person). There are also daily tours including a 1½-hour boat trip, sandwiches and transport to the lagoon, US$30 per person. ■US$3 entry to park watch between 0700 and 0900 and again at 1700. The road to the park has little whale signs at regular intervals. It is sandy in places, so drive with care.

Whale Conservation in Mexico

Mexico was the first country in the world to set aside habitat for whales. In 1971, Scammon's Lagoon was designated a grey whale refuge. A few years later, two more grey whale lagoons were protected - Guerrero Negro and San Ignacio. Whale watching and some fishing is still permitted in the lagoons under special regulations but other industrial activities are prohibited.

In 1988, a new biosphere reserve and world heritage site was created which included all of Laguna Ojo de Liebre,

Laguna Guerrero Negro and Laguna San Ignacio as well as the desert areas all around - a total area of more than 2.5 million hectares. Called the Vizcaíno Desert Biosphere Reserve, it is the largest nature reserve in Latin America. It is definitely worth visiting. Besides whales and dolphins, it is possible to see California sea lions, black and green turtles, osprey, brown pelicans, Caspian terns, great blue herons, great egrets and peregrine falcons.

With such habitat protection, the return of grey whale numbers, and the sightings of more and more humpback, blue, fin and Bryde's whales in the Gulf of California, Mexico's whales seemed to be in good shape compared to whale populations in many other countries.

In 1995, however, the Mexican government in partnership with Mitsubishi, the Japanese conglomerate, announced plans to build the largest salt mine in the world inside the reserve, greatly expanding existing salt factories. The US$120 million development, which would create 208 permanent jobs in a relatively underdeveloped area, was not part of the management plan for the biosphere reserve and would jeopardize the designation. A substantial percentage of the reserve (as high as 60% by some estimates) would experience direct impact from the construction of salt production facilities, roads, and new settlements, as well as the dramatic increase in barge and other boat traffic. The facility would be located on the shore of Laguna San Ignacio, the most pristine grey whale habitat, and water would be continuously pumped out of the lagoon to make the salt, thereby lowering the temperature and salinity of critical grey whale habitat. Since 1995, there has been considerable national and international outcry to the development plan led by the Grupo de los Cien (The Group of 100), Mexico's leading environmental organisation. The outcome remains uncertain, although a recent communication suggested that the plan was to be indefinitely delayed.

station. From here there is a coast road south to Punta Prieta, La Bocana and Punta Abreojos (93 km). A lonely road runs for 85 km back to Highway 1, skirting the Sierra Santa Clara before crossing the salt marshes north of Laguna San Ignacio and reaching the main road 26 km before San Ignacio.

San Ignacio

Phone code: 115
Colour map 1, grid B3
Population: 2,200

The Highway continues southeast on a new alignment still not shown on most maps and, 20 km from the Vizcaíno Junction, reaches the first of 23 microwave relay towers which follow Highway 1 almost to the Cape. They are closed to the public but make excellent landmarks and, in some cases, offer excellent views. The turn-off right for San Ignacio is 143 km from Guerrero Negro. Here the Jesuits built a mission in 1728 and planted the ancestors of the town's date palm groves. On the square is the beautifully preserved mission church, completed by the Dominicans in 1786. Near the mission is a small but interesting museum with information on nearby cave paintings. Trips to the caves are available. The town is very attractive, with thatched-roof dwellings and pastel-coloured commercial buildings; there is limited shopping but several restaurants, and a service station with mechanical assistance.

Sleeping **A** *La Pinta*, on road leading into town. A/c, pool, all facilities, built in mission style. Attractive but overpriced. **E** *Cuartos Glenda*, on highway east. With shower, basic but cheapest in town. **Motel D** *La Posada*, on rise 2 blocks from Zócalo (difficult to find). Well-maintained, fans, shower, best value in town, worth bargaining (owner can arrange trips to the cave paintings for US$25 per person).

Camping *San Ignacio Transpeninsula Trailer Park*, Government-run, on Highway 1 behind Pemex station at the junction. Full hook-ups, toilets, showers, US$4 per site, cheap restaurant nearby; basic campground on left of road into San Ignacio, grass, run-down, helpful owner, Martín, sells cheap dates in season. *El Padrino RV Park*, on same road on the right. Basic, cold water showers, sites on sand, decent restaurant.

Eating *Lonchería Chalita*, on Zócalo. Excellent value. *Restaurant Tota* has received poor reports.

Around San Ignacio

A 70-km road from San Ignacio leads to **Laguna San Ignacio**, one of the best whale viewing sites; mothers and calves often swim up to nuzzle boats and allow their noses to be stroked. The Cooperativa Laguna de San Ignacio, Calle Juárez 23, off the Zócalo in San Ignacio, takes fishermen to the lagoon every day and can sometimes accommodate visitors. The road is rough and requires a high clearance vehicle.

There are many cave painting sites around San Ignacio; colourful human and animal designs left by Baja's original inhabitants still defy reliable dating, or full understanding. To reach most requires a trek by mule over tortuous trails; Oscar Fischer, owner of *Motel La Posada*, arranges excursions into the sierras (about US$10 per person to Santa Teresa cave). The cave at the **Cuesta del Palmarito**, 5 km east of Rancho Santa Marta (50 km northwest of San Ignacio), is filled with designs of humans with uplifted arms, in brown and black; a jeep and guide (if one can be found) are required. A better road leads east from the first microwave station past Vizcaíno Junction up to **San Francisco de la Sierra**, where there are other paintings and petroglyphs in the vicinity.

Highway 1 leaves the green *arroyo* of San Ignacio and re-emerges into the arid central desert. To the north, the triple volcanic cones of **Las Tres Vírgenes** come into view, one of the most dramatic mountain scenes along this route. Dark brown lava flows on the flanks are evidence of relatively recent activity (eruption in 1746, smoke emission in 1857). The highest peak is 2,149m above the Gulf of California; the sole vegetation on the lunar-like landscape is the thick-skinned elephant trees.

Two and a half million hectares of the Vizcaíno Desert are now protected by the Reserva de la Biósfera El Vizcaíno, supposedly the largest in Latin America. It was decreed in November 1988 and has absorbed the **Parque Nacional Ballena Gris**. The reserve runs south from the state border to the road from San Ignacio to Laguna San Ignacio in the west and Highway 1 near Santa Rosalía in the east; it stretches from the Pacific to the Gulf. Encompassed by the reserve are the desert, the Vizcaína Peninsula, Scammon's Lagoon, Las Tres Vírgenes volcano, the Laguna San Ignacio and several offshore islands.

Reserva de la Biósfera El Vizcaíno

Santa Rosalía

Seventy-two kilometres from San Ignacio is Santa Rosalía squeezed into a narrow bottleneck valley running off the harbour. It was built by the French El Boleo Copper Company in the 1880s, laid out in neat rows of wood-frame houses, many with broad verandahs, which today give Santa Rosalía its distinctly un-Mexican appearance. Most of the mining ceased in 1953; the smelter, several smokestacks above the town and much of the original mining operation can be seen in the north of town.

Phone code: 115
Colour map 1, grid B3
Population: 14,500

Santa Rosalía's streets are narrow and congested; larger vehicles should park along the highway or in the ferry dock parking lot

There is a small **museum** off Calle Francisco next to the Impecsa warehouse, with historic exhibits of mining and smelting. The port was one of the last used in the age of sail. The church of **Santa Bárbara**, Obregón y Calle 3, a block north of the main plaza, was built of prefabricated galvanized iron for the 1889 Paris Worlds' Fair from a design by Eiffel. It was then shipped around the Horn to Baja. On the north Mesa, the broad forlorn-looking avenue, between the museum and *Hotel Francés*, is a line of rusting mine contraptions and locomotives. A car ferry leaves for Guaymas, from the small harbour, seven hours (T20014, fares are the same as for the La Paz-Topolobampo ferry, see schedule, page 717; tickets sold on day of departure). Immigration Office T20313.

Santa Rosalía

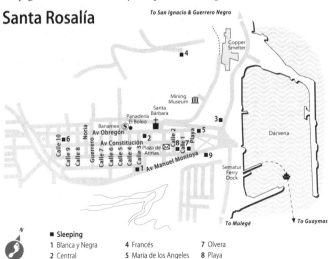

N
Not to scale

■ **Sleeping**
1 Blanca y Negra
2 Central
3 El Industrial
4 Francés
5 María de los Ángeles
6 Minas
7 Olvera
8 Playa
9 Real

The Pemex station is conveniently located on the highway, unlike the one at Mulegé (see below), so larger RVs and rigs should fill up here. There is a 24-hour store a couple of hundred yards south.

Sleeping **B** *Francés*, Jean Michel Cousteau on the north Mesa, T22052. A/c, restaurant, bar, pool not always filled, historic 2-storey wooden French colonial building overlooking smelter and Gulf, photos of sailing vessels on walls. Charming, lukewarm water. **C** *Minas*, Av Obregón and Calle 10, T21060. Dark, modern, large rooms, looks half finished from outside. **D** *María de los Angeles*, Av Obregón and Playa, T20075. Clean, a/c, TV, restaurant. **D** *El Morro*, on Highway, 2 km south of town, T20414, on bluff with Gulf views. Modern, Spanish-style, a/c, bar, restaurant (good food, generous portions, reasonable prices. **D** *Olvera*, on plaza at entrance to town, 2nd floor. A/c, showers, clean. Good value. **D** *Playa*, Calle 1, just west of Constitución Central. Fans, bathrooms, good budget hotel. **D** *Real*, Av Manuel Montoya near Calle 1. Similar to *Olvera*. Recommended. **E** *Blanca y Negra*, Calle 3 and Serabia. Basic but clean. *Central*, Av Obregón. Large rooms, shared bath. **D** *Motel El Industrial*, Transpeninsular Highway, at entrance to town, T21078.

Camping Possible on the beach under *palapas*, access via an unmarked road 500m south of *El Morro*, free, no facilities, a beautiful spot. Also trailer park *El Palmar*, 3 km south of town. US$5 for 2, showers, laundry, good value.

Eating *Balneario Selene*, T20685, on Highway opposite Pemex. *Panadería El Boleo*, widely noted for its delicious French breads.

Transport ABC bus/Autobus Aguila station (T220150) 400m south of ferry terminal; stop for most Tijuana-La Paz buses, several per day. To **La Paz**, 1100, US$24.

Directory **Communications** Post Office: only from here and La Paz can parcels be sent abroad; customs check necessary first, at boat dock. **Laundry** Opposite *Hotel Central*, wash and dry US$2.50 per load.

Excursions from Santa Rosalía Painted cave sites can be visited from the farming town of **Santa Agueda**. Turn off 8 km southwest of Santa Rosalía then it's rough dirt road for 12 km (four-wheel drive necessary, guide can be arranged at the Delegado Municipal, Calle Madero, Mulegé). The caves are in the San Borjita and La Trinidad deserts; the drawings depict animals, children and, some claim, female sexual organs.

The fishing village of **San Lucas**, on a palm-fringed cove, is 14 km south of Santa Rosalía; camping is good and popular on the beaches to the north and south. *San Lucas RV Park*, on beach, no hook-ups, flush toilets, boat ramp, ice, restaurant, US$5 per vehicle, 35 spaces. Recommended. Offshore lies **Isla San Marcos**, with a gypsum mine at the south end.

Just beyond **San Bruno** is a reasonable dirt road to **San José de Magdalena** (15 km), a picturesque farming village dating back to colonial days with a ruined Dominican chapel, attractive thatched palm houses and flower gardens. An awful road leads on for 17 km to **Rancho San Isidro**, from where the ruined Guadalupe Misión can be reached on horseback. At San Bruno, *Costa Serena* beach camping, no hook-ups, one shower, clean beach with good fishing and shrimping. Similar is *Camp Punta Chivato*, just before Mulegé, no hook-ups but clean toilets and shower, beautiful location.

Mulegé

Sixty-one kilometres south of Santa Rosalía, is another oasis community, a tranquil retreat outside of spring break. There are lovely beaches, good diving, snorkelling and boating in the Bahía Concepción. The old Federal territorial prison (La Cananea) has been converted into a museum. It became renowned as the 'prison without doors' because the inmates were allowed out during the day to work in the town. There is a good cheap fish restaurant 40 minutes walk along the river; the lighthouse, 10 minutes further on provides tremendous views. The beach is stony, but the tidal lagoons are popular for collecting clams. Just upstream from the highway bridge on the south side of the river is the Misión de Santa Rosalía de Mulegé, founded by the Jesuits in 1705. Above the mission there is a good lookout point over the town and its sea of palm trees. Looking the other way there is a fine view at sunset over the inland mesas. Locals swim at an excellent spot about 500m inland from the bridge and to the right of the track to the Mission. Tours to cave painting sites, US$30 per person including drinks; a guide is necessary; recommended is Salvador Castro, ask for him at the taxi rank in the plaza. There is no bank in Mulegé. **NB** One Pemex station is in Calle General Martínez, one block before plaza in the centre; not convenient for large vehicles, which also have a one-way system to contend with. But there is another Pemex station 4.5 km south of the bridge, on the road out of town towards Loreto, with restaurant and mini-market. There is good free **tourist information** at Ecomundo office (see kayaking under Santispac, below).

Phone code:115
Colour map 1, grid C3
Population: 5,000

Baja California Peninsula

A *Serenidad*, 4 km south of town near the river mouth on beachside road, may be closed because of long-running dispute with members of a local *ejido* who claim the land and have occupied the resort developed and run for many years by the Johnsons, T20111. **C** *Las Casitas*, Callejón de los Estudiantes y Av Madero. Central, a/c, showers, restaurant and bar, shady garden patio, fishing trips arranged, pleasant older hotel, well-run. **C** *Mulegé*, Moctezuma, near entrance to town, T30179. Large light rooms, a/c, TV. **C** *Vieja Hacienda*, Madero 3, T30021, F30340. Lovely courtyard, pool, rooms refurbished, bar, trips to cave paintings and kayaking offered (US$25 per person). Recommended. **C** *Las Casitas*, Callejón de los Estudiantes y Av Madero. Central, a/c, showers, restaurant and bar, shady garden patio, fishing trips arranged,

Sleeping

Mulegé

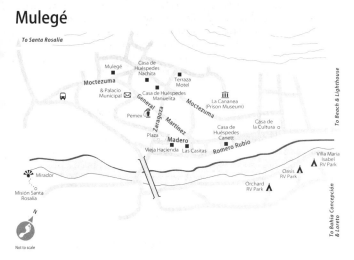

pleasant older hotel, well-run. **D** *Suites Rosita*, Av Madero near main plaza. A/c, kitchenettes, clean and pleasant, hot water, a bit run-down but good value. **D** *Terraza*, Zaragoza y Moctezuma, in business district, 35 rooms, rooftop bar, TV, parking, clean. Several **E-F** *Casas de Huéspedes*, eg *Manuelita*, *Nachita*, *Canett*, *Sorpresa*, behind Casa de la Cultura. Rents rooms by the week. All basic but reasonably clean. Difficult to find rooms during Semana Santa and at spring break.

Camping *The Orchard (Huerta Saucedo) RV Park*, on river south of town, partly shaded, off Highway 1. Pool, free coffee, book exchange, boat ramp, fishing, up to US$10.50 for 2, discount with AAA/AA membership. Recommended. *Villa María Isabel RV Park*, on river and Highway east of *Orchard*. Pool, recreation area, disposal station, American-style bakery. *Jorge's del Río Trailer Park*, grassy, on river at east end of Highway bridge by unpaved road. Hot water, clean, plenty of shade but watch belongings at night, seasonal residents only. *Pancho's RV Park*, next to *María Isabel*, off Highway 1. Little shade. *Oasis Río Baja RV Park*, on same stretch as those above. Reasonable. All have full hook-ups, flush toilets, showers, etc. Tent-camping just after start of dirt road to lighthouse, US$2. From here on down the Bahía Concepción coast and beyond are many *playas públicas*; some have basic facilities, most are simple, natural camping spots on beautiful beaches where someone may or may not collect a fee. At Mulegé is the Playa Sombrerito at the hat-shaped hill (site of Mexican victory over US forces in 1847); restaurant and store nearby. White gas is sold at the *ferretería* 'on the far side of town from the main entrance' in large cans only. Purified water in large bottles is sold at *La Misión*, General Martínez, T30380.

Eating *Patio El Candil*, Zaragoza. Simple outdoor dining. *Azteca* and *Vista Hermosa* at *Hotel Terraza*. Good food, budget prices. *Paco y Rosy's*, signed turn-off from Highway, 2 km south. Rustic, friendly, Chinese, open from 1800. *Tandil* and *Las Casitas*. Romantic and quiet atmosphere, good. *Equipales*, Zaragoza, upstairs. Recommended for good local cooking and for breakfasts. *Donna Moe's Pizza*, Zaragoza, on corner of plaza. Pleasant rooftop breakfast patio and bar. Opposite is *El Mezquite*, good burgers, live music. *Baja Burger*, between *Las Casitas* and *Hotel Vieja Hacienda*. Traditional burgers and *quesadillas*, ice cream. *Doney's Mely's Tacos*, at entrance to town. *Ramon's Asadero Tacos*, 2 blocks past *Las Casitas*. *Doney's Tacos*, Madero, end furthest from centre, good food and clean, closed Tue. There is a *taco* stand on the plaza most nights but the best one is *Alonso's*, 1 block past *El Candil*, on Zaragoza, open until 0200, closed Wed. Good pizza place under the bridge, on the river between *Jorge's Trailer Park* and town, reasonable prices, English book exchange, and nearby, on the way to the Misión, *La Cueva de Lagarto* does reasonable *mariscos* (seafood). Good fish restaurant, *Almeja*, on the beach near the lighthouse. In the plaza next to the *Hacienda* is a good *taco* stand in am and vendors selling chips and *churros* in pm. Next to *Doney's* on Madero is a Corona beer store, selling ice-cold beer with plastic bags of ice supplied.

Sport *Cortez Explorers*, Moctezuma 75 A, T30500, www.cortez.explorer.com, friendly, English spoken, US$60 for 2-tank boat dive. US$30 snorkelling from boat. Diving is off Punta Concepción or Isla Santa Inés. Also hires out 4 wheel motorbikes (must be 16 or over) and mountain bikes US$15 per day. Best snorkelling from shore is just past the point, opposite way up beach from lighthouse. There is a small sports fishing fleet operating out of the harbour here. Bicycle repairs near *Doney's Tacos*, 1 block before Casa de la Cultura, on left.

Transport Buses to the south do not leave at scheduled times. Allow plenty of time to complete your journey. Bus stop is on highway, north of bridge, at entrance to town. There is an airstrip for private planes beside the currently closed Hotel Vista Hermosa.

Communications Telephone and fax abroad at mini-supermarket *Padilla*, 1 block from Pemex station, also from video store, nearby, both on Zaragoza. Post Office and police in old city hall, 1 block up from Pemex. **Laundry** *Lavamática*, Doblado, opposite Tres Estrellas bus station.

Beyond Mulegé the Highway climbs over a saddle and then runs along the shores of Bahía Concepción for 50 km. This stretch is the most heavily used camping and boating area on the Peninsula; the water is beautiful, swimming safe, camping excellent and there is varied marine life. **Playa Santispac**, in the cove called Bahía Coyote, 23 km south of Mulegé, is recommended. There are many small restaurants (for example *Ana's*, which sells water and bakes bread, none other available, food good value, and *Ray's*, good food, bit pricey) and *palapas* (shelters) for hire (day or overnight, US$2.50). You can get to Santispac from Mulegé on the La Paz bus. Taxi about US$12. It is also quite easy to hitch. Just south of here, in the next cove, at Playa Concepción, kayaks can be hired at Ecomundo, T30409, Apartado Aerea 60, ecomundo@aol.com (office in Mulegé at *Las Casitas* hotel). There are also *palapas* (US$10 per person, US$12 if you are alone in a *palapa*), a bookshop, gallery, bar and restaurant. Idyllic place to hang out, run by an American couple. Kayak rental US$20 for half a day including snorkelling gear. Tent hire US$7 per day. Reductions for longer hire if you want to take off on a paddling expedition. At low tide you can walk on the rocky shoreline between this bay and Santispac, rather than walking up the highway over the hill in the heat. Just south of Santispac is Playa Burro and, beyond that, Playa Coyote. There is good swimming at Playa Escondida where the water is deeper. Further south from El Coyote is **Playa Buenaventura**, which has rooms at **A** *George's Olé*, *palapas* and three *cabañas* for rent (US$20), and an expensive restaurant serving wine, burgers and spaghetti. From the entrance to the beach at Requesón, veer to the left for Playa La Perla, which is small and secluded. In summer this area is extremely hot and humid, the sea is too salty to be refreshing and there can be midges.

A new graded dirt road branches off Highway 1 to climb over the towering **Sierra Giganta**, whose desert vistas of flat-topped mesas and *cardón* cacti are straight out of the Wild West. The road begins to deteriorate after the junction (20 km) to San José de Comondú and limps another 37 km into San Isidro after a spectacular drop into the La Purísima Valley. San Isidro (*Population: 1,000*) has little for the visitor; 5 km down the valley is the more attractive oasis village of La Purísima (*Population*: 800). The road leads on southwards to La Poza Grande (52 km) and Ciudad Insurgentes (85 km); it is now beautifully paved and is probably the fastest stretch of road in Baja. Two side roads off the San Isidro road lead down to the twin towns of San Miguel de Comondú and San José de Comondú (high-clearance vehicles are necessary); both oasis villages of 500 people each. One stone building remains of the mission moved to San José in 1737, and the original bells are still at the church. A new graded road leads on to La Poza Grande and Ciudad Insurgentes.

Loreto

Some 1,125 km from Tijuana, Loreto is one of the most historic places in Baja. Here Spanish settlement of the Peninsula began with Father Juan María Salvatierra's founding of the **Misión de Nuestra Señora de Loreto** on 25 October 1697. It was the first capital of the Californias. Nestled between the slopes of the Sierra Giganta and the offshore Isla del Carmen, Loreto has experienced a tourist revival; fishing in the Gulf here is some of the best in Baja California.

Phone code: 113
Colour map 1, grid C3
Population: 7,500

The Mission is on the Zócalo, the largest structure in town and perhaps the best-restored of all the Baja California mission buildings. It has a gilded altar. The **museum** beside the church is worth a visit: there are educational displays about the missions, Bajan history and historic horse and ranching equipment, book shop. ■ *0900-1300, 1345-1800, closed Mon, US$1.80*. An inscription over the main door of the mission announces: 'Mother of all the Missions of Lower and Upper California'.

Sleeping **LL** *Diamond Eden* T30700, F30377. All-inclusive, luxury, beachfront, 10 mins from airport, 224 rooms, a/c, 2 pools, fitness centre, 2 restaurants, 6 bars, golf, John McEnroe Tennis Centre, mostly package holiday business. **A** *Plaza Loreto*, Av Hidalgo, T50280, F50855, restaurant, bar. **A** *Oasis*, Playa y Baja California, T30112, F50795, on bay at south end of Loreto in palm grove. Large rooms, pool, tennis, restaurant, bar, skiffs (*pangas*) for hire, fishing cruises arranged, pleasant and quiet, a/c. **A-B** *La Pinta*, on Sea of Cortés 2 km north of Zócalo, T/F50026. A/c, showers, pool, tennis, restaurant, bar, considered by many the best of the original 'Presidente' *paradores*, 30 rooms, fishing boat hire. Recommended. **B** *Junípero*, Av Hidalgo, new. Recommended. **C** *La Siesta Bungalows*. Small, manager owns the dive shop and can offer combined accommodation and diving trips. **C** *Misión de Loreto*, Playa y Juárez, T30048, F50648. Colonial-style with patio garden, a/c, pool, dining rooms, bar, fishing trips arranged, very comfortable, but poor service, check for discounts. **D** *Villa del Mar*, Colina Zaragoza, near sports centre. OK, restaurant, bar, pool, bargain rates, on beach. **Motel** **C** *Salvatierra*, Salvatierra, on south approach to town, T50021, F50604. A/c, hot showers, clean, good value. **C** *Posada San Martín*, Juárez and Davis, 200m from beach, T50792. **E** *Motel Davis*, Davis. Friendly.

Loreto

N
Not to scale

■ **Sleeping**		● **Eating**	
1 Davis	4 Oasis	1 Café Olé	4 La Palapa
2 Junípero	5 Plaza Loreto	2 El Nido	5 Playa Blanca
3 Motel Salvatierra	6 Posada San Martín	3 Embarcadero	

Camping *Ejido Loreto RV Park*, on beach 1 km south of town. Full hook-ups, toilets, showers, free coffee, laundry, fishing and boat trips arranged, US$5 per person. Butter clams are plentiful in the sand. *El Moro RV Park*, Robles 8, T/F50542. Central – 1 block from plaza.

On Playa, *Embarcadero*. Owner offers fishing trips, average prices for food. *El Nido* and *El Buey*. Both good (latter barbecues); several *taco* stands on Salvatierra. *Playa Blanca*, Hidalgo y Madero. Rustic, American meals, reasonable prices. *César's*, Zapata y Juárez. Good food and service, candle-lit, moderate prices. *Café Olé*, Madero 14. Mexican and fast food, *palapa*-style, open-air breakfasts, budget rates. *La Palapa*, Av Hidalgo, ½ block from seafront. Excellent seafood. **Eating**

Diving Scuba and snorkelling information and equipment booth on municipal beach near the fishing pier; the beach itself stretches for 8 km, but is dusty and rocky. Beware of stingrays on the beach. **Fishing** *Arturos Sports Fishing Fleet*, T50409, F50022. **Sport**

Air: International, 4 km south; Aero California (T50500) daily to Los Angeles; Aerolitoral to Chihuahua, Ciudad, Obregón, La Paz and other destinations in high season. Charter flights to Canada. **Transport**

Buses: Bus station at Salvatierra opposite intersection of Zapata; to **La Paz** 6 a day, from 0700, US$10.75; to **Tijuana** 1500, 1800, 2100, 2300, US$30, 17 hrs. **Mulegé** with Aguila 1½ hrs, US$6.

Directory Bank *Bancomer* on southwest corner of plaza. **Communications Internet** at *Gigante*, estate agent above shoeshop, on Salvatierra.

Route south of Loreto

Just south of Loreto a rough road runs 37 km through impressive canyon scenery to the village of **San Javier**, tucked in the bottom of a steep-walled valley; the settlement has only one store but the Misión de San Javier is one of the best-preserved in North America; it was founded by the Jesuits in 1699 and took 59 years to complete. The thick volcanic walls, Moorish ornamentation and bell tower are most impressive in so rugged and remote a location. Near San Javier is Piedras Pintas, 16 km from the main road, close to Rancho Las Parras; there are eight prehistoric figures painted here in red, yellow and black. The road to San Javier Mission is in poor shape and requires a sturdy vehicle. In San Javier, you can stay in hostel and restaurant *Palapa*, close to the church, or in a **E** two-bed house with kitchen rented by Ramón Bastida in a beautiful, quiet garden, five minutes walk along the path behind the church.

The highway south of Loreto passes a picturesque stretch of coast. Fonatur, the government tourist development agency, is building a resort complex at **Nopoló** (8 km), which it was hoped would one day rival its other resort developments at Cancún, Ixtapa and Huatulco. An international airport, streets and electricity were laid out, then things slowed down; today there is the 15-storey **LL** *El Presidente Hotel*, T30700. International class, self-contained, on its own imported-sand beach; nearby is the lighted Loreto Tennis Center, half-finished foundations, weeds and an absence of people. Sixteen kilometres further on is **Puerto Escondido**, with a new yacht harbour and marina; although the boat landing and anchoring facilities are operating, the complex is still far from complete, slowed by the same diversion of funds to other projects as Nopoló. There is, however, the *Tripui Trailer Park*, claimed to be the best in Mexico (PO Box 100, Loreto). Landscaped grounds, paved roads, coin

Baja California Peninsula

laundry, groceries, restaurant and pool, lighted tennis court, playground; 116 spaces (most rented by the year), US$17 for two, extra person US$5 (T706-8330413). There are three lovely public beaches between Loreto and Puerto Escondido (none has drinking water): **Notrí**, **Juncalito** and **Ligüí**: palm-lined coves, which are a far cry from the bustle of the new resort developments nearby. Beyond Ligüí (36 km south of Loreto) Highway 1 ascends the eastern escarpment of the **Sierra Giganta** (one of the most fascinating legs of Highway 1) before leaving the Gulf to strike out southwest across the Peninsula again to Ciudad Constitución.

Ciudad Constitución
Phone code: 113
Colour map 1, grid C3

The highway passes by **Ciudad Insurgentes**, a busy agricultural town of 13,000 with two service stations, banks, auto repairs, shops and cafés (no hotels/motels), then runs dead straight for 26 km to **Ciudad Constitución**, which is the marketing centre for the Magdalena Plain agricultural development and has the largest population between Ensenada and La Paz (50,000). Although not a tourist town, it has extensive services of use to the visitor: department stores, restaurants, banks, public market, service stations, laundries, car repairs, hospital (see introduction to this section, **Insurance and Medical Services**) and airport (near Ciudad Insurgentes). Many businesses line Highway 1, which is divided and doubles as the palm-lined main street, with the first traffic lights since Ensenada, 1,158 km away.

Sleeping D *Casino*, Guadalupe Victoria, a block east of the *Maribel*, T20754. Quiet, 37 clean rooms, restaurant, bar. **C** *Conquistador*, N Bravo, just off Olachea, T21555, F21443. Dark rooms, a/c, TV. **D** *Conchita*, Blvd Olachea, with Hidalgo, T/F20266. A/c, TV. **D** *Maribel*, Guadalupe Victoria y Highway 1, T20155, 2 blocks south of San Carlos road junction. A/c, TV, restaurant, bar, suites available, clean, fine for overnight stop. **E-F** *El Arbolito*, Hidalgo. Basic, clean, central. **E** *Reforma*, Obregón, 2 blocks from the plaza. Basic, with bath. Friendly.

Camping *Campestre La Pila*, 2,500m south on unpaved road off Highway 1. Farmland setting, full hook-ups, toilets, showers, pool, laundry, groceries, tennis courts, ice, restaurant, bar, no hot water,

Ciudad Constitución

To Loreto

Nuevo Dragón   Pentatlón

Esgrima

Vicente Guerrero

Maribel   Casino
Guadalupe Victoria

Hermenegildo Galeana

Banca Serfín

Francisco Javier Mina

Banamex

Mariano Matamoros

Alvaro Obregón   Reforma

Nicolás Bravo
El Conquistador
Market

Miguel Hidalgo
Conchita   El Arbolito

Ignacio Allende

José María Morelos

Justo Sierra

Francisco I Madero

Pino Suárez

Emiliano Zapata

Francisco Villa

Boulevard Agustín Olachea Avilés

Av Benito Juárez
Av Rosaura Zapata
Ignacio Zaragoza

N

Not to scale   To La Paz

US$10-13 for 4. **RV Park Manfred**, on left of main road going north into town. Very clean, friendly and helpful, Austrian owner (serves Austrian food).

Eating *Nuevo Dragón de Oro*, Av Olachea with Esgrima, 5 blocks north of plaza. Chinese. *Panadería Superpan*, north of market hall. Excellent pastries.

Excursions Deep artesian wells have made the desert of the Llano de Magdalena bloom with citrus groves and a chequerboard of neat farms growing cotton, wheat and vegetables; this produce is shipped out through the port of **San Carlos**, 58 km to the west on **Bahía Magdalena** (40 minutes by bus from Ciudad Constitución). Known to boaters as 'Mag Bay', it is protected by mountains and sand spits. It provides the best boating on Baja's Pacific coast. Small craft can explore kilometres of mangrove-fringed inlets and view the grey whales that come here in the winter season. The best time to whale-watch is January-March, US$25 per hour for a boat for up to six persons. **C** *Hotel Alcatraz*. **E** *Las Palmas*, on same street as bus station. Clean, fan, hot water. **E** *Motel Las Brisas*, one block behind bus station. Clean, friendly, quiet.

'Mag Bay' is considered the finest natural harbour between San Francisco and Acapulco

On the narrow south end of Magdalena Island is Puerto Magdalena, a lobstering village of 400. Seven kilometres away is a deepwater port at Punta Belcher.

Whales can be seen at Puerto López Mateos further north (access from Ciudad Insurgentes or Ciudad Constitución); no hotel, but ask for house of María del Rosario González who rents rooms (**E**) or take a tent and camp at the small harbour near the fish plant. Alternatively, stay in Ciudad Constitución and take one of several daily buses. On **Isla Santa Margarita** are Puerto Alcatraz (a fish-canning community of 300) and Puerto Cortés (important naval base); neither is shown on the ACSC map.

Highway 1 continues its arrow-straight course south of Ciudad Constitución across the flat plain to the village of Santa Rita. Twenty-eight kilometres beyond Santa Rita, it makes a 45° turn east, where a road of dubious quality runs to the remote missions of San Luis Gonzaga (64 km) and La Pasión (49 km); there are plans to extend this road to the ruins of Dolores del Sur (85 km) on the Gulf of California, one of Baja's most inaccessible mission sites. South of Santa Rita there is a service station at the village of **El Cien**; meals and refreshments are available at the *Rancho San Agustín*, 24 km beyond.

La Paz

Capital of Baja California Sur, La Paz is a relaxed modern city, nestled at the southern end of Bahía La Paz (where Europeans first set foot in Baja in 1533). Sunsets can be spectacular. Prices have risen as more tourists arrive to enjoy its winter climate, but free port status ensures that there are plenty of bargains (although some goods, like certain makes of camera, are cheaper to buy in the USA). Oyster beds attracted many settlers in the 17th century, but few survived long. The Jesuit mission, founded here in 1720, was abandoned 29 years later. La Paz became the territorial capital in 1830 after Loreto was wiped out by a hurricane. Although bursting with new construction, there are still many touches of colonial grace, arched doorways and flower-filled patios. The early afternoon *siesta* is still observed by many businesses, especially during summer. The **tourist office** on Tourist Wharf at the bottom of 16 de Septiembre is helpful, English spoken, will make hotel reservations; they have some literature and town maps. Fax facilities here (send and receive worldwide), also noticeboard for rides offered, crew wanted, etc. ■ *Mon-Fri 0800-1500, Sat 0900-1300, 1400-1500, open till 1900 high season.*

Phone code: 112
Colour map 1, grid C2
Population: 1991: 168,000

Baja California Peninsula

Sights Heart of La Paz is the **Plaza Constitución**, facing which are the government buildings and the graceful **Catedral de Nuestra Señora de la Paz**, built in 1861-65 on or near the site of the original mission. The Post Office is a block northeast at Revolución de 1910 y Constitución. The street grid is rectangular; westerly streets run into the Paseo Alvaro Obregón, the waterfront **Malecón**, where the commercial and tourist wharves back onto a tangle of streets just west of the main plaza; here are the banks, Palacio Municipal, Chinatown and many of the cheaper *pensiones*. The more expensive hotels are further southwest. A must is the **Museo Antropológico de Baja California Sur**, Ignacio Altamirano y 5 de Mayo (four blocks east of the Plaza), with an admirable display of Peninsula anthropology, history and pre-history, folklore and geology. The bookshop has a wide selection on Mexico and Baja. ■ *Mon-Fri 0900-1700, free.* **The Museum of the whale** is at Navarro and Ignacio Altamirano, and a carved mural depicting the history of Mexico can be seen at the **Palacio de Gobierno** on Isabel La Católica, corner of Bravo.

Beaches There are many beaches around La Paz, the most popular on the Pichilingüe Peninsula; most have restaurants (good seafood restaurant under *palapa* at

La Paz

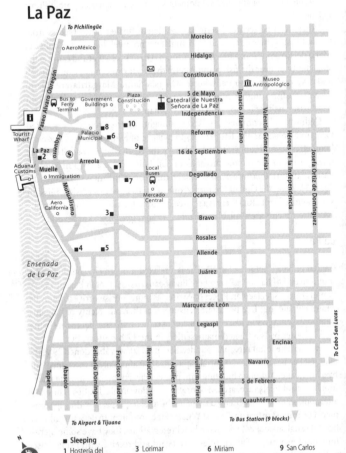

To Pichilingüe

Morelos
Hidalgo
Constitución
5 de Mayo — Museo Antropológico
Catedral de Nuestra Señora de La Paz
Independencia
Reforma
16 de Septiembre
Degollado
Ocampo
Bravo
Rosales
Allende
Juárez
Pineda
Márquez de León
Legaspi
Encinas
Navarro
5 de Febrero
Cuauhtémoc

Paseo Alvaro Obregón
Ignacio Altamirano
Valentín Gómez Farías
Héroes de la Independencia
Josefa Ortiz de Domínguez

Plaza Constitución
Bus to Ferry Terminal
Government Buildings
Tourist Wharf
Palacio Municipal
La Paz
Aduana/Customs · Muelle · Immigration
Esquerro
Arreola
Mutualismo
Aero California
Local Buses
Mercado Central

Ensenada de La Paz

Topete
Abasolo
Belisario Domínguez
Francisco I Madero
Revolución de 1910
Aquiles Serdán
Guillermo Prieto
Ignacio Ramírez

To Cabo San Lucas

To Airport & Tijuana   To Bus Station (9 blocks)

N
Not to scale

■ **Sleeping**
1 Hostería del Convento
2 La Perla
3 Lorimar
4 Los Arcos
5 Mediterráneo
6 Miriam
7 Pensión California
8 Posada San Miguel
9 San Carlos
10 Yeneka

Pichilingüe). Going north from La Paz to the ferry terminal on Highway 11 you will pass **Palmira**, **Coromuel** (popular with *paceños*), **El Caimancito** (admission fee) and **Tesoro**. Wind surfing and catamaran trips can be arranged. Buses to Pichilingüe run from 1000-1400 and 1600-1730, US$1.30 from station at Paseo Alvaro Obregón and Independencia; 100m north of ferry terminal is a *playa pública*. **Balandra** (rubbish bins, *palapas*, US$2) and **Tecolote** (same but camping free under *palapas*) are reached by the road beyond the ferry terminal (paved for some distance beyond this point; some buses on this route run beyond the ferry terminal at weekends). The road ends at a gravel pit at **Playa Cachimba** (good surf fishing), 13 km northeast of Pichilingüe; the north-facing beaches are attractive but can be windy, and there are some sandflies. **El Coyote** (no water or facilities), on the east coast, is reached by a road/track from La Paz running inland along the middle of the peninsula. Southwest of La Paz on the bay are the tranquil, no-surf beaches of Comitán and El Mogote. In October (at least) and after rain, beware of stinging jellyfish in the water.

Sleeping

- *on maps*

Price codes:
see inside front cover

AL *Los Arcos*, Paseo Alvaro Obregón 498 at Allende, T22744, F54313. A/c, pool, restaurant, coffee shop, across the Malecón from the beach, walking distance of centre, fishing trips arranged. Excellent value. **AL** *Cabañas de los Arcos*, opposite with shared facilities, T22297. A/c, pool, slightly cheaper. **AL** *Gran Hotel Baja*, 'the only high-rise structure south of Ensenada', so easy to find, T23844. Restaurant, bar, pool, disco, etc, on beach, trailer park adjacent. **AL** *La Posada*, on bay 3½ km southwest of centre, 5 blocks off Highway 1 on Colima, T20653. A/c, pool, tennis, bar, restaurant, quiet and relaxing, recommended but away from the centre. **AL** *El Moro*, 3,500m northeast on Palmira Beach, T/F52112. Moorish-style, a/c, TV, fridges, apartments with kitchenettes, pool, restaurant, bar. **AL** *El Presidente Sur*, 6,500m northeast at Caimancito Beach, T26544. Good location but furthest from town, a/c, pool, restaurant, bar, next door to Governor's mansion. **AL** *Misiones de La Paz*, on El Mogote sandspit. Isolated, accessible by launch from *Hotel La Posada*, T24021, a/c, showers, pool, restaurant, cocktail bar, quiet. **AL** *Palmira*, T24000, F16227, 3,500m northeast of Pichilingüe Rd. A/c, pool, tennis, restaurant, disco, convention facilities, fishing trips arranged, popular with families. **A** *La Perla*, Obregón 1570, on the water front, T20777, F55363, perla@lapaz.cromwell.com.mx; clean, a/c, friendly, restaurant expensive, swimming pool, locked garage.

C *María Dolores Gardenias*, Aquiles Serdán y Vicente Guerrero, T23088, F50436. A/c, pool, restaurant (good). Excellent value. **C** *Mediterráneo*, Allende 36, T51195 (**D** low season). A/c, beautiful setting, has outstanding restaurant. **D** *Lorimar* Bravo 10, T53822, F56387. Hot showers, clean, very helpful, run by a Mexican/American couple, popular, good place to meet fellow travellers, good-value restaurant, can organize trip to Tecolote beach. **D** *Yeneka*, Madero 1520, T54688. Nice, clean and friendly, safe parking, excellent *margaritas*, good restaurant, specials are recommended, chained monkey in courtyard, not recommended for animal lovers. **E** *Cuartos Jalisco*, Belisario Domínguez 251. Very basic. **E** *Pensión California*, Degollado 209, near Madero, T22896. Basic, fan, shower, garden patio, noisy, friendly, weekly deals, not too clean. **E** *Posada San Miguel*, Belisario Domínguez Nte 45, T21802, near Plaza. Colonial-style, bathroom, clean, hot water (limited), quiet. Recommended. **E** *Revolución*, Revolución 85, T58022. Basic. **F** *San Carlos*, 16 de Septiembre y Revolución, T20444. Clean but noisy, laundry upstairs. **E-F** *Hostería del Convento*, Madero 85, T23508. Basic, fans, clean, shower, tepid water between 0700 and 0900, beautiful patio. **F** *Miriam*, Av 16 de Septiembre, price per person.

Youth hostel On Carretera al Sur (Highway 1), Blvd Forjadores de Sudcalifornia Km 3, CP 23040, T24615. Dormitory bunk, open 0600-2300, good value, '8 de Octubre' bus from market.

Baja California Peninsula

Camping *El Cardón Trailer Park*, 4 km southwest on Highway 1, T40078, F40261. Partly shaded area away from beach, full facilities, US$11 for 2. *Aquamarina RV Park*, 3,500m southwest, 400m off Highway 1 at Calle Nayarit, on bay, T23761, F56228. Nicely landscaped, all facilities, marina, boat ramp, fishing, scuba trips arranged, US$17 for 2. *La Paz Trailer Park*, 1,500m south of town off Highway 1, access via Calle Colima, T28787, F29938. Deluxe, nearest RV Park to La Paz, very comfortable, US$12 for 2.

Eating *Palapa Adriana*, on beachfront. Open air, excellent service but beware overcharging.
• *on maps* *Antojitos*, next to *Pirámide* on 16 de Septiembre. Friendly, good value. *Rossy*, Av 16 de Septiembre. Good for breakfast, fish, cheap. *Café Chanate*, behind tourist office. Open evening only, good atmosphere, jazz music, sometimes live. *La Caleta*, on the waterfront. Recommended. *La Tavola Pizza*, good value. *La Revolución*, Revolución, between Reforma and Independencia. Cheap breakfast and lunch. Vegetarian restaurant *El Quinto*, Independencia y Belisario Domínguez. Expensive (whole wheat bread is half the price at the *panadería* in the market place). Excellent and cheap *tacos* at a restaurant with no name on Av 16 de Septiembre, near the bus station. Good *lonchería* and juice bars in the market. Superb seafood *tacos* at stand outside *Pensión California*.

Festivals *Pre-Lenten Mardi Gras* (carnival) in **February or March**, inaugurated in 1989, is becoming one of Mexico's finest. The Malecón is converted into a swirling mass of dancing, games, restaurants and stalls, and the street parade is happy and colourful. Well worth a visit, but book accommodation far in advance.

Shopping A duty-free port. *Casa de las Artesanías de BCS*, Paseo Alvaro Obregón at Mijares, just north of *Hotel Los Arcos*, for souvenirs from all over Mexico. *Centro de Arte Regional*, Chiapas y Encinas (5 blocks east of Isabel la Católica), pottery workshop, reasonable prices. *Fortunato Silva*, Highway 1 (Abasolo) y Jalisco at south end of town, good quality woollen and hand-woven cotton garments and articles. *Bazar del Sol*, Obregón 1665, for quality ceramics and good Aztec art reproductions. *Solco's*, Obregón y 16 de Septiembre, large selection of Taxco silver, leather, onyx chess sets. The *Mercado Central*, Revolución y Degollado, and another at Bravo y Prieto, have a wide range of goods (clothes, sandals, guitars, etc), plus fruit and vegetables. Tourist shops are concentrated along the Malecón between the Tourist and Commercial Wharves. **Bookshop** at the *Art House*, Belisario Domínguez with Juárez. The *ferretería* across from the main city bus terminal sells white gas stove fuel (*gasolina blanca*). *La Perla de la Paz* department store, Arreola y 21 de Agosto, sells general camping supplies. *CCC* Supermarket, opposite Palacio de Gobierno, is good for supplies.

Sports **Diving** *Baja Diving and Service*, Obregón 1680, T21826, F28644. Hires equipment and takes diving trips (US$320 for 4-day PADI course); snorkelling day trip about US$35, very good. *La Paz BCS Dive Centre*, Esquerro 1560, T/F57048.

Tour operators Sea-kayaking and whale-watching tours starting in La Paz, are offered by *OARS*, PO Box 67, Angels Camp CA 95222, T209-7364677, European office: 67 Verney Ave, High Wycombe, Bucks HP12 3ND, England, T01494-448901. *Katun Tours*, 16 de Septiembre, run by Hiram, www.imconn.com/katun; friendly, speaks English. Mountain bike hire US$19, kayak rental, hiking tours, open 0900-1300, 1700-2100, closed Wed.

Transport **Local** *Viajes Palmira*, Av Obregón, opposite *Hotel los Arcos*, T24030. Rents cycles and mopeds. *Budget, Avis, Hertz, Auto Renta Sol* and *Auto Servitur* booths at airport.

Air General Manuel Márquez de León International Airport (LAP), 11 km southwest on paved road off Highway 1. Taxi fare US$6, supposedly fixed, but bargain. Flights

Sematur ferry schedule

Route	La Paz - Mazatlán	Mazatlán - La Paz	La Paz - Topolobampo	Topolobampo - La Paz	Sta Rosalia - Guaymas	Guaymas - Sta Rosalia
Frequency and Class	Sun - Fri	Fri - Wed	Wed, Thur	Wed, Thur	Tues, Fri	Tues, Fri
	Salón US$21	Salón US$21	Salón US$14	Salón US$14	Salón US$14	Salón US$14
	Turista US$42	Turista US$42	Turista US$28	Turista US$28	Turista US$28	Turista US$28
	Cabina US$62	Cabina US$62	Cabina US$42	Cabina US$42		
	Especial US$83	Especial US$83	Especial US$55	Especial US$55		
	Wed	Thur	Fri - Tues	Fri - Tues		
	Load Ferry	Load Ferry	Load Ferry	Load Ferry		
	Salón US$21	Salón US$21	Salón US$14	Salón US$14		
Departure	1500	1500	2200	2200	2300	0900
Arrival	0900	0900	0800	0800	0800	1500

Fare pp sharing accommodation
Children under 12 ½ price
Children under 2 free
No pregnant women allowed on board
SALON - General seating
TURISTA - Cabin with bunkbeds & washbasin
CABINA - Cabin with bunkbeds & bathroom
ESPECIAL - Cabin with living room, bedroom, bathroom & closet

Routes on request for cars, motor homes, trailers, motorcycles etc

SEMATUR OFFICES:

Central reservation T 01-800-6969600
Terminal Pichilingue, La Paz T (112) 25005, F 55717
Terminal de Transbordadores, Mazatlán T (69) 817020/21, F 817023, www.ferrysematur.com.mx/sematur.htm
Muelle Fiscal, Topolobampo T (686) 20141, F 20035
Muelle Fiscal, Sta Rosalia T (115) 20014/13
Muelle Fiscal, Guaymas T (622) 23390, F 23393
Festival Tours, Texas 36, Col Nápoles, México DF, CP 03810 T 56827043, 56826213, F 56827378;I Allende Sur 655, Bajos del Hotel América, Los Mochis, T 183986; Ignacio Ramírez 2215 esq Benito Juárez, La Paz, T 53833, 54666

Baja California Peninsula

within Mexico to Chihuahua, Ciudad Juárez, Ciudad Obregón, Culiacán, Guadalajara, Guaymas, Hermosillo, Loreto, Los Cabos, Los Mochis, Mazatlán, Mexico City, Monterrey, Tijuana. US destinations include Anchorage, Los Angeles, Phoenix, San Antonio, Seattle and Spokane. Airline numbers at airport: Air Alaska T46131; Aero California T46344; AeroMexico T21636

Buses Local buses about US$0.50, depot at Revolución de 1910 y Degollado by the Mercado Central. Central Bus Station (Central Camionera): Jalisco y Héroes de la Independencia, about 16 blocks from centre (taxi US$2), terminal for Tres Estrellas de Oro and Autotransportes Aguila (a/c buses, video, toilet); Autotransportes de La Paz leave from Mercado Central. **Ciudad Constitución**, 13 per day, US$7.70; **Loreto**, 3 per day, US$11.50; **Guerrero Negro**, 6 per day, US$24; **Ensenada**, US$43; **Tijuana**, US$60.50, **Mexicali**, US$55. To the Cape: **San Antonio**, US$1.75, **Miraflores** US$5, **San José del Cabo**, US$6.60, **Cabo San Lucas**, US$8 (all 10 departures per day). **Todos Santos**, 6 per day, US$4.40; Cabo San Lucas via west loop US$7.70.

Try to book at least 2 weeks ahead (6 weeks at Christmas, Easter, Jul and Aug) **Ferry** For schedule to Mazatlán and Topolobampo, see page 717. Modern ferry terminal at Pichilingüe, 21 km north on paved highway. Tickets for the same day are sold at the terminal itself. In advance, tickets may be bought at Sematur, c/o Agencia de Viajes y Expediciones de Puerto, Ignacio Ramírez y Juárez, T53833/54666. Open 0800-1730 Mon-Fri, 0800-1300 Sat. Travel agents sell ferry tickets, eg *Turismo Express*, Esplanada Alvaro Obregón y 16 de Septiembre, 23000 La Paz, T56310-3, F56310. Tourist cards must be valid, allow 2 hrs as there are long queues, trucks have loading priority. It should be noted that many motorists have had difficulty getting reservations or having them honoured. If you have left booking to the last minute, get to the ticket office at 0400 and you may be able to get a cancellation. If cancelling 24 hrs before journey foot passengers are refunded ½ the fare, full refund with more than 48 hrs notice, ticket non-transferable, check for other types of ticket. **NB** Vehicles must have car permits, obtainable at ferry terminal and at Sematur, or at Registro Federal de Vehículos in Tijuana; automobile clubs will provide information. Service and conditions on the ferry are reported to have improved from the former 'cockroach haven'; toilets quickly get blocked and are then locked up, so make an early call and bring your own toilet paper. Restaurants on board are reasonably priced and food OK, but they sometimes close earlier than advertised, small *tienda* selling snack food. To get a tourist cabin, insist that you will share with strangers, a friendly chat may help. At busy periods, the queue for seats starts at 0630. On arrival, buses to Mazatlán may be full, ask about rides on the ferry. Bus to Pichilingüe ferry terminal from Medrita Travel Agency, Paseo Alvaro Obregón y 5 de Mayo, frequent departures on the hour until 1400, then 1600 and 1730; from terminal, Calle Ejido (1st on the left after leaving the ferry). Reasonable facilities at terminal but crowded; large parking lots, officials may permit RVs to stay overnight while awaiting ferry departures. Do not leave possessions on bikes in the car park; thefts have been reported. **NB** On all ferry crossings, delays can occur from Sep if there is bad weather, which could hold you up for 3 days; fog at the entrance to Topolobampo harbour is often a problem; mechanical breakdowns are not unknown! Keep a flexible schedule if travelling to the mainland. The most up-to-date site describing schedules and fares is www.mexconnect.com/mex/mexicoferryw.html; you might also try: www.trybaja.com/ferry.html, a little outdated but gives more flavour of the crossing.

Directory **Airline offices** *Aero California*, city office at Malecón y Bravo, T51023. *AeroMéxico*, T20091. **Banks** Banks will not exchange TCs after 1100. *Banamex*, Arreola y Esquerro. Two *casas de cambio* on 5 de Mayo off Obregón, 0800-2000, better rates than banks. **Communications** Internet: *Baja Net*, Madero 430, US$3.20 for ½ hr. *Katun Tours*, 16 de Septiembre near seafront, US$3.20 for ½ hr. **Laundry** *Laundromat Yoli*, 5 de Mayo y Rubio. Also at Marina de La Paz. **Useful addresses Immigration:** 2nd floor of large building on Paseo Alvaro Obregón, opposite the pier, reported to be very helpful, possible to extend visa here.

There are boat tours from the Tourist Wharf on the Malecón around the bay and to nearby islands like Espíritu Santo. Travel agencies offer a daily boat tour to **Los Lobos Islands** ranging from US$40 (basic) to US$80; the tour should include lunch and snorkelling, six hours, you can see pelicans, sea-lions and dolphins, with luck whales, too. About 17 km west of La Paz a paved road branches northwest off Highway 1 around the bay leading to the mining village of **San Juan de la Costa**, allowing a closer look at the rugged coastal section of the Sierra de la Giganta. Pavement ends after 25 km, the road becomes wide, rolling, regularly graded; OK for large RVs to San Juan, which is a company town of neat-rowed houses; phosphorus is mined and loaded by conveyor and deep-water dock, to be shipped to processing plants for fertilizer production. After San Juan (45 km), the road is passable for medium-size vehicles to Punta Coyote (90 km), closely following the narrow space between mountains and coast with wonderful untouched camping spots. From Coyote to **San Evaristo** (27 km) the track is poor and a rugged vehicle is recommended; travel time from Highway 1 is about 4½ hours. San Evaristo is a sleepy fishing village on a delightful cove sheltered on the east by Isla San José. It is an ideal boating area but is as yet undiscovered. Visit the salt-drying operations near San Evaristo or on San José. This is a rewarding excursion for those with smaller, high-clearance vehicles (vans and pick-ups) for the steep final 20-mile stretch.

State Highway 286 leads southeast out of La Paz 45 km to **San Juan de Los Planes** (*Population*: 1,350), a friendly town in a rich farming region. A fair road continues another 15 km to the beautiful **Ensenada de los Muertos**, where there is good fishing and swimming and 'wild' camping. A further 11 km is the headland of **Punta Arena de la Ventana**, with a magnificent view of the sterile slopes of Isla Cerralvo. (**LL** *Hotel Las Arenas*, resort overlooking Ventana Bay). Six kilometres before Los Planes, a graded road leads to the **Bahía de la Ventana** and the small fishing villages of La Ventana and El Sargento which have lovely beaches facing Cerralvo Island.

Excursions from La Paz

Baja California Peninsula

South of La Paz

South of La Paz and its plain, the central mountain spine rises again into the wooded heights of the Sierra de la Laguna and bulges out into the 'Cape Region', Baja's most touristically developed area. The highway winds up to El Triunfo, a picturesque village (almost a ghost town) where silver was discovered in 1862. The town exploded with a population of 10,000 and was for a while the largest town in Baja. The mines closed in 1926 but small-scale mining has resumed in places. There is a craft shop at the village entrance where young people make palm-leaf objects.

El Triunfo
Colour map 1, grid C2

Present-day miners are using arsenic in the old mine tailings; these areas are fenced & signed

Eight kilometres further on is the lovely mountain town and farming centre of **San Antonio** (gasoline, groceries, meals), which was founded in 1756 and served briefly as Baja's capital (1828-30) when Loreto was destroyed. Eight kilometres south of San Antonio was the site of Santa Ana, where silver was first discovered in 1748. It was from this vanished village that the Viceroy and Padre Junípero Serra planned the expedition to establish the chain of Franciscan missions in Alta California.

Highway 1 climbs sharply from the canyon and winds past a number of ancient mines, through the peaceful orchard-farming town of San Bartolo (groceries and meals) and down to the coastal flats around **Los Barriles**, a small town with fuel, meals and limited supplies. A number of resort hotels are situated near here along the beautiful **Bahía de Palmas** and at nearby **Buena Vista**; none is in the 'budget' class but all are popular (**AL** *Hotel Palmas de Cortés*. Nice beach location. *Víctor's* campground is clean, well-organized with all facilities; nearby is *Tío Pancho's* restaurant. Mediocre food but good atmosphere).

The Highway turns inland after Los Barriles (106 km from La Paz). An 'East Cape Loop' turns east off the Highway through La Rivera (**E** *La Rivera RV Park* in palm grove next to beach. Excellent swimming, hot showers, laundry, friendly. Recommended). A new spur leads towards **Cabo Pulmo**; it is being paved at a rapid rate and will eventually take a slightly inland route paralleling the coast to San José del Cabo. Off Cabo Pulmo, a beautiful headland, is the Northern Pacific's only living coral reef; fishing, diving and snorkelling are excellent (56 km from Los Barriles). There are many camping spots along the beautiful beaches of this coast.

Santiago
Colour map 1, grid C2
Population: 2,000

Santiago is a pleasant, historic little town 3 km off Highway 1 (bus stop at junction, two hours from La Paz). On the tree-lined main street are a Pemex station, café and stores grouped around the town plaza. One kilometre further west is the Parque Zoológico, the Cape's only zoo, modest but informative, free admission. The Jesuits built their 10th mission in Santiago in 1723 after transferring it from Los Barriles. The town was one of the sites of the Pericué Indian uprising of 1734. There are hotsprings (warm, not hot, some rubbish at site) behind a mini dam, in a pleasant setting, 12 km away along a dirt road at the foot of the mountains. Head towards the village of Aguascalientes (8 km) and the hotsprings are 4 km beyond this. You can walk on from the spring to a waterfall (**D** *Palomar*. A/c, hot showers, restaurant, bar, on main street, modest, good meals. Camping in hotel grounds US$5).

Some 3,500m south of the Santiago turn-off, Highway 1 crosses the *Tropic of Cancer*, marked by a large concrete sphere, and runs south down the fertile valley between the lofty *Sierra de la Laguna* (west) and the *Sierra Santa Clara* (east), to Los Cabos International Airport. San José del Cabo is 14 km further south.

San José del Cabo

Phone code: 114
Colour map 1, grid C1
Population: 10,000

The largest town south of La Paz and founded in 1730, San José del Cabo is now essentially a modern town divided into two districts: the very Americanized resort sectors and new Fonatur development on the beach, and the downtown zone to the north, with the government offices and many businesses grouped near the tranquil Parque Mijares. There are numerous shops and restaurants along Zaragoza and Doblado. San José also has a hospital, two service stations,

Los Cabos

Related maps:
A *San José del Cabo*,
page 721
B *Cabo San Lucas*,
page 723

auto parts and mechanical repairs. The attractive church on the Plaza Mijares was built in 1940 on the final site of the mission of 1730; a tile mosaic over the entrance depicts the murder of Padre Tamaral by rebellious Indians in 1734. Most of the top hotels are located west of San José along the beaches or nearby *estero*; the Fonatur development blocks access to much of the beach near town; best are Playas Nuevo Sol and California, about 3 km from downtown. Unofficial camping is possible on those few beaches not fronted by resort hotels.

LL *Palmilla*, one of the top resorts in Baja, 8 km west at Punta Palmilla (outstanding surfing nearby). Some a/c, showers, pool, beach, tennis, narrow access road, restaurant, bar, skin diving, fishing cruisers and skiffs for hire (daily happy hour allows mere mortals to partake of *margarita* and appetizers for US$3 and see how royalty and film stars live!) **LL** *Stouffer Presidente Los Cabos*, Blvd Mijares s/n, T20038, F20232. On lagoon south of town, a/c, all facilities, boat rentals, centrepiece of the Fonatur development at San José del Cabo. **L-AL** *Posada Real Cabo* (Best Western), next door, T20155, F20460. A/c, colour TV, showers, pool, tennis, restaurant, bar, gift shop, fishing charters. **AL** *Calinda Aquamarina-Comfort Inn*, next to *Posada Real Cabo*, T20077. US Comfort Inn chain, a/c, beach, pool, restaurant, bar, fishing, clean and comfortable. *Aston Cabo Regis Resort and Beach Club*, in hotel zone on Blvd Finisterra. A/c, colour TV, showers, kitchenettes, private balconies, pool, tennis, golf course, restaurant. **AL** *Castel Cabo*, on beach off Paseo San José south of town, T20155. A/c, another Fonatur hotel. **C** *Nuevo Sol*, on beach south of intersection of Paseo San José and Highway 1. Pool, restaurant, sports facilities, nicely landscaped, acceptable and good beachside value. **C** *San José Inn*, on last paved street north of beach. Clean, quiet, cool, comfortable, ceiling fans. Good value. **D** *Collí*, in town on Hidalgo above Budget Rent-a-Car, T20052. Fans, hot showers, 12 clean and adequate

Sleeping

Baja California Peninsula

San José del Cabo

To Airport, East Cape & La Paz

Carretera Transpeninsular

Pemex

A Obregón
Zaragoza
Manuel Doblado

Plaza

Municipal Buildings

Miguel Hidalgo

Valerio González Canseco

Blvd Antonio Mijares

Blvd Mauricio Castro

Blvd Finisterra

To La Playita

To La Playita

To Cabo San Lucas

Plaza Los Cabos

Calinda Aquamarina
Comfort Inn

Paseo San José

Posada
Real Cabo

Stouffer Presidente
Los Cabos

Estuary

Pacific Ocean

N

Not to scale

rooms. **D** *Pagamar*, Obregón between Degollado y Guerrero, 3½ blocks from plaza. Fans, café, hot showers, clean, good value. **E** *Ceci*, Zaragoza 22, 1 block west of plaza, T20051. Fans, hot showers (usually), basic but clean, excellent value, central.

Motel **D** *Brisa del Mar*, on Highway 1, 3 km southwest of town near *Hotel Nuevo Sol*. 10 rooms, restaurant, bar, pool, modest but comfortable, at rear of trailer park on outstanding beach.

Camping *Brisa del Mar Trailer Park*, 100 RV sites in fenced area by great beach. Full hook-ups, flush toilets, showers, pool, laundry, restaurant, bar, fishing trips arranged, popular, good location ('unofficial' free camping possible under *palapas* on beach). Recommended.

Transport **Air** To Los Cabos International Airport (SJD), 14 km, take a local bus, US$3, which drops you at the entrance road to the airport, leaving a 2-km walk, otherwise take a taxi. Airport to San José del Cabo in *colectivo*, US$7. Flights to Chihuahua, Ciudad Obregón, Culiacán, Guadalajara, Hermosillo, Los Mochis, Mazatlán, Mexico City, Monterrey, Puerto Vallarta. In the USA: Anchorage, Burbank, Dallas, Denver, Fort Lauderdale, Houston, Los Angeles, New York, Orange County, Phoenix, Portland, San Diego, San Francisco, Seattle, Spokane, Tucson.

Bus Bus station on Manuel Doblado opposite hospital, about 7 blocks west of Plaza. To **Cabo San Lucas** (Tres Estrellas) daily from 0700, US$1.25, 30 mins; to **La Paz** daily from 0630, US$9, 3 hrs.

Directory **Airlines** *Aero California*, T33700. *Mexicana*, T222722. *Alaska Airlines*, T95800-4260333. **Laundry** Self-service at Playa de California.

San José del Cabo to San Lucas All the beaches and coastal areas between San José del Cabo and Cabo San Lucas have become public after protests by local inhabitants against private developments. These include: *Hotel Cabo San Lucas*, *Twin Dolphin* (T30140), and *Calinda Cabo Baja-Quality Inn* (T30045), part of Cabo Bello residential development (all **LL**). At Km 25, just after the *Twin Dolphin*, a dirt road leads off to Playa Barco Varado (Shipwreck Beach), where a large ship rots on the shore. Five kilometres before Cabo a small concrete marker beside the highway heralds an excellent view of the famous cape. The Highway enters Cabo San Lucas past a Pemex station and continues as Boulevard Lázaro Cárdenas to the Zócalo (Guerrero y Madero) and the Km 0 marker.

Cabo San Lucas

Phone code: 114
Colour map 1, grid C2

Everything is quoted in US dollars and food is more American than Mexican

The resort town of Cabo San Lucas has grown rapidly in recent years from a sleepy fishing village of 1,500 inhabitants in 1970. It is now a bustling, expensive international resort with a permanent population of 8,500. There are trailer parks, many cafés and restaurants, condominiums, gift shops, discos and a marina to cater for the increasing flood of North Americans who come for the world-famous sportfishing or to find a retirement paradise. The town fronts a small harbour facing the rocky peninsula that forms the 'Land's End' of Baja California. Francisco de Ulloa first rounded and named the cape in 1539. The sheltered bay became a watering point for the treasure ships from the Orient; pirates sheltered here too. Now it is on the cruise ship itinerary. A popular attraction is the government-sponsored regional arts centre, located at the cruise liner dock. There is a Fonatur **tourist office** next to ferry landing, which has town maps.

Ringed by pounding surf, columns of fluted rock enclose **Lover's Beach** (be **Beaches** careful if walking along the beach, huge waves sweep away several visitors each year), a romantic sandy cove with views out to the seal colonies on offshore islets. At the very tip of the Cabo is the distinctive natural arch, **El Arco**; boats can be hired to see it close-up, but care is required because of the strong rips. At the harbour entrance is a pinnacle of rock, **Pelican Rock**, which is home to vast shoals of tropical fish; it is an ideal place for snorkelling and scuba diving or glass-bottomed boats may be rented at the harbour-side (45-minute harbour cruise in glass-bottomed boat to El Arco, Lover's Beach, etc US$5 per person; most hotels can arrange hire of skiffs to enable visits to the Arch and Land's End, about US$5-10 per hour).

Many firms rent aquatic equipment and arrange boating excursions, etc; the beaches east of Cabo San Lucas offer endless opportunities for swimming, scuba diving and snorkelling: **Cabo Real**, 5 km, has showers and restrooms, modest fee; **Barco Barrado** (Shipwreck Beach), 10 km, is a lovely beach.

In our **L** range *Finisterra*, perched on promontory near Land's End, T30000. A/c, TV, **Sleeping** shower, pool, steps to beach, poolside bar with unsurpassed view, restaurant, entertainment, sport-fishing cruisers. *Giggling Marlin Inn*, central on Blvd Marina y Matamoros. A/c, TV, showers, kitchenettes, jacuzzi, restaurant, bar, fishing trips arranged, lively drinking in attached cocktail bar. *Hacienda Beach Resort*, at north entrance to harbour. Some a/c, showers, pool, tennis, yacht anchorage, various water-sports, hunting, horse riding, restaurant, etc, claims the only beach safe from strong Pacific swells. *Marina Sol Condominiums*, high season 16 Oct-30 Jun, on 16 de Septiembre, between Highway 1 and Bay. Full-service hotel in 3 and 7-storey buildings. *Solmar*, T30022. The southernmost development in Baja California, a/c,

Cabo San Lucas

To San José & Airport
Old road to San José del Cabo
To Todos Santos & La Paz
Carretera Transpeninsular (Highway 1)
Narciso Mendoza
Leona Vicario
José María Morelos
Ignacio Zaragoza
A Obregón
Carranza
Revolución
20 de Noviembre
Niños Heroes
Cabo San Lucas
Hidalgo
Madero
Zócalo
Lázaro Cárdenas
Paseo del Pescador
Av Hacienda
Plaza Bonita
Marina
Playa Médano
Giggling Marlin Inn
Plaza Náutica
Hacienda Beach Resort
Bahía Cabo San Lucas
Plaza Las Glorias
US Consulate
Lover's Beach
El Arco
Land's End
Blvd Marina
Finisterra
Solmar
N
Not to scale

showers, ocean view, pool, tennis, diving, restaurant, poolside bar, fishing cruisers, beach with heavy ocean surf. **B** *Mar de Cortés*, on Highway 1 at Guerrero in town centre, T30032. A/c, showers, helpful, pool, out-door bar/restaurant, good value. **C** *Casablanca*, Revolución between Morelos y Leona Vicario. Central, ceiling fan (**D** in rooms with floor fan), hot shower, clean, but basic in cheaper rooms, quiet and friendly. **C** *Marina*, Blvd Marina y Guerrero, T30030. Central, a/c, restaurant, bar, can be noisy, pricey. **D** *Dos Mares*, Hidalgo. A/c, TV, clean, small pool, parking space. Recommended.

Motel C *Los Cabos Inn*, Abasolo y 16 de Septiembre. Central, 1 block from bus station, fans, showers, central, modest, good value. **D** *El Dorado*, Morelos (4 blocks from bus terminal). Clean, fan, hot water, private bath.

Youth hostel D Av de la Juventud s/n, T30148. Private bath, **F** per person in dormitory, not very central, but quite smart and clean.

Camping *El Arco Trailer Park*, 4 km east on Highway 1, restaurant. *El Faro Viejo Trailer Park*, 1,500m northwest at Matamoros y Morales. Shade, laundry, ice, restaurant, bar, clean, out-of-town but good. *Vagabundos del Mar*, 3,500m east on Highway 1. Pool, snack bar, laundry, good, US$15 for 2. *Cabo Cielo RV Park*, 3 km east on Highway 1. *San Vicente Trailer Park*, 3 km east on Highway 1. Same as *Cabo Cielo* plus pool, both reasonably basic, rates unknown. All have full hook-ups, toilets and showers.

Eating As alternatives to expensive restaurants, try the 2 pizza places just beyond *Mar de Cortés*, 1 next to the telephone office, the other in the block where the street ends; also *Flor Guadalajara*, Lázaro Cárdenas, on the way out of town a few blocks beyond 'Skid Row'. Good local dishes. Half a block uphill from *Hotel Dos Mares*, is *San Lucas*, Hidalgo s/n. Good food at very reasonable prices. Highly recommended. *Edith's*, 1 block from Medeno beach, evenings only, great views. *Mi Casa*, behind Plaza. *The Office Restaurant*, on Medeno beach. Good food, moderate prices, live dance show every Thu. Recommended. There is a good bakery in front of the large modern supermarket in the centre of town. The supermarket is stocked with a full range of US foodstuffs.

Transport **NB** There are no **ferries** from Cabo San Lucas to Puerto Vallarta. **Buses** Bus station at 16 de Septiembre y Zaragoza, central, few facilities. To **San José del Cabo**, 8 departures a day, US$1.25; **La Paz** 6 a day from 0630, US$8; **Tijuana** US$44, 1600 and 1800 daily via La Paz.

Directory **Communications** Post Office: Morelos y Niños Héroes.

Todos Santos

Phone code: 114
Colour map 1, grid C2
Population: 4,000

Highway 9, the western loop of the Cape Region, was not paved until 1985 and the superb beaches of the west coast have yet to suffer the development and crowding of the east. The highway branches off Route 1 just after San Pedro, 32 km south of La Paz, and runs due south through a cactus-covered plain to Todos Santos. This quiet farming town just north of the Tropic of Cancer is slowly becoming a tourist and expat centre rather than a working town. There has been a recent influx of expats from the USA and there is a community of artists and craftspeople. There is a Pemex station, cinema, stores, cafés, galleries, *artesanía* shops, a bank, market, and a Casa de la Cultura, Calle Topete y Pilar, with a museum. The Centro Cultural Siglo XXI has temporary exhibitions. Todos Santos was founded as a Jesuit mission in 1734; a church replacing the abandoned structure, built in 1840, stands opposite the Plaza Cívica on Calle Juárez. The ruins of several old sugar mills can be seen around the town in the fertile valley. Fishing is also important. There is a path to the beach, 20 minutes away through palm, mango and avocado groves. *El Tecolote*, on Juárez, has a selection of books in English, some on the region, and the US owner is helpful with essentials such as access to the Sierra de la Laguna.

Sleeping **L-AL** *Todos Santos Inn*, *Calle Legaspi*, 2 blocks north of Plaza T/F 50040; 19th-century house refurbished in that style, some *en suite* rooms, very tranquil. **B** *Hotel California*, formerly the *Misión de Todos Santos Inn*. Historic brick building near town centre, Juárez, a block north of Highway 9. Fans, showers, pool, a/c, dining room; opposite is **D** *Motel Guluarte*. Fan, fridge, shower, pool, good value. **C** *Way of Nature*, B&B, along dirt road signposted at southern end of Juárez, 2 blocks south of Hotel California. Large circular *palapa* with rooms. very quiet, **D-E** *Misión de Pilar*. Clean, good value. **E** *Miramar*, south end of village. New, with bath, hot water, fan, pool, clean, safe, parking. Recommended. Youth Hostel, **F,** along Degollado, 3 blocks up hill from park. **Camping** *El Molino Trailer Park*, off Highway at south end of town, 30 mins from beach. Full hook-ups, flush toilets, showers, laundry, American owner, very helpful, US$8 for 4. No camping here but apparently OK to use the beach (clean – but look out for dogs – see below). Several kilometres south is *Trailer Park San Pedrito* (see below), on the beach. Closed to camping, new hotel being built, full hook-ups, flush toilets, showers, pool, laundry, restaurant, bar, US$12 for RVs. Tent camping **(E)** at *Way of Nature B&B*.

Eating On main Plaza is *Café Santa Fe*. Gourmet Italian food, pricey but very highly rated restaurant. *Las Fuentes*, where main drag takes a right angle eastwards. Large portions.

Surfing Board hire at Todos Santos surf shop, Rangel and Zaragoza, US$10.50 per day, US$5.25 for body board. They have kiosk at Playa Los Cerritos beyond El Pescadero. They also hire out tents (US$5.50 per day) and mountain bikes (US$10) at the main shop.

Transport **Bus**: stop beside park on Juárez.

Directory **Banks** *Bancrecer*, doesn't change TCs, *Casa de Cambio* on Colegio Militar with Hidalgo does. **Communications** Fax from Message Centre on Hidalgo between Juárez and Centenario. **Laundry** El Zopilote, beside surf shop.

West coast beaches Two kilometres from Todos Santos is a stretch of the Pacific coast with some of the most beautiful beaches of the entire Baja California Peninsula. Nearest to the town is **Playa Punta Lobos** where the local fishermen shore up (the *pangas* come in early afternoon); it is a popular picnic spot, but with too much rubbish and too many unfriendly dogs for wild camping. Next comes Playa Las Palmas, good for swimming. Cleaner for camping is the sandy cove at **Playa San Pedrito** (4 km southeast). Backed by groves of Washingtonia fan palms and coconut palms, this is one of the loveliest wild camping spots anywhere; it is also good for surfing. Opposite the access road junction is the **Campo Experimental Forestal**, a Botanical Garden with a well-labelled array of desert plants from all regions of Baja; staff are very informative. Here too is the *Trailer Park San Pedrito* (see above), an open area on the beach and one of the most beautifully sited RV parks in Baja. Eleven kilometres south of Todos

Santos is **El Pescadero**, a fast-growing farming town with few facilities for visitors.

Seven kilometres south of El Pescadero is *Los Cerritos RV Park* on a wide sandy beach, with 50 RV or tent sites but no hook-ups, flush toilets, US$3 per vehicle. **Playa Los Cerritos** is a *playa pública*; there are several camping areas but no facilities, US$2 per vehicle. This is a good beach for both surfing and swimming. The succession of rocky coves and empty beaches continues to Colonia Plutarco Elías Calles, a tiny farming village in the midst of a patchwork of orchards. The highway parallels the coast to Rancho El Migriño, then continues south along the coastal plain; there are no more camping spots as far as Cabo San Lucas. Many now prefer the west Loop to the main highway; it is 140 km from the junction at San Pedro, thus cutting off about 50 km and up to an hour's driving time from the Transpeninsular Highway route.

Parque Nacional Sierra de la Laguna

In the rugged interior east of Todos Santos is the **Parque Nacional Sierra de la Laguna** (under threat and not officially recognized). Its crowning peak is the Picacho La Laguna (2,163m), which is beginning to attract a trickle of hikers to its 'lost world' of pine and oak trees, doves and woodpeckers, grassy meadows and luxuriant flowers; there is nothing else like it in Baja. The trail is steep but straightforward; the panoramic view takes in La Paz and both the Gulf and Pacific coasts. It gets cold at night. The park can be reached from Todos Santos by making local enquiries; three-day guided pack trips are also offered by the *Todos Santos Inn*, US$325 per person. Alternatively, take a taxi from Todos Santos to La Burrera, from where it is eight hours walk along the littered path to La Laguna.

Background

16

728

History

Pre-Colombian

The first humans arrived in Mexico some 20-25,000 years ago, having travelled from Asia across the temporary land-bridge that formed at the Bering Straits during the last Ice Age, and then migrated south overland.

First settlers

Background

These early peoples lived in small nomadic groups as hunter-gatherers, but from around 7000 BC they developed agriculture, planting and harvesting crops such as beans, avocados and fruit, but most significantly maize, which was to become their staple diet and spiritual source of life.

As farming took over from hunting, settled villages were built, fixed populations grew larger and the beginnings of a complex society were under way.

1 Pre-Classic/Formative (1400BC – 300AD)

In the midst of this scene of developing civilizations there emerged a culture – who they were or where they came from, no-one knows for sure – but the people who were known as the Olmecs became one of the most advanced cultures in Mexican prehistory, whose influence spread from the Gulf Coast into Central Mexico, and as far south as El Salvador. Material found at the important site of San Lorenzo dating from 1800 BC, confirms the Olmecs as the foundation on which all other known civilizations in Mesoamerica are based.

Olmecs

The principal achievements of the Olmecs were in creating the first permanently populated religious sites in Mesoamerica, as well as developing written hieroglyphics and a 365-day solar calendar. Their chief centres were at La Venta, San Lorenzo and Tres Zapotes, in present-day Veracruz and the neighbouring state of Tabasco. Here they built massive ceremonial pyramids and mounds, with carved stelae, statues and altars. La Venta and San Lorenzo, in particular, were powerful sacred sites. Above all, the Olmecs were superb artists and sculptors, producing tiny jade and serpentine figurines and, most intriguingly, enormous sculpted stone heads (see page 759).

However, the Olmecs declined after about 100 BC, at the end of the Formative Period. Their sacred sites had attracted many pilgrims and traders over the centuries, and the Olmecs were quick to adopt new ideas from neighbouring cultures with whom they had contact, both in war and in marriage. Gradually the symbiosis between the Olmecs and other peoples diminished their own influence and led to the emergence of other dominant cultures, including Teotihucán, the Zapotecs and, most notably, the Maya.

2 The Classic Period (200BC-900AD)

This transition led to the start of the Classic Period, which was marked by the growth of powerful urbanised empires, and the creative peak of the arts and science.

As Olmec influence was fading, 500 km or so to the west, in the Oaxaca Valley, the ceremonial centre of Monte Albán was being built. It was an impressive site

Zapotecs & Mixtecs

composed of pyramids, plazas and temples, strategically placed on a levelled hilltop overlooking the valley floor. Hieroglyphs carved into the stonework here are evidence of some of the earliest texts found in the region, as well as glyphs representing the 52-year cycle, known as the Calendar Round, used as the standard system throughout the Mesoamerican world (see page 757). The Zapotec people had occupied the site since its construction, and remained there throughout the Classic Period, during which time architectural influence from the Teotihuacán culture was apparent. After about AD 500 however, the site fell into decline, and in its later years was occupied by the Mixtec culture, which had merged with the Zapotecs by the time of the Spanish conquest.

Teotihuacán The Classic Period reached its crowning glory with the construction of the great planned city of Teotihuacán, near present-day Mexico City, in the Valley of Mexico, described by Michael D. Coe (Professor of Anthropology at Yale University and author of many books on the pre-Columbian cultures) as the "most important site in the whole of Mexico".

Teotihuacan was also the largest city in the pre-Columbian New World, covering more than 8 square miles (21 sq km), with a population of up to 200,000, which, by AD 600, made it the sixth largest city in the world. The dominant constructions at Teotihuacán are the Pyramids of the Sun and the Moon, overlooking the enormous Avenue of the Dead. The site is also filled with finely constructed temples, palaces and residential compounds. Besides their superb architecture, the Teotihuacán culture were also highly skilled artists, producing many beautiful murals, ceramics, and sculptures.

How Teotihuacán grew to be such a powerful and prosperous city remains largely a mystery. Examples of Teotihuacán-style artefacts have been found as far afield as Tikal and Kaminaljuyú in Guatemala, and to the NW at Chametla near present-day Mazatlán, some 1,400 km from Teotihuacán, evidence that it must have benefited from long-distance trade links.

Nevertheless, after thriving for almost 1,000 years, the culture dramatically collapsed around AD 600. The centre of the city was destroyed around AD 700, after which time all evidence of their regional influence suddenly disappeared. The invaders may have been the Totonac culture from Veracruz, or possibly the Totomí, a semi-barbaric culture from the north of Mexico.

Maya At around the same time that the Olmec and Teotihuacán civilizations were making their dramatic stage exits in the early Classic, the Maya were reaching the peak of their own magnificent dynasty. Although the heart of their culture lay outside of Mexico, the inclusion of the Mayas in this history is a reflection of the enormous influence they had throughout much of the country during and long after their days in power.

Maya-speaking people are thought to have inhabited a wide band of territory encompassing El Salvador, Guatemala, most of southeast Mexico and parts of western Honduras. As with other early Mexican cultures, the origins of the Maya is unknown, but remains of early fishing and hunting groups has been found in their westernmost territory, dating from 3000-2000 BC.

The Maya came into contact with the advanced pre-Classic cultures, particularly the Olmecs and Teotihuacán, from whom they learnt new skills and ideas. Agricultural developments allowed the growth of larger cities, especially around the Maya Lowlands of Guatemala, which became their heartland and the site of some of their greatest ceremonial centres: Tikal, Kaminaljuyú and El Mirador. The chief Maya sites in Mexico were Chichén Itzá in the Yucatán, as well as Palenque and Bonampak in Chiapas.

The architectural achievements of the Maya were exemplified in the superb temples, palaces and pyramids of their urban capitals. Again, they learnt from their predecessors, emulating Teotihuacán, for instance, in the massive scale of their most important constructions. All these buildings were decorated with highly artistic sculptures, murals, and glyphs.

Mayan society became increasingly hierarchical as their cities grew larger, with power concentrated in the hands of a hereditary elite. By the end of the Classic at the peak of the Maya civilization, there may have been as many as 14 million citizens living in the Maya heartland, with powerful urban centres across Mesoamerica, from Copán in Honduras, through Guatemala, Belize and to the Yucatán Peninsula. These centres never united into an organized empire however. Each was a separate city-state which, while sharing a common cultural background with its neighbour, was also often antagonistic, competing for power and status.

How did the Maya become such an advanced civilization? Their interaction with other Mesoamerican cultures – and probably with seafarers from South America – could quite easily have stimulated their growth. Theories of transatlantic contacts have long been proposed, but to date not one item made in the Old World has ever been found in a Mesoamerican site. However, many fascinating cultural similarities between Asian and Mayan cultures have been pointed out, including symbols used in both cultures' calendars. This is not to suggest that Old World cultures were at the roots of the New World civilizations, but some of the New World cultures may have come into contact with peoples from the East and from whom they could have adopted selective ideas.

Around AD 900, disaster struck, causing the abandonment of all the Mayan ceremonial centres. The cause of this sudden collapse, described by Michael Coe as "one of the most profound social and demographic catastrophes of all human history", remains unknown. Theories include famine brought on by drought, internal uprising, and massacre by invading foreign tribes. Whatever the truth, the downfall of the Maya marked the end of the Classic, and with it the end of the era of great imperial urban cultures in Mexico.

3 Post-Classic (AD900-1519)

The collapse of the Maya in southern Mexico was matched by the spectacular rise of new powers from the north, first among which were the Toltecs. The cultural standards reached by the Maya and the Olmecs in the Classic were never to be surpassed in this new era. Instead, a phase of military aggression and authoritarianism was beginning, which would reach its own tumultuous peak with the arrival of the Spanish conquistadors.

Huastecs

The peoples of the northeast coastal fringe of Mesoamerica, to the north of Veracruz and eastern San Luis Potosí, blossomed later than neighbouring cultures to the south and west, but they left a significant impression nevertheless. Originating from the Gulf Coast region to the north of the city of Veracruz, the Huasteca people were probably closely related to the earliest Mayas during the pre-Classic period, but after about 1500BC, their paths separated. The Huastecs produced some fine ceramics and painted murals, and built both large and small ceremonial centres (including Tamuin, near San Luis Potosí).

The most important site in the Veracruz area, however, was El Tajín, a large ceremonial centre, some 5 miles SW of Papantla, built during the early Classic period. The dominant building at El Tajín is the Pyramid of the Niches which, for its elaborate decoration and numerous niches (365 in total), ranks as one of the finest pieces of pre-Columbian architecture in all Mesoamerica. The construction of El Tajín reached its peak in the late Classic period, and included massive stone temples and at least 11 impressive ball courts (this was one of the founding regions of the cult 'sport' – see page 757).

The Huastecs later came into contact with the Aztecs, but despite some of their southern region falling to Aztec control, they mostly retained their own independence. Late successors to the Huastecs in the Veracruz region were the Totonacs, who arrived after the abandonment of El Tajín, in the 13th century, and who built their centres in Remojadas and El Zapotal.

Toltecs The Toltecs were originally a mixture of tribes dominated by Nahua-speaking Toltec-Chichimecas, from western Mexico, combined with the Nonoalca people from the Puebla and Gulf Coast regions. These early descendants had peacefully farmed the fringes of western and northern Mexico since ancient times, but by the post-Classic era they had been driven south by drought and starvation.

After AD 900 the Toltecs formed their capital, Tula (aka Tollan), in the state of Hidalgo, about 50 miles NW of Mexico City, under the leadership of a king named Topiltzin. Their characteristic feature was professional warmongering, glorifying militarism in mass rituals such as blood-letting, animal and human sacrifice, and the gruesome construction of *tzompantli* (racks of skulls), as a public display of their victims' heads.

Tula was the centre of the Toltec culture, which rose to dominate the whole of central Mexico, in northern and western Mexico almost as far as the border with New Mexico, and south through the Yucatán Peninsula, and even into parts of the Guatemalan highlands.

Topiltzin was driven out of Tula around AD 987, following an internal conflict. He invaded and conquered Chichén Itzá, followed by the rest of the Yucatán Mayan sites, eventually creating an alternative domain to the one he had lost at Tula. Toltec-style architecture was adopted in Chichén Itzá, but there is evidence of Toltec-Maya influence in the Yucatán long before the arrival of Topiltzin.

The Toltecs plunged into decline in the second half of the 12th century. Severe droughts provoked feuds between factions of the original Toltec-Chichimeca and Nonoalca tribes. The last Toltec ruler, Huemac moved the capital to Chapultepec (in the west of Mexico City), but failing to pacify the uprisings, he committed suicide. Some of the Toltec-Chichimecas stayed on at Tula for a few years, but others drifted south, even as far as Guatemala, where they clung to their memories of Tula's days of glory.

Independent states Post-Classic Mexico also saw the continuation of various independent states, who had resisted overthrow by the imperial civilizations, and who subsequently managed to hold back the Aztecs. Foremost among these states were the Mixtecs, from the Oaxaca region in SW Mexico, who united with the neighbouring Zapotecs to repel the invading Aztecs. They were a highly artistic people, renown as the finest craftsmen of gold artefacts and turquoise mosaics ever seen in Mexico, much of whose work has been uncovered in the earlier Zapotec site of Monte Albán.

The Tarascans, centred around Lake Pátzcuaro in western Mexico, were another redoubtable people who resisted the Aztecs, despite being eventually surrounded by their territory on all sides. They were highly accomplished artisans, in precious metals and stones and, with the finely cut stone pyramids of their capital, Tzintzuntzan, the Tarascans also showed their considerable skills as architects.

Aztecs The Aztec people were Nahuatl-speakers from the northwest of Mexico, from where they migrated to the Valley of Mexico during the 12th and 13th centuries AD. Here they conquered the Chichimeca people, who were living in relative peace, following the violent collapse of the Toltec Empire.

The Aztecs were first and foremost a supremely efficient military force, rapidly expanding their territory, extracting tribute and victims for human sacrifice as they went. They were also highly adept at adopting the artistic skills and styles of their conquered foes, and produced some fine works of art and architecture.

In 1344-45, they built their capital, Tenochtitlán, on an island in the middle of Lake Texcoco. The scale of this magnificent city, which at the time of the conquest may have been occupied by as many as 300,000 inhabitants, can be appreciated by the comparison with the contemporary London of King Henry VIII, which was only one-fifth the size.

By the late 1400s the Aztecs found themselves the most powerful state in the whole country. Not only that, but their ruler, Tlacaecel, rewrote the history books to declare the Aztecs as the chosen race, who would keep the sun moving through the sky, maintaining the Toltec mythology.

Following this declaration of divine destiny, the Aztecs began a wave of military conquests that expanded their borders across most of central Mexico and south as far as Guatemala, creating an empire to equal or surpass that of the Toltecs themselves.

The Aztec leader who presided over the boom period of their empire was Ahuitzotl (1486-1502), a dynamic and resourceful man. His successor was Motecuhzoma Xocoytozin (1502-1520). Motecuhzoma had the misfortune to come to power at the momentous time in history when the Spanish conquistadors arrived on Mexican soil. The dramatic ease with which these invaders overthrew the mighty Aztec Empire was partly explained by the mythical interpretations made of these bearded white-skinned foreigners. According to Toltec legends, the cult figure Quezalocoatl himself would return from the east and destroy the Mexicans, a theory which the Spanish were quick to propagate to help them win over their new subjects.

Spanish Conquest

Following Columbus' voyages of 1492-1504 the Spanish focussed their attention on the Caribbean islands but were disappointed by the lack of gold and silver. In 1517 the demand for labour to replace the indigenous population, killed off by disease and ill-treatment, led Diego Velázquez, Governor of Cuba, to send out an expedition which reached the Yucatán coast. The following year Velázquez commissioned Hernán Cortés to explore and conquer this new land. After landing on the island of Cozumel, Cortés founded the settlement of Veracruz and moved inland.

Reports reached Cortés of the powerful and wealthy Aztec Empire of Moctezuma, with its capital at Tenochtitlán, on an island on Lake Texcoco in the Valley of Mexico, nearly 400 km inland. To discourage desertion among his men Cortés destroyed his boats and marched inland making contact with the Tlaxcalans, traditional opponents of Moctezuma. Reaching Tenochtitlán Cortés was treated hospitably, but hearing rumours that the Aztecs were planning to massacre the Spaniards, he kidnapped Moctezuma. Relations between Aztecs and Spaniards worsened and Moctezuma was killed as he attempted to call off an attack by a much larger Aztec army. Under cover of night the Spanish broke out of the city, using portable bridges to cross the causeways. With support from the Tlaxcalans, Cortés led a large force, equipped with heavy cannons and boats, back to storm the Aztec capital in a battle which lasted several weeks. By the end of the battle in April 1521, the citys' fine buildings had been systematically destroyed by the Spanish to prevent the Aztecs using them as cover. The Spanish victory, the result of their superior weapons and armour, their use of horses, the spread of smallpox among the Aztecs and the support of the Tlaxcalans, gave the invaders control of Central Mexico and Cortés ordered the building of a new city on the site of Tenochtitlán. In the following decade expeditions were sent into the surrounding areas to conquer the other indigenous peoples throughout present-day Mexico and also further south in Central America.

Background

Colonial Period

As elsewhere in the Americas, the Spanish conquest of New Spain was carried out by soldiers of fortune who operated with permission of the Crown but outside its control. This led to tension between the Crown and the conquerors, due to the Crown's fear of the rise of powerful rivals which wanted to secure its share of the new territories' wealth. Accused of corruption and misuse of royal funds, Cortés returned to Spain to present his case to the Spanish monarch Carlos V; though the charges were dismissed and he was granted the title of Marqués de Oaxaca, Cortés was deprived of power by the appointment of a Viceroy to govern the territory on behalf of the monarch.

New Spain became one of the two great centres of the Spanish American Empire and of Spanish settlement, the other being Peru. Like Peru, it was attractive due to the discovery of precious metals and the availability of a large indigenous labour force, without which the wealth of the colonies could not be exploited by the small group of European settlers. Immediately after the conquest the key to controlling the natives was *encomienda*: under this system native villages and their inhabitants came under the control of an *encomendero*; in return for paying tribute and providing labour, the Indians were placed in the care of the *encomendero* who was supposed to ensure order and supervise their conversion to Christianity. Although many of Cortés' supporters had been granted *encomiendas*, this practice was opposed by the Crown which feared the growth of a powerful hereditary aristocracy, similar to that which had caused Carlos V so much difficulty in Spain. Throughout the colonial period an important role was played by the Church, which supported the Crown, providing schools and hospitals, establishing missions and working to convert the Indians. The latter role brought the missionaries into conflict with the *encomenderos* who wanted control over the Indians as a labour force. In 1542 the Crown issued the New Laws, which restricted the continuance of the *encomienda* system, but these restrictions were not enforced until the 1560s, when they provoked a revolt led by Martín Cortés, the conquistador's son, which was quickly suppressed.

By 1650 the Viceroyalty of New Spain included much of Central America, the Spanish Caribbean islands as well as northwards into California and New Mexico. Although the Viceroy possessed enormous powers, these were restricted in several ways: the Viceroyalty was subdivided into *audiencias*, administered by judges; the Crown sent *visitadores* to carry out inspections and at the end of an official's term a royal investigation occurred. At the local level each municipality was governed by the *Cabildo*, or town council; though initially elected, seats on it were later sold by the Crown.

The conquest devastated the indigenous population. Disease, harsh treatment (especially in the mines), and the disruption of traditional ways of life and belief systems all contributed to the decline of the native population of Central Mexico from an estimated 25 million in 1519 to around one million in 1650, after which a slow increase began. Miscegenation was widespread and a complex hierarchy of racial mixtures between the white, Indian and black African populations was established.

The economy was transformed by the discovery of large deposits of silver in the 1540s, which stimulated trade within the colony. By the 1650s the Bajío, the basins of Guanajuato and Jalisco, had become major grain-producing areas. Trade with Spain was hindered by distance and the danger of pirates; the defence against the latter, the organisation of an annual fleet protected by warships, restricted trade and provided opportunities for smugglers to evade Spanish commercial restrictions. By the 18th century the economy had received a further boost with new discoveries of silver and the reduction of import controls on mercury, used in silver-processing.

Along with the rest of Spanish America, the colony was affected by the decline of Spain in the 17th century: unable to produce the manufactured goods required in her colonies, Spain was forced to spend the wealth from the 'New World' on articles manufactured in northern Europe. Some improvement, however, took place in the 18th century and particularly during the reign of Carlos III (1759-1788). Attempts were made to improve colonial administration, the sale of government offices was ended and Creoles (whites born in the Americas) were replaced in the administration by Peninsulares (native-born Spaniards) since the latter were seen as being less corrupt. The administrative system was also reformed: New Spain was divided into 12 Intendencies, each headed by an Intendant appointed by the Viceroy. In 1767 the Jesuit order, considered too powerful, was expelled from Spain and the colonies, a move which led to rioting in New Spain. Restrictions on trade between the colonies were lifted and colonial defences were improved by the recruitment of regiments from the colonial population. To increase revenue, government monopolies were established over tobacco and mercury and new taxes were introduced on a range of goods.

While these changes benefited Spain, they alienated many Creoles. Further tensions were created by the growth of commercial agriculture in the Bajío which led to the expansion of haciendas at the expense of traditional farming communities. Despite these grievances, however, it was developments in Europe which would eventually produce the opportunity for Independence.

Independence

Spanish involvement in the European wars which followed the French Revolution of 1789 affected New Spain, its wealthiest colony, in several ways: Madrid attempted to meet the expenses of war by increasing taxes, eventually, in 1804 ordering the seizure and auction of non-essential Church property: since the Church operated as the colony's main banker and most of the wealthy owed it money, this threatened ruin. Napoleon's invasion of Spain in 1808 and replacement of King Ferdinand VII with his own brother, Joseph, provoked a crisis throughout Spanish America: did legitimate authority now lie with Joseph Bonaparte, with the Spanish resistance parliament in Cadíz, or with the Viceroy?

While this situation produced wars throughout Spanish America between those supporting Independence and those opposed, New Spain followed a very different route to Independence. On 16 October 1810 Miguel Hidalgo, parish priest in the town of Dolores, issued a call for Independence; the failure of his ally, Colonel Ignacio Allende, to rally local army units made Hidalgo dependent on the large mob of rural workers who rallied to his cause. After pillaging San Miguel and Celaya, the mob sacked the wealthy silver-town of Guanajuato. The insurgents seized several other towns before finally being defeated at Puente de Calderón, near Guadalajara; most of Hidalgo's troops deserted. Hidalgo and Allende were captured and taken to Chihuahua, where they were executed; their heads were hung on public display as a warning until 1821. After Hidalgo's death the insurrection continued, initially under the leadership of José María Morelos, another priest, though he was captured and executed in 1815.

Crucial to the failure of Hidalgo's rebellion were the fears of the Creoles: though many resented aspects of Spanish rule, Hidalgo's revolt raised the spectre of an Indian revolt in which they, as well as the Peninsulares, would be the victims. The situation was, however, transformed by events in Spain, where in 1820 a military revolt forced Ferdinand VII to adopt a constitution and convene a parliament. Hostile to the more liberal government in Madrid, Creole leaders backed General Augustín de Iturbide in putting forward a manifesto, the Plan de Iguala. This proposed Independence but with three guarantees to reassure the Peninsulares: a

Antonio López de Santa Anna

Many tales surround Santa Anna who occupied the Presidency no fewer than 11 times between 1833 and 1855. His taste for ostentation led to the furnishing of the presidential palace with European furniture. Orders were given for him to be styled 'His Most Serene Highness' instead of the usual 'His Excellency'; statues were erected and banquets were staged in his honour, and his arrival was announced by a 21 gun salute. The most bizarre incident, however, dates from 1842 when his left leg, amputated in 1838 after being smashed in a battle with a French army at Veracruz, was disinterred, paraded through the capital and placed in an urn on a huge stone pillar at a ceremony attended by high government officials.

Yet it would be wrong to see Santa Anna merely as a comic opera figure. With his lack of scruples and his use of political office for personal wealth, he set standards of political corruption which were followed by lesser officials. Moreover, his disastrous handling of the Texan issue contributed to war with the United States and the loss of over half the national territory.

European prince was to be found for the throne; Catholicism was to be the state religion and there was to be equality of Creoles and Spaniards. With Madrid unable to send troops due to unrest in the army, Independence was recognized by the Viceroy.

The 19th century

Independence did not, however, produce prosperity or political stability. The new government inherited large debts and an economy devastated by war. In 1822, with European princes understandably reluctant to accept the throne, Iturbide crowned himself emperor; when he was deposed a year later, Mexico became a federal republic with an elected president and Congress. During the years which followed, governments succeeded one another with bewildering frequency as rival leaders backed by irregular armies competed for power.

The dominant figure during this period was Antonio López de Santa Anna, a Creole army officer who became a national hero in 1829 by leading the Mexican army which repelled a Spanish invasion at Tampico. Elected president in 1833, Santa Anna tired of everyday politics and retired to his hacienda, leaving the vice-president, Gómez Farías to run the country. When the latter introduced controls on the church and reduced the size of the army, Santa Anna overthrew him and replaced the 1824 constitution, extending the presidential term from four-eight years and increasing the power of the central government over the states. This provoked conflict with the northern state of Texas, where settlers from the United States resisted. In 1835 Santa Anna led 6,000 troops into Texas in a campaign celebrated for the Battle of the Alamo. An old Franciscan mission outside San Antonio, the Alamo was defended by Texans including Davy Crockett and Jim Bowie: The mission was stormed and all the defenders killed. A few weeks later the Mexican army was defeated by Sam Houston at San Jacinto and Santa Anna was taken prisoner. After securing his release by signing a treaty agreeing to Texan independence, he returned to the capital where he denounced the treaty as extracted under compulsion. With Texas's independent status therefore not recognized by Mexico, the vote of the United States Congress in 1845 to annex Texas led to war in 1846. Within months US forces, their artillery proving too much for their opponents, had captured northern Mexico. In 1847 American troops seized Veracruz and occupied the capital. Peace talks resulted in the Treaty of Guadalupe Hidalgo, under which Mexico lost 55 per cent of her territory, including the present

Benito Juárez

One of the most famous political figures of 19th-century Mexico, Benito Juárez is celebrated as a symbol of Mexican nationalism and resistance to foreign intervention. The son of Zapotec Indian parents who died before he reached the age of four, Juárez worked in the countryside until the age of 12 when he moved to Oaxaca where he was educated by the Jesuits. Rejecting the priesthood, he became a lawyer and entered politics, being elected to the Oaxaca City Council and the Mexican Congress. Exiled by Santa Anna in 1853, he moved to New Orleans where he met other opponents of Santa Anna and made a living by making cigars. With the overthrow of Santa Anna in 1855, Juárez became Minister of Justice. As President of the Supreme Court from 1857, he was constitutionally first in succession to President Comonfort who was overthrown by a military revolt in 1858. He escaped to Guanajuato and subsequently to Guadalajara where he was captured by the Conservatives and narrowly escaped execution. Released, he made his way to Veracruz where he established a Liberal government which decreed the separation of church and state, seized church property and established civil marriage and civil registration of births and deaths.

Following the defeat of the Conservatives in 1860, Juárez was elected President in his own right, but was soon forced to flee by the invading French forces. With Maximilian established as emperor in Mexico City, Juárez established a government in El Paso del Norte on the United States frontier (now Ciudad Juárez). The defeat of Maximilian enabled Juárez to return to the capital. After the experience of civil war and foreign intervention he attempted to strengthen the presidency but this aroused opposition from many fellow Liberals. Re-elected President in 1867 and again in 1871, he resorted to extraordinary powers to maintain order and by the time of his death in 1872 he had become a controversial figure, seen by some as the embodiment of national independence and by others as increasingly dictatorial and arrogant in his use of presidential office.

Background

US states of Arizona, California, Colorado, Nevada, New Mexico and Utah in addition to Texas.

Santa Anna returned to the presidency in 1853 and promptly sold another strip of territory to the United States for US$10 million, before being overthrown in 1855 by a group of liberal leaders who launched a programme of reforms including the Ley Juárez, which reduced the privileges of the church and the army, and the Ley Lerdo, which ordered the sale of property held by the church and Indian communities. Opposition from the army and the Church, which threatened to excommunicate anyone swearing allegiance to the 1857 Constitution, led to a military coup and the resignation of President Comonfort. For the next three years civil war raged between the Conservatives, based in the capital, and the Liberals, led by Benito Juárez and based in Veracruz. In December 1860 the Liberals won a decisive victory, after which Juárez was elected President. With the economy ruined, Juárez proclaimed a two-year moratorium on payments of the foreign debt. This led to a joint military occupation of Mexican ports by the creditor powers, Britain, France and Spain, which proved to be a cover for a French invasion. With the French occupying Mexico City, Juárez was forced to retreat north again in 1863, and the following year the Austrian Archduke Maximilian arrived to take the throne offered by a group of Mexican conservatives. Within three years Maximilian was dead, executed by firing squad on the orders of Juárez: abandoned by the French armies who were needed in Europe, he had alienated Mexican conservatives by refusing to return church lands or declare Catholicism the state religion. Returning once again to Mexico City, Juárez was re-elected President in 1867 and 1871, but died shortly afterwards.

Emiliano Zapata

A peasant guerrilla leader from Morelos, Zapata has become the most famous symbol of the Mexican revolution and a symbol of the struggle for social justice. Born in 1879 in the village of Anenecuilco in Morelos, one of the 10 children of a peasant family, Zapata received little formal schooling but he did learn to read and write. He was soon involved in the local land disputes and in 1909 was elected president of Anenecuilco village council. In March 1911, responding to Madero's call for resistance to Porfirio Díaz, he formed a guerrilla band; in May they captured Cuautla, some 80 km south of Mexico City, a move which helped overthrow Díaz. However Zapata soon clashed with Madero and the latter's allies among the landowners of Morelos and by June 1911 the Mexico City press was attacking him as the 'Atilla of the South'. Madero sent federal troops under General Huerta to Morelos, but Zapata retreated into the mountains where he issued the Plan of Ayala, which called for the return of lands stolen by hacienda owners, the expropriation of one third of all hacienda holdings and their distribution to landless villages. As the conflict spread in 1912-13

Zapata's support spread outside Morelos into neighbouring states; in November 1914 his forces occupied Mexico City. After a meeting with his ally Pancho Villa, Zapata returned to Morelos, leaving his troops in control of the capital; in Morelos he began to redistribute land. In 1915 the defeat of Villa's troops and the expulsion of Zapata's forces from the capital was followed by the invasion of Morelos by forces loyal to Carranza. Zapata retreated again to the mountains but this time his ability to conduct a guerrilla campaign was weakened by defections and internal conflict. Like so many leaders of the revolution Zapata died violently, being tricked by President Carranza into an ambush at Chinameca in April 1919.

Zapata's death removed Carranza's most implacable opponent but Zapata's name lived on as a symbol of social justice. Many believed that Zapata did not die at Chinameca; a double had been sent to the fatal meeting and Zapata went into hiding in the mountains, to return when needed by the peasantry. His symbolic importance is shown by the use of his name by the Zapatista National Liberation Front.

From 1876 to 1911 Mexican politics were dominated by Porfirio Díaz who was President for the entire period except for 1880-1884. The *Porfiriato*, as it is known, was a period of rapid economic growth, much of it financed by foreign capital. Foreign companies built 15,000 miles of railroads, enabling Mexican goods to be exported and lands farmed by peasants to be seized and used for commercial crops. This was accompanied by a rapid growth in mining and manufacturing, based around the northern city of Monterrey. These changes led to the growth of a large middle class, but the fruits of economic growth were badly distributed. Peasants were hit particularly hard, often losing access to land farmed by their families for generations: by 1910 half of all peasants had become sharecroppers or wage labourers working on giant haciendas, such as those of Luis Terrazas who owned over seven million acres of land. Some estimate that by 1910 US citizens owned over 20 per cent of the country's land. This economic and social change was accompanied by political repression as elections were carefully controlled, the press censored and the army used to maintain order.

Mexican Revolution

Modern Mexican history is dominated by the legacy of the Revolution, a bloody upheaval between 1910 and 1917 which led to the deaths of nearly two million people, 1 in 8 of the population. In 1910 Díaz, aged 80, stood for re-election and was challenged by Francisco Madero, a northern landowner who ran under the slogan 'Effective Suffrage, No Re-election'. Defeated, Madero fled to the United States, from where he contacted other opposition groups before issuing the Plan de San Luis Potosí and calling for revolt. As rebellion spread throughout the country, Pascual Orozco seized Ciudad Juárez, which became the rebel capital and, in May 1911, Díaz resigned.

Though Madero became President in November 1911, he faced an impossible situation, between the supporters of Díaz who dominated the army, and radicals such as Orozco, Pancho Villa and Emiliano Zapata, who demanded land and labour reform. By February, 1913, Mexico was in chaos as rival groups revolted: after ten days street fighting in the capital, Madero was betrayed by one of his generals, Victoriano Huerta, and murdered. Huerta took over as president but he faced three main opponents: Zapata's peasant army from Morelos, Pancho Villa's peasant and worker forces from the north, and the troops of Venustiano Carranza, a reformer and landowner from Sonora. The three formed the Constitutional coalition, but it was Villa's Division of the North which defeated Huerta's forces in a series of battles and he was forced to resign in July 1914.

At a convention held in Aguascalientes in October 1914, the Constitutionalists split and war broke out between Carranza's supporters and the radicals who backed Zapata and Villa. Villa was defeated by Carrancista general Alvaro Obregón and was forced to retreat to Chihuahua where he carried on a guerrilla struggle until 1920. Carranza called a Congress of his supporters which met at Querétaro in November 1916 and which produced the 1917 Constitution. The key features of this included a commitment to agrarian reform, social protection for workers and hostility to the Church. Carranza was then elected president but as he met opposition from supporters of Villa and Zapata he turned for allies among the pre-revolutionary elite, to some of whom he returned lands which had been seized.

Mexico since the Revolution

Although the most violent period of the Revolution came to an end in 1917, political violence persisted and political life continued to be dominated by the leading Carrancista officers. In 1920 Carranza was assassinated after attempting to engineer the presidential victory of one of his supporters. His successor was Alvaro Obregón, who survived a full four years in office before handing over to Plutarco Elías Calles in 1924 but who was assassinated in 1928 after winning re-election. Calles was able to govern from behind the scenes during the three interim presidencies between 1928 and 1934. Under Calles the government came into conflict with the Church as it attempted to implement the anticlerical aspects of the Constitution; the Cristero Rebellion cost some 90,000 lives before it was ended by negotiation. The most important of Calles' initiatives was, however, the creation of a political party, the Partido Nacional Revolucionario (PNR) which, despite several name changes, has controlled the Mexican government since.

Though handpicked for the presidency by Calles in 1934, Lázaro Cárdenas isolated his patron to prevent his continuing influence. Cárdenas was to become the most popular Mexican president of the 20th century, remembered in particular for two policies, agrarian reform and oil nationalisation. During Cárdenas' six-year term 49 million acres of land were redistributed, twice as much as under all his post-Revolutionary predecessors combined. By 1940 one third of all Mexicans had received land, most of it in communal *ejidos* rather than as individual holdings. The nationalisation of all foreign-owned petroleum companies in March 1938, following years of disputes between workers and management, made Cárdenas a national hero, though it temporarily soured relations with the United States.

Background

The Partido Revolucionario Institucional (PRI)

Until its defeat in July 2000, modern Mexican politics had been dominated by the PRI, which had governed uninterruptedly since its creation as the Partido Revolucionario Nacional by Plutarco Elias Calles in 1929. Founded to unite the victors of the Revolution and composed of military leaders, pro-government labour and peasant leaders, and regional political bosses, it became a forum for resolving disputes and settling the crucial question of the presidential succession without resorting to violence. Between 1929 and the 1980s its dominance was so complete, that it controlled the presidency, most Congressional seats and all state governorships. Until the 1960s its presidential candidates regularly received over 90% of the vote and it polled over 80% of the vote in Congressional elections. From the 1960s, however, and especially after 1976, when the right-wing Partido de Acción Nacional's (PAN) refusal to run led to the embarrassing spectacle of a presidential election without any real opposition, attempts were made to encourage a limited role for opposition parties. In 1977 and in 1986 the electoral law was altered to guarantee opposition parties a percentage of Congressional seats.

The PRI domination was not merely due to fraud and corruption, as was often claimed. Almost inseparable from the government, the party was able to use the resources of the latter to secure support by offering jobs, services and other favours. Opponents were frequently co-opted with offers of favours and the press was influenced by its reliance on government advertising.

The rise of other parties in the 1980s,

however, highlighted some of the difficulties facing the PRI. As Mexican society became more urban and educated and embraced consumerism, it became more difficult to retain the old loyalties and the party was forced to rely on more blatantly fraudulent practices, such as overturning opposition victories in state governor elections. The adoption of a more liberal economic model to deal with the crisis of the 1980s also affected the party: as state industries were sold off, there were fewer jobs and contracts to offer in return for support. Since economic liberalisation was largely the work of the new type of PRI leader who emerged in the 1980s, namely gifted and highly trained specialists often educated in US business schools, opposition to economic and political change increased among the old-style PRI leaders, themselves veterans of years of party work and often labelled the 'dinosaurs'. The potentially violent consequences of this conflict were illustrated in 1994 by the assassination in mysterious circumstances of the party's presidential candidate, Luis Donaldo Colosio.

The party's ability to come to terms with its new role in opposition may depend on the outcome of such internal conflicts. Some observers suggest that defeat may strengthen the hand of the 'dinosaurs', who will point the finger of blame for the party's defeat at the modernisers for embracing economic reform and political liberalisation. How successful they are in this may, however, depend on whether the party's traditional supporters respond to the lead provided by the 'dinosaurs' or whether, faced with the loss of the benefits of power, they desert the party and switch

Since the Cárdenas years, Mexican governments have focussed on encouraging industrialisation. Manuel Avila Camacho, who succeeded Cárdenas, was a moderate Catholic who moved away from social reform and who encouraged foreign investment to stimulate industrial growth. The succeeding administrations of Miguel Alemán (1946-1952) and Adolfo Ruíz Cortines (1952-1958) continued these policies but under Adolfo López Mateos (1958-1964) there was a move back to agrarian reform, though this time in favour of individual holdings; welfare reform and rural education were promoted. The political calm of the previous administrations was broken under the presidency of Gustavo Díaz Ordaz (1964-1970). Demands for a liberalisation of the political system were rejected and several election victories by the opposition Partido Acción Nacional (PAN) were annulled. The most serious crisis came in 1968 in the run up to the Mexico City Olympics: on 2 October security forces opened fire, killing hundreds of students and bystanders at a protest in Tlatelolco in the capital.

Luis Echeverría, who succeeded Díaz Ordaz in 1970, tried to offset the political unrest caused by these events by emphasising economic nationalism and increased state involvement in social welfare and rural development, policies which involved the most rapid expansion in the state sector since the Revolution. By the end of his presidency these policies, combined with the worldwide inflation of the early 1970s, had contributed to an economic crisis which led to a 60 per cent devaluation of the peso in September 1976 followed by another of forty per cent a month later.

José López Portillo, who became president in 1976, began with the disadvantage of having been Echevarría's Finance Minister. Large oil discoveries mainly in the southern states of Tabasco and Chiapas and offshore in the Gulf of Mexico dated from the Echeverría administration, but under López Portillo oil production steadily increased and by 1981 Mexico was the world's fourth largest producer. This new wealth was not, however, to provide a solution to the country's problems which included a rapidly increasing urban population and rising unemployment. Increased government spending on public works, welfare schemes and subsidies on consumer goods were financed partly by international borrowing. A slump in world oil prices and an increase in global interest rates led to an economic crisis in early 1982: the peso was devalued, its rate against the dollar dropping from 26 to 100. In September 1982, in the dying months of his presidency, López Portillo nationalised the banks, a move which did little to hide his legacy of the country's worst economic crisis of the century.

Under his successor, Miguel de la Madrid (1982-1988), the depth of this crisis became apparent. Mexico was forced to re-negotiate its foreign debt, accepting severe cuts in government spending, which included sacking 51,000 federal employees and reducing the salaries of others. Nevertheless the peso continued to decline, especially after another drop in oil prices from 1986, falling against the dollar to 950 in January 1987 and 2,300 by December 1987. In 1987 the annual inflation rate was officially 159 per cent and by the end of de la Madrid's presidency Mexico's foreign debts was US$105 billion. In September 1985, in the middle of these economic disasters, an earthquake destroyed parts of the centre of the capital, leaving at least 8,000 people dead. However, de la Madrid's presidency had marked important changes in economic policy, with his Finance Minister, Carlos Salinas de Gortari, introducing cuts in state spending and selling state industries.

Against this background, opposition to the PRI grew in strength in the 1980s. While the PAN drew increased support in the north, conflict within the PRI led to the defection of Cuauhtémoc Cárdenas, son of Lázaro Cardenas, whose presidential ambitions were blocked by the party leaders. In 1988 Cárdenas ran for the presidency on behalf of the Frente Democrático Nacional, a coalition of leftist parties. In a shock result the PRI candidate, Salinas de Gortari, won only just over 50 per cent of the vote and unofficial results awarded victory to Cárdenas. Salinas continued the liberal reforms of the previous presidency and, in 1993, took Mexico into the North American Free Trade Agreement (NAFTA) with the United States and Canada. Cárdenas' supporters subsequently formed the Partido Revolucionaria Democrática (PRD) and attacked the PRI for abandoning many of its traditional policies. In 1989, for the first time, the PRI accepted the loss of a state governorship, to the right wing Partido de Acción Nacional (PAN).

Recent Politics

Background

The PRI's dominance was further rocked by a series of crises in 1994. On New Year's Day, at the moment when NAFTA came into force, a hitherto unknown guerrilla force, the Ejército Zapatista de Liberación Nacional (EZLN) briefly took control of several towns in the southern state of Chiapas. Demanding social justice, indigenous people's rights, democracy at all levels of Mexican politics, an end to government corruption, and land reform for the peasantry, the EZLN attracted international attention, helped by their use of modern communications technology; the government was forced to open peace talks. These, however, were overshadowed by the assassination, in March, of the PRI's appointed presidential candidate, Luis Donaldo Colosio. Further disquiet was caused by the murder of the Tijuana police chief and the kidnapping of several prominent businessmen in the following months. To replace Colosio, President Salinas nominated Ernesto Zedillo Ponce de León, a US-trained economist and former education minister. Further unrest in Chiapas enabled the PRI to portray its candidate as the defender of order; Zedillo won a comfortable majority in the July elections and the PRI retained control of congress. While the PRD and the PAN claimed fraud, attention centred on Chiapas where the state governorship had been won by the PRI in particularly dubious circumstances and on Tabasco where the governorship was also disputed. In September the General Secretary of the PRI, José Francisco Ruiz Massieu, was assassinated and in November his brother Mario, Deputy Attorney General and chief investigator into the murder, resigned, claiming a high level cover up of the assassinations of his brother and Colosio within the PRI. Zedillo's inauguration, on 1 December was soon upstaged by a major economic crisis and Zedillo devalued the peso. Though this move was forced on the government by a variety of economic problems, Zedillo blamed the move on capital outflows caused by political instability resulting from the situation in Chiapas. The decision, a few days after the devaluation, to allow the peso to float against the dollar caused a crisis of confidence and investors in Mexico lost billions of dollars as the peso plummeted in value. As the economic crisis worsened, the PRI was heavily defeated in a series of state elections. In Chiapas, Zedillo suspended the controversial PRI governor, but then allowed the army to launch a brief, but unsuccessful, campaign to capture the EZLN leader, Subcomandante Marcos. Resumed talks between the government and the EZLN led to the first peace accord being signed in February 1996. The pace of change was slow, however, and in 1997 the EZLN renewed its protests, accusing the government of trying to change the terms of the agreed legal framework for indigenous rights. Conflict continued in Chiapas with 60,000 troops heavily outnumbering the Zapatista guerrillas. In December 1997 45 civilians, mainly women and children, were massacred in Acteal, near San Cristóbal de las Casas, by paramilitaries linked to the PRI. Human rights groups and church leaders blamed the government for its failure to disarm paramilitaries and to negotiate an end to the Chiapas conflict. Although the local mayor was implicated and arrested along with 39 others, there were calls for more senior government officials to be removed and in 1998 the Minister of the Interior and State Governor were forced to resign. Despite this, tension continued in Chiapas, as the army increased its pressure on the EZLN and its civilian supporters in its searches for weapons in defiance of the 1995 Law of Dialogue, which forbade the harassment of the Zapatistas as long as they continued to engage in the peace talks.

The unsolved assassinations of Colosio and Ruiz Massieu caused further difficulties for the government. Zedillo appointed Antonio Lozano of PAN as Attorney General; the latter uncovered PRI involvement in Colosio's murder and ordered the arrest of Raúl Salinas, brother of former president Carlos Salinas, for masterminding the murder of Ruiz Massieu. This broke the convention under which former presidents were granted immunity from criticism or prosecution in return for their silence on the activities of their successors. Carlos Salinas left Mexico

Vicente Fox and the Mexican Earthquake of July 2000

By ending the PRI's 71 year uninterrupted control of Mexican government, the presidential elections of July 2000 mark a major turning point in the country's modern history. While opinion polls had shown the PRI candidate, Francisco Labastida, and the PAN's Vicente Fox, running neck and neck, few observers had predicted the scale of the opposition candidate's victory, winning 42.8 per cent of the vote against Labastida's 35.7 per cent. To some extent Fox may have benefitted from the switching of votes from the third candidate, Cuauhtémoc Cárdenas of the PRD who won 16.5%. The political reforms carried out under President Zedillo played a role, the independent status granted to the Federal Election Institute not only provided fewer opportunities for electoral fraud but also helped give voters the confidence to defy pressure from local political bosses who privately warned that that welfare benefits, particularly in the rural areas, would be withdrawn from voters who deserted the governing party.

Much of the credit for Fox's victory must, however, go to the candidate himself. A former Coca Cola executive and rancher, Fox swept aside the conservative leadership of the PAN to seize its presidential candidacy and build an alliance with a range of smaller political parties including the little-known Green Party. Campaigning across the country in cowboy boots, open-neck jeans and a thick belt with his name carved on the buckle, his flamboyant style contrasted with the sleek style of recent PRI presidential candidates with their educational backgrounds in the United States and their careers in the bureaucracy. Although PAN is usually seen as a conservative party and is close to business interests, Fox's campaign showed him to be a pragmatist; his critics accuse him of being all style and no substance, prepared to latch onto any issue to win votes.

Winning the presidency will proved easier than governing Mexico, however and Fox's skills on the campaign trail may be of limited value. Congressional elections held at the same time as the presidential poll made his Alliance for Change the largest party, but lacking a majority in either chamber. On many issues, such as privatisation of Pemex, the state oil corporation, the PRI and PRD can be expected to join forces in Congress and defeat the government. The PRI still controls 19 of the 32 state governorships, important power bases from which to resist change. Perhaps most important of all, the new government will have to work with government officials recruited on the basis of loyalty to the PRI. The new president's ability to govern at all may rest on his skill dealing with the bureaucracy and bargaining with the bosses of the PRI while fulfilling the expectations for change of his supporters.

---

acrimoniously, but this did not put an end to the scandals rocking the official party. Mario Ruiz Massieu was arrested in the United States on suspicion of covering up Raúl Salinas' involvement in the murder of his brother and of receiving money from drug cartels when he had been in charge of anti-narcotics operations. Raúl Salinas was investigated for alleged money laundering and illicit enrichment after his wife was arrested in Switzerland trying to withdraw US$84 million from an account opened in a false name.

Having come to power in the aftermath of assassination and scandal, Zedillo promised political reform. Despite a boycott of talks by the PAN, the other major parties agreed to introduce direct elections for the mayor of Mexico City and to alter the constitution to permit referenda as well as measures to guarantee party political broadcasts during election campaign. Perhaps the most important reform, however, was the abolition of government control over the Federal Election Institute (IFE). Reform of the political system was taken a step further by the July 1997 mid-term congressional elections: for the first time the PRI lost overall control of Congress, gaining only 239 of the 500 seats. The PRD became the second largest party with 125 seats and its leader, Cuauhtémoc Cárdenas, won the mayoral election for Mexico City, while the PAN won 122 seats. These results gave the opposition parties more leverage to push for political reform ahead of the presidential elections of July 2000 which proved to be a landmark in the history of modern Mexico, with the PRI losing the presidency to the PAN candidate, Vicente Fox. The PRI also lost heavily in the Congressional elections to Fox's centre-right Alliance for Change, which became the largest party in Congress.

Land and environment

Geography

In Latin America, Mexico is second only to Brazil in land area, just under two million sq km. This equates to four times the size of France and about a quarter the size of continental USA, with which it has 2,750 km of common frontier. To the south, Mexico has 1,020 km bordering Guatemala and Belize. It has 2,800 km of Gulf of Mexico and Caribbean coastline and 7,400 km on the Pacific side, of which 40 percent is represented by the long, thin peninsula of Baja California. This is a longer shoreline than any other Latin country. There are several islands near both coastlines and two small territories in the Pacific: Guadalupe, about 350 km west of Baja California, and the volcanic Islas Revillagigedo, 750 km west of Puerto Vallarta. The largest of these, Socorro, is 36 km long and 15 km wide and was at one time temporarily colonized by Australians.

Mexico's population is 96 million (1998), 10% of which lives in Mexico City, one of the largest agglomerations of people on the planet.

Structurally, Mexico mostly belongs to North America. The central highland block is a continuation of that of the USA – indeed Cretaceous rocks stretch, virtually uninterrupted, from mid-Mexico north to the Arctic Ocean.

Geology

This block is bordered to the east by the Sierra Madre Oriental, and to the west by the Sierra Madre Occidental, both rising to 3,000-3,500 m. Between them are the vast basins typical of the states of Chihuahua, Coahuila and Durango, semi-desert because of poor soils and lack of rainfall, creating both the hot, dusty, soporific scenery familiar as the location of many Hollywood movies, and spectacular areas of rugged mountains and deep canyons where the intermittent rivers end in *bolsones*, with water-bearing strata supporting oases on the surface.

Northern & Central Mexico

To the east, there are more recent strata and alluvial deposits bordering the Gulf of Mexico, a vast syncline which has been found to contain large reserves of oil and gas. The coastline is swampy with sand bars and lagoons that have inhibited exploitation for tourism, which is virtually non-existent north of Veracruz.

To the west of the central block, the geology is much more complex. It is the product of the continuing movement of the North American Plate westwards against the Pacific Plate (here the Cocos Plate), which has created the high mountain ranges from Alaska to Chile. Beyond, to the west, are the coastal plains, narrow in the south with natural harbours, coves and beaches such as Acapulco, Puerto Vallarta, Manzanillo and Mazatlán. North towards the US border, the plain grows wider, with richer soils supporting a prosperous agricultural development based on irrigation and the nearby US market. There are more bays and beaches along the coast but the very high summer temperatures limit the tourist-appeal.

Río Bravo – Rio Grande, whose is it?

One of the most contentious international frontiers in the Americas is between Mexico and the USA. Economic and cultural disparities, migration, contraband, drugs, and the expanding maquiladora industries have created many problems. [You will find references to these elsewhere in this book]. Not so well known are the difficulties associated with the border itself, especially the 60% which is along the Río Bravo, known as the Rio Grande in the USA.

The border was officially settled here in 1848 as 'the middle of the river following the deepest channel'. This was fine where the river goes through gorges as at Big Bend, but a problem in flatter country where gradual silting and storm flooding move the braided channels about laterally. The semi-desert conditions most of the way from Ciudad Juárez/El Paso to the Gulf make the flow very variable. In prolonged droughts and below irrigation dams, the river can disappear altogether. One of the features of the silting process is the formation of bancos or elongated sandbanks between channels. Land ownership problems emerged when the larger ones were colonised and then the river changed course. In 1899, a prize fight between Maher and Fitzsimmons was prohibited by both the Mexican and the US authorities. The fight was successfully staged on a banco while the two governments argued about which country it belonged to.

Water rights are even more of a problem. More people in the region means more water is needed for domestic, industrial and irrigation purposes. Several dams were built which helped to meet these requirements, to control erosion and provide for recreation. Above Ciudad Juárez, all the water comes from the US. Lower down, however, the Mexican tributaries produce more volume. At one point, the US offered to trade water from the Colorado to irrigate Mexican land on the Pacific for Río Bravo concessions.

Then there are the aquifers. In several places there are significant bolsones, holding long-established underground water resources, which straddle the frontier. As more wells are sunk to draw out the water, so the level falls below the rate of replenishment from water naturally seeping in. That water may be polluted.

There has been much progress since 1848. Treaties in 1906, 1944 and 1970 have amicably resolved many problems. Nevertheless there is still plenty of scope for argument. The 1998 storms created significant floods along the course of the river with damage to crops and property. Who pays? Who is responsible? Whose water is it anyway?

Further to the west is the Gulf of California, 1,000 km long. A brief look at the map will suggest a geological break here which stretches north into the USA. Baja California is indeed not part of the Cocos Plate, but is on a section of the Pacific Plate moving northward relative to the mainland with which the well-known San Andreas Fault is associated. Narrow ridges rising to over 3,000m run all the way down the peninsula which for most of its length is less than 200 km wide.

Volcanoes & Southern Mexico The Sierra Madre ranges come together in the south, where an east-west line of volcanoes known as the Sierra (or Cordillera) Volcánica crosses the country from Veracruz in the east, to Jalisco. This includes the highest points in the country, Orizaba (5760m), Popocatépetl (see Box), Iztaccíhuatl, Toluca, La Malinche and Paricutín, the latter appearing dramatically for the first time in 1943. Some are now active, and form part of the 'Pacific Ring of Fire' which continues south through Central and South America, and north, after a gap, in the Pacific states of the USA, for example Mt St Helens, which most recently exploded in 1980.

To the east, Mexico curves round the Bay of Campeche – more low-level

Popocatépetl

On a clear day, (which is not very often), this shapely volcano can be seen from Mexico City. At 5,452m it is Mexico's second highest mountain to Pico de Orizaba, about 100 km to the east. Its name in Nahuatl means "smoking mountain", which it has done from time immemorial helping to add to its mystery and fables (see page 172).

For many years it was considered 'dormant' and basically harmless. This however ignores its dramatic past including violent explosions, which have left layers of pumice and ash many meters thick over hundreds of square kilometres. In historic times there were major eruptions 5,000, 2,150 and 1,200 years ago, each time covering an area going well beyond Puebla, Tlaxcala and Mexico City. Many relics and artefacts have been found between the layers of material thrown out by the volcano evidencing settlements overwhelmed by the eruptions.

The resultant soils are some of the most productive of the country. The volcano itself, because of its height, creates a microclimate drawing moisture from the air, some of which it stores in the snow cover near the summit producing a good water supply for the slopes below. Hence it is very desirable farming land.

Recently 'El Popo' has been showing signs of greater activity, possibly as a by-product of the 1985 earthquake (which killed more than 10,000 people in the Mexico City area). Steam and gases have been produced in increasing quantities and by the end of 1994, small explosions in the crater were beginning to alarm the authorities. Now, serious attempts are being made by CENAPRED, a Federal Government disaster agency, to prepare for a possible major eruption which could affect the lives of about 20 million people living within the volcano's orbit. Particularly vulnerable will be those who live below the snows and glaciers, which, in past major eruptions, have melted creating catastrophic flash floods and mudflows.

The mountain is now ringed with instruments to give advance warning of problems to come. When the inevitable happens, it remains to be seen if effective evacuation will be possible, given the natural reluctance of those living there to leave.

shorelines with lagoons and a few beaches – to the Yucatán Peninsula, which has the best beaches and natural assets for coast tourism.

At this point, there is a fundamental break in the geological structure. Another line of mountains, named the Sierra Madre del Sur marks the zone where the North American Plate terminates and the Central American Bridge begins. This 'bridge' only appeared about 3.5 million years ago joining the Americas together, ending a period of at least 75 million years of separation. The Sierra Madre del Sur also rises to 3,000m, but is more rugged in character due to its more recent (late Tertiary) origin and the much greater rainfall here than further north. At the eastern end of this range is the Isthmus of Tehuantepec, about 220 km wide with a relatively low crossing point (250m). Several times it has been considered as a possible alternative inter-ocean canal site to Panama. James Eads, a US civil engineer, got closest in the 1880s, but his two attempts to obtain finance through the US Congress failed. Beyond, further mountain ranges go about 300 km southeast to the border with Guatemala.

Most of Yucatán is structurally a limestone platform, a feature that rings the Gulf of Mexico all the way round to Florida and is recognized as a separate chunk of the North American Plate. It is comparatively flat and characterised by natural caverns, wells and sinkholes (*cenotes*), and white, sandy beaches. The northeast corner of Yucatán is the point nearest to Cuba and where the Caribbean Sea meets the Gulf of

Yucatán

Mexico. It is the water passing north through this passage that initiates the current known as the Gulf Stream, with its dramatic effect on the climates of Europe, thousands of miles away. It is calculated that at times driven by strong trade winds, the surface water here is moving at as much as 6 km per hour.

Perhaps the world's most dramatic geological happening ever recorded is connected to Mexico, and concerned the Yucatán. It is now generally agreed that the cataclysm that almost ended life on the planet 65 million years ago was a small asteroid, weighing perhaps one billion tons colliding with the earth at 160,000kph. This left a hole many km deep and over 150 km wide in the Yucatán, known as the Chicxulub Crater. This event destroyed almost every living thing on the planet from the dinosaurs to ammonites (small crustaceans), leaving only the most primitive organisms. Fortunately for us, life was able to re-establish itself. Erosion has long since removed any surface features, but scientists assure us that Mérida is unlikely to be the site of another asteroid visit.

Climate

About half of Mexico is south of the Tropic of Cancer. Whilst there are seasons, monthly average temperatures change little near the coasts. Inland, however, variations are more pronounced where 'continental' style climate conditions prevail. Day/night temperature differences are much more significant the higher you go with agreeable climates in places like Guadalajara (1,650m) and Mexico City (2,240m). Temperatures below freezing are not uncommon above 3,000m especially in the winter months when northerly gales blow in from the USA. There is permanent snow on the highest volcanoes. The highest temperatures are at the head of the Gulf of California where the July average is around 35°C. One of the highest world shade temperatures (58°C) was recorded near San Luis Potosí in Central Mexico.

The deserts of southern California across to Texas continue south into Mexico. The easterly Trade winds bring a little rain to the Caribbean coast and increasing amounts from Tampico south and round the Yucatán Peninsula. Significant regular rainfall is only found near the borders with Belize and Guatemala. Most of the rain in these wetter regions comes between June and September. The highest mean annual rainfall is around 4,500mm in Chiapas, the least less than 200mm in Baja California.

Altitude plays an important part in the amount of precipitation. Each of the Sierra Madre mountain ranges receives more rain than the lowlands, frequently used to supply water to neighbouring cities and irrigation schemes. Much of the rain on the inside of the Sierra Madre ranges ends up in the *bolsones*. One of the largest is the Bolsón de Mayrán which receives water from two significant rivers and supplies sufficient water for Torreón and the surrounding area. However, much of the rain comes from storms running north up the Pacific coast and especially inwards from the Caribbean during the hurricane season (June to November). Mexico rarely escapes serious annual storms – for example Hurricane César struck southern Mexico in 1996, Pauline devastated Acapulco in 1997 and there were severe floods and mudslides on the Río Bravo (Rio Grande), in Chiapas and in central Mexico August – September 1998 and again in Veracruz and the southeast in 1999.

Flora and fauna

The diversity of Mexican flora and fauna should not be underestimated, and the space allocated in the present publication could never do justice to the subject. For those who wish to know more, and read Spanish, *Flora y Fauna Mexicana* by Leonardo and Jimena Manrique (1998), is a must, whilst those with an interest in bird life (over 1,000 species) should consult the excellent Peterson Field Guide, *Mexican Birds* by Roger Tory Peterson and Edward L Chalif (1973).

When studying the pre-Colombian history of Mexico, a knowledge of the flora and fauna of the region is useful, for the native peoples made use of the diverse natural environment within their art and architecture, and images of plants and animals can be found not only in sculptural and painted remains, but within the surviving books and maps, and within the calendar and the belief system.

Central Highlands

Despite extensive de-forestation, particularly in the Valley of Mexico, there are still large areas with tree cover. Pine forests cover the highlands to the northwest of the Valley of Toluca, home to the monarch butterfly, a rare but magnificent insect which migrates from the United States to winter in these woods, whilst evergreen oaks and piñon pines dominate the lower slopes, where band-tailed pigeons are hard to miss. great horned owls and Northern pygmy owls inhabit these forests as do the brightly coloured mountain trogons, though they are rarely seen, despite their green heads and brilliant red bodies. At lower elevations look out for the fig tree, with its distinctive exposed root system, used to make *amate* paper.

Large areas of the highlands are dry and denuded of tree cover, such as the states of Hidalgo and Puebla, and here the maguey (*agave*) cactus, is cultivated extensively.

Coyotes can still be seen in the mountains, though they are increasingly rare as pressure from man mounts. Amongst its prey are the local jackrabbits and long-tailed wood partridge, whilst the piñon mouse lives in the pine forests of the region. Turkey vultures, which appear everywhere in Mexico, can be easily spotted with their dark plumage and red heads, alongside their smaller cousins, the black vulture, scavenging the roadsides, and squabbling with each other, and anything else between them and their food. Alongside the common ground dove, little bigger than the ubiquitous sparrow, they are amongst the most frequently seen birds.

Baja California & the Sonoran Desert

The sahuaro, cardón and organ pipe cacti, long living columnar giants, are perhaps the best-known cacti species of this region; the cardón, at nearly 20m, is the tallest cactus in the world. Other plant species include yucca, ironwood, brittlebush, paloverde and ocotillo, one form of which is the endemic boojum tree, which grows into a 12-m-high candle shape. The compact form of the ocotillo has resulted in its use as a form of hedging by desert communities. The distinctive chaparral landscape of mesquite, oak, hollyleaf buckthorn and manzanita, dominates the dry mountain slopes of the peninsula's north and the desert's east.

The coyote is still a common sight, whilst the bighorn sheep, once found throughout northern Mexico, is confined to the interior of Baja and the El Pinacate National Park in Sonora. The metre-long chuckwalla, a type of lizard, is found on the islands in the Gulf of Cones, while the horned lizard inhabits the Sonoran desert, and desert iguanas are endemic to the region.

Elephant seals and fur seals are on the increase after years of persecution, and can be seen on the Guadalupe Island off the west coast of Baja, but Californian sea-lions can best be seen in the Gulf of Cortés. The Gulf is a haven for cetaceans, with several whale and dolphin species frequenting its waters. Pacific grey whales calve in the coastal lagoons of the peninsula, and can easily be seen from the coast, as can ospreys, catching fish with a feet-first plunge.

Pacific Coast & the Sierra Madre Occidental

Juniper, pine, and cedar forest dominates the higher elevations, where common turkeys still roam wild, whilst deciduous sub-tropical acacia and mesquite woodland dominate the lower slopes, where bromeliads and orchids grow. Several species of parrot, generally green in colour, trogons, hummingbirds of many types, and screech owls, inhabit the forests of this region.

It is believed the grey wolf is now extinct, though some may still live in the northern Sierra, but the mountain lion, or puma, is definitely still resident in the mountains, as is the bobcat and the lynx, but they are rarely seen during the day. Amongst the prey of the larger cats are the local pig, the collared peccary, and the common mule deer, found throughout Mexico, and the rarer white tailed deer, generally found above 1,500m. nine-banded armadillos, racoons and skunks frequent the lower regions, and white-tailed antelope squirrels inhabit the woodlands. The coatimundi, a relative of the racoon, is common throughout Mexico, but you are more likely to see one as a pet than in the wild.

Chihuahua Desert The flora of this area is dominated by typical desert scrub and cacti. With over two hundred cacti species few can be mentioned here, the most dominant being prickly pear. Peyote is used as an hallucinogenic by the Indian population in various religious rites. Amongst other plant species the crucifixion thorn, creosote bush and whitethorn acacia dominate, while stands of oaks and ash abound on the desert edges, and as one moves further south, grasslands, interspersed with prickly pear, yucca and barrel cacti, dominate. in this environment crested caracaras, large long-legged birds of prey, can be seen.

The coyote is common throughout the region, unlike the pronghorn, the fastest ungulate on earth, which is now a rare sight on the grasslands. The collared peccary survives around the margins of the deserts, and the nine-banded armadillo thrives here, as it does throughout Mexico. cottontail rabbits, adapted to desert life, are a relatively common sight, and rodents of all types abound, especially kangaroo rats, of which Mexico boasts several native species. Of course rattlesnakes are not uncommon, 18 species living in Mexico, though most are fairly harmless and rarely encountered, and scorpions, though highly venomous, are nocturnal creatures.

In Coahuila State, one area worth visiting is the Cuatro Ciénegas Natural Protected Area, a zone of natural oases, where permission is required to enter. Here some unique species live, such as the aquatic Coahuila box turtle, and the abundance of duck and fish is truly astonishing.

Gulf Coast, Sierra Madre Oriental & Chiapas In the north, the desert gives way to thorn scrub of mesquite, hackberry and acacia. One of Mexico's two coral snake species lives in the north-eastern deserts, the other being found in Yucatán, and though venomous, its bright colour makes it fairly conspicuous. The grasslands of the coastal plains, home to the common turkey, border the forests on the lower slopes of the Sierra Madre Oriental, inhabited by several species of nightjar, and the potoo, and stretch from the Texas border to Veracruz. The potoo is a large brown bird which, during the day, sleeps upright and motionless on branches, appearing to be part of the tree itself.

Cloud forests, with their distinctive Spanish moss (*pachtli*) formations, dominate the higher elevations further south, some of the best and easiest to see being along Route 175 from Oaxaca City to the Veracruz coast. One of the residents of the Chiapas cloud forest is the resplendent quetzal, a type of trogon, the most spectacular of birds, with its emerald and golden green body, red belly, and tail feathers that are white from below, but, depending on the angle of vision, green or blue from above. During pre-Colombian times its tail feathers were more valued than gold, but now it is so rare that one would be privileged to see it. The lower forests are home to several parrot species, whilst hummingbirds are frequently seen, the violet sabre-wing standing apart from the usual shimmering green varieties.

The lowlands of northern Chiapas are dense jungle, where huge ceiba trees can be seen, and where jaguars still roam, though being nocturnal, one is unlikely to see them. Other cat species include the spotted ocelot and its smaller (100cm long) cousin the margay, and the dark coloured 70-cm-long juagarundi, all rare and under pressure from habitat loss. Deep in the jungle lives the rarely seen baird's tapir, while the collared peccary gives way to the larger white-lipped peccary. The forest canopy resounds to the bellow of the howler monkey, and black-headed spider monkeys can be seen swinging through the trees, but one is unlikely to see the nocturnal american opossum.

The sight of military macaws, collared and keel-billed toucans and various parrot species is not uncommon when visiting the Mayan ruins along the Usumacinta River. Glossy blue, thrush-sized lovely coting, are a common sight, as are various species of the smaller manakin birds. On the forest floor leaf-cutter ants appear to be everywhere. These small insects travel along pathways carrying sections of leaf ten times their own size back to their nest, where the leaves are used as a fertiliser for growing the fungus that the ants eat. The jungle is full of colourful insects and arachnids too numerous to mention, but one is unlikely to encounter more than the odd harmless tarantula and occasional wasp colony if only visiting ruins.

American crocodiles and alligators live along the river banks, though one is unlikely to see either, since, like many large animals, they have suffered persecution from man for many years. However, it is possible to visit nurseries devoted to breeding these animals to re-populate the area.

Harpy eagles, though quite rare, may be spotted soaring over the coastal region, but one is more likely to see hook billed kites, king vultures and black hawks. Red-throated caracaras may be seen in large groups in the humid forests of southern Veracruz and northern Chiapas, particularly when visiting the ruins of Palenque.

The tinamou, a dull-coloured tailless bird with a long down-curving beak, can be seen in the undergrowth of the lower slopes of the mountains. Rarely flying, they will take to the wing if frightened. Smaller, but more common, are quails, several species occurring in the drier parts of Mexico, the most common, the bobwhite, being found throughout the southern and eastern parts of the country. In pre-Hispanic Mexico, the quail was valued as a sacrifice to the gods. The large turkey-sized crested guan and the similar great curassow are birds well worth looking out for on the forest margins.

Coastal waters used to be home to large numbers of manatees, but now their numbers are dangerously low, and they are rarely seen, either on the Gulf Coast or around the Yucatan Peninsula.

Yucatán Peninsula

The southern part of the peninsula is dominated by tropical rainforest, where the distinctive cough of the jaguar may be heard at night, but the animal will rarely be seen. The northern half is a distinct flat savanna landscape dominated by grasslands, trees and bushes, interspersed with *sisal (henequén)* plantations, once the mainstay of the local economy. The turkey-like (but half the size) plain chachalaca may be spotted early in the morning calling from the treetops, not to be mistaken for the much larger ocellated turkey, with its blue head topped by an orange-red knob, that can be seen in the dense scrubland, particularly in the east. Ovenbirds (horneros) and ant-birds, no larger than European blackbirds, are common in the forests and plains of the area. The latter can sometimes be seen at the head of army ant colonies, picking off insects flushed out by the ants as they travel across the ground in wide columns in search of insect prey. One might also encounter the tropical rattlesnake, the most venomous rattler after the large western diamondback, found in northern Mexico.

Flamingoes can be seen in large numbers at Celestún and on the north coast at Río Lagartos – named for the local crocodile population – where you can hire boats to the sandbars and islets to get closer to the birds. Several other bird species, such as long-legged grey-necked wood rails, and northern jacanas (easily mistaken for coots), may be seen in these coastal swamplands.

The coral reef off the east coast is part of the Belize reef, 250 km in length, and abounds in tropical fish, most easily seen by hiring snorkelling gear at Xcaret, Isla Mujeres and Akumal, the latter a breeding ground for green turtles. The best place to see green iguanas is along this coast, though they live in all of Mexico's humid jungles.

Whale & dolphin watching

More than any other animal, the grey whale has been associated with Mexico, particularly Baja California. Every year, in late December, grey whales begin arriving at a series of large lagoons along the west coast of Baja California, having travelled more than 3,000 km from their Arctic feeding grounds. Unlike other whale species which congregate in the open ocean to mate, calve and raise their young, the grey whales enter the protected salt-water lagoons and spend three months in sheltered waters.

In the mid-1800s, whalers led by Captain Charles M Scammon discovered the entrance to the Pacific coastal lagoon that would bear his name: Scammon's Lagoon. With nowhere to run, the grey whales were nearly all slaughtered in a few decades and by the early 1900s some scientists feared the species was on the brink of extinction. However, following a ban on hunting grey whales, the numbers have now returned. Today there are more than 20,000 grey whales – approximately their original numbers – in the eastern North Pacific.

The grey whale was the first whale to be watched on commercial tours, beginning in 1955 in southern California. In 1970 the first multi-day, long-range whale-watch cruises departed from San Diego to visit the grey whale lagoons on a self-contained ship. Today, the long-range trips are still offered from January to March from San Diego, as well as out of Mexican ports (such as Ensenada), usually lasting 7 to 10 days. The most popular trips go to San Ignacio Lagoon and Magdalena Bay; some visit both lagoons. Besides grey whales, it is possible to watch bottlenose dolphins mainly in the mouths of the lagoons, and often various other whale and dolphin species *en route* (in open waters), including common dolphins, Pacific white-sided dolphins, and even blue whales. Some trips feature camping beside the lagoons, while others utilise local Mexican boats, called *pangas*, which can approach fairly close to the whales.

For more information, contact: Baja Expeditions, 2625 Garnet Av, San Diego, CA 92109, USA, T619-5813311, F619 5816542. Pacific Sea Fan Tours, 2803 Emerson St, San Diego, CA 92106 USA, T619-2268224, F619-2220784. Baja Tours, Av Macheros y Calle Marina, Local G-3 – Plaza Marina, Ensenada, Baja California, México, T52617-781641, F52617-781045.

If you're already travelling in Mexico in winter and want to see whales, go to Puerto Adolfo López Mateos for grey whale watching on Magdalena Bay, or to Guerrero Negro for grey whale watching in Laguna Guerrero Negro. It is usually possible to join day trips within the lagoons, using *pangas*.

On the other (eastern) side of Baja California, the Gulf of California, or Sea of Cortés, offers a completely different whale-watch adventure which extends throughout most of the year in one of the most diverse whale-watch areas in the world. Access is through the southern Baja ports of San José del Cabo, La Paz, Bahía de los Angeles, and Loreto, as well as Rosarito. The whales include fin, humpback, sperm, short-finned pilot and minke whales as well as the difficult-to-identify Bryde's whale, the only truly tropical baleen whale (it does not migrate to cold temperate or Arctic waters). The main dolphins are common, bottlenose and Pacific white-sided dolphin. But most of all, the Gulf of California stands as one of the three or four best places in the world to see blue whales. Some of the above species are present throughout the year, others appear mainly in winter or summer. In general, the best time for most species is January until April. Day tours are possible, but most people take one- to two-week boat excursions with a small group of participants.

They live aboard the boat and are guided to a wide range of activities and adventures throughout their trip, with whales as the centrepiece.

For multi-day cruises and tours to the above areas (some of which also offer lagoon excursions), contact:

WildOceans/ WildWings, International House, Bank Rd, Kingswood, Bristol BS15 2LX, England, UK, T44(0)117-9848040, F44(0)117-9674444. Oceanic Society Expeditions, Fort Mason Center, Building E, San Francisco, CA 94123-1394, USA, T1415-4411106, F1415-4743395. Natural Habitat Adventures, 2945 Center Green Court, Boulder, Colorado 80301-9539 USA, T1303-4493711, F1303-4493712. Ecosummer Expeditions, 1516 Duranleau St, Granville Island, Vancouver, BC V6H 3S4, Canada, T1604-6697741, F1604-6693244. Discover the World, 29 Nork Way, Banstead, Surrey SM7 1PB, UK, T44(0)1737-218800, F44(0)1737-362341. Sea Quest Expeditions/ Zoetic Research, PO Box 2424, Friday Harbor, WA 98250 USA, T1206-3785767. ACS Whale Adventures, American Cetacean Society, PO Box 1391, San Pedro, CA 90731-0943, USA, T1310-5486279, F1310-5486950. Special Expeditions, 1415 Western Ave, Suite 700, Seattle, WA 98101, USA, T1206-6247750, F1206-3829594.

The Gobierno del Estado de Baja California Sur will provide whale-watching and other Baja tourism information. Contact: Coordinación Estatal de Turismo, Km 5.5 Carret, al Norte, Edificio Fedepaz, A P 419, La Paz, Baja California Sur, México. T52112 31702.

In recent years, whale watching for humpback whales has started up along the mid-Pacific Mexican coast. The tours are conducted only in winter, mainly from Punta Mita at Bahía de Banderas in the state of Nayarit. The tours visit Isabella Island.

It is also possible to see bottlenose, spotted and other dolphins on the Caribbean side of the Yucatán, especially on the southeast coast near the border with Belize, as well as from the offshore resort island of Isla Mujeres. Sometimes the dolphins are seen as part of diving trips. However, Belize has more developed dolphin-watching operations. Contact Oceanic Society, listed above, for more information on their excellent programme that combines science, conservation and a wonderful holiday with dolphins.

Erich Hoyt, marine ecologist and scientific consultant to conservation groups and governments, is the author of 12 books including *Insect Lives* (1999), *The Earth Dwellers* (1998), and *Seasons of the Whale* (1998).

National Parks

Mexico is the world's third most biologically diverse country, behind only Brazil and Colombia. It boasts between 21,600 and 33,000 of the 250,000-odd known species of higher plants (including 150 conifers, and around 1,000 each of ferns, orchids, and cacti), 693-717 reptiles (more than any other country), 436-455 mammals (second only to Indonesia), 283-289 amphibians (fourth in the world), 1,018 birds, 2,000 fish, and hundreds of thousands of insect species. Five Mexican vertebrates (all birds) have become extinct in the 20th century, and about 35 species are now only found in other countries; 1,066 of around 2,370 vertebrates are listed as threatened.

This is of course an immense country, with an immense range of habitats and wildlife; the far south is in the Neotropical Kingdom, with a wealth of tropical forest species, while the far north is very much part of the Nearctic Kingdom, with typically North American species, and huge expanses of desert with unique ecosystems. The greater part of the country is a transition zone between the two kingdoms, with many strange juxtapositions of species that provide invaluable information to scientists, as well as many endemic species. Many of these sites are now protected, but are often of little interest except to specialists; what's more Mexico's National Parks per se were set up a long time ago primarily to provide green recreation areas

Background

for city dwellers; they are generally small and often now planted with imported species such as eucalyptus, and thus of no biological value. However, the country does also have a good number of Biosphere Reserves, which are both of great biological value and suitable for tourism.

Starting in the far south, in Chiapas, **El Triunfo Biosphere Reserve** protects Mexico's only cloud forest, on the mountains (up to 2,750m) above the Pacific coast; the main hiking route runs from Jaltenango (reached by bus from Tuxtla) to Mapastepec on the coastal highway. Groups need to book in advance through the state's Institute of Natural History, on Calzada de Hombres de la Revolución, by the botanical garden and Regional Museum (Apdo 391, Tuxtla 29000; T23663, F29943, ihnreservas@laneta.apc.org).

From Jaltenango you need to hike or hitch a ride about 29 km to Finca Prusia and then follow a good muletrack for three hours to the El Triunfo campamento (1,650m). There are endemic species here, including the very rare azure-rumped tanager; the horned guan is found only here and across the border in the adjacent mountains of Guatemala. Other wildlife includes the quetzal, harpy eagles, jaguars, tapirs, and white-lipped peccary.

Turn left in the clearing for the route down to Tres de Mayo, 25 km away; this is an easy descent of five hours to a pedestrian suspension bridge on the dirt road to Loma Bonita. From here you should take a pick-up to Mapastepec, 25 km away.

Also in Chiapas is the immense **Lacandón Forest**, supposedly protected by the **Azules Biosphere Reserve** but in reality still being eaten away by colonization and logging. New plant species and even families are still being discovered in this rainforest, best visited either from the Bonampak and Yaxchilán ruins, or by the road/boat route via Pico de Oro and Flor de Café to Montebello.

In the Yucatán the **Sian Ka'an Biosphere Reserve** is one of the most visited in Mexico, being just south of Cancún; it's a mixture of forest, savanna and mangrove swamp, best visited on a day-trip run by Los Amigos de Sian Ka'an at Av Cobá 5, third floor, offices 48-50, Apdo 770, Cancún (T849583, F873080, sian@cancun.rce.com.mx). It is also well worth visiting the **Río Lagartos** and **Río Celestún** reserves on the north and west coasts of Yucatán, well known for their flamingoes. The **Calakmul Biosphere Reserve** is important mainly for its Mayan ruins, seeming to the layman more like scrub than forest.

Across the country's centre is the Transversal Volcanic Belt, one of the main barriers to Nearctic and Neotropic species; it's easiest to head for the **Izta-Popo National Park** (from Amecameca), the **Zoquiapan National Park** (on the main road to Puebla) or the **El Tepozteco National Park** (on the main road to Cuernavaca), and naturally the volcanoes themselves are well worth climbing.

Only small areas of the northern deserts and sierras are formally protected. The most accessible areas are in Durango state, including **La Michilía Biosphere Reserve**, with pine, oak and red-trunked Arbutus and Arctostaphylus trees typical of the Sierra Madre Occidental. A daily bus runs to San Juan de Michis, and you should get off at a T-junction two km before the village and walk west, first getting permission from the Jefe de Unidad Administrativo, Instituto de Ecología, Apdo 632, 34000 Durango (T121483); their offices are at Km 5 on the Mazatlán highway. The **Mapimí Biosphere Reserve** covers an area of desert *matorral* (scrub) which receives just 200mm of rain a year; it lies to the east of Ceballos, on the Gómez Palacio-Ciudad Jiménez highway. In addition to many highly specialized bushes and cacti, this is home to giant turtles, now in enclosures at the Laboratory of the Desert.

There is a great variety of protected areas in Baja California, all of considerable biological value: the highest point (3,000m) is the **Sierra de San Pedro Mártir**, in the north, which receives plenty of precipitation and has largely Californian fauna and flora. A dirt road starts at the Puente San Telmo, on the main road down the west coast, and leads almost 100 km to an astronomical observatory. Desert environments are, of course, unavoidable here, with 80 endemic cacti: the **Gran Desierto del Altar** is a dry lunar landscape, best seen from the main road along the US border, while the **El Vizcaíno Biosphere Reserve** protects a huge area of central Baja, characterized by *agaves* and drought-resistant scrub. However the main reason for stopping here is to see the migration of the grey whale to its breeding grounds. In the far south, the **Sierra de La Laguna** boasts a unique type of cloud forest, with several endemic species; to get here you have to cross about 20 km of desert from just south of Todos Santos to La Burrera, and then follow a trail for 11 km to a rangers' *campamento* at about 1,750m.

Limited information on National Parks and Biosphere Reserves can be obtained from SEDESOL (Ministry of Social Development), Av Revolución 1425, México DF (Barranca del Muerto metro), where you'll also find the National Institute of Ecology (INE), for more general information on conservation; their publications are stocked by the Librería Bonilla, nearby at Francia 17.

Non-governmental conservation organizations include Naturalia (Apdo Postal 21541, 04021 México DF; T56746678, F56743876, www.naturalia.org.mx), and Pronatura (Asociación Mexicano por la Conservación de la Naturaleza, Aspegulas 22, Col San Clemente, T56355054, www.pronatura.org.mx Information may also be obtained at www2.planeta.com/mader/ecotravel/mexico/mexparks.html

Background

Art and architecture

Pre-Hispanic archaeology By the time the Aztecs took over centre stage, the dominant cultures in Mexico had refined the customs, artistic skills and scientific knowledge acquired throughout nearly three millennia, much of which stemmed from the Olmecs on the Gulf Coast. A closer look at the more important aspects of life before the upheaval of the Spanish Conquest shows just how far they had come.

Religion The Mesoamerican pantheon of gods, each with their own identity and purpose, played a vital role in the people's everyday affairs. Many of these gods originated with the Olmecs and metamorphosed through various guises with subsequent cultures. By the Classic Period, a complete pantheon of gods had emerged, recognized and followed throughout the whole country. The best-known figures in the Mayan era included the following:

Itzamná – the supreme god, ruler of the sky, who together with his wife Chebel Yax, the creation goddess, begat all the other gods and goddesses.

Kukulcán – the ubiquitous feathered-serpent deity, originating from the Yucatán, rose to prominence with the Aztecs as Quetzalcoatl, and with the Toltecs in the post-Classic era. Feathered serpents were also common however, in earlier Classic sites, including Tikal, in Guatemala.

Yum Cimil – the god of death, often depicted with a fleshless skull and bare backbone.

Chac – the rain god (possibly derived from one of the Olmec were-jaguars. The most important of the gods of nature, who had a vital role in overseeing the seasonal cycles of agriculture and fertility. Chac was considered the centre of the universe as well as all points east, west, north and south, and was also the benefactor, creator and father of agriculture.

Kinich Ahau – the sun god, usually depicted with square eyes and filed teeth.

Ah Mun – the corn god, often portrayed as a handsome young man, with a maize plant sprouting from his head.

There were many lesser deities but most power was controlled by a few leading players. The gods were not generally gentle, charitable beings; they bestowed favours in return for exacting tributes in food, incense and blood sacrifice. The Aztecs were extremely devout and performed religious rituals for every daily activity, each of which was undertaken only after consulting the relevant gods, from deciding when to plant and harvest, to regulating marriages, baptisms and naming ceremonies, and even over when and where to trade, hunt and fish.

It was the role of priests and later on, of secular leaders, to interpret the gods' wishes. Aztec rulers in particular exploited the control the gods had over peoples' lives, by claiming divine descendency, and thus enhancing their own power and status.

The Aztec pantheon was incredibly complex, with over 200 gods, including some that had been adopted both from contemporary neighbours and from ancestral cultures. Many had several identities and most ceremonial rituals were devoted to several deities simultaneously. The concept of duality in the gods was also common (and ceramic masks found in Tlatilco in the Valley of Mexico, dating from 1400 BC, show dualistic features, suggesting that this belief ran throughout early Mexican history). Many deities seemed to have operated in pairs, sometimes embodying opposing elements. For instance, Quetzalcoatl (the Plumed Serpent) is both the double and the enemy of Tezcatlipoca (the Smoking Mirror), and both are often described as the gods of creation. To the Aztecs, there were two gods who had created the Universe: Two Lord and Two Lady. They had four sons, each of whom was a manifestation of the all-powerful Tezcatlipoca.

The Origins of humankind, according to Aztec beliefs

In a previous world, humans had already existed, but had perished. Quetzalcoatl ventured into the Underworld on a hazardous mission to recover human life, stealing their bones from Mictlantecuhtli, the 'Lord of the Realm of the Dead'. When Quetzalcoatl brought them back to Earth, the other gods gave them new life by dripping their own blood over them. However, they still lacked food to keep themselves alive, so again Quetzalcoatl supplied the demand and, turning himself into an ant, burrowed into the mountain and stole the maize which became their staple diet.

Background

Ball Game

Since the earliest days of the Olmecs, Mexican peoples had believed in a threshold linking life and death, the Earth and the Underworld. This threshold was symbolized by the court in the ritual ball game. In this team event that was similar to basketball, players would try to throw a solid rubber ball through large stone rings at either end of a specially constructed court. More than mere sport however, in the ball game players stood on the threshold between life and death, sometimes literally, as the losers in the game were often sacrificed as offerings to the gods.

Ball courts have been found in sites throughout Mesoamerica, but the oldest and most numerous have been found in the Olmec region of the Gulf Coast. At least nine courts have been found in El Tajín, the Classic site in northern Veracruz. Some of these are up to 60m long, I-shaped, with two facing stone walls, often elaborately decorated with bas-relief murals depicting the ceremonially dressed players. Because of the large number of ball courts found in this region, it is considered that the event probably orginated here. The biggest ball court found in all Mesoamerica, however, is at Chichén Itzá. It was built after the Toltecs took over the city in the 13th century, and its facing walls measure some 82m in length, by 8.2m in height.

Feeding the Gods

Human sacrifice was practised by most pre-Columbian cultures from the Olmecs onwards, as part of a customary tribute to the gods. It was taken to levels of mass slaughter by the warmongering post-Classic civilizations, however, particularly the Toltecs and Aztecs. In most cases, the victims were prisoners of war or slaves bought for that purpose, but also servants were often killed and buried with their masters in order to serve them in the afterlife (including one unfortunate Tarascan physician, who was buried with his lord, whom he failed to cure of his last illness!). The Aztecs, above all, sacrificed enemy warriors in order to appease the gods. Huitzilopochtli, the wrathful sun god, demanded the blood and hearts of human victims in order to make it through the Underworld every night and light up the Earth in the morning.

Time & space: astronomy & the calendars

The invention of a calendrical measurement of time is now credited to the Olmecs, after a stela was found in their site of Tres Zapotes, inscribed with a glyph that was interpreted as the representation of a date, 31BC. It was the Maya, however, who developed sophisticated systems of measurement of time, much of which was later adopted by the Aztecs, although not to such a high degree.

Calendar round

The basic unit of measurement was the single day. The 260-day cycle (known as the Tonalpohualli to the Aztecs, and as the Tzolkin to Maya scholars) was made up of 20 consecutive day signs, combined with prefix numbers from 1 to 13. Thus, for example, there would be the day 7 Ocelotl, or Jaguar, which would only come round again once 260 days had elapsed. It is not known what was the basis for this 260-day cycle, but it was not related to any natural pattern of events (although the period of human gestation is about 260 days, so this might have been one source of inspiration). The cycle was sacred to the Maya, forming the basis for all their religious rituals, some of which, like the Christian Easter, were 'movable feasts' that shifted from one year to the next. Each day was divine, symbolized by the god of that day 'carrying it' like a load.

There was also another cycle, probably devised more recently than the 260-day cycle and as common throughout Mexico during the Classic era, which ran at the same time, and which was similar to our own 365-day solar year. This cycle consisted of 18 named periods of 20 days each, equivalent to our months, plus five unlucky 'empty' days, totalling 365 days in total. The 360-day year was called the *Xihuitl* by the Aztecs and the *Haab* by the Maya, and the 5-day bad luck period was known as the *Nemontemi* by the Aztecs and the *Uayeb* by the Maya.

These two calendar cycles ran concurrently but they were also combined, in order to create a further cycle of 260 x 365 days, which equalled 94,900 days, or approximately 52 years.

Long Count The Maya also devised an extremely accurate system of counting time, called the Long Count, based on units of 20 days. This system was represented in glyphs on carved stone stelae, found in the Olmec region of the Gulf Coast as well as in the Maya lowlands. Numbers were arranged vertically, each subsequent level being 20 times greater than the previous. The third level however, was a multiple of 18, which made a total of 360, chosen in order to approximate the astronomical calendar year.

Each number level was named, as follows:
1 kin = 1 day
1 uinal = 20 days
1 tun = 360 days
1 katun = 7,200 days (about 20 years)
1 baktun = 144,000 days (about 400 years)

A dot was the symbol for one and a bar for 5, so that if a bar was used for instance on the third level (tun) shown above, it would indicate a figure of 1800 days (or about five astronomical years).

The Long Count was used to great accuracy to record the movement of the stars and planets, which the Maya observed with great interest. They calculated the paths of the Sun and the Moon, and made tables of lunar eclipses in their famous Dresden Codex. The measuring and recording of time was such an important task to the Maya that it is often considered to be the very soul of their culture, indeed the meaning of their name is 'cycle' so in fact the Maya can properly be called the 'People of Time'.

Art & writing As with every other aspect of their lives, the artistic output of the early Mexicans was inextricably tied to religion. Their magnificent temples and pyramids were richly decorated with murals, bas-relief scenes, sculptures, as well as beautiful treasures made of gold and precious stones. In spite of the ravages of time some fine paintings have survived, and can be seen today in sites such as Bonampak, Teotihuacán, Tepantitla, Atetelco, Cacaxtla, and Cholula, near Puebla.

The earliest and some of the most accomplished artists were the Olmecs. Fine murals, often depicting their cult figure, the were-jaguar, have been found throughout their region, mostly painted on stelae and temples, but also in caves.

Some fascinating Olmec paintings have been found in the Juxtlahuaca Cave, near Chilpancingo in Guerrero, and in another cave nearby, in Oxtotitlán.

Writing

As has been stated, the Olmecs were the first culture to use a system of writing in Mexico, although they did not develop anything like the level of sophistication reached by the Maya, whose system is recognized as the most complex of all Mesoamerican cultures. Other cultures, who developed their own forms of writing included Teotihuacán, Zapotec, Mixtec, Toltec and El Tajín. The earliest source of writing was in hieroglyphs, which were inscribed on upright stone monuments, or stelae. The predominant theme in the writing was the recording of time, particularly with regard to measuring and forecasting the seasons, on which agricultural production depended.

By the time of the Aztecs, writing had become a large-scale professional occupation. The *tlacuilo* was a highly respected and skilled craftsman, whose job it was to paint books, called *codices*, on parchment or native paper. Unfortunately, when the Spanish conquistadors saw these folded documents, they destroyed the vast majority as 'works of the devil'. Some of the Aztec codices have survived however, as well as several from the Mayan era, most important of which is the *Codex Dresden*, kept in Germany. As with the earlier Olmec glyphs, the Maya codices deal exclusively with religious and astronomical topics. Interpretations of the *Codex Dresden* have revealed that it is a kind of almanac, full of tables giving details of which gods are to be consulted on which dates, and giving explanations of how to interpret favourable or unfavourable signs, with regard to harvests, marriages, war, and hunting.

Sculpture

Despite the absence of technology and metal tools, the earliest Mexican cultures produced an enormous quantity of incredibly advanced stonework. The Olmecs carved the famous stone heads (see below) of La Venta, as well as beautiful small figurines and delicate jewellery made of jade, stone mask pectorals, and life-size figures sculpted in the round. Carved stone stelae, mostly dedicated to the gods, or to the lives and events of their rulers, were produced across Mexico from pre-Classic times onwards. Temple pyramids and palaces were often ornately worked with bas-relief carvings, such as the intriguing *Danzantes* of the Zapotecs in pre-Classic Monte Albán, depicting gruesome sacrificial victims and prisoners of war.

Olmec stone heads

Since the late 19th century, 17 massive sculpted stone heads have been discovered in the Olmec 'heartland', particularly in the swampy region by the Tonalá River, in La Venta, Veracruz. These stone heads, which were first excavated in the 1920s, measured up to 2.85m tall and weighed many tons. They have thickset, flattened faces, and typically wear headgear, nicknamed 'football helmets' which may have been used in the traditional Mesoamerican ballgame. The heads are thought to have been made as tributes to Olmec rulers. Recent studies have further suggested that they were in fact re-carved from the rulers' thrones, leading to the explanation that the stones which supported the rulers during their reign were thus re-fashioned to become 'portrait-memorials' to them after their death.

The features of the heads – 'negroid' flattened lips and nose – sparked off a spate of theories about their makers coming by sea from Africa. However, further study showed that these features were also common elsewhere in Olmec art, for instance depicting the broad snout and snarling mouth of the were-jaguar cult. Also, it has been argued that negroid features are common in peoples throughout Asia as well as Africa, and it is quite possible that some such people may well have been among the first settlers who crossed the Bering Straits and migrated throughout the Americas.

Post-conquest art and architecture

Art

The past five centuries have shown that those who have gone to the Americas, whether Anglo-Saxon or of Latin origin, have caused changes in language, especially accents, in music, literature, art and architecture, which demonstrate a certain freedom of expression that develops once the 'apron strings' binding them to the mother culture have been loosened. The rich body of literature produced in the Americas, particularly during the past century, has a robust and raw vitality resulting from the shedding of refinements inherent in the European model. The greater the gap, in space and time, between the model and its derivatives, the greater will be the expression of the differences between them. When the exiles or immigrants are exposed to a culture whose traits are completely alien to them, traits which they endeavour to eradicate and replace, the situation becomes more confused, a confusion that is aggravated by the necessity to utilize the skills and expertise of the craftspeople whose culture they are going to change. These, more or less, were the conditions that contributed to the emergence of Mexican art; and, despite the many restrictions imposed by exigent patrons, especially the Catholic Church (which meant that for many years the only art of any worth to be produced was religious and elitist), that created in Mexico during the past five centuries occupies an important position in the history of art.

When the Spanish discovered that the inhabitants of the territories they had conquered practiced a religion that was abhorrent to Christian sensibilities, down came pyramids, temples and sanctuaries; sculptures, when found, were smashed and paintings were disfigured or obliterated. To complete the total annihilation of everything that suggested paganism, they burned thousands of books in which histories, cosmogonies, calendrics, and social mores were registered. These books were great works of art, created by *tlacuilos* (painters/writers) who spent many years training for this prestigious post. However, one factor for which the historian will always be grateful is the interest certain friars took in what had existed in the land before their arrival, believing that before they eradicated it, they must first understand it. The *tlacuilos* recreated some of the books that had been destroyed, remembering vividly the gods, rituals, maps, and tribute lists of the Aztecs. They had no problem recalling the appearance of the gods; before the Conquest, the gods, impersonated by humans soon to be sacrificed in their honour, walked among the throngs in and around Tenochtitlán. How easy, then, was it for these people to accept images of saints in churches or carried through the streets on special days. But images of the saints had to be created and temples had to be built in which to house them. In this, the skills of the indigenous artisan were indispensable.

There is little evidence to suggest that the newcomers had brought with them painters, sculptors and others adept at creating buildings and images to be used in the indoctrination of the people. Linked to this was the need for somewhere to indoctrinate and cater for the spiritual needs of the indigene, and this brought into being the open-air chapel (see page 139). These structures had to be adorned; during the first years of the colony, the responsibility of this fell to the native artist. The façades of some churches were used to express the cult which was practised within, and many art historians point to the inclusion of non-Christian iconography in the general field of symbols used to adorn the church. Some open-chapels were painted with scenes from the Old and New Testaments. Unable to speak the language, in the early years the friars were dependent on visual aids and interpreters. Placards, which could be rolled up or opened at whim, somewhat like the screens used for projecting slides, were popular. Unfortunately, they were made from perishable materials and none is known to have survived the intervening years. The models for these placards, together with the walls of the open-chapels and the façades of the churches, were woodcuts and any other religious images that the friars carried abroad, interpreted by the indigenous sculptor or painter. This could be seen as the first manifestations of Mexican art, Old World imagery interpreted by New World sensibilities.

The problem of Old World models and New World interpretations was first addressed by the establishment of a school of arts and crafts in the capital by Fray Pedro de Gante between 1530-40. Fray Pedro, not an accomplished artist, with his assistant Fray Diego Valadés, who had a steady hand at sketching, instructed the young (most of whom were from an elite indigenous background), thus producing the first wave of masons, carpenters, blacksmiths, painters, and sculptors in New Spain. The children were taught to understand new forms that were alien to them. Nevertheless, they began to comprehend the meaning, in European art, of line, of foreshortening, of volumes, of colour, of costume, of symbolism. This enabled them to reproduce the images and objects essential for the new religion. These young people, in turn, went out to instruct local masons, sculptors and painters in the new style, while overseeing the adorning of churches and convents in the towns and villages of New Spain. Although adept at carrying out this work (writers of the period have commented on how quickly the indigenous artist copied the imported works) mistakes in interpretation were bound to occur. *Tequiqui*, in which low-relief sculpture became flat and angular, resulted from this interpretation of European forms. When used to adorn the façades of convents and churches, it is strikingly beautiful. And, despite the mistakes, these efforts constituted the beginning of Mexican art.

We cannot know how Mexican art would have developed had this combination of European models and native interpreters remained unchanged. However, changes took place.

Painters arriving from Europe brought the Renaissance style with them, influenced by trends in Italy, Flanders or Spain. Artists usually arrived in the entourage of Bishops or Viceroys, always appointed by the Spanish crown: Criollos, Mexican-born children of Spanish immigrants, were not eligible to fill high administrative or clerical posts. The most important painters to arrive from Europe in the late 16th century were Simón Pereyns, Andrés de la Concha and Francisco Zumaya. The subject of the paintings produced during this period was overwhelmingly religious, a fact that provoked Pereyns to remark that he would much prefer to paint portraits than the images of saints, an indiscretion that landed him in front of the Tribunal del Santo Oficio (Inquisition), and this notwithstanding the fact that many of these august men were not adverse to sitting for a portrait. Pereyns' paintings display a certain Flemish and Italian influence. Andrés de la Concha painted the main *retablo* of the Convento de Santo Domingo, Yanguitlán, Oaxaca (around 1575), which can be seen to be influenced by the Italian and Spanish schools. Francisco de Zumaya came to Mexico in or about 1565, but the only painting of his which survives is the superb study of San Sebastián in the upper part of the Altar del Pardón in Mexico City's cathedral. With these three artists, Pereyns, de la Concha and Zumaya, Renaissance painting had truly arrived in Mexico.

The newly arrived European artists instructed a talented group of Criollo artists how to paint according to Renaissance canons. However, even at this early stage in the evolution of Mexican art, commentators have noted a certain reticence in interpretation that almost echoes the hesitancy evident in the works carried out by the indigenous artists of the earlier period. But the students did learn from their masters, and were well prepared when the 'Golden Age' of Mexican art arrived.

The students who had been instructed by Pereyns, and their successors, imitated Francisco de Zubarán, José Ribera, Bartolomé Murillo, and other Spanish artists. But they were separated from the source of their inspiration. And dependent on engravings that were in short supply, they instructed students who had no knowledge of the background which had produced the art they studied, almost echoing the conditions experienced by the indigenous artists who, decades earlier, had adorned the façades of churches and painted murals. So these students responded to local tastes and created works that were based on European models but moving in a different direction.

Sebastián de Orteaga, born in Seville in 1610, is considered to be one of the best of the Colonial School; he was a great exponent of the *chiaroscuro* technique, in which he was clearly influenced by Rivera and Zurbarán. Though many of his paintings have been lost, his study of St Thomas touching the wounds of Christ demonstrate his mastery, both in the quality of its composition and its Raphaelesque tones. His disciple, José Juárez, son of Luis Juárez, benefited from the expertise of his master, creating works that were at times sombre, at others luminous. His speciality was flowers strewn on the floor. Another pupil to embrace the style of Sebastián de Orteaga was Baltasar de Echave Rioja, who imitated the style of Rubens, and created the Burial of Christ with great strength and dramatic effect. All these artists, while following the artistic styles and techniques developed in Europe, were separated from the source of their inspiration. Those arriving from Europe had broken contact with trends and tastes in the Old World, while the Mexican artists had never even seen the works they attempted to recreate. So Mexican art continued to develop in a direction different from that of its model, and an almost indefinable style came into being. The 'Golden Age' of Mexican painting closed with two artists distinguished for their prolificness: Cristóbal de Villalpando (born Mexico, 1649) and Juan Correa, flooded the churches and convents with their paintings.

But something else had been happening that was to alter the direction in which Mexican art would go. Excluded from high-ranking positions in both government and the Church, many of the Criollo elite began to explore pre-Hispanic and early colonial Mexico for models. This interest communicated itself to the artist, and led to the creation of the Portrait of Moctezuma and two enormous canvases of about 1653 depicting events in the history of the cult of the Virgin of Guadalupe. This has been described as the awakening of a Criollo, or Euro-Mexican consciousness, as distinct from the Spanish consciousness.

Miguel Cabrera is probably the best-known painter of the colonial period. It has been said that his works display a superficiality in execution and that his tones were limiting in scale. The style created by the Rodriguez Juárez brothers and Cabrera is clearly European in inspiration, but nevertheless manifests subtle distinctions of the Mexican school, among them a quiet sense of arrested motion, a certain naïveté, distinctive local pigments, distortions of physiognomy, occasional traces of Mannerism, and sweet yet observant realism. This departure from the European model echoes the political response to the plight of the Criollo elite, whose response to edicts emanating from Spain was *Obedezco pero no cumplo*, I obey but do not comply.

In the 18th century, the art of portraiture received much attention. The increasing wealth of the Creoles and Gachupines (Spaniards appointed to Mexico to fill high clerical or administrative positions) allowed them to indulge vanity and adorn their palatial homes with portraits, pictures that confirm their wealth and status in the imagery of luxurious drapery, jewellery and haughty expressions. But the 18th century also saw an awakening interest, albeit a romantic one, in the country they inhabited and the people with whom they shared it.

The Enlightenment tenet of knowledge being acquired through scientific observation and experience (Empiricism) reached Mexico; one area that it touched was that of racial mix, a process that had been going on since the Conquest, and the classification of each combination of groups. Miguel Cabrera, himself of mixed race, explored this topic in a group of 16 canvases dedicated to the depiction of the racial groups, whites, blacks, and Indians and the resulting *mestizaje* (mixtures of races) of these groups. They also portray the clothes used by each group and skilfully represent the quality of the fabrics as well as looking to the complicated social structure resulting from this racial mixture.

Others adopted this topic. Among them was José Joaquín Magón, who painted at least two series of 16 paintings devoted to the subject of *mestizaje*, one of which has a caption that reads: *Español y Mestiza producen Castiza*, which suggests that the Spaniard and mixed-race produce a new breed. Although the inclusion of flowers and fruits peculiar to Mexico does not imply a separation of Mexican art from that of Europe, it does show an increasing interest in local images.

During the 18th century the cult of the Virgin of Guadalupe, encouraged by the Jesuits' adoption of this very Mexican icon as their special patron, became a force that united the different groups, racial and economic, under one banner. The Jesuits were expelled in 1767, and some commentators believe that the close relationship between that Order and the Guadalupana was partly to blame for their fall from grace. Their expulsion could be interpreted as an attack on Mexican national identity, an attack that contributed to the Insurrection of 1810 in which the Guadalupana was the figurehead.

The school established by Fray Pedro de Gante which had made a great contribution to the evolution of Mexican art was not immediately followed by the establishment of an academy of art. The arrival of Jerónimo Antonio Gil in 1778 as supervisor of art standards and metallurgical techniques at the Mexico City mint stimulated interest and the Academy of San Carlos was established in 1781. This saw the beginning of the end of colonial art in Mexico.

The drama of the Insurrection and the First Empire was not reflected in the visual arts, which continued to develop from other impetus. Independence scarcely had a dramatic effect on the Academy of San Carlos, whose brighter lights continued to work in both the Romantic and Neoclassic manners, as well as the subsequent 19th-century academic style. The Academy offered a continuity of training, which was echoed by a continuity of patronage.

There was, however, increased interest in the pre-Hispanic cultures of Mexico. The growing middle classes could influence art, especially the secular subject matter. There was also a feeling of distancing from the European roots of Mexican art. Throughout the colony, there was a sense that distance blurs and distorts and that idea became more pronounced as the colonial years faded away. Yet, Rafael Jimeno Planes, of Valencia, continued to be the major teacher of painting at the academy. There are few Neo-classical elements to be detected in his works; he was more inclined to reveal influences from the Baroque and Rococo, and although Neo-classicism was in vogue, it co-existed with remnants of earlier ruling canons. Painters who had been exposed to several artistic traditions and who had never left Mexico created works often referred to as eclectic.

Results varied according to the models they had at hand. It has been observed that although the young Republic housed a few artists of unusual talent, the three decades following Independence were not particularly distinguished years for Mexican art.

However, the first Romantic movement in Mexico can be said to coincide with the achievement of Independence and it was expressed in Neo-classic forms. Foreign artists flocked to Mexico, recording the customs, dress and landscapes of the times. The response was increased interest in landscapes, customs and types, which focussed on the local, specific and unusual rather than the universal and timeless stressed by Neo-classicism. Engravers and lithographers continued to be inspired by the works of the visiting artists, and these they adapted to suit their visions or talents.

The introduction at the Academy of San Carlos of a course in landscape painting at mid-century was to bear a very rich fruit in later years. José María Velasco explored the possibilities in historical painting as well as natural subjects, drawing on events in the pre-Hispanic past for inspiration. Landscape painters were the forerunners of figure painters who would begin to move toward an examination of the Mexican past only with the definitive triumph of the liberal Republican Party in 1867.

The triumphant liberals adopted Positivism as their creed, the biblical themes gave way to those that were more secular, such as the Death of Marat by Santiago Rebull (1875) and in the same year, the painting by Rodrigo Gutiérrez of the Deliberation of the Tlaxcalan Senate Following a Message from Cortés, both magnificent works.

But probably the best-known artist of the epoch was Velasco, who painted the Valley of Mexico; he excelled when indulging in a style that was free in composition and a sincerity of expression. Each detail, be it a rock, the sky, clouds or the sparse vegetation is registered with great realism. Portraiture received the same treatment, and the tradition of including an emblem or legend identifying the subject's status was quietly abandoned.

This period also produced José Guadalupe Posada, whose caricatures were sharp and cutting, regularly hitting at the iniquities of politicians and leaders of society. Modernism in Mexico embraced eclecticism. Julio Ruelas, one of the greatest exponents of *Modernismo*, looked to the inner soul for inspiration, treating line and *chiaroscuro* with unprecedented freedom and transforming them into subtle instruments of his personal imaginative repertoire. The feeling of cynicism, decadence and disenchantment that pervades the *moderismo* works almost predicts the coming Revolution.

The anti-Positivism discernable in late 19th-century Mexican art can be attributed to the policies of the *Porfiriato*, that period (1876-1910) in which Porfirio Díaz held power. So much damage and suffering had been caused by the abuses of the administration that many intellectuals turned to *Modernismo* for solace. Solace, however, was to come with the convulsions of the Revolution, which brought in its wake the great muralists. José Clemente Orozco was influenced by Posada, whose work also affected Diego Rivera, winner of a state scholarship to travel to Europe, which allowed him to reside in Paris while the Revolution raged. David Alfredo Siqueiros, at the age of 13, was already serving one of his many jail sentences for political agitation. Rivera and Siqueiros met up in Europe in 1920. Prior to the Revolution, Mexican artists were exploring the possibility of reaching the uneducated and disaffected masses by means of mural painting. So the walls of the Secretaría Pública and the Escuela Nacional Preparatoria were offered to Siqueiros, Orozco, Rivera and about a dozen other artists. The great dream was to create an art that was identifiably Mexican.

With evangelical zeal, the muralists, working for the pay of ordinary labourers, covered the walls, external and internal, with the ideals that expressed the aims of the Revolution. The choice of location was determined by the status of the public who would view them. The poor would be inspired while the wealthy would be admonished. Although the political developments of post-Revolutionary Mexico were not those envisaged by the revolutionaries, the muralists achieved a success that was heroic in its scope. Aimed principally at Mexicans, the ideals expressed in these paintings reached the artists of post-war Europe and the United States. After centuries of importing styles and themes for their canvases, Mexican artists were now exporting the results of the first real wave of artistic innovation from the Americas. It was an exhilarating period.

As the Revolutionary years became, not the present, but history, and as disillusionment with the Revolution's achievements was felt by a new generation of artists aspiring to emerge from the shadow of the great muralist movement, a new style came into being. Frida Kahlo, wife of Diego Rivera and close friend of Trotsky, found inspiration in folk art rather than Parisian Surrealism. The Surrealist Movement opened Mexican art to approaches far removed from the heroic mural. Yet the fundamental drive of those who participated in post-Revolutionary artistic life remained constant. Artists still yearned both to establish a national identity through their work and to join the great modern Western tradition. This struggle has given their work a certain tension and freshness that remains as a defining factor in the Mexican art of the 20th century.

Architecture

Historians of Mexican art and architecture agree that there are no neat chronologies or easily definable styles available that adequately describe its colonial buildings. Many obstacles disturbed the flow of ideas from Europe to the lands entitled New Spain during the time of the viceroyalty (1521-1810). Problems of communication over the ocean between Madrid and Mexico City and across the vast territories beyond, as well as between the Spanish and their subordinates, enabled other influences to take hold. This resulted in an architecture enriched by the juxtaposition of cultures which fused to create modern Mexico. Formal influences from the diverse groups of indigenous Americans (Indians), such as the Aztecs of central Mexico and the Mayans of the Yucatán, are not easy to find. The most pronounced can be seen in the 18th-century strapwork in the Santa Isabel Church, Tepetzala and the Santo Cristo Chapel, Tlacolula, the atrial crosses at Cuautitlán and Huichapan, and the folk baroque churches at Acatepec and Tonantzintla near Cholula. Differences in the ways that spaces were made and used are discernible, especially in religious buildings, and the icons and other ornamental works adorning their interiors and façades had unprecedented meanings in an alien land of 'things never heard of, seen or dreamed of before.'

The first Franciscan priests arrived in Mexico in 1523, just two years after the arrival of Cortés at the Aztec capital of Tenochtitlán, later Mexico City. Their task and that of other Mendicant Orders soon to follow was to convert the Indians to Christianity, as a way of including them within the jurisdiction of the Spanish court. Their means was through the making of places of worship: a campaign of ecclesiastical construction spread wide across Mexico. On foot they reached the principal Indian centres, dismantling or building over their temples. Dominating the landscape, the *conjuntos* of religious buildings which replaced them consisted of large gardens and walled patios or atrios; a solid, single-aisled vaulted church; and friary buildings (*convento*) focused around a two-storeyed cloister and raised on a platform above the street level of the town. In a creative dynamic these buildings were improvised from memory by amateur priests and constructed by hastily trained Indian craftsmen, on site or at schools in the capital. Outstanding examples include *conventos* constructed by the Franciscans at Huejotzingo, the Augustinians at Acolman and Actopan, and the Dominicans at Teposcolula. A hybrid eclecticism characterises these early permanent buildings, which mix elements of many styles from Europe: Isabaline Gothic (arches, canopies and carving), Romanesque (structural form), Manueline from Portugal, Spanish Plateresque (ornament around doorways and windows), early Baroque, the art of the Moors under Spanish rule – Mudéjar (elaborate timber ceilings), and Tequitqui – the art of the Indian under Spanish rule. This latter term refers to strange bi-planar carving, thought to derive from an interpretation of European prints which were used to introduce images of religious icons to the Indian imagination.

After the 16th century the exotic and pagan presence of non-European influences was suppressed. The visionary friars with their dreams of a Christian utopia were replaced by more organized and politically ambitious priests who located themselves either in the capital of Mexico City, or new outlying cities such as Puebla, Oaxaca and Guadalajara. Spanish professionals often controlled the design of buildings, which became more sophisticated in their structural and ornamental objectives, and more tightly derivative of European models. The decoration of their façades reflected trends in the metropolis, and the contributions of Indian craftsmen were made by highly trained and specialised artisans. The consensus is that Mexican Baroque began in the mid-17th century. At this time a transition was made from the single-aisled church plan of the 16th century to a cruciform vaulted church with a dome over its crossing. This was, however, the limit of influence of the spatial experimentation that characterised Italian Baroque architecture. It was in the ornamentation of church interiors, where the seeds of a hybrid Mexican sensibility had been sewn in 16th-century altarpieces, that an opulence present only in the Iberian colonies developed. Despite some resistance to Baroque ideas in Spain and Mexico due to the sobering influence of Juan de Herrera, architect of the Escorial, social aspiration made the opportunity for grandeur and excess irresistible.

The Baroque in Mexico reached its culmination in the 18th century with the onomatopoeic Churrigueresque, the architecture of the *estípite*. This innovation was introduced from Seville by Jerónimo de Balbás, who first used it in the Altar de los Reyes in Mexico Cathedral, 1718-37. The *estípite* is a type of pilaster tapering towards its base, a characteristic that visually releases it from any structural role. Used in the huge and overwhelming *retablos* (vault-high altarpieces), and later the façades of 18th-century buildings, it embodies the gravity-defying nature of the polychrome and gilded ornament that swarms over their surfaces, and which was constantly remodelled and enriched until the arrival of Neo-classicism at the end of the century. Described as the pinnacle of Mexican religious art these assemblages were the sum of parts always individually derived from a codified European language. It is the act of synthesis, however, this sum of parts, which is quintessentially Mexican. There is a term in Spanish, *conjunto*, which refers to the assemblage of all the visual (plastic) works in a space experienced as intrinsic to the building's presence.

Mexico won Independence from Spain in 1821, but the spirit of its architecture by that time had been muted by an academic Neo-classicism promoted by the influential Academia de San Carlos in Mexico City. Despite the tendency towards unquestioning reproduction that the fashion of Neo-classicism required, explicit Indian references emerged alongside an increasing eclecticism towards the end of the 19th century. Drawn from a seemingly distant past this Indigenism was based on romantic mythologies that served nationalistic ends, rather than on contributions from contemporary Indian culture. Ideas from Europe continued to be transformed by the Mexican imagination, including Art Nouveau at the beginning of the 20th century and a post-Revolutionary attraction to Functionalism in the 1930s. The synthetic integration of architecture with other visual arts which blossomed during colonial times was to re-emerge later, alongside another rise in Indigenism during the middle of the 20th century. The campus of the University City (1950-2) in Mexico City self-consciously places itself within this tradition. Some of its buildings incorporate large murals on their exterior façades which narrate Mexican histories, notably the Olympic Stadium and the Central Library, whilst others seek through their pyramidal and massive form to connect with the land and its Indian legacy.

Culture

People

In 1900 the population was 12 million, a 100 years later it is pushing 100 million, and Mexico City is considered the most populace city on earth with 24 million inhabitants. About nine percent are considered white and about 30 percent Indian; about 60 percent are *mestizos*, a mixture in varying proportions of Spanish and Indian; a small percentage (mostly in the coastal zones of Veracruz, Guerrero and Chiapas) are a mixture of black and white or black and Indian or *mestizo*. Mexico also has infusions of other European peoples, Arab and Chinese. There is a national cultural prejudice in favour of the Indian rather than the Spanish element, though this does not prevent Indians from being looked down on by the more Hispanic elements. There is hardly a single statue of Cortés in the whole of Mexico, but he does figure, pejoratively, in the frescoes of Diego Rivera and his contemporaries. On the other hand, the two last Aztec emperors, Moctezuma and Cuauhtémoc, are national heroes.

Indigenous groups

Among the estimated 24 million Indians there are 54 groups or sub-divisions, each with its own language. Fewer than seven percent of the population now speak them: Oaxaca still has more than a million speakers of indigenous languages; Chiapas about 700,000; and Veracruz and Yucatán close to 500,000. The Indians are far from evenly distributed; 36 percent live on the Central Plateau (mostly Hidalgo, Puebla and México); 35 percent are along the southern Pacific coast (Oaxaca, Chiapas, Guerrero), and 23 percent along the Gulf coast (mostly Yucatán and Veracruz): 94 percent of them, that is, live in these three regions. There are also sizable concentrations in Nayarit and Durango, Michoacán, and Chihuahua, Sinaloa and Sonora. The main groups are: Pápago (Sonora); Yaqui (Sonora); Mayo (Sonora and Sinaloa); Tarahumara (Chihuahua); Huastec and Otomí (San Luis Potosí); Cora and Huichol (Nayarit); Purépecha/Tarasco (Michoacán); scattered groups of Nahua in Michoacán, Guerrero, Jalisco, Veracruz and other central states; Totonac (Veracruz); Tiapaneco (Guerrero); Mixtec, Mixe and Zapotec in Oaxaca state; Lacandón, Tzoltzil, Tzeltal, Chol and others in Chiapas; Maya in Campeche, Yucatán and Quintano Roo.

Land ownership

The issue of access to the land has always been the country's fundamental problem, and it was a despairing landless peasantry that rose in the Revolution of 1910 and swept away Porfirio Díaz and the old system of huge estates. The accomplishments of successive PRI governments have been mixed. Life for the peasant is still hard. The minimum wage barely allows a simple diet of beans, rice, and *tortillas*. The home is still, possibly, a shack with no windows, no water, no sanitation, and the peasant may still not be able to read or write, but something was done to redistribute the land in the so-called *ejido* system, which gave either communal or personal control of the land. The peasant was freed from the landowner, and his family received some basic health and educational facilities from the state. In 1992 new legislation was approved which radically overhauled the outdated agricultural sector with far-reaching political and economic consequences. Farmers now have the right to become private property owners, if two-thirds of the *ejido* votes in favour; to form joint ventures with private businessmen; and to use their land as collateral for loans. Private property owners may form joint stock companies, thereby avoiding the constitutional limits on the size of farms and helping them to raise capital. The failure of any agricultural reforms to benefit the peasants of Chiapas was one of the roots of the EZLN uprising in early 1994.

Migration There have been two major trends in migration. There has always been movement northwards to the United States which fed voraciously, and continues to do so, on cheap labour, and with the crash of the peso the upper classes also moved there in greater numbers. Towns like Tijuana and Ciudad Juárez grew rapidly as workers poured in to labour in the factories or to prepare for crossing the border. Over many years the poor have been migrating to the centre, to Estado de México whilst parts of Mexico City have close to shanty-town conditions. The states with least migration, either in or out, have been Chiapas, Yucatán, Guerrero and Oaxaca. The first three of these are often associated with past or present resistance to central government. The least stable demographically speaking have been Baja Norte, Baja Sur, Quintana Roo and Estado de México either because of tourism or economic unpredictability.

Religion Roman Church or 'other'. It's not so simple in Mexico. Today 90 percent of the population is Catholic, seven percent Protestant and three percent considered non-religious. But every belief is a hybrid concoction or a spin-off from the heavy hand of clerical authority – the Mexican people, ostensibly so orthodox, worship as they want.

The crux of this quiet rebellion is what Anita Brenner called 'Idols behind Altars' in her 1929 book about Mexican art and religion. Ancient beliefs did not die at the conquest under the Franciscan onslaught but went underground, or, more accurately, became the cornerstone of the new religion. The new temples – the chapels and cathedrals, frequently built from the stones of dismantled Aztec, Mixtec and Maya pyramids – often had hidden in their pillars and foundation stones the most sacred idols of the older religions. The most extreme examples of idol worship within Christian edifices were when effigies of ancient deities were concealed underneath or behind crosses.

Despite the intense missionary work of such priests as Fray Jacinto and the later zeal of the Jesuits, Catholicism in Mexico has resisted becoming strictly orthodox. Whereas the Franciscans unsuccessfully tried to convert and dominate, the Jesuits had to resort to translating indigenous myths into Christian stories. Quetzalcoatl, for instance, became St Thomas. This was a two-way thing: indigenous groups began to load their beliefs into Christian vessels. For instance, the taking of hallucinogenic mushrooms imitated the Eucharist and there were black Christs in abundance (black was considered a divine colour in pre-Columbian religions), many of which were known by the names of local deities such as Lord of Chalma or Lord of Amecameca. Our Lady of Guadalupe, Mexico's most miraculous Catholic apparition, was often known as the 'Dark Madonna'. The hill of Tepeyac, where the virgin was sighted by the *campesino* Juan Diego, was initially a shrine to the ancient earth goddess Tonantzin and many considered the Lady of Guadalupe to be her re-apparition. These are complex new idols that are grafted onto Christian stereotypes but which do not fit exactly – Nuestra Señora de Salud, a Madonna that appeared on Lake Pátzcuaro, was seen to perspire – hardly an unearthly figure.

The official Church came to accept this multi-layered Catholicism but remained tied to the state and the ideology of conquest – old allegiances with Spain persisted and later it did well under the Austrian Maximilian and the tyrant Porfirio Díaz. It was a bit of a shock, then, when the Liberal reformers of 1857 attempted to remove all of the Church's economic and cultural influence in the big cities, but a cataclysm of much larger proportions when the revolutionaries in 1917 went one step further and tried to uproot the priests from the countryside as well (see *The Lawless Roads* and *The Power and the Glory*, by Graham Greene). Priests are still not supposed to wear ecclesiastical dress. In many communities the *mayordomo*, a secular figure, organizes the local saint's feast day and often comes into conflict with the local priest.

Religion at grassroots level has fought back. The Cristero war 1926-29 (see page 739) was a rebellion against secular persecution. There are numerous Catholic 'charismatic' movements that act independently of the bishops. There has been a rapid growth of evangelical Protestant movements, particularly in Chiapas, Tabasco, Campeche and Quintana Roo. Protestantism, however, although taking root amongst the poorer socio-economic groups is often viewed with suspicion because of its 'foreigness'.

There has been a tentative rapprochement between State and Church in the 1990s and anyone seeing the millions who attend the passion play and crucifixion at Ixtapalapa during Easter week could not fail to consider Catholicism to be strongly supported. But even passion plays have been linked to pre-Columbian ceremonial rites and the athletic, televised, charge up the hill is as secular as a city marathon. Maybe it is better to go to the Day of the Dead rituals in November to appreciate the fascinating persistence of ancient rites, subtly concealed in a modernising religion.

Background

Cinema

It would be deceptively easy, after a walk past the cinemas near the Zócalo in Mexico City, to believe that Mexico has no indigenous tradition of its own, and that it simply relies on bringing in the latest Hollywood blockbuster for an undiscriminating public. But this would be a mistaken impression since Mexico has an enviable cinematic tradition stretching back to the turn of the century. Indeed, the first motion picture exhibited in Spanish America was shown in Mexico City in August 1896, at about the same time as elsewhere in the world (April 1896 is the equivalent date for the United States). In the early days, the camera was used to capture momentous historical events. Much of the Mexican Revolution was caught on film; one of the leaders of the Revolution, the cattle-rustler, Pancho Villa, signed an exclusive contract with the Mutual Film Corporation, thereby agreeing to have battles filmed, and even to change the time of execution of prisoners of war in order to give the cameramen better lighting. Mexico was producing talkies by 1930, and the first picture filmed in Mexico with direct sound was *Santa* (1931), based on the novel of the same title by Federico Gamboa.

Hollywood was in the ascendancy in the 1930s and few Mexicans in the film industry were able to avoid its pervasive influence. Actresses such as the gorgeous Dolores del Río, directors such as Emilio 'el Indio' Fernández, and cameramen such as Gabriel Figueroa, learned their craft in Hollywood. So it was that the Golden Age of Mexican Cinema, as it is now known, occurred between about 1935 and 1955. A major coup for Mexico, the first-prize winner at the very first Cannes Film Festival ever held (in 1947) was the Mexican film, *María Candelaria* (1943), directed by Fernández, and starring Dolores del Río. This was also the period in which Mexico became famous for its melodramas. In *Madre querida* (Dear Mother; 1935), directed by Juan Orol, we witness the melodramatic story of a young boy who goes to prison and whose mother dies of a broken heart precisely on 10 May, Mother's Day in Mexico. Another favourite stock character of the melodrama was the sexy temptress, fulfilled admirably in this role by María Félix in films such as *Doña Bárbara* (1943), directed by Fernando de Fuentes. Mexican cinema seemed unstoppable during this period. A staggering 124 films were produced in 1950, most of them melodramas.

In the 1950s and 1960s the iconoclastic film director, Luis Buñuel, exiled from his native Spain and applying for Mexican citizenship, made some of his most controversial movies in Mexico, including *Los olvidados* (The Young and the Damned; 1950), *Viridiana* (1961), and *El angel exterminador* (The Exterminating Angel; 1964). The Young and the Damned, in particular, offers a stark view of a group of adolescents in Mexico City who thrive on gratuitous cruelty. A particularly notable

●●

👉 *Mexico and the Western*

It was during the Mexican Revolution that Mexico first really caught the imagination of the US; Mexico was invariably depicted as a land of deserts, cacti, ruthless desperadoes (the fact the word is in Spanish tells us something), and beautiful, seductive women. In Saved by the Flag (1911), for example, a US army lieutenant falls in love and elopes with a sensual Mexican girl who is being pursued by a Mexican general. The films of this period overtly contrasted swarthy, uncivilized Mexicans with white, civilised Americans, and provided ideological justification for the United State's military interventions south of the border, a good example being Uncle Sam in Mexico (1914). A number of films were made in particular about Pancho Villa, the 'greaser' revolutionary who fascinated US audiences, an example of which was Jack Conway's Viva Villa! (1934).

During this early period, the Mexican,

whether exoticised or vilified, was always 'Other'; he represented the underbelly of the American dream. In the first major sound Western, In Old Arizona (1929), directed by Raoul Welsh, for example, the leading role was played by Warner Baxter as the Cisco Kid, a Mexican type on the run from a Texas ranger; Baxter won an Oscar for his performance and established in one fell swoop the South-of-the-Border Western. Other Westerns which took the theme of searching out hoodlums south of the border were Lambert Hillyer's South of the Rio Grande (1932), Mark Wright's Somewhere in Sonora (1933), starring John Wayne, George Sherman's South of the Border (1939), and Joseph Santley's Down Mexico Way (1941). In these films, Mexicans have thick moustaches, wear poncho hats, are lazy, deceitful and prone to unpremeditated, even motiveless, violence.

●●

film of the 1960s was *Tiempo de morir* (A Time to Die; 1965), directed by Arturo Ripstein, and based on a script written by Gabriel García Márquez and Carlos Fuentes, a Western which focuses on one man's obsession with death. By the 1970s Mexican cinema was a force to be reckoned with in the international arena. Important films of this decade include *Canoa* (Canoe, 1975), directed by Felipe Cazals, *Los albañiles* (The Building Workers; 1976), directed by Jorge Fons, *Cascabel* (Rattlesnake; 1976), directed by Raúl Araiza, and *María de mi corazón* (Darling Maria; 1979), directed by Hermosillo and based on a film-script by García Márquez. Of particular interest was Marcela Fernández Violante who produced a string of brilliant works during this period, including *Frida Kalho* (1971), based on the life and work of Mexico's best-known female artist; *De todos modos Juan te llamas* (Whatever You Do, It Makes No Difference; 1975), based on the War of the Cristeros in the aftermath of the Mexican Revolution; and *Cananea* (1977), a film which is set in pre-Revolutionary Mexico and which tells the story of a US mine owner who violently suppresses a miners' strike by calling in the Texan Rangers from across the border.

With the debt crisis of the early 1980s the Mexican government was unable to finance the film industry and encouraged foreign investment; many Mexican film studios, as a result, were bought out by US capital. Carlos Salinas de Gortari's presidency (1988-1994) ushered in an era of privatisation. The actor Héctor Bonilla, for example, invested his own money in Jorge Fons' controversial and widely acclaimed *Rojo amanecer* (Red Dawn; 1989), based on the Tlatelolco massacre of students in Mexico City in 1968 during the Olympic Games. The 1990s have seen some international success stories. *Cabeza de Vaca* (1990), based on the amazing story of Alvaro Nuñez Cabeza de Vaca, the first European ever to traverse the American continent, and directed by Nicolás Echeverría, explores the clash of Spanish and Amerindian cultures with great verve. María Novaro's *Danzón* (1991) uses a fairy-tale format to focus on the life-story of a single mother (played by

Como agua para chocolate

Como agua para chocolate, directed by Alfonso Arau, and based on the best-selling novel of his then wife, Laura Esquivel, was an instant international success when released in 1991. Set in an isolated ranch in northern Mexico near the Texas border, mainly during the Mexican Revolution (1911-19), it tells a story of star-crossed lovers. The authoritarian Mamá Elena (played by Regina Torne) offers Pedro Muzquiz (Marco Leonardi) Rosaura (Yareli Arizmendi), her eldest daughter, in marriage rather than her younger daughter, Tita (Lumi Cavazos), whom Pedro really loves, but who is destined to look after Elena until the latter dies. Pedro agrees to marry Rosaura just to be close to Tita. One of the intriguing features of the film is its use of the skeleton-in-the-cupboard motif (the father of one of the daughters, Gertrudis, is a mulatto and not Elena's husband). A stock technique of this film's varied repertoire is magical realism, such as when the house explodes into a fireworks display when Pedro and Tita finally make love, and the matter-of-fact way in which the appearance of ghosts is treated, some of whom are benevolent (Nacha the cook) and some not (Elena comes back from the grave to curse Tita). But the most striking effect of the film is produced by the metaphor of loving and eating, the best example of which is provided by the scene in which Tita prepares a sauce from the roses Pedro gave her in order to season the quail. The effect on the participants in the meal, particularly Gertrudis, is deliciously done.

Mexico's favourite film star, María Rojo), who is in love with an older man who makes his living out of dancing the *danzón*, a popular Caribbean music-and-dance genre. *Como agua para chocolate* (Like Water for Chocolate; 1991), Alfonso Arau's film version of Laura Esquivel's novel of the same title, a story about undying love, was an international hit, playing to packed audiences in Latin America, the United States and Europe. Other important films of the decade include Arturo Ripstein's *La mujer del puerto* (The Woman of the Port, 1991), a sordid tale in which Tomasa prostitutes her daughter (the abortion scene is not for the faint-hearted); Guillermo del Toro's *Cronos* (1992), a bizarre vampire movie about a time-altering device found in a junk shop in Mexico City; Paul Leduc's *Dollar Mambo* (1993), about the murder of a Panamanian woman by five US soldiers; María Novaro's *El jardín del Edén* (The Garden of Eden, 1994), based on the cultural paradoxes of Tijuana; and Arturo Ripstein's film version of García Márquez's *El coronel no tiene quien le escriba* (No-One Writes to the Colonel, 1999).

Mexican literature can boast that it has the longest, continuous literary tradition of any nation in the New World. Mexico, or New Spain as it was then called, was the first state to have a printing press; there was one operational in Mexico City by 1539, and possibly as early as 1535. Of all the states of Latin America it is the one which has the greatest wealth of Amerindian 'books', or the nearest equivalent to that western notion, namely, the codices which narrate the annals of the Maya and Aztec peoples and provide information in pictorial form about their gods and the divine rituals accorded them. Some of these can be seen in the Museum of Anthropology in Mexico City, and are definitely worth a visit. Mexico even had erudite conquistadors. While Hernán Cortés (1485-1547), the man who brought the mighty Aztec Empire to its knees in a devastatingly efficient campaign beginning in 1519, was able to regale his peers and the Catholic Kings with eloquent accounts of his exploits, in his *Cartas de relación de la conquista de México* (Letters of Account of the Conquest of Mexico; the five letters were written between 1519 and 1526), his equivalent in Peru, Francisco Pizarro, was illiterate and had to sign his name with a

Literature

Lawrence and Greene on Mexico

Attracted by the pantheism of the Aztecs, DH Lawrence (1885-1930), decided to go to Mexico in 1923. From March to May of that year he lodged at the Hotel Monte Carlo, which is located at Calle de Uruguay 69 in Mexico City, and he later stayed near the shore of Lake Chapala in a house which can still be visited. From November 1924 until February 1925 in Oaxaca, Lawrence wrote his Mexican masterpiece, The Plumed Serpent *(1926), a tense, brooding novel inspired by the Aztecs. We follow events through the eyes of the Irish girl, Kate, middle-class and aloof, as she strikes up a friendship with Ramón (who embodies Quetzalcoatl, the plumed serpent god of the Aztec pantheon) and Cipriano (who represents Huitzilopochtli, the corn god), whom she eventually marries. There are some brilliantly vivid descriptions of Mexico in* The Plumed Serpent, *particularly of the bull-fight in Mexico City, and the countryside surrounding Lake Chapala (called Lake Sayula in the novel).*

Graham Greene (1904-91) was sent as an unofficial envoy of the Foreign Office to Mexico from February to May 1938 in order to report on the persecution of priests in Tabasco and Chiapas. As a result, he wrote a travel book, Lawless Roads *(1938), describing his journeys through Laredo, Monterrey, San Luis Potosí, Mexico City, Veracruz and Chiapas. Greene also published a novel based on his Mexican experience,* The Power and the Glory *(1940), seen as his masterpiece, which describes the wanderings of a whisky priest who is attempting to fulfil his priestly duties despite the constant threat of death at the hands of the revolutionary government. The arid countryside and oppressively hot climate of southern Mexico provide an appropriate backdrop to Greene's portrayal of evil as a palpable force.*

cross. Just in case you thought Cortés' was the only version available of the conquest, though, there is a gripping account of the Aztecs' version of events now published in a handy English translation, Miguel León Portilla, *The Broken Spears*. It shows how the Aztec emperor, Moctezuma, was paralysed by fear at the thought that Cortés could really be Quetzalcoatl, the Plumed Serpent God, who had returned to Tenochtitlán in order to reclaim his empire.

During the Colonial Era, which lasted from 1519 until 1810, when Mexico was one of Spain's far-flung colonies, literature lived in the shadow of patronage. This did not stop some fine literary works being published, though, such as Bernardo de Balbuena's *Grandeza Mexicana* (Mexican Grandeur, 1604), which is intended to show to the rest of the world just how magnificent Mexico was. Mexico also boasts among its literary protégés Sor Juana Inés de la Cruz (1651-1695), the intellectually brilliant and breathtakingly attractive nun who wrote some of the most consummate poems ever written in the Spanish language. Her poetry so impressed the Viceroy's wife, de la Laguna, that she took it upon herself to ferry some of Sor Juana's works to Spain to have them published; the publication of *Inundación castálida* (The Castilian Flood, 1689) in Madrid made Sor Juana famous as the 'tenth muse' of the Americas. She is also renowned for being the first feminist in the new World; her *Respuesta de la poetisa a la muy ilustre Sor Filotea* (Reply to Sister Filotea) in which she – with devastating irony – rebuked the Bishop of Puebla for telling her to turn her mind away from literary matters, earned her this reputation. The Church was not amused, forced her to sell her library, which at that time had 4,000 books and was the largest in the New World, and obliged her to tend the sick in Mexico City during a plague which led – perhaps intentionally – to her death. One other important writer of the Colonial period was the dramatist Juan Ruiz de Alarcón (1581?-1639); though born in Mexico, he spent much of his life in Spain, and this has led to much flowing of ink

Mexico and the Beatniks

Mexico came to be something of a 'second home' for many of the US Beatnik writers. One of the foremost writers of the Beatnik generation, William Burroughs (b. 1914), for example, when arrested for the possession of drugs and firearms in 1949, escaped to Mexico City with his wife, Joan, where he lay low until the case was dropped. During a wild party in 1952 Burroughs accidentally shot and killed his wife in a William Tell act, for which he spent two weeks in a Mexican prison. He later wrote about his experiences as a morphine addict in Mexico City in Junkie: Confessions of an Unredeemed Drug Addict, 1953. A similar theme is relived in his autobiographical novel, Queer (1984). Jack Kerouac (1922-69), another of the Beatnik writers and a good friend of Burroughs, also had a Mexican connection. He spent the summer of 1950 with Burroughs at his house in Mexico City and this inspired part of his Beatnik classic, On the Road (1957), in which Sal Paradise (based on Kerouac) and the petty crook Dean Moriarty (based on Neal Cassady) drive across the border from the States into Nuevo Laredo, and then travel through Monterrey on their way to Mexico City. Marijuana and sex form an important part of their journey to personal illumination in Mexico.

Background

as to whether he is really Mexican or not. His claim to fame is his play, *La verdad sospechosa* (The Suspicious Truth, 1634), a witty work which shows how lies can eventually compromise the lives of apparently honest men.

Mexico is also famous for being the country in which the first Latin-American novel was published; this was *El Periquillo Sarniento* (The Itchy Parrot; 1816) written by José Joaquín Fernández de Lizardi (1776-1827), whose nickname was *El Pensador* (The Thinker) because his mission in life was to force his compatriots out of their lethargy which kept them cocooned in the swaddling clothes of Spanish colonialism. The novel describes the life of a picaresque figure who is attempting to earn a living in the society of his time. Its satiric view of life in New Spain earned its author social opprobrium, poverty and an early grave.

Mexico had something of a dry period in the second half of the 19th century. It was involved in the only really authentic literary movement of the time, called *Modernismo* (not to be confused with Anglo-Saxon Modernism, since it was an offshoot of the French Symbolist movement), producing poets such as Manuel Gutiérrez Nájera (1859-1895), but its main claim to fame came in 1911 when the Mexican poet Enrique González Martínez (1871-1952) famously said that the time had come for the swan (which was a favourite symbol of the *modernistas*) to have its neck twisted. The times of aristocratic leisure, as the Mexican Revolution (1910-1919) was to demonstrate convincingly, were definitively over. The best work written about this momentous historical event (the Mexican Revolution, as Mexicans are wont to tell you, preceded the Russian Revolution) was *Los de abajo* (The Underdogs; 1915) by Mariano Azuela (1873-1952). Azuela was a journalist and covered the war, especially during its early stages; he gives a frightening vision of war as a destructive, evil force which brings out the worse in men and women. The years after the Revolution were a time when Mexican writers began to brood on what it meant to be Mexican. To their credit, they refused easy solutions to this dilemma. Some writers, such as Rodolfo Usigli (1905-1979), suggested that Mexicanness was nothing more than a mask; his excellent play, *El gesticulador* (The Gesticulator, 1937), one of the classics of 20th-century Latin American drama, suggest that all Mexicans are forced into living a life of lies.

But perhaps the most important statement of all about what it meant to be a Mexican came from Octavio Paz (1914-1998), the Nobel Prize winner of 1990, and the only Mexican writer to date who has received this accolade. In 1950 he published an enormously influential essay, *El laberinto de la soledad* (The Labyrinth of Solitude), in which he argued that Mexicans are caught in a trap of their own making; living in the 20th century, but trapped by their past. Every Mexican, he suggested, is paying the sin for being the result of the rape of the Indian woman, La Malinche, by Cortés; they are all, therefore, *hijos de la Chingada*. Not every Mexican you meet in the street nowadays, of course, is likely to see his or her dilemma in these terms, but Paz's essay resonated beyond the decade in which it was written. One other particularly momentous literary event occurred in the 1950s, and this was the publication in 1955 of *Pedro Páramo* by Juan Rulfo, seen by many as Mexico's best writer of long and short fiction. *Pedro Páramo* tells the story of a society, in particular the village Comala, which has been ruined by the vindictiveness of a feudal landowner called Pedro Páramo. But what is remarkable about this novel is the manner in which it is told, since it presents the plot as if it were a series of stories told by dead people lying in their graves, thereby delving into popular Mexican beliefs about '*ánimas en pena*', that is, souls who are in purgatory as a result of their actions on earth, and who are never allowed to fully die.

Without doubt the single most significant living Mexican author is the Boom novelist, Carlos Fuentes (b. 1928). He made his name with his novel about the aftermath of the Mexican Revolution, *La muerte de Artemio Cruz* (The Death of Artemio Cruz, 1962) which reconstructs the events of Artemio's life from his death-bed, and has an at first disorientating use of person and tense. Fuentes' later works such as *Cristóbal Nonato* (Christopher Unborn, 1987) and *Diana, o la caza solitaria* (Diana, the Goddess who Hunts Alone, 1994), are masterpieces in their own right. Fuentes was awarded the Príncipe de Asturias prize in 1994 and is Mexico's best bet for a Noble prize in the hopefully not too distant future. Perhaps most significant, though, in the modern era has been the resurgence of interest in women's writing. Writers such as Rosario Castellanos (1925-1974), Elena Poniatowska (b. 1933), and Laura Esquivel (b. 1950), have now asserted themselves as serious contenders for the literary laurels once worn exclusively by men. In particular, Esquivel's novel, *Como agua para chocolate* (Like Water For Chocolate, 1989), has been the hit of the decade. Telling the story of the Mexican Revolution from the point of view of the women who bore the full brunt of its consequences (a version which has often been drowned out by masculinist, nationalist rhetoric), it is able to combine a vision of feminine sensuality with a sense of the uncanny side of life which has entranced readers all over the world. For more information see the relevant sections of Stephen M Hart, *A Companion to Spanish-American Literature* (1999).

The economy

Mexico is the 15th largest country in the world, but it is home to the 11th largest population, now at around 100 million people, twice the number living there in the 1970s. Meeting the needs of this growing population, two-thirds of whom are under 30, is an uphill struggle for the government. The demand for new jobs is enormous. Successive economic crises since 1980 have prevented real incomes from rising as fast as the population. Tight control of the fiscal purse strings in the 1990s, with limits on spending on education and health, has also limited improvement in social indicators. Infant mortality is 17.5 per 1,000 live births, compared with only 7.5 across the border in the USA, while 14 percent of the population over 15 has no primary education. Nevertheless, Mexico has one of the strongest economies in Latin America with a gross domestic product approximately the size of that of Australia, India or Russia. It is a founding member of the North American Free Trade Agreement (NAFTA) and is negotiating a free trade deal with the EU. Its proximity to the USA gives it a useful safety net as any financial crisis is reflected in a rise in illegal migration across the Rio Grande, a pattern Washington is keen to avoid. In the last two decades the US administration has been swift to organize financial rescue packages when required in conjunction with IMF economic programmes to enable Mexico to meet its foreign obligations and prevent a complete collapse of the peso.

Oil

Mexico has been an oil producer since the 1880s and was the worlds leading producer in 1921, but by 1971 had become a net importer. This position was reversed with the discovery in 1972 of major new oil reserves and the country is now the fifth largest producer in the world. Two-thirds of its output comes from offshore wells in the Gulf of Campeche, while much of the rest is produced in the onshore fields in the Chiapas-Tabasco area in the southeast. Mexico depends on fossil fuels to generate 100 percent of its electricity and crude oil, oil products and natural gas account for about a third of government revenues. The international price of oil is therefore a key indicator of the likely health of the Mexican economy.

Mining

Mexico's mineral resources are legendary. Precious metals make-up about a third of non-oil mineral output. The country is the worlds leading producer of silver, fluorite and arsenic and is among the major producers of strontium, graphite, copper, iron ore, sulphur, mercury, lead and zinc. Mexico also produces gold, molybdenum, antimony, bismuth, cadmium, selenium, tungsten, magnesium, common salt, celestite, fullers earth and gypsum. It is estimated that although 60 percent of Mexico's land mass has mineral potential, only 25 percent is known and only five percent explored in detail.

Farming

Agriculture has lost importance since the 1970s and now contributes less than six percent to GDP, although a quarter of the workforce is still employed on the land. About 13 percent of the land surface is under cultivation, of which only about a quarter is irrigated. Over half of the developed cropland lies in the interior highlands. Farming fortunes are almost always related to rainfall and available water for irrigation. On average, four out of every 10 years are good, while four are drought years. In 1999 the southeast suffered floods and mudslides, while elsewhere there was drought. Maize is the staple crop throughout Mexico, but others include sorghum, wheat, barley, rice, beans, tomatoes, a variety of fruit and livestock. There are 24,000 genetic strains of maize in Mexico, but this biodiversity is under threat from contamination by genetically modified corn from the USA, which is poorly regulated and supervised. There is concern that the traditional farming practice of saving the best seed for the following year, a tradition which has continued since corn was first domesticated 9,000 years ago, may be destroyed by commercialised transgenic seeds. Mexico is already growing 50,000 ha of genetically modified cotton and 6,000 ha of transgenic soya, the seeds of which will be sold abroad. Genetically modified, virus-resistant potatoes are being tested.

Manufacturing

There was a huge expansion in manufacturing (including oil refining and petrochemicals) in the latter part of the 20th century and it now contributes around 20 percent of GDP and 90 percent of exports. Mexico City used to be the focal point for manufacturing activity, followed by Guadalajara and Monterrey, but the pollution caused by heavy industry led the government to offer tax incentives to get companies to relocate. Target cities are Tampico, Lázaro Cárdenas, Coatzacoalcos, and Salina Cruz, while much of the manufacturing export activity takes place in the in-bond centres along the border with the USA. There are now over 3,000 *maquiladoras* (in-bond) in northern Mexico and they generate a considerable amount of employment, albeit at low wages with minimal labour rights and very poor conditions for workers.

Background

Tourism Tourism is now the largest single employer and generates billions of dollars in foreign exchange a year, more than petroleum in 1998-99. Over 20 million foreign visitors (mostly US) come annually, many to the purpose-built resorts of Cancún in the Yucatán or the beach hotels in Baja California, Acapulco and Puerto Vallarta, which help to make Mexico the eighth most popular tourist destination in the world. At the turn of the century there were 130 tourism projects in the works, worth some US$3.8 billion, designed to attract new visitors from South America and Europe.

Banking Mexico has suffered several financial crises since the initial debt crisis of 1982, each of which weakened the banking sector. In 1994-95 the devaluation of the peso and dollar flight caused many businesses to face bankruptcy as they could not service their bank loans. Bank deposits fell by 18.5 percent while non-performing loans trebled to 18 percent of banks total loan portfolios. Of the 18 banks privatized in 1992, seven collapsed. They and others had to be taken over by foreigners. Emergency schemes to keep banks solvent and provide interest relief for small debtors cost the government about US$70 billion by 1998. In 1999 the Institute for the Protection of Bank Savings (IPAB) was created to handle the legacy of the post-1994 crisis. The autonomous body lowered deposit insurance, raised capital and increased reserves against overdue loans to improve loan portfolios by 2003. Foreign banks were expected to increase their presence in Mexico and contribute to restoring the financial health of the banking system.

Government

Under the 1917 Constitution, Mexico is a federal republic of 31 states and a Federal District containing the capital, Mexico City. The President, who appoints the Ministers, is elected for six years and can never be re-elected. Congress consists of the 128-seat Senate, half elected every three years on a rotational basis, and the 500-seat Chamber of Deputies, elected every three years. There is universal suffrage.

Local administration The States enjoy local autonomy and can levy their own taxes, and each State has its Governor, legislature and judicature. The President has traditionally appointed the Chief of the Federal District but direct elections were held in 1997 for the first time.

Footnotes

17

Footnotes

Basic Spanish

Whether you have been taught the 'Castillian' pronounciation (all *z's*, and *c's* followed by *i* or *e*, are prununounced as the *th* in *think*) or the 'American' pronounciation (they are pronounced as *s*), you will encounter little difficulty in understanding either: Spanish pronunciation varies geographically much less than English. There are, of course, regional accents and usages; but the basic language is essentially the same everywhere.

Pronouns In the Americas, the plural, familar pronoun *vosotros* (with the verb endings – *áis*, – *éis*), though much used in Spain, is never heard. Two or more people, including small children, are always addressed as *Ustedes (Uds)*.

Inappropriate use of the familiar forms (*tú, vos*) can sound imperious, condescending, infantile, or imply a presumption of intimacy that could annoy officials, one's elders, or, if coming from a man, women.

To avoid cultural complications if your Spanish is limited, stick to the polite forms: *Usted (Ud)* in the singular, *Ustedes* in the plural, and you will never give offense. Remember also that a person who addresses *you* as *tú*, does not necessarily expect to be *tuteada* (so addressed) in return.

You should, however, violate this rule when dealing with a small child, who might be intimidated by *Usted*: he/she is, after all, normally so addressed only in admonitions such as *'¡No, Señor, Ud no tomará un helado antes del almuerzo!'* 'No, Sir, you will not have ice cream before lunch!'

Expressions of time Many misunderstandings about engagements stem from terminology rather than tardiness. Note that in Mexico, *ahora* is often a synonym for *hoy*, 'today', not the 'now', in the dictionary; 'now' or 'soon' are *ahorita*; 'right now' is *ahora mismo* or *enseguida*.

In Central America, *en la tarde*, while it could conceivably mean at 1230 or 1300 in the afternoon, is more likely to mean 1500 or 1600, even 1730 or 1800. A polite way of pinning down a vague commitment is to ask, with a smile, *'¿Como para a qué hora más o menos?'.*

Note also that a Spanish speaker, calculating the number of days until some future event, will count *today*; an English speaker starts counting *tomorrow*, one day hence. If an immigration official tells you you must wait *'tres días'* for some approval, he may well mean only until 'the day after tomorrow' (three days *including* today), not three days counting *from* tomorrow; a three-day hotel stay in Latin America consists of three days and two nights, not three days and nights as in English. (When asked how long you plan to stay, say *'tres noches'* to be clear.)

Hence a British fortnight is a *quincena*, from *quince* (15), not *catorce* (14). *Del lunes en ocho* (8) means the following Monday, not Tuesday; *de hoy en cinco* (5) means four days hence, not five; an event that occurs on alternate Sundays is said to take place *cada quince (15) días*. To clarify, ask *'¿el lunes 11 o el martes 12?'* ('Monday the 11th or Tuesday the 12th?').

Money The word *peso* has many meanings. In conversation along the US-Mexico border, *diez pesos oro* means US$10, as opposed to *diez pesos plata* (MN$10, or 10 Mexican pesos; MN = *Moneda Nacional*).

Terms of address Almost anyone qualified by credentials or custom to a title more elevated than *Sr, Sra*, or *Srta*, uses it. A physician, dentist, or veterinarian is always addressed as *Doctor(a)*, as is any holder of a doctoral degree. Primary school teachers, often not university graduates, are always *Maestro(a)*, as are some skilled crafts people, builders, etc. Secondary school and all university teachers, are always addressed as

Profesor(a), or, informally by their students, as *Profe*. Lawyers and university graduates in any of the arts or social sciences are addressed as *Licenciado(a)*; graduate engineers, and holders of any degree in a technical field, use *Ingeniero(a)*, abbreviated *Ing.* Architects use *Arquitecto(a)*, abbreviated *Arq.* Protestant clergy are always *Reverendo(a)*, never just *Sr(a)*.

Address male strangers over the age of 20 or so as Señor, or, if substantially older than you, as *Don*. Younger men may be addressed as *Joven*. Address female strangers over the age of 20 or so, or younger women if they are obvioulsy accompanied by (their own) children or a husband, as *Señora*. Younger women can safely be addressed as *Señorita*, or if younger than you, as *Joven*. Address middle-aged or older women as *Doña*.

Note that the terms *Señorita* and *Señora* have implications of virginity as well as marital status. An elderly woman who has no children and has never married may well correct you if addressed as Señora. So might a younger women whose escort is a friend, still a fiancé, or a relative. This is a grave matter for the women concerned, and the appropriate response is *'Disculpe, Señorita'*, *un*accompanied by a smile, which might be interpreted as a smirk.

Once you have learned a person's name young people among themselves, as everywhere, use given names or nicknames immediately. Whenever the person addressed is a few years older, however, use the form *Señora González*, or to imply respectful friendship, *Señor Juan*. Where the age difference is substantial, use *Doña Mercedes* or *Don Francisco*. Reply to officials' questions with *Sí, Señor* or *No, Señora*.

General hints Note that in Central America, the proper response to *¡Gracias!* is as often as not *¡A la orden!* ('Yours to command!') rather than the *'¡De nada!'* ("Tis nought!') taught in school.

Travellers whose names include *b's* and *v's* should learn to distinguish between them when spelling aloud as *be larga* and *ve corta* or *uve*. (Children often say *ve de vaca* and *be de burro* to distinguish between the two letters, pronounced interchangeably, either as *b* or *v*, in Spanish.)

Useful words and phrases

Greetings & courtesies	**Spanish**		
hello/	*hola/*	please	*por favor*
good morning	*buenos días*	thank you	*(muchas)*
good afternoon/	*buenas tardes/*	(very much)	*gracias*
evening/night	*noches*	yes/no	*sí/no*
goodbye	*adiós/chao*	excuse me/	*permiso*
see you later	*hasta luego*	I'm sorry	*lo siento/desculpe*
how are you?	*¿cómo está/*	I don't understand	*no entiendo*
	cómo estás?	please speak slowly	*hable despacio*
			por favor
I'm fine	*muy bien gracias*	what's your name?/	*¿cómo se llama?/*
pleased to	*mucho gusto/*	I'm called_	*me llamo_*
meet you	*encantado*	Go away!	*¡Váyase!*

Basic questions			
where is_?	*¿dónde está_?*	when does the bus	*¿a qué hora sale/llega*
how much does	*¿cuánto vale?*	leave/arrive?	*el*
it cost?		why?	*autobus?*
when?	*¿cuándo?/¿ a que hora?*	how do I get to_?	*¿por qué?*
			¿cómo llegar a_?

Basics			
police (policeman)	*la policía (el policía)/*	bank	*el banco*
	el carabinero	exchange house	*la casa de cambio*
hotel	*el hotel (la pensión,*	exchange rate	*la tasa de cambio*
	el residencial,	travellers' cheques	*los travelers/*
	el hospedaje)		*los cheques de*
room	*el cuarto/*		*viajero*
	la habitación	cash	*el efectivo*
single/double	*single/doble*	breakfast	*el desayuno*
with two beds	*con dos camas*	lunch	*el almuerzo*
bathroom/toilet	*el baño*	dinner/supper	*la cena*
hot/cold water	*agua caliente/fría*	meal	*la comida*
toilet paper	*el papel higiénico*	drink	*la bebida*
restaurant	*el restaurant*	mineral water	*el agua mineral*
post office/	*el correo/el*	beer	*la cerveza*
telephone office	*centro de llamadas*	with/without sugar	*con/sin azúcar*
supermarket	*el supermercado*	without meat	*sin carne*
market	*el mercado*		

Getting around			
on the left/right	*a la izquierda/*	train/train station	*el tren/la estación*
	derecha		*(de tren)*
straight on	*derecho*	airport	*el aeropuerto*
bus station	*la terminal*	aeroplane	*el avión*
	(terrestre)	ticket	*el boleto*
bus stop	*la parada/el*	ticket office	*la taquilla*
	paradero	luggage	*el equipaje*
interurban bus	*el bus*		
urban bus	*el micro*		
collective taxi	*el colectivo*		

Footnotes

Time

What time is it?	*¿Qué hora es?*	it's one o'clock	*es la una*
at half past two	*a las dos y media*	it's seven o'clock	*son las siete*
ten minutes	*diez minutos*	it's ten to seven	*son las siete menos diez*
five hours	*cinco horas*	it's 6.20	*son las seis y veinte*

Numbers Spanish

1	*uno/una*	11	*once*	21	*veintiuno*
2	*dos*	12	*doce*	30	*treinte*
3	*tres*	13	*trece*	40	*cuarenta*
4	*cuatro*	14	*catorce*	50	*cincuenta*
5	*cinco*	15	*quince*	60	*sesenta*
6	*seis*	16	*dieciseis*	70	*setenta*
7	*siete*	17	*diecisiete*	80	*ochenta*
8	*ocho*	18	*dieciocho*	90	*noventa*
9	*nueve*	19	*diecinueve*	100	*cien, ciento*
10	*diez*	20	*veinte*	1000	*mil*

Days/Months

Monday	*lunes*	March	*marzo*
Tuesday	*martes*	April	*abril*
Wednesday	*miercoles*	May	*mayo*
Thursday	*jueves*	June	*junio*
Friday	*viernes*	July	*julio*
Saturday	*sábado*	August	*agosto*
Sunday	*domingo*	September	*septiembre*
		October	*octubre*
January	*enero*	November	*noviembre*
February	*febrero*	December	*diciembre*

Key verbs

To go	*Ir*	To be	
I go	*voy*	(in a permanent	
you go	*vas*	state)	*Ser*
s/he/it goes	*va*	I am	*Soy*
you (unfamiliar		you are	*eres*
singular) go	*va*	s/he/it is	*es*
we go	*vamos*	you (unfamiliar	
they/you (plural) go	*van*	singular) are	*es*
		we are	*somos*
To have	*Tener*	they/you (plural) are	*son*
I have	*tengo*		
you have	*tienes*	To be (positional or	
s/he/it has	*tiene*	temporary state)	*Estar*
you (unfamiliar		I am	*estoy*
singular) have	*tiene*	you are	*estás*
we have	*tenemos*	s/he/it is	*está*
they/you (plural) have	*tienen*	you (unfamiliar	
		singular) are	*está*
		we are	*estamos*
		they/you (plural) are	*están*

See also Food and drink in Essentials, page 49

Index

Advertisers

Shorts

Footnotes

Map index

Footnotes

Sales & distribution

Footprint Handbooks
6 Riverside Court
Lower Bristol Road
Bath BA2 3DZ England
T 01225 469141
F 01225 469461
E Mail info@
footprintbooks.com

Australia
Peribo Pty
58 Beaumont Road
Mt Kuring-Gai
NSW 2080
T 02 9457 0011
F 02 9457 0022

Austria
Freytag-Berndt Artaria
Kohlmarkt 9
A-1010 Wien
T 01 533 2094
F 01 533 8685

Belgium
Craenen BVBA
Mechelsesteenweg 633
B-3020 Herent
T 016 23 90 90
F 016 23 97 11

Canada
Ulysses Travel Publications
4176 rue Saint-Denis
Montréal
Québec H2W 2M5
T 514 843 9882
F 514 843 9448

Europe
Bill Bailey
16 Devon Square
Newton Abbott
Devon TQ12 2HR. UK
T 01626 331079
F 01626 331080

Denmark
Nordisk Korthandel
Studiestraede 26-30 B
DK-1455 Copenhagen K
T 3338 2638
F 3338 2648

Scanvik Books
Esplanaden 8B
DK-1263 Copenhagen K
T 33 12 77 66
F 33 91 28 82

Finland
Akateeminen Kirjakauppa
Keskuskatu 1
FIN-00100 Helsinki
T 09 12141
F 09 121 4441

Suomalainen Kirjakauppa
Koivuvaarankuja 2
01640 Vantaa 64
F 08 52 78 88

France
L'Astrolabe
46 rue de Provence
F-75009 Paris 9e
T 1 42 85 42 95
F 1 45 75 92 51

VILO Diffusion
25 rue Ginoux
F-75015 Paris
T 01 45 77 08 05
F 01 45 79 97 15

Germany
GeoCenter ILH
Schockenriedstrasse 44
D-70565 Stuttgart
T 0711 781 94610
F 0711 781 94654

Brettschneider
Fernreisebedarf
Feldkirchnerstrasse 2
D-85551 Heimstetten
T 089 990 20330
F 089 990 20331

Geobuch Gmbh
Rosental 6
D-80331 München
T 089 265030
F 089 263713

Gleumes
Hohenstaufenring 47-51
D-50674 Köln
T 0221 215650
Globetrotter Ausrustungen
Wiesendamm 1
D-22305 Hamburg
F 040 679 66183

Dr Götze
Bleichenbrücke 9
D-2000 Hamburg 1
T 040 3031 1009-0

Hugendubel Buchhandlung
Nymphenburgerstrasse 25
D-80335 München
T 089 238 9412
F 089 550 1853

Kiepert Buchhandlung
Hardenbergstrasse 4-5
D-10623 Berlin 12
T 030 311880

Greece
GC Eleftheroudakis
17 Panepistemiou
Athens 105 64
T 01 331 4180-83
F 01 323 9821

India
Roli Books
M-75 GK II Market
New Delhi 110048
T (011) 646 0886
F (011) 646 7185

Israel
Geographical Tours
8 Tverya Street
Tel Aviv 63144
T 03 528 4113
F 03 629 9905

Italy
Librimport
Via Biondelli 9
I-20141 Milano
T 02 8950 1422
F 02 8950 2811

Netherlands
Nilsson & Lamm bv
Postbus 195
Pampuslaan 212
N-1380 AD Weesp
T 0294 494949
F 0294 494455

Norway
Schibsteds Forlag A/S
Akersgata 32 - 5th Floor
Postboks 1178 Sentrum
N-0107 Oslo
T 22 86 30 00
F 22 42 54 92

Tanum
PO Box 1177 Sentrum
N-0107 Oslo 1
T 22 41 11 00
F 22 33 32 75

Olaf Norlis
Universitetsgt 24
N-1062 Oslo
T 22 00 43 00

Pakistan
Pak-American Commercial
Zaib-un Nisa Street
Saddar
PO Box 7359
Karachi
T 21 566 0418
F 21 568 3611

South Africa
Faradawn CC
PO Box 1903
Saxonwold 2132
T 011 885 1787
F 011 885 1829

South America
Humphrys Roberts
Associates
Caixa Postal 801-0
Ag. Jardim da Gloria
06700-970 Cotia SP
Brazil
T 011 492 4496
F 011 492 6896

Southeast Asia
APA Publications
38 Joo Koon Road
Singapore 628990
T 865 1600
F 861 6438

Spain
Altaïr
Balmes 69
08007 Barcelona
T 93 3233062
F 93 4512559

Bookworld España
Pje Las Palmeras 25
29670 San Pedro Alcántara
Málaga
T 95 278 6366
F 95 278 6452

Libros de Viaje
C/Serrano no 41
28001 Madrid
T 01 91 577 9899
F 01 91 577 5756

Sweden
Hedengrens Bokhandel
PO Box 5509
S-11485 Stockholm
T 8 6115132

Kart Centrum
Vasagatan 16
S-11120 Stockholm
T 8 111699

Lantmateriet Kartbutiken
Kungsgatan 74
S-11122 Stockholm
T 08 202 303
F 08 202 711

Switzerland
Artou
8 rue de Rive
CH-1204 Geneva
T 022 311 4544
F 022 781 3456

Office du Livre OLF SA
ZI 3, Corminboeuf
CH-1701 Fribourg
T 026 467 5111
F 026 467 5466
Schweizer Buchzentrum
Postfach
CH-4601 Olten
T 062 209 2525
F 062 209 2627

Travel Bookshop
Rindermarkt 20
Postfach 216
CH-8001 Zürich
T 01 252 3883
F 01 252 3832

USA
NTC/ Contemporary
4255 West Touhy Avenue
Lincolnwood
Illinois 60646-1975
T 847 679 5500
F 847 679 2494

Footnotes

Footprint travel list

Footprint publish travel guides to over 120 countries worldwide. Each guide is packed with practical, concise and colourful information for everybody from first-time travellers to travel aficionados . The list is growing fast and current titles are noted below. For further information check out the website **www.footprintbooks.com**

Andalucía Handbook
Argentina Handbook
Bali & the Eastern Isles Hbk*
Bangkok & the Beaches Hbk*
Bolivia Handbook
Brazil Handbook
Cambodia Handbook
Caribbean Islands Handbook
Chile Handbook
Colombia Handbook
Cuba Handbook
Dominican Republic Handbook*
East Africa Handbook
Ecuador & Galápagos Handbook
Egypt Handbook Handbook
Goa Handbook
India Handbook
Indian Himalaya Handbook*
Indonesia Handbook
Ireland Handbook
Israel Handbook
Jordan Handbook*
Jordan, Syria & Lebanon Hbk
Laos Handbook
Libya Handbook*
Malaysia Handbook
Myanmar Handbook
Mexico Handbook
Mexico & Central America Hbk
Morocco Handbook
Namibia Handbook
Nepal Handbook
Pakistan Handbook

Peru Handbook
Rio de Janeiro Handbook*
Scotland Handbook
Singapore Handbook
South Africa Handbook
South American Handbook
South India Handbook*
Sri Lanka Handbook
Sumatra Handbook
Thailand Handbook
Tibet Handbook
Tunisia Handbook
Venezuela Handbook
Vietnam Handbook

* available autumn 2000

In the pipeline – Turkey, London, Kenya, Rajasthan, Scotland Highlands & Islands, Syria & Lebanon

Also available from Footprint
Traveller's Handbook
Traveller's Healthbook

Available at all good bookshops

Will you help us?

We try as hard as we can to make each Footprint Handbook as up-to-date and accurate as possible but, of course, things always change. Many people write to us - with corrections, new information, or simply comments.

If you want to let us know about an experience or adventure - hair-raising or mundane, good or bad, exciting or boring or simply something rather special - we would be delighted to hear from you. Please give us as precise information as possible, quoting the edition number (you'll find it on the front cover) and page number of the Handbook you are using.

Your help will be greatly appreciated, especially by other travellers. In return we will send you details about our special guidebook offer.

email Footprint at:
mex1_online@footprintbooks.com

or write to:
Elizabeth Taylor
Footprint Handbooks
6 Riverside Court
Lower Bristol Road
Bath BA2 3DZ
UK

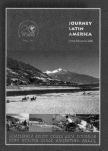

...the magic of all inclusive

...e ocean smiles... Mazatlan

...nega Oceano Palace

...e Oceano Palace is a beach-front resort located on the
...ious golden zone of Mazatlan "Now" offering the
...venience of an ALL-INCLUSIVE vacation. The Resort is
...own for its fun atmosphere and welcomes guests of all ages.
...t 30 minutes from the International Airport and 10 minutes
...n Mazatlan's revitalized downtown.

...exican atmosphere... Puerto Vallarta

...ega Las Palmas Beach Resort

...exciting Resort is nestled right on the beach in the heart
...e hotel zone. Only 15 minutes away from downtown, it
...rs an exciting atmosphere and exceptional beach front
...ommodations with a unique and authentic Mexican
...iance.

...mantic... Puerto Vallarta

...ega San Marino Plaza

...l Omega San Marino Plaza is located in the romantic
...on of Puerto Vallarta, also called Olas Altas or Los Muertos
...h. Surrounded by beautiful tropical mountains, restaurants,
...ping areas and cafés. The action is never ending in this
...t city of Puerto Vallarta

...utical atmosphere... Puerto Vallarta

...ega Nautilus Marina

...ted in Mexico's Pacific coastline, is nestled inside one
...largest protected bays in the world-Banderas Bay.
...m waters wash upon miles of beaches and provide playground
...ter activities of every type.

...w.omegaresorts.com

Francisco Medina Ascencio Km. 2.5 Tels (322) 40650
...322) 40543, Puerto Vallarta, Jalisco, Mexico.
...ctus@omegaresorts.com

Mexico

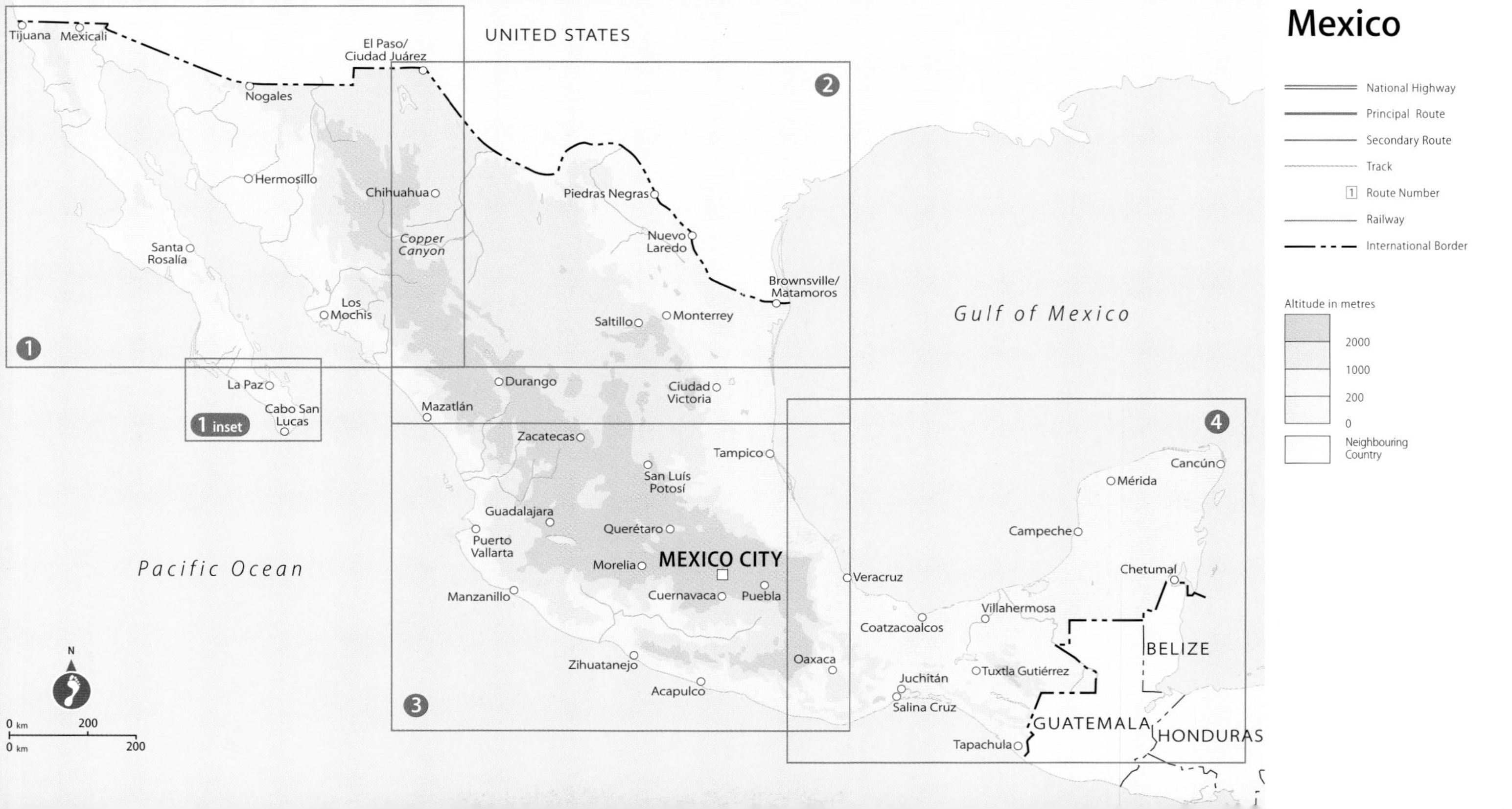

National Highway
Principal Route
Secondary Route
Track
1 Route Number
Railway
International Border

Altitude in metres

2000
1000
200
0
Neighbouring Country

UNITED STATES

1

Tijuana Mexicali
Nogales
Santa Rosalia
Hermosillo
El Paso/ Ciudad Juárez
Chihuahua
Copper Canyon
Los Mochis
La Paz
Cabo San Lucas
1 inset

2

Piedras Negras
Nuevo Laredo
Brownsville/ Matamoros
Monterrey
Saltillo
Ciudad Victoria
Durango
Mazatlán
Zacatecas
San Luis Potosí
Querétaro
Guadalajara
Morelia
Puerto Vallarta
Manzanillo
Tampico

3

MEXICO CITY
Cuernavaca
Puebla
Zihuatanejo
Acapulco
Oaxaca

Gulf of Mexico

4

Cancún
Mérida
Chetumal
BELIZE
Campeche
Villahermosa
Tuxtla Gutiérrez
GUATEMALA
HONDURAS
Veracruz
Coatzacoalcos
Juchitán
Salina Cruz
Tapachula

Pacific Ocean

N

0 km 200
0 km 200

Map 1

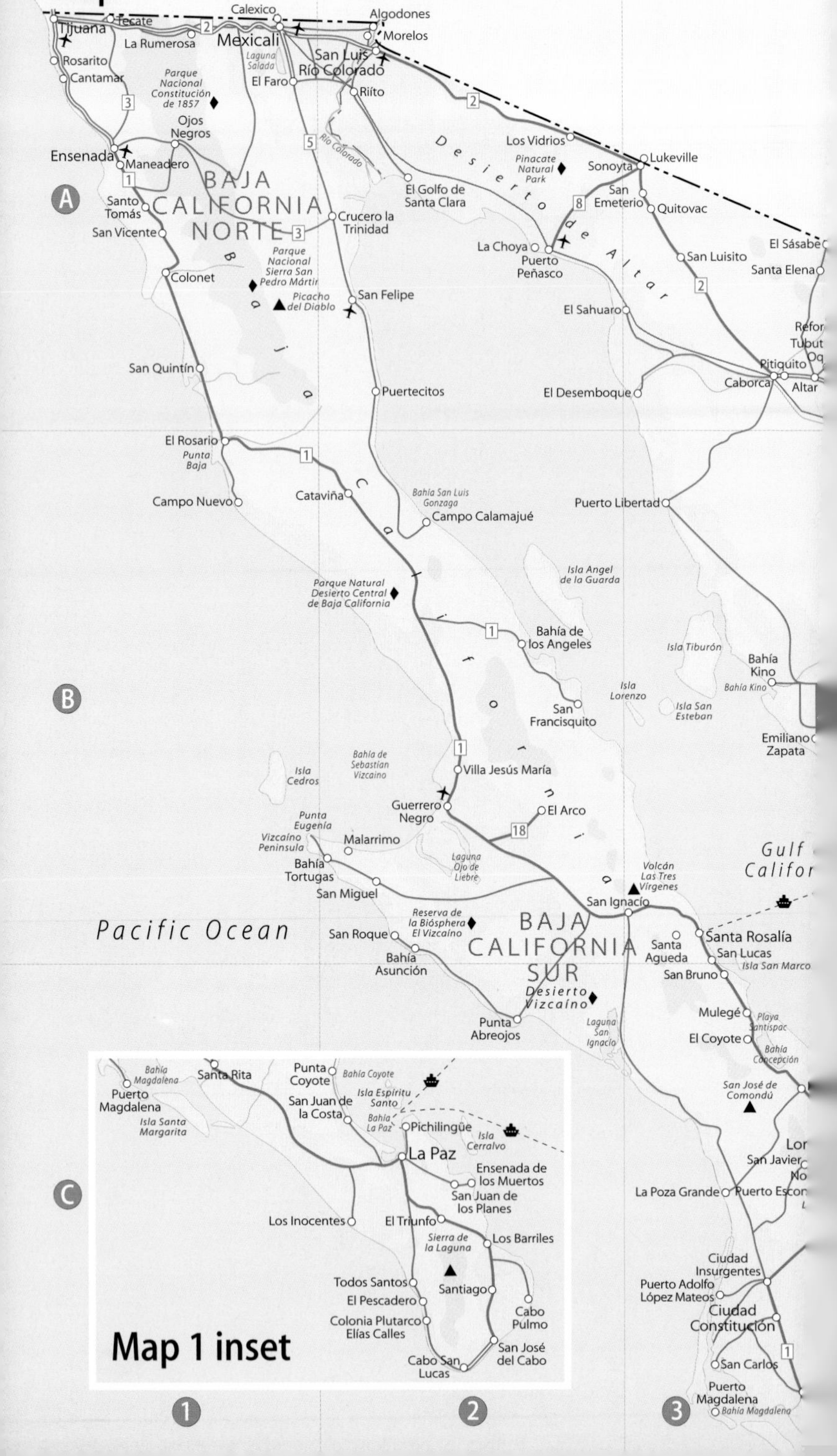

Tijuana
Tecate
Calexico
Algodones
Rosarito
La Rumerosa
Mexicali
Morelos
Cantamar
Laguna Salada
San Luis Río Colorado
El Faro
Riíto
Ensenada
Maneadero
Parque Nacional Constitución de 1857
Ojos Negros
El Golfo de Santa Clara
Los Vidrios
Pinacate Natural Park
Sonoyta
Lukeville
Santo Tomás
BAJA CALIFORNIA NORTE
San Emeterio
Quitovac
El Sásabe
San Vicente
Crucero la Trinidad
La Choya
Puerto Peñasco
San Luisito
Santa Elena
Colonet
Parque Nacional Sierra San Pedro Mártir
Picacho del Diablo
San Felipe
El Sahuaro
Reform Tubut Og
Pitiquito
San Quintín
Puertecitos
El Desemboque
Caborca
Altar

El Rosario
Punta Baja
Cataviña
Bahía San Luis Gonzaga
Campo Calamajué
Puerto Libertad
Campo Nuevo
Parque Natural Desierto Central de Baja California
Isla Angel de la Guarda
Bahía de los Angeles
Isla Tiburón
Bahía Kino
San Francisquito
Isla Lorenzo
Isla San Esteban
Emiliano Zapata
Isla Cedros
Bahía de Sebastián Vizcaino
Villa Jesús María
Punta Eugenia
Vizcaíno Peninsula
Guerrero Negro
El Arco
Gulf Califor
Malarrimo
Laguna Ojo de Liebre
Bahía Tortugas
San Miguel
Reserva de la Biósphera El Vizcaíno
BAJA CALIFORNIA SUR
Volcán Las Tres Vírgenes
San Ignacio
Santa Rosalía
Pacific Ocean
San Roque
Santa Agueda
San Lucas
Isla San Marco
Bahía Asunción
Desierto Vizcaíno
San Bruno
Punta Abreojos
Laguna San Ignacio
Mulegé
Playa Santispac
El Coyote
Bahía Concepción

Map 1 inset
Bahía Magdalena
Santa Rita
Punta Coyote
Bahía Coyote
Puerto Magdalena
San Juan de la Costa
Isla Espíritu Santo
San José de Comondú
Isla Santa Margarita
Pichilingüe
Bahía La Paz
Isla Cerralvo
La Paz
Ensenada de los Muertos
Lor
San Javier
Los Inocentes
San Juan de los Planes
La Poza Grande
Puerto Escon
El Triunfo
Sierra de la Laguna
Los Barriles
Todos Santos
Santiago
Ciudad Insurgentes
El Pescadero
Cabo Pulmo
Puerto Adolfo López Mateos
Colonia Plutarco Elías Calles
Ciudad Constitución
Cabo San Lucas
San José del Cabo
San Carlos
Puerto Magdalena
Bahía Magdalena

A B C

1 2 3

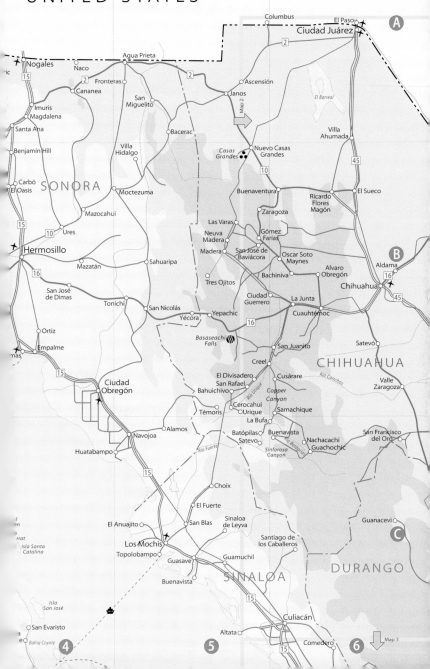

UNITED STATES

Columbus
El Paso
Ciudad Juárez
2

Nogales
Naco
Agua Prieta
15
Fronteras
2
Ascensión
El Barreal
Cananea
San Miguelito
Janos
Map 2
Imuris
Magdalena
Villa Hidalgo
Bacerac
Villa Ahumada
Santa Ana
Benjamín Hill
Casas Grandes
Nuevo Casas Grandes
Carbó
El Oasis
SONORA
Moctezuma
Buenaventura
10
45
Mazocahui
Ricardo Flores Magón
El Sueco
Las Varas
Zaragoza
Ures
10
Neuva Madera
Gómez Farías
Hermosillo
Madera
San José de Baviácora
Oscar Soto Maynes
B
Mazatán
Sahuaripa
Alvaro Obregón
Aldama
16
San José de Dimas
Bachiniva
Chihuahua
16
Tres Ojitos
45
Tonichi
San Nicolás
Ciudad Guerrero
La Junta
Ortiz
Yepachic
Cuauhtémoc
Empalme
Yécora
16
15
Basaseachi Falls
San Juanito
Satevó
Ciudad Obregón
Creel
CHIHUAHUA
El Divisadero
Cusárare
Río Conchos
San Rafael
Copper Canyon
Valle Zaragoza
Bahuichivo
Cerocahui
Samachique
Témoris
Urique
La Bufa
Batópilas
Buenavista
Nachacachi
San Francisco del Oro
Navojoa
Alamos
Satevo
Guachochic
Huatabampo
Sinforosa Canyon
15
Choix
Guanacevi
C
El Fuerte
El Anuajito
San Blas
Sinaloa de Leyva
Santiago de los Caballeros
Los Mochis
Guamuchil
DURANGO
Topolobampo
Guasave
Buenavista
SINALOA
Isla San José
15
San Evaristo
Bahía Coyote
4
5
Altata
Culiacán
Comedero
6
Map 3

N

0 km 50
0 miles 50

A

Río Urique
Río Batopilas
Río Fuerte

N

0 km 50
0 miles 50

UNITED STATES

A

Ciudad Acuña

Picas

Rio Sabinas

Piedras Negras
Allende
57

Nueva
Rosita
Palau

Sabinas

Melchor
Múzquiz

2

Nuevo Laredo   Laredo

Anáhuac

B

30

Monclova

Lampazos
de Naranjo

85

ociénegas
arranza

Castaños

Sabinas
Hidalgo

Ciudad
Guerrero
Mier

ue Nuevo

57   53

85

General
Treviño

Camargo

54

Reynosa

Brownsville

NUEVO LEON

Río Bravo   2   Matamoros

40

DL Garzas

40   China

Valle
Hermoso

101

Monterrey

Guadalupe

35

General
Cepeda

Saltillo

Agua
Nueva

Allende

Montemorelos

97

Santa
Teresa

Mezquital

Concepción
del Oro

San
Roberto

Linares

San Fernando
de Presas

La Carbonera

Map 3

San Carlos

TAMAULIPAS

C

54

an Tiburcio

Presa de las
Adjuntas

La Pesca

Santo
Domingo

Real de
Catorce

Ciudad
Victoria

70

Soto la
Marina

SAN LUIS

Matehuala

85

4

POTOSI

101

5

Tula

81

6

La Cruz

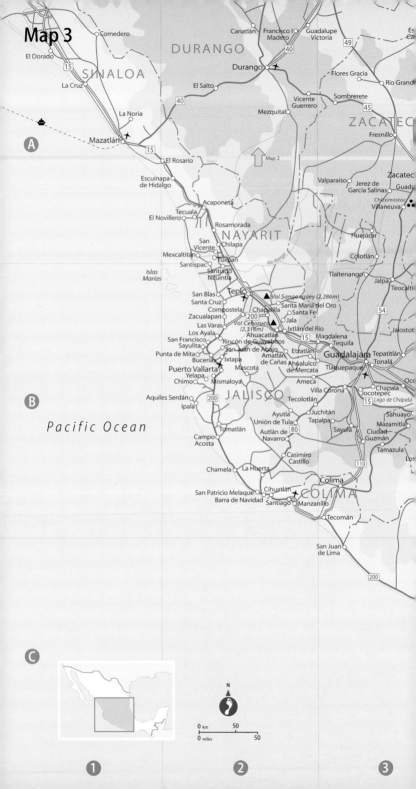

Map 4

Gulf of Mexico

Gulf of Tehuantepec

Mexico City metro

Ciudad Azteca
Plaza Aragón
Olímpica
Tecnológico
(Under construction)
Múzquiz
Río de los Remedios
Impulsora
Continentes
Bosque de Aragón
Villa de Aragón
ón
Deportivo Oceanía
Oceanía
mero Rubio
Terminal Aérea
✈
Hangares
z
is
oza
va
Puebla
Pantitlán
Agrícola Oriental
Canal de San Juan
Tepalcate
Guelatao
Peñón Viejo
Acatitla
Santa Marta
Cerro de la Estrella
Los Reyes
UAM
Constitución de 1917
La Paz

Line
1		
2		& Tren Ligero
3		
4		
5		
6		
7		
8		
9		
A		Metro Férreo
B		

Conversion tables

Weights and measures

Weight
1 kilogram = 2.205 pounds
1 pound = 0.454 kilograms

Length
1 metre = 1.094 yards
1 yard = 0.914 metres

1 kilometre = 0.621 miles
1 mile = 1.609 kilometres

Capacity
1 litre = 0.0220 gallons
1 gallon = 4.546 litres
1 pint = 0.863 litres

Temperature

°C	°F	°C	°F
1	34	26	79
2	36	27	81
3	38	28	82
4	39	29	84
5	41	30	86
6	43	31	88
7	45	32	90
8	46	33	92
9	48	34	93
10	50	35	95
11	52	36	97
12	54	37	99
13	56	38	100
14	57	39	102
15	59	40	104
16	61	41	106
17	63	42	108
18	64	43	109
19	66	44	111
20	68	45	113
21	70	46	115
22	72	47	117
23	74	48	118
24	75	49	120
25	77	50	122

What the papers say

"Footprint can be depended on for accurate travel information and for imparting a deep sense of respect for the lands and people they cover."
World News

"The titles in the Footprint Handbooks series are about as comprehensive as travel guides get."
Travel Reference Library

"Who should pack them – people who want to escape the crowd."
The Observer

"No-nonsense, succinct, authoritative."
National Geographic Traveler

"The guides for intelligent, independently minded souls of any age or budget."
Indie Traveller

Awards
Wanderlust Readers' Award for Top Guidebook Series
Bronze Award

Literati Club
Outstanding Achievement

Website
www.footprintbooks.com
Take a look for the latest news, to order
a book or join our mailing list.

Acknowledgements

Patrick Maher would like to thank the following for their considerable and invaluable contributions to this book.

Gavin Clark is a freelance journalist from London. He spent several months in the Yucatan Peninsula and Chiapas researching for this book. He has also contributed to Footprint's Cuba and South American Handbooks.

Hailing from Canada and Ecuador respectively, **Robert and Daisy Kunstaetter** have spent the past 17 years living and travelling throughout Mexico, South and Central America. They currently make their home in Ecuador, and are currently researching and writing Footprint's Ecuador Handbook.

John Gibbs lives in Mexico City where he runs his fine-art publishing business and contributes to *Amistad Británico-Mexicana*.

Apart from contributing to the South American Handbook, **Simon Harvey** has also worked on the Peru, Colombia, Ecuador and Chile Handbooks.

The late **Jim Hardy** graduated from college in Southern California, then travelled throughout Latin America by bus and spent ten years in Mexico, eight living in Guadalajara.

The author also wishes to acknowledge the specialist contributions made by: **S. Cameron** (Economy), **H. Clough** (Achaeology), **J. Gibbs**, **S. Hart** (Cinema and Literature), **E. Hoyt** (Whales and Tortillas!), **J.L. Juárez** (Food), **P. Pollard** (Land and environment), **C. Nurse** (History), **P. Stokes** (Flora and fauna), **H. Thomas** (Architecture), and neighbour **P. Richards**, for his invaluable computing help. A special thanks to editor **Felicity Laughton** (who has lived and worked in Mexico for 18 years and has contributed to several publications on the country) for all her hard work, and to all at Footprint.

The author is also very grateful to the many readers who took time out to email or write in with their comments and suggestions. E. Adams (Mexico), J. Adcock (USA), S. Alagaratnam & Y. Lien (Netherlands), C. Anderson, J. Anderson, I. Andersson (Sweden), M. Angst (Switzerland), M. Arden (Germany), B. Arenvall, G. Bates, J. Bauer (Germany), E. Bellini (Italy), M. Biechl (Austria), C. Boobbyer (UK), P. Bouchard (Canada), D. Bradley (UK), E. Brossin & M. Ciurea (Switzerland), A. Buchner (Israel), N. Covis, F. Cregan (Ireland), G. Dack & M. Retief, B. Desschanns (Belgium), M. Dulacki (USA), M. Eberl (Switzerland), U. Edenhofer, E. Erbe (USA), J. Erler (UK), N. Fellman (USA), H. Ferber (Mexico), L. Fullerton (Mexico), A. Graham (USA), J. Gruber (Germany), Y. Hadad & A.Rotem (Israel), I. Halling (UK), D. Harston (Mexico), V. Harvey (Mexico), N. & U. Hauser (Switzerland), F. Henle (Germany), L. Henne (USA), A. & B. Hess, J. Heward (UK), J. Hillet & E. Rohuer (Switzerland), M. James (USA), A. Johnson (Austria), G. & B. Klepkens, E. Kuzian (Poland), S. Lazar (UK), R. Loether & E. Schoener (Germany), D. López & D. Huneeus, I. Meere & J. Hakvoort (Netherlands), W. Meijnnckens, D. Meghani (UK), M. Menzies, A. Meyes (Switzerland), J. Middleton, T. Mohr (Germany), P. Moors (UK), M. Murphy (UK), P. Neumann (USA), Noam, P. Norman, G. Pariente (Ireland), C. Pirie, M. Potter (Honduras), P. Prowting & J. Ward, K. Reuter (Germany), H. & M. de Roo, S. Scott (UK), C. Sharp (USA), J. Shirley, R. Smit, F. Smythe (UK), M. St. John, (UK), C. Staubli (Switzerland), B. Van Tongerloo (Netherlands), D. Toporoski, G. Tudor & B. Marsh (UK), F. Vellema, J.Waits & J. Berry (UK), R. Werckenthien (Germany), Wichmann (Canada), J. & W. Walp, E. Zavala (Mexico), I. Zeilinger (Belgium), H. Zettl (Austria).

Selected bibliography

Adams, Richard E.W., *Prehistoric Mesoamerica*, University of Oklahoma Press (1991). Blanton, Richard E., *Monte Albán*, AP, New York (1978). Brotherston, Gordon, *Painted Books of Mexico*, British Museum Press (1995). Clendinnen, Inga, *Aztecs*, Cambridge University Press (1991). Coe, Michael D., *The Maya*, Thames and Hudson (1993); *Mexico*, Thames and Hudson (1997). Davies, Nigel, *The Ancient Kingdoms of Mexico*, Penguin Books (1990). Hammond, Norman, *Ancient Maya Civilization*, Rutgers University Press (1988). Kampen, Michael E., *The Sculptures of El Tajín, Veracruz, Mexico*, University of Florida Press (1972). McAndrew, John, *The Open-Air Churches of Sixteenth-Century Mexico*, Harvard University Press (1965). O'Neill, John P. (ed), *Mexico, Splendors of Thirty Centuries*, Bullfinch Press (1990). Porter Weaver, Muriel, *The Aztecs, Maya and their predecessors*, Academic Press (1981). Schele, Linda and David Freidel, *A Forest of Kings*, William Morrow and Co. (1990). Wright, Ronald, *Time among the Maya*, Abacus Travel (1997).

See also Further Reading pp. 72-3

Patrick Maher

Dublin born and bred, Patrick Maher worked in a market garden and in a haberdashery warehouse whilst indulging his taste for the stage. After touring with a small troupe of dancers in Spain, the Middle East and Africa, he settled in Madrid for three years working in theatre, films, tv and cabaret. Bored after a spell with BT while preparing to launch himself as an actor, Patrick finally found his true vocation and took a B.A. in Latin American Studies, followed by an M.A. in Maya Iconography and finishing with a Ph.D. in the Aztec Gods of Pulque (pulque is the fermented sap of the agave maguey), which involved spending five seasons of six months each exploring villages and towns in the states of Mexico, Puebla and Morelos. However, universities are not crying out for lecturers in the Aztec Gods of Pulque! So, in February 1999, Patrick took a TESOL (Teaching English to Speakers of Other Languages) course with the intention of returning to Mexico to teach when, out of the blue, he was offered the opportunity to edit this edition of the Mexico Handbook for Footprint.